BILINGUALISM AND THE LAT[...]

[...]COW

Bilingualism has become since the 1980s one of the main themes of sociolinguistics, but there are as yet few large-scale treatments of the subject specific to the ancient world. This book is the first work to deal systematically with bilingualism during a period of antiquity (the Roman period, down to about the fourth century AD) in the light of sociolinguistic discussions of bilingual issues. The general theme of the work is the nature of the contact between Latin and numerous other languages spoken in the Roman world. Among the many issues discussed three are prominent: code-switching (the practice of switching between two languages in the course of a single utterance) and its motivation, language contact as a cause of linguistic change, and the part played by language choice and language switching in conveying a sense of identity.

J. N. ADAMS is a Senior Research Fellow of All Souls College, Oxford and a Fellow of the British Academy. He was previously Professor of Latin at the Universities of Manchester and Reading. In addition to articles in numerous journals, he has published five books: *The Text and Language of a Vulgar Latin Chronicle (Anonymus Valesianus II)* (1976) *The Vulgar Latin of the Letters of Claudius Terentianus* (1977), *The Latin Sexual Vocabulary* (1982), *Wackernagel's Law and the Placement of the Copula* Esse *in Classical Latin* (1994) and *Pelagonius and Latin Veterinary Terminology in the Roman Empire* (1995).

BILINGUALISM AND THE LATIN LANGUAGE

J. N. ADAMS

Senior Research Fellow of All Souls College, Oxford

CAMBRIDGE UNIVERSITY PRESS

CAMBRIDGE
UNIVERSITY PRESS

University Printing House, Cambridge CB2 8BS, United Kingdom

Cambridge University Press is part of the University of Cambridge.

It furthers the University's mission by disseminating knowledge in the pursuit of education, learning and research at the highest international levels of excellence.

www.cambridge.org
Information on this title: www.cambridge.org/9780521731515

First published 2003
Reprinted 2005
First published in paperback 2008

A catalogue record for this publication is available from the British Library

Library of Congress Cataloguing in Publication data
Adams, J. N. (James Noel)
Bilingualism and the Latin language / J. N. Adams.
p.   cm.
Includes bibliographical references and index.
ISBN 0 521 81771 4 (hardback)
1. Latin language – History.   2. Languages in contact – Rome – History – To 500.
3. Latin language – Influence on foreign languages.   4. Latin language – Foreign
words and phrases.   5. Bilingualism – Rome – History – To 1500.   6. Code-switching
(Linguistics) – Rome.   I. Title.
PA2057 .A33   2002
470'.42–dc21   2002019278

ISBN 978-0-521-81771-4 Hardback
ISBN 978-0-521-73151-5 Paperback

To the memory of
H. D. Jocelyn
1933–2000

Contents

vii

Preface

I first began working on contact between Latin and other languages in an organised way when I had the good fortune to be Visiting Senior Research Fellow at St John's College, Oxford, in 1994–5. The project was given impetus by the invitation to deliver the J. H. Gray Lectures in the Faculty of Classics, University of Cambridge, in May 1999. The title of the lectures was the same as that of the present book. The subject turned out to have such ramifications, and the material relevant to it to be so scattered, that I might never have finished the book had I not had the even greater good fortune to be elected to a Senior Research Fellowship at All Souls College, Oxford, in 1997.

An account of the full range of bilingualism in the ancient world across the whole of the Mediterranean and Middle Eastern areas and at all recorded periods would be virtually unmanageable, unless a team of collaborators was assembled. I have restricted myself to the Roman period, from the early Republic to the late Empire (approximately the fourth century). I have not adopted a fixed cut-off point, but on the whole have avoided entering into the period of the barbarian invasions in the West. In the western Empire Latin came into conflict with a number of vernacular languages and eventually effected their death. In the East similarly the Romans behaved as if vernacular languages did not exist, but here by contrast they were prepared to use Greek as a lingua franca, and consequently Latin did not cause language death, since it remained very much in the background. The eastern Empire is represented in the book by case studies devoted to Egypt, where the evidence is far superior to that from other eastern regions, and to the trading community at Delos; various eastern languages are also dealt with in Chapter 2. But the full story of bilingualism in the East would not be the story of bilingualism and the *Latin* language, and I have left much of the area to others.

Bilingualism has become since the 1980s one of the major themes of sociolinguistics. It has also attracted some attention from classicists.

Students of bilingualism in the Roman world have tended to concentrate on the quality of upper-class Romans' knowledge of Greek, on loan-words (which as often as not are used by monolinguals and are thus not necessarily relevant to bilingualism), on anecdotal rather than primary evidence, and on the pretentious bilingual games played by the educated in genres such as epic (I refer, for example, to etymologising and to what has been called '(mis)translation by paronomasia' in a recent book by O'Hara (1996)). I have first and foremost looked for primary material, and have had at least as much to say about ordinary bilinguals as about the literary classes. Unlike virtually all previous writers on Roman bilingualism, I have not restricted myself to Latin in relation to Greek, but have collected for the first time most, if not all, of the evidence for contact between Latin and languages other than Greek. In Chapter 2 material is cited and discussed from about sixteen languages, though admittedly some of these are scarcely attested. The evidence for Oscan, Gaulish, Punic and Aramaic in contact with Latin seems to me to be particularly important.

Perhaps the best recent works about aspects of bilingualism in the Roman world are the book by Bruno Rochette (*Le latin dans le monde grec* (1997)), and various papers on code-switching by Otta Wenskus (1990s onwards). Both scholars confine themselves to Latin and Greek in contact. Rochette's approach is mainly historical, whereas that of the present book is mainly sociolinguistic. Wenskus uses literary evidence rather than inscriptions and papyri, and her work is thus complementary to mine, in which more attention is given to texts on wood, stone and papyrus, though I have also covered the literary texts of most importance (e.g. those by Plautus, Lucilius, Cicero, Varro, Petronius, Juvenal and Martial).

In this book I make one of the first attempts to deal systematically with bilingualism during a period of antiquity in the light of recent sociolinguistic discussion of bilingual issues. I consider a host of texts which may well be unfamiliar to many classicists, ancient historians and linguists. Three major topics (among others: see the next paragraph) have been identified and discussed in the book: code-switching (the practice of switching between two languages in the course of a single utterance) and its relationship to interference and borrowing, language contact as a determinant of linguistic change in the languages in contact, and the part played by language choice and language switching in the projection of a sense of identity. *Code-switching* has emerged in recent years as the most problematic feature of bilinguals' performance. There is a mass of evidence for the practice from Roman antiquity, in primary sources (inscriptions and papyri) and literature (e.g. Plautus, Lucilius and Cicero), and involving several languages in addition to Greek in contact with Latin, but it has scarcely been recognised as a phenomenon separate from borrowing (or 'grecism') by classicists (but see above on the work of Wenskus). I have assessed the determinants of code-switching partly in the light of recent explanatory models, and attempted to bring out the importance of the ancient evidence (neglected by linguists) to the general debate. Linguists have had little to say to date about code-switching in written form, and I have stressed the inadequacy of applying to a written text the same methodologies as those used by linguists investigating modern speech communities. *Language change* has usually been regarded by historical linguists as a response to pressures operating within a language itself, but there is now a growing awareness that outside contacts are influential. Latin was subject to influence from a variety of languages, and Greek and various vernacular languages for their part were subject to influence from Latin. As far as *identity* is concerned, there has been much written on the subject in recent years by classicists, but one will look in vain for a serious discussion of the bilingual dimension. Bilinguals can constantly be seen to be conveying types of identity by linguistic means when they speak or write in bilingual contexts (see the summary in the second section of Chapter 9).

An assortment of other topics familiar in current studies of bilingualism is discussed. Roman language policies and linguistic nationalism within the spheres of imperial administration and the army are dealt with mainly in the chapter on Egypt. I discuss second-language acquisition at social levels below that of the élite, in the Roman army, in various commercial communities and within the civil administration of Egypt. Related to this subject is the question whether there were pidgins or creoles in the period, and I have identified forms of communication conducted by means of what I call 'reduced language'. Diglossia is discussed particularly (but not exclusively) within the Egyptian context under Roman rule, and standard claims about the phenomenon questioned. Accommodation (whereby a speaker or writer modifies his language in some way to suit the addressee) is another topic which bulks large in recent sociolinguistic literature, and there is a good deal of interesting evidence for the practice from Roman antiquity which is assessed here. Regional variation in Latin as determined by contact with other languages is a major theme of Chaper 4; the definitive account of regional variation in the Roman period (anticipating the fragmentation of the Latin language into different Romance languages) has yet to be written, and this book has much evidence which has been little noticed, if at all. Inseparable from language shift (whereby a people moves from one language to another, as happened in Gaul, Spain, Africa, Etruria and the Oscan, Umbrian and Venetic territories in the material covered by this book) is the habit which speakers have of changing or modifying their names in response to the pressures of language contact. Names and name changing in a variety of languages are discussed. The tendency of scholars to treat lower-class Latin as monolithic is noted, and a sub-category of Vulgar Latin identified, which I call 'Greeks' Latin'. Themes such as bilingualism in the army, provincial élites and language learning, Jewish communities and bilingualism, bilingualism and slavery, language choice as a form of power or as an expression of solidarity, also come up. The bilingual dimension to literacy (usually disregarded in accounts of ancient literacy) is considered. What, for example, is the relationship between the acquisition of a second language, and the acquisition of literacy in that language? What is the significance of transliterated texts (e.g. Latin texts writtten in Greek script)?

The book falls loosely into two parts. The first four chapters are thematic, and the next four present case studies devoted to particular places and texts. It goes without saying that there are many places in the Roman world where bilingualism must have been commonplace (e.g. Sicily) which are passed over in silence here.

It must be acknowledged that there are many other ways of approaching bilingualism. A historian, for example, would presumably be more interested than I am in the chronology of language learning and language shift in particular areas, and in establishing linguistic boundaries across the Empire. Nevertheless, though the book is written from the viewpoint of a philologist, a good deal of it will, I hope, be of interest to historians, and much of the earlier part has to do with Latin literature.

I have made it a principle to cite the ancient evidence in the text. Much of the evidence on which this book is based (such as that to do with Aramaic and Punic) will be inaccessible to many readers, and it seemed sensible to bring together this little-known material in a form which would allow future readers to subject it to their own analysis. Evidence is a given, but modern ideas about that evidence come and go, and what seems a clever idea to one generation may well seem inept to the next; there can be no doubt that theories about bilingualism will continue to evolve. I have not followed the modern practice of translating every single word and passage in a foreign language into English, though I have used my judgment in translating selectively. Most of the material in languages other than Greek and Latin is translated, if, that is, it is translatable: some fragmentary texts in poorly attested languages simply do not admit of translations of the type found in the Loeb series. When I choose not to translate, the issues raised by the passage in question are made clear in the accompanying discussion.

I should point out here that in the transliterated Latin texts in Greek script which come up often in the book I have not attempted to accent the Latin. Therefore if a text in Greek letters is in a mixture of two languages (Greek and Latin) only the parts I consider to be in Greek will be accented.

I owe a considerable debt to many people. David Bain, Alan Bowman, James Clackson, Nicholas Horsfall, Nigel Kay, David Langslow and Harm Pinkster read all or substantial parts of the manuscript, and made many corrections and criticisms and provided me with items of bibliography. John Penney responded generously and with considerable learning to the numerous queries I sent him over a long period. Many others gave me bibliographical material or information and help of one sort or another, and to all of them I would like to express my gratitude: Frédérique Biville, Paul Brand, John Briscoe, Alison Cooley, Eleanor Dickey, Matthew Dickie, Andrew Dyck, Penny Fewster, Jane Gardner, Stephen Harrison, John Healey, Tony Honoré, Mark Janse, Joshua Katz, Christina Kraus, Csaba La'da, John Ma, Robert Maltby, Torsten Meissner, Fergus Millar, Stephen Oakley, Mark Pobjoy, Nicholas Purcell, Michael Reeve, Bruno Rochette, Donald Russell, Ian Rutherford, Simon Swain, Sarolta Takacs, David Taylor, Otta Wenskus. My old friend Harry Jocelyn sadly died while the book was being written. He would, I am sure, have found much in it to annoy him, and it would certainly have contained fewer errors and less jargon if he had been able to direct his caustic gaze at the manuscript. I dedicate the book to his memory.

J. N. Adams

Acknowledgments

The following translations are reprinted by permission of the publishers and the Trustees of the Loeb Classical Library:

(Chapter 1) Sidonius Apollinaris, *Epist.* 3.12.5, from SIDONIUS VOLUME II, Loeb Classical Library Volume L420, translated by W. H. Semple, E. H. Warmington and W. B. Anderson; Cicero, *Brutus* 259, from CICERO VOLUME V, Loeb Classical Library Volume L342, translated by G. L. Hendrickson and H. M. Hubbell; Cicero, *De Off.* 1.111, from CICERO VOLUME XXI, Loeb Classical Library Volume L141, translated by J. E. King; Cicero, *Tusc. Disp.* 1.15, from CICERO VOLUME XVIII, Loeb Classical Library Volume L030, translated by Walter Miller; Dionysus of Halicarnassus 19.5.1, from DIONYSUS OF HALICARNASSUS VOLUME VII, Loeb Classical Library Volume L388, translated by Ernest Cary;

(Chapter 2) Livy 22.13.5–6, from LIVY VOLUME V, Loeb Classical Library Volume L233, translated by B. O. Foster; Cicero, *Fam.* 7.1.3, from CICERO VOLUME XXVI, Loeb Classical Library Volume L216N, translated by D. R. Shackleton Bailey; Livy 9.36.2–4, from LIVY VOLUME IV, Loeb Classical Library Volume L191, translated by B. O. Foster; Livy 10.20.8, from LIVY VOLUME IV, Loeb Classical Library Volume L191, translated by B. O. Foster; Pliny, *Nat. Hist.* 18.22, from PLINY VOLUME V, Loeb Classical Library Volume L371, translated by H. Rackham; Livy 10.20.8, from LIVY VOLUME IV, Loeb Classical Library Volume L191, translated by B. O. Foster;

(Chapter 3) Lucilius 84–5, from REMAINS OF OLD LATIN VOLUME III, Loeb Classical Library Volume L329, translated by E. H. Warmington; Suetonius, *Claud.* 4, from SUETONIUS VOLUME II, Loeb Classical Library Volume L038, translated by J. C. Rolfe; Pliny, *Nat. Hist.* 29.17, from PLINY VOLUME VIII, Loeb Classical Library Volume L418, translated by W. H. S. Jones;

(Chapter 4) Plutarch, *Quaest. Rom.* 103, 288F, from PLUTARCH MORALIA VOLUME IV, Loeb Classical Library Volume L305, translated by Frank C. Babbitt; Cicero, *Brutus* 258, from CICERO VOLUME V, Loeb Classical Library Volume L342, translated by W. H. Semple, E. H. Warmington, W. B. Anderson; Quintilian 1.1.13, from QUINTILIAN VOLUME I, Loeb Classical Library Volume L124N, translated by Donald A. Russell;

(Chapter 5) Valerius Maximus 2.2.2, from VALERIUS MAXIMUS VOLUME I, Loeb Classical Library Volume L492, translated by D. R. Shackleton Bailey;

(Chapter 6) Babrius 11, 16, from BABRIUS AND PHAEDRUS, Loeb Classical Library Volume L436, translated by Ben E. Perry;

Cambridge, Mass.: Harvard University Press, 1965, 1939, 1913, 1927, 1901, 1929, 1945, 1926, 1926, 1950, 1926, 1938, 1979, 1956, 1936, 1939, 2001, 2000, 1990. The Loeb Classical Library ® is a registered trademark of the President and Fellows of Harvard College.

Abbreviations

For abbreviations of editions of papyri and ostraca, see J. F. Oates, *Checklist of Editions of Greek Papyri, Ostraca and Tablets*, 5th edn (Atlanta, 1995)

CEL	see Cugusi (1992)
CGL	G. Goetz et al. (eds.), *Corpus Glossariorum Latinorum*, 7 vols. (Leipzig and Berlin, 1888–1923)
ChLA	A. Bruckner, R. Marichal et al. (eds.), *Chartae Latinae Antiquiores* (Olten, Lausanne etc., 1954–)
CIE	*Corpus Inscriptionum Etruscarum* (Leipzig etc., 1893–)
CIL	*Corpus Inscriptionum Latinarum* (Berlin, 1862–)
CIS	*Corpus Inscriptionum Semiticarum* (Paris, 1881–)
CJI	J.-B. Frey (ed.), *Corpus of Jewish Inscriptions. Jewish Inscriptions from the Third Century B.C. to the Seventh Century A.D.* (New York, 1975)
CLE	F. Buecheler (ed.), *Carmina Latina Epigraphica*, 3 vols. (Leipzig, 1897–1926)
CPL	R. Cavenaile, *Corpus Papyrorum Latinarum* (Wiesbaden, 1958)
CSEL	Corpus *Scriptorum Ecclesiasticorum Latinorum* (Vienna, 1866–)
FEW	W. von Wartburg, *Französisches etymologisches Wörterbuch* (Bonn, 1928–)
FIRA	S. Riccobono et al. (eds.) *Fontes Iuris Romani Antejustiniani*, 2nd edn, 3 vols. (Florence, 1968–9)
GL	H. Keil (ed.), *Grammatici Latini*, 7 vols. (Leipzig, 1855–80)
ICUR	*Inscriptiones Christianae Urbis Romae* (vol. I, Rome, 1857; n.s., vols. II–IX, Vatican City, 1935–85)
ID	F. Durrbach et al. (eds.), *Inscriptions de Délos* (Paris, 1926–)
IG	*Inscriptiones Graecae* (Berlin, 1873–)
IGBulg	G. Mihailov (ed.), *Inscriptiones Graecae in Bulgaria repertae*, 5 vols. (Sofia, 1970–97)

IGLS	J.-P. Rey-Coquais (ed.), *Inscriptions grecques et latines de la Syrie* VI (Paris, 1967)
IGPhilae	see A. Bernand (1969)
IGPorto	see Sacco (1984)
IGRRP	R. Cagnat et al. (eds.), *Inscriptiones Graecae ad res Romanas pertinentes*, 3 vols. (I, III, IV) (Paris, 1901–27)
IGUR	L. Moretti (ed.), *Inscriptiones Graecae Urbis Romae*, (Rome, 1968–)
ILAlg	S. Gsell and H.-G. Pflaum (eds.), *Inscriptions latines de L'Algérie*, 2 vols. (Paris, 1922–76)
ILBulg	B. Gerov (ed.), *Inscriptiones Latinae in Bulgaria repertae* (Sofia, 1989)
ILCV	E. Diehl (ed.), *Inscriptiones Latinae Christianae Veteres*, 3 vols. (Berlin, 1925–31)
ILGR	see Šašel Kos (1979)
ILI	see A. and J. Šašel (1963)
ILLRP	A. Degrassi (ed.), *Inscriptiones Latinae Liberae Rei Publicae*, 2 vols. (I, 2nd edn, 1965, II, 1963) (Florence)
ILS	H. Dessau (ed.), *Inscriptiones Latinae Selectae*, 3 vols. (Berlin, 1892–1916)
IM	see Parlangèli (1960)
IMS	M. Mirković et al. (eds.), *Inscriptions de la Mésie Supérieure* (Belgrade, 1976–)
IPO	see Thylander (1952)
IPT	see Levi Della Vida and Amadasi Guzzo (1987)
IRB	see Mariner Bigorra (1973)
IRT	see Reynolds and Ward Perkins (1952)
ISM	D. M. Pippidi and I. I. Russu (eds.), *Inscriptiones Daciae et Scythiae Minoris antiquae* (Bucharest, 1975–)
KAI	see Donner and Röllig (1966–9)
Lewis and Short	C. T. Lewis and C. Short, *A Latin Dictionary* (Oxford, 1879)
LSJ	H. G. Liddell and R. Scott, *A Greek–English Lexicon* (revised and augmented by H. S. Jones, with a revised supplement, 1996) (Oxford, 1996)
MAMA	W. M. Calder et al. (eds.), *Monumenta Asiae Minoris Antiqua*, 8 vols. (Manchester, 1928–62)
OCD	*Oxford Classical Dictionary*, 3rd edn (Oxford, 1996)

OLD	*Oxford Latin Dictionary* (Oxford, 1968–82)
PAT	see Hillers and Cusini (1996)
PG	*Patrologia Graeca* (*Patrologiae cursus completus, series Graeca*, ed. J.-P. Migne) (Paris, 1857–)
PL	*Patrologia Latina* (*Patrologiae cursus completus, series Latina*, ed. J.-P. Migne) (Paris, 1844–)
PLRE	A. H. M. Jones, J. R. Martindale and J. Morris, *The Prosopography of the Later Roman Empire*, 3 vols. (Cambridge, 1971–92)
REW	W. Meyer-Lübke, *Romanisches etymologisches Wörterbuch*, 3rd edn (Heidelberg, 1935)
RIB	R. G. Collingwood, R. P. Wright et al. (eds.), *The Roman Inscriptions of Britain* (Oxford, 1975–)
RPC	A. Burnett, M. Amandry and P. P. Ripollès, *Roman Provincial Coinage* (London and Paris, 1992–)
SB	see Shackleton Bailey (1965–70)
SB	F. Priesigke (ed.), *Sammelbuch griechischer Urkunden aus Ägypten* (Strassburg, 1915–)
TLL	*Thesaurus Linguae Latinae* (Leipzig, 1900–)

Introduction

I INTRODUCTORY REMARKS; SOME ISSUES IN THE STUDY OF BILINGUALISM

It is thought that bilingualism is more common than monolingualism, and yet linguistics has traditionally operated as if the monolingual were the normal speaker.[1] Bilingualism across the Roman world cannot be quantified, but numerous languages survive in the written record (usually in a fragmentary state) or are attested in contact with Latin (Gaulish, forms of Hispanic, Oscan, Umbrian, Venetic, Etruscan, Hebrew, Aramaic, Egyptian Demotic and hieroglyphics, Coptic, Punic, Libyan (?), Thracian, forms of Germanic, as well as Greek),[2] and others were spoken without leaving any trace in our sources. In the vast expanses of the Roman Empire, where mobility was high among such groups as the army, administrative personnel, traders and slaves, language contact was a fact of everyday life. To survey bilingualism in the whole of the ancient world would be an immense task, but the Roman domain, particularly during the Empire, offers more manageable data.

Bilingualism has traditionally been of interest not only to linguists, but also to anthropologists, social and cultural historians and students of literature. As found in the Roman period it has received a good deal of attention, explicitly in some of the works of (e.g.) Dubuisson, Holford-Strevens, Horsfall, Leiwo, Millar, Neumann and Untermann, Rochette and Wenskus, and implicitly in virtually any work on Latin literary genres with Greek forerunners. The time seems appropriate for the topic to be taken up again, not least because bilingualism in modern societies has attracted much research by sociolinguists, psycholinguists and anthropologists in recent years. The issues have become clearer and methodologies

---

[1] See e.g. Milroy and Muysken (1995: 2–3), Romaine (1995: 1) on this point.

[2] When I say that such languages are attested 'in contact with Latin', I mean that we either have bilingual texts, or that there are *testimonia* recording or implying bilingualism of one sort or another.

have been developed. Those studying bilingualism in Roman antiquity have tended to concentrate on various subjects to the exclusion of others. Loan-words have been ceaselessly investigated to the neglect of code-switching,[3] learned imitation in one language of the syntax of another to the neglect of interference, the upper classes as second-language learners to the neglect of sub-élite bilinguals, lexical phenomena to the neglect of syntax, morphology and orthography, anecdotal evidence to the neglect of primary evidence, Romans as learners of Greek to the neglect of Greeks as learners of Latin,[4] and contact between Latin and Greek to the neglect of contact between Latin and other languages. Where Romans are concerned, much effort has been expended on an attempt to assess the extent of upper-class knowledge of Greek,[5] through the medium of ancient anecdotes about linguistic performance and through the study of literary translations mainly into the writer's first language. I will be trying to change the emphasis, by considering languages other than Greek in contact with Latin (though contact between Greek and Latin is the best attested, and must be given most space), by using primary material (inscriptions, ostraca and papyri) as well as anecdotal, and by dealing as much with sub-élites as with the upper classes. I will not be discussing (except in passing) the extent of bilingualism, the evidence for which is inadequate, nor will I be mapping language regions across the Empire and points of language contact.[6] Instead some of the major issues in current bilingual studies will be considered as they impinge on antiquity. These include the nature and motivation of code-switching, the related subject of the determinants of language choice, a topic which will be discussed particularly in relation to the place of Latin in Egypt, and bilingualism as an influence in language change. These issues, as we will see, in turn raise others, such as the part played by language choice and code-switching in the construction or perception of individual and collective identities, language choice as an expression of solidarity on the one hand and of power or dominance on the other, and the significance of topic or domain in language selection. Other themes of the book will include bilingualism in the army, and the relationship between second-language learning and the acquisition of literacy in a second language.

---

[3] Code-switching is now beginning to attract the notice of classicists: see Wenskus (1995, 1996, 1998), Jocelyn (1999), Dunkel (2000).
[4] But see now Dubuisson (1985), Holford-Strevens (1993), Rochette (1997a).
[5] See particularly Horsfall (1979), Dubuisson (1992).
[6] For which see Neumann and Untermann (1980).

In the present chapter I first introduce some terminology which is fundamental to the book, namely 'bilingualism' and the difference between 'élite' and 'non-élite' bilingualism, 'code-switching' as distinct from 'borrowing' and 'interference', and 'pidgins' and 'reduced' languages. Some of these topics will be dealt with at greater length in later chapters. I also consider here the main types of primary evidence which are relevant to bilingualism. It must be stressed that the primary evidence relating to bilingualism in dead languages is very different from that which modern linguists investigating bilingualism in spoken languages can call on. Written evidence raises its own problems of interpretation, and it would not do to accept uncritically all of the assumptions implicit in linguistic research on bilingualism in spoken forms. For that reason a good deal of space will be given to establishing a typology of texts with bilingual significance. Bilingualism as manifested in written form has been largely disregarded in the modern world. There is also a section on the concept of the 'authorship' of inscriptions, particularly bilingual and transliterated, since inscriptions will bulk large as evidence and their authorship is a complicated matter.

II BILINGUALISM

Bilingualism has been understood in many ways, and I begin with a discussion of the term leading to a definition on which this book will be based. Weinreich was content with a definition which does not even occupy two lines (1953: 1): 'The practice of alternately using two languages will be called BILINGUALISM, and the persons involved, BILINGUAL.' This would perhaps better serve as a description of code-switching (for which see below, v). Since then, the matter has been seen as more problematic. Hamers and Blanc (1989: 6–30), in a discussion of the difficulties inherent in such definitions, quote that of the *Webster Dictionary* (1961) for the word 'bilingual', as follows: 'having or using two languages especially as spoken with the fluency characteristic of a native speaker; a person using two languages especially habitually and with control like that of a native speaker'. There is embodied here an old and popular view that bilingualism is marked by equal and fluent competence in two languages. This view is found as well in earlier linguistic literature, notably in Bloomfield's assertion (1933: 55–6) that in cases 'where . . . perfect foreign-language learning is not accompanied by loss of the native language, it results in *bilingualism*, native-like control of two languages'. There are indeed bilinguals of this type, but equally there are speakers who have greater competence in one language than another, and it would seem perverse to exclude them from a study of bilingualism given that they might be perfectly capable of communicating fluently in the second language.

From the Roman period, for example, educated Latin writers can be found who, while working with complex Greek as the language of their source material, seem to have made mistakes from time to time in their understanding of the language;[7] but they should not merely for that reason be deemed not to have been 'bilingual'. An example of an apparent error in a literary text is at Livy 38.7.10, a passage based on Polybius 21.28.11, describing a confrontation between the Romans and Aetolians in a tunnel at Ambracia in 189 BC. Polybius says that both groups thrust shields in front of them (διὰ τὸ προβάλλεσθαι θυρεοὺς καὶ γέρρα πρὸ αὑτῶν ἀμφότεροι), but Livy, seemingly confusing θυρεοί with θύραι, has them holding forth doors (*foribus raptim obiectis*).[8] Another possible case is at Livy 33.8.13, where *hastis positis* corresponds to Polybius' καταβαλοῦσι τὰς σαρίσας (18.24.9). Note Briscoe (1973: 263): 'Polybius said that they were to lower their spears for the charge and L. took him to mean that they were to put them down on the ground.'[9] But errors of translation (into one's native language) are arguably of a different order from errors of what I will call 'positive performance' in the second language itself (on 'performance', see below). It might even be suggested that misunderstandings of the above sort are of no significance at all in assessing second-language competence, because even monolinguals reading their own language do not always read with the same concentration or comprehension.[10] In a strong sense a writer of, say, Latin who could not use passive verb-forms might be said to

---

[7] See in general Horsfall (1979: 80–4), and on errors of differing degrees of seriousness in a variety of Latin writers (Gellius, Pliny, Cicero, Terence, Virgil and Catullus), see Holford-Strevens (1988: 169–70). Also worth noting is Lucretius' account of the plague at Athens (6.1138–1286), which is largely based on Thucydides, but with some misunderstandings. See the notes of Bailey (1947), vol. III, on 1151–9, 1152, 1197–8, 1198–1204, 1230–51, 1235. For errors in Cicero's translation of Aratus, see Soubiran (1972: 88–9).

[8] See Walsh (1958).

[9] Walbank (1967) ad loc. takes the same view, but the case is far from established. Livy talks of the phalanx of the Macedonians laying down their spears, the length of which was a hindrance, and taking to their swords, which is radically different from Polybius' account of a charge. The possibility cannot be ruled out that Livy made a deliberate change to the nature of the event, for whatever reasons of artistry (see Briscoe ad loc. for additional bibliography on this point). Other possible examples from Livy cited by Briscoe (1973: 6, 1981: 2) are even less convincing, and some are purely speculative. Sometimes, if Livy did not alter the narrative of the original slightly for his own purposes, he might simply have lost the drift of his source.

[10] See Powell (1995: 273–9) for a discussion of the possible reasons why Cicero might sometimes have committed 'errors' of translation. Powell too seems disinclined to treat such errors as particularly significant.

have had imperfect knowledge of the language, but errors of translation may in fact be based on *knowledge* of the other language. Livy analysed καταβάλλω correctly, but (if the conventional interpretation is accepted) did not recognise the technical use of the word;[11] and in the other case it is well to remember that a writer's source in manuscript form might often have been either corrupt or difficult to read.[12] The presence of non-military objects in the context (γέρρα, πίθος) does indeed suggest the possibility that Livy's text might have had a different reading.

The errors of translation that have been found in Apuleius[13] similarly lack significance. I cite just one example. At *De mundo* 25 (343), *nec ambigitur eum praestantem ac sublimem sedem tenere et poetarum* **laudibus nomen eius consulum ac regum nuncupationibus praedicari** (of the supreme god: 'nor is it doubted that he occupies an eminent and lofty seat, and that in the eulogies of the poets his name is designated by the titles of consuls and kings'), the words in bold correspond to Περὶ κόσμου 397 b 25 ὕπατός τε [= *summus*] διὰ τοῦτο ὠνόμασται ('because of this he has been called supreme'). Note Beaujeu (1973: xii): 'le traducteur ignorait ce sens assez rare d'ὕπατος, mot qui, de son temps, servait presque uniquement à traduire *consul*'. Thus it is Apuleius' knowledge of the current language that leads him astray, if we accept that a genuine mistake has been made.[14] There is no point in attempting to assess the quality of Romans' knowledge of Greek on the evidence of translation errors alone. For one thing, the high Greek literary language in its various forms did not much resemble the varieties spoken during the Roman period, and even Greeks themselves may have had problems in understanding earlier literature. Romans did not have access to scholarly tools of the modern type (most notably bilingual dictionaries) to help them with the interpretation of classical genres full of archaisms.[15] I will here follow implicitly the principle that bilingual competence can only be seriously examined through examples of positive *performance* in a second language.

But what does 'performance' mean? The skills deployed by a language user (including a bilingual) may be said to fall into four types, listening, reading, speaking and writing.[16] Listening and reading are passive, speaking and writing active, and it is to the last two, as the positive skills,

---

[11] Similarly Walsh (1958: 85) is inclined to take a lenient view of this error.

[12] Compare Bailey's (1947) note on Lucr. 6.1198–1204: 'Lucr. again misunderstands or misrepresents Thuc., unless . . . he was using a corrupt version or even an inaccurate Latin translation.'

[13] See Beaujeu (1973: xi–xii).

[14] Beaujeu (1973: 330), in his note on the passage, appears not so confident that Apuleius had not made a deliberate change.

[15] See the remarks of Horsfall (1979: 82).   [16] See Romaine (1995: 13).

that attention should ideally be directed.[17] From antiquity we do not have equal access to all four activities. In corpus languages it is possible only to glean bits and pieces of information about the *listening* and *speaking* skills of 'bilinguals' in their second language, from anecdotes or by making deductions from narratives of events (see below, III on the shortcomings of anecdotes as evidence). Evidence of this type has its place in the study of ancient bilingualism, but it will not be the main focus of this book. *Reading* a second language is the skill required of translators such as Livy and Apuleius, but in an ancient language the assessment of this activity is made difficult by the literary translator's artistic licence, which allowed him to make deliberate changes to the content of his source, and also by momentary lapses of no necessary significance, as discussed above. It is *writing* a second language that is the most positive bilingual performance which can be observed from antiquity. On this view translations by Romans of literary Greek into Latin[18] would have less to tell us than specimens of Greek composed by Romans, whether by free composition (note the exercise in declamation at Cic. *Att.* 9.4.2; cf. 6.4.3, 6.5.1–2)[19] or as renderings of Latin originals (as for example the Greek translations of *senatus consulta*, as collected by Sherk (1969)).[20]

A distinction which is sometimes made is between the *balanced* bilingual, 'who has equivalent competence in both languages' (Hamers and Blanc (1989: 8)), and the *dominant* bilingual, 'for whom competence in one of the languages, more often the mother tongue, is superior to his competence in the other' (Hamers and Blanc (1989: 8)). Hamers and Blanc stress that balanced bilingualism 'should not be confused with a very high degree of competence in the two languages; it is rather a question of a state of equilibrium reached by the levels of competence attained in the two languages as compared to monolingual competence'. They go on to say that equivalent competence 'should not be equated with the ability to use both languages for all functions and domains. Dominance or balance is not equally distributed for all domains and

---

[17] For reading a foreign language as easier than speaking it, see the remarks of Jerome, *PL* 29, 23–6, cited below, 2.VII.5.

[18] As for example Catullus' translation of Callimachus (66), Cicero's translations of the *Timaeus* (see Poncelet (1957); also Mueller-Goldingen (1992)) and the *Phaenomena* of Aratus. Cicero also translated the *Oeconomicus* of Xenophon (see *Off.* 2.87). On translating from Greek into Latin, see Quint. 10.5.2–3, Cic. *De orat.* 1.155, *Opt. gen.* 23. See also Horsfall (1979: 83–4), and on Cicero, Powell (1995), Vitruvius, Lendle (1992), and Gellius, Steinmetz (1992). Note too the general discussion (with bibliography) of Traina (1989).

[19] The last two passages were ostensibly in Greek so that the courier could not read them (for code-switching as a form of coding, see below, 3.III.3).

[20] On the usefulness of translating into Greek, see Quint. 10.5.4–5.

functions of language'. Doubts have however been expressed about the value of the concept of 'balanced bilingualism'. Note Romaine (1995: 19): 'The notion of balanced bilingualism is an ideal one, which is largely an artefact of a theoretical perspective which takes the monolingual as its point of reference.'

Identifying fluent or balanced competence in two languages from the written record of antiquity is not easy, though where Greek and Latin speech is concerned there is anecdotal evidence of individuals competent *utraque lingua* (see further below, III).[21] As far as 'non-balanced' bilingualism is concerned, it is not difficult in inscriptions and elsewhere to find specimens of Latin that were written by Greeks with imperfect competence in Latin, and vice versa (see below). The Greekness or Romanness of the writers is revealed by interference from the first language (on interference, see V), and there may also be signs of a reduced morphology in the target language. The clearest evidence for this latter phenomenon is to be found in a Greek's attempted translation into Latin of parts of two fables of Babrius (*P. Amh.* II.26). This piece will be the subject of Chapter 8. I set out in section IX below some examples of such reduced or imperfect Greek and Latin, which take us into the world of Greeks and others struggling to acquire and communicate in a second language. Material from the hand of learners of Latin as a second language is perhaps the best evidence that we have for the problems of everyday cross-language communication in the multilingual Roman Empire. The evidence is relevant to such issues as the part played by language learning in inflicting change on a target language, the stages in the acquisition of a second language and the nature of learners' errors, the relationship between language learning and the acquisition of literacy in the second language, and more generally the linguistic policy of some groups such as the Roman army. Such evidence, which largely concerns social strata below the level of the highly educated Greco-Roman élites, has tended to be disregarded by students of ancient bilingualism, who have concentrated instead on what might be called *élite bilingualism* (see below, III).

In this book I will not be subscribing to the popular view of bilingualism referred to in the opening paragraph of this section. The bilingual's proficiency in the two languages, on my understanding of the term 'bilingual', may vary greatly across such areas as the phonological, morphological, lexical, semantic and stylistic.[22] The merchant who manages to

---

[21] See Horsfall (1979), Dubuisson (1981).   [22] See e.g. Romaine (1995: 12–13).

communicate in a foreign market place with a mixture of gestures and words of the foreign language shorn of some inflectional morphemes and articulated in a foreign accent may in a sense be described as a practising 'bilingual', but his proficiency in the second language is at a far remove from that, say, of a foreign ambassador who delivers a speech in Latin at Rome on a political subject.[23] It follows that I will be adopting an all-embracing definition of bilingualism. It will be assumed that speakers (or writers) of two languages may have an infinitely variable range of competences in the two languages, from native fluency on the one hand to imperfect competence verging on incompetence on the other. Even the speaker or writer with very poor command of a second language may be able to make himself understood in that language, at least within restricted domains, and is therefore worthy of study, particularly since language learners tend to turn up in important spheres of activity, such as the army and in trade, where their linguistic efforts, however inadequate, might have had considerable influence. Thus the term 'bilingual' will be used here to include even those whose second language is far from perfect. Setting up degrees of linguistic competence in a dead language is out of the question, and even in spoken modern languages is problematic.[24] Nevertheless the approximate opposites, competence and poor competence in the second language, are easy enough to distinguish.

I mention finally an obvious criticism to which the minimalist definition adopted here is exposed. Practically everyone knows at least a few words of a second language, and we are thus in danger of having to classify everyone as bilingual.[25] It is though intuitively clear that there is a difference between being bilingual, however that term is defined, and 'knowing a few words from a second language'. The bilingual 'performs', however imperfectly, in at least one of the areas listed above, whereas the 'non-bilingual' has at best a few bits and pieces of passive knowledge, which he may never use. The objection is not a real one for the student of ancient bilingualism, because of necessity attention has to be devoted to written sources, and these convey actual 'performance', or anecdotes about performance.

---

[23] Note the random list of fifteen types of 'bilinguals' given by Hoffmann (1991: 16–17), which include (e.g.) 'the two-year-old who is beginning to talk, speaking English to one parent and Welsh to the other', and 'the Portuguese chemist who can read specialist literature in his subject written in English'. Hoffmann (17) remarks: 'Many specialists would say that all the above individuals could be classed as bilinguals; but public opinion, and at least some of these people themselves, would probably disagree.'

[24] See e.g. Hamers and Blanc (1989: 14–25).   [25] Cf. Romaine (1995: 11).

III ÉLITE AND SUB-ÉLITE BILINGUALISM: ANECDOTAL EVIDENCE AND ITS SHORTCOMINGS

Those bilinguals who have attracted most attention among classicists, implicitly at least, might be called in the current jargon 'élite bilinguals', that is members of the educated classes who had freely chosen to become bilingual.[26] I say 'freely chosen' because there are other bilinguals who have no such choice. Upper-class Romans were by choice learners of Greek, and some are said to have achieved great competence in the second language. Quintilian asserted that the child (and he meant the upper-class child) should begin with Greek: 1.1.12 *a sermone Graeco puerum incipere malo, quia Latinum, qui pluribus in usu est, uel nobis nolentibus perbibet*. It might be said that a child had no choice, but in fact his father or parents were able to exercise such a choice on his behalf, and there is evidence that Quintilian's advice must often have been followed. Upper-class Romans who could not speak Greek (whether genuinely or allegedly) are sometimes disparaged, as Verres by Cicero: *Verr.* 4.127 *epigramma Graecum pernobile incisum est in basi, quod iste eruditus homo et Graeculus, qui haec subtiliter iudicat, qui solus intellegit, si unam litteram Graecam scisset, certe non sustulisset* ('it had a notable Greek inscription on its pedestal, which this learned exponent of Greek culture, with his delicate critical sense and unique appreciation of these matters, would certainly not (?) have removed if he had known a single Greek letter').[27] There is also a good deal of anecdotal and other evidence for fluent bilingualism (in Greek and Latin) among upper-class Romans, though opinions differ as to how it should be interpreted (see below). Here I select a few such anecdotes relating to Romans using Greek.[28]

According to Valerius Maximus, P. Crassus Mucianus as proconsul in Asia Minor in 131 BC was able to use the five Greek dialects: 8.7.6 *iam P. Crassus, cum in Asiam ad Aristonicum regem debellandum consul uenisset, tanta cura Graecae linguae notitiam animo conprehendit ut eam in quinque diuisam genera per omnes partes ac numeros penitus cognosceret*. The same anecdote is in Quintilian (11.2.50), perhaps taken from a common source: *Crassus ille diues, qui cum Asiae praeesset, quinque Graeci sermonis differentias sic tenuit, ut*

---

[26] See Hoffmann (1991: 46).

[27] There is obvious exaggeration here (so Dubuisson (1992: 188)), but it is of interest that elsewhere Cicero refers to an interpreter used by Verres, though allegedly for purposes other than interpreting (*Verr.* 3.84). The negative *non* in the final clause of the passage quoted may be wrong.

[28] Further details and evidence are discussed by Kroll (1933: II.118–19), Boyancé (1956), Kaimio (1979a: 94–110), Horsfall (1979: 84–7), Dubuisson (1982), id. (1992: 192), Weis (1992), Gruen (1993), chapter 6.

qua quisque apud eum lingua postulasset, eadem ius sibi redditum ferret.[29] Cicero on one occasion spoke Greek in the senate at Syracuse, an action for which he was criticised by an opponent, partly on the grounds that it was an improper act of deference for a Roman to speak Greek in public before a Greek audience: *Verr.* 4.147 *ait indignum facinus esse quod ego in senatu Graeco uerba fecissem; quod quidem apud Graecos Graece locutus essem, id ferri nullo modo posse.*[30] The Rhodian ambassador Apollonius Molo was allowed to speak Greek in the senate without an interpreter (Val. Max. 2.2.3). Atticus is said to have spoken Greek as if he were a native of Athens: Nepos *Att.* 4.1 *sic enim Graece loquebatur ut Athenis natus uideretur.* Much the same is said of L. Crassus: Cic. *De orat.* 2.2 *Graece sic loqui, nullam ut nosse aliam linguam uideretur.* Another who was more Greek than the Greeks was T. Albucius (Cic. *Brut.* 131 *doctus etiam Graecis T. Albucius uel potius plane Graecus . . . fuit autem Athenis adulescens*), who was mocked for his Hellenism by Scaevola in an incident reported by Lucilius (Cic. *Fin.* 1.8–9; Lucilius 88–94: see below, 3.IV.1). From the later Empire one may note, for example, the praetorian prefect Strategius Musonianus, who was famed for his knowledge of 'both languages': Amm. 15.13.1 *facundia sermonis utriusque clarus.*[31] Anecdotes on the other hand which portray Romans as either refusing to speak or use Greek themselves or to have it spoken directly to them cannot always be taken as evidence for an inability to use the language.[32] Greek, the language of high culture in Roman eyes, elicited in Romans a sense of cultural inferiority and in some of them a consequent linguistic aggression, particularly as Rome

---

[29] The division of the Greek dialects into five entailed classifying the koine as a dialect (along with Attic, Ionic, Doric and Aeolic): see Davies (1987: 14–15).

[30] For flattering remarks made by Apollonius Molo to Cicero after the latter had declaimed in Greek, see Plut. *Cic.* 4.4–5; also Rochette (1997a: 70–1).

[31] It has recently been argued (by Drijvers (1996)) that Musonianus knew Aramaic. The arguments advanced are convincing enough, but I would reject the tentative suggestion (537) that Ammianus might have meant by *facundia sermonis utriusque* 'those languages spoken in his hometown', viz. Greek and Aramaic. The phrase had long-standing literary associations and an accepted meaning, which could not possibly have been shed without very clear contextual pointers (contrast the example in Jerome, *PL* 29, 25–6, cited below, 2.VII.5, where there are such pointers). There are no pointers in the passage of Ammianus. On the contrary, it would be bizarre in the extreme if Ammianus had meant by *facundia* eloquence in any language other than Greek and Latin: these were the languages in which eloquence (*facundia*) in Greco-Roman culture could be displayed. Ammianus presumably meant that Musonianus was a gifted linguist, fluent of course in Greek and Latin, but by implication able to cope with other languages as well. A parallel can be found in the *protector* Antoninus, who defected to the Persians. He too was *utriusque linguae litteras sciens* (Amm. 18.5.1), but it emerges from the narrative that he could also communicate directly with Persians (see, e.g., 18.7.10–11 *dicere, auditis*), though Ammianus does not bother to tell the reader explicitly that he knew Persian (or Aramaic?). On Musonianus, see also 2.VII.5.

[32] See, e.g., Val. Max. 2.2.2, D.C. 57.15.2–3, Suet. *Tib.* 71.

established political control in the Greek world. On the one hand the educated Roman aspired to be fluent in Greek, but on the other hand it might be seen by some as humiliating to the Roman state if Greek was accepted on a public occasion. Attitudes were constantly changing, and what to Tiberius was unacceptable did not bother Claudius.[33]

It is worth dwelling a little longer on the diversity of anecdotal evidence about upper-class Romans and its interpretation. Not all anecdotal information is about fluent performance in the second language. Lesser degrees of competence are also occasionally acknowledged. Augustus, though he was interested in Greek culture and used code-switching into Greek in his letters (see Suet. *Tib.* 21.4–6), lacked confidence in the spoken language and was unwilling to speak extempore or to compose his own speeches in Greek: Suet. *Aug.* 89.1 *non tamen ut aut loqueretur expedite aut componere aliquid auderet; nam et si quid res exigeret, Latine formabat uertendumque alii dabat.* From the pages of Suetonius we are thus able to deduce a distinction between an individual's written and spoken Greek, or to be more precise between his writing of Greek to fellow Romans in private and his speaking of Greek to Greeks in public. Certainly Augustus did sometimes speak Greek before Greeks. After the battle of Actium he addressed the Egyptians and Alexandrians in Greek (D.C. 51.16.4),[34] but no doubt from a prepared text if we are to believe Suetonius. Claudius by contrast could reply to *legati* in extended speeches in Greek in the senate, and replies would not necessarily have been prepared in advance (Suet. *Claud.* 42.1 *ac saepe in senatu legatis perpetua oratione respondit*).

Another familiar story concerning poor competence has to do with the humiliation of Roman ambassadors to Tarentum in 282 BC under L. Postumius Megellus. The audience looked for errors in the Greek of Postumius and greeted his efforts with laughter. As the ambassadors left, someone excreted on the ambassadorial robe (D.H. 19.5).[35]

There is even found occasionally an attitude that mistakes in Greek might be made by a Roman deliberately, as a demonstration of Romanness: it would not do (in the eyes of some) to be considered too Greek. Thus, according to Cicero, Lucullus had inserted barbarisms and solecisms in his histories intentionally: *Att.* 1.19.10 *non dicam quod tibi, ut opinor, Panhormi Lucullus de suis historiis dixerat, se, quo facilius illas probaret Romani hominis esse, idcirco barbara quaedam et soloeca dispersisse.* Fluency in foreign languages may in some cultures arouse suspicion (see below 2 n. 381

---

[33] See, e.g., Suet. *Tib.* 71 alongside *Claud.* 42; see further Kaimio (1979a: 133–4).
[34] See Rochette (1997a: 98 n. 195) for bibliography.
[35] See Kaimio (1979a: 96), Dubuisson (1982: 196–7), Gruen (1993: 229–30), Rochette (1997a: 91).

for Roman suspicion of the linguistic skills of Carthaginians). Josephus
(*AJ* 20.264), for example, asserted that his people 'did not favour
those persons who had mastered the speech of many nations': παρ'
ἡμῖν γὰρ οὐκ ἐκείνους ἀποδέχονται τοὺς πολλῶν ἐθνῶν διάλεκτον
ἐκμαθόντας.[36] Cicero did not share the attitude of Lucullus. He sent
a copy of the *commentarius* on his consulship to Atticus, asserting that
any errors were not intended, and perhaps expecting Atticus to point
out any necessary corrections if there was anything un-Greek in it:
Att. 1.19.10 *in quo si quid erit quod homini Attico minus Graecum eruditumque
uideatur . . . me imprudente erit et inuito.*[37] Also relevant in the present context
are the Greek translations of *senatus consulta* written for circulation in the
Greek world and also of the *Res Gestae* of Augustus (some linguistic features
of which texts will be discussed in a later chapter (4.v.2.12)). These seem
to be aggressively Latinate in their idiom: translators rendered Latin
idioms literally into Greek, thereby producing a conspicuously peculiar
Greek which may have been meant to impress Greeks by its Romanness.
We should not (as has sometimes been done) take the translationese as
a sign of the translators' poor command of Greek (see further below,
4.v.2.12).

I stress a few points in conclusion. First, a distinction must be made between those anecdotes which relate to knowledge of the Greek language,
and those which relate to knowledge of Greek literature and culture.[38]
There were Romans who affected to disregard Greek literature and
culture (so Marius, Sall. *Iug.* 85.32, and L. Crassus, Cic. *De orat.* 1.82,
2.153), but that attitude should not be brought into discussions of the
extent of Greek–Latin bilingualism. It was not impossible that a Roman
fluent in Greek might parade a hostility to Greek culture. L. Crassus,
just mentioned, was said to be so fluent in Greek that some thought it
his native tongue (Cic. *De orat.* 2.2, cited above),[39] and Marius too knew
Greek.[40] Plutarch's remark about Marius (*Mar.* 2.2), to the effect that

---

[36] For a full discussion of this passage, see Sevenster (1968: 65–71).

[37] It would be wrong though to ascribe this Ciceronian ideal of achieving correctness in one's Greek
to Cato as well, on the basis of a well-known story. The fact that Cato rebuked A. Postumius
Albinus for inserting in the preface of his Greek history an apology for any errors which he might
have committed in Greek (Plb. 39.1, Plut. *Cato* 12.5) does not permit the conclusion that it was
Cato's view that 'Romans who try their hand at writing Greek should do so at least as well as
the Greeks themselves' (so Gruen (1993: 257)). The sources show that Cato was annoyed by the
man's hypocrisy: he was not compelled to write in Greek, and to do so of his own accord and
then to beg forgiveness for his barbarisms was ridiculous. Postumius' remark need have been no
more than a commonplace of a Roman writing in Greek (see Walbank (1979: 727)).

[38] For the distinction, see Plb. 39.1.   [39] See the discussion of Gruen (1993: 264–5).

[40] See Gruen (1993: 268–9).

it was said that he never studied Greek literature, and never used the Greek language for any matter of real importance, nicely brings out the distinction I am suggesting: he knew Greek, but disregarded Greek literature. I note in passing that on this evidence Marius would seem (in the terminology of diglossia, for which see 5.1.3) to have been assigning a 'low' role to Greek, while reserving Latin for the 'high' functions.

Secondly, it is not satisfactory to treat 'Greek' as a unity. The language of classical literature was at a far remove from the koine spoken in the Roman period, and some Romans might well have been fluent in the spoken language but relatively unversed in literary Greek. It would be illogical to argue from the errors made by a person in understanding literary Greek that he could not speak the language. Confusions arise in discussions of Roman bilingualism because the various categories of Greek (and the categories of performance) are not always distinguished.

Thirdly, it is necessary to give some consideration to the reliability of anecdotal information in establishing the extent and quality of Roman élite bilingualism.[41] There are shortcomings in such evidence, two of which I mention here; another will come up in the next section. First, it is possible that Romans in the Republican period were active in constructing for themselves a reputation for fluent control of Greek, in defiance of the reality. I am not inclined though to dismiss the evidence of these anecdotes *en masse*. Some of the stories in our sources are so circumstantial that they must be believed. Cicero undoubtedly addressed the senate in Syracuse in Greek,[42] and Apollonius Molo must have spoken Greek in the Roman senate, thereby exercising the comprehension skills of the senators. A second inadequacy of such evidence is that it concerns a limited number of individuals, and cannot give any real idea of the proportion of educated Romans who were fluent Greek speakers, or (e.g.) of the extent of bilingualism among women as compared with men.[43] I quote Jocelyn (1973: 64): 'Deductions about the general level of Greek knowledge among upper-class Romans on the basis of Cicero's correspondence with Atticus are ... dubious ... The tone of the prefaces to the philosophical dialogues suggests that, at the time these were written, Greek was a special accomplishment and that more men claimed than really possessed an effective knowledge of the language and its literature ... The many anecdotes related in extant literature about the

---

[41] Horsfall (1979) and Dubuisson (1992) to some extent take opposite sides on this issue.

[42] Cicero was also capable of writing an artificial literary Greek, as he did in two letters to Atticus apparently as a form of coding (see above, n. 19 and below, 3.III.3).

[43] For evidence concerning women, see below, 3.XII.6.

knowledge of individuals . . . have a tone indicating that such knowledge was not thought to be commonplace.'

It emerges from this section that, while anecdotal evidence concerning the bilingualism of the Roman élite has its interest, it is difficult to interpret, because tendentious assertions cannot always be distinguished from objective linguistic statements. It seems to me pointless to engage in a debate about the extent and quality of élite Roman bilingualism. Bilingualism existed, no doubt in many degrees of competence, but its extent cannot be determined.

III.1 Non-élite bilingualism

Bilingualism among those below the intellectual/social élite, whether involving Latin and Greek, Latin and another language, or other combinations of languages, has not received the same attention as the bilingualism of the upper classes. Yet it is well attested. It must be acknowledged that the notion of a 'sub-élite' is a vague one. I include within this category all speakers of Latin (and another language) who there is reason to believe did not belong to the small class which had received a literary education. The term is no more than a catch-all meant to embrace a diversity of educational and social levels.

A good deal of the non-literary evidence discussed in this book will concern such sub-élite bilinguals, and I merely introduce the category here without going into detail; as a preliminary illustration of the linguistic output of such persons I would cite the Christian inscription *ILCV* 4463 Βηρατιους Νικατορας [*sic*: = *Nicagoras*] Λαζαρίη καὶ ᾽Ιουλίη καὶ ᾽Ονησίμη κον φιλιους βενε μερεντες ὁ βίος ταῦτα, which, given its language mixture, was the work of a bilingual, and given its substandard Latin sections and the use of Greek script, was produced by someone who had not had a literary education (see below, v and 3.v.1 for a discussion of the inscription). The mass of bilingual speakers of less than the highest educational standards was not homogeneous. I will move between slaves on the one hand (though slaves too might be well educated) and local provincial worthies on the other, but without excluding educated bilinguals when the topic justifies their inclusion; there will however be no particular concentration on high literature as a source of information. It is my intention to be as wide ranging as possible in seeking out bilingualism beyond the literary classes, instead of restricting the scope of the book by imposing a rigid definition of the social classes to be included.

Concentration on anecdotal evidence for bilingualism (see further above) to the exclusion of primary sources can have the effect of portraying only the élite as second-language learners. Dubuisson's article (1992), for example, presents on the one hand upper-class Romans as learners of Greek, and on the other hand slaves as basically Greek-speaking (see 189 on Juv. 11.148, a passage which does indeed imply, no doubt with a degree of exaggeration, that slaves were often addressed in Greek (see also below, 3.V, n. 130 on this passage)). But if the Greek inscriptions of Rome (and indeed the Latin inscriptions) are examined in detail,[44] evidence emerges for ordinary Greeks learning Latin and showing some concern about the presentation of their linguistic identity.

IV ROMANS, GREEKS AND OTHERS AS LANGUAGE LEARNERS

In the material assembled in section III it was mainly Romans who were second-language learners (of Greek). But in the Roman period those who spoke or wrote Latin as their mother tongue and Greek as an acquired language represent only one of many categories of bilinguals. Latin speakers learnt languages other than Greek, and speakers of various languages other than Greek picked up some Latin. In the next chapter evidence will be discussed of Latin in contact with a variety of languages, and the discussion will introduce bilingualism of different types. For the moment, as a corrective to any false impressions which might have been created by section III, I offer a piece of evidence for language learning of another type.

I stress first that, just as there is evidence for Romans learning Greek, so there is abundant evidence for Greeks learning Latin (and I refer here to the élite as well as those lower-class Greeks at Rome mentioned in the previous section). It has long been the conventional opinion that Greeks were indifferent or hostile to the learning of foreign languages,[45] but recently it has been shown that that view is far from the truth. Latin in particular was widely known, as has been demonstrated by Holford-Strevens (1993) and on a massive scale by Rochette (1997a).[46] The whole of Rochette's book deals with the issue, but I would draw attention particularly to pp. 69–82 ('Les Romains et le latin vus par les Grecs'),

---

[44] Some such inscriptions will be discussed later in this chapter, and others in Chapter 3 (on code-switching).

[45] See the discussion of Rochette (1997a: 69–83).

[46] Note too Colvin (1999: 70): 'One thing that emerges from the *Anabasis* is that when their environment demanded it, Greeks were just as ready as anybody else to learn the languages of their neighbours' (some evidence cited).

pp. 83–143 ('Le latin dans les relations officielles avec l'Orient'), and above all Chapter 3 (pp. 211–56), a prosopographical study of Greeks known for their knowledge of Latin, from the Republic to the late Empire. The material bearing on this issue dealt with in the present book will be rather different from that of Holford-Strevens and Rochette: not (for the most part) anecdotal, but primary. Primary evidence richly documents Greeks using Latin.

I mention here just one anecdote which concerns knowledge of Latin among members of the Greek educated classes (Gell. 19.9). The passage has been discussed by Rochette (1997a: 267–9), but in connection with the Greeks' knowledge of Latin literature. It has as well a sociolinguistic dimension. Gellius tells of a dinner party, no doubt at Rome, attended by the Spanish *rhetor* Antonius Julianus, whose Latin had a Spanish accent: 19.9.2 *uenerat tum nobiscum ad eandem cenam Antonius Iulianus rhetor, docendis publice iuuenibus magister,* **Hispano ore** *florentisque homo facundiae et rerum litterarumque ueterum peritus.* Also present were some Greeks, described as expert in Latin literature: 7 *tum Graeci plusculi, qui in eo conuiuio erant, homines amoeni et nostras quoque litteras haut incuriose docti.* The Greeks turn on Julianus, attacking him as barbarous and *agrestis*, as of Spanish origin, and as a *clamator*. Given Julianus' *os Hispanum*, as already introduced by Gellius to the context, and the Greeks' concentration on his manner of speech, it is natural to see in the accusations an allusion to the man's regional accent. *Agrestis* is not unusual in reference to regional accents of Latin, as for example at *SHA, Hadr.* 3.1 *quaesturam gessit Traiano quater et Articuleio consulibus, in qua cum orationem imperatoris in senatu* **agrestius pronuntians** *risus esset, usque ad summam peritiam et facundiam Latinis operam dedit*[47] and Sen. *Contr.* 1 *praef.* 16 *nulla umquam illi cura uocis exercendae fuit: illum fortem et* **agrestem** *et Hispanae consuetudinis morem non poterat dediscere.*

There can be no doubting the Greeks' competence in Latin, but there is more to be extracted from the passage. It is a curiosity that Greeks, who will almost by definition have had an accent in their own Latin (on the Greek accent in Latin, see below, 4.v.1.1), should have felt no unease about mocking, if only obliquely, the accent of a man who was, after all, (unlike them) a native speaker of Latin. But it has been observed by sociolinguists that foreign accents are sometimes evaluated more highly than the regional accents of native speakers of a language. Hamers and Blanc (1989: 131) report a study which showed that 'English spoken with a French foreign accent was rated in a very favourable way, as superior to

---

[47] Note that the regional accent is mocked.

any regional accent and much superior to an Italian or German foreign accent.' The Greek accent in Latin probably had some prestige.[48]

The learning of languages other than Greek and Latin will come up in the next chapter, but here it is worth noting the model of second-language acquisition presented by Ovid in his exile poetry. The poems are full of curious linguistic assertions. He claimed variously not to be understood by the Getae and others or not to understand them (*Trist.* 5.10.37–40 *barbarus hic ego sum, qui non intellegor ulli, / et rident stolidi uerba Latina Getae; / meque palam de me tuto mala saepe loquuntur, / forsitan obiciunt exiliumque mihi*; cf. 3.11.9, 3.14.39–40, 4.1.89–90), to have partly forgotten his Latin (5.12.57 *ipse mihi uideor iam dedidicisse Latine*; cf. 3.14.45–6, 5.7.58),[49] to have been conscious or fearful of the intrusion of foreign words into his Latin (5.7.59–60 *nec dubito quin sint et in hoc non pauca libello / barbara*, 3.14.49–50 *crede mihi, timeo ne sint inmixta Latinis / inque meis scriptis Pontica uerba legas*), to have been afraid that the *barbara terra* in which he was might cause him to use incorrect Latin (3.1.17–18 *siqua uidebuntur casu non dicta Latine, / in qua scribebat, barbara terra fuit*), to have been compelled to say many things 'in the Sarmatian way' (5.7.56 *Sarmatico cogor plurima more loqui*), to have learnt to speak Getic and Sarmatian (5.12.58 *nam didici Getice Sarmaticeque loqui*), to be contemplating the possibility of writing 'in Getic measures', such was the din around him of Thracian and Scythian (3.14.47–8 *Threicio Scythicoque fere circumsonor ore, / et uideor Geticis scribere posse modis*), and finally to have written a *libellus* in the Getic language, with barbarian words 'in our measures' (*Pont.* 4.13.19–20 *a, pudet, et Getico scripsi sermone libellum, / structaque sunt nostris barbara uerba modis*). He also asserted that he had to use gestures to make himself understood (*Trist.* 5.10.35–6 *exercent illi sociae commercia linguae: / per gestum res est significanda mihi*).[50]

It is difficult to know what to make of these inconsistencies. Ovid does however seem to have been constructing an image of himself as a gradual learner,[51] eventually achieving mastery of a third language, though it is

---

[48] There are indeed a few bits of evidence for the affecting of Greek mannerisms by Latin speakers, or at least for a favourable attitude to Greek sounds. On this subject see the appendix to this chapter.

[49] A topos: see Solon frg. 36 West (drawn to my attention by David Bain). Note too Jerome, *Epist.* 29.7: so immersed was Jerome in Hebrew that his Latin was becoming 'rusty'. See further 2.IX for another example.

[50] It is of interest that, though Sittl devoted a chapter of his book on gestures (1890: 211–24) to sign language, he did not discuss this passage or the phenomenon of communication by gestures in a foreign country. For some allusions to the practice in Greek, see Aesch. *Ag.* 1060–1, Xen. *Anab.* 4.5.33.

[51] Cf. Lozovan (1958: 397); on the ethnic background to Tomi, see e.g. Lambrino (1958), but above all Syme (1978: 164); also Millar (1968: 126), id. (1993b: 10) (on Tomi as a Greek rather than a Getic town).

distinctly odd that various conflicting assertions about different degrees of competence seem to be presented in a cluster in book 5 of the *Tristia* (dated to AD 12).[52] Ovid's linguistic assertions in the exile poetry (and there are more of them) may be based on pure fantasy or fabrication,[53] and they certainly tell us nothing of substance either about the linguistic situation in Tomi (see further below, IX) or about Ovid's multilingualism, but they do reveal a Roman's attitudes to the problems of communication in a foreign place and to the possibility of second-language learning. They constitute a construct of the stages in second-language acquisition, with some recognition of the influence of those stages on the first language. We can distinguish (1) communication by gestures; (2) the picking up of some foreign words, which enter the first language; (3) the intrusion of non-specific 'interference' into the first language; (4) partial use of the second language (note *plurima* at 5.7.56); (5) fluent bilingualism. It will be an aim of this book to discuss most of these stages in action through the medium of primary sources. The idea, for example, that one language may be 'corrupted' by another will be seen in Chapter 4 (V.1.1, p. 435). It is of some interest how Ovid portrays his alleged new fluency in Getic.[54] He does not speak of linguistic skill as such, but rather of his literary skill in the second language. Élite Romans do from time to time show some interest in communication skills, pure and simple, in a second language, but they perhaps found it difficult to disentangle the ideals of fluency in the second language, and command of the culture expressed through that language. Thus, for example, Gellius (19.9) tells us nothing about the Latin of the Greeks at the symposium (see above), though manner of speech is partly at issue in the context, but concentrates on their learning in Latin literary culture. So Ovid's 'bilingualism' manifests itself not merely in an ability to communicate with the Getae, but in an impressive literary performance in the second language.

V CODE-SWITCHING, INTERFERENCE AND BORROWING

The terms 'code-switching', 'interference' and 'borrowing', which are used with variable meanings in linguistic literature, recur throughout this book, and some definitions must be given at the outset. The issues

---

[52] See Syme (1978: 39) on the date of *Trist.* 5.

[53] For the bibliography on Ovid's 'bilingualism', see Rochette (1997a: 54 nn. 29–31). Note in particular Della Corte (1976).

[54] Notice Syme's ironical observation (1978: 16–17): 'Ovid had been able to acquire a fluency in speaking foreign languages beyond parallel among the Romans in any age.'

involved are complex and little agreement has been reached among students of bilingualism. Note Romaine (1995: 180): 'Problems of terminology continue to plague the study of language contact phenomena with terms such as code-switching, mixing, borrowing not being used by all researchers in the same way or even defined at all.' Code-switching and its relationship to the other phenomena will be discussed in greater detail in Chapter 3, and I here merely introduce the term and offer a few comments.

Code-switching is usually described along these lines: 'the alternate use of two languages or linguistic varieties within the same utterance or during the same conversation' (Hoffmann 1991: 110): cf., e.g. Milroy and Muysken (1995: 7): 'the alternate use by bilinguals of two or more languages in the same conversation'. I generally use the term here to describe a full-blown switch from one language into another within one person's utterance or piece of writing.[55] The existence of code-switching is sometimes acknowledged in ancient anecdotes or comments.[56] Cicero seems to condemn the practice several times (*Off.* 1.111 *ut enim sermone eo debemus uti qui notus est nobis, ne ut quidam Graeca uerba inculcantes iure optimo rideamur, sic . . . ,*[57] *Tusc.* 1.15 [ostentatious refusal to quote Epicharmus in Greek] *dicam, si potero, Latine. scis enim me Graece loqui in Latino sermone non plus solere quam in Graeco Latine. – et recte quidem . . .* [Latin translation of Epicharmus] *. . . iam adgnosco Graecum.*),[58] though the first passage might just be taken as referring to borrowing (on the difference between code-switching and borrowing, see below).[59] Horace notes the presence of what I take to include code-switching in Lucilius (*Sat.* 1.10.20–1 *at magnum fecit, quod uerbis Graeca Latinis / miscuit,* 'but his achievement was great, in that he mingled Greek words with Latin'), and the discussion of language

---

[55] Other types of alternation have also been called 'code-switching', though they will not be of much significance in this book. Note Milroy and Muysken (1995: 7): 'Sometimes switching occurs between the turns of different speakers in the conversation [for which see below, 3.VI.1, p. 386 with cross references], sometimes between utterances within a single turn, and sometimes even within a single utterance.' It is this last type that will be my main concern.

[56] See also Jocelyn (1999: 89–94).

[57] Loeb: 'For as we ought to employ our mother-tongue [rendering *innatus* rather than the transmitted *notus*: the point of *notus* here has been questioned (see Dyck (1996: 282) ad loc.)], lest, like certain people who are continually dragging in Greek words, we draw well-deserved ridicule upon ourselves, so . . .'.

[58] Loeb: 'I shall give it [i.e. a *sententia* of Epicharmus] if I can in Latin: you know I am no more in the habit of using Greek in speaking Latin than of using Latin in speaking Greek.' A. 'Quite right. . . . Now I recognise the Greek.'

[59] Dyck (1996: 281) ad loc. suggests that when Cicero wrote these words he might have been thinking of T. Albucius, who, as we saw (above, III) was ridiculed in Lucilius (88–94, as quoted by Cicero himself at *Fin.* 1.9: see 3.IV.1) for his habit of using Greek. If so the allusion at *Off.* 1.111 would definitely be to full-blown switches into Greek, and not to integrated loan-words.

mixing goes on for some ten lines. The practice of Lucilius is compared with that of the bilingual people of Canusium (29–30 *patriis intermiscere petita / uerba foris malis, Canusini more bilinguis*, 'would you prefer to intermingle with native words words procured from abroad, in the manner of the bilingual Canusine?'), where Oscan and Greek (and Latin as well?) were presumably mixed (see below, 2.II.5).[60] Code-switching does occur in Lucilius, but there is evidence even in such a fragmentary text that some of it is not used by the poet in his own person, but put into the mouths of various characters and in fact ridiculed (see 3.III.2, IV.I)). Juvenal castigates women who switch into Greek at every opportunity (6.184–97). Martial writes disparagingly of an upper-class woman who switches into Greek in the bedroom (10.68) (see below, 3.V on these passages). Tacitus describes an altercation between two German brothers, one of whom kept switching into Latin as the exchange became more heated: Tac. *Ann.* 2.10.3 *cernebatur contra minitabundus Arminius proeliumque denuntians; nam **pleraque Latino sermone interiaciebat**, ut qui Romanis in castris ductor popularium meruisset* ('. . . he was interspersing many remarks in the Latin language, as one who had served in the Roman camp as the leader of his fellow-countrymen'). The fact that Arminius had served in the Roman army as an officer in charge of his own countrymen explains his knowledge of Latin (foreign units in which at least some men remained monolingual in their mother tongue could only be commanded by those who knew Latin as well as the mother tongue),[61] but it does not, as Tacitus appears to think, explain why he employed code-switching on this occasion. One can only guess about the circumstances. Of the two brothers, it was Arminius the code-switcher who was

---

[60] See below, p. 370 n. 314 for the continuing popularity of Greek names among some families in the town at a much later date, after the place was Romanised.

[61] It cannot be assumed that all soldiers in the Roman army, least of all auxiliaries, could understand Latin. Tacitus several times comments on the linguistic diversity as an impediment to cohesion: *Hist.* 2.37.2 *neque aut exercitus linguis moribusque dissonos in hunc consensum potuisse coalescere*, 3.33.2 *utque exercitu uario linguis moribus, cui ciues socii externi interessent, diuersae cupidines et aliud cuique fas nec quicquam inlicitum.* Similarly ps.-Hyginus *Met. castr.* 43 says that irregular units should receive orders in their own language, and orally: *symmacharios et reliquas nationes quotiens per strigas distribuimus, non plus quam tripertiti esse debebunt nec longe abalterutrum ut uiua tessera suo uocabulo citationes audiant.* There are also bits and pieces of evidence for some maintenance of their linguistic traditions by foreign units. Tacitus (*Hist.* 2.22.1) refers to a song of German cohorts (*aduersus temere subeuntes cohortes Germanorum, cantu truci et more patrio nudis corporibus super umeros scuta quatientium*), and it seems to be implied by the last clause of Tac. *Germ.* 3.1 that such *cantus* had words (*sunt illis haec quoque carmina quorum relatu, quem baritum uocant, accendunt animos futuraeque pugnae fortunam ipso cantu augurantur*), despite Anderson (1938) ad loc. Ammianus describes this song at 16.12.43 in terms that imply that it was without words, but at 31.7.11 the Goths are said to have praised their ancestors in this way. On the maintenance of Palmyrene by Palmyrenes serving in the Roman army, see 2.VII.2, p. 256.

anti-Roman; perhaps he wished to demonstrate that Romanisation (and the brother Flavus, who was still in the army, must have known Latin as well) did not necessarily entail the abandonment of pro-German feelings. Finally an anecdote in the *SHA* about the future emperor Maximinus Thrax has him using a form of Latin that was close to Thracian, a reflection no doubt of his constant switches into Thracian because he had poor competence in Latin (*Max.* 2.5; see 3.II for this passage and this type of code-switching).

Code-switching is sometimes classified into three types, tag-switching, inter-sentential and intra-sentential, as particularly by Poplack (1980).[62] 'Tag-switching involves the insertion of a tag in one language into an utterance which is otherwise entirely in the other language, e.g. *you know*, *I mean*, etc.' (Romaine 1995: 122). Exclamations or interjections fall into this category.[63] Speakers in Plautus (particularly slaves and other lower-class characters) and Petronius sometimes switch into Greek in such circumstances (see also below, 3.V on Juvenal's female code-switcher). Note, for example, in Plautus ναὶ τὰν Κόραν (*Capt.* 881), μὰ τὸν Ἀπόλλω (*Capt.* 880, *Most.* 973), ναὶ γάρ (*Bacch.* 1162, *Pseud.* 483) (not in Attic), ὦ Ζεῦ (*Cas.* 731, *Pseud.* 443).[64] At least one of the freedmen in Petronius (Hermeros) speaks a form of Latin which must have been meant to suggest a Greek or bilingual background. Hermeros switches into Greek especially in exclamations (37.9 *babae babae* < βαβαὶ βαβαί, 58.2 *io* = ἰώ, 58.3 *euge* = εὖγε, 58.7 *deuro de* = δεῦρο δή).[65] In epitaphs, particularly but not exclusively from Rome, it is not uncommon for a Latin text to be either preceded or followed by a Greek tag, the tag generally having formulaic status in Greek epitaphs; conversely, a Greek text may have a Latin tag or formula. There is perhaps a qualitative difference between at least some 'tags' of this type and (e.g.) single-word exclamations (the latter requiring no competence in the second language whatsoever), and for that reason it might be felt that tags should be classified as 'inter-sentential' switches (for which see below),[66] but I include them here because they are so distinctive in type and in their placement.

[62] See also e.g. Romaine (1995: 122).
[63] See e.g. Giacalone Ramat (1995: 47), Gardner-Chloros (1995: 85).
[64] Details about these various usages can be found in Shipp (1953).
[65] See Salonius (1927: 22–4), Boyce (1991: 92); also Smith (1975) on 37.9, 58.3. Exclamations do not exhaust the Greek words (some of which should probably be called 'borrowings') put into the mouth of Hermeros. Note 37.4 *topanta*, 37.6 *saplutus*, *lupatria* (on which see below 4.II), 37.9 *babaecalis* (apparently of Greek origin, but the details are obscure), 58.7 *Athana* (a Doric form, if the reading is right, and thus suggestive of the south Italian origin of the man: see 2.II.5).
[66] Hoffmann (1991: 104) indeed prefers to classify tag-switching as a whole as a form of inter-sentential switching.

Note, for example, *IGUR* 294 (Greek inscription with *dis manibus* at the end), 298 (long Latin epitaph, followed by ἀνθρ<ώ>πινα), 308 (Latin epitaph followed by transliterated Greek: *eupsychi <tecnon, udis athan>atos* = εὐψύχι τέκνον, οὐδὶς ἀθάνατος), 310 (as 308, but the Greek tag, with τέκουσα rather than τέκνον, is in Greek script), 489 (Latin epitaph, followed by χαῖρε, καὶ σύ), 564 (Latin epitaph, followed by νόθε μευ εὐψύχι), 728 (Latin epitaph, followed by *Palladi, tauta* = Παλλάδι, ταῦτα),[67] 762 (Προκόπι, ταῦτα), 804 (Latin epitaph, then Ἀφροδείσιε χαῖρε, καὶ σύ), 852 (θ(εοῖς) χ(θονίοις) instead of *dis manibus*, then a Latin epitaph), 893 (*cyria chere* = κυρία χαῖρε, then a Latin epitaph). Note too *IGPorto* 74 (Latin epitaph, followed by εἰρήνη αὐτῷ). In the transliterated Latin inscription *ILCV* 4908 = *CJI* 266 = Noy (1995), 287 (Αιλια Πατρικια Τουλλιο Ειρηναιο κονιουγι βενεμερεντι φηκιτ διὰ βίο), the last two words represent διὰ βίου. In Jewish inscriptions from Rome, whether in Greek or Latin script, διὰ βίου in various spellings commonly turns up.[68] Cf. *ILCV* 4908A *Tettius Rufinus Melitius uicxit annis LXXXV, ia biou* (*ia* = *za* = *dia?*), *ILCV* 4937; also *TLL* v.1.939 s.v. *diabius* (adjective). Sometimes, alternatively, a short formula in one language is embedded *within* an inscription, as distinct from placed at the beginning or end (for a discussion of this feature and another possible case, see below, 3.v.1). Thus in a Bulgarian inscription (*IGBulg.* iv.2116) the Latin expression *pos(u)it memoriam* turns up in a text that is otherwise entirely Greek: ἀγαθῇ τύχῃ. *posit memoriam* Επτ[α]κε[ν]θος Διζ[α]κενθου ζήσας καλῶ[ς] τὸν βίον...I note in passing that the phrase with which this last text begins is sometimes found at the head of Latin inscriptions in Greek-speaking areas (see below, vii.4.2 (8)). On 'formula-switching' of the type seen in *posit memoriam* see further below, 3.v.1, 7.iv.6.

Such tag- or formula-switching is also attested into ancient languages other than Greek and Latin. For example, in the Jewish funerary inscriptions from Venusia Hebrew tags are often attached to Greek or Latin texts (often 'shalom' in Hebrew characters). For Greek with a Hebrew tag, see Noy (1993), 48, 70, 71, 72 (σάλωμ, in this case Hebrew transliterated into Greek letters: see below, vii.2.4), 76, 77, 111, and for Latin with such tags, see 61 (Latin transliterated into Greek characters, the tag meaning 'peace to Israel, amen'), 63, 80 (here the name of the deceased as well as 'shalom' is in Hebrew characters), 85 ('peace to their resting place'),

---

[67] The name is a *signum*, and ταῦτα stands for ὁ βίος ταῦτα 'such is life' (see further 4.v.2.12). For this example and for other such *signa* in acclamations, see Kajanto (1966: 72). The *signum* is in the vocative not the genitive.

[68] See Leiwo (1995b: 299).

86 (more extended Hebrew formulae, this time in the middle of the Latin text), 87, 89 ('peace to her resting place'), 107 (much the same formula).[69] At Venusia Hebrew is virtually confined to tags (but see 82 and 82a). It is highly likely that Hebrew was no longer genuinely current. If so tag-switching may have lingered on as no more than a fading reminiscence of a lost language (see further below, 2.VIII).[70] Similarly Gardner-Chloros (1995: 85) implies that some Alsatians who scarcely know Alsatian retain a connection with their linguistic roots by stereotyped tag-switching when speaking French.[71]

Such switches are relatively straightforward and easy to interpret com-pared with some intra-sentential switches. They were facilitated by the highly formulaic character of epitaphs. The client/deceased will either have been monolingual (say in Latin) or bilingual. If he was monolin-gual or primarily Latin-speaking, then a switch into Greek might reflect a certain cachet attached to the presence in the epitaph of a formula from the language of high culture. Or a Greek might have a Latin tag attached to a Greek epitaph to associate it with the public language of the state. Code-switching is sometimes 'used to express group identity, i.e. belonging to a bilingual community' (Hoffmann (1991: 116); see further below, 3.IV–V), and that is one possible explanation for the addition of a tag in the second language. The client (on behalf of the deceased) might wish to advertise the bilingualism of the deceased, or his cultural/ethnic identity. By a switch into Hebrew Jews were effectively symbolising their Jewishness even if the language had been all but forgotten. If display was not the motive, it might have been felt that a speaker of both lan-guages would only be properly laid to rest if the funerary formulae of both languages were represented in the epitaph.

Inter-sentential switches occur at clause or sentence boundaries, such that, for example, one clause is in one language and the next in another. It is ob-vious that tag-switches of the type illustrated above from Greco-Roman epitaphs could be classified within this wider category. A good example from the Christian community at Rome, in which the switches come at

---

[69] On the significance of these various formulae, see Noy (1999).

[70] Note Sevenster (1968: 88) on such tags: 'My opinion is that such words and expressions, also in their Hebrew characters, quite possibl[y] had become sacred signs and sounds which were considered fitting in a funerary inscription, even though they were no longer used in everyday life.' See further Sevenster (1968: 102, 106, 136). In the last passage he comments (in reference to 'shalom' in an inscription) on the possibility 'that such a widely known Hebrew word was always preserved, even when that language was no longer properly known or regularly spoken'. See also Noy (1999).

[71] 'There are speakers in Strasbourg whose only form of switching consists in adding the Alsatian tag 'gel?' [= 'isn't that so, eh?'] to the end of each French sentence.'

the ends of clauses rather than sentences, can be found at *ILCV* 4463, which was quoted without discussion above, III.1: Βηρατιους Νικατορας [*sic*: = *Nicagoras*] // Λαζαρίη καὶ 'Ιουλίη καὶ 'Ονησίμη // κον φιλιους βενε μερεντες // ὁ βίος ταῦτα. There is a switch at every colon boundary, as marked by double obliques (see below).

Intra-sentential switches, finally, take place within the boundaries of the sentence or clause. Cicero's letters to Atticus are full of such phenomena, as for example *Att.* 1.14.3 *nosti illas* ληκύθους, where the switch is intra-phrasal. Switching may be so extensive in the speech of a bilingual that it is virtually impossible to assign an utterance to a base language (so *ILCV* 4463 above).[72] Poplack (1980: e.g. 589) describes switching of this type as 'intimate', 'since a code-switched segment, and those around it, must conform to the underlying syntactic rules of two languages which bridge constituents and link them together grammatically'. By contrast 'tag-like switches', such as fillers, interjections, quotations and idiomatic expressions (see above) are called 'emblematic'. They have sometimes been regarded not as true instances of code-switching, but rather as constituting 'an emblematic part of the speaker's *monolingual* style' (Poplack (1980: 589, my italics). Emblematic switches may be used to symbolise to outsiders (as distinct from members of a bilingual in-group, who are said to prefer switching of the more 'intimate' type among themselves)[73] an aspect of the identity which the speaker is claiming for himself. They can be used freely anywhere in a sentence without danger of violating any grammatical rules.[74] The notion of 'emblematic' switching has recently been applied to the study of Latin literature by Wenskus (1998) (see further below, 3.III.10).

Another recent classification, associated with Muysken (e.g. 1995: 177),[75] is between *alternation*, 'where a bilingual can best be seen as speaking now one language, now the other', *insertions*, 'where elements of one language are set within the framework provided by the other', and *leaks*, 'where relatively insignificant items from the psychologically dominant language infiltrate into discourse from [*sic*, = 'in'] the other one'.[76]

I illustrate these three types. First, the term *alternation* could be applied to the epitaph *ILCV* 4463 quoted above. The name of the dedicator of the inscription, Veratius Nicagoras, seems to be intended as Latin, to judge by the -ους ending, which is the standard transliteration of the Latin -*us*

---

[72] See the discussion of Romaine (1995: 144–9); also Wenskus (1995: 172).
[73] See e.g. Poplack (1980: 589–90, 595).   [74] See Poplack (1980: 589, 596).
[75] Cf. Bentahila and Davies (1998: 49).
[76] The quotations are taken from Bentahila and Davies, (1998: 49).

ending; the digraph ου was used to render either the short or long *u* of Latin in the imperial period (see e.g. below, VII.2.2, p. 51).[77] The next section, comprising the names of the deceased in the dative, has some non-standard morphology,[78] but is manifestly intended as Greek, as the connective καί shows. The third section is in Latin, though Latin with two odd features. First, *con* governs the accusative rather than the ablative, and that places the inscription well down the social scale (cf., e.g. *P. Mich.* VIII.471.22 *con tirones*, in a letter of Claudius Terentianus). Secondly, *filious* is inflected with the Greek accusative ending rather than the Latin (see further below, VII.2.3, 4.V.3.4 for this feature). The alternative transliteration of the Latin -*os* was by means of *omega* (which captured the length of the vowel) + *sigma*, as at *IGUR* 1671 κυι σηκου τουλιτ **αννως** XXV, *CIL* VI.15450 **ανως** βιξιτ μικου XXII. Finally, there is a Greek tag at the end = 'such is life'. Constant alternations of this type, apparently unmotivated, have been noted, for example, among fluent bilinguals in a Puerto Rican community of New York.[79]

Secondly, *insertions*. In Cicero's letters to Atticus the base language is overwhelmingly Latin, but there are frequent intra-phrasal insertions, the motivations of which I will discuss in Chapter 3. Note e.g. *Att.* 1.14.3, quoted above.

Thirdly, *leaks*. This phenomenon might be illustrated from a receipt (*SB* III.1.6304 = *CPL* 193) written in the Latin language but Greek letters which will be discussed at length later in this chapter (see VII.2.3). In the last but one line (ακτουμ καστρις κλάσσης πραιτωριαι = *actum castris classis praetoriae*) the word for 'fleet' does not have the correct Latin -*is* genitive ending. The word is Latin in origin, but it had been borrowed by Greek, and in Greek papyri it regularly has as here the -ης genitive (see below, p. 57). The writer of the text no doubt thought the word was Greek, and familiar with the established Greek inflection he in effect switched languages, using the Greek form instead of the Latin. One might say that in his attempt to copy out a piece of Latin, at this point his first language 'leaked' into the Latin. It must though be acknowledged that this type of 'code-switching' is virtually impossible to distinguish from (morphological) interference (on which see below).

The distinction between intra-sentential switching on the one hand, and *borrowing* and *interference* on the other, has proved difficult to define.[80] If a speaker/writer of language A introduces, say, a noun from language B

---

[77] See Gignac (1976: 217–18).
[78] See Gignac (1981: 3–4) on nouns originally in -α with forms in -ης, -η in later Greek.
[79] See Poplack (1980, 1988).   [80] See, e.g. Romaine (1995: 124).

and qualifies it with an adjective from language A, has he engaged in *code-switching* or *borrowing*? The answer to this question, it may be argued, will depend partly on the degree of integration of the transferred term into the receiving language.[81] Latin was full of Greek loan-words thoroughly integrated into the language, morphologically or phonetically or semantically or in all three ways, and freely used even by monolingual Latin speakers. It would be perverse, for example, to maintain that a Latin writer using the word *machina* was switching codes. The word is integrated morphologically, in that it has a full set of Latin endings, and phonetically, in that it displays in the second syllable the results of a Latin phonetic development (vowel weakening). If on the other hand someone writing Latin were to refer to his brother as ἀδελφός (using either Greek script or a transliteration), one might reasonably say that a switch of codes had taken place: in no sense had ἀδελφός been accepted into the Latin language. Morphological criteria are revealing in distinguishing a switch of codes from borrowing. If a Greek word is given a Greek inflection in a Latin text, it is usually in my opinion justifiable to refer to the phenomenon as code-switching: the writer has switched momentarily into a different linguistic system. If on the other hand the Greek word in the Latin text is given a Latin inflection, its integration is greater, and it may well have been widely current in Latin; the evidence of the distribution of the word in surviving texts can be drawn on to test this possibility. Another form of integration alluded to above was semantic. If a Greek word displays in its Latin incarnation a meaning not found in Greek itself, one possible explanation might be that it had taken on a life of its own in the second language. It must be stressed that these criteria are by no means infallible. It is well within the bounds of possibility that (e.g.) the very first person to transfer a word from Greek into Latin might have adapted it morphologically and phonetically to the recipient language, but it need not for that reason qualify to be described as an *integrated* loan-word. The absence of attestations of the word in earlier literature and in later writers might in such a case inform the observer that the term was an *ad hoc* transfer, and arguably therefore a case of code-switching. Hard and fast rules cannot be laid down for distinguishing between code-switching and borrowing, but I would maintain that the application of the criteria for determining integration listed above will usually allow a distinction to be made between a full-blown change of languages in a written text, and the employment of an integrated term

---

[81] This issue has been much discussed. See, e.g., Poplack and Sankoff (1984), Muysken (1995: 190–1).

of external origin. Where indeclinable words are concerned, such as the Greek exclamations put into the mouth of Hermeros by Petronius (see above, p. 21), the morphological criterion usually cannot be applied, but if an exclamation is rare or unattested elsewhere in the recipient language (as is the case with some of Hermeros' terms), then it may still be reasonable to speak of a switch of codes. Exclamatory words had a habit of entering Latin from Greek (a nice case in point is *sophos*, as e.g. at Petron. 40.1, Mart. 1.3.7),[82] and it is usually impossible to determine how speakers would have regarded them. Did the man who exclaimed *sophos* at a declamation feel that he was speaking Greek or Latin?: quite possibly Greek, as the adverbial ending is Greek.[83]

Integrated borrowings of the type referred to above are often used by those who do not even know the language in which the borrowed terms originated.[84] By contrast in the terminology that I will adopt the presence of *interference* phenomena (as indeed code-switching) in an utterance or text implies that the speaker/writer is bilingual, if only imperfectly so. If a speaker or writer of languages A and B in speaking or writing, say, language A imposes on a word or group of words of language A a morpheme or sound or syntactic structure or spelling from B, then it may sometimes be justifiable to say that morphological, phonetic, syntactic or orthographical *interference* has occurred, though even under these circumstances the terms *code-switching* or *borrowing* are sometimes more appropriate. Much depends on the direction of transfer, whether from the writer's second (L2) to his first language (L1) or vice versa. I explain the distinction with a few morphological examples, starting with code-switching/borrowing and moving on to interference.

If a writer who is a primary speaker of language A (say Latin) imposes a morpheme from B (Greek) on a word from A, the transfer may be described as a case either of intra-sentential *code-switching within a word boundary*[85] or alternatively of *morphological borrowing*. Cicero's humorous coinage *facteon* (*Att.* 1.16.13), formed on a Latin base with the Greek -τέος suffix, should be put in this class, as it is a deliberate creation in his first language by one who had a fluent command of a second language, Greek. The 'facetious hybrid' (Shackleton Bailey) in this case follows directly on a Greek verb of the same formation: φιλοσοφητέον, *id quod*

[82] See in general Hofmann (1951: 23–7).   [83] Cf. Wenskus (1998: 25).
[84] The Romans themselves were well aware of this. See Sen. *N.Q.* 5.16.4, and, on the concept of integrated loan-words among the Romans, see the discussion of Wenskus (1996: 234–6). An integrated Greek borrowing was sometimes (as in the passage of Seneca) referred to as having 'received the citizenship'.
[85] For this notion, see Romaine (1995: 123).

tu facis, et istos consulatus non flocci facteon. Similarly Ennius seems to have used the Homeric genitive -οιο in Latinised form *-oeo* in two Latin names: Quint. 1.5.12 *at in eadem uitii geminatione 'Mettoeo Fufetioeo' dicens Ennius poetico iure defenditur.*[86] Ovid in jest certainly did: Quint. 8.6.33 *at* οἴνοι' ἀγαθοῖο *ferimus in Graecis, Ouidius ioco cludit 'uinoeo bonoeo'.*[87] In these various cases the writer transfers into his primary (usually native) language a morpheme from the second language Greek. The process is conscious and deliberate, whatever the name we attach to it.

But equally the speaker/writer might be a learner of A with imperfect command of the second language, in which case the morphological switch may be a mark of incompetence (see below for examples) rather than of skilled transfer with literary pretensions; for this reason the term *interference* offers a useful contrast to *code-switching* or *morphological borrowing*. Morphological interference affects the writer's second language (in contrast to the borrowing or code-switching seen above in *uinoeo bonoeo*, which affects L1). Although one cannot with any confidence talk about the intention of a writer of an inscription, I see interference as unintentional and beyond the control of the writer, whereas code-switching (or borrowing, if we apply that term to the morphological phenomena cited in the previous paragraph) is often a manifestation of linguistic skill. There are many cases of morphological interference (in particular) in our material in texts written by Greek learners of Latin with imperfect competence in the second language.

What I mean by *interference* can be explained with a few further concrete examples. In connection with the receipt of Aeschines referred to above it was argued that, despite appearances, κλάσσης cannot (except historically) be treated as a Latin word with a Greek ending, because it was probably felt by Aeschines to be Greek. He inflected a 'Greek' word in a Latin text as Greek, and that I defined as code-switching (with some reservations). Earlier in the text, however, σεσκεντους (accusative plural) is a different matter. This is a Latin word in a Latin text with a Greek ending (see also above on φιλιους = *filious* for *filios*; contrast the phonetic transcription αυνως = *annos*, cited above). There has not been a full change of languages, which would have entailed the insertion of a Greek numeral, but rather Aeschines' dominant language has interfered morphologically with his attempt at Latin. See further below, 4.v.3.2–4.

---

[86] But see Mariotti (1988), and below, 4.II.

[87] I accept here the text of Radermacher (Teubner). Winterbottom (*OCT*) obelises liberally, while keeping the Ovidian phrase in the same form as Radermacher. But if we accept *uinoeo bonoeo*, the emendation to οἴνοι' ἀγαθοῖο is surely right.

I will return to code-switching in each of the next two chapters, and both interference and borrowing will come up frequently.

VI A FURTHER NOTE ON LOAN-WORDS

Loan-words from Greek into Latin and Latin into Greek have been extensively studied. On those of the first category the work of Biville (1990, 1995) has in some respects superseded earlier studies.[88] On Latin words in Greek I would cite the works of Wessely (1902), Meinersmann (1927), Cameron (1931), Cavenaile (1951, 1952), Rochette (1997a: 32–3), Cervenka-Ehrenstrasser and Diethart (1996–2000) and above all Daris (1991a) (cf. id. (1960)); see also the interesting remarks of Vaahtera (2000: 48), with some additional bibliography. For Latin loan-words in Greek veterinary writings, see Adams (1995b: 240 n. 2). Loan-words are relevant to bilingualism, in that the original transfer is usually effected by someone who knows the donor as well as the receiving language. But integrated loan-words, as was noted in the previous section, are also used by monolinguals who may not know the donor language and may even be unaware that a word is a borrowing.[89] These terms have little or nothing to tell us about the mechanisms of language contact. In this book only selective use will be made of the evidence offered by loans, partly because of the number of earlier studies, but mainly because of the limited relevance of lexical borrowing to what is intended to be an account of bilingualism in action. Loan-words will however sometimes be brought into the discussion for special reasons. For one thing, by no means all of the loans in Latin are from Greek, and a good deal will be said here about borrowings from a variety of other languages. Moreover in regions of the Empire at some remove from the centre, such as Britain, Gaul, Germany, Spain, Africa and Egypt, many loan-words from a variety of languages entered the Latin spoken locally, and these constitute evidence of regionalisms determined by local language contacts (see 4.V.2.2–6). Regional variation in Latin as brought about by bilingualism will be a theme of the book.

VII SOURCES OF INFORMATION

The question arises what primary material is relevant to the study of bilingualism in corpus languages, particularly the bilingualism of speakers down the educational scale. Here I introduce certain types of evidence,

[88] See Rochette (1997a: 19 n. 21) for some additional bibliography.
[89] Cf. Romaine (1995: 56).

which will come up again and again in the book. Among the categories
of texts there are four that should be singled out, namely bilingual texts,
transliterated texts, mixed-language texts, and finally texts which can be
described as implicitly reflecting bilingual situations. All of these categories will be introduced in the following sections with some illustration,
but it will be left to later chapters to exploit in full the evidence that they
have to offer. What I understand by *bilingual texts* is explained in detail in
the next section. *Transliterated texts* are written in a script appropriate to a
language different from the language of the text itself. Into this class fall
above all Latin texts written in Greek script. It is inconceivable that a
monolingual Latin speaker would have used Greek letters to write Latin.
A Latin text in Greek letters is bound to have been the work of someone
literate in Greek but using the Latin language, and as such it is virtually
certain to have been written by a bilingual, but perhaps a bilingual more
at home in Greek than in Latin. The determinants of transliteration
will be discussed at VII.2 below. *Mixed-language texts* combine two languages within a single utterance, often within a restricted space which
may be as short as the sentence, clause or even phrase (see above, V:
a 'mixed-language' text usually displays code-switching). There may be
multiple switches of language. It is though not always easy to distinguish mixed-language texts from bilingual texts. Texts *implicitly reflecting a
bilingual situation* are those written in one language but showing signs of
interference or influence from another language. It is the bilingualism
of the writer which is implicit. I take each of these types in turn. My
aim in the long section VII is to set up a typology of bilingual written
material. Bilingualism has been studied in recent decades by linguists
almost exclusively through speech; bilingualism as evidenced in writing
raises its own problems.

VII.1 Bilingual texts

Bilingual texts on my definition are texts written in two languages in
which the two versions are physically discrete and have a content which is
usually, at least in part, common to both. The degree of overlap need not
be complete, and generally is not. A distinction must be made between
mixed-language texts (see VII.3), in which the two languages are blended
together to form a single piece of discourse, and bilingual texts, in which
some sort of juxtaposition of two separate versions is the norm, and
there is an element of repetition, partial or complete, in the content of
the versions. The writer of a bilingual text for the most part sets out to

say at least some things twice, but alternatively he may present the two 'versions' as complementary contributions to the same theme, with few verbal correspondences.

Bilingual texts are a rich source of information about bilingual issues, but are not a straightforward subject of study. There is no comprehensive collection of the evidence from the Roman period, let alone from antiquity as a whole.[90] It would be out of the question in a work of this scope to attempt to present a full corpus of Greek–Latin bilingual texts, and the labour might not be worth the effort. I have though tried to take into account all bilingual texts in which Latin is in contact with languages other than Greek, namely Gaulish, Etruscan, Venetic, Oscan, Umbrian, Punic, Aramaic (particularly that of Palmyra), Hebrew, Egyptian Demotic and hieroglyphics and Coptic. Such texts are the subject of the next chapter. The Greek–Latin bilinguals are far more numerous than the others, but my material is selective.

Bilingual texts throw up an assortment of issues. Of two similar or identical versions it is sometimes possible to assign primacy to one: there may be internal evidence that one version is the original and the other a rendering of it. Texts of this kind may present us with 'dominant bilinguals' in action, that is with writers who were more at home in one language than the other, and who were prone to admit errors or interference phenomena in their second language. Such evidence opens the way to the study of the language use of imperfect learners, a topic which is relevant to bilingualism as a determinant of language change; for a language is under pressure to change in the hands of learners who have not fully mastered it. Above all partial or complementary bilinguals throw light on the writer's relationship to his potential readers, and that in turn may relate to the type of identity which he is attempting to construct for himself or for a referent. If one version omits elements which the other contains, what is the reason for the omission, and could it have to do with the impression which the writer wishes to create among readers of different types? What principles of selection can be extracted from these 'unequal' bilingual texts? I turn now to a selective discussion of some of the various types of bilinguals, and of the issues which they raise.

---

[90] This point is made by Touloumakos (1995: 79). There is an old collection of material in Zilken (1909), and a brief discussion of some general issues by Campanile (1988b). There is a useful collection of material in Kearsley and Evans (2001), but this book appeared too late for me to take account of it. Other works, dealing with specific issues or inscriptions, will be cited at the relevant points. I have not seen V. Bassler, *Inscriptiones Graecae-Latinae-bilingues* (Prague, 1934).

First, it should not be assumed that the aim of a bilingual inscription was always simply to reach the maximum readership.[91] If an edict were drafted in Latin and Greek and circulated throughout the Empire the intention might indeed have been to address as many readers as possible, but even official texts in the two languages cannot always be interpreted along these lines. Such public bilinguals as there are in Greek regions might sometimes have included Latin for symbolic purposes: the very presence of Latin, even if it is not understood, symbolises the Romanness of imperial power.

In some private bilingual texts it is even more obvious that one version would have been incomprehensible to most of the readers in the area in which the inscription was set up: it is therefore necessary to look for other motivations than the desire for maximum publicity. It is inconceivable, for example, that the Palmyrene Barates who commemorated his wife at South Shields in northern Britain in a combination of Latin and Palmyrene Aramaic (see *RIB* 1065)[92] was targeting a large Palmyrene readership. Since there will never have been many Palmyrenes at South Shields capable of reading the Aramaic text (no Palmyrene unit of the Roman army is known from Britain), that language must have been used for reasons other than the recording of the details of the woman for the sake of potential readers. On the one hand Barates might have had deep-rooted psychological reasons for commemorating his wife in his own language: he uses his native language for himself alone, as it were, at an intimate moment. On the other hand the Palmyrene text, even if it were never understood by a single reader, may be seen as a means of highlighting an aspect of Barates' identity which he regarded as important. In the Latin text he declares himself to be *Palmyrenus*, and the ethnic pride conveyed by the word is reinforced by the presence of the incomprehensible Palmyrene text. On this view a bilingual epitaph may be not only a means of imparting information about the deceased, but a form of display by the dedicator in which he expresses symbolically a feature of his identity or that of his referent. Bilingual inscriptions can often be interpreted along these lines. A Greek–Latin bilingual epitaph found at Rome is bound to be that of a Greek, just as for example a Celtic–Latin epitaph found in a Latin-speaking area such as Umbria is bound to be that of a Celt. No monolingual Latin speaker on home ground would set up a bilingual epitaph containing Celtic, but if his origin was Celtic he might well in his new home aspire to a bilingual

---

[91] Remarks along these lines can also be found in Touloumakos (1995: e.g. 80).
[92] This inscription is discussed from a different perspective in the next chapter, 2.VII.2.

monument.[93] Bilingual epitaphs of this kind, in which the ethnic origin of the dedicator or deceased (or both) finds linguistic expression alongside his or her secondary acculturation,[94] are not difficult to find in different combinations of languages from different parts of the Empire, as we will see.

I dwell on this point that the combining of two languages need not have the mundane function of addressing the largest number of readers in a mixed-language community. In the British text just mentioned the Palmyrene shows a desire to hold on symbolically to his roots in a Latin- and Celtic-speaking part of the Empire. On the other hand a Palmyrene who at Palmyra itself used Latin alongside Palmyrene would be making a rather different form of display, though a display which again involved the use of a language (Latin in this case) incomprehensible to the majority of readers in the region. A case in point is a trilingual inscription from Palmyra, dated AD 52, which I set out below with a translation of the Palmyrene.[95]

Haeranes Bonne Rabbeli
f. Palmirenus phyles Mithenon
sibi et suis fecit

Ἔτους γξτ' μηνὸς Ξανδικοῦ
Αἱράνης Βωνναίου τοῦ ῾Ραββήλου
Παλμυρηνὸς φυλῆς Μειθηνῶν ἑαυτῷ
καὶ Βωννη πατρὶ αὐτοῦ καὶ Βααλθηγα μητρὶ
αὐτοῦ εὐνοίας ἕνεκεν καὶ τοῖς ἰδίοις αὐτοῦ

byrḥ nysn šnt 3.100 + 60 + 3 qbr' dnh dy
ḥyrn br bwn' br rb'l br bwn' br 'tntn br
tymy tdmry' dy mn pḥd bny myt' dy bn' 'l
bwn' 'bwhy w'l b'ltg' brt blšwry dy mn
pḥd bny gdybwl 'mh wlh wlbnwhy lyqrhwn

In the month of Nisan of the year 363, this tomb of Hairan, son of Bonne, son of Rabbel, son of Bonne, son of Athenatan, son of Taimai, a Tadmorean from the tribe of the sons of Mita, which he built for Bonne his father and for Baalthega, daughter of Bolsori from the tribe of the sons of Gadibol, his mother, and for his sons, in their honour.

---

[93] I am thinking of the bilingual Latin–Celtic documents from Todi (see Lejeune (1988: 41–52), and below, 2.IV.2).

[94] Compare Touloumakos (1995: 89–90) on the implications of the bilingual *ID* 1802.

[95] For the text, see Rodinson (1950), Millar (1995: 409–10) (whose translation is quoted here), Hillers and Cussini (1996: 326), PAT 2801.

The Latin text can hardly be interpreted as primarily imparting information to Latin-speaking passers-by. Palmyra was coming within the orbit of the Roman province of Syria by this period,[96] but those who could have read Latin will have been few. Millar (1995: 412) observes: 'This is the earliest attested use of Latin by a native Palmyrene, and might be taken as a piece of exhibitionism by a prominent citizen in the early period of Roman domination.' Haeranes was parading an identity even for the eyes of those who could not read Latin: here was a local Palmyrene worthy who was *au fait* (up to a point: see below) with the language of the dominant power, a language which was hardly known in this region; Latin is included as the language associated with an imperial power, and it conveys the Romanisation of the man.[97]

But Haeranes gives the game away by the ineptitude of his Latin. Keen as he might have been to establish his familiarity with Latin culture, his command of the language was poor. The last line (*sibi et suis fecit*) is a correct funerary formula which Haeranes had picked up somewhere. The first four words ought to mean, as is shown by the Palmyrene version, 'Haeranes, son of Bonne, son of Rabbel'. The corresponding Greek has correct inflections, and expresses the meaning adequately.[98] In the Latin version *Rabbeli* is correctly Latinised as a genitive, but *Bonne* is not a satisfactory Latin masculine genitive form, and its function (without an additional case of *f(ilius)*) would be obscure without the other versions.

At the end of the second line of the Latin version *phyles Mithenon* represents a switch of languages within the Latin text (= φυλῆς Μειθηνῶν), presumably because the author could not translate the phrase or Latinise its inflections: this is a form of code-switching (see 3.11) motivated by the writer's ignorance of the target language. At this point the 'Latin' text can be seen as secondary to the Greek, but it is worth noting that *sibi et suis fecit* is not merely a rendering of the Greek version, which is fuller, but a genuine Latin formula. Haeranes was better able to cope with a fossilised formula than with the elements of the text specific to his own case.

My first point then arising from these examples is that the key to understanding the language choice of bilingual inscriptions need not necessarily be sought in the presence of a bilingual community in the area in which the text was set up. One of the versions might have been

---

[96] See Millar (1995: 408).

[97] On the desire to express Romanisation as a factor in language choice in some bilingual inscriptions, see Touloumakos (1995: 91).

[98] Palmyra was bilingual in Greek and Palmyrene Aramaic. For a collection of texts, many of them in Greek, see now Hillers and Cussini (1996).

included for symbolic rather than communicative purposes, with (e.g.) the presentation of a type of identity determining the inclusion of the second language.

The texts discussed so far are 'unequal' or partial bilinguals, in the sense that the two (or three) versions are not identical; one is longer than the other(s). I consider, secondly, some further aspects of such unmatched parallel texts.

In the Palmyrene trilingual above there is a descending order of length and detail, from Palmyrene through Greek to Latin, and that hierarchy reflects the linguistic competence of the writer, in that his Latin was imperfect. But the unequal length of the versions need not reflect the unequal competence of the writer in the languages of an inscription. He might have chosen to say more in one language than the other, for a variety of reasons. Consider, for example, the following partial bilingual from Rome:

IGUR 291
Θ(εοῖς) Δ(αίμοσιν)
Λ. Αἰλίῳ Μελιτίνῳ
τέκνῳ γλυκυτάτῳ
Φηλῖκλα μήτηρ καὶ Μύ-
ρων πατὴρ ἀτυχέστα-
τοι ἐπόησαν. ἔζησεν
μησὶν δέκα τρισίν,
ἡμέραις ἐννέα. **μὴ**
ἐνοχλήσῃς τῷ τάφῳ
μὴ τοιαῦτα πάθῃς
περὶ τέκνων. ne sis
molestus, ne patiarus hoc
et ollas inclusas caue.

It is only the warning at the end addressed to potential violators of the tomb that appears in Latin as well as Greek form.[99] The bilingual threat reveals an expectation on the part of the writer that a funerary inscription might be read by strangers, as well as the immediate family. Passers-by at Rome tempted to violate the tomb could of course have been either Latin- or Greek-speaking, and recognition of that fact prompts the writer to give the tomb maximum protection by addressing speakers of both types. But what is interesting, in view of this awareness of the mixed readership, is the fact that the deceased is commemorated exclusively in Greek. Latin speakers are excluded as readers of part of the text. This

---

[99] Latin though that is somewhat inept. There is nothing corresponding to τῷ τάφῳ, and *hoc* is not informative without any equivalent to περὶ τέκνων.

Greek family is inward-looking, and not concerned to project any sort of assimilation to Roman culture. There are large numbers of purely Greek funerary inscriptions at Rome which hint at the maintenance of a Greek identity by many Greeks at Rome, but this inscription is abnormal in that on the one hand it acknowledges the existence of Latin speakers but on the other excludes them from the personal part of the inscription. The family is thus presented as close knit and Greek speaking. The greater length of the Greek version has nothing to do with the writer's ignorance of Latin, but is the result of a decision to address Greeks for most of the inscription.

Another case from a different tradition has been discussed by La'da (1994). The text is a trilingual from Egypt (in Greek, Demotic and hiero-glyphics) in which the Greek and Demotic versions present the referent in different ways. I quote La'da (1994: 162): 'in the Demotic there are six priestly titles, in addition to three secular titles, in the Greek there are only two secular titles and no priestly ones at all. This can only be explained on the assumption that whoever was responsible for draw-ing up the Greek section of the inscription made a conscious selection as to which titles should appear in the Greek text. The complete ab-sence of Egyptian priestly titles from the Greek version suggests that these were not considered relevant for the Greek-reading public to whom this section was addressed. Furthermore, the public targeted by the Greek section seems likely to have been a secular and literate Greek-speaking group, presumably chiefly middle- and upper-class Greeks and to a lesser extent hellenised Egyptians, the majority of whom did not, or at least were not expected to, take much interest in the Egyptian priestly career of Ptolemaios.' By contrast priestly titles would have been of interest to readers of the Demotic version.

Thus unequal bilingual inscriptions may address different types of readers, with the different versions providing different types of informa-tion as considered suitable to the various readerships.

I would, thirdly, draw attention to another category of bilingual in-scriptions, that in which the two versions are identical word-for-word. Paradoxically, since no two languages are likely to have exactly equivalent idioms, and no two epigraphic traditions exactly equivalent formulae, the primary version may be easier to detect the more closely the ver-sions match. This point is demonstrated with particular clarity by those Greek versions of *senatus consulta* to which the corresponding Latin ver-sion survives. The Greek versions are full of literal renderings of Latin idioms which do not constitute idiomatic Greek, and it may be deduced that the Latin versions had primacy and that the Greek versions were as a matter of policy translated mechanically word for word, almost certainly by native speakers of Latin (see above, III, and below, 4.V.2.12).

Another such case, though this time involving a formulaic structure rather than idioms, can be quoted from Speidel's collection (1994a) of the epitaphs of the *equites singulares Augusti*, no. 688a:

m(emoriae) c(ausa). C. Iul. Proculum, eq. sing. impp. nn., natione Pannonium ... Q. Iul. Finitus ...
Μ(νήμης) χ(άριν). Γ. ᾽Ιούλιον Πρόκλον ἱππ[έ]α σινγουλάριν τῶν κυρίων αὐτοκρατόρων, γένει Παννόνιον ... Γάιος ᾽Ιούλιος Φινῖτος.

The structure of the Latin, with accusative of the honorand (for which see especially below, 6.III.3), absence of a verb, and a juxtaposed nominative of the dedicator, is not normal in Latin funerary inscriptions (other than those imitating or influenced by Greek; see further below, VII.4.2, IX (6), 2.VII.2, p. 254, 6.III.3; for a purely Greek honorific example, see the Greek doctor's dedication from Chester, quoted below, 3.V), and *memoriae causa* also was not a native Latin funerary formula but modelled on the Greek μ(νήμης) χ(άριν).[100] This inscription was set up at the unit's winter quarters in the Greek-speaking area of Anazarbos in Cilicia. In their numerous inscriptions at Rome the horse guards never used the accusative of the honorand. The Greek version, included for the local readership, is the primary one, and the Latin is modelled structurally on it. The result is a Latin text of slightly exotic flavour. Latin was apparently included as symbolising the deceased's membership of the Roman army. Funerary inscriptions of Roman soldiers are constantly in Latin or alternatively bilingual, even in Greek-speaking areas such as Egypt (see 5.VII.2.5; cf. 3.I), and even when the referent was a primary speaker of Greek; that is a reflection of the Roman identity that soldiers acquired or aspired to, whatever their place of origin. In the example quoted (by contrast, for example, with the short Egyptian text *CIL* III.8, quoted below) no effort was made to achieve conventional Latin phraseology. The dominant culture of the writer may have been Greek.

It must however be acknowledged that some inscriptions in which one version is influenced by the idioms or structures of the other language do not straightforwardly reveal the linguistic origins of the writer: influence from language A does not necessarily mean that the writer was a native speaker of A. An interesting case is discussed by Touloumakos (1995: 92), a bilingual from Leuke in Bithynia (*ILS* 9238):

---

[100] For further details see Zilken (1909: 25, 30), Kajanto (1963a: 23), Adams (1998).

Ioui Optimo Maximo tutori T. Marcius Gamus uotum reddidit eo loco quo et natus est
Διὶ κρατίστῳ μεγίστῳ φροντ[ιστῇ] Τίτος Μάρκιος Γάμος εὐχὴν ἀπέδωκεν τούτῳ τῷ τόπῳ οὗ καὶ ἐγεννήθη.

The dedicator was, as he tells us himself, a native of Leuke and therefore a native speaker of Greek. He was the freedman of a Roman. Despite his linguistic origins the title he gives to Zeus in the Greek version is Latinate and determined by the Latin text, which, interestingly, is placed first. Moreover the dative τούτῳ τῷ τόπῳ (without preposition) corresponds exactly to the idiomatic Latin ablative *eo loco* (also without preposition, as normally in the case of *loco* + adjective). It is suggested that Gamus had spent a long time in the service of a Roman master, perhaps in Rome or the west, and hence through long familiarity had adopted the formulae of his second language in his first. There are indeed some bilingual texts in which there is mutual influence of the one language on the other in the use of formulae, such that the primary language of the writer is difficult to determine; the reason may lie in his complete immersion in a bilingual culture. Note, for example, *CIL* I². 2259 = *ILLRP* 961: *Q. Auili C. f. Lanuine salue* Κόιντε ᾿Αουίλλιε Γαίου υἱὲ ῾Ρωμαῖε χρηστέ, χαῖρε. Here the the use of the vocative in addressing the deceased is more Greek than Roman (see below on *IGUR* 873), but the form of the filiation (with υἱέ corresponding to *f.*) is Latinate in both versions.[101]

Fourthly, in many bilingual inscriptions the formulaic conventions current in the two languages are adopted as appropriate in each of the versions, as a result of which an 'idiomatic' bilingual is produced, with the two versions not necessarily corresponding slavishly word for word. Thus, for example, at *CIL* III.8 the Latin version in Latin style has dative of the honorand and nominative of the dedicator, but the Greek in the Greek manner has accusative of the honorand rather than the dative: *Iuliae Augustae Cyrenenses*: ᾿Ιουλίαν Σεβαστὰν Κυραναῖοι.[102] Or again in the Roman bilingual epitaph *IGUR* 873 the Greek version has direct address of the deceased,[103] whereas the Latin merely names the deceased, a standard Latin pattern:

Papiria C. leib. Anthousa
Παπειρία Γαίου Παπειρίου ἀπελευθή(ρα) ῎Ανθουσα χρηστή, χαῖρε.

---

[101] On this text see further Poccetti (1984: 649).
[102] The distinction was observed by Zilken (1909: 52).
[103] For address in Greek epitaphs (entailing the use of the vocative and also χαῖρε), see Kajanto (1963a: 18). For χαῖρε see also Zilken (1909: 28–9) (also 21–2 for Latin equivalents) and (from a different perspective) Sourvinou-Inwood (1995: 180–216).

An example from a different linguistic area of this same practice, whereby separate conventions are followed in the two versions, can be found in the bilingual dedication set up on an altar by a veteran of the Roman army at Tilli in SE Turkey at the confluence of the rivers Tigris and Bohtan, published by Healey and Lightfoot (1991). The date is roughly the second or third century AD. It is plausibly suggested by the editors (3) that the veteran was a local who had served in the eastern (Greek-speaking) provinces and had retired to his *patria*. The text is in Greek and Aramaic, the latter fragmentary but well enough preserved to allow some comparisons between the two versions. The Greek text runs as follows:

Διὶ ᾿Ολυμπίῳ
Μαρη[α]λλη
[᾿Αν]τώνιος
Δομιτιανὸς
οὐετρανὸς
[ε]ὐξάμενος
ἀνέστησα.

I, Antonius Domitianus, a veteran, set up (this altar) to Zeus Olympius, Lord of the Gods, in accordance with my vow.

The fragmentary Aramaic text is published at p. 4. I report a few detailed comments by the editors. In l.2 *prk'* seems to be the Aramaic word for 'altar' (Healey and Lightfoot (1991: 5)), in which case there is a distinction between the two versions. The Greek, in common Greco-Roman manner, does not specify lexically the object which has been erected; the monument, as it were, speaks for itself. The two versions were not therefore identical word-for-word, but each followed the conventions of its own language.

mrlh' in line 6 (if the reading is correct) represents the Aramaic divine title *marallahe* = 'lord of the gods', which, interestingly, has been taken over directly into the Greek (l.2) as an additional oriental epithet of Zeus. A title such as this may inspire a switch of codes (see 3.v.5 for code-switching in titles); a rendering into Greek would not have had the same associations.

In the last line *'l ḥyyhy* means 'for his life' (Healey and Lightfoot (1991: 5)). Again there is not an exact correspondence between the two versions; the general content of the two dedications is much the same, but the formulae of the separate languages are used independently.

I summarise the points that have arisen: (1) at least one version of a bilingual text is likely to have been in the predominating language of the region in which the inscription was set up; (2) the presence of a second-language version need not imply that the area was widely bilingual; (3) bilingual inscriptions are often intended to confer a mixed cultural/ linguistic identity on the referent(s), and to that end one of the versions may have symbolic rather than communicative function; (4) sometimes a bilingual inscription deliberately excludes speakers of one of the two languages from some of the information which the inscription as a whole embodies; there may be various reasons for such exclusions; (5) verbatim equivalence of the two versions is not necessarily consistent with balanced bilingualism on the part of the writer; (6) the primary version of a bilingual inscription may be deduced from various hints, as for example from the relative competence of the two versions or from a comparison of their idioms and formulaic structure; but (7) there need not in every case be a 'primary' version. If the two versions are each idiomatic and formulaic within their language traditions, each must have been composed independently to convey predetermined information.

A good deal of Chapter 2 will concern bilingual texts, in a variety of languages. Further observations about such inscriptions will be made there.

VII.2 *Transliterated texts*

Numerous Latin inscriptions and other subliterary texts written in Greek characters survive, just as there are cases of Greek written in Latin script.[104] Such texts are of importance in the study of bilingualism, but their interpretation is not as simple as might be thought. The purpose of this section is not to offer a collection of transliterated texts, but to illustrate the types and bring out the problems which they raise. Several specimens will be analysed.

It has been said that the use of the inappropriate script to write Latin or Greek represents imperfect bilingualism or a stage in the learning of a second language,[105] but that is to confuse language learning with the learning of literacy in a language. In fact a fluent bilingual may be either illiterate in both scripts or literate in only one.[106] The use of, say, Greek script to write Latin does not necessarily imply imperfect bilingualism

---

[104] See in general Wouters (1976), Kramer (1983, 1984), Leiwo (1995b), Donderer (1995).

[105] Note the title of Kramer (1984); also Rea on *P. Oxy.* XXXVI.2772 (p. 63): 'Transliteration was a stage in the learning of a second language.'

[106] There are Panjabi-speaking bilinguals in Britain who have good listening and speaking skills in Panjabi, but cannot read the Gurmukhi script in which the language is written (Romaine 1995: 13). Such speakers may have attended school in Britain, and consequently have literacy only in

but may (at least under some circumstances: see further below) be due to imperfect literacy. A user of the wrong script might in theory be a 'language learner' (e.g. a lower-class Greek who had come into contact with Latin fairly late, picked up the language to a limited degree at a spoken level, but never learnt to write it), but equally he might be a fluent bilingual, born, say, into a lower-class Greek–Latin bilingual community at (e.g.) Rome, who had received limited instruction in the writing of only one of his two languages. But even that is not the whole story, as we will see: there is evidence that some writers used the wrong script deliberately.

VII.2.1 *Latin in Greek script: introduction*

Someone using Greek script to write Latin might have been unskilled in Latin script, as was suggested above. The Greek and Latin scripts in their various forms are closely related, and it might seem surprising that a bilingual should have been able to use one script but not the other. Greek capitals in particular have many letters identical to their Latin equivalents. We do however have some direct evidence for the difficulty encountered by Greeks literate in Greek script in learning to use Latin script freely (see the remarks below on an Egyptian alphabet). In cursive writing of the high Empire the two scripts, which diverge on many points,[107] would not have been as easy to master as capitals, and it is reasonable to suppose that some poorly educated writers with a degree of bilingualism in the spoken languages would have had to make do with just one script. Even in capitals the 'slow writer' might have had trouble in those areas where the two scripts did not correspond. I would maintain then that literacy in Greek script did not entail an automatic ability to use Latin script fluently, despite the evidence for a degree of convergence of the two scripts in bilingual communities.[108]

In this respect *ChLA* 4.259 (= *P. Ant.* 1 fr. 1, verso) is a revealing document. This is an alphabet of the fourth or fifth century consisting of the Latin names for the letters of the alphabet spelt in Greek characters, with the Latin letter written below the name.[109] The Latin script is described by Ullmann (1935) as a 'semi-formalised cursive'. A number

---

English script. But in no sense are they either imperfect bilinguals or learners of Panjabi (as a second language).

[107] Greek had letters not in Latin (ζ, η, θ, ξ, φ, χ, ψ, ω), and various other letters did not correspond closely in cursive to their Latin correspondents (α, β, γ, μ, π, ρ, σ). Latin for its part had *f*, and, where capitals are concerned, quite apart from the letters particular to Greek, H had a different value in the two scripts.

[108] See Rochette (1999), and below, 5.1.4.   [109] On this see now Kramer (1999).

of the letter names are incidentally of interest in themselves: e.g. ιφφε, ιλλε, ιμμε, ιννε, ιρρε, ισσε. These are anticipations of the names in some Romance languages, e.g. Italian *effe, elle, emme, enne, erre, esse*, Spanish *efe, ele*, etc. The Romance names were previously thought not to go back to antiquity, but their origin can now be taken back at least as far as the fifth century. The document is not a school exercise, but may be intended as a guide to scribes who might occasionally have had to write in Latin.[110] The Greek letters provide a phonetic representation of the sounds of the Latin names, apparently used as an aid in learning the form of the Latin letters themselves. We know that the names of letters were taught at the same time as their forms: note Manil. 2.755–6 *ut rudibus pueris monstratur littera primum / **per faciem nomenque suum**, tum ponitur usus*. On this evidence mastering Latin script was not a completely straightforward matter for a Greek, even a professional scribe.

There is evidence, quite apart from that to be derived from the inscriptions to be discussed later, that some Greek learners of Latin did not get very far in the process of learning Latin script. *P. Lond.* II.481 (= Kramer (1983), 13) is a bilingual Latin–Greek glossary of the fourth century consisting of Latin terms in the left-hand column, and their Greek equivalents in the right. Latin words as well as Greek are in Greek cursive characters. Perhaps the writer could not use Latin script, or he was making the assumption that potential users of the glossary would be unable to read Latin characters readily. The two possibilities are not mutually exclusive. The Latin which the author knew was manifestly that of colloquial speech rather than a literary variety of the language.[111] For example, ανσαρες (3) and πασαρες (4) show opening of *e* before *r*,[112] and the words for 'winter' (9 ειβερνος = *hibernus*) and 'summer' (10 στιβ[ος] = *aestiuus* > *estiuus* > *stiuus*) reflect various phonetic and lexical developments of substandard Latin.[113] On the other hand ουντε = *unde* (36) betrays (in the use of ντ for *nd*) Greek phonetic or at least orthographic interference (see 4.V.1.1; for morphological interference in the document,

---

[110] See Kramer (1999: 38).

[111] This is abundantly clear from Kramer's commentary (1983: 84–7); see also Kramer (1977).

[112] On this phenomenon see for example Adams (1977: 13–14).

[113] The circumlocution *hibernum tempus* = 'winter' was abbreviated to *hibernum*; here the aspirate has been lost and the neuter converted to masculine (cf. Fr. *hiver*). In the comparable circumlocution *aestiuum tempus* > *aestiuum* the initial diphthong (or rather the vowel deriving from it) has been treated as prothetic and deleted. For the form see Anthimus 50 *caulis uero hiemis tempore; nam stiuis diebus melancolici sunt* (see also Liechtenhan (1963: 76), index s.v.). See Kramer ad loc.

see 4.V.3.3). The Latin part of the document thus displays a mixture of colloquial Latin phenomena and interference from Greek.

The function of the glossary is not certain. It contains some basic vocabulary (names of plants, vegetables, fruit, birds, terms to do with the weather and seafaring), and one expression suggestive of a phrase book (36 ουντε βενιστε). The document was probably intended either as mnemonic (for the use of the writer himself), or as instructional (for the use of other Greeks). On either interpretation it implies the existence of non-élite Greek learners of sub-literary Latin who were not accomplished in writing or reading Latin script.

VII.2.2 The use of Greek script for Latin as a matter of choice
Some writers using Greek characters for the Latin language did so not because they were unable to use Latin script, but because they chose to transliterate on a particular occasion. An interesting case in point is a sixth-century fragment of the Lord's prayer (published by Harrauer and Sijpesteijn (1985), no. 184) written in Latin with interlinear transliteration into Greek script.[114] According to the editors (see pp. 177–8 for discussion), the same hand was responsible for the two versions. The Latin script is more assured and is likely to have been that of the writer's first language; this version also seems to have been written first. The lines start further to the left, and the Greek transcription, somewhat indented, is fitted into spaces between the lines. Clearly, if the editors are right, the writer could have restricted himself to Latin script, but chose as well to transliterate into Greek characters, perhaps as a form of exercise in the use of the second script.

A number of Latin *defixiones* survive from Africa (Carthage, Hadrumetum) in Greek characters.[115] The writers of these texts, or some of them, were bilingual (note particularly Audollent (1904), 252), but it would not do to maintain that they were forced by imperfect Latin literacy to use Greek script. *Defixiones* are often deliberately coded. Some are anagrams or palindromes. The *defixio* Vetter (1953), no. 7 is in a mixture of Oscan and Latin, not because the writer was a speaker of some sort of mixed language, but because the mixture made the text more obscure (see 2.II.3).

---

[114] I am grateful to James Clackson for this reference.
[115] See Audollent (1904), nos. 231, 252 (a mixture of Greek and Latin: for the latter, see especially lines 36ff.), 267 (lines 15ff.), 269 (B frg. I, lines 5ff., frg. II, 10ff.), 270. See further Donderer (1995: 99–103). There is now a transliterated *defixio* from Roman Britain (unpublished: information from Roger Tomlin).

The use of Greek letters for the writing of Latin *defixiones* can be interpreted as a form of obfuscation, perhaps to increase the power of the
magic.[116] A *defixio* from Autun (second century) has a list of names in Latin,
followed by magic words which are in Greek letters (*AE* 1979, 407).[117]

There are sometimes internal hints in a text that a transliterator into
Greek script was familiar with aspects of Latin orthography (and hence
with Latin script). The phenomenon of *graphemic interference* from Latin
script in transliterated texts written in Greek letters may point to the
writer's knowledge of Latin script. I illustrate this phenomenon here first
from Audollent (1904), 270, = *ILS* 8757, a *defixio* from Hadrumetum.
I quote most of the text, omitting the first few (fragmentary) lines, and
some meaningless magical words (text from *ILS*):

αδ[ιουρο]...περ σεπτεμ σθελλας, ουθ, εξ κουα ορα οχ comποσουερο, νον
δορμιατ Σεξτιλλιος Διονισιε φιλιους, ουραθουρ φουρενς, νον δορμιατ νεκουε
σεδεατ νεκουε λοκουατουρ σεδ ιν μεντεμ αβιατ με Σεπθιμαμ Αμενε φιλια.
ουραθουρ φουρενς αμορε ετ δεσιδεριο μεο, ανιμα ετ χορ ουραθουρ Σεξτιλι
Διονισιε φιλιους αμορε ετ δεσιδεριο μεο Σεπτιμες Αμενε φιλιε...φαχ
Σεξτιλιουμ Διονισιε φιλιουμ νε σομνουμ χονθινγαθ σεθ αμορε ετ δεσιδεριο
μεο ουραθουρ, ουιιους σιπιριτους ετ χορ χομβουρατουρ ομνια μεμβρα θοθιους
χορπορις Σεξθιλι Διονισιε φιλιους. σι μινους, δεσχενδο ιν αδυτους Οσυρις ετ
δισσολουαμ θεν θαπεεν [= τὴν ταφὴν?] ετ μιτταμ ουθ... α φλουμινε φερατουρ.
εγω ενιμ σουμ μαγνους δεχανους δει μαγνι δει Αχραμμαχαλαλα...

[= adiuro...per septem stellas ut, ex qua hora hoc composuero, non dormiat
Sextillios Dionisie filius, uratur furens, non dormiat neque sedeat neque loquatur
sed in mentem (h)abiat me Septimam Am(o)ene filia. uratur furens amore et
desiderio meo, anima et cor uratur Sextili Dionisie filius amore et desiderio meo
Septimes Am(o)ene filie ... fac Sextilium Dionysie filium ne somnum contingat,
sed amore et desiderio meo uratur, huius sipiritus [sic] et cor comburatur, omnia
membra totius corporis Sextili Dionysie filius. si minus, descendo in adytus
Osyris et dissoluam τὴν ταφὴν et mittam ut ... a flumine feratur; ego enim sum
magnus decanus dei magni dei Achrammachalala].

ε and ο are used throughout to indicate not only the short vowels, but
also the Latin long *e* and *o*: the Greek letters η and ω are not found,
apart from one instance of ω in εγω: e.g. ορα (*hora*), νον, με, Αμενε (genitive),
αμορε (*amore*), δεσιδεριο μεο, θοθιους (*totius*), νε, δεσχενδο. In theory
various factors might be invoked to explain these spellings, e.g.:

---

[116] Note Dessau on *ILS* 8757 (for which see below): 'Latina est, sed Graecis litteris scripta, ad
augendam speciem magicam.' Also of relevance here is the transliterated amulet, *CIL* XIII.5338.
On transliteration and magic, see Kotansky (1991: 121, 136 n. 103).
[117] See Biville (1989b: 106).

(1) The influence of the writer's pronunciation of Latin: could these be phonetic spellings? This is unlikely, because even in varieties of substandard Latin long *e* and *o* were not shortened in all positions. If (e.g.) ε for η and ο for ω were confined to final syllables, that might have been a reflection of vowel shortening in such (unstressed) syllables. But ε and ο occur under the accent (αμορε, often, θοθιους), in initial syllables (δεσιδεριο) and in monosyllables (με, νε), as well as in endings.

(2) The influence of later (koine) Greek writing conventions. In Greek papyri there is widespread confusion of ε and η and ο and ω reflecting a loss of phonemic distinctions of quantity in koine Greek.[118] But in the papyri such interchanges tend to be haphazard, whereas there is a regularity about the use of ε and ο in the *defixio* which suggests a different explanation.

(3) The graphemic influence of Latin. On this view the writer, though using Greek script, was unconsciously or otherwise influenced by Latin script, which used *e* and *o* to represent long and short vowels indifferently. If a feature (in this case a deficiency) of Latin script has influenced the way in which the writer transliterates into Greek script, then it would follow that he had some acquaintance with Latin script. This third possibility seems the most plausible to me. For possible cases of graphemic influence from Latin in transliterated texts, see *IG* xiv.698 (Sorrento)... Ειρηνα μαριτο βενε μερεντι φηκετ, *IGUR* 350 Αντονιο Ποτεολανο φιλιο δουκισιμο βενμερετι Τ(ιτος) Ατονιος Μαρινος πατερ φηκιτ, *ILCV* 4908 = *CJI* 266 = Noy (1995), 287 Αιλια Πατρικια Τουλλιο Ειρηναιο κονιουγι βενεμερεντι φηκιτ διὰ βίο. In these inscriptions there is repeated use of -ο in the dative. Similarly Latin speakers writing Greek (as distinct from transliterated Latin) sometimes used a dative in -ο, presumably on at least some occasions under the influence of the graphemic form of the Latin equivalent. This can be seen in the opening of the bilingual inscription (in which the Latin version comes first) *CIL* iii.555:[119] *Q. Calpurnio Eutycho Philetus*... Κ. Καρπουρνίο Εὐτύχο Φίλητος... Quite apart from the use of ο for ω twice, the Greek version has a Latinate abbreviation of the *praenomen*.[120] The writer was a primary speaker of Latin who seems to have been influenced by the graphemic forms of his first language. Similarly in Greek graffiti from the Syringes of Thebes

---

[118] See Gignac (1976: 242–6, 275–7).

[119] Discussed by Touloumakos (1995: 85–6). It should be noted that the type of dedication in Greek in which the honorand is expressed in the dative, as in this inscription, is Latinate (see Veyne (1962)).

[120] For the Greek treatment of *praenomina*, see Zilken (1909: 7–21).

there are various cases of Latinate graphemic intrusion which hint at the Roman origin of a writer (see 5.v.4). It must though be acknowledged that the material cited in this paragraph (if not the remarkably consistent *defixio* quoted above) is extraordinarily difficult to interpret. It is of course true, as noted above, that in koine Greek long and short *o* fell together as [o], and spellings of the type seen in *CIL* III.555 above could alternatively be interpreted as reflecting the pronunciation of Greek, just as o for ω in a piece of transliterated Latin might reflect the loss of quantitative distinctions in Latin. But the parallelism between the Latin and Greek texts in the above bilingual, and the primacy of the Latin version, suggest that the graphemic form of the Latin was the main determinant of the Greek dative endings, perhaps supported by phonetic developments in both languages.

Graphemic influence tends to go hand in hand with *character switching*, another phenomenon which will be dealt with later (VII.4.1). By this I mean the habit shown by some bilingual (and bi-literate) writers of switching, perhaps unconsciously, from one script into the other. As Audollent prints the above *defixio*, the prefix of *com*ποσυερο is written in Latin characters; but unfortunately Audollent's edition cannot be relied on in such matters, and I leave character switching for the moment.

The one example of ω in Audollent (1904), 270 above (εγω) is an interesting special case. In the Latin pronoun *ego* the *o* by this period was short. The spelling is not a phonetic transcription of Latin pronunciation, but represents a lapse into the Greek form of the pronoun ἐγώ. This is a switch of codes, if only at the level of writing. It suggests that the writer may have adopted Greek characters only as a means of coding, and that he was probably bilingual. In another place he seems to have used a Greek noun with the definite article, if Audollent's text can be trusted: δισσολουαμ θεν θαπεεν. Audollent interprets the last two words as equivalent to τὴν ταφήν. On this view various forms of obfuscation have been adopted in the word: the use of the aspirated stop θ for τ (a constant strategy throughout the text: e.g. σθελλας = *stellas*, ουραθουρ = *uratur*, θοθιους = *totius*; cf. χ for κ in χορ, χονθινγαθ = *contingat*, χομβουρατουρ = *comburatur*, χορπορις = *corporis*, δεσχενδο = *descendo*), and conversely the use of the unaspirated stop π to replace φ. It is true that such confusions between aspirated and unaspirated stops can be paralleled in the papyri,[121] but there is a systematic character to these substitutions which is suggestive of a deliberate ploy.

---

[121] See Gignac (1976: 86–95).

There are a few other traces of Greek interference (of a morphological kind) in the text. Σεξτιλλιος is given the Greek nominative -ος ending rather than the transliterated Latin ending -ους which is found (e.g.) in φιλιους (three times), σιπιριτους = *spiritus* and μαγνους. And the genitive form of Σεπτιμες arguably shows the Greek inflection in -ης, with η characteristically replaced by ε; the -ες ending will be dealt with in a later chapter (see 4.V.3.1, V.3.1.2).

Further acquaintance with Latin orthography can be seen in the constant use of final *-m*, e.g. in μαγνουμ, δεουμ, εουμ etc.; but note the inconsistency in Σεπτιμαμ... φιλια. Final *-m* had long since been lost in the speech of all classes. The writer would not have written it if he had merely been making a phonetic transcription of Latin speech as a Greek unfamiliar with conventions of Latin writing.

I conclude that the writer of the *defixio* was a bilingual with a knowledge of Latin script and orthography, as well as Greek. His motive in choosing Greek script is in this case obvious.

Another transliterated text which was probably written by someone who knew Latin script is the following:

IGUR 616 = *CIL* VI.20294[122]
Δις Μαν(ιβους). Γ. Ιουλους [*sic*] Τιλεσφορος φηκετ ετ σιβι ετ σουεις λειβ<ε>ρτεις λειβερταβουσκε εωρυμ. Τερεντια Ακτη φηκετ Τερεντιω Ανεικητω ετ λ<ει>βερ-τω ετ κονιουγει βενεμερεντει ετ σιβι ετ σουεις λειβερτεις λειβερταβουσκε εωρουμ. οκ μονομεντου ηδεφικατου ες κομουνε Ιουνιω Τελεσφορω ετ Τερεν-τια Ακτη.

This inscription is in assured Greek capitals carved in marble (for a photograph, see Moretti (1972: 189)). Many of the Greek letter shapes would have served for Latin as well, but the consistent use in the text of various distinctively Greek symbols (e.g. Δ, Ρ, Λ, Η, Φ, the lunate *sigma*, and also the *epsilon*, which is of distinctive form) shows that the writer was using Greek script, not Latin or a mixture of the two. It is likely that a stonecutter who could produce an expensive text of this quality in a script showing a high degree of overlap with Latin would have been able to use pure Latin capitals as well, but there is some additional evidence in this case that he was using Greek script by choice rather than necessity. There are signs that he was versed in the minutiae of Latin orthography, and I refer here not to letter forms but to subtle spelling

---

[122] Discussed by Leiwo (1995b: 297–8).

conventions. A striking feature is the use of the digraph ει to represent Classical Latin long *i*: σουεις (twice), λειβερτεις (twice), λειβερταβουσκε (twice), λειβερτω, κονιουγει, βενεμερεντει. In 11 (possibly 12) places long *i* is indicated by ει (some words have more than one case of the spelling), and there is only one long *i* in the text which is not rendered in this way; I deal with the Greek name Ανεικητω below. It will be argued here that these spellings reflect the influence of a Latin orthographic convention. The issue is, however, complicated by the tendency for ει (instead of *iota*) to be used in Greek as well to mark long *i*. I therefore deal at length here with the use of *ei*/ει in an attempt to establish the motivation of the writer.

In Latin there was a long-standing convention of using *ei* to distinguish long from short *i*. In the Gallus papyrus from Qasr Ibrîm, for example, long *i* is almost always rendered in this way (*spolieis, deiuitiora, tueis, deicere*).[123] The convention flourished, particularly in archaising and formal style, from at least the second century BC to the early Empire,[124] though it is not much in evidence in informal or substandard writings, such as the Vindolanda tablets, the Bu Njem ostraca or the letters of Claudius Terentianus.

In Greek papyri of the Roman period there is 'a very frequent interchange of ει and ι (whether long or short etymologically) in all phonetic environments throughout the Roman and Byzantine periods. This indicates the identification of the Classical Greek /ei/ diphthong with the simple vowel /i/' (Gignac 1976: 189).

Despite this apparent chaos in Greek papyri, there is in Greek inscriptions an increasing trend in the Roman period for ει to be written to mark long *i*. Note Threatte (1980: 198–9): 'In the second century A.D. and especially after 200 A.D. EI is the normal spelling for [i']: it is more than twice as frequent as I in texts dated securely to the second century; about ten times as frequent as I in texts certainly later than 200 A.D.' This tendency is in evidence in the Greek inscriptions of the city of Rome. In the Greek inscriptions in the first part of the second fascicule of Moretti's *IGUR* (inscriptions 264–728) I have noted about 69 examples of ει used for *iota* = long *i*, compared with only about 29 examples of *iota* itself. These figures suggest a fairly determined effort to employ the digraph to represent the original long vowel, though it has to be said that there are also in the inscriptions cases of ει for short *i*.[125]

---

[123] See Anderson, Parsons and Nisbet (1979).
[124] Full details can be found in Anderson, Parsons and Nisbet (1979: 132–3).
[125] See Moretti (1972) on nos. 547 and 832.

How do these figures compare with those for the *Latin* inscriptions of Rome written in Greek characters?[126] In these texts there are about 30 instances of ει = long *i*, and 29 of *i* (= long *i*). The incidence of the digraph is not as high in the Latin inscriptions as the Greek. On the face of it the Latin and Greek conventions might have combined to motivate the writing of ει for long *i* in Latin inscriptions written in Greek characters, with the Greek convention perhaps a stronger force than the Latin. This conclusion can be refined.

In the Greek inscriptions ει is particularly frequent in proper names. Of the 69 examples referred to above in inscriptions 264–728, 58 are in proper names, of both Latin (23 examples) and Greek origin (35 examples). Latin names spelt with ει include *Sabinus* (e.g. 312), *Acilius* (313), *Regina* (325), *Liberalis* (367), *Saturninus* (420), *Paulina* (463), *Peregrinus* (492), *Antoninus* (590), *Crispina* (626), *Caninius* (663), *Vitalius* (689).

It is revealing, with the help of the indexes to *CIL* VI, to compare the spelling of these proper names in *Latin* inscriptions written in *Latin* script at Rome. The names listed in the previous paragraph are found many hundreds of times, but there seems not to be a single example of an *ei* spelling. It follows, first, that in Greek inscriptions from Rome Latin names spelt with ει have this orthography because of a Greek convention, and not because writers of Greek inscriptions were imitating a Latin epigraphic habit. More importantly, any *Latin* name in a *Latin* inscription written in *Greek* characters which has ει for long *i* is likely to have been the work of a man versed in the local conventions of Greek orthography: either a Greek or a literate bilingual. There are indeed transliterated Latin texts containing such names. *IGUR* 346 not only has Σαβειναι (dative) but also the form Κλαυδειαι (= *Claudiae*), where the suffix is of Greek appearance. 773 has Μαρεινα (*Marinus* is never spelt with *ei* in the Latin inscriptions of Rome which are in Latin script), and 867 has Σατορνεινος, a form which also shows the Greek nominative morpheme (unless of course the writer has chosen to use *omicron* as a means of transliterating Latin short *u*: note the second vowel of the word), though the text is unambiguously Latin throughout. The indexes to *CIL* VI do not record any instances of *Saturneinus* or *Saturneina*, though there are hundreds of examples of the names. Clearly a *Greek* name containing ει = long *i* in a *Latin* text transliterated into *Greek* letters reflects the operation of the Greek spelling convention: thus Ανεικητω in our present inscription.

---

[126] I consider here *IGUR* 305, 346, 350, 417, 434, 570, 616, 718, 731, 773, 774, 793, 818, 867, 901, 979, 980, 1040. 475 also seems to be in Latin, but it is too fragmentary to be worth consideration.

In Greek inscriptions from Rome, therefore, the use of the digraph ει for long *i* seems chiefly to be a feature of the spelling of proper names. In Latin inscriptions transliterated into Greek script, on the other hand, the digraph is widespread in words of other types. Not only that, but the use of the digraph in transliterated Latin inscriptions can be exactly paralleled in Latin inscriptions from Rome written in Latin script. σουεις, for example, occurs twice in our inscription *IGUR* 616 and also in the transliterated texts 867 and 980. The index to *CIL* VI lists about 54 examples of *sueis* in Latin inscriptions, often in expressions similar to those in which σουεις occurs in the transliterated inscriptions. With σουεις λειβερτεις λειβερταβουσκε in our inscription compare, e.g. *CIL* VI.23770, A 5 *sibei et sueis liberteis conleiberteis*. In transliterated inscriptions λειβερτ- occurs four or five times in the present text, and once each in 818 (a mixed language text, but the word in question is in a Latin part) and 980. In Latin inscriptions from Rome *leibert-* is common (some 36 examples), and the dative/ablative plural ending is often, as in the transliterated inscriptions, written *-eis* (e.g. 21 examples of *liberteis*; there are also examples of *leiberteis* and *conl(e)iberteis*). The dative singular ending of *coniux* is written in transliterated form with ει in the present text 616, and also at 1040; for *coniugei* in Latin, see *CIL* VI.33921 (4). In 570 *dis* (*manibus*) is transliterated as Δεις; *deis manibus* is attested four times in Latin inscriptions from Rome, and there are also examples of *deis* in other collocations. *Maritus* is transliterated as μαρειτω at 346; for *mareitus* see *CIL* VI.15346 (4). *Filius* (*-a*) is sometimes transliterated with ει in the first syllable (346, 1040 twice); cf. in Latin *feil-* at *CIL* VI.12784 and elsewhere.

These constant correspondences between the use of ει in transliterated Latin words in Roman inscriptions, and of *ei* in the same words in Latin inscriptions in Latin script from the same area, make it virtually certain that those who used ει in the transliterated form of such words as *libertis*, *suis* and *filius* were familiar not only with the conventional formulae of Latin epitaphs, but also with the artificial Latin orthographic habit of using *ei* to mark long *i* in such words. The writer of 616, far from being unversed in Latin literacy, displays a knowledge not only of Greek formal orthography (hence ει in a Greek proper name), but also of Latin. It is hardly conceivable that such a person was unable to write Latin script. If he was a professional stonecutter, it is likely that he operated in both languages (and scripts). Whatever the case, he (or his client) apparently chose to use Greek characters in the writing of a Latin text; he was not compelled by his deficiencies in literacy to do so. It is revealing that in 616 ει is written a number of times in final syllables. In this position long vowels were subject to shortening; a phonetic transcription of (e.g.) *coniugi* would have been unlikely to produce ει at the end of the word. The spelling is not phonetic but artificial.

There are various errors in 616 which add to the picture of the writer/author. Whereas εωρουμ (found once in the text) is a conventional transliteration of *eorum* (with ου = short *u*), εωρυμ (also found once) reveals the graphemic influence of Lat. *eorum* (see 5.V.4), and is a further hint of the writer's familiarity with Latin script. He remembered to use the conventional transliteration in one place, but then was incapable of avoiding the more Latinate orthography. The omission of -μ in μονομεντου ηδεφικατου (= *monumentum aedificatum*) betrays the influence of Latin speech on the writer. Also of interest in this expression is the ε (for *i*) in the second syllable of ηδεφικατου. This perhaps represents the close *e* which resulted from the merger of CL long *e* and short *i*. The form *mono-* for *monu-* is attested in Latin (e.g. *CIL* VIII.1460.83), possibly in this case reflecting the merger of CL long *o* and short *u* as close *o*.

Twice φηκετ is written with ε rather than ι in the ending. Leiwo (1995b: 298) comments: 'I cannot give the reason for this, since there are no plausible phonological reasons. I can only suggest it was an idiosyncrasy of the engraver.' But such perfect-tense verb-forms are widespread in Latin inscriptions, including those transliterated into Greek script. At Pompeii, for example, *dixet* is attested, and there is an example of *fecet* on an amphora from Stabiae.[127] For *fecet*/φηκετ, see further *CIL* IX.648 (= 6220, *ILCV* II.4893, *CJI* 611, Noy (1993), 86), *IG* XIV.698 (transliterated Latin from Sorrento), *CJI* 615 (= Noy (1993), 67), *IPO* B.257, 261, A. and J. Šašel (1963), 184. There are 14 examples of *fecet* listed in the index to *CIL* VI. Differing determinants may lie behind such spellings. On the one hand, particularly in the later period, the merger of long *e* and short *i* as close *e* might have generated such forms. On the other hand the perfect ending in *-ed* is well attested in Oscan (cf. also *feced* in the Duenos inscription, *CIL* I². 4), with *t* sometimes replacing *d* (note the Oscan inscription in Greek letters, Vetter (1953), 191, containing δεδετ), and it is possible that at least some cases of *fecet* and other such perfect verb-forms are relics of an old dialectally determined spelling which had been Latinised to the extent that the final consonant had been changed. Whatever the case, the presence of the form in 616 is a further hint that the writer's spelling methods were rooted in Latin culture.

---

[127] See Väänänen (1966: 22).

The omission of τ in εσ = *est* may merely be a piece of carelessness. In koine Greek there is evidence for the occasional omission or assimilation of τ after σ (e.g. ἐσσί for ἐστί, γράσι for γράστιν),[128] but the similarities are not decisive enough to establish that interference has taken place from Greek to Latin in this case.

The form Τιλεσφορος, later in the same text written correctly with ε in the first syllable, is a curiosity. It cannot readily be explained as a Latin-based deviation (though it could of course be a mere slip). In koine Greek there was interchange of ε and ι mainly 'in specific phonetic conditions, namely before back vowels, nasals, liquids, or /s/' (Gignac 1976: 249). For ε > ι before a liquid, see Gignac (1976: 250*d*). Τιλεσφορος might be a representation of a Greek's (in this case a bilingual's) pronunciation of the name (with as well a Greek inflection: see below).

I turn finally to the inflection of the full name. In the name Ιουλ<ι>ους Τιλεσφορος the Latin *nomen* has been given a Latin (transliterated) nominative ending, whereas the Greek *cognomen* has a Greek ending.[129] The distinction might seem to imply that the writer knew both languages,[130] as indeed is likely. This however is not an isolated case but typical of a widespread phenomenon. In Latin funerary inscriptions from many areas (e.g. Ostia, Barcelona, to mention just two), persons from the servile classes with Latin *nomina* are regularly assigned a Greek inflection in their Greek *cognomina* (whereas their Latin names have Latin inflections). This mixture is particularly common in the case of females with Greek *cognomina*. It is dealt with below, 4.v.3.1.

I conclude. That Latin epitaphs should sometimes be written in Greek script may variously reflect the lack of assurance in Latin script of the deceased, or of his relative who commissioned the epitaph, or of his circle of acquaintances who were expected to read the inscription, or of the stonecutter. In *IGUR* 616 the choice of Greek script is not explicable from the illiteracy in Latin script of the drafter/stonecutter. He seems to have been a Latin speaker familiar with certain artificial aspects of Latin orthography. The graphemic form of a word in Latin script can sometimes be glimpsed through the Greek script (e.g. εωρυμ). On the other hand he knew a Greek convention of using ει in Greek names to indicate long *i*, and he could distinguish the Greek and Latin nominative singular endings. There are also some possible traces of Greek interference in his Latin. He was almost certainly bilingual, and able to use both scripts. That he used the wrong script shows that he had received

---

[128] See Gignac (1976: 66).   [129] See also Leiwo (1995b: 297–8).
[130] See Leiwo (1995b: 297–8).

a special commission. We can rule out the possibility that all Latin texts transliterated into Greek letters represent a phonetic transcription of Latin speech. 'Phonetic transcriptions' may exist (see the next section), but that is not the whole story. I return below (VIII) to the question why someone capable of using Latin script might have chosen to use Greek.

VII.2.3 Latin written in Greek script by possible illiterates in Latin script
I turn now to those who seem to have had no choice but to use Greek script when writing Latin, either because they were only partially literate (i.e. in one script but not the other), or because they were unsure of their ability to use Latin script. If they were unversed in Latin script and orthography, they might be expected to produce something resembling a phonetic transcription of their Latin speech, with orthographic and perhaps other forms of interference from Greek. Texts of this kind ought in theory to take us into the world of an important but shadowy group, whose non-standard Latin differed from the 'Vulgar Latin' of monolinguals in various ways, and who may have engaged in code-switching or even used a mixed language.

The following is a receipt of the second century AD written by a slave trader Aeschines Flavianus from Miletus, recording the sale of a female slave to a soldier of the Ravenna fleet, T. Memmius Montanus. The receipt was written in Ravenna, but found in the Fayûm, where it must have been carried by Montanus. Aeschines may not have been a Roman citizen,[131] but it would seem that he was in the habit of conducting business with Latin speakers:

SB III.1.6304 = *CPL* 193 = *AE* 1922, 135
Γαιω Κουρτιω Ιουστω Πουπλιω Ιουλιω Ναυτωνε
κωνσουλιβους σεξστουμ *νωνας* οκτωβρης.
Αἰσχίνης Αἰσχίνου Φλαουιανὸς Μιλήσιος **σκρι-**
ψι μη ακκηπισσε α Τιτω Μεμμιω Μοντανω
μιλιτε πεντηρω Αυγιστι δηναριους σεσκεντους βιγεντι κινκυε **πρετιουμ** πουελλαι Μαρ-
μαριαι βετρανε, **κουαμ ει δουπλα οπτιμις κον-**
δικιωνιβους βενδιδιτ [*sic*] ετ τραδιδι εξ εντερρογατιωνε φακτα ταβελλαρουν σιγναταρουμ.
ακτουμ καστρις κλασσης πραιτωριαι Ραβεν-
νατους.

---

[131] See Eger (1921: 455).

The text is transliterated into Latin letters at the end of this section (p. 63).

In the consulship of Gaius Curtius Iustus and Publius Iulius Nauto, 2 October. I, Aeschines Flavianus, son of Aeschines, a Milesian, wrote that I have received from Titus Memmius Montanus, soldier of the quinquireme 'Augustus', 625 *denarii* as the price of a Marmarian (?) girl, a 'veteran' [i.e. a slave of more than a year's standing], whom (I) [lit. 'he'] sold to him, with a liability to double repayment, on excellent terms and handed over after inspection of the sealed tablets. Transacted at the camp of the praetorian fleet of Ravenna.

The wording and structure of the receipt are formulaic. Numerous such documents survive from Pompeii (*CIL* IV.3340),[132] most of which concern sales by auction. Two types of document predominate in the Pompeian material. First, there are texts written by the banker Iucundus or a secretary, stating that the vendor has received before witnesses the money due to him.[133] The second type is that to which the above text belongs. Such texts are written by the vendor or a representative in the first person, with a formulaic structure beginning *L. Titius scripsi me accepisse...*[134] One of the Pompeian documents of the same form as the above text from the Fayûm is also written in Greek letters (*CIL* IV.3340, xxxii). It was clearly a requirement that the correct form of wording should be used, and that the vendor should if possible write the receipt in his own hand (but see further below, 5.VII.2.2). If he used Greek letters that could only mean that he felt unable to write in Latin script, particularly since free composition was not needed. An exemplar must have been copied out with a certain number of gaps to be filled in, or alternatively a text might sometimes have been taken down from dictation. It is not clear whether the text which Aeschines copied was in Latin or Greek script (see further below). If he was ignorant of Latin, both in its spoken and written forms, it is possible that someone first wrote the text out for him in Greek letters. But it seems a reasonable supposition that he did understand Latin up to a point. Some of his errors betray an awareness of the morphological structure of the language. There are also variations in the distribution and nature of the errors across the fixed and the variable parts of the document, which, as we will see, would be explicable if he were filling in gaps himself, perhaps with dictated assistance.

The text is an important specimen of the Latin of a learner. It reveals the types of deviations from the standard language which might have been heard from an imperfect bilingual. It also provides evidence that

---

[132] See Mommsen (1877), Andreau (1974).   [133] See Andreau (1974: 19).
[134] See Mommsen (1877: 103), Andreau (1974: 19).

even a text copied from a correct model will not necessarily be free from bilingual interference and code-switching, if the copier had imperfect command of the second language. This evidence is relevant to the interpretation of the errors to be found in inscriptions on stone. Many inscriptions must have been composed by one person and carved by another, but it cannot be assumed that errors are exclusively those of the drafter (see below, VIII).

The document contains parts which are particular to the sale in hand (such as the date, the names of the parties to the transaction, and the sum of money received), as well as formulaic phraseology. The formulaic words (transliterated back into Latin) are: *scripsi me accepisse a . . . pretium . . . qu- ei . . . optimis condicionibus uendidi[t] et tradidi ex interrogatione facta tabellarum signatarum. actum . . .* I have printed these formulaic parts in bold (above). The underlining in the text as set out above indicates errors of one sort or another (on which see below).

The formula *scripsi me accepisse* occurs repeatedly in the wax tablets published at *CIL* IV.3340; and for *ex interrogatione facta tabellarum* see *CIL* IV.3340, xxxii in Greek script. In the following discussion the distinction between the formulaic and the variable parts will be kept in mind. Statistics showing the distribution of errors will be given later in the section.

The document displays linguistic and orthographic features which can be classified into several categories.

First, there is an element of correct and artificial orthography which could derive from a written exemplar, or perhaps from very close supervision of the writer by a Latin-speaking expert, but not from the act of writing down the sounds of the language. Both in the date, which is conspicuously correct, not only in its naming of the consuls but also in its specification of the day of the transaction, and in the formulaic parts, final -*m* is consistently written even though it would not have been pronounced: σεξστουμ, πρετιουμ, κουαμ, σιγναταρουμ, ακτουμ; on ταβελλαρουν see below. In the date, σεξστουμ also reflects the artificial Latin spelling *xs* for *s*;[135] it is not phonetically determined. In κωνσουλιβους the *n* would not have been pronounced, and the long *o* in the first syllable is also correct. If Aeschines had had the date written out for him in Latin letters, would he have known when to write *omega* and when to write *omicron*? He also correctly distinguishes between long and short *e* in the date. I stress the correctness of the date. There is abundant evidence that the Latin dating system, particularly that by the day, was poorly

---

[135] On *xs* see Adams (1995a: 90–1). For the intrusion of *xs* into Greek (mainly in Latin words), see Gignac (1976: 141).

understood under the Empire by those whose education fell short of the highest standards, and that it caused special trouble to learners of Latin as a second language.[136] I conclude that Aeschines had in front of him a written text, certainly of the date and probably of the fixed sections (see further below). A Greek incapable of using Latin letters could not conceivably have written these various words correctly by free composition or from dictation, unless they were dictated letter by letter.

Secondly, there is an element of Greek interference in the text, not only in the original parts, but also in the formulaic sections. I take first errors of this type in the formulaic parts.

In εντερρογατιωνε it is possible that the initial ε reflects the Vulgar Latin merger of long *e* and short *i* as a close *e*, but it is more likely that the prefix *in-* has been replaced by the corresponding εν- of Greek. A case of such morphological interference, but of the inverse kind (i.e. of Latin on Greek in a Greek text), is to be seen in the form ἰνγόνιν (<ἐγγόνιον)[137] in an inscription, meant to be in Greek but heavily Latinised, from the Jewish community at Venusia (*CIL* IX.6230 = *ILCV* 4895 = *CJI* 590 = Noy (1993), 62). A scribe overseeing the legalistic dealings of members of the Ravenna fleet, a man who could compose dates with accuracy and who knew when to write *-m*, is unlikely to have committed the slip seen above. It must represent Aeschines' own input into the copying of the text.

The only other comparable slip in the formulaic sections is ταβελλαρουν (= *tabellarum*), which shows orthographic interference. Here Aeschines failed to write -μ but fell instead into the -ν which in final position was natural to a Greek.[138] An exact parallel is at *ILCV* 4919 (Αυρηλιους Διονυσιους Ιουδεους Τιβε<ρ>ιηνσις αν. XXXXX, **φιλιωρουν** τριουν πατερ).

Greek interference and also code-switching are found in the variable parts of the document as well. Aeschines writes his name and patronymic with Greek inflections in 1.3. The genitive Αἰσχίνου is not Latinised, as it could readily have been, and the nominatives in -ος are Greek rather than transliterated Latin. Αἰσχίνου is a Greek word with a Greek inflection in a Latin text, and it fits the definition of code-switching given at p. 26. Aeschines has used Greek in writing what is in effect his signature.

The accusatives δηναριους σεσκεντους exhibit morphological interference (see above, V, p. 25). The phonetic rendering of Lat. long *o* in

---

[136] See Adams (1994a: 92–5, 108–9).

[137] Noy (1993: 83) cites also *CJI* 92 ἐγγόνιν, where the prefix is correct.

[138] I refer to 'orthographic' rather than 'phonetic' interference, because in Latin final *-m* was not pronounced. Its replacement by the Greek final ν thus represents a phenomenon of writing rather than of pronunciation.

a Greek text was ω, as e.g. in 2 κωνσουλιβους, Νωνας and Οκτωβρης. The digraph ου, as we have seen, was used to transliterate both the short and long *u* of Latin, as e.g. in line 1 Ιουλιω (representing long *u*) and line 2 σεξστουμ (representing short *u*), but here it belongs instead to the Greek accusative plural ending. For further examples of Greek endings in Latin words in transliterated Latin texts, see below, IX (5). It was no doubt all too easy for someone using Greek letters in the writing of Latin to slip into such mistakes (cf. 4.V.3.2, V.3.3). The Greek script (associated by definition with Greek morphemes) triggers by association the switch into Greek morphology. It is therefore necessary to see such morphological interference as a feature particularly of the written language; a Greek need not have been so prone to morphological mistakes when speaking Latin. The error in our text would in any case seem to imply a degree of bilingualism on Aeschines' part. If he was copying a text written in Latin letters, he must have recognised *-os* as accusative. If on the other hand a clerk was dictating the Latin to him, he was able to interpret the spoken form of *denarios* as an accusative plural.

κλάσσης in line 10 is not a transliteration of *classis* (genitive); as was noted earlier (V), the form displays the regular Greek genitive inflection of the Latin loan-word as it had been integrated into Greek. *Classis* is declined κλάσσα, -αν, -ης, -η in Greek papyri.[139] It was argued above (V) that Greek has momentarily 'leaked' into Aeschines' attempt at Latin (a type of code-switching, or, possibly, interference). The switch again implies a degree of bilingualism on Aeschines' part. Whether he was copying a written Latin text (in Greek or Latin script) or receiving dictation, he must have understood the case of the Latin *-is* ending. If on the other hand he was composing this (variable) part of the text himself, he was by definition using a variety of Latin, if only one marked by code-switching and interference.

The third feature of the text is the presence, in the original but hardly at all in the formulaic parts, of phonetic spellings representing the sounds of colloquial Latin speech. The spelling κινκυε reflects the dissimilation of the labio-velar at the start of the word under the influence of that in the next syllable.[140] βιγεντι = *uiginti* must show the effects of the merger of CL long *e* and short *i* as close *e*, in this case probably in an unaccented syllable, since *uiginti* seems to have been stressed on the initial syllable.[141] βετρανε displays syncope, and also the effects of the monophthongisation of *ae* in the final syllable. The diphthong had the same outcome in the Romance languages as the classical short *e*,[142] and here it is rendered as a

---

[139] See Gignac (1981: 7). [140] Cf. Fr. *cinq*, It. *cinque*, and see Schopf (1919: 127).
[141] See Väänänen (1981: 35, 119). [142] See the comprehensive discussion of R. Coleman (1971).

short vowel. Aeschines has given a phonetic transcription in Greek letters of how the word would have sounded in spoken Latin, particularly that of lower social classes. The Greek letters make the spelling more revealing than it would have been if Latin letters had been used, because the Greek alphabet allowed a distinction between long and short *e*.

Fourthly, in the original sections there are inexplicable errors. The last word in the document, Ραβενναrous, represents the Latin adjective *Rauennas, -atis*, but the ending is a mistake. In line 5 the phrase μιλιτε πεντηρω Αυγιστι presents some problems. What is the second word? The most obvious interpretation is that it stands for πεντήρης 'quin-quireme', a word which very occasionally turns up in Latin in the form *penteris*;[143] the sense would be 'a soldier of [or 'from'] the quinquireme "Augustus" '. Either a genitive or an ablative would in theory have been possible in such an expression (cf. *ala/alae* used interchangeably in mili-tary inscriptions of the *ala* to which a man belonged: see below, 5.VII.1, n. 142). The genitive *Augisti* (*sic*) would be a genitive of definition (cf. Claudius Terentianus, *P. Mich.* VIII.467.25 *in liburna N[e]ptuni* 'on the ship "Neptune" '). If the expression is to be interpreted along these lines, then it is of interest, first, that the Greek term has been used rather than *quinquiremis*. Given the rarity of *penteris* in Latin (two examples in the ps.-Caesarean corpus and one in Isidore), it is unlikely that the word would have been used officially in the Ravenna fleet itself. Aeschines rather than a scribe was probably responsible for the choice of the word. The ending would also be a mistake, because it is neither a correct Greek inflection (the expected Attic genitive would have been -ous) nor a Latinised ab-lative or genitive. It is possible that Aeschines chose to use the Greek word, and made an unsuccessful attempt at Latinising it. πεντηρω is taken differently at *TLL* X.1.1120.20, as a derivative adjective *penterus, -a, -um* from the Greek noun, supposedly with the meaning 'ad penterem pertinens'. The sense would thus roughly be 'a quinquireme-soldier of the "Augustus" '. No other example of *penterus* is attested either in Latin or Greek, and the expression would be an extraordinary one, with *Augisti* tacked on in the genitive without a supporting noun (such as *liburna* in the passage of Terentianus cited above). Such an expression could not repre-sent official usage, but would have to be considered a bizarre form of free composition by Aeschines himself. Another possible explanation of the form is that it reflects a number of developments in vulgar Greek. Perhaps the second-declension genitive ending -ου has intruded into a third-declension word (for which see Gignac (1981: 43)), and ου has been misspelt

---

[143] See *TLL* X.1.1120.13ff.

as ω (for which see Gignac (1976: 208)). On this view the form would have to be classified as a Greek-based error rather than as 'inexplicable', as it is here.

Αυγιστι also contains an anomalous misspelling. The word would normally have been spelt in Greek characters with ου in the second syllable.[144] Gignac (1976: 217–26) in his account of the use of ου and variants in the transliteration of Latin words in the papyri does not record a confusion of ου with ι.

Finally, there is just one example of another type of mistake, which I would call a 'comprehensible' slip. I refer to the ending of *bendidit* (8). The verb should be in the first person, like the juxtaposed *tradidi*, but it has been mistakenly put in the third person. Such a mistake is not difficult to understand. Formal texts are often in the first or the third person indifferently, and a writer will sometimes mechanically switch from one person to the other, having lost the drift of the text for a moment. In funerary inscriptions we sometimes find first and third persons conflated in this way. There is though a significance to this mistake. Considered in isolation the form itself is neither non-existent nor meaningless, and its presence implies that Aeschines knew some verb endings, and that he was even aware of the variable use of first and third persons in some types of texts. If he knew some verb endings, he knew some Latin, and was not therefore simply a copyist writing in a language incomprehensible to him. The possibility must however be left open that the 'error' was in the exemplar which Aeschines had.

In the original parts of the text there is thus an accumulation both of phonetic spellings derived from spoken colloquial Latin, and of errors/anomalies which cannot be accounted for on normal linguistic grounds. Table 1 shows the distribution of the various types of errors.

Table 1

	Interference errors	Phonetic spellings	Other
formulaic parts	2	1	1 = 4
non-formulaic	3	7	4[145] = 14

---

[144] See Gignac (1976: 218).

[145] I include *Augisti* under this heading, and also the lexical choice of *penter-* instead of the proper Latin *quinquiremis*. It is immaterial for our purposes whether the ending of πεντηρω represents an intrusion from vulgar Greek, or is an inexplicable slip: the point is that it occurs in a non-formulaic part of the document.

After the date I have noted 18 errors, no fewer than 14 of which are in the non-formulaic parts. This unequal distribution is the more striking in that the two components of the text from line 4 onwards, that is the formulaic and the non-formulaic parts, are virtually identical in length, 18 words as against 17.

Some further comments on the distribution of the various types of mistakes as shown by the table might be worthwhile. First, phonetic spellings overwhelmingly predominate in the original, non-formulaic sections, by 7:1, with the only possible phonetic error in the formulaic parts to be seen in the *b* of *uendidit*. I would conclude from this that Aeschines had a written exemplar in the formulaic parts, but that an element of dictation or free composition went into the non-formulaic parts other than the date.

Secondly, the incomprehensible errors to which I referred (shown in the table under 'other') are found only in the non-formulaic parts. The one error under 'other' which appears in the table in the formulaic parts is the ending of *bendidit*, which, as I have argued, is not really incomprehensible at all. Here, then, in the exclusive appearance of pointless errors in the non-formulaic parts, is further evidence that in these Aeschines did not have a full written exemplar to follow.

Finally, interference errors are found as well in the formulaic parts as in the non-formulaic. The obvious conclusion to be drawn from this is that, whether at a particular moment Aeschines was following a written text or dictation, he filtered his perception of Latin through the eyes of a first-language speaker of Greek, a language which was by so far his stronger that he was incapable of avoiding lapses into the sounds and endings of that language.

The evidence suggests that the document was put together through a mixture of dictation and copying of an exemplar. It is likely that someone wrote out the date for Aeschines perhaps even in Greek letters, and that he either copied it accurately himself or even used the other person's version. He then wrote his name in Greek without error. Next he proceeded to the document proper. The virtual absence of phonetic errors in the formulaic parts suggests that there was an exemplar available, with blanks. The preponderance of phonetic spellings in the non-formulaic parts implies that an element of spoken Latin lies in the background here. Either Aeschines used free composition, putting the sounds of his Latin speech into writing, or alternatively, and this seems more likely, there was a Latin-speaking assistant on hand to help him fill in the blanks, employing mainly dictation. It is inconceivable that he filled in the blanks entirely on his own. The individual words of the non-formulaic parts may be original to this particular case, but the structures into which they fall are formulaic, and he must have been told how to proceed. The description of the slave as βετρανε, for example, represents technical legal usage (*ueteranus* indicated a slave of more than one year's standing, in contrast to *nouicius*). But the expression μιλιτε πεντηρω Αυγιστι in particular looks like the free composition of someone with a poor grasp of Latin.

Did Aeschines know Latin, if only in a reduced form, or was he entirely dependent on a model and the dictation of an assistant? We have seen signs that he did have some understanding of Latin. If the original parts of the document were composed to the same high level of accuracy as the formulaic parts, it would be hazardous to argue that Aeschines was doing anything other than copying out a text. But the intrusion of errors into these variable sections of a sort which a professional Latin-speaking scribe would not have committed suggests that Aeschines was up to a point attempting to use the language himself; μιλιτε πεντηρω Αυγιστι, however it is to be taken, cannot but be a Greek's 'creative' composition. The lapse into the Greek accusative form in δηναριους σεσκεντους, which syntactically meets the requirements of the sentence, shows that, whether Aeschines had *denarios* before him in a written exemplar, or had heard *denarios* spoken as dictation, he was able to interpret the case correctly. The case of *classis* was also understood.

Aeschines, though a Milesian, was himself at Ravenna doing business with the Ravenna fleet. As a trader who travelled on business to the west, he is bound to have had a working knowledge of Latin. Basing myself on the presence of peculiar errors and substandard phonetic spellings in the variable sections of the document and the absence of such deviations from the formulaic sections, I would maintain that it is justified to treat the text as something more revealing than a scribally determined collection of formulae. Though the text is formulaic, Aeschines' own input can be detected, and this input provides evidence for the language use of a Greek with imperfect command of Latin as a second language. I list the main features of Aeschines' Latin:

(1) His Latin was heavily influenced by Greek, particularly in morphology. He could not avoid Greek morphological/orthographic interference even when copying out formulae. On this evidence poorly educated Greek learners of Latin would constantly have transferred Greek morphemes into their Latin, though it would not do to argue from such mistakes in transliterated written documents that interference was as

common in their speech. The Greek inflection of Aeschines' name and patronymic is not a case of interference, but of code-switching. Even Greeks assimilated to Latin culture tended to revert to the Greek inflection of their Greek names when writing Latin (see 4.v.3).

(2) Certain inflections are aberrational, that is neither Greek nor genuinely Latin. Such errors are symptomatic of a less than total control of Latin inflectional morphology. The speaker, uncertain of the correct morpheme, may make something up. To what extent are there wrong inflections in learners' Latin? Are there particular areas of Latin inflectional morphology which gave learners problems? These questions will be considered in Chapter 8 (also below, IX).

(3) The speech of Aeschines – who can scarcely be described as an 'élite' bilingual – will have been influenced by the lower social dialects of Latin (note βιγεντι, κινκυε, and particularly βετρανε). The existence side-by-side of Greek interference and colloquial Latin features in the Latin of lower-class Greeks is a phenomenon which will come up again.

Thus Aeschines was a Greek who was illiterate in Latin, and who, if he ever spoke the language, would have used a variety of Latin recognisable as 'Greeks' Latin'.[146] 'Foreigner talk' is well attested, as we will see, though disregarded in accounts of subliterary Latin. It must have been

---

[146] The subscription by a witness to the receipt is also of interest in this respect: *idem cosulubus aeadem diem Domitius Theophilus scrisi me in ueditionem puellae Marmariae supra scriptae pro Aescine Aescine philium Flauianum secumdum auctorem exstitisse. acctum.* Theophilus' Latin writing combines Greek interference with phonetic spellings based in Latin speech. *ph* (in *philium*) was the correct transliteration of Greek φ as used in the Latin versions of Greek words. But if it is transferred to a Latin word in a text in the Latin language then there has been a form of interference. Such a spelling is unlikely to have been committed by a first-language speaker of Latin. The spelling also implies that the sound represented by φ was now a fricative rather than an aspirated stop (see Gignac (1976: 99) on φ for Latin *f*). There is another example of this spelling of *filius* at *IPO* A 198. It is possible that both writers were familiar with the transliteration of the word into Greek letters (φιλιους), which is not uncommon (note for example κον φιλιους βενε μερεντες at *ILCV* 4463; cf. *IGUR* 350, Audollent (1904), 270.6, 9, 12, 13, 16, 21), and that *philium* represents a transliteration of that form. For Latin phonetic spellings, note *scrisi* (for which see 4.v.1.3), *ueditionem*, with omission of the nasal before a stop (see e.g. Väänänen (1966: 67–8)), *cos-*, with banal omission of *n* before *s*, and *acctum* (this may be an attempt to represent the long *a* and the syllabic arrest that it caused). There is hypercorrection (*aeadem* – see e.g. *O. Wâdi Fawâkhir* 1.12 *aeorum* –, *diem = die*, and perhaps *secumdum*), a 'genitive' inflection (*Aescine*) that is neither Greek nor Latin (cf. the various inexplicable forms in the receipt of Aeschines), and a fossilisation of *idem* (equivalent to an ablative plural) of a type which does not seem to be attested (for various possible fossilised uses of *idem*, though not of this kind, see Konjetzny (1906–8: 306–7), Sturtevant (1907)). The use of the accusative seen in *philium* is open to several explanations within the norms of substandard Latin. The first possibility is that it is a sort of 'accusative of apposition', a usage which, though by no means as common as the nominative of apposition, does exist: both cases are sometimes treated as unmarked base-forms into which a writer slips when strictly the apposition requires an oblique case (for the accusative used thus, see p. 227; cf. 447). See e.g. *RIB* 1064 *D.M. Victoris natione Maurum, CIL* VI.3454 *D.M. Aurelie Gorsile coniugi bene merenti, . . . natione Acuicesem, CIL* III.371 add. p. 977 *Thalarioni puerum sum.* In this last text another

an important form of communication particularly among traders. The strangeness of the form of Latin used by Aeschines can be seen from the parts printed in bold in the following transliteration of the text back into Latin:

C. Curtio Iusto P. Iulio Nautone
consulibus sexstum nonas octobres.
Aeschines **Aeschinu Flauianos Milesios** scripsi me accepisse a T. Memmio Montano
milite **pentero Augisti denarious sescen-**
tous bigenti cinque pretium puellae Marmariae betrane quam ei dupla optimis condicionibus bendidit et tradidi ex **enterro-**
gatione facta **tabellarun** signatarum.
actum castris **classes** praetoriae **Raben-**
natus.

Transliterated Latin texts are thus a mixed bag, ranging from those in which the use of Greek script was not, as far as we can tell, forced on the writer by his unfamiliarity with Latin script but was a matter of choice, to those in which the writer had no choice: he was either illiterate or of low competence or confidence in Latin script.

VII.2.4 Some other scripts

I have dealt in detail here only with Greek in Latin script, but transliteration of other types survives from antiquity, and the phenomenon is known in more modern times. I mention a few examples, and make a distinction between transliteration of the type seen so far, and the loss of a script which sometimes accompanies the disappearance of a culture.

possible example (*presentibus collegibus suis, id est Perulam et Frontinum . . .*) is open to a different explanation: *id est* could govern an accusative as if it were a preposition. Secondly, the writer may have switched unconsciously in mid-phrase from the correct prepositional case (ablative) to the new substandard prepositional use of the accusative: note e.g. *CIL* III.6122 add. p. 1336 *ex equtibus siculares*, *CIL* VI.880 *pro filiis suis A. Perelium Nymphium, A. Perelium Nymphodorum*. The two explanations are not mutually exclusive. The last example cited is exactly parallel to the example in Theophilus. The accusative of apposition, which scarcely finds its way into the literature (but see the cursory and somewhat unsatisfactory remarks of Svennung (1935: 175–6)), could do with proper treatment. Some of the examples cited by Konjetzny (1906–8: 319) would have to be brought into a discussion of the accusative as a 'default' case. It may tentatively be suggested that Theophilus was a Greek speaker of colloquial Latin, who had received some instruction in the writing of Latin (note particularly the hypercorrect use of -*m* and of *ae*), but was not so sure of the Latin inflectional system that he could readily Latinise Greek endings and avoid blatant errors of inflection.

There are examples of Greek written in Latin script, though the reverse phenomenon is much more common;[147] the unequal distribution probably reflects the greater numbers of poorly educated Greeks learning Latin under the Empire as compared with poorly educated Romans learning Greek. Some cases of Greek transliterated into Latin were seen above, v, in the tags at the end of Roman funerary inscriptions. Or again, *PSI* vii.743 (= *CPL* 69) is a fragmentary conversation in transliterated Greek between Alexander and the gymnosophists. *P.Tebt.* ii.586 is part of 'a contract for a loan of money from Gaius Julius Fuscus to Psenkebkis, the creditor having a right of ἐνοίκησις in place of interest'. The verso contains the title of the contract in Greek, and then some Greek in Latin letters: *enegoisis Psengebgis Marheus* (i.e. ἐνοίκησις Ψενκήβκιος Μαρρήους). On the embedding of the Greek verb ἐπιδέδωκα in Latin letters in a piece of Latin at *P. Oxy.* ii.244, see 3.ii (5). A curious example of such transliteration is found in a Demotic–Greek bilingual from Edfu (*O. Warsaw* 139802), published by Zauzich (1984). The main part of the text is in Demotic, but the name (of the contributor of a tax) and the date are then given in Latin script (*Pachombechis Petestheo[s] Payni XI*). The numeral as well as the letters is Latin, but the syntax and morphology of the filiation are Greek transliterated into Latin. See further 5.i.i.

Two specimens of Greek written in Latin letters (*BGU* xi.2116 as read by Browne (1969), and also J. Rea in a note on *P. Oxy.* xxxvi.2772 (p. 63 n. 1)), and *P. Oxy.* xxxvi.2772) illustrate again the point made in the previous sections, that not all cases of transliteration are open to the same explanation. Transliteration may be a matter of necessity or choice.

In the first a Roman called Cosmus writes to a certain Petermuthis in Greek. The Greek is done by a professional scribe, and a reason is given: διὰ τὸ βραδύτερα γράφειν of Cosmus. Then Cosmus attempts some Greek himself at the end of the document, but using Latin script: *Cosmus [. . . d]edanica ṭas proc̣iṃ[enas argyriu drachma]s hebdẹmeconta* [sic] *dio* (= Κόσμος δεδάνεικα τὰς προκειμένας ἀργυρίου δραχμὰς ἑβδομήκοντα δύο. Noteworthy here is the phonetic spelling of the sounds represented by diphthong spellings in 'correct' Greek: *i* is written for ει in *dedanica* and *procimenas*; and there is also *i* for *u* in *dio*.[148] Phonetic spellings of this type suggest that the writer knew Greek in a spoken form, but had not been formally trained in its writing. The statement of his 'slow writing' is probably a reference to virtual illiteracy in Greek. The reason for this illiteracy,

[147] See Kramer (1984: 1381), citing Sijpesteijn (1980: 104), who offers a few remarks on such transliteration; also Donderer (1995: 104–8).
[148] Cf. Gignac (1976: 267).

unusually, emerges from the other part of the document: the writer was literate in Latin, and therefore only a second-language speaker of Greek.

But *P. Oxy.* XXXVI.2772 is a different matter. It is a letter from Julius Lepus to Archibius the banker instructing him to pay 1,953 drachmas to another banker Harpocration: *Iulios Lepos Archibio collybiste chaerein. poeson moe para Arpochrationi collybiste argyriu drachmas chilias [.]enacosias penteconta [trei]ş g(inontae) dr(achmae) MCMLIII [.] etoş XL [.] Caẹsaros Pachon III* (= Ἰούλιος Λέπος Ἀρχιβίῳ κολλυβιστῇ χαίρειν. πόησόν μοι παρὰ Ἁρποχρατίωνι κολλυβιστῇ ἀργυρίου δραχμὰς χιλίας ἐνακοσίας πεντήκοντα [τρεῖ]ς. γ(ίνονται) δρ(αχμαὶ) 1,953. ἔτους 40 Καίσαρος Παχὼν 3).[149] The assumption has been made that Julius Lepus was a Roman citizen and a native speaker of Latin who had learnt Greek orally without studying the language formally.[150] This view does not entirely stand up to examination. The writer does not use phonetic spellings for the old diphthongs at all.

Particularly striking is the spelling *moe* = μοι. The pronoun was pronounced with a monophthong in Greek at this period, as is established by the extremely common interchange of οι with υ in Greek papyri from the first century onwards: see Gignac (1976: 197) 'There is a frequent interchange of οι with etymologically long or short υ in various phonetic environments, indicating the identification of the classical short diphthong /oi/ with the simple vowel /y/.' In no sense is *moe* a phonetic spelling such as might have been perpetrated by someone who spoke Greek but had not been instructed in its writing. The spelling implies that the writer knew (1) that the Greek word was correctly spelt μοι and (2) that in learned orthography *oe* was the conventional representation in Latin of Greek οι. His knowledge thus concerns both the non-phonetic representation of Greek vowel sounds, and the relationship between the digraphs of Greek and those of Latin.

Similar conclusions may be drawn from the form *chaerein* = χαίρειν. Unlike the writer of *BGU* XI.2116, our writer had not merely heard the vowel sound in the second syllable. He knew the correct written form, with digraph, of the Greek word. He also was familiar with the αι spelling of the first syllable (which will also by this time have represented a monophthong in speech),[151] and again he effected a Latinate conversion αι to *ae* to suit the Latin script (cf. *Caesaros*). This is a salutary case, which serves as a warning against the automatic assumption that every

[149] See Kramer (1984: 1381 n. 21).
[150] So Wouters (1976: 181), quoted with approval by Kramer (1984: 1381 with n. 22); also J. Rea, the editor of the letter in *P. Oxy.*
[151] See Gignac (1976: 191).

instance of transliterated Greek or Latin must be attributed to the writer's illiteracy in the target language.

I move on to some different languages and scripts. A funerary inscription from the Jewish community at Venusia (Noy (1993), no. 72) runs: τάφος ῎Ανα διὰ βίου σάλωμ. The last word is a transliteration into Greek of *shalom* 'peace',[152] which is regularly used at Venusia in Hebrew characters (see above, v). Conversely, the text no. 75 starts in Hebrew (and Hebrew characters) with a familiar formula (= 'peace to his resting place'), then continues in Greek transliterated into Hebrew. Origen's *Hexapla* contains Hebrew in Greek letters in one column.[153] An amulet from Sicily is in the Hebrew language but Greek script (Noy (1993), 159; see further below, 2.VIII for this and a comparable text). The Cairo Genizah texts (see de Lange (1996)) are all in Hebrew characters but a mixture of Hebrew and Greek Language. There are some south Oscan inscriptions written in Greek script (Vetter (1953), 180–94, 195a–199). From the Memnonion at Abydos there is an Egyptian Demotic graffito in Greek letters,[154] and at the temple of the Palmyrene gods at Dura-Europos there survives a dedication in the Aramaic language but Greek letters.[155] For a Phoenician graffito in Greek script, see 2.V.9, and for a Punic inscription in Greek letters, see *KAI* 177, discussed at 2.V.9. An Egyptian papyrus containing Greek in Armenian script and dating perhaps from the fifth to the seventh centuries AD has recently been published in full with commentary by Clackson (2000). At a much later date (the Arab period in medieval Spain) we have Spanish texts written in Arabic characters, as the so-called 'poem of Yúçuf', which is dated to about 1300.[156]

From Tripolitania there are some late neo-Punic inscriptions written in Latin script; these texts will be discussed in the next chapter (2.V.6). These come from the period when Punic must have been in decline, and suggest the hypothesis that during a period of language death literacy in the old language may be lost before the language itself dies out completely. As education in Latin literacy spread, local literary culture must have died out, leaving a limited number of speakers with a residual ability to speak Punic but literate only in Latin. Similarly the Etruscan alphabet gave way to the Latin as Romanisation took place in Etruria, and Etruscan was sometimes written in Latin script (see 2.III.6). The same thing happened to Venetic (see 2.II.3, p. 143), Oscan and Umbrian. Similarly, on (e.g.) a late Republican mosaic from Spain a fragmentary Iberian inscription

---

[152] For this type of transliteration, see also Donderer (1995: 104).
[153] See J. Barr (1966–7: 281).   [154] See Pestman (1977), 11.
[155] See Milik (1967) for the text and discussion; also Hillers and Cussini (1996), PAT 1117.
[156] See Gifford and Hodcroft (1966: 110–11), no. 54.

survives written in Latin characters;[157] further Spanish material of this type will be cited below, 2.x.

These last cases all represent stages in the Romanisation of provincial regions, with vernacular scripts replaced by Latin before the vernacular languages were ousted completely. The use of the new script to write the old language is not quite the same as transliteration as it was seen in the previous sections, because neither the Greek and Latin languages nor their scripts were ever lost. Both languages and both scripts were current side by side, but not everyone had received training in the script of his second language, though training was available.

The Jewish case for its part is different from the others just mentioned. The Hebrew language may not have been genuinely current at (e.g.) Venusia; it is, as we saw (v, p. 23), restricted to a few tags, most of them very short. If it is right to suggest that the language was all but defunct, then in this case the Hebrew *language* had been lost before the Hebrew *script*. How could that be? It is possible that Jews held on to their identity by passing on down the generations the script of their language, even if it was never used for anything but a few formulae. There is a parallel to this symbolic use of Hebrew script in the case of Yiddish, which is a form of German written in Hebrew characters. For Hebrew, see further 2.viii. On the use of a distinctive script as a marker of identity once the language associated with that script is defunct, see also below, p. 91.

I mention finally a different case again, some Greco-Babylonian tablets of the third century AD, which have recently been discussed and edited by Geller (1997).[158] These texts are written once in Sumerian or Akkadian, and then on the reverse a transliteration is written in Greek letters. Geller (1997: 47) describes the function of the Greek transliteration thus: it 'was intended to show how the cuneiform is to be read, probably read aloud'. It served a phonetic purpose, at a time when knowledge of the old script clearly still survived, though the languages which it recorded were no longer spoken.

VII.3 Mixed-language texts

Mixed-language documents do not have parallel versions in different languages of the same or similar material, but embody changes of language within one and the same text. These changes usually represent code-switching (see v). Sometimes the base language is easy to identify,

[157] See Gómez Pallarès (1991: 81–2).
[158] I am grateful to James Clackson for this reference.

in that a switch into a second language is brief and represents merely a momentary insertion or 'leak' (on these terms see v) from the dominant language of the text, but alternatively the switching may be so constant that it is difficult or impossible to assign the text to one language or the other. Switching of this type I have called 'alternation'. Here I merely illustrate a few types of such mixed-language texts, leaving detailed discussion to the chapter on code-switching.

The following inscription (on which see also below, 3.XII.1, 4.V.3.1.2) is from the Jewish community at Venusia:

CIL IX.6230 = *ILCV* 4895 = *CJI* 590 = Noy (1993), 62
τάφως Μαννίνες πρεσβιτέρες τιγάτερ Λονγινι πατερις ἰνγόνιν Φαοστινι πατερις ἐτ[ῶν] λη'.

The script is Greek, and it might be argued that the base language too is Greek. Unambiguously Greek is the statement of the age of the deceased, which has ἔτος rather than *annus* and a Greek numeral symbol. Also Greek are τάφως (with a Greek confusion of o and ω),[159] τιγάτερ (misspelt for θυγάτηρ; the use of ε for η must be explained from the loss of quantitative distinctions in Greek), and ἰνγόνιν. This last has the Greek diminutive ending in its reduced form (-ιον > -ιν). The word has however been subject to Latin morphological interference, in that the prefix has been Latinised, as we saw above (VII.2.3). The inflections in Μαννίνες and πρεσβιτέρες will be dealt with in detail in another chapter (4.V.3).

If the inscription is mainly in Greek, it has two switches into Latin of the same type (the genitive expressions Λονγινι πατερις and Φαοστινι πατερις). The language changes about four times in eleven words. The cluster of examples of the Latin masculine genitive names, and of *pateris*, seems to be associated with one family.[160] That family may have been, and perceived itself as, primarily Latin-speaking. Venusia, the birthplace of Horace, had received a Latin colony as long ago as 291 BC, and it was a Roman stronghold on an important route. Not much Greek will have been spoken there by this time, and even Jews may have been holding on to the language only in limited domains, such as the formulaic language of epitaphs (see 4.V.3.1.2). The family may have bowed to the Jewish convention of setting up its epitaphs in Greek, but not to the extent of giving up its Latin identity as expressed by the language in which masculine names were inflected. Arguably the title was inseparable from the name, and hence goes into the same language.

It might reasonably be objected that the interpretation set out in the preceding paragraph assigns an excessively subtle ability to the drafter

---

[159] See Gignac (1976: 275–7).   [160] On which see now Williams (1999).

to switch between the two languages. Greek the inscription may be intended to be, but one must stress the signs of poor competence in that language. The only inflectional endings which are correct both in morphology and syntax are those in the Latin phrases Λονγινι πατερις and Φαοστινι πατερις (though πατερις has an intrusive vowel). Both τάφως and τιγάτερ have a vocalic misspelling in their endings, and τιγάτερ also embodies a syntactic error in that it does not agree in case (genitive) with the name to which it stands in apposition; this error it shares moreover with ἰνγόνιν. The ending of ἔτος is lost. To these errors of Greek must be added the Latinised prefix of ἰνγόνιν.

An alternative interpretation of the mixed language of the inscription therefore suggests itself. The drafter may have set out to write an epitaph in Greek in keeping with an old Jewish convention. But his control of the target language was so poor that he both made errors and was forced to keep switching into Latin morphology. The text would thus display code-switching motivated by lack of control of the target language (on which see 3.II).

Also difficult to interpret are various short inscriptions in two languages, which fall neatly into two halves, e.g:

ILCV 2534 Picen<ti>nus et Panteris i pace, Δουλκιτίου κὲ Μελίσσης τέκνα

IG xiv.678 Heraclas Heraclidu Alexandreus uixit an(nis) L h(ic) s(itus).

It can however be argued in these cases that different languages are selected for different types of information (see 3.v.1, 2). There is no one base language, but an alternation related to the different components of each text. The first text (for which see below, 3.v.1) has the additional interest that it is in a mixture not only of languages but also of scripts. The other code-switching material discussed in this section is in a single script. The educated however would have been capable of using the appropriate script for each of the languages when they engaged in language mixing; the change of script displays the writer's dual competence, and explicitly presents his code-switching as a skilled performance (see e.g. 3.I below). Cicero probably used Greek script in his letters when he switched into Greek. Such bi-literate code-switching in written form can be found in other cultures. In Bulgarian magazine advertisements code-switching from Bulgarian into English is sometimes accompanied by a switch of scripts.[161] There are Egyptian Demotic ostraca from Medinet Madi which have switches into Greek marked by a change of script. The

---

[161] See McClure (1998: 143–4) on the use of the Latin alphabet in code-switching into English in Bulgarian advertising.

Greek is usually either a name or title associated more with Greek than Egyptian culture, as for example names of Roman emperors (e.g. *OMM* 1370 ḥz.t-sp 16 θεοῦ Τραιανοῦ),[162] or a culturally specific Greek technical term, as for example the legal terms αντικατηκωριν = ἀντικατηγορεῖν and αγωκιη = ἀγωγή embedded in the long Demotic texts published by Bresciani, Pernigotti and Betrò (1983) as 26 and 28 respectively.[163] A curiosity is Bresciani, Pernigotti and Betrò (1983), 5, where the writer first declares in Demotic that he will not write in Greek letters, then says in Greek that he is stubborn, gloomy or the like (στυφιν = στύφειν). This is a joke, which interestingly seems to reflect a situation of language (and literacy) learning among primary speakers of Demotic.[164] In several cases the Demotic *ir* 'make' is combined with a Greek infinitive,[165] an anticipation of a Coptic construction.

In this introduction I have used the phrase 'mixed-language text' to describe a text with code-switching. In the survey of languages in contact with Latin which will follow in the next chapter other such texts will be discussed. There the terminology will have to be refined somewhat, in that I will suggest that the term 'code-switching' is not always appropriately applied to mixed-language texts. A distinction will be made between code-switching and what I will call 'language mixing'.

The bilingual issues raised by the texts considered in this section are obvious: the fundamental problem of what motivates code-switching can only be considered for antiquity in the light of evidence of this kind. I return to the subject in Chapter 3.

VII.4 *Texts which implicitly reflect a bilingual situation*

A text, though in a single language, may reveal by various tell-tale signs that its writer was bilingual. The clues may lie in orthography, formulaic content or some other features, such as morphological interference. This is not the place to deal with interference as a whole, a subject which will come up particularly in Chapter 4, but I will say something about orthography, which overlaps to some extent with morphological interference. I take in turn various signs of the implicit bilingualism of the author of a text.

---

[162] See Bresciani and Pintaudi (1987: 124) for this and other examples.
[163] Other examples can be found in the texts discussed by Gallo (1989).
[164] For a brief discussion of the bilingualism of such documents, see Bresciani and Pintaudi (1987), a paper which fails to treat adequately the mixing of languages and scripts.
[165] See for example Bresciani, Pernigotti and Betrò (1983: 29) on no. 21; also Bresciani and Pintaudi (1987: 124).

VII.4.1 Orthographic interference and alphabet-switching

Cross-language orthographic interference falls into two types: (1) spellings typical of one language and script are transferred to the other; (2) Greek letters intrude into Latin script or vice versa. I call this latter phenomenon alphabet- or character-switching.[166] I take the two phenomena separately.

(1) A list of soldiers of the *ala III Assuriorum* (on which see also 5.VII.3), dated to AD 319–29 (*ChLA* 18.660), contains (col. ii, line 2) the expression *prigceps I turmης*. On -ης see below, 5.VII.3. In *prigceps* the writer has failed to convert the Greek representation of the velar nasal (i.e. γ in certain environments) into the Latin representation (i.e. *n*),[167] and has used *g* because it usually corresponds to γ. The writer's script of primary literacy must have been Greek. He had learnt the equivalence g = γ = [g], and made the false assumption that the two graphemes were also equivalent when one of them had another phonetic value [ŋ]. He must have been a literate Greek recruited into the Roman army and employed as a military scribe in his second language.

The same text also has other cases of orthographic interference, which will be discussed in a later chapter (5.VII.3). On the basis of the one item discussed here it may be concluded that the writer could not cope with the multiple phonetic values that a single letter could have. He was probably literate in Latin only in the sense that he had learnt the letters of the alphabet and a single phonetic value for each.

A Latin epitaph from Rome (*IGUR* 728) begins: *D.M.**Cointo** Aug(usti) lib(erto) a frum(ento)* ... The text ends with a transliterated Greek tag (*Palladi, tauta*: see above, V), but is otherwise in correct Latin. But the spelling of *Quintus* in Latin letters was determined by one of the Greek transcriptions of the name, i.e. Κόιντος.[168] The writer/drafter was presumably literate in both scripts, and in one place he fell into a misspelling of category (1). Unlike the soldier who wrote the list above he did not use Greek letters in a Latin text.

It may be conjectured that among some Greeks attempting to write Latin there were several stages in the acquisition of literacy in Latin script: (i) Latin was written in Greek letters; (ii) Latin was written in a mixture of Greek and Latin letters (see below); (iii) Latin was written in Latin letters, but with certain spellings typical of Greek script as used for

---

[166] A few examples of alphabet-switching are cited by Donderer (1995: 101 n. 39).
[167] See Allen (1974: 33); for πρίγκιψ in Greek papyri, see Daris (1991a: 94).
[168] See Gignac (1976: 225) for numerous examples, with the observation: 'The name *Quintus* is variously transcribed Κο-, Κου-, Κυ-, with the Κο- spellings tending to be earlier and the Κυ- later.'

the writing of Greek transferred into Latin script; (iv) Latin was written in Latin script without errors of types (ii) and (iii). The epitaph *IGUR* 728 just discussed has an error only of type (iii), whereas the list of soldiers has errors both of types (ii) and (iii). Its author was further down the scale of literacy in a second language. For an expansion on this hierarchical description of learners' errors, see below, 5.VII.3.

The Latin epitaphs of soldiers of the *Legio II Parthica* found at Apamea in Syria[169] also contain errors belonging to stages (ii) and (iii) above. Note, for example, text no.9: *D.M. Aur(elius) Moucianos mil. leg. II Pat.* [= *Parthicae*]. *Moucianos* is a Grecising spelling, not only in the ending (morphological interference), but also in the first syllable. With *Moucianos* cf. e.g. *CJI* 226 = Noy (1995), 247 *Doulcitia* (with which compare the transliterated δουλκισειμε at *CJI* 264 = Noy (1995), 332). For alphabet-switching in the Apamean epitaphs, see below.

Some of the spellings discussed in earlier sections, though superficially of this same type (1), are in fact different, and it is worthwhile to explain the difference. Take, for example, λειβερτεις = *leiberteis* at *IGUR* 616. In this (see VII.2.2) a spelling typical of one language (Latin) and script (that of Latin) has been transferred into another script (that of Greek), *but not into another language*. By contrast in (e.g.) *prigceps* a spelling typical of one language (Greek) and script (that of Greek) has been transferred both into another script (that of Latin) *and into another language* (Latin). Spellings such as *prigceps*, *Cointo* and *Moucianos* are mistakes determined by the writer's language of primary literacy, whereas λειβερτεις is not a mistake, but shows the deliberate retention in a different script of a spelling convention used in the writing of Latin. We have seen several spellings comparable to λειβερτεις, whereby the graphemic form of a word as it would have been written in Latin script is retained in Latin texts written in Greek script (e.g. ο for ω in the dative/ablative, ξσ for ξ, *upsilon* rather than ου for Lat. long or short *u*). These spellings have a certain interest as revealing the writer's acquaintance with Latin script, but they are not relevant to the present phenomenon.

(2) I turn now to the intrusion of Greek letters into Latin writing or vice versa (alphabet-switching). If someone writing (e.g.) Latin in Latin script adopts Greek letters from time to time, he was not in total command of Latin script and is likely to have been a Greek with imperfect Latin literacy. Note the following:

---

[169] See Balty and van Rengen (1993).

ILGR 30
DIOGENHS PISCINAM
BETEREM NOBAM
[F]HCIT TOTAM.

This inscription comes from Andros. What caused Diogenes to have the restoration of his *piscina* commemorated in Latin in a Greek-speaking area is obscure, but it is clear that the stonecutter was more used to writing in Greek script than Latin. He was unable to resist the urge to write *eta* for long *e*, though one case is in a nominative morpheme; hence it may represent morphological interference, or code-switching, in that a Greek name has been given a Greek ending in a Latin text: see below, 5.VII.3. I consider further examples to see if a pattern emerges.

Alphabet-switching is sometimes closely associated with morphological interference. Note for example *IPO* B.27 *D.M. Aurelios Hliodorus et Aurηlia Trofime fecerum Aurelio Teseo filio bene merenti.* Twice *eta* is used instead of *e*; and in the first name a Greek morpheme has been employed instead of *-us*, which the writer remembered to use in the second name. On this evidence alphabet-switching is to literacy learning what morpheme-switching is to language learning: the language learner or imperfect bilingual who is at the stage where he tends to adopt morphemes from his dominant language is also likely to fall into letters from his first script when using the second.

Several cases of alphabet-switching so far noted have involved the intrusion of *eta* into Latin script. It is possible that some imperfect learners, aware that the Latin alphabet possessed H, interpreted the letter as *eta*, particularly since H no longer had a phonetic value in spoken Latin.

The same form of switching is found on an ostracon from a military environment in the Eastern Desert of Egypt:[170]

COH I APA-
MHNORUM
] ... ONI BABI-
]. PPA ...

A Jewish inscription from Venusia (*CIL* IX.648, 6220 = *ILCV* 4893 = *CJI* 611 = Noy (1993), 86) not only has η in a Greek word transferred into Latin (*trηnus* = θρήνους), but also in *mηnsurum*. In the same text the name *Asellus* is spelt with a Greek *sigma*, according to editors.

---

[170] See Schwartz (1956: 118).

The inscriptions at Apamea in Syria relating to the *legio II Parthica* have already been mentioned as showing Greek errors of type (1). Alphabet-switching (or confusion) is also found in the inscriptions. Note Balty (1988: 102): '... the stone engravers who inscribed the texts were no doubt Apameans and not accustomed to write Latin words, as is indicated by numerous confusions between P and R, C and S, uncial C and E, and by the introduction of a Δ in words such as *Gordiana* or *decurio*' (cf. Balty and van Rengen (1993: 20)). A critical edition of the whole corpus is needed before the extent of the character-switching can be determined.

Quite apart from alphabet-switching, papyrologists and others often report that the letter shapes of either a Greek or Latin text show some sort of influence from the other script. Precise details are not always given. I list here without further comment a few such claims. In the archive of Successus at Mons Claudianus (*O. Claud.* I.124–36) the writing (in Greek) of Ponticus the *duplicarius* shows the influence of Latin script, e.g. in the form of δ (Bingen et al. (1992: 112)). Price (1955–6: 160–1) has noted in one of a set of eight ostraca (no. 1) held by University College London that '[t]he handwriting ... shows Latin characteristics. The slanting sweeping lines of many of the letters give a general effect not unlike that of Guéraud's Latin ostracon No. 3 [= *O. Wâdi Fawâkhir* 3].' Evidence of the same type has also been noted recently in the second volume of ostraca from Mons Claudianus. For example, the lists of names in 193–210 are in the same hand, which has Latin characteristics: see p. 22 'Les listes **193–210** sont toutes de la même main ... qui pourrait être celle d'un latiniste peu accoutumé à écrire le grec.' Various latinate features of the script are listed, including 'le ductus des μ, aux jambages très écartés, qui évoque certains *m* de la cursive latine'. Welles, Fink and Gilliam (1959: 394) on document 123 from Dura-Europos note that the 'use of the Latin *item*, as well as the ductus of the *alpha*, suggests that the writer was more accustomed to that language than to Greek'. On one of the ostraca from Wâdi Fawâkhir Guéraud (1942: 191) says that the Greek hand is influenced by Latin. In a Greek text from Myos Hormos 'the μ particularly shows influence from Latin cursive', according to Bülow-Jacobsen, Cuvigny and Fournet (1994: 33). A Latin document dealing with a dowry (*P. Mich.* VII.442, = *ChLA* 5.295) has crudely written signatures in Greek by witnesses who were scarcely capable of using the script. The editor (H.A. Sanders) on *P. Mich.* VII.442 (p. 63) remarks: 'the scrawls that pass for signatures are even worse than would be expected ... there seem to be Latin cursive tendencies in most of the signatures of this document, and in some cases understandable names can be formed only by assuming a Latin form of a letter rather than a Greek'. Similarly one

of the witnesses to the marriage contract published at *P. Mich.* VII.434
(+ *P. Ryl.* 612; cf. *ChLA* 4.249), attempting to sign in Greek, 'seems to
have used a Latin cursive *s* for ς at the end of the cognomen' (*P. Mich.*
VII.434, p. 26). In a Greek text with Latin date published at *ChLA* 3.207
(*P. Lond.* 820) the hand has 'strongly marked Latin characteristics'. All of
these cases suggest the difficulty of achieving mastery of the two scripts.[171]

A more complex type of character-switching involves numerals (see
further below, 3.VIII). If a text in one language and script has a numeral
symbol belonging to the script of another language it is usually impossible
to determine whether a code-switch or merely a switch of scripts (akin to
an alphabet-switch) has taken place. If the writer associated the symbol
with the relevant numeral of the other language, then he has changed
languages (if only mentally). But it is just as likely that he was counting
mentally in the language of the rest of the text, in which case it is only a
change of scripts that has taken place.

The following two examples are special cases:

Ruppel (1930), Gr 1 Τίτος Σερούλιος στρα[τιώτη]ς λεγεῶνος **III** Κυρηναικῆς
χωρογραφήσας. ἐμνήσθη τῶν γονέων παρὰ τῷ κυρίῳ Ἑρμῇ. *vac.* κα΄ ἔτος
Τιβερίου Καί[σ]αρος Σεβαστῆ Με̣[σο]ρὴ β΄

A. Bernand (1989), 35 obscure first line, then:
στρατιώ[τ]ης λ(εγεῶνος) **II** [ἥκ]ων μέτ[α]λλα ἐπαιτῶ Φαρμοῦθ[ι] . . . (ἔτους)
ια΄ Ἀδριανοῦ τοῦ κ[υρί]ο[υ].

These are military inscriptions in Greek in which the number of the
legion is written by means of a Latin numeral symbol. It is striking that
in both cases the numeral symbol in the (Greek) date is Greek. Thus the
writers were not compelled by some inadequacy in their literacy to use the
Latin symbol. It is obvious what has happened. They associated Roman
numerals with the Roman army and the naming of legions, but otherwise
followed convention in using the Greek symbol in a Greek context. There
is an exact parallel between the numeral use in these texts and that in two
other military documents which will be discussed below, 3.VI.3 (*O. Claud.*
II.320, *O. Amst.* 8, frg. *e*, col. I). Both texts contain a date at the start in
Greek numeral symbols. The first then has Latin numeral symbols in the
assigning of the order of the watch, whereas the second, more revealingly,
uses fully written Latin ordinals for the same purpose. On the evidence of
this latter text it is tempting to argue that when a Roman numeral is found
in a Greek text of Roman military provenance the symbol actually stands
for a Roman numeral: that is, it represents a code-switch. Whatever

---

[171] It is possible though that in some communities there had been a convergence of letter shapes
in the writing of the two languages: see 5.I.4.

the case, such switches of script in military documents are heavy with symbolism. In the text from Mons Claudianus, for example, the Roman numerals assigning the watch give the order an official Roman flavour, particularly since the writer otherwise used Greek numeral symbols. It looks as if a convention was at work here.

Various examples of inconsistent numeral use in transliterated texts represent a special case of a different type. I refer to Latin texts written in Greek script. The writer of such a text was faced with a dilemma. If he chose a Greek symbol, his choice was consistent with the script of the text but not with its language, because a Greek speaker seeing the numeral symbol would be likely to interpret it as standing for a Greek numeral. If on the other hand he chose a Roman symbol, his choice was consistent with the language of the text, but not with its script. The dilemma seems to have been insoluble, in that we find now one choice now the other.[172]

For a funerary inscription (*IGPorto* 43) with a haphazard mixture of Greek and Latin numeral symbols see below, 4.V.4.1.3.

I offer finally a few conclusions about the trends to be observed in alphabet-switching.

We have noted the frequency with which *eta* intrudes into Latin texts, and have related this to the fact that Latin had a letter which could be mistaken for *eta*. Fleeting, non-systematic switches, say from Latin into Greek script, may be attributed either to the poor literacy in Latin of a writer whose language of primary literacy was Greek, or sometimes merely to carelessness, if the writer was a constant user of both languages in written form in a bilingual community. The two scripts were similar, and lapses therefore became possible.

A number of the texts discussed are from military contexts. The Apamean epitaphs are perhaps a special case, because they may have been commissioned from local stonecutters who were Greeks unused to writing Latin. Other texts seem to imply at least a half-hearted policy in the army of doing things in Latin, such that mere learners sometimes had to write in their second language.

VII.4.2 *Translations of clichés, formulae, etc.*

'Implicitly bilingual texts' may reveal themselves as such through their formula use. It is often the case that in non-literary documents in one language clichés, phraseology, formulae and the like are translated out of or derivable from the clichés etc. of another language. Patterns of

---

[172] Roman numerals: *IG* XIV.844, *IGUR* 1671, *ILCV* 3391, 4118B, 4919, 4954; Greek numerals: *IG* 14.698, *ILCV* 4952.

expression and thought are transferred from one language to the other. If it is possible to detect the pattern of another language behind an expression it may be deduced either that the writer was bilingual, or that he came from a bilingual society in which the phraseology of one language had passed into the other.

A case in point is the inscription *ILBulg.* 155: *D. M. Mucianum mil. leg. [. . . de]ceptum a barba[ris] Durazis fra(ter) eius memoriam [ca]usam posuit. ualete uiatores.* Here there is not only an accusative signifying the honorand (a feature of Greek rather than Latin funerary inscriptions: see above, VII.1), but also the expression *memoriae causa*, a formula which found its way into Latin funerary inscriptions in some (Greek-speaking) areas under the influence of μνήμης χάριν (see above, VII.1 and below, (4)). Moreover the form of the expression (with *causam* rather than *causa*) betrays the influence of the Gk. χάριν. The writer could not avoid leaving traces of his Greek background. Either he rendered the Greek expression into Latin himself, with interference of case from the Greek, or he had found the expression around him in Latin form in an area in which Greek was prevalent. If the latter were the case, it could not positively be concluded that he himself was bilingual. Even if a sceptical view is taken in a particular case of the possibility that the writer himself was responsible for translating a Greek formula, the presence of Greek-derived phraseology in a text at least contributes to our picture of the bilingual culture of a region. In this example the accusative form of *causam* is strongly suggestive of a direct rendering by the writer himself. The inscription records a military man; military inscriptions often bear tell-tale signs of the second-language learning of their referents.

Comparable phenomena, but with different determinants, are sometimes found in literary Latin. Writers sometimes allude to a Greek expression or word by translating it into Latin. At *Fam.* 1.6.2, for instance, Cicero uses a Greek proverb in Latin form (*a teneris, ut Graeci dicunt, unguiculis,* = ἐξ ἀπαλῶν ὀνύχων), but in this case flags the Latin expression as of Greek origin. Or again, whereas Lucilius (231) used the Homeric tag τὸν δὲ ἐξήρπαξεν Ἀπόλλων in the Greek form, Horace (*Sat.* 1.9.78) rendered it (with modifications) into Latin (*sic me seruauit Apollo*), no doubt expecting his readers to recognise the allusion. Similarly Celsus at 8.1.23 alludes obliquely to the Greek term κτείς through the Latin *pecten* (*a quibus oritur os quod **pectinem** uocant*), as Langslow (2000: 181) has demonstrated. There is something of a literary or learned game here,[173] whereas in the

---

[173] This sort of game, in which the Roman reader of a literary work is expected to spot in a Latin usage an allusion to a Greek expression, usage, etymology or the like, had taken firm root. Thus,

above inscription the use of Greek-inspired formulae is an unpretentious reflection of the bilingualism of the writer or his background.

Another difficulty encountered in the interpretation of such evidence is that in bilingual communities it is not always possible to place the origin of a cliché in one language rather than the other. It may be justifiable sometimes to speak of convergence of two languages in the use of formulae. I list below some variable examples, attempting to face the various problems that have just been raised.

(1) The Latin funerary formula *dis manibus* was rendered into Greek as θεοῖς καταχθονίοις in bilingual communities. It is found, for example, in the inscriptions of Italy and Sicily, but never in Attic inscriptions.[174] Examples in Greek-speaking areas tend to be special cases, with some sort of Roman connection likely. For example, six of the seven funerary inscriptions from Nicopolis ad Istrum and its environs in Bulgaria published by G. Mihailov at *IGBulg.* II.687–93 begin with the expression θεοῖς καταχθονίοις, and significantly they have as well other Latinate patterns, such as the dative ἔτεσιν expressing duration of time (II.692) (on this, see 4.v.4.1.3) and the use of υἱός in an expression of filiation (II.693) (see e.g. 6.v.1). Nicopolis was founded by Trajan, and though Greek speaking, was subject to Roman influence, and the Greeks responsible for inscriptions such as these may sometimes have been bilingual. But it is unlikely that every user of the Greek expression was aware of its Latin origin.

(2) An epistolary structure at Terentianus, *P.Mich.* VIII.467.18 (*nem[i]nem habeo enim karum nisi secundum deos te*) is of Greek origin. It is found in the Abinnaeus archive: 34.7 μετὰ τὸν θεὸν οὐδίναν ἔχομεν ἡμῆς βοηθὸν ὑμῶν. Also from Karanis is *P. Mich.* VIII.466.4 [σέβομ]αί σε μετὰ τοὺς θεούς; cf. *P. Giss.* I.68.8–9 οὐδένα <ἔ>χω [μ]ετὰ τὸν θεὸν εἰ μή σε. The presence of the expression in Terentianus suggests the primacy of Greek culture in the circles in which he moved.[175]

(3) At *P. Abinn.* 1.6 the following phrase in bold (*ducere Blemniorum gentis refuga[s]* **ad sacra uesti<gi>a** *pietatis uestrae*)[176] is based on a Greek original.[177] The ambience of the Abinnaeus archive is overwhelmingly

for example, Virgil, in calling Styx *tristis... palus inamabilis undae* (*Aen.* 6.438–9), was expecting his readers to recognise the association of *Styx* with στυγερός 'hateful' (see O'Hara (1996: 70)). A rich collection of material of this type can be found in O'Hara's book; see earlier Bartelink (1965), and also (e.g.) the note of Harrison (1994). See further below, 3.III.1, p. 315 on Cicero's letters to Paetus.

[174] See Schwarzlose (1913: 14), Kajanto (1963a: 9), Leiwo (1995a: 105–6), Robert (1989: 313).
[175] See also Daris (1991a: 64); also below, 5.VI.2.
[176] Cf. *ChLA* 11.469 *ideo a[d] sac[ra] uest[ig]ia ue[s]tra comf[u]gio.*
[177] See Bell et al. (1962: 36) ad loc. citing e.g. *P. Oxy.* XVII. 2130.19 πρὸς τοῖς θείοις ἴχνεσι τοῦ κυρίου ἡμῶν Αὐτοκράτορος.

Greek; on an occasion when, unusually, formal Latin was attempted, the writer fell into a Greek mode of expression in his second language.

(4) *Memoriae causa*, as noted above, is based on μνήμης χάριν. It occurs, for example, in bilingual inscriptions, and in some Latin inscriptions from Greek-speaking areas. For a Latin example from Asia Minor (Katin Serai, Lystra) in an area where μνήμης χάριν is constant in Greek inscriptions, see *MAMA* VIII.15 *Q. Laitilio Nepoti Annia Vettia uxor eius memoriai causa et sibi restituit*. The names are Latin, but the digraph of *Laitilio* is of Greek form (see 5.VII.3). *Memoriai* could be explained in two ways: it may have a grecising ending, or the writer may have used a Latin archaism.

(5) An introductory formula in a Latin letter of Claudius Terentianus, *P. Mich.* VIII.468.3f. *ante omnia opto te bene [u]alere, que m[ihi ma]xime uota [su]nt*, corresponds closely to one in a Greek letter by the same man: *P. Mich.* VIII.476.2 πρὸ μὲν πάντων εὔχομαί σε ὑγιαίνειν καὶ εὐτυχεῖν μοι, ὅ μοι εὐκταῖόν ἐστι. Much the same formula is also found in one of the Latin ostraca from Wâdi Fawâkhir: *opto deos ut bene ualeas que mea uota sunt*.[178] Even the dative pronoun μοι (with εὐτυχεῖν) has its equivalent in a variation on this formula in Terentianus, at 467.2 *an[te omn]ia op[to te] fortem et h[i]larem [e]t saluom **mihi** esse*.[179] The combining of *ualeo* and *opto* is attested already at Vindolanda,[180] where Greek influence does not seem likely. On the other hand the other components of the formula (such as the relative clause, the opening expression and the dative pronoun) do not appear to be attested in contexts uninfluenced by Greek.

(6) The problem is compounded by Terentianus 468.64, which has a similar (closing) expression *bene ualere te opto multis annis* corresponding to that at 477.44f. in one of the Greek letters: ἐρρῶσ]θ[αί σε] εὔχομαι πολ[λοῖς χ]ρό[νοις]. Though the text of the latter passage is fragmentary, the conjectured verb-phrase (ἐρρῶσθαί σε εὔχομαι) is found in another place in Terentianus where the reading is certain (VIII.481.36). It is striking that the word order of the verbal formula in the Greek letters of Terentianus is the same as that in the Latin (with the dependent construction preceding the main verb and the infinitive preceding the accusative pronoun: see 477.44, 479.22–3). The expression occurs frequently elsewhere in Greek papyri. It has been argued by Parsons, *P. Rainer Cent.*, no. 164 (pp. 488–9) from *P. Qasr. Ibrim* inv. 78-3-21/24 (Tafel 117) (first century BC), which he reconstructs (p. 488 l.15) as *ual[ere te hilarem et sa]luom cupimu[s]*, that the 'infinitive valediction is now attested for Latin, well before it appears in Greek; it is a natural inference that Greek took it

---

[178] See further Adams (1977: 5).   [179] See Adams (1977: 5).
[180] See Adams (1995a: 117–18), with Cugusi, *CEL* II.37.

from Latin'. Thus 'the common Latin *ualere te opto* became the common Greek ἐρρῶσθαί σε εὔχομαι; the less common *ualere te cupio* became ἐρρῶσθαί σε βούλομαι for Romans writing Greek' (p. 488). There remains the temporal expression *multis annis*, which has a typical later Latin ablative of extent of time. There is evidence suggesting that the dative of duration of time in Greek was originally a Latinism, though it may have become established widely in later Greek (see 4.v.4.1.3). πολλοῖς χρόνοις is common in the papyri, usually in the above formula. If the Latin expression influenced the Greek, certainly in Greek the formula had become well established (for further details about this expression, see below, 4.v.4.1.3). For the plural use of χρόνοι, but in the expected accusative (of duration), see *MAMA* viii.252b συνζήσασά μοι χρόνους ὀλίγους. It is incidentally of interest that the equivalence of the Latin and Greek expressions in Terentianus, with *annis* corresponding to χρόνοις, allows a decisive interpretation of the meaning of χρόνοι. This is the late use of the word, = 'year',[181] which in its turn was to inspire a loan-shift in Latin: e.g. *ILCV* 2125 *uixit in pace tempora III*, *CIL* vi.1080 (= *CLE* 274) *felicia tempora quattuor*.[182]

Youtie and Winter (1951:31) on Terentianus 468.64–5 took the formula *bene ualere te opto* to be Greek-inspired, but they did not have the Vindolanda evidence available (on which see n. 180; for the infinitival construction at Vindolanda, as distinct from *ut* + subjunctive or the plain subjunctive, see *Tab. Vind.* ii.248). In military communities in Egypt and elsewhere in the east epistolary formulae as used by bilingual soldiers might have passed indifferently from one language to the other. There might indeed have been input from native-language speakers of both languages in the establishment of the formulae used in letters.

(7) Another possible case of convergence of the two languages in the phraseology of military epistles is also to be found in one of the passages just cited: Terentianus, *P. Mich.* viii. 468. 65 *bene ualere te opto multis annis / felicissime* **im perpetuo**. Similarly in a Greek letter Terentianus writes (481.36) ἐρρῶσθαί σε εὔχομαι εἰς **αἰῶν[α]**. There is nothing unusual about either expression, but it is the combination of elements in the two passages that is of note.

(8) The southernmost Latin inscription extant, from Musawwarat es Sufra in Ethiopia (*CIL* iii.83; also Hintze (1964)), adopts formulae used in Greek. It may have been written by a Latin-speaking African who had visited Rome, perhaps as an official representative. He states that he had

---

[181] See E. Löfstedt (1956: ii.442), id. (1959: 117–18).   [182] See Löfstedt (1959: 117).

been to Rome (?:*urbs*: often used on its own for Rome in the late period), possibly in a boastful spirit, though it has to be said that the boast would have been lost on virtually everyone in such a remote region. The display consists at least as much in the ability to use the language of the Romans. The inscription runs as follows: *bona fortuna. Dominae reginae in multos annos feliciter! uenit e urbe mense Apr. die XV* . . . (followed by miscellaneous letters, with TVS visible at the end).

Bona fortuna corresponds to ἀγαθῇ τύχῃ, and *domina regina* to κυρία βασίλισσα which is used in the inscriptions of nearby Dakka.[183] On the expression ἀγαθῇ τύχῃ, see Gomme and Sandbach (1973: 305): 'The original meaning, "may good fortune follow", was sometimes more or less forgotten, and the phrase does hardly more than indicate consent, cf. *Sam.* 297.' In inscriptions the expression is nearer to 'good luck' (cf. *feliciter* in the same inscription). It is common all over the Greek world. See, for example, from Samothrace, Fraser (1960), nos. 39, 45, 46, 49, and the bilingual no. 54, which begins with the Greek phrase, then switches into Latin (a consular date is all that survives of a text that would originally have contained a list of initiates); for other mixed-language inscriptions which begin with the Greek phrase then switch into Latin, see *IGBulg.* II.496, IV.2116 (on which see above, v). ἀγαθῇ τύχῃ is common (e.g.) in Bulgarian inscriptions and in those of Asia Minor (as published in *MAMA*).

For *bona fortuna*, see *TLL* VI.1192.70ff., with cross references; several times in Greek-speaking areas: *CIL* III. 249, 251 (Galatia), etc. An example of the Latin phrase occurs at the head of a decree of Gordian from Scaptopara in Bulgaria (*IGBulg.* IV.2235). The long inscription begins with a short Latin preamble, then switches into Greek for its main content. Thus even the Latin part betrays the influence of the Greek formulaic conventions operating in the area.

If the circumstances behind the Ethiopian inscription are along the lines of those suggested above, the writer is likely to have been a speaker of Greek, who adopted Greek-style phraseology when setting up an inscription in Latin.

(9) *P. Mich.* VII.442 = *ChLA* 5.295 is a second-century document from Karanis dealing with a dowry. There is a significant expression in the second line: *corpore fusco, fa[c]ię [d]ęd[u]cta, naso recto,* **lentigo malo d̦[e]xtrọ.** The nominative *lentigo*, in a series of descriptive ablatives, appears to be syntactically unconstrued. It might be interpreted in various ways, for

---

[183] See Ruppel (1930: 49), Gr. 61, and Hintze (1964: 297).

example as a parenthetical clause with the copula understood, or as a nominative absolute (see *ChLA* 5, p. 37), but in fact, however it is taken, it is an imitation of a Greek formulaic structure. A close parallel is found at *P. Ryl.* II.160b.11 ο(ὑλὴ) μήλωι ἀριστερῶι (see also line 10 of the same document, and *P. Ryl.* II.160c, col. ii, 1. 9 Ὀνν[ώ]φρις ὡς ἐτῶν πεντήκοντα οὐλὴ κνήμη κὲ ποτὶ δεξ[ιῶ]ι, where the structure is particularly clear). Here οὐλή, exactly like *lentigo*, stands as part of a 'nominatiuus pendens' construction. A second (and decisively important) feature of the Latin lies in the use of *malo* = 'cheek' (which ought to have been feminine, *mala*). The usage represents a loan-shift based on μῆλον (see 4.V.2.11). Given this lexical influence from Greek, it is certain that the structure of the phrase as well is Greek determined. The writer must have been either thoroughly familiar with the Greek formula, or (and this is likely) translating from a first version in Greek. The context is eminently Greek (see Sanders, *P. Mich.*, p. 59).

(10) The Latin *uiuus sibi* formula turns up frequently in Greek form. Note, for example, *IGPorto* 29 ζῶ[ντες ἑαυ]τοῖς ἐποίησα[ν κὲ ἰ]δίοις = *uiui sibi fecerunt et suis*, *IGUR* 387 ζῶν ἑαυτῷ ἐποίησεν = *uiuus sibi fecit* (cf. 414). See Sacco (1984) on the first example for the use of ἴδιος = *suus*, citing *IGUR* 292, 333, 999.[184] Thus, e.g. at *IGUR* 292, καὶ αὐτῷ καὶ τοῖς ἰδίοις is equivalent to *sibi et suis* (ἰδίοις has taken on the sense 'relative' under the influence of Lat. *suus*),[185] and at *IGUR* 552 ἐκ τοῦ ἰδίου is equivalent to *ex (de) suo*. Funerary formulae in bilingual communities seem to have been particularly prone to pass from one language to the other. Note, for example, *IGUR* 1005 ἀπελευθέροις τε καὶ ἀπελευθέραις καὶ τοῖς ἐκγόνοις τούτων, = *libertis libertabusque posterisque eorum*,[186] and *IGUR* 947 γῆ σοι κούφη = *terra sit tibi leuis*. This last expression in its Greek form is found only at Rome in prose inscriptions, according to Moretti (1972, ad loc.).

(11) An inscription from Beirut (*AE* 1957, 118; also Mouterde (1956: 45)) runs thus: *regi deo I(oui) o(ptimo) m(aximo) H(eliopolitano), Veneri, Mercurio, C(aius) Cornelius stra(tor) c(onsularis) (?) cum suis omnibus u(otum) l(ibens) a(nimo) s(oluit) cum magna gratia*. Of interest here is the expression *regi deo*, which according to Mouterde (1956: 46) is a 'formule unique dans l'épigraphie latine'. Mouterde compares Aramaic titles such as *Melqart* (*Milik-Qart* 'king-city' = 'king of the city'). The oriental expression-type may have influenced the Latin in the placement of *regi* at the head of the expression.

---

[184] See also Viereck (1888: 73).   [185] See also Leiwo (1995a: 54).
[186] See Moretti (1972: 486).

(12) The Jewish Greek funerary formula μετὰ τῶν δικαίων ἡ κοίμησίς σου (e.g. *CJI* 118 = Noy (1995), 342) appears in Latin form as well (e.g. Noy (1993), 174 *dormitio eius cum iustis* (Sardinia)). Of particular interest is *CJI* 210 = Noy (1995), 343 (Rome) *dormitio tua inter dicaeis*, where the formula has not been fully Latinised, and thus betrays not only its Greek origin but also the exposure of the writer to the Greek expression.[187] The inscription also contains an error of Latin morphology (*omniorum amicus*).

The evidence discussed in this section is mixed in character. If a formula associated with language A is found in translation in language B, various possible relationships between its two manifestations must be considered. First, a native speaker of A, thinking, as it were, in his first language, may have translated a formula of that language literally when using language B, perhaps unaware that it was not usual in the second language. That was perhaps the case in nos. 2 and 3 above. The mental processes involved are presumably much the same as those behind loan-shifts (see 4.V.2.11) and renderings of idioms (see 4.V.2.12), except that the expressions that have just been discussed happen to fit easily into the second language and are not abnormal in the manner of over-literal idiom renderings. I have however stressed that not all formulae of one language when used in another will have been creatively translated by the writer of a particular text; once a formula passes into a second language, it may gain currency in the usage of monolingual speakers of the recipient language. Secondly, a native speaker of A may consciously seek to translate a formula of language B into his first language, perhaps to demonstrate a partial acculturation to the society which language B represents. Greeks at Rome or Nicopolis ad Istrum who used the expression θεοῖς καταχθονίοις were following a convention of Latin funerary inscriptions, but not to the extent of abandoning their own language; see also in particular the material collected at (10). Thirdly, in societies in which fluent bilingualism was well entrenched (and the Roman army in units with significant numbers of Greeks is a case in point) the two languages may have converged to some extent, such that the same formula became established in both languages, perhaps with components derivable separately from the two languages (see the material in (5)–(6) above). Fourthly, in some cases (as perhaps that of (9) above), though a surviving text is monolingual, there may once have been another version in the other language.

---

[187] See the discussion of Sevenster (1968: 89).

Formula transfers of the types discussed here are a persistent phenomenon of bilingual societies. Further cases will come up in Chapter 2.

This concludes the classification of the types of texts which betray the
bilingualism of the writer. Many similar texts will be discussed in detail in
the next chapter. I now turn to a few further general issues which ought
to be addressed in a book on bilingualism in written form.

VIII THE AUTHORSHIP OF INSCRIPTIONS

In this book I will refer constantly to the 'writer' or 'drafter' (*et sim.*) of an
inscription or non-literary text. But the concept of the 'authorship' of an
inscription or other non-literary text is far from simple, and it is appropriate to consider the possible circumstances behind the composition of
such a text. The complexities of authorship in the case of a text which
contains a formulaic element and in the composition of which the writer
may have received assistance have already emerged from the receipt of
Aeschines (VII.2.3).

In the production of any inscription on stone (I am thinking particularly of epitaphs) there were potentially three main participants:[188] (1) the
person who commissioned the inscription; (2) the person who composed
the text (a category which would include the author(s) of any examplars
used); and (3) the person who cut it into the stone. Some inscriptions
may well have been the work of three different persons, but that was not
necessarily the case. I consider the possibilities.

In some cases just one person might have been responsible for the
inscription. A relative of the deceased, for example, could both draft an
epitaph and carve it. Note, for example, *ILI* 561 *D. M. Flauia Seuera uix.
an. XXXV, M. Vlpius Bassus mil. leg. IIII Fl. coniugi pientissime posuit.* **manu
mea scribsi**. The husband of the deceased declares that he wrote the
inscription with his own hand, switching from the third to the first person
to underline the claim. He may of course have taken advice on its wording, or consulted a manual or copied the formulae of other gravestones
in the vicinity. Similarly the Palmyrene who set up a bilingual epitaph at
South Shields for his British wife (*RIB* 1065) is likely to have drafted and
carved the inscription himself, since the hand in the Palmyrene part is
assured but that in the Latin uncertain (see below, 2.VII.2).

---

[188] There is a good deal of literature on this matter (and some controversy). Note e.g. Susini
(1973: 9–10) on the difference between the procedures apparently described by the verbs *ordinare*
and *sculpere*, though these do not directly concern me here. See further Mallon (1952: 55–73),
Panciera (1967: 100–8); note too the interesting remarks of Horsfall (1983: 87–9) on the role of
the stonecutter.

It is rare to find explicit reference to the writing/authorship of a non-official inscription/graffito.[189] The author of a Pompeian verse inscription (*CIL* IV.4966) wrote his name beside the verses (*Tiburtinus epoese* (= ἐποίησε)), using a Greek verb associated with the signatures of Greek sculptors and artists (see 3.V, p. 360). Another interesting case is found at the Syringes of Thebes (Baillet (1920–6), no. 1733): Ἀλέξανδρος ἔπαρχος κάστρων Θηβῶν, ἶδον καὶ ἐθαύμασα. καὶ ὧδε ὁ τούτου νοτάριος Ἰσὰκ Ἀλεξανδρεὺς ὑπερεθαύμασα θ(ε)ιότατον ἔργον. The military officer speaks, as it were, in the first person, but since he was accompanied by his scribe, who records his own greater amazement at the wonders of the syrinx, it is highly likely that the scribe wrote on behalf of both of them. Or again, É. Bernand (1981), no. 124 is a rare case of an inscription in which the writer is explicitly stated to differ from the dedicator. The inscription is a dedication of a sanctuary to Ammon by a veteran (C. Valerius Cottus) of the third Cyrenaic legion. Greek is used. Following the inscription is [Νί]κανδρος ἔγραψε. Cf. (from Dakka) Ruppel (1930), Gr 28 *Deo magno Mercurio adorauit ue.xillus leg(ionis) II Traiane Fortis nonas Febr(uari)as anno XI Imp(eratoris) Traian(i) Hadri(ani).* **scripsit C. Cossutius Nigrinus.**

In the second and third of the four cases in the last paragraph (particularly the third) it might be said that there were two participants in the construction of the text. The dedicator C. Valerius Cottus must have expressed his views on the desired content of the text, and then left it to another to do the writing. When two persons were involved, their roles might have been variable. For example, the processes implied in stages (2) and (3) of the above list could have been performed by just one person. It is easy to imagine a client going to a stonecutter with general requirements, and the stonecutter both drafting and carving a text. The client might often have been illiterate; and whether he was literate or not, it would have been open to him to specify the script to be used. If however the stonecutter was competent in only one script, he, rather than the client, will have determined the script, if not the language, of the text. Alternatively, stages (1) and (2) might have involved just one person. For example, a client wishing to commemorate a deceased relative will sometimes have drafted an epitaph and passed the written text on to someone else for carving.

There is some further evidence for the production of a text by two participants. At *CLE* 477.2 (= *CIL* XIV.2605) a certain T. Flauius Hermes records in verse how he dictated verses for his own epitaph to an unnamed

[189] Relevant material (some of it cited here) from *carmina epigraphica* is collected by Cugusi (1996: 23).

person and instructed him to write them out (*scribere*, presumably in this context of the incising of the verses: cf. *ILI* 561 above): *quos ego dictaui et iussi scribere quendam*. It is well known that persons often ordered their own funerary monuments and epitaphs during their lifetime,[190] and in such cases the text will often have been of their own composition. The best evidence for this procedure is at Petron. 71.5–12, where Trimalchio composes his own epitaph and issues instructions to the stonemason Habinnas.

A Roman funerary monument dedicated to a soldier (*CIL* VI.2938) has an inscription written partly in prose, partly in verse. Embedded in the text towards the end is the sentence *heredes titulum uersiculos Cornelius epoi*. The verb (*epoi* for ἐποίει) again alludes to the Greek artistic tradition (see above). The sentence seems to tell us that the heirs composed the prose part, and a certain Cornelius the verses, though it is just possible that *titulum* indicates the monument itself, constructed at the expense of the heirs. The second clause is though unambiguous; and it is also clear that there was more than one participant, because however *titulum* is taken Cornelius does not lay claim to the authorship of the whole inscription.

There is an interesting passage of Sidonius Apollinaris which is relevant here. Sidonius, having just composed a funerary inscription in verse, gives his friend Secundus instructions that he should have it engraved on the stone. Secundus is to supervise the stonemason to make sure that no errors creep into the text: otherwise there may be readers who will attribute the errors to Sidonius himself: *Epist.* 3.12.5 *quod peto ut tabulae, quantulumcumque est, celeriter indatur; sed uide ut uitium non faciat in marmore lapidicida; quod factum siue ab industria seu per incuriam mihi magis quam quadratario liuidus lector adscribet* (Loeb: 'But, for what it is worth, I should like you to have it promptly cut on the slab: and see that the mason makes no blunders on the marble: because if such a thing is done, whether from perversity or from carelessness, the malignant reader is sure to put it down to me rather than to the engraver'). Not only is the drafter of the text distinguished from the man who inscribed it, but there is clear recognition of the part which might be played by masons in importing errors into a text. They would of course not always have been supervised in the way envisaged here.

---

[190] Hence the frequency of the formula *se uiuo* (and variants) on tombstones indicating that the deceased had had the monument made himself. Sometimes there is a space for the age at death of the deceased (see on *KAI* 142, discussed below, 2.V.5.3), a fact which shows that the text was incised in advance of the death of the referent and that at a later date no one bothered to insert the age.

An inscription discussed by Priuli (1984) gives some insight into one of the ways in which client and stonecutter might have interacted. The stonecutter, no doubt at the time when the tombstone was purchased, wrote the text on the verso in small letters; the text was then transferred to the recto, presumably not until it was approved by the client. Priuli cites other evidence for the same process.[191]

Also of interest are two inscriptions edited by Sotgiu (1961: nos. 107–8). These are two versions of the same epitaph, one in correct Latin (107), the other with peculiarities and errors:

107 bonae (me)moriae. homini bono Ireneo rari exempli, qui uixit annis XLVI, m. VIII, d. XVIII, h. [= *horis*] V. Perpetua marito incomparabili et Ireneus patri contra uotum fecerunt.

108 b(onae) m(emoriae). Homo bonus innox et incomparabilis Munatius Ireneus, uixit in XP(isto) annis XXXXVI, m. VIII, d. XVIII, hor. V. Perpetue [*sic*] uxor coniuge [*sic*] uirgino [*sic*] dulcissimo item Ireneus qua et patri carissimo con. uotum sum [*sic*] fecerunt.

It is of interest that the rough copy is on stone. The first version must have been scrutinised, either by the client or an overseer, then improved. The revision not only eliminated errors, but improved the sentence structure (note the neat dative *homini* in 107, which establishes the dedicatee at the outset, followed by a relative clause; the other version begins less elegantly with a nominative construction). There must also have been some discussion of the appropriateness of various epithets.

A revealing bilingual epitaph of a centurion was found at Tarsus in Cilicia (*CIL* III.222):[192]

Iulio Seuero (centurioni) leg. V Maced. dulcissimo marito Iulia Hermione Ytale matrona memoriae cauza [*sic*]
Ἰουλίῳ Σευήρῳ [*sic*] (ἑκατοντάρχῳ) λεγ. πέμπτης Μακεδ. Μαρίτων γλυκυτάτ(ῳ) συνβίῳ Ἰουλία Ἑρμιόνη Ἰτάλη ματρῶνα μνήμης (χάριν).

A feature of this inscription establishes that more than one person took part in the process that brought the text to publication. The Latin text is correct in syntax, morphology and and vocabulary, but that cannot be said of the Greek. γλυκυτάτῳ συνβίῳ is a literal rendering of *dulcissimo marito*, but before the Greek phrase Μαρίτων is added. The word is superfluous and meaningless, and it could not have been put there by someone who knew Latin; indeed its ending suggests that the author thought of it as a name, grecised from Latin -*o* to Greek -ων.

---

[191] He discusses the dealings between client and *lapidarius* at 55–6.
[192] Discussed by Adams (1999: 131–2).

The sequence of events would seem to have been roughly as follows. A Latin text was written, either by the widow or by a drafter. This was then translated into Greek, by someone who knew the meaning of *marito*. Then another person (perhaps the stonecutter), who did not know what this word meant, thinking that a name had been left out of the translation, added Μαρίτων.

The degree of error which found its way into a text on stone would have been partly dependent on the circumstances of its production. If 'client', drafter and carver were one and the same person, then the script, spelling and language of the final inscription would reflect the educational level of that person, even if he had a model to follow: we have seen in the receipt of Aeschines that those with imperfect literacy were not necessarily capable of copying out an exemplar accurately. If the client drafted the inscription himself and then handed it to a carver, any ineptitude on his part in the writing of the language would find its way into the inscription if the carver followed his instructions to the letter. But the scope for error would probably be reduced if the drafter and/or stonecutter were 'professionals'. One assumes that many of those who made a living out of setting up funerary monuments were capable of establishing a fairly correct text. They would have had at their disposal exemplars and formulae which could be used over and over again.

The above account is oversimplified. Variations could be suggested on the circumstances which have been sketched. For example, members of humble (illiterate) communities would not necessarily have had access to competent drafters/stonecutters. An illiterate wishing to commemorate a deceased relative would by definition be incapable of influencing the written form of the epitaph himself (by 'written form' I refer in this context not to the wording of the inscription, but to the orthography and script by which that wording was conveyed), and he might also only be able to employ a drafter or stonecutter of limited skills in literacy. Under these circumstances errors would readily be committed by the stonecutter, who could not be supervised by the client.

We have now seen that the notion of the 'writer' of an inscription is a difficult one to pin down. In an earlier section (VII.2.3) I discussed Latin texts which were in Greek script because the 'writer' apparently had no choice but to use that script. In the light of the distinctions set out above between client, drafter and stonecutter, what does it mean to say that on occasion Greek script *had* to be used?

If the person wishing to set up the inscription were himself to compose the text and incise it, then the situation is relatively straightforward. If he were a bilingual or learner of Latin who was fully literate in Greek script but not Latin, then he would be compelled by his imperfect literacy to use Greek characters if he wanted the text to be in Latin. The difficult question is not why the writer used Greek script, but why he chose to write the text in the Latin language rather than Greek. The vendor Aeschines had to use Latin in his receipt, because that was the language of such Roman documents. But there was no such compelling reason, even in the west, why an epitaph should be in Latin if the writer could use Greek script but not Latin script. Large numbers of epitaphs in the Greek language survive from Rome and elsewhere in Italy. Epitaphs in Latin language but Greek script imply a general context of bilingualism, since monolinguals, if literate, would write epitaphs, whether in Latin or Greek, in the appropriate script.

The hypothetical stonecutter might have been capable of using either Greek characters or Latin, or both. If he could write only Greek script, and if the client, say an illiterate Latin speaker, commissioned a Latin text, the text would have to be in Greek characters because of the stonecutter's incompetence in Latin.

If on the other hand the stonecutter could write Latin in Latin script but nevertheless produced a text in Greek letters, the compulsion acting upon him was not his imperfect literacy, but some extraneous factor such as the requirements of the client. In this case we might say that the writer *had* to use Greek script only in a very restricted sense, that is because someone had requested him to do so. The question why a client might have demanded from a bilingual and bi-literate stonecutter the use of Greek characters for a Latin text is an interesting and important one which must be commented on here. It is much the same question as that raised by *IGUR* 616 (see above, VII.2.2), a Latin text in Greek script which, as we saw, contains hints that the writer could alternatively have used Latin script.

I suggest some circumstances which might have caused a client to commission a Latin epitaph in Greek characters, even if the stonecutter had the ability to use Latin characters.

(1) The client is a Greek native speaker, illiterate in Latin, the deceased a native speaker of Latin. The client chooses Latin on behalf of the deceased, but commissions it in Greek letters so that he/she can read the text. In this case the choice of language expresses the ethnic (or, perhaps better, 'linguistic') identity of the deceased, whereas the choice of script is a reflection of the ethnic/linguistic identity of the client. Such a circumstance may lie behind *IG* XIV.698 (Sorrento), in which a veteran

of the Misenum fleet is commemorated in Latin but Greek script by his wife, who had a Greek name:

Δι Μ (= *dis manibus*)
Αυρηλιους
Ιυπετρατους
β. κ. μ. (= *beteranus classis Misenensis*)
βειξ ανο υ΄ μησις σ΄ δει (= *deies?*)
η΄
κοζους ιμβεια (= *coniux impia?*)
Ειρηνα μαριτο βενε μερεντι
φηκετ.

A Greek married to a first-language speaker of Latin and living in a Latin-speaking area would perhaps wish to commemorate her spouse in his native language and in that of the community where the epitaph was to be erected, even if she was illiterate in Latin script.

(2) The client is a Latin speaker, the deceased a native speaker of Greek. The client is unwilling to commission an epitaph in a language which is not his/her mother tongue, but goes part of the way in acknowledging the linguistic/ethnic origin of the deceased by commissioning a Latin inscription in Greek characters. In this case it is the choice of script that expresses the identity of the deceased. Relevant to this hypothetical situation is the fact that there are some Latin inscriptions extant written in Latin script, which contain names written in Greek script (see further below, 3.V.2): e.g.

IGUR 1528 Μιλτιάδης, / qui Persas bello uicit Marathonis in aruis / ciuibus ingratis et patria interiit [on the base of a bust of Miltiades; the text then switches into Greek]

ILCV 1352C Ἀλεξαμενὸς fidelis

ILCV 3977B Συρᾶς, anima innox

Such curious texts[193] show that the use of Greek letters, quite apart from the use of the Greek language, might help to convey information about the identity of the bearer of a (Greek) name. In this connection four oculist's stamps from Gaul (Seine-et-Oise) written in the Latin language but Greek script are worth citing:[194] (*a*) Αιλει Ρουφει κυκνινουμ αδ ιμπετουμ, (*b*) Αιλει Ρουφει διασμυρνης αδ ασπριτουδινημ, (*c*) Αιλει Ρουφει διαμυσου ατ ουετερης κικατρεικης, (*d*) Αιλει Ρουφει πυξινουμ αδ

---

[193] See further *IMS* VI.178, *ILCV* 2951.   [194] See Wuilleumier (1963), 543.

κλαριτατε. The writing is in reverse so that it would come out clearly in an impression. Western doctors were conscious of the Greekness of their profession (see below, 2.V.5.1 on trilingual doctors' inscriptions from Africa), and for that reason they sometimes wrote in Greek, even using Ionic forms in allusion to the Hippocratic tradition (see 3.V). The oculist did the next best thing to writing in Greek: he used Greek script.[195] Thus Greek script could symbolise Greekness, even if the language it was conveying was not itself Greek. It is a professional rather than an ethnic identity that is expressed in this case. Similarly the use of Hebrew script for Hebrew tags in texts otherwise in Greek or Latin might have been as close as the writer could get to the use of the Hebrew language: see above, V, VII.2.4 (particularly p. 66 on Noy (1993), 75), and below, 2.VIII. The difficulty experienced by Jews at Venusia in the late period in writing Greek (for which see above, VII.3 on Noy (1993), 62) suggests that some of the Latin epitaphs transliterated into Greek at the site represent the writers' best attempt at 'Greek' itself. See further below, 2.III.6, p. 175 for a case of Etruscan script used as a substitute for the Etruscan language, and 5.I.1 for Latin script used for the writing of Greek by an Egyptian Demotic speaker attempting vainly for some reason to use 'Latin'.

(3) Both client and deceased are bilinguals, possibly first-language speakers of Greek who had been assimilated to Latin culture, perhaps as they rose in social status, from, say, servile origins. The Latin language is used for the epitaph as a mark of their acculturation, but Greek script as a mark of their bilingualism or ethnic/linguistic origins. I emphasise that the writing of either Latin or Greek in the wrong script would be an effective way of laying claim to membership of a bilingual community.[196] The use of Greek script can be seen as a form of display which symbolises the bilingualism of deceased and dedicator, and conveys their pride in this state.[197] The alien script also sets up a distinction between ordinary monolingual Latin speakers and the referents of the inscription, and portrays the latter as members of an exclusive group.

(4) So far I have stressed that the client may have chosen Greek script to express his/her own cultural identity, or that of the deceased. But whatever the origins of the client or deceased, the expected readership of the inscription also has to be taken into account, at least as a

---

[195] See Donderer (1995: 103).

[196] See also the remarks of Kajanto (1980: 96–7) and Donderer (1995: 103–4).

[197] Kajanto (1963a: 6) argues that the Greek language (at Rome) was often used in epitaphs 'to lend the gravestone greater distinction'. Presumably Greek script might also have had the effect of conveying Greekness.

complementary determinant of the choice of language/script. If we make the assumption that funerary inscriptions were meant to commemorate and thus by definition to be read, Latin texts in Greek script imply the existence of bilinguals who could understand Latin but not read Latin script fluently.

I turn now to a different topic. A feature of the texts considered in section VII.2 is that they have bilingual interference, code-switching and irrational errors. Now that we have made explicit the fact that there may have been as many as three contributors to any one inscription, the question arises whether errors of these types can be ascribed to one contributor or the other in inscriptions produced by collaboration.

The client, as we have stressed, will sometimes have been illiterate. In this case orthographical errors determined by cross-language interference could only be those of the drafter or stonecutter. In such circumstances it is the stonecutter's errors, rather than those of the client, which could be used to make deductions about the linguistic situation in our bilingual community.

Morphological interference and code-switching are a different matter. In theory an illiterate, dictating a text to the drafter or stonecutter, could have such marks of his bilingualism recorded in the text.

If the client was literate, then Grecising errors even of an orthographical kind might imply a degree of complicity between client and stonecutter, and a similar cultural background. If the literate client were not himself given to cross-language orthographical and morphological interference and code-switching, he would be unlikely to accept these from a drafter or stonecutter. Would a client who could read tolerate in the epitaph he had commissioned Latin words with Greek inflections, unless the mixture were a reflection of his own habits? And it is reasonable to think that a competent stonecutter capable of distinguishing Latin from Greek would at least be uneasy about writing 'Latin' of this form. It follows that, if a text such as the epitaph *IGUR* 718 discussed below at IX (5), which has Greek inflections imposed on Latin words and is written in Greek script, were the product of collaboration between at least two persons, they must have come from the same social milieu and have shared features of speech and literacy. It would not be plausible to suggest that such a text was incised by a professional, fluent in Latin and Greek and versed in both scripts, on behalf of a client of a lower cultural level.

I conclude that, although the establishing of a funerary inscription might have involved the decisions of several persons, such variables do not undermine the linguistic evidence which the inscription can provide about language use in a lower-class bilingual community. Crass interference errors in a text compiled by two or three persons are more likely than not to reflect a common cultural background of the collaborators.

IX PIDGINS AND 'REDUCED' LANGUAGES

It was stated earlier (II) that some bilinguals have poorer competence in one language than another, and it was noted that examples of imperfect command of a second language are easy to find in the ancient material. It is as well though to make clear that in speaking of 'imperfect competence' I am not referring to Latin- or Greek-based pidgins or creoles. Some of the inscriptions that we will see might be described as being of 'mixed language' in various senses (on the term 'mixed language' see below, (5), and 3.XII.1), and pidgins are indeed 'mixed languages', in that they tend to draw some of their resources from two or more different languages. But the distinctive features of pidgins as they have been described are as follows:[198] (1) they lack inflectional morphology; (2) while they may take most of their vocabulary from a single source language, their grammar is not merely a simplification of the grammar of the source language(s); (3) they have to be learned; those who speak the native languages of users of the pidgin cannot understand the pidgin merely from their knowledge of the languages in contact, nor can they produce the pidgin merely by making an *ad hoc* simplification of one of these languages.[199] The evidence available from antiquity of imperfect 'Greek' and 'Latin' does not, as far as I know, include genuinely uninflected texts (but see below on Aristophanes), or texts that would not have been understandable as Greek or Latin. If some of our texts do indeed manifest 'reduced' forms of communication, then that reduction does not seem to have been institutionalised to such an extent that the outcome can be described as a new contact language distinct from Greek and Latin, i.e. a pidgin which would not have been comprehensible to Greek and Latin speakers. I prefer then to speak of 'reduced' or 'learners'' or 'foreigners'' Greek or Latin. But specimens of such Greek and Latin are by no means a unity, and accordingly in this section I attempt to

---

[198] See e.g. Thomason and Kaufman (1988: 168–70), Hock and Joseph (1996: 423); on certain ancient texts, see Adams (1994a: 90).

[199] Leiwo (1995b: 299), commenting on certain Jewish inscriptions which will be discussed later, states that they are manifestations 'of a mixed language' which he calls a 'Greek based pidgin'. But the inscriptions to which he refers are inflected by means of recognisably Greco-Latin morphemes, and the introduction of the term 'pidgin' merely confuses the issue.

describe some of the different types that are attested. 'Reduced' Greek has received more attention than its equivalents in Latin, but there is more to be said about its features. The best example extant of the Latin of a learner is a translation of parts of two fables of Babrius (*P. Amh.* II.26); it is so revealing that a separate chapter (8) will be devoted to it.

Various examples of 'foreigners' Greek' survive, partly as primary material and partly from the hand of dramatists attempting to portray barbarians. This Greek evidence nicely illustrates the difficulty of dealing with poor performance in a second language in any stereotyped way. I begin this section with a discussion first of a real-life letter and secondly of Aristophanes' representation of the speech of barbarians. Despite the differences between them, one significant similarity will emerge.

(1) The letter of Phonen to Aburni, found in 1976 at Qasr Ibrîm,[200] is a document of the fifth century AD written by a king of the Blemmyes to a king of the Nubades. Aburni is apparently the successor of Silco, who left an inscription in bad Greek at Kalabcha (Talmis) boasting of three defeats inflicted on the Blemmyes (*SB* v.8536).[201] Current opinion is that the Blemmyes and Nubades spoke separate languages,[202] and it would seem to follow that the use of Greek in such a communication represents the employment of a lingua franca. It has been observed by Rea (1979: 150) that the Greek of Phonen is marked by misuse of case endings and particularly of verb-forms. But it is possible (thanks to Rea's convincing interpretation of the document, which he renders into 'correct' Greek) to be more precise about the nature of the errors. I concentrate here on errors in the morphology of the verb, which are particularly marked and admit of a comparison with the more usual errors in papyrus texts.

One example will bring out the character of the mistakes, and from this I will move on to a statistical assessment. Line 12 is printed by Rea as follows: πρῶτον Σιλκω ἔλαβα καὶ ἐκώλυσα τὰς χώρας ἡμῶν, σήμερον [δὲ] ἐνικάσης καὶ ἔλαβα Τάλμεως. This seems to mean 'first Silco took and kept us off our lands, but today you have conquered and taken Talmis' (Rea). Of the four verbs here, only one (ἐνικάσης) approaches correctness. If ἐνίκησας is intended, there has been an unremarkable transposition of the last two vowel graphemes, despite which there remain a recognisable second-person ending and an aorist marker (the sigmatic

[200] For a text, interpretation and translation of the letter, see Rea (1979).
[201] For a discussion of the Greek of Silco, see Kapsomenos (1953). Kapsomenos shows convincingly that one should see in the language of the text not Greek influenced by Coptic, but conventional vulgar Greek.
[202] See Rea (1979: 149).

suffix). The papyri are full of phonetically determined errors in verb forms, of a sort which cannot be classified as morphological mistakes. Thus the Dioscorus who wrote ὀγνήσεται = ὀκνήσητε in the Egyptian letter *O.Claud.* II.228 was obviously using classical morphology, but developments in the pronunciation of vowels caused him to misspell the ending. I am not concerned here with such superficial phonetic spellings occurring in verbal morphemes, and hence I disregard as relatively insignificant the form ἐνικάσης. Far more significant is the fact that ἔλαβα is used in the same sentence both as a third- and second-person verb. It is of course extremely common in the papyri for first-aorist endings to intrude into the second aorist (note e.g. ἔλαβα at *O.Claud.* II.228.15, a first-person form),[203] but while that may account for the presence of an *alpha* in our examples, it does not explain why ἔλαβα should have been used outside the first person singular. The use of this verb-form with first-person function does not represent a genuine error but is a reflection of a systematic change in the verb system; however, the extension of the form to other persons is highly anomalous and has nothing to do with the norms of koine Greek. In Modern Greek the first- and second-aorist personal endings have been conflated in the singular (-α, -ες, -ε), but the persons are distinguished.

In the letter of Phonen there is a striking difference between the general correctness of the personal endings in present-tense indicative verbs, and the degree of error to be found in the endings of aorist indicative verbs. I have counted 22 correct present-indicative forms,[204] spread across a variety of persons, both numbers, and the middle as well as the active (though the latter is far more common). The distribution is as follows: first-person singular forms 13 (including two cases of the middle), second-person singular 1, third-person singular 6 (including one middle), first-person plural 1 (middle), third-person plural 1. I have included as 'correct' one or two banal phonetic misspellings, as ἀκούις (1.9). The one error is ἔχι (6), used apparently for the first person singular of the verb 'to be'. The mistake does not however seem to be morphologically based. The writer several times used the verb ἔχω in the immediate context, and

---

[203] On the general phenomenon see Mandilaras (1973: 148–54), who deals with this verb at 152.

[204] I base myself on Rea's interpretation of the text. It should be allowed that not everything is clear; but while statistical precision cannot be achieved, the general tendencies which I shall bring out are obvious enough. One or two of these correct present forms may not strictly have present functions. Rea glosses θέλω (7) as ἤθελον, and at 28 εἰρηνεύουσιν appears to be a future equivalent. There is nothing particularly remarkable about such usages. On the other hand the form παραμίνομεν (at 11 and 25) probably represents a subjunctive and future respectively, with vocalic misspellings.

this would seem to have been a mechanical writing error by association. There is thus virtually 100 per cent correctness in the personal endings of the present indicative.

The endings of the aorist indicative (active, middle) present a stark contrast with those of the present. I have counted some 45 examples in all,[205] of which 29 are incorrect and 16 correct. Thus about 65 per cent of examples are incorrect, and there is good reason to believe that most of the superficially correct endings are right only by accident (see below). I have not classed as erroneous cases of confusion between the first and second aorist, provided that the personal ending is the right one for the context (thus κατῆλθα = κατῆλθον (17), and the inverse case ἔγραψον = ἔγραψα (14)).

28 of the 45 aorist forms have the ending -α. 11 of these have first-person function,[206] but the others are anomalous in having either second-person (thus two examples of ἔλαβα at 12 and 13) or third-person function (15 examples).[207] The writer obviously had a penchant for -α as the aorist personal ending, regardless of the person expressed. No fewer than 62 per cent of aorists have this ending. It therefore follows that in the 11 places where he appears to have used the ending correctly, he may have achieved correctness purely by chance, on the principle that by writing -α mechanically most of the time as the singular aorist ending he was likely on average to be right once in every three attempts to produce a past-tense form.

It will be seen that if we eliminate from consideration the 11 correct forms which may be right for the wrong reason, there remain only 5 correct aorist forms (i.e. those which do not simply have an -α ending: 6 γενόμεθα = ἐγενόμεθα, 12, 13 ἐνίκασης = ἐνίκησας (with transposition of the last two vowels: see above), 24 ἐρήμωσεν = ἠρήμωσεν, 14 ἔγραψον = ἔγραψα). Thus only about 11 per cent of aorists (i.e. 5 out of 45) show a more or less correct personal ending (but note that not a single one is correct in every respect) of a sort which might perhaps be attributed to *deliberate choice* rather than the mechanical attachment of an *alpha* to the aorist stem. This low success rate in aorists (if we leave aside the 11 cases which do not definitely derive from the writer's understanding of the form) is at an almost polar remove from the total correctness in present indicative endings.

---

[205] A few problematical examples have been left out: 17 ἐλυπήσας, glossed by Rea with ἐλυπήθην, and 20 εὐρήθημεν, glossed with εὔρομεν.

[206] The examples are found in lines 8, 14 (twice), 17, 20, 25, 26, 27 (three times), 32.

[207] The examples are in lines 8, 11, 12 (3 times), 14, 15 (twice), 16, 18, 23, 24 (twice), 26, 27.

It should also be noted that not all of the incorrect aorists comprise the -α ending used for the wrong person. There are other errors, such as ἔγραψεν = -ας (4, 10), ἐδήλωσεν = -ας (20), ἐνίκησες = ἐνίκησε (25); for further anomalies, see 11 φιλῆσαι = ἐφίλησα, 17 πολεμῆσαι = ἐπολέμησα, 14, 15 ἐκχλευάσης = -ε, 16 χλευάσης = -ε.

How are these oddities to be explained? Clearly Phonen was using Greek rather than a pidgin, because the text is highly inflected and comprehensible as Greek. But it is very imperfect Greek, particularly in the verb system. The simplest explanation is that Phonen was a second-language learner who had set about acquiring verb morphology in a certain order, starting with the present tense. He had a past tense, in that he regularly used forms that are marked for aorist in the stem, usually by the sigmatic suffix, and by the augment. But the system of aorist personal endings was a closed book to him. He had some knowledge of the actual endings, but had not learnt their functions, and repeatedly contented himself with the *alpha* form. It is entirely plausible that a learner who was being taught would proceed in this order. The present tense is likely to be learnt first by any learner of any language. The first step in the learning of the Greek aorist is the acquisition of the stems, because there are two sets of endings which are dependent on the nature of the stem. Phonen had advanced as far as reducing the aorist stems, but the next step he had not mastered. His chaotic use of existing personal endings with the wrong functions displays a typical feature of second-language acquisition. Learners may pick up morphemes before they are able consistently to give them the correct functions.[208] Phonen's aorist endings cannot, as we have seen, be explained as an anticipation of modern Greek.

(2) The 'foreigner talk'[209] in Aristophanes (in the speech of the Scythian archer in *Thesm.*, of Pseudartabas at e.g. *Ach.* 104 and of the Triballian at *Aues* 1678–9) cannot be interpreted in quite the same way as representing partial learning. On the one hand Aristophanes puts a good deal of correct Greek into the mouth of his major barbarian character (the Scythian archer),[210] no doubt to make him mainly comprehensible, but on the other hand he uses what are clearly intended to be markers of foreigners' Greek. I would draw attention to four such markers.[211]

---

[208] See Hamers and Blanc (1989: 218).

[209] For 'foreigner talk' as a quasi-technical term, see Hock and Joseph (1996: 420), citing e.g. *no-speak-Spanish* as an example.

[210] See Friedrich (1919: 286–8, 293–4).

[211] A full discussion can be found in Friedrich (1919), Brixhe (1988) and Colvin (1999: 287, 294).

First, in two different plays there are recognisable Greek words with a non-Greek ending -αυ: *Ach.* 104 οὐ λῆψι χρυσό, χαυνόπρωκτ' Ἰαοναῦ. Greeks were called 'Ionians' by orientals, and the Greeks were aware of this (Aesch. *Pers.* 899);[212] the last word therefore strikes an authentic note. The origin of the ending is unknown, but is clearly meant to be foreign.[213] There seems to be a comparable example at *Aues* 1628–9 σαυ νακα βαταρι κρουσα. The meaning of these words is obscure,[214] but the first may be intended as the second-person pronoun, in which case the same ending would have been assigned to a Greek root. Finally, lines 1678–9 of the same play run (Dunbar's text) καλανι κοραυνα καὶ μεγαλα βασιλιναυ / ὀρνιτο παραδίδωμι. Dunbar tentatively glosses the first five words as καλὴν κόρην καὶ μεγάλην Βασίλειαν, and takes ὀρνιτο as a dative-equivalent ('to the bird(s)'). Whatever the case, the same ending -αυ seems to be present, in βασιλιναυ. The speakers have thus been made to impose a 'foreign' morpheme (probably not from a real language) on a Greek word. This is a form of interference which was no doubt well recognised in antiquity as a mark of foreigners' performance in a second language; examples from the linguistic output of real second-language users will be seen below (see also above, VII.2.3 on Aeschines).

Secondly, one case form is sometimes used for another, as for example nominative for accusative or genitive, accusative for dative.[215]

Thirdly, alongside correct nominal morphology, nouns are often given an -o ending which fulfils several case roles, such as nominative, vocative, accusative, genitive.[216] Brixhe argues (e.g. (1988: 118)) that the peculiarities of the Greek of foreigners in Aristophanes can be largely traced to various developments (attested in inscriptions and the like) in popular Attic,[217] including the loss of final -ν and -ς, and it is to this last phenomenon that he attributes the -o case form. This explanation sometimes fits the use of the form, as at *Thesm.* 1176 κῶμό τις ἀνεγείρί μοι (nominative singular, and thus explicable from loss of -ς) or *Ach.* 104 χρυσό (accusative, and thus derivable from loss of final -ν),[218] but in general it is not sufficient in itself. The form is not only found in the *o* declension. Note for example ὀρνιτο (a dative singular or plural?) at *Aues.* 1679, τὴ

---

[212] See Colvin (1999: 58, 77, 289).   [213] See Brixhe (1988: 116–17), Colvin (1999: 290).
[214] For different approaches, see Brixhe (1988: 116–17) and Dunbar (1995), ad loc. Brixhe takes νακα as a negative, whereas Dunbar relates it to νάκη. It is worth noting that snatches of gibberish can have dramatic point on stage. It is highly likely that Aristophanes put nonsense from time to time into the mouths of foreigners; it is therefore perhaps misguided to look for real languages in all such utterances. See Colvin (1999: 289).
[215] See Friedrich (1919: 287–8).   [216] See Friedrich (1919: 289).
[217] See also Sier (1992: 67–8) for a similar approach.   [218] See Brixhe (1988: 128–9).

γέροντο (acc. sing.) at *Thesm.* 1123, and γύναικο at *Thesm.* 1097.[219] To explain this last case Brixhe (1988: 132) resorts to the suggestion that the form may be explained from loss of -ς in the genitive. But the word does not have genitive function in the context. Aristophanes may possibly have got the idea for such an -ο form from nominative and accusative singulars in popular Attic lacking a final consonant, but it could not conceivably have been attached in the real popular language to all of the roots with which Aristophanes uses it, nor could it have had such a diversity of case functions. Aristophanes has attempted to catch the non-inflecting character of 'foreigner talk' by using a single base-form in nouns, though not of course all nouns. The smattering of -ο forms alongside some correct noun endings is merely meant to confer a general barbarian colour, without the undermining of comprehensibility which the consistent use of the form might have caused. Despite this lack of consistency, the usage does reveal a conception on Aristophanes' part of what constituted 'foreigner Greek': that is, the use of an invariable noun-form, whatever the case role in question. A form of Greek which had a single form for nouns would not necessarily qualify to be described as a pidgin, in the sense in which that term is applicable to the slaves' and workers' languages which have evolved in recent centuries. Pidgins tend to have a distinctive grammar which cannot be directly derived from the grammars of the languages in contact, and an absence of inflectional morphemes. If Aristophanes was basing himself on something which he had heard, it would be rather the imperfect Greek of foreigners (as distinct from some sort of institutionalised pidgin, i.e. a separate language) as marked by a certain amount of unchanging forms.

Fourthly, in verbs there is a comparable multi-purpose ending, in -ι.[220] Note e.g. *Thesm.* 1104 κἀγὼ λέγι, 1118 οὐ ζηλῶσί σε (both first-person equivalents). If this morpheme also (cf. -ο above) is to be derived from an Attic form or forms (and Friedrich (1919: 294) sees its origin in the -ει third-person singular ending),[221] it had spread into persons (such as the first singular) in which a direct derivation from an Attic form is out of the question.

It is possible that the -ο and -ι endings originated in popular Attic and that Aristophanes took them from there, but I am not inclined to dwell on their origin but would rather stress their use as unchanging forms with a variety of functions which popular Attic correspondents could

---

[219] This last is perhaps a nominative singular (Sier (1992: 68)), but see Friedrich (1919: 288 n.13).
[220] For examples see Friedrich (1919: 294).   [221] See further Brixhe (1918: 127).

not fully have shared. If popular Attic had lost various final consonants in certain environments and suffered various vowel mergers, it would nevertheless have remained systematic. The use of -o in (e.g.) γύναικο and -ι in a first-person verb could not have been part of that system but would represent the extension of a noun- or verb-morpheme from the appropriate case/declension or person to a different case/declension or person. It is in this respect that the letter of Phonen provides important comparative evidence. We saw that he used the (correct) morpheme -α in the wrong persons. If Aristophanes' -ι in verbs was a popular Attic form of, say, the third person singular, its extension to (e.g.) the first person singular would be paralleled exactly in type by Phonen's chaotic use of -α; and I would also draw attention to a comparable phenomenon noted above as my second point, that is the tendency for one (correct) case form to be used for another. Viewing the practice of Aristophanes in the light of the evidence of Phonen, we may deduce that Aristophanes had observed that foreigners, even if they did use Greek-like endings, had a tendency to use those endings with the wrong function.

Thus Phonen would seem to have been a systematic learner of Greek who had not completed the process of learning and was able to achieve consistent correctness (in indicative verbs) only in the tense with which he had begun, whereas the Scythian archer is a literary confection who is given on the one hand some correct Greek, but on the other hand chaotic verb- and noun-forms which cannot be related to any order of acquisition of the morphology. Nevertheless the two forms of foreigners' Greek are not completely unrelated. I move on now to a few other examples of 'reduced' languages.

(3) In various ostraca from Bu Njem (mid-third century AD), a military base in the African desert staffed at least in part by African recruits with African names, there are some striking uses of the nominative for the accusative, even after prepositions. The nominative serves up to a point as the base form. I have discussed these texts in detail elsewhere (Adams (1994a)), and also briefly at 2.V.7 below. For the nominative as an all-purpose form, see 2.V.7 and also 5.IX, p. 633 with cross references.

(4) It has been pointed out by Meiser (1987: 112, n. 48) that the Umbrian text Vetter (1953), 234 has Umbrian words with Latin inflectional morphemes. The text is quoted and discussed in the next chapter (2.II.3, p. 140). Language learning (in the conventional sense of that term as indicating the gradual acquisition of a second, current, language) is not at issue here, so much as language death or shift. Umbrian morphology

had been all but forgotten by the time when the text was written, at an advanced period in the Romanisation of the area, and the writer in an attempt to use the language had to adopt the only inflections that he knew (from Latin).

(5) The inscription *IGUR* 718 –

Σέξστος Κλώδιος
Δεκόμου λιβερτῖνος
αντι διον τερτιον νωναις –

is one of a set of funerary inscriptions on *ollae* from the *uinea s. Caesarii* near the Appian Way (*CIL* I¹, p. 210, I².1015–1201 = VI.8211–934) offering an early glimpse[222] of a lower-class community which, though Romanised, shows a marked Greek presence. Sixteen of the names are Greek. There is also one Greek inscription, which, interestingly, reveals a trace of the influence of the Latin inscriptions at the same site.[223] On the other hand, various Latin inscriptions show Greek orthographic or morphological interference: thus the spelling of *Dekem(bris)* (1038) with *k*, the name *Quintus* spelt *Cun(tus)* (1139),[224] and *Alfenos* (1024) with a Greek morpheme. The graveyard was that of a bilingual community. The text quoted raises acute problems of interpretation. Is it in Latin, Greek or both languages? Mommsen (*CIL* I, p. 210) was of the opinion that the language was Latin, though the work of a foreigner. The three names in lines 1–2 are all inflected as Greek, including the genitive of the patronymic. *Libertinus* is a Latin word, but it was borrowed by Greek (see LSJ s.v.), and it therefore cannot be used to diagnose the intended language of the piece. In the Imperial period Latin *u* was regularly transliterated as ου (see above, p. 25), but earlier there had been a convention of using Greek ο for Latin short *u*.[225] It would not do to find this earlier convention of transliteration at work in *IGUR* 718: the genitive ending of Δεκόμου is unambiguously Greek, and it is likely therefore that the nominatives as well are intended as Greek. But while the two lines are in Greek, that does not mean that the whole piece was necessarily conceived as Greek. It will be shown later that Greek names may retain their Greek form in a Latin text (see e.g. 4.V.3.1).

---

[222] The texts are usually dated to the second half of the second century BC: see Solin (1971: 94).
[223] See Kajanto (1963a: 21). The inscription is *IG* XIV. 1737 = *CIL* I². 21 Καρνεάδ(ης) πρὸ είδῶν δ' Μαρτίων. Latinate here is the nominative structure, and also the abbreviation of the name. The -*is* masculine nominative singular, possibly reflecting Gk. -ος > -ις, is also common in the Latin texts. On the Greek character of the corpus, see also Kaimio (1969: 25, 29).
[224] See above, VII.4.1 (1).   [225] See Dittenberger (1871: 282).

The date on the other hand is obviously intended to be Latin,[226] but it is a strikingly imperfect Latin. In αντι the writer has replaced the expected Latin word *ante* with its nearest phonetic equivalent in Greek, but unfortunately for him the Greek word did not have the same meaning as the Latin. τερτιον is a Latin word, but it is given a Greek inflection instead of the transliterated accusative in -ουμ. διον is not inflected in the Latin manner. A Greek masculine accusative of the -*o* declension has been attached to the root *di*-. Straightforward Greek transliterations of *diem* are usually in the form διεμ.[227] Compare however *IGUR* 1040 δηφουνκτους αννωρουμ ν[.] μησουμ γ΄ διου[μ...]; here the -ουμ of αννωρουμ seems to have been interpreted as a genitive marker, and it has accordingly been added to μησ- and δι- (see 4.v.3.2). The formula *ante diem* was often abbreviated *a.d.* As a fifth declension noun (a type with only a few members), *dies* may have caused problems for Greek learners. There is a mistake in the inflection of a fifth declension noun in the translation by a Greek into Latin of two fables of Babrius (see 8.1, p. 728).[228] Finally, νωναις represents the Latin ablative *nonis*. Again the writer has used a Greek (dative) inflection instead of transliterating the Latin.

It is a remarkable fact that the seven inflected words of this inscription are all of Latin origin, but every single one has been given a Greek ending, and the preposition too, though intended as Latin, has a Greek form. Was the text written fluently in a 'mixed language', or was it perhaps the hesitant effort of a Greek learner of Latin who had no control whatsoever over Latin morphology? Are there other possibilities? In connection with the first possibility note Romaine (1995: 67): 'In some long-term situations of intensive language contact far-reaching structural changes can take place so that the product can be a mixed language. In extreme cases, *the language may share lexical affiliation with one language, while having the structural traits of another*' (my italics). Accordingly it might be suggested that in lower-class Greek communities at Rome a mixed language had developed, with a Latin lexicon on which Greek inflections tended to be imposed. It would however be hazardous to accept such a possibility in the absence of far more extensive evidence (on this issue, see further below, 3.XII.1). The language mixing in the inscription, if it is genuinely such, may not be

---

[226] The dating by day alone is strikingly characteristic of the graveyard: cf. e.g. 1015, 1017, 1018, 1019, 1020, etc.

[227] See *TLL* v.1.1022.63ff.

[228] The fifth declension was not recognised as a distinctive type even by Donatus: see Law (1997: 72, 102).

representative of the language use of a whole community, but only of an individual (or a few individuals). On this (second) interpretation the language of the text would be a specimen of our reduced (learners') Latin. It would be 'reduced' not in the sense that it is without inflections (as is the case with most pidgins), but in the sense that the inflections of the target language are never used. It is a tempting hypothesis that lower-class first-language speakers of Greek at Rome attempting to communicate in Latin without any real knowledge of Latin morphology may sometimes have resorted to the combination of Latin lexemes with Greek inflections. This might have been an *ad hoc* strategy adopted occasionally by very imperfect learners (see above, VII.2.3 for Aeschines' occasional use of Greek endings); I can find no evidence that mixing of this kind had been institutionalised into a genuine mixed language.

There is another way of looking at the inscription. It may well be that the writer considered himself to be using Greek, and that the names in lines 1 and 2 just happen to be of Latin origin. If the writer was a Greek and was using Greek in his own eyes, then manifestly what has happened in the second part of the text is that he has attempted to code-switch into Latin for the recording of the date. Dates belong to the public, transactional domain of language use; parallels are considered elsewhere for code-switching in dates (see above VII.4.1, p. 75, and below, 3.VI.2). On this interpretation the inscription belongs primarily in the discussion of code-switching. But it is also relevant to the present chapter, because the writer, when he changed languages to note the date, was unable to get the endings right and produced a bizarre variety of the Latin language with Latin lexemes and Greek morphology.

(6) A comparable piece of Latin to that just discussed can be seen in an inscription from Kara Agac in the Pisido-Phrygian borderland: *MAMA* VIII.348 *G. Iuliun Verun Maximun Caesara Aug. P(ium) F(idelem) ciu(i)tas Cillanensium*. The language is intended as Latin, but the syntactic structure (nominative + accusative of the honorand) is of Greek inspiration (see above, VII.1). Four of the six complete words have incorrect inflections, reflecting both direct interference from Greek, and the conflation of Greek and Latin morphemes (for which phenomenon see also 4.V.3.2, 5.V.3). *Iuliun*, *Verun* and *Maximun* have partially Latinate accusatives, in that the vowel in the ending is *u*, but the writer has used the Greek nasal in final position: the endings are thus hybrid, at least in their written form. This is the sort of spelling which might have been perpetrated by a Greek who was familiar mainly with spoken Latin: he would have heard the close back vowel in the ending, but not the *-m*,

which belonged to the written language. *Caesara*, finally, has a pure Greek accusative ending, though the Latin digraph is correct.

(7) I cite finally *IGBulg.* III.1777:

1 [. . . coniu]ge sua (*sic*) bene merita (*sic*) et sibi uius (*sic*) e(t) sapiens tumulum fecit
2 [. . . μ]νημεῖον ἑαυτῷ καὶ τῇ συμβίῳ ἑ(α)υτοῦ Σατρί(ᾳ) Μαρκίᾳ βιωσά(ση) σεμνῶς ἔτη κέ
3 [. . . κατεσ]κεύασεν.

The Latin version of this bilingual could not be described as being of mixed language, because the inflectional morphology is purely Latin. However, only the nominative and accusative forms are correct; ablative forms are used where the dative seems to be required (on the assumption that the opening words of the Latin as extant were intended to be syntactically parallel to the coordinated *sibi*). It may tentatively be concluded that the writer could not match Latin morphemes to their correct syntactic function. The endings are 'correct' in form, but not in function. The same phenomenon was noted above in the speech of the Scythian archer. It will be shown later that the Greek who translated some fables of Babrius into Latin committed errors of this type several times.

The texts considered in this section display various features. First there is a text the intended language of which was probably defunct in the community in which it was written: the 'Umbrian' text will have been written at a time when the language shift from Umbrian to Latin was well advanced. It is a feature of the document that Latin morphology is imposed on Umbrian words. A comparable feature was seen in two Latin inscriptions in which the inflectional morphology is almost exclusively Greek or hybridised; and in Aristophanes there was the 'morpheme' αυ attached to Greek roots, which may have been intended as foreign. We may conclude that in situations of language death or imperfect learning of a second language the morphology of the speaker's or writer's primary language may sometimes be used in the target language. A second feature of learners' Greek and Latin is that correct morphemes are often used with incorrect functions. In at least one case (the letter of Phonen) the writer's variable comprehension of the function of a variety of morphemes can be related to the order of his acquisition of the morphology: that which is learnt first is best understood. This approach to the interpretation of errors will be elaborated in Chapter 8. A related phenomenon was seen in the use of a single morpheme with a variety of functions. In the letter of Phonen the repeated use of the *alpha*

ending in the aorist reflects imperfect learning of the personal endings
of the aorist, in that the ending is genuinely Greek even if it is often
used incorrectly. In Aristophanes on the other hand the repeated use of
-o in nouns and -ı in verbs is not so easy to relate directly to imperfect
learning of Greek, and it is possible that Aristophanes was attempting in
these cases[229] to portray his barbarian as not inflecting Greek with Greek
morphemes (misunderstood or not) at all, but as inflicting multi-purpose
endings of indeterminate origin on Greek roots. If this interpretation of
the data were accepted, it would follow that in Aristophanes we come
closest to finding pidgin-like characteristics, though only as one element
of barbarian speech.

I mention finally some non-primary evidence for reduced language.
There is some anecdotal evidence for the grossly imperfect use of Latin
by foreigners, though by its very nature it does not convey any detailed
information. Note, for example, Apuleius' description of the 'broken
Latin' of a Punic speaker (see also 2.v.8): *Apol.* 98.8–9 *loquitur numquam nisi
Punice . . . Enim Latine loqui neque uult neque potest. audisti, Maxime, paulo ante,
pro nefas, priuignum meum, fratrem Pontiani, diserti iuuenis, uix singulas syllabas
fringultientem* ('he never speaks anything but Punic . . . As for Latin, he has
neither the inclination nor the ability to speak it. You heard just now,
Maximus – what a disgrace – my stepson, the brother of that eloquent
young man Pontianus, scarcely stammering out individual syllables').
And according to the *SHA*, the future emperor Maximinus Thrax used
a form of Latin that was 'almost Thracian' (see above, v, p. 21).

I note finally that there may possibly be allusions to an institutionalised contact language of some sort in Ovid, in his remarks about the
linguistic situation at Tomi. I conclude this section with a brief account
of that situation as he presents it. First, Ovid is aware that Tomi was
of Greek origin (see *Trist.* 3.9, especially 1–4 and 33–4, where a Greek
etymology of the name is given). Secondly, he makes a clear distinction
between Greek inhabitants of the place, and various barbarian tribes (see
5.7.11–14, 5.10.27–8), notably the Getae, Sarmatae and Bessi (see 3.10.5
for the three), with the first most frequently mentioned. At 5.10.27–8, for
example, Greeks and barbarians live together within the fortifications,
and at 5.7.13–14 Getae and Sarmatae ride *per medias uias*. Alternatively,
the Getae are shut out (3.14.41–2), or they threaten the town (with the
Bessi at 4.1.67–78). Thirdly, we hear that traces of Greek remain, but
rendered barbarous by 'Getic sound' (5.7.51 *in paucis remanent Graecae*

---

[229] *pace* Brixhe and Sier as cited above.

uestigia linguae, / haec quoque iam Getico barbara facta sono). Greek is also said
to be overlaid with Getic sound at 5.2.67–8 (*Graecaque quod Getico uicta
loquela sono est*). The most obvious interpretation of these remarks is that
Greek was still spoken (and it should be noted that the epigraphy of the
place is Greek: see below, 2.XII), but that it had taken on a distinct regional form (presumably in the matter of accent, to judge by the double
occurrence of *sono*) which, if Ovid's complaints are anything to go by,
made it difficult to understand. The regional dialect, if Ovid is right,
was determined by contact with another language. Fourthly, Greeks and
barbarians can communicate together by *sociae commercia linguae* (5.10.35
exercent illi sociae commercia linguae),[230] whereas Ovid has no shared language with the barbarians (3.11.9 *nulla mihi cum gente fera commercia linguae*).
What does *commercia linguae* mean? It could hardly refer to the local Greek,
because then Ovid could presumably have made himself understood. Alternatively it may have been some sort of contact language, with elements
not only of Greek and Getic, but also of other languages. Conditions in
fact were ideal for the development of such a language, if there were genuinely three or more ethnic groups present, distinct from one another
and thus almost certainly having their own languages. Pidgins historically have developed when groups of speakers of a variety of languages
and sharing no lingua franca have been brought together. Sarmatians,
however, should not have been in this area, and Ovid is not to be trusted
in any of the detail he gives.[231] Ovid does seem to have been telling the
reader that a 'shared language' different both from Greek and the barbarian languages was available as a means of communication across the
various ethnic groups, but unfortunately no confidence can be placed in
his remarks. The poems are of more interest for the linguistic concepts
that they present than for their particular linguistic assertions.

X SOME CONCLUDING REMARKS

I do not attempt a summary of this chapter, but I stress points of
importance.

As was observed earlier, bilingualism in modern societies has been
studied by linguists almost exclusively in speech. Fluent bilinguals are
reported for example as switching backwards and forwards between two
languages even without being fully aware that they are doing so. Bilingual
performance as it appears in a written text is a very different matter from

---

[230] Those of Greek origin are the subject of the verb here.
[231] See Syme (1978: 164).

bilingual performance in speech. A single text, as we saw, may be the work of as many as three collaborators. Much preparation must go into the production of a public inscription, not least if it is to have versions or elements of one kind or another in different languages. If a bilingual text on stone presents different information to different categories of readers, conscious decisions about what to include and what to omit have to be taken by at least one person. A text of this kind is a far cry from the informal utterance of a bilingual made off the cuff. While modern research on bilingualism in speech cannot be neglected, a work such as this must pay particular attention to the special problems raised by the interpretation of written sources. Code-switching, for example, in an inscription on stone cannot simply be assumed to have the same determinants and functions as code-switching in informal speech. Literacy learning is a different matter from language learning, and imperfect literacy has the potential to influence a written text at least as much as does imperfect language learning. 'Morphological' interference in a written text, for instance, may on occasions be a consequence of poor literacy in L2 rather than a genuine morphological phenomenon. I have therefore devoted a good deal of space in this chapter to discussing the character of written texts with a bilingual dimension, and have dealt to some extent with literacy acquisition in its relationship to language acquisition, a subject which will be developed further in Chapter 5 (VII.3). In studies of ancient literacy insufficient attention has been paid to what might be called 'bi-literacy': that is the ability (or, in some cases, inability) of the writer to vary scripts to suit the language being written.

At the outset I adopted an all-embracing definition of bilingualism, and included among 'bilinguals' those with only limited competence in a second language. It should now be clear from the discussion of the receipt of Aeschines, from some of the inscriptional material discussed in the chapter, and from the evidence assembled in IX, that users of reduced forms of Latin and Greek as L2 are a well-attested category of language users, well recognised in antiquity itself, and that their efforts in L2 played a significant role in spheres such as commerce and the army. Varieties of 'Greeks' Latin' showing input from substandard Latin as well as from the speakers' (or writers') L1 constitute a neglected sub-category of Vulgar Latin.

I have not spoken explicitly about language attitudes in this chapter, but these have surfaced in passing, particularly in III. The alleged hostility of Greeks to learning other languages is simply an irrelevance in a study dealing with the Roman world. Greeks who came within the Roman sphere of influence, such as immigrants to Rome (servile or otherwise), recruits into the army, and traders, were of necessity learners of Latin, and their efforts at language learning can often be observed in action, as for example in the transliterated bilingual glossary cited earlier (VII.2.1), in the alphabet with the names of the Latin letters transliterated (VII.2.1), in exercises such as the translation of Babrius (see Chapter 8), and in texts with heavy Greek interference. Where the Romans themselves are concerned, a linguistic insecurity in their relations with Greek speakers emerges from some of the material discussed in III. On the one hand the educated classes admired Greek culture and language, and aspired to fluency in Greek; but as the Romans gained political ascendancy over the Greeks they became keen to assert the dominance and superiority of their own language. But this is not the place to dwell on the Romans' linguistic insecurity and their consequent nationalistic assertiveness; both topics will come up again, particularly in the chapter on Egypt (5).

APPENDIX: ATTITUDES TO THE GREEK ACCENT IN LATIN

It was observed above (p. 16) that foreign accents are sometimes more highly esteemed than the regional accents of native speakers of a language, and it was suggested that the Greek accent in Latin probably had a certain prestige. In this appendix I collect some evidence for attitudes to Greek sounds as heard in Latin. Occasionally the Greek pronunciation of Latin is mocked, as we learn for example from the anecdote told by Quintilian (1.4.14) about a Greek witness in Cicero's case *pro Fundanio* who could not pronounce the fricative *f* but replaced it with an aspirate (see Biville (1990: 190); see below, 4.V.1.1). But usually Greek sounds are positively evaluated. Quintilian talks of the sweetness of some Greek sounds compared with the harshness of some Latin (12.10.33) (cf. Biville (1990: 70–1)), and refers to the way in which Latin poets 'adorn' their verse by these sounds, through the medium of Greek names, employed no doubt in Greek form. Another passage (12.10.27–8) deals with two Greek sounds (those represented by *upsilon* and *zeta*), which, if used in Latin (in Greek words) make the *oratio hilarior* (Biville (1995: 17, 409)). It may be deduced from Quint. 12.10.57 that names of Greek origin might sometimes be pronounced with Greek prosody even if Latinised morphologically: the name *Amphionem* pronounced in the Greek manner (but apparently with a Latin inflection) had to be repeated in Latinised form (with an unaspirated stop and a short *i*) by the speaker because a 'rustic' witness had at first not understood (Biville (1990: 158); see 4.II).

The 'rusticity' of the witness is of particular interest here: there was clearly a difference between the way in which the name was pronounced by the educated orator (with Greek prosody) on the one hand and by the uneducated witness on the other. The Greek pronunciation was an educated affectation. Sergius, *GL* IV.526.14–19 utters a warning against the accentuation of the Latin *cuspidis* on the second syllable in the Greek manner; he compares Αὐλίδος: *cauendumque hoc unum, ne quem Graecorum nominum similitudo a praescriptis regulis deducat, ut si quis dicat 'cuspidis' acuens quamuis breuem paenultimam, eo in fraudem inductus quod quorundam simile est Graecorum, ut Phyllídos Aulídos*. Again, there is the matter of the aspiration of stops in some Latin words, such as *pulcher, triumphus* (borrowed ultimately from Greek, but through the intermediary of Etruscan: see 2.III.2), *Cethegus, Carthago*. These were originally unaspirated, but the aspirated forms were coming into vogue at the time of Cicero (*Orat*. 160: cf. Quint. 1.5.20). This trend may be related to a habit among Latin speakers dateable to about 150 BC onwards of aspirating both in writing and speech Greek aspirated stops in Greek words and names used in Latin (Leumann (1977: 162–3), Biville (1990: 139)); in the early period such stops had passed into Latin in Greek words in unaspirated (and sometimes geminated) form (as Livius Andronicus' *struppus* < στρόφος) (on the whole issue see Biville (1990), chapter 7). The introduction of aspiration into stops in some *Latin* words (as distinct from Greek loan-words) may possibly be seen as a Greek affectation motivated by the prestige of the new 'correct' aspiration of the Greek stops. Note Sihler (1995: 142): 'The correct pronunciation of the aspirates [of Greek aspirated stops] was so highly esteemed in polite circles . . . that aspirated stops were introduced into a number of native Latin words' (but for a more sceptical view, see Allen (1965: 26–7)). Finally, I would draw attention to the curious passage Cic. *Brut*. 259: *Cotta, qui se ualde dilatandis litteris a similitudine Graecae locutionis abstraxerat sonabatque contrarium Catulo, subagreste quiddam planeque subrusticum* (translation of Loeb: 'Cotta from his habit of using broad vowels was as far removed as possible from resemblance to Greek enunciation, and, in contrast to Catulus, his speech had a rural, downright rustic sound'). Cotta famously affected a 'rustic' accent, and had certain 'broad' sounds, particularly it would seem in his pronunciation of vowels (see Cic. *De orat*. 3.46). *Dilatandis* in the passage quoted has a correspondent in *illa lata* (of Cotta's speech) at *De orat*. 3.46. By speaking in this way Cotta obviously avoided any resemblance to a Greek manner of speech. The allusion in *Graecae locutionis* is considered obscure by Douglas (1966), ad loc., but Dubuisson (1982: 196–7) claims that Greek did not lengthen long vowels

to the same extent as Latin; accordingly Romans speaking Greek are
said to have lengthened Greek vowels excessively. Dubuisson finds an
allusion to this practice at D.H.19.5.1 (the story of the Roman ambassador who addressed the Tarentines in bad Greek and was humiliated
as a result: see above, III) πρὸς τὰς ἀναστάσεις ἐτραχύνοντο, which is
translated in the Loeb edition as 'became exasperated at his truculence';
but, according to Dubuisson, 'Ils sont mis en joie . . . par la façon dont
l'accent romain allonge les voyelles grecques.' On this view Cicero at
Brut. 259 above might be thought to have been referring to a Grecising
truncation of Latin long vowels by some Romans. It would not do to
be too dogmatic about the meaning either of Cicero or of Dionysius,
but there must be an allusion in the passage of the *Brutus* to some sort of
Roman affectation whereby a Greek sound or mannerism was imitated in
Latin by urbane Latin speakers (in contrast to the self-appointed 'rustic'
Cotta, who made a point of avoiding it). There is implicit here the same
sort of contrast between rustic and sophisticated practice as that seen
above in the story about the pronunciation of *Amphionem.*

CHAPTER 2

Languages in contact with Latin

I INTRODUCTION

In this chapter I review the languages (other than Greek, which will be
dealt with from various points of view in later chapters) attested in contact
with Latin. It is not the aim of the chapter to identify all of the languages
spoken in the Roman Empire; for that the comprehensive volume edited
by Neumann and Untermann (1980) can be consulted.[1] The emphasis
here is rather on language contact as it is attested in direct form. The evidence consists partly of inscriptions and other documents in which two
or more languages (one of them Latin) stand side by side in one form or
another, and partly of *testimonia* which refer to speakers of Latin (whether
as their first or second language) using another language as well. I avoid
speculating from historical events (as for example visits by embassies from
one place to another) about the language or languages which might have
been used in an exchange.[2] Where narratives of events are concerned
I restrict myself to cases which make direct mention of bilingual language
use. But it is primary evidence, in the form of inscriptions and the like,
which is the main concern of the chapter. On the whole the evidence is
allowed to speak for itself in bringing out the issues raised by language
contact, but in the conclusion an attempt will be made to summarise the
major points which have emerged, and to bring together related phenomena presented in scattered places throughout the chapter. Certain
questions and themes will recur. To what extent were primary speakers
of Latin learners of other languages? Were the attitudes of Latin speakers to foreign languages uniform, or were different languages evaluated
differently? Can degrees of Romanisation be plotted through language
use? In what ways could one language 'influence' another in a situation
of contact? Is there evidence for regional variation in Latin determined

[1] See also the general survey of Harris (1989: 175–90).
[2] There is a good deal of information of this kind in Snellman (1914–19).

111

by language contact? What are the different relationships which the two versions of a bilingual inscription might have to each other (a topic raised in the first chapter), what determines that relationship, and why might an inscription be set up in two languages in any case? What is the nature of code-switching in a written text? Some of these questions will be dealt with more systematically in other chapters, mainly in connection with Latin in contact with Greek, but there is a good deal of evidence which concerns languages other than Greek.

As far as I know the primary evidence for Latin in contact with languages other than Greek has never been systematically collected, and I have therefore set out to make the scattered evidence accessible by quoting many of the relevant inscriptions in full before considering the issues which they raise.

II OSCAN, UMBRIAN, VENETIC, MESSAPIC

There was a considerable variety of languages spoken in the early period in Italy, including not only Greek and Latin but Etruscan and Italic languages such as Oscan, Umbrian and Venetic (if, that is, the last *is* Italic). In the south there was also Messapic (see II.5). In this section (II) I will be concerned mainly with Oscan, Umbrian and Venetic, of which for our purposes Oscan is the best attested. There were extensive contacts between Latin, Oscan and other Italic speakers, which show up for example in the regional loan-words which found their way into Latin (e.g. *popina* alongside the native *coquina*, and the adjective *rufus* alongside *ruber*).[3] As far as concrete evidence for bilingualism is concerned, the early period from, say, the seventh to the fourth centuries BC is a closed book. In the last two centuries BC, when inscriptions proliferate in (e.g.) Latin and Oscan and *testimonia* relevant to bilingualism begin to appear, the Latinisation of the peninsula is well under way, and much of the evidence concerns attitudes to Latin as the prestige language of Italy, forms of influence of Latin on Oscan, and the marginalisation of Oscan leading eventually to its death. Inscriptions showing code-switching, perhaps the most distinctive bilingual characteristic of written texts, are found. There is though some complexity to the language attitudes embedded in the inscriptions, and it would not be satisfactory to maintain without reservation that by the last centuries of the Republic Latin was the prestige language in relation, say, to Oscan, in all areas and all strata

---

[3] See e.g. Ernout (1909: 218, 222) on these cases.

of society. An attempt will be made to look more closely at the various kinds of evidence and to extract whatever general trends might lie behind them.

II.1 Testimonia *and literary evidence*

There is a story in Livy that in 180 BC the people of Cumae applied to Rome to be allowed to conduct certain forms of public business in Latin: 40.43.1 *Cumanis eo anno petentibus permissum ut publice Latine loquerentur et praeconibus Latine uendendi ius esset* (presumably *publice Latine loquerentur* refers to the use of Latin in public assemblies). Whatever else it might be taken to mean,[4] the passage certainly shows that by this time the upper classes of the town were bilingual (or multilingual). Cumae was a Greek foundation, but was conquered by the Oscans *c.* 421 (Diod. Sic. 12.76.4).[5] It was Oscanised, but retained some Greek culture (Strabo 5.4.4). The story of Livy is conventionally taken to indicate that Oscan gave way to Latin,[6] but it is possible that Greek had lingered on alongside Oscan.[7] In the epigraphy of the town there are Greek inscriptions (*IG* XIV. 860–72) as well as Oscan (for which see Vetter (1953), 108–14), though the dates of these are usually unclear.[8] At Delos at exactly the time of the event referred to by Livy (179 BC) a Cumaean is recorded in Greek as making a dedication (*ID* 442 B.147), with no indication that the inscription was in any language other than Greek (contrast the Delian text referred to at 3.III.3, n. 61). A sudden switch to Latin in some public affairs could not have been made unless Latin was well established already in private usage among the élite. The desire to make the switch (which the Cumaeans could have made without the permission of Rome)[9] must reflect the degree of linguistic Romanisation that the town had undergone by this

---

4 There is an extensive literature on the passage. See e.g. Kaimio (1975: 99–100), Prosdocimi (1989: 59–60), Campanile (1991b: 10), Rochette (1997a: 89 with n. 160) (with further bibliography), and also the works cited in n. 6.

5 See Oakley (1998: 631–3.)

6 See e.g. Salmon (1982: 175, 207 n. 526), Brunt (1988: 104), Balsdon (1979: 116). Harris (1971: 172) does not commit himself. Lomas (1993: 175) allows that although Oscan was the principal language Greek was still spoken.

7 However according to Dion. Hal. (15.6.4) the Campanians expelled the Cumaeans. Diodorus (12.76.4) talks of the Campanians plundering the city, and selling into slavery those who were captured.

8 The *defixio IG* XIV.872 = Audollent (1904), 198 may be as late as the second or third century AD (see Audollent (1904: 271)).

9 Note Brunt (1988: 104 n. 25): 'The inference sometimes drawn that Rome had hitherto forbidden Cumae the official use of Latin seems absurd. Presumably the Cumaeans, to ingratiate themselves, intimated their wishes and Rome gave a sanction that was not required legally.'

date. We will also see (II.3, p. 139) evidence that Latin had made inroads into Cumae at a lower social level by the second century BC.

The anecdote brings out the background to the linguistic Romanisation of at least part of the peninsula. There is no suggestion that the Romans were attempting actively to wipe out the local language or languages of Cumae. The initiative was taken by the Cumaeans themselves. The story is meaningful only if the Cumaeans were attaching such prestige by this time to the use of Latin that they wanted to adopt it as their public language, and to make Rome aware that they had done so (on the status of one language in relation to another as a factor in language shift, see below, II.6, XIV.3).[10] Similarly, as we will see (6.III.2), at much the same time on the island of Delos the Italian *negotiatores* who styled themselves collectively as *Italici* made a point of using Latin in their public inscriptions, even though they were based in a Greek-speaking region, and many of them were Greek speakers, or fluent bilinguals, or Campanians from old Oscan families. By the second century BC, long before the Social War, Latin was clearly acquiring status among Italian upper classes, such that they might wish to be seen to be Latin-speaking. There is moreover an analogy between these cases, in which Italians set store by presenting themselves as Latin-, rather than or as well as, Greek- or Oscan-speaking, and those cases of Italian Latin speakers from regions outside the city of Rome who, either before or not long after the Social War, were keen to be seen as speakers of city, as distinct from Italian regional, Latin. Plautus (*Truc.* 688), Lucilius (*apud* Quint. 1.5.56) and Cicero (*De orat.* 3.43), all of whom originated outside the city, made disparaging remarks about non-city varieties of Latin,[11] thereby betraying the outsider's desire to advertise his assimilation to the language or dialect of what was seen as the cultural centre.

The abandonment of Oscan probably did not take place without some sort of nationalistic reaction. We will see some evidence for local pride in Italic and even of an attempt to elevate the cultural level of writing in Oscan (II.3, p. 142, II.4, p. 148). Where Cumae was concerned, the change of languages was at an official level, but in private, informal usage Oscan need not have been dropped so abruptly. A *defixio* thought to be from Cumae which is generally dated to the Sullan period will be discussed below (II.3); this contains an element of Oscan, though it has some

---

[10] See also Bradley (2000: 210–11), taking much the same line as that adopted here.

[11] It has to be said though that these passages are in literary works in which the writer need not have been speaking in his own person. But general attitudes can nevertheless be deduced from such *testimonia*.

Latin as well. The anecdote in Livy, if it can be accepted as true, points to an early stage in the Romanisation (in the linguistic sense) of Italian élites. But on the eve of the Social War, when the independence of Italians was more of an issue, one might expect to find something of a revival of Oscan. A relevant text in this respect is the *Lex Osca Tabulae Bantinae*.[12] This was probably written locally not long before the Social War.[13] On the choice of the Oscan language, note the remarks of Crawford (1996: 276): 'We suspect that the preparation and engraving of the text was intended to symbolise independence from Rome. Would an élite which wished to demonstrate its loyalty have put up a charter in Oscan? We also suspect that our text is the work of an élite which normally spoke and wrote Latin and which in any case used the Latin script and wrote from left to right, which became desperate to assert an Oscan identity. That élite perhaps did not enquire too closely about the ultimately Roman origin of a text adapted from a model at Venusia, which was after all to join the rebels in the Social War.' On this view the authors were fully Latinised, and the Oscan represented some sort of revival made for symbolic political reasons. This interpretation of the authors' motives is plausible, but it would not do to argue that the ineptitude of the Oscan engraving reflects the ineptitude in the Oscan language of the composers themselves. Vetter (1953: 21; see also 14) argued in reference to line 11 of the Naples fragment (where *exeic* is written *ex.elg.* because the writer mistakenly associated the first part of the word with the Latin preposition) that the engraver did not know Oscan, but obviously the composer did, even if he was heavily influenced not only by principles of Roman law but also by the Latin phraseology in which those principles were expressed.[14] The linguistic competence of the composer of a text is to be strictly distinguished from that of an engraver who is merely copying it out. The members of the upper classes responsible for the text may well have moved over to Latin in their everyday life, but there was clearly still a residual knowledge of Oscan that they could call on. What is interesting is that it is now Oscan which is capable (on the interpretation quoted above) of conveying a political symbolism, whereas at the time of the Cumae affair local élites were resorting to Latin apparently for a comparable purpose.

---

[12] For which see Vetter (1953), 2, and particularly Crawford (1996), 13.

[13] The date is much disputed, but see the detailed discussion of Crawford (1996: 274–6) arguing for the period before the Social War. Note too A. W. Lintott (*OCD* 3rd edn, *s.v.* 'tabula Bantina'), stating that the Oscan statute almost certainly 'antedates the incorporation of Bantia into the Roman *res publica* at the end of the Social War'; and see also Brunt (1988: 119).

[14] See Porzio Gernia (1970), *passim* on the influence of Latin phraseology on the Oscan text, and see below, II.3.

In this connection it is interesting to note that at the time of the Social War the Italian rebels issued large numbers of coins, more than 900 of which survive.[15] Some of these have the legend ITALIA, but others the Oscan equivalent **víteliú** (or **vítelliú**).[16] Others again are bilingual, with Latin on one side and Oscan on the other.[17] There are also rare coins with the Oscan **safinim** (= Samnium).[18] Not all of the rebels were Oscan speakers, but those who spoke Oscan will in most cases have known Latin as well. The Oscan legends were not therefore a necessary element of the coinage, as is particularly clear in the case of those coins which have Latin as well. The Oscan has symbolic significance. There would be little point in arguing that Oscan was used only on issues from areas in which Oscan was understood.[19] It was not after all a complex sentence which had to be understood: the point of a single-word Oscan name would not be lost even on monolingual Latin speakers, who would soon pick up its meaning. As Burnett (1998: 170) observes, 'the Italian coins have a good case for being regarded as the first coins produced as propaganda, in the sense that their existence and the symbols they bore were intended to convey a simple and strong message, of common identity and hostile distinction from a specific enemy'. These are not the only coins which we will see on which a vernacular language is used in a Roman area to express a distinctive identity for a subordinate people. Neo-Punic (v.3) and Iberian coin legends (x) of comparable significance will be discussed in later sections. It is incidentally worth recalling that coinage with Oscan legends was also issued by Italian rebels at an earlier period. During the rebellion of Capua and satellite towns (Atella, Calatia) in the Hannibalic war coin issues (probably 216–211) carried the names of the towns exclusively in Oscan form and script (e.g. **kapv**, **kalati**, written *sinistrorsum*).[20] In this case the choice of language probably had a different determinant: at this early date Oscan was the language of the towns in question. The fact that in the Social War Oscan appears on only some issues hints at the language shift which had occurred in the intervening period.

The poet Ennius was tri- or multilingual, possibly in Oscan as well as Greek and Latin: note Gell. 17.17.1 *Quintus Ennius tria corda habere sese dicebat, quod loqui Graece et Osce et Latine sciret.* The passage as it stands hints at the esteem in which in the early period Italic languages must have been held by their speakers. Ennius is presented in the anecdote

[15] See in general Burnett (1998). I have not seen A. Campana, *La monetazione degli insorti italici durante la Guerra Sociale (91–87 a.C.)* (Soliera, 1987).
[16] See Burnett (1998: 166).   [17] See Burnett (1998: 170). This is Campana's type 2.
[18] See Burnett (1998: 167). On the name, see Untermann (2000: 641).
[19] See the discussion of this point by Burnett (1998: 169–70).
[20] See Giard (1965), and particularly the catalogue at 246–59; also Frederiksen (1984: 242–3).

as evaluating the three languages equally. There is though a problem of interpretation here. Ennius was a native of Rudiae, a Messapic foundation in Calabria, and it is therefore puzzling that he should be described here as an Oscan rather than a Messapic speaker.[21] Jocelyn (1972: 991) thought that Gellius was wrong and that Ennius knew Messapic not Oscan.[22] Oscan inscriptions do not happen to survive from the heel of Italy, but Skutsch (1985: 749) argues that 'the poet's sister's son, born at Brindisi, bears the Oscan name Pacuvius, and *Osce* therefore is not to be questioned'; he also observes that the name *Ennius* belonged to the Oscan dialect region. It could however be readily countered that names have a habit of travelling. Ennius might have known Messapic as well as Oscan,[23] but continued speculation in the absence of any hard evidence is pointless. Certainly bilingualism in Greek and Messapic must have been common in this area, and we will see later (ii.5) a Messapic inscription with possible code-switching into Greek (IM 2.24). Any attempt to find the influence of Oscan or any other vernacular language on the Latin of Ennius would not incidentally be fruitful. *Tongeo*, quoted from Ennius at Paul. Fest. p. 489 L. (*Var. 28*) (*alii rhetorica tongent*), is cognate with Osc. **tanginúd**, but the verb was probably in use in early Latin. The Praenestines are said (Paul. Fest.) to have used *tongitionem* for *notionem*. *Tongeo* occurs nowhere else in Latin.[24] It is possible that *famul* (*Ann.* 313) represents Oscan *famel*, but the form is open to other explanations.[25] Skutsch (1985: 278) is sceptical about *homonem* (*Ann.* 125) as an Oscanism (but cf. Untermann (2000: 329)). As for Ennius' Latin, though he served in the army, he is unlikely to have acquired the language in such an archaic and artificial form there.[26]

Strabo (born about 64 BC) makes the claim (5.3.6) that in his day (or should we rather say that of his source?)[27] plays (Atellane farces) were performed in Oscan at Rome; note ἡ διάλεκτος μένει παρὰ τοῖς Ῥωμαίοις. If this story could be taken at its face value,[28] it would be

---

[21] The problem has been much discussed. See e.g. Prosdocimi (1979: 1036–7), id. (1989: 62–3, 66–7) (with earlier bibliography), and the works of Jocelyn and Skutsch cited henceforth.

[22] I quote his comment: 'It is often said that he knew the language of the neighbouring Sabellian peoples as well as his native Messapian, without, however, very good cause.' For a critique of this view, see Skutsch (1974: 78). Kearns (1990: 41 n. 3) bizarrely claims that the 'native tongue [of Ennius] was likely Umbrian'.

[23] Salmon (1967: 123), noting that Rudiae was Messapic in origin, suggests that Oscan was an *acquired* language for Ennius. It is perhaps worth asking whether a language 'Messapic' was recognised as a separate entity by anyone (such as Gellius) outside the area in which it was spoken.

[24] See further Vetter (1953: 377).

[25] See Skutsch (1985: 492); but also Rix (1994: 41), taking the word as an 'Oscanism'.

[26] See Jocelyn (1972: 993 with n. 60), noting his military service in the context of Latin learning.

[27] See Brunt (1988: 118 n. 85).

[28] As it is taken, for example, by Petersmann (1995: 536 n.10); so too Salmon (1967: 119), Prosdocimi (1978: 1038–9).

evidence for a lingering use of Oscan, and hence for Oscan–Latin bilingualism, in some communities in the city. This is not the only evidence
of its kind. There are references in Suetonius to spectacles in the city in
which *histriones* 'of every language' participated, and a passage of Cicero
considered alongside these suggests that Oscan must have been included;
the allusion is to Atellane farce. The passages are as follows: Suet. *Iul.* 39.1
edidit spectacula uarii generis: munus gladiatorium, ludos etiam regionatim urbe tota
et quidem per omnium linguarum histriones, *Aug.* 43.1 *fecitque
nonnumquam etiam uicatim ac pluribus scaenis* **per omnium linguarum
histrionum** <...> *non in foro modo, nec in amphitheatro, sed et in circo et in
Saeptis,* Cic. *Fam.* 7.1.3 *non enim te puto* **Graecos aut Oscos** *ludos desiderasse,
praesertim cum Oscos uel in senatu uestro spectare possis.*[29] In reference to the
last, Rawson (1985: 22, n. 12) notes that *Graecos aut Oscos ludos* 'is neater if
language is referred to in the second case [i.e. *Oscos*] as well as the first'.
Tac. *Ann.* 4.14.3, where the phrase *Oscum ludicrum* is used, is taken to refer
to the type of drama (Atellane farce), not to the Oscan language. It is of
course possible that 'Oscan' farces were still performed in the Empire
from old texts learnt by heart which virtually no one understood; the
performance might have relied purely on slapstick and the audience's
familiarity with unchanging plots for its effect.[30]

   In the context of the possible survival of Oscan drama (in the Oscan
language) at Rome, it is worth recalling that Pomponius, the late
Republican author of literary Atellane farce in Latin form, has sometimes
been taken to have admitted an item of Italic morphology into lines of
Latin.[31] Note 141 R. *quot* **laetitias insperatas** *modo mi inrepsere in sinum.*
Here the *-as* endings of what appears to be the subject of the verb can be
variously interpreted. One possibility is that they are accusatives of exclamation and that the construction breaks off after *insperatas*. But *-as* was
the (inherited) feminine nominative plural ending in Oscan, and an alternative explanation would be that the usage is a reflection of the Oscan
origin of farce. There is another such case at 150: *ego quaero quod comedim;*
has *quaerunt quod cacent: contrariumst.* Emendation has been resorted to
(by Ribbeck), but *has* can be defended,[32] not least because *hasce* occurs at
Cato, *Agr.* 134.1 (where it has usually been emended away)[33] and at *CIL*

[29] Translation of Shackleton Bailey (Loeb): 'As for the Greek and Oscan shows, I don't imagine you
   were sorry to miss *them* – especially as you can see an Oscan turn on your town council.'
[30] For the way in which gibberish can be presented on stage so that the dramatic meaning is made
   clear, see Gratwick's discussion (1971) of the Punic in Plautus' *Poenulus.*
[31] See E. Löfstedt (1956: II, 333–4), Devoto (1968: 169); cf. Palmer (1954: 150).
[32] See Löfstedt (1956: II, 333–4), Bakkum (1994: 34–6).
[33] Mazzarino retains the reading in the second edition of his Teubner text.

1².2685.[34] Two possible examples of -*as* at Pisaurum (*CIL* I². 378, 379), both showing *matrona* as nominative plural, apparently with loss of final -*s*, might seem to accord with an Italic origin of the morpheme.[35] However, it is not only at Pisaurum that the form is attested in inscriptions (see also *CIL* I². 1342 (Rome), 2520 (*defixio* said to have been found at Rome), 2685);[36] and the presence of *hasce* in Cato (see above) further weakens any attempt to pin the ending down exclusively to Oscan-influenced Latin. Moreover Bakkum (1994), in his comprehensive discussion of the -*eis* second-declension masculine plural ending (as e.g. in *magistreis*) and of -*as*, has argued persuasively that in function the latter cannot be entirely separated from the former,[37] which (on the basis of a large collection of evidence) he states cannot be assigned to any dialect in particular.[38] The precise source of the -*as* plural in Latin texts[39] such as Pomponius in my opinion remains uncertain.[40]

In fact the influence of Oscan on non-standard Latin has been exaggerated,[41] and alleged phonetic manifestations of such influence in particular are usually explicable in other ways.[42] It is mainly in the matter

---

[34] See Bakkum (1994: 35–6).

[35] Devoto (1956–7: 449) refers to the word as having an 'Umbrian' form.

[36] See Bakkum (1994: 35).

[37] A distinctive function of the usage he terms the 'resumptiveness-parameter' (see further 6.v.2).

[38] See Bakkum (1994: 19).

[39] It is worth noting that the -*as* plural is well attested in imperial inscriptions (e.g. *CIL* III. 2386, 13374, V.5078), and that it is reflected in some Romance languages.

[40] Another morpheme attested in Latin which has been assigned a 'dialectal' origin is the second-person singular ending -*rus* as seen e.g. at *P. Rainer Cent.* 164.5 *misererus* (cf. Cato *Agr.* 157.8, *CIL* VI.10736). But see now Parsons on *P. Rainer Cent.* 164.5. (citing J. H. W. Penney), arguing that the form is rather a Latin archaism.

[41] The evidence produced by Devoto (1933) cannot be taken at its face value.

[42] For example, much of the evidence bearing on the matter in Coleman (1990) is unconvincing, and little attention is paid to bibliography. The same goes for Moltoni's (1954) account of alleged 'Oscanisms' in the Latin inscriptions of Regio I; this is a work which calls for a detailed refutation, but there is no space for that here. Väänänen's view (1966: 67) that the assimilated spelling in the single item *Verecunnus* = *Verecundus* at Pompeii (*CIL* IV.1768) is 'without doubt an Oscanising form' is not compelling. The comparable *Secunnus* occurs at Rome (*CIL* VI.3607), and there is the possibility in such cases that the name had been deliberately deformed for humorous or other purposes to incorporate *cunnus*. The assimilation *nd* to *nn* is attested both in Oscan and Italian, but it does not make its appearance in Italian until the medieval period, and may be an independent innovation rather than a direct continuation of something found in a local Oscan-influenced form of Vulgar Latin. For various views, see Rohlfs (1966: 357–61), Tekavčić (1972: 276–80), Hall (1974: 63), De Simone (1980: 76), Polomé (1983: 521 n. 29). Eska (1987) reaches negative conclusions about the possible influence of Oscan on the Latin of the Pompeian inscriptions. He argues that many of the alleged 'Oscan' features of Pompeian Latin 'are attested to some extent in the non-standardised Latinian dialects of the provinces in pre-classical times and that some also are found in the Latin of the distant parts of the empire' (158). Wachter too tends to be sceptical about such substrate influence in Latin (e.g. (1987: 426; see further below); but cf. id. (1987: 422, 474)). The monophthongisation seen in *cedito* and *cedre* = *caidito*, *caidere* in a Latin inscription from

of the lexicon (as distinct from phonetics, syntax and morphology)[43] that good evidence is to be found for the intrusion of Oscan elements (words and word-forms) into Latin (but see further below on a passage of Lucilius, and also the concluding remarks at II.6.2 below). It. *bifolco*, for example, reflects *bufulcus rather than CL *bubulcus*.[44] This is a case of the borrowing by Latin of a regional word rather than of phonetic interference in a Latin word. Some further evidence could be added to that of Ernout (1909): see e.g. Rohlfs (1959: 178–80), noting for example that CL *gleba* survives in Calabrian dialects with intervocalic *f*.[45]

There are two possible cases in Lucilius of (single-word) switches from Latin into Oscan (or Oscan-influenced Latin), one of more interest than the other.[46] At 138 there seems to be an example of the Oscan word *sollo*:[47] *uasa quoque omnino dirimit* [*redimit* Marx, following Dousa] *non sollo, dupundi*.[48] Unfortunately the line itself is obscure, and has no context, and it is impossible to be sure that *sollo* represents a piece of code-switching. Marx (1904–5: II, 423) asserts: 'Quod Oscum posuit uocabulum poeta id

the Umbrian territory (Spoletium: *CIL* I².366 = *ILLRP* 505) on the face of it may appear to be an Umbrianism, but caution is advisable. It is possible that monophthongisation had occurred in the Latin of Latium and been carried further afield (see Wachter (1987: 430–2, 481–2). It is just possible (see Flobert (1995)) that there is some substrate (Oscan) influence in the Murecine tablets which bear the name of Novius Eunus. The anaptyxis (see Flobert (1995: 148–9)) seen in such misspellings as *ominis*, *octoberes* and *septeberes* can be related to the distinctive Oscan types of the phenomenon (for which see Buck (1904: 50): 'If it [the liquid or nasal] precedes [the adjacent consonant], the quality of the new vowel is that of the vowel preceding, while if it follows, the new vowel has the quality of the following vowel'). At least two of the examples cited could be explained as falling into the second category, but it has to be said that the anaptyxis in e.g. *omnis* can be found in other areas (see Adams (1990b: 232)). Wachter (1987: 396–401) plays down the possibility of Oscan influence in some early inscriptions (*c.* 200 BC) from Campania. See however Vine (1993: 133–4) (with the speculative but interesting discussion that follows, 134–41). At *ID* 2628, III.36 the name *Vlcius* appears in Greek in the form Ὀλόκιος (but with dots under the first three letters). If the reading is right, this form would display an Oscan anaptyxis of the first type. Perhaps the spelling was allowed in a Greek text because in Greek there would not have been the same pressure as in Latin to preserve the 'correct' written form.

43 Morphological interference of Oscan in Latin has sometimes been seen in the verb forms *fundatid* and *parentatid* found in the so-called *Lex Lucerina* (*CIL* I². 401). Wallace (1988: 215), among others, relates these to the Oscan formation seen e.g. in **tríbarakattíns** (third person plural perfect subjunctive), arguing that both have a stem ending in -*a*, a perfect morpheme (-*tt*-/-*t*-), a subjunctive morpheme and an ending (see further e.g. Wachter (1987: 422), Lazzeroni (1991b)). This explanation may well be right, but such an analysis is not however the only one possible: see Leumann (1977: 571). The classic study of the lexical evidence is that of Ernout (1909).

44 See Ernout (1909: 131) and note *REW* 1355 'Das -*f*- scheint auf osk.-umbr. Herkunft zu weisen'; see also De Simone (1980: 76), Polomé (1983: 521).

45 See further De Simone (1980: 76).   46 See further Petersmann (1999: 308–9).

47 See Festus 384 L. on *sollo*: *Osce dicitur id quod nos totum uocamus*. Cf. Untermann (2000: 714–15), s.v. **sullus**.

48 Vetter (1953: 374) argues that *sollodupundi* is to be taken as a compound word of Greek type (cf. *moechocinaedi*). See further Lejeune (1949: 106–7).

consulto fecit ut hominem opicum, figulorum Campanorum qui utatur sermone, describeret.' This however is no more than guesswork.

The second case of what seems to be an Oscan (or Oscanised Latin) word embedded in the Latin text is at 581: *primum Pacilius tesorophylax pater abzet.*[49] The line is quoted in a gloss (*CGL* IV, p. XVIII, VI, p. 11) which equates *abzet* with *extincta* or *mortua*. An explanation of the word has been offered by Mras (1927–8: 80–1). He interprets it as equivalent to *abiit*, citing e.g. (81, n. 9) *CIL* VI.28044 for the use of *abiit* in the sense *mortuus est.* The palatalisation of *j* in such environments is characteristic of some Oscan dialects (cf. Vetter (1953), 2 for *Bansae* = *Bantiae*; see further Maniet (1972: 548)), and the spelling with *e* is reminiscent of such Oscan perfect forms as **deded** = *dedit.* On this view *abzet* could be an Oscanisation of *abiit* (cf. Pael. *afded* at Vetter (1953), 213),[50] presumably intended to express the pronunciation of the referent.[51] *Pacilius* is a *gentilicium* corresponding to the Oscan **Paakul** (for which see Vetter (1953), 116). This explanation, though speculative, nicely takes account of the context and of the form of the spelling. Lucilius' interest in regional Latin[52] and in language in general is well documented. The passage is suggestive both of regional bilingualism and possibly also of the Latin speaker's contempt for Oscan or at least Oscan-influenced Latin. Lucilius was from Suessa Aurunca, a Latin colony founded in 313 BC in central Italy. The town itself will not have been primarily Oscan-speaking, but it is in just such a provincial, Latin-speaking, environment that Lucilius might have acquired a condescending attitude to the Oscan spoken in neighbouring areas.[53] If

---

[49] Terzaghi (1966), line 617 punctuates *primum Pacilius: tesorophylax, pater, abzet.* There is no way of determining whether this is right.

[50] On which see e.g. Zamudio (1986: 28, 51–2, 88, 105), Untermann (2000: 57–8). The form is problematical in meaning and etymology.

[51] Note Mras (1927–8: 81): 'Den Pacilius wollte er, wie bereits bemerkt, wegen seiner Aussprache karikieren; der wird *abiit* wie *abzet* . . . ausgesprochen haben.'

[52] Note for example his sneering reference to the rustic speech of one Caecilius at 1130, and the story at Quint. 1.5.56 that he rebuked a certain Vettius for his use of Praenestine words (see next footnote).

[53] Harris (1971: 170) puts the question how the Romans regarded the use of the local Italian languages, and at 171 he states: 'Such second-century references as there are, by Titinius and Lucilius, suggest that Romans looked down on the Italian languages.' The passage of Titinius (104 *qui Obsce et Volsce fabulantur, nam Latine nesciunt*) has no context, but it is probably, as Harris suggests, a disparaging reference to non-Latin speakers (see Skutsch (1974: 78); but cf. Prosdocimi (1989: 63)). The fragment of Lucilius which he cites, however (*apud* Quint. 1.5.56), has no place in the discussion, because Lucilius was criticising one Vettius for using non-urban words in Latin; it is about regional *Latin.* After saying that Lucilius criticised Vettius for using *Praenestinis (uerbis)*, Quintilian revealingly adds *quem ad modum Pollio reprehendit in Liuio Patauinitatem*, a clause which Harris does not quote. This makes it obvious that separate *languages* are not at issue. Moreover Lucilius was not a Roman. The passage which we have just discussed in the text is far better evidence for an attitude embedded in Lucilius' work to an Italic *language.*

the passage has been correctly interpreted, it complements Livy's story about the Cumaeans. The Cumaean upper classes in the second century BC were by implication conceding to Latin a higher prestige than to Oscan, while on the other hand native speakers of Latin from provincial regions at roughly the same time might have looked down on Oscan (or Oscanised Latin). It is worth recalling that the adjective *Opicus* means not only 'Oscan', but also 'Ignorant (esp. of Latin), uncultured, barbarian' (*OLD*, s.v., 2). The two attitudes, of contempt for Oscan by Latin speakers, and admiration for Latin by Oscans, go hand-in-hand, for if Italian élites from Oscan areas were aware of Roman disparagement of their language that will have increased the pressure on them to switch to Latin.

If the attempt to find decisive evidence for phonetic influence (particularly in the long term) of Oscan on Latin has been unsuccessful, this last example suggests that such interference must have occurred, but *in the Latin of first-language speakers of Oscan* rather than in that of monolingual Latin speakers. That is precisely what might have been expected, for interference (from L1) typically affects those speaking L2. Much of the Latin which has traditionally been examined for Oscan interference was probably written by native speakers of Latin, and in this interference is unlikely to have taken place. In discussing bilingualism and its consequences it is always worth attempting to distinguish between first- and second-language speakers of the languages in contact (see 1.v for a discussion of this distinction in relation to interference).

There are two possible Oscanisms in Plautus (perhaps *rustix* for *rusticus* at *Most.* 40,[54] and *Campans* (*genus*) at *Trin.* 545, which is confirmed by Nonius p. 781 L.),[55] but of these certainly the first is not compelling. *Campans* has to be interpreted in the context as neuter nominative singular. Were it masculine nominative singular it would represent a straightforward Oscan form, as the *o* of the original *-os* was regularly lost in Oscan.[56] But *Campans* is not an Oscan neuter form. One possibility is that in the first instance *Campans* entered a variety of Latin as a masculine nominative, and was then subject to reinterpretation within Latin

---

[54] See Vetter (1953: 373). Some editors are not happy with the *rusticus* of the manuscripts (and also Donatus); see also Leo (1912: 263).

[55] See Vetter (1953: 373). I mention as a curiosity the view of Sheets (1981) that there are 'dialect glosses' in Livius Andronicus. This notion has been rejected effectively by Kearns (1990), though Kearns' article itself is not without oddity. He argues (47–8) that Andronicus avoided Grecism. The possible presence of adverbial *multa* (= πολλά) in the fragments (*Od.* 22 Morel) is not discussed.

[56] See e.g. Buck (1904: 116).

as a neuter, on the analogy of Latin neuter adjectives (e.g. *elegans*) and participles with the ending *-ans*.[57] There is a comparable form in the old expression for 'elephant', *Luca bos*, lit. 'Lucanian ox'. *Luca* must derive from *Lucan(u)s*, which, with the regular loss of *n* before *s*, would have produced *Lucas*. This in turn must have lost its final *s* in the manner of *Aeneas* > *Aenea* etc. in early Latin.[58] *Campans* (at least in its hypothetical original masculine form) and *Luca*, as their own semantics show, will have originated in Oscan areas, among (L2) Latin speakers.

On the Oscan-speaking spies mentioned by Livy at 10.20.8, see below, III.5 n. 241.

II.2 Bilingual texts

Bilingual coins were mentioned in the previous section. There are a few other bilingual texts in Latin and an Italic language. I cite first Poccetti (1979), 9 = *ILLRP* 1206:

(a) Numesier. Varea. Polenia
(b) Nomesi. Varia.

This is the text printed by Poccetti; Degrassi (*ILLRP*) has *Folenia*.[59] The inscriptions, said by Poccetti (1979: 30) to be in different hands, are on a bronze vessel ('poêle en cuivre jaune avec patine noire', Lejeune (1952a: 98)), the first in Umbrian (with rhotacism at the end of the genitive form *Numesier*, but not within the word; Poccetti compares *Tab. Ig.* Va 2, 14, 15 **plenasier**, **urnasier**), the second in Latin. The inscriptions indicate the ownership of the object (for a similar bilingual, in Punic and Latin, on a domestic object, see below, V.5.1 on *IPT* 91). *Nomesius* is a *praenomen* which precedes the rest of the onomastic formula, in a manner typical of servile naming patterns.[60] For a genitive (of a *praenomen*) at the head of an inscription, see the next text discussed below. In the absence of any information about the circumstances in which the two inscriptions were incised, nothing can be made of them, though they do seem to locate Latin–Umbrian bilingualism in a domestic setting. Lejeune (1952a: 99–100), on the evidence of the names as well as the language, is inclined to see the provenance of the text

---

[57] See further Leumann (1977: 324, 432).   [58] See Leumann (1977: 324, 454).
[59] See Lejeune (1952a: 98–9) on the names and the readings.
[60] See Poccetti (1979: 30), citing nos. 21 and 269 in his own collection. It is clear from his note on 269 that he would take the name in the genitive as that of the patron (owner of the slave). Degrassi on the other hand takes *Nomesius* to be the name of the husband, following Lejeune (1952a: 98), who suggests the alternative possibility that the name may be that of the father.

as Umbria. The date is probably second century BC.[61] If so the text shows the spread of Latin among Umbrian speakers before the Social War.

It is of note that in this inscription the name is given two different inflections determined by the language in which it is being used. The following inscriptions present a contrast in this respect.

Poccetti (1979), 21 is bilingual in Oscan and Latin:

(a) **hn. sattiịeís detfri**
    seganatted. plavtad
    (= H(erenni) Satti Detfri / signauit planta)
(b) Herenneis. Amica
    signauit. qando
    ponebamus. tegila.

These two inscriptions are on a terracotta tile discovered at Pietrabbondante in Samnium in 1975. They may be dated to the first decade of the first century BC.[62] The two persons responsible for the inscriptions (Detfri (?), Amica) seem to have been fellow (female?) slaves perhaps working in a tile factory.[63] They impressed the soles of their feet in the soft clay and then added inscriptions.[64] The inscriptions are in different hands.

Both inscriptions begin with a name in the genitive (cf. above); the name (in its Latinate form) is Herennius Sattius. *Herens* must have been an Oscan *praenomen*,[65] and the Latin inscription uses this name alone in the Oscan genitive form without the *gentilicium*. Herennius will have been the owner of the other persons named, or their patron if they were freed, and it is possible that he was the proprietor of a tile factory.[66]

Various things stand out in the inscriptions. First, this type of code-switching, whereby a name is inflected according to its language of origin or to the mother tongue of its bearer rather than to the language of the text in which it is used, is commonplace (see e.g. 1.VII.2.3 on the inflection of Aeschines' Latin name *Flauianus*), and the failure of the Latin writer to Latinise the form strongly suggests that Herennius was perceived as an Oscan speaker. The Oscan form in an otherwise Latin text is used as appropriate to the referent's identity.

---

[61] See Bradley (2000: 210), with bibliography.   [62] See La Regina (1976: 287).
[63] See La Regina (1976: 283–8). On **plavtad**, see Mura and Prosdocimi (1978: 205 n. 2), Untermann (2000: 563). Untermann (1979: 303 n. 41) took *tegila* to be a misspelling of *tegulum* 'roofing', but it is more likely to represent *tegula* (see Rix (1994: 36), interpreting the form as = *tegila(m)*, but equally it might be a hypercorrect neuter plural).
[64] See Lejeune (1976a: 290).   [65] See Lejeune (1976a: 291) on the name.
[66] See La Regina (1976: 287).

Secondly, the two persons responsible for the scratching of the texts before the tile was dry,[67] on the same day and in the same place, were clearly speakers on the one hand of Oscan and on the other of Latin, and they almost certainly worked together. The pair of texts is suggestive of artisans' bilingualism. The Latin writer's use of an Oscan inflection in an Oscan name in a text in Latin hints further at her bilingualism. The Oscan Herennius had at least one slave of Latin background, and her care to grant him an Oscan genitive inflection in his name would seem to imply an attitude of deference or accommodation. In the absence of precise details about stages in the linguistic Romanisation of Italy it is tempting to hold on to generalisations about the prestige of Latin and the consequent death of Oscan, but there is no reason why in specific communities, particularly at lower social levels, such general attitudes should have been so clearly formulated. In this case the Oscan Herens would seem to have been in the position of dominance, and it is the Latin speaker who defers to him linguistically.

The name *Amica* poses no problems,[68] but **detfri** is a mystery. La Regina (1976: 286) thought that it might either be a servile name, or the designation of a trade, but the consensus now seems to be that it is a name: note Poccetti (1979: 43) 'Il confronto speculare con *Amica* e ragioni morfologiche rendono più probabile per DETFRI un nome servile di origine orientale . . . che un appellativo.'[69]

The verbs in the two versions, **seganatted** and *signauit*, clearly mean 'left a mark/seal' (with the foot). The Oscan verb is a denominative based on **segúnú** = *signum*, but since the Oscan noun is attested only in the meaning 'statue', the verb, though a genuine Oscan formation, may have been semantically influenced by the Latin (a loan-shift: see 4.V.2.11).[70]

There also survives a partially bilingual text in Venetic and Latin (Pellegrini and Prosdocimi (1967), Es 27):[71]

[vza].n.vo.l[.tiio.n.]mno.s.zona.s.tokela.χ.[../ śa.i.]nate.i.re.i.tiia.i.o.p
[.vo.]l[.]tiiole[no]
(= *[vda]n Vol[tion]mnos donasto ke lag[. . . ?] Śainatei Reitiai op [vo]ltio le[no]*)
[d]o[nom] dedit libens merito.

---

[67] *qando ponebamus tegila* must refer to the laying of the tiles out in the sun or in a kiln.
[68] See La Regina (1976: 286). Untermann (2000: 172) though takes the word as a common noun, as does Rix (1994: 36), who has the Oscan genitive dependent on *amica*.
[69] Further speculations can be found in Lejeune (1976a: 290–1), Pisani (1977: 347). See further Untermann (2000: 172), with additional bibliography. Rix (1994: 36) is not convinced that **detfri** is a name. He declares the form to be not only ἅπαξ but also a 'monster'.
[70] See Untermann (2000: 661).
[71] See also Lejeune (1974), no. 12 A–B, with divergences from the text of Pellegrini and Prosdocimi.

This text is on one of the bronze votive plaques from the Venetic sanctuary at Este, and is probably to be dated to the first century BC.[72] *Libens merito* seems to be equivalent to the prepositional phrase at the end of the Venetic (*op voltiio leno*).[73] The verb phrase of the Latin (*donom dedit*) corresponds loosely to *donasto*.[74] In the Venetic *Voltionmnos* is the name of the dedicator, and *Śainatei Reitiai* (dative) the name of the goddess.[75] *vdan* is problematic.[76] Below the Latin there is a series of Venetic consonant clusters, and on the edge of the document a fragment of a Latin alphabet, in jumbled order (these letters are not printed here). Tablets from Este often have alphabets, which must have been of magical significance.[77] Prosdocimi (1983: 95–8) explained the order of the Latin letters thus: the first letter of the alphabet is followed by the last, the second by the second last, and so on.[78] It is interesting that two different writing systems are in existence side by side. In the manner which will later be seen to be typical of the process of Romanisation, locals have acquired Latin script, but they still retain their native script, though there are signs of uncertainty about Venetic practice, as the Venetic consonant clusters are 'wrong' (see Langslow (forthcoming), sect. 3.3). Conditions were obviously right for a switch of scripts to take place.

Most of the information of the inscription is conveyed by the Venetic alone; it is only there that the names of the participants are expressed. The Latin on its own would not allow the reader to determine what the situation was, and it has nothing which the other version does not have. This is not then even a text with complementary versions.

A rough parallel in type can be found, for example, in the trilingual Palmyrene–Greek–Latin inscription from Palmyra of the first century AD (see I.VII.1), in which the Palmyrene is fuller than the Greek, and the Greek than the Latin. The Latin is in no sense intended to convey information to potential readers, but is a token presence meant to impress on passers-by that the referent was *au fait* with the language of the imperial power. The primary language of the writer/referent is used to

---

[72] See Lejeune (1953b: 77).   [73] See Pellegrini and Prosdocimi (1967: II, 207).

[74] On which (= *donauit*) see Lejeune (1952b: 206).   [75] See Lejeune (1952b: 210).

[76] See Pellegrini and Prosdocimi (1967: II, 194).

[77] See Lejeune (1952b: 199–203). Similarly the Etruscans considered their model alphabet decorative and even magical (see e.g. Bonfante (1990: 15)).

[78] Quintilian (1.1.25) notes that after teaching their pupils the letters of the alphabet in the prescribed order, teachers reversed the order and jumbled the letters to ensure that pupils knew their form rather than merely their order. The order here may reflect a system or systems of instruction. Exactly the same order of Latin letters as that in the Venetic inscription is sometimes found on coins (AX, BV, CT, DS etc.); on the significance of these (apparently control marks) see Burnett (1998: 167–8).

express the totality of information, whereas the alien language is there to add a cultural nuance to his identity. On this analogy the dedicator of the Venetic inscription might have been primarily a Venetic speaker, but with some reason for displaying his Romanisation. The Latin formula associates the text with a familiar Latin type of dedication, and perhaps reveals the writer's aspiration to be seen as a participant in Latin as well as Venetic culture.

I conclude this section. The most interesting text discussed here is that on a tile which shows slaves in Samnium in the first century BC writing different languages alongside each other, perhaps in parody of official record keeping. They were communicating together and at least one of them must have been bilingual. Their patron had an Oscan identity, which would suggest that he was an Oscan speaker, and the Latin writer defers to his identity linguistically. The text offers a contrast to the story of the official abandonment of Oscan by the élite at Cumae, and brings home the point that language death which has taken place at a public level may be slow to spread to ordinary people. Among these artisans it is a person of Oscan identity who is dominant. There was clearly not a regular progression from Oscan to Latin all over Italy; as Latin ousted Oscan there will have been pockets of resistance, particularly among the lower classes.

II.3 'Mixed language' texts, 'Latinised' Oscan and 'Oscanised' Latin (?)

The evidence discussed in this section is of three main types: texts in which there is a switch of languages, those in which there is imitation in one language of the syntax, phraseology or structures of the other, and those which are apparently intended to be in one language but have inflections from the other (i.e. morphological interference). Orthographic imitation or interference will also come up briefly at the end of the section. I have not tried to set out the material under such headings, because constantly the categories overlap. The categories will however be distinguished as far as possible in the discussion (and see also the conclusions below, II.3.1, II.6).

The *defixio* Vetter (1953), 7 = *ILLRP* 1146 is in a mixture of Latin and Oscan. It is thought to have originated at Cumae, and may be dated roughly to the period of Sulla. If this provenance is correct, it complements the evidence of the story in Livy about the official adoption of Latin, because it is more than a century later than the event referred to by Livy, but implies that there was still a residual knowledge of Oscan. I print the text following Mancini (1988):

l. harines. her. m^{aturi}
c. eburis
pomponius
m. caedicius m. f.
n. andripius n. f.
pus. olusolu. fancua
rectasint. pus. flatu
sicu. olu. sit.

There is some dispute about the interpretation of the names in line 1, with Buecheler (1907), Degrassi (*ILLRP* 1146), Vetter and Mancini offering different views. Vetter (1953: 45) suggests the possibility *Charines Her(ii) Maturi (seruus)*, whereas Degrassi prints *L. Harines Her(i) (f.)* ... According to Mancini (1988: 215–16) the first line has two names, *L. Harines* and *Her. Maturi(us* or *s)*, without patronymics (which is claimed to be consistent with the Italic character of the two persons). Mancini (1988: 217) argues that the name *Harines* is of Etruscan origin, with an *-es* nominative ending found in Oscan in a few non-native names. The other names in the text are inflected as Latin, with the exception of *Eburis*, which has the Oscan nominative inflection of *gentilicia*.[79] This name also is not accompanied by a patronymic. The repetition of *f(ilius)* in two of the other names shows that these were conceived as Latin. In effect the Oscan name on the one hand, and the Latin names on the other, are in two different languages. The mixing of languages in the expression of names, with the inflection frequently determined by the language of origin of the name itself, is an aspect of code-switching which will figure largely in this book.

The curse which follows the names is in a mixture of Latin and Oscan (see below). It cannot be deduced from evidence of this kind that any sort of institutionalised mixed language existed, reflecting (for argument's sake) the mixed or changing linguistic culture of Cumae.[80] Such a text can be seen as displaying code-switching. *Defixiones* are special texts, in which obfuscation was often deliberately sought to enhance the power of the magic (see I.VII.2.2, with n. 116), and it is that fact which probably lies behind the language mixing in this case.[81] As a parallel I would cite the *defixio* of Amélie-les-Bains (see below, IV.4).[82] This appears in part to

---

[79] See Mancini (1988: 215), and, on the ending, Lejeune (1976b: 75–7).
[80] In this I agree substantially with the discussion of Mancini (1988: 205–7, 209–11) (who was followed by Lazzeroni (1991a: 182)), whose opinion, however, of the nature of the mixing differs somewhat from mine (see below). For further bibliography on the language mixing in this *defixio*, see Mancini (1988: 205 n. 12).
[81] This point is made by Mancini (1988: 208–11).
[82] See *CIL* XII.5367, Whatmough (1970: 142), Audollent (1904: 173–5, nos. 114–20).

be in a Celtic language, with snatches of Latin. Mancini (1988: 209–10) also compares Audollent (1904), 253, a *defixio* in a mixture of Greek and Latin; and to this could be added nos. 252 and 270 which, as we have seen (I.VII.2.2), employ transliteration as an analogous means of obscuring the language of the text. Utterances which show heavy code-switching are often difficult or impossible to assign to a base language, and that is certainly so of Vetter (1953), 7. I am though sceptical about the view of Mancini (1988: 211) (followed by Lazzeroni (1991a: 182) and Poccetti (1993: 79, 80)) that the text is basically in Latin, with an Oscan formula inserted within the Latin text. After the names, which, as we saw, have a rational form of code-switching (if the problematic first line is left aside), the switches are too complex to admit of such an interpretation, as the following will show.

The curse begins with an Oscan subordinating conjunction *pus*,[83] the equivalent of *ut*, which in the manner of archaic Latin introduces a wish.[84] In Latin *defixiones*, *ut* sometimes comes at the head of the curse (e.g. *Tab. Sulis Mineruae* 5.5, 31.4).[85] Code-switching after a subordinating conjunction can be paralleled in other languages.[86] Within both *pus*-clauses the verb-forms are Latin rather than Oscan (*sint*, *sit*; the Oscan forms would have been *sins* and (probably) **sid*).[87] Thus the framework of the two clauses (i.e. the subordinator + verb) is a mixture of Latin and Oscan.

The lexical components of the clauses are, in the first, Oscan, and in the second, apparently a mixture of Latin and Oscan. *olu*, which is in both parts, is the genitive plural (without *-m*) of the (Oscan) demonstrative pronoun (cf. Umbr. **ulu**, Osc. **ulas** genitive singular feminine, **úlleís** genitive singular masculine).[88] The omission of *-m* could be explained from the phonetics of either Latin or (less plausibly) Oscan.[89] For the Oscan character of *sol(l)u*, again genitive plural without *-m* (= *omnium*), see Festus p. 384 L., and above, II.1, on the presence of the word in Lucilius. *fancua*, which also occurs at Vetter (1953), 3, is obviously not Latin; it seems to signify 'tongue'.[90] The ending must be the Oscan feminine nominative

---

[83] Osc. **puz**: see Untermann (2000: 627).

[84] One might reasonably ask whether the Oscan construction was modelled on the Latin. Some other uses of *pus* are demonstrably based on Latin: see Porzio Gernia (1970: 135).

[85] See Adams (1992: 6–7). For another example, see Hassall and Tomlin (1993: 312–13).

[86] See (e.g.) some of the examples given by Muysken (1995: 181).

[87] See Mancini (1988: 223).

[88] In Latin the cognate was *olle* (see Buck (1904: 143), which had long fallen out of use except as a high poeticism (see Skutsch (1985: 65)). On the Oscan pronoun, see Untermann (2000: 793–4).

[89] See Mancini (1988: 219–20, Buck (1904: 71). Final *-m* is usually written in Oscan, except at Pompeii, where it is usually omitted.

[90] See Vetter (1953: 30), Mancini (1988: 226–7), Untermann (2000: 264).

plural -*as*, this time with omission of final -*s*.[91] There is the same omission in the next word *recta*, which precedes the verb 'to be' in a form beginning with *s* (*rectasint*). Mancini (1988: 220–2) discusses several cases in Oscan of such omission before the copula,[92] but it is also found in Latin (as part of a wider phenomenon whereby *s* might be omitted before any type of word beginning with *s*: see below, 8.1, p. 734 on line 5).[93] It is not therefore clear whether it is the enclitic character of *sint* which determines the omission on Oscan principles (so Mancini (1988: 222)), or whether the spelling represents a Latinate simplification of *ss* across a word boundary. *recta(s)* seems to be the Latin form of the word (which might in Oscan have been **rehtas*: the consonant cluster *kt* is found in Oscan as a secondary phenomenon, as in *factud* < **faketod*, rather than as a primary survival),[94] but it does not have the Latin meaning; a sense such as that of Lat. *rigidas* would be better suited to the context.[95] There has been Latinisation of the spelling, but the word might have an Oscan meaning. Finally, in the second *pus*- clause, *flatu(s) sic(c)u(s)* has every appearance of being Latin, with Latinate morphology (-*u* for -*us* where Oscan had zero + *s*).[96]

I would prefer to see in this text a haphazard mixture of Latin and Oscan, with some Latinising of the spelling of Oscan,[97] rather than a basically Latin text with an Oscan formula. This though is an issue admitting only of subjective judgments which are often encountered in the attempt to interpret the base language of an utterance with code-mixing. It is likely that the writer of the curse deliberately mixed the languages to make the interpretation of the curse more confusing. That he was able to do so is a reflection either of the coexistence of the two languages in the community in which he was writing, or at least of the limited survival of Oscan, perhaps as a traditional language now restricted to certain domains, alongside a dominant Latin. We will see below (IV.4) from a different area evidence for a degree of maintenance of a dying language in the sphere of magic.

[91] See Mancini (1988: 220–2), Buck (1904: 74–5) on final -*s* in Oscan, which is retained, except before forms of the verb 'to be' beginning with *s*. In *fancua* for *fancuas* Mancini (1988: 222) sees 'un'interferenza con la competenza latina del trascrittore', whereas in the second case of such omission (considered next in my discussion) he invokes instead an Oscan tendency (i.e. the omission of final -*s* before the copula beginning with *s*).
[92] Cf. Buck (1904: 75): *h* replaces *s* in this environment.
[93] See Väänänen (1966: 79); cf. E. Löfstedt (1956: II. 82–3) on what appears to be an analogous phenomenon, whereby *qui* replaces *quis* before *sit*.
[94] See Mancini (1988: 223), Untermann (2000: 633), s.v. **rehte**. Untermann notes that *recta* is Latinate.
[95] See Vetter (1953: 46).   [96] See Mancini (1988: 222).
[97] Mancini (1988: 222) speaks of someone 'incapace di dominare le regole morfofonologiche della lingua osca'.

Various other inscriptional texts can be described as in a mixture of Latin and Italic in one sense or another. A case in point is provided by a pair of dedications to Hercules in different hands written on a *cippus* found in the territory of the Paeligni near Castelvecchio Subequo (Vetter (1953), 217, *ILLRP* 143, *CIL* I². 2486, Zamudio (1986), 43; discussed by Wachter (1987: 409–10)). Both inscriptions bear the names of members of the *gens Seia*:

(a) sa(luios). seio(s). l(ouci). f(ilios) herclei. donom ded(it) brat( ) datas;
(b) [l(oucios)] seio(s). sa(lui) f(ilios) herclei uicturei.

Vetter dates the second inscription to later than 89 BC, that is to after the Social War, but there is some controversy about the time gap between the two texts.[98]

The version in the *CIL* reads *p(uer)* instead of *f.* in both places, but this seems unlikely to be right on grounds of normal usage. With the exception of two elements, both texts are in Latin.[99] A notable indicator of Latinity is the inflectional form of *Herclei*, and the absence of a vowel between *r* and *c*.[100] The name belonged to the *o*-declension in Oscan (**hereklúí** at Vetter (1953), 147, Poccetti (1979), 36),[101] and also in marginal areas such as the territory of the Marsi (Poccetti (1979), 219), the Vestini (Vetter (1953), 220) and the Paeligni.[102] Also Latinate is the filiation with *f.* (if the reading is right) (on filiations, see below). The non-Latin features of these texts are the vocalism in *uicturei* (cf. Poccetti (1979), 16 **víkturraí** = *Victoriae*), but more interestingly *brat. datas*. This is an Oscan formula which is now attested a number of times (e.g. Poccetti (1979), 152 βρατηις δατας (Paestum), 164, 182, Vetter (1953), 203, 220; see also Poccetti (1979) on 33).[103] Despite the vocalism referred to above, the consonant cluster of *uicturei* is Latinate, because only Latin preserved the primary group *kt* (see also above).[104] Finally, the *o* of *donom* is Latinate.[105]

---

[98] See Poccetti (1993: 75–6).   [99] See Poccetti (1993: 75).

[100] Note Untermann (2000: 318) on this and two other forms: 'Im Ms., P. und Vs. stärker latinisiert'.

[101] See Untermann (2000: 318, 319). In Latin the vocative form embedded in *(me)hercle* is a trace of the *o*-stem form (Untermann (2000: 319)).

[102] See Vetter (1953: 153) on no. 217, citing an inscription, from the same findspot as 217, in pure Latin but containing the form *Hercolo* (quoted below, p. 133).

[103] 'Because of a favour given': see Untermann (2000: 150), with the full collection of material at 149–51; also 177. See further Poccetti (1979: 48), Durante (1978: 796, 808). The case is genitive, in an absolute construction (Durante (1978: 808), or loosely dependent on *donom* and indicating the reason for the gift (the 'matter involved': see perhaps the cases discussed by Buck (1904: 197)).

[104] See Buck (1904: 89), Zamudio (1986: 42, 101–2), Untermann (2000: 856), the last arguing from the consonant cluster that the word was borrowed from Latin.

[105] So Untermann (2000: 191). Cf. O. **dunúm**.

It is thus the case that in a Latin dedication an Oscan formula is included right at the end. This type of code-switching recalls those Latin inscriptions of Rome which have a Greek formula tagged on at the end, or Greek inscriptions which have a Latin tag (see I.V). The ability to add to a text a formulaic tag in a second language does not establish the bilingual fluency of the writer, any more than does the inclusion in an utterance of exclamations from another language (see above. I.V); such insertions are not a mark of creative language use. In this case the tag is probably no more than a relic of a remembered earlier culture, included as a claim to a certain type of regional identity. The distinctive feature of the text is that it is in Latin. We saw earlier a Latin tag placed at the end of a Venetic text, and drew a different conclusion from its presence. Clearly the Latin expression there was not carried over from an earlier period of Venetic culture, but was a sign of the new influences to which Venetic speakers were subject. A single model will not therefore explain the incorporation of second-language tags in a text; each case must be assessed against its cultural background.

A more problematic text is Vetter (1953), 220, where the declension class of the divine name is Italic, but the dative ending Latin (see e.g. Durante (1978: 808); also Poccetti (1993: 76, n. 13)). The inscription runs as follows: *t. uetio duno didet herclo iouio brat data* ('T. Vettius gives a gift to Hercules son of Jupiter because of a favour given'). This is a rare item from the territory of the Vestini (from Navelli), said to belong to the third century BC.[106] The verb has a local appearance, with redoubling as in Pael. *dida* (reduplicated present).[107] The final Oscan formula *brat data* has been seen above. The nominative inflection of *Vetio* looks to be Latinate, with omission of final -*s* in the Latin manner and a Latinate vowel; in Oscan, -*ios* > -*is*, and in Umbrian there was rhotacism of -*is* to -*ir*.[108] *duno* has a mixed character. The first vowel is Italic in appearance (see above). The vowel in the inflection is though Latinate. The omission of final -*m* is in accord both with Latin and Umbrian tendencies.[109] Thus the verb and final two-word formula are Italic, but all of the other inflections in the inscription are Latinate. Could it be that in this area a 'mixed language' was in use? A simpler hypothesis is that the writer set out to compose an Italic inscription, but that at a time of language shift his command of Italic nominal inflections (outside a fixed formula) was

[106] For a discussion of this text and its date, see Durante (1978: 807–8); also Wachter (1987: 410).
[107] See further Buck (1904: 82, 157), Untermann (2000: 175).
[108] See Buck (1904: 119).   [109] For the latter, see Buck (1904: 71); on Oscan, see n. 89 above.

so poor that he had to use Latin inflections instead. This phenomenon would be classifiable as morphological interference from the writer's stronger language in his weaker. We will see a very similar pattern below in an inscription aspiring to be in Umbrian (p. 140; see also above, 1.IX (4)).

This text may usefully be compared with the Paelignian Latin inscription mentioned above (n. 102), cited by Vetter (1953: 153) (= Zamudio (1986), 44): *L. Seius C. f. Hercolo donum dat Burus*. The structure of the inscriptions is much the same, but here the verb form is not Italic, *donum* is pure Latin, and the final Oscan formula is lacking; the text is unambiguously intended as Latin. But both have virtually the same form of the god's name, which is neither pure Latin nor Italic, in that it is of the *o*-declension as in Italic, but has a Latin inflection (see above on the inflection of the god's name) and Latinate structure (note the *o* between *c* and *l* and the absence of a vowel between *r* and *c*); this must be a regionalism of the local Latin introduced under Italic influence.

The linguistic mixture of Vetter (1953), 220 above contrasts with the purely dialectal (Italic) character of an inscription from nearby S. Benedetto in Perillis (Poccetti (1979), 207, territory of the Vestini). Durante (1978: 807), noting that the mixed language text is a private dedication and that the dialectal text records the construction of a public building, suggests that in the third century in this region the everyday language was being Latinised, whereas the pure dialect was reserved for public documents. This view, though interesting, is scarcely compelling given the paucity of the evidence on which it is based. It is simpler to suppose that the writer of the one text had better competence in the Italic language than the writer of the other.

Some Italic texts have been described in one sense or another as 'Latinised'.[110] The term 'Latinised' is too vague to be satisfactory, and I attempt to define more precisely in the following pages the different phenomena which are at issue. Those who have used the term have more often than not been referring to a cultural rather than a linguistic phenomenon, as we will see.

A case in point is Poccetti (1979), 34, from Chieti (in the territory of the Marrucini) and dated by Poccetti to the period between the second century BC and the Sullan era:

ṃ[.] t[.] ṇị[.] dekitiúd[.] ṃịṃ.[.]pụ̣d̤ ṿ. ụ̣pṣ̣t. legú. tanginúd/
aamanafed. esídum. p[rú]fa[tt]ed. úpsed. g. paapii[.] g[.] f[.].

---

[110] See Campanile (1976), Porzio Gernia (1970), Lazzeroni (1965: 75–7); but cf. the cautious discussion of Meiser (1987: 111–12).

This is rendered into Latin by Poccetti as *M(eddice) T(utico) N(umerio) Decitio Mi( ) f. . . . . sententia/faciend( ) curauit idem probavit fecit G( ) Papius G( ) f. /.*

Notable here, first, is the ablative form **dekitiúd**, which reveals the initial construction to be an ablative absolute of the eponymous magistrates. This construction is probably an imitation of the Latin ablative absolute (so Poccetti (1979)).[111] It is not a case of code-switching, as in the *defixio* discussed above, or of morphological interference, as in Vetter (1953), 220, but constitutes a third phenomenon (see the classification at the start of this section), syntactic imitation, which is a form of borrowing (syntactic imitation as borrowing is discussed in a later chapter (4.II). A parallel can be found in later Greek, where in imitation of the Latin ablative absolute in consular dates the dative is used absolutely, not least because in some forms (notably the singular of second declension names such as Τίτῳ) it is homonymous with the Latin ablative if the iota sub-/ adscript is disregarded (see 4.V.4.1.2). It is noteworthy that these cases of syntactic imitation are found in official expressions. Similarly dates often inspire code-switching, particularly into the language of an imperial power (e.g. from Greek into Latin in Egyptian papyri: see 3.VI.2). Clearly the Latin dating construction is given an official status if it is imitated by an Oscan writer; the implicit prestige of Latin, which was an essential background to the eventual death of Oscan, is brought out by such a usage.

A second Latin feature of the inscription lies in the final *f.*, interpreted by Poccetti as a filiation on the Latin pattern. This by contrast represents a change of languages (code-switching).[112] The normal Oscan method of filiation was to attach a genitive to the name (*gentilicium*) (see below,

---

[111] Buck (1904: 203) gives the ablative absolute as an Osco-Umbrian construction, on the basis of one Oscan and one Umbrian example. The Oscan case is in the highly Latinate *Tabula Bantina* (on which see further below): Vetter (1953), 2 = Crawford (1996), 13 line 21 *toutad praesentid*, = Lat. *populo praesente*. What is revealing here is the Latinate *ae* diphthong for the expected *ai*, and it may reasonably be suggested that the construction as well as the spelling is taken from Latin. There is another example (*oisa aetate*) in the Latinate text Vetter (1953), 214, discussed below (note again the *ae* diphthong, and also the Latin ablative form: see below). The Umbrian example is at *Tab. Ig.* Ia.1 **aves anzeriates** (= *auibus obseruatis*). The status of this example is more difficult to assess, but certainly as far as Oscan is concerned Latin influence seems to be the determinant of the construction. There is also an example in a Volscian inscription, Vetter (1953), 222, *toticu couehriu sepu*, = *publico conuentu sciente* (a text discussed by Durante (1978: 812)). See too Planta (1892–7: II, 436), noting the rarity of the construction in Oscan and Umbrian, and relating the Umbrian example to a Latin expression.

[112] Alternatively, if the formula had become integrated into varieties of Oscan, it might be described as borrowing (on borrowing as representing the integration of alien elements into another language, see 1.V, p. 26); see also below, n. 118.

pp. 511–12), but the Latin formula is found,[113] for example, in inscriptions of the Marrucini (Poccetti (1979), 206 *Pa. Petroni Pom. f. bea ecan. fec medix*, = *Pacius Petronius Pom( ) f. cisternam [fontanam?] hanc fecit meddix*)[114] and Paeligni (Vetter (1953), 210c *u. loucies ob. f.*, = *V(ibius) Lucius Ob(elli) f.*).[115] Similarly Vetter (1953), 123b contains the words ... **min(ieis)**. **futír**, where **futír** is the equivalent of Lat. *filia* (not code-switching this time, but syntactic imitation).[116] The inscription from the territory of the Marrucini just cited also has another possible Latinism, viz. the use of *fec* = (probably) *fecit*. Italic usually employed **úpsa-** in the required sense.[117] In fact the inscription is basically in Latin, with the object of the verb apparently an alien element.

Expressions of filiation in one language not infrequently influence in one way or another those of another in contact with it (see 3.V.4, 4.V.4.3). Several Umbrian grave tiles (Vetter (1953), 232) appear to show a change of practice within a single family across several generations. Bradley (2000: 205) notes that whereas 'the Umbrian naming formula was used for the father ... two generations later his grandson's grave was marked using the Latin formula with the patronymic coming after the gentile name: *ca puplece ma fel*, i.e. C. Publicius son of Ma(rcus)'.[118] We will see (6.V.1) cases of the infiltration of (genitive +) υἱός into Greek under the influence of Latin (genitive +) *filius*. A comparable phenomenon can be found in a small group of Oscan inscriptions from a restricted area (region of Teggiano). In Oscan the filiation (plain genitive) is regularly placed in the Latin manner *after* the *gentilicium*, whereas in Umbrian (patronymic adjective) it is placed *before*. There are however several Oscan inscriptions in which the filiation has the Umbrian position, no doubt as a result of a contact situation.[119] On

---

[113] See also Campanile (1976: 110–11), Poccetti (1979: 154).

[114] Zamudio's interpretation of this text (1986), 45) differs slightly from that of Poccetti. He renders *bea* as *uiuam*, without saying how he takes the word. On *bea* see now Untermann (2000: 148), s.v. **bio** (etymology unknown, but apparently indicating some sort of water source). On *f.* as a Latinism here, see also Durante (1978: 806), and on the phenomenon elsewhere, id. (1978: 796).

[115] Cf. Zamudio (1986), 11. There are other Paelignian texts with *f(ilius)*: e.g. Vetter (1953), 215r = Zamudio (1986), 36, Vetter (1953), 215u = Zamudio (1986), 39.

[116] On **futír** see Untermann (2000: 306).

[117] See Durante (1978: 806). On **úpsa-** see Untermann (2000: 801–3).

[118] On the interpretation of *fel* (borrowed from Latin), see Untermann (2000: 270–1).

[119] See Rix (1996: 257), citing e.g. Poccetti (1979), 149 Πλατορ. Σι. Αλαπονιες (= *Plator Si( ) f. Alponius*); see also Poccetti (1979: 112). For Rix's hypothesis to account for the phenomenon, see id. (1996: 258): the Samnites originally used the Latin order; the few examples of the inverse (Umbrian) order are due to the influence of the pre-Samnite substrate, in that after the invasion of the Samnites into Campania some of the pre-Samnite families adopted Oscan but retained the inherited order of their onomastic formula.

the other hand a case in which the Oscan pattern seems to have influenced Latin may be seen in the archaic Campanian (Latin) inscription *CIL* I².400:

R. Vedo[
V. Autrodiu C.
S. Racectiu. S.
S. Teditiu.S
statuendos
locauerunt.

Vine (1993: 293) notes 'the remarkable patronymic expressions without *f(ilius)*, "ex more Oscorum" ', and in addition draws attention to the fact that 'lines 2 and 3 end not with the letter abbreviating the patronymic, but with line-final puncts, which can be compared with the same practice in Oscan'. He compares Vetter (1953), 25.4 **mr. spuriíeís l.**, an *eituns*-inscription from Pompeii which shows this practice 'in at least three of its six lines'.

Analogous to the Latin form of filiation seen above as intruding into Oscan is the Latinate statement of the relationship of freedman to patron in inscriptions of the Paeligni (e.g. Poccetti (1979), 209 *S. Acaes. L.l*, where *l.* = *libertus*).[120]

There is a striking case of code-switching in a filiation in another inscription from Chieti. A text of the inscription (originally published at *CIL* IX.3032) can now be found in Poccetti (1979), 204. Earlier it had been discussed by Durante (1978: 806). Poccetti's text and translation are as follows: *sacracrix herentatia. Vara Sonti.salas.uali,* = *sacerdos ueneria Vara Sonti f. saluus uale.*[121] Durante takes *Sonti* to be a name in the genitive inflected in Latin. If so it is not the only case in our material of code-switching in the genitive of a filiation. In a Sicilian *defixio* there is a switch from Greek into a Latin inflection (3.v.4), and in an inscription from Delos (*ID* 2440 = *ILLRP* 289) from Latin into Greek (3.v.4). See also below, III.6 (p. 177) on *CIE* 2860.

Filiations are such a distinctive area of language switching and formulaic imitation that they will be discussed several times in later chapters. I move on to some further cases of 'Latinisation'.

---

[120] See further Poccetti (1979: 158). The text is printed also by Zamudio (1986), as 41 D 2. Other Paelignian texts with *l(ibertus)* are Vetter (1953), 215m = Zamudio (1986), 31, Vetter (1953), 215o = Zamudio (1986), 33, Vetter (1953), 215s = Zamudio (1986), 37.

[121] Details of all of the words in this inscription can be found (s.vv.) in Untermann (2000). Presumably the last two words (which include a masculine nominative singular *salas*, despite the gender of the honorand of the inscription) are intended as an address of the reader.

The inscription Vetter (1953), 11 is notable for the construction usually called *attractio inuersa* (**eítiuvam paam ... deded eísak eítiuvad**, = *pecuniam quam ... dedit, ea pecunia*), of a type found several times in old Latin and later (e.g. Ter. *Eun.* 653 *eunuchum quem dedisti nobis, quas turbas dedit!*, Petron. 134.8, *Per. Aeth.* 13.4).[122] The construction can be paralleled in Hittite and Vedic Sanskrit,[123] and its presence in the Oscan text may therefore represent an inherited feature of Italic rather than the influence of Latin on Oscan. Poccetti (1982a: 238–9), however, draws attention to the attestation of the construction in the Latin legal and bureaucratic styles, and in view of other Latinisms in the text (see below) there is a distinct possibility that imitation of Latin legal syntax was the decisive determinant.[124]

Some of the evidence for the alleged 'Latinisation' of Oscan cited by Porzio Gernia (1970) and Campanile (1976) consists of the presence in Oscan of formulae translated from equivalents in the Latin official language ('imitation' of phraseology, in our terminology set out at the start of this section; see also above, 1.VII.4.2 on translations of formulae). Campanile (1976: 113) compares, for example, Vetter (1953), 11 (the text discussed immediately above) **v. viínikiís. mr. kvaísstur. púmpaiians. trííbúm. ekak. kúmbennieís. tanginud. úpsannam. deded. ísídum. prúfatted** (= *V. Vinicius M(a)r(aei f.) quaestor Pompeianus domum hanc (de) conuentus sententia faciendam dedit, idem probauit*) with *CIL* I².1563 *L. Cemoleius L. f. L. Statius L. f. Q. Paccius M. f. aid(iles) d(e) s(enatus) s(ententia) portas faciundas dederunt eisdemqe probauerunt*. In the same text **trístaamentud deded** is based on the commonplace Latin expression *testamento dare*.[125] In the *Tabula Bantina* (Vetter (1953), 2, = Crawford (1996), 13)[126] there are various formulae which have an exact equivalent in the Latin juridical language: e.g. 3 *maimas carneis senateis tanginud, am[pert nei mins pam] XL osins pon ioc egmo comparascuster* (= *maximae partis senatus sententia, dumtaxat [ne minus quam] quadraginta adsint cum ea res consulta erit*) compared with *Lex Ursonensis* (*CIL* I². 594) III.3.18 *de m(aioris) p(artis) decurion(um) sententia cum*

[122] See further E. Löfstedt (1956: II.114–15).
[123] See e.g. Watkins (1995: 541), Penney (1999: 251 n. 3). Watkins rightly questions the use of the term *attractio inuersa*. He assigns such examples to the category of Indo-European bipartite relative sentences, in which the antecedent appears twice, in the preposed relative clause and in the postponed matrix clause. So in the Oscan example there is such repetition. The antecedent may be deleted in the matrix clause (or replaced by a pronoun) and fronted (as in the Oscan case) around the relative in the relative clause (see Watkins, loc. cit., n. 2).
[124] See also Porzio Gernia (1970: 137). Note too the analogous material cited from Latin laws by Kroll (1912: 8–9).
[125] See Poccetti (1982a: 244 with n. 27).
[126] Here I cite Crawford, using the numeration in his text.

non minus L aderunt, cum e(a) r(es) consuletur;[127] or 17 *suae pis contrud exeic fefacust ionc suae pis herest meddis moltaum { licitud} ampert mistreis aeteis eituas licitud* (= *si quis aduersus ea fecerit eum si quis uolet magistratus multare dumtaxat minoris partis pecuniae liceto*) compared with a law from Luceria (*CIL* I². 401) *sei quis aruorsu hac faxit [in] ium quis uolet pro ioudicatod ni (?) manum iniect[i]o estod seiue mac[i]steratus uolet multare [li]ceto.*[128] In *Tab. Bant.* 3 just cited I would also draw attention to *ioc egmo* as an exact equivalent to *ea res*. This is not the only legalistic expression in which *egmo* corresponds to *res*.[129] For example, *egm[as touti]cas amnud* at *Tab. Bant.* 5 corresponds to *rei publicae causa*, a phrase found in legalistic contexts in Plautus (*Pers.* 65; cf. *Mil.* 103 *magnai rei publicai gratia*), and *dat eizac egmad* in the same document (10) corresponds to *de ea re*, which is attested in laws (e.g. *Lex Repet.* 3). Also of note in *Tab. Bant.* 17 above is the Latinate diphthong in *aeteis*. The word is found in the *Cippus Abellanus* (Vetter (1953), 1) with the Italic spelling (cf. above, n. 111 on *praesentid*).

Formulaic structures in a looser sense in Oscan legal texts can often be closely paralleled in Latin laws, as Porzio Gernia (1970: 126–42) has shown. For example, conditional sentences with a future perfect in the protasis and an imperative in -*to* in the apodosis, found, for instance, in the *Lex Repet.* (e.g. 76–7 *sei quis . . . detolerit . . . esto . . . sunto*), can be paralleled in the *Tab. Bant.*, with *suae pis* of the Oscan corresponding to Lat. *si quis:* 4 *suae pis pertemust, . . . deiuatud,* = *si quis prohibuerit, . . . iurato.*[130] The construction which Porzio Gernia (1970: 127) calls the 'costrutto indiretto libero' can be found in the *Cippus Abellanus* and in Latin in the *S.C. de Bacch.* The *facito ut* construction (e.g. *Lex Repet.* 12 *facito uti . . . legat*) has a parallel in *Tab. Bant.* 9: *factud pous . . . tanginom deicans,* = *facito ut . . . sententiam dicant.*[131] Porzio Gernia gives a good deal more illustration of correspondences between Oscan texts and Latin laws.

The obvious explanation of these correspondences is that there has been imitation in Oscan of the Latin legalistic formulae,[132] and that would reflect the prestige of Roman legal practices and of the language in which they were expressed.[133] The correspondences are also indicative of the bilingualism, in Latin and Oscan, of the educated Oscan speakers who drafted the documents. Note Gabba (1994: 109) on the general background to the transfer of such formulae: 'the assimilation of the behaviour of the Italian elites to Roman norms . . . had gone beyond language and culture to affect the political systems and magistracies of the allied cities'.

[127] See Campanile (1976: 115–16).   [128] See Campanile (1976: 117).
[129] See Porzio Gernia (1970: 124–5) for details. On *egmo* see Untermann (2000: 198).
[130] See Porzio Gernia (1970: 133).   [131] Porzio Gernia (1970: 135).
[132] See the remarks of Campanile (1976: 112–13).   [133] See, for example, Brunt (1988: 119).

But the 'Latinisation' of Oscan in these senses is not the whole story. It has been pointed out by Poccetti (1993: 79–80) that *defixiones* appear much earlier in Oscan (i.e. from the fourth or third centuries BC: Vetter (1953), 5, 6 and Poccetti (1979), 189, 190 are cited in this connection)[134] than in Latin (in which they do not occur until the second century), and that some of the earliest Latin specimens come from Oscan-speaking areas such as Cumae (*CIL* I². 3128, 3129) and Pompeii (*CIL* I². 2541 = *ILLRP* 1147). It is therefore of interest that various formulae in Latin *defixiones* correspond exactly to formulae in Oscan texts. Poccetti (1993: 80) compares the Latin expression (*CIL* I². 1012 = *ILLRP* 1144, Rome) *nec loqui nec sermonare possit* with the Oscan Vetter (1953), 4 (Capua) **nep deíkum nep fatíum pútíad** (= *nec dicere nec fari possit*), and the general structure seen here (negative + *possit*, **pútíad**) also recurs in texts of both languages (for Latin see *CIL* I². 3129, from Cumae, and for Oscan, see Vetter (1953), 4). The chronology of the *defixiones* in the two languages would suggest that the influence in this case was in the direction Oscan to Latin (i.e. 'Oscanisation' of Latin), and that would accord with the tendency in Latin literature for certain magical practices to be associated with Italic peoples such as the Sabelli, Paeligni and Marsi.[135] Shared formulae in Latin and Oscan curses reflect a general bilingual culture which must have existed at a social level below that of the élite; a slave is involved in the Pompeian curse *ILLRP* 1147. The Latin *defixiones* from Cumae and Pompeii reveal the penetration of Latin into Oscan-speaking areas at a low social level already in the second century BC.

It is worth making some general observations at this point about the nature of the phenomena which have been, somewhat loosely, referred to as 'Latinisation' (of Oscan) and 'Oscanisation' (of Latin). The transfer of formulae from one language to another, which is akin to the loan translation of single lexical items, is not uncommon in conditions of contact, and, where corpus languages are concerned, may be valuable evidence not only for bilingualism, but also for the dominance of one culture over another in a particular community (see I.VII.4.2 for a detailed discussion). If, for example, in letters written in Egypt in Latin under the Roman Empire Greek epistolary formulae are used, that suggests the bilingualism either of the writer or of his community, and a subservience to Greek practice (see I.VII.4.2); and that subservience in its turn could indicate either that Greek was the writer's primary or preferred language, or that the influence of Greek culture was overwhelming in the area in which he was writing.

---

[134] See Poccetti (1993: 79 n. 23).   [135] See Poccetti (1993: 81).

But while the transfer of formulae from one language to another ('imitation') has its interest and even importance, particularly to students of dead languages, it is a cultural rather than a strictly linguistic phenomenon. The recipient language is in no sense influenced or changed, as it might be for example if it received instead alien morphemes or syntactic patterns from the other language which caught on. Latin poets could imitate at will Greek syntactic structures, but that does not necessarily mean that the language even of the educated was permanently changed. In Greek translations of Latin legal texts Latin idioms were translated literally, but that did not cause the introduction of new idioms into the Greek language in general (see 4.v.2.12). It is less than satisfactory to talk of Oscan as 'Latinised' merely because in some legal texts Latin legal formulae and constructions were imitated. If a vague term such as 'Latinisation' is to be used at all, it must at least be clearly subdivided into its diverse constituent phenomena. The imitation by Oscan writers of Latin formulae does not constitute Latinisation in the linguistic sense, of the type observable for example when one language suffers heavy interference from another. I will return in the conclusion to this section (II.6) to such notions as 'influence', 'interference' and 'Latinisation', and attempt to make some distinctions (for interference see 1.v; also the next paragraph).

I now turn to a rather different piece of evidence, of a morphological kind, this time showing interference from Latin in Umbrian. It has been pointed out by Meiser (1987: 112 n. 48) that the Umbrian text Vetter (1953), 234 has a number of Umbrian words with Latin inflectional morphemes. The text is printed by Meiser as follows: *bia(m) opse(n)t marone(s) t. foltonio(s) se. p(e)tr(o)nio(s).* Vetter translates thus into Latin: *fontanam fecerunt marone(s) T. Foltonius, Se(xtus?) P(e)tr(o)nius).* The Latinate *opse(n)t* has been used for **opsens, marone(s)* for **marons, foltonio(s)* for **foltonir,* and *petronio(s)* for **petronir.* This text then shows a far more profound Latinisation than those in which formulae are merely translated from Latin; the writer knew some Umbrian lexemes and stems, but not it seems Umbrian endings. There are at least two ways of looking at the 'influence' of Latin on Umbrian in this text. If it reflects the state of the Umbrian language at a particular time and place, then the language had for so long been under the shadow of Latin that its inflectional system had been modified. An alternative (and more plausible) possibility is that the individual drafter had imperfect competence in Umbrian, and that his attempt at writing is not a true indication of the state of the language as it might have been used by others at the same time. But if it was falling to those with imperfect competence to write documents in Umbrian, that would suggest that the language was in terminal decline, and at a time of language shift there may have been others too who could no longer use the old language in pure form. We saw a comparable case above (Vetter (1953), 220) of an 'Italic' text in which the nominal endings were all Latinate. Indeed the form of the personal name in *-io(s)* in that inscription (*Vetio*) was the same as that of the two comparable names in the above inscription. On the imposition of alien morphemes on a language either during a period of language death or as a consequence of imperfect second-language learning, see in general 1.IX.

I now consider *orthographic* transfers between the two languages. We noted above the spellings *praesentid* and *aeteis* in the *Tabula Bantina* (p. 138). Similarly a bronze *lamina* now found in the Museo Nazionale at Bari (Poccetti (1979), 202) contains the Oscan onomastic formula *Pac Caedcies Pac,* = *Pac(ius) Caedicius Pac(ii) f.* This too is notable for the presence of the Latin diphthong spelling *ae* in the syncopated form of the name *Caedicius.* This same name is found with its correct Latin spelling in the mixed Latin–Oscan *defixio* Vetter (1953), 7. In each case the writer, though using the Oscan language (either exclusively, or partly in the case of the *defixio*), must have been familiar with the written form of the name in Latin, and that implies that he was literate in both languages. The spelling adopted may represent a type of orthographic code-switching, motivated by the language of origin of the name; or perhaps it merely reflects the writer's inability to stick consistently to the correct Oscan spellings because Oscan was now his second language.

A comparable example occurs in a Paelignian inscription published by Poccetti (1979), 208: *L. Anies. Pet. Graex. Graex* (in the form of its ending) represents an Oscanisation of the Latin *Graecus*, which is often attested in Latin as a name. But even in this modified form the name retains the Latinate diphthong, and that again reveals the writer's acquaintance with Latin orthography. For the expected *ai* form of the diphthong in Oscan (or Oscanised) inscriptions from the territory of the Paeligni, see e.g. Vetter (1953), 204 *aisis*, 211 *Scaifia* (= *Scaefia*), 213 *praicime* (on which see further below).[136]

Another Paelignian inscription is worth quoting in full: Vetter (1953), 214 *pes. pros. ecuf. incubat casnar. oisa. aetate c. anaes. solois. des. forte faber,* = *pius probus hic incubat, senex usa aetate, C. Annaeus, omnibus diues, fortunae faber.*[137] To what extent the idiom of this text (in *oisa aetate* and *forte faber*) is determined

---

[136] See further Lazzeroni (1965: 76).
[137] I print here the rendering of Vetter. The translation of Durante (1978: 798) is as follows: *pius (?) probus (?) hic endo cubat senex consumpta aetate, C. Annaeus, omnibus diebus fortunae faber.* Zamudio's interpretation ((1986), 19) is closer to that of Vetter (with *perfecta* substituted for *usa*).

by Latin is controversial,[138] but certainly the *ae* diphthong in the name looks Latinate,[139] as does that in *aetate*; for Oscan *ai* in this word, see the inscription from Teanum Sidicinum, Vetter (1953), 123, containing the genitive form **aítateís**. The morphology of *aetate* has also apparently been Latinised.[140] The expected Oscan ablative would have been *-ud* (cf. perhaps Vetter (1953), 213 *aetatu*: see below); that of Umbrian was also *-e*.[141] In syntax *oisa aetate* is an ablative absolute,[142] which may represent another Latinism (see n. 111). Another Paelignian text, Vetter (1953), 213, the so-called 'Herentas' inscription, has the expression *sua aetatu*, which is interpreted by Vetter as an accusative singular, but by Lazzeroni (1965: 73), Durante (1978: 800, 802) and Zamudio (1986: 27) as an ablative; Untermann (2000: 57, 70) is non-committal about whether the form is accusative or ablative. Note that the Latinate *ae* again appears. Poccetti (1980: 93–4) suggests that the writer of this inscription deliberately used *ai* in the Oscan word *praicime* but *ae* in the Latin borrowing *aetatu*. This is possible: the different spellings would have been determined by a feeling for the language of origin of the two terms. The 'Herentas' inscription displays signs of Greco-Latin cultural influence, as Poccetti (1980, 1981) has shown,[143] and the writer was probably multilingual in the manner of Ennius.

It will be observed that several of the orthographic Latinisations noted in the previous paragraphs are found in Paelignian inscriptions. The original language of the Paeligni (together with that of the Marsi, Vestini and Marrucini), whether it be Oscan or a continuation of the dialect

---

[138] See on the one hand Lazzeroni (1965: 75–6), id. (1976: 391), Durante (1978: 798) and Untermann (2000: 790 (on *oisa aetate*), 254, 304 (on *forte(s) faber*, perhaps reflecting the Latin proverbial expression *suae quisque fortunae faber*)), and on the other, for a more sceptical approach, Meiser (1987: 112). *incubat* is something of an oddity here. Durante (1978: 798) and Poccetti (1981: 260) point out that the simplex *cubare* is attested in central Italic and dialectal (Latin) epitaphs from central Italy, including the area of the Paeligni (see further Untermann (2000: 418), s.v. **qupat**). The *in-* of the prefix gives the compound a Latinate look (contrasting with Italic *en-*). However, *incubo* is not used in Latin in the sense 'lie dead' (contrast *cubo*, *OLD*, s.v. 3), as can be seen from the articles in the *TLL* and *OLD*. It is possible that the writer has switched into Latin for some reason, perhaps because of cultural aspirations of some sort, but used the Latin word incorrectly. Similar misuse of English words in French is usually referred to as 'franglais'. An alternative possibility is that the compound is genuinely Italic, with the expected *en* changed to *in* because of the closing effect of *n* + velar (see Meiser (1986: 41, 112) for this phenomenon). In the same text *pes. pros.* is probably Latin-inspired (see Untermann (2000: 554). The combination *pius probus* is found in Latin (see Poccetti (1981: 266)).

[139] See Meiser (1987: 112) on the Latin character of the diphthong (also Durante (1978: 803–4)).

[140] See Untermann (2000: 71): 'Stark latinisierter Text; wahrscheinlich lat. Endung'.

[141] See Lazzeroni (1965: 74).

[142] See Untermann (2000: 790); the first word is equivalent to Lat. *usa*, but has a passive meaning.

[143] See also Durante (1978: 800–1).

seen in the South Picene inscriptions,[144] has been very heavily Latinised in the extant inscriptions from the region.[145]

It will be worthwhile to comment briefly on further aspects of the 'Latinisation' of Venetic (already touched on above, p. 125). This consists partly in the adoption under Roman influence of the Latin alphabet, but there are also some cases of language mixing, for the most part from the period when Latin had been adopted and isolated Venetic elements were incorporated in Latin inscriptions. There is for example a small group of inscriptions in which the name of the local divinity Trumusiatis (sometimes spelt *Trib-*) appears with a Venetic inflection (dative in *-atei*, accusative in *-atin*) in a text which is otherwise wholly Latin:[146] e.g. Pellegrini and Prosdocimi (1967), Ca 60[147] *L. Apinius L. f. Trum[sia]tei u(otum) s(oluit) l(ubens) m(erito)*, Ca 59[148] *T]ribusiatin d(onauit) L.[.M.].* The dative ending is of course not as remarkable as the accusative, which cannot be interpreted as Latin in form. Whereas in some Latin texts Venetic personal names are completely Latinised, in others they retain their Venetic form.[149] Thus, for example, note Ca 58[150] *V. Olsomnos. Enniceios*[151] *V.S.L.M. Trum* alongside Ca 60 (quoted above) *L. Apinius L. f. Trum[sia]tei V.S.L.M.* It is constantly the case, as we have seen, that personal names either inspire a switch of codes, or, from another perspective, retain their original form. The Latin formula in these inscriptions, *uotum soluit libens merito*, is very similar to that seen in the Venetic bilingual text discussed above (II.2) (*donom dedit libens merito*). Clearly those who used the formula in these dedications could present themselves as either completely Romanised (if they used a Latin form of their names), or as of mixed culture (if they retained the Venetic form of their names, alongside the Latin formula). An alternative combination of elements is present in Pa 6: *[M'. Galle]ni*

---

[144] See Meiser (1987), Penney (1988: 731–2).

[145] The inscriptions of the Marsi similarly are more or less pure Latin: see Peruzzi (1962: 137–40). Note however Poccetti (1979), 219, where the non-Latin *o*-declension form of the name of Hercules (*Herclo*) is retained in a Latin text. On this form, see also above, p. 132.

[146] See Lejeune (1954: 121–2).   [147] Cf. Lejeune (1954), 13 (= id. (1974), 221).

[148] Cf. Lejeune (1954), 14 (= id. (1974), 218).

[149] I note in passing that Lejeune (1953a: 150–5) argues that female names could be accompanied in Venetic by a gamonymic adjective in *-na* (as supposedly at Lejeune (1953a), LV *Canta Loxina*) or a patronymic in *-ya* or *-aca* (as at LVI *Canta Upsedia*), but came to be complemented either by genitive + *uxor* (e.g. Lejeune (1953a), LXV bis *Canta. Paphia. c. [ ]ni. uxor*) (on the text here see Untermann (1961: 48)) or genitive + *filia* (e.g. LXIII *Nerca. Vanticconis. f.*). Untermann (1961), however, merely takes these second Venetic names as 'Nachname' (see pp. 46, 47 on the names in question). He questions the alleged function of *-na* names as gamonymics (see 88). See too id. (1968: 145), noting that some names in *-na* occur on their own; it is inconceivable that a gamonymic could be used thus.

[150] Cf. Lejeune (1974), 217.   [151] On this name see Untermann (1961: 5, 146).

M'. f. Ostialae Galleniae equpetars.[152] The syntax and morphology of the onomastic formula are pure Latin. The case of the names is genitive, instead of the dative expected in a purely Venetic text of this type (contrast Pa 2).[153] The Latinate names are combined with the local word *equpetars* apparently signifying a tomb, stele or the like.[154] The referents had Latinised their names, but in part were adhering to the local form of funerary inscription. Perceptions of identity seem to be at issue here, and varying degrees of Romanisation.

Other Venetic texts appear to contain Latin words, though it is possible that the words were shared by Venetic. I quote such texts without further comment, merely noting that code-switching of this type, if it is such, need cause no surprise during a period in which Venetic was being ousted by Latin; Paelignian inscriptions, for example, provide parallels. See Es 111 [155] *Fougontai. Egtorei.* **filia**. *Fugenia. Lamusioi,* Ca 11 *e.s. kaivali*ϕ*er.tos a. rs. leticako.s. zona[. . . .]o śaina[. . . .]sicate.i,* Es 113 [156] *Gavis Ravpatnis* **miles** *Poltos Ostinobos fri[. . . t]er.*[157]

II.3.1 Conclusions

We have seen in this section several types of code-switching. Magical texts are often composed in more than one language, presumably to increase the obscurity and enhance the power of the magic (see below, IV.4). The insertion of a formula or term of one language into a text in another (as in *brat data, VSLM, donum dedit libens merito, equpetars*; see also below, II.5 on the curious Messapic text IM 2.24) may be intended to imply that the writer or referent had links with another culture, either one which was almost defunct or one which was gaining hold. The inflection of the referents' names reveals their preferred linguistic identity, whereas the inclusion of formulae from another language is apparently made in deference to a competing linguistic or cultural influence in the region. A momentary change of languages may also be appropriate to the subject matter or the identity of the referent, as for example when the posited owner of a tile factory (II.2) was given an Oscan inflection of his name. The Latin

---

[152] Discussed briefly by Untermann (1980b: 52).

[153] On which see Pellegrini and Prosdocimi (1967: I, 331; also 346 on the genitives of the quoted text).

[154] For a discussion of this word (which is also found in purely Venetic inscriptions at Pa 2, 3, 3bis), see Pellegrini and Prosdocimi (1967: II, 74–8).

[155] Cf. Lejeune (1953a), xxxv.   [156] Cf. Lejeune (1974), 110 bis.

[157] For a discussion of this text, with bibliography, see also Lejeune (1972). He is inclined (p. 9) to play down the possibility that *miles* here is Latin, but the overall interpretation of the text does not inspire confidence. Lejeune's paraphrase is *Gauius Rauipatnius miles afflictus ossibus Friui pater.*

filiation formula sometimes intruded into non-Latin texts; expressions of filiation seem to have been a sphere in which forms of cross-language influence were particularly commonplace (see below, 3.v.4).

Heavy morphological interference from Latin in two texts apparently intended as 'Italic' points to a declining knowledge of Italic, and suggests that in the last stages of Oscan and Umbrian there will have been some speakers who could only use a reduced form of the languages, with some Oscan/Umbrian lexemes but an abundance of Latin inflections.

Where 'imitation' is concerned, the evidence assembled in this section points overwhelmingly in one direction. Oscan texts, particularly of a legalistic kind, are heavily influenced in phraseology and formulaic structure by their Latin counterparts. The prestige of Roman law affected the way in which Oscan speakers phrased their own legal documents. The presence of this imitation obviously points to the bilingualism in Latin and Oscan of Oscan élites, but it can also be seen as a step in the direction of the death of Oscan. Once bilingual Oscan speakers had begun to draw heavily on the form of Latin official phraseology, they were succumbing to the dominance of Latin culture, and it was only a matter of time before, as is explicitly attested in the case of the Cumaeans, they adopted Latin itself as the language of their official business.

But curse tablets add a different dimension to the picture. Here the imitation seems to operate in the reverse direction, no doubt because of the potency of Italian regional magic in the sub-culture of regions in which Latin and Italic existed side by side.

Names, both divine and personal (for the latter type, see *Olsomnos Enniceios* in the Venetic text Ca 58 cited above), frequently show a resistance to change, such that after a regional language was largely abandoned the new Latin speakers of that region might retain the original form of names. The conservatism of names often causes code-switching when a person is named, from the language of the text as a whole into the primary language of the name or its bearer. This phenomenon was seen, for example, in the spelling of Latin names in Oscan texts with the Latin *ae* diphthong, as well as in the use of the genitive form of an Oscan name in a Latin text from Samnium.

II.4 Bilingual areas: some remarks about Pompeii

Many of the areas from which Oscan inscriptions survive also turn up Latin inscriptions as well. This fact is not in itself decisive evidence for bilingualism, because in many cases the inscriptions will have come from different periods. A particularly rich source of Oscan (and indeed Latin) inscriptions is Pompeii,[158] and some of the Oscan inscriptions undoubtedly come from a relatively late period when Latin was already well established. They may then be evidence for the coexistence of the two languages. Some of these inscriptions are of particular interest, and it is worthwhile to examine some specific cases as possible evidence for forms of bilingualism.

The town received a Sullan *colonia* of veterans some time after 89 BC, and the transition to Latin following that date is generally assumed to have been rapid. I would draw attention particularly to Vetter (1953), 29 and 30, which are electoral recommendations of a type found in greater numbers in Latin after the Romanisation of the town. No. 29, for example, runs as follows: **mr. perkden[iúm] IIII. ner. d . . . labiku. niel. . . . seis aphinis altinúm**, rendered into Latin by Vetter as *M(a)r(aeum) Percennium IV uir(um) . . . Afinius -orum*. Opinions vary about the interpretation of these texts. Castrén (1975: 44–5) remarks: 'Some electoral notices written in Oscan probably belong to the autonomous period or to the first years after the occupation, when, during a transitional stage, both languages were used in the election propaganda. The magistracy recorded in these texts is that of the **IIIIner**, evidently *quattuoruir*,[159] and the closest parallel is thus the earliest Latin election-notices in which this magistracy appears.' Mouritsen (1988: 85), however, states that none of the Latin electoral notices mentions quattuorviral candidates, and he rejects the idea that the Oscan notices form part of the same election campaign. Instead he argues that they belong to a separate (short-lived) Pompeian *municipium* (c. 89–80 BC) administered by *quattuoruiri*. On this view the inscriptions could not be taken as showing Oscan speakers participating in elections along with Latin speakers amid mutual understanding of the different forms of propaganda. It has to be said though that Mouritsen does not deal with Vetter (1953), 30, where an Oscan notice seems to have a correspondent in Latin referring to the same candidate (**ma. herenni / IIII.i.i.d.e.n.d.eiú**; for the Latin see Garrucci (1853: 149)).

A Latin inscription by one Vibius Popidius (*CIL* X. 794) commemorating the construction of a portico is of interest for its language choice, for Popidius was of an old Oscan family, and an earlier Popidius had used Oscan for an identical purpose (Vetter (1953), 13). The later Popidius'

---

[158] For a survey of the Oscan inscriptions from Pompeii, see Antonini (1977).

[159] **IIIIner** is manifestly a calque on the Latin official term: see e.g. Poccetti (1993: 89). Cf. too *[tr]ium nerum* in the *Tabula Bantina* (29 (Crawford (1996)). Of note is the Roman numeral symbol, with which may be compared (e.g.) Vetter (1953), 70 **akun(um) CXII** (= Lat. *annorum CXII*; the figure may be a mistake).

move to Latin brings out again the prestige which local élites were quickly to give to Latin, and their desire to be seen to be using that language for public purposes.

Something of an antiquarian interest in Oscan at Pompeii in the middle of the first century AD may be deduced from the inscription Vetter (1953), 11, if one accepts the interpretation of the text and its context by Poccetti (1982a). The text records a legacy by Vibius Adiranus to the *vereiia Pompeiana*, and the setting up of a hall with the legacy by the quaestor Vibius Vinicius in response to a decree of the assembly. I print the text in the form noted by Poccetti, which shows a type of paragraphing marked by the intrusion of the initials of the two participants into the left-hand margin:

V. Aadirans. V. eítiuvam. paam
veraiiaí. púmpaiianaí. tristaa
mentud. deded. eísak. eítiuvad
V. Viínikiís. Mr. kvaísstur. púmp
aiians. trííbúm. ekak. kúmben
nieís. tanginud. úpsannam
deded. ísídum. prúfatted.[160]

Poccetti (1982a: 242–3) argues that the text was recopied after the earthquake of AD 63, in accordance with modern graphic trends evidenced in (Latin) inscriptions of the Imperial period. The date of the original text will have been late Republican (second century BC).[161] This interpretation puts an interesting complexion on changing attitudes to Oscan in relation to Latin. When the Cumaeans switched in public to Latin, they were no doubt responding to the status of the Latin language. But when Latin was well established in former Oscan areas, there may have emerged a local pride among Oscan families in their Oscan origins, such that old inscriptions were preserved or recopied.[162] Such antiquarianism or local patriotism is consistent with a residual knowledge of Oscan in such areas in the early Imperial period, though bilingualism in a fluent spoken form cannot be assumed. It has been argued that the highly stylised 'Herentas' inscription (Vetter (1953), 213) and Vetter (1953), 214 from the territory of the Paeligni display the influence of Greek forms of

---

[160] 'Vibius Adiranus son of Vibius, the money which he gave in his will to the *vereiia Pompeiana*, with that money Vibius Vinicius son of Maraeus quaestor of Pompeii granted and also approved the making of this house in keeping with the decision of the *conuentus*.'

[161] See Poccetti (1982a: 244).

[162] As evidence for an antiquarian interest in Oscan may be cited the presence of an Oscan inscription dealing with two quaestors in the house of Cornelius Rufus (Vetter (1953), 16: see Poccetti (1982a: 243)).

expression.[163] One way of explaining this feature would be to see it as an attempt to upgrade Oscan culturally, and that again would be indicative of regional pride: the language is not to be lost, but brought into line with Greco-Latin culture.

It is possible that a more systematic assessment than I am able to offer here of the Latin, Greek and Oscan of Pompeii would have light to throw on language attitudes, language change and possible diglossia in the town.

11.5 Greek and Italic

The mention of a connection between Greek and Oscan raises the final topic of this section. It was noted earlier that Ennius claimed a Greek as well as an Oscan (and Latin) heart. In the preceding pages a good deal has been made of evidence for bilingualism in Oscan and Latin, but it would be misleading to pass over the bilingualism which must also have been widespread in Oscan and Greek. I offer below a few observations, without attempting to achieve anything like a complete coverage of the subject.

Contact between Italian Greeks and Oscan speakers was of long standing and considerable influence. Greek settlements were in some cases invaded by Oscans and subjected to Oscanisation, and there must have been periods of bilingualism. Paestum, for example, 60 km south-east of Naples, was originally a colony of Sybaris but in 410 it fell to the Lucanians and was Oscanised. An Oscan inscription discovered in 1977 in a large circular building which was possibly the ἐκκλησιαστήριον of the original foundation (Posidonia) was published for the first time as Poccetti (1979), 152.[164] It can be dated to the end of the fourth century BC, and certainly antedates the Latin colony of 273. Significantly, like many Oscan inscriptions (see below), it is in Greek script, and is thus an early sign of the impact of cultural contacts between the Oscan invaders and Greeks. Similarly Cumae fell to Oscans in 421, and, as we have seen (II.1), there survive from the town both Oscan and Greek inscriptions. Naples was another Greek foundation in which there were contacts between Greeks and Oscans. A recent study (Leiwo 1995a) has turned up evidence for families in the area with a mixture of Oscan and Greek names, writing in Greek; presumably many Oscans infiltrating the town had been Hellenised.[165]

---

[163] See Durante (1978: 800–1), Poccetti (1981).   [164] See also Del Tutto Palma (1990: 52).
[165] See e.g. Leiwo (1995a: 60, 64).

The bilingualism of the *bilingues Bruttaces* (the Bruttii were the inhabitants of Calabria, and this was another name for them)[166] was referred to by Ennius (*Ann.* 477 S.), according to the lexicographical tradition, which has it that they were bilingual in Greek and Oscan: Paul. Fest. p. 31 L. *bilingues Bruttaces: Ennius dixit quod Brutti et Osce et Graece loqui soliti sunt.* Similarly the *bilingues Canusini* of Hor. *Sat.* 1.10.30 were presumably bilingual in Greek and Oscan.[167] The Hellenisation of these southern Oscans is nicely evidenced by their use of the Greek alphabet to write Oscan.

An example was cited above of an Oscan inscription written in Greek characters. The use of the Greek (Ionic–Tarentine) alphabet for the writing of Oscan in the south (see e.g. Vetter (1953), 180–94, 196–9) dates from the fourth century BC.[168] But various earlier inscriptions in the archaic Achaean alphabet testify to a very early cultural influence of Greeks on Italic speakers.[169]

Further evidence for this influence may also be seen in the numerous Greek loan-words in Oscan.[170] An interesting case in point is provided by the name of the goddess Athena, which may appear at Vetter (1953), 192A, republished with alterations by Poccetti (1979), 151. The crucial phrase is ασανας μεταποντινας. If the reading is correct,[171] the *s* would derive from the Laconian of Tarentum (σ for θ), with the *a* also Doric. A freedman in Petronius, Hermeros, is apparently attributed a comparable form *Athana* at 58.7 (see above, 1.v). It is possible that the form had spread among Greek, Latin and Italic speakers in contact in southern regions.[172]

Vetter (1953), 22 (with now Poccetti (1979), 109) lists a series of weights and measures (on a *mensa ponderaria*) which are predominantly loan-words from Greek: **ka[.]íks** = κάδδιξ,[173] **kúiníks** = χοῖνιξ,[174] **sehsík**.[175] **limu(m)** at Vetter (1953), 6 is another borrowing (Gk. λιμός).[176]

A partially bilingual text in Greek and Oscan is published at Poccetti (1979), 120. This consists of a name in Greek on a terracotta lamp (Διόφαντος), with the start of its Oscan equivalent (**díú**).

---

[166] On the formation, see Skutsch (1985: 637–8).
[167] See e.g. De Simone (1980: 75), Jocelyn (1999: 192).   [168] See in general Lejeune (1970).
[169] See Vetter (1953), 186, 195a, Poccetti (1979), 153, 263, 264, with Rix (1996: 245).
[170] On this subject see in general Prosdocimi (1976), id. (1978), though not all of his evidence is equally compelling.
[171] This has been disputed. Campanile (1985: 11) cites La Regina as having demonstrated that the true reading is καμπσανας, but Del Tutto Palma (1990: 42–5) maintains that ασανας is correct. Untermann (2000: 365–6) accepts καμπσανας.
[172] See Biville (1995: 447–8), and above, 1.v, n. 65.   [173] See Untermann (2000: 361).
[174] See Untermann (2000: 406).   [175] On this problematical term, see Untermann (2000: 664).
[176] See Untermann (2000: 436).

The following text, attributed by Vetter to the territory of the Lucanians or Bruttii, displays again through its use of the Ionic alphabet the close association in the south between Oscans and Greeks (Vetter (1953), 190): σπεδισ μαμερικιες σαιπινσ ανα:fακετ (= *Spedius Mamercius Saepinus* ἀνέθηκεν, in Vetter's rendering). There are various possible explanations of the verb-form. The base is an Oscan perfect without reduplication (= *faced*).[177] The prefix is probably *an-* (cf. Lat. *anhelo*),[178] with Oscan anaptyxis.[179] Alternatively it might just possibly be the Greek ἀνα-. The verb ἀνέθηκεν in this position would be formulaic in a Greek inscription, and it may be that the verb in the inscription is a hybrid, with Greek prefix and Oscan root. Comparable hybrids will be discussed elsewhere. Note e.g. Horace's *depugis* (*Sat.* 1.2.93), which is a partial Latinisation of ἄπυγος (see 4.II).

It was not only Oscan that was in contact with Greek. It has been noted by De Simone (*OCD* 3rd edn, s.v. 'Messapic language') that a 'recent inscription of Arpi (Daunia) from the 3rd cent. BC has *Artos pinave* "Artos painted", the signature of the artist who decorated the tomb; the form of the name (*Artos* and not *Artas*) shows Greek influence; yet the verb *pinave* is Messapic'.[180] Note too the Messapic inscription IM 2.24 *artos atotios taiθoi tai günakhai pensklen oυpave.*[181] Arena (1969: 438) takes the first two words as the name (in the masculine) of a dedicator, and the next three as equivalent to τᾶι θεῶι τᾶι γυναικείαι. The last two words must be a Messapic verb phrase of some description. An alternative might be to take *taiθoi* as a female name (in the dative), followed by a representation of τῇ γυναικί. On this view the names and kinship term would be in Greek (note the *-os* ending of the first two words, and see above on *Artos*), and the dedicatory formula in Messapic. The switch of languages would be exactly the same as that seen earlier (II.3) in the Venetic inscription comprising names in Latin and the Venetic term *equpetars*.

Some alleged Messapic traces in S. Italian Greek are not however decisive.[182]

II.6 Conclusions

Oscan went on certainly into the late Republic, and possibly beyond that to the Augustan period, though the Augustan evidence is difficult

---

[177] See Buck (1904: 170, also 51).   [178] See Buck (1904: 193), Untermann (2000: 257).
[179] See Buck (1904: 51).
[180] I have not been able to track this inscription down in any publication.
[181] See Parlangèli (1960: 46).   [182] See Rohlfs (1958), id. (1959: 173–5).

to interpret. Oscan and Latin speakers were not discrete groups; even in the limited material available it is possible to find speakers of the two languages in contact, as in the proposed tile factory at Pietrabbondante. The application to Rome by the people of Cumae in 180 BC is a guarantee that there were speakers of Oscan who had learnt Latin. The same conclusion can be drawn from the imitation of Latin legalistic phraseology in the *Tabula Bantina* and elsewhere. But whether there were primary speakers of Latin who learnt Oscan (or Umbrian) is another matter. It was probably the prestige attached to Latin and the growing power of the Romans which motivated Italic speakers to learn Latin (see below), but Latin speakers by contrast were never great learners of languages other than Greek. Lucilius' apparent disparagement of Oscan-influenced Latin shows an awareness of the existence of regional variation in Latin determined by language contact, but the attitude implicit in the passage, that the Italic language in question was inferior, would not have been conducive to language learning by Romans. There is no evidence that Romans tried to stamp out regional languages; the initiative was probably taken by the Italian upper classes themselves in acquiring the language of the dominant power. But the lower classes such as the tile makers seen earlier may have been slower to shift languages.

An attempt has recently been made (by Mouritsen (1998)) to play down the amount of Latin learning in allied communities in the second century BC.[183] There is the complicating factor, according to Mouritsen, of 'the lack of comprehensive studies of the use of Latin in pre-Roman Italy' (80); the works of Wachter (1987) and Vine (1993) do not appear in the bibliography. It is stated (p. 70) that the 'political power of a large, hegemonic state is not in itself a valid explanation of why smaller neighbours should spontaneously assume its language and culture; the opposite reaction has more often been the case. Small nations often react quite differently when put under such political pressure.' There is an element of exaggeration here, particularly in the sentence 'the opposite reaction has more often been the case'. *Cultural assimilation* has historically been an important factor in language death: 'one culture is influenced by a more dominant culture, and begins to lose its character as a result of its members adopting new behaviour and mores' (Crystal (2000: 77)). Cultural domination has often been associated with urbanisation, which produces 'cities which act as magnets to rural communities' (Crystal (2000: 77)), as a result of which incomers learn the language of the cities

---

[183] Mouritsen (1998), sect. II.3 (especially 80–1).

and abandon those of the outlying rural areas. We know that the city of Rome during the Republic was a magnet to speakers of other languages and of non-city varieties of Latin itself (Cic. *Fam.* 9.15.2, *Brut.* 258): every literary author of the Republic moved to Rome from outside. It is also one thing to argue (with Mouritsen) that the adoption of Latin by Italians is difficult to explain, and quite another to suggest that, because it is difficult to explain, therefore it did not really happen (at least in the second century). Mouritsen cites little of the specific evidence[184] relating to the use of Latin (alongside Oscan, Umbrian and Venetic) in making the claim (81) that no 'generalised Latinisation can . . . be demonstrated in allied Italy'. Here is a very brief review of some of the evidence which we have seen (and some which has not been mentioned) for the spread of Latin in the second century; I would not wish to argue that Oscan and Umbrian were ousted by Latin before the Social War, but rather that Latin was in vigorous rivalry with the local languages and that bilingualism was well entrenched.

The story about the Cumaeans implies that long since Latin had been adopted in informal use. The evidence of Latin *defixiones*, and of a Latin–Oscan *defixio*, suggests the spread of Latin in the town of Cumae in mundane contexts. Bradley (2000: 294–300) has collected the Latin inscriptions extant from Umbrian regions which antedate the Social War (see also id. 203–17 for discussion). The death of Umbrian had not yet taken place (see id. 281–93 for a collection of the Umbrian material from the same period), but however one interprets the data Latin was making inroads. Some Gauls who set up a bilingual inscription at Todi in Umbria, *c.* 150–100, chose Latin rather than Umbrian to use alongside their native language (see 2.IV.2). The Gaulish version was purely symbolic and personal, but the other version must have been intended for local readers. Bradley (2000: 210–11) draws some interesting conclusions from a comparison of the Latin inscription *CIL* I².2112 from Asisium with an Umbrian border cippus (Vetter (1953), 236) from the same place. The Latin inscription is a monumental building inscription from a prominent place in the centre of the town, whereas the Umbrian text belongs to the domain of religion. We will see further evidence in this chapter for linguistic conservatism in the religious sphere. Bradley (2000: 210–11), making a comparison with the Cumae affair of 180 BC, sees in the use of Latin for official purposes (in the public building inscription) a symbol of 'the new affiliations that some of the Umbrian élite wished

---

[184] But see 80–1.

to establish at this time'. There is even evidence for the early intrusion of Latin into religious dedications (*CIL* I².2101).[185]

Distinctive features of 'Campanian' Latin have been detected. For example, there is good evidence that duplication of vowels (*Maarcus*, etc.) to mark length first entered Latin writing in areas where Oscan was spoken, under the influence of an Oscan convention.[186] Whether primary speakers of Latin imitated Oscan writing, or primary speakers of Oscan introduced the Oscan convention into their Latin writing, clearly Latin was in use in some form alongside Oscan in the area in question, and literacy practices in the two languages were not immune from mutual influence. We saw too an archaic Campanian Latin inscription in which the Oscan pattern of filiation was used. Again, Vine (1993: 134–41) discusses at length a Capuan Latin inscription dated to the late third century BC belonging to a set of inscriptions on Campanian Cales ware. The Latin inscriptions of Delos, which date from about 150 BC onwards, were set up by a group styling themselves *Italici*, which embraced at least some Campanians and members of old Oscan families (see Chapter 6).

The poet Ennius, who, as we saw, evaluated Greek, Latin and Oscan (?) equally, could not have acquired his learned variety of Latin in the army. He is likely to have been an early learner of the language, possibly at a Latin colony. Latin colonies will have given Italic speakers access to Latin, and the line of Lucilius with the form *abzet*, which can be paralleled in Paelignian, implies the existence of a local variety of Latin (in the region of a Latin colony) with Oscan interference. The various mixed-language texts considered in this section, such as that from the territory of the Vestini which appears to be of early date, attest Latin in close contact with Italic. The Marsi must have abandoned Oscan early; the texts of the Paeligni for their part are markedly mixed in language.

Another significant literary figure was the (probable) Umbrian Plautus. He was a master of all of the formal and colloquial styles of Latin, and also (through one of his characters, Truculentus), disparaging of 'rustic' Latin (see e.g. *Truc.* 689–91). His career and attitudes hint at a desire on the part of outsiders to be assimilated linguistically to Roman ways. That same desire surfaces during both the second and first centuries BC. Lucilius, as we have seen (see particularly n. 52), mocked the inclusion of Sabine, Praenestine and Etruscan words in Latin (Quint. 1.5.56), and the use of a non-urban monophthong for *ae* (frg. 1130) as well as the use of the

---

[185] See the discussion of Bradley (2000: 209).
[186] See Vine (1993), chapter 11, and below, p. 661.

Oscanised *abzet*, and Cicero esteemed city Latin above that of the provincial periphery (see *De orat.* 3.42–4), just as Pollio sneered at the *Patauinitas* of Livy (Quint. 1.5.56, 8.1.3). These scattered anecdotes (and more material of the same kind could be added) and remarks point to a distinctive attitude on the part of Latin-speaking outsiders to Rome (and all of those mentioned were from outside). By implication they themselves were not exposed to the linguistic charges they made against other outsiders, and hence they had adapted their speech to an esteemed Roman norm. I see no reason why the attitude of an outsider who spoke Latin should not have been shared by outsiders who were originally Oscan-, Umbrian- or Venetic-speaking. The language of Rome was esteemed (witness again the story about Cumae), and that esteem will have been enough to motivate the acquisition of Latin by some Oscan and Umbrian speakers alongside their original language. The Romans actively attempted to enhance the *dignitas* of their own language, as can be seen from a well-known passage in Valerius Maximus (2.2.2, discussed below, 5.IV.3). The commercial, political and military influence of Rome, along with the positive evaluation of its own language and disparagement of the speech of outsiders, will have put pressure particularly on upper-class Italians to acquire the language (or the 'Roman' variety of Latin). The stages of acquisition cannot be documented in any sort of detail, and an exact account cannot be given of the language situation in any one area at a particular time, but the evidence is consistent with a spread of Latin in the second century, and its considerable influence on Oscan before language death took place (see below).

In the first chapter (v) a distinction was made between interference, which usually consists of the influence of a speaker's (writer's) first or stronger language (L1) on his second (L2), and borrowing (sometimes referred to as 'imitation', a term which has the advantage that it can embrace borrowing of non-lexical kinds: see 4.II), which consists of the adoption in L1 of elements from L2. It is though not always easy to draw such a distinction when the evidence is sketchy and the primary language of the writer unclear. The Latinate formulae and structures found in Oscan legal texts such as the *Tabula Bantina* represent borrowing of patterns established in Roman law. It is perverse to speak of this phenomenon as a 'Latinisation' of Oscan (unless it is made clear in what sense the term is being used), because the Oscan language as it was spoken by ordinary speakers (and by the upper classes when they were not trying to imitate the usages of Roman law) need not have been affected at all. It would be preferable to speak of the Romanisation of local legal practices. Nevertheless from the linguistic point of view it is important to recognise the presence in Italic texts of such imitation of Latin structures, if only so that the pitfall may be avoided of always assuming that a parallel between, say, Oscan and Latin is due to the joint retention by both languages of an inherited feature. *Attractio inuersa*, for example, was an Indo-European construction, but it cannot be concluded from its use in an Oscan text of official character that it had survived independently in Oscan from the Indo-European period; the writer may simply have been imitating Latin official inscriptions, in which the construction also appears. On the other hand the fact that Oscan structures seem to have been imitated in Latin *defixiones* shows that cultural interchange operated in both directions. Roman law was dominant, but in the sphere of magic it may have been Italic practices which were more influential.

The 'influence' of Latin on Italic is more marked than that of Italic on Latin; I use the general term 'influence' to embrace both interference and borrowing. That is only to be expected at a time when there was a shift in progress from Italic languages to Latin. I list here the main manifestations of such influence in the two directions. But crude lists on their own tell us little, particularly if no distinction is made between borrowing and interference. The lists, which are meant to be rough and ready and to embrace uncritically much of the material discussed in this section, will therefore be accompanied and followed by an attempt to bring out the implications of the various phenomena.

11.6.1 Latin 'influences' Italic

(1) The writer of the *Tabula Bantina* committed Latinate errors and spellings, as for example *ex.elg.* for *exeic* and the use of the digraph *ae* for *ai*.

(2) This Latinate digraph is not uncommon in other texts. I would draw attention to its appearance in a number of Paelignian texts which do not seem to be in Latin as their matrix language (Vetter (1953), 213, 214, Poccetti (1979), 208).

(3) The Latin formula of filiation (genitive + *f(ilius)*) intruded into Italic, as in the text Poccetti (1979), 34. Another case is in a Paelignian inscription (Vetter (1953), 210c) which, to judge by the form of a name, is not in Latin. The use of *fel* in the patronymic in an Umbrian text (Vetter (1953), 232c) appears to be modelled on the Latin filiation formula. There is even a non-Latin text (Poccetti (1979), 204) in which a Latin genitive morpheme is used in a filiation. Genitive + *f(ilius)* in an Italic text represents

code-switching, or perhaps borrowing.[187] Code-switching though is a special phenomenon which is usually irrelevant to the structural influence of one language on another; it is rather a mixing of two discrete languages.

(4) We saw a calque from Latin in Oscan (**IIIIner**).

(5) Similarly **seganatted** may have been influenced semantically by *signauit*.

(6) The use of *incubat* in the sense 'lies dead' (see n. 138) may represent a 'creative' or erroneous borrowing, in that the verb does not have this sense in Latin itself. The text is Paelignian. Reference was made to 'franglais', in which borrowings from English often do not reproduce English usage accurately (e.g. 'le parking' for a parking area). But this is not the only possible explanation of the form, as we saw.

(7) The ablative absolute seems to be imitated in a dating formula in the Oscan text Poccetti (1979), 34.

(8) The expression *oisa aetate* is not only ablative absolute, but it has Latin orthography (*ae*) and morphology (the ablative form).

(9) The Umbrian text Vetter (1953), 234 has Latin morphology imposed on Umbrian lexemes, and the Vestinian inscription Vetter (1953), 220 is comparable in this respect. The writers (like the engraver of the *Tabula Bantina*) had poor competence in the vernacular languages, which had probably been all but forgotten, and they could only inflect them by resorting to Latin inflections. This may represent interference (from their L1 Latin), or perhaps it might be classified as an unusual form of borrowing (from L1 into L2). Interference is often probably unconscious, but borrowing from L1 into L2 would be deliberate, and motivated by an inability to come up with the correct morphology in the target language. Whether we speak of 'interference' or 'borrowing' in these inscriptions, the determinant of the alien morphology is the same.

(10) Oscan borrowed legal terms from Latin, as e.g. *dolo malo*, which appears several times in the *Tabula Bantina* with Oscanised morphology. We also saw several words of Latin appearance in Venetic texts (*filia, miles, libertus*). In the Paelignian text Vetter (1953), 212 the verb *locatin(s)* is perhaps a borrowing from Latin.[188] I have not dealt here with Latin borrowings into Italic, because it is sometimes difficult or impossible to determine whether words found in Latin and (say) Oscan were borrowings into one from the other, or part of a shared stock of inherited Italic terms.

---

[187] It might alternatively be suggested that a mere graphic symbol of Latin inscriptions, (name +) *f*, has been transported into Italic inscriptions; *filius* is not written in full, and perhaps should not be treated as a 'word'.

[188] See Vetter (1953: 145); but see Untermann (2000: 351) on the reading.

II.6.2 Italic 'influences' Latin

For the sake of completeness I include in this list various phenomena the relevance of which to this issue has been rejected in the previous discussion.

(1) The *-rus* verb ending did not enter Latin from Italic (see above, n. 40), and the *-as* nominative plural morpheme as it occurs in Latin is not conclusively dialectal.

(2) The possible Oscanisms in the Latin of Pompeii have been effectively dismissed by Eska (1987).

(3) Phonetic features of Oscan (such as the assimilation of *nd* to *nn*) which can be paralleled at a much later date in Italian dialects are likely to have been medieval innovations in Italian rather than continuations of features of an ancient variety of Oscan-influenced Vulgar Latin.

(4) Possible Oscan morphological influence on the Latin of the *Lex Lucerina* (in *fundatid, parentatid*: see n. 43) can be explained in other ways, though it has to be said that there are scholars who hold firmly to the view that the morpheme is Oscanising. If Oscan influence is to be allowed, the writer can only have been a first-language speaker of Oscan who had acquired some Latin.

(5) The anaptyxis in Novius Eunus is arguably partly of a type which can be paralleled in Oscan, but Oscan influence (surely not 'interference', because Eunus, a freedman with a Greek name, is unlikely to have been a speaker of Oscan as his L1) is not the only possible explanation. Anaptyxis operates haphazardly and can be idiolectal. If Oscan influence is to be allowed, Eunus had presumably picked up regional pronunciations in Puteoli which had spread from L2 speakers of Latin (with Oscan as L1) into local Latin.

(6) The monophthongisation of *ai* seen in a Latin inscription from Spoletium in Umbria (see n. 42) cannot securely be attributed to Umbrian influence.

(7) Lucilius' implied criticism of the verb-form *abzet* suggests that an Oscan speaking Latin as his L2 showed signs of interference from L1 in his Latin. Similarly *Luca* and *Campans* must have originated in the Latin of Oscan speakers.

(8) There are loan-words from Italic languages in Latin many of which may date from an early period.

(9) The hybrid dative *Herc(o)lo* is found in a Latin text of the Paeligni (Vetter (1953: 153), and in an inscription of the Marsi (Poccetti (1979), 219) (see p. 131).

(10) The Paelignian inscription Vetter (1953), 217b has a partially Oscanised spelling *uicturei* in what looks like a Latin text; the word also has a Latinate consonant cluster *ct*.

(11) The Paelignian inscription Vetter (1953), 217a has an Oscan formula at the end of a Latin text.

(12) There is one early Latin text in which the Oscan pattern of filiation is found (*CIL* I².401). If this were written by a native speaker of Oscan, it might be a case of interference from L1. But expressions of filiation represent a special area of cross-language influence, with distinctions between interference, code-switching and borrowing not always easy to make.

(13) An Oscan formula in *defixiones* seems to have been imitated in Latin.

Doubts have thus been raised about the relevance of the first five or six items in the second list. In the first list two types of evidence are worth distinguishing. First, there is evidence of imitation of or borrowing from Latin in Italic (see (4)–(8), (10)). Secondly, the material listed at (1) and particularly (9) can be classified as interference (but see above (9) on the difficulty of classification). The L1 of the various writers must have been Latin. In other words, a language shift had already all but taken place and the writers were incapable of producing the vernacular language without interference from L1. These examples represent the most profound influence of one language on another which we have seen in this section.

In the second list one item stands out (7). The referent in the passage of Lucilius was probably a first-language speaker of Oscan who had adopted Latin to some extent. His competence in L2 is not such that he can avoid interference from L1. This evidence, paradoxically, though it has been set out in a different list, points to much the same development as that highlighted in the previous paragraph from the first list. I refer to the adoption by Oscans and Umbrians of Latin. At a time of language learning, their new language (Latin) is subject to interference from L1. When the language shift is further advanced but not yet complete, they still admit interference from L1, but this has now become Latin, with the vernacular languages scarcely remembered. The evidence of the two lists taken together thus brings out stages in the death of Oscan and Umbrian.

It is striking that Paelignian inscriptions come up constantly in the two lists. The evidence is difficult to assess because the inscriptions are mostly short, but it is clear that during Romanisation the Paeligni found it difficult in writing to keep the two languages apart.[189] When they were

---

[189] On the nature of the original language of the Paeligni and its Latinisation, see Meiser (1987).

writing 'Paelignian' they fell into Latinate spellings and the like, and when they were writing 'Latin' they retained some formulae and forms from their traditional culture (code-switching). Not all Latinate 'misspellings' in 'Paelignian' texts represent interference from Latin. We have noted a tendency for the *ae* digraph to be used in words of Latin origin in Paelignian texts (pp. 141–2), and that must have been due to a deliberate policy of spelling a word according to its language of origin. This phenomenon is best seen as a show of learning, taking the form of 're-nativisation' of the loan-word. So Cicero in the letters sometimes used Greek script for loan-words (e.g. *philosophus*) which had long since been integrated into Latin.

The other major element in the material discussed in this section comprises texts in a mixture of languages. These do not all fall into the same class, and there is not in every case a clearcut distinction between a text in a mixture of languages (i.e. one displaying code-switching), and a text in a single language with borrowing or interference from another. The types of code-switching which have so far come up in this chapter are summarised above (II.3.1).

Finally, at the start of this chapter the question was asked whether there was regional variation in Latin determined by language contact. We have now seen clearcut examples, in the partly Italic form of the dative *Herc(o)lo* in certain regional Latin inscriptions, in the Oscanised pronunciation of Latin apparently castigated by Lucilius (*abzet*), and in the spelling of *uicturei* in a text from the area of the Paeligni. All of these usages reflect varieties of Latin used by provincials who were either learners of Latin as a second language themselves, or were from a background in which Italic speakers had shifted to Latin and imposed some marks of the earlier language on the new in the process of the language shift. This is the phenomenon which Thomason and Kaufman (1988) call 'interference through shift'. Learners of L2 inflict interference from L1 on the acquired language, and that interference may become a defining feature of a whole regional variety of the language. Indian English, for example, has distinctive features which reflect interference from Indian languages.

III ETRUSCAN

The evidence concerning language contact between Etruscan speakers and speakers of Italic languages including Latin falls into two parts, that of the archaic period, and that of the later Republic when Romanisation of the Etruscan population was well under way. For the early period there is anecdotal material (but written at a later date), indirect evidence (in the form for example of loan-words from Etruscan into Italic, and of evidence for the free movement of the upper classes across different language areas), and a few archaic inscriptions from which deductions can sometimes be made. The later evidence, comprising both Latin and Etruscan inscriptions of mixed linguistic character and a small corpus of bilingual inscriptions, is more revealing of the background to the language shift in Etruria from Etruscan to Latin.

In the early period (seventh and sixth centuries BC) issues relevant to bilingualism which have attracted recent attention are that of the possible presence at Rome of an Etruscan community speaking a regional form of the language, and the extent of so-called 'horizontal mobility' across the various language communities in central Italy. Both possibilities, if accepted, would imply a functional bilingualism. Unfortunately the evidence is very limited.

III.1 'Roman' Etruscan

I take first the Etruscan community at Rome. There is a small number of Etruscan inscriptions from Rome (perhaps four) belonging to the regal period, of which three are on votive offerings. Such texts might in theory have been the work of visitors to Rome; and if that were so, they would tell us little. But Cornell (1995: 157) notes that 'two of the texts show dialectal peculiarities that have been plausibly interpreted as a distinctly Roman form of Etruscan', and he concludes that, if this is genuinely the case, 'we have evidence that Etruscan speakers were a well-established group within the Roman upper class, and that their presence goes back a long way'. This conclusion may be correct, but it is worthwhile to demonstrate the flimsiness of the evidence. The two inscriptions are as follows:

ni araziia laraniia[190]

araz silqetenas spurianas[191]

In the first inscription the first word *ni* is a variant form or misspelling of the pronoun *mi* (= *ego*) (see below). It is probably followed by a genitive

---

[190] The text is datable to the sixth century BC, and comes from the Capitol. It can be found in Pallottino (1968), 24, and has been extensively discussed, for example by De Simone (1968), id. (1988), 31–2.

[191] See Pallottino (1979a, 1979b); from the sanctuary of Fortuna and Mater Matuta in the Forum Boarium, and dated 580–560 BC.

of the common masculine *praenomen* Arath (*Araθ*)[192] and a problematic genitive ending in *-ia* of a masculine *gentilicium*.[193] With *ni* is understood the verb 'to be' ('am'). At the head of the second inscription is the same *praenomen* in the nominative, followed by two appositives in the genitive.[194] Attention has been drawn to the presence of *z* for *θ* in the first name in both inscriptions,[195] which is paralleled in the Caeritan text *mi hulus larziia*,[196] where *larziia* is genitive of the equally common masculine *praenomen Larθ* and *hulus* is genitive of the *gentilicium Hulu*.[197] The order of *praenomen* and *gentilicium* is also reversed in this last inscription,[198] a phenomenon not found anywhere else in the abundant archaic inscriptions of Caere, according to Colonna (1987: 58). There may therefore be some grounds for arguing that the inscription is peculiar and perhaps from the hand of an Etruscan from Rome;[199] and if this view were accepted, the case for taking the palatalisation as a 'Roman' feature might gain support. But the matter is not straightforward. An archaic inscription from Vulci (dated to the end of the seventh century BC) of relatively recent publication (*mi Arusia Meitunas*)[200] has also been taken as showing such palatalisation,[201] with the first name a genitive of the masculine *praenomen Arnθ*, which, it is said, could also have been written as *Arunθia*. On this view the palatalisation is indicated by *s* rather than *z*. De Simone (1968: 209) cites some other cases of palatalisation in Etruscan (Ἀρκαδία > *Arχaza*, Διομήδης > *Zimaite*), mostly of later date.

Colonna (1987: 58–9) also notes that the spelling *n* for *m* (in *ni*: see above) is attested in the archaic period (some seven times) in what he calls 'un ambito tipicamente tiberino' (i.e. from Veio, Bomarzo, Orvieto and

---

[192] See De Simone (1968: 208), comparing (for the genitive form) *mi hulus **larziia*** (from Caere, second half of the sixth century BC) (for which text, see Vanoni (1965: 502–3)).

[193] On the interpretation of and difficulties raised by *laraniia*, see De Simone (1968: 210–12); also Colonna (1987: 59). Normally in Etruscan a masculine *praenomen* in the genitive (in *-(i)a*) is followed by a *gentilicium* in *-nas* (*-nies*) (see De Simone (1968: 210 with n. 4)). De Simone (1968: 210–11) discusses two possible parallel cases of genitives in *-ia* in masculine *gentilicia*, only one of which is accepted by Colonna (1987: 59 with n. 31) (see below). The rejected case is at Pallottino (1968), 154.

[194] On the interpretation of which see De Simone (1988: 33–4). Note too Colonna (1987: 59 n. 33); also Pallottino (1979a: 11).

[195] See particularly Colonna (1987: 58). Note too De Simone (1968: 208) and Pallottino (1979b: 322).

[196] For the inscription, see above, n. 192.

[197] See De Simone (1968: 208), Colonna (1987: 58, especially n. 29).

[198] See De Simone (1968: 208–9).

[199] Note Colonna (1987: 58), suggesting that, given the connections between Caere and Rome, the inscription 'potrebbe benissimo riportarsi ad un etrusco di Roma'.

[200] Note Martelli (1982), (1984).   [201] By De Simone (1988: 32).

Chiusi).[202] Moreover the masculine genitive of the *gentilicium* in *-ia* seen in *laraniia* (instead of *laranas*) is, according to Colonna (see n. 193), securely attested only once (*mi aviles laucieia*),[203] at Orvieto, and the content of the text is perhaps significant, in that the name *laucie* is equivalent to Lat. *Lucius*. Colonna suggests that the man might have been an Etruscan from Rome who had moved to another area and adopted the *praenomen Avile* while retaining an attachment to his original dialect.[204]

In the second Roman inscription quoted at the start of this discussion there are other interesting features. The *koppa* before the vowel *e* in *silqetenas* has no parallel in Etruria,[205] but is perhaps found in an archaic Latin inscription (in the name *sqetios* or *qetios*) (*ILLRP* 5).[206] Also unusual, but supposedly of 'Faliscan' type, is the structure of the inscription, with two appositives attached to the *praenomen* in the nominative (see above).

Views will vary about the quality of this evidence, but it is at least suggestive, particularly given that the corpus of Etruscan inscriptions is so large. Aberrant spellings have much more interest if they can be set against a very well established norm. If it is accepted that there was a distinctive variety of 'Roman' Etruscan,[207] then it must follow that there was a settled population of Etruscans at Rome (as distinct from a population of temporary and changing outsiders) such that their language was able to develop along independent lines, and under these conditions contact between Latin and Etruscan speakers, and forms of bilingualism, will have been inevitable. But in my opinion the evidence does not amount to much.

Much has been made in recent years of the existence of 'horizontal social mobility' in the archaic period.[208] Towns supposedly maintained an open-door policy which facilitated movement across the different language areas of central Italy, and this (if true) will have fostered bilingualism. In Etruria there is evidence for the presence of wealthy persons of Greek, Italic and Latin origin,[209] such as one Titus Latinus (rather

---

[202] There is a list of examples of the spelling in Colonna (1981: 170). See also De Simone (1968: 207–8).

[203] For another possible case, see above, n. 193.

[204] Note id. (1987: 59): 'Il "Vornamegentilicium" Laucie, equivalente al latino Lucius, rende in questo caso pressoché certo che si tratti di un etrusco di Roma, entrato nella cittadinanza volsiniese assumendo il prenome Avile, ma conservando l'attaccamento alla propria parlata.'

[205] See Colonna (1987: 59).   [206] See Prosdocimi (1979: 385).

[207] See the discussion of De Simone (1988: 31–6).

[208] See for example Ampolo (1981), De Simone (1988: 35), Cornell (1995: 158), Watmough (1997: 16).

[209] See for example Cornell (1995: 158).

than Latinius)[210] attested in an Etruscan inscription at Veii (*mi tites latines*) on a rich tomb of the seventh century.[211]

III.2 *Loan-words and calques*

Loan-words and calques are a source of information about languages in contact in the early period,[212] though borrowing does not establish anything about the quality of the bilingualism of those in contact (see further below). Borrowing in early Italy does of course involve Etruscan and Latin, but not only those two languages, and sometimes indeed a third language may act as an intermediary when a word passes from one language to another.

As far as borrowings from Etruscan to Latin are concerned, from the abundant material available I give just a few examples. Borrowings into Latin of terms to do with stage performances attest a particular type of Etruscan cultural influence on Rome. A case in point is the term *subulo* 'flautist',[213] the Etruscan origin of which is explicitly noted by Latin sources (Fest. 402.2 L. *subulo Tusce tibicen dicitur*,[214] Varro, *Ling.* 7.35 *subulo dictus, quod ita dicunt tibicines Tusci*; the word occurs in Latin already in Ennius, *Sat.* 65 v., cited by Varro). Particularly revealing of the complexity of linguistic contacts in the early period are those borrowings from Greek into Latin which on phonetic, orthographical or morphological grounds can be deduced to have entered Latin through Etruscan as intermediary. For example *catamitus*, which in Plautus has not yet become a common noun but is a name (*Men.* 144 *enumquam tu uidisti tabulam pictam in pariete/ubi aquila Catameitum raperet aut ubi Venus Adoneum*), derives from Gk. Γανυμήδης (or *Γαδυμήδης) via Etr. *catmite*.[215] The Latin form displays instead of the original voiced stops the voiceless stops typical of Etruscan.[216] The Plautine context (in which a painting is described) suggests the route by which the name might have entered Latin. Various names from Greek myth and tragedy are found in Etruscanised form in Etruscan works of art, and the name might have been picked up by Latin speakers from such works. *Triumphus* (attested first in the form *triumpe*) is

---

[210] On the form of the name, see De Simone (1988: 35, n. 52).
[211] See *Civiltà del Lazio Primitivo*, Exhibition Catalogue (Rome, 1976), 376 no. 131.
[212] See for example De Simone (1988: 37–40), id. (1991), Breyer (1993), Watmough (1997).
[213] See De Simone (1988: 38), Breyer (1993: 300–1) and Watmough (1997: 53) on the Etruscan origin of the word.
[214] An item which no doubt reflects the Etruscan learning of Verrius Flaccus.
[215] See De Simone (1970: 189–90), id. (1988: 37), Breyer (1993: 155–6).
[216] On this matter, see Pfiffig (1969: 26, 36–8).

from θρίαμβος (θρίαμβε) via Etruscan.[217] It has been argued that various theatrical terms (*scaena, persona, ludius/ludio*) are of Greek origin but mediated through Etruscan.[218] Various other Latin words with a Greek etymology show phonetic or morphological features suggestive of an Etruscan intermediary, such as *lanterna* (cf. λαμπτήρ: note the suffix)[219] and *amurca* (cf. ἀμόργη: note the voiceless stop).[220] Some toponyms at Rome, such as *(porta) Ratumen(n)a*, which by tradition was named after a youth from Veii who had been a victor in a chariot race (Fest. 340.31 L.), also seem to have been of Etruscan origin.[221] There was also a *uicus Tuscus* in the city, a name which may preserve a folk memory of an Etruscan settlement.

Some of the Etruscan elements in Latin are more telling than simple loan-words. The abnormal Latin numerals *undeuiginti* and *duodeuiginti*, which entail a subtraction (one from twenty, two from twenty), are calqued on the Etruscan *θunem-zaθrum* (one from twenty) and *eslem-zaθrum* (two from twenty).[222] Lat. *res publica* seems to correspond to Etr. *meχ rasnal*.[223] Calquing implies a more profound level of bilingual contact than mere borrowing, which (as was observed in the previous chapter, e.g. VI) can be effected by speakers who know little or nothing of the language from which they are borrowing.[224] Also indicative of contact between some Latin and Etruscan speakers is the presence in Latin of several Latin–Etruscan hybrids.[225] Etruscan suffixes (familiar from Etruscan borrowings into Latin) are sometimes attached to Latin roots. *Dossennus*, for example, the name of a character in farce (e.g. Pompon. 109), has

---

[217] See Versnel (1970: 48–55), who does however admit a slightly different possibility. Note 55: 'Etruria is the link connecting θρίαμβε and *triumpe, it being possible that a pre-Greek word was taken over by Etruscan and, independently, by Greek*' (my italics). See further De Simone (1970: 276), id. (1988:40), Breyer (1993: 232–4).

[218] See Szemerényi (1975: 307–16). On *persona*, see the detailed discussion of De Simone (1970: 293–8); also id. (1988: 32–3), Breyer (1993: 373–7).

[219] See De Simone (1970: 190–1, 279–80).

[220] See De Simone (1970: 276–7, 278), Breyer (1993: 173–4).　　[221] See De Simone (1988: 30).

[222] See Pfiffig (1969: 124).　　[223] See Rix (1984: 466).

[224] Perhaps at the time of the war with Pyrrhus, for example, Latin speakers picked up the Greek word for 'elephant', but in a debased form derived from the Greek genitive (*elephantus*; cf. ἐλέφας, ἐλέφαντος). The deformation reflects the original users' poor understanding of Greek; it is easy to see how the word might have been introduced to Latin through superficial contacts between Greeks, and Latin speakers who knew no Greek at all. It was left to educated Latin speakers at a later period to seek to replace the popular borrowing with the 'correct' Greek form *elephas*. For a collection of such 'popular' borrowings (nouns) showing deformations of one sort or another, see e.g. Kahle (1918: 16). Verbs too were sometimes borrowed in a form which reflects poor competence in Greek on the part of the borrower (e.g. *pauso* derives from the aorist form of παύω, and *camsare* from that of κάμπτω (on this last, see E. Löfstedt (1911: 109–10)).

[225] See e.g. Ernout (1930 = 1946: 27, 29).

the Latin root *dorsum* (*dossum*, *dossus*) with Etruscan suffix. The sense is perhaps 'hunchback' (so *OLD*). The same suffix is found in *sociennus* (Plaut. *Aul.* 659 *illi socienno tuo iam interstringam gulam*). *-enna* is attached as a nominal masculine suffix to *leuis* in the term *leuenna*, which is quoted by Gellius (16.7.11) from Laberius (80¹) (*atque item in mimo, qui Saturnalia inscriptus est, botulum pro farcimine appellat et hominem leuennam pro leui*).²²⁶ These various hybrids are in farce, mime and comedy. In popular stage performances they might go back to a time when there were Etruscan actors at Rome.²²⁷

There are in general two main types of hybrids in Latin. If a foreign root is given a Latin prefix or suffix, the 'hybridisation' is merely a reflection of the integration of the borrowed term into the language (e.g. *con-technor* at Plaut. *Pseud.* 1096). If on the other hand (as in some of the cases just discussed) a foreign suffix (or prefix) is attached to a Latin root, then the formation is the more striking in that it is a morpheme rather than a lexeme which has been borrowed, and has taken on some sort of productive life (if only in a limited sense) in the recipient language. It is less common for morphemes to be borrowed than words themselves. When the phenomenon turns up in Latin it is a sure sign of the close contacts between Latin speakers and the speakers of the other language. Most morpheme borrowing into Latin is from Greek (see 4.II; cf. V.3.5), but in the early Republican period Etruscan achieved an influence which only Greek was to match (and of course outstrip) at a later date.

III.3 *Greeks and Etruscans*

Greeks (for example slaves) are explicitly attested in Etruria. For a slave name of Greek origin (*murila* = Μύριλλα) in an Etruscan inscription, see *CIE* 10007 (third to second century BC) *cn. turce. murila. hercnas: θuflθas. cver:*²²⁸ A notable text is a short bilingual found on an Attic *skyphos* at Gravisca, published as *CIE* 10339 (also Rix (1991), Ta. 4.7) and described as the only specimen of a dedication with the god's name in Etruscan and that of the dedicator in Greek:²²⁹ *mi Turuns* Δειάκος τε. *Turan* is the Etruscan equivalent of Ἀφροδίτη,²³⁰ here in the genitive (= 'I (*mi*) (am) (the object of) . . . Turan').²³¹ The dedicatory formula *mi turuns* is

²²⁶ On these hybrids, see Breyer (1993: 255–6, 461–2, 463–4).
²²⁷ See Livy 7.2.4–13 on the story of the summoning in 364 BC of actors from Etruria to Rome, with Oakley's long discussion of the passage (1998: 40–71).
²²⁸ On the name, see De Simone (1970: 232–3).   ²²⁹ See Pandolfini (1983: 265), 143.
²³⁰ See Rix (1981: 105).   ²³¹ On the form *Turuns* see De Simone (1975: 167), 94.

common at Gravisca (cf. *CIE* 10312, 10335, 10391). Then follows the dedicator's name both in Greek characters and inflected as Greek (though τε is problematic). Here then is a case where a personal name inspires a switch of languages. The dedicator, though participating in the local culture, was holding on to his personal identity as symbolised by the language and script of his name. For a parallel to this type of language and alphabet mixing, see the Greek–Punic text *CIS* I.191 discussed below, v.5 (p. 220).

There are one or two other pieces of direct evidence for Greek speakers in Etruria apparently retaining a mark of their identity as expressed in the use of Greek (script and language). An inscription (see Pandolfini (1983: 257), 89) from Tarquinia has an apparent name in Greek characters, followed by a change of script: Ζηνω *cu.* A fragment (see Martelli (1981: 245), 16) has the Greek letters εστ.[232] And at the temple of Hera (Etr. *Uni*)[233] at Caere a vessel of secure Etruscan make is inscribed in Greek letters with the name HPA.[234] Nothing much can be made of evidence of this type.

III.4 *Etruscan and Italic*

It was of course not only Greeks, Etruscans and Latin speakers who were in contact in the early period. The Umbrian **kletra** 'litter' (see *Tab. Ig.* 3.13, 14, 24), a word with Indo-European cognates[235] and therefore not of Etruscan origin, occurs in Etruscan presumably as a result of borrowing from Umbrian.[236]

III.5 *Etruscan and Latin: anecdotal evidence*

There is a limited amount of anecdotal material in historical sources about Romans learning Etruscan and vice versa, but it is unreliable and may reflect the perceptions of a later age. Under the year 310 BC Livy tells the story of the brother of a consul who offered to go on a mission of reconnaissance in the impenetrable Ciminian forest because of his linguistic accomplishments. He had been educated at Caere *apud hospites* where he had learnt Etruscan *litterae* and also the language, and thus was equipped to travel into Etruscan territory. Livy (9.36.2–4) quotes

---

[232] The editor ad loc. (p. 246) gathers some evidence for Greeks in Etruria.
[233] See Rix (1981: 106).   [234] See Mengarelli (1936: 84).
[235] See Poultney (1959: 300), De Simone (1991: 134–5), Untermann (2000: 400–1).
[236] See Pfiffig (1969: 174).

unnamed sources to the effect that at the time Roman boys were trained in Etruscan 'letters', just as in his day they were trained in Greek: *tum ex iis qui aderant consulis frater (M. Fabium, Caesonem alii, C. Claudium quidam matre eadem qua consulem genitum, tradunt) speculatum se iturum professus breuique omnia certe adlaturum. Caere educatus apud hospites, Etruscis inde litteris eruditus erat linguamque Etruscam probe nouerat. habeo auctores uulgo tum Romanos pueros, sicut nunc Graecis, ita Etruscis litteris erudiri solitos; sed propius uero praecipuum aliquid fuisse in eo qui se tam audaci simulatione hostibus inmiscuerit.*[237] The reference to the learning of Etruscan has sometimes been taken at its face value.[238] The story may perhaps be related to the tenuous evidence that on one occasion six (?) sons of Roman (?) *principes* were sent to learn the Etruscan *disciplina* (see Cic. *Diu.*1.92, Val. Max. 1.1.1).[239] As for the tale that the Roman had learnt the Etruscan language at Caere, that at least accords with the notion of 'horizontal social mobility' in multilingual early Italy. It is possible that some members of the Roman nobility might have taken steps for cultural and political reasons to see that their offspring learnt some Etruscan. Their interest in the 'Etruscan discipline',[240] which was to last for centuries, might have acted as a particular spur to language learning in the early period.

It is of note that, despite the indifference of ancient historians in general and Romans in particular to problems of communication between peoples speaking different languages, this is not the only early Republican

[237] I have quoted the text of Walters and Conway (OCT), glossing over the difficulties raised by the first name. The following translation is that of the Loeb, modified at the start: 'Then one of those present, the brother of the consul – Marcus Fabius, or some say Caeso, others Gaius Claudius, a son of the same mother as the consul – offered to explore and return in a short time with definite information about everything. He had been educated at Caere in the house of family friends, and from this circumstance was learned in Etruscan writings and knew the Etruscan language well. I have authority for believing that in that age Roman boys were regularly wont to be schooled in Etruscan literature, as nowadays they are trained in Greek; but it seems more probable that this man possessed some exceptional qualification to induce him to venture amongst enemies in so daring a disguise.' The passage goes on to say that he was accompanied by a slave, brought up with him, who also knew the language.

[238] See e.g. Homeyer (1957: 435), Heurgon (1964: 238–9), De Simone (1988: 35).

[239] See Harris (1971: 9, with n. 7). He says (10 n.) of the passage of Cicero (the relevant words are *senatus tum cum florebat imperium decreuit ut de principum filiis sex* [MSS; usually changed to *X ex*: see Pease (1920–3), ad loc.] *singulis Etruriae populis in disciplinam traderentur)* that '[o]pinion is divided as to whether Cicero was referring to the sons of Etruscans or Romans; the latter is what the text seems to say'. But everything depends on how the crux is resolved. Rawson (1978: 139), without discussing the Latin, produces evidence for thinking that the *principes* concerned might have been Etruscan. Note in particular her remark that one 'of Cicero's proposals in the conservative and archaizing *de legibus* is that "Etruria principes disciplinam doceto" – clearly her own *principes*'. She also cites Tac. *Ann.* 11.15.1 *primoresque Etruriae sponte aut patrum Romanorum impulsu retinuisse scientiam et in familias propagasse.*

[240] For which see e.g. Rawson (1978).

story concerning Romano-Etruscan affairs in which spies or interpreters have a place. It is possible that because Etruscan (unlike, for example, Greek) was so inscrutable to Romans of later generations historians were induced to speculate about methods of communication in the earlier period.[241]

There is another such anecdote at Livy 10.4.8–10. The setting is the Etruscan town of Rusellae (302 BC). Some Etruscans, in hiding among ruined buildings, send out cattle as an enticement to the Romans. The narrative continues as follows (§8): *ad quam inlecebram cum moueretur nemo ab Romana statione, pastorum unus progressus sub ipsas munitiones inclamat alios, cunctanter ab ruinis uici pecus propellentes, quid cessarent cum per media castra Romana tuto agere possent. haec cum legato Caerites quidam interpretarentur et per omnes manipulos militum indignatio ingens esset nec tamen iniussu mouere auderent, iubet peritos linguae attendere animum, pastorum sermo agresti an urbano propior esset. cum referrent sonum linguae et corporum habitum et nitorem cultiora quam pastoralia . . .* [242] Here Caerites are again implicated; some of them, apparently serving in the Roman army, interpret the words of Etruscan *pastores* to the Roman *legatus*, and are able (on the instruction of the Roman commander) to deduce from the accents of the Etruscans that they were not true *agrestes* but *urbani* (and hence that an ambush was intended). It was in the late Republic that inhabitants of Rome (most notably Cicero among extant writers) became interested in the differences between 'urbane' and 'rustic' accents in *Latin* (see e.g. Cic. *De orat.* 3.43, Varro *Ling.* 5.97), and this anecdote seems to impose on early Etruscan speech the sort of model that was later applied in certain quarters to Latin. In both anecdotes Caere is presented as (indirectly) affording Romans access to the linguistic mysteries of Etruscan. There may be buried here some sort of later tendentious annalistic elaboration, its motivations obscure. In the second anecdote it is the Etruscans rather than Romans who are the language learners.

---

[241] Or it may simply be that Livy had a mild interest in communication in the early period. At 10.20.8 (under the year 296) he talks of spies who were *gnari Oscae linguae* being sent among the Samnite enemy to find out what was happening.

[242] 'But when this tempting bait failed to lure any of the Romans from their post, one of the shepherds came out under the very works and called out to the others, who were hesitating to drive out their flock from amongst the tumble-down buildings, asking why they were so slow, for they could safely drive them through the midst of the Roman camp. Some men from Caere interpreted these words to the lieutenant, and great was the indignation aroused through all the maniples of the soldiers; yet they dared not stir without the orders of their leader, who commanded those familiar with the language to mark whether the shepherds' speech were more like that of rustics or of city-folk. On their reporting that in accent, in carriage, and in complexion they were too refined for shepherds . . .' (Loeb).

III.6 Inscriptions

There are some 10,000 inscriptions in Etruscan, though their linguistic value is not as great as their bulk might imply, because they are usually extremely short and consist only of names. Nevertheless they do convey some information about the relationship between Latin and Etruscan in the period of Romanisation; names, as we have seen, may be an index to a person's sense of identity, and the names in many funerary inscriptions are of considerable interest. The small number of bilingual texts has been collected, with bibliography, by Benelli (1994).[243] Issues relating to bilingualism have been discussed by Rix (1956) and Kaimio (1975). Both of these discussions are of some length, and I here merely set out the main issues. The bilinguals come from one area, north-east Etruria, which was enfranchised in 90 BC.

I take as a starting point a bilingual published for the first time in 1954 (Benelli (1994), 3):

Cn. Laberius A.f.
Pom.
a. haprni. a
aχratinalisa.

This inscription was found on a funerary urn from Arezzo, dated to the second half of the first century BC. In the Latin version *Pom.* is the abbreviation of the Latin tribe name *Pomptina*. In the Etruscan the first *a.* is the abbreviation of the forename *aule*, and the second *a*, standing for the same name (*aules*), is the patronymic. In typical Etruscan manner the final word in the Etruscan version is the matronymic. The differences between the Latin and Etruscan are thus substantial. The only name that is the same in the two versions is that of the father. The Latin lacks the matronymic, and the Etruscan lacks the tribe name. In the bilinguals, as Rix (1956: 148) illustrates, the relationship between the two versions often seems to be similar to that seen here, in that there is not a total or obvious correspondence between the two parts. In such cases, if the inscription is on a gravestone which might have been intended for more than one person, there is inevitably some doubt whether the text is a genuine bilingual, because it is possible that two different persons are commemorated. The Arezzo urn therefore takes on some importance, because it is out of the question that it should have contained the remains of more than one person.[244] The discovery of the urn therefore allowed

---

[243] For some general remarks to do e.g. with dating, see Harris (1971: 175–7).
[244] See Rix (1956: 150).

the correct interpretation of the other texts, which can now be seen to be bilingual commemorations of single persons.

What are the implications of the divergences between the two versions of the inscription quoted? Each version gives information pertinent to the respective cultures. The deceased was a Roman citizen, as can be seen from his membership of a tribe and also from the presence of the filiation in the Latin.[245] Clearly when the citizenship was obtained Etruscans chose Roman names which might have little or no correspondence with their Etruscan names. The number of *praenomina* in particular available to Roman citizens was severely restricted,[246] and in many cases inevitably the Etruscan would be forced to take a forename which did not resemble his Etruscan name. Note, for example, Benelli (1994), 4:

velχe fulni velχes
ciarθialisa
Q. Folnius A.f. Pom.
Fuscus.

Here *velχe* has been replaced by *Quintus* in the nomenclature of the deceased, but in the nomenclature of the father a different Latin *praenomen* corresponds to the same Etruscan name.[247] *Folnius* on the other hand was probably a new Latin *nomen* based on the Etruscan name.[248]

The significance of such cases is that they show the referents hanging on to their Etruscan names even a generation or so after their families had obtained the citizenship. The retention of the name, as expressed in formal terms with patronymic and/or matronymic, also suggests at least a limited survival of the Etruscan language, with its different sound system (note the letters χ and θ), not to mention morphology. It also in more general terms implies an attempt on the part of the writers/referents to retain their original Etruscan identity even though their families had been Roman citizens for some time, and such an ideal was possibly associated with some degree of maintenance of the Etruscan language. The possession by individuals of double names (belonging to two languages) will be noted in other mixed, bilingual communities (see the sections on Punic and Aramaic later in this chapter, and also 3.v.2, n. 133), and is analogous, for example, to the inflection of a Greek name as Greek in

---

[245] But see Harris (1971: 176) for some reservations about the acceptability of arguing from the presence of a filiation in such material that the referent was a citizen.
[246] See Rix (1956: 156).
[247] See Rix (1956: 155) on the variable choice of Latin *praenomina* to replace particular Etruscan names.
[248] See Rix (1956: 162, 165).

a Latin text. A name not only serves to identify an individual within a crowd, but it may also by means of its formal characteristics convey background information about the person.

These are bilingual texts of a type already identified in the first chapter (VII.1), in which the versions are complementary. It is unlikely that the Etruscan version was provided primarily for the information of mono-lingual Etruscan speakers, as by the late Republic such will scarcely have existed. The inscription is intended for a bilingual readership,[249] with the different information given in the two versions determined by the funer-ary traditions of the two cultures. The presence of the Etruscan version will also have made a point to monolingual Latin readers, namely that the referent, though Romanised, had an older, non-Roman, identity.

The Etruscan versions of the bilinguals show different degrees of ac-commodation to Roman practice in conventions of naming,[250] and thus (potentially) different stages of a process of Romanisation which would ultimately result in the death of the Etruscan language itself.

First, whereas in the inscriptions cited so far the Etruscan version as well as the Latin has an expression of filiation, it was by no means obligatory in Etruscan to indicate the filiation in formal naming, and it has been calculated from an examination of about 500 inscriptions at Clusium that only about 2 inscriptions in 5 have it.[251] In some bilinguals in which the Latin version has a filiation (that is, a patronymic) the Etruscan does not. Note, for example, the following:

Q. Scribonius C. f
vl. zicu. (Benelli (1994), 10)

arθ. canzna
varnalisla
C. Caesius C. f. Varia
natus. (Benelli (1994), 12)

cuinte. sinu. arntnal
Q. Sentius L. f. Arria. natus. (Benelli (1994), 13)[252]

It would be going too far to suggest that the omission of the filia-tion was more natural than its expression in Etruscan, but it is certainly true to say that there was a choice available; and the omission in those

---

[249] I would not wish to imply that there was much active bilingualism; but there must have lingered on an ability to understand at least the elements of a funerary inscription in Etruscan.
[250] The discussion which follows draws particularly on Rix (1956).   [251] See Rix (1956: 154).
[252] For a list of further examples, see Rix (1956: 153). In the last two examples the last word of the Etruscan is a matronymic, not a filiation (in the conventional sense of that term).

bilingual inscriptions in which the Latin version has a filiation is perhaps a purist attempt to distance the Etruscan from the Latin and to keep it as free as possible from the influence of the formulaic structure of the other language, though other explanations could be suggested. It is tempting to see such inscriptions as reflecting a stage of language contact in which efforts were still being made to preserve the integrity of Etruscan, at least in the highly restricted domain of the funerary inscription. It should however be stressed that funerary inscriptions which have Etruscan alone vastly outnumber the bilinguals, as do those from the same area in Latin alone. The proportionately insignificant bilingual inscriptions seem to take us into the world of a small group of families which were sensitive to their new Romanness, but at the same time keen to express their Etruscan roots. The first inscription cited above (10) incidentally displays one of the ways in which Etruscans on acquisition of the citizenship went about selecting a Latin *gentilicium*. The Etruscan *zic-* is of a root meaning 'write';[253] a Latin name of equivalent root (*Scribonius*) has therefore been assumed. Alternatively an Etruscan name was sometimes mildly Latinised in form (as in the case of *Folnius* above).[254] Or again, in the inscription Benelli (1994), 8 (not quoted here), the relationship between the two names (*arntni/Arrius*) is merely one of assonance: the bearer has taken on a Latin name which sounds vaguely similar to his original name.[255]

Into a second category among the bilinguals may be placed one which has not only a filiation in the Etruscan version, but one comprising name + *clan* (= 'son') in direct imitation of the Latin structure genitive + *filius*. Note:

C. Cassius C. f.
Saturninus
v. cazi. c. clan. (Benelli (1956), 2)

This pattern is extremely unusual in Etruscan, whether in bilingual or monolingual epitaphs,[256] and its rarity leaves no doubt that it was Latin-influenced: *c. clan* is a rendering of *C. f.*[257] The inscription is late (*c.* AD 10–15),[258] and may well come from a period when the Etruscan language

---

[253] See Rix (1956: 168–9), Pfiffig (1969: 311).
[254] See Rix (1956: 162) on *Cafatius, Folnius* and *Scarpius*, which occur only in Etruria as *gentilicia*; these were Latinisations of Etruscan names.
[255] See the very detailed discussion of Rix (1956: 160–71) on the relationship between the Latin *gentilicia* of Etruscans and their original names.
[256] See Rix (1956: 155), citing a few other examples.   [257] See Rix (1956: 155).
[258] See Benelli (1994: 15).

was no longer living and fully understood. On this view the referent's Etruscan roots are no longer receiving secure and fluent linguistic expression, and an advanced stage of Romanisation is reflected.

Between the extremes represented by the two categories of filiation just seen there lie the bilingual inscriptions in which both versions have a filiation (whatever their other features), the Latin in Latin style, the Etruscan in Etruscan (i.e. without *clan*). Since the evidence of monolingual Etruscan inscriptions does not prove that the inclusion of such a filiation was alien to the funerary conventions of the language (see above for the figures from Clusium), these inscriptions, at least in so far as their filiations are concerned, do not have positive information to impart about the degree of Romanisation that they represent. It is the first and second categories distinguished above that are interesting for our purposes. Inscriptions of the intermediate type can be found at Benelli (1994), 3, 4, 5, 6, 7.

The above evidence concerns differing degrees of accommodation of Etruscan to Latin, and is consistent with Romanisation in progress, but accompanied by an attempt on the part of a few Etruscan families to maintain their old identity along with the new. Some inscriptions on the other hand allow us to observe developments from a different perspective, in that they display in their Latin versions imitation of an Etruscan pattern. The inscription Benelli (1994), 12, quoted above, has a matronymic in the Etruscan version but no filiation; the Etruscan version is free from any Latinate input. The Latin version has an alien element by normal Latin standards, namely a Latin rendering of the matronymic.[259] The lack of the filiation in the Etruscan and the presence of the matronymic in the Latin are complementary features, in that both imply a dominant position for Etruscan conventions: no concession is made to the Latin pattern in the Etruscan, but a concession is made to the Etruscan in the Latin version. Other bilinguals in which the Latin has a matronymic (though usually a filiation as well) are Benelli (1994), 7, 11, 13 (another case where the Etruscan has no filiation), 14, 15, 16, 17, 23. Moreover in Latin inscriptions also from Etruria (as distinct from bilinguals) the matronymic is not unusual: e.g. *CIE* 3498 *Aros Rufis Atinea natus*, 3501 *L. Rufis Cotonia natus*,[260] 3337, 3340, 3545. One variant on the typical pattern ablative + *natus* is also worth noting: e.g. *CIE* 3514

---

[259] See the remarks of Rix (1956: 154).

[260] Benelli (1994: 26) says of these inscriptions that they are in 'un latino fortemente etruschizzante'. It would be more accurate to say that their formulaic structure was of Etruscan type. On the name *Rufis* see Kaimio (1975: 153).

(Perusia) *C. Sulpicis C. f. Velthuriae gnatus*, 3622 (Perusia) *L. Pomponius L. f. Arsniae gnatus Plautus*, 3657 *C. Saluius Cassiae gna.* In these three cases the name of the mother is in the genitive, presumably because *natus* has been interpreted as a noun; the Etruscan construction in matronymics (genitive of the mother's name,[261] as for example at Benelli (1994), 7) might have favoured this reinterpretation of *natus*, which would normally be participial. It should be noted that the last example quoted (3657) has a feature seen above in the Etruscan version of Benelli (1994), 12, that is the presence of a matronymic but absence of the filiation. Outside Etruria in Latin funerary inscriptions such a pattern would be virtually unthinkable, and the inscription nicely illustrates the way in which substrate cultural influences may colour the highly formulaic language of epitaphs.

Of the bilinguals listed above in which the Latin version has a matronymic I single out two as special cases:

C. Treboni Q. f.
Gellia natus
cae
trepu. (Benelli (1994), 15)

ar mesi
Mesia Arun.
L. f. Tetia gnata. (Benelli (1995), 23)

Here the Latin versions have both filiation and matronymic, but the Etruscan versions neither. The Etruscan consists entirely of the names of the deceased. While it may be true to say that in some of the material collected in the previous paragraph the Latin version has in a sense been subordinated to the Etruscan, that is not so here. Latin alone in these cases is expressing information which traditionally would have been given in Etruscan in a funerary inscription in Etruria. Presumably the writer's knowledge of Etruscan did not go beyond an ability to write names in the old alphabet; it is likely that the epitaph was written at a time when Etruscan was virtually dead. The old custom of formally naming the deceased by means of a matronymic was remembered, but could no longer be effected in the Etruscan language (hence also the numerous purely Latin epitaphs from the area which have a matronymic: see above).

I summarise to this point. The Etruscan–Latin bilingual funerary inscriptions commemorating Etruscans who were Roman citizens and had no doubt been heavily Romanised display accommodation in their formulaic structure in both directions. One concession is made in Latin to

---

[261] See Pfiffig (1969: 197–8) on the 'gen. genealogicus'.

Etruscan (in that matronymics tend to be included). In Etruscan expressions of filiation have more than one form. Usually (if they are present at all) they consist of a plain genitive, but in a bilingual of Augustan date we have seen an Etruscan filiation which mimics exactly the Latin pattern (see further below on this phenomenon). During this period (roughly the first century BC) there were some families which were keen to give some sort of linguistic expression to their Etruscan roots while parading their Romanness, but the shift to Latin that was in progress is much in evidence, in the imitation of a Latin formula in Etruscan, in the use of Latin alone to convey traditional Etruscan information, in the survival of numerous purely Latin epitaphs in the region of Etruria, and in the use of Latin script to write Etruscan (on which see below). It should be stressed that what we have seen so far is the transfer of *formulae* from epitaphs in one language to those of the other; it is not the case in the material hitherto cited (but see further below) that either language influenced the other in any linguistic sense. The translation of formulae associated with one language into another was identified in the first chapter (VII.4.2) as a mark of written texts in bilingual societies; and the same phenomenon turned up earlier in this chapter (II.3) in Oscan areas of Italy.

I turn now to two complementary inscriptions:

l. pvrni l. f.
L. Purni L. f. (Benelli (1994), 31)

larza
capru
catlial
L. Capro
Catlial. (Benelli (1994), 33)

Both of these inscriptions involve transliterations. The first is throughout in the Latin language, with the italicised part transliterated into Etruscan script.[262] This is the only case extant of Latin transliterated into Etruscan (see Benelli (1994) on 31). The second inscription is in the Etruscan language, which in the second half of the text is transliterated into Latin script. The second version of the second inscription is mildly Latinised, in the form of the final vowel of the name *Capro*. The circumstances behind the two inscriptions are obscure, but it is probably true to say that the writers by means of such double versions were attempting to place

---

[262] The part in Latin script is written *dextrorsum*, that in Etruscan script (in the traditional way) *sinistrorsum*. On this inscription see Pfiffig (1969: 22).

the referents in two different cultures. The first writer almost certainly knew nothing of Etruscan other than the script, and resorted to that alone to give the referent a residual Etruscan identity. Etruscan script thus serves the same function as the Etruscan language in a genuine bilingual. The use of a distinctive script as a substitute for the language normally associated with that script at a time when the language was all but dead was mentioned in the previous chapter (VIII, p. 91).

Whereas the use of Etruscan script to write Latin (as in the first inscription above) is all but non-existent, the use of Latin script to write Etruscan is much more common (see e.g. *CIE* 1577, 1600). The general phenomenon (whereby Latin script is used for the writing of a language which traditionally had its own script or at least a script other than the Latin) will turn up again in this chapter (see also above, 1.VII.2.4), as for example in Gaul (in the writing of Gaulish) and Africa (in the writing of Punic). One instrument of Romanisation consisted of giving instruction in Latin literacy to provincials (in the western provinces), accompanied perhaps by some sort of suppression of local literacy practices. The old languages came for a period to be written in Latin script, before dying out. A nice example from Etruria can be seen in the pair of inscriptions at *CIE* 714 and 715. These commemorate two brothers from Montepulciano, one in Latin, the other in Etruscan:[263] 714 *ar. spedo thocerual clan*, 715 *vel. spedo Thoceronia natus*. Both texts are in Latin script, and that in Etruscan language has a matronymic consisting not of the plain genitive (for which see above, with n. 261), but of genitive + *clan* (a Latinate usage parallel in type to the use of *clan* in a filiation seen above). The Etruscan text seems to represent the last throes of the Etruscan language, with the traditional script abandoned and the formulaic language Latinised (by the inclusion of *clan*).[264]

Much of the onomastic material discussed so far has involved the transfer of formulaic structures from one language to the other. In bilingual communities we have elsewhere seen forms of code-switching in names, in the sense that a name will sometimes be inflected in the language not of the text as a whole, but in that to which the name originally belonged (see e.g. above, II.2, II.3). Similar phenomena are found in the inscriptions of Etruria: an inscription with Latin elements will sometimes retain a name

---

[263] See also Pfiffig (1969: 22).

[264] For some further remarks about the intrusion of Latin script and literacy practices into Etruscan, see Pfiffig (1969: 22). At *CIE* 280, for example, an Etruscan text in Etruscan script is written partly *dextrorsum* and partly *sinistrorsum*. Note the comment of the editor ad loc., 'sculptor haud dubie linguae etruscae ignarus'.

with an Etruscan inflection. Since such inscriptions are always short, to appearances they may be in a mixed language, part Latin, part Etruscan, but the reality is probably that the referent was Latinised and the epitaph conceived as being in the base language Latin, with the retention of an Etruscan morpheme serving as a residual claim to membership of Etruscan society.

An interesting case (from Clusium) is at *CIE* 2860: *Vel Tite Larisal f. Cainai natus.*[265] Here *Tite* is not put into the Latin nominative form, but has the Etruscan ending -*e* (which may however derive from the Latin vocative: see below, 4.v.4.4). Comparable examples are common in the Latin inscriptions of Etruria:[266] e.g. *CIE* 735 *L. Venete Vel f. Arria n.*, 989 *Vel Aule A. f.*, 1015 *C. Latinius C. f. Ladile*, 1538 *C. Odie C. f. Lartia gnatus*, 2822 *A. Tetie Philotimus*, 5593 *L. State L. f. anno [u]ixit LX, CIL* XI.2979 *Sex Gegani*[267] *P. f. Galle a. u. LXX.* The matronymic in 2860 above is of Etruscan type, but in the Latin language, with the name in the genitive rather than the ablative in the manner noted earlier. It is the filiation *Larisal* that is of primary interest here, because it retains the Etruscan genitive inflection -*al*,[268] dependent on the Latin *filius.* Kaimio (1975: 164) sees in this inscription the 'first stage of the Latinization process', but in fact the text is predominantly in Latin. Parallels can be found in other languages for the retention in the genitive of filiation of an inflection belonging not to the language of the text as a whole but to that of the culture to which the referent originally belonged (see above II.2 (p. 136) on Poccetti (1979), 204; see too 3.v.4).

Another similar 'mixed' text is *CIE* 729 *Annia C. f. Cetisnasa.*[269] *Cetisnasa* is an Etruscan genitive form of the name *Cetisna*, and in this case is a gamonymic.[270] The genitive is not made to hang on a Latin word (contrast *CIE* 728[271] *Annia N. f. Maxsimi uxor*, which displays a complete Latinisation of the Etruscan formula), and it thus differs from the filiation seen in the previous paragraph in that it is purely Etruscan. Alongside it however stands a filiation of the Latin type. In this text it is the gamonymic which stands out as an alien thing. However it is to be explained, it brings out the mixed culture of the family.

Just as names ending in -*e* are sometimes embedded in Latin texts (see above), so there are names ending in -*i* which at least sometimes may

---

[265] On various aspects of this inscription, see Kaimio (1975: 149, 164).
[266] See Kaimio (1975: 149–50).
[267] On this name, which also has an Etruscan inflection, see Kaimio (1969: 35).
[268] See Kaimio (1975: 157, 164).   [269] On which see Kaimio (1975: 168).
[270] See Kaimio (1975: 157).   [271] As read by Kaimio (1975: 169 n.1).

represent switches of code.[272] There are apparent cases, for example, in the bilinguals numbered 20 and 21 in Benelli's edition (1994):

20 *au fapi larθial*
A. Fabi. Iucnus

21 *aθ trepi θanasa*
Ar. Trebi. Histro.

The problems surrounding forms of this type are such that they cannot yield evidence fruitful to the issues under discussion here.

Sometimes a Latin text displays signs of poor competence in the language, and suggests that the writer's choice of Latin might have been made not because that language was his first tongue, but because he wanted to confer a Roman identity on the referent. A case in point from Clusium is the inscription *CIE* 2075 *L. Varius Oglinia f.* Kaimio remarks (1975: 167) that a 'speciality of Clusium is the use of *filius* in the metronymikon', but it is not that regional feature, interesting though it is, which concerns us here, so much as the case with which *filius* is accompanied. *Filius* + ablative would be an inconceivable construction in the speech/writing of a fluent native speaker of Latin. The motivation for the case here is however clear. The normal method of expressing the matronymic in Latin inscriptions in Etruria, as we have seen, comprised *(g)natus* + ablative. The writer of 2075 has inserted *filius* into that syntagm as a replacement for *natus*, apparently unaware that the ablatival construction with *filius* was unacceptable because, unlike *natus*, it was not a participle. Another bizarre use of the ablative lies in those matronymics which comprise name + ablative (of the mother's name), without *natus* or *filius*: e.g. *CIE* 3742 *C. Cascellius Cauthia.*[273] These may be seen as an attempt to imitate an Etruscan form of expression in Latin, but the construction is not an established Latin idiom. A more satisfactory Latinisation consists in the ablative of the name accompanied by *matre* (*CIE* 1586, 2592).[274]

Similar are one or two instances in Latin inscriptions of syntactic imitations of Etruscan. At *CIE* 713 *Vel Spedo Caesiae* the matronymic takes the form of a Latin genitive attached directly to the name without the support of *natus* or *filius*.[275] The construction was not natural for Latin.

---

[272] Names with this ending are however difficult to interpret, because the ending is also sometimes found in Latin Republican inscriptions from outside Etruria, sometimes perhaps as an abbreviation. The problem of interpretation has been studied by Kaimio (1969) (cf. also (1975: 152)).
[273] Further examples are at Kaimio (1975: 166).
[274] See Kaimio (1975: 166).   [275] See Kaimio (1975: 166).

On the other hand at *CIE* 3733 *Ursia A. f. Quarta Aconi* the genitive *Aconi* is a gamonymic, again obviously taken from Etruscan constructions of the type seen above in *Cetisnasa* (*CIE* 729).[276] Without a specifying head noun the function of the genitive is unclear. These various non-Latin constructions inflicted on 'Latin' inscriptions show the keenness of the writers to use that language; they were not *au fait* with standard Latin. I will return to some of these examples in the conclusion to this chapter in reference to regional variation (in Latin) determined by language contact (XIV.1).

III.7 The prophecy of Vegoia

The second prophecy of Vegoia in the gromatic texts has often been thought to contain genuine Etruscan material.[277] I quote the full text:

scias mare ex aethera remotum. cum autem Iuppiter terram Aetruriae sibi uindi-cauit, constituit iussitque metiri campos signarique agros. sciens hominum auari-tiam uel terrenum cupidinem, terminis omnia scita esse uoluit. quos quandoque quis ob auaritiam prope nouissimi octaui saeculi data sibi < . . . > homines malo dolo uiolabunt contingentque atque mouebunt. sed qui contigerit moueritque, possessionem promouendo suam, alterius minuendo, ob hoc scelus damnabitur a diis. si serui faciant, dominio mutabuntur in deterius. sed si conscientia do-minica fiet, caelerius domus extirpabitur, gensque eius omnis interiet. motores autem pessimis morbis et uulneribus afficientur membrisque suis debilitabuntur. tum etiam terra a tempestatibus uel turbinibus plerumque labe mouebitur. fruc-tus sepe ledentur decutienturque imbribus atque grandine, caniculis interient, robigine occidentur. multae dissensiones in populo. fieri haec scitote, cum talia scelera committuntur. propterea neque fallax neque bilinguis sis. disciplinam pone in corde tuo.

Harris (1971: 39) states that 'it is difficult to resist the idea that the pecu-liarities of its language result from a translation (and not from Greek [i.e. from Etruscan]) by a person with imperfect Latin', and this despite his acknowledgment (38) that not a single linguistic feature of the work has been convincingly attributed to Etruscan influence. It is important not to fall into the trap of explaining the odd vulgarism (such as the inflec-tion of *aethera* (ablative singular) and the spelling of *caelerius*)[278] as due to

---

[276] Further examples are cited by Kaimio (1975: 168).
[277] See Valvo (1988) for a full account of the issues, with extensive bibliography; also Harris (1971: 32–6). Harris (1971: 31–2) quotes the text from Lachmann (1848: 348–50).
[278] This last Harris (38) says is 'quite unknown elsewhere', but it could only be claimed to be unparalleled if one narrowly sought cases of the misspelling in this same word. Once the *ae* diphthong became a monophthong, the *e* was shortened and produced the same outcome

imperfect command of Latin. Imperfect command of a second language may manifest itself in forms of ignorance of the language (see above, 1.IX), but in no sense is the employment of current vulgarisms a mark of ignorance. Far from being imperfect Latin, the piece is stylish and literary, though it does contain the odd colloquialism. The author shows some concern for the rhythm of the clausula. Twice *atque* is placed before a consonant in the clausula in Ciceronian manner, once apparently to achieve an artificial heroic clausula (*atque mouebunt*). The same rhythm is found in *afficientur, alterius minuendo*, and also in *damnabitur a diis*, if, as is likely, the last word were pronounced as a monosyllable; the last two examples are in successive clausulae. In line 5 *mouebunt* is linked to *contingent* by *atque*, but in the next clause the same two verbs are linked by *-que* (*contigerit moueritque*), perhaps not simply as a means of variation, but to achieve the highly favoured double trochee. The literary pretensions of the piece are illustrated by the fact that there is only a single instance of the mundane connective *et*: *-que* and *atque* are used throughout (nine times in all). Also worth noting is the frequency of passive verbs, particularly in the second half of the piece, where, from the sentence beginning *si serui faciant*, passives outnumber actives by 11:6. The artistry of the writer can be seen in the variation of active with passive in two parallel clauses (*si serui faciant, sed si conscientia dominica fiet*). In *promouendo suam, alterius minuendo* a double cretic clausula is followed (as we saw) by a heroic clausula, and there is also a chiastic word order. The expression *terrenum cupidinem*, in which the adjective has the function of an objective genitive (= *terrae cupido*, 'desire for land'), may be compared with *conscientia dominica*, 'with the master's knowledge', where *dominica* plays the part of a *subjective* genitive. These two examples show an awareness of the potentialities of such adjectives as substitutes for different types of genitive, and are not the work of a writer with imperfect Latin. Harris (1971: 39) notes that *dominicus* occurs once in comedy under the late Republic (Afran. 282 *gannire ad aurem numquam didici dominicam*; the usual early adjective was *erilis*), but there the adjective has the role of a *possessive* genitive. More to the

---

in the Romance languages as the CL short *e* (see above, 1.VII.2.3 on βετρανε in the receipt of Aeschines). From the time when this shortening had been achieved, the way was open for the hypercorrect use of the diphthong spelling to express short *e*. It is moreover unacceptable to make the assumption that a banal misspelling of this kind was the work of the writer of the Latin prophecy rather than of a medieval scribe. It should further be noted that, even if the spelling were due to the original writer rather than a later scribe, the hypercorrect use of *ae* for short *e* is overwhelmingly of imperial date. When *ae* changed into a monophthong, it went through several stages (long open *e* followed by short open *ẹ*), and it is out of the question that a hypercorrect representation of the final outcome (i.e. *short* open *ẹ*) could be used to establish an *early* date for the piece. See in general R. Coleman (1971) on the development of *ae*.

point are the extensive attestations of *dominicus* for the genitive *domini* in later (Christian) Latin in various other roles, including that of subjective genitive.[279] At *TLL* v.1.1888.83ff. more than two columns of examples of *dominicus* as equivalent to a subjective genitive are cited, dating from Tertullian onwards.[280] In non-Christian Latin the earliest example of the usage is Neronian (Petron. 28.7 *sine dominico iussu*); I have not been able to find clearcut examples other than this before the time of Tertullian. Harris (1971: 38) states that '*terrenus cupido* for "desire for land" is quite unparelleled, but is the sort of difficulty that is covered by the translation hypothesis'. In fact the use of *terrenus* functioning as an equivalent of the objective genitive is not a difficulty, and is far from unparalleled, but it does not seem to turn up until the imperial period. There is an example in the Vulgate (*Sap.* 9.15 *deprimit* **terrena inhabitatio** *sensum multa cogitantem*), and another in [Apuleius]: *Asclepius* 9 *ut et* **terrenum cultum** *et diuinitatis posset habere dilectum*. The usage can be illustrated from late Christian Latin: e.g. Caesarius of Arles, *Serm.* 1.9 *timeo tamen, ne forte sit magis praesumptio, si aliqui pro praeparandis conuiuiis, quam pro dandis eleemosynis,* **terrenae culturae** *se occupare uideantur*.[281] Far from being suggestive of crude translationese, the use of an adjective for an objective genitive represents stylish Latinity of a type to which E. Löfstedt devoted a whole chapter (VII) of the first volume of *Syntactica*.

Harris (1971: 37) dates the piece to the period 150–88 BC.[282] and others have also assigned it relatively early dates,[283] but it may not be early at all. The noun *motor* is rare and first attested in Martial. An interesting item of Latinity is to be found in the clause *dominio mutabuntur in deterius*, '(slaves) will be put into a worse situation by their masters' power'. The *TLL* (v.1.1893.1) makes the acute observation that *dominium* here is virtually equivalent to *domini*, and that is indeed the implication of the usage: if slaves act in a certain way, they will be punished by their *masters*. The writer of the *TLL* article had in mind the fact that various abstracts, including for present purposes a number denoting power or subservience

---

[279] See the discussion of E. Löfstedt (1911: 76–8), quoting such expressions as *praecepta dominica, dominica passio, dominica repromissio, tactus dominicus, dominicus aduentus* from late Latin; also id. (1956: I, 117–19).

[280] For the use of the word as equivalent to an objective genitive (again from Tertullian onwards), see *TLL* v.1.1890.73ff.

[281] I have collected these examples from chance reading and have not attempted to be systematic. A full survey of the distribution of this use of *terrenus* would be needed in a serious discussion of the date of the prophecy.

[282] See also Rawson (1978: 139 n. 55).

[283] For a full discussion of opinions, see Valvo (1988: 19–53). Valvo inclines to an early first century date (BC) (see e.g. 135). See also MacBain (1982: 76–7).

(e.g. *regnum, imperium, principium, dominatio, ministerium, obsequium*), tended to be personalised, either in the singular as collectives (thus e.g. *ministerium* = *ministri*, from Livy onwards and often in later Latin;[284] *dominium* here may be compared with the use of *dominatio* from Florus onwards),[285] or in the plural of collections of individuals (e.g. Stat. *Theb.* 12.380 *etsi regna uetant*), from which developed a singular usage designating a single person. In the case of the words listed above these developments take place to an overwhelming extent in the imperial period;[286] it is only *imperium* which can be traced back into the Republic, where it occurs in the late works of Cicero.[287]

I conclude that the text cannot be taken as the work of an imperfect speaker of Latin, and that the linguistic evidence provides no grounds for seeing an Etruscan original behind the Latin text. The piece on linguistic grounds appears to be imperial, and has no place in a discussion of Latin–Etruscan bilingualism.

III.8 Conclusions

As Etruria was Romanised and its inhabitants acquired the citizenship, there was a shift to Latin. We can merely glimpse that shift in progress through funerary inscriptions. At one extreme there are texts purely in Etruscan, and at the other those purely in Latin. The transitional stage shows up in various ways. Some Etruscan inscriptions, as we saw, are in Latin script, and that hints at a decline in levels of literacy in the native script. Other epitaphs are bilingual, a reflection of their writers' sense of a double identity. Some 'Etruscan' epitaphs consist merely of the name of the deceased, without any inflected material such as filiations or matronymics. These were not necessarily written by locals still fluent in the old language: possibly all that lingers is a knowledge of the script. Some Latin texts have bits and pieces of Etruscan morphology, and some Etruscan texts have Latinate features (such as a filiation with *clan*). The Etruscan morphemes in Latin texts suggest that when the language shift had taken place some Etruscans held on to the old Etruscan morphology of their original names as a mark of identity; but they need not have used Etruscan in any other domain. The intrusion of *clan* into Etruscan filiations is in overt imitation of the Latin formula. The

---

[284] See Hofmann and Szantyr (1965: 747).   [285] See Hofmann and Szantyr (1965: 747).
[286] There is an extensive discussion of the matter in Hofmann and Szantyr (1965: 747–9), with bibliography.
[287] See *TLL* VII.1.581.31 ff.

intrusion of matronymics into Latin epitaphs certainly reflects imitation of a traditional Etruscan formula; but some of those who included the matronymic in the Latin version of bilinguals were apparently unable to write its equivalent in Etruscan, and that is a nice reflection of language death on the one hand, and, simultaneously, of some sort of cultural continuity on the other.

I list various general points which will come up later in different contexts:

(1) In a period of language shift, the target (i.e. new) language may be imperfectly learnt. Imperfect learning, if institutionalised, may produce a distinctive local form of the target language. Such imperfect learning was seen in the use of the ablative with *filius*, which for a period might have constituted a regionalism in the Latin of Etruria. The plain ablative of the matronymic was also a construction with no place in Latin. The plain genitive in a matronymic represents interference in L2 from L1.

(2) But L2 also influences L1, as in the use of *clan* in a filiation. The phenomenon may on one interpretation be classed as borrowing or imitation. Borrowing is often a feature of stable bilingualism rather than of language shift preceding language death, but here it seems to be found during a period of shift. But there is another way of looking at this example. From an historical perspective the writer's 'first' language would have to be regarded as Etruscan, because no non-Etruscan would aspire to use Etruscan in a funerary inscription. But in reality the writer/referent might have been born into a Latin-speaking environment, with his 'Etruscan' origin merely a memory. On this view his first language might in a practical sense have been Latin, and his knowledge of Etruscan highly imperfect. Thus it might be more reasonable to class the usage as interference in Etruscan (L2) from Latin (L1), though that 'interference' affects the formulaic structure of epitaphs and not the Etruscan language itself.

(3) Names are worthy of study at a time of language shift. As they pass to a new language and culture speakers may acquire new names, translated for example from their original language into the new (cf. *Scribonius* above), or chosen because their form is reminiscent of the original. But they may be unhappy about what is in effect the loss of an aspect of their identity. The old names may therefore be retained for a period alongside the new, and in the new language these may even be given their original morphology. The question arises how one should classify the inflecting in L2 of a name belonging to L1 with the morphemes of L1 rather than of the language being used. I have called the practice 'code-switching', but see further below, pp. 376, 415, 478.

(4) In various parts of the Empire peoples undergoing Romanisation were taught Latin script. The writing of the old language in the new script represents a break with the culture of the past, and may reflect the suppression of the means by which training in the old literacy was imparted. We will see hints from Gaul and Africa that imply the use by the Romans of instruction in Latin literacy as a form of Romanisation. Which comes first in a language shift, loss of the original language or loss of the original script? Given the survival in different parts of the Empire of vernacular languages written in Latin script, it would seem that some knowledge of the original languages lingered on after the scripts had been abandoned. The pair of inscriptions cited earlier commemorating two brothers, one text in Etruscan, the other in Latin, but both in Latin script, hints at the sequence of events. First the Etruscan script is lost, and then the language. The one Latin inscription seen earlier written in Etruscan script is a freakish case. The writer had managed to learn some Etruscan letters, but it is fairly certain that he did not know the language, because he would otherwise have composed a genuine bilingual text, given that he went to the trouble of using Latin script as well in the inscription.

IV CELTIC (GAULISH)

IV.1 Introduction: loan-words and interpreters

The long-standing contacts between Latin and Celtic (Gaulish) speakers, particularly in Gallia Cisalpina, are bound to have generated forms of bilingualism at differing social levels. Latin had many loan-words from Gaulish, some transferred at an early period (e.g. *raeda, esseda, carrus*: see further Quint. 1.5.57), others, such as Catullus' *ploxenum* (97.6; cf. Quint. 1.5.8), and items such as *ceruesa, bracis* and *tossea* at Vindolanda (see 4.v.2), borrowed at a later date. Cicero tells us (*Brut.* 171) that in the Latin of Cisalpine Gaul words not current in the city could be heard, and he must be referring to Gaulish words which had been picked up by Latin speakers in the area (see 4.v.2). Latin took a considerable number of terms to do with transport and horsemanship from Celtic,[288] a reflection of Gaulish expertise in such matters and of trading contacts between Gauls and Latin speakers. The goddess of horsemen, Epona, was of Gaulish origin. Even in the late period Latin was still acquiring Celtic borrowings

---

[288] Palmer (1954: 53) cites *benna, couinnus, carpentum, petorritum* and *ueredus* apart from those listed above.

belonging to the same semantic area (e.g. *carruca, burdo*).[289] Nor is this the only semantic field represented in Gaulish borrowings into Latin.[290] A Gaulish loan-word appears in Latin literature as early as Ennius (*ambactus*, at Paul. Fest. p. 4 L., *Ann.* 610 Sk.: *ambactus apud Ennium lingua Gallica seruus appellatur*). Skutsch (1985: 739) cites Caes. *Gall.* 6.15.2, where the social structure of the Gauls is commented on: *(equitum) ut quisque est genere copiisque amplissimus, ita plurimos circum se ambactos clientesque habet*. Skutsch remarks: 'One might guess that Ennius used the word in a similar context.' This was not an integrated loan-word, but a term which retained an exotic flavour and was only used in reference to Gallic society. The fact that it was picked up so early testifies to the length of the contact between speakers of the two languages, and to an ethnological curiosity on the part of the Romans which was favourable to the reception of foreign terms.

Given the subordinate status of Gaul for part of the historical period, and the fact that language death was to occur in much of the Gallic territory, there would have been greater pressure on Gauls to learn Latin than on Latin speakers to learn Gaulish, though in border regions, as around the Po, bilingualism might have been commonplace. Certainly it is possible to cite evidence for the acquisition of Latin by Gauls. The most important evidence of this type comes from the pottery at La Graufesenque in southern Gaul, to which a separate chapter (7) is devoted. Here I concentrate on miscellaneous bits and pieces of primary and secondary evidence.

Caesar had interpreters with him during his campaigns in Gaul (*Gall.* 1.19.3). Their nationality is not specified, but they are bound to have been locals who had learnt some Latin. He was also able on a special occasion to make use of the interpreting ability of a Gallic chieftain (*Gall.* 1.19.3: see below, 7.II). Caesar's use of Greek (*Gall.* 5.48.4) in a letter to Q. Cicero as a form of coding (see 3.III.3) implies a fear that Gauls might be able to understand an epistle written in Latin if it were intercepted.

IV.2 Gaulish and bilingual texts

Latin–Gaulish bilingualism on the part of Gauls is attested by a small group of inscriptions from Italy which are either bilingual or have an

---

[289] On the second, see Adams (1993).

[290] For an extensive collection of Celtic terms borrowed by Latin, see Lambert (1995: 200–3), and other words could be added (see below, IV.4 for example, on Marcellus of Bordeaux). Lambert also has a long account (1995: 185–200) of Gaulish terms surviving in French, at least some of which (as he brings out) had already entered Latin.

obvious bilingual dimension. I consider first an inscription (possibly funerary) in Gaulish from S. Bernadino di Briona (Novara), which was discovered in 1859 and is published (e.g.) by Lejeune (1988: 19–20) and by Lambert (1995: 72), with full commentary in each case:

TANOTALIKNOI
KUITOS
LEKATOS
ANOKOPOKIOS
SETUPOKIOS
ESANEKOTI
ANAREUIŠEOS
TANOTALOS
KARNITUS

(a)]N[-]K[–]ESASOIOIKAN[-]
(b) TAKOS.TOUTAS.

The text is in a script inherited from Lepontic epigraphy, a variety of the north Etruscan alphabet called the 'alphabet of Lugarno'.[291] I translate the main part of the inscription, after Lambert (1995: 72): 'The sons of Dannotalos, Quintus the legate, Andocombogios, Setubogios, and (the sons) of Essandecot(t)os, Andareuiseos, Dannotalos, have erected (this mound?).' The name in the first line has the Celtic patronymic suffix *-ikno-*.[292] The last word of the main text (*karnitus*) is a third-person plural preterite verb possibly derived from a Celtic noun **karno-* 'heap of stones' (see also the inscription from Todi, below).[293] But what stands out for our purposes is the Latin name of the first-named son, *Quintus*, and his designation as *legatus*. We saw earlier (III.6) an Etruscan who had 'translated' his original name into Latin (*Scribonius*), and in a later chapter we will see that at the Gaulish pottery of La Graufesenque various Celtic names derived from ordinals stand side by side with their Latin equivalents (e.g. *Tritos* alongside *Tertius*). Quintus, who had clearly rendered some service to the Romans (hence his Latin title),[294] had abandoned his native name and adopted a Romanised identity. He is likely to have been bilingual. The change of name is a sure sign of a desire to be seen as assimilated to a different culture.

From Todi and Vercelli there are bilingual inscriptions in Latin and Gaulish:

---

[291] See Lambert (1995: 71).   [292] See Lambert (1995: 73).
[293] See Lejeune (1988: 21).   [294] See the discussion of Lejeune (1988: 21–2).

(1) Todi

Version A (notation of Lejeune, alluding to ARTUAŠ):
(Latin)   [ATEGNATEI · DRV]
             [TEI · F · . . . . . .]
             [COI]SIS
             DRVTEI · F · FRATER
             EIVS
             MINIMVS · LOCAV
             IT · ET · STATVIT
(The tomb) of Ategnatos son of Drutos, his youngest brother, Coisis son of
Drutos, placed and set up.

(Gaulish)   ATEKNATI · TRUT
             IKNI · KARNITU
             ARTUAŠ KOISIS · T-
             RUTIKNOS
Coisis son of Drutos has erected the tomb of Ategnatos son of Drutos.

Version L(OKAN):
(Latin)   [ATEGNATI]
             [DRVT]I[·] F[· . . .]
             [C]OISIS [·] DRVTI · F
             [F]RATER · EIVS
             [M]INIMVS · LOCAV[I]<T>
             [ST]ATVITQV<E>
(Tomb of Ategnatus) son (of Drutus) Coisis son of Drutus, his youngest brother,
placed and set up.

(Gaulish)   [AT]EKNATI TRUTI[K]NI
             [KAR]NITU · LOKAN · KO[I]SIS
             [TR]UTIKNOS
Coisis son of Drutos has erected the tomb of Ategnatos son of Drutos.

Todi is in Umbria. This text (found in 1839) is on a stele, both
faces of which for some reason[295] are inscribed with bilingual funerary
inscriptions. These are virtually the same on the two faces, with one or
two discrepancies. The designation of the burial place/type differs in the
two Gaulish versions (ARTUAŠ, LOKAN),[296] and might have differed
in the Latin versions as well, but the start of the Latin has not survived

---

[295] For some speculations, see Lejeune (1988: 43–4).
[296] On these two terms, see Lejeune (1988: 43–4, 49).

intact.[297] The Latin versions are fuller, and are given pride of place over the Celtic, perhaps in deference to the expected readership. The potential significance of the ordering of the versions in a bilingual inscription should always be considered. Note for example the remarks of Levick (1995: 398) in a different context: 'of all the grave inscriptions and private dedications in Asia Minor that offer two versions, an infinitesimal number put the Greek version above the Latin. Inscribers knew the superior status of Latin and, like governors and city councils, normally put it first.' Lejeune's view (1988: 49) that the Latin of the above inscription is not the original version because 'pour les informations communes aux deux versions, le latin traduit le celtique' is unconvincing. Either could be interpreted as a translation of the other, or each could have been composed separately. How Celts came to have established themselves in Umbria, far from Celtic territory, is a mystery. Are they perhaps to be taken as traders who had come there and stayed on, becoming up to a point assimilated?[298] Whatever the case, the use of Gaulish in a public monument in an area in which that language would scarcely have been understood is reminiscent of the use of Palmyrene by Barates in South Shields (see above I.VII.1 and below VII.2). The Celtic text can be seen either as a form of exhibitionism (cultural pride), intended to impress non-Celtic speakers by its very alienness, or as an attempt by the families to hold on to a symbol of their ethnic identity, in disregard of what outsiders might think.

(2) Vercelli (Lejeune (1988: 31, 37), Lambert (1995: 76–7)):

(Latin)   FINIS
            CAMPO · QVEM
            DEDIT · ACISIVS
            ARGANTOCOMATER
            ECVS · COMVNEM
            DEIS · ET · HOMINIB
            VS · ITAVTILAPIDES
            IIII · STATVTISVNT

Delimitation of the space which A. A. has given as common to gods and men, (a space defined) in such a way as the four stones have been placed.

(Gaulish)   AKISIOS · ARKATOKO{K}
            MATEREKOS · TO[-]O
            KOT[-A]TOS TEUOΨ
            TONI[O]N EU

---

[297] So Lejeune (1988: 43).   [298] See the discussion of Lambert (1995: 76).

A. A. (has given) the ATOS (?) belonging to gods and men; [EU possibly represents the Latin *ex uoto*].[299]

This inscription records the consecration of a sacred place, apparently in keeping with a Celtic practice.[300] The date is uncertain, though Lejeune (1988: 25) speaks of any period from the time of the Gracchi to the end of the Republic as *a priori* possible. The Latin text is rather more detailed than the Gaulish, and it is placed first. We have already seen (1.VII.1) a trilingual inscription from Palmyra in which the Aramaic version is fuller than the Greek, and the Greek fuller than the Latin. It was argued that the writer knew little Latin, and therefore placed the Latin version last and was able to give it less detail than the other versions. It would not do though to argue on that analogy that the present Gaulish text is merely an abbreviated translation of the Latin, perhaps made at a time when Gaulish was hardly remembered.[301] In contrast to the *legatus* Quintus discussed above, the dedicator has retained a Gaulish name and designation (*Argantocomaterecus* in the Latin text)[302] even when using Latin. Moreoever Lejeune (1988: 36) has brilliantly explained TEUOΨTONION as a dvandva compound, < *devo-ghdonioi*, in the genitive plural, = 'of gods and men'. The Latin expression *comunem deis et hominibus*, which is perfectly idiomatic Latin, is rather more long-winded than the Gaulish merely because Latin made little use of such compounds; it should not be interpreted as crude or as an indication that the Latin version was in any sense secondary to the Gaulish. Lejeune (1988: 34) states: 'Il est clair en effet qu'à Verceil le texte d'origine n'avait rien de romain.' But there is an assumption here that of the two versions of a bilingual inscription one must be primary and the other a translation of it. The above two texts have the appearance of idiomatic or complementary bilinguals, which need not have been put together by a wholesale act of translation in one direction or the other (see in general 1.VII.1, and particularly point (7) in the conclusion to that section; idiomatic bilinguals will come up throughout the present chapter). The composer has given some additional information in the Latin version, and there is a good reason why this should have been done. The area was Latin-speaking, and the dedicator might have felt the need to draw the attention of non-Celtic passers-by with no knowledge of Celtic practices to the sacred nature of the spot, and its extent, as a means of safeguarding the place. Celtic is

[299] See Lambert (1995: 78).   [300] See Lejeune (1988: 31–2), Lambert (1995: 79).
[301] See the telling discussion of Lejeune (1988: 33–4) on this point.
[302] On the problematical interpretation of this term (which is however undoubtedly Celtic), see Lejeune (1988: 33), Lambert (1995: 78).

included as well because a Celtic religious observance was at issue, and it is reasonable to assume that Celts who had found their way into Latin territory would have been keen to maintain their language in connection with inherited cults (see further below, IV.5, V.4, and VII.2 on the maintenance by Palmyrenes at Rome of Palmyrene Aramaic in the context of their native cults). The Gaulish compound may have been traditional in such a context.

IV.3 Interference from Gaulish

I next consider some evidence of different kinds for the interaction of Gaulish and Latin. In a Vindolanda writing tablet there is a bizarre term *souxtum*, the reading of which is absolutely clear (*Tab. Vind.* II.301.3):

souxtum saturnalicium
(asses) iiii aut sexs rogo frater
explices.

The spelling seems to be Celticised. The inherited consonant cluster *pt* became *xt* in Gaulish, as in *sextametos* ('seventh') at La Graufesenque (cf. Lat. *septimus*) (see 4.V.1.3). Gaulish (unlike Latin) retained to some extent the digraph *ou*.[303] If therefore two conversions are made, *suptum* emerges (= *sumptum*, with a banal omission of the nasal before a stop).[304] The sense (of Saturnalian contributions) is ideal in the context. It is to be assumed that a Celt Celticised his pronunciation of the Latin word, and represented the pronunciation in Gaulish manner with the typical Gaulish consonant cluster and digraph. If this is accepted we have evidence for a Gaul serving in the Roman army and now using Latin, but with some interference from his first language. There are various Celtic terms in the Vindolanda tablets (see 4.V.2, V.2.6).

There is possibly indirect evidence of interference in Latin and/or Greek from Gaulish to be extracted from Virg., *Cat.* 2. I quote the poem in full:

> Corinthiorum amator iste uerborum,
> iste, iste rhetor, † namque quatenus † totus
> Thucydides, tyrannus Atticae febris,
> tau Gallicum, min et sphin ut male illisit,[305]
> ita omni ista uerba miscuit fratri.

---

[303] See Lambert (1995: 42).   [304] For this interpretation, see Adams (1995a: 93–4), id. (1996).
[305] *et male illisit* is obelised by M. Winterbottom in his edition of Quint. 8.3.28.

The subject of the poem was T. Annius Cimber, as emerges from Quint. 8.3.28–9. He was a rhetorician and a native of Marseilles, whose father had a Greek name (Cic. *Phil.* 11.14) and was no doubt a freedman. He was apparently (in Greek) an imitator of Thucydides and a lover of archaisms (note *min* and *sphin* in the second last line),[306] and the same charge was also made against his Latin style (see the epigram of Sallust quoted by Quint. 8.3.29, and also Suet. *Aug.* 86.3). Marseilles was a trilingual city, in Greek, Latin and Gaulish (see Varro *apud* Isid. *Etym.* 15.1.63), and it can be deduced from the evidence so far cited that Cimber declaimed in both Greek and Latin (like various other rhetoricians), in a distinctive style.[307]

The allusion to *tau Gallicum* would seem to imply that he had some sort of Gaulish pronunciation of a phoneme which might loosely be referred to as *t*. Gaulish writing has a variety of distinctive graphemes (e.g. θ, θθ, Đ)[308] which presumably represented the 'Gallic *tau*', but the phonetics remain obscure.[309] It has been noted that the poem has a striking accumulation of instances of *iste*.[310] Since Continental Celtic seems to have had the same demonstrative *iste*,[311] Cimber may have had a distinctive 'Gallic' pronunciation of the central consonant cluster of the Latin word.[312] It is possible that he was trilingual, and that Gaulish had coloured his Greek and Latin (?) speech in one noticeable way.[313] Or could it simply be that he had a regional accent in Latin and/or Greek, without necessarily speaking Gaulish? On either interpretation Gaulish would seem to have been perceived by the poet as having some effect, direct or indirect, on Latin and/or Greek in this trilingual community.

IV.4 Marcellus of Bordeaux

Marcellus of Bordeaux preserves in his medical work a good deal of material relevant to language contact in Gaul in the later period. This material, consisting partly of plant names and partly of medico-magical

---

[306] See Westendorp Boerma (1949: 37) for some Greek epigrams which have parallels to the use of *min* and *sphin* here. The passage is highly literary.

[307] See Westendorp Boerma (1949: 25).

[308] See e.g. Evans (1967: 410–20), Meid (1983: 1031 n. 33), id. (1996: 17), Eska (1998: 115).

[309] See Frank (1935), Watkins (1955: 15), Evans (1967: 410–20), Eska (1998), Katz (2000: 343–4).

[310] See Frank (1935), Watkins (1955).   [311] See Eska (1989), id. (1991).

[312] See Frank (1935), Watkins (1955).

[313] Killeen (1974) takes a completely different view of the matter. He suggests (58) that 'the expression *tau Gallicum* was a derisory way of designating an atticizing speaker's imitation of the Attic δασύτης' (i.e. the speaker had an aspirated voiceless dental stop in Greek, unlike most Latin speakers). See further along similar lines O'Sullivan (1986). But what is the point of *Gallicum*?

incantations and the like, has recently been investigated by Meid (1996), to whom I am indebted in this section.

Frequently a plant is named in Latin, and then its Gaulish name is given, as at 3.9 *trifolium herbam quae Gallice dicitur* **uisumarus** *aqua frigida macerato*.[314] See further e.g. the comments on *odocos* (7.13, with Meid (1996: 13–14; the page references which follow in brackets are to Meid), *vernetus* (9.131, pp. 14–16), *blutthagio* (10.132, pp. 17–18), *gigarus* (10.58, pp. 18–19), *gilarus* (11.10, p. 19), *calliomarcus* (16.101, pp. 19–22), *calocatanos* (20.68, pp. 22–3), *ratis* (25.87, pp. 23–4), *bricumus* (26.41, pp. 24–5), *halus* (31.29, pp. 25–9), *baditis* (33.63, pp. 29–30). There are two ways of interpreting this evidence. Either the words listed were in use in Gaulish itself at the time of Marcellus or his source(s), in which case we would have evidence for the continued vitality of Gaulish under the Empire;[315] or Marcellus merely recognised the Celtic terms as of non-Latin origin and loosely described them as 'Gaulish', without necessarily meaning that he had heard them used in the Gaulish language itself. On this second interpretation such words (or some of them) would have been in use in the local Latin, and would thus constitute regionalisms in Gallic Latin determined originally by contact between Celtic and Latin speakers. A good deal will be said in this book about vernacular words entering Latin around the margins of the Empire and no doubt giving local varieties of the language a regional flavour (see 4.V.2). I introduce the topic here by citing a few terms from Marcellus which belong unambiguously to this category of Gallic Latin regionalisms.

Note first 36.51 *adpones herbam, quae in aquae iugis decursu nascitur, quam* **Latine berulam**, *Graece cardaminen uocant*. Berula ('cress') is a Celtic term (MIr. *biror*, Welsh *berwr*),[316] but Marcellus describes it as Latin, a clear indication that it had entered Gallic Latin and that its origin had been forgotten. This is confirmed by its survival in Gallo-Romance (Fr. *berle*, OProv. *berla*; also Sp. *berro*).[317] At 16.33 (*salis quantum intra palmam tenere potest qui tussiet in potionem ceruisae aut* **curmi** *mittat et calidum bibat*) there is an example of a Celtic word for 'beer', *curmi*;[318] the term is also found on one of the so-called Gallo-Latin 'spindle whorls' to which we will come (IV.5). Meid notes (1996: 32) that unusually Marcellus does not describe the word as Gallic, but embeds it without comment in the text: that is

---

[314] See Meid (1996: 10–13).
[315] Gaulish certainly lasted on into the Empire, at least in country districts. Further *testimonia* will be discussed in a later chapter (7 n. 8).
[316] See Meid (1996: 35).   [317] See *REW* 1054, and particularly *FEW* I.338–9.
[318] See Meid (1996: 32–4); cf. OIr. *cuirm*, Welsh *cwrw*.

because it had been borrowed by the regional form of Latin. Also of note in the same passage is a second Celtic word for 'beer', *ceruisa*,[319] which had certainly been taken over into Gallic Latin, as we will see below; Marcellus' silence about its origin can safely be taken to mean that he thought of it as Latin, because we have other evidence for its currency in that language. The term *gaitano* at 8.27 (*dolorem oculorum ut anno integro non patiaris, cum primum cerasia erunt idonea esui, id est quasi matura, de tribus cerasiis lapillos pertundes et **gaitano lino** inserto, pro phylactyerio uteris..*) is of problematic etymology,[320] but is likely to have been Gaulish. Again Marcellus is silent about its origin. It is also of note that *odocos*, which, as we saw in the previous paragraph, was described by Marcellus as Gallic, has reflexes exclusively in Gallo-Romance (*REW* 6039). It too had clearly entered the Latin of Gaul.

There are also magic formulae in the text, the language of which is of some interest. These may be in Latin alone,[321] but are sometimes in Gaulish, as for example at 8.171 (Meid's word division) *in mon dercom argos axati-son*.[322] Others are in mixed language, as at 8.170 *tetunc resonco bregan gresso*. The first word probably = *te tunc*, and is either Latin or Latinised Gaulish.[323] *Resonco* looks like a hybrid verb-form. The preverb seems to be Latin, the verbal lexeme Gaulish and the ending Latin. The remaining two words look Gaulish. *bregan* is an accusative singular, indicating apparently the foreign body (referred to in the Latin as *sordicula aliqua*) to be removed from the eye (etymology obscure).[324] *Gresso* has a Latin instrumental ablative ending, perhaps from a Gaulish dative-instrumental *crissu* 'through rubbing'; note the Latin *percurrens et pertractans oculum* in the same passage. On this interpretation the sense is something like 'you, the particle, I rinse out through rubbing'.[325] Meid (1996: 50) takes the root of the verb to be that of the I.-E. term for 'juice' (cf. Lat. *sucus, sugere*), with nasal infix; it would be a first person singular present form (*su-n-k-u*). This interpretation is somewhat speculative, but it is at least clear that the formula contains both Latin and Celtic elements. How is the mixture to be regarded? Is it evidence that there was a sort of mixed language in use in Gaul in the Imperial period? It would be wrong to come to such a conclusion. The point is that the formula belongs to magic, and the

[319] See Meid (1996: 34).
[320] See Meid (1996: 36–8). Helmreich (the editor of Marcellus) emended to *Gaditano*.
[321] See Meid (1996: 40–3). [322] Discussed by Meid (1996: 45–6).
[323] See Meid (1996: 49); on the passage as a whole, see also Meid (1983: 1026–8).
[324] See Meid (1983: 1027), id. (1996: 49 n. 100).
[325] Meid (1996: 50) translates 'dich, somit, Partikel, schwemme ich heraus durch massierendes Reiben'.

language of magic often makes use of hocus-pocus. We have already seen that the *defixio* Vetter (1953), 7 is in a mixture of Latin and Oscan (II.3); and another Gallic document, the *defixio* of Amélie-les-Bains (for which see above, II.3, p. 128), seems to be in Celtic with snatches of Latin, as in the words *rogamos et de*. The Greek magic papyri contain switches into Egyptian. A late antique Latin translation of Origen, *Comm. in Matt.* (*PG* 13.1757), refers to the use by Christians in incantations adjuring demons (in exorcism) of pieces of Hebrew. The relevant sentence is: *quibusdam autem et de Hebraeo acceptis adiurant daemonia* ('they adjure demons by means of certain (adjurations, words, things) taken even from Hebrew'). The reference is presumably to the inclusion of Hebrew in the usual Greek. An Ethiopic amulet intended to protect a woman contains the words *sâdor, 'alâdor, dânât, aderâ, rodas*, which represent the Latin palindrome *sator arepo tenet opera rotas*.[326] And a recently published magical spell in Coptic from Kellis in the Dakhleh Oasis of Egypt (*P. Kell. Copt.* 35) has a few words of Greek, though this may be an attempt to give the text a 'professional' status, if the argument of Mirecki, Gardner and Alcock (1997: 17) is accepted ('The use of the Greek language in the spell appears to be a rhetorical device by which the Coptic writer makes a sympathetic connection with the revered and authoritative tradition of the Greek-language magic').[327] Whatever the case in this last document, since magic also employs words which have no meaning,[328] it may be misguided to attempt to find a precise meaning for the above text from Gaul. It may just be acceptable to use the term 'code-switching' of the language mixture, but if so it is code-switching of a very special kind. Whereas (as we have often stressed, and will see again) code-switching may be a mark of fluent and creative bilingualism, magic relies for its effect on an element of obscurity, and the presence of the Celtic may even be taken to imply that the words were no longer understood.

The view that one should not seek a real language in such formulae is confirmed by the appearance of some formulae which have bits and pieces of Greek alongside Latin or Gaulish. Note 8.192 κυρια κυρια κασσαρια σουρωρβι. The third word, which also occurs in a formula in Latin letters in the same section (*uigaria gasaria*), appears to be of a Celtic root *kass- (which is found in OIr. as *casair* 'thorn, needle'), with a Latin suffix *-arius*.[329] The root (ultimately = 'cut') may be the same

[326] See Cohen (1985: 150).
[327] I am grateful to Matthew Dickie for the last three references.
[328] The so-called Ἐφέσια γράμματα: see e.g. Heim (1893: 525–42), with e.g. his text no. 201 (Cato, *Agr.* 160); also Jordan (2000).
[329] See Meid (1996: 55).

as that in Lat. *castrare*.[330] κυρια on the other hand is obviously Greek. σουρωρβι is the Celtic word for 'barleycorn', > 'sty' (in the eye), in the dative plural.[331] Thus 'mistress, mistress, cutter out of the sty'.[332] The mixture of elements from three languages cannot possibly represent an institutionalised mixed language.

29.45 *trebio potnia telapaho* is a mixture of Greek and Celtic. *potnia* (πότνια) means 'mistress' (cf. κυρία above), *telepaho* must reflect θεραπεύω or a similar form ('I heal'),[333] and the final word can be analysed as Celtic *tre bio* 'durch Lebendiges', through the living one (the healing power of the living lizard,[334] according to Meid (1996: 58)).[335] Meid sees here the Celtic *tre bivon or *tre bivu*, comparing OIr. *tre*, *tri*, Welsh *trwy* and OIr. *béo*, Lat. *uiuus* 'living'. In a partly Greek formula the Gaulish would be suggestive also of βίος.[336]

Finally, at 15.105–6 (*heilen prosaggeri uome si polla nabuliet onodieni iden eliton*) there is again a mixture of languages, though the words were probably never intended to be meaningful. *uome* is Latin, *pros-* and *polla* (πολλά) and the spelling *-gg-* seem to be Greek, *heilen* and *eliton* are suggestive of ἑλεῖν and ἑλετόν, *nabuliet* must be a verb form, and *onodieni* and *iden* are possibly Gaulish.[337] The last is probably pronominal, and perhaps equivalent to *idem*. Meid (1996: 59) suggests renderings of various parts of the text. It has to be acknowledged, however, that a good deal of imagination must be used to establish connections between some of the terms in this text and the classical languages, and I would not wish to press these interpretations.

What emerges from the material in Marcellus is that (1) there were some Gaulish words which had entered local Latin and were no longer recognised as Celtic by Marcellus (though for the most part in his linguistic observations he makes a distinction between Latin and Gaulish and thus seems to have known some of the words he comments on in Gaulish, an indication that the language lingered on); those words which are embedded without comment in the Latin text can be regarded as regionalisms; (2) in magical formulae there was mixing of Latin, Greek and Gaulish elements, sometimes in a mélange that is arguably

---

[330] See Meid (1996: 55).
[331] See Meid (1996: 52–3). This usage has a parallel in Gk. κριθή and Lat. *hordeolum* (for which see *TLL* VI.2–3.2966.37), and one wonders about the relationship between the various languages in this respect.
[332] See Meid (1996: 55).
[333] See Meid (1996: 57–8); also id. (1983: 1025–6). There seems to be some confusion over the spelling of the word.
[334] A *lacertum uiridem* is used as part of the remedy.   [335] Cf. Meid (1983: 1026).
[336] See Meid (1996: 58).   [337] See Meid (1996: 58–9).

comprehensible, but sometimes with a meaning which is obscure to us and might have been obscure to users of the formulae themselves. The mixture at least reflects the original trilingualism of part of Gaul, and the mixing considered to be comprehensible may perhaps be seen as the relic of code-switching which in the transitional period of Romanisation might have been common at lower social levels; though one must also reckon with the deliberate obfuscation of magic formulae. Code-switching (if it is to be called that) sometimes takes place within the boundaries of a single word.

IV.5 The spindle whorls from eastern France

Not unlike some of the above language mixing, at least at first sight, is that found in the Gallo-Latin inscriptions on so-called 'spindle whorls' (Fr. *pesons de fuseau*), the language of which has been elucidated by Meid (1983: 1029–43).[338] These are weights of metal, slate or bone for attachment to the spindle, found in the east of France and dating from about the third or fourth century.[339] The inscriptions are greetings addressed to girls (unnamed), with vocatives such as (in Latin) *puella, soror, domina* or (in Gaulish) *nata* (*gnatha*). There is usually an imperative verb, and often some sort of epithet of the girl. The speaker, real or imagined, is intended to be male. The inscriptions are light-hearted in tone, sometimes suggestive or risqué, and reflect the rituals of flirtation and the drinking party.[340] Meid (1983: 1030) divides them into three groups, those in Latin alone, those in Celtic, and those in what appears to be a mixture of the two languages, the last group being of most interest here. The Latin texts are: *salue tu puella; salue soror; aue uale bella tu; accede urbana;*[341] *aue domina sitiio.*[342] A pure Gaulish text is *moni gnatha gabi buddoton imon.*[343] *moni* is an imperative meaning 'come' (cf. *accede* in the Latin text above), *gnatha* is the Gaulish for 'girl' (which also appears in the form *nata*: see below), *gabi* is another imperative of a Celtic verb = 'take', and the last two words are taken to mean 'my kisses'.[344]

---

[338] For the texts, see also Whatmough (1970: 359, 495–6), Wuilleumier (1963), 523–36; and for a selection of texts with one or two new interpretations, see Lambert (1995: 122–5).

[339] Some illustrations may be found in Meid (1983: 1029).   [340] See Meid (1983: 1030).

[341] For the suggestive 'amatory' use of *accedo*, see Adams (1982: 175–6).

[342] The verb in the last is probably not meant to be sexual in implication; a number of the texts have to do with drinking (see below).

[343] See Meid (1983: 1031). I use *dd* in the second last word for the *tau Gallicum* which is represented in different ways in Gaulish texts (see Meid (1983: 1031 n. 33)).

[344] For a full discussion, see Meid (1983: 1031).

Of the mixed texts[345] I cite two. Several of the others are of uncertain interpretation: (1) *nata uimpi curmi da*; (2) *nata uimpi pota ui(nu)m*. The vocative expression *nata uimpi* is Gaulish (*uimpi* = 'beautiful';[346] *nata* = 'girl': see above, and further below). *Curmi*, as we have seen, was a Gaulish word for 'beer' which had probably been borrowed into the Latin of the region. In (1) the imperative *da* is probably Latin.[347] (2) has a Latin verb phrase.[348]

These texts spring from a society to some extent bilingual, but the domain of use is so restricted that one must be cautious in making generalisations about the language situation. There are certainly no grounds for setting up a mixed language, neither fully Latin nor fully Gaulish, which might have become established at a transitional stage in the process of Romanisation. After all, in some of the other texts, as we have seen, Latin and Gaulish are clearly differentiated, and that establishes that there were two languages in use, which might from time to time have been mixed together for special purposes. In other words, code-switching was an option. Code-switching in the context of flirtation and sexual relations we will see again in Roman society (where the switching was from Latin into Greek: see 3.v, p. 360), and I would suggest that it is that type of code-switching which may lie in the background here. At a time of advanced Romanisation, when Gaulish was fading from use, code-switching into Gaulish or the use of simple Gaulish phrases might have offered a sort of language of intimacy, a language which has become fossilised in semi-public form in the banter of the spindle whorls. It should be noted that the terms of affection are in Gaulish, and the verb phrases at least partly in Latin. Given the firmly established place of Latin in the genre, the phenomenon is best seen as belonging to a late stage in the language shift, with switching into Gaulish representing a reversion to speakers' roots. It seems less likely that in an earlier stage of the process first-language speakers of Gaulish would have seen switching into the language of the imperial power as a potential form of intimacy. Meid (1983: 1034) treats the jargon of the spindle whorls as a 'typisches Kompromißprodukt', which made it easy for the Gauls to speak 'Latin' and the Romans to understand, and even speak, 'Gaulish' in limited domains, and which therefore facilitated communication in a region that was still bilingual. But there is in my opinion no need to introduce

---

[345] For which see Meid (1983: 1032) and the discussion which ensues there.
[346] See Meid (1983: 1032–3), Lambert (1995: 123).
[347] See Meid (1983: 1034), Lambert (1995: 123).
[348] Lambert (1995: 124) retains the reading *uim*, translating 'Belle fille, bois ma force'.

Romans into the picture. The producers of these objects were surely Gauls communicating among themselves, and sometimes choosing to do so partly or wholly in their dying inherited language.

Another text discussed by Meid (1983: 1028) can be interpreted along similar lines. When the martyr Symphorianus was being led to his death, it is said that he was addressed by his mother in the following terms: *nate nate Synforiane, mentobeto to diuo.*[349] The utterance is basically in Latin. The verb *mentobeto*, however it is to be spelt, is an imperative form from *mente habere* and a clear regional usage. The expression survived directly only in OFr. (*mentevoir*) and Prov. (*mentaure*), though from French it was borrowed by Italian and from there by a few other Romance dialects (*REW* 5507). *to* could represent the reduced form *tum* deriving from the Latin possessive *tuum*. The nominative form *tus* is already attested in a letter of Claudius Terentianus (*P. Mich.* VIII.471 *pater tus*), but *to* is also the Celtic possessive.[350] But the most interesting item in the present context is the use of *diuus* for *deus*. This may represent a switch into Gaulish, which inherited *deuos* > *diuos*. The switch would perhaps be related to a tendency of bilinguals to hold on to their primary language in the context of religious observance (see above, IV.2). An alternative possibility is that Gallo-Latin had adopted *diuus* = *deus* because of the coincidence of form between the Gaulish noun and the recherché Latin term *diuus*,[351] though it has to be said that *diuus* does not survive in any of the Romance languages. A final possibility is that the mother used the Latin term itself, but that would seem unlikely in ordinary speech. On balance *to diuo* looks like pure Gaulish.[352]

It may also be significant that the woman used *nate* rather than the usual *fili*.[353] Gaulish *natos* had the sense 'child', and the identity of form between this and the Latin *natus* (which we saw earlier in Etruria with the meaning 'son') may have caused *natus* to catch on in the Latin of Gaul, not only indeed in the literal meaning but also in the slightly extended sense 'child'.[354] Indeed in Provençal the reflex of *natus* (*nat*) means 'child',[355] though it must be acknowledged that the same meaning attaches to Rumanian *nat*[356] and therefore cannot entirely be attributed to Celtic

---

[349] For the wording, see Thurneysen (1923: 11), suggesting the text given here on the basis of the readings in two corrupt manuscripts of a passage of the *Vita Symphoniani Augustodunensis*.
[350] See also Fleuriot (1991: 7, 31).   [351] This is the view of Meid (1983: 1028).
[352] So Fleuriot (1991: 7).
[353] For the interpretation that follows, see Meid (1983: 1029), and earlier, *FEW* VII. 23 n. 27 (s.v. *nasci*).
[354] But note that the plural *nati* can mean 'children' in classical Latin (*OLD* s.v. *natus*).
[355] See *FEW* VII. 21, b.   [356] See *REW* 5851.

influence. Nevertheless it is of note that the feminine *nata*, which occurs in the sense 'girl' on several of the spindle whorls in mixed language,[357] and was, as we saw, the Gaulish term for 'female child',[358] is reflected in Gallo-Romance in this sense (OFr. *nee*, Prov. *nada*).[359] It is of particular interest that in the Old French material cited by Godefroy (1888: 483) the expression *bel(l)e nee* occurs no fewer than five times in a restricted number of citations (e.g. *B. de Seb.* VII.78 *ma soer qui tant est belle nee*). This expression corresponds exactly in meaning to *nata uimpi*. There is a hint here that the coexistence of *natus* (*-a*) in both Latin and Gaulish gave it some currency in the Latin of Gaul alongside the more usual terms *filius* and *filia*, and *puer* and *puella*, particularly in the feminine.

IV.6 Conclusions

Several types of code-switching or language mixing have been seen in this section. In magical incantations haphazard mixing seems to reflect the power of incomprehensible verbiage in magic. The amatory inscriptions on the spindle whorls are closer to real life, and here there is a hint that switching into Gaulish could be a strategy of intimacy and solidarity in a bilingual society in which Gaulish was being overwhelmed.

Evidence for regional variation in Latin determined by contact with the substrate language has been noted in the survival of *nata* into Old French and Provençal. The expressions *belle nee* and *nata uimpi* are equivalents. *Nata* as used in Latin was not a borrowing from Gaulish, because Latin had always had this word; but its currency in Gallic Latin (as evidenced by Gallo-Romance) in the sense 'girl' may have been determined by its identity of form with the Celtic word. Further regional (lexical) features of Gallic Latin can be extracted from Marcellus of Bordeaux. The interference, if such it is, in Cimber's Latin (and/or Greek?), and that seen in the Vindolanda tablet, also hint at the distinctive features which Gallic Latin must have had. We will return to this subject in the chapter about La Graufesenque (7).

The Gaulish inscription in which a Gaul is referred to as KUITOS LEKATOS brings to light one of the factors which lay behind the language shift in Gaulish-speaking regions. This man (unlike his brothers) had given himself a Latin name, presumably by translating his original name, and he also had a Latin title which he must have picked up through

[357] See the material at Meid (1983: 1032). [358] See Meid (1983: 1032).
[359] See *REW* 5851, and the material collected from Old French by Godefroy (1888: 483), s.v. *nee*. The *Nouum Glossarium Mediae Latinitatis* (ed. F. Blatt), s.v. *nata*, 2, gives an example = 'jeune fille'.

contact with Latin speakers. His esteem for the Romans had caused him to modify his identity, and such esteem must have been a potent force in motivating Gauls to learn the new language. We will see later that names at La Graufesenque also point to a sense of changing identity among the local potters.

Finally, a bilingual text with complementary versions was discussed (IV.2). An act of translation need not have taken place in the composition of such a text; the writer(s) may simply have decided what had to be said in the separate languages. It is not surprising that the longer version should have been that in the local language; its length indicates that the composer wanted to convey information to local readers. On the other hand we will see cases later of inscriptions whose writers were indifferent to the local readership; sometimes an inscription in a language alien to the area in which it was set up was intended to carry symbolism, not detailed information.

V PUNIC

V.1 Introduction

In 1968 Millar wrote that the 'very numerous Punic (or rather neo-Punic) inscriptions of Roman Africa, many with parallel Latin texts, are effectively impossible to survey with confidence, for they have never been assembled in any modern edition' (1968: 131). He noted that *The Inscriptions of Roman Tripolitania* printed the Latin versions of bilingual texts from Tripolitania, but not the Punic. The situation has improved considerably, at least on the Punic side. For Tripolitania there is now Levi Della Vida and Amadasi Guzzo, *Iscrizioni puniche della Tripolitania (1927–1967)* (1987) (= *IPT*), in which the bilingual and trilingual texts (nos. 5, 9, 12, 13, 16, 21, 24, 25, 26, 27, 30, 91) are set out in full, with commentary on the Punic versions. Another bilingual text from Tripolitania is published by Rossi and Garbini (1976–7). For Italy (Sardinia, Sicily) we have Amadasi Guzzo, *Iscrizioni fenicie e puniche in Italia* (1990), a volume which again has bilinguals (13, 15, 31, 38 (Pyrgi: see below)). Amadasi Guzzo also published in 1967 *Le iscrizioni fenicie e puniche delle colonie in occidente*, which overlaps partly with the last-mentioned work (it too contains the inscriptions of Sardinia and Sicily), but also has texts from Malta and Spain. From Malta there is a bilingual in Greek and Punic (1). The late so-called 'Latino-Punic' inscriptions, written in Latin script, have been collected by Vattioni (1976) (though this cannot be treated as a definitive edition:

see further below, v.6), and there is further discussion of some of the texts in question by Garbini (1986: 72–81). A general survey of work done on 'Latino-Punic' can now be found in Amadasi Guzzo (1989). Finally, in *KAI* various bilinguals are published which are not found in the collections of Levi Della Vida and Amadasi Guzzo (nos. 117, 140, 142, 152, 160, 165). In this section I will be concentrating particularly on the bilingual (trilingual) texts, though some anecdotal evidence will also be dealt with.

V.2 The early period

Punic continued to be spoken in north Africa well into the Imperial period (see below, v.8),[360] but at a much earlier date the Carthaginian influence was more widespread, in for example Spain, Sicily and Sardinia. The Carthaginians had commercial and military associations with the Etruscans, and they made treaties with the Romans of a type which imply trading activities in Latium. At the battle of Alalia (Hdt. 1.166–7) in about 535 BC the Phocaeans fought a combined force made up of Carthaginian and Etruscan fleets.[361] Aristotle (*Pol.* 3, 1280a.36) refers to agreements between Carthage and the Etruscans, and the first treaty between the Romans and Carthaginians as described by Polybius (3.22.3–13) regulates (among other things) Carthaginian trading activities in Latium.[362] Polybius speaks of the treaty as being in difficult archaic Latin, but it is unlikely that there was not a Punic version as well of this and the later treaties, even if such versions were not kept at Rome. The existence of written treaties demands the assumption of bilingual negotiations in drawing up the texts. Although Romans were not much given to learning languages other than Greek, and although they later administered their empire through a combination of Latin and Greek, in disregard of the numerous vernacular languages spread around the Mediterranean world, there is, as we will see, evidence that some Latin speakers acquired expertise in Punic during the Republic, and even in the Empire Punic was not as a rule belittled by those who came into contact with it. Etruscan and Punic occupy a special place among the languages with which Romans came into contact. These were both languages associated with ancient literate cultures which in different ways exercised influence on Rome, and as such they possessed a certain prestige in Roman eyes.

[360] See e.g. W. Green (1951), MacMullen (1966), Millar (1968), Vattioni (1968), Cox (1988). There is a very good general survey of Punic in the Roman period by Röllig (1980), and an excellent discussion of various bilingual issues by Amadasi Guzzo (1988).
[361] See for example Heurgon (1966: 3). [362] See Walbank (1957: 341).

Mention must briefly be made of the Pyrgi tablets, though the relevant text in the present context is not in Punic but in Phoenician.[363] At Pyrgi, modern Santa Severa, one of the harbours of Caere, there were discovered in 1964 three gold tablets, one inscribed in Phoenician, the other two in Etruscan. They may be dated to about 500–480 BC, and concern a dedication in a temple by the Etruscan ruler at Caere to the Phoenician goddess Astarte.[364] The fact that the Etruscan king claims to be responding to a request from the goddess hints at the influence which the Phoenicians had achieved in the region, perhaps through resident merchants. Gibson (1982: 152) states that the 'most plausible explanation of the composition of the inscr. seems . . . to be that the king of Caere allowed himself, for obvious reasons of state, to be associated with the establishment of a place of worship within an Etruscan temple at Pyrgi for the use of a community of Phoen. traders who had settled in the port'. The Phoenician text as printed by Amadasi Guzzo (1990: 95) (cf. Pfiffig (1965: 9), Fischer and Rix (1968: 68)) is as follows:

1 lrbt l'štrt 'šr qdš
2 'z 'š p'l w'š ytn
3 tbry' wlnš mlk 'l
4 kyšry' byrḥ zbḥ
5 šmš bmtn 'bbt wbn
6 tw . k 'štrt 'rš bdy
7 lmlky šnt šlš by
8 rḥ krr bym qbr
9 'lm wšnt lm'š 'lm
10 bbty šnt km hkkbm
11 'l

1 'To the lady Astarte. This holy place
2 (is that) which was made and which was given by
3 TBRY' WLNŠ, king over
4 KYŠRY',[365] in the month of the sacrifice

---

[363] See Röllig (1980: 287), with bibliography, on the language. According to Donner and Röllig (1966–9: 332), the text was probably written by a Phoenician from Cyprus. Gibson (1982: 152–3) supports this view in some detail, arguing that it does not concern Carthaginians but Phoenicians who came originally from northern Cyprus.

[364] Texts (mostly with full commentary and translation) can be found in Pfiffig (1965), Fischer and Rix (1968: 68), *CIE* 6314 (the longer Etruscan), 6315 (the shorter Etruscan), 6316 (the Punic), *KAI* 277, Amadasi Guzzo (1967: 158–69) (with commentary and bibliography), ead. (1990: 95), Gibson (1982: 151–9) (with very full commentary and bibliography). For the general background, see Cornell (1989: 256–7). Further bibliography is at *KAI* 277, Röllig (1980: 286 n. 10).

[365] On *Cisra* as the original name of Caere, see e.g. Pfiffig (1965: 13).

5 to the sun-god, as a gift (and) as a temple. I built
6 it, because Astarte requested (it) of me
7 in the third year[366] of my reign, in
8 the month of KRR, on the day of the burial
9 of the deity. So (may) the years (granted) to the statue of the deity
10 in her temple (be) years like the stars
11 above!'[367]

The Etruscan texts are even more problematic,[368] but the first appears to correspond fairly closely with the Phoenician.[369] The name of the dedicator is the same (*Thefarie Velianas* in the Etruscan), and *unialastres* in line 3 of the Etruscan seems at least to contain *uni* (the Etruscan name corresponding to *Iuno*, = *Astarte*), however the second part of the word is to be explained.[370] Also recognisable in the Etruscan is *ci avil* 'three years', which shows the known Etruscan numeral *ci*, and matches the Phoenician.[371] Despite the problems of interpretation it is generally agreed[372] that the first Etruscan and the Phoenician are only 'quasi-bilinguals', 'in the sense that both refer to the same event in the same context, but each uses the phrases and formulae proper to its own language and religious tradition' (Ridgway (1990: 521)); in my terminology they are 'idiomatic' bilinguals.[373] For that reason the Phoenician version is only of limited help in elucidating the Etruscan.[374] The circumstances of composition cannot be established, but idiomatic or complementary bilinguals (as distinct from bilinguals corresponding word for word and sometimes showing interference or translationese inflicted by one language on the other) imply either good mutual understanding of the two languages by the various drafters, or competent bilingualism on the part

---

[366] On the dating formula ('year three') here (the word for 'year', *šnt*, is plural), a feature of Phoenician rather than Punic, see Pfiffig (1965: 19).

[367] I print here the translation of Gibson (1982: 154). Translations can also be found at (e.g.) *KAI* 277, Fischer and Rix (1968: 68), and Amadasi Guzzo (1990: 95), with some divergences from that of Gibson, who acknowledges (151) that there is little agreement about the detailed interpretation of the inscription.

[368] Ridgway (1990: 519) prints the following translation of E1, but it has to be stressed that on various points this can be treated as no more than speculative: 'This is the shrine and this is the place of the image dedicated to Uni(-Astarte): Thefàrie Vèlianas gave it, as a thank-offering, because he had been raised to be king for three years . . . stars . . . (?).' Fischer and Rix (1968: 88) collect various suggested translations, stressing the divergences.

[369] See for example the list of correspondences given by Fischer and Rix (1968: 74).

[370] On the problem of this word, see Fischer and Rix (1968: 78; also 74).

[371] See for example Heurgon (1966: 10).

[372] See e.g. Heurgon (1966: 8–10), Ridgway (1990: 521).

[373] Cf. along the same lines Gibson (1982: 151), stressing that the Etruscan has not been elucidated.

[374] See e.g. Fischer and Rix (1968: 75).

of a single drafter. The Pyrgi tablets, if nothing else, serve to underline the linguistic diversity of early Italy, and its reception of outside cultural and linguistic influences.

That there were some Romans in the Republican period who had picked up Punic emerges from a story about a Punic agricultural treatise. After the destruction of Carthage in 146 BC the Roman senate voted that the work in twenty-eight books by the Carthaginian Mago should be translated into Latin. The episode is described by Pliny, *Nat.* 18.22 (cf. Columella 1.1.13): *Poenus etiam Mago, cui quidem tantum honorem senatus noster habuit Carthagine capta, ut, cum regulis Africae bibliothecas donaret, unius eius duodetriginta uolumina censeret in Latinam linguam transferenda, cum iam M. Cato praecepta condidisset, peritisque Punicae dandum negotium, in quo praecessit omnes uir clarissimae familiae D. Silanus.*[375] This was to be translation by a committee of experts in Punic (*peritis Punicae*), with D. Silanus the most prominent in the enterprise. Here there is specific evidence for a knowledge of Punic among members of the Roman educated classes in the second century BC.[376] There was possibly greater knowledge of foreign languages (other than Greek) among the Latin-speaking upper classes in the early Republic than was the case in the Empire. That would be a reflection of close ties between Romans and outsiders whose culture had standing.

On the interpretation proposed by Gratwick (1971)[377] of the duplicate Punic speeches of the Carthaginian Hanno at Plaut. *Poen.* 930–9, 940–9 (which are followed in the textual tradition by a Latin equivalent, 950–60), it might be argued that some scholarly knowledge of Punic still existed among Romans at the end of the Republic or beginning of the Empire. Gratwick (1971: 37) points out that the version which he calls text I must have been written at or after the time of Varro, because it uses certain features of orthography alien to the time of Plautus (*y, th, ch, ph*); text II on the other hand uses spelling resources of the type available to Plautus. He concludes that 'text II is the genuine version, clearly desperately corrupt in the early Empire, and . . . text I is a scholar's repair,

---

[375] Translation of Loeb: 'the Carthaginian Mago, on whom indeed our senate bestowed such great honour, after the taking of Carthage, that when it gave away the city's libraries to the petty kings of Africa it passed a resolution that in his case alone his twenty-eight volumes should be translated into Latin, in spite of the fact that Marcus Cato had already compiled his book of precepts, and that the task should be given to persons acquainted with the Carthaginian language, an accomplishment in which Decimus Silanus, a man of most distinguished family, surpassed everybody'.

[376] On Mago and his translators, see Heurgon (1976). Mago was later translated into Greek, by Cassius Dionysius of Utica (originally a Punic city), and this work was abridged by Diophanes of Bithynia (see Varro, *Rust.* 1.1.10); see further Heurgon (1976: 441–2). The *libri Punici* mentioned at Sall. *Jug.* 17.7 were not necessarily consulted by Sallust himself in Latin (or Greek) form: see Paul (1984: 74), with bibliography.

[377] Accepted by Röllig (1980: 288).

made up independently, but with reference to text II, in the contemporary Neo-Punic and Roman orthography of his time'. The genuine version may or may not have been in the original (of Alexis ?)[378] which Plautus was following. The 'scholar', if his existence is accepted, must have been an educated Latin speaker, to judge by the form of the script he uses; but some doubts about his knowledge of Punic inevitably remain, because it is possible that he had access to the original of Alexis(?) which he might simply have transliterated into Latin with the help of the corrupt text of Plautus.

Röllig (1980: 288) notes that in the fifth act of the *Poenulus* there are a further fourteen short verses or *sententiae* in Punic without an accompanying translation, and he suggests on this evidence that there must have been some members of the audience at this period shortly after the Second Punic War who had some familiarity with Punic, either because they had been in Africa with Scipio and heard the language there, or had encountered it in Italy. This is a possibility, but not an inevitable deduction from the evidence. Gratwick (1971: 33–4) well shows that even gibberish (in small doses) can be given dramatic point on stage (see further above, 2.II.1 on 'Oscan' stage performances at Rome).

It is possible that the Latin greeting *aue* represents a borrowing from Punic, with Latinisation of the inflection. *Auo = uiue* occurs as a greeting in a Punic section of the *Poenulus* (e.g. 998 HA. *auo*. MI. *salutat*; for the Punic verb see below, p. 231).[379] But a borrowing of this sort would not require any knowledge of Punic on the part of those Latin speakers who effected the loan. Romans hearing Punic speakers, whether soldiers or ambassadors, using the greeting could have deduced its function and taken it up as a form of humour.

There is though a story in Livy (22.13.5–6) which hints at the existence of Italians in the Hannibalic period who knew some Punic, but the passage does contain a textual problem: *ipse (Hannibal) imperat duci ut se in agrum Casinatem ducat, edoctus a peritis regionum, si eum saltum occupasset, exitum Romano ad opem ferendam sociis interclusurum; sed Punicum abhorrens ab Latinorum nominum <locutione os, Casilinum>[380] pro Casino dux ut acciperet, fecit, auersusque ab suo itinere per Allifanum Caiatinumque et Calenum in campum Stellatem descendit . . . uocatum ducem percontatur ubi terrarum esset. cum is Casilini eo die mansurum eum dixisset, tum demum cognitus est error et Casinum longe inde alia regione esse.* The translation of the Loeb edition is as follows: 'He [Hannibal] then ordered his guide to conduct him to the territory of Casinum, for he had

---

[378] On the problem of the authorship of the Greek original, see Arnott (1996: 31, 284–6).

[379] See e.g. Ernout and Meillet (1959: 55).

[380] Some such addition is needed. Weissenborn suggested *pronuntiatione* instead of *locutione* (which is printed by Walters and Conway).

been told by those who knew the country that if he occupied that pass he could keep the Romans from marching to the aid of their allies. But the difficulty experienced by Carthaginians in pronouncing Latin words caused the guide to understand Casilinum instead of Casinum; and quitting the proper road he led him down through the districts of Allifae, Caiatia and Cales into the plain of Stella. (There Hannibal ...) called up the guide and asked him where in the world he was. And only when the guide had answered that he should lodge that night in Casilinum, did he perceive at last how the man had blundered, and that Casinum lay far off in another direction.'

The anecdote turns on a misunderstanding by Hannibal's guide, who confused two place names and led Hannibal to the wrong place. It is the *Punicum os* (?) which causes the misunderstanding, that is the pronunciation by a Punic speaker of the Latin name. The Punic speaker was presumably Hannibal, and on this assumption the guide may have been a primary speaker of Latin who had difficulty understanding the Punic rendering of the name. This evidence is of low quality and tells us nothing about the nature of the bilingualism of the guide, but the man seems to be presented as a Latin speaker with some rudimentary knowledge of Punic. One wonders though how much thought Livy gave to the linguistic details of the incident and to their presentation. Could it be, for example, that the guide as well as Hannibal was thought of as Punic-speaking, and that the pair were imagined as having difficulties in their native language with Latin place names? Against this it must be objected that, given the guide's role, he must surely have been an Italian with local knowledge.[381]

---

[381] On the general subject of bilingualism in Hannibal's armies, see Rochette (1997b). There is good evidence at this period for some knowledge of Greek among the Carthaginian upper classes (from the various pieces of evidence cited by Rochette I mention Livy 28.46.16, which refers to a bilingual inscription, *Punicis Graecisque litteris*, set up by Hannibal; note that *litteris* here refers to language and not simply script: see 3.III.3, n. 61; see further the early transliterated Phoenician inscription discussed in sect. V.9, and also above, n. 376 on the Greek translation of Mago), but not much for a knowledge of Latin. But note the Carthaginian stratagem reported by Livy 26.6.11, whereby Hannibal has some of his men who are Latin speakers dress up in the Italian manner and attempt (by the use of Latin) to persuade the enemy that they were transmitting orders of the consuls to flee: *fraudem quoque super tumultum adiectam, immissis ab Hannibale qui habitu Italico gnari Latinae linguae iuberent consulum uerbis quoniam amissa castra essent pro se quemque militum in proximos montes fugere*. On the stratagem, see Rochette (1997b: 157). There is Republican evidence that Romans regarded Carthaginians with some suspicion as gifted linguists, and stories such as this might well have got into the annalistic tradition as a consequence. At *Poen.* 112 Plautus represents Hanno as knowing 'all languages' and capable of concealing that knowledge: *et is omnis linguas scit, sed dissimulat sciens / se scire: Poenus plane est*. Later in the play Hanno suddenly switches from Punic into Latin, as a result of which he is abused for his linguistic deceitfulness: 1029–34 *at ut scias, nunc dehinc latine iam loquar. / ... at hercle te hominem et sycophantam et subdolum, / qui*

From this point onwards I turn to inscriptional and other primary evidence for the use of Punic alongside Latin. Bilingual texts will be assessed in the manner adopted elsewhere in this chapter for the light they throw on the character of the bilingualism of the composers, on perceptions of linguistic identity, on code-switching and its motivations, and on the possible influence of the one language on the other. There is in fact under the Empire one clearcut case of a regionalism in African Latin which can be attributed to the indirect influence of Punic, and that involves a use of the vocative. The matter will be dealt with in detail in a later chapter (4.v.4.4), but I will lay the foundations here for that discussion.

V.3 Coins

I begin with some coin legends, which offer the advantage that their symbolism is relatively straightforward. An insight into the symbolic potential of code-switching can be obtained from some of the coinage of Africa and also Spain in the early Imperial period. Various coin issues of towns of Punic or Phoenician foundation have portraits of the emperor's head with a Latin legend, accompanied by the ethnic of the town in neo-Punic.[382] Note for example *RPC* I.1, 208: 'Lepcis [an ancient Phoenician settlement] struck coinage under Augustus and Tiberius; the Augustan coins have only the ethnic in neo-Punic, LPQY; under Tiberius, the coins are bilingual.' Thus for example the Tiberian no. 848 has DIVOS AVGVSTVS with the laureate head of Augustus, along with LPQY, and an image of Dionysus holding a cup and thyrsus, with a panther. The Augustan and Tiberian coinage of Sabratha (an ancient Tyrian or Carthaginian settlement) is all bilingual: 'the ethnic of the city is in neo-Punic [SBRT'N], the name of the princeps in Latin' (*RPC* I.1, 204–5). The coinage of Oea (Tripoli) again sometimes combines a neo-Punic ethnic (WY'T) with the name of the emperor in Latin (e.g. 832), but here Augustan coins have further neo-Punic elements, reported as

---

huc aduenisti nos captatum, migdilix, / *bisulci lingua quasi proserpens bestia.* He has the double tongue of the snake. Herein is expressed the suspicion of multilingualism which might be held by the monolingual (compare the passage of Josephus cited at 1.III). Along these lines there is an account in Livy (27.28.4) of Roman fears on one occasion that the Carthaginians might attempt to write letters in Latin in the name of a dead consul in order to deceive the locals; see further Front. *Strat.* 3.2.3. Signs of knowledge of Greek in Africa at a later period will come up below, v.5.1, v.9.

[382] For references see *RPC* I.2, index p. 749 (obverse legends, neo-Punic), p. 768 (reverse legends, neo-Punic). See also Vives (1924: 9–12), Grant (1946: 173), Garcia y Bellido (1972: 488).

S'VQ ThThE and M'QR PYLN. These are names representing pairs of suffetes.[383] Variations on these patterns are found. From Abdera (*RPC* I.I, 86) 125 has TI CAESAR DIVI AVG F AVGVSTVS, and also (I quote) 'ABDERA; tetrastyle temple, of which two columns are in the form of fishes, pediment containing Punic legend 'BDRT.' Here the name of the town is expressed in a contrived way in neo-Punic as well as Latin. The coinage of Bocchus II (*RPC* I.I, 213–14) struck between 38 and 33 BC is bilingual in a slightly different way. Note e.g. 873 REX BOCCHVS SOSI F . . . BQŠ HMMLKT. The name and title of the king are given in both languages. From Spain note e.g. 479, from Ebusus, which was a Punic foundation (*RPC* I.I, 144–5): TI CAESAR AVG P P / INS AVG(V) 'YBSHM.[384]

This material is not all of exactly the same type. The coins of Bocchus contain bilingual inscriptions, in the sense that the legends say the same thing in the two languages. On the other hand those legends which have an emperor's name in Latin but the ethnic of the town in neo-Punic express completely different information in the two languages, with no overlap except in the special case of Abdera. There is a switch of languages as the topic changes, and that phenomenon is classifiable as code-switching or language mixing (on the question of terminology, see further below, v.10; here for convenience I refer to switching without addressing the problem of definition directly). Whereas code-switching in speech may be natural, scarcely (if at all) noticed by the speaker, and therefore unmarked, a coin legend cannot possibly be composed without a good deal of thought and preparation. The code-switching cannot be haphazard. And it almost inevitably represents the decision of a committee rather than an individual's linguistic practice. I stress these points because code-switching in written form should not simply be assessed according to the criteria applied in linguistics to the assessment of code-switching in informal speech. We must assume that the language switching in these coin legends is deliberate, and look for the motivation of the composers. The motivation is obvious. Roman control of Africa (and Spain) is expressed by the Latin legend which accompanies the portrait of the emperor, whereas the Punic origin of the towns is symbolised by the Punic ethnics. Clearly the towns retained some pride in their past, and were keen to convey that by using the old names in Punic form. The switching, brief as it is, thus expresses a double identity for the places

---

[383] See *RPC* I.I, 206. However, the transliterations printed by *RPC* are not entirely convincing.
[384] For the coinage of another Spanish city, Gades, see the works of Vives, Grant and Garcia cited in n. 382.

issuing the coins. By changing languages the composers were able to make a few words express a lot. The use of Latin for the emperor's name recalls various bilingual texts in which only the Latin version has information of this type. A case in point to be discussed later in this chapter (VII.2) is a Palmyrene–Latin bilingual inscription set up at Rome; later in this section (V.5.2) we will see examples in Punic–Latin inscriptions from Tripolitania. A nice parallel for language switching of this type is found in Palestinian milestones which have the imperial titulature in Latin and then a distance in Greek (or Greek and Latin): e.g. Thomsen (1917: 83), 300: *Imp(erator) Caes(ar) L(ucius) Septimius Seu[erus] Pertinax A[ug(ustus)] pont[ifex] max(imus) tr[ib(uniciae)] pot(estatis) co(n)s(ul) II . . .* ἀπὸ Κολ(ωνίας) Αἰλ(ίας) Κ[απιτ(ωλίνας)] μίλ(ια) III.[385]

What a town could do, so too could an individual. Code-switching (in written form) will emerge throughout this book as a distinctive way of conveying a double identity of one sort or another for the referent.

On code-switching and coins, see II.1 above, and below, X.

V.4 Sardinia

Sardinia was under the control of Carthage from about 500 BC. It was captured by Rome in 238/7 BC, but was isolated and apparently despised by the Romans, and Romanisation was not rapid.[386] The island is notable for a considerable number of Phoenician and Punic inscriptions dating from the end of the ninth century BC to the second century AD.[387] The linguistic remains along with other archaeological evidence reflect both the depth of the Phoenician/Punic penetration, and the isolation of the place. A monolingual Punic inscription set up as late as the second half of the second century AD or first half of the third at Bitia near a temple of Bes (Amadasi Guzzo (1990: 81), 14), which mentions in its dating formula the emperor Marcus Aurelius Antoninus, is still in the Punic (as distinct from neo-Punic) script, at a time when in North Africa the old script had been modified.[388] Amadasi Guzzo (1990: 48) points out that the persistence of Punic tradition is to be seen not only in the structure of the formulae of the inscription, but also in the political organisation implied by the mention of suffetes (see further below). The names of the

---

[385] For other such cases, see Thomsen (1917), 266, 267, 276, 288, 279(a), 303, 305 (distance bilingual).
[386] So e.g. Wilson (1996: 445).
[387] See Amadasi Guzzo (1990: 39); there is also a brief discussion of the Roman period by Röllig (1980: 289, 294–5).
[388] See Amadasi Guzzo (1990: 48).

referents (quite apart from those of the emperor) however are predominantly Latin, a fact which suggests that the original nomenclature might have been abandoned before the language itself.

From Sardinia there is the trilingual *CIS* 1.143 = Cooke (1903), 40 = *ILLRP* 41 = *KAI* 66.[389] I quote the three versions:

Cleon salari(us) soc(iorum) s(eruus) Aescolapio Merre donum dedit lubens merito merente

'Ασκληπίῳ Μηρρη ἀνάθεμα βωμὸν ἔστησε Κλέων ὁ ἐπὶ τῶν ἁλῶν κατὰ πρόσταγμα

1 l'dn l'šmn m'rḥ mzbḥ nḥšt mšql ltrm m't 100 'š ndr 'klyn šḥsgm 'š bmmlht šm['
2 q]l' rpy' bšt sptm ḥmlkt w'bd'šmn bn ḥmlk

To the lord šmn m'rḥ: – the altar of bronze, in weight a hundred 100 pounds, which Cleon (slave) of ḥsgm, who is over the salt mines (?), vowed; he heard his voice (and) healed him, in the year of the suffetes ḥmlkt and 'bd'šmn, son of ḥmlk.'[390]

The date of the inscription must be after the capture of the island from Carthage in 238/7 BC. It has conventionally been attributed to the first half of the second century BC in the period 180–150 on the evidence of the Greek and Latin letter forms.[391] The text of the Latin printed above is that usually adopted, but there are uncertainties about the completion of the second to fourth words; *salari*, for example, might stand for *salariorum*.[392] Salt mining was an important local industry, to which there are other inscriptional references.[393] A member of the *salarii* is seen as practising the cult of Eshmun Merre, who is equated with Aesculapius;[394] this is one of a number of Punic cults which lasted into the Roman period in Sardinia, in association with which the Punic language may have been maintained longer than it was for everyday purposes (cf. IV.2 above on the Vercelli inscription, with cross references). On the evidence of this inscription though it would seem to have still been Punic which was the dominant language in this area.[395] The inscription is one of

---

[389] See also Amadasi Guzzo (1967: 91), 13, ead. (1990: 82), 15. The Latin text is found at *CIL* I².2226, x.7856.

[390] See also Donner and Röllig (1966–9: 81–2) on the interpretation of the Punic. The translation into Latin in *CIS* is: 'Domino Esmuno Merre: altare aereum ponderis librarum centum c, quod uouit Cleon, [seruus seruorum] qui in re salaria; audit uocem eius, sanauit eum. anno suffetum Himilcati et Abdesmuni, filii Himilci.' See further Amadasi Guzzo, locc. cit. for renderings into Italian.

[391] See *CIS* 143 (p. 189), *ILLRP* 41, Amadasi Guzzo (1967: 91), ead. (1990: 82).

[392] So Mastino (1985: 54 n. 142).   [393] See Mastino, loc. cit.

[394] See Mastino (1985: 78 with n. 291).

[395] Note Rawson (1985: 22 n. 19): 'Sardinia was a backward place, where Punic, and perhaps some Greek, was spoken alongside Latin.'

those bi-/trilingual texts in which there is a descending order of detail (see the trilingual from Palmyra discussed earlier, I.VII.1), ranging in this case from the Punic through the Greek to the Latin, which is the least informative version of all, though it is placed first. Indeed the Latin on its own would permit few deductions about the circumstances lying behind the setting up of the inscription. The Punic alone gives the information that the god had heard the voice of Cleon and healed him, and that as a result Cleon had set up an altar. The altar is mentioned as well by the Greek (βωμόν), but only the Punic states the weight and material of the object. The Latin on the other hand is at a high level of generality, in that it makes use of a formula *donum dedit lubens* which tells the reader nothing about the nature of the *donum*. There is no more than lip-service to Latin, and indeed Greek. There are moreover signs of uncertainty in the handling of the Latin formula system. *merito* and *(bene)merenti* are usually interchangeable (for the most part in funerary inscriptions), but here both are used together, and, what is worse, *merente* is not correctly inflected as a dative. Finally, it is only the Punic version which has a date. Since the island was no longer Carthaginian, the suffetes cannot be those of Carthage; they were presumably officials of some local town.[396] It was through the medium of Punic that the drafter set out to convey the circumstances of the dedication, whereas in the Latin and to a lesser extent the Greek he was content to string together a few non-specific formulae. One of the few concrete details in the Latin version concerns the (secular) profession of the dedicator. Either the writer did not have sufficient control of Latin to use the language creatively, or religious conservatism prompted him to reserve the most important details about the dedication for the traditional language. However one looks at it, there is evidence here for a degree of Romanisation on the one hand, but persistence of the older language on the other some time after the island had passed to the Romans.[397] The form *merente* implies imperfect language learning at a time of incipient language shift, though the writer had some familiarity with Latin dedicatory formulae. I stress that there is no evidence here that one version was the primary one and the others renderings of it. Bilingual (and trilingual) inscriptions seem rarely to have been put together in that way (though see below on the next inscription). The Latin version has conventional phraseology of its own, and there are Punic formulae in the Punic version. For Latin as a mere token presence

---

[396] See *CIS* (p. 190).
[397] Van Dommelen (1998) stresses the continued vitality of Punic culture during the first centuries of Roman rule, but he disregards the linguistic evidence entirely.

at a period of incipient Romanisation in a provincial region, see the inscription of Haeranes (I.VII.I) and the Venetic text Es 27 discussed at II.2.

There is also a Latin–Punic bilingual from Sardinia, in this case from Sulci (Sant'Antioco) on the south coast of the island (*CIS* I.149, Cooke (1903), 60, *KAI 172, ILLRP* 158; Latin text also at *CIL* I². 2225, X.7513):[398]

Himilconi Idnibalis f.[ ] quei hanc aedem ex s(enatus) c(onsulto) fac(iendam) coerauit, Himilco f(ilius) statuam [posuit]

1 [(l)ḥ]mlkt bn 'dnbʻl bn ḥmlkt
2 hprṭ ʻl myṭb 'rš' hslkẙ
3 lbn't t hmqdš st lhrbt l'lt
4 ṭyn' t hm'š st bn' ḥmlkt

'[To ḥ]mlkt, son of 'dnbʻl, son of ḥmlkt, who decided on the consent of the 'senators' (?) of Sulci[399] to construct this sanctuary for the mistress, the goddess. Set up this statue his son ḥmlkt.'[400]

This inscription is dated by Degrassi (*ILLRP*) to the Sullan or Caesarian periods. It too was composed long after the island was taken over by the Romans, and is further evidence for the maintenance of Punic culture in this isolated place. There is a close correspondence between the two versions, which permits, if only through guesswork, a rough interpretation of some of the obscure parts of the Punic text.[401] There are three obvious differences between the versions, all of which take the form of additional detail in the Punic. The honorand Himilco has his ancestry given to two generations in the Punic (a typical Semitic feature, which will be seen elsewhere in this section (V.5.1) and also in the section on Aramaic (VII.2)) but to one in the Latin; the Latin refers only to a decree of the 'senate', whereas the Punic seems to have made it clear that it was a council of the Sulcitani which was responsible for the decision; and the Punic ascribes the temple (merely *hanc aedem* in the Latin) to a 'goddess', who is perhaps not explicitly named.[402] It is again clear that Punic was a living language. The formulation though is not typically Punic but follows to some extent that of the Latin.[403] The expression corresponding (line 2) to *ex senatus consulto* is not a Punic formula,[404]

---

[398] See also Amadusi Guzzo (1967: 130–1), ead. (1990: 80).
[399] For this interpretation of line 2, see Amadusi Guzzo (1967: 130–1), ead. (1990: 81).
[400] Translations with slight variations are offered by Cooke, Donner and Röllig (*KAI*), *ILLRP*, Amadusi Guzzo.
[401] See Donner and Röllig (1966–9: 157), Amadusi Guzzo, locc. cit.
[402] See Donner and Röllig (1966–9: 157); cf. Amadusi Guzzo (1967: 131). But on the other hand Amadusi Guzzo (1990: 80) translates 'alla signora Elat', taking the word *'lt* as a name.
[403] See Amadusi Guzzo (1990: 47).   [404] See Amadusi Guzzo (1990: 47).

but is an attempt to render the Latin.[405] This is the first example of several which show the influence of Latin formulae on the form of a Punic text (a type of cultural influence which has already been illustrated from Oscan and Etruscan material), though we will repeatedly see as well cases in which the different versions of a bilingual inscription stick to formulae current in the respective languages. In no sense is the Latin for its part in the above inscription linguistically inferior: it is on the contrary idiomatic and archaising (note the forms *quei* and *co-erauit*), and was the work of someone well versed in the forms of official Latin.

In the late Republic in Sardinia Latin was beginning to be used along-side Punic, but in both of the inscriptions quoted Punic still carries in-formation not in the Latin, even if Latinate formulations were creeping in; and there is evidence in monolingual inscriptions for the survival of Punic far beyond the relatively early period.

V.5 *Africa*

What emerges from the bilingual and neo-Punic inscriptions which have survived from Africa is a prolonged vitality of the Punic language well into the Empire, not only in rural areas but also in the cities.[406] But to talk of 'resistance' to Romanisation would be misleading. The bilingual inscriptions reveal tell-tale signs of a developing sense of a double iden-tity among Punic speakers, who remained African but were sometimes concerned to present themselves as Roman as well. Names in particular have a good deal to tell us about stages of Romanisation, sometimes across the generations in particular families.

V.5.1 *Bilingual texts and names*
I start with some texts which raise the issue of naming practices. The neo-Punic/Latin bilingual funerary inscription set out below is from Guelaat bou Sba in Numidia (*KAI* 165, *CIL* VIII.17467).[407] The first four lines of

---

[405] See Amadasi Guzzo (1990: 81) for the details; also p. 47, stating that the literal sense must be 'with the approval of the select of Sulcis' ('su beneplacito degli scelti di Sulcis'). In North Africa *senatus* is rendered by another Punic word, *'drm* 'the grandees'. The variation indicates that among Punic institutions there was not an assembly exactly like the Roman senate.
[406] See in general the discussion of Mattingly (1987) on the persistence of Punic culture in other forms as well.
[407] See also Chabot (1917: 23–9), Février, (1951–2a), Levi Della Vida (1965: 62–8), Garbini (1974: 33), id. (1986: 68).

the Punic version are problematic,[408] and I therefore concentrate on lines 5–8, which are transliterated by Garbini as follows:

tsdt bn mtʻt bn gwṭʻl
hngry dl ʻṭrt wdl šm
tʻṣmt ʻwʼ šnwt ʻmšm skr
drʼ lʼlm
tsdt, son of mtʻt, son of gwtʻl, the n.g.-ri, decorated with the crown and decorated with the title of greatness. He lived fifty years. Memorial of his family for ever.[409]

Rufo Metatis f(ilio)
Num(idae) honor(ato)
uix(it) anni(s) L fecer(unt)
fili. h(oc) l(oco) s(epultus) e(st)
o(ssa) t(ibi) b(ene) q(uiescant).[410]

The two versions are to some extent complementary or idiomatic (but see further below). Both as quoted contain much the same information (though it must be remembered that this is only half of the Punic version, which on grounds of length alone must be considered the primary text), but expressed up to a point according to different formula systems.

Whereas the name of the father, *mtʻt*, has been transferred into Latin in the Latinised genitive form *Metatis*, the name of the son, *tsdt* (Tisdat), has been replaced in the Latin version by a completely different (Latin) name (*Rufus*). Such replacement was seen, for example, in Etruria; its consequence was that in some bilingual communities certain individuals had two different names, each appropriate to one of the languages of the community. It is likely that the degree of Romanisation of the family had advanced with the generations, such that the (grand)son, unlike his two forbears, had assumed a second name as a mark of his integration into Latin-speaking society. This integration is reflected also in the provision of a Latin epitaph alongside the Punic version.

The last three lines of the Latin (as it is printed here; but see n. 410 on the last line) consist entirely of Latin funerary formulae. The Punic version, in a manner typical of Semitic funerary inscriptions (see above, v.4), records more than one generation of the deceased's ancestors, whereas the Latin version, in the correct Latin manner, has only a filiation. The use of *honorato* has caused some comment. It should first be noted that this single word corresponds to two rather more specific epithets in the

[408] See Donner and Röllig (1966–9: 154); also Chabot (1917: 25–6) for discussion, Février (1951–2a) loc. cit., and in particular Levi Della Vida (1965: 62–8) and Garbini (1974: 33) and (1986: 68).
[409] The translation given here is based on that of Garbini. The text of *KAI* is different.
[410] The letters *o*, *t*, *b*, and *q* are found at the four corners of the inscription.

Punic, one of which, translated 'decorated with the crown', no doubt embodies a reference to some sort of local mark of honour.[411] That this is not rendered literally into Latin might on one view be taken as an indication that the drafter was at ease in Latin only in the use of out-and-out funerary formulae, and that creative use of the language was beyond his powers. That would probably be an unwarranted conclusion. An alternative possibility is that the drafter wanted to use the idioms or formulae appropriate to the two languages, instead of aspiring to a word-for-word correspondence. The ideas embedded in the Punic would have required a long-winded Latin translation. The absolute use of *honoratus* was well established in Latin,[412] and cannot be taken as a sign of poor competence in the language.[413]

Finally, the formula (in the Punic) stating the number of years lived is not a Punic type, but derives from Latin.[414] Here, as in the second Sardinian inscription discussed in the previous section, we see the beginnings of an intrusion of Latinate formulaic methods of expression into Punic, though the Latinate formula stands alongside traditional Punic expressions.

On the whole, the inscription provides an illustration of two languages being used to convey the same basic information in independent ways appropriate to the conventions of the two funerary traditions. The marks of honour, whatever they were, were specific to one culture, and no real effort was made to find an exact Latin correspondent at this point. When one version of a bilingual inscription is a servile rendering of the other there may be reason to think that it does not reflect a living bilingualism, but such a conclusion could not be drawn from an inscription of the present type. Linguistically the family was being Romanised, but was still well able to make claims on its own behalf in Punic. The names of the various members of the family are of special interest, and I stay with that theme.

It is possible to find other Punic speakers (like Tisdat above) possessing both a Punic and a Latin name, and using each in the appropriate language. Two fragmentary bilingual dedications to Apollo from Oea (Tripoli) (for the Latin see *IRT* 229, 246, and for the Punic and Latin, *IPT* 5A–B) assign the dedicator different names in the two versions. The Latin of *IRT* 229 (see also Levi Della Vida and Amadasi Guzzo (1987:

---

[411] See Donner and Röllig (1966–9), 154 ad loc., citing from their own collection of texts nos. 60 and 126, 8.

[412] See *TLL* VI.3.2949.25ff.   [413] As Février (1951–2a: 39–40) is inclined to take it.

[414] See Amadasi Guzzo (1988: 24).

28 n. 1)) runs thus: *Apollini sacrum Aurelius Epagri f(ilius) d(e) s(uo) d(edit)*. The Punic versions are very fragmentary, but it is clear that the man was *ʿbdmlqrt* son of *mtnbʿl*.[415] It has been demonstrated by Amadasi Guzzo (1988: 27–9) that the (partially) Romanised Punic-speaking inhabitants of Tripolitania often had two names, one traditional, the other Roman. These could be used together in the same inscription, or alternatively distributed between the different versions of a bilingual text, as in the above cases.[416] This form of mixed naming reveals with particular clarity the referents' sense of a double, or changing, identity.

A case in which a Punic and Latin name belonging to a single person stand side by side in the same text can be found in the trilingual inscription (in Latin, Greek and Punic) honouring a doctor (*IRT* 654, *IPT* 13). Only the Latin version is now (largely) legible: *Boncar Mecrasi Clodius medicus*.[417] Of the Greek version only the first two letters survive, but it is reconstructed thus: Βω[νχαρ Μεχράσι Κλώδιος ἰατρός]. The Punic version can no longer be read, but it was once copied as: *bdʿlqrt ḥmqr . . qlʿʾy ḥrpʾ*. The first name has been miscopied: it ought to be *bdmlqrt*, which would correspond to the form *Boncar* of the Latin.[418] The next word is of uncertain meaning. *qlʿʾy* represents *Clodius*, and the last word is the term for 'doctor'. This man (or the dedicator) was happy to have both the Latin and the Punic names used in both languages in juxtaposition.

There is an additional interest to this inscription, namely that it contains a Greek version. Even in the western parts of the Roman world Greek was the professional language of doctors (see above, 1.VIII (p. 90) on the oculist's stamps from Gaul), and in inscriptions which doctors set up or which commemorate them some Greek was often included in recognition of the connection felt beween the Greek language and medicine. There is another Tripolitanian trilingual inscription commemorating the mother of (the same?) doctor, who, in setting the inscription up, had taken care to underline his professional identity in the same way (*IRT* 655, *IPT* 12):

brkt bt bʿlšlk ʾm qlʿʾʾy ḥrbʾ
brkt, daughter of bʿlšlk, mother of qlʿʾʾy (Clodius) the doctor.

Byrycth Balsilechis f(ilia) mater Clodi medici

Βύρυχθ Βαλσιάληχ θυγάτηρ μήτηρ Κλωδίου ἰατροῦ.

---

[415] See *IPT* 5B.   [416] See in particular Amadasi Guzzo (1988: 29).

[417] Levi Della Vida and Amadasi Guzzo (1987: 38 n. 1) report that the second line, which begins after the *i* of *Clodius*, is now illegible.

[418] See Levi Della Vida and Amadusi Guzzo (1987: 38) on this point.

In the Greek version the name of the mother's father is not inflected, perhaps because the writer was incapable of drawing on analogy in order to achieve an appropriate genitive ending. In Punic/Greek inscriptions transliterated into Greek letters Greek names are sometimes not inflected in filiations (as Greek) (see v.9).

This is also the place to mention a third trilingual inscription in the name of a doctor, though the names are not significant in this case. The inscription is from Henchir-Aouin (prov. procos.), and is Republican (91 BC) (*CIL* I².707, VIII.24030, Warmington (1940: 176)). The inscription is fragmentary, and the word for 'doctor' does not survive in the Greek and Latin versions, but it can be restored in both on the evidence of the Punic. The text of the Greek and Latin is printed as follows by Warmington:

Q. Marci[us] Protomacus [medicus]. facta L. M.[419] cos. m[ense]
Κουίντος Μάρκιο[ς Πρωτό[μαχος] Ἡρακλείδο[υ ἰατρός].

The professional status of Greek as a doctors' language is a topic which will recur at various places in this book (see particularly 3.v).[420]

Another Punic–Latin bilingual, from El Amrouni in the Gefara, a coastal plain stretching south-west from Sabratha and Tripoli, is also particularly interesting for the forms of its names (*KAI* 117, Berger (1895)).[421] It is dated on the evidence of its Latin lettering to the late second or early third century.[422] Millar (1968: 132) observes that the inscription 'illustrates graphically the Romanization of a prosperous local family, presumably of farmers':

D(is) M(anibus) sac(rum)
Q. Apuleus Maxssimus
qui et Rideus uocaba-
tur Iuzale f(ilius) Iurathe n(epos)
uix(it) an(nis) LXXXX Thanubra
coniunx et Pudens et Se-
uerus et Maxsimus f(ilii)
piissimi p(atri) amantissimo s(ua) p(ecunia) f(ecerunt)

1 l'l[nm] 'r'p'm š 'pwl'ẙ
2 m'k[šm]' ryd'y bn ywbz'l'n

---

[419] Taken to be Lucius Marcius.
[420] I do not of course mean that Latin-speaking doctors made a habit of using Greek when they were behaving as doctors, but only that snatches of Greek from time to time might have lent the doctor authority. See in general Langslow (2000: 28–41). On 'authority' and code-switching, see e.g. above, IV.4, p. 194.
[421] The inscription is discussed at length by Ferchiou (1989); see also Millar (1968: 132), Röllig (1980: 292).
[422] See Millar (1968: 132).

3 bn ywr˚[t]ʿn hmtʾby bʿnʿ tʿnb-
4 rʿ ʾšt[ʾ] ʾl pwdnš wšʾwʾ(wʾ)-
5 rʾ wmʿk[šm]ʾ bʿn[nm(?)]

To the gods, the Rephaim[423] of Apulei Maxime Ridai, son of ywbzʿlʿn (Iubalaan), son of ywrʿ[t]ʿn (Iurathan), the hmtʾby.[424] Thanubra, his wife, for Pudens and Sevevere [*sic*] and Maxime, their sons, built (this mausoleum).[425]

The deceased Q. Apuleius Maximus Rideus has a largely Latin name.[426] His sons Pudens, Severus and Maximus have exclusively Latin names. On the other hand his father, grandfather and wife have African names.[427] It would appear that Apuleius, of Punic origin and married to a Punic speaker, had Latinised his identity, the degree of Latinisation being more advanced than that seen above in (e.g.) the inscription from Guelaat bou Sba, in that here the man has the same Latin names in both versions, whereas Rufus/Tisdat had a different name in each version. This inscription nicely brings out the change in nomenclature which had occurred in time within a single family. Four generations of the family are named in both versions. The first two generations have African names, the later two Latin names.

In the Punic version the names of Latin origin all reflect the Latin vocative form rather than the nominative, a feature which is the norm in Latin names (of nominative function) in neo-Punic inscriptions.[428]

---

[423] The spirits of the dead: equivalent to *dis manibus* (see Röllig (1980: 292)).

[424] This term is obscure: see Röllig (1980: 292).

[425] The translation is based largely on Donner and Röllig (1966–9: 122), but see also Berger (1895: 76), Ferchiou (1989: 51).

[426] The *signum* Rideus is not Latin, and is of obscure origin (see Ferchiou (1989: 57)). It is possibly a Latin transcription of a Punic name; if so, it might have been the original name of the man (Ferchiou (1989: 60)).

[427] See Röllig (1980: 292).

[428] See Donner and Röllig (1966–9) on 117, Friedrich (1947: 120–2), id. (1953: 110–11), Röllig (1980: 292), Amadasi Guzzo (1986: 31–2, with the list at 30); also Février (1953b), taking a different line. The ending -*e* instead of -*us* is represented by -ʾ, and -*i* instead of -*ius* by -*y* (Amadasi Guzzo, loc. cit.). The vocative origin of these forms is particularly clear in the 'Latino-Punic' inscriptions written in Latin script. From Vattioni's corpus (1976) of texts I cite some examples using his numeration: 1 *Rogate*, 4 *Amice*, 6 *Licini*, 22 *Flabane*, 32 *Flabi*, 56 *Flabi*, *Macrine*. Almost all Latin names in neo-Punic inscriptions are derivable from the vocative. Exceptions to this rule are mainly of a particular type (see Friedrich (1953: 110)): in relatively early formal inscriptions names of members of the imperial family are sometimes written with a representation of final -*s*, as for example *grmʾnyqs* = Germanicus at *IPT* 22.1, 2 and *drʾss* = Drusus at *IPT* 22.1, 2. This no doubt reflects in part the lack of currency of such names in ordinary speech, and also a desire to get imperial titles absolutely right in formal inscriptions; but there was a chronological development, with such names tending in time to be 'Punicised' (i.e. given a 'vocative' ending) (see Amadasi Guzzo (1986: 31)). In one rare case an African individual is given the Latinate form of his Latin name: *rwps* = *Rufus* at *IPT* 21, line 3 (8 BC): see Levi Della Vida and Amadasi Guzzo (1987: 52), 'il mantenimento della terminazione -*us* è spiegato con la recente adozione del nome in Africa' (see also below, n. 442). Finally, in the late period when there was a marked

This is to be explained from the fact that the vocative is the form of a name most commonly heard,[429] and if a Latin name were picked up by Punic speakers from Latin speech rather than written texts, it is that form which might well have been borrowed. The presence of such vocative borrowings in Punic obviously hints at the existence of a genuine spoken bilingualism, as distinct from a learned type practised largely at the level of writing; for in the latter case one might have expected the correct (written) nominative forms of Latin names to have been transferred. The vocative forms are the more interesting because in African Latin inscriptions a tendency has been noted for names to be used in the vocative case where the nominative might have been expected; I will return to this matter in a later chapter (4.v.4.4), where an alternative explanation of the apparent vocatives in neo-Punic will be considered (and rejected). It should be noted that in the above inscription the Latin names have the correct nominative inflections in the Latin version; it is only in the Punic that the vocative form appears. From this distinction it can be deduced that the two different types of 'nominative' of Latin names were separately current in the two languages.

The Latin version has several formulaic elements which are not in the Punic (the *qui et X uocabatur* formula, the epithets *piissimi* and *amantissimo*, and the concluding formula *s.p.f.*), but the Punic has nothing which is not in the Latin (apart from the obscure *hmt'by*). In one respect it is the Latin version that has determined the form of the Punic, in that an attempt has been made in the latter to render the Latin formula *dis manibus*, in a form which will have sounded odd in Punic. The Latin version seems therefore to have primacy, which would be consistent with a fairly advanced Romanisation within the family. We have frequently stressed that the two versions of a bilingual inscription may be idiomatic within their own traditions, but later in this section further signs will be seen of the growing influence exerted by Latin structures on Punic.

A different relationship between the names in the two versions of a bilingual text can be found on an inscribed bronze spatula (?) from Lepcis (*IPT* 91) which bears the names of the possessor of the object. This type of text we saw earlier from Umbria (II.2); it is a curious indication that even in a domestic setting a bilingual may wish to give expression to his double linguistic identity. The Punic reads *mtnb'l bn ṣdq* (= 'M. son of S.'). The Latin has *Diodoru[s]*. The first Punic name means 'gift of

---

intrusion of Latin elements into 'Latino-Punic' inscriptions there is extant a corpus of texts in which the Latin nominative ending is commonplace (see below, v.6).

[429] See e.g. Février (1953b: 467), and in general Wackernagel (1926: 309–10).

Baal'; *Diodorus* is thus a translation (into Greek, but presented in Latin form) of the Punic;[430] for a Latin rendering of this or a similar Punic name, see below, v.8 on the name of Augustine's son. The translation of names in bilingual societies we have seen before, in Etruria (see III.6 on *zicu* = *Scribonius*), and it will come up again, for example in Gaul (see 7.IV.2). The pure Latin translation of the name here might have been expected to be *Saturninus*, since *b'l* was equated with Saturn (see below v.5.3 for a bilingual inscription in which the equation is explicit).[431] *Saturninus* is well attested in Tripolitania (see the editors of *IPT* on 91),[432] but whoever was responsible for this rendering must have been trilingual.

Evidence for a degree of Greek culture in the early period at Carthage was mentioned above (n. 381). The doctors' inscriptions discussed earlier are a special case, in that Greek is a 'professional' language. A Christian catacomb from Sirte which will be introduced below (v.6) contains short epitaphs from what appears to be a fairly humble social level, in Greek, Latin and neo-Punic. There is a small corpus of Punic inscriptions written in Greek letters (see below, v.9);[433] literacy in the Greek alphabet may imply a knowledge of the language, and one or two of these transliterated texts have other indications that the writer was bilingual (see v. 9). The Punic translation of *consul* might have been modelled on that of Greek (see v.5.2 below). The inscription *CIS* I.191 (Carthage) is in a mixture of scripts. As extant it appears to run Εὐκλέα ʼš *ndr* 'which vowed Euklea'.[434] Most of the dedication, which was probably to Tanit and Baal (see *CIS*), is missing. It is observed by the editor that the inscription is notable for the fact that a 'femina pia, serva videlicet, nomen suum graecum graecis litteris scribi voluit'. There is a distinctive type of language mixing or code-switching in evidence here, which has a close parallel in a Greek–Etruscan inscription seen earlier (III.3). The dedicator uses the local language in making a religious dedication, but holds on to her identity as symbolised by the Greek script used for the name. There were clearly polyglot speakers about with a knowledge of Greek, and not merely at the highest social level. Greek literary culture as manifested for example in the persons of Apuleius (note too the quotation from a Greek letter written by a woman at Apul. *Apol.* 82) and Septimius Severus was perhaps a different matter,[435] in that the wealthy educated classes in any

---

[430] See Levi Della Vida and Amadasi Guzzo (1987: 141), Amadasi Guzzo (1988: 29).

[431] See Levi Della Vida and Amadasi Guzzo (1987: 141).

[432] See also Amadasi Guzzo (1986: 37).   [433] See Vattioni (1976: 534–6).

[434] On the problem of the reading, see Vattioni (1976: 535), 8.

[435] Sandy (1997: 9) claims that 'Greek culture does not appear to have put down deep roots there [i.e. in North Africa] until after Apuleius' formative years.' Augustine (at a rather later date)

part of the Empire could afford to have access to Greek teachers and instruction.

V.5.2 *Punic borrowing from and imitation of Latin*

A fragmentary bilingual from Tripolitania (Lepcis Magna) raises the question of the treatment of Latin titles in Punic (*KAI* 125, *IRT* 305, *IPT* 30; I adopt here the text of the last):

Neptu[no] Aug(usto) s[ac(rum)] C. Sossius [...]nus IIIIu[ir...] pot(estate) de sua [pecunia posuit]

...] 'ydls qw'ṭrbr lmb̊[.]pkḥ bt[m]
... aedile, quattuoruir ... [erected it] at his own cost.

In the Punic text both the reading and meaning of the third word are uncertain.[436] The Punic contains two loan-words from Latin, namely *aedilis* and *quattuoruir*, the latter in a form which reflects Vulgar Latin *quattorbir*.[437] In spoken Latin a back vowel or [w] following a stop was lost before another back vowel (*antiquus* > *anticus, sequondus* > *secundus,* etc.), and the form of the first part of the borrowing thus reveals its passage into Latin at the level of speech.

It is in these borrowings that the interest of the inscription lies. Punic speakers made some effort to translate Latin titles such as 'consul', 'proconsul' and 'censor' into Punic,[438] but later the practice of borrowing set in. Previously *aedilis* was rendered by *mḥz*, a term of the same root as *mḥwz* = 'market'.[439] The date of the present inscription is uncertain, but it may belong to the second half of the first century AD.[440] Although the two versions were clearly very similar, there are structural differences. The Latin seems to have had the abstract ablatival expression *aedilicia potestate* after *IIIIuir*, whereas the Punic is more concrete, in that it has instead two personal nouns, *aedilis* and *quattuoruir*.[441]

---

made out that his Greek was not good (see *Contra litteras Petiliani* 2.91, *CSEL* 52, 75 *et ego quidem Graecae linguae perparum assecutus sum et prope nihil; non tamen impudenter dico me nosse* ὅλον *non esse 'unum', sed 'totum'* (see e.g. W. Green (1951: 184)). But since the time of the Carthaginians there had clearly been some Greek-speaking bilinguals in Africa.

[436] See Levi Della Vida and Amadasi Guzzo (1987: 73).

[437] See Donner and Röllig (1966–9: 131), Levi Della Vida and Amadasi Guzzo (1987: 73). *Quattuoruiri* are not otherwise known at Lepcis, according to *IRT* ad loc.

[438] For examples, see Donner and Röllig (1966–9: 123) on 118.2, citing also 62.4 and 83 in their collection; see also Février (1953a: 358), and, in particular, for discussion with further bibliography, Levi Della Vida and Amadasi Guzzo (1987: 73), Amadasi Guzzo (1988: 30–2).

[439] See Levi Della Vida and Amadasi Guzzo (1987: 72–3) (with bibliography), and Amadasi Guzzo (1988: 32) (discussing this inscription).

[440] See Levi Della Vida and Amadasi Guzzo (1987: 72).

[441] See Levi Della Vida and Amadasi Guzzo (1987: 73).

The most striking effort to translate titles is to be seen in a long bilingual building inscription of 8 BC from Lepcis (*KAI* 120, and now *IPT*
21; for the Latin see also *IRT* 319). In this Hannibal Tapapius Rufus
son of Himilcho[442] states that he has built and has dedicated a structure at his own expense. Both versions begin with a Latin-style dating
formula which names the emperor (in the nominative in the Latin)[443]
and gives a full list of his titles; this is followed (in the Latin) by an
ablatival consular date. The titles in the Punic version do not consist of the
Latin words transliterated, but are rendered into Punic: the translator,
who must have been a native speaker of Punic, has attempted to identify
the titles with pre-existing Punic institutions.[444] *Imperator* is replaced by
mynkd, a Libyan term of debatable meaning,[445] *consul* by *rb mḥnt* ('chief
of the army'),[446] *pontifex maximus* by *'dr khnm* (something like 'priest in
chief'), *flamines* by *zbḥm* (= 'sacrificers'),[447] and *tribunicia potestate* by a circumlocution, *tḥt mšlt 'sr hmšlm*, rendered by Amadasi Guzzo (1988: 31)
as 'al posto dell'autorità dei 10 aventi autorità'. There seems to be a linguistic ideology behind this inscriptions. Punic is kept free of Latin words
even in reference to distinctively Roman institutions. But the history of
many languages shows that linguistic nationalism which takes this form is
rarely influential for long. Borrowing is far easier than the establishing of
equivalences.

It is not only the fact of translation which is of interest in this last inscription. Latin words may be avoided, but the presence of the emperor
at the head of the Punic as well as the Latin version with his titles marks
the text out as exceptional. In similar formal bilingual dedications the
emperor is usually named and described only in the Latin version (see

---

[442] *Tapapius* is a local *cognomen* used by a famous family of Lepcis (see Levi Della Vida and Amadasi
Guzzo (1987: 52)). It is of interest that this man also now has a Latin name, *Rufus*, which retains
the Latin ending -*us*, in contrast to the names of vocative form seen earlier (see above, n. 428).

[443] This is unusual: see Levi Della Vida and Amadasi Guzzo (1987: 49 n. 1).

[444] See Amadasi Guzzo (1988: 31) for details; also Levi Della Vida and Amadasi Guzzo (1987:
49–51).

[445] By contrast in the Sardinian Punic inscription, Amadasi Guzzo (1990: 81–2), 14, *imperator* is
borrowed. Amadasi Guzzo (1990: 82) renders *mynkd* as 'un capo con poteri straordinari'.

[446] Levi Della Vida (1935: 8) (cf. id. (1951: 67)) notes that the Punic expression used to render *consul*
stresses the military role of the office, like the Greek rendering στρατηγὸς ὕπατος. He puts this
similarity down to coincidence, but it is not impossible that the rendering is Greek-inspired; on
Greek knowledge in Africa see v.5.1 above.
   The practice of translating Latin titles is well illustrated by the ponderous equivalent of
proconsul found at *IPT* 76, a Punic text (15–17 AD) which contains a dating formula referring to
the proconsul Lucius Aelius Lamia, a friend of Horace. The title is rendered *rb t'ḥt rb mḥnt*,
literally 'chief instead of the chief of the army' (see Levi Della Vida and Amadasi Guzzo (1987:
111); also Röllig (1980: 292)).

[447] See Levi Della Vida and Amadasi Guzzo (1987: 51).

IPT 24, a dedication of a theatre in AD 1–2,[448] *IPT* 26, of 54–3 BC, and *IPT* 27, of AD 92).[449] The view must have been that the imperial titles were so Roman in character that they should be expressed only in the Latin version; it is a case then of a category of information which was more suited to one language than the other.[450] This attitude inevitably produces 'unequal' bilingual texts. We will later discuss evidence from Egypt and elsewhere for the use of Latin in imperial or consular dating formulae in texts the remainder of which is Greek (3.VI.2, 5.IV.6). A parallel from Africa was seen earlier (V.3) in certain bilingual coin legends in which the name of the emperor is given only in Latin; and we also cited some Palestinian milestones with the Imperial titulature in Latin and the distances in Greek; see further below, VII.2 on a Latin–Palmyrene bilingual text. On the other hand in the *monolingual* Punic inscription from Bitia in Sardinia discussed earlier (V.4) there is a date by regnal year of the emperor, alongside the earlier style of dating by the suffetes. A bilingual inscription allowed the different categories of information to be expressed in the appropriate language.

[448] The Latin version (*IRT* 321) has a highly formal date (*Imp. Caesare diui f. Aug. pont. max. tr. pot. XXIV cos. XIII patre patr.*), followed by a statement that Hannobal Rufus set the monument up (*d(e) s(ua) p(ecunia) fac(iendum) coer(auit) idemq(ue) dedicauit*). Between the date and the verb phrase there are recorded five titles of the dedicator and a filiation. The Punic on the other hand is without the date, but it otherwise corresponds closely to the Latin. Again the man is given five titles. Among these are *ornator patriae* and *amator concordiae*, with Punic equivalents. In *IPT* 27 the Latin has comparable titles, *amator patriae, amator concordiae, amator ciuium, ornator patriae*, which are again in most cases found in Punic form in the other version. In Punic this type of titulature occurs only in these two inscriptions, but in Latin it is common in North Africa (*IRT*, index). The origin of the phraseology might well be Latin (see Amadasi Guzzo (1988: 32)), in which case there has again been translation from Latin into Punic. Mattingly (1987: 74) asserts without discussion of the issues that such phrases in Latin are 'direct translations of Neo-Punic titles'.
  One typical difference between the two versions of *IPT* 24 above is that whereas the Latin has a filiation (*Himilchonis Tapapi f.*) the Punic records two generations of the subject's ancestors ('son of *ḥmlkt ṭabaḥpi* Rufus, son of *'rm*').

[449] See the remarks of Amadasi Guzzo (1988: 25–6). Two other fragmentary building inscriptions should be mentioned here. *IRT* 481, *IPT* 16 is trilingual, in Latin, Greek and Punic. The Latin and Greek versions are fragmentary, and the Punic more so, and the texts are not worth quoting here. It would seem though that the Punic as well as the Greek and Latin contained imperial titulature (see Levi Della Vida and Amadasi Guzzo (1987: 42)). Another bilingual which presumably recorded works of some sort (*IRT* 349, *IPT* 9) is badly damaged because of the *damnatio memoriae* of Domitian. There are remnants of the imperial titulature in the Latin, and in the fragmentary neo-Punic apparently a reference to the provision of works. No worthwhile observations can be based on the inscription in its present state, but it does seem to have been the case that major building dedications tended to be bilingual (or trilingual) (cf. 5.IV.7 for bilingual building inscriptions in Egypt).

[450] A comparable phenomenon is to be seen in official inscriptions set up in Greek areas in which the text is basically in Greek but preceded by a Latin preamble. The information is conveyed in Greek but the presence of Latin at the start establishes the official nature of the text. See e.g. *IGBulg.* IV.2235, cited above, 1.VII.4.2, p. 81.

The bilingual building inscription *IPT* 27 just referred to has another feature of interest. Amadasi Guzzo (1988: 26) observes that the Punic version renders the Latin word for word with syntax inappropriate to a Semitic language.[451] Thus *aram et podium* in the Latin has as its correspondent in the Punic *mzbḥ wp'dy* (the second word borrowed from the Latin), an expression which is notable for the lack of determiners (either articles or demonstratives).[452] This anomaly by Punic standards is explained from the faithful adherence of the translator to the structure of the Latin.[453] Thus, whereas some of the texts we have considered are idiomatic bilinguals, here the Latin version seems to be dominant, with the Punic in some respects a non-idiomatic rendering of it. Once structures characteristic of Latin start to intrude into Punic, Romanisation is well under way. This text, along with *IPT* 24, as we saw (n. 448), also has titulature in the Punic version which is probably Latinate.

v.5.3 *Miscellaneous*

I now move on to some miscellaneous texts from which bits and pieces of information relevant to our present purposes can be extracted.

A neo-Punic–Latin bilingual which apparently concerns a corporation of dealers in spices (*KAI* 160, Février (1951–2b); Latin text at *CIL* VIII.27774) is so fragmentary and full of difficulties, and the surviving parts of the two versions so unrelated, that it cannot be lingered over, but an observation may be made about the Latin version:

fragment 1 of Latin:
quod bonum fau[stum fe-]
[l]ixque sit sod[alibus (?)]
[tur]is igne(i)[454] quis [uelit]
[   ]isa Iouis [   ]
[   ]templo po[nere]
[   ]difici[   ]

Fragment 2 of the Latin is even more incomplete, though *animo* and *Iouis* can be discerned. There are six lines of Punic, all of them incomplete on the right.

The inscription seems to have been set up by the members of a *collegium* or the like. The one feature which stands out in the Latin text is the

[451] 'Ricalcando parola per parola il testo latino con una sintassi impropria a una lingua semitica'.
[452] See Amadasi Guzzo (1979: 33–4). For determiners in such a context, see Friedrich and Röllig (1970: 152).
[453] See further Amadasi Guzzo (1988: 26–7) on the unusual rendering of the Latin dative relative pronoun *cui*.
[454] The restoration *turis ignei* was suggested by Février (1951–2b: 23).

presence of the old quasi-religious formula *bonum faustum felixque*, complete with *-que* attached to the third member of the list in the manner of old prayers (see e.g. Cic. *Mur.* 1 *fauste feliciter prospereque*). The inscription contains Latinity of old formal style which hints at the existence of bilingualism among the fairly well educated. The Latin text can only have been composed by someone competent in the traditional formulae of the religious language, and even if he were an outsider not necessarily fluent in Punic a sophisticated communication must have taken place between him and the (Punic-speaking) commissioners of the inscription.

A bilingual epitaph (from Henschir Brigitta in Tunisia) has an accumulation of formulae in the Latin version which are appropriate to the language as it was used in Africa (*KAI* 142, Latin at *CIL* VIII.793):

Dis manib(us) sacr(um). Gadaeus Felicis fil(ius) pius uix(it) annis LXVI hic sit(us) est. Secunda Secundi fil(ia) u(ixit) a(nnis) [ ]. Saturio et Gadaeus patri piissimo posuerunt

1 g'[d]'y bn plkš bn pḥl'n 'qyl'
2. 'wh š'ṅ'[t] š['š]m wš'š wšhqnd
3. ' bt šqṅd' 'š̊[t]' 'w' š'nt
4. phl' l'b'nhm mt̊ qbr š'ṭry wg'dy
5. '-tṅb'bdmwn-"ph'mtr'q̊-"t̊m
6. bt̊ḥṅmphl'ṅg̊s̊g̊ 'w' š̊t hnm--wb mšyt̊
7. ḥ'[...]-[.]'---š̊'ṭṙb[...]--'qbr bšlm

Gadaeus, son of Felix, son of pḥl'n Aquila lived 66 years. And Secunda, daughter of Secunda, his wife, lived ... years. For their ... father Saturius and Gadaeus made a grave ... the grave, in peace.

There are here at least three typical Latin funerary formulae (with African connections) which are not rendered in the Punic version, *dis manibus*, *pius uixit* and *hic situs est*.[455] The epithet of the father (*piissimo*), while typical of such Latin texts, appears to have no correspondent in the Punic. On the other hand the Punic, unlike the Latin, records the ancestry of the deceased to two generations in the Semitic manner. The end of the Punic version is difficult to read and has not been fully explained,[456] but it is certain (since there is nothing equivalent in the Latin text) that this section will have contained further material contributing to the 'complementarity' of the two versions. The Punic records the parentage of the wife on the mother's side, whereas it is on the father's side

[455] For the last two formulae as widespread in Africa, see Mastino (1985: 87). *Dis manibus* is said to be relatively late (from the start of the second century AD) in Africa (Mastino (1985: 87)).
[456] See Donner and Röllig (1966–9: 140).

in the Latin. All of these variations, minor though they might be, show that separate conventions of presenting epitaphs were surviving to some extent in the two languages in Africa; such complementarity is consistent with a living bilingualism. It is incidentally of interest that the age of the wife is not completed in either version. At the time of the death of Gadaeus Secunda was still alive, and no one remembered to fill in the gap when she died. The names are virtually the same in the two versions.

The following bilingual funerary inscription from Mactar has a Latin version which is formulaic and differs slightly from the Punic (*KAI* 152):

Iasucta Selidiu f(ilius) uixit annis LXIII honeste

1. yʿsktʿn bn sʿldyʾ bʿl hmktʿrm
2. hnkt qybr tḥt ʾbn zt ʿbn
3. t bn ššm št wšlš tm bḥym

Iasuctan, son of Selidiu(s), citizen of Mactar...was buried, under this stone...[457] (He was) 63 years old, upright in life.

The second line of the Punic, whatever its interpretation, has no equivalent in the Latin, nor is there any reference in the Latin to the deceased's *patria*. The names are the same in both versions. The Latin is notable for the fact that the name of the father is not inflected; *Selidiu* seems to have been written for *sʿldyʾ*.[458] The final word *honeste* strikes a slightly odd note for a Latin text.

The following inscription from Dschebel Mansur (Gales) shows a greater agreement between the two parts (*KAI* 140):

Quarta Nyptanis [f(ilia) G]
a[l]e(n)sis uxsor Celeris
Mantis (?) f(ilii) sacerdos magna
conditiu(m) s(ua) p(ecunia) f(ecit) cu[ra]torib-
us Saturum Rogato Bruti-
ione Maniu [N]am[f]amone
Valente Celer[is f(ilio)] stru(ctoribus) [R]uf[o]
Imilcone-ul-ses ui[xit]

1. bnʾ b[t] z [q]wʾr[ṭ]ḥ bt npthn
2. bʿl gʿl [ʾš]t qlr bn hmʿn/tt/n hknt
3. bʾ[...]ṭ hḷ[...]yḥn/tk/bʾ/ šʿs/šym
4. šʿṭr rgʿṭʾ brṭʾ hmʿ/tt/n nʿmp
5. [ʾm wʾ]ls/š bn ḍlṛ bn hmʿn/tt/n bʿlʾ

---

[457] On this problematical line, see Donner and Röllig (1966–9: 136) on no. 136, lines 1–2.
[458] See Février (1953b: 470).

6. [gʻl] bʻynm rẘp' whmlkt bʻ
7. [l' . . .] whw' šʻnt ʼm̊šm w[   ]

This (building) Quarta erected, daughter of npthn, the citizen of Gales, (wife) of Celer, the son of hmʻnt (?), the priestess . . . Satur, Rogatus, Brutus, hmʻnt (?), Namp[hamo, V]alens, son of Celer, sons of hmʻnt (?), citizen [of Gales]. Builders (were) Rufus and hmlkt, (citizen) . . . And she lived fifty . . years.

There are only minor differences between the two versions, as for example in the absence from the Latin of anything between *Celeris filio* and *structoribus*; also the Latin formula *sua pecunia fecit* does not have an exact correspondent in the Punic. A few other features in the Latin are of note. The name *Maniu* does not seem to have a Latin inflection, but is probably intended as an accusative, with omission of the final *-m*. This possibility is suggested by the form of the first name in the list (*Saturum*). The complete list of names may therefore have been conceived as standing in the accusative. Certainly the first name is unambiguously accusative, and that syntactically is a matter of interest, because the writer has clearly lapsed into the substandard construction 'accusative of apposition' immediately after writing the ablative *curatoribus* (on which construction see p. 62 n. 146). The presence of this usage locates the Latin version somewhat down the educational scale. The Latin versions of Latin–Punic bilinguals are sometimes in a formal, archaizing language, whereas in other cases they display colloquial or substandard characteristics. This diversity suggests that bilingualism was spread across a fairly broad social/educational spectrum. The names are again the same in the two versions, but here again there is evidence for a change in naming practices between two generations, this time in two families. The dedicator has a Latin name, but her father a Punic; similarly her husband has a Latin name, but his father too a Punic name.

The following inscription is from the forum at Lepcis. It is dated to the first century AD on the basis of the neo-Punic script (*KAI* 127, *IRT* 294, *IPT* 25; the last work is cited here):

Libero Patri sac(rum)
Boncarth Muthumbalis f(ilius)
Sobti IIIuir macelli ex multis
LXII quibus adiecit de suo LIII

Various bits and pieces of the neo-Punic survive, but it is only the first line that is securely legible:

m'š z ṭyn' l'dn šdrp' bd̊mlqrt bn mtnbʿl šmkẙ

This statue has erected to lord šdrp' bdmlqrt, son of mtnbʿl šmky . . . .'

The names of the dedicator are the same in the Latin version as in the Punic, and are Punic throughout. *Boncarth* is equivalent to *bd-mlqrt* (see above, v.5.1 on *IPT* 13), and *Muthumbalis* to *mtnbʿl.* The next word in the Punic, *šmky*, is interpreted by Levi Della Vida and Amadasi Guzzo (1987: 62) as some sort of *cognomen*; *Sobti*, which has the corresponding position in the Latin, must represent this same *cognomen*.[459] The first word of the Punic, which may = 'statue' (see the editors of *IPT*), corresponds to *sacrum* in the Latin, but the two are not equivalents. The composer of the Latin has used a genuine Latin formula, whereas the Punic is abnormal by Punic standards but not in ways which have been determined by the Latin. It is usual in Punic for the dedication to the divinity to precede mention of the object dedicated; if the name of the object does come first, the name of the dedicator precedes the name of the divinity.[460] However the abnormalities of the Punic are to be explained, it is clear that slightly different structures have been adopted in the two versions, with the Latin structure idiomatic.

From Sabratha (Tripolitania) Rossi and Garbini (1976–7: 7–19) have published a bilingual votive inscription to Baal/Saturn inscribed on a marble basin, presumably a sacred object. The Latin inscription is incised on the outside of the rim of the vessel, whereas the neo-Punic version (in neo-Punic script) is incised in parallel to the Latin on the inside. From this it appears that the composer wished to give the Latin greater prominence (see Rossi, 8). The texts are as follows:

domno Sapurno [*sic*] uico Ṃ[. . . . .]no u(oto) s(uscepto) Iu[. .]hn [?]giaduris f[il]ius f(ecit)

ndr lbʿl bšʿnṭsty [y]ẘn̊t̊ḥn bn 'g'dr ks dḥ'. . . . .'t qlm

Has dedicated to Baal of bšnṭst [or 'to Baal in the settlement of tst/tsn] ywntḥn son of 'g'dr the vessel of ablution . . . (since he has heard) his voice.

The content of the two versions seems to have been substantially the same, though there are lacunae in the Punic. *uico* M . . . must have indicated the precise site (probably in a rural region of Sabratha) in which Saturn was venerated (see Rossi, 11), and there might have been

[459] *sobti* has been taken as a local variant of *sufes* (see *IRT*, p. 92 n. 2, Donner and Röllig (1966–9: 132)), but that view is effectively disposed of by the editors of *IPT*, p. 62.
[460] See Levi Della Vida and Amadasi Guzzo (1987: 61).

something equivalent in the Punic. The misspelling of the god's name in the Latin is curious, and not explicable by linguistic hypotheses. Had the Latin name been misunderstood for some reason in an out of the way place, or has there been some sort of carver's slip? The names of the dedicator and of his father seem to be the same in the two versions, and of non-Latin origin. There are enough minor differences between the versions to show that different formulaic traditions were being followed. For example, *domno, u.s.* (surely the normal expression *u(otum) s(oluit)* is preferable here, against Rossi, 12) and *fecit* do not have exact equivalents in the Punic, the structure of which is characterised by Garbini (18) as 'assai tradizionale'.

In the inscriptions quoted in this section the referents are not given different names in the two versions. Most of the names are Punic. This evidence should be set against that seen at v.5.1 above. Clearly some Punic speakers had learnt Latin before it occurred to them to take on Latin names either alongside or instead of their original names. But on the other hand the adoption of Latin names did not necessarily entail the complete abandonment of the Punic language; we noted in Sardinia (v.4) an exclusively Punic inscription (that from Bitia) in which the local referents have Latin names. We have now seen a remarkably large number of families (given the small size of the corpus) in which the older generation(s) have Punic names but the younger generation Latin, with no cases of the reverse type.

The other recurrent feature of these inscriptions lies in the constant subtle distinctions between the versions.

V.5.4 Conclusions

Various points which arise from these bilingual or trilingual texts should be stressed:

(1) To a considerable extent the different versions are idiomatic or formulaic within their own traditions, as in the case of those seen in the last section (v.5.3). The formula *pius uixit*, for example, which has no correspondent in the Punic version, is a cliché of African funerary inscriptions.

(2) There is though imitation of Latin formulae in some Punic texts.[461] *Dis manibus* is imitated in one Punic funerary inscription. *IPT* 27 follows the structure of the Latin exactly. The formula 'lived so many years' is Latinate. *Ex senatus consulto* is imitated in the Punic version of a Sardinian inscription. Imitation of formulae is a cultural rather than a linguistic

---

[461] See the remarks of Amadasi Guzzo (1988: 26).

phenomenon. The dominant culture influences the form of the wording on funerary and other public monuments, without necessarily altering the language itself in any permanent way.

(3) But imitation of formulae can shade into syntactic interference. The failure of the writer of *IPT* 27 to provide determiners with the Punic equivalent of *aram et podium* is modelled on Latin but non-idiomatic for Punic. But again *ad hoc* translationese need not affect the language as a whole, unless it is very obtrusive and its idioms taken over in other domains of use.

(4) There is by contrast virtually no sign of imitation of Punic formulae in Latin. The greater influence of Latin formulae on Punic than vice versa hints at the advancing Romanisation of North Africa (and Sardinia).

(5) There are signs of an ideological shift in Punic texts, in that translation of official Roman titles gives way to borrowing. The shift is again consistent with increasing Romanisation.

(6) Also suggestive of different stages of Romanisation are certain changes in naming practices. Punic names came to be complemented by Latin names, and then were replaced entirely. The shift can be plotted in various families over several generations. But there were some Punic speakers who retained their Punic names even when writing Latin.

(7) A prominent urban Tripolitanian with the name *Tapapius* went to considerable lengths to express a double identity. To put it another way, he was no doubt Romanised but keen to hold on to his earlier linguistic identity. Many of the bilingual texts can be interpreted along these lines.

(8) The doctors' inscriptions which have a Greek version well illustrate the special status of Greek in the eyes of the medical profession.

V.6 The 'Latino-Punic' inscriptions

An interesting group of texts are the so-called 'Latino-Punic' (previously called 'Latino-Libyan') inscriptions from the interior of Tripolitania (from places such as Ghirza, Bir Scemech, Bir ed-Dreder), the most notable feature of which is that they are written in the Latin script but in the neo-Punic language.[462] That language was originally thought to be 'Libyan'

---

[462] See the general introduction to the inscriptions by Goodchild (1950). There is an extensive recent bibliography on this corpus: see Levi Della Vida (1963), Vattioni (1976: 536–55) (a full collection of the texts), Coacci Polselli (1978), Garbini (1986: 72–81) (with bibliography at 72), Elmayer (1983, 1984, 1985) (though these last three papers must be treated with caution), Amadasi Guzzo (1989) (an overview of the state of the question).

(not Punic), but it is now clear that they are in neo-Punic, though with borrowing and interference from and code-switching into Latin.[463] The texts are difficult to read and have many obscurities. There has been some speculation about the reason for the choice of script,[464] but, as we have abundantly seen, transliteration is a feature of bilingual communities in which there is only partial literacy. The inscriptions represent a late stage of neo-Punic language and culture (roughly from the third to the fourth centuries AD),[465] by which time Latin literacy practices will have spread in Tripolitania and been adopted for the writing of Punic. Parallels have already been seen in this chapter, in the writing of Etruscan and Venetic in Latin script.

A few of the inscriptions have a mixture of Latin and Punic elements, for example *IRT* 894:[466]

D(is) m(anibus) s(acrum) Nabor Surṇiạ auo sanu n(umero) LXXX ny sath fo . . milim e . . duo . . s.

auo is the well attested Punic verb = 'he lived',[467] and *sanu* = 'years'.[468] The phrase is equivalent to and no doubt calqued on *uixit annis*. The structure of the first part of the inscription is not unlike that of various Greek–Latin mixed-language texts dealt with elsewhere (see *ILCV* 4463, discussed at 1.V and 3.V.1), in that it consists of a series of formulae with switches of language at formula-boundaries ('formula-switching'), though after the numeral obscurity sets in. The base language of the text would appear to be neo-Punic, but with two pieces of Latin, the introductory formula, and the formula for age at death (*numero* LXXX); there is too the Latinate expression *auo sanu*. An interesting feature of this expression in such inscriptions is that it is sometimes abbreviated (*auos* for *auo s(anu)*: Bartoccini (1928: 193, 198), 40). The abbreviation is probably modelled on the commonplace abbreviation of *uixit annis* in Latin,[469] and this imitation further underlines the dominance by this period of Latin literacy practices.[470] It should not be argued on the basis of evidence

[463] See Levi Della Vida (1963) for a convincing interpretation of the language.
[464] See Goodchild (1950: 142–3).
[465] On the problematical date of such texts, see Amadasi Guzzo (1989: 101).
[466] On this text see also Vattioni (1976: 552), Coacci Polselli (1978: 240).
[467] See Donner and Röllig (1966–9: 167), Levi Della Vida (1963: 85).
[468] See Donner and Röllig (1966–9: 167), Levi Della Vida (1963: 85).
[469] See Coaci Polselli (1978: 240).
[470] For *auo* abbreviated as *au*, see the inscription quoted below, p. 233, with Garbini (1986: 74) on *IRT* 855a, who counters a suggestion of Levi Della Vida that *au* cannot for phonetic reasons be equated with *auo*: it is in an orthographic tendency, not in the phonetics of the language, that the explanation of the form must be sought.

such as this that a 'mixed language' was current in Africa at this time. It would probably be more reasonable to say that users of Punic in its last days tended to switch into Latin if Latin had a convenient phrase or word for their purposes.

IRT 877 is rather different in its combination of elements:[471]

centenare mu felthi ana Marci Cecili bymupal fesem a pero y nbanem bucu buoms ayo nema.

The first word is of Latin origin. The adjective *centenarius* (= 'That is or contains a hundred': *OLD*) is commonplace, but the substantival neuter *centenarium* which lies behind the borrowing here is much rarer in Latin. The neuter is confined to African Latin, where it seems to have indicated a small fort on the African *limes*.[472] There are examples (in Latin) at *CIL* VIII.22763 (*centenarium Tububuci, quod Valerius Vibianus . . . initiari . . . curauit*), 8713, 9010, 20215, and also in another Latino-Punic inscription from Bir Scemech (*IRT* 889, *KAI* 179).[473] Whatever its precise meaning, this was clearly a regional Latin word which had entered the local Punic language.[474]

Vattioni (1976: 543) translates the first six words of the inscription as it is printed here as 'the *centenarium* which I Marcus Cecilius have made'.[475] The interpretation of the rest of the inscription seems hopeless. It is enough to note that the language is neo-Punic, but that a Latin term from the region has been taken over. That is a feature of the Latino-Punic inscriptions. We should in this case speak of 'borrowing'.

Such borrowing can also be seen at *IRT* 901, which I quote with the word division of Vattioni (1976: 552):

mmemoria mu fela Thualath? buth nasif mu fela lyruthi abi linema.

The first four words mean 'memorial which Thualath has made'.[476] The first word is Lat. *memoria* used with the concrete meaning 'memorial' familiar from funerary inscriptions and elsewhere. The last three inscriptions

---

[471] The text I print here is that of Vattioni (1976: 543), who discusses the numerous difficulties found particularly in the second two-thirds of the inscription.

[472] So Donner and Röllig (1966–9: 166). *TLL* III.814.60 is more circumspect (= 'genus aedificii, fort. castri uel burgi').

[473] This last inscription is notoriously difficult to interpret, and there is no need to get bogged down in the details here. Various possibilities are set out with bibliography by Garbini (1986: 77).

[474] The speculations of Elmayer (1985) do not contribute to an explanation of the usage, and the derivation of the word from *centuria* is plain nonsense.

[475] See also Garbini (1986: 75) for approval of the word division adopted by Vattioni.

[476] For bibliography and discussion of the difficulties of the rest of the inscription, see Garbini (1986: 78–9).

quoted all begin with a Latin word or words before switching into Punic.

A text possibly showing a switch into Latin is presented and translated by Vattioni (1976: 542) as follows:[477]

iu flau sanu au LXVI hoc fillyth mia sanu au XXXIII
Julius Flavius years lived 66. This has done (this is the work of) Mia: years lived 33.[478]

Hoc is generally taken to be the Latin demonstrative pronoun.[479] If so, it is hardly likely that a word of this kind had been borrowed by Punic, in the sense of being integrated into the language. It is more likely to have been an *ad hoc*, momentary switch adopted by one particular writer for reasons which are obscure.

We have several times seen a Punic expression (*auo sanu*) which was calqued on a Latin formula. Another case of imitation of a formula appears in the Latino-Punic inscription *IRT* 828 (= Vattioni (1976: 538), 2)). This is a funerary text of three lines, the last three words of which are *fel baiaem bithem*. The first of these is the verb 'made'. *Baiaem* is Punic *bhym*, meaning 'during his own life'; it represents Lat. *se uiuo*. *Bithem* 'at his expense' corresponds to Lat. *de sua pecunia* or *de/ex suo*.[480]

In the Latino-Punic texts the prevalence of vocative forms (for the nominative) is the more obvious because the texts are in Latin script (see above, v.5.1 with n. 428, and below on the Christian catacomb at Sirte). It is though of note that in the necropolis of Bir ed-Dreder, the inscriptions of which were first published by Goodchild (1954), Latin names, along with the title *tribunus*, are usually given the correct Latin ending *-us* in texts which are overwhelmingly in Punic. I cite, for example, the start of no. 6 (= Vattioni (1976), 37), a text of eleven lines: *Iulius Nasif tribunus* (cf. in Vattioni nos. 32, 33, 34, 35, 36, 44, 45). Here again we see the intrusion of Latin elements into these late texts.[481] The writers were countering a pattern of Punic in dealing with Latin names, and using the 'correct' Latin morpheme not only in the names but also in a common noun. Inflecting Latin names as Latin in a Punic text, like the inflecting

---

[477] See further Garbini (1986: 80), with bibliography. The inscription was first published by Oates (1954: 115).

[478] Here we see again the apparent abbreviation of the verb *auo* 'lived' (see Garbini, (1986: 80)).

[479] See Oates (1954: 115), Levi Della Vida (1965: 59–60), Garbini (1986: 80). Vattioni (1976: 542), while translating as if this were the Latin word, raises the possibility that *Hocpillyth* may be a name.

[480] See Levi Della Vida (1963: 78), Vattioni (1976: 538).

[481] On Latin words in the texts, see Bertinelli Angeli (1969) (but offering no distinctions between borrowing, interference and code-switching).

of Greek names as Greek in a Latin text, might arguably be seen as a form of code-switching (see further 4.V.3.1).

Various other texts have apparent language mixing as they are quoted by Vattioni (1976), but his readings are arbitrary. I cite several problematic (or cautionary) cases:

(1) The Latin text (in eight lines) Vattioni (1976), 71 ends *Masirann pronepos hoc opus super patris aedificium addidit fel*. The last word is taken by Vattioni to be the Punic verb = 'made', in which case there would have been iteration of the final Latin verb by a near-equivalent in Punic. But Brogan (1964: 53), who first published the text, prints the last two words as *addidit fe* ... The last word is as likely to be *fecit*.

(2) Vattioni (1976), 72, another Latin text, has towards the end the expression *u(ixit) anos XXX pate(r) ana f(elthi?)*. On the interpretation implicit here the last two words consist of the first-person pronoun and the verb 'made'. Di Vita (1966: 97) completes the last word as *f(ecit)*, but here the presence of *ana* (for which see above, p. 232 on *IRT* 877) lends some support to Vattioni.

(3) Vattioni (1976), 73 is printed as follows: *d(is) m(anibus) s(acrum)*. . . . *natus sanu VII*. As it stands, the text is in Latin, but with the word for 'years' in Punic. But Di Vita (1966: 99) prints the text thus:

D. M. S.
. . .] natus
. . .]V VII.

It is not clear whether Vattioni has emended the last line without using brackets, or examined the original inscription and come up with a new reading. This case in particular highlights the need for a proper re-edition of these texts. The emendation, if it is such, is not implausible in view of the first inscription quoted in this section, but more information is needed about the text.

Perhaps the most notable evidence for African multilingualism in action at a relatively low social level comes from a Christian catacomb of the fourth century AD discovered near the forum at Sirte in Tripolitania and reported by Bartoccini (1928). The short inscriptions from the catacomb, some fifty-three in number (published by Bartoccini (1928: 195–200)),[482] are in three languages, Latin, Greek and neo-Punic (written in Latin letters, and thus 'Latino-Punic'). Almost all of them, whatever the language, have the structure *Y uixit annos X*, with various

---

[482] *IRT* 855 records the find but does not print the texts.

abbreviations. For Latin examples, note e.g. 1 *Bernu u(ixit) ann(os) XXV*, 28 *Iambart uixit an(nos) LXX*. The most complete Greek text is 5 ἔζεσεν Φαῦ[σ]τος ἔτηα Δ. The Punic texts (for which see 8, 15, 39, 40, 43, 46, 50) tended to be misconstrued by Bartoccini in such a way as to suggest that they were in a mixture of Punic and Latin. Thus 15 is printed as *Mercuri auos ann(os) VI*, along with a suggestion that *auos = uixit*. It is now known that *auo sanu* is equivalent to *uixit annis* (see above), and hence with a different word division and the change of the second *n* to *u* the text is converted from a mixed-language type to pure Punic, though in the Latin alphabet and with a Latin numeral symbol: *Mercuri auo sanu VI*.[483]

Despite the consequent elimination of the mixed-language texts, the whole find is revealing evidence of the language situation in what must have been a relatively closed community. Of the names in Latin inscriptions, not a single one has the correct nominative inflection; it is the vocative form which is for the most part used with this function. I will return to this find and to the use of the vocative in a later chapter (4.v.4.4).

v.6.1 Conclusions

The 'Latino-Punic' inscriptions are few, brief and full of problems, but they throw up some interesting information. In the later Empire at humble social levels in Africa there were communities in which Punic, Latin and Greek were in use. Literacy in Punic had been lost, and the Latin script and to some extent also Greek script (see below, v.9) were used for the writing of the language. Latin formulae were imitated in Punic, and at least one Latin writing convention (the abbreviation of the formula for age at death) was adopted in Punic written in Latin letters. Latin words continued to be borrowed into Punic, and at least one Latin morpheme was retained in Latin words in Punic texts. And there are signs of code-switching into Latin in texts of which the matrix language is Punic. All of these features point to the influence of Latin culture, and they are consistent with a language shift in progress, though that can only be asserted with the benefit of hindsight, for it is in theory possible that Punic could have continued indefinitely without its own script and in forms marked by borrowing from and code-switching into the other language.

---

[483] For the correct interpretation see Donner and Röllig (1966–9), 180, with the commentary on this and a few other of the Punic inscriptions on p. 167.

v.7 Bu Njem

From the military outpost of Bu Njem in Tripolitania there survives a collection of ostraca dated to the third century AD.[484] The auxiliaries based there had in many cases African names, and the ostraca abound in African words otherwise unknown in Latin (see below, 4.V.2.5). Some of the texts are formulaic in structure, such that those dispatching messages merely had to fill in gaps. But there are signs that even that was a struggle for them.[485] Everything points to the presence in the camp of Africans who were learners of Latin as a second language and who had not achieved fluent competence in that language.[486] Here I would draw attention to a peculiar feature of the ostraca, which I have discussed in detail elsewhere,[487] namely the frequent use of the nominative for an oblique case in contexts in which even in substandard texts the construction is not found. For example, the nominative is found after the preposition *per*, and more than once (e.g. 77 *transmisi at te domine per kammellarius*; cf. 78, 80.5, with Adams (1994a: 92, 101)). *Muli* at 72 stands as object of *ferentes*.[488] At 99.4 *cuis* (*sic*: it introduces a relative clause) is used where *quem* would have been normal (*un asinu cuis nobis atulisti*). And there are also cases of the nominative for accusative in the accusative + infinitive construction (73.2–3, 101).

The most obvious explanation for these abnormalities is that the writers, as imperfect learners of Latin, were constantly lapsing into the 'uninflected' base-form of nouns, presumably the form which they had learnt first (cf. above, 1.IX, and, for further examples of the nominative as a base-form, below, 5.IX, p. 633, with cross references to that chapter). They were using in effect a type of 'reduced' Latin.

As a further parallel I here cite examples of nominative for oblique cases in Greek documents which there is reason to think were written by foreigners who were attempting to use Greek as a second language. In the Egyptian tax receipts published as *O. Bodl.* II there is a frequent formula of the structure 'tax collectors to X son of Y. We have received the tax . . .'. (e.g. II.676).[489] About 90 per cent of the inflections in the patronymic are right, but only 60 per cent of those in the first name. When the inflection

---

[484] For the texts see Marichal (1988), and for a discussion of the language, Adams (1994a).
[485] See Adams (1994a: 96).
[486] See also Adams (1999) on the poem of a centurion Iasuchthan, whose Latin is far from idiomatic and probably that of a language learner.
[487] Adams (1994a: 96–102).   [488] See Adams (1994a: 98).
[489] See Fewster (forthcoming).

is wrong in either name it is overwhelmingly the nominative which is used for dative or genitive. Cf. *O. Ont. Mus.* 1.21 Χεσφμόις πράκ(τωρ) ἀργ(υρικῶν) Πικῶς νεω(τέρῳ) Ἀπολώδωρος = 'Chesphmois, collector of money taxes, to Pikos the younger son of Apollodoros.' See the editor (n. 2): 'As happens frequently, oblique cases are rendered by the nominative, Πικῶς for Πικῶτι, Ἀπολώδωρος for Ἀπολλοδώρου'.

V.8 Later literary evidence

There is plentiful literary evidence from the Empire for the continued currency of Punic into the fourth century. The important *testimonia* are set out by Millar (1968: 130),[490] though a passage of Statius (*Silu.* 4.5.45–6) which he cites concerning the avoidance of *sermo Poenus* by a Septimius Severus almost certainly refers to the avoidance of an African accent in Latin rather than of the language Punic (see further 4.v.1.2).[491] Both Apuleius (*Apol.* 98.8–9: see above, 1.IX, p. 105) and the *Historia Augusta* (*Sept. Seu.* 15.7 *cum soror sua Leptitana ad eum uenisset uix Latine loquens, ac de illa multum imperator erubesceret . . . redire mulierem in patriam praecepit*) refer to Africans of some social standing allegedly unable to speak Latin except in a broken form, for which they are disparaged.

But the best evidence comes from Augustine. Augustine's works have more than twenty references to Punic (not Libyan)[492] implying or stating openly that it was still widely used. These passages have been elucidated by W. M. Green (1951), Vattioni (1968) and Cox (1988). Green and Cox collect the *testimonia*, and there is no need for me here to repeat their collections. The main conclusions to arise from these discussions are the following:

(1) Some Christian congregations knew Punic but little Latin (*Epist.* 66.2, *CSEL* 34, 236 (Green (1951: 181)), *Epist.* 108.14, *CSEL* 34, 628 (Green (1951: 182)), *Epist.* 209.2–3, *CSEL* 57, 348 (Green (1951: 182–3)). For a congregation not all of which knew Punic, see *Serm.* 167.4, *PL* 38, 910 (Green (1951: 183)).

(2) Augustine himself, while not fluent in Punic, had some sort of passive knowledge of the language.[493] He discusses the meanings of various words (see further below), knows the similarity between Punic and

---

[490] See also Vattioni (1968), Röllig (1980: 294).
[491] See K. Coleman (1988), ad loc. It is also taken as referring to the Punic language by Röllig (1980: 294 n. 59).
[492] Despite Courtois (1950).   [493] See the conclusions of Cox (1988: 98).

Hebrew,[494] and appears capable of quoting a Punic proverb in the original language.[495]

(3) Most importantly, though he was an educated primary speaker of Latin, Augustine shows some sort of respect for the Punic language (see below).

Augustine's son *Adeodatus* ('given by god') had a name which is calqued on a Punic name (Mutunba'al 'gift of Baal' or Iatanbaal 'Baal has given').[496] The first of these Punic names we have already seen calqued by the Greek *Diodorus* (v.5.1); it was possibly fashionable in some circles in Africa to translate Punic names in this way. Adeodatus himself knew some Punic (more, it would seem, than his father), and Augustine reports a dialogue between father and son on a question of Punic word-meaning (*De magistro* 44, *PL* 32, 1219).[497] Possibly the mother was a Punic speaker.

Augustine's esteem for Punic, in a man who was undoubtedly a first-language speaker of Latin (on his Greek see above n. 435), provides a background to the survival of the language for so long under Roman rule. There is no suggestion that Latin-speaking Christians should attempt to stamp Punic out. On the contrary, there is even evidence for a view that in out of the way Punic-speaking regions bishops should know Punic. Note Green (1951: 182–3) on a passage from the *Epistles*: 'Fussala, a fortified settlement of Augustine's diocese, had been a scene of violence between Donatists and Catholics. Because of its distance from Hippo, Augustine decided to appoint a bishop for the place. One of the requirements was that he must know Punic, and Augustine had a presbyter who was thus prepared' (*Epist.* 209.3, *CSEL* 57, 348 *quod ut fieret, aptum loco illi congruumque requirebam, qui et Punica lingua esset instructus, et habebam, de quo cogitabam, paratum presbyterum*). Augustine refers here to the need for someone who had been *instructed* (*instructus*) in Punic; there is a hint that Latin speakers within the Church might learn Punic as a second language. The reason for the respect in which Punic was held by Christians (or at least some of them) is obvious: there was an

---

494 This emerges particularly from several of the detailed discussions of words in Cox (1988). For example, Augustine recognises as a Hebraism in his Latin Bible the expression (Gen. 8: 9) *et extendit manum suam* (where the reflexive adjective is redundant for Latin), because it is 'very familiar to the Punic language' (*Loc. Hept.* 1.24, *CSEL* 28.1, 511–12 *locutio est, quam propterea hebraeam puto, quia et punicae linguae familiarissima est, in qua multa inuenimus hebraeis uerbis consonantia*). Notable in this passage is the last clause, which is a general recognition of the close relationship between Hebrew and Punic. See Green (1951: 183), Cox (1988: 90).

495 See *Serm.* 167.4, *PL* 3, 910 *prouerbium notum est Punicum, quod quidem Latine uobis dicam, quia Punice non omnes nostis*. See Green (1951: 183), Cox (1988: 90).

496 See Cox (1988: 88), Kajanto (1963b: 102–3).

497 See Green (1951: 185), Cox (1988: 88).

awareness that Punic was related to the Biblical language Hebrew (see above).[498]

Augustine's attitude to Punic emerges from a passage of the *Epistles*. I quote Green (1951: 180) on the background: 'Maximus, a teacher of Madaura, is defending [*Epist.* 16.2, *CSEL* 34, 37–8] the pagan gods and ridiculing the Christian cult of martyrs. Against the venerable names of Jupiter, Juno, Minerva, Venus, and Vesta he sets the Punic Miggin, Sanam (?), Namphamo, and Lucitas, names which he regards as "hateful to gods and men". Latin was evidently the language of the cultured class and Punic the mark of the low-born.' Augustine responds as follows *Epist.* 17.2, *CSEL* 34, 41):

neque enim usque adeo te ipsum obliuisci potuisses, ut homo Afer scribens Afris, cum simus utrique in Africa constituti, Punica nomina exagitanda existimares. nam si ea uocabula interpretemur, Namphamo quid aliud significat quam boni pedis hominem? id est, cuius aduentus adferat aliquid felicitatis, sicut solemus dicere secundo pede introisse, cuius introitum prosperitas aliqua consecuta sit. quae lingua si inprobatur abs te, nega Punicis libris, ut a uiris doctissimis proditur, multa sapienter esse mandata memoriae; paeniteat te certe ibi natum, ubi huius linguae cunabula recalent.

Nor could you have so forgotten your identity, as an African writing for Africans, as to think that Punic names should be criticised. If I may interpret these words, what else does "Namphamo" mean than "man with the good foot"? That is, one whose arrival may bring some good luck, just as we are accustomed to say that the man whose entrance has been followed by some good fortune "entered with favourable foot". If this language is repudiated by you, deny that many wise instructions have been handed down in Punic books (as is revealed by learned men); you should certainly regret being born in a place where the cradle of this language remains warm.

Green (1951: 180–1) summarises Augustine's position thus: 'both Maximus and Augustine were born in Africa, the home of the Punic language, hence they should not be ashamed of it. Namphamo, he [Augustine] adds, was a respectable name,[499] meaning "the man with the good foot", a phrase similar to one which Vergil applies to Hercules. Furthermore, there were Punic books which, in the judgment of the learned, contained a store of ancient wisdom; this fact should command some respect for the language.' Cf. id. 190: 'Augustine himself belonged to the educated class, but felt that no African should scorn Punic names, or the sound of Punic words, for these were, after all, a part of his native heritage.'

[498] See Cox (1988: 97).
[499] Augustine here in effect derives the name *Namphamo* from Pun. *nˤm* 'good' and *pˤm* 'foot'.

Although Augustine is on the defensive here, in that he is arguing against someone who clearly held the view that Punic was uncultivated, his own attitude seems to have been genuinely felt,[500] and if shared by others in influential positions would have lent some support to the Punic language. In any case it was a remarkable attitude for a primary speaker of Latin to maintain in a Romanised part of the Empire.

V.9 Punic (Phoenician)–Greek code-switching or language mixing

Several times in this section we have commented on the use of Greek in North Africa alongside Punic, both in the early Republican period and under the Empire (see V.5.1). There are in fact several inscriptions which display the two languages in contact through the presence of code-switching or language mixing. One such text is relatively early, and another Imperial. These texts are worthy of brief discussion not only because they throw light on states of literacy, but also because they present interesting forms of code-switching which can be paralleled in written form in other languages.

I take first a graffito quoted and discussed by Milik (1954), Sznycer (1958), *KAI* 174, Vattioni (1976: 536), 11:

ΑΦΕ-
ΘΕΝΝΑΥ
ΥΙΟΣ ΑΦΕ-
ΣΑΦΟΥΝ
ΝΕΣΕΟ Θ
ΑΜΑΘΗ
Δ ΕΣΑΘ
ΛΑΦΑΕΜΑ.

The graffito was found in a grotto of Astarte on the route from Sidon to Tyre in Syria.[501] It is thought to be predominantly in Phoenician, but the meaning of the last four lines is disputed.[502] The first four lines are clear enough. They name the dedicator in an interesting form ('Aphethennau son (of) Aphesaphoun').[503] What stands out here is the presence of the Greek υἱός in the filiation in an inscription which is definitely not in Greek. We have already seen cases of code-switching in filiations (II.3, III.6). By contrast with the above case, a short inscription from El-Hofra

---

[500] See in particular Cox (1988: 91–2).   [501] For which see Beaulieu and Mouterde (1947–8).
[502] For differing opinions, see Milik (1954), Sznycer (1958); also *KAI* ad loc.
[503] On the problem of the Semitic character of the names, see *KAI* ad loc.; also Milik (1954), Sznycer (1958).

at Constantine in North Africa (Algeria) written in Greek letters and containing two names of Greek origin (one of them uninflected) has the *Semitic* word for 'son' in the filiation (Berthier and Charlier (1955: 172), 8, Friedrich (1957: 283), *KAI* 177, Gratwick (1971: 42), Vattioni (1976: 535), 7): Σωσιπολις **βυν** Ειερων (or Σωσίπολις βυν Είέρων). It is not immediately clear whether this text is meant to be in Greek or Punic. If the text is in Greek, the writer switches into the other language in the filiation, as in the Syrian graffito above, and also shows imperfect competence in the target language, in that the name of the father is not inflected in the genitive. If it is in Punic, the interest lies in the transliteration. It should in my opinion be taken as Punic. There is another inscription in Greek letters from the same site (Berthier and Charlier (1955: 167), 1, *KAI* 175, Vattioni (1976: 534), 1 (but with a misleading misprint)) which is definitely in Punic but has an identical naming formula Σωσιπατ(ρ)ος βυν Ζωπυρος, where again the names are Greek and that of the father is in the nominative (or base) form rather than the genitive as expected in Greek.

The above graffito from Syria is attributed by Milik (1954: 11–12) (followed by Sznycer (1958)) to the second century BC (at roughly the time of the *Poenulus* of Plautus). The writer is said to have been a North African who had come to Syria for some reason, perhaps as a trader; and it is asserted that the syntactic structure (subject-predicate) also shows Greek influence. The obscurity of the second half of the text, which is well brought out by *KAI*, does not encourage over-confident speculation, but it can be accepted that the filiation contained in an apparently Semitic inscription has a switch into Greek. Also of interest is the transliteration into Greek letters. Possibly the writer was more at home in Greek; if so that might account for the obscurity of part of the text, in which he attempted another language.

I mention finally another text from El-Hofra (Berthier and Charlier (1955: 169), 3, Friedrich (1957: 283), *KAI* 176, Vattioni (1976: 535), 4):

ΚΡΟΝѠΙ ΘΕΝ
ΝΕΙΘ ΦΕΝΗ Β
ΑΛ ΕΘΣ[ΕΝ Α]
ΑΚΙΜΗΔΗ[Σ]
ΚΑΙ ΕΠΗΚ[Ο]
[ΣΕ] ΤΗ[Ν   ].

From line 3 onwards this inscription is in Greek, with verbs of 'offering' and 'hearing' recognisable, along with the connective καί and a Greek name; it is assumed by editors that φωνήν is to be supplied in the last line).

The first two lines (with the first part of the third) are more complex. The meaning is 'To Kronos (and) Tannit, "face of Baal".' Baal-Hammon was equated with Kronos. The god's name has obviously been Grecised. The goddess, however, who was equated with Artemis, retains both her original name and her epithet (*pane ba'al* is a common epithet of Tannit).[504] Sometimes a text in one language will contain a word or phrase from another language which is more strictly appropriate to the subject matter. Despite the language of the inscription as a whole, the offering was made within a Punic cultural context, and the writer alluded to the Punic background by merely transliterating the name of the goddess and her title. Names and titles associated originally with a particular language have a marked tendency to be expressed in that language even in a text which is otherwise written in a second language. Such terms are so culturally specific that speakers and writers may be resistant to adapting them to suit another language, though the present case well shows that consistency was not necessarily sought or achieved. Code-switching or language mixing which consists in the retention of the original form of a name or title when another language is being used will be discussed further in a later chapter (on retention, see 3.v.3, XII.5).

V.10 Conclusions

The attitudes to Punic held by Latin speakers were mixed. Implicit in the passages of Apuleius and the *Historia Augusta* referred to at v.8 is a view that Punic had lower status than Latin, and the same opinion was clearly held by Augustine's opponent in the controversy over Punic names. Punic was associated in the later period with 'rustics' (see Aug. *In Rom. Imperf.* 13, *PL* 35, 2096f.),[505] and rustic varieties of language were traditionally not held in high esteem by educated Latin speakers. But that is not the whole story. There was a belief among Latin speakers that 'Punic books' with literary qualities existed or had once existed (Sall. *Jug.* 17.7; cf. also the reference to such works, supposedly marked by *sapientia*, at Aug. *Epist.* 17.2 cited at v.8 above), and the Roman senate bestowed *honor* (in the words of Pliny) on the Carthaginian Mago because of his writings. Roman experts on the Punic language existed, at least in the Republic, and in Africa itself in the Imperial period there were those such as Augustine who actively espoused the cause of Punic, particularly because it was known to be related to Hebrew. There is slight evidence

[504] For details, see *KAI* ad loc. [505] Discussed by Green (1951: 186).

in Augustine for Latin speakers within the Church who had received instruction in Punic. It is highly unusual under the Empire to hear of Latin speakers learning a vernacular language.

Punic speakers themselves must have esteemed their language or it would not have persisted so long under Roman domination. Nor was it only the lower classes in remote places who continued to use the language. The prominent urban family the *Tapapii* made a point of using Punic alongside Latin in highly formal public inscriptions, and we saw evidence of the effort which went into the translation into Punic even of Roman titles in one of these texts. The Punic language was to be adapted to the new political situation by using its own resources instead of merely borrowing from Latin. The mild form of linguistic nationalism implicit in this act of translation is in contrast to the attitude displayed by the Cumaean upper classes in making a show of their desire to abandon Oscan completely in certain types of public business.

That said, even the texts in Punic discussed in this chapter betray tell-tale signs of the effects of Romanisation. I refer to (1) the abandonment of the attempt to translate Latin titles; (2) the intrusion of Latinate formulae into Punic texts (with little or no sign of the intrusion of Punic-style formulae into Latin); (3) occasional signs of interference of Latin in Punic; (4) the adoption by Punic speakers of Latin names alongside and then instead of their Punic names, with repeated evidence for a change of naming practice within particular families; (5) the intrusion of Latin loanwords into Punic; and (6) the eventual abandonment of Punic script in the writing of Punic. If all of these signs can collectively be described as forms of 'influence' of Latin on Punic, then it has to be said that parallel influence in the reverse direction, of Punic on Latin, is scarcely to be found. There is no question in which direction events were moving, but the death of Punic was to be long drawn out, largely for the reasons set out in the first two paragraphs above.

Various forms of code-switching or language mixing have come up in the discussion, and it will be worthwhile to run through the types. If code-switching usually consists of a short-term switch from a base language into another language (as for example in Cicero's letters to Atticus, where the base language to an overwhelming degree is Latin), then it would seem appropriate to find a different name (such as language mixing) for the phenomenon whereby a short text is half in one language and half in another. The coin legends discussed in v.3 fall into this category; there is no base language, but two languages are used in equal proportions for different purposes. Short as these legends are, they are particularly revealing. In the case of the emperors' names information which is specific to one culture is expressed in the language of that culture. There is nothing more 'Roman' than Roman imperial names and titles, and Latin language and script were used to convey those elements. There was of course nothing obligatory about the use of Latin for this purpose. Imperial names and titles could be expressed in any language, including, as we have seen, Punic, but the choice of Latin for this type of information alongside another language has the effect of symbolising most powerfully the Romanness of imperial rule. If in these legends the names of the issuing towns were written in Latin rather than neo-Punic, the absence of a contrast between the two languages and scripts would effectively remove the symbolism which emerges from the choice of Latin for expressing just one part of the message. And as far as the names of the towns are concerned, if they were merely expressed in Latin the casual reader would have no reason to think of their Punic origins. The use of neo-Punic symbolises their original identity as Punic foundations without the need to resort to anything so long-winded as a descriptive clause. Implicit in the language mixing there are therefore perceptions of identity and power. I stress that there are no 'rules', grammatical or otherwise, which necessitate language mixing (or code-switching) under particular circumstances. Mixing should be looked on as a stylistic resource which may or may not be exploited for its symbolic effects by individuals or groups as they see fit.

Switching related to the special association which a type of information might have with a particular culture was also seen in v.9 in the Greek inscription which switches into transliterated Punic in stating the name and epithet of a goddess. Again a perception of identity is at issue. The goddess is so eminently Punic in the dedicator's eyes that he cannot help changing languages, even though the change produces an inconsistency.

A writer's sense of his own identity might also be involved in code-switching. This was seen in the inscription *CIS* i.191 (v.5.1), where a woman making a dedication in Punic to Punic deities has her Greek name written in Greek letters. Her Greekness thus receives far more effective expression than it would if the name were merely transliterated into Punic.

In all of the cases so far discussed names are involved, and code-switching and names will be a recurrent theme of this book. Names by their very nature express identity, and code-switching has the power to make more explicit nuances implicit in a name. The original Greekness of a Romanised Greek with a Greek name will be more forcefully conveyed if he gives his name a Greek inflection even when using Latin. A nice example in the previous chapter was seen in the receipt of Aeschines, who uses Greek throughout his long naming formula in a Latin text (I.VII.2.3).

Closely related to personal names are filiations. Code-switching of a particular type in a filiation was seen in v.9 (a switch from Punic into Greek in the word for 'son'). This type of code-switching came up in Italic and Etruscan material, and will be discussed again.

'Formula-switching', already mentioned in the first chapter, was also alluded to at v.6. In highly formulaic forms of writing in a bilingual community there may be switches from one language to the other at formula boundaries.

Finally, there are miscellaneous and rather haphazard switches into Latin in the late 'Latino-Punic' inscriptions written in Latin script (v.6). I would tentatively suggest that in the last days of Punic, when a language shift was well under way and literacy of the traditional kind dead, those attempting to write the old language in the new script found it difficult to avoid convenient switches into the now dominant language Latin. Heavy code-switching has been observed as characteristic of speakers of a language in the throes of death.[506]

The question whether there are regional features of African Latin which are determined by contact with Punic will be dealt with in a later chapter (4). Relevant are the use of the vocative for the nominative (4.V.4.4), and the presence of some localised loan-words in African writers of Latin (4.V.2.5).

I would stress finally the subtle evidence that has emerged here for some knowledge of Greek in Africa among those who were not members of the literary classes. The doctors' inscriptions are of special interest in that in these the presence of Greek symbolises a professional identity.

VI LIBYAN, BERBER

There was another language spoken in Roman Africa which is represented by inscriptions in a script comprising geometric symbols.[507] The language is usually referred to as 'Libyan'.[508] Some of the inscriptions

---

[506] See e.g. Crystal (2000: 22).
[507] For the inscriptions, with discussion of the script, see Chabot (1940), Galand (1966).
[508] For discussion of the nomenclature and of the distribution of the inscriptions see Millar (1968: 128–9), showing for example that on the evidence of the inscriptions the language covered the whole length of Latin North Africa (129).

are bilingual, either in Punic and Libyan (e.g. Chabot (1940), 1–5, 7, 10, Galand (1966), 9) or in Latin and Libyan (e.g. Chabot (1940), 146, 151, Galand (1966), 1–4).[509] Some of the honorands of such inscriptions bear exotic names in the Latin version, as *Nabdhsen Cotuzanis f.* (*ILAlg* 1.138). Others, in the traditional manner seen all over the western Empire, had taken on Latin names, at least as they presented themselves in the Latin version of bilingual inscriptions. Thus, for example, the veteran (*ILAlg* 1.137) *C. Iulius Ge[tu]lus, uet(eranus), donis donatis torquibus et armillis, dimissus et in ciuit(ate) sua Thullio flam(en) perp(etuus). uix(it) an(nis) LXXX. H.S.E.* Nothing much can be made of these inscriptions because of the obscurity of the script, but it would appear that speakers of the language were subject to typical patterns of linguistic Romanisation, as can seen from the adoption of Latin alongside the vernacular language, and the adoption of Roman names.

The question arises whether the language represented by this strange script is the forerunner of Berber. The caution of Millar (1968: 128) on this matter is fully justified, given the obscurity of 'Libyan'. If we know virtually nothing of the ancient language, we cannot begin to attempt to relate it to the modern.

There is though slightly more to be said about the possible ancient precursor of Berber and contact between its speakers and speakers of Latin. Berber is said to have considerable numbers of Latin loan-words. The evidence is discussed, for example, by Laoust (1920: 291–300), Wagner (1936), Basset (1952: 43), Rössler (1962) and Kossmann (1999: 24–5). If this could be established, it would mean that speakers of an ancient form of the African language had acquired some knowledge of Latin and, as a consequence of at least a degree of bilingualism, had been able to transfer Latin terms into their native language. Since on this hypothesis the posited Latin terms must by definition have been picked up from the Latin of Africa, the 'Latin' element of Berber ought in theory to have light to throw on the old question of whether there was a distinctive form of 'African' Latin.[510] There are though in my opinion two problems raised by the evidence which have not received proper discussion. First, it is by no means obvious to a sceptical non-expert in Berber that all of the alleged Latinisms are definitely of Latin origin. Thus, while there is no reason why the Latin feminine *sagmaria*, a derivative of *sagma* 'pack saddle', should not have acquired the sense 'mare', is it necessarily

---

[509] Some of the latter can be found also in *ILAlg* (1.137, 138, 145, 147, 153, 156, 162, 169).

[510] Note Rössler's attempt (1962) to use this sort of evidence to get at the vowel system of African Latin.

the case that Berber *tagmart* 'mare' reflects this Latin word?[511] But the second difficulty is even more fundamental to our present purposes. Even if it is allowed that Berber is full of words of Latin origin, there is the chronological question of when they entered the language. An early borrowing, from the period of the Roman Empire, might indeed be brought into a discussion of African Latin. But the problem is that most of the alleged Latin words in Berber are also reflected in Romance languages around the Mediterranean, as for example Italian dialects, Spanish and Sardinian dialects. The question therefore arises whether they were borrowed in the Roman period itself, or at a later date from one of the Romance languages. Unless this chronological problem can be addressed and criteria established for distinguishing between early (Roman period) borrowings, and later borrowings from Romance,[512] the Berber evidence cannot be assumed to have anything to contribute to our knowledge of language contact in Africa under the Romans.

VII ARAMAIC

VII.1 *Introduction*

In the last chapter (VII.1) two bi-/trilingual inscriptions containing Palmyrene Aramaic were discussed, one from Palmyra itself set up by a local, Haeranes, to commemorate himself and his family, the other from South Shields in Britain (see further below, VII.2). These two inscriptions, both of which have a Latin version, encapsulate important features of the linguistic behaviour of Palmyrenes in their relations with Latin and the Romans. Palmyrenes were clearly ready language learners, and there is good evidence for the acquisition of Latin by some of them. On the other hand, unlike many of the speakers of the vernacular languages who came into contact with the Romans, they held on to their original linguistic identity, even when they were far from home and participating in Roman institutions. These two sides to their linguistic activity explain two different forms of display which can be detected in Palmyrene/Latin inscriptions. At Palmyra itself the use of Latin by a local worthy (such as Haeranes above) or soldier displays to their countrymen familiarity with the culture of the imperial power. On the other hand at South Shields

[511] See Wagner (1936: 35).
[512] Colin (1926, 1927) shows an awareness of the problem, as e.g. at (1927: 86), where he offers a Latin etymology, but allows that the word may have come via Ibero-Romance. See too Kossmann (1999: 24–5).

the use of Palmyrene alongside Latin makes a symbolic display of the writer's ethnic identity, which would not have been missed even by those who could not understand the language. The inscription of Haeranes was dealt with at length in the previous chapter; that of Barates at South Shields will come up again below. Most of the material in this section concerns Palmyrene rather than other forms of Aramaic (but see VII.4).

VII.2 *Palmyrenes abroad*

There was a Palmyrene community in the city of Rome. The surviving inscriptions associated with this group are in various mixtures of Greek, Latin and Palmyrene.[513] In a lower class quarter of the city (Trastevere, southern sector), outside the Porta Portuensis in what might have been the 'Long Street of the Eagle' (*Vicus longus aquilae*),[514] there is evidence for a Palmyrene sanctuary and the local practice of the cult of the Palmyrene Sun god.[515] Two Palmyrenes, Heliodorus and C. Licinius,[516] in a pair of bilingual inscriptions in Greek and Latin (*CIL* VI. 50, 51), record the setting up of one or two temples to Bel and Malakbel. I quote here *CIL* VI.50 (= *ILS* 4334, *IGUR* 117), which is better preserved than the other. The inscriptions are numbered in bold for ease of cross reference (**1**):[517]

pro salute imp. [Caesaris. . . .]
C. Licinius N[. . . . et Heliodorus]
Palmyrenus [aedem Belo . . .]
constitu[erunt]
Ἡλιόδωρος ὁ [Παλμυρηνὸς καὶ Γ. Λικίνιος Ν . .]
τὸν ναὸν Βή[λῳ. . . . . θεῷ. .]
Παλμυρην[ῷ ἀνέθηκαν. . . . .].

Heliodorus (if not, on this evidence alone, Licinius) was possibly a speaker of Palmyrene Aramaic, given the apparent application to him of the adjective *Palmyrenus*.[518] Before coming to Rome he might well have been bilingual in Aramaic and Greek, and now uses Latin as well. The Latin version precedes the Greek in both of these inscriptions (photographs in *IGUR*, p. 100). There is often, as we have seen, a significance to the

---

[513] Palmyra was bilingual, in Palmyrene and Greek, as the numerous bilingual inscriptions (which can be conveniently found in Hillers and Cussini (1996)) show.

[514] See R. Palmer (1981: 369–70).   [515] See Palmer (1981: 375–6).

[516] Licinius was a name favoured by Palmyrenes: see Moretti on *IGUR* 117. See further Palmer (1981: 375–6).

[517] I quote here the text of *IGUR*, which has a commentary and bibliography. The other inscription of the pair, *CIL* VI.51, is printed as *IGUR* 118.

[518] His name is also significant: see Palmer (1981: 375), and below, p. 252.

ordering of the languages in a bilingual inscription (see IV.2, p. 188). In the above inscription (and, by conjecture, its pair) it is only the Latin version which refers to the emperor (for this phenomenon in bilingual inscriptions, see above, V.3, V.5.2). The inscriptions are not only to do with Palmyrene gods, but are explicitly linked to the *salus* of the emperor. This imperial dimension seems to have determined both the choice of Latin as one of the languages, and its pride of place. Greek on the other hand is present as one of the languages of Palmyra, though it was not the language which expressed most forcefully a Palmyrene identity (see below). By admitting it here the dedicators were able to pay lip service to their origins without presenting themselves as out and out aliens, given that Romans too were devotees of Greek culture and that the city abounded in Greek inscriptions of one sort or another.

There is also an altar on the slopes of the Janiculan hill set up by workers apparently associated with the *horrea Galbana* (see below), the text this time in Latin and Palmyrene (*CIL* VI.710 = *ILS* 4337) (**2**):[519]

Soli sanctissimo sacrum
Ti. Claudius Felix et
Claudia Helpis et
Ti. Claudius Alypus fil. eorum
uotum soluerunt libens merito
Calbienses de coh. III.

The Palmyrene text (Hillers and Cussini (1996: 55), PAT 0248, *CIS* II.3903) is as follows:

'lt' dh lmlkbl wl'lhy tdmr
qrb ṭbrys qlwdys plqs
wtdmry' l'lhyhn šlm.

The last is translated thus by Teixidor (1979: 47) (followed by Houston (1990: 190)): 'This is the altar (which) Tiberius Claudius Felix and the Palmyrenes offered to Malakbel and the gods of Palmyra. To their gods. Peace!'

Houston (1990: 192–3) lists six differences between the two versions, of which I will mention the main ones. The Latin version names three dedicators, a man Claudius Felix (presumably a freedman), his wife and their son, whereas the Palmyrene names only the first. It is significant that the man has the same name in the two versions; we will see below a Greek–Palmyrene bilingual text in which a referent has different names

[519] See Palmer (1981: 376), Houston (1990), MacMullen (1993: 62–3).

in the two languages; he was projecting a sort of double identity, like some of the Punic speakers seen earlier. Claudius Felix used a Latin name even when addressing his countrymen in their native language, thereby stressing his assimilation, even if he was still holding on to his first language.[520] Next, the Latin text mentions the place where they live and/or work (they are 'Galbienses from the third court': see below), whereas the Palmyrene does not. The Palmyrene mentions Palmyrenes, whereas the Latin does not; if we had only the Latin text it would not be clear that Palmyrenes were involved in the dedication. The Palmyrene version refers to gods of Palmyra as well as Malakbel, whereas the Latin text names only the Sun, which does not come across in this version as distinctively Palmyrene at all. Finally, there is no equivalent in the Palmyrene to the Latin formula *uotum soluerunt libens merito*, and no equivalent in the Latin to the final two acclamations of the Palmyrene.

Houston (1990: 193) rightly concludes that neither text is a translation of the other. This is in fact a classic bilingual text of the type which has what we have already referred to several times as 'complementary' versions. The drafter gave different types of information to the different categories of readers. There is no other bilingual inscription discussed in the present book in which this is more clearly the case. He presented the participants in the dedication as Palmyrenes only in the Palmyrene version, and did not complicate the Latin version with a reference to 'Palmyrene gods' which might have been lost on local readers. On the other hand the reference to local topography (*Calbienses de coh. III*), which will have been immediately comprehensible to Roman readers from the quarter, and which no doubt had the effect of giving the referents a local identity and roots, is found only in the Latin version. They are locals in the Latin version, outsiders in the Palmyrene, and of mixed identity to those bilinguals who could read both versions. The absence of any attempt to render a formula of one language into the other displays an awareness that idioms or formulae of one language are not necessarily translatable word for word into another language. It goes without saying that the main dedicator was bilingual. He shows an attachment to his roots, but also clear signs of acculturation (notably in his complete

---

[520] Noy (2000: 243), noting that the man has the same name in both languages, states: 'presumably he did not have a Palmyrene name, which suggests that he may not have been an immigrant himself'. The weakness of this argument is obvious from a good deal of the material discussed in this chapter. Those who adopted a new language might go all the way in changing their names, or retain a link with the past.

adoption of a Latin name). It is possible that the Palmyrene language had some role in the cult.[521] We have already seen examples of the retention of an older language in the domain of religion (see IV.2, V.4, and below on *IGUR* 119).

It is assumed that *Calbienses* contains a reference to the imperial warehouses called *horrea Galbana* (or *Galbae*),[522] but opinions have differed about the implications of *de coh. III*.[523] MacMullen (1993: 62) takes the reference to be to one of the courtyards in the warehouse where the Palmyrenes worked, whereas Houston (1990: 191) thought that the courtyard was the living quarters of workers at the *horrea Galbae*.[524] The issue probably cannot be resolved, but I quote MacMullen's view of the matter (1993: 62–3): 'They were all workers in one or another courtyard of the warehouse. Where the altar was found, thirty-odd dedications define the place as a shrine to eastern worships, Syrian, Arabian, Lebanese. The texts are in Latin, Greek, and Palmyrene, the latter suiting the district's community of that language. The whole of this vast Regio of the city was largely from the eastern Mediterranean.'[525]

Here then was a remarkable polyglot community of workers. Whereas the above text is in Latin and Aramaic, others are in Greek and Aramaic, a further testimony to the mixing of the three languages. In AD 236 a relief was given to the Moon Aglibol and the Sun Malakbel by a certain Heliodorus, and inscribed in Greek and Palmyrene (*IGUR* 119, Hillers and Cussini (1996: 54), PAT 0247, *CIS* II.3902) (**3**):[526]

Ἀγλιβώλῳ καὶ Μαλαχβήλῳ πατρῴοις θεοῖ[ς]
καὶ τὸ σίγνον ἀργυροῦν σὺν παντὶ κόζμῳ ἀνέθη[κε]
Ἰ. Αὐρ. Ἡλιόδωρος Ἀντιόχου Ἁδριανὸς Παλμυρηνὸς ἐκ τῶν ἰδίων ὑπὲρ
σωτηρίας αὐτοῦ καὶ τ(ῆς) συμβίου καὶ τ(ῶν) τέκνων ἔτους ζμϛʹ μηνὸς Περιτίου

l'glbwl wmlkbl wsmyt' dy ksp' wtṣbyth 'bd mn kysh yrḥy br ḥlypy br
yrḥy br lšmš š'dw 'l ḥywhy wḥy' bnwhy byrḥ šbṭ šnt 5. 100 + 40 + 5 + 2.

---

[521] Cf. Noy (2000: 243–4).
[522] On which see e.g. MacMullen (1993: 60 with n. 31, 62).
[523] See e.g. Houston (1990: 191), MacMullen (1993: 62–3). Houston did not know of Palmer's article (1981). MacMullen (1993: 63 n. 35), however, cites Houston.
[524] MacMullen (1993: 63 n. 35) slightly misrepresents Houston when he says that he took *horrea Galbae* to be 'apartment houses'. Houston's words (191) are: they 'all lived on "Courtyard Number Three" of an apartment complex used by families some of whose members worked in the imperial warehouses, including the *horrea Galbae*'.
[525] The inscriptions are collected by Palmer (1981: 372 n. 50).
[526] See Palmer (1981: 376) for discussion.

The Palmyrene is translated by *CIS* (cf. also Moretti, *IGUR*)[527] as follows: 'To Aglibol and Malakbel: both the silver relief and its decoration Iarhai son of Haliphi, son of Iarhai son of Lišamš (son of) šoʻadu made from his purse for his own safety and that of his sons; in the month Shebat of the year DXXXXVII.' Heliodorus had been born Iarhai. It is easy to discern in the detailed statement of ancestry a certain ethnic pride, of a type which we will also come across below in another Palmyrene (see also v.4 above on this Semitic feature, which has been encountered several times already). In the light of such a pronounced consciousness of ancestry, and given the presence in the area of a community of easterners, it is not difficult to see why Aramaic lingered on. Heliodorus, like some of the Africans seen earlier, has a double name (the Greek form used in the Greek version, the Palmyrene in the Palmyrene). That in Greek has a solar connection which is found in other names in documents relating to the same community.[528] Unlike Claudius Felix in the above inscription, he had not dropped his Palmyrene identity; but like Felix, he apparently did not find Latin appropriate in a religious dedication to named Palmyrene deities.

In another bilingual document in Greek and Aramaic (*IGUR* 120, Hillers and Cussini (1996: 55), PAT 0249, *CIS* II.3904) Maqqai son of Male son of Lisams and Soʻadu son of Taime son of Lisamsei honour Bel, Iaribel and Aglibol. In this case the Palmyrene version is above the Greek, whereas in the previous text it was the Greek which had that position (photographs in *IGUR*, pp. 101, 103) (**4**):

[. . . . lšm]š wšʻdw br tymʼ lšmšy wqrbw
[To Bel, Iarhibol and Astarte: made (this) Maqqai son of Male (son of) Lišam]š and Šoʻadu son of Taime (son of) Lišamšai, and offered (it).

θεοῖς πατρῷοις Βήλωι ᾽Ιαριβώ[λωι καὶ ᾽Αγλιβώλωι . . . . .]
ἀνέθηκαν Μακκαῖος Μαλῆ τ[οῦ Λισάμσου καὶ Σόαδος Θαίμου τοῦ Λισαμσαίου].

The most aggressively 'Palmyrene' religious texts – those in which both gods and dedicators retain Palmyrene names – do not have Latin versions. There would seem to be a reflection here of the distinctively

---

[527] Translations in this section taken from *CIS*; I have translated from the Latin renderings given there.

[528] Palmer (1981: 375 with n. 69) mentions (e.g.) Anicetus, after Helius Anicetus, *Sol inuictus* (*CIL* VI.52).

Palmyrene character which the dedicators accorded the religious obser-
vances. Perhaps too different degrees of integration into Roman society
on the part of the participants are represented in the various inscriptions,
with Claudius Felix standing out for his assimilation and desire to present
a Roman identity alongside the Palmyrene.

There is also a bilingual funerary inscription at Rome in Palmyrene
and Latin (Hillers and Cussini (1996: 55), PAT 0250, *CIS* II.3905, *CIL*
VI.19134) (**5**):

D. M.
Habibi Annu
bathi f. Pal
murenus u(ixit) an(nis)
XXXII m(ensibus) V d(iebus)
XXI fecit heres
frater

npš ḥbyby bř
mlkw ʼnbt ḥbl
Monument of Habibi son of Malku Annubat, [529] alas.

The Palmyrene is only a token presence, though the ethnic pride of the
deceased emerges even in the Latin in the use of *Palmurenus* (see further
below). Both versions are of formulaic type within their own languages.
This Palmyrene type will be seen in other inscriptions quoted below; it is a
characteristic of the Latin–Palmyrene bilingual funerary inscriptions that
the formulaic conventions operating in the two languages are followed
in the separate versions.

Various bilinguals (or partial bilinguals) in Palmyrene and Latin are
known from other areas, including one found in Britain, at South Shields.
A certain Barates set up an epitaph for his wife in both Latin and
Palmyrene (*RIB* 1065, Hillers and Cussini (1996: 54), PAT 0246) (**6**):

D.M. Regina liberta et coniuge Barates Palmyrenus natione Catuallauna ann.
XXX

rgynʼ bt ḥry brʻtʼ ḥbl
Regina, the freedwoman of Barate, alas.

Barates is a mysterious figure. No Palmyrene military unit is evidenced
in Britain, though Barates might possibly have been (e.g.) a centurion

---

[529] On this last name, see the note of *CIS* : 'nomen gentis, ut uidetur. Hic autem cognomen esse
Malchi e titulo latino elicere licet.'

serving in another unit.[530] Another possibility is that he was a trader, since South Shields is a port of entry. Whatever his origin, he would appear to have settled in Britain and to have taken a British wife.[531] The relationship between the two versions is similar to that in the previous example, in that more information is given about the deceased in the Latin version than in the Palmyrene.

The composer of the Latin text is unknown, but it must be significant that the monument has a correct Palmyrene text, alongside a Latin text which is less than correct in spelling (see below). The lettering is also revealing. At *RIB*, 2nd edn, addenda p. 778 attention is drawn to 'the contrast between the confident lettering of the Palmyrene inscription and the erratic lettering of the Latin', and it is concluded that 'the sculptor was Palmyrene, but under western influence'; it is also suggested that he was probably the same man as the sculptor of *RIB* 1064. Thus whether the Latin was composed by Barates himself (which is by no means unlikely) or by the sculptor, it was probably the work of a first-language speaker of Palmyrene; there may well have been a small Palmyrene group at South Shields.

The Latin text is remarkable for its case usage. The editors state that *Regina, liberta, coniuge* and *Cataullana* are in the ablative, instead of the normal dative case. This statement is erroneous. There are three cases regularly found in this position (expressing the dedicatee) in such Latin texts, nominative (e.g. *RIB* 11), dative (e.g. *RIB* 15) or genitive (*RIB* 12). The forms of *RIB* 1065 cannot be interpreted as any of these cases, and an 'ablative' in this context would be impossible to construe syntactically. In fact the four words are accusatives, with final *-m* omitted, and recognition of that provides an interesting insight into the linguistic background of the composer. The accusative is the normal case into which the name of the honorand is put in Greek honorific inscriptions, usually when there is an accompanying statue of the person honoured (see 6.III.3). The (probable) sense originally was 'so-and-so (sets up a statue of) x' (for a name standing as object of the verb of setting up which is here assumed to be understood, see below, 6.n.49). From there the construction spread to funerary inscriptions (see above, 1.VII.1 with cross references to Chapter 1, and also below, 6.III.3). The accusative of the honorand is a standard construction in the Greek inscriptions of Palmyra

---

[530] There is another Palmyrene of the same name in *RIB* 1171 (perhaps the same man), who is said to be *uexil(l)a(rius)*.

[531] She is of a local British tribe.

itself.[532] Barates was presumably bilingual in Aramaic and Greek, and he imitated here in Latin the Greek construction which he knew from his place of origin;[533] it is also of note that the tombstone contains a carved representation of the deceased, and thus there is a point of connection between the use of the construction in honorific inscriptions on statue bases, and its use here in an epitaph. Latin is made to behave as Greek would have behaved in a bilingual Greek–Palmyrene honorific text at Palmyra; the syntactic structure of the Latin shows that this is one of those texts 'implicitly reflecting a bilingual situation' (see I.VII.4 above).

Barates' motivation in using Palmyrene in an area in which it would not have been understood was discussed in the previous chapter (I.VII.I). He was keeping an aspect of his identity, whatever else is to be made of the text.

One category of Palmyrene speakers who will have acquired some Latin and hence varieties of bilingualism were those serving in the army. From Karánsebes in Hungary there is a bilingual Latin–Palmyrene funerary inscription probably dating from the late second or early third century. It was dedicated to an *optio* Guras who had belonged to a *numerus Palmyrenorum*, and was set up by his heir, who bears a Palmyrene name *Habibi*.[534] The text runs as follows (Hillers and Cussini (1996: 55), PAT 0251, *CIS* II.3906, *CIL* III.7999) (**7**):

D(is) M(anibus) M. Fl(auius) Guras Iiddei [op]tio ex n(umero) Palmur(enorum) [ui]xit ann(is) XXXXII mil(itauit) [an]n(is) XXI Ael(ius) Habibis [pon]tif(ex) et h(eres) b(ene) m(erenti) p(osuit)

gwr̊' ydy hptyn
Gura (son of) Iaddi, *optio.*

For a *numerus Palmyrenorum* in a purely Latin inscription from the same area (Dacia; Porolissum = Mojrád), see *CIL* III.837,[535] and for Latin inscriptions from Karánsebes itself, see *CIL* III.1548, 1549. Various aspects of the above inscription are worthy of mention. First, the filiation in the Latin version consists of the genitive alone (editors tend to add *(filius)* after *Iiddei*), as it does in the Aramaic, and this may be taken as interference from the writer's primary language (but see further below); we have repeatedly seen that expressions of filiation are particularly susceptible

---

[532] See for example Hillers and Cussini (1996), 0263, 0266, 0267, 0271 (a Greek–Palmyrene bilingual), 0274 (another bilingual), 0277 (bilingual), 0278 (bilingual), etc. Cf. Adams (1998).

[533] See for details Adams (1998).

[534] For the name, see the bilingual inscription from Rome quoted above.

[535] Note too *CIL* III.7693 for the expression *ex n. Palmur.* in a Latin inscription commemorating Palmyrenes.

to cross-language interference. Secondly, the Aramaic is no more than a mark of (ethnic) identity; Latin is used in the conventional way to present a military identity for the referent (see below, 3.I, 5.VII.2.5), though there is one brief allusion in the Palmyrene to the man's military status, in that the Latin term *optio* has been borrowed. Nevertheless the mere presence of Aramaic, however brief, in such an inscription is of considerable interest. In inscriptions by soldiers in the Roman army Greek as well as Latin is of course common, but Palmyrenes alone of barbarian auxiliaries made use of their own language in such public documents (alongside Latin).[536] This may be taken as an indication of 'the strength of Palmyrene local culture' (Millar 1993a: 328). It is a sign on the one hand of ethnic pride, but also of a particularly well developed literary culture; some regional languages had virtually no convention of writing associated with them. The proportion of Latin to Palmyrene in the inscription just quoted and in that (e.g.) of Barates in Britain is much higher than in that of Haeranes from Palmyra discussed in the first chapter. There are two possible reasons for this. First, Habibi and Barates were both far from home, in regions in which Palmyrene would not have been understood; a token expression is enough to make a point. Secondly, the command of Latin on the part of both Barates and the dedicator of the inscription of Habibi was no doubt greater than that of the composer of Haeranes' text. At Palmyra it is Latin that is the mere token presence.

A rather fuller Aramaic text is found in another soldier's bilingual epitaph, this time from El-Kantara in Algeria (late second, early third century), now published at Hillers and Cussini (1996: 56), PAT 0253; cf. *CIS* II.3908, *CIL* VIII.2515 (**8**):

D(is) M(anibus) s(acrum) Suricus Rubatis Pal(myrenus) sag(ittarius) (centuria) Maximi (uixit) ann(is) XLV mi[lit]auit ann(is) XIIII

npš' dnh dy
šrykw br rbt
tdmwry' qšt'
qtry' mksmws
br šnt 40 + [5]
ḥbl

This (is) the monument of Soraiku son of Rubat, a Palmyrene, *sagittarius*, of the century of Maximus, forty (five) years old, alas.

The only detail which is not in the Palmyrene text is the length of service of the soldier; in contrast to the last inscription discussed above a good deal of military information is presented in the Aramaic version.

---

[536] See Millar (1993a: 328). We should modify this statement slightly. At VI above a bilingual inscription commemorating a former soldier was cited which has a *Libyan* version as well as a Latin.

Again in the Latin the filiation is expressed without *filius*, but in this case direct influence of the Aramaic version has to be ruled out, because in that *br*, the word for 'son', is used. Aramaic inscriptions sometimes have this word, sometimes not. The omission of *filius* here can only be due to the writer's uncertainty about the Latin convention, and such uncertainty might well have been generated by the variability of the Aramaic practice.

This is not the only bilingual military inscription from El-Kantara. Chabot (1932) (= Hillers and Cussini (1996: 158), PAT 0990) published a pair of juxtaposed epitaphs in both Latin and Aramaic for Palmyrenes who were undoubtedly serving as auxiliaries in the Roman army. The second Latin text is too fragmentary to be worth quoting, but the other has one or two interesting details (**9**):

Ierhobo
les. Iedd
ei. mil. Pal
uix. an. xlv

(A) npš' dh dy
yrḥbwl' ydy
ḥbl
(B) npš' dh dy
'stwrg' brh
ḥbl.

The two Palmyrene texts are translated by Chabot (1932: 266) as follows: (A) 'This (is) the monument of Iarhibolei (son of) Iaddaei. Alas'; (B) (This (is) the monument of Astorga his son. Alas.' It is obvious that the Latin text had some military information (note *mil.*), and was formulaic in the Latin manner (note the expression for age at death). In the Palmyrene texts on the other hand there is no reference to the army. The Latin explicitly identifies the referent as a Palmyrene for potential Latin-speaking readers, whereas the Palmyrene text did not need to do so for those who could read it. Latin emerges as the deceased's professional voice, while Aramaic is his mother tongue.

Another bilingual text in Latin and Palmyrene from Algeria (Lambaesis) can be found at Hillers and Cussini (1996: 56), PAT 0255; cf. *CIS* II.3909, *CIL* VIII.3917 (**10**):

D. M. S.
Mocimus S
umonis fil(ius)
Palmurenus

uixit annis
xxx h(eres) p(osuit)

npš' dnh
mqymw bȓ
šm'wn ḥbl
šnt 4.100 + 60 + 1
'This (is) the monument of Moqimu son of Sim'on, Alas. In the year CCCCLXI.'

In this case it is not clear whether the referent was a soldier. The two versions adopt structures typical of funerary inscriptions in the separate languages (as was also the case in the previous two inscriptions). Again it is obvious that bilingual inscriptions were often put together by two separate acts of composition, not by composition in one language followed by translation into the other.

A bilingual epitaph for a member of a *numerus Palmyrenorum* has also turned up at Tibiscum in Rumania, dated AD 158. It is published by Sanie (1970) and Hillers and Cussini (1996: 159), PAT 0994. The Latin runs as follows (**11**):

D(is) M(anibus)
N[e]ses Ierhei [f(ilius)]
[7?] n(umeri) Pal(myrenorum) uixit
[a]n(nis) XXV Malchus et Ier
f(ratri) b(ene) m(erenti) p(osuerunt).

The Palmyrene text is fragmentary,[537] but is tentatively translated by Sanie (1970: 408) as: 'fait par Malchus pour Nese w wh [en] l'an 470 au mois Teveth'. In this case it is made explicit that fellow Palmyrenes took the trouble to commemorate their 'brother' in Aramaic (as well as Latin). In no sense is the form of the Latin determined by the phraseology of the Aramaic; it is formulaic funerary Latin, with dedicator as well as deceased named in a typical Latin manner.[538]

The role of Latin in these various military inscriptions is clear, but it would not do to imply that any inscription concerning a Palmyrene soldier in the Roman army would of necessity include a Latin component. There are various bilinguals in Greek and Palmyrene at Palmyra which mention members of the Roman army. Hillers and Cussini (1996: 205), PAT 1397, = Starcky (1949), 81), dated AD 135, accompanies a statue of a legionary centurion Julius Maximus. The statue and inscription were set up by Marcus Ulpius Abgar and members of his caravan in honour

---

[537] 'bd mlkw / lnš' [....] [?ḥ?]w?h? / šnt 4.100 + 60 + 10 / byrḥ ṭbt.
[538] On this feature of Latin funerary inscriptions, see Meyer (1990).

of Maximus, who had presumably escorted the caravan.[539] The Greek version has the Greek accusative of the honorand which is commonplace in Greek inscriptions at Palmyra (see above). Presumably Greek and Palmyrene are used in this inscription rather than Latin because the dedication does not have a Roman military context. Also at Palmyra is a statue and inscription honouring Tiberius Claudius, prefect of the *cohors I Augusta Thracum equitata*, tribune of the *legio XVI Flauia Firma* and prefect of the *ala I Vlpia dromedariorum Palmyrenorum*, and set up by Marcius Ulpius Yarhai son of Hairan son of Agbar, to his friend (Hillers and Cussini (1996: 209), PAT 1422, = Starcky (1949), 128). The military titles of the man are set out in full in the Greek version, but there is no Latin. He was a citizen of Palmyra (note εἴλης πρώτης [Οὐλπί]ας δρομεδαρίων Παλμυρη[νῶν καὶ **πολείτη]ν τῆς Παλμυρη[ν]ῶν πόλεως**). The inscription is essentially a private one (the dedicatee is described as τὸν ἑαυτοῦ φίλον) rather than the product of a military environment, and that is no doubt why the dedicator did not use Latin, though the inclusion of all of the referent's military titles in their correct Greek form does show that there must have been considerable prestige attached to service in the Roman army. Again, when in AD 259 the local council (ἡ βουλὴ καὶ ὁ δῆμος) honoured someone who was a Roman cavalryman (Hillers and Cussini (1996: 67), PAT 0281), that fact is mentioned but does not influence the language choice (the text is bilingual in Greek and Palmyrene), because the dedication was local and civilian with no military dimension whatsoever. Similarly the dedicator of a statue in AD 251 to his patron, one Septimius Hairan, son of Odainat, a Palmyrene senator (see Hillers and Cussini (1996: 69), PAT 0290), describes himself as a soldier in both the Palmyrene and Greek texts (the Greek has the expression στρατιώτης λεγ[εῶνος Κυρηνα]ικῆς, while the Palmyrene refers less technically to him as a 'soldier in the legion of Bosra'), but refrains from the use of Latin because the inscription was a private act of devotion.

What is significant about the military epitaphs seen earlier in this section is not so much the presence of a Latin version (for this feature of soldiers' epitaphs see the next section, and also below, 5.VII.2.5) as the inclusion of Palmyrene as well. Palmyrenes were reluctant to abandon their identity entirely when serving in the Roman army. On the other hand the absence of Latin from certain inscriptions at Palmyra which mention Roman soldiers is to be put down to the non-military character of the dedications; moreover the inscriptions referred to in the last

---

[539] See Starcky (1949: 52).

paragraph are all honorific rather than funerary, and it was above all epitaphs of soldiers which attracted the use of Latin.

VII.3 Palmyra

There is a trilingual inscription from Palmyra which raises the same issues as the trilingual dedication of Haeranes discussed in the first chapter.[540] A dedication of a statue to the same Haeranes (AD 74)[541] again has a Latin version which is clearly secondary to the Greek (**12**):

Bu[le et civi]tas Palmyrenorum Hairanem
Bo[nnae f.] qui et Rabbilum
pium [et phi]lopatrin

Ἡ [βουλ]ὴ καὶ ὁ [δῆμος] Αἱράνην Βωννέο[υς]
[τὸν καὶ Ῥ]άββηλο[ν]
κ[οσμητ]ὴν εὐσε[βῆ] καὶ [φιλ]όπατριν, τειμῆς χάριν
[ἔ]τους ἑπτ' μηνὸς Ξανδικοῦ

bwl' wdms lḥ[y]rn br bwn[' dy mtqr' rb'l]
mṣbth bbnyny [']l[ḥy'] wrḥym
mdynth 'qymw lh ṣlm' dnh lyqrh
byrḥ n[ys]n [šnt] [3.100] + 20 + 20 + 20 + 20 + 5
The boule and demos, to Hairan, son of Bonne, who is also called Rabbel, decorator of the buildings of the gods (?), and lover of his city, erected to him this statue, to honour him, in the month Nisan of the year 385.[542]

No attempt is made to translate φιλόπατριν (a common word in the Greek inscriptions of Palmyra), which retains as well in the Latin its Greek accusative ending; and ἡ βουλὴ καὶ ὁ δῆμος is dealt with partly by means of code-switching (*bule*), caused perhaps by an inability to find the appropriate Latin word (see below, 3.II for this phenomenon), partly by translation (*ciuitas*). The syntactic structure of the Latin (nominative + accusative of the honorand) is determined by the Greek. The writer of this text, as of that discussed in the first chapter (I.VII.I), had a firmer grasp of Greek than of Latin. The inclusion of a Latin version in such an imperfect state can only be interpreted as a form of display, with the Latin wording less important than the ostentatious use of that language alongside the other two.

Another trilingual text from Palmyra, dated AD 176 (Hillers and Cussini (1996: 330), PAT 2824), is poorly preserved (**13**):[543]

---

[540] This is also discussed by Millar (1995).
[541] See Cantineau (1933: 174–5), Millar (1995: 410–11).   [542] Translation of Millar (1995: 411).
[543] See also Al-As'ad and Teixidor (1985), 9, Millar (1995: 412).

[ἔκτι]σεν Λούκιος
[. . .]λῷου τοῦ ζπυ′

[. .du]arum gub
[. .pecun]ia sua
[. .Polli]one II et Apro II cos

qby᾿ ᾿ln tr[y᾿ . . .]
᾿nṭnys q[lsṭrṭs].[544]

The Latin text has a Roman consular date corresponding to the remnants of a Greek date, but again there is code-switching in the Latin, this time apparently into Palmyrene (*gub*, possibly = 'craters').[545] The same man, L. Antonius Callistratus, turns up in the last but one inscription discussed in this section.

In the last two inscriptions the Latin versions contain Greek or Palmyrene words for which the writers were unable to find a Latin equivalent. The aspirations of the writers to display their familiarity with Latin culture can thus be deduced from the fact that they were using Latin, though ill equipped to express themselves in the language, and were doing so in an area in which there would not have been many readers for a Latin text.

A bilingual funerary text from Palmyra commemorates a centurion (*CIS* II.3962 = Hillers and Cussini (1996: 73), PAT 0308). The Latin is very fragmentary (**14**):

[. . .]OH I GEBASIS
[. . .]VPRAVI[. . .]T HIERAPOLI
ELABELVSQVIETSATVRNINVS MALICHI F[546]

ṣlm qlsṭqs qṭrywn᾿
dy mn lgywn᾿ dy ᾿rb῾t᾿ dy ῾bd
[l]h ᾿lhb[l . . .]
[. . . .]
Statue of Celestici (?) centurion from the legion which (acts at) Arba῾ta;[547] which made [for him] Elahbê[l, son of Maliku].

The Latin term for 'centurion', like other technical military terms in such Palmyrene inscriptions, is taken over into the Aramaic text, but it is the Greek form of the word which lies behind the borrowing (note *CIS* II.3962

---

[544] Al-As῾ad and Teixidor (1985: 279) translate: 'Ces deux cratères. . . / . . . [Lucius] Antonius Callistratus. . '.
[545] See Millar (1995: 413–14).
[546] This line should obviously be printed *Elabelus qui et Saturninus Malichi f.*
[547] There is some uncertainty about the reading and interpretation here. Starcky (1949: 17) took the reference to be to the 'fourth legion', not to a legion at Arba῾ta.

'vox lat. centurio, sed e Graeca transcriptione κεντουρίων inlata').[548] It was seen earlier (VII.2) that at Palmyra there are references in inscriptions written in Palmyrene and Greek to Palmyrenes who had served in the Roman army. Full military details are given but still Latin is not used. Though the present inscription was also set up at Palmyra, what makes it different from the texts just referred to is that it is probably funerary. The funerary inscription represents a final fossilisation of a person's memory, and there was a strong convention all over the Empire for Roman soldiers to be commemorated in Latin (or, in the case of Palmyrenes, Latin with the vernacular language), even in areas where Latin was not spoken, and even when the referent was a speaker of another language (see 5.VII.2.5). Latin is used to symbolise a feature of the soldier's identity.[549] There is, for example, a remarkable series of three stones from Caesarea Mazaca in Cappadocia (*AE* 1984, 893) which show 'a leading centurion receiving a Latin grave monument from his wife and son, the wife herself getting one in Greek from her daughter, and the son getting one in Greek from his sister' (Levick (1995: 400)). Here there is clear evidence that the family language of the referents was Greek, but that a Latin commemoration was still considered essential to express the Romanness of the centurion's identity. As Levick (1995: 398) puts it, 'the use of Latin is one of the most crisply assertive and unmistakable ways of expressing Romanness . . . especially in the ultimate utterance of the gravestone'.

I conclude this section with two trilingual inscriptions from Palmyra which are difficult to interpret. First, L. Antonius Callistratus (for whom see above) is recorded in an inscription dated AD 174 (Hillers and Cussini (1996: 208), PAT 1413).[550] I quote the text in full (**15**):

L. Antonio Callis-
strato manc. IIII merc.
Galenus actor.

Λ. ᾽ Αντωνίῳ Καλ-
λιστράτῳ τεταρτώ-
νη Γαληνὸς πραγ-
ματευτὴ[ς] ἴδιο[ς]

ṣlm' dnh dy (l)wqys 'nṭwnys
qlsṭrṭs dy rbᶜ dy
'qym lh lyqrh glnws
prgmṭṭ' dydh byrḥ' 'b šnt 4.100 + 80 + 5

[548] On this phenomenon see also Millar (1995: 405).
[549] See further Adams (1999: 131–2).
[550] See also Seyrig (1941), 25, Millar (1995: 411), Starcky (1949: 68–9), 113. The Palmyrene is obscure without the Latin and Greek (so Starcky).

This is the statue of Lucius Antonius Callistratus 'of the quarter', which erected to him, to honour him, Galenus, pragmateutes, his agent, in the month Ab(?) of the year 485.[551]

L. Antonius Callistratus was a Roman citizen of Greek origin.[552] He was a 'tax-collector, concerned with a 25% tax, apparently on goods being traded or transported' (Millar 1995: 413). Here then we seem to have an outsider to Palmyra, if not a first-language speaker of Latin, who presumably was Aramaic-speaking to carry on his affairs; recognition of that is apparently embedded in the inscription in the use of Aramaic alongside the other two languages. Nevertheless this cannot be taken as a case of a Latin speaker learning Aramaic, because an eastern Greek may well have been bilingual in Greek and Aramaic long before he came into contact with Latin. Millar shows that the various versions complement each other. The Palmyrene reference to the tax will not have been comprehensible without the Greek, and the Greek πραγματευτής and Latin *actor* are independent equivalents.

Another trilingual inscription from Palmyra (AD 58) throws up the same ambiguities concerning the origin and primary language of the referent (Hillers and Cussini (1996: 110), PAT 0591) (**16**):[553]

[L. S]pedius Chrysanthus
[ui]uos fecit sibi et suis.

Λούκιος Σπέδιος Χρύσανθο[ς]
ζῶν ἐποίησεν ἑαυτῷ καὶ τ[οῖς]
ἰδ[ίοι]ς ἔτους θξτ´ μηνὸς Γ[ορ]π[ιαίου].

byrḥ 'lwl šnt 3.100 + 60 + 5 + 2 + [2] bnh [lwqy]ws
'spdy[s] krystws mks' bḥywhy [qbr' dnh]
lh wlbnwhy wlbny byth ly[q]rh[wn]
In the month of Elul of the year 369, Lucius Spedius Chrysanthus, tax-collector, during his life built this tomb for himself and his sons and the sons of his house, in their honour.[554]

This man too was a tax-collector, but it should not be assumed that he was a Roman *publicanus*. Millar (1995: 412) notes also that it 'is quite uncertain whether [the inscription] reflects a degree of attachment to Graeco-Roman culture by a native Palmyrene or the presence of an immigrant Greek who is already in possession of the Roman citizenship'. Since the inscription was composed during the lifetime of the deceased, it is likely that he was trilingual, and he may even have been an immigrant, possibly of Greek origin. On the face of it the Latin version looks to be

[551] See Millar (1995: 411).   [552] See Millar (1995: 413).
[553] See also *CIS* II.4235, Millar (1995: 410).   [554] See Millar (1995: 410).

secondary to the other two versions. It consists only of the name and of a single Latin funerary formula, in the second line. Dates are given in the Greek and Palmyrene versions but not in the Latin, and the Palmyrene also records the man's profession.[555] However we cannot deduce from this imbalance that the writer's command of Latin was poor, because there would have been no point in putting great detail into the Latin version at Palmyra. The inclusion of the brief piece of Latin probably carries some sort of symbolic intention, but we cannot say what.

VII.4 Nabataean

Also worth mentioning is a Nabataean–Latin bilingual at Rome (*CIL* VI.34196, *CIS* II.159). The dedicator was apparently an immigrant from Petra who used formulaic Latin to commemorate his *cognatus*: *Abgarus Eutychi f. Petraeus Abdaretae cognato suo Estechi f. uixit an. XXX b. m.* The Nabataean is shorter but of typical Aramaic form (translated at *CIS* as 'hoc est monumentum τοῦ Abdharetat'). This inscription, with its (rare) ethnic, illustrates the speed with which outsiders to Rome might take up Latin, while not, in the first generation, abandoning their native language. So the original names have been Latinised in inflection but not exchanged for Latin names.

VII.5 Native speakers of Latin and contact with Aramaic

Given the power of Rome, it is not surprising that Aramaic speakers should sometimes have been learners of Latin, particularly if they moved to the West for some reason or joined the army. A more complicated question concerns the extent to which Latin speakers might have learned Aramaic. When a guardsman (*candidatus*) mentioned by Jerome (*Vita Hilarionis* 13) set out for the area of Gaza to find the holy man Hilarion, he was accompanied by military interpreters who knew only Latin and Greek, though Hilarion, whom he wanted to consult, was an Aramaic speaker. The guardsman himself spoke only Frankish and Latin (not Greek). Hilarion had to switch into Greek so that communication could take place with the interpreters: 13.8 *et ut interpretes eius intelligerent, qui Graecam tantum et Latinam linguam nouerant, Graece quoque eum interrogauit.* The main importance of this anecdote for our purposes is that the soldier is imagined as making his journey not with Aramaic speakers, but with

---

[555] See Millar (1995: 412–13) on the force of *mks'*.

interpreters who must have intended to use not Aramaic as the eastern lingua franca, but Greek.[556] The information and attitudes embodied in the story can be further elucidated by a roughly contemporary passage from the *Peregrinatio Aetheriae* (47.3). Aetheria notes, first, that in Jerusalem part of the population spoke Greek only, part Aramaic only, and part were bilingual in both languages: *in ea prouincia pars populi et grece et siriste nouit, pars etiam alia per se grece, aliqua etiam pars tantum siriste.* Secondly, when Greek was spoken in Church, an Aramaic interpreter was used for those who knew that language only (47.4). Finally, Latin speakers who, like the *candidatus* in Jerome, did not know Greek or Aramaic, had to rely on the translation of *fratres et sorores grecolatini* (47.4), that is Latin- and Greek-speaking outsiders (monks and nuns).

There is an implication in both of these stories that Latin speakers who found their way to the Near East would be unlikely to communicate in the lingua franca of the area, Aramaic, but would tend rather to use Greek as a lingua franca, either themselves (if they knew Greek), or through Greek–Latin bilinguals (if they did not know Greek).

Nor do we only have anecdotal information about Romans making do with Greek in these eastern regions. There is documentary evidence from the so-called Cave of Letters in Judaea in the second century AD for the use of Greek by Latin speakers in their contacts with speakers of Aramaic (see Lewis (1989)). Many of the documents record the dealings of a woman Babatha and members of her family, clearly Aramaic speakers, with the Roman authorities. Text no. 11 (6 May 124) concerns a loan of sixty denarii received by one Judah, the second husband of Babatha, from a centurion Magonius Valens of the *Cohors I Miliaria Thracum*. Lines 29–30 run as follows: ἑρμηνεία· Ἰούδας Ἐλ[αζάρου] Χθο[υσίων]ος τὰ α[...]μην[ ] ὑπέθηκα ἀκολούθω[ς τοῖς προγεγρ]αμμέν[οις]. ἐγράφη διὰ] Ἰουστείνου. These lines declare themselves to be a translation of Judah's acknowledgment of the loan, written by a scribe Justinus ('I, Judah son of Elazar Khthousion . . . have hypothecated according to the aforementioned terms . . . It was written by Justinus'). The original words of Judah at this point will of course have been in Aramaic. The

---

[556] It is interesting to be told that the *candidatus* was accompanied by interpreters. Interpreters must have had an important role in the army and provincial administration, though we hear relatively little about them. Interpreters are mentioned in the *Notitia Dignitatum* (*Or.* XI.52 *interpretes diuersarum gentium*, *Oc.* IX.46 *interpretes omnium gentium*; note too *Or.* XIX.12–13 *magister epistolarum graecarum eas epistolas, quae graece solent emitti, aut ipse dictat **aut latine dictatas transfert in graecum***; see further Lee (1993: 41, 48 n. 151, 67)), and also occasionally in inscriptions and elsewhere. For an interpreter of the Dacians, see *AE* 1947.35 (see Lee (1993: 66)), and for further inscriptional evidence, see below, IX.

original version was retained by the centurion as the ultimate confirmation that the loan had taken place;[557] he need not have had any understanding of Aramaic to know the significance of the debtor's acknowledgment, which was basically a signature. The whole of the rest of the document (both the extant copy and the original) was in Greek. Clearly Judah could not write Greek, but he could presumably understand it, and the centurion conducted the affair through the medium of Greek.

Even more remarkable is the document no. 16, dated 2 and 4 December 127, a registration of land by Babatha in connection with a census return ordered by the Roman governor. I quote the editor (p. 65): 'Accompanied by her husband Judah . . . who served as her transactional guardian and wrote her attestation for her at the end of the return, Babatha appeared in person at a government office in Rabbat . . . There she hired a clerk to write out the return in the proper form . . . Judah wrote on the original return, in Aramaic, Babatha's sworn attestation to the bona fides of the foregoing declaration; a Greek translation of the Aramaic followed, ending with the words ὑπὲρ αὐτῆς (line 36 in this copy). In that form the return was submitted to the office of a *praefectus equitum* on 2 December. Two days later in that office a notation of receipt, written in Latin, was appended at the bottom of the return, which was then posted in the basilica.' The extant document is a copy of the original which appeared in the basilica. The most important section of the text for our purposes is that at 33ff.: ἑρμηνεία ὑπογραφῆς. Βαβαθα Σίμωνος ὄμνυμι τύχην κυρίου Καίσαρος καλῇ πίστει [= *bona fide*] ἀπογέγραφθαι ὡς προγέγραπ[τα]ι. Ἰουδάνης Ἐλαζάρου ἐπιτρόπευ[σ]α καὶ ἔγραψα ὑπὲρ αὐτῆς. [2nd hand] ἑρμηνεία ὑπογραφῆς τοῦ ἐπάρχου. Πρεῖσκος ἔπαρχος ἱππέων ἐδεξάμην τῇ πρὸ μιᾶς νωνῶν Δεκεμβρίων ὑπατίας Γαλλικ[αν]οῦ [καὶ Τιτιανοῦ].[558] This is the Greek translation of the attestation in Aramaic written by Judah for Babatha, and a Greek translation of the Latin subscription of the prefect.

The three languages Greek, Latin and Aramaic are in contact here, in that Babatha's husband wrote in Aramaic and the Roman official Priscus wrote in Latin. Both the Aramaic and the Latin are rendered into Greek, which thus serves as the lingua franca. It is clear again that

[557] See Lewis (1989: 42).
[558] See Lewis (1989: 68) for a translation: 'Translation of subscription: I, Babtha daughter of Simon, swear by the *genius* of our lord Caesar that I have in good faith registered as has been written above. I, Judanes son of Elazar, acted as guardian and wrote for her. [2nd hand] Translation of subscription of the prefect: I, Priscus, prefect of cavalry, received [this] on the day before the nones of December in the consulship of Gallicanus and Titianus.'

Babatha and her husband were Aramaic speakers, though they may have understood Greek but not been literate in that language. Priscus must have understood Greek, but there is no evidence that he knew Aramaic.

There are a few signs of interference from Aramaic in the Greek version of the passage quoted. At line 34 (ὄμνυμι τύχην κυρίου Καίσαρος) the normal formula would have contained the words τὴν τοῦ κυρίου τύχην.[559] The omission of the article seems to represent interference from Aramaic;[560] the writer of the Greek was translating literally from Aramaic, and he may have been a first-language speaker of Aramaic. In this case an Aramaic text lies behind the Greek, but earlier there is apparent interference from Aramaic in a purely Greek part of the document: line 14 ἐν αὐτῇ Μαωζα (= 'in the said Maoza'). Here again there is omission of the article in the Aramaic manner.[561] Since the interference here is not direct, in that it was hardly determined by a written Aramaic text which was being translated, it offers some insight into the linguistic characteristics of the scribe. He was presumably an Aramaic speaker.

There is possibly also evidence in the archive for a first-language speaker of *Latin* writing Greek for the benefit of an Aramaic speaker. If our interpretation of the data is accepted, it would follow that we have cases of an Aramaic speaker on the one hand, and a Latin on the other, resorting to Greek as a common linguistic denominator. The evidence is in text no. 12. Babatha's orphaned son had had two men appointed by the town council of Petra to act as his guardian. The purpose of document 12 'was to copy from the minutes (*acta*) of the Petra town council ... the names of the two men appointed' (Lewis 1989: 48). Lewis notes that from beginning to end the text reads like a Greek translation of the original Latin minutes, and it thus incidentally provides evidence for Latin record keeping in the province. I note a few of these Latinate elements, not all of which have been pointed out by Lewis. The inner text has the phrase ἀπὸ ἄκτων βουλῆς Πετραίων, which as Lewis notes has a threefold omission of the definite article (by contrast for variants of the expression with one or more articles, see 13.21, 14.25, 15.5: see further below, 4.v.4.5 on this phrase). It was seen above that elsewhere such an omission might be put down to Aramaic influence, but here it is more likely to be Latin which is the determinant.[562] The Greek is a word-for-word rendering of

[559] See Lewis (1989: 14).   [560] So Lewis, (1989: 14).   [561] See Lewis (1989: 69) ad loc.

[562] Cotton (1993: 95 n. 12) quotes the expression ἀπὸ ἄκτων βουλῆς from a different region (Tyre), but that does not rule out the possibility that Latin may lie behind the absence of the article here.

ab/ex actis senatus Petraeorum. Behind lines 8ff. (ἐπράχθη ἐν Πέτρᾳ μητροπ-
όλει τῆς Ἀραβ[ία]ς πρ[ὸ τεσσ]άρων καλανδῶν ... ἐπὶ ὑπάτων
(names) . . .) can be observed *actum* along with a Latin date indicating both
day of the month and the consular year. Lewis (1989: 50) observes that in
lines 1 and 4 ἐγγεγραμμένον καὶ ἀντιβεβλημένον renders *descriptum et
recognitum.* I would finally draw attention to lines 6f. of the outer document,
where a filiation has the following form: καὶ Ἰασσούου Ἰουδαίου υἱοῦ
Ἰασσούου. Here the form of the Greek has probably been determined by
the Latin type of filiation comprising genitive + *filius* (though the order is
not Latinate here), a structure which, as we have seen and will see again,
was also influential in other bilingual communities. Elsewhere in the
archive of Babatha filiation in Greek is regularly expressed by the plain genitive with or without τοῦ (e.g. 5a col. i, lines 5, 14.21, 23, 28, 36ff., 15 (numerous filiations in the inner and outer text, all of them without υἱός), etc.).

   Either a word-for-word translation technique was deliberately used,
or the translator (a Latin speaker) was not completely *au fait* with the
subtleties of Greek idiom. Whatever the case, the Romans were taking
care in the necessary circumstances to make sure that the subject people
understood their official transactions, and to do this they were prepared
to use Greek, but not Aramaic, as a lingua franca.

   Thus at least some Latin speakers will have communicated with
speakers of Aramaic through Greek. But not all speakers of Latin of
non-Palmyrene origin will have been unable to speak Aramaic. It has,
for example, been argued by Drijvers (1996) that the praetorian prefect Musonianus, described by Ammianus (15.13.1) as *facundia sermonis
utriusque clarus,* must have understood Aramaic in order to investigate
Manichaeism as he had been instructed to do (see further above, 1.III).
Musonianus might have known Aramaic as well, but such indirect evidence is less than satisfactory, because, as we have seen in the preceding paragraphs, communication in such cases might easily have taken
place through Greek (or through interpreters). According to John (19:19),
Pontius Pilate 'wrote' the trilingual inscription (in Aramaic – Ἑβραιστί:
see Geiger (1996) – as well as Greek and Latin) placed on the Cross
(Ἰησοῦς ὁ Ναζωραῖος ὁ βασιλεὺς τῶν Ἰουδαίων), but that would only
mean that he 'had it written'. If the story were true, it would incidentally be an unparalleled case of a quasi-official (but ironical) use by the
Romans of a vernacular language (an act of offensive accommodation
(see 5.V) meant to annoy the Jews).

   There is explicit evidence for the efforts of one man to learn Aramaic
(Jerome).[563] At one point Jerome speaks as if he were fluent in the

---

[563] See the discussion of Brown (1992: 82–6).

language: *Epist.* 17.2 (*CSEL* 54, p. 72) *plane times, ne **eloquentissimus homo in Syro sermone** uel Graeco ecclesias circumeam, populos seducam, scisma conficiam.* But this passage is so much at variance with the other evidence on the matter that Brown (1992: 83) must be right in suggesting that Jerome was being ironical. In the preface to his commentary on Daniel (*PL* 28, 1292) he gives some insight into his difficulties with the language. As a youth he laboured hard and had begun with difficulty to pronounce some words with their distinctive sounds, but then he flagged: *multo sudore multoque tempore uix coepissem anhelantia stridentiaque uerba resonare.* He began again, but makes the admission that even at the present time he is better able to read and understand the language than to speak it: *et ut uerum fatear, usque ad praesentem diem magis possum sermonem Chaldaicum legere et intelligere quam sonare.* More details are found in the preface to the commentary on Tobit (*PL* 29, 23–6). There Jerome reveals his method of translating from Aramaic. Since Hebrew (which he knew quite well)[564] and Aramaic were similar, he found a man who knew the two languages. The man translated into Hebrew, and Jerome then dictated a translation into Latin to a scribe: 25–6 *et quia uicina est Chaldaeorum lingua sermoni Hebraico, utriusque linguae peritissimum loquacem reperiens, unius diei laborem arripui, et quidquid ille mihi Hebraicis uerbis expressit, ego accito notario sermonibus Latinis exposui.* It follows that Aramaic was a struggle for Jerome. He could certainly not speak the language. He may have had a limited reading knowledge, but was nonetheless unhappy translating a written text. It is worth mentioning the four types of language 'performance' identified in the first chapter (1.II). Jerome is quite explicit about the greater difficulty of speaking Aramaic than reading it; it will be recalled that speaking was described earlier as a form of positive performance, whereas reading was said to be passive.

VII.6 Conclusions

Palmyrenes are one of the most interesting groups of vernacular speakers in their contacts with Latin. As we have seen, soldiers in the Roman army adopted Latin, but did not abandon their native language, and they virtually alone of all ethnic groups in the army (other than Greeks) sometimes adopted a double linguistic identity in funerary inscriptions.

At Rome there is good evidence that Palmyrenes maintained the languages of Palmyra, Palmyrene and Greek, at least in connection with native religious cults. The four bilingual inscriptions (1–4) present some interesting variations suggestive of differing degrees of acculturation. Two of these texts (3, 4) are exclusively in the languages of Palmyra, and

---

[564] See Brown (1992: 71–82), and below, VIII.

they also show other signs of the maintenance of a distinctively Palmyrene identity on the part of the dedicators. The names of the deities retain their Palmyrene form in both the Palmyrene and Greek versions. The dedicators too keep their Palmyrene names, at least in the Palmyrene versions; in (4) this is the case too in the Greek version. The dedicator of (3) did make a limited accommodation to his new Romanness, in that he has a Greco-Roman name in the Greek version. In (4) there is a long Palmyrene-style genealogy of the dedicator in both versions, and this is also so in the Palmyrene version of (3). The other two texts (1, 2) both have a Latin version, one of which (1) is accompanied by Greek, the other by Palmyrene. The presence of Latin can be seen to go hand in hand with a diminution of the other Palmyrene elements of the types just listed. The dedicators now exclusively have Greco-Latin names. Palmyrene genealogies are abandoned. The Latin versions come first or are given prominence. In (2) the deity is not given his Palmyrene name in the Latin version, though it is kept in the Palmyrene. And some distinctively Roman elements are introduced in the Latin versions. The emperor is honoured in (1), along with the Palmyrene gods, and in (2) the dedicators give themselves a local Roman identity in the Latin version, in that their place of residence and/or work is named. There is thus visible in (1) and (2) considered alongside the other two texts what must have been a gradual loosening of ties with Palmyra. The old cults and languages are still being held on to in the first two inscriptions, but there is a noticeable accommodation to Romanness. That same accommodation is also to be seen in the bilingual military inscriptions, which by definition display as well a continuing attachment by the referents to their Palmyrene roots. At Rome the changes we have just seen no doubt occurred across several generations in various families.

We have repeatedly seen that in bilingual (or trilingual) inscriptions the various versions use formulae appropriate to the respective languages. The assumption should never automatically be made that a bilingual inscription was first composed in one language and then translated into another. There are just two Latin inscriptions in this section of which the structure is modelled on a pattern favoured in another language (6, 12). It is likely that the composers of these two texts were not thoroughly *au fait* with Latin culture. Moreover in (12) there are two code-switches into Greek in the Latin version (*bule, philopatrin*) which are also suggestive of poor competence in Latin.

As far as the learning of Aramaic by Latin speakers is concerned, we are in the unusual position of having the explicit comments by Jerome about his difficulties in the matter. Evidence was presented to suggest that, while there might have been individual Romans who picked up the language, communication with primary speakers of Aramaic will usually have been effected through the medium of Greek in the typical Roman way, unless of course the Aramaic speakers concerned had themselves learnt some Latin.

VIII HEBREW

In Rome, Italy and the west there is no reason to think that there was much knowledge of Hebrew among Greek or Latin speakers, apart from the odd Jewish scholar. Italian Jewish communities used Greek or Latin or both.[565] Hebrew, as we saw in the previous chapter (V), turns up in Jewish inscriptions at Venusia and elsewhere in the west almost exclusively in the form of short formulaic tags attached to texts in Greek or Latin.[566] The tags are *šalôm, yiśra'el* and *šalôm 'al yiśra'el*.[567] 'Israel', written either on its own or as part of the formula 'peace upon Israel', is always written in the Hebrew alphabet at Rome.[568] Clearly the Hebrew script, if not in practical terms the language itself, was of symbolic importance for Jews in the west, and inextricably associated with the name of Israel itself. As Noy (2000: 264) puts it, Hebrew at Rome 'seems to have been inscribed [in a few formulae] as much for its symbolic and visual effect as for any linguistic reason'. A revealing text is the Venusian inscription Noy (1993), 75, which begins with a tag in Hebrew script (= 'peace upon his resting place'), then switches into Greek, but written in Hebrew characters. It may be deduced that the writer was aspiring to write a Hebrew text, but knew nothing of the language other than a tag or two, and was therefore forced to make the script serve for the language. Earlier we saw a text from Etruria which repeated its Latin version in Etruscan script (III.6: Benelli (1994), 31). It was presumably intended as bilingual, but the writer knew nothing of Etruscan other than the script (see further 1.VIII (p. 91)). These examples highlight an interesting cultural phenomenon. When a language shift has occurred speakers may be proud of their linguistic heritage without knowing much or anything of the earlier language. They may therefore make do with whatever linguistic scraps they can muster

---

[565] This is not the place to enter into the question of the relative currency of Greek and Latin among Jews at Rome and elsewhere in Italy. See the discussions of Solin (1983: 701–11), Rutgers (1995: 176–84), Noy (2000: 263–4). Some of the Greek in Jewish catacombs at Venusia is 'Greek' only in lexicon (with Latin inflections imposed on Greek lexemes, a comparable phenomenon to that seen in some of the 'Italic' inscriptions discussed in II above) or alphabet (see 4.V.3.1.2).

[566] See Noy (1999: 140–1).   [567] See Solin (1983: 701).

[568] See Noy (2000: 264). But *Israel* sometimes appears in Latin script in other places (see Noy (1993), 174 (Sardinia), 187 (Spain)).

to symbolise their earlier identity. Even the vernacular script might be pressed into service by those who knew it as a substitute for the vernacular language itself. It is possible that some of the Latin inscriptions in Greek characters (for example, those in Jewish catacombs) were written thus not because the writers were illiterate in Latin script, but because they were adhering to a tradition of using 'Greek' for such texts (usually epitaphs) in the only way that they could manage. Even the use of the Hebrew alphabet in a few formulae was a struggle for Jews at Rome. Noy (2000: 178) notes that Hebrew 'lettering is generally of a much lower standard than it is for the Greek or Latin parts of the same inscriptions: smaller, irregular, with uneven alignment, and lacking serifs'.[569] The only exception is the Roman inscription Noy (1995), 58, from the Monteverde catacomb, and apparently in the Aramaic language. It is 'entirely in the Hebrew alphabet, with no Greek or Latin. The standard of the lettering is much higher, with reasonable alignment . . . and some use of serifs' (Noy (2000: 264)). This inscription is exceptional among Roman inscriptions in Hebrew script in that it does not merely contain a short formula.[570] In some other places, most notably Tarentum and Spain, there are longer Hebrew inscriptions, sometimes using Biblical quotations, but these are mainly early medieval, and reflect some sort of literary revival.[571] They are outside the period covered by this book. Finally, at Venusia there are slightly more varied uses of Hebrew than at Rome, but again it is only short tags which are at issue.[572]

There is some Hebrew on western amulets and the like.[573] A notable case from Sicily (Sofiana) is an amulet in the Hebrew language but Greek letters (Noy (1993), 159). There is also a Hebrew phylactery in Greek letters from Wales (*RIB* 436). The interest of such objects in the present context is limited, because they could be transported and might have originated anywhere in the Mediterranean world. A rather more intriguing item from a magical context is the opening phrase of one of the Bath curse tablets (*Tab. Sulis Mineruae* 98): *seu gens seu Chistianus* [*sic*] . . . *Gentes* (plural)

---

[569] See further Noy (1999: 139–40).   [570] See Noy (1999: 140).

[571] For details see Noy (1999: 141–2). A particularly notable text is the trilingual from Tortosa in Spain, Noy (1993), 183, which is perhaps to be dated to the sixth century. The Greek and Latin are identical, and the Hebrew somewhat different from them. In the Latin version the filiation of the deceased runs *filia Iudanti et cura Maries*. The genitive ending of the last name is the same as that in the Greek version (Μάρες), a sign of convergence between Greek and Latin in this respect; we will later see that in the Jewish community at Venusia the same convergence in feminine nouns/names had taken place ((4.v.3.1.2). *Cura* (uninflected) must represent κυρία, a rather odd word to find in a Latin text given the wide currency of *domina*. It is to be assumed that in this respect Greek usage had influenced Latin in this community.

[572] See above, 1.v, and also Noy (1999: 143–4).   [573] See Noy (1999: 142–3).

was well established in the sense 'gentiles', but here the singular is strikingly used of an individual non-Christian. The singular usage has an exact parallel in Hebrew (*goi* singular = 'nation', *goyyim* plural = 'gentiles'; the singular came to mean 'gentile'),[574] and it is just possible that the phraseology in some way derives from a Semitic speaker.

The most famous case of a Latin speaker learning Hebrew is of course Jerome. J. Barr (1966–7: 283) remarks that 'Jerome is one of the few men in antiquity, or perhaps the only man of substantial historical importance, of whom we know that he learned a language of structure and family quite unlike his own . . . and whose steps and stages in language learning can in part be followed from written remarks of his own.' Whether he had any command of a spoken variety of the language is less clear.[575]

One category of Latin speakers who might have had some access to written Hebrew were the one or two Africans with some knowledge of Punic who could use that knowledge to read at least short passages of the Hebrew Bible. A case in point is possibly Tyconius (late fourth century), but the interpretation of the evidence is controversial and not to be entered into here.[576]

It is likely that there were easterners with a knowledge of Hebrew who had acquired some Latin, perhaps through moving to the west. In this connection it is worth drawing attention to a remarkable Old Latin version of the Psalms preserved in a manuscript of Monte Cassino.[577] At least part of the text was translated directly from Hebrew, and the Latin accordingly contains an abundance of Hebraisms,[578] such as the use of *cum* to render the Hebrew 'signum accusativi' (the preposition *'et*), new Latin words created as calques, and changes to the gender of Latin words based on that of the Hebrew equivalents (e.g. *gressus* (plural), *carbones* and *pauores* are all used as feminines).[579] There are also various Hebrew words in the text, transliterated rather than translated.[580] Clearly the translator knew both languages. The imitation of Hebrew should not be put down to his incompetence in Latin, but reflects a deliberate policy of translation: the form of the Latin is meant to suggest that of the Hebrew original, which had of course the status of a sacred text (on

---

[574] See Adams (1992: 11–12, with n. 41).

[575] See J. Barr (1966–7: 289–93), and in general on Jerome's Hebrew, Brown (1992: 71–82).

[576] For the evidence and discussion, see Cox (1988: 98–102).

[577] See Ammassari (1987). I owe this refrence to Nicholas Horsfall.

[578] See the discussion of Ammassari (1987: 25–31).

[579] Ammassari (1987: 10) claims to have found 301 such 'calchi latini sintattici, grammaticali, talvolta fonetici dell'originale'.

[580] See Ammassari (1987: 8, 10).

this form of translation, which permits the recovery of the wording of an authoritative original, see below, 4.V.2.12).[581] Ammassari (1987: 21) argues that the translator wrote for Christians in the west, probably indeed in Rome itself, but that his cultural and linguistic origins were eastern. He was presumably a learner of Latin as a second language.

Attempts have also been made to find the influence of Semitic on the Latin of some of the freedmen in Petronius.[582] Some of the evidence is indecisive, but the following expression (spoken by the narrator's neighbour) seems to me convincing, and it is not alone in that respect: 41.3: *plane etiam hoc seruus tuus indicare potest* (= 'your humble servant', i.e. *ego*).[583] This form of reference is not Latin, but standard Hebrew usage (cf. Gen. 44:18 *loquatur seruus tuus*).[584] Petronius must surely have intended the speaker to sound exotic. If he had heard the idiom in Rome, it will probably have been in the mouth of a Semitic speaker (perhaps slave or freedman) who had learnt Latin as a second language, or a Greek speaker from a Semitic-speaking area whose Greek, and thence Latin, was coloured by Semitic.

IX GERMANIC

The Romans first came into close contact with Germans following Caesar's conquest of Gaul and the establishment of the Rhine as the imperial frontier. Trier became an important frontier city and the Romanisation of this frontier zone was an important policy. Contacts between Latin and Germanic speakers (I use this general term without attempting to distinguish varieties of 'German') took place over a number of centuries in several spheres: (1) through trade; (2) in frontier areas where Germans underwent Romanisation and learnt Latin as a second language; (3) in the Roman army; and (4) in the later period as a result of Germanic invasions into Latin-speaking areas. All of these forms of contact had the potential to influence Latin in various ways, mainly (as it turned out) through the introduction of Germanic loan-words into Latin. The superiority of Roman culture and the military dominance of the Romans for several centuries meant that it was chiefly Latin which influenced Germanic in this way; the influence of Germanic on Latin was slight.[585] It was no doubt also the case that Germans were more extensive learners of Latin than Latin speakers were learners of Germanic.

---

[581] See Ammassari (1987: 30).
[582] See Hadas (1929), Bauer (1983); also Petersmann (1995: 538–9).
[583] See Smith (1975) ad loc.   [584] See Hadas (1929: 380); also Svennung (1958: 18–19).
[585] See D. Green (1998: 183), with the whole of chapters 10 and 11.

Bilingualism in Latin and Germanic would mainly have been found in the Roman army, where Germanic-speaking recruits would inevitably have picked up some Latin. Anecdotal evidence bears this out. The German Arminius (Tac. *Ann.* 2.10.3), who was commander of a unit of his own countrymen, on one occasion used a mixture of Latin and Germanic in addressing his brother: *cernebatur contra minitabundus Arminius proeliumque denuntians; nam pleraque Latino sermone interiaciebat, ut qui Romanis in castris ductor popularium meruisset* (see above, 1.v). The phrasing here is of some interest. Arminius' ability to use Latin is explicitly related in the *ut qui* clause to the fact that he was *ductor* of his own compatriots in the Roman army (rather than to the mere fact of his serving in the army). It seems to be implied that a German who was not an officer might serve in a Germanic unit without necessarily learning Latin. There is nothing implausible about this possibility. The army was recognised as polyglot and subject to problems of communication (see 1.v, with n. 61); it could certainly have functioned even if only the officers in foreign auxiliary units were bilingual in Latin and a vernacular language.

Another (implicit) reference to Germanic–Latin bilingualism can be found at Ammianus 18.2.2. The emperor Julian in his dealings with some kings of the Alamanni sent a certain Hariobaudes, a tribune, ostensibly as an envoy but really as a spy to one Hortarius. The reason for Julian's choice is expressed in the phrase *sermonis barbarici perquam gnarus*. The name of the tribune reveals his Germanic origin; he will have been another Germanic officer who had learnt Latin as well through his service in the army.

In Jerome's *Vita Hilarionis* there is the story about a *candidatus* (a member of the imperial bodyguard) who was afflicted with an evil spirit (see above VII.5). His origin was Germanic: 13.2 *inter Saxones quippe et Alemannos gens eius, non tam lata quam ualida, apud historicos Germania, nunc Francia uocatur*. Since a point of the story was that he began to speak in a language which he did not know (Aramaic), Jerome was forced to state those languages which he did know. He too was bilingual in Germanic (Frankish) and Latin: 13.7 *uideres de ore barbaro, et qui Francam tantum et Latinam linguam nouerat, Syra ad purum uerba resonare*.

In the Latin Anthology (285; 279 Shackleton Bailey) there is a two-line epigram with a sentence of Gothic embedded, but unfortunately there is no context or date: *Inter 'eils' Goticum 'scapia matzia ia drincan'/non audet quisquam dignos edicere uersus* (possibly = 'salutem, procura et cibum et potum': cf. *heil, schaffen, Messer, jah*).

The Vindolanda writing tablets may present us with the linguistic consequences of service by Germanic speakers in the Roman army, but unfortunately the evidence is tantalising rather than enlightening. The Batavians serving there under the prefect Cerialis corresponded among themselves and kept records exclusively in Latin. That is not surprising, given their relatively high status, but their Latin betrays not a single sign of a possible Germanic substrate beneath the surface of the official language,[586] although Germanic names turn up (e.g. *Chrauttius*). Nevertheless it is worth recalling Tacitus' remark, discussed above, about the linguistic behaviour of the Germanic officer Arminius, with its implication that his *populares* will still have been German-speaking, and also another of his observations, that Batavian units in the Roman army were commanded by their own nobles (*Hist.* 4.12). If this is correct Cerialis must have been a Romanised Batavian native.[587] The documents at Vindolanda come from the hand partly of the (Romanised) officer class and partly of their military scribes, who were probably trained in (Latin) literacy in the Roman army. If one could make the assumption that the Batavian rank and file were still holding on to their native language, at least to some extent, what would most stand out in the Vindolanda material would be the degree of Romanisation of the officers. Cerialis in particular writes a good literary Latin. We may tentatively suggest that Vindolanda presents us in practice with the sort of linguistic situation hinted at by Tacitus in his anecdote about Arminius.

It was no doubt much less usual for native speakers of Latin, whether in the army or outside, to learn a form of Germanic, but two possible cases are known. The following inscription, from Boldog in South-West Slovakia, records the career of a centurion who was also, presumably at the end of his military career, a *negotiator*: *Q (uintus) Atilius Sp(urii) f(ilius) Vot(uria tribu) Primus inter(p)rex leg(ionis) XV, idem (centurio)negotiator an(norum) LXXX h(ic) s(itus) e(st). Q (uintus) Atilius Cog(i)tatus Atilia Q (uinti) l(iberta) Fausta Priuatus et Martialis hered(es) l(iberti)? p(osuerunt).*[588] It will be seen that Atilius was a legionary interpreter, a fact which no doubt facilitated his activities as a *negotiator.* In this area he can only have been an interpreter between Romans and Germans, presumably Marcomanni and Quadi.[589] His tribe suggests that he was from North Italy, in which case he will have been a native speaker of Latin.[590] If so he must have

---

[586] Or were Batavians Celtic-speaking? There are Celtic words in the tablets, as we will see (4.V.2), but these might have been borrowed from the local Celts.

[587] See Bowman and Thomas (1994: 25).   [588] See Kolník (1978).

[589] See Kolník (1978: 66, 68).   [590] See Kolník (1978: 67).

reversed the normal pattern and acquired not Latin but a barbarian language through service in the Roman army, but his illegitimacy (note *Sp. f.*) does raise doubts about his linguistic origins.

Rather more interesting is Sidonius, *Epist.* 5.5. This is a remarkable letter from Sidonius to his friend Syagrius, described as the great-grandson of a consul (and thus of good Roman stock) and as highly educated in the Latin classics (§2). Sidonius remarks at length on Syagrius' rapid acquisition of fluent German. Note e.g. 1 *immane narratu est quantum stupeam sermonis te Germanici notitiam tanta facilitate rapuisse* ('I am therefore inexpressibly amazed that you have quickly acquired a knowledge of the German tongue with such ease' (Loeb)). He goes on to imply that this was in spite of the fact that Syagrius had from boyhood been schooled in Latin liberal studies (note *atqui* at the start of 2), as if education in the superior culture would preclude mastery of the barbarian language. Syagrius has mastered the sounds of the language (2 *euphoniam gentis alienae*). Various jokes follow, with the distinct implication that such an accomplishment was so unusual that it was bound to occasion comment and amusement. So competent is Syagrius in German that (3) 'the barbarian is afraid to perpetrate a barbarism in his own language'. So astonished are the Germans that they adopt Syagrius as an 'umpire and arbitrator in their mutual dealings' (*negotiis mutuis arbitrum te disceptatoremque desumit*). Sidonius ends on a characteristically Roman note, somewhat reminiscent of some of the remarks in Ovid's exile poetry. Syagrius is advised (4) to maintain a balance between the two languages, so that, fluent as he may become in German, he retain his Latin (*ut ista tibi lingua teneatur, ne videaris, illa exerceatur, ut videas*, 'retain your grasp of Latin, lest you be laughed at, and practise the other, in order to have the laugh of them'). Here is the view that exposure to a foreign language (other of course than Greek) may have an adverse effect on one's native language (for which topos see above, Chapter 1, n. 49).

The particular interest of the passage lies in the fact that Sidonius expresses considerable surprise at Syagrius' accomplishment, and even finds it funny. He also hints at the dangers of such an activity. It may be deduced that Syagrius was in a very small minority among the educated classes in learning the barbarian language.

Some other interpreters are known (presumably vernacular speakers who had learnt Latin to a competent level). See *CIL* III.10505 (an interpreter 'of the Germans': a plausible restoration of *Ge[rmanoru]m*). III.14349.5 (possibly an interpreter of the Sarmatians, but the text has only *interprex S* . . . , and the *s* could even be the last letter of *interprexs*) I mention only in passing. So, for an interpreter of the Limigantes of Sarmatia, see Amm. 19.11.5. The languages are obscure.

The entry into frontier varieties of Latin of Germanic words which will have given the local Latin a regional flavour (see the opening paragraph, above, (2) for this category of influence) will be discussed in a later chapter (4.V.2.3). The period of the barbarian invasions (which merges into the early medieval period) is beyond the scope of this book, but I will nevertheless comment briefly later (4.V.2.3) on contact with Germanic as a determinant of regionalism in the Latin of one particular late writer, Anthimus (category (4) in the list of forms of influence given at the start of this section). There remains from our list above the influence on the Latin vocabulary of trade with Germans and of Germans serving in the army.

One should not exaggerate the impact of either of these factors. If for example Roman traders acquired from Germans certain exotic objects for import to Rome and if they used the Germanic names for those objects, the influence on the Latin language could only be described as minimal; the influence is more cultural than linguistic. And in any case the number of Germanic loan-words directly attested as entering Latin through trade or warfare is tiny (no more than a dozen items).[591] There is of course in addition the evidence of Germanic words reflected in the Romance languages but not attested in Latin itself,[592] but these entered Romance (to an overwhelming extent Gallo-Romance, which has 600 Frankish loan-words)[593] in the post-Roman period largely as a result of the Frankish invasion of Gaul, and they form a specialised subject of their own which is well beyond the scope of this book.

Nevertheless it will be worthwhile to mention one or two cases of Germanic (or Germanic-influenced) terms which found their way into Latin through trade or via Germans in the army.

Pliny (*Nat.* 37.42) describes how Romans became acquainted with the Germanic word for 'amber', *glaesum*. Soldiers serving in the fleet with Germanicus encountered the substance and the word, on the basis of which they named an island, presumably one on which amber was found, *Glaesariam*. Pliny goes on (43) to describe a trade route by which the substance (and the word) may have reached Rome. It was taken by the Germans to Pannonia, and from there the Veneti seem to have picked it up. This was merely a technical term for a rare luxury item, and it probably had little currency in Latin. It is not reflected in the Romance languages.

---

[591] See D. Green (1998: 184), with the detailed discussion on the subsequent pages.
[592] See most recently D. Green (1998: 189–200).   [593] See D. Green (1998: 196).

Ganta 'wild goose' is also mentioned by Pliny (*Nat.* 10.53). The soft feathers of the animal were prized: *mollior quae corpori proxima, et e Germania laudatissima. candidi ibi, uerum minores; gantae uocantur.* This looks to be *par excellence* a borrowing effected within a trading context.[594] The word survives in some western Romance languages (OFr. *jante*, Prov. *ganta*, Cat. *ganta*).[595]

Some Latin military terms of possible or certain Germanic origin (*carrago, drungus, framea*) are discussed by D. Green (1998: 185–6). Here however I mention two loan translations (calques; see 4.V.2.11 for the term) rather than mere loan-words. At *CIL* VIII.9060 (Africa) there is a soldier's epitaph which contains a unique word *concibones*, a compound comprising *cum* + *cibus*, with personal suffix, which obviously means 'messmates' or the like: *D(is) M(anibus) s(acrum). Titulus Itamoris Ituueri (?) ex p(rouincia) G(ermania) S(uperiore) n(umeri) Melenuens(ium) st(ipendiorum?) XIII. concibones f(ecerunt) et d(e)d(icauerunt).* What stands out here is that the referent was a German. There is a structural parallel for *concibo* in OHG *gimazzo* 'table companion' (WG *gimato*),[596] the second part of which, cognate with Eng. *mate*, is formed from the word for 'meat, food', while the first is a collective prefix. The calque is likely to have been made by German soldiers as they learnt Latin. Very similar to *concibo* is the term *companio*, which has as its base the word for 'loaf', *panis*. Old High German had a comparable compound *gileibo*, which may again have prompted a calque.[597] *Companio*, which is quoted by the *TLL* only once, from the *Lex Salica* (63.1), survives in all of the western Romance languages. In this case we cannot say whether the calque was made in the Roman army, or later in that of the Franks (see *FEW* II.2, 968).

X HISPANIC LANGUAGES

The linguistic situation in pre-Roman Spain and during the period of Romanisation has been elucidated particularly by Untermann (e.g. 1980a, 1983), not least in his monumental *Monumenta Linguarum Hispanicarum*. What little is known about the pre-Roman languages (mainly through names) comes from epigraphy. There are traces of three main languages, referred to as Iberian, Celtiberian and Lusitanian,[598] the first

[594] See D. Green (1998: 186).   [595] See *REW* 3678.
[596] See Brüch (1913: 82), D. Green (1998: 194).   [597] See Green (1998: 194).
[598] See Untermann (1980a: 5), with a map showing the areas in which the languages have been identified. The Iberian inscriptions are collected by Untermann (1990), and the Celtiberian and Lusitanian by id. (1997).

of which is not an Indo-European language.[599] One piece of anecdotal evidence for the survival of a vernacular language into the Empire is found in Tacitus. In AD 25 a peasant (*agrestis*) from Termes in Hispania Citerior was accused of murdering the *praetor prouinciae* L. Piso. Under interrogation he replied in a loud voice in his native language that it was useless for the authorities to question him: Tac. *Ann.* 4.45.2 *et repertus cum tormentis edere conscios adigeretur, uoce magna sermone patrio frustra se interrogari clamitauit.* It is significant that he was *agrestis*: linguistic Romanisation all over the west was no doubt slower in rural areas. The man's unprovoked act of violence towards the Roman official shows his hostility to the Roman occupation, and that hostility is further symbolised by the defiant use of the *sermo patrius* under torture. The latest attestations of Iberian script (and language) are on coins of Osicerda (period of Caesar) and in a bilingual inscription on stone from Saguntum, possibly to be dated to the early years of Augustus.[600]

In a later chapter some neglected evidence (a passage from Pliny the Elder) for contact between Hispanic and Latin will be dealt with in detail, and some remarks will be made about lexical regionalisms in Iberian Latin determined by the substrate language or languages (4.V.2.4). In this section I discuss various pieces of evidence relevant to language shift and the local sense of identity which can be extracted from Untermann's collections of material.

First, some of the coin issues of Spanish towns have bilingual legends, usually showing the name of the town in two languages and scripts.[601] Thus, for example, some of the coins of Saguntum have both *Saguntinu* (possibly the old Latin genitive plural with omission of *-m*)[602] and *arse*, the earlier name.[603] Others have *Sagu* (for *Saguntum*) and *arse*, and there are others again with these same names as well as the names of pairs of officials, either in Latin (where the names are Latin: *M. Acil. Q. Popil.*) or in Iberian (where the officials have Iberian names: *biulakoś, balkaltuŕ*).[604] There is a close association here between the language and script on the one hand, and the identity which is expressed of the referents. The town itself is given a double identity, its origins still not forgotten, and the officials are named in the language appropriate to their origin. Similar forms of language mixing were seen on the coins of towns of

[599] See e.g. Untermann (1990: 1, 150).
[600] See in general Untermann (1990: 1, 125). For the inscription from Saguntum, see id. (1990: 2, 410), F.11.8.
[601] See Untermann (1980a: 8–9).   [602] See Untermann (1975: 231).
[603] For examples see Untermann (1975: 230), A.33.
[604] Details can be found in Untermann (1975: 230, 232).

Punic/Phoenician origin not only in Africa but also Spain itself (see above, V.3).

Secondly, sometimes Latin script is used for the writing of Iberian[605] and of Celtiberian (for which the Iberian script was usually used).[606] Here again we see evidence for the decline of native literacy practices prior to the death of the language itself. Lusitanian is written only in Latin script.[607]

Thirdly, inscriptions occasionally have language mixing consistent with a language shift in progress. A double inscription on stone from Castulo (Untermann (1990: 2, 651–2), H.6) written throughout in Latin script is in the Iberian language in part A, whereas part B is largely in Latin. The letter forms suggest a date in the second half of the first century BC. I quote part B:

PCORNELIVS.P.L.
DIPHILVS
CASTLOSAIC.

It would seem reasonable to take *Castlosaic* as composed of the place name + an Iberian suffix (otherwise unattested) -*saic*, the whole presumably meaning 'from Castulo'.[608] Thus the man's new (?) name and freed status are expressed in Latin, but his origin in Iberian; his dual and changing identity is aptly symbolised.

Various filiation formulae display typical traces of language mixing or cross-language imitation. The so-called 'Bronze of Ascoli', a list of thirty members of a Spanish auxiliary unit of the first century BC, the *turma Salluitana*, is of interest because of the form of the names.[609] The text is in Latin. Of the thirty men, twenty-seven have Iberian names. Three have instead a Latin *praenomen* and *gentilicium* (e.g. *Q. Otacilius. Suisetarten. f.*). It is the form of the fathers' names that particularly concerns us here. Every name is Iberian, including those of the fathers of men who had taken on Latin names (see above for an example). Each precedes *f(ilius)*, but none has a Latin genitive marker. No concession was made to Latin in naming members of the earlier generation, but signs of Romanisation in the next generation include not only the partial adoption of Latin *praenomina* and *gentilicia* but also occasional Latinate endings in some of the Iberian names (*Sosimilus, Elandus, Turinnus*). There are hints here of the changing linguistic identity of certain families across two generations.

---

605 See Untermann (1980a: 8), id. (1990: 1, 125 with n. 94, 133 with n. 9).
606 See Untermann (1997: 725).   607 See Untermann (1997: 725).
608 See Untermann (1990: 1, 169 with n. 111, 2, 653).
609 For the text and discussion see Untermann (1990: 1, 195–7).

In Celtiberian inscriptions the naming formula consists of an individual name, a family name with a suffix and genitive plural ending (occasionally the singular is used instead), and sometimes a filiation in the genitive singular following the family name.[610] In five cases this last element comprises instead genitive singular of the father's name + the Celtiberian word for 'son', *kenti-*,[611] sometimes abbreviated in the Latin manner as *ke* or *G* (e.g. Untermann (1997), K.0.2, 3.14). There can be no doubt that this is a Latinism. A telling case is K.26.1 (Untermann (1997: 716):

]LICVIAMI
GMONIM
AM.

LIC may be an abbreviation of the ending of a family name in the genitive plural. *Viamus* is a local name known from a Latin inscription (*CIL* II.5719). *G* probably stands for *gente* 'son', and *monimam*, a word found elsewhere, may be equivalent to *memoria* or *monumentum*.[612] Not only is the inscription in Latin script, but the genitive of the father's name has a Latin inflection. The filiation formula with *G*, if such it is, is thus bound to have been determined by imitation of Latin. The first line of K.3.20 (MARCOS.MASMI F) shows comparable language mixing. *Marcos* is attested as a Celtiberian form of the Latin name, and the assimilation and syncope seen in *-xim- > -sm-* can also be paralleled in Celtiberian, as Untermann notes, but the morphology and lexicon (*f(ilius)*) of the filiation formula are both pure Latin. Also of note is part of K.18, this time in Iberian script and transliterated as **loukio.kete**. The name, in the genitive singular, is equivalent to Lat. *Luci*, and the whole expression corresponds to *Luci fili*.[613] Again, in K.3.18, in Latin script (TVROS CARORVM.VIROS.VERAMOS), *Carorum* seems to be a Latin genitive plural form, possibly of a family name without suffix. VIROS VERAMOS is taken to be equivalent to *uir supremus*.[614] The various cases discussed in the last few paragraphs show the intrusion of Latinate elements into traditional naming formulae.

Fourthly, there are various bilingual or mixed-language inscriptions, in Iberian and Latin (see Untermann (1990), part 2, for C.18.5, 18.6, D.8, E.1.335, F.11.8, F.11.27, H.6) and Celtiberian and Latin (see Untermann (1997), for K.5.4).

---

[610] See Untermann (1997: 422).   [611] For which see Untermann's lexicon (1997: 509).
[612] For details see Untermann (1997: 716).
[613] See the discussion of Untermann (1997: 699). *kete* is genitive singular.
[614] Details in Untermann (1997: 640).

Finally, there is a Lusitanian inscription from Portugal (the inscription of Lamas de Moledo) which is introduced in Latin with the words *Rufinus et Tiro scripserunt.*[615] The writers must have been bilingual. They clearly wanted to identify themselves in Latin rather than the vernacular language, perhaps because they felt that Latin offered the better medium for drawing attention to their achievement. If so readers of Lusitanian might have been diminishing in number while those of Latin were anticipated to increase.

XI EGYPTIAN

A separate chapter is devoted to Egypt (5; see especially 1.1).

XII GETIC AND SARMATIAN

The epigraphy of Tomi, Ovid's place of exile, is Greek, and were it not for Ovid's exile poetry we would not know of the 'Getic' and 'Sarmatian' which were allegedly spoken there, or of the form of Greek said to have been influenced by the local language(s).[616] Ovid's linguistic observations have been discussed elsewhere (1.IV, IX). Getic and Sarmatian were not in any real sense ever in contact with Latin, but Ovid's account of his experiences has a certain interest as describing the problems of communication faced by a Latin speaker in an area where neither Latin nor, it seems, ordinary Greek had everyday currency. Not everything which he says is easy to believe, but he does at least present his idealised pattern of language learning. The one other figure from Roman antiquity who discusses the problems of learning a vernacular language is Jerome (see above, VII.5).

XIII THRACIAN

The Indo-European language Thracian was spoken in the Balkan provinces, but it has disappeared virtually without trace.[617] Thracians were numerous in the Roman army, and they must have been learning Latin all the time. There is an interesting piece of what looks very much like code-switching into Thracian in a Roman inscription set up by citizens of the province of Thrace (*CIL* VI.32567): *uotum quod uouimus*

---

[615] See Hernando Balmori (1935) for the inscription; also Untermann (1980a: 11), citing a parallel example, and id. (1997: 751–3; also 749).
[616] See the remarks of Millar (1968: 126). [617] See Detschew (1957), Katičić (1980: 111–13).

ciues prou(inciae) Tracie, reg. Serdicens., **midne** *Potelense, saluo coll(egio) Martis et Herculis* (AD 266). In this position one might have expected the Latin *(ex) uico*. Thracians in the third century were particularly fond of indicating their village of origin in Latin inscriptions,[618] and it is therefore likely that this is the Thracian equivalent of *uicus*.[619] Detschew (1957: 304) compared Lith. *mintu* 'live' and OBulg. *mêsto* 'locus, habitatio'. If the interpretation is correct, this would be the type of code-switch adopted as particularly appropriate to the subject matter or object referred to. Some objects or concepts are so culturally specific that a speaker or writer might switch into the language of that culture when referring to the thing. There is of course nothing obligatory about such a switch; in this case there seems to have been a good Latin equivalent. But a particular writer in a particular context may feel so strongly about the associations of the object, or so desirous of conveying symbolically its alienness, that he is moved to change languages.

There is also a story in the *Historia Augusta* (see above, 1.v) about a future Thracian emperor attempting at an early stage of his military career to communicate with the emperor in a mixed language, part Latin but mainly Thracian. He was learning Latin as a second language.

XIV CONCLUSIONS

XIV.1 Regional Latin and language change

Discussions of language change in Latin determined by contact with another language have usually concentrated on the influence of Greek. In this chapter some evidence has been seen for the influence of languages other than Greek on Latin. Since that influence was exerted in provincial areas of Italy and further afield in the west it can be seen to have determined regionalisms in Latin, or alternatively usages peculiar to particular communities (e.g. of soldiers) without a fixed abode. Here I summarise the evidence, starting with a glance forward.

Some of the clearest examples of regional forms of Latin emerging under the influence of vernacular languages will be discussed in later chapters: I refer to certain features of the Latin attested at the pottery of La Graufesenque in Gaul (see 4.v.1.3; cf. 7.v) and to the use of the vocative for the nominative in Africa (4.v.4.4; cf. above, v.5.1).

---

[618] See Noy (2000: 219).

[619] It was interpreted as such by the editors of *CIL*. See also Mateescu (1923: 133), Detschew (1957: 304), Noy (2000: 219).

In outlying parts of the Empire where Latin was in contact with other languages the most obvious contribution made by these languages to Latin was in the lexicon. Local words from vernacular languages entered Latin either in the speech of those whose primary language was other than Latin, or even of those who knew little of the vernacular language. Words of this kind which remained restricted in currency to the region of contact can be regarded as contact-induced regionalisms. The study of such words is a subject in itself. In a later chapter (4.v.2) examples will be discussed from Africa, Germanic regions, Celtic regions, Spain and Egypt. In this chapter some material from Marcellus of Bordeaux was presented (iv.4).

But it was not only the lexicon which was influenced by language contact. In Italy itself there are signs of morphological and phonetic interference in Latin, as for example in the form of the dative *Herc(o)lo* in regional inscriptions, the Oscanised pronunciation castigated by Lucilius, and in the form *uicturei* in an inscription from the territory of the Paeligni (see ii.6.2). From a different area (Britain) the spelling *souxtum* is Celticised (iv.3). In the sphere of syntax we saw an archaic Campanian inscription (*CIL* i². 400: see ii.3) with an Oscan type of filiation. These usages from Italy almost certainly sprang from communities which were primarily or at least originally Oscan-speaking. They represent interference in L2. In assessing regional variation in Latin it is essential, if language contact is at issue, to attempt to make a distinction between first- and second-language speakers (writers) of Latin.

In a period of language shift the target language may be imperfectly learnt, and if imperfect learning produces a usage which becomes institutionalised that usage may constitute a regionalism. A rule of the target language may, for example, be overextended. In Etruscan Latin the typical Etruscan matronymic of funerary inscriptions was often expressed by the ablative of the mother's name + *natus* which, in perfectly correct Latin style, is construed as a participle. But *natus* was also sometimes construed (again in acceptable Latin manner) as a noun, with a genitive rather than the ablative attached. At Clusium however *filius* was used for *natus*, sometimes, on the analogy of the participial interpretation of *natus*, with an ablative instead of a genitive (iii.6, 8). But *filius* was not a participle, and thus the rule by which *natus* could take an ablative was extended to its synonym *filius*. This usage must have been perpetrated initially by someone who did not have native fluency in Latin. If it caught on in the whole community it would be a regionalism of Clusium. Again, those matronymics in Etruscan Latin which comprise mother's name in the ablative without either *natus* or *filius* reflect on the one hand interference from Etruscan (which did not as a rule use a term for 'son' in either matronymic or patronymic, except occasionally under Latin influence), and on the other some input as well from Latin, in that the ablative case has to be explained from the deletion of *natus* rather than from imitation of the Etruscan case (genitive) in such expressions.

These various peculiarities of Etruscan Latin during language shift represent the interaction of several factors: interference from L1 and the drawing of false analogies in L2. Another possible case of a false analogy was incidentally seen in an Oscan text with Latinate features (Vetter (1953), 214: see II.3 n. 138, II.6.1 (5)). *Incubat* is used for the simplex *cubare*, possibly because the writer knew that under some circumstances the compound and simplex were interchangeable. But they were not interchangeable in the sense 'lie dead', and the writer has thus possibly overextended the use of *incubare*, which might have been chosen for its distinctively Latinate appearance (the prefix in this form is not Italic). Alternatively there could have been an Italic compound in *en-* which has been Latinised, or modified according to an Italic phonetic development.

The survival of *nata* 'female child' in early Gallo-Romance was seen as a possible reflection of the fact that Gaulish had a homonym *(g)nata* (IV.5) with this sense.

At the start of this section I referred to usages which might be peculiar to communities without a fixed regional base. A case in point is the calque *concibo* 'mess-mate', calqued on a Germanic term and no doubt current in German units of the Roman army. *Companio* might have had the same distribution (see IX).

The phenomena discussed in this section, apart from the purely lexical, were almost certainly located in the writing of users of Latin as L2, at a time of language shift. For the most part they were ephemeral usages, which could only be said to have given a regional flavour to the local Latin for a short period. But contact-induced regionalisms did occasionally have a long life. Regional loan-words often survived into the Romance language of the region, as we will see. A phonetic feature of the Latin of La Graufesenque leaves its mark in Gallo-Romance (see 4.V.1.3). And *nata* in the sense 'female child' lasted into the early Romance of Gaul.

It goes without saying that Latin for its part had some influence on the vernacular languages with which it came into contact. The influence of Latin on Italic has been summarised at II.6.1; I draw attention here to the two texts referred to at II.6.1 (9) which are intended to be in Italic but have morphemes which are almost exclusively from Latin. These texts were presumably the work of writers with only a residual knowledge of the vernacular language: they could make a show of using the language only if they resorted to Latin morphology. In Etruscan, expressions of filiation (or matronymics) were sometimes modelled syntactically on the Latin pattern name + *filius*; name + *clan* in Etruscan is determined by Latin (III.6). And we saw, in Punic, loan-words and loan translations from Latin, and a syntactic pattern (*IPT* 27 *mzbḥ wp'dy*, without determiners, = *aram et podium*) taken over from the Latin version.

XIV.2 *Code-switching*

Code-switching was introduced in the first chapter, and it has come up repeatedly in this chapter (see particularly II.3.1). The subject is so important that a separate chapter will be devoted to it. Here I merely summarise the general aspects of the subject which have arisen in the present chapter. Frequently when the language of an inscription changes, the information expressed in the second language has a special connection with the culture to which that language belongs. We have used the expression 'culturally specific' in reference to such information; Poplack (1980: 596), similarly, has referred to 'ethnically loaded' items. Perhaps the most striking case of the phenomenon was seen in the first chapter (VII.3), where various Egyptian Demotic ostraca from Medinet Madi were cited in which there is a switch into Greek language and script when a name, title or technical term associated specifically with Greek (or Greco-Roman) culture (as for example a legal term) had to be used. As for the present chapter, the Thracians who referred to a Thracian village as a *midne* (XIII) clearly thought that the local name for such a habitation was more appropriate than any Latin word, even though they were using Latin as the matrix language in the inscription. The writer of the Latin text on a tile (Poccetti (1979), 21, II.2) used the Oscan genitive *Herenneis* presumably because the referent was an Oscan speaker and liked to be named in his native language. If one prefers to use the term 'language mixing' (for the introduction of which, see above, V.10) rather than code-switching of the phenomenon whereby a text displays two languages in roughly equal proportions without having an identifiable matrix language, then such language mixing may assign different types of information to the two languages. Thus there are coin legends which have the emperor's name in Latin but the name of the issuing town in neo-Punic, and milestones in which the imperial titulature is in Latin but the distances in Greek (V.3; on switches into Latin in dates, see 3.VI.2, 5.IV.6–7). The Venetic funerary inscription Pa 6 (II.3) uses Latin to name the deceased, presumably as appropriate to the preferred identity of the referents, but Venetic *equpetars* of the monument, because it was the local word (cf. also *CIL* II.6342, = F 11.8, above, p. 282, in which the name of the deceased is in Latin and Latin script, but the funerary formula in Iberian and Iberian script). In the case both of code-switching and of language mixing in these senses it might be said that there is a connection between the language chosen and the *topics* contained within the text. But while there is a relationship of sorts between language and topic, the nature of the topic is not on its own the decisive determinant of language switching (see also above, V.10 on this matter). The African towns named on the coinage mentioned above had perfectly good Latin names, and Latin could have been used for the whole legend. The name *Herenneis* could easily have been given a Latin form. There is thus more to the matter than mere topic. The use of neo-Punic to express the town names conveys by means of symbolism a good deal of information which, had Latin been used throughout, could only have been conveyed by a full sentence or clause: whereas the emperors were Roman, the towns were originally Punic or Phoenician foundations, and their origins were not only remembered but a source of pride. The switch of languages tells the reader something about the *identity* of the towns. Code-switching or language mixing was thus an evocative resource which was available as an optional means of adding a nuance to the message, and it is con-stantly an aspect of the referent's identity which is underlined in this way. Expressions of identity are an issue in almost all of the texts referred to so far in this section. In the dedication made by a group of Thracians mentioned above the identity of the dedicators is explicitly stated in the Latin; but the single switch of codes makes their alien identity far more vivid. Since the material at our disposal is written not spoken, switches of script could also be used to enhance the implication of a switch of languages. This phenomenon was seen with particular clarity in two inscriptions discussed in this chapter (and cf. the ostraca from Medinet Madi referred to above). There is an Etruscan–Greek dedication to a deity in which the name of the Etruscan goddess is in Etruscan language and script, and the name of the dedicator in Greek script (III.3). And a Punic–Greek religious dedication from Carthage (*CIS* I.191, above, V.5.1) has the (Greek) name of the dedicator in Greek script. In both inscrip-tions the contrasting identities of deities and dedicators are eloquently brought out by the changes of script (and language). Given the locations and nature of the two inscriptions, the unexpected element in both is the use of Greek script for the personal names. It may be deduced that it was important to both dedicators to express their Greek identity in an alien environment.

A special type of code-switching, that in magical texts, was discussed at II.3 and IV.4. We have also seen further evidence for what I have called 'formula-switching' (V.6).

It was argued that some cases of switching seem to reflect a last-ditch attempt to hold on to a dying language (see II.3 on the Paelignian text Vetter (1953), 217, and V.6, 9 on the formula-switching in some Latino-Punic texts). It was suggested that the writers, though aware of their linguistic heritage, might have known insufficient of the old language to use it consistently without lapsing into Latin. It is though difficult to interpret the switches in such short texts, and the interpretation offered here is only tentative.

Users of L2 may sometimes be lost for a word, and forced to switch into L1 momentarily. This phenomenon is obvious in some Palmyrene Latin inscriptions (VII.3).

Finally, switching in filiations was mentioned as a special case which will be dealt with later in the book.

XIV.3 *Language death and Romanisation*

In many of the areas which have come up in this chapter (Italy, Gaul, Spain, Africa) local languages receded before Latin and eventually died. It is incumbent on those with an interest in the (linguistic) Romanisation of any one of these areas (such as the Oscan area: see above, II.6) to examine the full picture and not to concentrate on a particular region to the exclusion of the others. Comparable phenomena are found in the different regions, and although these may have little to tell us in detail about (e.g.) Roman linguistic policies and local attitudes to Latin and vernacular languages they nevertheless give some idea of the factors behind language death.

Comparable to the story about the Cumaeans is the anecdote about the African emperor Septimius Severus (V.8). The poor competence in Latin of his sister caused him such embarrassment that he had her sent home. There are linguistic attitudes to be deduced from this story. In the eyes of an upper-class African Punic was felt to be lower in status than Latin, and fluency in Latin was a necessary accomplishment of an African of high ambition in the wider Roman world. Local upper classes in western provinces are likely to have shared the attitude of Septimius.

We saw, for example, that Caesar was able to use a Gallic noble to interpret for him in Gaul (IV.1), and that suggests that members of the Gaulish élite might have been early learners of Latin. They were perhaps assisted in any such linguistic ambitions by the Romans themselves. In a later chapter (7.II) we will discuss evidence for the setting up of schools in various western provinces (Britain, Gaul and Spain) by the Roman authorities for the offspring of the local upper classes.

Indeed we have repeatedly seen evidence for the learning of Latin literacy by vernacular speakers, in Etruria, the Venetic territory, Gaul (see Chapter 7), Spain and Africa. The Latin alphabet was used to write local languages. Since Romans are unlikely to have taught, say, Africans to write Punic in Latin script, it may be deduced that either some instruction was given in the writing of Latin (with the new script then adopted by the locals to write their own language), or that locals were themselves taking the initiative in making themselves literate in the script. Literacy learning implies an element of language learning as well.

Two other recurrent developments were seen. Name changing can in some cases be plotted across several generations in the families mentioned in funerary inscriptions. In Etruria, Africa, Spain and in Palmyrene inscriptions (see also Chapter 7 on La Graufesenque in Gaul) vernacular speakers first took on Roman names alongside their native names, and then dropped the old names completely. Since patterns of name changing are particularly apparent in bilingual inscriptions, it may be deduced that changing names went hand in hand with changing languages. At La Graufesenque, as we will see, potters continued to use Gaulish names to a considerable extent in the pottery itself, but in the makers' stamps on the products distributed in the wider world Latin names were exclusively used. I draw much the same conclusion from this distinction as from the story about Septimius Severus and his sister. Latin names conferred a cachet on the products; they had higher status than the local Gaulish names. Given the close connection between name changing and language changing noted above, it is likely to have been the case that those who esteemed Latin names also esteemed the Latin language. This esteem of Latin, combined with an ambition to get on in a world that was now Roman, I see as the primary determinant of language shift in the western provinces, where there was no competing language of culture to rival Latin. Greek by contrast was most definitely a language of culture, so much so that the Romans themselves were prepared to use it as a lingua franca, and for that reason it was not exposed to the same pressures as western languages without a literature.

The second development lies in the imitation in vernacular inscriptions of Latin ways of expressing things. We saw, for example, the imitation in Africa of Latin funerary formulae, and the imitation in Oscan of Latin legal formulae. Such imitation implies the dominance of Roman culture, and again points to the same determinant of language shift.

XIV.4 Bilingual inscriptions

Some aspects of bilingual texts were introduced in the first chapter (I.VII.I). We have now reviewed a much larger body of material, and some further observations can be made. What motivates a person to set up an inscription in two languages? Some obvious determinants emerge from the material assembled in this chapter. Some inscriptions were the work of immigrants to an area in which a language different from their L1 predominated. The Gaulish–Latin bilingual from Vercelli (IV.2 (2)) belongs to this category, as do a number of Palmyrene–Latin bilinguals, such as the Roman inscription discussed at VII.2 (**2**). The immigrant from (e.g.) Gaul, Palmyra or a Greek-speaking region who used Latin alone in an inscription in Rome or Italy would either be assimilated completely to the new linguistic environment, or at least desirous of claiming such assimilation. Recent immigrants were probably less likely to abandon their old language entirely, particularly if they were part of a community of immigrants. It would be an extreme form of non-assimilation to use, say, Palmyrene alone in a public inscription at Rome, whereas a bilingual inscription allowed the writer to address locals in their own language while retaining a Palmyrene identity. The two versions of the Roman Palmyrene–Latin bilingual referred to above contain significantly different types of information relevant to the two types of readership. The writer was conscious of his membership of two different communities, and did not want to cut himself off from either group; his complex identity is conveyed linguistically. *Topic* in the sense of the word as used in XIV.2 above is also a subsidiary factor behind the language choice in this inscription. One language was considered appropriate for expressing certain topics, and the other for various other topics. But it is again not topic on its own that can explain the language choice. The composer was taking account also of the potential readership, and of the context of the inscription. It is also worth noting that both this inscription and the Gaulish–Latin text mentioned above are religious in content. Immigrants may be strongly motivated to hold on to their native language in the sphere of religion (see also the Sardinian inscription discussed at V.4).

Not all migrants move to a region where there is a group speaking their native language. If they set up a bilingual inscription in such an area they are obviously not addressing a readership and conveying information through the medium of their native language, but are using the language symbolically as a marker of their identity, and also attempting to cling on to their linguistic roots. Palmyrenes had a habit of behaving in this way. Soldiers wrote Palmyrene–Latin bilinguals in scattered parts of the Empire, and a certain Barates left a bilingual inscription at South Shields.

But those who composed bilingual inscriptions had not always migrated to a new area. Etruscans, for example, wrote in Etruscan and Latin in Etruria, Veneti in Latin and Venetic in the Venetic territory, Africans in Latin and Punic in Africa, and Spaniards in Latin and Iberian in Spain. Latin was spreading in all of these places, and those who used two languages together were sensitive to their mixed and changing linguistic identities. Just as they were taking on Latin names alongside their original names, so they took up Latin but had not yet reached the stage of completely dropping the vernacular language.

We have seen various relationships between the different versions of bi- or trilingual inscriptions. Sometimes the main information is in one version and another is a mere token presence, either because the writer was not adept in one of the languages (so the Palmyrene trilingual at VII.3 and possibly the Sardinian inscription at V.4; see also I.VII.1 for another text with Palmyrene), or because there was no local readership for it (so the inscription of Barates and various others). Often the two versions are complementary and/or idiomatic or formulaic in the manner appropriate to the separate languages. This sort of relationship is the norm, and it undermines any assumption that a bilingual text was usually written in one language and then translated literally into another. Those setting up even humble funerary inscriptions seem to have felt that they should use the idioms and formulae appropriate to the individual languages, and translationese was usually avoided. One should therefore think of separate acts of composition rather than of composition followed by translation. We have seen complementary or idiomatic bilingual texts in virtually every section. Finally there are, despite what has just been said, some bilinguals in which one version imitates the phraseology of the other, even if the result was not normal in the second language. In Etruria (III.6) matronymics in Latin were modelled on those in Etruscan, and if there was a plain ablative unaccompanied either by *natus* or by *filius* the phraseology was unidiomatic. Filiations with *clan* in Etruscan and *kenti-* in Celtiberian were modelled on the structure of the Latin filiation formula. We saw particularly in Punic–Latin bilinguals a good deal of Latinate formulae in the Punic. The imitation of the formulae of one language in another implies the increasing dominance of one culture over another, such that those using the old language cannot avoid falling into the patterns of the other.

XIV.5 Language learning

The question was asked in the introduction to this chapter to what extent primary speakers of Latin were learners of other languages (apart from Greek). The material assembled here has pointed overwhelmingly in one direction. There is abundant evidence for primary speakers of Oscan, Venetic, Etruscan, Punic, Gaulish, Germanic, Hispanic, Aramaic and Thracian learning Latin, but virtually none for Latin speakers learning any of these languages. Some exceptions have been seen, but they do not amount to much. An exception moreover may prove the rule: Sidonius presents it as a striking anomaly that his friend Syagrius should have learnt German. In the Republican period there is literary evidence for Latin speakers learning Etruscan and Punic. The *disciplina Etrusca* was admired and influential at Rome, and it is not unlikely that in the early period, when no one language had established dominance in Italy, upper-class Romans in contact with Etruscans should have learnt (or had their offspring learn) some Etruscan. It is admiration for an alien culture that will motivate some learning of the language associated with that culture. Tradition has it too that Etruscan stage performers came to Rome, and here again is to be seen a form of cultural contact conducive to mutual language learning. But by the late Republic Etruscan was swamped by Latin as Etruria was Romanised. Carthage for its part was a military power, and it had a literate culture which elicited some admiration from Romans. The long military conflicts between Rome and Carthage and the negotiations entailed in establishing treaties will have prompted some learning of Punic by Latin speakers, and there is explicit evidence in the story about the translation of the work of Mago for the existence of Punic experts among the Roman upper classes. But in Plautus (and, later, Livy) there are signs of suspicion among Latin speakers of the bilingual capacities of Carthaginians, and that attitude implies a feeling that Carthaginians were more adept at Latin than Romans at Punic. One should not therefore exaggerate the extent of Punic learning by Romans. In the Empire we have observed the acquisition of Latin by

Punic speakers in Africa, but Punic was not suddenly wiped out. Some prominent Africans were keen to parade a double linguistic identity, though the story about Septimius Severus' embarrassment at his sister's ignorance of Latin shows clearly enough the relative status of Latin and Punic in the eyes of upper-class Africans. The Latin Church, however, displayed a tolerance of Punic, and that was partly because Punic was known to be related to Hebrew. A more pragmatic consideration was that some congregations in rural areas were almost entirely Punic-speaking. There are signs that acceptance of that fact even prompted some learning of Punic by clerics who were primarily Latin-speaking. Language learning inspired by Christianity was also seen in the person of Jerome, who aspired to learn both Aramaic and Hebrew because of the task which he had set himself of translating the Old Testament (and because he had chosen to live in a region where Aramaic was the standard language). But this is very much a special case; and Jerome, a remarkable linguist, testifies to the extreme difficulty he found with Aramaic. It is of some interest that the military interpreters who accompanied the Germanic *candidatus* when he visited the Aramaic-speaking holy man Hilarion knew Greek but not Aramaic, and other evidence was presented which showed members of the Roman army communicating in the east through Greek rather than Aramaic. That is not to say that there would not have been military interpreters who spoke Aramaic, but these are likely to have been primary speakers of Aramaic who had been recruited into the army rather than primary speakers of Latin who had learnt a second language. As we saw, Palmyrenes learnt Latin in the army but retained their native language, and these will have been well equipped to serve as interpreters. It would be rash therefore to argue from narratives of events which do not make explicit mention of language use that such-and-such a Latin speaker must have known (e.g.) Aramaic because he had dealings with Aramaic speakers (I am referring particularly to the praetorian prefect Musonianus). Aramaic speakers often knew Greek, which could be used as a lingua franca. And a praetorian prefect would have had access to native speakers of Aramaic serving in the army who could interpret for him. And what is true of communication between Latin speakers and speakers of Aramaic is bound to have been true also of communication between Latin speakers and speakers of the other vernacular languages of the Empire. There is evidence in Ammianus, for example, of German soldiers with Latin as their second language acting as interpreters or spies in Germanic-speaking regions. A centurion recorded in an inscription as an interpreter in a Germanic area *might* have picked up a Germanic language as a second language, but it is not impossible that Latin was his second language.

The evidence for language learning by primary speakers of Latin after the Republican period is thus very slight. We cannot know anything of the linguistic accomplishments of individuals who lived in border regions or moved around the Empire for the purposes of (e.g.) trade, but certainly the two major Roman institutions of the Imperial period, the army and the civilian administration, acted as if only two languages, Latin and Greek, existed. The army used interpreters who knew other languages, but what is lacking is evidence that these sometimes acquired not Latin but a vernacular language as their second language.

XIV.6 Accommodation

A term which has been used from time to time in this chapter is 'accommodation'. I conclude with a few introductory remarks about the term, which will come up again later in the book (see particularly 3.IV.1, 5.III, V; also 6.V.1, VII). Accommodation in the strictest sense may be defined as the act of modifying an utterance in some way in deference to the addressee. Accommodation is relevant to the study of bilingualism, because the desire to be accommodating to an addressee may determine a speaker's language choice on a particular occasion, or determine a switch of codes. A nice instance of accommodation lying behind a code-switch was seen above, II.2, in the Oscan–Latin bilingual text written by tile makers. The writer of the Latin version switched momentarily into Oscan in naming the owner or patron (in the genitive *Herenneis*). The switch was an act of deference to the referent. It will be seen that the definition just given of accommodation would have to be modified slightly to embrace this example, because Herens was not the addressee of the inscription but a referent. In a looser sense then accommodation is the act of modifying language use (whether in speech or writing) to suit the addressee, the referent or the circumstances. Accommodation in this wider meaning might be argued to lie behind the adoption in one language of the formulae or clichés current in another in a bilingual community. If for example someone composing a funerary inscription in Latin in Etruria attaches a matronymic to the name of the deceased, lip service has been paid to the local Etruscan practice of naming persons formally in Etruscan by name + matronymic. Latin has been adapted to the local Etruscan way of expressing things, in deference to a long tradition in the region. At various points in this chapter I have applied

the term 'accommodation' to comparable modifications of forms of expression to match the norms of those obtaining in the other language
of the region. Usually the modification is made not in Latin (as in the
Etruscan example) but in the vernacular language, which in its formula
use is brought into line with the dominant language, Latin. Writers thus
'accommodate' their phraseology to the forms of expression they know
in Latin. They are responding in many cases not to an individual addressee and his preferences, but to the subtle pressure applied by the
Latin language itself which they hear around them.

3

Code-switching

I INTRODUCTION

In a previous chapter code-switching was defined, and distinguished from borrowing and interference (1.v). Some testimonia were cited which established that the phenomenon was recognised in antiquity. Code-switching is common both in literary texts and primary material, particularly inscriptions. I turn in this chapter to its determinants.

There is now a variety of opinion about the nature and motivation of code-switching. An old view was that the 'ideal bilingual switches from one language to the other according to appropriate changes in the speech situation (interlocutors, topics, etc.), but not in an unchanged speech situation, and *certainly not within a single sentence*' (Weinreich (1953: 73), my italics). Weinreich goes on to 'visualize two types of deviation from the norm' (i.e. the norm whereby the ideal bilingual is resistant to switching). The second of his 'deviations' is 'in the direction of insufficient adherence to one language in a constant speech situation' (1953: 74). He observes that this 'tendency (abnormal proneness to switching) has been attributed to persons who, in early childhood, were addressed by the same familiar interlocutors indiscriminately in both languages'. Switching is thus acknowledged to exist, but is seen as an aberration, or, as Weinreich puts it (1953: 74), a 'deviant behaviour pattern'. Such claims have now been rejected as a result of study of bilingual communities in which in unchanged speech situations speakers have been observed to switch languages with considerable freedom even within sentence or clause boundaries.[1] Far from reflecting 'oversight', incompetence (but see below, II) or deviant behaviour, code-switching, particularly of the 'intra-sentential' type, has been said to carry a high degree of 'syntactic risk', and in consequence

---

[1] See in general Milroy and Muysken (1995: 8) on possible reasons why code-switching was relatively invisible to early researchers such as Weinreich. For detailed studies of code-switching, see e.g. Gumperz (1982), Poplack (1980, 1988), Myers-Scotton (1993), and many of the papers in Milroy and Muysken (1995).

to be avoided by 'all but the most fluent bilinguals'.[2] On this view code-switching may involve a good deal of linguistic skill.[3] Poplack (1980: 600) points out that in her corpus of 1,835 switches recorded in a Puerto Rican community in New York 'there were virtually no instances of ungrammatical combinations of L_1 and L_2'. Code-switching raises questions of the following types:[4] what motivates a speaker of languages A and B to switch from one language to the other in mid-utterance? Can patterns ever be detected? Is such a question itself based on a misconception, implying as it does that language differentiation is a sort of unmarked option?[5] Are there factors, syntactic or otherwise, which restrict or prevent certain types of code-switching (generally referred to as 'constraints')?[6] Do the different types of switching (e.g. tag switches, intra-sentential, etc.) have different functions? And is code-switching ever mechanically triggered? I stress that I will be dealing here mainly with functions and motivations of code-switching, rather than with constraints placed upon it (but see below, III.10, 4.V.4.1, p. 499). It seems to me perverse that some linguists have shown a desire to establish 'universal' constraints on code-switching when there is as yet so little empirical data available about a practice which is undoubtedly familiar all over the world, particularly in this age of globalisation, when English is intruding heavily into dozens of languages.

The evidence of corpus languages may seem inadequate as a vehicle for studying code-switching in action, because code-switching is bound to be at its most creative in speech rather than writing. The formality of writing may elicit extra care from the writer in differentiating languages. On the other hand the written text does offer some advantages for the would-be analyst of code-switching.[7] Whereas two bilinguals may

---

[2] See Romaine (1995: 123); also Hamers and Blanc (1989: 148–9).

[3] The skilful performance of fluent bilinguals in code-switching is now often brought out in the literature. For example, Poplack (1988: 230, 237) stresses this aspect of the bilingual speech of some Puerto Ricans in New York ('For Puerto Ricans, code-switching *per se* is emblematic of their dual identity, and smooth, skilled switching is the domain of highly fluent bilinguals'). Jacobson (1998b: 68) in reference to Malays bilingual in English and Malay states that the 'knowledge of English becomes . . . a matter of intellectual pride. The speaker attempts to blend or fuse the two languages into a single mode of manifestation to demonstrate this versatility.'

[4] See the introduction to Milroy and Muysken (1995) for an account of the current issues in the study of code-switching.

[5] See e.g. Gardner-Chloros (1995: 68).   [6] See e.g. in general Romaine (1995: 125–30).

[7] Horsley remarks (1989: 8), that the 'issue of **code-switching** appears to have little practical application to the study of dead languages . . . since it can really only be tested and observed in oral communication', but he appears to disregard the sheer extent of code-switching in written texts, and the interesting question of what might have motivated a writer to change languages within a piece of writing. Some idea of the extent of the corpus of Latin literary texts which show code-switching emerges from Wenskus' various works (1995, 1996, 1998), and the diversity of the phenomenon has already been seen in the first two chapters.

in informal speech switch haphazardly in and out of two languages, inscriptions on stone cannot possibly have been composed without a good deal of thought. As we have seen (1.VIII), as many as three persons could be involved in the establishment of any one text, the client who commissioned the inscription, the drafter and the stonecutter. Spontaneous switches of code are not to be expected in such a text, but a deliberate switch may allow deductions to be made about the motives of the writer on a particular occasion. Code-switching as it is attested in inscriptions, papyri and also some literary texts from the Roman period is by no means chaotic, and I will be identifying various types and factors determining switches. Code-switching in writing has indeed begun to attract some attention recently, namely from McClure (1998), who shows that switching into English from Mexican Spanish, Spanish and Bulgarian in magazines, newspapers and advertising in the three countries is overwhelmingly motivated by a desire to claim association for a product or the like with the all-powerful English-speaking consumer and pop culture. In Bulgarian code-switching there is sometimes a change from the Cyrillic alphabet into the Latin, much as some of the texts to be discussed here show changes of script.

Code-switching often has an obvious symbolism, and I begin with a distinction which will be of some importance in this chapter. Consider first the advertisement for a low-cost Channel crossing, 'At this price it's rather bon, non?'.[8] The Channel crossing entails a crossing of linguistic boundaries, and the transition is nicely symbolised here by the passage from English to French in a single sentence. The advertisement reflects the perspective of an English speaker, who will pass from the English-speaking area to the French. Note on the other hand *CIL* III.125 Κλ. Κλαυδιανὸς οὐετ(ρανὸς) Θεοφάνου **leg**(**atus**) **p**(**ro**) **p**(**raetore**) **ex leg**(**ione**) **III K**(**yrenaica**) ἐποίησεν τὴν στήλην ἰδίαις αὐτοῦ δαπάναις.[9] The soldier who set up this inscription for himself in a Greek-speaking area (Zorava in Syria) used the Latin language and script only for the military rank. The code- and alphabet-switch symbolises the Romanness of his profession as a soldier, alongside the Greekness that he still retains.[10]

---

[8] Quoted by Gardner-Chloros (1991: 4).

[9] This inscription is not straightforward. The editor completes the abbreviation *leg.* as *legati*. If Θεοφάνου is a filiation, it is in an odd place, if, that is, ουετ = οὐετρανός. However the difficulties are to be resolved, it remains true that there is code-switching in the inscription, and that the military rank is in Latin.

[10] A comparable example of the use of Latin (though not in the form of code-switching) to convey a Roman military identity in a Greek area was seen in the previous chapter (2.VII.3) in an inscription from Caesarea Mazaca in Cappodocia (*AE* 1984, 893). The referent's own epitaph is in Latin,

There is though a difference between the functions of the code-switching in these two cases. The military text characterises a *person* (as having a particular, partially Romanised, identity) for the sake of potential readers in a Greek part of the Empire, whereas the other text characterises a hypothetical *event* (as involving a movement from one speech area to another). The military inscription is thus interpersonal, interactional, or in a word *social*, whereas the advertisement carries an interpretation of an abstract activity, and there is no relationship implied between a specific writer, with a particular perception of himself, and a reader. Code-switching (in our written texts) often expresses social meanings in one sense or another.[11] The writer often seeks to create an impression of himself in the eyes of an addressee or reader, and perhaps to set up a particular relationship with the addressee. He may (e.g.) wish to establish a sense of solidarity with the addressee, or alternatively to create a distance from him. The code-switching may be directly interactional, in that it is triggered by a perceived taste or characteristic of the addressee. In Plautus' *Pseudolus*, Pseudolus, who likes to code-switch himself, arguably prompts code-switching at one point when another character refers to him (IV.1). And at least two persons who were more Greek than the Greeks, Atticus and T. Albucius, inspired code-switching for that reason in their interlocutors (and Atticus not only in Cicero's letters but also in Varro's *Res rusticae*: see IV.1); this phenomenon might be called code-switching as a form of *accommodation* (see below, IV.1). If on the other hand the readership (as for example that of a funerary inscription in a public place) does not consist of individuals known to the writer but of undifferentiated passers-by, the aim of the writer may be to present a special identity for himself to all and sundry (as in the military inscription *CIL* III.125 above). A good deal of this chapter will concern code-switching with social intention in these various senses. The other type of code-switching distinguished above, that which characterises events, activities, material etc., is sometimes found, for example, in texts in which the identity of the writer is not a major issue in the text. A momentary switch of languages in such a context may evoke another world (see below, IX). Just as Lucretius uses (integrated) Greek loan-words 'to conjure up for the readers a Greek or an otherwise exotic context' (Sedley (1999: 238)), so code-switching could serve the same purpose. In this role it is one of those stylistic resources such as archaism, poeticism,

but that of his wife and son are in Greek. The family was Greek-speaking, but the soldier is given a Latin inscription.

[11] The social functions of code-switching have been studied particularly by Gumperz (e.g. (1982)).

vulgarism, metaphor etc. which the linguistic virtuoso can exploit to make his speech or narrative more evocative.

A mass of detailed evidence will be presented in this chapter, but I will be dealing mainly with four general issues, several of which have already been identified. I list all four issues in the interests of clarity. First, there is code-switching as a means of establishing a relationship with an addressee, as for example a sense of solidarity, or a position of dominance or aloofness. A speaker may diverge occasionally from the addressee's preferred language as a means of distancing or partial exclusion (something which happened from time to time, for example, in hearings before Roman officials in Egypt: see below, VI.I), or he may converge with the addressee by adopting as far as he is able the first language of the second person, though his ability to do so may be limited. Convergence can also be described as accommodation. Divergence and convergence by code-switching may represent language use as symbolising power on the one hand or solidarity on the other.[12] Or again a mixed discourse, where speaker and interlocutor are equally bilingual, can reinforce the feeling of a shared, mixed identity or culture. This type of code-switching may often be interpreted as a mark of solidarity or as a demonstration of shared membership of an in-group. Gumperz (1982) memorably used the term 'we-code' to describe the language or variety of speech used by such in-groups. It is sometimes the case that a code-switching variety establishes solidarity. It is reported that while Italian-Australians have little concern for preserving literary standard Italian, they do make use of oral family languages for everyday communication within restricted social groups.[13] Family languages have different forms. They may consist of an Italian-English 'mix', comprising 'either . . . a dialect base overlaid with English usages, or an English language structure interspersed with dialect words and phrases' (Smolicz (1981: 76)). These 'mixed languages' (on this term see below, XII.I) are code-switching varieties either of English or of Italian expressing solidarity within Italian-Australian communities; they mark out their users as belonging to a distinctive group. To educated Romans Greek was the language of high culture, but it would have been an extreme act for two educated Romans to communicate purely in Greek to express their joint possession of the trappings of that culture (and hence their sense of belonging to an exclusive group). But they could (at least in theory)

---

[12] For this opposition, see Brown and Gilman (1968), Myers-Scotton (1993: 93–4). See further below, VI, XII.4.

[13] See Smolicz (1981: 76).

code-switch from time to time into Greek for that purpose. So it is that Cicero's correspondence with the new Epicurean Cassius is larded with Epicurean Greek,[14] used of course satirically on Cicero's part, which suggests that the coterie of late Republican Epicureans represented by Cassius code-switched to underline their direct adherence to Epicurus, their rejection of attempts to Latinise Epicurean terminology, and hence their special status as a group (see further below, p. 317); Cicero for his part in these letters was accommodating himself humorously to the linguistic practices of his addressee as a member of that group.

Secondly, there is code-switching for the expression of different types of identity. The author of the military inscription quoted earlier took on a military identity merely by recording his military rank, but by switching out of Greek into Latin for that purpose he gave that identity additional impact. The soldier emerges as a Greek who had been Romanised through service in the army, and as such he acquires a mixed identity;[15] the Romanness of his professional identity is expressed not only by the meaning of the words, but also by the symbolism of the shift into Latin. It must be stressed that code-switching of the types described in the previous paragraph (those which put a person on a certain footing with an addressee) and that used to convey an identity cannot always be clearly distinguished. Consider, for example, the following hypothetical example reflecting linguistic conditions in part of Africa. A Kenyan who speaks a minority African language and English, but who, in conversation with a person from the same homeland, refuses to speak anything but English, may be presenting himself as educated, ambitious, indifferent or hostile to his roots, and aloof from the other speaker. If on the other hand he switches between the minority language and English, he may take on a dual identity: educated and Europeanised on the one hand, but still attached to his origins and wishing to display some solidarity with the other person, if not the total solidarity that would be conferred by exclusive use of the minority language. This example fits into both of the categories distinguished here, and that is frequently the case, as we will see: the person who seeks to present a type of identity will often in effect be establishing a certain relationship with his interlocutor, and vice versa. The example also brings out the fact that 'solidarity' is not a single entity, but admits of differing degrees of closeness. By modifying his language choice and language mix the Kenyan is potentially able

---

[14] See Baldwin (1992: 2–4).
[15] On code-switching and dual identity, see e.g. Appel and Muysken (1987: 119, 130), Myers-Scotton (1993: 70, 122, 147), and also Poplack (1988) as quoted above n. 3.

to express different degrees of solidarity with his addressee. Similarly the code-switching Italian-Australians also give themselves a distinctive identity. Though I have separated these two social determinants in the last two paragraphs, I will not in practice be enforcing such a distinction in the discussion that follows.

The jargon used in the last two paragraphs (terms such as 'solidarity' and 'in-group') has typically been used in sociolinguistics by those investigating spoken languages in modern communities. It will become apparent later in the discussion that, though such terminology offers a framework for the consideration of written code-switching in a dead language, it is too vague to capture precisely the very special determinants of written code-switching in upper-class Roman society of the late Republic. I will not be doggedly trying to subordinate unsuitable data to a view or views of code-switching which may have proved appropriate for the analysis of modern speech communities, but will keep in mind the special conditions of Rome. The notion of the 'in-group' as it is applicable to upper-class late Republican society will have to be refined.

The categories of code-switching so far mentioned fall under the general heading of code-switching with social meaning as referred to earlier. It is to Gumperz that we owe the insight that code-switching may represent interactive strategies.[16]

Thirdly, I will say something about code-switching as a possible response to the topic of part of an utterance, though I will be suggesting that a change of topic is usually not enough on its own to generate a switch. This is a subject which came up from time to time in the previous chapter: various cases of 'culturally specific' terminology in a language different from that of the rest of the text in which it was embedded were noted (see 2.XIV.2). Solidarity, identity and topic are not mutually exclusive, and will turn out to be difficult to separate. The general point that will be implicit is that in our written material code-switching seems to be a marked activity (see further below and also XII.3 on 'markedness') frequently expressing social meanings, and deriving from the rationality of the user and his desire to make a special impression. The code-switcher in a written text is not the slave of particular topics as determining switches of language, but like all users of marked forms of discourse is conscious of the effects of his code choice.

Finally, code-switching as a stylistic resource evocative (e.g.) of the exotic will be dealt with (see above, and below, III.8, IX). Appel and

---

[16] For a summary of Gumperz's contribution in this respect, see Milroy and Muysken (1995: 9–10).

Muysken (1987: 120) refer to switching which is said to serve the 'poetic function of language', and they appear to mean by that what I call 'stylistically evocative' switching.

Early in the chapter (III) Cicero's letters will be discussed as a special case, and in this discussion a variety of issues will come up, not all of them falling under socially determined code-switching; but it would be confusing to split the discussion of Cicero into different parts. Our account of Ciceronian practice will allow some miscellaneous issues which have not yet been mentioned to be introduced, and will also bring out the futility of relying too much on the jargon and categories of sociolinguistics in analysing a written corpus from a distinctive society.

The question arises whether code-switching should be described as 'marked', 'unmarked' or both, depending on the circumstances.[17] As I have emphasised, almost all work done on code-switching to date has dealt with spoken language, whereas our material is written. It is possible that unmarked code-switching (that is, code-switching as a 'normal' form of communication) is not uncommon in the speech of particular communities. But if that could be established, it would not necessarily follow that one should expect to find code-switching with a comparable role in written texts. The military inscription quoted above, for example, is by no means normal. There are hundreds of military inscriptions from the Empire in which soldiers state their rank, but these are overwhelmingly in either Greek or Latin. One deduces therefore from the norms of what is a fairly stereotyped genre that the above case has code-switching in a marked stylistic role. The writer may have been particularly proud of his acquired Romanness in a closed community of Greek speakers. The advertisement too is highly unusual, and represents the inventive effort of a skilled composer. His or her composition is every bit as marked as it would have been if a novel metaphor or neologism had been inserted instead of the French. In both epigraphy and Latin literature code-switching is a resource used only sparingly for symbolic purposes, and is therefore necessarily to be classified as marked in most cases. There are however a few inscriptions which have such intensive code-switching that the base language is indeterminate, and these may have originated in communities in which code-switching was an unmarked option. There is usually though an alternative explanation (see I.V and V.I below on *ILCV* 4463). And finally there are the letters of Cicero to Atticus. Would the pair have regarded the code-switching Latin of the correspondence as their

---

[17] I allude here to the work of Myers-Scotton (e.g. 1993). I will return to her 'markedness model' later in the chapter (XII.3).

'normal' way of communicating in private? I will come to this question later.

It has been assumed so far in this chapter that code-switching expresses intentional meanings and that it is a skilled linguistic performance; it is the merit of Gumperz and Poplack in particular that they have highlighted these aspects of the phenomenon. But there is also another type, namely code-switching reflecting poor competence in a second language, and I begin with that.

II CODE-SWITCHING AND IMPERFECT COMPETENCE

A distinction can be made between 'code-switching which results from the bilingual's competence and code-switching resulting from a speaker's lack of competence' in the second language (Hamers and Blanc (1989: 149)).[18] Switching through imperfect competence may be committed, for example, by second-language learners such as, at Rome, slaves of foreign origin or other immigrants. It has been observed that 'language shift typically takes place over three generations, the first being monolingual or dominant in L_1, the second differentially bilingual, and the third dominant or monolingual in L_2' (Hamers and Blanc (1989: 176); but see below, n. 130). In the early stages of a shift within a family switches are likely to be made back into the mother tongue.[19] Language shift across various generations and its relevance to code-switching will come up later in this chapter (V.1).

Code-switching motivated by limited competence is well attested from the Roman period, both in inscriptions and in anecdotes. I cite a few pieces of evidence (see also the first two cases discussed at 2.VII.3 above).

(1) As we have seen (1.V, 2.XIII), the Thracian emperor Maximinus, according to the *SHA (Max.* 2.5), following his recruitment to the Roman army and before he was fluent in Latin, once addressed the emperor Septimius Severus in a language that was virtually Thracian: *hic adulescens et semibarbarus et uix adhuc Latinae linguae, prope Thraecica imperatorem publice petiit ut . . .*[20] The context makes it clear that he was attempting to speak Latin, but that he was forced to keep switching into Thracian.

(2) A marriage contract from Egypt, re-published at *ChLA* 4.249 from *P. Mich.* VII.434 and *P. Ryl.* IV.612, was obviously written by a Greek with

---

[18] See too Poplack (1980: 583).

[19] Code-switching against the background of language shift within immigrant families has been studied (e.g.) by Milroy and Wei (1995).

[20] For a brief discussion of this passage, see Kaimio (1979a: 154).

a limited command of Latin (see below, 5.VIII for a detailed discussion of the document). The text contains a dowry list, many words of which are Greek, some of them not integrated morphologically into Latin. It is likely that the scribe simply did not know the appropriate technical terms of Latin; the list he was copying was presumably in Greek, into which language he switched when he was lost for a word. I mention here just one case, *enotion* 'earring' at line 8 of the Michigan fragment. The word is not otherwise attested in Latin.

(3) A translation on papyrus of part of two fables of Babrius (*P. Amh.* II.26) seems to be the work of a Greek learner of Latin whose competence in the second language was imperfect (see below, Ch. 8). For example, the translator knew the form of some Latin participles, but not their function.[21] Occasionally he came up with the *mot juste*, but his *infra aruras* (line 13) represents a transfer into Latin of a Greek term in the original (Babrius 11.5 εἰς τὰς ἀρούρας) of which he presumably did not know the Latin equivalent.

(4) We saw in the first chapter (1.VII.1) a trilingual funerary inscription from Palmyra set up by a local Palmyrene in commemoration of himself, in Aramaic, Greek and Latin. The writer could find no Latin equivalent to φυλῆς Μειθηνῶν, which he rendered as *phyles Mithenon*. His failure even to Latinise the endings makes it justifiable to treat the expression as a piece of code-switching.

(5) A more complicated case can be found at *P. Oxy.* II.244, which is a letter by a slave Cerinthus written in Greek, probably by a professional scribe. The letter is addressed to the *strategus* Chaereas. At the end in another hand, almost certainly that of the slave himself (see below, VII, on autograph *subscriptiones* in letters), there is a subscription containing a date in Latin script and basically the Latin language, but with two switches of code: *Ceri[nthus] Antoniae Drusi ser(uus) epid[e]doca anno VIIII Tib(eri) Caesaris Aug(usti) Mechir die oct(auo)*.

The month is not Roman but the Egyptian Μεχίρ; whether we classify this as a code-switch, as I am doing here, or a borrowing is for once immaterial. The second switch lies in the technical verb *epidedoca*, which is not an integrated borrowing but a Greek verb inflected as Greek, and unequivocally a switch of code. Why did Cerinthus insert these two words?

Kramer (1984: 1383) makes the assumption that the two insertions reflect Cerinthus' imperfect knowledge of Greek: he wanted to use Greek,

---

[21] On the acquisition by learners of the form, but not the function, of morphemes, see Hamers and Blanc (1989: 218).

but knew only the two technical terms ('In questo caso è evidente che Cerinthus vuole servirsi del greco, ma *le sue conoscenze non sono sufficienti; conosce solo il termine tecnico* ἐπιδέδωκα *ed il nome del mese* Μεχίρ') (my italics). This explanation is implausible, for it fails to explain why he used Greek in the body of the letter (or at least had it used on his behalf). Are we to assume that Cerinthus dictated to or instructed a Greek scribe, even though he might hardly have been able to understand the Greek letter produced by the scribe? Is it conceivable that he knew the verb ἐπιδέδωκα (and its inflection) but could not put *Antoniae Drusi seruus* into Greek, particularly since the phrase appears in Greek form in the body of the letter? It is more likely that he had a good understanding of Greek, even if he was not necessarily literate in that language. There is often a deliberate language shift in the subscription of a letter, marking (e.g.) the shared bilingualism of the writer and addressee (see below, VII).

It is significant that the two alien words in the Latin section are Greek (or Greco-Egyptian) *technical* terms. It is more plausible to suppose that a primary speaker of Greek attempting to write in Latin should be able to cope with names in the target language but not know the Latin equivalents of technical terms, than that a fluent speaker of Latin attempting to use Greek should only know Greek technical terms. There is also in the Latin syntactic interference from Greek. The first four words mean 'Cerinthus slave of Antonia daughter of Drusus'. The filiation lacks the expected *filiae*, and is a syntactic calque on the Greek construction found at the start of the Greek part of the letter: παρὰ Κηρίνθου ᾿ Αντωνίας Δρούσου δούλου. The direction of the interference (Greek influences Latin) points unmistakably to the primacy of Greek. Filiations, as we have seen and will see again (below, V.4), often contain tell-tale signs of cross-language influence or interference.

I conclude that Cerinthus was a Greek (as his name would suggest), who as the slave of a Roman had learnt some Latin. At the end of a letter in his first language, Greek, he switched into Latin, perhaps to mark his bilingualism and his acquired Romanness,[22] but was uncertain both of the Latin equivalent of ἐπιδέδωκα and the Latin system of months, and for that reason was forced to make two switches of code. Dating systems often caused uncertainty in language learners. When a date is given in two different languages, the two versions do not always correspond

---

[22] It is possible that the switch into Latin was intended to give authority to Cerinthus' request. In Egypt, as we will see in Chapter 5, the Romans used Greek as the everyday language of administration, but switches into Latin were sometimes made to underline the Romanness of the imperial power.

exactly (see n. 140). Second-language learners sometimes reverted to their original language when recording a date. Parallels can be cited for this last form of code-switching in Egypt. Note A. Bernand (1972), 51 *L(ucius) Lon(ginus)* (ἔτους) αʹ Τίττου, Μεσουρή, A. Bernand (1977), 64 *C. Numidius Eros hic fuit anno XXIIX Caesaris exs Inda redes menos Pamen(oth)*. This second graffito is on the wall of a cavern at Wâdi Menih on the road from Coptos to Berenice. The writer gives the date by month in Greco-Egyptian form only, with code-switching into Greek not only in the name of the month, but more interestingly in *menos*, which bears a Greek inflection.

Imperfect competence is only one determinant of code-switching, and it is by no means the most important. I turn now to a variety of more positive influences.

III CICERO'S LETTERS

III.1 Introduction

I begin with Cicero's letters, the largest body of material from Roman antiquity displaying forms of code-switching. They are however unrepresentative, because not all code-switching attested in the Roman period comes from so far up the social scale. If (for argument's sake) Cicero was interested in presenting a type of identity through code-switching, this identity could in theory have differed radically from that which a lower-class Greek at Rome might have hoped to project. Code-switching by native speakers of Latin was not homogeneous, as I hope to make clear in this chapter. To some extent the present section will deal with code-switching as socially determined, in that (it may be argued) Cicero was attempting to establish types of relationships with his addressees (particularly Atticus), but there is more to Ciceronian code-switching than that, and I will bring out the diversity of the phenomena. In this introduction I allude to some recent accounts of code-switching in Cicero, and consider selected passages in an effort to summarise the essential features of the practice.

Switching into Greek in Latin literary texts is related to genre. In the formal literary genres such as historiography, oratory and epic poetry switching as a rule does not take place. On the other hand in some less formal genres such as the plays of Plautus, early satire and epistolography it is admitted more or less frequently. In both comedy and satire it occurs in representations of speech. In the genre in which it is most common

(private correspondence) it is most marked in letters to particular intimates, as for example in the Ciceronian corpus in letters to Atticus,
Cicero's brother Quintus and his freedman Tiro.[23] By contrast in more
formal or official letters of the type found particularly in the *Ad familiares*
it is absent or rare,[24] particularly if Cicero was not on easy terms with
the addressee. There is at least one obvious reason for this distribution.
The public attitude to Greek was ambivalent. Greek culture might be
secretly admired, but Roman cultural insecurity made it advisable to
avoid excessive shows of Greekness in public. Cicero, for example, got
into trouble for speaking Greek to the senate of Syracuse (see above, I.III).
In public Greek and Greek culture were as likely to be disparaged as
praised. Greek words (borrowings, not switches of code) in public oratory,
for example, are sometimes used with contemptuous tone.[25] If one were
not on close terms with the addressee of one's letter, or if alternatively the
subject of the letter were highly serious and the tone formal, one would
inevitably use the 'public' language, that is Latin without any (or much)
code-switching. Hence the more formal letters in the correspondence
Ad familiares are largely without Greek. The code-switching variety of
Latin was by contrast essentially a private language, which could not be
flaunted before an indiscriminate audience without danger of ridicule
or rebuke. Of necessity we know of this private code-switching form
of Latin mainly from private letters, but it was probably used in private
conversation as well (see the reported conversation at *Att.* 13.42.1; Lucilius
and Varro (in the *Res rusticae*), as we will see, put code-switching into
conversations).

Code-switching into Greek by Cicero and other upper-class Romans
has often been spoken of as a form of intimacy or even as a language
of intimacy. Dunkel (2000: 128) states that '[p]sychological and emotional life...provoke [*sic*] clusters of Greek'. For Jocelyn (1999: 187)
(in reference to a specific case in Plautus) '[t]he use of Greek asserts
a degree of intimacy'. Note id. (1999: 194), '[code-switching] tended
to occur in circumstances of intimacy, relaxation or merriment and to
be avoided on occasions requiring formality and the maintenance of
dignity'. Wenskus (1998: 8) relates the phenomenon to genre, but makes
much the same point: within the genre of the private letter integrated
code-switching serves to indicate the sub-genre of lively letters to

[23] See e.g. Cugusi (1983: 84), Wenskus (1998: 8).   [24] See e.g. Cugusi (1983: 84).
[25] See for example Laurand (1936–8: 72–4); also Courtney (1999: 119) on the contemptuous use of
the Greek term *chirodyta* instead of the Latin *manicata* in a fragment of Scipio Aemilianus (frg. 17
Malcovati).

close friends ('So dient integrierter Codewechsel innerhalb des Genus "Privatbrief" zur Kennzeichnung des Subgenus "Muntere Briefe an enge Freunde"'). The case has been argued most forcefully by Dubuisson (1992: 193), dealing not explicitly with code-switching from Latin into Greek but with the use of Greek itself by upper-class Romans (in effect code-switching, because there is of necessity a switch from Latin in every case). Several times he uses the expression 'la langue de l'intimité' of Greek, and he stresses that the language was used to express high emotion. It is also, for example, the language 'des paroles bienveillantes que l'on adresse à son interlocuteur pour le mettre en confiance ou lui manifester sa sympathie'. Both Dubuisson (1992: 193)[26] and Dunkel (2000: 128) argue that the reason why there was often a switch to Greek under such circumstances was that Greek was in effect the first language of upper-class Roman boys, and that they were therefore in later life prone to revert as it were to their childhood language in expressing intimacy or emotion. This idea is, though, not entirely plausible, at least as I have expressed it here. The Greek used by such Romans is not the Greek of the nursery, but to a considerable extent, as we will see, that of the rhetorical schools, the philosopher's lecture room, and of high literature. If there is a reversion here to the writer's roots, these roots are to be sought not in early childhood, but at an advanced stage of the educational system. One should not take too literally claims that children became speakers of Greek before they spoke Latin. A salutary case is provided by recent literature on Caesar's last words. Dubuisson (1992: 193) (cf. id. (1980: 888)) quotes Caesar's καὶ σύ, τέκνον (Suet. *Iul.* 82.3) with the comment that Caesar on the point of death 'retrouve sa langue maternelle ou du moins sa langue première'. But Wenskus (1993: 215 n. 27) cites evidence that Caesar was taught by his mother, who is highly unlikely to have used Greek to her children. She points out moreover (1993: 214–15) that in many cultures last words are considered to have magical power, and argues that Caesar's words are probably to be taken as a curse.[27] Earlier Russell (1980: 126, 128) had pointed out that καὶ σύ was a common apotropaic formula, and he translated the words as 'to hell with you too, lad'. On this view the code-switch has nothing to do with the language of childhood, but is related to a type which was identified in the last chapter (code-switching for magical purposes: see 2.II.3, IV.4).

---

[26] See also Dubuisson (1980: 888).

[27] The same view is expressed by Dubuisson himself in a footnote (1992: 203 n. 55), following Russell (1980).

There are further problems with any attempt to explain code-switching in Cicero as exclusively determined by the intimacy of an exchange or some related phenomenon such as the need to express high emotion or the like (on the related issue of code-switching and frivolity, see below). First, by no means all of the switches into Greek in, say, Cicero's letters to Atticus are associated explicitly with what can reasonably be called 'intimacy' or with expressions of emotion. It would in my opinion be perverse to see the use of Greek technical terms (such as those of rhetoric or grammar: for which see below, III.2) in Greek form in a Latin letter as a mark of intimacy, except in a very special sense: two Romans who fall into Greek rhetorical terms are in effect mutually acknowledging their common educational background, but there must be a more appropriate term than 'intimacy' to describe this phenomenon (see further below). Secondly, code-switching into Greek is without question sometimes adopted by Cicero and others as a form of distancing or euphemism, that is as a means of making more acceptable the discussion of unpleasant matters or of being tactful (see below, III.4); a letter of Augustus to Livia is particularly revealing in this respect. There is a conflict here: how can a 'language of intimacy' also be a language of 'distancing'? The conflict can in fact be resolved. It may well be that Greek was sometimes used when (e.g.) emotions were conveyed, precisely because it had the effect of *distancing* the emotion. Thus C. Cassius Longinus, who 'always expressed himself in Greek when he wished to display affection [Plut. *Brut.* 40.1 [28]]' (Jocelyn (1999: 178)), may have done so because he was uncomfortable about the direct expression of personal feelings, and not because he found Greek a more 'intimate' language. Should the idea of Greek as the 'language of intimacy' therefore be replaced by Greek as the 'language of distance'? Thirdly, a good deal of the evidence cited by Dubuisson (1992: 193 with the relevant footnotes) and Jocelyn (1999: 178) for switching into Greek at moments of tension, emotion or the like does not involve the creative use of Greek at all, but the citation of Greek literary tags or proverbs. To bring this point out I quote in part Jocelyn (1999: 178), with omission of footnote numbers and textual references: 'P. Cornelius Scipio Aemilianus . . . cited two verses of Homer . . . as he contemplated the ruins of the Carthage he had sacked in 146 and another on being told of the death of Ti. Sempronius Gracchus in 133. When C. Iulius Caesar . . . announced to his companions his decision to lead his forces across the Rubicon in 49 he cited

---

[28] ὥσπερ εἰώθει φιλοφρονούμενος, Ἑλληνικῇ φωνῇ.

the end of a comic trimeter. . . . As they prepared themselves for death
C. Pompeius Magnus . . . and M. Iunius Brutus . . . cited tragedy.' If this
is code-switching, it is code-switching of a very special type, and it has
more to do again with the educational background of the disputants than
with any inherently intimate character of Greek in upper-class Roman
eyes. Romans trained in the grammatical and rhetorical schools were
able to sum up virtually any situation succinctly by the citation of an
appropriate Greek tag, and there is little connection between this rather
contrived literary practice and code-switching of the forms studied in
modern speech communities by linguists. Dunkel (2000: 128), for example, in the context of switching into Greek as an alleged form of reversion
to childhood at moments of emotion or intimacy, cites Cic. *Att.* 13.42.1
(SB 354), where a report of a conversation between Cicero and his nephew
Quintus *filius* begins with two snatches of Greek.[29] But the two pieces of
Greek are almost certainly partial quotations of comedy, probably of
Menander (see Shackleton Bailey ad loc.).[30] If so one speaker uses an
unflagged literary quotation which the other is expected to recognise
and perhaps be able to respond to. This is the sort of game which takes
place between two members of a self-conscious cultural élite. If there
is an intimacy here, it is the intimacy of a shared cultural background
and not merely of mutual affection, and at issue as well is membership
of an in-group. Such disputants are conscious of their common Greek
education and keen to use literary allusion which draws on that
education. This is a highly artificial form of intimacy or solidarity.
The final point which I would make about Greek as the 'language
of intimacy' is that various endearments in Greek put into the mouths
of women by two writers (for which see below, v) should not be spoken of
in the same breath as the types of utterances of upper-class males which
have been alluded to so far. They are special cases, and involve a special
type of role play.

   Closely related to the perception of Greek as a language of intimacy is
the view that code-switching into Greek (in Cicero's letters in particular)
is motivated by a sense of humour, frivolity or lightheartedness. Jocelyn
(1999: 194) refers to the 'specifically frivolous associations which switching from Latin to Greek had for members of the Roman upper classes'
(cf. 193 for the same point; also 183, on 'code-switching of the kind in
which Cicero and his correspondents indulged when letting their hair

---

[29] See also Wenskus (1998: 14).

[30] Dunkel was aware of this possibility, and should therefore probably not have cited this example
in the context in which it is used.

down, so to speak'). Wenskus (1998: 31) finds that Greek 'Einschaltun-gen' are a mark of good humour. Dunkel (2000: 128) expresses himself in much the same way as Jocelyn: 'many switches are due to the desire for humor . . . Sheer human playfulness . . . should not be underestimated as a motivation for code-switching, despite the inherent difficulty of cold philological proof.' It is certainly true that switches are often associated with frivolity, and they may even be flagged as humorous. Thus in a letter to Varro (*Fam.* 9.7.2) soon after a partial quotation of Homer (*Il.* 10.224) Cicero remarks 'away with such jests', *sed ridicula missa* (but see further below). But there is a potential circularity in this sort of argument. Letters to intimates are bound to have a good deal of frivolity or lightheartedness, and therefore if switches into Greek are adopted in such letters some of them are bound to be in jocular contexts. Is the switching due to the de-sire to inject an element of humour, or is the humorous use to which the Greek is put simply a consequence of the generally flippant tone of many private letters in which it is embedded? Moreover many switches are not jocular (see in particular the material collected in III.2 and III.4 below, and also the discussion which follows of the letters to Paetus),[31] and much of the frivolity in the letters is conducted not in Greek but in Latin.[32] Thus, for example, the light-hearted passage in the letter to Varro referred to above (*Fam.* 9.7.1) has not only a partial quotation of Homer, but two Latin tags as well, and Cicero's comment *sed ridicula missa* is to be taken as referring to the whole section of the letter and not merely to the Greek. If the personal letters are full of banter and jokes expressed not merely through Greek, and if not all Greek is bantering in tone, then it becomes difficult to sustain the view that a major or the sole motivation of code-switching was 'sheer human playfulness'. The fact that Cicero did not code-switch at times of crisis (when joking was out of the question: see III.9)[33] does not mean that code-switching was inherently jocular; during crises *serious* code-switching as well as *jocular* is avoided. It was the artificiality of the practice, the fact that it was a type of showing-off, which made it inappropriate under such circumstances (see below, III.9).

The letters to Paetus (*Fam.* 9.15–26) are worthy of study in connection with frivolity and code-switching. Paetus was on intimate terms with

[31] A switch in a letter to Terentia could not be described as 'frivolous' (see below, III.4). The occasional single-word switches in a letter to Varro (*Fam.* 9.2) are in no sense flippant. One could go on.
[32] On joking and the like in the letters, see von Albrecht (1973: 1280–1).
[33] Jocelyn (1999: 179) says that '[n]one of those [letters] . . . which give voice to a mood of depression depart from Latin'. Dunkel (2000: 128) refers to Cicero's avoidance of Greek 'when he was feeling down'.

Cicero, as is made particularly clear in the opening section of 15 (1). He was also a notable wit, and is fulsomely praised for this characteristic by Cicero at 15.2, in a passage which ends with a linking of the man's *amor* (for Cicero) with his *lepores*. Given this combination of qualities, is it any wonder, Cicero asks, that he worries about the man's welfare? The corpus of extant letters is full not only of light-hearted banter (e.g. 15.5, 16.8, 17.2, 19.1, 20.2, 26.2) and puns (18.3, 19.1, 20.1) but also of explicit reference to the jesting which took place between the pair (16.7 *nunc uenio ad iocationes tuas*, 16.9 *superiora illa lusimus*, 24.3 *sed mehercule, mi Paete, extra iocum moneo te*, 24.4 *quod iocosius scribam*, 25.2 *sed iocabimur alias coram*). If code-switching was closely related to the intimacy of a relationship and to the frivolity of an exchange, then here is a corrrespondence which ought to be full of code-switching. But it is not. Cugusi (1983: 84) oddly puts the letters to Paetus on a par with those to Atticus and to Quintus *frater* for their adundance of Greek, and von Albrecht (1973: 1274) makes much the same point, but this is wide of the mark. In the twenty or so pages of the corpus there are only eleven or twelve non-integrated Greek words (that is about five every ten pages; in the letters to Atticus, as we will see, there are sometimes as many as sixty Greek words per ten pages of Shackleton Bailey's edition), most of them used singly, and most of them special in one way or another. Two do not even qualify to be described as switches of code (see below). Four of the twelve letters (15, 17, 19, 23) have no switches at all, and another five have just a single Greek word (16, 18, 20, 21, 26; I am referring to code-switching as it has been defined here, and not to integrated borrowings). A few comments on the nature of the Greek will show that it is not overwhelmingly associated with frivolity or intimacy, but may be quite mundane. The famous letter 22 on obscenity is a disquisition on the Stoic maxim that the wise man will call a spade a spade, and it is no surprise that the maxim is quoted in Greek (5 ὁ σοφὸς εὐθυρρημονήσει). At 24.3 two Greek words are discussed and translated: *qui [sermo familiaris] est in conuiuiis dulcissimus, ut sapientius nostri quam Graeci; illi* συμπόσια *aut* σύνδειπνα, *id est compotationes aut concenationes; nos 'conuiuia', quod tum maxime simul uiuitur.* This is not code-switching at all, but philological (or philosophical) discussion of Greek terms. At 25.1 a book title is given its Greek form (Παιδείαν Κύρου), a quite common phenomenon which has nothing to do with intimacy; the usage is rather technical (see III.8). ἀποφθεγμάτων (16.4) (possibly not a code-switch at all),[34] προλεγομένας (18.3)[35] and ζήτημα

---

[34] It is by no means certain that Cicero wrote this word in Greek form. Shackleton Bailey prints *apopthegmatorum* (see the note ad loc., no. 190 in his edition).
[35] Understand θέσεις? See Shackleton Bailey ad loc. (no. 191). The usage is not found elsewhere.

(26.1) are literary/philosophical terms; finally there are ὀψιμαθεῖς (20.2) and ἀπότευγμα (21.1). Of these last five single terms, some may be in bantering contexts, but others seem to be used neutrally.

There is then not much code-switching to speak of at all, and very little of it is frivolous in a way which might have suited the addressee, given Paetus' reputation and his closeness to Cicero. Moreover there are two places where Cicero might have code-switched if he had behaved true to form, but where instead he translates a piece of Greek into Latin. Particularly notable is 26.2: *sed tamen ne Aristippus quidem ille Socraticus erubuit cum esset obiectum habere eum Laida: 'habeo' inquit, 'non habeor a Laide.'* [= ἔχω καὶ οὐκ ἔχομαι] *Graece hoc melius; tu, si uoles, interpretabere* (Shackleton Bailey: 'But after all, even Aristippus the Socratic did not blush when someone twitted him with keeping Lais as his mistress. "Lais is my mistress," said he, "but I'm my own master" (it's better in the Greek, make your own rendering, if you care to)'). The remark was better in Greek than in Latin, Cicero says,[36] but he leaves it to Paetus to translate it. The context is conspicuously light-hearted, and on the view of code-switching under discussion here the use of Greek would surely have been especially appropriate, particularly if the Greek sounded better. The other instance is at 18.3, where *sus Mineruam* (sc. *docet*) is a rendering of ἡ ὗς τὴν Ἀθηνᾶν.[37] In this case Cicero does not explicitly draw attention to the Greekness of the expression.

The question arises why there is so little code-switching in the letters to Paetus. Even if we reject the narrow idea that among upper-class Romans of the time a code-switching variety of Latin was exclusively a 'language of intimacy', it remains true that switching into Greek occurs overwhelmingly in letters to intimates, and Paetus was certainly an intimate of Cicero's. The answer may lie in the attitudes of Paetus, and in the role which he had chosen to play. A significant passage is Cicero's description of the wit of Paetus (15.2): *accedunt non Attici sed salsiores quam illi Atticorum Romani ueteres atque urbani sales.* His wit is not Attic, but something more pungent, the traditional old wit of the city of Rome. This, according to Cicero, is a quality which has now been swamped by outside influences, and Paetus' wit remains as a relic of the past, reminiscent for example of that of the auctioneer Q. Granius, which is elsewhere mentioned by Cicero as characteristic of the old ways. Paetus was of course educated in Greek culture like Cicero himself (see the previous paragraph for passages in which he was expected to pick up Greek allusions; note too 26.1 for his philosophical interests), but he must have chosen

---

[36] *Habeor* does not exactly correspond in meaning to ἔχομαι.
[37] See Shackleton Bailey (no. 191) ad loc.

to emphasise his old-fashioned Romanness. It is to him that Cicero addresses his letter on Latin obscenity, in response to Paetus' use of the basic Latin word *mentula* in a letter, a usage quite out of keeping with normal educated Latin epistolography. It is possible that such a person would have disapproved of the excessive use of Greek in Latin, even in private. The practice of code-switching frequently into Greek in private in correspondence with an intimate of the same educational background in frivolous contexts should not be seen as inevitable; the attitude of the addressee was also a factor. A man such as Atticus resident in Greece and presenting himself as more Greek than the Greeks would use much Greek himself and inspire its use in others addressing him, whereas someone playing the role of a Roman of the old school would be less likely to inspire heavy code-switching. On this view code-switching in a letter (or its absence) is partly a form of accommodation to the role which the addressee was attempting to play.[38] We see similar forms of accommodation in the letters to Varro and Cassius.

A short letter by Cicero to the scholar Varro (*Fam.* 9.4) contains a cluster of Greek words and phrases, 'all technical terms from and about the sages Chrysippus and Diodorus'.[39] Shackleton Bailey notes ad loc. that 'this badinage is . . . a compliment to Varro's expertise in Greek philosophy'. On this interpretation the code-switching has social intention, in that it is meant to flatter Varro for his philosophical expertise;[40] the topic itself (Greek philosophy) is not enough on its own to explain the use of Greek, because it could no doubt have been dealt with in Latin or by means of Greek loan-words integrated morphologically into Latin or by a mixture of both.[41] Cicero thus accommodates his usage to the identity which he knew Varro liked to adopt. There may be an element of light-hearted banter in the letter, but lightheartedness pure and simple is not the determinant of the code-switching. If it were not for a specific attribute of the addressee (his Greek learning and pride in that learning)

---

[38] Greek is also largely avoided in the correspondence with Caelius (just two cases: *Fam.* 2.8.1 πολιτικώτερον *enim te adhuc neminem cognoui*, 2.13.2 κωμικὸς μάρτυς; Caelius for his part has just one switch into Greek in his letters to Cicero, *Fam.* 8.3.3 διδασκαλίαν). Are we to see here an accommodation on Cicero's part to Caelius' attitudes to such practices? It is also conspicuous that Greek is almost completely absent from the letters in *Fam.* 14 to Cicero's wife Terentia, with the exception of the medical term χολὴν ἄκρατον at 14.7.1. On this evidence she could understand Greek, but perhaps Cicero felt that the form of showing-off which epistolary code-switching constitutes was not appropriate in writing to his wife (on code-switching and gender, see below, XII.6).

[39] Baldwin (1992: 10).   [40] See also Cugusi (1983: 84).

[41] Thus on the whole Cicero avoids code-switching in the strict sense in the philosophical works, except when he states the Greek word for a certain idea. Note the statement of principle at *Fin.* 3.15.

the switching might have been pointless or even offensive. But there is more to it even than this. Cicero is not only flattering Varro; he is also parading his own knowledge of such matters before Varro, and thereby putting himself on an equal footing with his learned addressee. The code-switching thus establishes Cicero's (as well as Varro's) membership of an élite group, comprising those educated Romans with expertise in Greek philosophy; or, to put it another way, it gives Varro and Cicero a shared identity or cultural solidarity. At issue in the code-switching is thus a combination of factors: the common education of the interlocutors, the role Varro had chosen to play, Cicero's desire to be associated with him as a cultural equal, and the topic of the discussion. Frivolity is only one of the elements in the passage. Varro's sense of his identity was apparently different from that of Paetus.

Also revealing in this matter of philosophical code-switching is the correspondence referred to earlier (p. 302) between Cicero and the Epicurean Cassius (Cicero: *Fam.* 15.16–18; Cassius: *Fam.* 15.19), dated December 46–January 45, the very period at which Cassius took up Epicureanism.[42] The group of letters is full of Epicurean Greek, both single words and longer quotations, used not only by Cassius (note 15.19.2 *difficile est enim persuadere hominibus* τὸ καλὸν δι' αὐτὸ αἱρετὸν *esse*; ἡδονὴν *uero et* ἀτ<αρ>αξίαν *uirtute, iustitia,* τῷ καλῷ *parari, et uerum et probabile est*; there then follows an explicit quotation of Epicurus himself), but also (in a light-hearted and satirical vein) by Cicero himself (e.g. 15.16.1 *neque id* κατ' εἰδ<ώλ>ων φαντασίας, *ut dicunt tui amici noui, qui putant etiam* διανοητικὰς φαντασίας *spectris Catianis excitari*). Baldwin (1992: 4) was no doubt right to refer to these late Republican Epicureans (*tui amici noui*) as 'a coterie with [a] shared culture and wit'. To judge from Cassius' own letter and the nature of Cicero's disparagement, the group rejected the efforts of the Latin translators of Epicurus, Catius and Amafinius (Lucretius is passed over in silence), who are explicitly criticised by Cassius as 'bad translators of terms' (15.19.2 *omnes Catii et Amafinii, mali uerborum interpretes*), but instead looked directly to the master Epicurus himself, and laced their philosophical discourse with appropriate code-switching to demonstrate that direct adherence. Such a coterie was by definition an in-group, and code-switching was a mark of identity and a means of expressing in-group membership. Cicero for his part was obviously well aware of the role of code-switching within the group, and he entered into the spirit of things with his own code-switching in dealing jokingly with Epicurean

---

[42] For a discussion of this correspondence, see Baldwin (1992: 2–4).

matters. Indeed at one point he took it upon himself to remind Cassius of certain facts about an Epicurean term, εἴδωλα, 'in case he had forgotten' (15.16.1 *ne te fugiat*), namely that it was rendered into Latin by Catius as *spectra*, after being used by Democritus as well as Epicurus. Thus Cicero is not allowing a monopoly of knowledge to Cassius and his group, but is making a demonstration of his own knowledge, despite the fact that he portrays himself as an outsider. Similarly, as we saw above, the flatterer of another's expertise may by the very nature of his flattery contrive to suggest that he too is in possession of the same knowledge. Or again, unflagged quotations of Greek literature (which are very common in Cicero's letters) may be a way of flattering the recipient by assuming his knowledge of Greek literature, particularly if the quotation is unfinished and needs to be completed by the reader if the full point is to be understood;[43] but they have another function, because they allow the writer to display his easy mastery of the classics and put pressure on the addressee to recognise the allusion. In-group membership is again at issue. Code-switching of these types involves the establishment of relationships, and is thus eminently social.

Cicero constantly panders in light-hearted spirit to Atticus' identity as a virtual Athenian, as for example at *Att.* 1.16.8 (*quem* ἀγῶνα **uos** *appellatis*), where the use of the plural has the effect of including Atticus among the Greeks, and 2.1.3, where Demosthenes is described as Atticus' 'fellow citizen' (*tuus ille ciuis Demosthenes*). Cicero's use of code-switching to Atticus can thus be seen on one level as a form of accommodation to the role that Atticus was playing. Atticus used the same code-switching variety of Latin in his letters to Cicero. Cicero often picks up words of Atticus, and these are both Greek (e.g. 12.5.1)[44] and Latin (e.g. 12.34.3). There are also citations of Atticus which themselves embody code-switches (e.g. 16.7.3). Thus Cicero's code-switching can be looked on as a type of reciprocity. But Cicero was not simply showing accommodation to Atticus' chosen identity, with the desire to flatter. He was also constructing a persona for himself: he portrays himself as possessed of certain forms of expertise and culture, and thus claims possession of the same cultural trappings as Atticus.

A revealing switch can be found at *Att.* 4.4a.1 *quos uos Graeci, ut opinor,* σιττύβας *appellatis*. The presence of the comment *quos uos Graeci appellatis*

---

43 E.g. *Att.* 1.1.4 (*Il.* 22.159), 1.12.1, 2.16.4 πρόσθε λέων, ὄπιθεν δὲ, incomplete quotation of Hom. *Il.* 6.181, 4.7.2 (Homer again), 5.10.3 (Aristophanes). See further Steele (1900: 394–5, 397), Dubuisson (1992: 192), Baldwin (1992: 12).

44 See Steele (1900: 390) for Cicero's (frequent) citation of Greek words that had been used by Atticus.

marks the Greek as what can be called a 'flagged switch' (so 1.16.8 above). Switches of this type 'are marked by pauses, hestitation phenomena, repetition and metalinguistic commentary, which draw attention to the switch and interrupt the smooth production of the sentence at the switch point' (Romaine (1995: 153)). Flagging is not unusual in Cicero, as for example at *Att.* 2.3.3 *uenio nunc . . . ad* ὑπόστασιν *nostram ac* πολιτείαν, *in qua* Σωκρατικῶς εἰς ἑκάτερον, *sed tamen ad extremum,* ***ut illi solebant****,* τὴν ἀρέσκουσαν. Shackleton Bailey ad loc. notes that this is a 'jocular reference to the dialectical procedure often employed by C. and in his dialogues variously imputed to Socrates, Plato, the New Academy and others'. Cicero not only uses the appropriate Greek technical terminology, but underlines its connection with a Greek school, and thus, by implication, his own familiarity with Greek philosophy.[45] In the passage quoted at the start of the paragraph Cicero both flatters Atticus by drawing attention to his assumed Greekness (see above for this phenomenon), and associates himself with his addressee by his own ability to say what the Greeks say. This example has the additional interest that the word σιττύβαι (an emendation of Tyrrell's, but almost certainly correct, to judge by the forms of the corruption of what must be the same word in two other letters of the same period: 4.8.2, 4.5.4) does not belong to high literature at all (Shackleton Bailey, basing himself on an entry in Hesychius, translates 'bit of parchment for the labels', i.e. 'tongues of parchment for book labels'), but was presumably a technical term of cultured life current in Athens; it can only have been the preserve of men of letters as distinct from the masses, since it denoted an object used in libraries (see *Att.* 4.8.2). Cicero thus demonstrates to Atticus his familiarity with a technical Greek word which he could not have picked up from literature. A good deal of Cicero's Greek words, some of which he is the first or only writer extant to attest,[46] belonged not to the old literary language but to current Greek,[47] and by this means he signalled his acquaintance with contemporary Greek life for the benefit of one who was part of it.[48]

But while Cicero uses a good deal of contemporary Greek, that is not the whole story. A glance through any group of letters will show that a fair proportion of switches belongs to a general type. Many of Cicero's Greek

---

[45] For Cicero's use of Greek words to convey his own expertise, see also Hutchinson (1998: 155).

[46] See e.g. Steele (1900: 406, 408) for examples.

[47] Some examples can be extracted from Shackleton Bailey (1962, 1963).

[48] It was noted above (n. 3) that among contemporary Malays the display of a knowledge of English is a matter of intellectual pride. There is possibly an element of such intellectual pride in Cicero's fairly contrived use of Greek in the letters.

words consist of philosophical, literary, rhetorical, medical or scientific terms: that is, they are suggestive of high Greek culture and technical disciplines.[49] Cicero and Atticus by this type of code-switching present themselves as fellow members of an élite group. By using a culturally marked code-switching variety of Latin Cicero was in effect asserting joint membership with Atticus of the group of educated Romans who liked in private to play the role of hellenophiles, often in a bantering tone.

Several times at the end of letters Cicero has his son Marcus address Atticus in Greek: e.g. *Att.* 2.9.4 *Terentia tibi salutem dicit* καὶ Κικέρων ὁ μικρὸς ἀσπάζεται Τίτον τὸν ᾽Αθηναῖον. The greeting from Terentia by contrast is in Latin. At 2.12.4 in a similar greeting the boy is face-tiously called ὁ φιλόσοφος: καὶ Κικέρων ὁ φιλόσοφος τὸν πολιτικὸν Τίτον ἀσπάζεται ('on the . . . principle of "like father, like son"', accord-ing to Shackleton Bailey ad loc.).[50] Dunkel (2000: 128) notes that Cicero often switches into Greek when he mentions his son, and he suggests that this is another sign of the reversion to Greek (as the 'language of intimacy') at emotional high points. No attention is paid to the content of the Greek. In fact it is the boy's literary training which is at issue in a number of these passages, not intimacy pure and simple between father and son. Cicero shows persistent concern that Marcus should achieve a certain level of Greek literary culture, and he typically lapses into Greek terms when alluding to his son's (alleged) classical style. Note *Att.* 14.7.2 *a Cicerone mihi litterae sane* πεπινωμέναι *et bene longae. cetera autem uel fingi pos-sunt,* πίνος *litterarum significat doctiorem* ('I have had a letter from Marcus, really classically phrased and pretty long. Other things can be assumed, but the style of the letter shows he has learned something': Shackleton Bailey) (cf. the similar passages 15.16, 15.17.2).[51] Quintilian indeed noted the attitude Cicero adopted towards Marcus of *recte loquendi asper quoque exactor* (1.7.34). He was attempting to mould Marcus to his own image, and the acquisition of Greek literary culture was essential to this identity.

---

[49] The following examples have been chosen completely at random: literary/rhetorical: *Att.* 1.14.4 *si umquam mihi* περίοδοι ἢ καμπαὶ ἢ ἐνθυμήματα ἢ κατασκευαὶ *suppeditauerunt, illo tempore. quid multa? clamores. etenim haec erat* ὑπόθεσις, *de grauitate ordinis* . . . , 1.19.10 *quamquam non* ἐγκωμιαστικὰ *sunt haec sed* ἱστορικὰ *quae scribimus,* 2.6.1 *et hercule sunt res difficiles ad explicandum et* ὁμοειδεῖς *nec tam possunt* ἀνθηρογραφεῖσθαι *quam uidebantur;* theatrical:1.16.12 *consul autem ille* δευτερεύοντος *histrionis similis suscepisse negotium dicitur;* philosophical: 2.17.2 *neque tam me* εὐελπιστία *consolatur ut antea quam* ἀδιαφορία. Other examples have already been seen in this section, and many others will come up below.

[50] For another such passage, see *Att.* 2.15.4, and see Shackleton Bailey p. 373 on the possibility that the Greek was added by Marcus himself.

[51] See Shackleton Bailey's note (no. 361): 'πίνος is literally patina on bronze. In a literary context it denotes an agreeably old-fashioned quality of style . . . or, with a slightly different nuance, classical correctness without slang or neologisms'.

By having him greet the 'Athenian' Atticus in Greek, and by referring to him in Greek as the 'philosopher', no doubt at the very period when he was undergoing education in Greek disciplines, he implies that the boy is entering into a relationship of cultural equality with the hellenophile Atticus. He is becoming a member of an in-group, from which Terentia is apparently excluded.

I attempt to sum up the view of code-switching in the letters which has been advanced so far.

(1) A code-switching form of Latin was a private language. Since code-switching was a private form of communication used in informal circumstances with those with whom the writer/speaker was on close terms, it is inevitably often found in light-hearted contexts. But jocularity is at least as likely to be expressed in Latin. Frivolity on its own did not necessarily generate code-switching. I stress that I am not denying that code-switching is often frivolous, or that it occurs in intimate letters; but to invoke frivolity and intimacy as the main determinants of code-switching is not an adequate explanation of the phenomenon.

(2) A shared educational background of writer and addressee was a *sine qua non* if this type of code-switching was to be adopted in private. An extraordinary number of Greek words in Cicero's letters to Atticus are what might be called rhetorical terms (see below, III.2), and many of these were probably in use in the rhetorical schools. There would be little point in using such language in addressing someone who had not had a rhetorical education. Many switches of code in the letters also consist of literary quotations from the Greek classics, some of them incomplete and requiring the addressee to recognise the allusion. There is an acknowledgment here of a common background, a sense of belonging to an exclusive group.

(3) But a shared cultural background was not on its own sufficient to generate code-switching in a private letter between intimates. There is also accommodation to the tastes and chosen identity of the addressee to be taken into account. If Plutarch was right about Marius' attitude to Greek (see I.III), Marius would not have attracted much code-switching. Paetus too was of the old Roman school. On the other hand a man famous for his *doctrina* in Greek (Varro), or one residing in Greece and playing the Greek (Atticus; also the disputants in the second book of Varro's *Res rusticae*: see below, IV.1), would no doubt have been flattered to have his assumed Greekness acknowledged by code-switching. And the code-switcher himself by his use of allusive Greek to such persons was able to put himself on a par with his addressees.

(4) There is an element of in-group communication about the code-switching variety of Latin at which we have been looking. But such socio-linguistic terms as 'in-group' and 'solidarity' are too crude on their own to capture the character and motivations of Roman epistolary code-switching. Upper-class Romans with the same education no doubt saw themselves as an élite, but that feeling and any feeling of solidarity with their peers do not go far in explaining the nature of their private code-switching. It is reasonable to talk of 'solidarity' only if it is specified that the solidarity was that springing from a joint exclusivist culture and shared attitudes to that culture. There is something of the cultured game about upper-class Roman code-switching. This is in no sphere clearer than in the incomplete quotation of Greek verses. There is a world of difference between such contrived use of the second language, and code-switching which merely makes use of the contemporary collo-quial varieties of the two languages in contact. It is often said that a good deal of Cicero's Greek belonged to the current koine, but that is only part of the story.[52] Many of the Greek words in the letters are either learned technical terms, or literary phraseology which had no currency at the time of writing. The artificial character of such code-switching is nicely reflected in the fact that it is dropped at times of crisis (see below, III.9). The game is played with the full resources of the Greek language as pro-vided by many centuries of the language's development, from Homer to the Roman Republic. Code-switching as in-group communication in modern speech communities has little in common with such a phe-nomenon. The notion of the 'in-group' also needs to be refined in refer-ence to Roman society. Membership of the educated élite did not make one a code-switcher, or make one the ideal recipient of code-switching. Greeks and the Greek language inspired strong and mixed feelings in Romans of the period. They could not view Greek in neutral terms as merely another language, but associated it with the long-standing Greek cultural superiority. The use of the language by an upper-class Roman was not a culturally unmarked act. Opinions of one kind or another are constantly expressed by Romans about the propriety of using Greek or a Greek word or words under particular circumstances (see e.g. Suet. *Tib.* 71). To some educated Romans a switch into Greek might smack of cultural subservience, whereas to others it might display an assured mastery of an admired language (and culture). Thus the educated upper

[52] See above, nn. 46, 47; also e.g. Dubuisson (1980: 887). In my opinion there is scope for a detailed study of the element of koine in Cicero's Greek. Too often it is merely asserted to be an important component, without detailed discussion and definition, and without a statistical account of its place in relation to more literary or technical terminology.

classes did not constitute a coherent in-group with a uniform attitude to the second language, and in assessing acts of code-switching (or its avoidance) one must as far as possible take into account the attitudes of the individuals in question. Some were willing players of the game, but others were not. The in-group therefore cannot simply be defined in social or educational terms (as for example comprising those who belonged to a certain stratum of society or who had received a rhetorical education).

I now consider in more detail some of the categories of code-switching in the letters, particularly those to Atticus. Where appropriate I will go beyond Cicero and bring in relevant material from other sources.

III.2 *Critical terms*

It is a striking fact that the most common type of switching in the letters (at least those to Atticus) consists of brief characterisations (usually by a single Greek adverb or sometimes by a short phrase) of someone's words. This point has been made of the Greek in Augustus' letters by Gelsomino (1959: 121). It is usually Cicero's own words or discourse in the letters that attract this method of description, but sometimes Atticus' words or those of other correspondents may be so characterised. Alternatively Cicero may switch into Greek in categorising aspects of his other writings, or in reference to someone's speech. This phenomenon has been called the 'metalinguistic function' of code-switching.[53] To bring out its frequency I list below classified examples mainly from the letters to Atticus (with selective translation). This collection is by no means exhaustive. When translations are given in this section, they are from Shackleton Bailey.

Characterisations of Cicero's words in the letters
1.16.1	*respondebo tibi* ὕστερον πρότερον, Ὁμηρικῶς
1.16.2	*ut iam* πρὸς τὸ πρότερον *reuertar*
2.3.3	Σωκρατικῶς εἰς ἑκάτερον
2.7.4	*non me abs te* κατὰ τὸ πρακτικὸν *quaerere*
2.19.5	*quid enim* ἀκκιζόμεθα *tam diu* ('why go on mincing words?')
2.19.5	*cetera erunt* ἐν αἰνιγμοῖς
2.20.3	ἀλληγορίαις *obscurabo*
4.15.3	*multis quidem de rebus* ἡμερολεγδὸν *perscripta omnia*
5.20.1	*quae cognosce* ἐν ἐπιτομῇ
5.21.7	*non* ὑπερβολικῶς *sed uerissime loquor*
5.21.13	*in quo quidem,* ὁδοῦ πάρεργον …

[53] Appel and Muysken (1987: 120).

6.1.8   *ego* ἀφελῶς *scripsi*

6.1.16   τὸ παραδοξότατον: *usuras eorum . . . seruauit etiam Seruilius* (of a surprising revelation by Cicero)

6.1.25   *haec te uolui* παριστορῆσαι ('I thought I'd tell you this *en passant*')

6.2.4   *non loquor* ὑπερβολικῶς

6.7.1   *Graece* ἐν αἰνιγμοῖς

7.1.5   *nam* ὁδοῦ πάρεργον *uolo te hoc scire*

7.3.5   '*quid fiet cum erit dictum "dic, M. Tulli"?*': σύντομα, "*Cn. Pompeio adsentior*"'

9.7.3   εἰδώς σοι λέγω; *nihil ille umquam minus obscure tulit* ('*experto crede*')

10.11.5   θυμικώτερον *eram iocatus*

12.3.1   *audi igitur me hoc* ἀγοητεύτως *dicentem* ('So listen to what I tell you *sans blague*')

13.25.2   *fui fortasse* ἀσαφέστερος (of a letter to Brutus which Atticus had read)

13.25.3   *ne Tironi quidem dictaui, qui totas* περιοχὰς *persequi solet*

13.32.3   *credo quia* διὰ σημείων *scripseram*

13.51.1   *nec mehercule scripsi aliter ac si* πρὸς ἴσον ὁμοιόν*que scriberem*

13.51.1   *itaque scripsi et* ἀκολακεύτως

15.27.1   *scriptas* πάνυ φιλοστόργως

ad Brut. 1.1.1 (SB 13) *ut* ἐμφατικώτερον *dicam*

Q. fr. 3.7.3   (SB 27) ἐν παρέργῳ: *de dictatore tamen actum adhuc nihil est*

Characterisations of the words of Atticus or other correspondents

2.5.3   *omnia, quem ad modum polliceris,* ἐπὶ σχολῆς *scribe*

2.18.2   *ac ne forte quaeras* κατὰ λεπτὸν *de singulis rebus*

5.11.7   *ualde scripta est* συμπαθῶς

5.21.3   *etsi bellum* ἀκροτελεύτιον *habet illa tua epistula*

6.1.7   ἀκοινονοήτως *solet scribere*

6.1.11   *te enim sequor* σχεδιάζοντα ('I am following your impromptu')

6.7.1   ἀφελῶς *percontando*

10.1.3   *tuaque ista crebra* ἐκφώνησις 'ὑπέρευ'

10.10.1   *uide quam ad haec* παραιν<ετ>ικῶς ('This is his wise-acre reply', of a letter from Antonius)

10.11.5   *quod* ἀποτόμως *ad me scripserat* ('he had written to me brusquely')

12.44.1   *Hirtium aliquid ad te* συμπαθῶς *de me scripsisse facile patior*

13.10.1   *sed illud* παρὰ τὴν ἱστορίαν, *tu praesertim, me reliquum consularem*

13.22.2   *de Marcello scripserat ad me Cassius antea,* τὰ κατὰ μέρος *Seruius. o rem acerbam!*

14.7.2   *a Cicerone mihi litterae sane* πεπινωμέναι *et bene longae* . . . πίνος *litterarum significat doctiorem* (see above, p. 320); cf. 15.16 *sed mehercule litterae* πεπινωμένως *scriptae*

14.16.3   *mandaram ut mihi* κατὰ μίτον *scriberet*

15.17.2   *litterae sic et* φιλοστόργως *et* εὐπινῶς *scriptae* (a letter of Marcus so elegant that Cicero would like to read it in public)

Q. *fr.* 2.16.5 (SB 20) *reliqua ad quendam locum* ῥαθυμότερα *(hoc enim utitur uerbo)* (of Caesar's criticism of Cicero's verses, in a letter)

Q. *fr.* 2.15.2 (SB 19) *quae tu in hac eadem breui epistula* πραγματικῶς *ualde scripsisti* (of a letter of Quintus)

Characterisations of Cicero's other writings

1.19.10   *non* ἐγκωμιαστικὰ *sunt haec sed* ἱστορικὰ *quae scribimus*

2.6.1   *etenim* γεωγραφικὰ *quae constitueram magnum opus est*

2.6.2   *itaque* ἀνέκδοτα *a nobis* . . . *pangentur*

4.16.3   *reliqui libri* τεχνολογίαν *habent*

6.1.15   *ego tamen habeo* ἰσοδυναμοῦσαν *sed tectiorem ex Q. Muci P. f. edicto Asiatico* (of a clause of an edict: see below, p. 328)

12.44.4   *ego hic duo magna* συντάγματα *absolui*

12.52.3   ἀπόγραφα *sunt, minore labore fiunt*

13.12.3   *postea autem quam haec coepi* φιλολογώτερα, *iam Varro mihi denuntiauerat magnam sane et grauem* προσφώνησιν

13.16.1   *deinde, quia* παρὰ τὸ πρέπον *uidebatur* (of the assignment of speeches in one of Cicero's philosophical works)

14.17.6   *librum meum illum* ἀνέκδοτον *nondum* . . . *perpoliui*

15.27.2   *excudam aliquid* Ἡρακλείδειον

Characterisations of speech

1.14.2   *tum Pompeius* μάλ᾽ ἀριστοκρατικῶς *locutus est*

1.14.4   *si umquam mihi* περίοδοι ἢ καμπαὶ ἢ ἐνθυμήματα ἢ κατασκευαὶ *suppeditauerunt*

4.19.1   *ille Latinus* ᾽Αττικισμὸς *ex interuallo regustandus?*

10.9.1   *id enim* αὐθεντικῶς *nuntiabatur*

13.52.2   σπουδαῖον οὐδὲν *in sermone,* φιλόλογα *multa* (of conversation at a dinner party)

15.12.1   *noster uero* καὶ μάλα σεμνῶς *in Asiam*

Q. *fr.* 1.2.3 (SB 2) *quam multa autem ipsum* ἀφελῶς *mecum in sermone ita posuisse* . . .

This type of code-switching can be traced back in Latin to a passage
of Lucilius. I print the text of 181–8 M. as convincingly emended by
Housman (1907,[54] = 1972: 686–8):

> quo me habeam pacto, tametsi non quaeris, docebo,
> quando in eo numero mansi, quo in maxima non est
> pars hominum . . .
> ut peri<i>sse uelis, quem uisere nolueris, cum
> debueris. hoc 'nolueris' et 'debueris' te
> si minus delectat, quod atechnon et Isocration
> ληρῶδεςque simul totum ac sit μειρακιῶδες,
> non operam perdo, si tu hic.

Housman also supplies <*neque enim tam te mihi credo inimicum*> after
hominum, not as a conjectural addition to the text but as an aid to its
interpretation.

The passage, which is quoted and to some extent explained by Gellius
(18.8), is at once an attack on an acquaintance and on Isocratean
homoeoteleuta.[55] According to Gellius, Lucilius was complaining to a
friend who had not come to visit him when he was ill. I translate the
passage as printed with Housman's addition: 'Although you do not ask
as much, I will tell you how I am, since I have remained among the
number of those who do not make up the majority. <For I do not think
that you are so hostile to me> that you would want me to have perished,
though you were unwilling to visit me when you should have done so. If
you are by no means pleased by (my use of this homoeoteleuton) *nolueris*
and *debueris*, on the grounds that (you think) it undeserving of the name
of art and Isocratean and at the same time wholly silly and childish, then
I am not wasting my efforts, if you are this sort of person.'

Because he has been let down, Lucilius takes pleasure in the irritation
he causes his friend by using the Isocratean jingle. It is presented as a
form of revenge, though the revenge lies not only in the infliction of an
offensive stylistic trick on the ears of the friend. The *quod*-clause is of
crucial importance. Whether or not there is a subjunctive verb (*sit* is an
emendation), the words which the clause contains must surely have been
attributed to the friend (as his thoughts). The key words are not only of
Greek origin, but are inflected as Greek in every case (whatever script is
adopted), if we accept Housman's change to *Isocration* on the strength of
his observation that many Greek adjectives in Lucilius are inflected as

---

[54] 'Luciliana', in *CQ* 1 (1907), 148–59.   [55] On this second topic, see Fiske (1920: 110).

Greek whereas many Greek nouns are inflected as Latin (1907, = 1972: 687).⁵⁶ Embedded in a Latin text and bearing Greek inflections, they obviously represent code-switching. Lucilius may be suggesting that this was the way in which the friend spoke: he was given to the use of Greek critical terms⁵⁷ in Latin discourse. At one level Lucilius uses code-switching to ridicule the man. At another level he is ridiculing the man's use of a type of code-switching in critical debate. And even if the above interpretation were rejected, it would remain true that Lucilius in his own person had switched into Greek when making metalinguistic comments.

Another passage of Lucilius with a Greek critical term (though its inter-pretation is problematic) is at 15f.: *porro 'clinopodas' 'lychnosque' ut diximus* **semnos** / *ante 'pedes lecti' atque 'lucernas'*. With the use of *semnos* here, cf. at a later date Plin. *Epist.* 2.11.17 *respondit Cornelius Tacitus eloquentissime et.* . . . σεμνῶς.

There are other examples of the same phenomenon in Pliny: *Epist.* 1.2.1 *eodem* ζήλῳ *scripsisse uideor*, 6.22.2 *egit autem carptim et* κατὰ κεφάλαιον. And a letter of Augustus to Livia (Suet. *Claud.* 4.6) uses two adverbs in -ῶς in describing the delivery of Claudius in both speech and declamation: *nam qui tam* ἀσαφῶς *loquatur, qui possit cum declamat* σαφῶς *dicere quae dicenda sunt, non uideo*.⁵⁸

I return to Cicero. There is a close similarity between Cicero's use of such Greek critical terminology, and that in Donatus, who has Greek words in similar contexts on virtually every page of his commentary on Terence. I list below a selection of terms:

Andr. 30 *haec* δεικτικῶς . . . *bene* ἀντέθηκεν τῷ '*nempe*' τὸ '*immo*'
37 *MIHI* ἔμφασιν *habet* (cf. 384, *Eun.* 53, 459, 994)
96 ἐμφατικώτερον '*fortunas*' *quam* '*fortunam*' (cf. *Eun.* 168, 307, and ἐμφατικῶς at *Eun.* 626, *Phorm.* 120)
Eun. 924 *figura* ἐπιμονὴ *per* ἐκφώνησιν *facta*
Eun. 593 *it lauit rediit* συντομίᾳ

⁵⁶ There is corruption in the manuscripts of Gellius at this point, but the various readings share the *-ium* ending. Housman's observation is worth dwelling on. The phenomenon which he observes is not difficult to explain. It has often been noted that nouns are the part of speech most readily transferred from one language to another and integrated into the recipient language (see e.g. Poplack (1980: 589), Wenskus (1998: 15)). Lucilius would appear to have been more ready to integrate Greek nouns into Latin than adjectives; there is a hierarchy of transferability.
⁵⁷ Examples of ἄτεχνον and ληρῶδες are quoted and discussed briefly by Charpin (1978: 254). For μειρακιῶδες as a critical term, see D.H. *Isoc.* 12 and Marx (1904–5) ad loc. The *Rhet. Her.* 4.32 uses *puerilis* of the same 'Isocratean' figures.
⁵⁸ Adverbs of this type were readily transferred into Latin: see Wenskus (1998: 10–11); also ead. (1996: 239).

Eun. 426 ἀλληγορικῶς *intelligimus* (cf. *Ad.* 958 ἀλληγορία)

Andr. 676 *MANIBVS et PEDIBVS* ὑπερβολικῶς (cf. *Eun.* 231, 310)

Andr. 696 παραδόξως *locutus est*

Andr. 702 *intulit* παράδοξον

Eun. 14 *se* παρὰ προσδοκίαν *dicitur, sed* ἠθικῶς *addidit* (cf. *Phorm.* 208 παρὰ προσδοκίαν)

Eun. 123 *haec dicuntur* ἰσοδυναμοῦντα (cf. Cic. *Att.* 6.1.15 *ego tamen habeo* ἰσοδυναμοῦσαν *sed tectiorem ex Q. Muci P. f. edicto Asiatico*, 'I have a clause to the same effect, only more guardedly phrased...': see above)

Andr. 436 εἰρωνικῶς *'uirum' dixit defessum senem* (cf. 505, *Eun.* 224)

Andr. 192 μεταφορικῶς (cf. *Eun.* 312)

Andr. 533 μεταλημπτικῶς (cf. 674)

Eun. 44 *nos* ἐλλειπτικῶς *dicimus*

Andr. 147 ἀρχαισμός

Eun. 310 ἠθικῶς *et* ἱλαρῶς *nimis*

Ad. 729 ἀφελῶς... *respondendum.*

Baldwin (1992: 8) notes that the one Greek word used by Cicero in the letters to Brutus (1.1.1 = SB 13; quoted above, p. 324), ἐμφατικώτερον, is illustrated by LSJ only from Hesychius,[59] but that it 'actually recurs in Aulus Gellius 13.29.4, suggestively also in the context of Roman style and accompanied by a part of the verb "dicere"' (*'cum multis mortalibus' Metellum in Capitolium uenisse dixit* ἐμφατικώτερον *quam si 'cum multis hominibus' dixisset*). It might be added that the term is constant in Donatus' commentary, and is likely therefore to have been a critical term of the schools. Other terms which Donatus shares with Cicero are ἀφελῶς, ἐκφώνησις, ἀλληγορία, παράδοξ-, ὑπερβολικῶς, σύντομος/συντομία, ἰσοδυναμέω, but there is also the general similarity to be seen in the proliferation of adverbs in -ῶς.

There would seem to be a distinctive form of educated code-switching in evidence here, with a history extending from the second century BC into the Empire. The Greek terms are rhetorical and critical, and as such their use represents a form of cultured code-switching. To account for the frequency of the type one must look for a special determinant, and that surely lies in a convention of the rhetorical schools of using a Greek critical vocabulary. Two educated Romans who use such terminology constantly in private may be seen as alluding to their common

---

[59] It is true that the comparative form is cited by LSJ only from Hesychius, but it should be noted that ἐμφατικῶς is quoted from Galen and Philodemus; the positive, as we have just seen, is also found in Donatus.

rhetorical education. There is perhaps an 'intimacy' of sorts here,[60] but it is the intimacy of using a special vocabulary which the correspondents have jointly acquired in an exclusive educational environment, and has nothing to do with any intimacy conferred on Greek in early childhood. It is also worth noting that such terminology can be used in contexts of any type, serious or light-hearted.

III.3 Code-switching as a form of coding or exclusion

I would next draw attention to a remark of Cicero's at *Att.* 2.20.3: *de re <publica> breuiter ad te scribam; iam enim charta ipsa ne nos prodat pertimesco. itaque posthac, si erunt mihi plura ad te scribenda,* ἀλληγορίαις *obscurabo.* There was a concern about the security of letters in antiquity, in the absence of a formal postal system, and here Cicero expresses his fear that letters may betray him. Caesar on one occasion wrote in Greek to Q. Cicero so that the courier could not understand the letter (*Gall.* 5.48.4 *hanc Graecis conscriptam litteris mittit, ne intercepta epistola nostra ab hostibus consilia cognoscantur*).[61] Cicero says that he will obscure his meaning by code terms (ἀλληγορίαις).[62] He means partly but not exclusively the use of Greek substitute terms for proper names. Shackleton Bailey cites ὁ Κροτωνιάτης for Milo at 6.5.1, and also the frequent use of βοῶπις for Clodia (2.9.1 with Shackleton Bailey's note, 2.12.2, 2.14.1). There is extensive use of such coding in two letters of 50 BC (*Att.* 6.4.3, 6.5.1–2). The purpose of the switch of languages is flagged in the first letter (6.4.3

---

[60] See Wenskus (1998: 11).

[61] Here *Graecis litteris* means 'in the Greek language', though it is taken by Donderer (1995: 98) as meaning that Caesar wrote the letter in the Latin language but in Greek script. That is unlikely in itself, given the old Gaulish custom of using Greek script for the writing of Gaulish. If a language had a distinctive script, a text could be described as being in that script when the writer meant that it was in the language associated with the script. Note *Dig.* 14.3.11.3 (on the public display of a legal document) *litteris utrum Graecis an Latinis? puto secundum loci condicionem*. There is no ambiguity here: the text had to be in the language appropriate to the place. Note too Livy 40.29.4 *litteris Latinis Graecisque utraque arca inscripta erat*, Cic. *Verr.* 4.103 *itaque in iis scriptum litteris Punicis fuit regem Masinissam imprudentem accepisse, re cognita reportandosque reponendosque curasse*; see also Livy 28.46.16, discussed above, p. 206 n. 381. Greek had the same idiom. In the inscriptions of Delos offerings made in Latin are several times described as written 'Ρωμαικοῖς γράμμασιν (*ID* 443, face B. fr b.58, 1439, face C. fr a.8). Note too Josephus, *AJ* 14.197 ἐγκεχαραγμένην γράμμασιν 'Ρωμαικοῖς τε καὶ 'Ελληνικοῖς, with Sevenster (1968: 115). A particularly revealing example is at *P. Oxy.* VI. 907, where it is stated that a will was 'dictated' in Greek letters (τόδε τὸ βούλημα 'Ελληνικοῖς γράμμασι κατὰ τὰ συνκεχωρημένα ὑπηγόρευσεν). The expression can only mean 'in the Greek language'.

Dubuisson (1992: 203 n. 48), in defiance of Caesar's own words, asserts: 'ce n'est assurément pas pour ne pas être compris, en cas d'interception, par l'ennemi gaulois, à qui le grec était plus familier que le latin'.

[62] There is a discussion of this phenomenon in the dissertation of Font (1894: 42–6).

illud praeterea μυστικώτερον *ad te scribam, tu sagacius odorabere*), and in a later letter (6.7.1) Cicero comments on his use of riddling Greek in the earlier letters: *bis ad te antea scripsi de re mea familiari, si modo tibi redditae litterae sunt, Graece* ἐν αἰνιγμοῖς. In both epistles the subject is a possible case of fraud by Philotimus, freedman of his wife, who sometimes carried Cicero's letters (see 6.3.1). The coding takes the form not only of switching into Greek, but also of the use of literary or allusive terminology within the Greek, as for example the replacement of γυναικός by δάμαρτος and ξυναόρου at 6.4.3 and 6.5.1,[63] and of the name *Milo* by τοῦ Κροτωνιάτου τυραννοκτόνου at 6.4.3 (see also above for this usage). There is a hint here that if the bearer knew Greek, he would not know literary Greek. The ability to use such coded reference depends of course on the shared Greek literary culture of Cicero and Atticus.

Further examples are cited by Dunkel (2000: 128), who remarks that 'Greek was felt to be the proper language of conspiracy'. Since Greek could not be used freely in public, its use might readily have taken on an air of the conspiratorial.

III.4 Code-switching as distancing or euphemism

A switch into a second language which is not the native language of the addressee may have a distancing effect.[64] Thus switches into Greek are sometimes made for euphemistic purposes. I start with a revealing passage of Lucretius.[65]

Lucretius 4.1160–70 to some extent exemplifies code-switching in the expression of endearments (for which see below, and also v on Juv. 6.187–97), though there is more to the passage than that. It deals with the blindness of a hypothetical lover in the face of his mistress's faults. These are concealed usually under a Greek endearment or euphemism, with the Greek words often unambiguously inflected as Greek (1160 *melichrus, acosmos*, 1161 *dorcas*, 1162 *chariton mia*, 1163 *cataplexis*, 1166 *ischnon eromenion*, 1167 *rhadine*, 1169 *philema*. The most notable example is that at 1164, *balba loqui non quit*, **traulizi**. The woman who stammers is described in Greek as 'having a lisp' = τραυλίζει. Lucretius gives the Greek verb a Greek inflection (for the Greek third person singular form transliterated

[63] See Font (1894: 45) for these and other such literary terms that Cicero clearly believed would not be understood by the carrier.
[64] On the use of Greek as distancing in Cicero's letters, see von Albrecht (1973: 1275). He observes that such distancing can often lead to irony.
[65] The passage is discussed from a different point of view by Jocelyn (1999: 182–3).

in this way, see Cic. *Fam.* 9.22.3 *bini*, and also the comparable *laecasin* at Petron. 42.2). Bailey ad loc. remarks that 'the use of a Greek verb goes farther than most of Lucr.'s grecisms', and suggests that he was following a Greek original. This is inadequate as a description of what is at issue in this passage. Lucretius has not used a 'Grecism' in his own person, but has put the verb, in quotation marks as it were, into the mouth of the hypothetical lover. Lucretius does provide evidence of a sort for a belief that Roman lovers tended to switch codes into Greek when expressing endearments (cf. Juv. 6.187–97, Mart. 10.68),[66] but the real point of the discussion is that the foolish lover will not acknowledge the woman's faults for what they are but will attempt to play them down by the use of euphemisms. It is significant that not all of the euphemistic terms are Greek (note 1162 *paruula, pumilio . . . **tota merum sal**,* 1163 *magna atque immanis . . . **plena . . . honoris**,* 1164 *muta **pudens** est*), and it is not therefore the use of Greek as such that is castigated but the use of euphemisms. The passage thus exemplifies in its Greek parts not primarily code-switching for the expression of endearments, but code-switching as one form of euphemism.[67]

So at Cic. *Att.* 10.13.1 (*postridie redire iussit (Antonius); lauari se uelle et* περὶ κοιλιολυσίαν γίνεσθαι) Antony is described as making an excuse not to see certain persons who had come to visit him. He wanted to wash and to devote himself to certain bodily functions, with κοιλιολυσίαν a discreet term for the act. The term has the additional interest that it is medical, and medical subject matter is sometimes implicated in switches of code (see III.7).

A letter of Augustus to Livia preserved by Suetonius (*Claud.* 4) switches into Greek in discussing the mental and physical infirmities

---

[66] These passages will be discussed below, sect. v. It should be noted that the passage of Lucretius does not concern first-person address of the woman by her lover, but seems to deal with references to her in the third person (see Wenskus (1998: 38)). It therefore differs from the passages of Juvenal and Martial, as we will see.

[67] It is worth observing in passing that while Greek could be exploited for its distancing effect, Latin in contrast with Greek could on occasions be exploited for its harsh directness. This is a point made by Sedley (1999: 242–3) in a discussion of Lucr. 2.410–13, where there is 'an implicit contrast of Roman and Greek noises'. 'The almost pure Greek . . . line contrasts with the pure Latin which precedes. Where Greek has given us sublime music, Rome's more characteristic noise is the shrieking sawblades of a workshop.' See also Rudd (1986: 166) on Lucilius 540–6, where 'the reader is warned not to idealise the female beauties of the past'; he observes that the 'point is sharpened by using Greek for the ladies' perfections and Latin for their defects'. Even a first-language speaker of Greek might switch into Latin to achieve harsh effects. According to Cic. *Nat.* 1.93 Zeno the Epicurean once used the Latin word *scurra* (in Greek) in abusing Socrates. In these three passages considered as a whole Greek words are treated as pleasant, cultivated or laudatory, and Latin as harsh in sound or in meaning. Implicit here is an attitude that Greek words, as belonging to the language of culture, can achieve pleasant effects, whereas Latin words are potentially harsher and appropriate (e.g.) to abuse.

of Claudius,[68] and the possibility of their being publicly derided: §1 *sin autem* ἡλαττῶσθαι *sentimus eum et* βεβλάφθαι καὶ εἰς τὴν τοῦ σώματος καὶ εἰς τὴν τῆς ψ<υ>χῆς ἀρτιότητα, *praebenda materia deridendi et illum et nos non est hominibus* τὰ τοιαῦτα σκώπτειν καὶ μυκτηρίζειν εἰωθόσιν.[69] The only code-switch in Cicero's letters to his wife Terentia (see above, n. 38) consists of a Greek medical phrase used in the context of Cicero's vomiting of undiluted bile: *Fam.* 14.7.1 χολὴν ἄκρατον *noctu eieci*. Baldwin (1992: 13) comments on this passage: 'Perhaps [this phrase] was intended as a kindly bowdlerisation, to spare Terentia's sensibilities. Vomiting bile is not the pleasantest of topics.' The use of code-switching as a form of tact and also exclusion has been detected in another of Augustus' letters (Suet. ap. *Tib.* 21.5).[70] I need hardly point out that tact is not invariably a subdivision of frivolity.

Cicero refers to certain 'unmentionable things' about Quintus in an interesting way: *Att.* 13.9.1 *multa* ἄφατα, ἀδιήγητα. They are not mentioned, and not mentioned as unmentionable except in Greek. Note too the way in which Cicero refers to an error that he has made: 13.44.3 μνημονικὸν ἁμάρτημα (cf. 14.5.1). This phrase follows *erratum meum*, and seems to tone down the mistake.

Not all switching of this general type is overtly euphemistic. Sometimes it seems more appropriate to speak of 'distancing'. Criticism, for example, might be rendered more polite by a switch into Greek. This function of code-switching is nicely brought out by Hutchinson (1998: 15) in reference to two usages in Cicero's correspondence. I quote: 'A letter of Caesar's own used a Greek term, technical, distanced, discriminating, to express and to moderate a criticism of part of Cicero's poem (ῥαθυμότερα, "rather spiritless", *QF* ii.16.5). Cicero employs a Greek word to soften somewhat a possible description of his addressee Appius as "prone to find fault", in an unusually strong yet carefully modulated passage ("si autem natura es φιλαίτιος" *Fam.* iii.7.6). He uses a Homeric quotation to describe exactly the same quality in Varro, whom he wants the reluctant Atticus to help him with (*Att.* xiii.25.3). The Greek again lends some graceful distance, but of a different kind: the neatness

---

[68] On the Greek here as distancing the unpleasant, see Birch (1981: 161), Cugusi (1983: 85), Wenskus (1995: 175), (1998: 32).

[69] Loeb: 'But if we realize that he is wanting and defective in soundness of body and mind, we must not furnish the means of ridiculing both him and us to a public which is wont to scoff at and deride such things.'

[70] See Birch (1981: 161): 'the use of Greek in 21.5 to refer to "such great lack of morale among the troops" suggests a more specific purpose. It may have been employed out of tact in what can be read . . . as a refutation of criticism of Tiberius which may have been Augustus' own. Another purpose may have been to ensure that this Imperial frankness about army morale did not spread too far in the camp to which the letter was presumably sent.'

and humour lighten Cicero's pressing, worried depiction of the prickly polymath.'

Not infrequently Cicero switches into Greek in alluding to characteristics of his own which might be construed as faults:

Att. 2.17.2   *quin etiam quod est subinane in nobis et non* ἀφιλόδοξον *(bellum est enim sua uitia nosse) id adficitur quadam delectatione* ('Indeed a certain foolish vanity to which I am somewhat prone (it's a fine thing to know one's failings) is actually gratified in a way')

5.20.6   *recte* πεφυσίωμαι ('I have a right to a swollen head')

9.7.4   *ut* ἀχαριστίας *crimen subire non audeam*

10.8A.1   *quae magis a* ζηλοτυπία *mea quam ab iniuria tua nata est* ('more from jealousy on my part than from any injury on yours')

13.13–14.1   *nisi forte me communis* φιλαυτία *decepit* ('unless my share of *amour propre* deceives me')

13.19.3   *in Varrone ista causa me non moueret, ne uiderer* φιλένδοξος (again in reference to Cicero's own faults, but in this case the word had been used by Atticus, obviously as a form of toned-down criticism: '. . . the consideration you mention, that I might look like a tuft-hunter, would not influence me')

15.29.2   *tum ego, etsi* ἐβδελυττόμην, *tamen negaui putare me illa esse uera* (of an unpleasant emotion on Cicero's part, disgust)

16.5.5   *ea quibus maxime* γαυριῶ *legenda non putet* ('notwithstanding his opinion that those [works] on which I most plume myself are not worth reading'; Cicero does not want to refer openly to his pride in certain of his works which have been criticised).

More generally, criticisms of others (or references to their possible defects) are softened by switches into Greek:

Att. 1.14.6   ἀπρακτότατος; *sed uoluntate . . .* καχέκτης

6.1.7   *contumaciter, adroganter,* ἀκοινονοήτως *solet scribere* (of Brutus) (cf. 6.3.7 *in quibus non inesset adrogans et* ἀκοινονόητον *aliquid*)

6.1.17   *erratum fabrile putaui, nunc uideo Metelli. o* ἀνιστορησίαν *turpem*

6.2.10   εὐήθειαν *Semproni Rufi cognoui ex epistula tua*

9.10.4   *faciet omnino male et . . .* ἀλογίστως (a quotation of a letter of Atticus)

9.13.4   *quos Matius* ἐλάπιζεν, *ut puto . . . sed sit hoc* λάπισμα

10.10.6   *nihil ego uidi tam* ἀηθοποίητον *. . .* ἤθους ἐπιμελητέον (the character of a certain youth needs attention; the discussion is notably discreet)

10.11.1   *habent nihil* ὕπουλον, *nihil fallax*

10.15.2 ὦ πολλῆς ἀγεννείας

12.9 *nisi paulum interpellasset Amyntae filius.* ὦ ἀπεραντολογίας ἀηδοῦς

13.30.1 *istae autem* κολακεῖαι *nec longe absunt a scelere*

13.16.1 *nota non illa quidem* ἀπαιδευσία *sed in his rebus* ἀτριψία (of the lack of expertise of certain persons whom Cicero had considered including in a philosophical treatise)

14.11.1 ἀκολασίαν *istorum scribis.*

Of a slightly different type is the criticism of Tiberius' character made prophetically by his teacher for rhetoric Theodorus and reported by Suetonius, *Tib.* 57.1: *saeua ac lenta natura ne in puero quidem latuit; quam Theodorus Gadareus rhetoricae praeceptor et perspexisse primus sagaciter et assimilasse aptissime uisus est, subinde in obiurgando appellans eum* πηλὸν αἵματι πεφυραμένον, *id est lutum a sanguine maceratum* ('mud kneaded with blood', of the cruel character of Tiberius). There is presumably again some distancing of the criticism by the choice of Greek, but this case differs from the euphemistic use of Greek synonyms for individual Latin lexical items in that Theodorus used a proverbial-type *expression* which had to be interpreted. A proverb or proverbial expression has the characteristic that it allows a whole situation to be encapsulated in a few words, and there is extensive evidence that educated Romans including Cicero often resorted to Greek for this purpose (see below, III.5). It is of some interest in this case that it is a Greek rhetorician who is responsible for the *mot*; could it be that the Roman taste for the practice stemmed from the rhetorical schools?

Finally, the same distancing effect might sometimes have been sought in the expression of sophisticated praise. Note for example:

10.8.9 *est* στοργή, *est summa* σύντηξις ('She combines natural affection with the most delicate sympathy')

13.9.1 *nihil possum dicere* ἐκτενέστερον, *nihil* φιλοστοργότερον ('I must say he could not have been more forthcoming or more affectionate').

The use of code-switching for euphemistic or distancing purposes is sometimes determined by the nature of the relationship between writer and addressee, as is implicit in Hutchinson's characterisation (1998: 15) of Cicero's letter of recommendation to Caesar, *Fam.* 13.15: 'The Greek in the letter to Caesar . . . enables Cicero to write with the distance, and the community, of cultured discourse about his difficult political relationship with his addressee' (see further below, n. 71, on this letter). But code-switching of this type does not only have social function in this sense. Code-switching as a form of distancing represents the exploitation of a stylistic resource, and it thus falls into the fourth category of code-switching as listed above, pp. 300–1, 303–4.

Many of the utterances quoted in this section are to do with feelings and human qualities, and they can be described as personal remarks. Nevertheless evidence of this type would not justify the description of Greek as a language of intimacy without further specification: it is rather a language of euphemism or distance which makes intimate or embarrassing matters easier to cope with. Such distancing may merge into irony (see below, and n. 64), but some of the remarks quoted are non-flippant.

This potential distancing effect of Greek in my opinion lies behind a number of the functions which have tended to be attributed to code-switching in Cicero. Most obviously, it explains the use of Greek as coding or conspiratorial. Again, when writer and addressee mutually recognise that less is being said than implied (through, e.g., a partial quotation, or a proverb or citation the relevance of which to the context has to be deduced), that recognition establishes a sense of irony, which is not far removed from frivolity, humour or the like.[71] A Greek quotation or formula uttered at a time of crisis or disaster makes the reality slightly more remote. And we commented in the previous paragraph on the role of Greek in the expression of feelings.

III.5 Code-switching and proverbial or fixed expressions

It has been observed by McClure (1998: 134) that Mexicans (in certain forms of writing) sometimes switch into English because of a desire to play with well-known English phrases, and this type of code-switching can also be heard in speech in other languages.[72] The ready made phrase offers several advantages for the code-switcher. First, because it is ready made it need require no creative skill for its use,[73] and hence is not unlike oaths and exclamations as providing an easy method of claiming familiarity with another culture. Secondly, clichés from one language

---

[71] It is worth returning to Cicero's letter of recommendation to Caesar, and quoting Shackleton Bailey's interpretation of the Greek at *Fam.* 13.15.2 (SB 317, p. 458). The passage indirectly concerns certain calumnies apparently made against Cicero to Caesar by young Quintus: 'How was Cicero to react? He preferred not to recognize what seems to have been the real implication, that he might be plotting in secret. Nor did he choose to write directly and seriously to Caesar, giving Quintus the lie; such a letter would have 'dignified' the calumnies and perhaps defeated its purpose. So he put his denial in semi-serious form' (by means of quotations of Homer and Euripides). The subject is serious, but the Greek distances the problem and, because more is implied than said (through literary citation), creates a degree of light-heartedness.

[72] 'Formula-switching' in epitaphs as seen several times in previous chapters involves the use of familiar phrases transferred into a second language.

[73] But even a cliché can be used creatively. Recently a letter to the *The Times* drew attention to a Paris shop called *Homme sweet homme*, which depends for its point on the familiarity of Parisians with the English original.

may be known even to monolingual speakers of another, and thus if worked into speech by a bilingual even when addressing a monolingual they may serve to establish the solidarity of joint understanding.

It is above all (in our material) proverbs and proverbial-type expressions which belong in this category. Familiar literary tags have much the same character, as e.g. τὸν δ' ἀπαμειβόμενος at Mart. 1.45.2; also Lucil. 231–2 <*nil*> *ut discrepet ac* τὸν δ' ἐξήρπαξεν 'Απόλλων *fiat* ('so that it may be all the same and become a case of "and him Apollo rescued"') with Hom. *Il.* 20.443.[74] As we remarked in the previous section, educated Romans had a taste (perhaps stemming from the rhetorical schools) for Greek proverbial expressions, which allowed a neat (symbolic) summing up of the implications of virtually any situation. Proverbs or literary tags might be used for serious purposes, but equally they could be exploited in double entendre as a form of jest. Suetonius (*Vesp.* 23.1) records a joke of Vespasian, who on seeing a well-endowed man once quoted the Homeric verse μακρὰ βιβάς, κραδάων δολιχόσκιον ἔγχος (*Il.*7.213; 'with long strides, brandishing his far-shadowing spear'). Similarly Martial at 7.57 exploited some Homeric tags for sexual double entendre: *Castora de Polluce Gabinia fecit Achillan:*/πὺξ ἀγαθός *fuerat, nunc erit* ἱππόδαμος ('Gabinia has made Achillas a Castor out of a Pollux; he was *pyx agathos*, now he will be Hippodamus'). Achillas is converted from a passive to an active lover.[75] I mention this risqué side to code-switching by formula because the phenomenon has sometimes been treated over-selectively. Dubuisson (1992: 193), as we have seen, argues that Greek was used by Romans as a 'language of intimacy', as 'la langue du retour sur soi, des mots qu'on se dit à soi-même', and as a means of expression natural to exclamations 'qui lui échappent sous l'emprise d'un sentiment violent'. Thus, for example, we saw (III.1) that he interprets καὶ σύ, τέκνον (Suet. *Iul.* 82.3) as representing a return by Caesar to his mother tongue. He also discusses Caesar's ἀνερρίφθω κύβος[76] in the context of code-switching as a form of self-address. I would prefer to stress that tags or formulae could be used to characterise virtually any situation, and were not restricted to the circumstances identified by Dubuisson. Suetonius, for example, is a rich source of information about the use of Greek proverbial or literary expressions uttered in a variety of contexts.[77]

---

74 By contrast Horace even more allusively puts the tag into Latin (see above, 1.VII.4.2).

75 On the interpretation of this passage (and for similar material) see Adams (1981: 200); also the note ad loc. in Shackleton Bailey's Loeb.

76 The expression appears in Latin form *iacta alea est*<*o*> at Suet. *Iul.* 32, 'translated from the original Greek by some intermediate Latin writer' (Townend (1960: 99)). The words were uttered in Greek, as emerges from App. *B.C.* 2.5.35, Plut. *Caes.* 32.8, *Pomp.* 60.4.

77 See *Aug.* 25.4, *Tib.* 57.1, *Cal.* 22.1, *Claud.* 43, *Nero* 40.2, *Galba* 20.2 (another jesting use of a Homeric tag).

Greek proverbs are very common in Cicero's letters.[78] Sometimes, like literary allusions, they are left unfinished (see n. 78), and for the same reason (both to flatter the addressee, and to establish writer and addressee as joint possessors of a body of Greek knowledge). Code-switching by proverb or formula could be widely illustrated from a variety of other writers: note for example the punch line to Mart. 1.27. 7 μισῶ μνάμονα συμπόταν, *Procille* ('I don't like a boozing-partner with a memory, Procillus') and also Varro, *Men.* 27 Cèbe = 30 B. *aurum enim non minus praestringit oculos quam* ὁ πολὺς ἄκρατος ('for gold blinds the eyes no less than an abundance of unmixed wine').[79]

It was stated above that clichés from another language may be used even by or to those with little knowledge of that language. There can of course be no doubting Cicero's (or Atticus') knowledge of Greek, and they had no need to rely on existing Greek phrases or even words. But proverbs, particularly in the form of literary tags, in many cases belonged to Greek literary culture, and their use had much the same function as the use of technical terms from the various *artes* or of phrases from Greek literature: they placed the user and recipient within the hellenophile cultural élite. It is though worth stressing again the general point that familiar phrases do seem to have an appeal to code-switchers.

III.6 Code-switching and the mot juste

A recent study of code-switching (in written texts) from Mexican Spanish into English (McClure (1998: 134)) describes two motivating factors as the lack of a set Spanish word or phrase for the expression of a particular idea, and the greater explicitness of an English term in conveying an idea. Similarly Appel and Muysken (1987: 118) note that 'a specific word from one . . . of the languages involved may be semantically more appropriate for a given concept', and they go on to say that this type of switching 'is the one that bilingual speakers are most conscious of' (cf. Romaine (1995: 143)).[80] Poplack (1980: 589) refers to certain words

---

[78] For examples, see the discussions of Font (1894: 47–54) and Steele (1900: 400–3): e.g. 1.18.6, 1.19.2 (τὸ ἐπὶ τῇ φακῇ μύρον, with a pun on Lentulus' name), 2.12.3, 5.20.3, 15.5.1 (ὁ γναφεὺς ἄνθρακας; a partial proverb; the reader is left to supply the rest).

[79] See Cèbe (1972: 122–3). Two Greek proverbs are combined by Varro here. See too Venini (1952: 266) on the letters of Pliny.

[80] The British press in April–May 1999 carried several letters and articles concerning the abolition of Latin words and phrases in English legal language effected by the Civil Procedures Rules. A correspondent to *The Times* on 4 May wrote: 'Latin has not been over-used in a procedural context . . . And since the new rules do not actually forbid its use, the few Latin phrases in regular use, *useful because they summarise a concept more accurately and less ambiguously than the nearest equivalent*

(mainly nouns) as 'heavily loaded in ethnic content', and as 'placed low on a scale of translatability'. In the previous chapter we saw cases of what were described as 'culturally specific' terms (see in general 2.XIV.2). Dunkel (2000: 127) refers to '"need-filling" code-switching', and Wenskus sometimes makes the assumption that certain Greek terms could not be translated (1995: 175–6; 1996: 239–40). Font (1894: 77) heads one of the chapters (x) of his monograph on the Greek in Cicero 'De Graecis uocabulis ob subtiliorem sensum usurpatis'. The Romans were well aware of the existence of Greek words difficult to render into Latin. When ἔμβλημα was used in a senatorial decree (Suet. *Tib.* 71), Tiberius ordered it removed even if a single native word could not be found to replace it. At Cic. *Acad.* 1.25 Atticus is made to state that Greek words can be employed (in philosophical discourse) if Latin words are lacking (cf. *Fin.* 3.15).

There are many Greek words in Cicero which could be described as filling gaps in the Latin language; some of the critical terms discussed above, III.2, may have been difficult to replace with Latin. But the existence of such gaps cannot be invoked as the ultimate determinant of the code-switch, because in the speeches Cicero would never have allowed himself to switch into Greek simply because Greek offered the *mot juste*. There was also an alternative option in some but not all cases, of using the Greek word in a form integrated into the Latin morphological system, thereby rendering it less obtrusively alien: it became a 'borrowing'. This is an important, and neglected, point: those using a Greek word (particularly a noun) were not compelled to use it with overtly Greek morphology. Nevertheless, the special appropriateness of a Greek word to the topic might often have determined a code-switch, *but only within the private language of letters exchanged by hellenophile intimates wishing to display a cultural solidarity with each other*. Font (1894: 70–6), for example, has another chapter entitled 'De uocibus graecis ob breuitatem electis', in which he collects numerous Greek words in the letters which could only have been replaced in Latin by circumlocutions. Compounds bulk large among such words, as was noted also by Steele (1900: 391), and their prominence accords with the greater facility of the Greek language in compounding (see Livy 27.11.5 *faciliore ad duplicanda uerba Graeco sermone,*

---

in English, will no doubt continue to be used wherever clarity and accuracy of expression count for anything.' This is a defence of code-switching based on the alleged expressiveness of certain tags. On the other hand, Anthony Scrivener, a former Chairman of the General Council of the Bar, appeared to argue in an article in *The Independent* (26 April 1999) that the use of Latin tags was a means by which lawyers established themselves as an exclusive in-group ('Legal jargon, including the use of Latin, has helped to create the mystic and protect lawyers from invasion by the ordinary people').

Quint. 1.5.70 *res tota magis Graecos decet, nobis minus succedit*). The advantages of brevity provided by some Greek formations might be seen, for example, at *Att.* 1.6.2 *tu uelim, si qua ornamenta* γυμνασιώδη *reperire poteris quae loci sint eius quem tu non ignoras, ne praetermittas*, 'If you succeed in finding any *objets d'art* suitable for a lecture hall, which would do for you know where, I hope you won't let them slip.' Cicero was to repeat the word at 1.9.2, but when at 1.10.3 he expressed the idea purely in Latin (presumably for the sake of variation), he was compelled to use a circumlocutory relative clause: *maxime quae tibi palaestrae gymnasique uidebuntur esse.*

Some such Greek *uoces propriae* which offered advantages of expressiveness became key words in Cicero's discussions of various subjects, and hence tended to recur. For example, after the death of his daughter Tullia in February 45, Cicero planned to deify her by means of a *fanum*, and the compound ἀποθέωσις became a thematic word (12.12.1, 12.36.1, 12.37a) in his references to the plan. Another, much rarer, compound, ἐγγήραμα, also impressed itself on Cicero in connection with an associated scheme (12.25.2, 12.29.2, 12.44.2). Following Tullia's death Cicero became tired of life in Rome, and he conceived the idea of acquiring a suburban estate which might be a site both for the *fanum* and for a residence for himself. ἐγγήραμα, which is attested elsewhere only at Plut. *Cat. Mai.* 24, means in this context 'place for growing old in'.[81] To judge by the first two of these passages, the word was first used by Atticus, and then taken up by Cicero. There is a game being played between the two correspondents, whereby each from time to time seeks a recherché Greek word to designate something for which there was no obvious Latin term. Cicero demonstrates some skill in coining Greek words particularly for the purpose of making puns.[82] I stress once again this aspect of code-switching as a game played between self-conscious members of an intellectual élite. But such switching was certainly not exclusively frivolous (ἀποθέωσις, for example, could not be explained thus).

Among educated Greek terms which filled a gap in the Latin language were above all technical terms from philosophy and rhetoric. That is not to say that many such words could not have been replaced by Latin equivalents. In the first century BC (as for example the works of the anon. *ad Herennium*, Lucretius and Cicero attest) much effort was devoted to establishing Latin technical vocabularies, by calquing, loan-shifts, metaphor and borrowing. But the business of finding Latin

[81] See Shackleton Bailey's discussion of 'Tullia's fane', at Appendix III (404–13) of vol. V of his edition of the letters to Atticus.
[82] See Steele (1900: 405).

substitutes was a burdensome one (see above on Suet. *Tib.* 71), as can be deduced from discussions of the problem at the time (e.g. Lucr. 1.136–45, Cic. *Acad.* 1.24–6). Whereas the effort might be worthwhile in a formal philosophical or rhetorical treatise for public consumption, in private letters it was simpler to use the Greek terms themselves in addressing a sympathetic correspondent. Sometimes Greek offered not merely a single word appropriate to Roman concerns, but a whole group of cognate terms, nominal, verbal, adjectival and adverbial, which allowed a topic to be discussed in a more economical and varied way than might have been possible in Latin. A case in point are the derivatives of πόλις. πολιτεύομαι, πολιτεία, πολίτευμα, πολιτικός and πολιτικῶς are all more or less common in the letters to Atticus.[83] It is not the topic that required the use of such words; after all, the topic 'politics' bulks large in the speeches, but Cicero does not have to resort to Greek. It was the nature of his relationship with the addressee and the medium of the discourse (private correspondence) that permitted the exploitation of this lexical convenience. Or again, when Atticus used the verb ἐπέχω in a letter to Cicero (see *Att.* 6.6.3, 6.9.3), Cicero was moved to exploit the existence of a cognate noun ἐποχή to continue the discussion of Atticus' 'suspension of judgment'. Other such lexical groups are συμπάσχω, συμπάθεια, συμπαθῶς and φιλοσόφως, φιλοσοφέω.

III.7 Code-switching and medical terminology

Cicero often uses Greek medical terms in Greek form: *Att.* 6.1.2 ἐξ ἀφαιρέσεως (but used metaphorically),[84] 7.7.3 *tua* λῆψις *quem in diem incurrat nescio*, 10.10.3 δυσουρία *tua mihi ualde molesta; medere, amabo, dum est* ἀρχή, 12.10 *et, si quid habet collis* ἐπιδήμιον, *ad me cum Tisameno transferamus*, 13.52.1 ἐμετικὴν *agebat, Fam.* 7.26.1 *sane* δυσεντερίαν *pertimueram . . . (2) tanta me* διάρροια *adripuit ut hodie primum uideatur coepisse consistere*, 14.7.1 χολὴν ἄκρατον, 16.23.1 *Balbus ad me scripsit tanta se* ἐπιφορᾷ *oppressum ut . . .*

Whereas some disciplines, most notably rhetoric and philosophy, were being actively Latinised in the Republican period, medicine preserved its Greek identity longer. Pliny asserted that 'Roman *grauitas*' did not yet practise this alone of the Greek arts, and went on to maintain that even the ignorant who did not know Greek would accord no prestige to a

---

[83] See the index volume (1970) to Shackleton Bailey's edition for examples.
[84] On this as a medical term, see Shackleton Bailey (1963: 88).

practitioner who did not use that language: *Nat.* 29.17 *solam hanc artium Graecarum nondum exercet Romana grauitas, in tanto fructu paucissimi Quiritium attigere, et ipsi statim ad Graecos transfugae, immo uero auctoritas aliter quam Graece eam tractantibus etiam apud inperitos expertesque linguae non est, ac minus credunt quae ad salutem suam pertinent, si intellegant.*[85] We saw cases in the last chapter of doctors commemorated in Latin-speaking regions in Greek in deference to their professional identity (see 2.v.5.1). The use of medical Greek in the letters evokes the Greekness of the *ars*,[86] though that said Cicero would hardly have code-switched under such circumstances in a public speech; the topic or domain is only influential within the framework of the hellenising mixed language in which Cicero and Atticus communicated in private. Cicero was not alone in the correspondence in switching into Greek in medical contexts. His brother Quintus does so in a letter to Tiro in speaking of an illness of the latter: *Fam.* 16.8.1 ἀκίνδυνα μὲν χρονιώτερα δὲ *nuntiant*; cf. Cicero's own letter to Tiro (*Fam.* 16.18), which contains all of the following: διαφόρησιν, πέψιν, ἀκοπίαν, περίπατον σύμμετρον, τρῖψιν, εὐλυσίαν κοιλίας. Given that Cicero even used a Greek medical expression to his wife Terentia, who was not normally a recipient of code-switching (but see p. 416), and given that we have evidence for such code-switching within a family group comprising Cicero, Quintus, Terentia and Tiro, it may be deduced that the educated had a tendency to toss Greek medical phraseology around among themselves, perhaps within the family; such phraseology, as we have seen (III.4), also had the advantage that it could effect the distancing of unpleasant topics. I have treated medical terminology separately because it should probably not be put on a par with the cultured code-switching as seen in the use of (e.g.) philosophical and critical terms; medical technical terms might well have been in widespread use among the educated in the late Republic.

III.8 Special cases: the evocativeness of code-switching

The use of code-switching as a stylistic resource for evocative purposes has already been mentioned (pp. 300, 303), and it will come up again (IX).

---

[85] Loeb: 'Medicine alone of the Greek arts we serious Romans have not yet practised; in spite of its great profits only a very few of our citizens have touched upon it, and even those were at once deserters to the Greeks; nay, if medical treatises are written in a language other than Greek they have no prestige even among unlearned men ignorant of Greek, and if any should understand them they have less faith in what concerns their own health.'

[86] Note Holford-Strevens (1988: 109) on a passage of Gellius (18.7) in which Favorinus is quoted: 'Favorinus, when discussing Insanus' ailment, drops repeatedly into Greek with every sign of quoting from a treatise.'

There are some special cases of the use of the proper Greek term by Cicero to evoke an object or the like. At *Att.* 6.1.17 Cicero refers to a statue of Hercules by the sculptor Polycles, using the Greek form of the sculptor's name in the genitive: *in illa autem (statua) quae est ad* Πολυκλέους *Herculem*... There is an allusion here to the practice whereby Greek sculptors signed their work in Greek even when the object was for a Roman client and contained a Latin inscription as well. Note for example the following statue base from Delos: *ID* 1699 = *ILLRP* 343 *[C. Marium C. f. lega]tum Alexandreae Italicei quei fuere [uirtut]is beneficique ergo.* Ἀγασίας Μηνοφίλου Ἐφέσιος ἐποίει.[87] The statue referred to by Cicero almost certainly had an inscription in Greek, and by his code-switch Cicero is able to bring the object more vividly before Atticus. Similarly Cicero often gives the titles of Greek literary works in Greek (e.g. *Att.* 12.38a.2, 12.40.2, 13.8, 13.32.2; so too Varro, *Rust.* 1.5.1), thereby showing a taste for accuracy. Rather different is the reference to his own *De finibus* as περὶ Τελῶν at 13.19.4. This perhaps had the effect of stressing the essential Greekness of such a treatise.

III.9 *The chronology of code-switching in Cicero*

The Greek in the letters to Atticus is not evenly distributed chronologically.[88] At some times Cicero made much greater use of code-switching than at others. I have calculated the number of Greek words (by which, for the sake of simplicity of calculation, I mean words printed in Shackleton Bailey's edition in Greek script and therefore inflected as Greek) per ten pages of Shackleton Bailey's text, as used annually from 68 BC to 44. No attempt has been made in this rough and ready survey to distinguish between literary quotations and other types of words, though it might have been worthwhile not only to make such a differentiation, but also to analyse the incidence of different parts of speech (most notably verbs and nouns; in general, as we have seen, it has been observed that code-switches are more often nominal than verbal, though in Cicero Greek verbs are not uncommon), and, where nouns are concerned, the relative frequency of the various case forms. Nevertheless, despite their crudity, the figures do reveal some significant variations. In the early

[87] For some Greek artists' signatures in the Roman world, see further Zevi (1976: 60), Becatti (1954: 33). Note too *SEG* 44 (1994), 644 = *ILBulg.* 9, cited below at 5.IV.7. On artists' signatures at Delos, see 6.II n. 18. See also *IGBulg.* II.503 *I.O.M. pro s(alute) imp(eratoris) uic(ani) Trullens(es) per mag(istros) P. Ael. Attalum et T. A(el.) Secu[n]dum.* Ἀγαθοκλῆς ἐποίει.

[88] This point was made in brief by Font (1894: 23–4), and regularly comes up in the literature.

letters switches are not particularly common, but by 60 BC the incidence of Greek words per ten pages has risen to 47. In the first half of 59 (say, from letter 24 in Shackleton Bailey's ordering down to 40, dated to mid-July) the incidence is as high as 60, but then in the remaining letters of the year (nos. 41–5, the last dated to September) the figure falls dramatically to 6.3. This was a period of gathering crisis for Cicero (as he repeatedly makes clear in the letters, as SB 39.1 = 2.19.1 *multa me sollicitant et ex rei publicae tanto motu et ex his periculis quae mihi ipsi intenduntur*), which was to culminate in his flight into exile in 58. In the letters of 58 (nos. 46–70 in Shackleton Bailey) there is not a single switch into Greek, and in 57 (nos. 71–5), for much of which he was still in exile, there is just one Greek word, and that in October, soon after his return from exile on September 4 (SB 74.7, = 4.2.7). The word is at the end of a long letter, and appears to mark symbolically a return to normality.

It is thus a remarkable fact that during his exile and in the period leading up to it, Cicero avoids code-switching into Greek entirely, but that within a month of his return to Rome he is falling back into his old ways. Indeed in the letters of the next year, 56 (nos. 76–82), the incidence of Greek words per ten pages is back up to about 63 (though there is not much correspondence extant from this period, and the figures are not statistically sound), and it stays high in 55 (nos. 83–7) at 40.

There was clearly a psychological dimension to Cicero's code-switching. Since at a time of crisis he seemed unable to contemplate switching into Greek, it is justifiable to treat his code-switching as contrived and artificial, and (as has been stressed repeatedly here) as a game played with Atticus. It would obviously be inappropriate to describe code-switching of this type as 'unmarked', or as something of which Cicero was not conscious.

This interpretation is confirmed by some further variations in the later correspondence. First, in the letters of 48 (nos. 211–19) and 47 (nos. 220–37) there is once again a total absence of Greek (in about thirty pages of text, a substantial portion which at other times might have contained well over 100 Greek words). This was again a period of political crisis (the high point of the Civil War), and again Cicero must have felt that the pretentiousness of insertions of Greek was out of keeping with the gravity of the situation. In the later 40s Cicero proceeded once more to use a good deal of switching (for example, in 45 (nos. 250–354) there are 28 Greek words per ten pages, and in 44 (nos. 355–426) there are 33). To the period 45–44 belongs Cicero's composition of the philosophical treatises, works that drew on Greek sources. In this period code-switching in the letters may be seen as a parallel to his concentration on Greek philosophy. If political worries could cause a diminution in the amount of Greek, a retreat into philosophy might have had the opposite effect.

Secondly, in the days immediately after his daughter Tullia's death in February 45 Cicero again dropped all Greek. The year 46 had marked a high point in the incidence of Greek in the letters to Atticus (some 63 examples per ten pages of text), but in the letters between 7 March and 15 March 45 (nos. 250–8) there are no Greek words at all. There are some Greek words in the next letter (259), of 16 March, but significantly some of them are in connection with Cicero's current philosophical writings, which seem to have occupied his attention particularly after Tullia's death, and another is the new key-word ἀποθέωσις (see above). The incidence of Greek in the few months following Tullia's death is of some interest. In March (nos. 250–73) there are 11 Greek words in twenty pages, an incidence of 5.5 per ten pages. In May (nos. 274–307) there are 57 in twenty-three pages (25 per ten pages), in June (nos. 308–327) 66 in fourteen pages (47 per ten pages), in July (nos. 328–36) 26 in seven pages (37 per ten pages) and in August (nos. 337–52) 39 in ten pages.

It was observed above that in the later 40s Cicero resumed his code-switching, and for the year 45 the global figure of 28 Greek words per ten pages was given. It can now be seen that this year presents a more complex picture. There was first an abandonment of Greek immediately after the death of Tullia, a gradual increase in its use in the later part of March and in May, and then a levelling out at a substantial figure between June and August.

III.10 *Some concluding remarks*

I have in this section not entirely confined myself to Cicero, but have cited some other material to illuminate phenomena found in Cicero. Certain functions of code-switching I would stress here. A good deal of Cicero's code-switching terms are culturally marked, and their employment underlines Cicero's and Atticus' shared culture and hence their joint membership of an élite. Code-switching in this role has social intention, in that it establishes a special type of cultural solidarity with hellenophile addressees,[89] but it is also linked to the topic of the utterance,

---

[89] Much the same point is made by von Albrecht (1973: 1275), who at the same time points out the distancing effect of Greek in the letters. Note too Dunkel (2000: 127), who summarises von Albrecht's observations thus: 'Greek provided both a low-key solidarity with the addressee [though von Albrecht stressed the point that the addressees were highly cultured] and an urbane distancing from the subject matter.'

in that it was clearly felt in such circles to be appropriate to switch into Greek when making (for example) metalinguistic observations; but since the topic alone would not have generated the switch if the addressee and circumstances of composition were not suited to the use of Greek, we must conclude that social function and the influence of topic were complementary determinants. On the other hand code-switching has been seen to be a stylistic resource which has similar functions to other stylistic or linguistic resources such as euphemism or evocative metaphors. So it is that Cicero uses code-switching as a form of distancing (a function that euphemism in all of its forms has) or evocation.

To some extent code-switching of this type is an artificial game played by two intimates using what is in effect a secret language which fosters a conspiratorial air. Both parties must have the same attitude to such pretentiousness. The game is played with the cultural resources supplied by a literary/rhetorical/philosophical education in Greek, as well as with current Greek. It involves coining words, exploiting the derivational properties of Greek, seeking the *mot juste*, displaying expertise in various technical disciplines and flattering the expertise of the other correspondent. The game is abandoned not so much when serious subjects are addressed (note, for example, the context in which ἀποθέωσις is used; see also above, n. 31) as when there is an external crisis which causes the code-switcher to lose his taste for showing off. Since this type of code-switching was a game, and since it took place in private between intimates, it is often light-hearted, but there is also a good deal of Greek in the letters used neutrally, as e.g. technical terms, critical terms and forms of distancing.

Much remains to be done on Ciceronian code-switching. In the previous section, for example, it was suggested that a statistical survey of the parts of speech and inflectional forms admitted might be revealing.[90] Ideally too a distinction should be made between the different forms which Greek takes in the letters: literary quotations, partial quotations, proverbs, single words, words from the koine, coinages, etc. What distinctions of function can be discerned between the various types?

It is appropriate to mention Wenskus' recent monograph (1998) on 'emblematic code-switching' in Latin, particularly that of Cicero. The terminology (as we saw above, I.V, p. 24) comes from Poplack (1980: e.g. 589), who makes a distinction between an 'intimate' type of switching, which involves 'a high proportion of intra-sentential switching', and a

[90] For this approach to code-switching in a modern speech community, see Poplack (1980: 602).

less intimate, 'emblematic' type, which is characterised by 'relatively more tag switches and single noun switches'. The elements to which Poplack was referring under 'emblematic' are made clear at e.g. 596 (fillers, interjections, vulgar idiomatic expressions, quotations, 'segments which are less intimately linked with the remainder of the utterance, insofar as they may occur freely at any point in the sentence'). The distinction is clearcut as it is applied to the speech community (a Puerto Rican group in New York) studied by Poplack. It is a distinction which is made elsewhere in the literature, in that, as we saw (1.v), linguists have frequently noted the difference between tag-switching and the intra-sentential type. For Poplack, the non-intimate type is emblematic of the Puerto Ricans' dual identity (see above, p. 298, n. 3), and it is adopted in communication with non-group members; the intimate type is used among members of the in-group.[91]

There are some difficulties in applying Poplack's distinction lock, stock and barrel to the letters of Cicero. First, Cicero does not use Greek at all with 'non-group' members (those with whom he was not on close terms). Secondly, fillers, interjections and the types of idiomatic expressions Poplack had in mind are not to be found in Cicero. And thirdly, since all code-switching is symbolic in some sense, what is the point of describing just one type as emblematic; and of what is it emblematic? Wenskus (1998: 5) distinguishes emblematic switching, the elements of which are are only loosely inserted in the sentence, from a syntactically integrated type. The components of an emblematic switch are left rather vague (but see Wenskus (1998: 12)), but are usually to include literary citations and proverbs (Wenskus (1998: 19)). Wenskus (1998: 19) does acknowledge the difficulty of making the distinction between emblematic and integrated switches. In my opinion if this approach is to be followed more rigorous definitions are needed, and a full-scale statistical survey of the distributions of the different categories of Greek (see above) undertaken. For Wenskus (1998: 5, 6) the function of an emblematic switch is to make an otherwise monolingual utterance bilingual. But (e.g.) literary citations in Cicero surely have a more precise function than merely to mark the interlocutors' bilingualism. They establish a particular type of cultural equality.

Wenskus (1998: 12–15, 17–20, 23) makes the interesting observation that code-switching of the types which she calls emblematic has a special tendency to take place at the opening of a conversation or at the end

---

[91] See Poplack (1980: 589–90, 595, 601).

of a letter, in which positions it neatly expresses the bilingualism of the interlocutors (or, we might say, their shared literary culture and hence sense of cultural solidarity). At these points the citation or proverb often occurs in a jocular context (note for example the passages of Varro, *Rust.* 2.5.1 discussed by Wenskus at p. 13, and of Cicero writing to Varro, *Fam.* 9.3.2, discussed at p. 19; the latter contains a proverb which flatters Varro's philosophical expertise). Code-switching at the end of (non-literary) letters will come up in a later section (VII).

In the matter of syntactic constraints on code-switching in the letters Dunkel (2000: 126) draws attention to the complete absence of subordinate optatives. I quote his remarks in full: 'This is quite striking in comparison to the frequency of subordinate infinitives and indicatives . . . and is evidently due to friction between the two systems of temporal "sequence" of subordinate subjunctives when the main verb is preterital: in Greek they are replaced by a different mode (the optative), but in Latin by a past tense of the same mode. This annoying difference . . . led to the avoidance of such constructions.' Demonstrative adverbs and pronouns tend not to be put into Greek,[92] nor do subordinating conjunctions such as conditionals.[93] Constraints on Ciceronian code-switching will come up again in the next chapter (4.V.4.1).

IV SOLIDARITY: SOME INSCRIPTIONAL AND OTHER EVIDENCE

It may be true to say that under conditions when there is pressure on bilinguals to use a public language (the dominant language of the state), code-switching into the mother tongue is available as a means of expressing solidarity with fellow members of a minority group. Consider, for example, a hypothetical family of Greek servile immigrants living in Rome. For a time they are likely to have retained Greek in the family as a 'we-code', while attempting outside, at least under certain circumstances, to employ Latin. But the potential for variations on this simple distinction between family language and outside language (the 'they-code') was considerable. Within the family one can imagine members of the younger generation switching into Latin to mark their solidarity as a group now beginning to be linguistically distinct from the older generation. On the other hand outside the family code-switching from the base language Latin into Greek in the hearing of Latin speakers could be used with the complementary aims of marking solidarity with fellow bilinguals

---

[92] See Wenskus (1996: 248).
[93] See Wenskus (1996: 249). Further relevant material can be found at Wenskus (1996: 250, 252–3).

of Greek origin, of partially excluding monolingual Latin speakers from the group, and of conveying a sort of mixed identity which not everyone shared. Thus it is that under differing circumstances either the family language in unmixed form, or different types of code-switching varieties, could be employed as the languages of solidarity.

In this connection I turn to an inscription written in Greek script: *IGUR* 570 Ἡρακλέων Ἡλιοδώρῳ ἀδελφῷ φηκιτ βενεμερετι Δεις Μανιβους. This is a typical product of the Greek community at Rome. Many of the funerary inscriptions from this community are in Greek alone (as published in *IGUR*), some are in Latin though not infrequently in Greek script, and others are in Latin language and script. This inscription seems to be in a mixture of Latin and Greek. The last four words are unequivocally in Latin, and are formulaic in funerary inscriptions. The name Ἡλιοδώρῳ, which would not have had an iota subscript or adscript on the stone (which does not survive), cannot be assigned decisively to Greek, though it is probable that it was intended as such. The first name on the other hand is arguably Greek not only in origin, but also in inflection, since the -*n* would have been dropped if the name had been Latinised (Quint. 1.5.60; see below, v.2). Finally, there is ἀδελφῷ, which is as Greek as *fecit benemereti* [sic] *dis manibus* is Latin. There is no evidence that ἀδελφός was ever domiciled in Latin.

How is one to explain what is going on in the text *IGUR* 570? The inscription is to some extent in the Latin language, yet it may not have been easily readable by monolingual Latin speakers who by definition would not have been literate in Greek script. The readership expected could only have been bilingual Greeks literate in Greek. That readers of this type should have been addressed partly in the Latin language suggests that the person who ordered the inscription was aware and even proud of his family's degree of Romanisation, and that he was, whether consciously or unconsciously, constructing a double identity for his brother and himself for the sake of fellow Greeks. The one unambiguously Greek word in the text, ἀδελφῷ, belongs to the sphere of the family, and its presence conveys the impression that Greek was the mother tongue of the family. This impression is enhanced by the Greekness of the names. The first part of the inscription, which contains the personal element, that is the names and the statement of a family relationship, is in Greek, whereas the second part, which is impersonal and formulaic, is in Latin. The writer, by his use of formulaic Latin in Greek letters for part of the epitaph, implies to fellow-Greek readers that the family was to a degree assimilated to the language of Rome. On the other hand the use of the Greek word for 'brother' introduces an intimate note which is suggestive of the private life of the pair. The writer cannot bear to refer to his relationship to the deceased in the language of the state or of formality, but reverts to the more emotive language of their family background.

But while code-switching is available as a strategy for expressing solidarity when there is a need felt to use a second, more formal language (in this case the public language of the city of Rome), it is not only solidarity that is at issue at *IGUR* 570. Provided that we can allow rationality to the writer of the inscription, he does not merely want to commemorate his brother as a Greek for fellow Greeks. He is expressing as well a Romanised identity for the family, or, to be more exact, a dual identity. The writer seems to have felt the conflict set up by his Greekness in a Latin-speaking city, and the code-switching is distinctly different from that in Cicero.[94]

Similar to the above text is *AE* 1989, 196, from Brundisium:[95] *Cresces Euplunis threptus u(ixit) a(nnis) XV. h(ic) s(itus) e(st)*. Again the kinship term (*threptus* = θρεπτός (Lat. *alumnus*)) is Greek, in a Latin text, though the morphology has been Latinised in this case.[96]

Further light is thrown on *IGUR* 570 by the material assembled in VIII below, where a distinction will be made between the personal and 'bureaucratic' parts of various inscriptions, and the notion of 'diglossia' introduced in defining the difference of status and function between the two languages mixed together in such texts. Communities in which diglossia has been argued to exist may have two languages (or varieties of the same language) which are functionally distinguished, with one having H(igh) function, the other L(ow). The H language or variety, for

---

[94] On code-switching as a marker of double identity see above, n. 15. It is very much the subject of Myers-Scotton (1993).

[95] See Solin (1992: 183).

[96] This inscription is worth contrasting with *IGPorto* 28: Θ(εοῖς) Κ(αταχθονίοις). ᾽Αννία Δάφνη καὶ Αρτεμιδωρους Καρω αλουμνω ἰδίῳ μνίας χάριν· ἔζησεν ἐνιαυτόν, μῆ(νας) δ, ἡ(μέρας) κγ΄. I have followed the punctuation of the editor, Sacco. Whereas in the inscription just cited θρεπτός is found in an otherwise Latin text, here its Latin equivalent αλουμνω is found in a Greek text. This inscription is very much a mixed linguistic production. The man's name, though of Greek origin, is inflected as Latin (with the -ους transliteration for -*us*). The *alumnus* has a Latin name. The formula for age at death (expressing years, months and days) is of Latin type, as is the opening formula (= *dis manibus*). The family may have been of mixed language and culture: is there perhaps an accommodation to the preferred linguistic identity of Artemidorus and to the identity of the *alumnus*? However the inscription is to be explained, code-switching in kinship terms does seem to have taken place in these bilingual families, and that may reflect the emotive character of such terms and the unwillingness of some bilinguals to translate them into their second language. Similarly native speakers of French using English within the family would be unlikely to translate *maman* or *papa*.

example, may be the language of bureaucracy, the L that of family life. A diglossic opposition between Greek (L) and Latin (H) seems to lie behind the language mixing in the present inscription. Diglossia will be dealt with in greater detail later (below, v, p. 365, v. 2, VIII, 5.1.3, VI).

IV.1 Accommodation as an act of solidarity and as a form of disparagement

One means of expressing solidarity is through 'speech accommodation'. Accommodation in this sense is the act of modifying one's speech (or writing) in some way to make it more acceptable or appropriate to an addressee (or, we might add, the circumstances of the exchange, such as its location; on accommodation, see above 2.XIV.6, and below, 5.III, 5.V, and Chapter 6 *passim*).[97] For example, if speaker A adopts the language of speaker B in an exchange, he may be accommodating his language choice to the linguistic competence of his addressee. But sometimes accommodation is not so extreme. There may be subtle modifications of the speaker's or writer's language use in deference to the addressee. Augustine (*Doctr. Christ.* 4.10.24), for example, envisages the possibility of 'talking down' to the uneducated so that they will understand what is being said:

cur pietatis doctorem pigeat imperitis loquentem ossum potius quam os dicere, ne ista syllaba non ab eo, quod sunt ossa, sed ab eo, quod sunt ora, intellegatur, ubi Afrae aures de correptione uocalium uel productione non iudicant?

Why should a teacher of piety when speaking to the uneducated have regrets about saying *ossum* ('bone') rather than *os* in order to prevent that monosyllable (i.e. *os* 'bone') from being interpreted as the word whose plural is *ora* (i.e. *ōs* 'mouth') rather than the word whose plural is *ossa* (i.e. *ŏs*), given that African ears show no judgment in the matter of the shortening of vowels or their lengthening?[98]

Accommodation is worthy of recognition in its own right, but it is also sometimes related to the phenomenon discussed in previous sections whereby a speaker or writer seeks to set up by linguistic means a relationship of solidarity with an addressee (see below, 6.V.1 (3)).

Code-switching, as we have seen, is often to be interpreted as an act of *convergence* with an addressee (see above, I, p. 301), and as such it may sometimes be a form of accommodation. Giacalone Ramat (1995: 49), discussing code-switching in interchanges between speakers of Italian

---

[97] See for example Giles and Smith (1979) for the general issues.
[98] On this matter see in general Herman (1991).

and of (Italian) dialects, observes that (in rural communities) the 'amount of CS towards Italian may ... vary considerably according to the interlocutor and tends to increase where the latter prefers to speak Italian'. It will be recalled that we suggested above (p. 316) that code-switching in Cicero's letters is partly related to the tastes of the addressee: those proud of their Greek *doctrina* or literary culture, such as Atticus, Varro and Quintus, attract more Greek than others.[99] Giacalone Ramat's remarks are directly relevant to this tendency. She notes (using the expression 'speech accommodation theory') that 'in general, when speakers desire each other's approval they tend to adapt to each other's speech in order to narrow the social distance between them'. Similarly Gardner-Chloros (1991: 57) relates code-switching as 'convergence' to speech accommodation, while observing that, as far as she is aware, 'code-switching has not as yet been considered in any detail in relation to accommodation theory'.

Code-switching as accommodation can be illustrated from the plays of Plautus. It is usually slaves and lower-class characters who switch into Greek in Plautus.[100] In the *Pseudolus* the slave Pseudolus regularly

---

[99] Cf. von Albrecht (1973: 1274).

[100] A full account of the interpretations so far advanced of this distribution can be found in Jocelyn (1999: 169–73). Jocelyn for his part does not accept that the distribution reflects servile practice. The statement (175) that '[i]n such a community it would have been scarcely possible to think of the use of Greek as characteristic of a slave', if it is meant to be taken literally, represents an extreme position. From a later period (the first half of the second century BC onwards, when there is relevant material from Delos) the evidence is overwhelming that large numbers of slaves were of Greek origin and that they tended to hold on to their language or to use code-switching. From the Plautine period it is true that evidence about slaves is hard to come by (Jocelyn (1999: 174)), but there is the evidence of Plautus himself. Not only do slaves in his plays indisputably code-switch into Greek, but it is also the case, as Jocelyn himself admits (1999: 175), that 'Greek words [i.e. borrowings] apparently domesticated in Latin mass in the utterances of comic slaves, soldiers, pimps and cooks.' Jocelyn (loc. cit.) plays down the significance of their distribution as follows: 'If upper-class Latin-speakers did tend to avoid them in certain situations it was not because of Greek or servile or low-class associations but because they belonged to various technical registers of the language of which a man of standing and education had to feign ignorance or disdain.' A Greek loan-word to which this remark is irrelevant is *colaphus* 'blow' (κόλαφος). This is a word which is absent from mainstream Greek (Shipp (1979: 327)), but is found in the Sicilian Epicharmus (frg. 1 Kaibel), where it is the name of a slave. Beatings are overwhelmingly in Plautus associated with slaves (such that, for example, *statua uerberea*, 'statue made of blows', could designate a slave). Alongside the native *uerbera* we also find *colaphus* in both Plautus and Terence, used by or addressed to lower-class characters (see Martin (1976) on *Ad.* 200). Plautus, like Epicharmus, in one place uses the word as a slave name (*Capt.* 657). Here is a word which *par excellence* is likely to have entered Latin via the slave trade, and given its Sicilian connection and absence from Attic it must have arrived at Rome from the south (see Shipp (1979: 327)), brought by slaves or slave dealers. Its profile suits the period. Before the establishment of Rome's eastern empire some slaves will have been acquired from the south, and some of them will have been Greek speakers (such as Livius Andronicus, from the Greek settlement at Tarentum). *Colaphus* might well have been picked up by Latin because it was first

code-switches (443, 483, 484, 488, 654, 712), but at 700 it is the *adulescens* Calidorus who does so: *nimium est mortalis graphicus,* εὑρετὴς *mihist.* Shipp (1953: 110) convincingly explains this utterance as follows: 'Calidorus is here praising the inventiveness of Pseudolus, who him-self... is much given to using Greek. The young master, the only *iuvenis* in Plautus who does so, seems to have caught the trick from the slave he admires so much.'[101] On this view Calidorus is not accommodating

heard uttered to southern Greek-speaking slaves. Another revealing Greek word in Plautus is *badizas*, which is used in an interesting way by a slave but is found nowhere else in Latin literature (*Asin.* 706, with Shipp's fascinating discussion (1979: 123)). If it were true (Jocelyn (1999: 174)) that '[d]own to 184 many more non-Greek than Greek populations suffered enslavement', that is not relevant to the issue. The point is that at least some slaves at Rome in the Plautine period will have been Greek speakers, and these will inevitably have been heard (and understood) mixing Greek with their second language, unless they were very different from their later counterparts; by contrast those switching from and into languages other than Greek would not have been understood, and their code-switching would have gone largely unremarked. Jocelyn wishes to establish that the Greek in Plautus, whoever the speaker, does not reflect servile or lower-class usage but is in fact a reflection of *upper-class* usage. Note e.g. (1999: 172): 'I shall... argue that a switch from Latin into Greek helped to present the personage as speaking in a way one of the better placed and more sophisticated members of the contemporary Roman citizen body might have done in a similar situation or real life.' In this connection he states (189) of certain passages, including *Capt.* 880–3, where the parasite Ergasilus utters a series of Greek oaths, that it 'is much easier to associate [the utterances] with the way gentlemen spoke to each other in the relaxed atmosphere of the *conuiuium* than with the everyday dealings of slaves with their fellows and their masters'. There is a flaw in this argument as applied to the passage of the *Captiui*. Shipp (1953) showed that some of the Greek in Plautus is not conventional Attic but can be associated with Magna Graecia, either directly or by conjecture, and the passage in question has the most conspicuous Doricisms in Plautus. The expression ναὶ τὰν Κόραν (881), with its two instances of long *a*, is put into the mouth of a woman from Sybaris in Magna Graecia by Aristophanes (*Vesp.* 1438). This is not the type of Greek that an upper-class Roman educated in Greek would have used, but is precisely of the sort which might have been heard in the mouth of a native speaker of Greek, such as a slave, from the south of Italy. There is in my opinion no point in trying to locate the use of Greek (and code-switching) in one social class to the exclusion of all others. At least some slaves were of Greek origin and first-language speakers of Greek, whereas some upper-class Romans were learners of Greek as a second language. Greek was thus spoken at the two opposite ends of the social spectrum: it was, paradoxically, both a lower-class and an upper-class language within the same society. This point is well made for a later period by Dubuisson (1992: 189) and Leiwo (1995a: 51).

[101] Jocelyn (1999: 185) finds Shipp's explanation unconvincing, and offers an alternative of his own at 187: 'It is to a friend... given like himself to verbal wit... that the young man of *Pseud.* 700 describes the slave trying to help him out as a εὑρετής.' We have already discussed in this chapter Jocelyn's view that among upper-class Romans of the late Republic code-switching was associated with frivolity. Here, basing himself on that belief, he would transfer to the Plautine stage a form of behaviour found in private correspondence of a later date. It was argued above that such a view of code-switching in Cicero is in any case one-sided, but the main point that I would make here is that free young men in Plautus do *not* otherwise engage in frivolity among themselves in Greek. It therefore seems preferable to me to look for a special motivation in the context, rather than introducing the general determinant 'code-switching as frivolity' in a single passage in the whole of Plautus in an exchange of this type. There is a good deal of subjectivity required in interpreting evidence of this type, but Shipp's view seems the more plausible to me, particularly since there is another place in Plautus (see below) where accommodation seems much more explicitly to be at issue.

himself linguistically to the addressee face-to-face as a mark of politeness (Pseudolus, though present, has not yet revealed himself), but is approximating his speech to that of another character out of admiration for him, significantly at the moment when he is named.

But politeness or deference is not necessarily the motivation of all such accommodation. Accommodation – in the form of code-switching – may on occasions be humorous, sarcastic or even threatening. I illustrate this contention from passages of Lucilius and Plautus.

T. Albucius, who aspired to be more Greek than the Greeks, was once addressed by the praetor Scaevola in Athens. The story is put into the mouth of Scaevola himself in a passage of Lucilius (88–94), quoted at some length by Cicero (*Fin.* 1.8). Scaevola explains that, since Albucius preferred to be described as Greek rather than Roman or Sabine, he greeted the man in Greek when he approached, and was followed in this by the lictors and praetorian cohort:

> 'Graecum te, Albuci, quam Romanum atque Sabinum,
> municipem Ponti, Tritani, centurionum,
> praeclarorum hominum ac primorum signiferumque,
> maluisti dici. Graece ergo praetor Athenis,
> id quod maluisti, te, cum ad me accedis, saluto:
> chaere, inquam, Tite. lictores, turma omnis chorusque:
> 'chaere, Tite'. hinc hostis mi Albucius, hinc inimicus.'

Scaevola goes on to explain (to a jury?) that thus he earned the hatred of Albucius: *hinc hostis mi Albucius, hinc inimicus*. The context is full enough to bring out the irony of Scaevola in using the words *chaere, Tite*, but the exchange certainly at a superficial level displayed accommodation, because Scaevola says so explicitly: *Graece ergo . . .* **id quod maluisti**, *te . . . saluto*. The incident can loosely be described as manifesting code-switching, because there is no suggestion that Greek was used beyond the initial greeting. The reason why address of an hellenophile in the language he liked to use could cause offence is not hard to see. Code-switching forms of address, as we have seen, were appropriate only in private between intimates. But this was a public occasion, and the participants were not intimates. Albucius was addressed by a whole crowd. The circumstances were unsuitable for code-switching, and Albucius' tastes were in effect publicly mocked.[102]

There is another passage of Lucilius which may be relevant here (84–5). It is printed as follows by Marx: *quam lepide lexis compostae ut tesserulae*

---

[102] See also Wenskus (1998: 14).

omnes / arte pauimento atque emblemate uermiculato (Warmington, Loeb: 'How charmingly are *ses dits* put together – artfully like all the little stone dice of a mosaic in a paved floor or in an inlay of wriggly pattern'). The lines are quoted by Cicero *De orat.* 3.171, from which passage it is clear that the speaker is again Scaevola and the victim of the criticism Albucius (note *quae cum dixisset in Albucium inludens...*). It is Albucius' style that is criticised (see Marx ad loc.), and it is hard to believe that the Greek term *lexis* (λέξεις) is not part of the criticism.[103] Again Scaevola may have accommodated his own usage to that of Albucius as a form of humorous rebuke: that is, he switches momentarily into Greek in imitation of a practice of Albucius himself. The point would be enhanced if the word were written in Greek script. The passage has the additional interest that the Greek word is a critical term.

At Plaut. *Cas.* 728 the slave Olympio switches into Greek in mid-sentence: *haec res. etiamne astas? enim uero* πράγματά μοι παρέχεις. His addressee, the old man Lysidamus, replies in kind: 729f. *dabo tibi* μέγα κακόν. Here he has translated the Latin *magnum malum* (referring to a beating) into Greek as a form of accommodation to the linguistic habits of the slave.[104] But the accommodation is anything but deferential or conciliatory. It is a joke, motivated directly by the code-switching of the slave, which is meant to reinforce the threatening nature of the utterance. Shipp (1953: 106) again well brings out the character of the exchange: 'The slave starts it and the master falls into his humour, substituting the corresponding Greek phrase ... for the *magnum malum* perpetually on the lips of slave owners, in order to give Olympio tit for tat. A jest is never out of place in a threat.'[105]

---

[103] Cf. the use of *lexidia* (λεξείδια) with contemptuous force in words cited by Gellius (18.7.3): see Holford-Strevens (1988: 108).

[104] On the Greek phrase as a translation of the Latin, see Shipp (1953: 106 n. 4). He argues that, though the expression is found in Athens, it is not as fixed and stereotyped as the Latin; it is here modelled on the mundane Latin and has not been taken over from the original. See further below, 4.v.2.12.

[105] Jocelyn (1999: 185) again finds the explanation unconvincing. Interestingly, his own explanation (188 'At *Cas.* 729–730 ... an old man is so non-plussed by the brazen familiarity displayed by his slave in addressing him partly in Greek ... as to reply similarly, something he would normally do only with a social equal') is in effect an acknowledgment that a form of accommodation has taken place, with the addition of some contentious assertions about the acceptability or otherwise of code-switching within and across the social classes. On Jocelyn's own statistics (187) as many as 33 per cent of the switches in Plautus (7 of 21) have the speaker addressing a social superior, and it is therefore unclear why the old man should be non-plussed on purely social grounds. The small number of the switches in Plautus (which may be related to the need felt to keep the plays comprehensible to a largely monolingual audience rather than reflecting genuine linguistic practices among bilinguals of the time (see Jocelyn (1999: 172–3)) does not in my opinion permit one to establish rules about what might or might not have been socially acceptable in the matter of language mixing in exchanges between equals or non-equals. The

Curiously, as in Lucilius so in Varro there is a case of the Greek greeting χαίρετε (along with a Homeric tag) which can be taken as a form of humorous (but not in this case offensive) accommodation: *Rust.* 2.5.1 *at Quintus Lucienus senator, homo quamuis humanus ac iocosus, introiens, familiaris omnium nostrum, Synepirotae, inquit,* χαίρετε: *Scrofam enim et Varronem nostrum,* ποιμένα λαῶν, *mane salutaui* ('At this point Quintus Lucienus, the senator, a thoroughly kindly and jovial person, and a friend of all of us, entered and said: "Greetings, fellow citizens of Epirus; for to Scrofa and to our friend Varro, shepherd of the people, I paid my greetings this morning" '). It is important to note that this conversation takes place in Epirus.[106] Among Lucienus' addressees are Atticus and Cossinius, who had estates there. In the other books of the dialogue, which are set in Rome, there is nothing of this sort. There is accommodation here both to the setting of the exchange and to the role as virtual Greeks which the disputants were playing. An element of the same sort of accommodation is also, as we saw, found in Cicero's letters to Atticus: Cicero sometimes when using a Greek word alludes to the Greekness of his addressee and his residence in Greece. It is worth stressing again that location is one of the factors which inspires linguistic accommodation (see p. 321), as this is not, as far as I am aware, a factor which receives much recognition in accounts of accommodation. There is an even more explicit case of accommodation at *Rust.* 2.1.2, where the same men are referred to as *semigraeci pastores*, and that characteristic of virtual Greekness is humorously used to justify a switch into Greek: *ut semigraecis pastoribus dicam graece,* ὅς πέρ μου πολλὸν ἀμείνων.

What these various cases show is the sensitivity of some Latin speakers in the late Republic to the nature of the linguistic and cultural identities which some of their bilingual contemporaries were keen to present. Code-switching into Greek as a form of convergence with or accommodation to the self-consciously Greek persona which an addressee cultivated might well on occasions have been expressive of solidarity or admiration, but there was clearly a fine line then as now between polite

---

one statistic in the whole case which may have some validity – that which shows that most of the code-switchers belong to the lower classes – may have a very mundane explanation, namely that upper-class Romans tended to be reluctant to be presented as speaking the private language, Greek, in public. One can believe that most of the limited switching in Plautus is done by lower characters without accepting as a consequence 'the notion that there was something essentially lower-class about code-switching in the early second century' (Jocelyn (1999: 189), apparently taking this second view as an inevitable concomitant of the first). The reality, as I suggested earlier, is probably that code-switching was polarised at the two social extremes, and for good historical reasons: Greek-speaking slaves were imported to Rome, and the upper classes were avid learners of Greek. Nothing in Plautus is inconsistent with this view.

[106] On this point and for a good discussion of the passage see Wenskus (1998: 13).

accommodation and ironical over-accommodation. Code-switching could become offensive if it was ostentatiously used to mock the linguistic propensities of an interlocutor. Similarly speech accommodation in general will cease to be deferential if the addressee senses that an aspect of his speech is being mimicked. It would not do to address a Yorkshireman in a stage Yorkshire accent.

V IDENTITY

We saw above (IV) in connection with *IGUR* 570 that the aim of expressing solidarity through code-switching may overlap with that of conveying a particular identity. Identity and code-switching will be dealt with in detail in this section.

For the sake of clarity I start with language choice in general rather than with code-switching specifically. In a multilingual society one language may have a particular association with a domain or activity or profession, and the choice of that language may be seen (e.g.) as a claim by the user to be working in the relevant activity: it marks his professional identity. Medicine, for example, had long been regarded at Rome as a profession appropriate to Greeks, and there is evidence even in the west (as we saw in the last chapter, 2.V.5.1) that the Greek language might be considered a sort of professional language of doctors (see also above, III.7). The reason for this attitude lies partly in the fact that from an early period Greek doctors had been prominent at Rome, and partly in the reputation of the Greek Hippocratic corpus. Numerous inscriptions from the western provinces associated with doctors are written in Greek (some sixty in number).[107] In later antiquity the father of the poet Ausonius, a doctor at Bordeaux, allegedly knew Greek better than he knew Latin (see Auson. *Epicedion* 1.9–10 *sermone inpromptus Latio, uerum Attica lingua / suffecit culti uocibus eloquii*). This claim cannot be taken at its face value. As a native of Aquitaine (Vasates),[108] Iulius Ausonius will have been a native speaker of Latin, but he might perhaps, like others, have had a Gaulish accent (on the uncultivated or 'rustic' nature of Gaulish Latin, see e.g. Pacatus, *Pan. Lat.* 1.3, Sulp. Sev. *Dial.* 1.27.2).[109] As a doctor, he made a parade of his knowledge of Greek.

---

[107] See Gummerus (1932) for a collection of evidence.

[108] See *PLRE* I.139.

[109] This view, which is undoubtedly correct, is close to that attributed by Hopkins (1961: 241 n. 5) to A. H. M. Jones ('this was a polite way of saying his Latin was not literary; and in Gaul his medical Greek would probably have passed muster'). R. P. H. Green (1991: 276), however, takes Ausonius as meaning that his father's native language was not Latin but Celtic, and that his 'Greek was evidently not much better'. Neither of these assertions is plausible. Gaulish might

The 'professional' choice of Greek by a doctor can be seen in an honorific inscription, set up by two doctors to an emperor Antoninus, at Narbonne: *AE* 1914, 251 (*CRAI* 1914, 224–5) [Αὐτοκράτ]ορι Ἀντω[νείνῳ Σε]βαστῷ [Π]ομπεῖος ᾽Ε... [καὶ .. Πομ]πεῖος Φορ[τουνᾶτος] **ἰητροί**. What is of interest here is the use of the Ionic form of the word for 'doctor'. The doctors here advertise, if only for their own satisfaction, the fact that they are educated in traditional Greek medicine, that is the Ionic works of Hippocrates.[110] There is another example of the Ionic form in an epitaph of *L. Lucilius Lupi l. Hiero medicus*, from the *columbarium* of C. Annius Pollio at Rome (*CIL* VI.7408 = *IG* XIV.1813 = *IGRRP* 298):[111] [εἰμὶ] Λύπου, ῾Ιέρων πολύχους ἐμ πᾶσιν **ἰητρός**, [εὐδοκ]ίμου[112] πάσης εὑρέσεως κάτοχος. Note too *MAMA* VIII.118 ἐνθάδε γῆ κατέχι Αὐρ. Πρίσκον **εἰητρόν**... The same form is at *MAMA* VIII.404, whereas the Attic form is found at 208 and elsewhere in the area. The Ionic form also occurs at *IGBulg.* III.1776. Also worth noting is the Greek inscription set up on an altar at Chester by a doctor Antiochus, first published at *JRS* 59 (1969), 235 no. 3:[113]

πανυπείροχας ἀνθρώπων σωτῆρας ἐν ἀθανάτοισιν Ἀσκληπιὸν ἠπιόχειρά <θ᾽> ῾Υγείην <καὶ> Πανάκειαν **εἰητρὸς** [Ἀ]ντί[ο]χος

The doctor Antiochus (honours) the allsurpassing saviours of men among the immortals, Asclepius, Hygeia of the soothing hands, and Panakeia.[114]

Here too is to be seen the Ionic form of the same word, but this case is more complex in that part of the inscription (beginning after πανυ-) is metrical (hexameters), and thus the epic as well as the Hippocratic tradition lies behind the text.

By using Greek with Ionic elements these various doctors were behaving in character for their profession, and by demonstrating their ability to use the professional voice of medicine were no doubt contributing to their professional 'identity', if only in their own eyes. I would stress that

have been lingering on, but mainly among country speakers (for the evidence, see below, Ch. 7 n. 8). And Ausonius certainly does not intend us to think that his father's Greek was poor. Green compares *suffecit* with *sufficiens sermo* at Amm. 16.5.7, of Julian's Latin, but it is important to note that in our passage *suffecit* is complemented by *culti uocibus eloquii*, which can only be taken as a claim that the man had a certain eloquence in the language. Ausonius is no doubt exaggerating. In my opinion the implications of the passage would be captured if we added to Jones' remark after 'not literary' the phrase 'but a regional variety of the language'. On this view the father had some 'doctor's Greek', which need not have amounted to much, and regional Latin.

[110] For the significance of the Ionic form, see Fischer (1977).
[111] See Gummerus (1932), 31.   [112] [ἐλλογ]ίμου *IGRRP.*
[113] See now Clackson and Meissner (2000), proposing two emendations to make the text metrical. See also Nutton (1968).
[114] See J. and L. Robert, *Bull. Ép.* 1970, no. 667 on this text and on the Ionic form in inscriptions.

in at least some of these inscriptions the doctors seem to have been using Ionic-coloured Greek for their own sake alone, since it is unlikely that passers-by would have been able to pick up the nuance. On this view a person may seek to project a certain identity in an inscription while well aware that there may never be a reader who will appreciate its subtleties. The Greek in, say, the doctors' dedication at Narbonne operates on several levels. The mere presence of the Greek inscription advertises the culture of the writers, even if it cannot be understood (and one thinks again of Pliny's assertion (*Nat.* 29.17) cited above (III.7) that patients wanted their doctors to speak in Greek even if they did not know the language). To those who could understand it the Ionic form would have been significant. And to the dedicators themselves it obviously had a point.

It would be easy to multiply cases in which the choice of language is related to the formal or professional identity which the author of the text is attempting to convey for the referent. Sometimes code-switching is used for the same purpose. A doctor, as we have seen, may choose Greek to bolster his identity as a doctor in a community which is Latin-speaking, but alternatively he might in theory merely hint at the linguistic aspect of his professional identity by an appropriate switch of languages. Or on the other hand another person may characterise the professional status of someone by such a switch.

This practice can be seen at *IGUR* 707 (= *CIL* VI.2210 = *ILS* 4499). Here a woman Claudia commemorates her *paedagogus* and tutor Julius Hymetus *ob redditam sibi ab eo tutelam*:

diis propitis
Clauda Ti(berii) f(ilia) Quinta
C. Iulio Hymeto aedituo
Dianae Plancianae
paedagogo suo καὶ
καθηγητῇ item
tutori a pupillatu,
ob redditam sibi
ab eo fidelissime
tutelam et C. Iulio
Epitynchano fratri
eius et Iuliae Sporidi
mammae suae f(ecit)
lib(ertis) libertabusq(ue) poste(risque) eor(um).

The text is in Latin, but the man's roles, while partly described in Latin, also inspire a switch into Greek. I take it that there is an implication not only that he was a Greek speaker, but also that he was able to give instruction in one of the disciplines traditionally associated with Greeks and the Greek language (καθηγητής = 'teacher'; cf. καθηγέομαι = *uerbis praeeo*, of one of the activities of a *grammaticus* in explicating a text).[115] The presence of καί is significant. The writer seems to have used the Greek connective to flag the switch into Greek. There is a difference between the isolated use of a Greek noun in a Latin text, and the introducing of that noun by καί. The latter strategy leaves no doubt that the reader is intended to register a change of languages, as distinct from a mere borrowing from Greek.[116]

Another text in which the deceased's professional voice seems to be briefly acknowledged is *IGUR* 460:

Γλύκωνι διδασκάλῳ
C. B. Theaetetus et
C. B. Acaphtus et
B. Fellica Glyconis
patri pientissimo
libertis libertabusque
p(osterisque) suis f(ecerunt).[117]

Here various offspring of Glycon set up an inscription to him, in Latin, but the opening dative expression suggests his Greek origin and the Greek character of the instruction that he must have given.

Note too *IGUR* 746:

Licinia M. Crassi lib. Selene
choraule
Σελήνη χοραυλίς.

The woman was a chorus flute-player, a profession with Greek associations (the normal form of the Greek word is χοραύλης; χοραυλίς is said to occur only here: not in LSJ). The switch here is not intra-sentential, but consists in the repetition of the name and professional designation in Greek. Code-switching often takes the form of the repetition in a second

[115] The editor, L. Moretti, draws attention to the Roman Greek inscription *IGUR* 675 dedicated to a doctor Alcimus by a woman ' Ρεστιτῦτα, to her πάτρωνι καὶ καθηγητῇ. The woman must have been a *medica* and Alcimus her teacher (see Moretti ad loc.). For honorific inscriptions and epitaphs set up by pupils to their καθηγητής, see J. and L. Robert, *Bull. Ép.* 1958, 552, with literature cited there; also Moretti on *IGUR* 675.
[116] It might alternatively be said that the decision to use the Greek noun 'triggered' the switch in the connective as well. On such phenomena see Holford-Strevens (1992), and particularly Wenskus (1995: 179) (the latter on καί triggered by a Greek word which follows).
[117] On the abbreviation *B.* note the editor (pp. 110–12) '*B.* est compendium nominis gentilis quod gesserunt Glyconis filii . . . necnon Fellica.'

language of what has just been said in another (cf. VIII below on *ICUR* 4025 = *ILCV* 3999, with cross-references).[118]

In these cases it is a code-switching noun that is suggestive, but a verb too may be used with a similar symbolic function. The Arretine potter who wrote his name on a pot in Latin form and Latin script and then added *epoi* for *epoiei* rather than *fecit* (see Oxé and Comfort (1968), 297:*[Aui]l(ius) Romanus epoi conlegae et amico*), was associating himself (and he was not alone in this in sigillata wares)[119] with the Greek artistic tradition whereby Greek artists signed their work by means of name + a form of ποιεῖν, as can be seen for example at *ID* 1699 = *ILLRP* 343, quoted above, p. 342. This is code-switching which makes a professional claim on the writer's behalf by attempting to place him in that tradition. Similar are *CIL* VI.2938 *heredes titulum uersiculos Cornelius epoi* and *CIL* IV.4966 *Tiburtinus epoese* (alongside some Latin verses: see above, I.VIII), though in these cases it is Latin poets who use the strategy.[120]

It is not only a 'professional' identity that may be conveyed by code-switching. There are endless possible roles and activities which may be alluded to by code-switching employed as a method of characterising an individual. Sometimes a person uses code-switching as a form of role play. Martial at 10.68.5 (κύριέ μου, μέλι μου, ψυχή μου *congeris usque*; cf. 6–7 *lectulus has uoces, nec lectulus audiat omnis, / sed quem lasciuo strauit amica uiro*) castigates the upper-class woman Laelia for using Greek endearments and terms of address. This, he says, should be the language of the bedroom, but not every bedroom, only that which an *amica* has prepared for a *lasciuus uir*. The point is that Greek terms of endearment are appropriate for a prostitute, because prostitutes were often Greeks, but not for an upper-class Roman woman. Laelia then was using switching into Greek to suggest a particular persona for herself, or at least that is what Martial is alleging.

A passage of Juvenal (6.187–97) has similarities to that of Martial:

> omnia Graece:
> cum sit turpe magis nostris nescire Latine
> hoc sermone pauent, hoc iram, gaudia, curas,
> hoc cuncta effundunt animi secreta: quid ultra?
> concumbunt Graece. dones tamen ista puellis:
> tune etiam, quam sextus et octogesimus annus
> pulsat, adhuc Graece? non est hic sermo pudicus
> in uetula. quotiens lasciuum interuenit illud

---

[118] See e.g. Romaine (1995: 162).   [119] See Oxé and Comfort (1968: xxx), Donderer (1995: 107).
[120] See Donderer (1995: 107–8).

ζωὴ καὶ ψυχή, modo sub lodice loquendis[121]
uteris in turba. quod enim non excitat inguen
uox blanda et nequam?

There is however a slightly different emphasis here.[122] Those women are portrayed as intolerable to their husbands who use Greek at every opportunity. They express fear, anger, joy, cares and also the secrets of the heart in that language, even if they are of Italian provincial origin: pure Attic is the ideal. But they also use Greek during intercourse (191 *concumbunt Graece*). This is tolerable in a girl (191 *dones tamen ista puellis*), but not in an octogenarian (note 193 *non est hic sermo pudicus / in uetula*). There does seem to be a recognition that the use of Greek endearments would be normal during intercourse, and even acceptable in the young. The section *quotiens . . . nequam* (despite its textual difficulties) suggests that the *uetula* not only uses Greek endearments, but does so in public (note *uteris in turba*). Martial and Juvenal have in mind different categories of women, Martial the upper-class woman who behaves beneath her status in using Greek terms, and Juvenal the *uetula* who behaves beneath her age in doing so, but both categories are presented as code-switching during intercourse and flirtation, and that code-switching may be seen in both cases as a form of titillating role-play suggestive of the world of prostitution. It is worth pointing out that Greek obscenities (either as borrowings or switches of code) sometimes intrude into obscene Latin graffiti or literary texts, perhaps as a reflection of the Greekness of prostitution. A notable case in point is *AE* 1980, 262: *Floronius binet ac miles leg(ionis) VII hic fuit, neque mulieres scierunt nisi paucae et ses erunt*. This is the graffito of a soldier boasting of his sexual exploits at the door to a brothel (see *AE* ad loc.). *Binet* is presumably a present indicative, and *ses* is the numeral *sex*. Note too Lucil. 303–4 *cum poclo bibo eodem, amplector, labra labellis / fictricis compono, hoc est cum* ψωλοκοποῦμαι ('when I drink from the same cup and embrace the clever pretender, pressing her lips to mine, that is, when I'm racked with tension': Rudd (1986: 166)). The verb, no doubt an obscenity, is attested in the active in a causative sense in the margin to *P.Lond.* 604 B col. 7 (ψωλοκοπῶ τὸν ἀναγιγνώσκοντα; for the sense, see LSJ Suppl. (Glare-Thompson)).[123] I note in passing that while such Greek words were obscene in Greek, and while they might have been evocative of

---

[121] So Nisbet; emendation adopted by J. Willis (Teubner).

[122] Pabón (1939: 129) has some remarks on this passage and on Lucr. 4.1160ff., but he fails to bring out the differences between the passages (see III.4 on the passage of Lucretius), and does not deal with Martial.

[123] For another Greek term in a Latin graffito of sexual content, see Adams (1982: 172–3) on *calas*.

low commercial sex (the world of which Martial certainly was trying to evoke), it is possible that they also had a distancing effect; it is of note, for example, that while Ausonius never admits the Latin obscenity *cunnus* (or various other words of equivalent status) in his epigrams, he does once use its Greek equivalent κύσθος (*Epigr.* 82).[124] *Cunnus* would not have been possible in this context, but Ausonius' willingness to admit Greek obscenities but not Latin in Latin epigrams suggests that to the Latin speaker they were more oblique.

Juvenal's woman uses Greek for a wider range of purposes than the expression of endearments. Where emotions are concerned, Juvenal might partly have had in mind the type of person who was given to Greek exclamations.[125] As we saw (III), it has often been pointed out that high emotion is sometimes expressed in Greek, though it was suggested that the interpretation of this factor as the major determinant of upper-class code-switching is an exaggeration. The use of Greek to express *cuncta animi secreta* recalls Greek as 'conspiratorial' (III.3), and as a form of distancing (III.4); distancing may also be behind the use of Greek to express emotion.

The passage of Lucretius discussed at III.4 I do not take to be relevant to the above passages of Martial and Juvenal, though superficially all three concern the use of endearments in Greek. I will be returning briefly to all of these passages in the next chapter (4.V.2.11), because some of the Greek they contain is of a special type: it is 'Roman' Greek calqued on Latin idiom.

IGUR 974 (= *CIL* VI.27285/6 = 34179) is an epitaph dedicated to an imperial freedwoman by her *collibertus* and husband:

[. . .]ae
Tertiae Aug(usti) lib(ertae)
νύμφη δρακαίναι
coniugi sine exemplo . . .

Embedded in the Latin text is a strange Greek expression. The word order does not favour the possibility that the Greek was some sort of private epithet used by the husband of the wife.[126] It has recently been suggested that the woman might have been a devotee of a dragon- or snake-cult,[127] the terminology of which made use of Greek. If so the

---

[124] A Greek term is also inserted into what is generally taken to be an allusion to a sexual act at Lucil. 306: *et cruribus crura diallaxon* (= διαλλάξων or διάλλαξον). For this type of expression, see e.g. Tibull. 1.8.26 *femori conseruisse femur*. But the context is obscure, and it is unclear why Lucilius switched into Greek.

[125] See the edition of J. D. Duff on *pauent* (189), 'crying ὤμοι and the like'.

[126] As has been suggested by Leiwo (1995b: 300–1).   [127] By Aronen (1996).

practice of the cult could not in any conventional sense be described as a profession, but it will have been an institutionalised activity which, even if it did not employ a language different from that of Roman society at large, must at least have had Greek technical terms. The switch of languages within the inscription again contributes to the definition of the referent's identity.

A comparable inscription is the Roman epitaph *IGUR* 397:

πατὴρ χαῖρε
D(is) m(anibus) s(acrum)
Aurel(io) Diogeneti
sacerdoti uene-
merenti fecit
Aurelia Caenis
coiux con quem
uixit annis XXX.

Here a woman Aurelia Caenis sets up an inscription to her husband Aurelius Diogenes. Why did she address him as πατήρ in Greek? It has been suggested that the word was the cult title of Diogenes as a priest of Mithras, who might himself have intitiated his wife into the cult.[128] On this view the woman uses the language of the cult in which the pair were apparently initiates, thereby hinting at an aspect of her husband's identity and also perhaps implying her own membership with him of an in-group. An alternative possibility is that πατήρ is simply a familial term of affection, in which case Greek might have been the family language of the pair (see on the next example). But the presence of *sacerdoti* is surely significant.

The identities discussed so far in this section are either professional, or specialised in that the person is commemorated allusively by code-switching as a participant in a special activity. But many epitaphs for humble persons using code-switching are not intended to express anything so grand as a professional identity. Some inscriptions convey by such methods no more than a mixed cultural or linguistic identity of the referents. Note for example *IGUR* 501:

χαῖρε Ἐλπιδία
χαῖρε κύριε
d. m.
Faeniae Elpidiae
dominae meae feci
T. Iulius Syriarcha.

---

[128] This was the view of Orelli. See Moretti (1972: 74) ad loc., with a full account of opinions. For πατήρ used thus, Moretti cites *IGUR* 106–8, 179, 181.

Here the two languages are not blended together, but set apart physically and by the change of script, and it is difficult to decide how the
phenomenon should be described. The writer or client must have made
a deliberate decision to mix languages.[129] The Greek takes the form of
mutual address between the man and his consort, who is made to address
him as κύριε, whereas the Latin is more formal, in that it gives the full
names both of the commissioner, who is not named in the Greek, and the
deceased. The Greek and Latin parts are separately typical of epitaphs
in the two languages, but when they are juxtaposed as here the contrast
between the personal address in the Greek and the formality of the Latin
creates a presumption that Greek was the family language of the pair.
On the other hand the inscription conveys formal information about
them (their full names) through the Latin language and Latin script for
Latin speakers who might only have been literate in Latin. They are thus
presented as at least aspirant members of Latin-speaking society on the
one hand, but as having Greek roots on the other. The mixing can be
seen as a means of presenting a double cultural identity.

A remarkable example of switching for the same purpose in a Roman
inscription can be seen at *IGUR* 972:

D(is) m(anibus)
T(erentiae) Marciae coiugi
dulcissime Ter(entius) Zoticus
dignae et merite fecit cum
qua uixit m(enses) XI, hec que uixit ann(os) XXI et m(enses) VI λέγει δὲ
Ζωτικὸς ὀμνύων ἀληθῶς·
Μαρκία μόνη καλὴ καὶ σεμ-
μνὴ καὶ πρὸ πάντων σο-
φή. et Myrineti liberte eius
dignissime fecit.

A certain Terentius Zoticus sets up a monument to his wife Terentia
Marcia. The information about her life is in Latin and in the third
person, but then some compliments, in Greek, are put into the mouth
of Zoticus, introduced by the explicit verb phrase λέγει Ζωτικός. This

[129] Also worth noting here is a group of Latin funerary inscriptions from Lyons in which the Latin
is accompanied by acclamations of the χαῖρε/ὑγίαινε type, and address by *signum* (in Greek
letters) rather than by the referents' primary names: e.g. *CIL* XIII.1854, where alongside the
Latin the following occur: χαῖρε Βεναγι, ὑγίαινε Βεναγι and χαῖρε Εὐψύχι, ὑγίαινε Εὐψύχι.
Décourt (1993) has plausibly argued that the Greek addresses have no mystical significance (as
has sometimes been argued). The referents must however have sought to portray themselves as
of mixed culture and identity, perhaps as a mark of belonging to an educated élite.

inscription does not belong to a formulaic type, and it must have been commissioned in this form by Zoticus himself, who wanted to have his own words recorded. That they are in Greek and at some length makes it certain that Zoticus was a Greek speaker, and proud of the fact; the verb-phrase λέγει ... ἀληθῶς could after all have been left out, in which case Zoticus would not have been unambiguously presented as the speaker. Zoticus gives himself a continuing Greek identity in a Latin-speaking society, but he also underlines his membership of that society by choosing to have himself and his wife named formally in Latin.

I offer a few conclusions to this section. Most of the texts considered display code-switching as a marker of a special or professional identity, but in the last few inscriptions the writers seem rather to have given the referents a dual identity, presumably because they were immigrants undergoing Romanisation. As has been mentioned (p. 349), in VIII below (cf. V. 2) a distinction will be advanced between the 'personal' and the 'bureaucratic' elements of funerary inscriptions, and the term 'diglossia' discussed. The first type of information is in Greek, the second in Latin. This distinction is relevant to the inscription of Zoticus above, because it is only in the Latin that factual details about the deceased are expressed.

These last inscriptions considered alongside various other categories throw light on the degrees of integration of the undifferentiated mass of Greeks resident at Rome. In terms of language choice and switching, four types of epitaphs of Roman Greeks can be identified, reflecting different degrees of integration.

First, there are Greek epitaphs in Greek language and script, indicating non-integration. At the other extreme are Latin epitaphs in Latin language and script. In reference to those inscriptions of Greeks which make no concession to the Latin-speaking character of the area in which they were set up, I would refer again (see above, II with n. 19) to the evidence that some immigrant groups may take three generations to make a language shift. On this model some purely Greek epitaphs at Rome might be the work of first-generation newcomers, or might commemorate immigrants of the first generation.[130]

---

[130] It must however be allowed that the matter is not straightforward, and that different families might have been assimilated at different speeds. It has been shown (see Smolicz (1981: 87)) that different ethnic groups who have migrated to an area where another language is spoken may show different degrees of tenacity in their maintenance of the mother tongue. For example, in Australia 'Greek-born Australians have the smallest language shift (3 per cent), while the Dutch are the most willing of all the groups to change to English, with a 44 per cent swing in the first generation ... Italians, Yugoslavs, Poles, Germans and Maltese occupy intermediate positions on such a scale' (Smolicz (1981: 87)). It may well be that Greeks at Rome were given

In between the two extremes stated above two categories of texts can be separated. First, there are Latin texts in Greek script, perhaps with code-switching (see e.g. *IGUR* 616, discussed above, 1.VII.2.2). These are likely to have commemorated Greeks who, while wishing to be recorded in Latin, were not looking beyond the Greek (bilingual) community for their readers. A greater degree of assimilation, finally, is implied by texts in a mixture of the two languages and the two scripts, because these address both Greek and Latin speakers. But the referents are still, up to a point, holding on to their roots. Every text must be considered on its own merits, because the mixing of script and language need not have the same motivation in every case.

In reference to those inscriptions which seem to express a double identity of the referent(s), I would take up a suggestion of Hamers and Blanc (1989: 124). They argue that 'the harmonious integration of two cultures into [a person's] identity calls for a social setting that allows dual cultural or ethnic membership', and that the development of what has been called 'additive bilinguality' is 'dependent on social factors that lead to the valorization of both languages and cultures'. That is, if members of a society which is mixed, culturally and linguistically, are to acquire dual membership of the two cultures, 'the society in which [they live] must not present these two cultures as conflictual and mutually exclusive, as is the case with apartheid for example'. The two languages must be esteemed, and neither of the two language groups can be exclusivist, if immigrants are to acquire a mixed identity. These conditions were met in Rome. Slaves from Greek or Grecised cities were the most expensive and highly prized at Rome,[131] and that is partly because Romans were comfortable with Greeks and Greek, not least because Greek was admired as a high cultural language. And from the point of view of the slaves themselves there was an avenue of integration into Roman society via manumission. An immigrant slave who aspired to be manumitted would be motivated to esteem the Latin language and to attempt to become fluent in it, while the Romans themselves were not exclusivist towards the servile population.

to prolonged language maintenance. Their language was, after all, esteemed even by Romans, and upper-class Romans liked to expose their children to native speakers of Greek. It must have been considered desirable by some Romans to have slaves in the household continuing to speak Greek. On the use of Greek within households note Juv. 11.148 *cum posces, posce Latine.* The reference is to the address of a *uerna* who did not speak Greek (see Courtney (1980: 509)). The implication of this line and of the passage in general is that one would have to address other slaves (of Greek origin) in Greek (see Dubuisson (1992: 201 n. 21)). Moreover the Greeks who flooded into the city were of diverse ethnic backgrounds, and were unified only by the use of the Greek language. Greek was a lingua franca, and as such its potential for survival was enhanced.
[131] See Gordon (1924: 99). The greatest outside source of slaves was Asia Minor (Harris (1980: 122)).

This is the general background to mixed language inscriptions of the sort which have been discussed in this section, inscriptions which on the one hand reveal degrees of integration on the part of their subjects into the Latin-speaking population, and on the other a continuing solidarity with fellow Greeks.

v.1 Identity: language shift across several generations

It must have been common in the Greek community at Rome, as in immigrant communities elsewhere, for some members of the older generation to hold on to their mother tongue, while the younger generation adopted Latin more readily (but see the reservations expressed in n. 130). In this connection I note *ILCV* 2534 *Picen<ti>nus et Panteris i pace,* Δουλκιτίου κὲ Μελίσσης τέκνα (see also above, 1.vii.3). The shift of languages is made explicit by the switch of scripts. The offspring, who are deceased, are named in Latin, but the parents in Greek. The Greek expression is in effect a filiation, and has a Greekness which is established not only by the script and the inflections but also by the connective and by the word τέκνα.

It must have been the case here that the parents were Greek, and as such preferred Greek in naming themselves. Their offspring, however, who may well have been born and brought up in Rome, were perhaps mainly Latin-speaking; or, alternatively, their parents might have wished to see them commemorated in Latin, aware that a language shift was bound to have taken place. A general point of some importance here is that the direction of language change hinted at is that which we would expect. Greek families at Rome would normally have moved from Greek to Latin, and it would have been peculiar if the parents had been named in Latin but the offspring in Greek.

I return briefly to the inscription *ILCV* 4463, quoted in an earlier chapter (1.v) as an example of a text in which there are alternations of language at every colon boundary: Βηρατιους Νικατορας [*sic:* = *Nicagoras*] Λαζαρίη καὶ ᾿Ιουλίη καὶ ᾿Ονησίμη κον φιλιους βενε μερεντες. ὁ βίος ταῦτα. The complexities of this inscription are considerable, and one could not hope to explain the alternations decisively without any context. I offer a few speculations which in the first instance are based on the interpretation of *ILCV* 2534 given above.

It is possible that the named deceased were members of a bilingual family or families with Greek as their mother tongue, and that Greek was therefore used for naming them. On this view it would not be the origins of the names as such which caused the choice of Greek (on this principle, see below, v.2), but the recognised Greekness of the bearers of those names. The tag at the end is typical of bilinguals' funerary inscriptions (see 1.v), and it can be excluded from the discussion. The real curiosity is the Latin κον φιλιους βενε μερεντες alongside the names. It will be noted that the 'Greek' names on the one hand and the Latin formula on the other are applied to different generations, with Latin used to refer to the younger generation. This case then may be a parallel to that discussed above. Similarly we will see later that filiations, which by definition name a member of the generation prior to that of the bearer of the name to which the filiation is attached, are sometimes in a different language from that of the name (see v.4); so in the above inscription it is possible that Latin was felt to be the appropriate language for referring to the younger generation, because a language shift had taken place between the generations.

But for the sake of completeness I would offer an alternative approach to the inscription, aware that the interpretation suggested in the previous paragraph may be over-subtle and that in the absence of a context it is impossible to be certain what lies behind the switches. One might make no attempt to explain the rationale behind the different parts of such formulaic inscriptions, and instead take a more global approach to their mixed character. If, for example, a Latin inscription has a Greek tag at the beginning or end, such as ὁ βίος ταῦτα, one would not necessarily seek to analyse in detail the function of the tag in the context. Instead it might be interpreted in general terms as a low-level claim that the referent was of mixed culture, so uncreative in its language use that it could not be taken as evidence for fluent bilingualism on the part of the writer; indeed it might even be consistent with ignorance of the second language. Such tags are not unlike Greek oaths and exclamations put into the mouths of Latin-speaking characters (such as Hermeros in Petronius and one or two characters in Plautus: see 1.v). For the dramatist exclamations are an easy form of symbolic characterisation, just as for a real speaker they are an easy gesture indicating allegiance to a language or culture but requiring no real competence in that language.[132] The tag or exclamation may even constitute a claim to continued membership of a culture or speech community which scarcely exists any more. If for example an Oscan tag is tacked on to an inscription that is mainly in Latin (see 2.II.3 on Vetter (1953), 217(a)), it would be hazardous to deduce that the speaker was a

---

[132] See Gardner-Chloros (1995: 85; cf. 81).

fluent bilingual in Latin and Oscan. Similarly Hebrew tags at the end of Greek or Latin epitaphs do not establish any real knowledge of Hebrew on the part of the writer or referent (see I. V, 2.VIII). The tag might be no more than a relic of a vaguely remembered culture which had all but disappeared.

On the analogy of switching in the form of tags or exclamations of this type, it might be argued that the embedding of a second-language formula within, as distinct from at the beginning or end of, an epitaph (so here κον φιλιους βενε μερεντες), should be regarded not as precisely functional but as no more than a symbolic gesture which either recalls the referent's linguistic roots, or, if the switch is into Latin within a Greek text, asserts his new linguistic identity alongside the old. I have referred to the phenomenon several times in the first two chapters as 'formula-switching'. See e.g. above, I.V on *IGBulg* IV.2116.

V.2 Identity: code-switching and names

I turn now to a special type of code-switching as a marker of identity, code-switching in personal names. In Latin texts it is often the case that Greek names are inflected as Greek; alternatively, the name of a person perceived as being a Greek may sometimes be inflected as Greek (in a Latin text), even if the name itself is not Greek in origin (see above, V.I).

A case in point is to be found in the receipt of Aeschines discussed in an earlier chapter (I.VII.2.3). In line 3 Aeschines not only inflects his names and ethnic in the nominative in Greek in a transliterated Latin text, but also the filiation Ἀισχίνου in the genitive. Of the nominatives particularly noteworthy is Φλαουιανός. The name is not of Greek origin, and it must therefore be the Greekness of the names *en bloc*, and indeed their bearer's perception of his own Greekness, which determines the use of the Greek ending. This case is typical of a multitude of examples in inscriptions and elsewhere. If a name of language A is inflected in language A in a text of language B, code-switching of a particular type has taken place (see p. 478). Many such switches can be interpreted as bound up with the identity of the bearer of the name. The name is such an inseparable part of a person's identity that it may retain its grammatical characteristics when it is transferred into another language; it is as if the referent's personal identity may be diminished if his name is integrated into an alien morphological system. It must however be acknowledged (as we saw in the last chapter) that there are bilingual communities attested in the ancient world in which names belonging to the region's primary culture were either dropped, modified or supplemented by names from a secondary culture,[133] but this happened when a secondary culture was becoming dominant and a language shift was taking place. Greek names though were particularly tenacious of their morphological features when they were used in Latin, and this may reflect the age-old significance attached by Greeks to names, the prestige of their language particularly in the eyes of Romans, and an unwillingness to abandon entirely a Greek identity.[134]

This section will be about code-switching in names as indicated by the alienness of their inflection to the language in which they were being used. The Greekness of a name (or of its bearer) is sometimes blatantly marked in a Latin text by a switch into Greek script even if the text is otherwise in Latin script (see also above, 1.VIII). I cite a few examples: *ILCV* 2716A *Marciano karissimo fecit* Πριμακιανα *mater en* ἡρήνε (here the name in Greek letters seems symbolically to perform the role of the signature of the woman), *ILCV* 3366 *Kallimachus koiugi karissimae'* Ἰουλία ἐν θεῷ, *ILCV* 3391 A *spi. Ilara.* Ειλαρα *ispiritum tuum santum*, *ILCV* 3962A Εὐέλπιστος *Euelpistus*. In the last two cases the name is written in two scripts, presumably because the writer wished to emphasise the mixed identity of the referent, or to identify the person clearly to both Greeks and Romans.

As noted, at least one of these code-/alphabet-switches is in effect a signature of the person concerned (as is literally the case in the document of Aeschines). One cannot use the term 'signature' when someone writes the name of another person (for example on stone) in the language

---

[133] For example, from Egypt the list of names dated to the early third century AD at *P. Amst.* 1.72 indicates that the persons listed once went by different names. Van Minnen (1986) noticed that some of the new names were translations into Greek of earlier Egyptian names (e.g Ἰσχυρίων was formerly called Νεχθερωοῦς, which 'stems from the Egyptian meaning *il est puissant contre eux*' (Van Minnen (1986: 89)). Bagnall (1995: 37) observes that such a change of nomenclature 'would be an aspect of the process whereby the bilingual upper classes of the cities became fully absorbed during the course of the third century into political and social structures common to Greek cities throughout the Roman East'. At the potters' community at La Graufesenque in Gaul some of the potters' names in Latin seem to be translations of Gaulish names (e.g. *Primus* of *Cintusmos, Tertius* of *Tritos, Albus* of *Vindulos*: see Marichal (1988: 94)). Relevant Etruscan (2.III.6), Gaulish (2.IV.2), Punic (2.V.5.1) and Aramaic (2.VII.2) material was discussed in the last chapter.

[134] A nice illustration of the importance attached by Greeks to Greek names in the Roman period comes from the album of Canusium (*CIL* IX.338). Garnsey (1974: 246) points out that among the *praetextati* in the list is a certain T. Aelius Nectareus, who was presumably the son of one of the TT. Aelii higher in the album, all of whom have Latin *cognomina*. He remarks that this 'appears to be an instance of reversion from a Latin to a Greek *cognomen* in the younger generation', and he refers to other cases of the retention of Greek or 'servile' *cognomina*. On this view upper-class Canusini in the third century AD (223) had not forgotten their distant Greek roots, and were apparently proud of their old Greek names.

appropriate to the referent, but again there is a recognition that the form of the name, whether graphically or morphologically, expresses an aspect of the referent's identity.

The examples discussed so far are not literary but from real life. I mention in passing that there was a controversy among the Roman literary classes about the way in which Greek names (mainly of gods, heroes and the like) should be inflected in literary texts. Varro (*Ling.* 10.70) asserts that Ennius had Latinised the inflection of names such as *Hectorem* and *Nestorem* (to which he gave a long *o* as well as the Latin accusative ending),[135] but that Accius in his tragedies began to 'take such words from early usage' (*a prisca consuetudine mouere coepit*) and to inflect them as Greek, as for example *Hectora*. There is another discussion of the matter at Quint. 1.5.58–64, which in some respects is similar to that of Varro. Quintilian too sees the use of Latin inflections in Greek words as characteristic of the ancients, or more precisely of the hypothetical grammarian who is *ueterum amator* (59). Such a grammarian would praise the attempts of the ancients to 'increase the power of the Latin language' (60). Various examples of Latinisation are cited, some of them attributed to specific persons such as Cicero and Messala. But, says Quintilian, more recently there has been a trend to use Greek inflections in Greek names, though he himself remains a Latiniser, as far as *decor* allows (63): *nunc recentiores instituerunt Graecis nominibus Graecas declinationes potius dare, quod tamen ipsum non semper fieri potest. mihi autem placet rationem Latinam sequi, quousque patitur decor.*

The issue is complicated. Despite Varro's assertion about Accius, there are certainly places where Accius Latinised, if the tradition is to be trusted:[136] e.g. *trag.* 137 *quanto magis te isti modi esse intellego,/tanto,* **Antigona**, *magis me par est tibi consulere et parcere,* 240/2, 642 *Semela* (abl.), 667 *Hectorem* (for various other Latinate accusatives, see 55 *Orestem*, 212 *Thyestem*, 653 *Ancisem*). On the other hand there are a few Grecising forms ((116 *Perseu* (vocative), 243 *Cithaeron*, 400 *Triton*). The form *Agamemno* is in an unattributed[137] fragment of early verse found at Cic. *Att.* 13.47 (for the dropping of *-n* as a Latinisation, see Quint. 1.5.60). Another early

---

[135] On Ennius, see Jocelyn (1999: 179–80), making a distinction between the tragedies (where Latinisation is the norm) and the *Annales* (where there are some Greek inflections). *Mettoeo . . . Fufetioeo* is not the same as the other examples of Greek morphemes listed, because here the endings are in *Latin* names, and the ending may even be Italic (see further below, 4.II).

[136] But manuscripts cannot be trusted, at least where some Greek endings minimally different from the Latin equivalents are concerned: see Housman (1910, = 1972: 817–39). The original paper, 'Greek nouns in Latin poetry from Lucretius to Juvenal', is in *JPh* 31, 236–66.

[137] See Shackleton Bailey on Cic. *Att.* 13.47.

writer who seems to have Latinised Greek names was Naevius in the
Bellum Punicum. At 23 he has the nominative *Aenea* without an *s* (*blande et
docte percontat, Aenea quo pacto / Troiam urbem liquerit*), and at 25.1 *Anchises* is
given the form *Anchisa*. This is a phenomenon commented on explicitly by Quintilian (1.5.61).[138] There is an interesting non-literary case in
a bilingual inscription written in a cave on the Berenice road (in the
Eastern Desert of Egypt):[139] Λυσᾶς Ποπλίου ᾽Αννίου Πλοκάμου ἥκωι
Λ̣ε Καίσαρος ᾽Επείφ η᾽ (2 July, AD 6); *Lysa P. Anni Plocami ueni anno XXXV
III Non. Iul.* (5 July, AD 6 (?)).[140] Lysas spells his name differently in the
two versions. He was undoubtedly a Greek and a slave in origin, but he
must have been Romanised, and is able to give himself the two forms of
the name in keeping with the language used.

I would suggest that the inflection of Greek names in Latin poetry, an
interesting subject which deserves a comprehensive study,[141] should not
be confused with the use of Greek inflections in private inscriptions. In
a private inscription written or commissioned by a Greek speaker the
Greek inflection (or indeed its Latinisation, as in the inscription of Lysas
above) contributes to the identity of the referent, whereas Latin poets
(who by contrast were primary speakers of Latin rather than Greek)
in elevated genres were probably more interested in using the sounds
and inflections of Greek to evoke an exotic world (on code-switching
and the evocation of the exotic, see below, IX).[142] Moreover Greek was

---

[138] See further Leumann (1977: 454). Such forms seem still to have been in popular use by the
Augustan period. Horace, for example, has *Apella, Dama, Mena*, and Quintilian, loc. cit., notes
Pelia from Caelius, *Euthia* from Messala, and *Hermagora* from Cicero.

[139] See Meredith (1953).

[140] It will be noted that the dates differ slightly. Meredith (1953: 38) suggests that Lysas visited the
cave twice, once on his way somewhere (perhaps the Roman station at Wâdi Menihel-Heir)
and again on his way back, but it is at least as likely that he failed to make the two dating systems
correspond exactly. A parallel case can be found at *P. Vindob. Lat.* 1 a = *CPL* 247 = *CEL* 8) (see
VI.1 p. 388).

[141] It was for example noted by Bentley on Horace, *Epodes* 17.17 that there is generic variation in
Horace, with Greek endings preferred in the higher genres, but Latin in the lower. Housman's
paper, cited above, n. 136, is important. The inflection of foreign place names in Latin in the
classical period might also be worthy of study. It is, for example, of note that in the trilingual
inscription set up at Philae by the first prefect of Egypt, Gallus (for which see below, the Appendix
to Chapter 5), place names are inflected partly as Latin in the Latin version but mainly as Greek:
IGPhilae II.128 *V urbium expugnator, Bore[se]os, Copti, Ceramices, Diospoleos Meg[ales, Op]hieu*. The Greek
version of the inscription has the accusative instead of the genitive at this point. It is possible
that Coptos was the most familiar of these places, and that the name was therefore felt to be
suitable for integration into Latin. One recalls Quintilian's dictum (1.5.63) that Greek names
should be Latinised in inflection in so far as *decor* allowed; it was the overly exotic that could not
readily be Latinised.

[142] Conversely those early poets who persistently Latinised such names might have been motivated
by a sort of linguistic nationalism (that is the view of Quintilian, whose hypothetical grammarian

supposedly 'sweet' in sound, Latin 'harsh' (Quint. 12.10.27–8),[143] and the poet who wanted his *carmen* to sound *dulce* should adorn it with Greek *nomina*: Quint. 12.10.33 *itaque tanto est sermo Graecus Latino iucundior ut nostri poetae, quotiens dulce carmen esse uoluerunt, illorum id nominibus exornent.* It was a Greek word that had not been integrated morphologically or phonetically into Latin which would be most capable of retaining the 'sweet' sounds of Greek, and into that class fell *par excellence* Greek proper names. Quintilian meant 'names' by *nominibus* in this passage.[144] Whereas here Quintilian appears to accept the use of Greek *nomina* with their 'sweet' Greek sounds retained, in another passage just referred to (1.5.63) he had advocated the integration of Greek *nomina* into Latin morphology. The two positions are not inconsistent, because in the present passage he is talking about poetry, whereas the other can be taken to refer to prose (or speech) as well; Cicero, Caelius and Caesar are all referred to in the discussion.

I return to inscriptions, and in particular to the variable inflection of the names of one and the same person. In the transliterated Roman inscription *IGUR* 616 = *CIL* VI.20294 quoted and discussed in the first chapter (1.VII.2.2) it was seen that the Latin *nomen* of the dedicator Γ. Ιουλους [for Ιουλιους] Τελέσφορος is given a Latin nominative inflection, as ου is the standard transliteration of Lat. *u* in the Imperial period, whereas the *cognomen* is inflected as Greek. It must be said that the distinction between the Greek and Latin nominative singular forms in the *o*-declension is trifling, and if this example stood alone little could be made of it. I would however argue that the Greekness of the *cognomen*, contrasting with the Latin origin of the *nomen*, has inspired a switch of codes. Other, more striking, evidence can be added to support this interpretation.

Numerous relevant examples could be cited from the inscriptions of Ostia. Consider the following two:

IPO A.54 D(is) M(anibus) Caesenniae Galenes m(atris) d(ulcissimae) Italicus f(ecit).
IPO A.121 D(is) M(anibus) Fulciniae Callistes.

would praise the ancient poets, *qui potentiorem facere linguam Latinam studebant nec alienis egere institutis fatebantur*), or at least by a desire to establish a specifically Roman literary language. It is noteworthy that Livius Andronicus not only uses the Latinised accusative *Calypsonem*, a form which Quintilian says he would not allow himself, though Caesar, following the ancients, did so (1.5.63 *neque enim iam 'Calypsonem' dixerim ut 'Iunonem', quamquam secutus antiquos C. Caesar utitur hac ratione declinandi*), but also Romanises (by substitutions) Μοῦσα (1 Morel *Camena*), Μοῖρα (11 *Morta*) and Μνημοσύνη (23 *Moneta*).
[143] See Biville (1990: 71), are the Appendix to Ch. 1 above.   [144] See Austin (1948) on 12.10.27.

Here the deceased have double names in the genitive dependent on *dis manibus*. In each inscription the Latin *nomen* is inflected with a Latin genitive and the Greek *cognomen* with a Greek genitive, transliterated into Latin in a normal way as *-es*. This pattern is constant at Ostia, and indeed in various other corpora of inscriptions from the western provinces (e.g. the inscriptions of Barcelona) where there were Greeks living in Latin-speaking areas and Romanised (it may be conjectured) in differing degrees. The writers were responding to the Greek origin of the *cognomen* (and probably also that of its bearer or at least of her family) and separating inflectionally the Latin *nomen* from the Greek *cognomen*. Problems associated with the interpretation of these endings (and the related *-aes*) will be discussed separately in the next chapter, and a good deal of further evidence cited (4.v.3.1). The code-switching in these cases arguably has the effect of introducing a new morpheme to the language, and thus bringing about a linguistic change within a particular social stratum.

Inscriptions of the type just cited spring from the population of freedmen in the western provinces. Many such persons were of Greek origin; they added a Latin *nomen* to the old Greek name on manumission. The preservation of the Greek ending in the Greek name could be taken as a hint of the continuing bilingualism of such freedmen or of their families, but it is preferable not to put too strong an interpretation on the practice. Such forms may be no more than a concession to the remembered origins of the deceased's family; they do however show that families of this type tended to retain a hold linguistically on their roots.

In the material just discussed a bearer of two names is given a mixed identity by the variable inflection of the names. I turn now to another pattern of code-switching involving names. At *IGUR* 570 discussed above (iv) the names and a kinship term are in Greek, whereas certain formulae from funerary inscriptions are in transliterated Latin (Ἡρακλέων Ἡλιοδώρῳ ἀδελφῷ φηκιτ βενεμερετι Δεις Μανιβους). The same is true of the inscription from Brundisium, *AE* 1989, 196, discussed in the same section above. It is common in funerary inscriptions for the name to be in one language, but the details of the death in a second. The most frequent pattern in Rome and other parts of Italy is that Greek is used for the names and Latin for the rest of the information, such as dates (on which see below, viii), age at death and units of time. Consider, for example, *IG* xiv. 678 *Heraklas Heraklidu Alexandreus uixit an(nis) L h(ic) s(itus)*. Here the full name, comprising name, filiation and ethnic, is in Greek, and even the transliteration makes little concession to Latin practice, in that *k* is kept. The name retains its final -*s* (see above on the Latinisation of such names by deletion of the *s*). The filiation is not only inflected as Greek (= Ἡρακλείδου), but in the Greek manner it also lacks an equivalent of Latin *filius* (cf. e.g. above, II (5) on the Cerinthus inscription for this form of interference; also below, v.4 on *P. Amh. Lat.* = *CPL* 172); on filiations see below (v.4). *Alexandreus*, which in Latin would have been replaced by *Alexandrinus*, is not a Latin word. Then follow typical funerary formulae in Latin. As in *IGUR* 570, the personal part of the inscription, that identifying the deceased, is in Greek, but the details of his life and burial, such as they are, are in Latin. The deceased was unambiguously a newcomer to Rome. If the commissioner of the inscription (who might have been the deceased himself) was true to the character of the man, the choice of Latin for part of the text would imply that he had adopted Latin, while not abandoning a feeling for his Greek origin as expressed by the choice of Greek for the name and by the inclusion of *Alexandreus*. I would refer again to the view mentioned earlier (II) that it may take three generations for an immigrant family to abandon its language of origin. Heraclas is a first-generation immigrant who would seem to have had a mixed linguistic identity. The formula is part of this inscription is in what might be called the 'bureaucratic' language of the city of Rome, that is the official, public language of the state (cf. above, v, p. 365). The question is worth asking whether among bilinguals code-switches might sometimes have been motivated by the 'bureaucratic', official or formal nature of part of an utterance. This is a question to which I will return below (VIII).

V.3 Identity: code-switching in names in some other languages

Code-switching in names is a widespread practice and by no means confined in our material to inscriptions in Greek and Latin. Comparable examples were seen in the last chapter from a variety of language communities. I list some of them together here to bring out just how influential the origin of a name and/or the linguistic identity of its bearer can be in determining a change of languages. Sometimes there is a switch of script as well as language (for which phenomenon see also the previous section). An Attic *skyphos* found at Gravisca, the port of Tarquinia in Etruria, has a Greek name in Greek letters alongside the name of the goddess in Etruscan (see 2.III.3). Similarly a Greek name in Greek letters is embedded in an otherwise Punic dedication at Carthage (*CIS* I.191; see 2.V.5.1). In the Oscan–Latin bilingual from Pietrabbondante in Samnium (Poccetti (1979), 21) the Latin version inflects the name of an Oscan speaker in Oscan (*Herenneis*). We saw (II.3) a Venetic–Latin bilingual (Ca. 58 *V. Olsomnos. Enniceios V.S.L.M. Trum.*) in which the votive formula is Latin, but the names have their Venetic form. The distribution of languages in this inscription is much the same as that seen in some of the texts in the previous section: the language associated with the referent's roots is used in the name, whereas the formula is in another language. It is worth introducing the term *retention* (which came up briefly at 2.V.9) at this point as an alternative to or subdivision of 'code-switching'. During a language shift the original form of a name may be *retained* for a period and used within the new language (on the term 'retention' see further below, XII.5), thereby creating a special type of code-switch.

Also of interest are the onomastic formulae in the *sententia Contrebeensium*, a Latin text from Hispania Citerior of the period of Sulla.[145] The masculine genitive plural is usually in *-orum* as expected, except in partly Latinised onomastic formulae of indigenous structure: e.g. *Lubbus* **Urdinocum** *Letondonis f. praetor . . . Babbus* **Bolgondiscum** *Ablonis f. magistratus.* These are names of clans retaining the Celtiberian genitive plural, whereas the personal names and filiations have been Latinised. Such examples (like some of those discussed above) show that the Latinisation of onomastic formulae in provincial areas in the west was a gradual process.

V.4 Identity: filiations

Filiations often show a switch from the main language of a text to the family or original language of the referent, as we have seen from time to time already (e.g. 2.II.3, 2.III.6; see also below, 5.VII.1). Again it may be appropriate to speak of a 'retention'. I treat filiations separately, alluding to a few cases mentioned already and adding some others.

Sometimes the alien filiation is part of a name which in its entirety is in a different language from that of the rest of the text. Two cases in point are the inscription *IG* XIV. 678, discussed above (*Heraklas Heraklidu Alexandreus . . .*), and the receipt of (Aeschines 1.VII.2.3). Alternatively it may be only the filiation that has an inflection alien to the text. A *defixio* from Lilybaeum, recently republished by Curbera (1997a), begins (lines 1–2) Γάιος Ούείβιος υ[ίὸς] Λούκι Ούείβι . . . The whole *defixio* is in Greek, and the names in the nominative, though of Latin origin, have the Greek inflection. The filiation, however, seems to be inflected in the genitive as

---

[145] See Lejeune (1992: 53).

Latin. Curbera argues that the ending is the Greek -ι found sometimes as the genitive of the -ις nouns that derive from -ιος, but these normally have an -ου genitive; the -ι form is late.[146] The inscription is dated to the first century BC or first century AD by Curbera (1997a: 219). In view of the parallel examples of switching/retention in filiations, it is simpler to take the endings as Latin. Curbera suggests that the persons cursed were Africans who had come to Sicily for some reason, and if that were accepted they would probably have been Latin speakers. That possibility, along with the fact that the names in the document are of Latin origin,[147] provides a background of sorts to the switch/retention, though it does not explain it.

The following is a list of names, mostly of freedmen, from the Greco-Italian community of traders operating on the island of Delos in the last two centuries BC (*ID* 2440 = *ILLRP* 289): *L. Pumidius L. l.*, vac. *M. Castricius Q. l.*, *Cn. Otacilius Q. l.*, vac. *A. Claudius Sex. l.*, *Cn. Mescinius M. l.*, **Philologus Aprodisiu**, *Dositheus, A. Granius Q. l.*, **Archibius Aprodisiu**, *C. Nerius M. l. hisce signum Volcani merito statuerunt.* Here again the nominatives of the names of the two Greeks have been given the form appropriate to the primary language of the text itself, whereas the filiation[148] is a transliteration of the Greek genitive. As a parallel for the form Degrassi refers to one of the Capitoline bilingual inscriptions (*ILLRP* 178a; for this corpus, see below, 6. III.3), which contains the expression *[Z]enodoti Apoloniu* (Gk. Ἀπολλωνίου). The text printed by Degrassi, *ILLRP* 178a is as follows: *[. . .]es [uirtutis et benef]ici ergo. [Legati Pasicrates . . . d]ori f(ilius), [Mnesitheus Asclep . . . f(ilius), Z]enodoti Apoloniu*; [ὁ δῆμος ὁ . . .] ἐλευθερωθεὶς ὑπὸ [τοῦ δήμου τοῦ Ῥ]ωμαίων ἀρετῆς ἕνεκεν κ[αὶ εὐεργεσίας πρε]σβευσάντων Πασικράτ[ους . . . δωρου,] Μνησιθέο[υ] Ἀσκληπι[. . . , Ζηνοδότου] Ἀπολλωνίου. The Greek version has a genitive absolute, beginning at πρεσβευσάντων and continuing with a string of names in the genitive in agreement with the participle (for which construction see e.g. *ILLRP* 179). The structure of the Latin is less clear. Degrassi prints a nominative plural *legati* with appositional names in the nominative, no doubt with various formulaic texts such as *ILLRP* 176, 180 in mind, but a glance at these 'nominatives' in the present text will show that not a single one of them is extant, whereas there are two juxtaposed

---

[146] Gignac (1981: 25) gives the genitive ending as -ίου, with -ι quoted (1981: 26) from the sixth/seventh century.

[147] Note Curbera (1997a: 222): 'What strikes one in this text is the abundance of Roman names'; four names have an -ι ending.

[148] See Degrassi, *ILLRP* ad loc., n. 1, interpreting the expressions as = Ἀφροδισίου scil. *filius*. But see further below, 6.V.1 (4) for an alternative possibility.

genitives surviving which cannot both be filiations. Clearly the restoration *legati* + nominatives is difficult to sustain. The genitive *Apoloniu* is almost certainly a filiation dependent on *Zenodoti*, because in this corpus of texts (*ILLRP* 174–81) the *legati* are regularly given filiations both in Greek and Latin versions. If so the first name must be genitive because of the construction (corresponding to the genitive absolute in Greek: e.g. *cura* (ablative) with or without *legatorum*) in which it is embedded.

Note too *ILI* (1963), 373: *C. Sp(ectatius) Secundinus u(iuus) f(ecit) s(ibi) et Tut(oriae) . . . et Rusticio Tutori nepoti . . . et Rusticium [sic]* **Albinu** *f(ilium)*.

For the possible intrusion of a Latin genitive inflection into a filiation in an Oscan inscription from Chieti in the Marrucine territory, see Poccetti (1979), 204, cited above, 2.II.3, p. 136.

At 2.III.6 (p. 177) the Latin–Etruscan text *CIE* 2860 (*Vel Tite Larisal f. Cainai natus*) was discussed. The ending in the filiation (*-al*) is the Etruscan genitive inflection, dependent on the Latin *f(ilius)*.

Further (salutary) light of a different order is thrown on the phenomenon of switching in filiations by a papyrus text from Egypt (*P. Amh. Lat.* = *CPL* 172). The text, discussed with a translation by de Ricci (1904), is a *manumissio inter amicos*. A citizen of Hermopolis frees a female slave born in his house and now aged thirty-four. He receives the price of the manumission from a third person. The Latin text is impersonal and in the third person, whereas the Greek part contains a chirograph declaration in the first person by the manumitter, and also a declaration by the man who put up the money (one Aurelius Ales), this last in the hand of another, because Ales was illiterate.

The Latin text begins *Marcus Aurel[iu]s [A]mmonion* **Lupergu** *Sarapionis*, with which may be compared from the Greek of the manumitter (lines 16–17) Μᾶρκος Αὐρήλιος Ἀμμωνίων **Λουπέργου** Σαραπίωνος (='son of Lupercus son of Sarapion'). The treatment of the two filiations in the Latin version is not consistent, with one Greek genitive retained in transliterated form, but the other integrated morphologically into Latin. Syntactically the Latin version shows Greek interference, in that the genitives do not hang on *filius* (for this type of interference, see above, and also v. 2 above on *IG* XIV.678, and 2.II (5) on the letter of Cerinthus).

Elsewhere too the Latin section displays the writer's indifference to the integration into Latin of oblique-case forms of names. Note lines 7–10 *et accepit pr[o] liber[t]ate eius ab Aurelio Aletis Inaroutis a uico* **Tisicheos** *nomi* **Hermupolitu** *dr(achmas) Aug(ustas) dua millia ducentas quas et ipse Ales Inaroutis donauit*. Again there is inconsistency. *Hermupolitu* (from Ἑρμοπολίτης) reflects a Greek genitive ending in -ου,[149] and *Tisicheos* (nominative *Tisichis*)[150] also has a Greek inflection.

How are the various cases of switching in filiations discussed in this section to be explained, and are they all of the same type? The last should be separated from most of the others. The Latin part of the document is conspicuously bad (note the incorrect genitive (for ablative) *Aletis* in the passage just quoted), with several switches into Greek inflections as well as interference. Such features are commonplace in Latin texts of the Roman period from Egypt (5.VII.2.2, VII.3, VIII, IX). 'Learners' Latin' I have identified as a neglected subdivision of subliterary or Vulgar Latin. It may be deduced that there were not always fluent writers or speakers of Latin available for the drafting or copying of Latin legalistic texts, and that Greeks, with poor training in Latin literacy, sometimes had to be employed for the purpose. The switches into Greek inflections may be due to poor command of Latin on the part of the Greek drafter, much as Aeschines (2.VII.2.3) lapsed into Greek inflections (e.g. κλάσσης for *classis* (genitive)). The Latinisation of the genitive form of Greek names is probably more difficult to effect than that of the nominative, and the complexity of the conversion might have caused more switches/retentions in this case than in the nominative. Thus there is not necessarily a rationale to the switch or retention (on code-switching and imperfect competence, see above, II).

As far as the other texts are concerned, various factors have to be considered as determinants of the inflections in the filiation. First, whereas the name of a person in an inflecting language will be regularly used in a variety of cases and thus will have an inbuilt variability, the filiation is always in the genitive and by definition of fixed form. Its lack of variability might have prompted its fossilisation. Secondly, the filiation in any language will belong to formal written registers, not to everyday speech, and its formality might have contributed further to the fossilisation. Thirdly, and most importantly, in bilingual immigrant communities it is not unusual, as we have seen (above, V.I), for a language shift to take place over several generations. Under circumstances of language shift within a family the primary language of the older generation may therefore remain, say, language A, when that of the next generation has changed to language B. Members of the later (assimilated) generation, writing in the new language B, might on occasions have kept the inflection of

---

[149] The expected form would be *Hermopolitu*: see de Ricci (1904: 191).
[150] See de Ricci (1904: 191) on this village.

their father's primary language in a filiation in accommodation to his perceived or preferred linguistic identity. On this interpretation the presence of an alien inflection in a filiation might sometimes have reflected the changing linguistic identity of a family over a couple of generations. It was seen earlier in connection with other situations of language contact (e.g. Latin–Punic (2.v.5.1), Latin–Greek–Aramaic (2.vii.2)) that during a language shift, while new names belonging to the acquired language may eventually be adopted, change is gradual and affects different members of the same family differently. It was pointed out above (v.1) on *ILCV* 2534, a text in a mixture of languages and scripts, that there are types of code-switching in inscriptions which may be accounted for on the principle that a family's linguistic identity takes a few generations to change. But the phenomenon of code-switching in filiations cannot always be neatly related to perceptions of linguistic identity, as the *manumissio inter amicos* illustrates.

It may be stressed in conclusion that in bilingual communities expressions of filiation in one language seem to have been particularly subject to influence from the other. I have confined myself here to the inflection of the filiation because of the subject of the present chapter, but interference of various types has also come up from time to time, such as the addition of *filius* in Italic texts, the omission of *filius* in Latin texts or the inclusion of υἱός in Greek, and the use of *clan* in Etruscan on the model of Latin *filius*.

v.5 Identity: official titles

At the beginning of this chapter a soldier's epitaph from the east was quoted in which the military rank was stated in Latin within a Greek inscription. The code-switch underlines the soldier's professional identity as a member of the Roman army. Roman military terms or titles are often in this way inflected as Latin in Greek texts.

For example, *O. Flor.* 4 begins as follows:

Ἰούλις Ἀπολινάρις
τύρμα Ἀπωνίου.

Bagnall (1976: 44) states: 'The Greek formula calls for τύρμης [for which see *O. Flor.* 5.7], but τύρμα is probably meant as a dative in imitation of the Latin formula.' That is, the writer was aware that the Latin ablative (either descriptive or indicating source) *turma* might have been used in Latin in such a context, and he chose a Greek dative as resembling the Latin ablative. That is possible (the relationship between the Greek dative and Latin ablative in texts with a bilingual dimension will be dealt with in the next chapter, 4.v.4), but equally he might have felt that he was keeping the Latin ablative of the formulaic expression, a procedure which would constitute code-switching. It is significant that there is *upsilon* in the first syllable rather than ου, the normal Greek transliteration of Latin *u*; this suggests that the form of the word reflects its appearance in Latin.[151]

A revealing graffito from the Frankincense road in Judaea belonging to a group of graffiti written by members of the *ala ueterana Gaetulorum* (Jaussen and Savignac (1914: 648), 16) runs as follows:

Φολσκιανὸς Σεουέρος
ἐκύης δὶς
αλε Γετουλῶν.

Here αλε can only be the Latin genitive *ale* (with monophthongisation of the diphthong: see below), and it therefore follows that another inscription from the same corpus (p. 647, 14 μνησθῆ... ἐκκύης **αλα** Γετουρῶν) probably has the Latin ablative rather than a Greek dative. On this analogy one is more inclined to take the example above from the Florida ostraca in the same way.

At the Colossus of Memnon (also in Egypt) there can be found titles inflected wholly or partly in Greek in Latin texts: e.g. A. and É. Bernand (1960), 41 *[Aq]uila [epistr]ategus Thebaidos fecit* (cf. 67 ἐπιστράτηγος Θηβαίδος.[152] Here it is not a military identity that is at issue, but that of a civil functionary. The local Egyptian administration of the nomes was conducted in Greek, and titles such as this were intimately associated with the Greek language; the title is thus left in Greek form in a Latin text.

The most extensive code-switching (or interference?) in a Greek military document is to be found in *P. Hamb.* 1.39. This will be dealt with in a later chapter (5.vii.1). Also worth noting are some of the genitive plural forms in *proskynemata* at Kalabcha (discussed below, 5.v.3).

Not all code-switching in titles need be deliberately connected with the writer's sense of identity. Some examples may rather reflect poor

---

[151] There is some uncertainty shown in the handling of the case inflection of the Latin terms *turma* and *ala* by Greek speakers attempting to write Latin, and by Greek speakers attempting to use the words in Greek. The Greek writer of a Latin list of soldiers of the *ala III Assuriorum* (*ChLA* 18.660), stationed at Oxyrhynchus, on the one hand gave *turma* a Greek inflection (*turmης*), and on the other used a mixed genitive-ablative expression *ale tertia*. See 5.vii.3(1).

[152] See the editors on 78 (p. 174).

competence on the part of the writer in the target language, or even the difficulty of integrating certain terms into another language. In the Abinnaeus archive (see Bell et al. (1962)) from Dionysias in Egypt note 1.13 *[p]raefecturae alae Dionusados*. It is possible that the writer did not know how to Latinise the name. In the same letter, which is in formal style, there is a curious error at line 10: *[promo]uere me clementia praefectum alae* **Dionusada** *prouinciae Aegupt[i] uestra dignata est.* The inflection is Greek, but it is in the wrong case. However one is to explain the mistake, there is a hint that the writer was having difficulty in dealing with the title in Latin. Accuracy and consistency are not always achieved in the attempt to move into the language considered proper for the expression of a title. Note, for example, Bell (1937: 33), lines 14–15 *contra Apollonos poli magna*[153] *Thebaidis*, where one name is given a Latin inflection and the other is not. For a further case of the difficulty experienced by a writer in Latinising a name forming part of a title, note, in a bilingual receipt for goods dated AD 220 (*ChLA* 41.1198 = *CEL* 205), *Tito Flauio Valeriano euteṇiarca [O]xsoricito* **poleis**, *qui . . .*, which is meant to be equivalent to τῆς Ὀξυρυγχιτῶν πόλεως.[154] The expression is described by Cugusi, *CEL* 205.21–2n. as a 'pure Grecism',[155] but whereas the first name perhaps represents the Greek genitive plural with omission of *-n*, *poleis* is neither pure Greek nor a correct Latinisation (contrast *CPL* 216.6 *ciuitatis Oxyrhynchitarum* for a complete Latinisation).

I have put the material in this section under the general heading 'identity' because Roman soldiers were eminently conscious of the Romanness of the institution in which they were serving, and they often alluded to that fact, either by using Latin in Greek areas in funerary inscriptions which mentioned their military profession, or by switching into Latin at points where the institution was referred to. From another perspective, military or civilian titles or the names of military units, though translatable into the other language, can be seen as 'culturally specific', in that they are associated with a particular military or political institution which had its own public language. A switch into Latin when a unit of the Roman army is named represents a switch into the 'proper' language for that name; the procedure is much the same as switching from Latin to Greek when the title of a Greek literary work is given (see III.8 above). But poor competence in the target language may also generate switches into L1.

---

[153] Accusatives without *-m*.   [154] This expression is restored at lines 5–6 of the Greek part.

[155] So too *ChLA* 41.1198 ad loc.

VI CODE-SWITCHING, LANGUAGE CHOICE AND POWER

Language practices (including code-switching and language choice in bilingual settings) may be 'bound up in the creation, exercise, maintenance or change of relations of power' (Heller 1995: 159). A particular language choice as symbolising the power of the speaker *vis-à-vis* his addressee can be seen at Apul. *Met.* 9.39 (see 5.IV.3), where a soldier in a Greek-speaking region aggressively addresses a local peasant, who could scarcely have been assumed to be a Latin speaker or even bilingual, in Latin. I discuss here code-switching/language choice as a possible display of power. Whereas code-switching expressing solidarity displays what I have called 'convergence', code-switching which symbolises exclusion, superiority, power or the like represents the other side of the coin, that is the phenomenon referred to earlier as 'divergence' (see above, I, IV.1).

VI.1 Bilingual transcripts of hearings

J. Rea (*P. Oxy.* LI.3619) lists some thirty-nine (largely fragmentary) documents recording hearings before Roman officials.[156] Such documents, which are mainly but not exclusively found in Egypt (see below), have interesting bilingual structures of slightly different types which raise several issues to do with bilingualism and code-switching. This is not the appropriate place to discuss the whole subject but I begin with a couple of categories which are not strictly relevant here in order to bring out the character of the texts with which I am concerned.

Roussel and de Visscher (1942–3) published the fragmentary remains of the inscriptional transcript (found at Dumayr in Syria) of a hearing held before Caracalla at Antioch in AD 216. The advocates and the emperor himself speak Greek, but the transcript is headed by a Latin passage and each speaker in introduced in Latin by formulae such as *Aristaenetus d(ixit)*. Interesting though the question is why Latin is used for the framework of the report (see below, p. 390), the text is of no relevance to a discussion of code-switching and power, and I mention it here only because it provides a sort of base form on which various modifications were to be imposed. Significantly, the emperor, by using Greek in a Greek-speaking area, displays accommodation rather than the form of arrogance observed in the soldier at Apul. *Met.* 9.39 (see VI above).

---

[156] These are discussed at length by Coles (1966). A few further examples published since then are listed at *P. Oxy.* LXIII.4381 (p. 82); see also below, n. 158.

A slight but striking variation on the above pattern can be seen in *P. Ross.-Georg.* v.18 (AD 213).[157] The text records proceedings before the prefect Baebius Iuncinus. Once again the speeches, both by the prefect and the advocate, are in Greek, but the framework in this case is only partly in Latin: the advocate's words are introduced in Greek, those of the prefect in Latin. This inconsistency calls for explanation (see p. 387). Note Coles (1966: 37): 'In this particular case . . . the use of Latin must be simply a stylistic method of emphasising the distance between presiding officials and parties.'

Sometimes the code-switching was in the hearing itself rather than merely in the document, and it is transcripts of hearings of this type which belong in the present section. As Rea (*P. Oxy.* li.3619) remarks, the 'judge in these cases usually speaks Greek, but he may address his staff in Latin . . . and give judgements in Latin'. A collection of documents which have Latin at some point, whether in the framework or in the speeches, can be found at *CPL* pp. 431–7, though Cavenaile only prints the Latin parts, which are difficult to interpret without the Greek in which they are embedded. A list of these bilingual texts can also be found at Coles (1966: 59–63).[158]

It seems likely that, if the transcripts do justice to the actual hearings, the code-switching did, on occasions at least, have the nature of stressing the judge's power. The official who in the presence of Greek speakers in a Greek-speaking region addresses other officials in Latin excludes monolingual Greeks, and thereby places them in a position of momentary uncertainty. Similarly in informal settings code-switching by bilinguals in the presence of monolinguals will cast the latter as outsiders.

One of the most common forms of instruction to court personnel in such reports (whether in Greek or bilingual) was the order to beat one of the participants, 'not as a punishment but generally to elicit information' (Coles 1966: 48). There was such an instruction in Latin at *P. Oxy.* li.3619, where the expression *quo uexato* occurs in a fragmentary text:

23–4 . . . πῶς ἐπράθη ὁ σῖτος. Apollọṇius ex[
    ]. um. (*vac.*) quọ ụẹxato.

This is undoubtedly the use of *uexo* = 'beat'. Rea (*P. Oxy.* li, p. 51 and line 24) comments: 'I take it that the *praeses* spoke here to his staff in Latin,

---

[157] Discussed by Coles (1966: 37), Kaimio (1979a: 146).
[158] To the material cited there may be added *P. Wisc.* ii.48.42–3, but unfortunately the context is too fragmentary to be comprehensible. It is though clear that there was some Latin in a speech. See also *P. Oxy.* lxiii.4381, discussed below, 5.iv.2.1.

saying something like *uexa] eum*, and that "*quo uexato*" means "when he had been beaten".' If this reconstruction is correct (and it is undoubtedly along the right lines: see below), the instruction to beat a witness delivered in a language that the witness might not have understood would probably have been threatening, the more so since the uncertainty of the witness about the meaning of the words would only have been cleared away as the beating was administered.

A similar, and particularly interesting, text is found at *P. Lips.* 40 (fourth/fifth century, Hermopolis). Here the speeches are (largely) in Greek, but are introduced in Latin in the manner described above (e.g. col. ii, line 2 *Fl(auius) Leontius Beronicianu(s) u(ir) c(larissimus) pr(aeses) Tebaei(dis) d(ixit)*). Though Beronicianus usually speaks Greek, at col. ii, line 7 he gives orders in Latin that a witness be stripped: '*expolia'. c[u]mque expoliatus fuisset, d(ixit)*... It is of note that after the order of the *praeses* is quoted, the commentary continues in Latin, with the verb *expoliare* repeated. Thus Rea's reconstruction of *P. Oxy.* LI.3619 above must be correct. Again the switch of codes seems to humiliate the witness as an object whose comprehension or otherwise of the proceedings is, momentarily at least, immaterial.

But the matter is complicated by col. iii, lines 20–3, the salient parts of which I quote:

20 Fl. Leontius Beronician(us) u. c. pr. Tebaei(dis) dixit: τίνος ἕνεκεν ἐπῆλθες τῷ βουλευτῇ; et ad officium d(ixit): τυπτέσθω. et cum buneuris caesus fuisset,
21 Fl. Leontius Beronicianus u. c. pr. Tebaei(dis) d(ixit): ἐλευθέρους μὴ τύπτητε. et ad officium d(ixit): parce. cumque pepertum ei fuisset . . .

The *praeses* puts a question (in Greek) to the witness, and orders the staff in Greek to beat the witness (interrogation under torture). The *praeses* then forbids in Greek the beating of freemen,[159] and instructs the staff (in Latin) to spare the witness. It will be seen that the *praeses* addresses his staff in both Greek and Latin, but that his instruction to administer the beating is in Greek, and that to stop the beating is in Latin. This pattern obviously does not fit that suggested above for *P. Oxy.* LI.3169, because the *praeses* uses τυπτέσθω rather than a Latin verb. Nor is there a neat division between the formal speeches (in Greek) and address to or between members of the staff. Exchanges of the latter type are indifferently in Greek and Latin rather than in Latin alone. But the code-switching does not occur in the formal speeches by president or advocates. In those, in which all details had to be understood by the

---

[159] The interpretation of the text at this point is problematical: see *P. Lips.* 40, p. 133 n.

parties in question, accommodation (to a Greek-speaking society) was absolute. The code-switching between the members of the staff might on the other hand have expressed a degree of solidarity among outsiders in a non-Latin speaking society. Even if Latin was not used consistently in these exchanges, its presence, if only in moderate doses, must have created an element of uncertainty among Greek-speaking monolinguals, and promoted in their eyes the mystique of the officials. And even if there was no significant uncertainty on a particular occasion, occasional switching into the language of the imperial power would have effectively symbolised the Romanness of that power, and have left no doubt that this was a Roman hearing, whatever the linguistic accommodation being made to the Greek-speaking participants. The use of Greek reflects the need for comprehensibility, that of Latin or mixed-language utterances the exclusion of some hearers for a moment from the proceedings, and a desire on the part of the officials to present themselves symbolically as representatives of Rome and as an exclusive group. Linguistic exclusion may under differing circumstances be (e.g.) offensive or threatening or a cause of anxiety; in other words, it can be an expression of power. Both convergence and divergence need only be partial to achieve symbolic effects: a small amount of Latin links the officials together, and sets them apart from monolingual Greeks.

PSI 1309, the report of a hearing before the *praeses* of a *prouincia*, shows a further development in these hearings. As usual the framework is in Latin (note col. I, line 1 *R]ufinus prot/d(ixit)* εἰ Μανίκιος δύναταί τι εἰπεῖν). But what is different here is that the *praeses* (referred to in the text as *u(ir) c(larissimus) pr(aeses)*) seems regularly to have *spoken* in Latin, as well as being introduced in that language. This is particularly clear at col. II, line 7, where one of the advocates, Rufinus, takes up the words of the president, but translates them into Greek: *u(ir) c(larissumus) pr(aeses) Rufino d(ixit)* **confides negotio tuo**? *Rufinus d(ixit)* πέποιθα τῷ ἐμῷ πράγματι ... Nor is this an isolated case of the use of Latin by the *praeses*. Note too col. II, line 3 *u c pr d(ixit) transeunt eloquentissi[m]i uiri in partem [..., col. II, line 10 *u c pr d(ixit) hoc praecepi*, line 15 *[u c pr d(ixit) ...] propterea confundis iudis et ... sic uter [...*

This is the form of code-switching which consists of changes of language as different speakers take their turn (on which see above, I.V. n. 55, and below, VI.2, p. 393). The effect here is to render the president aloof from the participants, who are allowed to use Greek, but required to understand what is said to them in Latin. The *praeses* must have understood Greek, but have chosen not to speak it. The different linguistic behaviour of *praeses* and participants here recalls the way in which at *P. Ross.-Georg.* v.18 the prefect is introduced in Latin in the documentary framework but the other participants in Greek (see above). There is a subtle symbolic use of Latin at work in both cases. The Latin language in a Greek setting is exploited to establish a distinction between the chairman, who is in the position of dominance, and the others. In the one document it is his own use of Latin in speech that has this function, whereas in the other it is in the written record that his introduction by means of Latin sets him apart from the others. There is a parallel to the language use of *PSI* 1309 above in an incomplete passage of the Theodosian Code (8.15.1). A plaintiff speaks in Greek, but the judge in Latin: *Agrippina d(ixit):* τῷ τόπῳ ἐκείνῳ οὐκ ἐπαγάρχει. *Constantinus A. d(ixit): sed iure continetur* . . . Constantinus continues at some length in Latin, then Agrippina speaks again in Greek, and finally there is more Latin from Constantinus. It may be deduced that this procedure was common.

Decisions were also sometimes given in Latin. An early example of this type is *P. Oxy.* XLII.3016 (AD 148), 'an extract from the prefectoral daybook' (Parsons ad loc.) which presumably records proceedings in the prefect's court. The surviving part takes the form of a genitive absolute in Greek, meaning 'when the decisions of the *xenokritai* (who are listed by name) had been read out', followed by fragments of the decisions quoted verbatim in Latin:

4–5 ἀναγνωσθεισῶν ἀποφάσεων ξενοκριτῶν. . .
13] mulier de qua agitur . . . (further fragmentary Latin)

Parsons observes (58): 'The *xenokritai* in this document number fifteen; they are Roman citizens; they return a decision in Latin. It is obviously likely, though not to be proved, that they functioned in Egypt.' The switch into Latin to give (or record) a decision looks like an attempt to symbolise the Romanness of power even in circumstances in which, for practical purposes, there was no alternative but to conduct proceedings in Greek.[160]

---

[160] As far as recorded (as distinct from spoken) decisions are concerned, it is worth noting the official subscription *edantur* 'let a summons be served' which is attested several times at the end of records in which the speeches are in Greek. *P. Oxy.* XVI.1877, a report of proceedings for debt dated *c.* 488, has a Latin framework and Greek speeches, including a judgment of the *praeses* (lines 12–13), to the effect that some of the participants were 'either to discharge their obligations or to make a formal defence' (p. 74). Then there follows the Latin *edantur*. The same usage is found at Zilliacus (1941: 35), 4 = *CPL* p. 433 no. 8. I quote sect. B, lines 26–8: *Strategi(us) u(i)r p(erfectissimus) comes pres(es) Thebei(dos) d(ixit):* εἰ παραστήσειας αὐτὸν τοῖς ἀπαιτηταῖς οὐκ ἐνοχληθήσει ὑπὲρ αὐτῶν. *edantur. Fl(auius) Antirus exceptor obtuli.* See now also Kramer (1990).

At *P. Ryl.* IV.653 and *P. Thead.* 13, both of which record hearings in the 320s before the same man, Q. Iper, *praeses Aegypti Heracleae*, the plaintiffs speak Greek and the *praeses* Latin, but here the Latin states decisions, and it is not certain that Iper (like the *praeses* at *PSI* 1309 above and the official in the passage of the Theodosian Code) used only that language throughout the hearing. The judgment, in formal and difficult Latin, is followed by a translation (in a different hand) of that judgment into Greek in both documents (Coles (1966: 36–7)). The translation is a form of accommodation motivated by the need to make things clear to the participants, but it need not have been provided in the spoken proceedings. Whatever the case, the switch into Latin can be interpreted as a symbolic move into the language which, though it was that of only a minority in Egypt itself, was nevertheless that of the imperial power. The use of Latin before Greek speakers to reveal an official decision, followed by the condescending provision of a Greek translation, is an act which can be paralleled in the second century BC in another part of the Greek world (see below, 5.IV.3). Language use and language choice as acts of power will be dealt with in greater detail in the chapter on Egypt (5.III–IV), and it will become possible to observe the function of the Latin in the present documents in a wider context.

I note in passing that there is another type of code-switching in the written record of *P. Ryl.* 653 above. The date (col. i) is given in Latin as well as Greek: *die III nonas Iunias* Παῦνι θ´. As we have seen (see above, V, on *IGUR* 746, with the bibliography at n. 118), code-switching in bilingual societies often takes the form of the repetition of a remark in a second language for the sake of clarity or emphasis. The need for such bilingual elucidation is particularly obvious where two different dating systems coexist, and for that reason it is no surprise that bilingual dates are quite common. I cite in passing some examples:

(1) *P. Vindob. Lat.* 1a, *CPL* 247, *CEL* 8.

This is a private letter in Latin from Egypt of relatively early date (24–21 BC), of military provenance to judge by line 12 *contubernales mei te salutant.* One Paconius writes to Macedo. The letter ends with a bilingual date giving the day of the month both in Latin (and Latin script) and in Greco-Egyptian form (in Greek script): *XIIII K(al.) August(as)* Ἐπεὶφ κζ´.

The Latin date (19 July) differs slightly from the Greek (21 July), but that is undoubtedly because of a mistake rather than of an attempt to distinguish between date of dispatch and date of receipt.[161]

---

[161] So Sijpesteijn (1984: 95); cf. above, V.2, on the bilingual from the Berenice road.

(2) *P. Fior.* II.278 = *CPL* 145, col. II (part of a very fragmentary military text): *X Kal. Aug.* Ἐπεὶφ κθ΄ (23 August; the period is late second or early third century).

This text is uninformative because of its poor state of preservation, but light is thrown on such double dates by a substantial number of cases in one particular type of document (birth certificates), to which I turn.

(3) *CPL* 148 = Cairo 29812 = *P. Mich.* III.167 *app.* is a birth certificate which contains the following date as part of the interior text: *P. Mario L. Afinio Gallo cos.* **X K. Augustas** *anno VIII Neronis Claudii Caesaris Augusti Germanici Imp.* **mense Epiph die XXIX**. Here the month and day of the month are stated according to both systems. There is not a change of language and script in the Egyptian date as there is in the previous examples, but cases such as this do illuminate the motivation of double dates. The nature of the document is significant: it is above all in a birth certificate that exactitude of dating must be achieved, and the effect is to remove any possibility of misunderstanding in a society in which not everyone was *au fait* with the Roman system. The first date is in line with formal Roman practice and helps to confer official status on the document, whereas the second is for the benefit of locals.

Numerous such dates are attested in birth certificates of more or less identical form. For simplicity I give references only to *CPL*: 150, 151, 152, 153, 154, 155, 156, 157, 162. All of these documents are from the second century. The last has the official text in Latin, with a Greek résumé. The double date is in the Latin part but not the Greek, a fact which illustrates the relative status of the two parts.

(4) It was not only birth certificates which employed this method of dating. Another example is found in the *manumissio inter amicos*, *P. Amh. Lat.* = *CPL* 172, discussed in another connection above, v.4. The Latin part has the following date (there is nothing equivalent in the Greek declarations): **VII Kal. Augustas** *Grato et Seleuco cos. anno IIII Imp. Caesaris Marci Aureli Antonini Pii Felicis Aug.* **mense Mesore die I**.

I conclude this section. It is assumed in the above discussion of the records of hearings that the language switching in the speeches in these documents is a reflection of what actually happened in the hearings themselves. Another interpretation might be to see the switching as a purely clerical device characterising the *written* record alone. To take this view would in my opinion be extreme. The Latin framework (whereby speakers are introduced) is obviously a written convention, but the switches of language in the speeches themselves are of a different order. I have suggested that two determinants were at work in the switching in speeches.

The code-switcher on the one hand diverges from the normal language use of some of the other participants in the case as an act of exclusion or symbolic power, and on the other hand converges with his fellow officials as an act of solidarity. The *praeses* at *PSI* 1309 adopted an extreme means of detaching himself from the advocates, by addressing them only in Latin and expecting them to understand him, though they themselves were using Greek. We also saw various symbolic uses of Latin in the framework of the reports; in general the Latin framework in a report of proceedings conducted in Greek underlines the fact that this is Roman record keeping.

There is a partial parallel between Roman linguistic policy in legal hearings in Egypt and that of the legal profession in South Africa in recent years under the old regime.[162] Advocates could address a judge in either official language (English or Afrikaans) since the judge was expected to know both, but for many years judgments were always given in English, until Afrikaner nationalists began to make a point of giving judgments in Afrikaans. English was chosen not as the language of law (which was basically Roman-Dutch), but as the language of the conqueror, as it were. Its role was very much the same as that of Latin in Egypt. It is also possible to parallel the use by a professional class in court of a language alien to that of many of the participants in such legal actions. In later medieval England (say, of the thirteenth century) there is evidence that proceedings were conducted in Norman French, though at least some of those who appeared in court were English-speaking only.[163] I quote Brand (2000: 66): 'there were advantages to the professional elite who came to dominate legal practice in using a language which needed to be learned and mastered by outsiders and which enhanced their mystique'.

One of the most interesting mixed-language reports of hearings is *P. Oxy.* LXIII.4381, which will be discussed in the chapter on Egypt (5.IV.2.1). The hearing in this case was military, and it took place before the *dux Aegypti*.

VI.2 Code-switching and dates

Examples of code-switching to express dates have just been cited. Earlier, in other connections, a letter by a Roman slave Cerinthus (*P. Oxy.* II.244), containing a switch from Latin to Greek in the date, two Egyptian Latin inscriptions with dates in Greek, and a Republican inscription of

---

[162] I owe the following information to Tony Honoré.   [163] See Brand (2000).

indeterminate language in Greek script (*IGUR* 718), with the Latinate date αντι διον τερτιον νωναις, were discussed (3.II (5), I.IX (5)). The motivations of these various switches are not all the same. I now add some further comments on code-switching and dates (for which, in a slightly different connection, see also below, VIII), in the general context of code-switching as underlining political power. There is a use of Latin in dates in Greek official documents in Egypt which sometimes seems to serve as a means of validating the document itself.

The hearing before Caracalla at Antioch in Syria (see Roussel and Visscher (1942–3), and above, VI.1) begins with some Latin comprising a consular and calendar date, and full titles of the emperor and a detailed preamble. It is the content of the Greek speeches that would be of interest to readers in this area, but the Latin date and titles have a symbolism. This use of Latin recalls that (expressing imperial titulature) in various texts discussed in the last chapter (see 2.V.3, V.5.2).

P. Oxy. XLIII.3129 was addressed in AD 335 by the prefect Flavius Philagrius to the *strategus* of the Oxyrhynchite nome, one Synesius, instructing him to make an investigation. The letter has the particular interest that 'it is an original issued from the prefect's chancery' (J. Rea ad loc., p. 99). The letter is in Greek, but the consular date at the end is in Latin (*[Iulio Consta]ntio u(iro) c(larissimo) pat[r]icio fratre d(omini) n(ostri)* ...), and there is also a Latin calendar date in the margin, *dat* (for *data* = 'issued') *kal. octobr.*, possibly with traces of *Alexandriae* as representing the place of issue (so Rea at a later date on *P. Oxy.* L.3577 (p. 195)). This sort of marginal notation (possibly in this document in a different hand from that of the consular date, according to Rea (p. 100), though on *P. Oxy.* L.3577 (p. 195) he expresses greater uncertainty) seems to represent an old Latin convention; it is found at *P. Dura* 56, B, C = *ChLA* 6.311 (a document concerning the *probatio* of horses, and entirely in Latin).[164] It is of note that ἔρρωσο at the end of the document *P. Oxy.* XLIII.3129 above (placed without spacing right at the end of the text, presumably, as Rea suggests on *P. Oxy.* L.3577 (p. 193), as a means of preventing unauthorised additions and hence serving as a validation), which is likely to be the autograph of the prefect,[165] is in the language of the text as a whole, and this makes the use of Latin for both parts of the date particularly striking.

P. Oxy. L.3577 shares many of the features of the above text. Again it is an original letter from a chancery, this time of a governor (Flavius Julius Ausonius) of Augustamnica. It is dated 28 January 342, and addressed

---

[164] See Rea on *P. Oxy.* L.3577 (p. 192). See also *P. Oxy.* L.3579.   [165] See Rea ad loc. (p. 99).

to Aetius and Dioscorus, leading citizens of Oxyrhynchus, in a rather peremptory tone on a matter to do with the improper collection of a tax on traders. Again the letter is in Greek but the date in Latin, and that in two parts, a consular date at the end of the document (*d(ominis) n(ostris) Const[ant]io Aug(usto) ter et Constante Aug(usto) iterum co(n)s(ulibus)*) and a marginal note in the form *dat(a) V Kal(endas) Febr(uarias) Heracl(eopoli)*, the place name indicating the place of issue. Rea (ad loc., p. 195) notes that the 'Latin consular date is obviously in a very different script [from the body of the text of the letter], but also the ink is lighter and the pen was perhaps thinner, so that there is good reason to believe that a second person wrote it, perhaps a senior clerk'. Rea does not express a firm view about the hand of the marginal notation, but he does put forward the possibility that it might be equivalent to a countersignature.

ChLA 5.285 is a fragment, perhaps an official proclamation in the form of a letter, issuing from a certain Proclus. The content in unclear. There is a Latin consular date (AD 357) at the end of the Greek text: *]d(ominis) n(ostris) Constantio Aug(usto) VIIII et Cl. Iulian[o II]*.

ChLA 3.207 is an order 'from the centurion Domitius Annianus to the elders and public officials of the village of Taurinus to see that the usual guard is kept' (p. 89), dated to the second or third century. The text, in Greek, is followed by *III Kal(endas) Apriles*. The editors insist that the whole document is the work of a single hand with 'strongly marked Latin characteristics' in its Greek portion (for which phenomenon they cite as parallels *P. Oxy.* 1.122, *BGU* 815). This letter is of a particular type, in that it expresses an order, and the Latin date perhaps confers something of an official status on the text.

The examples cited are mainly from the post-Diocletianic period. Dates readily take on official status, in that they confer, particularly on a legalistic document, a precision and authenticity which an undated agreement cannot have. From the period after Diocletian the distinctively Roman type of date, that by the names of the consuls, becomes very common in Egypt,[166] usually, it is true, translated into Greek in Greek documents rather than put into Latin, the second language. Nevertheless it is easy to understand why code-switching might sometimes have taken place. The presence of a Roman-style date in an official document emanating from the Roman administration is symbolic in a sense of Roman domination, and if that date is also in the Latin language the symbolism is enhanced. Code-switching in this sphere is not so common that

---

[166] See Bagnall and Worp (1978: 150).

there was necessarily an official policy at work, but certain individuals were clearly attached to this method of distancing themselves from their addressees. It must be stressed that two general types of texts are at issue here. There are those in which the first writer himself changes languages in the date, and those in which the date is in a second hand. The second phenomenon is only loosely classifiable as code-switching, though it is analogous to that form of switching in speech which involves a change of languages with a change of speaker (generally described as code-switching).[167] It is possible that some documents were authenticated by the insertion of a date or other marginal notation by a second person.

In Chapter 5 some documents, largely from Egypt, will be discussed in which, though code-switching is not on the whole at issue, Roman dates have bureaucratic significance (see 5.IV.6). There are, for example, petitions addressed to Roman officials such as the prefect in Latin or Greek or both which contain Latin-style consular dates, even though there is internal evidence in the document that the petitioner would normally have used the Egyptian dating system. The incorporation of the consular date must be seen as an official requirement in texts which involve Roman citizens or Roman law, and is evidence of the importance attached by officials to Roman dates in certain contexts. The attitude inherent in the requirement may sometimes have inspired a switch of codes (into Latin) when a date was given, as in some of the texts discussed in this section; see also below, VIII.

VI.3 Power: code-switching and passwords and the like

Among the ostraca from Mons Claudianus in the eastern desert of Egypt (see further, 5.VII.2.1) there are (to date) twenty-five lists of *uigiles* designated for duty at Mons Claudianus (II.309–36), written predominantly in Greek. The following is a typical example:

O. Claud. II.320
ιαʹ
I Νεῖλος
III Παμῖνεις
IIII Ἡρακλίδης
II Διόσκορος
II Ἑρμίας

---

[167] See e.g. Romaine (1995: 122–3), and above, I.V, n. 55 and p. 386.

Ι Ψε<ν>ταῆσις
ΙΙΙΙ ᾽Απολινάρις
ΙΙΙ Σαραπίων ᾽Απολ( )
ιβ ́ φρυγονατο
Σαραπίων ᾽Απολ( )
σίγνεν
Μαρτις.

Note the remarks of the editor (Bülow-Jacobsen), p. 166: 'The lay-out is everywhere the same: the first hand writes the date [in Greek form, comprising a Greek letter with a stroke superscript], then eight names [in Greek], then the date of the following day [again in Greek form] and φρυγονατο(ι) [an unknown word which must, according to the editor, derive from φρύγανα = 'firewood'] and one more name, which was often already on the list, but sometimes chosen among those who were not on duty. Hand 2 then adds Roman numerals in random order opposite the eight names, first from 1 to 4 and then again from 1 to 4. Hand 2 finally adds σίγνεν (= *signum*) and writes the password. It must somehow have been important to keep an element of surprise in which number (i.e. presumably which watch) was given to each man.' The Greek dates represent days of the (Egyptian) month; in two texts (335, 336) the month is named (Μεσορή, Φαρμοῦθι).

The numerals assigning the order of duties are Roman, whereas that in the date is a Greek symbol. There must be significance to this distinction (for which see above, 1.VII.4.1). The password at the end, though written in Greek characters, is in the Latin language (*Martis*). The passwords in the group of documents include the following: Κονκορδια, Φορτουνα, Μαρτις, Μινερουα, Πακε, Πιετατις, Σαλουτις Εινπερατ(ορις), Ουεστα, Ουικτορι, some of them with unambiguously Latin inflections, such as the genitive and the ablative. They are not therefore loan-words into Greek, but represent a switch of languages. There is good evidence that in the Byzantine army some stereotyped orders were given in Latin,[168] though the army was Greek-speaking, and this document would appear to offer a partial anticipation of that convention.

---

[168] The evidence is found e.g. in ps.-Mauricius, *Strategicon* 3.5, 12 B.14, and is discussed in detail by Zilliacus (1935: 126–40), Lot (1946) and Reichenkron (1961). Orders include *aequaliter ambula*, *largiter ambula, ad latus stringe, ordinem seruate*. 3.5, for example, begins thus: δεῖ μανδάτορα παραγγέλλειν οὕτως· σιλεντιον, νεμο δεμιττατ, νεμο αντεκεδατ βανδουμ... The writer's awareness of the language shift involved is explicitly noted at 3.5, 10–11 (Dennis), where the instruction is given that, if the squadron is to be moved, one should do so through the verb *mouere* rather than κινεῖν: καὶ εἰ μὲν θέλει κινῆσαι, σημαίνειν τῇ φωνῇ· μοβε, αντὶ τοῦ κίνσον. For further bibliography, see Rochette (1997a: 143 n. 354).

A near parallel to the use of Latin passwords at Mons Claudianus can be found at *O. Amst.* 8 frg. *e. O. Amst.* 8–15 have to do with the assignment of posts in *stationes*, that is the posts of military police stationed in the Egyptian countryside.

8 frg. *e* 'appears to contain two different items. In Column I a list is given by date (16th – 21st) of *stationes*. Most of the names are lost, which were clearly written in Greek, but the *stationes* are numbered 1–4, first in transliterated Latin ordinals, then with Roman numerals I–IV. A similar list is preserved in *9*, where four numbered stations again appear [with Roman numerals I–IV]' (*O. Amst.*, p. 6).

For example, the start of 8 frg. *e*, col. I is as follows:

[σ]τατίωνες ιϚ′
[Πετοσῖ]ρεις **πριμα**
['Απώ]νεῖς **σεκονδα**
[Αἴλε]ις **τερτια**
[. . .]ωφεις **κορτα**.

In a second hand there is another list like this, with full Roman ordinals (one of which, σεκουντα, betrays phonetic interference from Greek: see 4.V.I.I), but thereafter in the same fragment (Column I) Roman numeral symbols are used instead.[169] At Mons Claudianus we saw above the use of Roman numerals in handing out duties, but this document is the more revealing because the Latin ordinals are not mere symbols but are spelt in full: they represent a change of languages.[170] Again, as at Mons Claudianus, Greek numeral symbols are used for the date. It is to be assumed that the personnel in these documents were not speakers of Latin as their primary language, and the fact that the assignments are in Greek script points to the nature of their literacy. In these two sets of texts then there is a hint that the assignment of watch duties was partly carried out in Latin by means of key words with Latin morphology even in units where Greek was the predominating language. The switch into Latin at the moment when instructions were transmitted might be seen as symbolising the fact that this was the Roman army and that Latin was the language of Rome, however liberal might have been the linguistic attitudes generally prevailing in the remote outposts of Egypt. We know moreover from Vegetius (*Mil.* 3.5.4) that the passwords had to be *spoken*

---

[169] On the other hand in Col. II in a third hand *Greek* numeral symbols are used.
[170] Some unclassified references to Latin ordinals in Greek papyri can be found in Meinersmann (1927: 49, 96, 99), cited by Clarysse and Sijpestein (1988: 95). For our purposes it is necessary to know in any given case whether the ordinal represents code-switching or borrowing, and Meinersmann's material needs closer examination.

by members of the watch, in these cases apparently with the correct *Latin* inflections; in some cases the member of the watch would presumably embed the Latin word in Greek speech. The code-switching in these cases symbolises authority.

I would call code-switching of this type 'institutionalised', in that it is a formal method of communication used under restricted circumstances in an institution (see below, XI).

VII A SPECIAL CASE: CODE-SWITCHING IN THE *SUBSCRIPTIO* OF LETTERS

What appears to be one and the same form of code-switching may have different motivations, depending on the circumstances. A form of expression which in one context might constitute an act of convergence might on another occasion be seen as an act of divergence (see also above, IV.1). Unfortunately we often do not know much of the context of a code-switch from antiquity, and a lot of material is difficult to interpret. I illustrate such complexities of interpretation in this section in a discussion of second-language *subscriptiones* in papyrus letters. The section is placed here because there do seem to be cases of the phenomenon which represent mild assertions of power, but there is rather more to such *subscriptiones* than that, and it is necessary to allow all possible determinants.

In letters on papyrus a *subscriptio* is sometimes in a different language from that of the rest of the letter (see above, II (5) on the letter of Cerinthus). If the conventional view is accepted, such *subscriptiones* will usually have been in the hand of the author.[171] While it is understandable that the *subscriptio* should be written by the sender himself to add a personal touch if he had used a scribe for the main body of the text, it is not immediately clear why a switch of languages should have taken place. One obvious possibility is that the sender might have been illiterate in the other language, but if so the question arises why he had had the body of the letter written in a language which was not his first choice when he took up a pen himself. Perhaps sometimes the linguistic competence of the addressee was the determinant of the language chosen for the main part of the letter; but if the addressee lacked competence in the other language, why send the personal greeting in that language? It is not clear that scholars who have noted the phenomenon have considered its implications sufficiently. For example, Bagnall (1993: 232), commenting

---

[171] See J. D. Thomas on *P. Mert.* III.115 for bibliography. See too Youtie (1981–2: 757, index s.v. 'Subscriptions').

on *P. Abinn.* 16 (see below), points out merely that the letter comes from an archive connected with the military, and the editor of *P. Oxy.* LV.3793 observes (p. 66) that the Latin *subscriptio* 'suggests that [the sender] was a soldier'. Cf. p. 63 'His farewell is in Latin, which makes it probable that he was a military subordinate of the *dux*' (cf. n. 2). That is not, in itself, enough to explain the switch of languages. Many soldiers could write Greek (far more Greek than Latin survives in the name of soldiers), and if the two soldiers in question here could not it is strange that they should have had the main body of their letters written in that language. I cite the evidence of some letters, and then discuss the problem further. To the evidence cited here might be added *ChLA* 3.207, a letter in Greek with a Latin date at the end, which has been discussed briefly above, VI.2.

(1) *P. Abinn.* 16. Sakikas, *praepositus* of a *uexillatio*, writes in Greek to Abinnaeus, with a Latin greeting in what is taken to be his own hand (*et te per multos annos be[n]e ualere*). The archive of Abinnaeus is in both languages, and there is explicit evidence that Abinnaeus knew both (see 5.IV.2). It would not do to suggest that Sakikas chose Greek because of the limited linguistic abilities of the addressee.

(2) *P. Oxy.* LV.3793. This is a letter about the supply of craftsmen for government works. 'The sender ... had been ordered by Flavius Valacius, the *dux Aegypti*, to inspect all the military forts in the province and to report back to him any repair or renovation that any of them might need.' The letter is to the Oxyrhynchite *curator*, asking that he send a craftsman. The greeting is as follows: *opto bene ualeas per multos ann[os]*. In another hand there are the remains of a consular date in Latin: *[u] (iris) c(larissimis) cons* (on this phenomenon, see above, VI.2).

(3) *P. Mert.* III.115 is a private letter 'to a person addressed by the writer as his son, though there was clearly no blood relationship between them. After a familiar complaint by the writer that he has received no letters he goes on to offer the recipient fatherly advice about his behaviour' (J. D. Thomas, p. 52 ad loc.).

There is then a greeting in Latin (*opto te fili bene ualere*), in a second hand. Thomas notes (p. 52): 'Although we must suppose that he used Latin because this was his native tongue, the letter makes it plain that he was also well-versed in Greek, and the style is that of an educated person.'

It should first be noted that it cannot be deduced from such a greeting that Latin was necessarily the native language of the sender. We have seen (II (5)) that the letter of Cerinthus (*P. Oxy.* II.244) has a Latin greeting with two switches into Greek and Greek interference in the syntax of the filiation, features which imply that Cerinthus' Latin was imperfect. Greek was his first language, and he chose his weaker language for the greeting.

I review various possible explanations for such code-switching in letters.

(1) The sender was illiterate in Greek (see further above), and when he came to add a greeting he was forced to use Latin. This explanation would not hold for the letter of Cerinthus, but it cannot be ruled out in all cases. It is not, however, particularly compelling in any of the examples that have been cited above. It was observed that the Greek body of the private letter *P. Mert.* III.115, which was presumably dictated to a scribe, is in an educated style of Greek. Is it conceivable that the sender could speak educated Greek but not be able to use it in written form?

(2) A more mundane determinant was the linguistic competence of the scribes who happened to be available at the time (on this factor, see 5.1.4). If the scribe on hand was illiterate in Latin script, then a letter would have to be written in Greek (or at least Greek script), and the *subscriptio* might then be put in Latin if that was the sender's preferred language. It would not do though to fall back on this factor as the only or main determinant of the language choice in private letters from bilingual communities. Sometimes there are clues in a text that, though, say, language A was being used, the scribe was also competent in the writing of language B. In the Latin letters of Claudius Terentianus (*P. Mich.* VIII.467–71), which were certainly written by a variety of scribes, there are traces of the graphemic influence of Greek, and these suggest that the scribe was also familiar with the writing of Greek (see 5.1.4). And there are many documents in Greek or Latin on materials such as papyrus in which letter shapes show the influence of the other language (see 1.VII.4.1, 5.1.4), and these were probably the work of bi-literate scribes.

(3) The sender assumed that his addressee was more fluent in Greek than in Latin, and reserved his Latin (perhaps his mother tongue) for the greeting. The sender was thus bilingual, but his language of primary literacy (or mother tongue) was Latin, so that when he took up a pen it was more natural for him to use that language, almost as his signature. This would seem to be roughly the view of Thomas in relation to *P. Mert.* III.115. This explanation might well hold good in some cases, but not that of the letter of Cerinthus, who was forcing himself to use Latin when he did not have complete facility in it.

(4) Another possibility is that the switch of languages was an implicit acknowledgment that both sender and addressee were bilingual, a mark

of shared membership of an in-group. Greek-speaking Roman soldiers (like Sakikas in the Abinnaeus archive) might well occasionally have written Latin *subscriptiones* for this reason, as an acknowledgment that they belonged to the Roman institution *par excellence*. I refer here again to Wenskus' observation (1998) that what she calls 'emblematic' code-switching is often found at the end of literary letters (see above, III.10), presumably as a mark of shared bilingualism.

(5) But sometimes the switch into Greek might have been an act of divergence, that is a deliberate and symbolic departure from the pre-ferred language of the addressee, and here I return to the general theme of code-switching and power. Why did Cerinthus, who had some trouble with Latin, add a *subscriptio* in that language to his letter to a local nome official, who is likely to have been a native speaker of Greek, the language indeed of the body of the letter? The Latin will undoubtedly have given Cerinthus a partly Romanised identity, and hence might have been intended to place him in a position of superiority in relation to a local Greek (to whom he was giving instructions). On this view (which is admittedly speculative) code-switching as an expression of identity and code-switching as symbolical of power come together. The categories set up in this chapter constantly run into one another.

Factors (4) and (5) are in my opinion probably the most important.

VIII CODE-SWITCHING AND THE EXPRESSION OF BUREAUCRATIC INFORMATION: SOME REMARKS ON 'DIGLOSSIA' AND THE LANGUAGE OF AUTHORITY

Various inscriptions have already been noted in which personal details about the deceased, such as the name and complimentary epithets, are in one language (usually Greek), but what I have called 'bureaucratic' details, such as date of death, burial formulae (for the term see above, V.2; note too the discussion of *IGUR* 570 at IV) are in another, for our purposes Latin. Into this category fall e.g. *IG* XIV.678 (see V.2) and *IGUR* 972 (the inscription in the name of one Zoticus: see V). Sometimes indeed in such inscriptions there is a change of script as well, and this fact underlines the deliberateness of the change of languages.

I now offer a few more examples in which the bureaucratic or formulaic parts of a funerary inscription are in one language, but a name or names (and also in some cases complimentary epithets) in another. Note, for example, *ILCV* 2939 (Rome, AD 345) Σωκράτης, ἀείμνηστος φίλ[ος? . . .], δηποσειτους θ΄Κ. Ωκτβ. Ἀμ[αντίου . . .] αννους τριγιντα ιν πακε. The name and epithet are in Greek, but the verb, the date and the age at death are in Latin. The mixed culture of the writer is apparent in one or two details. The numeral with αννους is in Latin, but the numeral symbol earlier in the Latin section is of Greek type. And whereas the ending of the verb δηποσειτους is transliterated Latin, that of αννους is not a transliteration of *annos* but displays the transfer into a Latin word of the Greek accusative ending (cf. δηναριους σεσκεντους in the receipt of Aeschines (I.VII.2.3), and κον φιλιους βενε μερεντες at *ILCV* 4463 (above, V.1); contrast αννως at *IGUR* 1671 (above, I.V)). The inscription reads like the effort of someone wishing to have the deceased partly commemorated in Latin, but less than assured in his control of the Latin language and its transliteration.

At *ILCV* 2953 (ἀγείᾳ θεοσεβεῖ μόνῃ φιλάνδρῳ ᾿Απολλωνείαι τῇ καλῇ ὁ εἴδιος ᾿Απολλόδωρος. *deposita VII Kal. Maias* (Rome)) the bureaucratic section is of a more restricted type (a date accompanied by a verb of laying to rest).

The following inscriptions, all from Rome or its environs, have units of time expressed in Latin, with the rest of the text in Greek:

ICUR 4440
Συνφόρῳ αἴζησεν a[n]nu[s] XXV.

The verb is in Greek and in Greek script, but the age of the deceased consists of the Latin term *annus* (whether transliterated or not)[172] and a Roman numeral.

IG Porto 78
[. . .]ρῖνος Σερ<α>-
[πιοδ]ώρου ANV
[ἐνθ]άδε κῖτ[ε].

The inscription is in Greek, but the age of the deceased has again generated a switch of codes. *ANV* represents either *an(norum) V* or αν(νωρουμ) V.

ICUR 1867 = *ILCV* 3375A
῾Ερμαείσκε φῶς ζῆς ἐν θεῷ κυρείῳ Χρειστῷ αννωρουμ X μησωρουμ septe.

A striking inscription mainly in Greek but with the age at death expressed completely in Latin, with a switch into Latin characters not only in the numeral symbol but in the Latin word *septe*. The presence side by side

---

[172] There is some doubt about the text here. Leiwo (1995b: 299) prints the second last word in Greek characters as αιvu. If this is correct, the word would presumably still be an attempt at the same Latin term.

of the symbol X and the full Latin numeral suggests that in other Greek inscriptions which contain Roman numeral symbols the symbol may sometimes stand for a Latin numeral rather than a Greek (i.e. it may represent a switch of codes rather than a change of alphabets: on this matter, see I.VII.4.I). But it is usually impossible to know what a writer had in mind when he used such a symbol.

The following example is slightly different, but I quote it here because of its general interest:

ICUR 4025 = *ILCV* 3999
Παυλινα αννωρων κδ΄ XXIIII.

Two points may be made about this short text. First, though αννωρων obviously represents *annorum*, it is not a transliteration: the ending has been subject to Greek interference (see 4.V.3.2 for this phenomenon). Secondly, the age of the deceased is given in both Greek and Latin numerals. As has been noted, one of the most common functions of code-switching is to express the same idea in two languages (see above, V, on *IGUR* 746, and VI.I on the double date in *P. Ryl.* 653; also below, XI). A language cannot be assigned to this inscription, given that several instances have already been seen in this section of the intrusion of *annus* into Greek inscriptions. But it is certain that the writer's Latin was subject to Greek morphological interference, and that his typical bilingual's desire to achieve clarity by expressing part of an utterance in both languages implies a feeling that the text would be read by speakers of both Greek and Latin.

It does not seem to be the case, at least at Rome, that language switches of the opposite type to that just discussed occur: that is, we do not find names and personal details written in Latin but bureaucratic information in Greek.[173] If this observation is along the right lines,[174] it supports the contention that such switches are not haphazard, but reflect the social situation. Some Greeks undergoing assimilation in Rome were holding on to their names and having Greek script used to record themselves, but were sometimes adopting Latin formulae for their commemoration (cf. above, IV, on the inscription *IGUR* 570, which also falls into this category). On the other hand in the Greek-speaking city of Naples there is a funerary inscription dated AD 59 in which the deceased is commemorated in Latin but the date is given in Greek (*CIL* X.1504 = *IG* XIV.794):

[173] But see n. 96 on *IGPorto* 28.
[174] I cannot claim to have carried out an exhaustive examination of the evidence.

M. Cominio M. f. Mae(cia) Verecundo Quintia Dia filio piissimo
ἐπὶ ὑπάτων Γ(αίου) Οὐειψτανοῦ Ἀπρωνιανοῦ καὶ Γ(αίου) Φοντείου
Καπίτ(ωνος).

Leiwo (1995a: 145) comments: 'The inscription shows also the official nature of the Greek language in the city. Greek is clearly the language of bureaucracy.' The situation was the reverse of that in Rome. On this evidence at Naples Latin speakers might switch into Greek to express bureaucratic information.

Superficially we seem to get close in some of these inscriptions to a change of topic within the utterence as determining the switch. Dates and units of time are by their very nature bureaucratic, and the topic 'bureaucratic information' might, it could be argued, have helped generate the selection of Latin for part of a text which was otherwise in Greek. But there is more to the matter than that. Those Greek speakers who changed languages when writing a date were not merely responding to the topics embedded within their texts, but were assigning a particular status and function to Latin. Dates and units of time can take on an official status, as we have seen (VI.2), and Greeks who regarded Latin as appropriate for the recording of such information in a Greek text were treating Latin as the language of authority. Whereas the Roman official in Egypt who switched into Latin in a public hearing was adopting Latin to underline his own authority, the Greek at Rome who switched into Latin in a date was acknowledging the authoritative status of Latin.

If 'topic' pure and simple is not enough to explain the language mixing, the writers of the above inscriptions, and also of certain others dealt with earlier and cross-referenced at the start of this section, do seem to have been setting up a 'diglossic' opposition between Greek and Latin, with Greek, the language of 'home', having Low status, and Latin, the language of bureacratic information or authority, having High (see also above, IV). This is not the place to deal with diglossia, which will be discussed in greater detail (with bibliography) in the chapter on Egypt (5.1.3, VI). There reservations will be expressed about the applicability of a polar opposition H versus L to the use of Latin versus Greek in Egypt by the Roman authorities. But humble Greek immigrants to Rome may well have treated Greek as the L language (of family, home, etc.; note the inscription *IGUR* 570, above, IV, where ἀδελφός is used in a Latin text in explicit recognition of the family character of Greek) and Latin as the H.

But in these inscriptions perceptions of identity as well must have played their part in the language mixing. Greek could surely have been used instead of *annus*, etc. were the writers not bothered by the mixed identity of the referents in this particular society. Those conscious of a conflict of identity, in that they were Greeks in a Latin-speaking state, might well have been unhappy about expressing a purely Greek persona, and for that reason they might have seized on the bureacratic part of the text as an appropriate place to switch in order to symbolise their belonging to the Roman state.

I would offer a final speculation of a different kind about the above mixed-language inscriptions with Latin numerals and the like. Bilinguals do not necessarily count or reckon in both languages. Note Mackey (1968: 565), commenting on what he calls the 'internal' use by a bilingual of his languages: 'Some bilinguals may use one and the same language for all sorts of inner expression . . . But such is by no means always the case . . . Some count in one language and pray in another; others have been known to count in two languages but to be able to reckon only in one.' Welsh speakers speaking Welsh in shops regularly use the English numeral system, and that is at least partly because the numeral system of English is dominant all over Britain since English is the language of finance and the banking system. It is possible that an alternative or complementary factor behind the code-switching here was the tendency for some Greeks at Rome to abandon Greek numerals and measures of time entirely.

IX CODE-SWITCHING AND THE EVOCATION OF THE EXOTIC

It has already been observed (see above, III.8) that code-switching is sometimes used as evocative. As such it can be called a stylistic resource (see pp. 300, 303). If a writer dealing with the Greek world switches into the proper Greek term for something in that world, he might be said to have evoked the exotic by that means. Integrated loan-words can have the same function: it has been shown, for example, by Sedley (1999: 242–3) that Lucretius constantly uses Greek borrowings in this way. Baldwin (1992: 8) notes that in two letters of Cicero to the provincial administrators Thermus and Servilius (*Fam.* 13.53.2, 13.67.1) 'Cicero drops the technical Greek term for an assize district, διοίκησις.' The word is evocative of the Greek provinces, but it also has additional significance in this case, because Cicero demonstrates his own expertise in the technical terminology.

The phenomenon can be further illustrated from Varro. A fragment of the *Menippea* has a switch into Greek apparently in allusion to a view that provincial governors might be tempted to have affairs with local women in their provinces, a temptation which was to be resisted:[175] 176 *multi enim qui limina intrarunt integris oculis strabones sunt facti: habet quiddam enim* ἑλκυ[ι]στικὸν *prouincialis formonsula uxor.* The 'attraction' or 'drawing power' of the provincial wife is economically expressed by the Greek word, for which there might have been no ready Latin alternative.[176] But the idea could have been expressed in Latin in some other way, and the notion of the 'lexical gap' would not be compelling as an explanation of the usage. The advantage of the Greek is that it is suggestive of the exotic world in which the man might find himself, vulnerable to the charms of foreign, particularly Greek, women.[177] This then too would be a case of code-switching to evoke another world. I would suggest that a good deal of code-switching in our written texts could be described in these terms, even though it might be classified in other ways as well. A case in point is the inflecting of Greek mythological names as Greek in Latin poetic texts (see above, v.2). It is likely that such names were felt by some writers to be more suggestive of a heroic world if they did not bear everyday Latin inflections.

Varro also seems to exploit the evocativeness of a code-switch in another fragment of the *Menippea*: (98 Cèbe = 99) *Socrates, cum in uinculis publicis esset et iam bibisset* κώνειον *in exodio uitae.* Latin had its own word for 'hemlock' (*cicuta*), which was famously avoided (as mundane?) by Tacitus at *Ann.* 15.64.3 through substitution of a circumlocution. Varro's choice of the proper Greek word relocates the story, which had no doubt become thoroughly familiar to Latin speakers, back in Athens.[178] On the other hand at *Men.* 65 Cèbe (= 70) the evocation is rather of a mythical world: *non Hercules potest, qui Augeae agessit* [?] κόπρον. Cèbe (1974: 268) cites Lucian, *Fug.* 23 τὴν κόπρον ἐκκαθᾶραι αὖθις τὴν Αὐγέου. The Greek phrase may have been a familiar one; by retaining part of the Greek expression Varro was possibly also engaging in that form of literary allusiveness so common in Cicero's letters to Atticus, whereby familiar Greek phrases were quoted only in part and the reader expected to recognise the whole. Or was the Greek euphemistic in this case (see above, III.4 on Cic. *Att.* 10.13.1)? At Varro, *Men.* 210 Cèbe (= 205) *moechas* (μοιχάς) is inflected as Greek in reference to a sexual act, though the word had long since

[175] Cèbe (1980: 817) cites a good deal of evidence relevant to this supposed pattern of behaviour.
[176] Nigel Kay suggests to me that there may be some sort of medical or magical pun in this passage. The Greek adjective is used of drugs. On an interpretation along these lines *strabones* might have literal significance as well.
[177] Or was the word used as euphemistic, as a means of avoiding saying openly what was at issue? See Cèbe (1980: 818), and, on the interpretation of the fragment, id. (1980: 816–17).
[178] Cèbe (1975: 442) refers to an 'effet par évocation', following L. Deschamps.

been Latinised (*moecha*): *et rex/et misellus ille pauper amat habetque ignem intus acrem;/hic ephebum mulierauit, hic ad moechada adulescentem/cubiculum pudoris primus polluit.* This is possibly meant to evoke the 'Greek' nature of the behaviour, or alternatively of the referent, the setting or some such;[179] unfortunately there is not much context.

Greek sexual terms were capable of special resonances for Latin speakers, because of a Roman tendency to regard certain 'vices' as characteristic of the Greeks. Whereas in the private language of the correspondence between Cicero and Atticus Greek culture and language are esteemed, in public, as we have seen, things Greek were as likely as not to be disparaged by upper-class Romans, and Greek words too could take on a pejorative tone (see above, III.1 with the bibliography at n. 25). Various terms referring to passive homosexuality are borrowings from Greek (*pathicus, cinaedus, catamitus, malacus* in Plautus), with the implication that effeminacy was distinctively Greek (on the association of a Greek morpheme with types of sexuality, see below, 4.II). Whereas some Greek loanwords in Latin could readily be used pejoratively, a code-switch, because it would tend to pass between fellow hellenophiles, was less likely to take on such a tone.[180]

X UNMOTIVATED CODE-SWITCHING?

Sometimes a switch of codes may have no obvious motivation. This contention may be graphically illustrated from the veterinary writer Pelagonius, who used Greek sources but wrote in Latin. At 268.3 the manuscripts have: *nitri* ὁλκὴν *unam,* ὁποῦ Κυρηναικοῦ κυάμου μέγεθος. The source (Apsyrtus) is extant at this point: *Corpus Hippiatricorum Graecorum* I, p. 178.8–9 νίτρου ὁλκὴν μίαν, ὁποῦ Κυρηναικοῦ ἡλίκον κυάμου.

It could not be argued that Pelagonius did not know how to translate the passage, because the Latin equivalents of the expressions recur in the text. *Drachma* is used for ὁλκή; ὀπὸς Κυρηναικός appears in Latin guise at 200 (*lasere Cyrenaico*), and κυάμου μέγεθος had a standard Latin equivalent: note particularly 214 *laser magnitudinis fabae* (which would have been suitable as a rendering of Apsyrtus at this point), and cf. 303. There is a slight discrepancy between Apsyrtus' Greek and that of Pelagonius

---

[179] Cèbe (1983: 938) describes the content of the passage as follows: 'l'un a fait d'un éphèbe une femme, l'autre, chez une jeune adultère, a le premier souillé la chambre à coucher, sanctuaire de la pudeur'.

[180] Thus it is that while in the speeches of Cicero *philosophus* was used disparagingly (see Laurand (1936–8: 73)), in the private letters φιλόσοφος could by contrast be a term of praise, as we saw in a passage in which the word is used of Cicero's son (above, III.1).

at this point (ἡλίκον in the one but μέγεθος in the other), but that need not be significant, because the extant extracts of Apsyrtus come from a late compilation, and it is likely that often Pelagonius' (much earlier) text of Apsyrtus was different from that which has survived.

Was Pelagonius even aware that for once he had changed languages? It is repeatedly reported that those who switch codes are often unaware that they have done so.[181] The Greek phraseology which Pelagonius had before him was completely hackneyed. Could it be that a bilingual thoroughly familiar with a technical vocabulary in two closely associated languages might occasionally switch codes inadvertently? Not that this would be a conventional switch of codes: it is rather a momentary failure to translate.

XI FURTHER INSTITUTIONALISED CODE-SWITCHING

Code-switching in speech and a good deal even of that in writing has an *ad hoc* character: it takes place in unpredictable ways as an individual's response to situational factors. It is often inventive. On the other hand some code-switching is uninventive and stereotyped, in that it has a conventional place within certain institutions and is formulaic. The Latinate passwords which we saw at Mons Claudianus fall into this category (see above, VI.3). Equally formulaic were the Latin orders in the Byzantine army as described in the *Strategicon* (see n. 168). The Greek adverb *sophos* 'bravo' was a conventional audience response at imperial recitations (Mart. 1.3.7).[182] This last example fits a general type, in that it was a Greek critical term used to express a judgment of literary texts; but it had formulaic status, and could no doubt have been used by speakers who did not know Greek.

A nice parallel is provided by the constant use of *nica* (νίκα, imperative) even by western theatre and circus spectators as a congratulatory acclamation.[183] This turns up as early as the first century AD in Latin acclamations to gladiators at Pompeii (*CIL* IV. 1664 *nica Glaphyrine*, 3950 *Nicanor nica*), and is commonplace in the west, where it alternates with *uincas*; the two verbs are used quite indifferently, with no discernible principles of selection.[184] Cameron (1973: 79) states that the 'first professionally-trained theatre claques were introduced into Rome by Nero from Alexandria' (citing Suet. *Nero* 20), and that 'they will surely

---

[181] See (e.g.) Heller (1988: 6).   [182] See Biville (1996).

[183] There is an excellent discussion of this usage by Alan Cameron (1973:45–6, 76–80); cf. Donderer (1995: 106).

[184] See the discussion of Cameron (1973: 78–9).

have used Greek'. The usage may have come to the west in some such way, and then become institutionalised as a formulaic code-switch among Latin-speaking spectators. Some would no doubt prefer to call *nica* and the military passwords 'borrowings', but they are unlike most Greek borrowings into Latin (or Latin into Greek) in that they retain their original inflections; on a scale of alienness they are more alien than integrated loan-words.

Another such Greek formula institutionalised in the west was *zeses* (ζήσης/-αις) and the fuller *pie zeses* (πίε ζ.).[185] These occur particularly in Latin texts on gold-glass memorials found in the Catacombs:[186] e.g. Morey and Ferrari (1959), 15 *anima dulcis, fruamur nos sine bile. zeses*, 48 *dulcis anima, pie zeses uiuas*.[187] Noteworthy in the second example is the juxtaposed *uiuas* (cf. e.g. 42). This is another case of the juxtaposition of equivalents from two different languages (cf. VIII above, with references).

The code-switching seen in this section recalls an observation made earlier (III.5) about the frequency not only at Rome but in other cultures as well (including those of the modern world) of code-switches consisting of the insertion into the base language of a ready-made phrase (such as a proverb). But proverbs can be used creatively, and the would-be code-switcher has a vast store of such expressions on which he can draw. The formulae in this section had all established a connection with a particular cultural or institutional context.

XII CONCLUSIONS

In this concluding section I attempt to bring out certain themes of the chapter, to raise a few issues which need to be addressed, and to offer some further generalisations about the nature of code-switching and its motivations.

XII.1 Code-switching and the notion of the 'mixed language'

The question might be asked whether or in what sense some of the inscriptions discussed are in a mixed language. The expression 'mixed language' raises problems of definition (see also 1.IX (5) and below, 7.III). Many languages diachronically are mixed, in that they are made up of elements of more than one language. It is reported, for example, that

---

[185] See the illuminating discussion of Donderer (1995: 105–6), with bibliography; also Biville (1989b: 106–7) for this and some other similar formulae.

[186] And in funerary material from the north and the east of Gaul (Biville (1989b: 106)).

[187] For numerous examples, see the index of Morey and Ferrari (1959: 78, 79).

the variety of Aleut spoken on Mednyj, one of the Commander islands off the north-eastern coast of Russia, preserves Aleut noun morphology and non-finite verb morphology, whereas its finite verb morphology has been replaced by Russian (Romaine (1995: 69)). But it is a moot point whether synchronically such a language should be described as mixed. If there are monolingual speakers of a 'mixed' language (such that in this case, for example, they do not speak Russian), they need not necessarily be aware of its mixed origins and hence may only be speakers of a mixed language in a historical sense.

When on the other hand speakers are conscious that their speech is a 'mixture', it may not be an institutionalised language that they have to use, but a mixture whose elements they vary to suit the circumstances. Heller (1995: 168) discusses the speech of Francophone working-class women married into an Anglophone area in northern Ontario. English they value as the language of social mobility, but in the home French is used. However, among other women and in some family networks they may speak a variety which they call 'mélangé'. This though is a code-switching French–English variety rather than a language in its own right, and it may well be that the nature of the mixture varies from speaker to speaker and from occasion to occasion.

In the case of Greek–Latin mixtures, it is safer to think of code-switching in differing degrees rather than to attempt to set up some sort of formalised mixture. The Jewish community at Venusia is worthy of study in this respect. In the extant inscriptions the two alphabets are used, and there are inscriptions on the one hand unequivocally in Greek, and on the other unequivocally in Latin. Among those inscriptions in Greek script which have components from the Latin language as well as Greek, the mixture varies in a way that is consistent with code-switching (particularly of the type motivated by imperfect competence in a second language), as distinct from an institutionalised 'mixed language'. For example, the text Noy (1993), 59 (τάφος Βερενικενις πρεσβιτερες ετ φιλια Ιωσετις) makes an interesting comparison with a text quoted earlier from the same community (1.VII.3): Noy (1993), 62 τάφως Μαννίνες πρεσβιτέρες τιγάτερ Λονγινι πατερις ἰνγόνιν Φαοστινι πατερις ἐτ(ῶν) λη'. There are superficial similarities, most notably in the use of τάφος and of πρεσβιτερες, but whereas 62 has the Greek word for 'daughter', in the other we find the Latin φιλια, and both Βερενικενις and Ιωσετις are unambiguously inflected as Latin (on the form of the genitive of βερενικενις see below, 4.V.3.1.3), unlike Μαννίνες, which is more difficult to interpret (see 4.V.3.1.2). 59 is basically in Latin, if the first word is left aside, whereas the other is an

attempt at Greek with some switches into Latin and also Latin interference (see I.VII.3 for details). Jews at Venusia presumably spoke Latin
like the rest of the population, but there was a tradition of using Greek
in funerary memorials. One writer was only able to use Greek script
(might this have passed muster as 'Greek' once the language itself had
died?: see on this issue I.VIII, p. 91, 2.III.6, p. 175, 2.VIII), whereas the
other managed some Greek language, but with errors of inflection and
syntax, switches into Latin and morphological interference from Latin.
It would clearly not do to argue that, because some of the Jewish epitaphs
at Venusia are in a mixture of Greek and Latin, there was therefore a
'mixed language' current in the Jewish community.

XII.2 *The significance of funerary inscriptions*

A good deal of the evidence used in this chapter consists of funerary
inscriptions. The genre may seem inadequate for deducing attitudes to
code-switching, but I would argue on the contrary that such inscriptions
carried information which was considered highly important not only to
the dedicator but also to the deceased. It was recognised that a funerary
inscription conferred an identity on its subject in perpetuity. Funerary
inscriptions were often composed by the deceased themselves during
their lifetime, as we know not only from the scene in Petronius' *Satyricon*
where Trimalchio declaims his own epitaph (71.12), but also from the
numerous inscriptions which state explicitly (through the formula *se uiuo*
and variants) that the deceased prepared the monument during their
own lifetime. There are also one or two particularly revealing cases, such
as the epigraphic poem (*CLE* 477) in honour of T. Flavius Hermes which
claims that the man dictated the epitaph himself before death (see I.VIII).
The most important evidence for attitudes to funerary inscriptions is to
be found in the longest of all epigraphic poems, the memorial of the
Flavii of Cillium (Kasserine) in Africa (*CIL* VIII. 212, 213 = *CLE* 1552 A
and B = Courtney (1995), 199). This asserts that the dedicatee is now
immortal because of the *scripta nomina* (55–9):

> sic immortalis haberi
> iam debet pater ecce tuus Ditisque relicti
> tristem deseruisse domum, dum tempore toto
> mauolt haec monumenta sequi scriptisq(ue) per aeuom
> uiuere nominibus.[188]

---

[188] Courtney's translation: 'in this way your father now deserves to be considered immortal and to
have departed from and abandoned the gloomy halls of Dis, namely that through all time he
prefers to accompany this monument and to live for eternity in the inscribed record'. I would

There follows an interesting discussion of the possibility that the composition of an epitaph before the referent's death might shorten his life, a superstition which shows that the practice was commonplace and a subject of discussion (62–8):

> forsitan haec multi uano sermone ferentes
> uenturae citius dicant praesagia mortis,
> si quis dum uiuit ponat monimenta futuris
> temporibus. mihi non tales sunt pectore sensus,
> set puto securos fieri quicumque parare
> aeternam uoluere domum certoque rigore
> numquam lapsuros uitae defigere muros.[189]

The theme of the immortality conferred by *monimenta* recurs here. Finally, the hope is expressed that the deceased will live for many years to read his monument (B 19–20):

> opto, Secunde, geras multos feliciter annos,
> et quae fecisti tu monimenta legas.

There can be no doubting the significance to the deceased and his family of the wording of his memorial. If code-switching is embedded in an epitaph, or an alien script used for part or the whole of the inscription, it must be assumed that the form of the text had been the subject of thought and that it conveyed some message for its writer. On this assumption funerary inscriptions are an eminently suitable vehicle for the study of code-switching in writing.

XII.3 Code-switching and markedness

Myers-Scotton (1993) proposes a 'markedness model' of code-switching, based largely on the study of African languages. I do not intend to discuss this model in detail or to attempt an account of its complexities, but in view of what has been said in III.9 and earlier in the introduction to this chapter (I) it is worthwhile to take up some of Myers-Scotton's arguments.

Myers-Scotton (1993: 75) states that the 'theory behind the markedness model proposes that speakers have a sense of markedness regarding

---

prefer though to render *scriptis nominibus* at the end of the passage literally. The referent lives on for ever because his names have been written.

[189] Courtney: 'Perhaps many people, commenting in empty words, say that it is a presage of death destined to arrive sooner if a man during his lifetime establishes a monument for time yet to come. Such opinions are not in my heart, but I believe that freedom from care comes to those who have resolved to prepare an eternal abode and with unswerving rectitude of life to establish walls that will never fall.'

available linguistic codes for any interaction, but choose their codes based on the persona and/or relation with others which they wish to have in place. This markedness has a normative basis within the community, and speakers also know the consequences of making marked or unexpected choices. Because the unmarked choice is 'safer' (i.e. it conveys no surprises because it indexes an expected interpersonal relationship), speakers generally make this choice. But not always. Speakers assess the potential costs and rewards of all alternative choices, and make their decisions, typically unconsciously.' One cannot take exception to this statement, but aspects of the attempt to relate code-switching to it cause some unease.

It is the view of Myers-Scotton that code-switching may be either a marked or an unmarked choice, depending on the circumstances. I will quote at length her answer to the question 'when and where does unmarked CS occur?' (1993: 119): 'Certain conditions must be met for unmarked CS. First, the speakers must be bilingual peers; such switching typically does not happen when there is a socio-economic differential between speakers or when they are strangers. Second, the interaction has to be of a type in which speakers wish to symbolise the dual memberships that such CS calls up. Typically, such interactions will be informal and involve only ingroup members. Third, proficiency in the languages used in the switching is not a sufficient condition; perhaps the most important criterion is that the speakers must *positively evaluate* for their own identities in this type of interaction the indexal values of the varieties used in the switching.'

The conditions listed here exactly match those obtaining in the correspondence between Cicero and Atticus. The pair are bilingual peers, they symbolise their membership of a bilingual hellenophile group of educated Romans by the use of the code-switching variety, they are loosely speaking part of an in-group (but see above, III.1, p. 322), their interaction is informal, and they positively evaluate 'the indexal values of the varieties used in the switching'. On the face of it then Cicero and Atticus would seem to have been engaging in code-switching as an unmarked option. But were they? Evidence presented earlier in the chapter suggests that they were not. I refer to the startling variations in the incidence of code-switching at different times in the correspondence (III.9), with switching dropped entirely at periods of crisis. It seems incontrovertible that to Cicero code-switching even in private to a peer was a form of show that he found intolerable at times when he had more pressing things to worry about. It has moreover been noted that the flagging of switches is typical of marked code-switching,[190] and we have observed that such flagging is not uncommon in Cicero's letters. I would suggest on the strength of this evidence that *code-switching into Greek by educated Romans was always a marked choice, even if carried out in private with a sympathetic peer.* The obvious reason why this should have been so lies in the cultural markedness to educated Romans of Greek and things Greek, such that it was impossible for a Roman to switch into Greek other than self-consciously. There may well be societies in which code-switching can be unmarked, but there are hazards in constructing a model from the evidence of one society and making the assumption that it is applicable to another. Moreover, as we have often pointed out (see e.g. 1), most code-switching attested from the Roman world is in written texts,[191] and there is a fundamental difference between a written text, which has an inherent formality, and informal speech.

I stress that the markedness of switches into Greek at Rome refers only to switching as performed by educated Romans. The switches into Greek by (e.g.) Hermeros in Petronius are of a different order, in that to a Roman readership familiar with a Greek servile population such characters would readily have been assumed to be of Greek origin rather than Roman, and it was one thing when a Greek speaking Latin switched back into his native language, and quite another when an upper-class native speaker of Latin switched into Greek.

I take up another remark of Myers-Scotton (1993: 132). She states that, diverse as are the manifestations of marked code-switching, they can be 'subsumed under one general effect: to negotiate a change in the expected social distance holding between participants, either increasing or decreasing it'. If an attempt is made to apply this assertion to the material collected in the present chapter, the dangers will readily be seen of making generalisations based on the study of one culture and seeking to impose them as 'universals' on another. We have, it is true, seen evidence that code-switching may set up a 'social distance' between speaker and addressee: I refer to the use by Cicero and his correspondents of code-switching as a method of what I called 'distancing' (though, paradoxically, this form of code-switching is located in a form of discourse which, as we have just pointed out, fits Myers-Scotton's criteria for the identification not of marked but of unmarked code-switching).

---

[190] See Myers-Scotton (1993: 141).

[191] I say 'most' rather than 'all', because some of the code-switching in written texts occurs in representations of speech (most notably that in Plautus, but also in Lucilius, Lucretius, Petronius and Martial).

But how is the phenomenon which I have called the 'stylistically evocative' use of code-switching to be subsumed under Myers-Scotton's definition of marked code-switching? It is, I would maintain, marked, but has nothing to do with the 'negotiation of social distance' between identifiable participants in the process of switching. If it is accepted that the stylistic virtuoso may use a range of stylistic resources to enhance the suggestiveness of his discourse, and that such stylistic resources as novel metaphors, changes of language, striking colloquialisms, coinages, deliberate mismatches of register,[192] etc. are marked rather than unmarked, then clearly Myers-Scotton's statement of the defining characteristic of marked code-switching must be revised, for the exploitation of stylistic resources in a narrative text is not illuminated by the claim that 'social distance' is in any way at issue.

XII.4 Code-switching and social intention: power and solidarity/accommodation

It has been argued throughout this chapter that code-switching frequently has social intention, in a variety of senses. The code-switcher associates himself with or dissociates himself from his addressees in varying degrees, to convey solidarity, shared culture, aloofness, power, etc., or constructs an identity for himself or another, whether e.g. cultural or professional, for the sake of addressees, specific or assumed. Solidarity (accommodation) and power can be treated as polar opposites.[193] The opposition can be seen in its most extreme form in certain aspects of language choice. The Roman soldier who addresses a Greek in Latin, well aware that the Greek does not know the language, is using language as a demonstration of power (see 5.IV.3). On the other hand the Latin speaker who chooses Greek for the sake of such an addressee is acting deferentially and accommodating his language choice to the linguistic competence of the addressee. A good deal of code-switching can be loosely related to this opposition.

Texts in Latin with code-switching into Greek are not homogeneous. One thing that is now stressed in sociolinguistic literature is the variability of code-switching behaviour.[194] Some upper-class Romans switched languages in private to present themselves as belonging to a cultured minority capable of exploiting the distancing, evocative and expressive resources of Greek (qualities of the language which could scarcely be acknowledged in public). But upper-class Romans either switching into

---

[192] On this phenomenon see Powell (1999).   [193] See above, I, with the bibliography at n. 12.
[194] See e.g. Treffers-Daller (1998: 178).

Greek or commenting on the procedure have been only part of the subject of this chapter. Quite different are the Greeks, many no doubt of slave origin, who have left numerous epitaphs at Rome, some of them in mixed language (and even script). Some Greeks were conscious of a conflict of linguistic identity. Two features of these inscriptions have been stressed. First, Greeks tended to retain the Greek form of their names even when writing in Latin (see also the next chapter, 4.v.3.1), and along with the name there is also sometimes other personal material in the mother tongue, as for example kinship terms or laudatory epithets. Secondly, they sometimes used Latin in mixed-language inscriptions for the recording of what I called 'bureaucratic' information, such as dates. There is reflected here a Greek perception of the status and role of Latin *vis-à-vis* Greek. Loosely speaking, we might say that Latin is treated as the language of authority. In bilingual societies one language may be associated with authority, and code-switching into that language may symbolise an assertion of authority. The Roman Greek who switches into Greek under the circumstances described is not asserting his own authority, but acknowledging that Latin, as the language of the dominant element in society, is appropriate for the expression of information that has a public function, as for example the formal details of someone's life. It was suggested that such Greeks were acknowledging a diglossic opposition between Greek (L) and Latin (H). This opposition was by no means the same as that which might have been assumed by some upper-class Romans, who treated Greek (in private) as the language of high culture, without however (in public) treating Latin as L. These complications will be discussed further below (5.1.3, VI). The status and function of Greek differed according to the background of the code-switcher. It was a language of the family on the one hand, but of culture on the other.

If Greeks at Rome accorded Latin a bureaucratic status, so Romans in the Greek world treated their own language as marking authority. The most extreme case of this phenonenon alluded to in this chapter was the bilingual soldier's selection of Latin in Apuleius' *Metamorphoses* to address a Greek peasant as a means of humiliating the man (see above, VI), but the attitude is inherent in more subtle ways in other material. I leave this subject until the chapter on Egypt (5.IV.3).

In the previous paragraph a case was cited of the choice of Latin in unmixed form as appropriate to the assertion of power, but code-switching (into Latin from Greek) could have the same function. This we saw in the reports of hearings of a legalistic kind which have turned up on papyrus in Egypt (VI.1). Here the Roman officials allowed the business to be conducted in Greek (they had no choice in a society in which Latin had virtually no place), but they switched into Latin among themselves, and when (the symbolism is obvious) a decision was given. It makes no difference that the decision might have been translated into Greek: it will have been given first in Latin as underlining Roman authority.

'Universal' constraints on code-switching have sometimes been proposed, but soon abandoned as more evidence came to light. There are some syntactic restrictions on code-switching in Cicero (see above, III.10, and also below, 4.V.4.1 on restrictions placed on 'ablatival' uses of the Greek dative), but the nature of the evidence is not on the whole conducive to the study of this subject.

XII.5 'Retention': some further observations about the code-switching of Roman Greeks

The term 'retention' is perhaps more appropriate than 'switching' to account for the presence of at least some of the Greek in mixed-language inscriptions of Roman Greeks. The base language of these inscriptions might be looked on as Latin, written either in Greek script or Latin depending on the desired readership or some other factor, but with the retention of some Greek elements which the writer is not yet able psychologically to regard as translatable into another language (eg. names, kinship terms). Such retentions, I would suggest, are particularly likely to turn up in situations of language shift. In Etruria, for example, there was in the Republican period a massive shift from Etruscan to Latin as the population was Romanised. In some attempts at Latin in the transitional period there are Etruscan names and onomastic formulae.

There is evidence in some of the texts of the effects of a language shift across several generations among Greeks at Rome. In *ILCV* 2534, for example, there is a hint that Latin was the language of the younger generation, Greek that of the older (see V.1, and also V.4 on filiations). Language shift among immigrants across various generations has sometimes been discussed in the modern literature as the background to patterns of code-switching. Funerary inscriptions are highly formal and brief; if in such a succinct genre code-switching reflecting the different linguistic identities of members of the different generations of an immigrant family can be found, it is highly likely that in the speech of such people code-switching was commonplace, and related in type and frequency to the age of the speaker.

XII.6 Code-switching and gender

There is not much evidence about bilingualism and code-switching among women in the sources.[195] Nothing should be made of the relative absence of code-switching in Cicero's letters to Terentia. The distribution of the Greek in the letters hints, as we saw, at the pretentiousness of the practice even in the eyes of Cicero himself. It is therefore possible that the constant use of Greek to his wife would have been interpreted as pompous. The one (medical) expression that Cicero does use (χολὴν ἄκρατον) is of some interest. It is not the sort of phrase that would have had everyday currency, designating as it does not a disease but a cause of disease; its use implies that the addressee must have had some familiarity with the humoral theory which lies behind it. Cicero could hardly have used such an expression to Terentia if she was ignorant of things Greek. Moreover we no doubt have only a fraction of the letters which passed between the pair.

There is of course evidence for women knowing Greek. A letter in Suetonius from Augustus to Livia (_Claud._ 4) is full of code-switching into Greek, motivated apparently by the desire to distance unpleasant topics (see above, III.4). On the Greek culture of Sempronia, see Sall. _Cat._ 25.2 _haec mulier genere atque forma, praeterea uiro liberis satis fortunata fuit; litteris Graecis [et] Latinis docta._[196] Women are castigated in both Juvenal and Martial for code-switching (see above, v). In a bilingual school exercise probably from Gaul edited by Dionisotti (1982) girls are explicitly included among the pupils.[197] Apuleius' _Apology_ includes a letter in Greek by Pudentilla (82.2).[198] Both Fronto and Favorinus (as reported by Gellius) used Greek to women.[199]

---

[195] See the discussion of Wenskus (1998: 34–8); also her recent paper (2001).
[196] See Rochette (1997a: 63).   [197] See Dionisotti (1982: 107).   [198] See Hunink (1997), ad loc.
[199] See Wenskus (1998: 37). On the insignificance of Pliny's failure to code-switch in extant letters to women, see Wenskus (1998: 36–7).

4

Bilingualism, linguistic diversity and language change

I INTRODUCTION

Works on historical linguistics have tended to concentrate on factors internal to a language as determining linguistic change,[1] but external factors may also be influential, though perhaps mainly in the short term (see below, VI.4). This chapter will be about language contact as a cause of language change, in either or both of the languages in contact. I make the assumption that most bilinguals will have a first or 'native' language and a second language. There are 'balanced' bilinguals, but these are probably in a minority except in some special communities. In the material available from antiquity it is usually possible to identify a writer's first language.

The chapter has several aims. First, in general accounts of bilingualism and language change evidence from antiquity has been neglected, though it is extensive. Thomason and Kaufman (1988), for example, range all over the world but pass over antiquity in silence. This chapter will present evidence relevant to the general debate. Secondly, discussions of cross-language influence in the Roman world (such as that of R. Coleman (1975)) have dealt above all with the literary languages, and non-literary evidence has not been fully exploited. The present chapter will not be restricted to the non-literary evidence, but that will occupy a significant place. Thirdly, in keeping with a general theme of the book I will be attempting to identify the effects of bilingualism on the regional diversification of Latin. Fourthly, while the main focus of the chapter will be on Latin as exposed to Greek influence, the influence worked in the other direction as well. Just as there were varieties of 'Greeks' Latin', so there was 'Roman Greek'. To avoid presenting a one-sided picture, I will

---

[1] See the remarks of Thomason and Kaufman (1988: 57). An exception to this tendency is provided by the works of Hock (1986) and Hock and Joseph (1996), which have lengthy discussions of bilingualism and language change. See now also Harris and Campbell (1995: 120–50).

offer some case studies concerning contact with Latin as a determinant of change in Greek, though this subject will not be treated systematically. Finally, where Latin is concerned, contact was not only with Greek but with a variety of other languages, as we have seen, and these as well as Greek will be taken into account, though the non-Greek evidence is not extensive. It is not the purpose of the chapter to provide a summary of all of the changes which have been identified in Latin and Greek as prompted by language contact. The main types will be covered, but the material is selective.

In the literature on the relationship between Greek and Latin terms such as 'influence' and 'Grecism' abound.[2] Serviceable as these terms may be, they are inadequate. Borrowing and interference are usually distinct phenomena, the difference between which is blurred by the use of such catch-all terms as 'influence'. There is a difference between the imitation by a learned Latin author of a feature of Greek syntax (borrowing), and the imposition by an imperfect language learner of a morpheme or idiom of his first language on a second (interference). Nor does 'influence' operate in only one direction. There follow a few remarks about terminology which will complement those in Chapter I.

II BORROWING AND ITS DIVERSITY

At I.V borrowing, interference and code-switching were defined. Since borrowing and interference will occupy a good deal of this chapter, I begin with a few further comments on aspects of the two phenomena. We saw that bilinguals usually borrow from a second language into their first. Borrowing is defined by Thomason and Kaufman (1988: 21) as 'the incorporation of foreign elements into the speakers' native language'. Borrowing of the reverse type does occur, as we will see (see in particular p. 424), but a transfer from a speaker's first language into his second is as likely as not to represent something different, interference (see further below, III, and above, I.V).

The term 'borrowing' in ordinary usage is applied mainly to lexical loans, but borrowing may affect any part of a linguistic system.[3] Words are usually the most prominent foreign elements to enter a borrowing

---

[2] See e.g. R. Coleman (1975), *passim*, E. Löfstedt (1959: 88–119).

[3] Note the remark of Harris and Campbell (1995: 149), based on a series of case studies, that 'given enough time and intensity of contact, virtually anything can (ultimately) be borrowed'. In their view, 'borrowing must be accorded a significant position in the ranks of mechanisms of syntactic change'.

language, but under conditions of close contact phonetic, phonological, syntactic and morphological elements may be borrowed.[4] Latin is full of Greek loan-words, but borrowing into the language by native speakers goes well beyond the lexical. Even the sounds of Greek were sometimes adopted. Quintilian (12.10.57) tells of a *rusticus testis* who when asked in court whether he knew a certain *Amphionem* replied that he did not, but when the speaker removed the aspirate (of *ph*) and shortened the *i* he said that he knew him well: *prudenter enim qui, cum interrogasset rusticum testem an Amphionem <nosset>, negante eo detraxit aspirationem breuiauitque secundam eius nominis syllabam, et ille eum sic optime norat.* The name seems to have been Latinised morphologically by the speaker (to judge by the accusative form in the text), but was pronounced with a Greek aspirated stop and probably a Greek accentual pattern. The implication of the passage is that the use of Greek phonetic features (in a Greek name) was a mark of an educated speaker of Latin. Phonetic (or phonological) borrowings of this sort are most likely to be found in loan-words and names from the source language,[5] but there is some evidence as well for the affecting of Greek phonetic mannerisms in Latin by educated Latin speakers (see Chapter 1, Appendix).

Borrowing may also be morphological (see above, 2.III.2 for the borrowing of various Etruscan suffixes by Latin in the early period).[6] For example, the Greek masculine suffix -της (manifesting itself as -ιώτης, -ίτης, -έτης, etc.) is on the one hand found in Latin (in the forms *-ta*, *-tes*) in numerous loan-words from Greek,[7] but more interestingly it is sometimes attached to Latin roots, as in *hamiota* (Plaut. *Rud.* 310, Varro *Men.* 55). Greek words in Latin showing this suffix should be described as lexical loans. But once the suffix is used on a Latin base, it has taken on a life of its own in the borrowing language; it is now the suffix which has been borrowed. Not that this suffix enjoyed any real vitality in classical Latin. But in later Christian Latin there are other such hybrids, denoting members of heretical sects (e.g. *Rogatistae*, 'disciples of Rogatus').[8] Most such terms have a Greek base, but once the suffix had become associated in the language of the Christians with the names of sects it was applied to Latin roots as well. Conversely Greek sometimes made use of the Latin

[4] See Thomason and Kaufman (1988: 37), and Harris and Campbell, cited above, n. 3. A vast amount of material is assembled by Thomason and Kaufman.
[5] Thomason and Kaufman (1988: 74) place phonological borrowings restricted to loan-words at point (2) on a 'borrowing scale' of (1)–(5) (= 'slight structural borrowing').
[6] See, for example, the remarks of Hofmann and Szantyr (1965: 763).
[7] These are discussed by André (1971: 73–103).
[8] See André (1971: 100; also 101 for a set of six words with Latin base).

suffix -*ianus* for the same purpose, as for example in Χριστιανοί, Ὀφιανοί, Σηθιανοί, Ἀπελληανοί.[9] The two suffixes -*i(s)tae* and -*iani* became interchangeable in both Greek and Latin for the designation of such sects.[10] On -*ianus* see further below, v.3.5.

The Greek feminine suffix -τρια occurs in various Greek loan-words in Latin,[11] but in *lupatria* (Petron. 37.6) it is attached to a Latin base (on the model of πορνεύτρια); the term is not in André (1971).[12] Greek feminine nouns of agent in -τρια (which correspond to the masculine -της) are usually (unlike *lupatria*) based on a verbal root (so πορνεύ-τρια).[13] It is to be assumed that among some bilingual speakers of Latin the normal Greek process of derivation was forgotten once the suffix -*tria* had acquired an association with female purveyors of sex (cf. λαικάστρια). Thenceforth the suffix could be applied to a Latin base (even one which was non-verbal) provided that the semantic field was appropriate;[14] on Greek terms adopted by Latin to designate types of sexual activity, see above, 3.ix. In *lupatria* the suffix is redundant, in that the base *lupa* carries the same meaning. The same suffix in a sexual term is to be seen in Latin in a coinage of Tiberian date, *spintria* (Tac. *Ann.* 6.1.2, Suet. *Tib.* 43.1).[15]

Structurally not unlike *lupatria* is Augustus' humorous coinage *betizo*,[16] which according to Suetonius was modelled on *lachanizo* < λαχανίζω: Suet. *Aug.* 87.2 *ponit assidue (Augustus)... betizare pro languere, quod uulgo lachanizare dicitur*. The root of the Greek term is again replaced by a Latin root of similar meaning, but the Grecising suffix retained.[17] A partial translation of a different kind is to be seen in Horace's *depugis* (*Sat.* 1.2.93), which is based on ἄπυγος. Here the prefix has been replaced with a Latin morpheme but the root left unchanged. Such hybrids seem to have been potentially a source of humour or used for self-conscious

---

[9] See André (1971: 101). On the -*ianus* suffix in general, see Leumann (1977: 325–6), Schnorr v. Carolsfeld (1884: 185–7), and on its borrowing by Hellenistic and later Greek, see Chantraine (1933: 197). On Latin suffixes in general as taken over into Modern Greek (usually in lexical loans, but occasionally in attachment to Greek roots), see G. Meyer (1895: 73–7), Thumb (1901: 155), Palmer (1946), cited below, v.3.5.

[10] See André (1971: 101).   [11] See André (1971: 103–6).   [12] But see Biville (2000: 91–2).

[13] See Biville (1991: 48).   [14] See Biville, loc. cit.

[15] On the origin of this term, which is not straightforward, see André (1971: 104–5), Biville (1991: 48). It designates someone engaged in an act of copulation involving three participants. The word is masculine in Suetonius, but may originally have been coined as a feminine (since one female can participate in such an act). It may have been generalised to embrace all three members of the sexual chain, passing into the generalising masculine in the process.

[16] Discussed also by Biville (2000: 94).

[17] *Lachanizare* must incidentally in this sense have belonged to 'Roman Greek'. The word is not used thus in extant Greek, though the middle is found in the meaning 'gather vegetables'.

linguistic display.[18] In each case there is a Greek model which is partially Latinised. The Greek word became familiar to Latin speakers, who then transferred its suffix to Latin bases when there was a semantic association with the Greek model.

There are other Plautine coinages (apart from *hamiota* above) which make use of Greek morphemes on a Latin base. For example, several compounds with Latin components are formed with the Greek linking morpheme *-o-* rather than the Latin *-i-*: *merobibus* (cf. ἀκρατοπότης), *sescentoplagus*, *speculoclarus* (note also the fully Greek *tympanotriba* (< * τυμπανοτρίβης), etc.[19] An inventive coiner of words like Plautus might have adopted the morpheme if he had in mind a specific Greek model for a humorous Latin coinage (such as *merobibus*). Superficially similar is the form *primopilo* (= *primipilo*) in two inscriptions from Baalbek, *IGLS* 2786 and 2787, but if the writers were Greeks they might have been subject to lexical interference from their first language (for the form which the Latin loan-word had acquired in Greek, see A. Bernand (1984), 102 πριμοπιλάρ(ιον) λεγ(εῶνος) ζ). Humorous morphological borrowing in literary texts (equally describable as morphological code-switching: see p. 27) can also be seen, possibly in Ennius' *Mettoeo Fufetioeo* (*Ann.* 120 Skutsch = Quint. 1.5.12),[20] and certainly in Ovid's *uinoeo bonoeo* (Quint. 8.6.33) and Cicero's *facteon* (see above, 1.V, pp. 27–8).[21] Not that morphological borrowing need be exclusively literary, artificial and humorous: note the hybrid *epitogium*, with Greek prefix ἐπί and Latin base *toga*, a word discussed by Quintilian (1.5.68) along with other interesting material: *aut ex nostro et peregrino, ut 'biclinium', aut contra, ut 'epitogium' et 'Anticato', aliquando et ex duobus peregrinis, ut 'epiraedium'; nam cum sit 'epi' praepositio Graeca, 'raeda' Gallicum (neque Graecus tamen neque Gallus utitur conposito), Romani suum ex alieno utroque fecerunt.* On Quintilian's interpretation *epiraedium* would be an exact parallel for *epitogium* (given that *raeda*, despite its Celtic origin, was a thoroughly integrated term in Latin), but it is alternatively

---

[18] Further miscellaneous suffix transfers can be found in Schulze (1894 = 1958: 112).

[19] Details of all of these words can be found in Lindner (1996).

[20] That the ending here is Greek is disputed by Mariotti (1988), who argues that it is an archaic Latin genitive. See further Heraeus (1930), Wachter (1987: 79 with n. 201), and Leumann (1977: 412). At Ardea (Latium) there is attested a form *Titoio* (see Vetter (1953), 364a). On *Mettus* as the correct form of the name, see Skutsch (1985: 273).

[21] The reverse phenomenon, the imposition of a Latin (ablative) morpheme on a Greek word, can be seen in a letter of Fronto to Marcus Aurelius (3.8.2 *in hac* εἰκόνε). We will later (5.V.4) see an example of this sort which can be put down to interference from the writer's first language in his second, but unconscious interference is out of the question in a learned bilingual such as Fronto: Fronto must have produced the macaronic form deliberately, perhaps in jest. The same word occurs repeatedly earlier in the letter, correctly inflected as Greek; this case may be a humorous variation. See Wenskus (1995: 177–8) for various possible explanations of the form.

possible that the first part of the compound derives from Gaulish *epos* 'horse' (so *OLD* s.v.).[22] Hybrids such as *epitogium*, where the Greek prefix lends a semantic nuance which could not be so readily conveyed by a Latin correspondent, reflect the profound and prolonged contact between Romans and the Greek language, in its many forms. Bilinguals were prepared to borrow morphemes from Greek for *ad hoc* coinages in Latin, whether because of the utility of a Greek element, or because of its special semantic associations (*-tria, -ta*), or for humorous purposes.

There are other hybrids in late Latin. *-issa*, which was productive from the Byzantine period in Greek (see, e.g. *P.Oxy.* III. 478.27 πατρώνισσα (πατρωνείσης), cited by Cavenaile (1952: 195)), is not only found in words of Greek root in Latin, but also occasionally attached to Latin bases (e.g. *sacerdotissa*).[23] In a Jewish inscription from Venusia (Noy (1993), 63 *hic requescet Alexsanra pateressa) pateressa* is the feminine correspondent of the masculine title of the synagogue *pater*, which sometimes retains the *e* of the nominative in oblique cases in the same corpus (e.g. Noy (1993), 61 πατερις). *Pateressa* does not appear in André (1971). On suffixation, see further below, V.3.5.

In high literature, particularly poetry, there is a good deal of imitation of Greek syntax,[24] and that is a form of borrowing.[25] Those poets who used, for example, constructions such as *formam pulcherrimus* (R. Coleman (1975: 126)),[26] the gnomic 'aorist' (Coleman (1975: 134)), and the nominative + infinitive instead of the (reflexive) accusative + infinitive (Coleman (1975: 139)) were deliberately introducing Greek syntax into their native language. Quintilian (9.3.17) makes an observation on this practice in Sallust and Horace.[27] A tradition of Grecising Latin poetic syntax can be traced back to Ennius (e.g. *Ann.* 48 Skutsch *quamquam **multa** manus ad caeli caerula templa / tendebam);* the adverbial use of the neuter plural adjective has its inspiration in the use of πολλά

---

[22] Cf. *CGL* III.623.26 (*epocalium idest ungula cabalina*) for the prefix.

[23] See Schulze (1894 = 1958: 112), Palmer (1946: 93), André (1971: 108).

[24] On the Greek 'influence' on Latin poetic language see e.g. Lunelli (1980), index p.184, s.v. 'grecismo', Maurach (1995), index p. 273, s.v. 'Gräzismus', and especially pp. 87–92. There is a classic chapter in E. Löfstedt (1956: II, 406–57); see also Leumann (1947: 127–8), Hofmann and Szantyr (1965: 764–5). Commentaries on poetic texts are full of references to 'Grecisms' of this sort (e.g. Fordyce (1961: 100) on Catull. 4.2, Austin (1964: 159) on Virg. *Aen.* 2.377); the list could be greatly extended.

[25] Rosén (1999: 21) makes (and modifies) a distinction between borrowing as literary imitation and naturalised Greek features in Latin.

[26] On this construction in Latin see also the discussion of E. Löfstedt (1959: 94).

[27] On Grecising syntax in Sallust, see E. Löfstedt (1956: II, 412–14). In this way Sallust might have been attempting to display his connection with Thucydides.

in Greek.[28] This procedure had its origin in the subservience of Latin culture to Greek, and was one of the strategies whereby a Latin 'poetic' language was artificially created. By a distinctive Greek usage a Latin writer might subtly advertise his indebtedness to a Greek predecessor.[29] Not that syntactic *imitatio* was exclusive to poetry (or poeticising prose, such as historiography:[30] see above on Sallust, and below, III on Ammianus). Syntactic Grecisms are found occasionally in Cicero's letters[31] and in the philosophical works. The speeches were another matter, but in the more private sphere of epistles and philosophica bilingual linguistic display was more acceptable.[32] Parallels can be quoted for the influence of a prestigious literary language on the written form of another language. In India, for example, Sanskrit is said 'to have influenced literary Dravidian languages both phonologically and morphosyntactically' (Thomason and Kaufman (1988: 79); cf. 78, 84 for other such examples).

I stress that not all syntactic borrowing or imitation represents literary affectation. When Greeks at Delos introduced υἱός into the filiation of Romans (see below, 6.v.1) they were not engaging in literary affectation. Aware of the Latin construction with *filius*, they deliberately introduced an equivalent into their first language in naming Romans, undoubtedly as a form of deference: they wanted to get the honorand's formal name 'right' in both languages. The direction of the transfer is again that emphasised at the start of this section as typical of borrowing.

The complexity of such transfers is highlighted by some further examples of the same type which by contrast cannot be explained as due to accommodation in this sense. In the Latin versions of *senatus consulta* produced probably at Rome for circulation in the Greek world, it is

[28] See Hofmann and Szantyr (1965: 37–8). For Ennius' imitation of Greek usages, see Maurach (1995: 87–8), with bibliography; also Rosén (1999: 21 with n. 28), Jocelyn (1999: 180).

[29] See above, n. 27 on Sallust; also Löfstedt (1956: II, 436) on Homeric precedents for some Virgilian Grecisms.

[30] See e.g. Draeger (1882: 124) for a list of places where Greek syntax in Tacitus is discussed in the book.

[31] See von Albrecht (1973: 1278).

[32] There is a good discussion of one particular syntactic Grecism in Cicero by Laughton (1964: 43–5). He discusses the Greek idiom, very common in Plato (43), 'in which a participle bears the main weight of a clause or sentence'; 'when, as often, the clause is interrogative or relative, it is to the participle, not to the finite verb, that the relative or interrogative pronoun or adverb is attached'. Cicero provides eight examples in the later writings (44), only one in a speech (*Phil.* 2.86 *supplex te ad pedes abiciebas* **quid petens**?), the others in letters and philosophica. Laughton (44) argues that the number of attestations 'suggests that Cicero was deliberately trying to make a syntactical innovation'. That examples are found in the philosophical works is easy to understand, given the place of the construction in Plato. That there should be even a single example in a speech shows that the hellenising of Latin by the Roman upper classes was not entirely restricted to special genres.

also standard for υἱός to be used in the naming of Romans (and indeed Greeks) (see 6.v.1). The translations were almost certainly the work of Latin speakers,[33] and it is thus (in contrast to the case in the previous paragraph) into their second language, Greek, that the Latinate construction is introduced. Some of the translators, unfamiliar with the Greek pattern, might simply have rendered the Latin version word-for-word, and on this view the form of the filiation in the Greek could be seen not as borrowing but as interference. The possibility cannot however be ruled out that some of the translators knew the Greek construction, but chose to inflict the Latin construction on the Greek, that is on their second language. This would be an unusual case of borrowing by the writers into their second language, perhaps for political purposes (to underline the Romanness of the decrees, and the Roman indifference to correct Greek idiom: on this translation technique see further below, v.2.12). It is necessary to examine syntactic transfers closely to determine whether they are due to imitation, i.e. borrowing (mainly affecting the writer's first language), accommodation (affecting the first language again and a subdivision of borrowing), borrowing (deliberately) into the second language (a rare phenomenon which may be difficult or even impossible to distinguish from (unconscious) interference), or interference itself (affecting the second language).

This rarer type of borrowing, that from a speaker's first into his second language, has some well-documented cases. There are some classic examples of peoples shifting from one language to another and importing into their new language extensive loans from the old. The Norman French in medieval England, and the Franks when they abandoned Germanic and adopted the Latin/Romance of Gaul are two cases in point.[34] Similarly Indian English has loans from native languages.[35]

III INTERFERENCE AGAIN: A PROBLEM OF INTERPRETATION

A speaker's (or writer's) first language may influence his second. We have allowed the possibility several times in the previous section that such influence may sometimes be classifiable as borrowing, but usually the phenomenon is best seen as interference (see also above, 1.v). Interference is

---

[33] See Viereck (1888: 82) (on the possible use of glossaries by translators), Sherk (1969: 13–16); see also Rochette (1997a: 86–7).

[34] See Thomason and Kaufman (1988: 121, 123). On the Germanic loans in Gallo-Romance, see *FEW*, vols. xv–xvii, Gamillscheg (1970), Pfister (1972, 1973), D. H. Green (1998); a few brief remarks may be found in Gaeng (1968: 9–11). See also below, v.2.3.

[35] See Hock and Joseph (1996: 375).

most obviously found in the speech or writing of imperfect learners of a second language; examples have already been cited in the first chapter (I.V, I.VII.2.3). It is worth stressing again here that one and the same phenomenon may have to be classified in one case as borrowing and in another as interference, depending on the circumstances (see above on υἱός in filiations). For example, the nominative and infinitive construction if used by a Latin poet is, as we saw, an instance of (deliberate) borrowing (into his first language). But the same construction as used in Latin by Ammianus (e.g. 14.2.9 *arbitrantur enim nullo impediente transgressi inopino accursu apposita quaeque uastare*) is arguably of a different kind. Ammianus was a first-language speaker of Greek, and in the passage cited he used a construction from his first language in his second, possibly as a momentary lapse through interference. But interference and borrowing are difficult to disentangle in this case. Ammianus was familiar with the language of Latin poetry, and he was capable of deliberately introducing the Greek pattern on the model of examples which he had observed in Latin literature. On this view he would have been borrowing from his first into his second language. On Ammianus, see further below, V.2.11.

I return to borrowing and interference in section V.

IV SECOND-LANGUAGE ACQUISITION AND REGIONAL VARIATION IN LANGUAGE: SOME INTRODUCTORY REMARKS

Many factors were responsible for variation in the Latin language, such as the choice of a register and style appropriate to the circumstances of composition, the educational level of the writer or speaker, and the area from which he originated. Another was bilingualism or language contact. I intend among other things in this chapter to bring out the part played by bilingualism in contributing to the regional diversification of Latin (see also above, 2.XIV.1), in line with my general aim of establishing that subliterary Latin was far from unified and monolithic. Here I make some general observations on the matter.

Latin is an example of a 'supraregional' or 'link' language.[36] As the Roman Empire spread, Latin was carried to different parts of Europe. There might have been no aggressive policy of Latinisation, particularly in eastern areas, but, as we saw in the second chapter, speakers of various languages found it in their interest to acquire some Latin (as a link language), and the process of acquisition effected changes in the link

---

[36] For the terminology, see Hock and Joseph (1996: 369).

language itself (see the summary at 2.XIV.1). Note Hock and Joseph (1996: 369): 'Adoption of [a second] language [in our case Latin] . . . generally leads to changes in the adopted link language, or even in the native language of the speaker, and thus can have profound effects on linguistic change.' The link language may be said to be 'indigenised', as it takes on features in the different regions which may to some extent be due to interference from the first languages of the new speakers. Indian and West African English are examples of indigenised varieties of a link language.[37] The process of language learning produces changes in the language learnt, and these changes in some cases constitute regionalisms. In the discussion of the regional diversification of Latin little attention has been paid to the place of bilingualism as a determinant of variation, though there is some interesting evidence bearing on the matter, some of which was seen in Chapter 2.

Various things are axiomatic in the study of second-language acquisition.[38] First, the target language will be subject to modification (see above). Secondly, not all modifications can be straightforwardly explained as due to interference from the first language of the learner.[39] Thirdly, modifications may be 'relatively short-lived or limited to individual learners'.[40] Fourthly, different learners show different modifications. Finally, 'in cases where the second language serves as a link language and is used in that capacity over an extended period, there is a greater chance that interlanguage phenomena [i.e. our 'modifications' above] may become a permanent feature . . . (they) can become cumulative and the results tend to become INSTITUTIONALIZED as the linguistic norm of an entire speech community' (Hock and Joseph (1996: 379)).

Of these five points I stress particularly the third and fourth, that is the transitory and individual character of a good deal of contact-induced change. In this chapter the focus will be above all on transitory, localised or individual modifications, chiefly to Latin, and for a good reason. Contact-induced change is more realistically identifiable in the micro-context, that is in individual speakers or small communities where there is explicit evidence of bilingualism and language contact. It is probably true to say that, in so far as bilingualism has been studied in the ancient world as a determinant of language change, the emphasis has rather

---

[37] See Hock and Joseph (1996: 373) for the terminology, and for detailed discussion of the phenomenon, (1996: 375–80).

[38] See the discussion of Hock and Joseph (1996: 377–9).

[39] See Hock and Joseph (1996: 377): 'Modifications of the "target" language in second-language acquisition . . . are not always explainable as resulting exclusively from interference or transfer.'

[40] See Hock and Joseph (1996: 379).

been on the identification of changes affecting a language as a whole (whether Latin or Greek).[41] Such studies have had to face a recurrent problem. If Latin and Greek show a syntactic correspondence in, say, the later period (such as that of the Roman Empire and the koine in Greek), was the correspondence due to the influence of Greek on Latin or of Latin on Greek, or had the two languages undergone parallel development?[42] If the perfect in Greek takes on an aoristic use which it did not have in the classical period (see below, V.4.5), is that because of the influence of Latin, in which the perfect had had this function from the beginning of the historical period, or is it alternatively possible that Greek underwent the change independently? Was the acquisition by the demonstratives *ille* and *ipse* in later Latin of an article-function motivated by the existence of the Greek article? Were the constructions ἔχω λέγειν and *habeo dicere* expressing futurity independent of each other? The quality of the evidence is generally not such that definitive answers to questions of this sort can be given, and scholars have not infrequently adopted the compromise of admitting external influence as accelerating a native tendency.[43] I do not intend to deal systematically here with the large-scale convergences between later Greek and Latin (but see the special case discussed below, V.3.1.2), partly because there are long and judicious studies already available (most notably R. Coleman (1975) for Latin and Dubuisson (1985) and Horrocks (1997: 73–8) for Greek), and partly because the study of widespread trends in a language or languages, even if they were arguably contact-induced, has little to tell us about the effects of bilingualism in action, particularly in the ancient languages, which are poorly documented in their regional varieties. It is regional varieties, as distinct from a literary standard, which are more likely to show up evidence for linguistic change related to bilingualism. Moreover while it may well be (for argument's sake) that bilingual Greeks such as Polybius and Appian were influenced by Latin, it is difficult to generalise from them to the mass of monolingual Greeks and to assume that those Latinate features found in the writings of bilingual authors are necessarily Latinate if they turn up as well in the Greek written by monolinguals. In this chapter I will concentrate rather on more detailed cases in which changes in one language can only be attributed to contact

---

[41] Two classic accounts are those of R. Coleman (1975) and Dubuisson (1985).

[42] An early discussion of this problem is that by Schulze (1894 = 1958).

[43] See for example Dubuisson (1985: 240–3) on changes in the use of the Greek perfect, and R. Coleman (1975: 117) on factors behind the emergence of the definite article in Latin/Romance. Note too the material discussed by E. Löfstedt (1932).

with the other, and will attempt from there to establish something about the circumstances which generate change. The limitations of contact-induced change will gradually emerge (see below, VI.4). The chapter will be mainly about what Hock and Joseph (1996: 375) call 'interference' and 'interlanguage' phenomena. By 'interlanguage phenomena' (see also above) I mean mainly modifications made to a second language under the influence of the writer's or speaker's first language.

I repeat (see the second of the five axiomatic points made above) that, while many modifications may be caused by direct interference from the first language, the new structures cannot always be explained as simple transfers from one language to the other. Whereas, for example, the Indian English compound *Godlove* seems to have been formed on the model of the native *deva-bhakti-* ('god' + 'devotion'),[44] the compound *keybunch* 'cannot be motivated in terms of an existing indigenous compound. Rather, the word must result from an '*overextension* [my italics] of the English process of compounding or, possibly, of its indigenous counterpart' (Hock and Joseph (1996: 377)). Hock and Joseph stress that 'the resulting structure is the product of a creative process, not simple (or simple-minded) transfer or interference'.

A good example of overextension as producing a 'creative' change was seen in the Etruscan material in Chapter 2 (see 2.XIV.1). *Filius* (in filiations) was sometimes in Etruria construed with an ablative, on the (false) analogy of *natus*, which historically was a participle and therefore correctly used with the ablative.

A few examples from Greek will clarify what is meant by direct interference on the one hand, and creative interference on the other. First, at *Quaest. Rom.* 103, 288F Plutarch uses the expression σίνε πάτρις in an attempt to explain the Latin *spurius*: *Quaest. Rom.* 103, 288F γράφουσι δὲ διὰ τούτων καὶ τοὺς ἀπάτορας σίνε πάτρις οἶον ἄνευ πατρός, τῷ μὲν σ τὸ σίνε τῷ δὲ π τὸ πάτρις σημαίνοντες.[45] He has construed the Latin preposition *sine* with a genitive instead of the ablative on the model of the equivalent preposition in Greek, ἄνευ, which itself took a genitive, and is indeed used in the same passage as an explicit equivalent of the Latin word. This is a case of direct interference. I refer again to a point made above, that the effects of interlanguage may be short-lived or restricted to individual learners. It would not do to suggest that there was

[44] See Hock and Joseph (1996: 375–6).
[45] Loeb: 'And by these two letters they also denote children of unknown fathers, *sine patre* [the editor emends the Greek at this point], that is "without a father"; by the *s* they indicate *sine* and by the *p patre*.'

ever an institutionalised form of 'Greeks' Latin' in which *sine* + genitive was an established construction. It is more likely to be an *ad hoc* error, but an error of a type which, even if it were only ever heard once in speech, would contribute to a feeling among native speakers who happened to hear it that there existed a variety of Greeks' Latin which was marked (among other things) by strange syntax which the hypothetical native speakers present might, but need not necessarily, have recognised as determined by interference from Greek. Given the paucity of material from antiquity, it would be absurd to eliminate cases such as this from the discussion simply because they are transitory and affect individual usage rather than the language as a whole. The pressures exerted by language contact on individuals may result in changes to a language itself (or one of its varieties) as more individuals are affected; the study of the individual case takes us to the very genesis of a potential linguistic change.

An example of the creative type, again involving prepositional usage, is arguably to be found in a bilingual inscription from Palermo in Sicily, though the problems of the text are considerable: *CIL* x.7296 = *IG* XIV. 297 στῆλαι ἐνθάδε τυποῦνται καὶ χαράσσονται ναοῖς ἱεροῖς σὺν ἐνεργείαις δημοσίαις, *tituli heic ordinantur et sculpuntur aidibus sacreis cum operum publicorum*. This is an advertisement for a stonemason's workshop, which states that monuments are impressed (?)[46] and engraved for sacred buildings as well as public buildings. There are several oddities in the inscription,[47] particularly in the prepositional expression at the end. In the Greek σύν is construed with the correct case, but the phrase is nevertheless odd.[48] σύν links one noun to another, and the whole phrase is thus equivalent to a structure of the type A καὶ B. This function is normal in Latin for *cum*, but not, it seems, in Greek for σύν. σύν can mean 'in company with, together with' (LSJ s.v. 1), but it complements verbs rather than coordinating one noun with another. It would seem that in a bilingual community in Sicily σύν had extended its range by acquiring a function of its near-synonym *cum* (a loan-shift: see v. 2. 11). In the Latin the prepositional expression *cum* + genitive (*cum operum publicorum*) is grossly incorrect. Clearly direct interference of Greek on Latin cannot account for the error. The synonymous μετά does take the genitive, but obviously here the writer associated *cum* with σύν, not with μετά. What then has happened? One possibility is that the writer was aware that the case selected by Latin prepositions did not always correspond exactly to

---

[46] For some speculations about the meaning of *ordinantur* in this context, see Susini (1973: 10–12).
[47] See the discussion of Kruschwitz (2000).   [48] As was pointed out by Kruschwitz (2000: 239).

that of their Greek counterparts. Thus, for example, ἐκ and ἀπό in Greek govern the genitive, but *ex* and *ab* in Latin the ablative. Historically the genitive of Greek and the ablative of Latin are connected (in that in Greek it was the genitive which subsumed the functions of the I.-E. ablative), but synchronically speakers might not so readily have made the connection. Like other Greeks (and indeed Latin speakers: see below, v.4.1) the writer of the inscription might have felt that the Latin ablative corresponded most closely to the Greek dative. *cum* + ablative would on this assumption have been the correspondent of σύν + dative, but perhaps because he had been taught or was aware that exact correspondence was not always correct, he *overextended* the 'rule' which only sometimes could be said to operate (i.e. the rule that one should not assume that Greek and Latin prepositions always took the 'same' case). The overextension led him to use a case which was not only wrong for *cum*, but also for all other Latin prepositions as well, other than the few examples of nominal origin (such as *causa*). On this interpretation[49] the error (a form of hypercorrectness) illustrates our second point, that interlanguage errors are not always due to straightforward interference from the speaker's or writer's first language, but may be creative overextensions of a rule perceived to operate in the second language.[50] There is also a vague 'Greekness' about the error, in that the genitive was a prepositional case in Greek but not in Latin, but the direct influence of a specific Greek construction on the Latin has not taken place.

I note in passing that there are other peculiarities in the Greek inscription. The abstract noun ἐνέργεια has been used in a concrete sense '(public) building, building works', a meaning which is not, it seems, otherwise attested. It might be said that the word has undergone an extension of meaning (a loan-shift: see below, v.2.11) on the analogy of the Latin *opus*, which combined the abstract meaning 'work' with the concrete 'building, building works'. But even so the use of the Greek word is puzzling, because it is ἔργον rather than ἐνέργεια which might have been expected as the equivalent of *opus*. ἐνέργεια corresponds more closely to Latin *opera*, and it is therefore possible that the writer has confused *opus* and *opera*,[51] as well as inflicting a loan-shift (based on *opera*) on ἐνέργεια. The Latin of the last part is conspicuously bad, and the Greek conspicuously influenced by Latin in direct ways. Was there a local variety of Greek showing Latin features, and was our writer a speaker of

---

49 Which is admittedly speculative. See Kruschwitz (2000: 240) for further discussion.
50 The term 'overgeneralisation' has also been used of such phenomena. See Adams (1994a: 91).
51 See Kruschwitz (2000: 240).

that without really knowing Latin itself? If we make this assumption, we must account for the general correctness of both inscriptions down to the prepositional expression (note the use of the passive, and the correct archaising Latin orthography). Is the prepositional expression perhaps an afterthought, composed by someone else? Was the writer a native speaker of neither Greek nor Latin?[52] The problems raised by this inscription may be insoluble.

A different type of creative change is to be seen in a late use of *potare*. The verb is used in Biblical Latin (e.g. Vulg. *Sir.* 29.32) and Latin influenced by the Bible as an equivalent of ποτίζειν, with an animate accusative object. The sense is 'give someone a drink' (e.g. *Per. Aeth.* 20.11 *puteus ille, ubi sanctus Iacob potasset pecora*).[53] In classical Latin *potare* means 'drink', and is not used causatively in this way. If ποτίζειν had meant 'drink' as well as 'give to drink' in Greek, then the semantic change in the Latin verb would have represented a classic loan-shift (see below, V.2.11). But the Greek verb did not have the first meaning. *Potare* has been forced to bear a new meaning on the basis of nothing more than its phonetic similiarity to the Greek verb.[54] Translators, finding no single verb in Latin which took the appropriate construction to render ποτίζειν, went to the verb that most resembled the Greek and simply inflicted on it the necessary construction. This process is neither direct borrowing nor interference, but creative borrowing (of a construction taken by the near homonym).

V BORROWING AND INTERFERENCE: TYPES AND CASE STUDIES

In this, the main section of the chapter, I discuss some categories of borrowing and interference, phonetic, lexical, morphological and syntactic, which contributed to the diversity of Latin in particular but also of Greek. Greek and Latin were in such close contact over a long period that it would be misleading to discuss the influence in one direction only. To some extent the chapter might be described as dealing with 'Romans' Greek' and 'Greeks' Latin'. I discuss as well some usages in Latin which might have been determined by languages other than Greek. My principle of selection is that the interference or borrowing must be clearcut;

---

[52] See Susini (1973: 10).   [53] See e.g. Rönsch (1874: 376).

[54] Cf. in Latin poetry the phenomenon which O'Hara (1996: 63) calls 'translation with paronomasia' or 'sound imitation'. The poet sometimes deliberately mistranslates, choosing instead of a correct rendering the word which is phonetically closest to the model (thus *fagus* 'beech' for φάγος 'oak' in Virgil's *Eclogues*). But this is another of those bilingual games played by learned Romans; the reader is meant to recognise the 'mistranslation' for what it is.

phenomena which can be put down to independent development in two languages will be excluded, or in a few cases discussed with the problems made explicit.

I will not put borrowing and interference in separate sections, partly because it is not always possible to separate one from the other, and partly because one and the same usage may under some circumstances be classified as borrowing, and under others as interference (see above, III). Much depends on the direction of transfer. Nevertheless the two will be distinguished as far as possible.

V.1 Phonetic interference: accent

V.1.1 Greeks' Latin: some evidence concerning phonetic interference and accent
A 'foreign accent' (a type of interference) is by many seen as the most obvious characteristic of the speech of a second-language learner, however fluent.[55] We would not expect written texts to carry the marks of a particular accent, but there is some anecdotal evidence bearing on the matter. Quintilian states in general terms that 'foreign nations' (*nationes*) could sometimes be recognised by their particular 'indescribable' sounds (1.5.33 *sunt etiam proprii quidam et inenarrabiles soni, quibus nonnumquam nationes deprehendimus*). He must have been thinking of different foreign accents in Latin. Would he have meant that we can recognise foreigners from distinctive 'sounds' of their *native* languages? Foreigners speaking their own languages are recognisable from the alienness of those languages in their entirety, not from their phonetic characteristics, whereas foreigners speaking a second language may indeed give away their origins only by certain *inenarrabiles soni*. For *nationes* in this context, see Consentius, *GL* V.395.17, quoted at V.1.2 below.

There is also anecdotal evidence for interference (phonetic) from Greek in the Latin spoken by Greeks. Quintilian (1.4.14), for example, records that a Greek witness in a case of Cicero's could not pronounce *Fundanius* with its initial fricative but substituted an aspirate (**Hundanius*): *nam contra Graeci adspirare f solent, ut pro Fundanio Cicero testem, qui primam eius litteram dicere non possit, inridet.*[56] On the other hand an obscure passage of Cicero's *Brutus* (259) quoted and discussed in Chapter 1 (Appendix) seems to turn up the other side of the coin, that is imitation (i.e. borrowing) by some Latin speakers of a Greek way of pronouncing certain unspecified

---

[55] On the general features of a foreign accent (affecting intonation and articulation), see further Mackey (1968: 577, 579).
[56] See further Biville (1990: 190).

Latin sounds. It was suggested earlier that there might have been prestige attached by some speakers to Grecising affectations in Latin.

There are several pieces of evidence comparable to the above passage of Quintilian in the grammarian Consentius, though not all of them are easy to understand. Note first *GL* v.394.22 (= Niedermann (1937), 16.5)[57] *labdacismum uitium in eo esse dicunt, quod eadem littera uel subtilius a quibusdam uel pinguius ecfertur, et re uera alterutrum uitium quibusdam gentibus est. nam ecce Graeci subtiliter hunc sonum efferunt. ubi enim dicunt 'ille mihi dixit', sic sonant duae ll primae syllabae, quasi per unum l sermo ipse consistat.*[58] This passage is notoriously difficult.[59] Superficially it is about 'thin' and 'fat' *l*. Since the double realisation of the phoneme, apparently so marked in Latin,[60] seems not to have been so obvious in Greek,[61] it is possible that in the Latin speech of some Greeks the distinction between the two types was not made in the native Latin manner. The problem is that in Latin *i exilis* (i.e. *subtilis*, in the terminology of Consentius) would be expected in *ille* in any case, and Consentius seems to have shifted ground and to be talking about simplification of the geminate.

Secondly, there is *GL* v.395.3 (= Niedermann (1937), 17.2): *ecce in littera t aliqui*[62] *ita pingue nescio quid sonant, ut, cum dicunt 'etiam', nihil de media syllaba infringant. Graeci contra, ubi non debent infringere, de sono eius litterae infringunt, ut, cum dicunt 'optimus', mediam syllabam ita sonent, quasi post t z grae-cum ammisceant.*[63] The palatalisation of *di/ti* to (graphically) *z*, *dz*, *tz* (with

---

[57] Niedermann's edition makes use of two manuscripts, M (the *codex Monacensis*) and B (the *codex Basileensis*), whereas only M was available to Keil (*GL*). I quote Keil here without commenting on discrepancies between the two editions unless they are directly relevant to the point.

[58] 'Labdacism is a vice which they say is as follows: certain speakers pronounce the same letter [*l*] either more "thinly" [than the norm] or more "fatly". In fact the one vice or the other is characteristic of particular peoples. The Greeks pronounce the sound thinly, for when they say *ille mihi dixit*, the two *l*s of the first syllable sound as if the word has a single *l*.'

[59] See Kohlstedt (1917: 63).

[60] See Sihler (1995:174): 'The distinction was as follows: *l* exilis was found before the vowels -*i*- and -*ī*-, and before another -*l*-; *l* pinguis occurred before any other vowel; before any consonant EXCEPT *l*; and in word-final position.'

[61] See Biville (1990: 65).

[62] *in littera t aliqui* is an emendation by Keil. M has (after *ecce* and before *ita*) *ut in tali uerbo*. B on the other hand has *ut itali*. Niedermann prints *ecce ut <in t> Itali ita pingue . . . Itali* (contrasted with *Graeci*) must surely be right, whether or not one accepts Niedermann's insertion.

[63] '. . . so that when they say *optimus*, they sound the middle syllable as if introducing a Greek *z* after the *t*'. The passage with all its problems is discussed at length by Vainio (1999: 97–107). She takes *infringere* to mean 'to break, to cause a friction in the teeth' (99). Thus the *Itali*, when they say *etiam*, do not palatalise the middle syllable, whereas Greeks do so, though they ought not to. An additional problem is that whereas M has *z* (*graecum*), B has *y*. And since the passage seems to be about the 'vices' of various races (Niedermann, largely following B, prints the sentence which precedes the passage I have quoted thus: *sed et in aliis litteris sunt gentilia quaedam quorundam uitia*, 'in other letters too there are vices particular to particular races which are committed by some

further spelling variants) took place in Latin from about the second century, but seems to have become the norm by the fourth or fifth century.[64] Spellings such as *zabulus* for διάβολος or *amphizatru* (Audollent (1904), 253.17)[65] for *amphitiatrum* (< *amphitheatrum*) could therefore be the result of a purely Latin development, but alternatively some such Greek words borrowed by Latin may already have undergone the evolution in Greek. δι is not only represented by ζ in certain Greek dialects,[66] but in the papyri there is a general confusion of δ and ζ before ι.[67] It is then possible that a Greek would have pronounced *optimus* in the manner apparently described by Consentius, but Consentius was perhaps exaggerating the distinctive 'Greekness' of the pronunciation, since palatalisation did take place in native Latin as well.

Another passage has to do with the simplification of *ss*: *GL* v.395.13 (= Niedermann (1937), 17.14) *item s litteram Graeci exiliter ecferunt adeo, ut, cum dicunt 'iussit', per unum s dicere existimes.*[68] In Modern Greek geminates have been lost.[69] Consentius' observation may be relevant to this development. In Latin double *s* was subject to reduction from an early period after a long vowel or diphthong (thus *caussa > causa* at some time after Cicero and Virgil but before Quintilian: see Quint. 1.7.20), but it was more persistent after a short vowel. The constant spellings *iussus* and *iussit*, alongside the classical scansion of *iubeo* with short *u*, suggest that *iussus/iussit* had a short vowel in the classical period (though the verb is attested in the early period with diphthongal spellings, such as *ioubeatis, iousiset*).[70] If so, a Greek who simplified the geminate in this position might have sounded conspicuous (note Quintilian 1.7.21 *nos gemina dicimus 'iussi'*).

Two of Consentius' remarks concern semi-vowels. The first is at *GL* v.395.15 (= Niedermann (1937), 17.16): *u quoque litteram aliqui pinguius[71] ecferunt, ut, cum dicunt 'ueni', putes trisyllabum incipere.*[72] *Graeci* is the subject of the preceding sentence, and it is clear that Consentius is still talking about Greeks. The background to the remark is the fact that Lat. [w] was regularly transcribed in Greek letters as ου. Since Greek had lost both the digamma and the phoneme [w] that it represented (except as

people'; *gentilia* is his own (plausible) emendation; M has *genitalia*, B *generalia*), the question arises wherein lies the vice of the Italians themselves. This and other matters are discussed by Vainio.

[64] See Pompeius, *GL* v.104.6–7, 286.12–15, Biville (1990: 277–8), Wright (1982: 60).

[65] This last word is printed by Audollent with a Greek *zeta*.

[66] See Biville (1990: 107, 278).   [67] See Biville (1990: 278), Gignac (1970: 190).

[68] '. . . so that when they say *iussit*, you would think they were saying it with a single *s*'.

[69] See Gignac (1976: 154–65), Biville (1990: 65), with bibliography.

[70] See Lindsay (1894: 111), Ernout and Meillet (1959: 325) s.v., Leumann (1977: 541).

[71] B has *pinguis*. Niedermann here prints an emendation *exilius*.

[72] '. . . so that when they say *ueni*, you would think that a trisyllable is beginning'.

the second element of certain diphthongs), it is not unlikely that Greeks speaking Latin, whether influenced by the transcription or not, would have substituted a vocalic *u* for [w]. Or is it possible that Consentius has confused transliteration with pronunciation and deduced a Greek pronunciation from the 'Greek' spelling?

The other passage is at *GL* v.394.14 (= Niedermann (1937), 15.17): *Graeci exilius hanc proferunt, adeo expressioni eius tenui studentes, ut, si dicant 'ius', aliquantulum de priori littera sic proferant, ut uideas disyllabum esse factum.* Again the observation (that *ius* was pronounced as disyllabic) is plausible. During the classical period in Greek *yod* is not attested as a separate phoneme, though it is found in Attic as the second element of some diphthongs and may arise also from synizesis.[73] The lack of semi-vowels in Greek may therefore have caused some Greeks speaking Latin to substitute for the Latin semi-vowels the corresponding vowel.[74]

There remains in Consentius a passage (*GL* v.395.7–13, = Niedermann (1937), 17.6) in which various allegedly Greek features of the pronunciation of the 'letter *c*' are discussed (e.g. the pronunciation of *sic ludit* in such a way that it may be taken as *si cludit*). The authenticity of such claims is impossible to judge, but they do at least demonstrate the Latin speaker's perception of the distinctiveness of the Latin spoken by Greeks.

One or two more general pieces of evidence about foreign accents can be cited. Note first Cic. *Brut.* 258 *aetatis illius ista fuit laus tamquam innocentiae sic latine loquendi . . . sed omnes tum fere, qui nec extra urbem hanc uixerant* **neque eos aliqua barbaries domestica infuscauerat**, *recte loquebantur.*[75] Douglas (1966:189) observes that the oxymoron *barbaries domestica* seems emphatic, and asks: 'is there an allusion to the influence of foreign slaves in the upbringing of Roman children?'. This suggestion is plausible; on the potentially bad influence of the speech of slaves on children, see Quint. 1.1.3–5. If this view is accepted, the slaves (presumably Greeks) will have pronounced Latin with a foreign accent, which, it is hinted, might be passed on to young children.

Similarly Quintilian (1.1.13) argues that, though pupils should begin with Greek, Latin should soon be taken up as well, or else their Latin speech will be corrupted by 'foreign' sound: *non tamen hoc adeo superstitiose*

[73] See Allen (1974: 49).
[74] See Vainio (1999: 103) for a slightly different interpretation of the passage.
[75] Loeb: 'pure Latinity, not less than righteousness of character, was the mark of their time . . . still, practically every one, unless his life was passed outside Rome, or some crudeness of home environment had tainted his speech, in those days spoke well and correctly'.

fieri uelim, ut diu tantum Graece loquatur aut discat, sicut plerisque moris est. hoc enim accidunt et oris plurima uitia in peregrinum sonum corrupti et sermonis, cui cum Graecae figurae adsidua consuetudine haeserunt, in diuersa quoque loquendi ratione pertinacissime durant.[76] This passage was taken over almost verbatim by Jerome: *Epist.* 107.9 *sequatur statim et latina eruditio; quae si non ab initio os tenerum composuerit, in peregrinum sonum lingua corrumpitur et externis uitiis sermo patrius sordidatur.* The point is that interference from the first language (Greek) might persist in the second (Latin) if pupils are forced to speak mainly Greek for too long.

Further indirect evidence for interference in Greeks' Latin can be extracted from Quintilian's discussion (1.5.29–30) of what he calls an 'old linguistic law' of Latin (29 *uetus lex sermonis*). He is referring to the rules for the placement of the accent in Latin, as emerges from the next section (30).[77] It is difficult, he tells us, for Greeks to observe this law: 29 *cuius difficilior apud Graecos obseruatio est, quia plura illis loquendi genera, quas* διαλέκτους *uocant, et quod alias uitiosum, interim alias rectum est.* Their difficulty supposedly arises from the fact that they have various dialects, and what in one is wrong is in another right (an anachronistic view?). In general it is possible that since the Greek accent (at least for a time) differed in nature from that of Latin, Greeks speaking Latin had trouble with the Latin accent.

Not all evidence for phonetic interference from Greek in Greeks' Latin is anecdotal. It is sometimes possible to make deductions from misspellings. A Greek–Latin glossary of the fourth century written in Greek characters throughout (containing Latin terms in the left-hand column and their Greek equivalents on the right) (*P. Lond.* II.481, = Kramer (1977), id. (1983), 13) has the form ουντε at line 36, = *unde* (ουντε βενιστε). For a parallel see *O. Amst.* 8, frg. e, col. I (for this text, see above, 3.VI.3), where one hand writes a Latin ordinal (in transliteration) as σεκονδα and another as σεκουντα. ουντε and σεκουντα betray Greek phonetic interference in the writers' Latin. Whereas Latin admits the contrast *nt* / *nd* (e.g. *amanti, amandi*), Modern Greek shows a falling together of νδ and ντ as [nd], and this spelling foreshadows (by hypercorrection) that development.[78] It is impossible to know why the glossary was written, but it

---

[76] Loeb (D. A. F. M. Russell): 'However, I do not want a fetish to be made of this, so that he spends a long time speaking and learning nothing but Greek, as is commonly done. This gives rise to many faults both of pronunciation (owing to the distortion of the mouth produced by forming foreign sounds) and of language, because the Greek idioms stick in the mind through continual usage and persist obstinately even in speaking the other tongue.'

[77] This whole passage is extraordinarily difficult to understand. See D. Russell (2001) ad loc.

[78] See Kramer (1983: 87), ad loc.

is interesting to find that it has not only Greek interference in the Latin (see below, V.3.3), but also an input from colloquial substandard Latin, as we saw in an earlier chapter (I.VII.2.I). We may deduce that the writer was unskilled in Latin script (or that he was writing for the benefit of other Greek learners of Latin who lacked aptitude in the script), that he knew some Latin as a spoken language, and that his spoken Latin was subject to Greek phonetic (and morphological) interference. If our sole evidence for the learning of Latin by Greek speakers consisted of learned Latin texts in correct Latin written by Greeks, we might be tempted to conclude (implausibly) that the learning of Latin among Greeks was an accomplishment only of the educated élite. But this text shows that there were Greeks who had picked up Latin as a colloquial spoken language, and is suggestive of an element of language learning beyond the narrow circles of the highly educated.

This section has not been about linguistic change in Latin in any broad sense, but about the diversity of the language. It is a myth that Greeks did not learn Latin. Communities of Greeks in the west (particularly at Rome) will have used forms of Latin with Greek interference, as has been established by the evidence cited here. Relevant material has already come up earlier, for example at I.VII.2.3 and I.IX.

V.1.2 *Some other accents*

It was not only Greek which was perceived as imparting a foreign accent to Latin. The African accent of the emperor Septimius Severus as reported by the *Historia Augusta* (*Sept. Seu.*19.9 *canorus uoce*, **sed Afrum quiddam usque ad senectutem sonans**) would have been determined by interference from Punic, if the presentation given by the *Historia Augusta* of the linguistic situation in the emperor's family is accepted. His sister, we are told, scarcely spoke Latin, and that suggests that Septimius will have been a first-language speaker of Punic: *Sept. Seu.* 15.7 *cum soror sua Leptitana ad eum uenisset uix latine loquens ac de illa multum imperator erubesceret . . . redire mulierem in patriam praecepit*. Similarly the addressee of Stat. *Silu.* 4.5.45–6 is complimented for not using *sermo Poenus* (*non sermo Poenus, non habitus tibi,/externa non mens. Italus, Italus*), and that phrase in the context does not mean 'the Punic language' but 'a Punic accent (in Latin)'.[79]

Consentius also makes observations on the distinctive features of the Latin of Africans (*GL* v.392.4, 12) and Gauls (394.12), without indicating whether he thinks bilingual interference is at issue; and for

---

[79] See above, 2.v.8.

general recognition that *nationes* might have such 'vices' (in their Latin), see id. V.395.17:*fortasse sint etiam alia generalia quarundam nationum <uitia>, quae obseruare et animaduertere debent qui suae linguae puritatem uolunt custodire diligenter, ut euitare ipsi possint* (for *nationes* in such a context, see Quint. 1.5.33, above, V.I.1).[80] There is also a suggestion here that native speakers should be on their guard against picking up these vices.

Also relevant is the allusion to the *tau Gallicum* of T. Annius Cimber at Virg. *Cat.* 2, discussed earlier (2.IV.3).

V.1.3 Phonetic interference: Celtic interference in Gallic Latin

There is some direct evidence for the phonetic influence of Gaulish on the Latin of first-language speakers of Gaulish. A notable item in the Latin and Gaulish documents from the pottery of La Graufesenque (for which see Marichal (1988), and below, Chapter 7) is the vessel name (plural) *paraxidi (-es)*, which is derived from the Greco-Latin *paropsides* (παροψίδες). The second vowel (*a* for *o*) does not concern us here, though it must be due either to assimilation, or to the constant graphic confusion of *a* and *o* at La Graufesenque.[81] The spelling with *x* is overwhelmingly preferred in the corpus (Marichal (1988: 274) lists some fifty-four examples), with a variant *parasidi* found about fifteen times. It is this *x* which is significant here. Gaulish had a velar spirant, indicated by χ in Greek script and *x* in Latin, which was notable for its displacement of the first element of various inherited consonant clusters (*kt, pt, ps*). Thus, for example, the inherited *pt* of Latin *septem* corresponds to the *xt* of Gaulish *sextan-* (cf. the ordinal *sextametos* at 19.1).[82] The modification of *ps* to *x(s)* (> *x*) is illustrated by *Uxello-dunum* 'high fort' alongside ὑψηλός, which is cognate with *uxello-*; so, at La Graufesenque, *uxsedios*, which is of the same root (see below, V.2.6). *Paraxides < paropsides* could be explained thus if the assumption is made that Gaulish at this late stage still converted *ps* to *x(s)*. The legacy of this Celtic-inspired sound change in Gallo-Romance is perhaps to be seen in Fr. *caisse < capsa*. The presence of *i* here may be explained through the influence of a Celticised intermediary **caxsa*.[83] Similarly *captiuus > *caxtiuus >* Fr. *chétif* (< earlier *chaitif*; Prov. *caitiu*);[84] also perhaps *factum > *faxtum >* Fr. *fait* (alongside the assimilated Italian form

---

[80] Niedermann, following B, prints the first clause of the passage quoted as *fortasse sint etiam alia gentilia quorundam uitia*. In the section introduced by the following *quae* Niedermann prints a text which radically differs from that of Keil in the order of its elements, but does not make clear in his apparatus how the manuscripts differ.

[81] See Marichal (1988: 35).   [82] For details, see Lambert (1995: 44).

[83] See Lambert (1995: 46–7).

[84] Note *FEW* II. 332: 'Alle gallo-rom. formen beruhen auf einem **caχtivus* (oder **cactivus*)'.

fatto).[85] Further evidence for the operation of such conversions in Celtic (or Celtic-influenced Latin) may perhaps be extracted from the bizarre form *souxtum* (juxtaposed with *Saturnalicium*) at Vindolanda (*Tab. Vind.* II.301: see above, 2.IV.3). *Su(m)ptum* 'expenses' would fit the context perfectly. Note too at La Graufesenque (in a Celtic text, 6.10) *inbrax[tari?]*. The Latin root seems to be *brattea* ('thin sheet of metal, gold leaf'), which had an alternative spelling in Latin, *bractea*. The latter would seem to be at the base of the Celticised word (*kt* > χ*t*).[86] This development also seems to be in evidence in various Latin inscriptions from Celtic territories:[87] note *CIL* XIII.11774 (Stockstadt, AD 212) *Deae Fortunae superae aarmipotenti Sacconius Iustus* **Ambaxtus** *aedem cum ara de suuo f. . . .*,[88] *CIL* XIII.8481 **oh** *[tum]olo requiescet in pace bone memorie Leo uixet annus XXXXXII transiet nono id(us)* **ohtuberes** (*h* here seems to be an attempt to represent the velar spirant).

What is significant about *paraxidi* (*-es*) is that it is attested not only in Celtic texts, where its presence is perhaps to be expected, but also in Latin texts (30, 47, 66). Here then there seems to be evidence that language contact in an area of Gaul had caused the emergence of a regional feature in the Latin of that area, a regional feature which was moreover to leave its mark on Gallo-Romance (see above on *captiuus* and *capsa*). It would have been Gaulish speakers learning Latin who were responsible for the form, using it both in their first and second language. It is of interest that the correct form does not turn up at La Graufesenque. That suggests that the community was cut off from native speakers of Latin, who would surely have reintroduced *paropsides*.

For completeness I mention an alternative explanation of the form. It might be argued that the misspelling *paraxidi* has nothing to do with substrate influence, but is explicable from within Latin itself. On this interpretation *ps* might have been assimilated to *s(s)* and then by hypercorrection reconstructed as *ks*, given that the assimilation of the two consonant clusters *ps* and *ks* would have had the same outcome. Thus on the one hand *scripsi* was assimilated to *scrisi* (as for example in the second, Latin section of the receipt of Aeschines (see 1.VII.2.3) written by a certain Theophilus in bad Latin: see Chapter 1, n. 146),[89] and on the other hand (e.g.) *uixit* often is spelt *uissit* (cf. *dixi* > Fr. *dis*).[90] A spelling *ixi* for *ipsi* is

---

[85] For further details and bibliography, see Marichal (1988: 70); also Flobert (1992: 108). On the complexities of *ct* from Latin to Romance, see Väänänen (1966: 63–4).

[86] See Marichal (1988: 70).   [87] See Tovar (1980: 333).

[88] On the name *Ambactus* (of Gallic origin), see Kajanto (1965: 313).

[89] On *ps* > *s(s)* see e.g. Väänänen (1966: 65–6), id. (1981: 64).

[90] See Väänänen (1981: 65). For *uis(s)it* see *ILCV*, vol. III, index p. 609.

attributed to a *legatus consularis* in an anecdote at Suet. *Aug.* 88, and that
might be interpreted as due first to an assimilation *ps > ss*, and then to a
subsequent hypercorrect reconstruction *ss > ks*.[91] But against this interpretation of *paraxidi* stands the fact that assimilation of *ps* to *(s)s*, though
it is revealed by the Romance languages to have taken place, is poorly
attested in Latin,[92] particularly in the early period.[93] In the Pompeian
graffiti of much the same date as the graffiti of La Graufesenque the
notable examples of *isse*, *issa* and *issus* have been treated by Väänänen
(1966: 65–6) as a special case rather than as representing a general phonetic development (id., 66 'le pronom *isse, issus, issa* semble être un dou-
blet familier de *ipse (ipsus), ipsa*, ayant une valeur hypocoristique, plutôt
que représentant l'aboutissement phonétique de ce dernier'). Otherwise
Väänänen (65) is able to quote only one example of the assimilation,
namely *scriserunt* at *CIL* vi.22579, to which can be added the example
of *scrisi* cited above. Moreover if *parax-* were a hypercorrect reconstruction of *paras-* < *paraps-*, one would not expect the hypercorrection to be
the predominating form; hypercorrections are usually only occasional.
The appearance of *x* (and of *h* apparently representing the velar spirant) in Latin inscriptions of the area (see above) also points strongly to a
Celticising pronunciation of various Latin consonant clusters in Gaulish
regions. The issue is somewhat confused by the fact that this type of
assimilation is attested in Oscan, and the Pompeian examples thus raise
the old question of the possible substrate influence of Oscan on Latin at
Pompeii.[94]

The matter is not clearcut, but however one looks at it *paraxidi* must
be a regional deformation. On one view (the more plausible, in my
opinion) it originated in this one area as a result of substrate influence;
on the alternative view that it was not necessarily determined by a sound
pattern of Gaulish, but was nevertheless restricted in distribution and
probably not found elsewhere in the Empire.

It emerges from this section that there was a feeling among native speakers of Latin that there existed distinctive Greek, Gaulish and
African accents in Latin, much as there is an Indian accent in English.
Some phonetic details have been given. Occasionally a misspelling in
a written text has as its motivating force an indigenised feature of non-
native Latin speech.

---

[91] Or was the man of Celtic origin?   [92] See Väänänen (1981: 64).

[93] Note Väänänen's discussion (1966: 65) of *ixi* for *ipsi* in the passage of Suetonius. He plays down
its significance: 'Mais il peut n'y avoir qu'une faute d'orthographe: le pauvre homme se sera
mépris sur la valeur de la lettre *x* (la confondant avec gr. Ψ?).'

[94] See in general Eska (1987), rightly taking a sceptical line.

V.2 *Vocabulary*

With vocabulary we come firmly to borrowing. Borrowing from Greek affected many areas of the Latin lexicon, particularly scientific vocabularies, just as borrowing from Latin affected Greek, particularly in the fields of administration and the army,[95] but this is not the place to attempt a systematic coverage of loan-words, which would be irrelevant to the present discussion. I am concerned here not with learned borrowings effected in the written language by first-language speakers of Latin, but with borrowing as influencing the character of regional speech. Did loanwords entering Latin in remote parts of the Empire give the Latin of those parts a regional flavour? The answer is that they did; there is a surprising amount of evidence on the matter, by no means all of it to do with loans from Greek (see also above, 2.IV.4 on Celtic loan-words in Marcellus of Bordeaux). It is sometimes even possible (in admittedly very general terms) to locate the place of composition of a text on the evidence of its regional loan-words. A school exercise published by Dionisotti (1982) has been plausibly attributed to Bordeaux on the grounds partly of the occurrence in it of the Celtic terms *bracis* and *ceruisia*.[96] Pliny (18.62) attributes *bracis* to the 'Gauls', and *ceruisia* (*Nat.* 22.164) to 'Gaul and other provinces'. It is obviously likely that a text with two such words comes from one of the Celtic provinces; but one can only place it so precisely on the basis of additional clues (there was a strong school tradition in Bordeaux which might well have produced such a text). It is interesting that both of these Celtic terms also turn up in the Vindolanda writing tablets (*bracis* three times to date and *ceruesa* seven times, along with an example of *ceruesarius*).[97] The attestation of the words on the one hand in Gaul (on Pliny's evidence, quite apart from the school text; see also above, 2.IV.4 on *ceruisa* in Marcellus of Bordeaux) and on the other in Britain shows the limitations of such evidence as a criterion for placing a text precisely, but it remains true that the presence of such vernacular loan-words in the texts at least would allow their assignment to the Celtic fringes of the Empire, and offers a glimpse of one of the ways in which a regional flavour will have been acquired by Latin in peripheral areas in which vernacular languages were spoken. In using such evidence in this way one must take account of the complete pattern of attestation of the word. If a vernacular word has made its way from the fringes to the centre (and many Celtic words, such as *sagum* and *raeda*,

---

[95] See above, 1.VI for bibliography on Latin borrowings into Greek.
[96] See Dionisotti (1982: 123).   [97] See Adams (1995a: 127–8).

became thoroughly domiciled in Latin: see 2.IV.1), it can tell us nothing about regional diversification or the area of composition of a text. In this section I will restrict myself to loan-words which had not caught on in Latin as a whole. In the Vindolanda tablets again there is an account (*Tab. Vind.* II.192) which has two such Celtic terms, *bedocem* and *tosseas*, both of them attested elsewhere only in Celticising contexts.[98] The second of these, for example, occurs otherwise only in a Gallic inscription (*CIL* XIII. 3162, II, line 12; the form is *tossim*) recording a letter of Tiberius Claudius Paulinus, governor of Lower Britain, from an unidentified British town Tampium. In the letter the word has the epithet *Brit(annicam)*, which primarily characterises the origin of the object, but equally is suggestive of a regionalism which had developed in Britain under the influence of the local Celtic. We will see below another case of a formal inscription in a provincial region in which a local vernacular term was admitted.

It is interesting to note that there is an implicit recognition in Cicero that substrate loan-words in outlying regions of the Roman sphere of influence might give a regional flavour to the Latin of the area. At *Brut.* 169–70 there is a review of provincial oratory, at the end of which Cicero tells Brutus that the orators he has listed lacked one thing, *urbanitas*: 170 *praeter unum, quod non est eorum urbanitate quadam quasi colorata oratio.* When asked about the meaning of the word, Cicero replies that Brutus will understand when he goes to Cisalpine Gaul. There he will hear words not current at Rome, which however can easily be 'unlearned': 171 *id tu, Brute, iam intelleges, cum in Galliam ueneris; audies tum quidem etiam uerba quaedam non trita Romae, sed haec mutari dediscique possunt* (see also above, 2.IV.1). What did Cicero mean by 'words not current in Rome'? Since the addressee, Brutus, is a Latin speaker about to go to Gaul as provincial governor, and since the passage deals explicitly with provincial Latin oratory, these words can only have been in use in Latin; that is, there can be no question of any allusion to the speaking of a foreign language (Gaulish) in the area. But there is little doubt what type of non-urban words heard in the *Latin* of Cisalpine Gaul Cicero must have been thinking of. These will have been loan-words from Celtic. Catullus' *ploxenum* (97.6) is a case in point, a word which, according to Quintilian, Catullus *circa Padum inuenit* (Quint. 1.5.8; see below, V.2.8).[99] The Ciceronian passage is by implication an early allusion to the presence of substrate words as marking the Latin of a particular region. Recognition of regional peculiarities in Latin was always sparse, but there was something of a tradition among

---

[98] See Adams (1995a: 128).   [99] For a discussion of this word, see Breyer (1993: 269–70).

writers of various types of commenting on substratum words which had found their way into the Latin of particular regions (see the passages of Pliny cited above; further such evidence will be cited throughout this section). Cicero probably had in mind Celtic words borrowed into Latin by first-language speakers of Latin, but it is in theory possible that he was referring as well to Celts who had acquired Latin.

V.2.1 'Regional' loan-words

Language contact in different parts of the Empire resulted in the transfer of local terms belonging to other languages into the Latin of those language learners, bilinguals or first-language speakers of Latin in the areas in question. Such loans constitute an important, but largely neglected, regional feature of provincial varieties of Latin.

I deal in turn with loans from several languages.

V.2.2 Greek

Various Greek words current in Egypt entered Latin texts written in the region.[100] Such loans fall into various classes: (1) words for which there existed a Latin equivalent; the writer was so familiar with the local Greek term that he adopted it in response to local conditions; (2) local Greek technical terms for which it might have been difficult to find a Latin equivalent; and (3) transfers determined by a writer's lack of fluency in Latin, as a result of which he either adopted Greek words because he was unaware of their Latin equivalents, or did so unconsciously because of his poor command of Latin. In this last group we would expect to find transfers not integrated into Latin, and thus classifiable as code-switching on the definition adopted in this book. But the distinction between borrowing and code-switching in such cases is so fine that I include such terms here. I take each of these categories in turn.

(1) *Loncha* 'lance', a word not attested elsewhere in Latin, was used in one place by Claudius Terentianus of Karanis (*P. Mich.* VIII.467.20) instead of the commonplace *lancea*. It was *lancea* that lived on in the Romance languages,[101] and the word was in use in the Roman army.[102] It is inconceivable that Terentianus, as a Roman soldier, did not know the Latin word. This presumably is the sort of transfer that might occasionally

---

[100] See the brief but informative remarks on such regionalisms by André (1971: 127).
[101] See Adams (1977: 77–8).
[102] See Tomlin (1998), 16 for a military text about some missing lances.

be made by a fluent bilingual; the soldiers with whom Terentianus was associating were perhaps predominantly Greek-speaking.

In a Latin letter found at Mons Claudianus (*O. Claud.* 2) a certain Antistius Flaccus announces that there is now an abundance of water: *aquam copiosissimam creuisse **ydreuma**, unde non minimam securitatem te consecuturum spero*. ὕδρευμα had the senses 'water source, well, tank', but it probably refers here to a well (see the editor, p. 26), and could no doubt have been replaced by a Latin term (*puteus, fons*).[103] The writer of the letter has used the local term current in Greek, and probably the Latin of bilinguals. At *TLL* VI.3.3133.24f. it is stated that in Latin the word is found only in proper names (of water sources) between Coptos and Berenice on the Red Sea ('non nisi in nom. propr. fontium quorundam inter Coptum et Berenicen in mari Rubro'), a statement which can be modified, in that a case of the common noun is found near Coptos: A. Bernand (1977), 68 *anno IIII . . L. Iulius Vrsus [praef(ectus) Aeg(ypti) . . .] hoc loco hydreuma [ampl]iauit et cum esset in[secur]um praesidium [forti]us aedificari iussit curam agente operis M(arco) Trebonio Valente praef(ecto) Bernic(idis)*. These attestations of *ydreuma*, at Coptos and now Mons Claudianus, tie in with the observation of the *TLL*, and explain why it is only in one area that the word is the basis of proper names.

At *O. Wâdi Fawâkhir* 5.15 (from the same region) *amaxe* (= *amaxae*) is used in the sense 'wagons' (cf. Gk. ἅμαξα). This loan-word is virtually unknown in Latin (apart from *SHA, Max.* 6.9), which had its own comprehensive set of terms for varieties of vehicles. Its occurrence at Wâdi Fawâkhir in a Latin text falls into place when it is observed that ἅμαξα is found in Greek ostraca in the same corpus (9.4–5, 17.10). ἅμαξα was the current term in Greek for the wagon in use in the region; note too *amaxitem* (ἁμαξίτης) at 1.6.[104] Also in the same corpus there is a unique attestation in Latin of *chiloma* (χείλωμα), = 'box, coffer' (2.13);[105] for the term in the Greek of Egypt, see e.g. *P. Oxy.* X.1294.5.[106] Mundane practical affairs forming the *raison d'être* of such bilingual (military) communities in the desert of Egypt could be handled more effectively by speakers of the two languages if the languages had converged partially in the use of technical terminology appropriate to the region. *ydreuma, chiloma* and *amaxa* were no doubt part of the pool of common terms; such transfers would have given the Latin a distinctive regional flavour in the eyes of outsiders.

[103] There is a bilingual inscription on a granite altar at Mons Claudianus (Bernand (1977), 37 = *ILS* 5741 in which *fons* is used as a translation of ὕδρευμα (see below, 5.IV.7).
[104] See André (1971: 77).   [105] On last word, see Daris (1991b: 60).
[106] See further Cugusi, *CEL* II, pp. 65–6.

Several other words which strictly belong in this section will be included in the next, for reasons that will become apparent.

(2) In the Latin letter *O. Claud.*131 a certain Athenor writes: **zeucterias** *quattuor pernecessarias iube mitt[i]*. There is no other attestation of *zeucteria* in Latin, according to the editor (p. 118), 'but ζευκτηρία is well known. In P. Oxy. VI 934, 5 and elsewhere it is evidently made of rope and from P. Mert. II 79, 3 it becomes clear that it was a necessary part of a μηχανή. It is thus uncertain what exactly is involved, but it must have been a piece of harness or a special piece of rope used in the transportation of the stones.' *Zeucteria* had a highly specialised meaning, and a Latin equivalent was probably not available, and it is a different type of loan-word from those which had a Latin correspondent.

At *P. Lips.* 40 (fourth/fifth century, Hermopolis) there is an account of a hearing before an official (see 3.VI.1). Within the Latin framework there is a Greek word at col. iii, line 20: *et ad officium d(ixit):* τυπτέσθω. *et cum* **buneuris** *caesus fuisset. Buneurum* (?) (< βούνευρον, 'whip of ox hide') had no currency in Latin, but it will have been a local term, impossible to translate into Latin except by a periphrasis.

In an account of payments (*P. Tebt.* 686, frgs. a and b; cf. *ChLA* 5.304, from which I quote here) the form ̣chalkiotheḳis occurs at frg. a, 14. This is the only example of the word quoted at *TLL* III.984.11 (*chalciotheca*), and the Greek original itself is marked with an asterisk: '*χαλκιοθήκη, fort. i. q. cistula aenea (cf. χαλκοθήκη Atheniensium) uel cista aeneorum nummorum?'. Though the account has numerous technical Latin words (e.g. *aciscularis, fabris materiaris, musaris, adplumbatoribus*), it also has several Greek terms with no currency elsewhere in the Latin language; these reflect the influence of local conditions on the Latin of the place where the account was produced. I mention here two further terms which strictly belong in the previous section, but it is useful to bring out the Grecising character of this document by dealing with it in one place. Twice the expression *ligna causima* occurs (frg. a, 29, b, 4). This represents the Greek ξύλα καύσιμα, = Lat. *cremia. Causimus* is quoted by the *TLL* only from this document. And at frg. b, 12 ̣potamịt (incomplete) must represent ποταμίτης, 'water-finder'. The borrowing is not noted in the *TLL* (X.2, fasc. II). The Latin equivalent was *aquilex*. Also in this document there is a case of interference of gender in a Latin word (see below, V.4.6).

At the sanctuary of Samothrace the Greek expression for initiates, μύσται εὐσεβεῖς, is only partly translated into Latin in Latin inscriptions (as *mystae piei*: see Fraser (1960), 31, 34 (c), 33.II; also *ILLRP* 211, 214). The partial translation reflects the unavailability of an obvious Latin term for the first word. The Greek word might have been distinctive of the Latin used in formal inscriptions at Samothrace, but it was picked up too by Latin poets (see *OLD* s.v. *mystes*).

(3) Into this class fall the Greek words in the dowry list in the marriage contract from Karanis (*P. Mich.* vii.434 (*scriptura exterior*), *P. Ryl.* iv.612 (*scriptura interior*), = *ChLA* 4.249) referred to in the last chapter (3.ii (2)) and discussed below, 5.viii (1), and *arura* in the translation of Babrius (3.ii (3)).

It is worth noting that in the Latin letters of Claudius Terentianus there are numerous Greek words (some twelve examples: see below), but in his Greek letters just one word of Latin origin, and that with a Greek diminutive ending (478.47 φοῦνδιν, 'dimin. of φοῦνδα, "money-bag, purse"'; so the editors). I list the Greek loans (to which should be added *loncha*, discussed above): 467.5 *anaboladium* (a kind of cloak, a word not found in Latin before this time),[107] 467.27 *colymbas* (of an olive swimming in brine; already in Columella and Pliny the Elder), 467.31 *tocas* (a breeding animal, τοκάς, equivalent to the Latin *matrix*; the word is not previously attested in Latin), 468.10f. *sabanum* (a Semitic word for a linen cloth, but found in Greek as well; not attested before this time in Latin),[108] 468.16 *suntheseis* (*synthesis*, of a set of matching articles, is not uncommon in Latin), 468.17 *phiala* (a broad shallow dish; the word is well established in Latin, most notably in satire and epigram), 468.18. 19 *charta* (commonplace in Latin), 468.19 *calamus* (also commonplace), 470.13 *bussinus* (= 'made of fine flax'; cited by the *OLD* from Apuleius and Pliny the Elder), 471.29 *xylesphongium* ('a stick with a sponge attached used for the same purpose as mod. toilet-paper', *OLD*; the expected Greek form would be ξυλοσπόγγιον; this is a real rarity, but there is an inscriptional example at *AE* 1941.5).[109] I would not see any ideological significance to the unequal frequency of Latin and Greek loan-words in the two groups of letters (such as, for argument's sake, a desire to keep the 'High' language free of borrowings from the 'Low' language). The Greek loan-words in the Latin letters are in no sense uniform in type. Some are commonplace terms well established in Latin. But others were not current elsewhere in Latin, and these can be treated as regionalisms which reflect the dominance of Greek in the life of Karanis; the local

---

[107] See Cugusi, *CEL* ii, p. 135, citing an example from the *Vetus Latina*.

[108] See Cugusi, *CEL* ii, p. 147. The word occurs at *ChLA* 1.12.10 (AD 167).

[109] Seneca describes such an object, but does not use the word: *Epist.* 70.20 *ibi lignum id quod ad emundanda obscena adhaerente spongia positum est totum in gulam farsit.*

words fall variously into the above categories (1) (*tocas* as well as *loncha*) and (2) (*xylesphongium*, and perhaps *anaboladium* and *sabana*).

The Greek words discussed so far in this section are attested in a region where Greek was spoken (Egypt). Curiously, in a western province, at La Graufesenque, there is also found a word of Greek origin which may be classified as a regionalism. At the pottery *canastr-* is the regular spelling of the Greek term κάναστρον.[110] Otherwise in Latin the word shows vowel weakening (*canistrum*). Had κάναστρον been independently borrowed (into Gaulish) in Gaul from local Greek speakers, and then taken over into Latin in this form in the bilingual potters' community after vowel weakening had stopped operating?[111] Or did *canistrum* undergo vocalic assimilation (like, apparently, *paraxidi*)? On either interpretation the form is specific to one region in Latin.

It is necessary to be precise about the meaning of the term 'regionalism' in reference to the sorts of words discussed in this section. Many Greek words had entered Latin speech in Egypt. This though is not to say that they were features of a 'regional dialect' of Egypt. Latin speakers in Egypt will in many cases not have been born and brought up there; they came (particularly if they were members of the army) from many parts of the Empire, bringing no doubt their own regional dialects with them. But to outsiders coming to Egypt for the first time the currency of local Greek words in forms of Latin speech might well have attracted attention. These may be seen as a special category of regionalisms, imposed in one area on the Latin speech of immigrants with a variety of (non-Egyptian) regional dialects.

V.2.3 *Germanic*

Some Germanic borrowings into Latin hint at the existence of speakers bilingual in Germanic and Latin. A case in point is *socerio / suecerio*, which is attested just five times in inscriptions (*CIL* III.5622, Noricum, III.5974, Rhaetia, V.8273, Aquileia, XIII.8297, Cologne, *AE* 1945, 101, Ramasse in the province of Gallia Lugdunensis).[112] The discussion of Deman (1981) has made it clear what the word means. Note Deman (1981: 205): 'SOCERIO, dans les cinq inscriptions latines où le mot est attesté, désigne *le frère ou la soeur du mari ou de la femme*, et, le plus souvent…, *le frère de la femme*' (i.e. 'brother-in-law'). The word is attested either in Germanic regions or their environs. Deman (1981: 208) has

---

[110] For a list of examples, see Marichal (1988: 273).   [111] See Biville (1989b: 102).
[112] See Wuilleumier (1942) on the Ramasse inscription.

argued that *suecerio* 'serait un nom germanique à thème consonan-
tique en -*io(n)*- correspondant à l'indo européen **swekuryo*-'. The spelling
suecerioni is found in one of the inscriptions (*CIL* III.5974). It is no doubt
a close reflection of the Germanic form; the alternative *socerio* has been
Latinised under the influence of *socer*. Examples of the word tend to
be in sepulchral inscriptions originating from the families of military
men. Germanic speakers who had learnt Latin in the army might have
been responsible for the introduction of the term to Latin (their second
language).

Suecerio is not the only Germanic kinship term to have entered
Latin in provincial regions. *Brutes* (*bruta*), which, like *suecerio*, is attested
only in inscriptions in significant regions (Noricum, Aquileia and the
Balkans, areas which were Germanic-speaking or bordering on German
regions),[113] was a Germanic word (Frankish *brûd*)[114] meaning 'daughter-
in-law' or 'young married woman, jeune mariée', reflected for example
in OE *brÿd*; cf. OHG *brût*. It came into French (*bru* 'belle-fille'), probably via the Latin borrowing from Germanic. In Latin it was a rival of
nurus.[115] The word did not fill a gap in Latin, and it is likely to have been
introduced by Germanic speakers who spoke some Latin.

A text which could tentatively be assigned to a Germanic-speaking
area on the evidence of the Germanic loans which it contains is the dietary monograph of Anthimus.[116] In this case we possess other information about the author and the place of composition of the text. Anthimus
was a Greek doctor who took refuge in Italy at the court of Theodoric
the Great, the Gothic king of Italy, 493–526. The *De obseruatione ciborum*
was written some time after 511. There could be no more vivid illustration of the effects of language contact on a form of Latin, because
Anthimus' Latin is influenced by two different languages. Anthimus was
not exposed to the grammatical tradition in Latin, and his Latin is suggestive of the language as it would have been spoken at this period.[117]
But there is more to it than that. Anthimus' Latin has one characteristic
that does not derive from the area in which he was writing, but from his
Greek background: the work has Greek syntactic and other interference

---

[113] See *FEW* XV, s.v. *brûdi*, 304. See *CIL* III.4746, 12377, 12666.
[114] See Gamillscheg (1970: 415).
[115] For details, see *FEW*, loc. cit. Note (304) 'Das got. wort hat sich in den nördlichen grenzgebieten
des Römischen Reiches festgesetzt, während sonst die Romania an NURUS festhielt (dieses auch
im occit.).'
[116] See Liechtenhan (1963).
[117] Some details can be found in Mras (1943–7); see also Liechtenhan's Index grammaticus (1963:
48–61).

(see below, V.4).[118] Various other late medical texts translated from Greek originals (e.g. Hippocratic treatises) also show syntactic interference,[119] but the feature is of less interest in a translation text in which it can derive from a servile translation technique. Anthimus' text by contrast reveals something of the interference which might have been heard in the Latin of a Greek who had not been formally trained in Latin but had picked up the language as a spoken medium. But the effects of language contact of another type are also visible in the text, and it is these which are relevant in the present context. In the Gothic territory Latin was coloured by Germanic loans, and that feature of regional Latin is reflected in Anthimus. At 64 (p. 24.1) Anthimus distinguishes between a Greek term (acknowledging his Greekness in the process) and its Latin and Gothic equivalents, in which case one could not securely deduce that the Gothic word had entered local Latin: *fit etiam de ordeo opus bonum, quod nos Graece dicimus alfita, Latine uero polenta, Gothi uero barbarice fenea*. But in other cases the Germanic word is embedded without comment in the Latin, and in these we may see local usages: e.g. 14 (p. 8.11) *si assatum fuerit ad hora quomodo* **bradonis**,[120] 43 (p. 19.5) *in* **brido** *assentur*,[121] 78 (p. 29.4) *oxygala uero Graece, quod Latine uocant* **melca**, *quod <est lacte quod> acetauerit*,[122] 3 (p. 4.16) *de carnibus uero uaccinis uaporatas factas et in* **sodinga** *coctas utendum*.

There are numerous Germanic loans in the Latin law codes of Germanic tribes, which mark in general terms the provenance of such texts. The Salic Law, for example, is full of Frankish terms, some of which were to pass into Romance, particularly Gallo-Romance.[123] These belong to a period later than that covered by this book, but it is worth noting just one such word, *baro*, which occurs four times in the Bath curse tablets in opposition to *mulier*, in the sense 'man' (e.g. *Tab. Sulis* 44.3 *si mulier si baro*; cf. 44.8f., 57.4, 65.7f.). Previously the word had been known in various Germanic law codes in this sense, but its attestation on the Celtic fringes of the Empire must be due to the influence of German

---

[118] See Mras (1943–7).

[119] See e.g. Mazzini and Flammini (1983: 28–9), Mørland (1932: 111), and see below, V.4.6.

[120] Glossed by Liechtenhan (1963), index p. 64 with *sura*. See *FEW* I.489, citing e.g. OFr. *braon*, OPr. *brazon*. One sense of the term is given as 'morceau de viande propre à être rôti'. See also *FEW* XV.234–5, Gamillscheg (1970: 315) (Frankish *brado*).

[121] Tentatively equated with *ueru* by Liechtenhan (1963), index p. 64.

[122] But of controversial origin: see Janko (1910).

[123] See for example Eckhardt (1962), index, s.vv. *ambascia, bannire, baro, faidus, fredus, grafio, leodes, mallus, mannire, raubare, texaga, trustis*. See also Schramm (1911: 70–1). On Germanic loans in Latin and the Romance languages, see above, n. 34, and especially D. Green (1998), cited earlier, 2.IX.

soldiers serving in the Roman army, who will have introduced it into their second language.[124]

V.2.4 *Hispanic languages*

CIL II.2660, an inscription from León partly in verse set up by a member of the *Legio VII Gemina* (which was stationed there) on the four sides of a marble base and headed *Dianae sacrum. Q. Tullius Maximus leg. Aug. Leg. VII. Gem. Felicis*, reads on side III (see *CLE* 1526C) *ceruom altifrontum cornua / dicat Dianae Tullius, / quos uicit in* **parami** *aequore / uectus feroci sonipede*. *Paramus*, which was obviously a local word and no doubt of Hispanic origin (cf. *TLL* X.1.310.78 'vox peregrina, fort. hiberica'), was to produce Sp., Pg. *páramo*. For another Latin example in a Spanish context, see Julius Honorius, *Cosmogr.* B 20 p. 36 *currit per campos Hispaniae inlustrans paramum*. The word indicated a high plain. On side I (*CLE* 1526A) it seems to be glossed by its Latin equivalent: *aequora conclusit* **campi**. The Latin-speaking reader would have been able to deduce the meaning of the word from this expression.[125] On side I (line 6) there is also an unexplained word *disice*, which is conceivably another local term.[126] The inscription is relatively early (second century AD) and literary; the intrusion of the regionalism (if it is not a place name) into such a formal text is remarkable. The writer had presumably been struck by the local usage, and he dignified it by the poetic context. Poets occasionally inserted regionalisms into their work, perhaps to mark their origins (see below, V.2.8). In the provinces terms to do with the land and its measurement were particularly successful in finding their way from vernacular languages into local varieties of Latin.[127] Further examples will be noted later in this section (see V.2.5, 2.6, 2.7).

But the best evidence for Hispanic words colouring Spanish varieties of Latin comes from Pliny the Elder. Between 72 and 74 Pliny was procurator of Hispania Tarraconensis, and the *Natural History* contains information about the area which Pliny seems to have derived from autopsy.[128] Syme (1969: 218) notes that Pliny displays a knowledge

---

[124] See Adams (1992: 15–16).

[125] Courtney (1995), 141 ad loc. raises the possibility that the word may be a local place name ('El Páramo'), following a suggestion of Mariner Bigorra (1952: 71). On the equivalence which may be deduced of *paramus* to *aequora*, see Tranoy (1981: 35).

[126] See Holford-Strevens (1988: 11 n. 17); but the word could be given a Latin etymology (see Courtney (1995), 141 ad loc.).

[127] Note, for example, that such terms are included by Corominas (1956: 41) among the main categories of Celtic terms to have passed into Spanish (i.e. by being borrowed from the original languages by Latin and thence passing into Romance).

[128] See Syme (1969: 216–19).

of mining in the north-west, particularly gold-mining in the regions of Cantabria, Callaecia and Lusitania (e.g. *Nat.* 33.80, 34.148, 149, 156–7, 158, 37.163). The whole area is replete with Roman gold mines, and those which have been examined by archaeologists reveal traces of the types of processes described by Pliny.[129]

As evidence for Pliny's acquaintance with north-western mining Syme might have used the passage *Nat.* 33.66–78, which has been related to the archaeological evidence by various scholars.[130] There Pliny goes into considerable detail about mining. He does not make it absolutely explicit that he is dealing with Spain, but it gradually emerges from the context that Spanish mines are his subject. He refers to Spain in 33.67 and 76; that he was writing particularly about the north-west is suggested by 78: *uicena milia pondo ad hunc modum annis singulis Asturiam atque Callaeciam et Lusitaniam praestare quidam prodiderunt, ita ut plurimum Asturia gignat.* The conventional view (see e.g. Domergue (1972–4), (1990: 482), Healy (1999: 91)) is that the passage concerns Spanish mining. The linguistic evidence, as we will see, confirms this opinion.

Scattered throughout the passage there are technical terms and linguistic observations. I set out the evidence below:

Pliny, *Nat.* 33. 66–77

67 aurum qui quaerunt, ante omnia *segutilum* tollunt; ita uocatur indicium (the earth that indicates the presence of gold)

67 cum ita inuentum est in summo caespite, *talutium* uocant (gold found on the surface)

68 quod puteis foditur, *canalicium* uocant, alii *canaliense* (gold mined in shafts)

69 farinam a pila *scudem* uocant (the flour that results from pounding)

69 argentum, quod exit a fornace, *sudorem* (the white metal sublimed from the hearth is called 'sweat')

69 quae e camino iactatur spurcitia in omni metallo *scoria* appellatur (the refuse cast out of the furnace)

69 catini fiunt ex *tasconio*, hoc est terra alba similis argillae (a white earth like clay from which hearths are made)

---

[129] See O. Davies (1935: 101), Lewis and Jones (1970), Bird (1984: 357–8).
[130] See Lewis and Jones (1970), Bird (1984), and the very detailed work of Domergue (1990).

70 *arrugias* id genus uocant
   (galleries dug into mountains)

72 est namque terra e quodam argillae genere glarea mixta –
   gangadiam uocant – prope inexpugnabilis
   (earth consisting of gravel mixed with clay)

74 *corrugos* uocant, a conriuatione credo
   (pipe-lines to wash fallen material)

75 id genus terrae *urium* uocant
   (a kind of clay)

76 fossae, per quas profluat, cauantur – *agogas* uocant
   (trenches to carry off the stream to wash the material)

77 *palagas*, alii *palacurnas*, iidem quod minutum est *balucem* uocant
   (names for types of nuggets and gold-dust).

There are sixteen technical terms here.[131] One (*scoria*) and possibly two (cf. *agoga*) are Greek (i.e. Greco-Latin).[132] *Sudor, canalicium* and *canaliense* are Latin. The remaining eleven terms are of non-Latin origin, and are no doubt Hispanic in some sense. I offer some comments on these terms.

First, in the linguistic atlas of the pre-Roman Hispanic languages (Celtiberian, Iberian, Lusitanian) based on the survival of inscriptions, the far north-western region is empty.[133] Here however in Pliny is a cluster of words which must have been in use.

Secondly, the accuracy of Pliny's information is confirmed in a number of cases by the evidence of the Romance languages. *corrugus* survives only in the Iberian peninsula, in Burgos (*cuerrego*) and Portugese (*corrego*), = 'ravine, gully'.[134] The masculine correspondent of *arrugia* also goes into both Spanish and Portuguese (*arroyo, arroio,* 'stream');[135]

---

[131] I know of no comprehensive treatment by an Indo-Europeanist of these terms, but discussions of some of them may be found in Bertoldi (1931a (*arrugia*), 1931b (particularly *gangadia*), 1937: 142, 1950: 100), Domergue (1972–4: 516–18, 1990: 482–6), Corominas and Pascual (1980–91) (e.g. I, 359, V, 438), Healy (1999: 91–3).

[132] *agoga* looks to be Greek (ἀγωγή), but the possibility that it is Hispanic cannot be ruled out (see Bertoldi (1937: 142)).

[133] See Untermann (1983: opp. 808).

[134] See *REW* 2260b; also Corominas and Pascual (1980–91: II,276–7), s.v. *cuérrago*, describing the word as pre-Roman (277 col. b), and ruling out any connection with Lat. *ruga*.

[135] See *REW* 678, Corominas and Pascual (1980–91: I, 359), Machado (1967: I, 321); Corominas (1961) *s.v.* describes the word as a 'Vocablo hispánico prerromano'. Corominas and Pascual (I, 359, col. b) express doubts about any connection of *arrugia* with the Indo-European root seen in Gk. ὀρυγή, ὀρυχή etc., a view discussed also by Domergue (1990: 483, 485–7). It is virtually certain that *arrugia* and *corrugus* are of the same root (see e.g. Corominas and Pascual, loc. cit.),

the feminine form has North-Italian reflexes, the relationship between the two groups being unclear.[136] *balux* (*-ucem*) survives only in Spanish (*baluz*;[137] note too in the Spaniard Martial, 12.57.9 *balucis malleator Hispanae*: see below, v.2.8).[138] *segutilum* is another word reflected only in Spanish.[139] For *tasconium*, see Corominas and Pascual ((1980–91: v, 438), Bertoldi (1931b: 100–2). *Talut(i)um* is reflected only in French (OFr. *talu*, Fr. *talus* 'high place'), from where it is said to have been borrowed by Spanish (*talud*) and Portuguese (*talude*).[140] The word is Celtic.[141] If the Spanish and Portuguese terms were indeed borrowed from French, it must nevertheless have been the case that the word was in use in the Iberian peninsula at the time of Pliny.

Thirdly, although most words are non-Latin, there are hints that Latin was the language, or one of the languages, of the mines at the time of Pliny. Pliny derives *corrugus* from *conriuatio*, a derivation which implies that he thought of the word as Latin, and that suggests that he had heard it used in Latin (as distinct from presented as a curiosity of foreign origin). Then there are the Latin terms themselves, and the Greco-Latin *scoria*. Another mining term from Cantabria, noted at *Nat.* 34.148 as a regionalism, seems to be of Latin origin: *hic lapis et in Cantabria nascitur, non ut ille magnes uerus caute continua, sed sparsa* **bulbatione** *[bullatione?]* – *ita appellant.*

Another Hispanic mining term found in a Latin text from Spain (the *Lex Vipascensis*, written on a bronze tablet found at Aljustrel in Lusitania) is *ternagus* (*FIRA* 1.104, 7, 8), which is defined by the *OLD* as an 'exploratory shaft'.

In the exploitation of foreign mines an outside power may make use of pidgins to communicate with local miners. But the lexical basis of a pidgin is almost invariably the language of the dominant group,[142] whereas here it is the local languages which supply the terminology. It would not do therefore to posit the existence of a pidgin. There are two possible

---

a connection which is reinforced by the fact that the Spanish and Portuguese terms *arroyo* and *arroio* reflect a masculine form. It is of interest that the only examples in extant Latin of *arrugia* apart from that in Pliny are in the African medical writer Cassius Felix (so *TLL*, s.v.), a fact which suggests the origin of the term in a marginal, substrate language; local words passed easily between Spain and Africa, as could be demonstrated by the presence in Berber of certain Latin (or early Romance) loan-words which have correspondents only in the Romance of the Iberian peninsula (see above, 2.vi, with the bibliography cited). On *arrugia* see also Bertoldi (1931a).

[136] See *REW* 678.   [137] See *REW* 920.
[138] On *balux* (and also *palacurna*), see Breyer (1993: 406).
[139] *segullo: REW* 7790.   [140] So *REW* 8545b. See also *FEW* xiii. 68–71.
[141] See *REW, FEW*, locc. cit.; also Tobler and Lommatzsch (1975: 68).
[142] See for example Hock and Joseph (1996: 424).

explanations of Pliny's detailed (and clearly accurate) knowledge of such terms. The words might have been borrowed by native speakers of Latin into their first language, perhaps through the intermediary of Romanised Spaniards bilingual in Latin and the local language(s). Alternatively, if the locals had given up the indigenous language(s) and moved to Latin, they will have taken over the indigenous words into their second language. On either hypothesis Pliny would have heard the words used in Latin, much as Brutus was about to hear local words in the Latin of Gaul (see V.2). I stress that, though I have used the expression 'technical term' of these words, most denote surface phenomena of the local topography, as distinct from things particular to underground mining. That explains why some of them survive in Romance languages: they were everyday words which happened to be used as well by searchers after gold. I would draw attention again to the observation made on *paramus* above, that terms to do with topography often pass from one language to another (cf. also *ydreuma*).

V.2.5 Punic and Libyan

The medical text of Cassius Felix is believed on various grounds to have been composed by an African.[143] Linguistic observations of the type found at p. 32.12 (*herbam putidam quam punice aturbis dicunt*) and p. 176.17 (*coloquintidis interioris carnis, quam uulgus gelelam uocat*)[144] are consistent with this view, but of greater interest is Cassius' insertion without comment into his text of the Semitic word *girba*, which was an equivalent of the Latin *mortarium* (pp. 63.5, 70.20, 174.5, 186.6).[145] It is likely that the word had entered Latin in the area in which Cassius wrote. Another explanation for its presence in the text might be that Cassius had used an African source, but given the other indications of his African origin as assembled by Sabbah the simplest hypothesis is that Cassius' Latin was influenced in this respect by local usage.

The legal documents known as the *Tablettes Albertini* from Vandal Africa exemplify in the same way the entry into a regional form of Latin of loan-words from a local vernacular.[146] Two such terms are *gemio* (e.g. 8.5) ('parcelle enclose par un mur en pierre sèches ou en toub')[147]

---

[143] See the discussion of Sabbah (1985).
[144] On *gelela* see André (1985: 109), comparing the Arabic *gelala* of the same sense.
[145] See Sabbah (1985: 285).
[146] A partial text and discussion of the language of the documents can be found in Väänänen (1965).
[147] See Väänänen (1965: 48).

and *maforsenum* (1.6) ('sorte de vêtement de femme, couvrant la tête et les épaules').[148]

In the military outpost of Bu Njem in Tripolitania soldiers dealing with local camel drivers imported into their Latin a range of local (Punic, Libyan or dialectal?) quantity terms, *selesua, sbitualis, siddipia, asgatui* and *isidarim* (cf. also *gura* at *O. Bu Njem* 86.4, 87.4).[149] At *O. Bu Njem* 77, for example, the *camellarius* who transports seven *sbitualis* of *triticum* is called *Iassuchthan*, a Libyan name. The African terms are glossed in the documents by equivalences in *modii*, a fact which shows that the local words were not fully integrated. But clearly to carry out commercial transactions with the locals the soldiers had had to acquaint themselves with the native terms. In this case then we are able to observe the circumstances under which the regionalisms entered Latin. Marichal (1992: 101) notes (basing himself on the measures in *modii*) that *siddipia, asgatui, selesua* and *sbitualis* designated the same amount; the existence of the four local synonyms is suggestive of regional (dialectal or tribal) variations. The soldiers sent out to deal with local transporters (one of whom is suggestively called *Aemilius Aemilianus*, a name which might have been a Latinisation of the Punic *Himilis*), must have been able to communicate in the local language(s), and the entry of the terms into Latin thus reflects a bilingual background. Soldiers recruited locally who were native speakers of the African language(s) will have been responsible for the borrowings into their second language, Latin, which, as the supraregional language of the Roman army, can truly be described as a link language.

V.2.6 Celtic

Latin had acquired numerous loan-words from Celtic over a long period, and many of these had become domiciled in the language (see 2.IV.1). Words which had entered mainstream Latin cannot be described as regionalisms, as was stressed earlier, but we now have evidence for a Roman military community on the Celtic fringes of the Empire (that at Vindolanda) which had taken up Celtic words, perhaps from local contacts, that had no place in the literary language (see above v.2). Two of these (*bedocem, tosseas*) occur in the same account (192), listing goods supplied by a man with what appears to be a Celtic name (*Gauo*). It is in just such contacts with local entrepreneurs in the provinces that loan-words will have entered Latin and given it a regional flavour. Whether

---

[148] See Väänänen (1965: 49).
[149] For a discussion of the first set of terms, see Marichal (1992: 101).

these words were borrowings into the soldiers' first or second languages is unclear, because the units of Batavians and Tungrians at Vindolanda might have contained speakers of Celtic.

Various *testimonia* allow us to observe the infiltration of Celtic terms into regional Latin. Eucherius, bishop of Lyons in the fifth century, comments at *Instr.* 2, p. 155.25 on a word for 'owl': *sunt qui ululas putent aues esse nocturnas ab ululatu uocis quem efferunt, quas uulgo* **cauannos** *dicunt.* With this should be compared the note of the Berne scholia on Virg. *Ecl.* 8.55:[150] *quam auem Galli* **cauannum** *nuncupant.*[151] It is to be assumed that both writers had heard the term in Gallic Latin, as distinct from Celtic. *Cauannus* was almost certainly a Celtic word (cf. e.g. Welsh *cuan*), = 'owl'. It is extensively reflected in Gallo-Romance (e.g. OPic. *coan, c.* 1180, MFr. *chouan*, Ronsard, O. Jewish Fr. *javan*),[152] but scarcely found outside this region (Comelico *cavanel*).[153]

A Celtic term to do with land measurement which came into Latin in the Celtic-speaking regions is recorded as a regionalism by Columella: 5.1.6 *semiiugerum quoque* **arepennem** *uocant (Galli)* (cf. Ir. *airchenn*;[154] with Romance reflexes, OPr. *arpen*, OFr. *arpent*, OSp. *arapende*, all deriving from a form *arependis).[155] Examples of the word in Gregory of Tours and the Salic Law evidence its continued use in the Gallic region (see *TLL* II.506.42ff.).[156] But it was more widespread than that, and is attested in other regions with a Celtic substratum. An example has turned up in a stilus tablet dated 14 March 118 in the City of London: *cum uentum esset in rem praesentem, siluam Verlucionium,* **arepennia** *decem quinque....*[157] Terms such as this (cf. also *bracis, ceruesa*) may either have entered 'British' Latin (i.e. Latin spoken in Britain, but not necessarily by native Britons) from British Celtic, or have been brought to Britain by Latin speakers from mainland Celtic areas.

Further evidence for the entry of Celtic terms into Latin comes from the community of potters at La Graufesenque (see further below, 7.IV.6). In the expression *mortariji uxe[di]*, found in the Latin text 66, the Latin noun is qualified by the Celtic adjective *uxedios*, which, as we saw above (V.1.3) is cognate with Greek ὑψηλός (but with a different suffix).[158] The same phrase is common in Celtic texts.[159] Since *mortari* had been borrowed by Gaulish in the pottery, the occurrence of the phrase in a Latin

---

[150] On the *scholia Bernensia* see M. Geymonat in *Enciclopedia Virgiliana* IV. 711 ff.
[151] See also André (1967: 161–2).   [152] See *FEW* II.1.548.   [153] *FEW* II.1.550.
[154] Cf. Walde and Hofmann (1938: 66).   [155] *FEW* I.135f.
[156] See also Beszard (1910: 88) on the formulae of Sens.
[157] See M. W. C. Hassall and R. S. O. Tomlin, *Britannia* 25 (1994) 303, no. 34.
[158] On *uxedios*, see Marichal (1988: 100).   [159] Examples are listed by Marichal (1988: 274).

text represents the transfer of a whole formula from one language to the other, possibly into the second language of the potters. Another formula containing *uxedios* is *summa uxedia* (5 examples listed by Marichal (1988: 100; cf. 278), all of them in Celtic texts; most are abbreviated, but note 18.2 for the full expression), which seems to have meant *summa summarum*, 'le total le plus élevé par opposition aux totaux de chaque catégorie de vases' (Marichal (1988: 100)). The phrase was probably used in Latin as well as Celtic, but on the evidence as it stands the potters would seem to have taken a Latin word into their first language, Gaulish.[160]

A Latin inscription from Trier (*CIL* XIII.4228) contains the Gaulish name for a judge or official, *dannus*: *Deo Mercurio coloni Crutisiones ferunt de suo per dannum Giamallum*. A compound with this same element, *casidanos*, occurs several times in Gaulish texts from La Graufesenque.[161]

Perhaps the best evidence for Gaulish loan-words colouring the Latin of Gaul (but at a later period) comes from Marcellus of Bordeaux; this evidence was discussed in a previous chapter (2.IV.4).

V.2.7 Miscellaneous

Various technical writers (most notably Columella) record as regionalisms words of substrate (e.g. Celtic, Venetic) origin. There is usually no statement of the language in which the word was heard, but it may be assumed in each case to have been Latin, given that the writers were unlikely to have known the substrate languages, even if these still survived; Venetic, for example, was no longer spoken by the time of Columella. These then were words which had entered Latin in provincial regions originally in the speech of native speakers of the substrate language, and not spread beyond their area of origin; they were perceived by others (such as Pliny and Columella) as regionalisms. I cite a few examples without further comment: Plin. *Nat.* 18.141 *secale Taurini sub Alpibus* **asiam** *uocant* (or *sasiam?*),[162] Col. 6.24.5 *melius etiam in hos usus Altinae uaccae probantur, quas eius regionis incolae* **ceuas** *appellant*, Col. 5.1.5 *sed hunc actum prouinciae Baeticae rustici* **agnuam** *uocant, itemque XXX pedum latitudinem et CLXXX longitudinem* **porcam** *dicunt* (these last again have to do with local land measurement; for *agnua*, see the inscription *CIL* II.3361, from Hispania Tarraconensis).

---

[160] A more complicated case is that of the word *panna*, which is common at La Graufesenque. Its origin (Latin or Celtic?) is controversial (see Marichal (1988: 88–90), Flobert (1992: 106, with n. 6), the latter assigning the word a Gaulish rather than a Latin (or Greco-Latin) origin.

[161] For a full discussion of the word see Marichal (1988: 98); see also below, 7.III.

[162] On the reading see Lambert (1995: 11–12).

v.2.8 The use of regional words as a marker of regional identity

The potential of localised words to confer a regional flavour on the Latin of an area is suggested by several passages in poetry in which poets of provincial origin use a substrate word from their own region, apparently as a marker of their roots. Martial (12.57.9) introduced the word *palux* (*balux*), qualifying it by *Hispanus*; cf. Plin. *Nat.* 33.77, quoted above, v.2.4. Catullus' use of *ploxenum* at 97.6 (*gingiuas uero ploxeni habet ueteris*) might have had the same motivation (cf. Quint. 1.5.8, quoted above, v.2). At *Sat.* 1.5.78 Horace inserts the word *atabulus* from his native Apulia: *incipit ex illo montis Apulia notos /ostentare mihi, quos torret atabulus* (note Plin. *Nat.* 17.232 *flatus alicuius regionis proprius, ut est in Apulia atabulus*). Finally there is the ostentatious insertion by the soldier-poet at León of the Hispanic word *paramus* into high-flown Latin verse (V.2.4).

v.2.9 Latin loan-words as regionalisms in Greek

Similarly, the entry of Latin words into Greek in particular communities will have given some varieties of Greek a regional flavour. A systematic collection of such evidence is beyond the scope of the present discussion, but an interesting example can be cited from a military environment; it is in military units *par excellence* that loans will have come into Greek from Latin.[163] In Latin military strength reports the term *aegri* was used of those who were sick and unfit for service at a particular time (see *Tab. Vind.* II.154.22; numerous examples in the Bu Njem ostraca: see Marichal (1992: 265, index s.vv. *eger, egri*)). This is rendered into Greek as ἄρρωστοι at *O. Claud.* I.86–94, 96. But in some other Greek texts from the same site the Latin word αἴγροι is used instead (see *O. Claud.* II.191, 192). This can be classified as a localised loan-word (see further below, 5.VII.1, p. 607).

v.2.10 Conclusions

The material assembled earlier in this section is different from that which usually figures in discussions of the influence of Greek on Latin. I have disregarded the learned scientific vocabularies into which educated Latin speakers transferred Greek technical terms, and concentrated instead on words confined to particular regions. A good deal of the evidence is new (such as that from Vindolanda and Mons Claudianus), non-literary or virtually unnoticed (such as that of mining terms in Pliny). There was a feeling among educated Latin speakers that foreign words in use in the Latin of provincial regions constituted regionalisms: this can be seen not

---

[163] For bibliography on such loan-words, see above, I.VI and Rochette (1997a: 32–3).

only in the passage of Cicero cited at v.2, but also in the comments about regional usage found in writers such as Pliny and Columella, and in the insertion into verse by various provincial poets of terms marking their regional identity. It has been possible to speculate in some cases about the direction of borrowing, and we have seen probable examples of the introduction of foreign words into Latin by second-language speakers of Latin (see v.2.3 on Germanic kinship terms, v.2.4 on mining terms, and v.2.5 on measures of quantity at Bu Njem); these represent borrowings into the link language, and are different from the borrowing by learned Latin writers of Greek words into their first language. Borrowing into Latin as a link language contributed to the regional diversification of the language.

But it is not only loan-words which display the influence of bilingualism on the Latin language. I am concerned in this chapter not only with regional variation, but more generally with language change determined by bilingualism. I turn now to some other ways in which language contact affects the lexicon of a language, using illustrations particularly from Latin but also Greek.

V.2.11 Calques and loan-shifts

Calquing 'consists of translating morphologically complex foreign expressions by means of novel combinations of native elements that match the meanings and the structure of the foreign expressions and their component parts' (Hock and Joseph (1996: 264)).[164] Calques from modern languages include Germ. *Wolkenkratzer* and Fr. *gratte-ciel* based on Eng. *skyscraper*. In technical fields calquing was one of the strategies used to create Latin technical terminologies. Thus for example Cicero's coinage *qualitas* (*Nat. Deor.* 2.94) corresponds morpheme by morpheme to ποιότης.[165] Such words 'do not introduce foreign elements into the language; but they do introduce new forms' (Hock and Joseph (1996: 264)). Calques in Latin are for the most part learned formations which are severely restricted in distribution; calquing did not as a rule generate innovation in the language in general, but only in particular registers. Calques occur in Latin partly in the technical languages of such disciplines as rhetoric, grammar, philosophy and medicine,[166] and partly in

---

[164] Cf. R. Coleman (1975: 106): 'the compounding of lexical material in the recipient language to replicate a lexical compound in the source language'.

[165] See e.g. R. Coleman (1989: 80).

[166] See e.g. R. Coleman (1989). For a medical calque, see Langslow (2000: 56 n. 180) on *imminere* (+ dative, = 'persist (with treatment)') = ἐπιμένειν in Theodorus Priscianus.

high poetry, where some artificial compounds are element-by-element renderings of Greek terms. Calquing in this second sphere had begun as early as the time of Ennius (see e.g. *Ann.* 76 Sk. *altiuolantum*, < ὑψιπέτης, 554 *altitonantis*, < ὑψιβρεμέτης). It is found in the early period also in Plautus, as an aspect of his linguistic inventiveness. *Falsidicus* (*Capt.* 671), for example, seems to be based on ψευδολόγος (cf. *falsiloquus* at e.g. *Mil.* 191),[167] though Plautus did not need a specific Greek model to justify his coining of compounds, whether in passages of abuse (e.g. *Mil.* 191), high style or parody (cf. *caelipotens* at *Pers.* 755). For an unusual, mundane calque of a technical kind attested from Plautus onwards, see on *inaures* 'earrings', below, 5.VIII. A particularly interesting group of calques has recently been elucidated by Kajava (1999). These comprise denominative verbs derived from animal names, as for example Varro's *uulpinor* (*Men.*327) 'play the fox' alongside Gk. ἀλωπεκίζω. Kajava notes (1999: 62) that such denominatives without a Greek model are very rare in Latin, and that, while they are common in Greek in many types of literature, in Latin they predominate in technical literature (Pliny the Elder and medical writers); in poetry they are 'almost non-existent' (id. (1999: 62)).

A comprehensive account of calquing in Latin would require a book of its own, and the subject is not strictly relevant to my purposes because this is not a work exclusively about the high literary language. Nevertheless I offer here several observations. First, compounding was not so readily acceptable in Latin as in Greek, as the Romans were well aware (see 3.III.6, p. 338), and even within technical registers unease is sometimes expressed about some calques. Cicero coined *ueriloquium* as what he calls a *uerbum ex uerbo* rendering of ἐτυμολογία,[168] but he 'shrank from' using it because of the *nouitatem uerbi non satis apti* (*Top.* 33; cf. Quint. 1.6.28, also using *uerbum ex uerbo*), and adopted instead *notatio*. Of course not all compounds were equally alien to Latin: if the Greek term had a preverb (i.e. prepositional prefix) as its first element, it might be easily rendered into Latin (see Quint. 1.4.18 on *coniunctio* and *coniunctio* as renderings of σύνδεσμος). Secondly, phrasal renderings of Greek compounds were sometimes adopted. Ennius' *dicti studiosus* (*Ann.* 209) is a translation of φιλόλογος.[169] An expression of this type engages the learned reader with the text in a way which we have seen

---

[167] See Lindner (1996: 70).

[168] It should however be noted that Cicero does not consistently use *uerbum ex uerbo* of calquing alone, but is capable of using the phrase rather more generally. On this point see Powell (1995: 276–7).

[169] See Skutsch (1985: 374).

in other connections. Just as Greek tags, proverbs or quotations were sometimes rendered allusively into Latin without flagging in communication between two learned Romans (see 1.VII.4.2, 3.III.1 (on Cicero's letters to Paetus)), so here the reader would be expected to identify the Greek word in the background (for such an expectation, see also below, n. 272). A number of descriptive genitives containing *multus* would be taken as renderings of Greek compounds by the bilingual reader (e.g. Cicero's *plurimarum palmarum* at *S. Rosc.* 17 (πολυστεφής)).[170] Similarly various adnominal *cum*-expressions particularly in early Latin can be seen as equivalents of Greek compounds: thus Ennius' *cum pulcris animis* (*Ann.* 563 *optima cum pulcris animis Romana iuuentus*) alongside εὔθυμος,[171] and *audaci cum pectore* (*Ann.* 371 *Hannibal audaci cum pectore de me hortatur*) alongside θρασυκάρδιος.[172] Rosén (1999: 24) suggests that phrases of this type which were coined as direct equivalents of Greek compounds 'may have enhanced a later attributive use of *cum*-phrases'. On this (rather speculative) view a usage which had begun as a form of high literary *imitatio* became established in the literary language in general. It might equally be argued that a structure natural to Latin was sometimes pressed into service to create equivalents of Greek compounds. See further Plaut. *Mil.* 16 *illum . . . cum armis aureis, Pseud.*158 *te cum securi caudicali,* Cic. *Mur.* 64 *te . . . cum ista natura*. Thirdly, not all calques in Latin remained tied to the technical discipline in which they were formed, or to the Greek term on which they were based. *Substantia* seems to have been coined in the early Imperial period as a calque on ὑπόστασις 'existence, essential nature' (so for example in Seneca the Younger). But it then took on a life of its own in Latin (particularly the later legal language), and came to acquire the concrete meaning 'possessions' which the Greek word did not have. Finally, not all calques in Latin are based on Greek. We saw in an earlier chapter (2.IX) two terms (*concibo, companio*) calqued on Germanic originals. These differ in one way from the other terms discussed here. If, as seems likely, they were coined by German soldiers serving in the Roman army, they were calqued on usages not of the speakers' second language but of their first. It is to be assumed that sometimes learners of Latin as a second language will have introduced to their Latin calques from the first language.

'Loan-shifts' are similar to calques, and are not always distinguished from them. By this process 'the semantic field of a lexeme in the recipient

[170] See the rich collection of material by Landgraf (1914: 47).
[171] See Rosén (1999: 28).　[172] See Skutsch (1985: 538), and in general Rosén (1999: 24–5).

language is adjusted to replicate that of an already partially equivalent one in the source language' (R. Coleman (1975: 106)).[173] Coleman cites Sallust's use of *amare* (as noted by Quintilian 9.3.17) with the meaning 'to be in the habit of', a usage modelled on φιλεῖν, with which it already shared the meaning 'to love' (for Greek influence on Sallust, see above, II). Loan-shifts again are found in the technical vocabularies created in Latin on Greek models, and again they will often have been introduced into the language by native speakers (of Latin) as distinct from language learners.[174] Nicolas (1996: 93–117), for example, discusses at length the semantic development of *casus* as a grammatical term, which underwent a semantic extension on the analogy of πτῶσις.[175] Or again, the use of *iudicium* of the turning point of an illness (e.g. Cael. Aurel. *Chron.* 4.113) is based on Gk. κρίσις.[176] Numerous other examples could be cited from the Latin medical language. Various late Latin medical writers (Caelius Aurelianus, Soranus Lat.) use *pinnae, pinnacula* 'wings, little wings' in the sense 'labia minora'.[177] These uses are based on that of πτερυγώματα, which has this meaning in (e.g.) Galen, Soranus and Rufus, *Onom.* Several such loan-shifts have also been noted in Cassius Felix.[178] *Carnifico*, which usually means 'torture' (see *TLL* III.480.1), is used by Cassius on the model of σαρκόω, in the sense 'make fleshy' (e.g. p. 31.20 *et postquam uideris bene fuisse purgatam, collyriis ad horam factis ex melle pastillato admixto cephalico medicamento diligentissime carnificabis*).[179] But unlike calques, loan-shifts are not entirely restricted in Latin to learned technical vocabularies. Even in the non-technical usage of educated Romans the occasional case turns up. Cicero uses the verb *conquiro* at *Rep.* 1.17 (*Rutilius quidem noster etiam sub ipsis Numantiae moenibus solebat mecum interdum eiusmodi aliquid conquirere*) in the sense 'dispute with'.[180] This meaning is based on the use of συζητεῖν.[181] The usage might seem to be a calque, but the Latin compound existed before it was used in the 'Greek' sense, and we should therefore rather speak of a loan-shift affecting a pre-existing Latin

---

[173] See also Hock and Joseph (1996: 263). This phenomenon, under the name 'calque sémantique', has been studied in detail (though not with a very wide range of evidence) by Nicolas (1996).

[174] Native speakers of Greek who were bilingual will have introduced loan-shifts based on Latin models into Greek. Examples from Appian can be found in Famerie (1998: 213–39).

[175] See also E. Löfstedt (1956: II, 433). Löfstedt discusses various other loan-shifts at 433–5.

[176] See E. Löfstedt (1959: 92). In the passage of Caelius Aurelianus just cited the connection is explicitly made between *iudicium* and κρίσς.

[177] See E. Löfstedt (1959: 100), Adams (1982: 99).   [178] See Giuliani (1985); also Migliorini (1981).

[179] The *TLL* glosses an example of the word in Cassius with *carne implebis*.

[180] See *TLL* IV.356.66, 'quaerere cum aliquo, disputare, gr. συζητεῖν', citing this example. For συζητεῖν used thus, see LSJ, s.v. II. On the other hand the *OLD*, s.v., 3, merely gives the meaning 'investigate'.

[181] See E. Löfstedt (1956: II, 434–5), id. (1959: 102), as well as the *TLL* cited in the previous note.

word.[182] *Hiems* shared with χειμών the meaning 'winter', but under the influence of the Greek word it also took on the sense 'stormy weather'. This meaning is particularly common in poetry, but is not excluded from ordinary prose (see *OLD*, s.v. 3): note Nep. *Att.* 10.6 *(gubernator) qui nauem ex hieme marique scopuloso seruat.*[183] There is a use of *alius* based on ἄλλος which on the one hand occurs in the Latin of the first-language speaker of Greek, Anthimus, and on the other in an earlier period was occasionally taken over into literary Latin by first-language speakers of Latin. On Anthimus p. 29.15f. *(quia exsucata alia pinguedo lapides puras efficitur)* Mras (1943–7: 101) notes that this is not the normal use of *alius*, but is Grecising ('Hier ist *alia pinguedo* etwa τὸ ἄλλο λίπος = *das übrige, nämlich das Fett*'); he cites (n. 9) e.g. Xen. *Hell.* 2.4.9 τοὺς .. ὁπλίτας καὶ τοὺς ἄλλους ἱππέας. The same usage occurs at Anth. 23, p. 12.13: *nam inter diuersa bona commixta in prandio si unus cibus non congruus et crudior fuerit,* **illa alia bona** *dissipat et non bonam digestionem permittit uentrem habere* (= 'the rest, namely the good things').[184] The usage, treated as a Grecism, has been well discussed in reference to a passage of Juvenal and literary Latin in general by W. Barr (1973).[185] For literary examples, see e.g. Virg. *Aen.* 6.411 (with the note of Austin (1977) ad loc.), Livy 4.41.8; note too Apul. *Met.* 3.8 *inter haec quaedam mulier per medium theatrum lacrimosa et flebilis atra ueste contecta paruulum quendam sinu tolerans decurrit ac pone eam* **anus alia** *pannis horridis obsita paribusque maesta fletibus.* The sense is not 'another old woman', but 'another woman, namely one who was old' (or, more accurately, 'an old woman, another woman'). Though *mundus* 'female adornment' and *mundus* 'universe' are sometimes in lexica treated as distinct words (so the *OLD*, but not Lewis and Short or Ernout and Meillet (1959)), κόσμος had both meanings in Greek, and the sense 'universe' which *mundus* came to acquire represents a loan-shift based on the analogy of the Greek word.[186] The secondary meaning is not restricted to technical genres. Other terms which would repay investigation are *silua* in its relationship to ὕλη and *uirtus* in relation

---

[182] Similarly *ambitus* 'period' (rhetorical technical term) corresponds exactly in structure to περίοδος, but the word was probably already in use in Latin before it acquired this meaning, and it would thus be more accurate to say that a semantic extension of an existing word has taken place (see R. Coleman (1989: 84)). Or again, *translatio*, used by the *Rhet. Her.* 4.45 to render μεταφορά, might already have existed in Latin (see R. Coleman (1989: 84)).

[183] Ernout and Meillet (1959), s.v. suggest that this usage might have belonged to the nautical language.

[184] See Liechtenhan (1963: 63), s.v., glossing as 'reliqui, scilicet'.

[185] Cf. E. Löfstedt (1956: II, 188–90), under 'pleonasm', and expressing reservations about the status of the usage as Greek-inspired, Hofmann and Szantyr (1965: 208), *TLL* I.1625.75ff., *OLD* s.v., 5.

[186] See Ernout and Meillet (1959), s.v.; also Holford-Strevens (1988: 166).

to ἀρετή. Loan-shifts were also coined in poetry,[187] as for example at Virg. *Aen.* 6.411 *inde alias animas, quae per iuga longa sedebant, deturbat. Iuga* here has the highly unusual meaning 'thwarts' (= the usual *transtra*). The semantic extension is modelled on the range of meanings of Gk. ζυγά (for this plural in the sense 'thwarts', see LSJ, s.v. III).[188] Notable too is Statius' use of *castior* of a river (*amnis*) at *Silu.* 4.7.12: note K. Coleman (1988: 201) ad loc.: 'since καθαρός (*purus*) means both 'physically unsullied' and 'chaste', St(atius) makes *castus* (= 'chaste') a synonym for καθαρός (= 'unsullied')'. Catullus' use of *nutrix* not in its usual sense 'nurse' but of the breasts at 64.18 (*nutricum tenus*) probably reflects the fact that τίτθη combines both meanings. Onomastic practices too may be affected by loan-shifts.[189] The Latin name *Spes*, for example, is a loan-translation of Gk. Ἐλπίς. I have concentrated here on loan-shifts in Latin, but it must be stressed that the phenomenon is also represented in Greek, as we will see further below. Recently, for example, Dickey (2001) has argued that the vocative use of κύριε which emerged in later Greek did so on the model of Lat. *domine*.

In the Latin of Ammianus, whose first language, as we have seen, was Greek, loan-shifts have been detected.[190] For example, at 14.6.6 (*populique Romani nomen circumspectum et uerecundum*), rendered into Greek by De Jonge (1935: 91) ad loc. as τὸ περίβλεπτον ὄνομα καὶ αἰδέσιμον, *circumspectus* (= 'ab omnibus cum admiratione spectatus, magnificus': *TLL* III.1171.77) is a loan-shift based on περίβλεπτος (again not a true calque, because *circumspectus* already existed). The usage is found almost exclusively in Ammianus (see the *TLL*, loc. cit.). But not all alleged examples of loan-shifts in Ammianus are equally convincing, or of the same type. Ammianus was a student of earlier Latin literature, and some of his supposed lexical 'Grecisms' were already long since domiciled in literary Latin (cf. the remarks above, III). For example, the metaphorical use of *supercilium* (of the bank of a river) at 14.2.9 cannot plausibly be dubbed a Grecism (cf. ὀφρῦς) as it is used by Ammianus (so De Jonge (1935: 71) ad loc.), because the metaphorical use had already had a long history in Latin (it is even found at *B. Afr.* 58.1: see *OLD*, s.v., 3, though not of a river), and Ammianus may merely have been drawing on Latin literary usage.

The cases of *circumspectus* above in Ammianus and *alius* in Anthimus underline the fact that loan-shifts are not only effected by speakers

---

[187] See e.g. the material collected by Kroll in Lunelli (1980: 13–15); also E. Löfstedt (1956: II, 436).
[188] See Austin (1977: 149) ad loc. ('a remarkable Grecism'; cf. Maurach (1995: 89)).
[189] See Solin (1971: 83–4) on loan-translations in Latin names.
[190] See e.g. Schickinger (1897: 28–30), den Boeft, den Hengst and Teitler (1991: 152).

(or writers) extending the semantic range of words in their first language. Those using a second language may introduce into that language new meanings of old terms based on the analogy of the semantic range of partially overlapping words in their native language (cf. also 2.IX on Germanic calques in Latin). Good examples can be cited from 'Roman Greek', that is the Greek acquired as a second language by native speakers of Latin. Martial 10.68.5 alleges that an upper-class Roman woman Laelia had a habit of using Greek endearments in the bedroom (see above, 3.V). One of these, κύριέ μου, is well represented in Greek (but see above on its Latinate character), but another, μέλι μου, does not seem to be attested in Greek.[191] It is based on the Latin endearment *mel meum*, and thus represents a loan-shift which had either genuinely taken place in the Greek used by educated Romans, or was invented on the spot by Martial. There is a very similar example at Juv. 6.195, again attributed to a woman, ζωή (another endearment) (see 3.V). Once again the use of the word cannot be paralleled in the Greek of Greeks, but it has an obvious parallel in the Latin (*mea*) *uita*, on which a loan-shift appears to have been based. The presence of two different but comparable loan-shifts in two different writers suggests that the usages were not *ad hoc* creations by the poets themselves, but taken from real Roman Greek. Jocelyn (1999: 182 with n. 91) has pointed out that in the passage of Lucretius (4.1153–70) which was discussed in the previous chapter (3.III.4) not all of the Greek terms put into the mouth of a hypothetical lover can be paralleled in Greek literature, and he invokes Roman Greek in explanation. The use of φίλημα, for example (usually written by editors as *philema*), at 1169 'resembles that of *sauium* at Plaut. *Cist.* 247, *Poen.* 1366, *Pseud.* 180, Ter. *Eun.* 456'.

There are comparable examples in the Greek put into the mouths of lower-class characters from time to time by Plautus. At *Pseud.* 210 δύναμιν is used in the sense 'quantity': *oliui /* δύναμιν *domi habent maxumam*. Shipp (1953: 109) observes: 'There is no evidence for any similar use of the noun in Attic, and the only example quoted from any source by Liddell and Scott, Hdt. 7.9 χρημάτων δύναμιν, is not very close, the meaning being rather "financial strength" of a country.' He suggests that CL *uis* in this sense (a use which is not found in OL) may be a loan translation of a technical use of δύναμις current in Magna Graecia. There is though another, more straightforward, possibility. It may be true that *uis* does

[191] I owe this information to Dr Eleanor Dickey, who has recently herself discussed the topic raised in this paragraph (at Dickey (2002: 162)).

not occur in this sense in old Latin, but that is perhaps merely due to chance, because the usage is very well established in the later Republican period (see *OLD* s.v., 8), where, significantly, it is often accompanied by the adjective *magna* (see *OLD*, loc. cit.). The presence of *maxumam* in the passage of Plautus is thus suggestive of the later Republican use of *uis*. On this view one need not invoke the influence of southern Italian Greek; the Greek usage could simply be a loan-shift from Lat. *uis*, with a parallel (in type) in (e.g.) μέλι μου.

An example of a non-literary loan-shift in the Latin of a Greek can be found at *P. Mich.* VII.442 = *ChLA* 5.295, a second-century document from Karanis dealing with a dowry (see 1.VII.4.2 (9)). In the second line the expression *corpore fusco, fa[c]iȩ [d]ȩd[u]cta, naso recto, lentigo malo d[e]xtro̧* contains a use of *malum* = 'cheek', whereas the appropriate word in Latin ought to have been feminine (*mala*). A revealing parallel (both structurally and lexically: on the structure, see 1.VII.4.2 (9)) is found at *P. Ryl.* II.160b.11 ο(ὑλὴ) μήλωι ἀριστερῶι (see also *P. Ryl.* II.160c, col. ii, line 9). μῆλον 'apple' was used in the metaphorical sense 'cheek' in Greek, as here. *Malum* 'apple' has by a loan-shift been given a new sense based on the semantic range of μῆλον (see also *OLD*, s.v. *malum*, 6). If there is often something artificial about a loan-shift (or calque) introduced into a writer's (or speaker's) first language from his second, those introduced into a second language do not derive from conscious effort: they represent interference, whereas a self-conscious loan-shift or calque effected in a first language represents borrowing.

Not all loan-shifts in Latin are based on Greek. E. Löfstedt (1950: 47–50) discusses (though from a much later period) the interesting case of Adamnanus' use of *alius* in his *Vita S. Columbae*: e.g. p. 112.27ff. Fowler *et sic per aliquot dies eodem in loco eademque uespertina sentiebant hora. fuit autem iisdem in diebus sanctus Baitheneus inter eos operum dispensator, qui sic ad ipsos* **alia die** *est prolocutus, inquiens . . .* Here, as often elsewhere in the work, *alius* is equivalent to *quidam*, as Löfstedt shows in detail. Behind this usage lies the fact that in Irish *araile* combines the meanings of *alius* and *quidam*; the semantic range of *alius* has thus been extended by an Irish writer to replicate that of the Irish word.[192]

It must be acknowledged finally that many possible loan-shifts in Latin, particularly of the later period, are (like various syntactic developments) open to the alternative explanation that later Latin and Greek had developed independently along the same lines. For example, in later Latin

[192] See E. Löfstedt (1950: 49).

nomen often has the meaning 'person' (e.g. *Vitae Patrum* 6.2.8 *quando eram in Scythi cum abbate Macario, ascendimus metere cum eo* **septem nomina**). In later Greek ὄνομα can have this meaning, and examples of *nomen* used thus may in some cases be taken as loan translations of the Greek usage; the *Vitae Patrum*, for example, is translated from Greek. But E. Löfstedt (1950: 42–4) has shown that *nomen* was already showing much the same development in Latin itself. Or again, there is the case of Ammianus' use of *transtulerunt* intransitively at 21.12.8: *contra munitores, licet pauore discriminum anxii, pudore tamen, ne socordes uiderentur et segnes, ubi parum uis procedebat Marte aperto temptata, ad instrumenta obsidionalium artium* **transtulerunt**. The passage has been variously emended (e.g. <*se*> *transtulerunt* Bentley, *transiuerunt* Gardthausen). E. Löfstedt (1936: 208) draws attention to the same usage in the *cod. Bob.* of the *Vetus Latina* at Matth. 13.53, which is based on μετῆρεν ἐκεῖθεν. Did the intransitive use of μεταίρω in Greek influence Latin? There is again an alternative explanation. Many reflexive verbs in later Latin developed an intransitive use, as E. Löfstedt (1936: 207–8) demonstrates in the case of this verb.[193] Parallel development of the two languages is thus a possibility.[194] The chronology of the attestations of *ficatum* (sc. *iecur*) and συκωτόν (sc. ἧπαρ) of the liver (first that of animals stuffed with figs, then eventually of humans in general) does not make it clear whether one was a loan-translation of the other, or both emerged at the same time in bilingual communities among cooks and those raising animals for consumption.[195] Similar ambiguities of interpretation must also be confronted in the classical period. For example, *caulis* 'stalk, cabbage stalk' has the sense 'penis' at Lucilius 281, as later in Celsus, for whom it was the standard word in this meaning.[196] Celsus will have had before him the Greek medical metaphor, καυλός, = 'stem of a plant' > 'penis', particularly given the fact that the two terms were virtually homonyms. He probably introduced a loan-shift, but must the same be said of Lucilius, given that botanical metaphors for the male organ are so commonplace in Latin?

I mention here a comparable phenomenon to lexical loan-shifts, that is the analogical extension of the function of a suffix based on the functional range of a suffix in the other language. Latin adjectives of material in *-eus* (e.g. *aureus*) correspond to the Homeric type in -εο- (e.g. χρύσεος).[197] But -εος was also used in epic language to form adjectives based on personal

---

[193] See the very full monograph of Feltenius (1977), particularly at 81–2 on this usage.
[194] A good deal of material of the same kind is assembled by E. Löfstedt (1936: 197–216).
[195] For the attestation of the two, see André (1991: 152); see also Schulze (1894 = 1958: 115).
[196] Details can be found in Adams (1982: 26).   [197] See Leumann (1977: 286).

names (Νεστόρεος). So in Latin poetry -*eus* was extended in function to form such adjectives on Latin bases (e.g. *Romuleus* in Virgil, Ovid, al.).[198]

It has been shown in this section that loan-shifts in Latin, mainly based on Greek, were not confined to technical vocabularies. They can readily be found in technical writings, but are also attested in the educated language in general, in epic, in colloquial speech (indirectly: see above on Plautus and Martial), and in substandard texts (see above on the Egyptian document). They were variously introduced by native speakers of Latin and of Greek; a distinction has been drawn between the two different directions of transfer. A systematic account of loan-shifts in Latin is yet to be written; the Republican period from Plautus and Cato onwards would perhaps prove particularly fruitful.

V.2.12 Translations of idioms

Comparable to loan-shifts but involving more than one word are word-by-word renderings of idioms from the speaker's (or writer's) primary language into a second language. Such a rendering will not necessarily capture the meaning of the original idiom. By 'idiom' here I mean a combination of words such that the meaning of the whole cannot be deduced from the meanings of its component parts.[199] Foreigners notoriously have a habit of translating idioms literally from their first language into a second, with results that are often less than satisfactory. A good example in late Greek is the expression ἀπ' ὀμμάτων = 'blind'.[200] This is a translation of the Latin expression *ab oculis* (> Fr. *aveugle*), the sense of which is not deducible from a literal rendering (*ab* does not mean 'without'). It was shown by Rohlfs (1954: 34–5) that the Latin expression is derived from phrases of the type *orbus ab oculis* 'bereft of eyes',[201] a phrase which was abbreviated both into *orbus* (> It. *orbo*)[202] and *ab oculis*.[203] Later Greek simply took over (in the form of a translation) the Latin idiom. Or again, it has been observed by E. Löfstedt (1950: 46) that in the late text *Vita sanctae Melaniae iunioris* the expression *uerbum dare alicui* sometimes means 'to promise' (e.g. 2.36 *periclitaberis modo,*

---

[198] See Leumann (1947: 130), id. (1977: 286–7).

[199] The translations of formulae discussed in the first chapter (I.VII.4.2) were not necessarily non-idiomatic in the second language.

[200] See E. Löfstedt (1959: 101).

[201] For *orbus* in various collocations used of blindness, see *TLL* IX.2.927.48ff.; also E. Löfstedt (1956: II, 374–5).

[202] There are reflexes in other languages as well: see *REW* 6086.

[203] E. Löfstedt (1959: 101) mistakenly argued that the Latin expression was derived from the Greek, without satisfactorily explaining how the Greek acquired this meaning.

nisi **pollicita fueris** *mihi quod hinc non recedas. tunc puella perterrita* **dedit uerbum** *et dixit*). Löfstedt explains this idiom as a rendering of the late and Byzantine Greek use of λόγον διδόναι in the same sense. The *Vita* has other signs of Greek interference, and may even be translated from a Greek original.[204] Literal renderings of idioms are a feature of inartistic translation literature, and may be of quite complicated history. For example, corresponding to the Vulgate at Num. 14: 31 (*terram,* **quam** *uos abscessistis* **ab ea**), where the case of the relative pronoun is conveyed later in the clause by an otiose demonstrative + preposition, the LXX has ἣν ὑμεῖς ἀπέστητε ἀπ' **αὐτῆς**; but it is a Hebrew construction, not a Greek, which lies at the root of the idiom in the Latin (as well as the Greek).[205] That said, this resumptive use of a pronoun in a relative clause is not unknown in substandard Latin.[206]

Further examples of idiom-translations may be found in the Greek of Romans. At Plaut. *Cas.* 729f., as we saw in another connection in the last chapter (3.IV.1), the old man Lysidamus, addressing a slave, says: 729f. *dabo tibi* / μέγα κακόν. He has translated the Latin *magnum malum* into Greek, mimicking the habits of the slave (who has just used a Greek expression). Whereas the use of the Greek expression at Athens, such as it is attested (Shipp (1953: 106 n. 4) cites e.g. Men. *Per.* 208–9), was not stereotyped, *magnum malum* in this specialised meaning was an idiom of Plautine Latin, and the audience must have been expected to hear the Latin expression behind the Greek. On this occasion then the idiom-translation was meant to be funny.

Clear examples of idioms rendered literally are to be found in the Latin translations of *senatus consulta* (see Sherk (1969)) and in that of the *Res Gestae* of Augustus.

Holford-Strevens (1993: 207) draws attention, for example, to the expression ᾧ ἔλασσον θεραπεύει in Sherk (1969), 5, lines 29–30 (of 164 BC), a rendering of *quominus curet*. Or again, in the *Res Gestae* (25.2), ὤμοσεν εἰς τοὺς ἐμοὺς λόγους is equivalent to *iurauit in mea uerba*.[207]

I list further examples from the same two works:

(1) At *Res Gestae* 9.1 *uota suscipere* is translated by εὐχὰς ἀναλαμβάνειν, whereas the expected Greek verb would have been ποιεῖσθαι.[208]

---

[204] See E. Löfstedt (1950: 47).   [205] See E. Löfstedt (1959: 91).
[206] See below 5.VII.2.2 on *ChLA* 3.204 (with Ahlquist (1909: 114–15), Hofmann and Szantyr (1965: 556–7)).
[207] See Holford-Strevens (1993: 208 with n. 33). On Latinate elements in the *Res Gestae*, see also Wigtil (1982a: 628–31). The numeration from the *Res Gestae* given here is that of Gagé's second edition (1977).
[208] See Meuwese (1920: 112).

(2) Several times in the *Res Gestae deducere colonias* is rendered literally by κατάγειν ἀποικίας (e.g. 16.1, 28.2). This is not the normal Greek idiom (which would have been ἀποικίαν ἐκπέμπειν or ἀποστέλλειν ἀποίκους).[209]

(3) At *Res Gestae* 10.2 (*sacerdotium*) *deferre* is rendered by καταφέρειν, which is not idiomatic Greek.[210]

(4) At Sherk (1969), 22.7 (*senatus consultum de Asclepiade*) ἐργασίαν ἔπανδρον καὶ πιστήν. [. . παρεσχηκέ]ναι is translationese, rendering *operam fortem et fidelem . . . nauasse.*[211]

(5) In the same *senatus consultum* (cf. (4) above) line 14, εἰς ἀκέραιον ἀποκατασταθῇ corresponds to the Latin *in integrum restituere.*[212]

On the face of it these various renderings might seem to reflect the incompetence in Greek of the translators, and they have indeed been taken in this way.[213] On this view the expressions quoted would show interference from L1 (Latin), and would be manifestations of Roman Greek, that is of a regional form of the language with features determined by language contact. There is though good reason for treating such renderings as special cases, not as ineptitudes. In various cultures texts of which the wording is sacrosanct, particularly from the spheres of religion and law, have been shown to inspire word-by-word renderings into a second language, and for an obvious reason: if the text is translated with dead literalness, the wording of the original can be recovered from the translation.[214] The technique of translation is so well established that it has a modern technical name ('word-for-word translation').[215] The early Latin Bible translations and various other Biblical translations fall into this category (for a specific example, an Old Latin version of the Psalms translated directly from Hebrew, see above, 2.VIII). There is a heavily Grecised form of Syriac which turns up between the sixth and eighth centuries in translations of Greek Biblical, theological and philosophical writings, at a time of christological controversy. Those who were engaged in such debates had to have access to 'authoritative' translations, that is translations which were as

---

[209] See Meuwese (1920: 116–17).   [210] See Meuwese (1920: 117).   [211] See Viereck (1888: 83).

[212] See Viereck (1888: 83); also Dubuisson (1985: 151, 319 n. 12).

[213] For example by Jocelyn (1999: 177 n. 49), following Holford-Strevens (1993). On the debate about this issue, see Wigtil (1982b).

[214] The word-for-word translation technique in religious and legal texts from antiquity has been well treated by Brock (1979). Note his comment on our texts (74): 'in the Republican administrative documents from the east, the Greek version always points the reader to the official original in Latin'. See also Bartelink (1980: 36, 46–7, 52) on different types of translation as discussed in Jerome's monograph on the subject.

[215] See Delisle, Lee-Jahnke and Cormier (1999: 200), s.v.

close to the originals as possible.[216] Similarly Gershevitch (1979) coined
the term 'alloglottography' for what was in effect the Elamite writing of
Old Persian. On his view certain documents of the Achaemenid dynasty
of the Persian Empire were written by scribes bilingual in Elamite and
Old Persian who, working from the the King's dictation in Old Persian,
wrote the texts in a form of Elamite from which the original Old Persian
could be exactly recovered. Alloglottography is defined (p. 138) as
'the use of one writable language for the purpose of writing another
language'. But we need not go so far afield for this process. Justinian
(*Cod.* 1.17.2.21) prescribed a single method of translating Roman laws
into Greek, which he called the 'foot-by-foot' method (κατὰ πόδα): *eas
(leges) in Graecam uocem transformare sub eodem ordine eaque consequentia, sub
qua uoces Romanae positae sunt (hoc quod Graeci* κατὰ πόδα *dicunt).* The word
order and structure of the original Latin were to be kept.[217] It would
therefore be hazardous to assume that the translations of the *Res Gestae*
(recording the words of Augustus himself) or of *senatus consulta* were done
by translators who were 'incompetent' in Greek, or that their efforts
reflected a genuine variety of foreigners' Greek current at Rome; indeed
Wigtil (1982b: 190–1) has plausibly argued that the translator of the *Res
Gestae* (if not those of the *senatus consulta*) was a Greek, not a native Latin
speaker (though he would have been closely supervised by Romans). It is
far more likely that the translators deliberately stuck (or were instructed
to do so) as closely as possible to the wording of the originals, in disregard
of the nature of Greek idiom.[218] If the documents were given in this way
a distinctive Romanness, so much the better: the non-Greek idioms
bring out the Roman indifference to the sensibilities of their subjects.
Similarly it will be recalled (see above, 1.III) that Lucullus deliberately
included errors of grammar in his Greek history (Cic. *Att.* 1.19.10).

An example of the reverse kind to those which have just been seen,
that is of an idiom translated out of Greek into Latin with consequent
lack of clarity, can be found in an inscription from the region of Histria

---

[216] See Brock (1979: 74), noting that sometimes the Syriac translations are unintelligible without the Greek. I am indebted here to observations by Taylor (forthcoming).

[217] See Maclean (1992: 51, 115).

[218] Various other types of (deliberate) Latinisms could be cited from the Greek translations of official Roman documents discussed earlier. I mention a few. In the *senatus consultum de Asclepiade* (Sherk (1969), 22) the reflexive (subject) pronoun has been admitted at line 8 of the Greek version in imitation of the Latin accusative + infinitive construction (see Viereck (1888: 68)): τούτους ἑαυτὸν κατὰ τὸ τ<ῆ>ς συγκλήτου δόγμα εἰς τὰς πατρίδας ἀπολῦσαι βούλεσθαι. The connective relative, which is especially characteristic of literary Latin, if not completely unknown in Greek, is found in the *Res Gestae* from time to time on the model of the Latin version: e.g. 8.4 Gagé ἐν ᾗ ἀποτειμήσει ἐτειμήσαντο, = *quo lustro censa sunt.*

(in modern Rumania), dated to the second or third century. In this case we may more reasonably speak of incompetence: *ISM* 1.301 *[...] m[emoriae caus]e ti[tulum po]suerun[t]. aue uiator et uale.* **hec sunt.** The editor plausibly explains the peculiar *hec sunt* from ὁ βίος ταῦτα, a funerary formula (= 'such is life') which is sometimes found in the reduced form ταῦτα;[219] this latter forms the basis of the Latin expression. The inscription is one of a group of three from the same area, all of which share certain characteristics.[220] I quote the other two: *ISM* 1.273 *[... uixi]t an(nis) [...]X Titinius Seuerinus, sescuplicarius ales II Arabacorum, et Titinius Iamuaris, fili, tituli memoriae cause posuerunt. aue uiator et uale, ISM* 1.338 *d(is) m(anibus). Claudia Dusia ui[xit an(nis). ... Aur(elii) Cocceius et Genialis et] Claudis et Vindix, fili Erculani et eredes, matri pientisime uiuo titulum posuerunt, bene merite, memoriae cause. aue uiator et uale.* There are signs of imperfect competence in Latin here, notably in 273 (note *tituli* for *titulum*), and also hints of a Greek background to the texts. In all three the expression *memoriae cause* (sic) occurs. This is based on the Greek μνήμης χάριν (with the ending of *cause* perhaps intended as a dative (of purpose),[221] and perhaps inflicted on the word by a non-native speaker of Latin). Similarly in 273 *ales* has a Greek genitive inflection. The area was Greek-speaking. These inscriptions may originate from families with members in the Roman army (so definitely 273) who had picked up some Latin during service, without giving up Greek. It is in just such a social milieu that Greek idioms might have been rendered literally into the second language (a phenomenon classifiable in this case as interference).

Latin idioms rendered into Greek are a feature of the work of Appian, as has been abundantly demonstrated by Hering (1935).[222] For example, the expression ἐς γάμον διδόναι (i.e. διδόναι τινά τινι ἐς γάμον) is not the normal Greek method of conveying the giving away of a woman in marriage, but is derived from the Latin idiom (*in matrimonium aliquam alicui dare*: e.g. Caes. *Gall.* 1.3.5).[223] In this case, in contrast to that discussed in the previous paragraph, the 'alien' element is in the writer's first rather than his second language, and it may be seen as borrowing, possibly done deliberately to suit the 'Roman' subject matter.

---

[219] For ταῦτα see e.g. *IGBulg.* II.872, IV.2085, with the note of G. Mihailov ad loc., and L. Moretti on *IGUR* 367 with bibliography.

[220] These inscriptions were drawn to my attention by Iveta Mednikarova.

[221] For bibliography on the Latin expression *memoriae causa* as determined by the Greek, see p. 37 n. 100.

[222] Famerie (1998) to a considerable extent deals with technical vocabulary for Roman institutions, but there are some remarks about Latinisms of idiom in Chapter 3 (213–39).

[223] See Hering (1935: 16).

V.3 Morphology

V.3.1 Greeks' Latin: dative and genitive singular of female first-declension names in Latin

The next sections (down to and including v.3.1.5) will present a series of case studies, all of them interrelated, in that they deal with the feminine genitive singular, and all to do with morphology. Creative or indirect interference will be partly involved, as well as direct interference and code-switching (or possibly borrowing). I will on the basis of this material offer some comments on one of the ways in which a morpheme may pass from one language to another. Another subject which will come up is convergence.

A primary aim will be to explain the origin of the problematic *-aes* genitive singular ending, which is common in first-declension words, particularly female names, in inscriptions, but is not as far as I know attested in literary sources (e.g. *CIL* IV.2457 *Cominiaes*, 3123 *Liuiaes*, 5782 *Benniaes Sabinaes*).[224] This would appear to be a case of distinctive morphology found in inscriptional language, though it is not to be put down to the existence of an inscriptional language as such. It is rather because persons of a certain social milieu are represented in inscriptions, but scarcely in literature. I am referring to lower-class Greeks who had acquired or were acquiring Latin as a second language. The *-aes* genitive belongs very much to this social stratum. How did the ending originate? I will be arguing that it is a secondary phenomenon, secondary that is to an *-es* genitive, and that it has no real relevance to the spoken language. I will point out in passing the confusions which the ending has caused in the works of reputable scholars, and will be sounding a warning about the hazards of disregarding old dissertations and paying attention exclusively to more modern works.

My argument will begin not with the genitive, but with the dative in first declension names in inscriptions. The dative is relevant to the interpretation of the genitive, and it allows us into the world of the partially Romanised Greeks to whom I just referred. I intend to concentrate particularly on one corpus of inscriptions (those of Ostia), which presents coherent material from a relatively early date. The discussion will lead through code-switching to borrowing/interference and then to convergence.

---

[224] There is an example of Augustan date, not in an inscription but in a papyrus letter, published by V. Brown in *BICS* 17 (1970), 136–43, line 3 (*de inprobitate Epaphraes*).

In inscriptions, papyri and other types of texts there is constant and random variation between the digraph *ae* and an *e*-spelling which arises from monophthongisation of the diphthong, as for example at *CIL* III.2233 (*Iulianae puellie* [sic] *innocentissime*), where the writer used the digraph in the first word but then changed to -*e* in the third. When therefore one encounters a double name in the dative, such as *Veianiae Iotape* (*IPO* A. 5), it is tempting to conclude that the writer first wrote the 'correct' form and then shifted inconsistently to the phonetic spelling. But a closer examination of the whole corpus of inscriptions in which this name turns up shows that the variation is not haphazard but systematic, and that a spelling convention among stonecutters was in operation. It would no doubt be possible to support this contention from the inscriptions of many areas, but I largely restrict myself here to Ostia (*IPO*), and, for the sake of comparison, to the funerary inscriptions of Barcelona. The main aim of this first section is to eliminate, by means of an argument based on detailed statistics, the possibility that a dative such as *Iotape* might simply be a Latin inflection reflecting the monophthongisation of *ae*.

There are some 628 funerary inscriptions from Ostia, numbered by Thylander (1952) A.1–342 and B.1–286.[225] Many of the female dedicatees bore two names, which are usually, but not always, in the dative case. Those inscriptions in which the *cognomen* belongs to the third declension have been largely disregarded here; I have concentrated on texts in which the deceased has two names, both admitting of an -*ae* ending.

There is a total of 114 women whose two names are of the first declension, and who are commemorated in such a form that the names are in the dative. The distribution between the A-series and the B is: 81 examples in the first group and 33 in the second.

In 110 of the 114 the first name is given the 'correct' ending (that is, the *ae* digraph). This overwhelming tendency to correctness in the *nomen* is even more obvious if those double names are added of which only the first belongs to the first declension. There are 39 such names in the A-series and 7 in the B, every one of which displays *ae* in the *nomen*. Thus of 160 double names in the dative case, 156 have the digraph as the ending of the *nomen*. Despite the monophthongisation of *ae* in speech, in the area of Ostia stonecutters or the drafters of funerary inscriptions were able to hold rigorously to the historically correct dative form of the Latin names.

---

[225] For a classification of the types of inscriptions in the collection, see Thylander (1952: xi). The A-series inscriptions come from the left side of the canal of Trajan, the B-series from the right.

Table 2

first name	second name	A-series	B-series
-ae	*-ae*	54	24
-ae	*-e*	25	7
-e	*-e*	2	2
-e	*-ae*	0	0

But the second name is by no means so frequently spelt with *ae*. Table 2 shows the distribution of the various possible combinations of *ae* and *e*.

There are thus 36 cases in which the *cognomen* (i.e. the second name) ends in *-e* (taking the central four figures together), compared with 78 in which it ends in *-ae*. We may convert the figures into percentages thus. There are 114 potential cases of the sequence *-ae . . . -ae*. In 96 per cent of cases the first name has *-ae* (110 out of 114), whereas in 32 per cent of cases (36 out of 114) the second name has *-e*.

Was it merely a matter of chance that engravers used the digraph proportionately more often in the first name than in the second? It might seem tempting to say simply that *-e* was common in *cognomina*, as Thylander (1952) remarks on A. 163: 'e = ae . . . , terminaison très habituelle au datif sing. des surnoms'; also on A. 240: 'Très souvent on trouve la terminaison *-ae* dans le gentilice et *-e* dans le surnom.'

But why should this be? The answer lies in the nature of the *cognomina*: very often they are of Greek origin. For example, in the B-series the following are the *cognomina* inflected with *-e* when the *gentilicium* has *-ae*: 28 *Aphrodite*, 84 *Callytyche*, 93 *Hermione*, 142 *Euterpe*, 142 *Theodote*, 154 *Aegle*, 166 *Chreste*. In all seven cases the *cognomen* is Greek; note, for example, that the Greek *cognomen Euterpe* in 142 is juxtaposed with the Latin *nomen Tertiae*, which has a digraph ending. These figures clearly suggest that *-e* is not a monophthongisation of *-ae*, but represents the Greek feminine dative *-η*.

This conclusion may be checked by an examination of those *cognomina* in the B-series which are inflected in *-ae*. There are 24, *of which 21 are of Latin origin*.

I turn now to the A-series. There (see the table above) there are 25 examples of the pattern *-ae . . . -e*. About 15 of the *cognomina* inflected with *-e* are of Greek origin: 5 *Iotape*, 5 *Deutere*, 15 *Melitine*, 24 *Tyche*, 60 *Phoebe*, 69 *Eutychiane*, 113 *Aphrodite*, 119 *Tyche*, 148 *Arsinoe*, 188 *Pontice*, 222 *Callityche*, 234 *Izotice*, 243 *Acte*, 276 *Naphame*, 314 *Filume*.

Table 3

| | origin of *cognomina* in *-ae* | | |
	A-series	B-series	Totals
Greek names	14	3	17
Latin names	40	21	61

Table 4

| | origin of *cognomina* in *-e* | | |
	A-series	B-series	Totals
Greek names	15	7	22
Latin names	10	0	10

By contrast, of the 54 *cognomina* inflected with *-ae* (in the A-series), about 40 are in Latin names. Tables 3 and 4 reveal the situation.

Latin names thus account for about 78 per cent (61 out of 78) of dative *cognomina* ending in the digraph.

Greek names account for about 70 per cent (22 out of 32) of *cognomina* in *-e*. It should be stressed that these figures are not absolutely complete, because I have restricted myself to the pattern *-ae* . . . *-e* as offering a useful sample, and have not taken into account other patterns such as *-e* . . . *-e*.

The conclusion is inescapable that the frequency of *-e* in *cognomina* is due to the fact that in some areas in lower-class society *cognomina* of Greek origin were common. The Greek morpheme -η tended to be retained in the Latinised form of such names.

As a secondary phenomenon a habit of writing *-ae* in the *nomen* and *-e* in the *cognomen* may have become almost mechanical, at least in the work of some stonecutters, even when the *cognomen* was of Latin origin.[226] When the *-ae* . . . *-e* alternation found its way into Latin names, the *-e* spelling could be interpreted simply as the representation of a monophthongised Lat. *-e*.

There are other reasons for seeing *-e* in Greek names as usually representing -η. In Greek *cognomina* in the same corpus of inscriptions other Greek inflections are to be found. For the genitive in *-es*, see A. 54

---

[226] Note particularly A. 240, where there are three cases of *-ae* . . . *-e* in which both first and second name are of Latin origin.

Caesenniae Galenes (note the alternation -*ae* ... -*es* (see above, 3.v.2) which matches exactly that of the type -*ae* ... -*e* in the dative), 121 *Fulciniae Callistes*, 272 *Beianiae Iotapes*, 279 *Zosimes*, B. 23 *Atiliae Politices*, 133 *Ramenniae Chlides*. In all six cases the *cognomen* is Greek. Note too B.32: *concessam sibi partem monumenti a Corneliis Zotico et Epictetiano et* **Corneliam Draucen.** Here there is a Greek accusative in the Greek name. The ablative would have been grammatically correct, but the accusative is sometimes used at the end of a list of items in other oblique cases as a sort of unmarked case (see above, I.VII.2.3, n. 146, and below, 5.VII.2.2), for example:

ILI (1963), 373 C. Sp(ectatius) Secundinus u(iuus) f(ecit) s(ibi) et Tut(oriae) Auitae ... et Rusticio Tutori nepoti ... et *Rusticium Albinu f(ilium)*

ILI (1963), 397 Nundinus Respecti u(iuus) f(ecit) sibi et Secundinae. . et *Firminam fil(iam) an(norum) XL et Iun(ius) Lucillianus an(norum) LX.*[227]

For another (Greek) accusative form in a Greek name where an ablative would have been expected, see A. 254 *ab Attia Helenen*.

Also of note are Grecised nominatives in -*e*, not only in Greek names (e.g. A. 274 *Zosime*), but also in Latin (e.g. A. 237 *Saturnine*, 214 *Saluiane*, B. 301 *Marciane*; on the form of the last two, see V.3.1.4 below).

The tendency which we have seen for Greek morphemes in the nominative, genitive and dative cases to be retained in Greek names, and to be transferred occasionally even into Latin names, produced in bilingual communities what has been called a *declinatio semi-graeca*.[228]

The conclusion reached above about the origin of the -*e* dative in *cognomina* can be confirmed from another relatively coherent corpus, the inscriptions from Barcelona (*IRB*). In these, double names in the dative with the endings -*ae* ... -*ae* occur some 37 times, and in 29 cases the *cognomen*, inflected correctly in the Latin manner, is of Latin origin. On the other hand there are 13 double names of the -*ae* ... -*e* type, and in 9 of these the *cognomen* is of Greek origin: 79 *Iuliae* ... *Coene*, 111 *Clodiae Pephilemene*, 122 *Mariae Telete*, 127 *Aemiliae Philumene*, 142 *Corneliae Cosme*, 149 *Fabiae Psyche*, 160 *Flauiae Theodote*, 189 *Pedaniae Ariste*, 194 *Iuliae Callyroe*; for the remaining 4 cases in Latin names, see 74 *Verane*, 78 *Fidentine*, 131 *Fortunate*, 157 *Celtibere*. -*e* is also used as the dative of Greek names in a few places where there is not an accompanying *nomen* in -*ae*: 143 *Terpsicore*, 146 *Eutychie*, 203 *Euche*.

---

[227] Presumably Lucillianus is also a dedicatee of the inscription, in which case the writer has switched from a 'default' accusative to a 'default' nominative.
[228] See Dessau, *ILS* III.852–7 (dealing with the dative in -*e* at 853–4), Carnoy (1906: 236). Cf. Pirson (1901: 128–32), Gaeng (1977: 28).

Predictably, in a social setting of the type reflected here, the -*es* genitive is also attested, in a Greek name (135 *Caletyches*). And whereas the masculine name *Agathio* at 135 is a Latinisation of Ἀγαθίων, at 136 *Thallión* retains its Greek ending (and the length of the final vowel is indicated by an apex). The Greek nominative in -*e* is found in Greek names at 196 (*Chreste*) and 197 (*Philumene*), but, as in Ostia, it was occasionally extended to Latin names (59 *Liuiane*, 62 *Clementiane*: see below v.3.1.4).[229]

The question whether the endings in -*e* or -*es* represent borrowing or interference or something else is not a straightforward one. The persons in question were Greeks (with Greek original names) who had been Romanised. They were probably slaves in origin who had been freed and had acquired Latin *nomina*; Ostia is famous for its large freed population. Could it be said that Greek has 'interfered' with their second language, Latin?[230] That is hardly the case in the material seen so far, because they (or, we should more accurately say, those writing on their behalf) systematically used the Latin *ae* ending (dative and genitive) in *Latin* names; it would be more appropriate to speak of 'interference' if the Greek endings had been inserted randomly, in Latin as well as Greek names (but see further below). One might loosely say that they had 'borrowed' a Greek morpheme in their Latin, but that too is a not entirely satisfactory way of explaining the phenomenon, because the Greek forms were not consistently used in all Greek names; there are rather frequent but not invariable changes of language. Arguably the practice is best seen as a form of code-switching: in Greek names in Latin texts Greek inflections have sometimes been used, and that constitutes code-switching as that term has been used in this book (see above, 3.v.2). Code-switching of this type was described as 'retention' in the previous chapter (3.v.3, xii.5). This though is a switch of codes which has wider implications relevant to language change. So common in bilingual societies were these Greek inflections that they seem to have caught on and spread to other feminine words, as we will see (v.3.1.2). I have therefore chosen to treat the phenomenon in detail in this chapter rather than in that on code-switching.

In addition to the -*es* genitive at Ostia seen above, there are two examples of an -*aes* genitive, both in Latin *nomina* (A. 43 *Axiaes*, 48 *Aureliaes*). Here is an interesting fact. Whereas the -*es* ending mentioned above occurs in Greek *cognomina*, the -*aes* genitive occurs only in Latin *nomina*.

---

[229] See Mariner Bigorra (1973: 74).

[230] They may no longer have been fluent speakers of Greek, but if a language shift had taken place among such freedwomen they clearly remembered their Greek origins and were capable of using some Greek inflections.

This is a distinction which, if it turns out to be supported by other evidence, must be explained, and accordingly I am now going to move on to this genitive. I would stress two conclusions which arise from the material considered so far:

(1) In typical names of the type *Veianiae Iotape*, *ae* can be seen as the Latin correspondent to the Greek *e*. The digraph defines Latin, the single *e* defines Greek. This principle of correspondence will become relevant later.

(2) There is evidence here for freedwomen of Greek origin retaining to some extent their Greek identities, though undergoing Romanisation. Greek names of this type could have been readily adapted to the Latin inflectional system (and indeed frequently were), but in our material such integration is often resisted. This resistance, repeated all over the western Empire, indicates the desire of such people to keep a hold on their roots.

v.3.1.1 The genitive in *-aes*

The *-aes* genitive ending has been variously explained,[231] but several views (such as the notion that it is a combination of *-ae* and Oscan *-as*: see below) can be disregarded. Väänänen (1966: 83), cited with approval by Gaeng (1977: 29), sees the form quite reasonably as a conflation of -ης and *-ae*[232] (but the matter is more complicated than that: see below), and he supports this view with the assertion that *-aes* occurs only in *cognomina* of slaves, 'dans lesquels l'influence du grec peut le plus facilement se faire valoir, en raison de la provenance étrangère de ceux-ci'. This view, that *-aes* appears above all in (Greek) slave *cognomina*, is wide of the mark. We have already seen reason for doubting it, in that at Ostia *-aes* occurs only in Latin slave *nomina*, though so far we have not had many examples to go on. A typical name encountered in inscriptions of such women of servile origin has the form seen (e.g.) at *CIL* VI.20509 *Iuliae Hermiones* (genitive), with a *cognomen* of Greek origin (inflected here as Greek), and a *nomen* of Latin origin (inflected as Latin). Names of this kind can be found on almost any page of Solin's collection (1982b), with the same combination of Greek and Latin inflections. It is not *-aes* but *-es* that is found in the Greek *cognomen*, and that is a crucial point.

Solin (1982b) has now made available a massive amount of data concerning Greek servile names at Rome. I begin by stressing on the basis of this material that *-aes* is comparatively very rare in Greek *cognomina*.

---

[231] See Gaeng (1977: 27 n. 2, 29–30) for reference to the various theories.
[232] 'Les gén. lat. en *-aes* … s'expliquent par un compromis entre *-ae* du latin et -ης du grec'; see also (e.g.) Battisti (1949: 201).

I list below sixteen names of Greek origin with nominative in-*e* chosen at random from Solin (1982b), giving the relative frequency in the material collected there of the -*es* and -*aes* forms in the genitive of such *cognomina*:

	-*es*	-*aes*
Acte	3	–
Berenice	1	–
Calliope	4	–
Calliste	5	–
Chreste	5	–
Chrysogone	1	–
Daphne	5	–
Epigone	1	–
Hagne	10	–
Hedone	5	–
Hermione	4	–
Irene	12	1
Nice	6	–
Philete	4	–
Semne	3	–
Tyche	24	–

The -*es* form predominates in this selection by 93: 1. That is not to say that -*aes* does not occasionally occur in *cognomina* of Greek origin,[233] but it is clearly -*es* that is preferred. We can say on the basis of this evidence that primacy belongs to the -*es* forms in Greek *cognomina*, and that is because they tended to be inflected as Greek, with -*es* the straightforward representation of -ης.

-*aes* on the other hand is often found in Solin's material in *Latin nomina*, sometimes indeed in juxtaposition with -*es* in the Greek *cognomen*: e.g. *CIL* VI.10561 *Acutiaes Tyches*, 26695 *Marciaes Tyches*, 11600 *Amulliaes Nices*, 36476 *Turpiliaes Agnes*, 12763/4 *Attiaes Cyrenes*, 18033 *Flauiaes Hermionis* (= -*es*?), 12306 *Volusiaes Phoebes*, 20795 *Iuniaes Ariadnes*, Solin (1982b), I.533 s.v. *Beroe, Iuliaes Beroes*. For further examples in *nomina*, see e.g. 9576 *Piliaes ... Callistenis*, 4521 *Cusiniaes Chrestenis*, 18453 *Flauiaes Capitolinaes uernae*, 5454 *Nouiaes Niceni* (*sic*: there has been an omission of final -*s*), *CIL* IV.5782 *Benniaes*, 3123 *Liuiaes*, 5909 *Vibiaes*. Not only that, but it is also found in *Latin cognomina*, as in *Capitolinaes* quoted above. See also (e.g.) *CIL* VI.9506 *Faustinaes*, 9616 *Primaes*, IV.5782 *Sabinaes*, 5636 *Plantaes*.

---

[233] Some examples may be found in Hehl (1912: 21) and Bindel (1912: 14, 15, 17).

The evidence suggests that while -*es* was the pure Greek ending located *par excellence* in Greek *cognomina*, -*aes* must have been felt in some way to be 'Latinate', and appropriate in the Latin *nomen* of a Greek with a Greek *cognomen*. It is a curious fact that at the very point at which Väänänen (1966: 83) makes the incorrect assertion that the barbarism (i.e. the use of -*aes*) does not occur outside the *cognomina* of slaves ('ce barbarisme n'apparaît guère en dehors des *cognomina* d'esclaves'), he cites Hehl (1912: 22ff.), who on this very page (22) correctly stresses the *non-Greek* character of the names which bear this ending. Hehl gives detailed statistics, based on a reading of many volumes of *CIL*. In his material there are 57 examples of Greek names with the -*aes* ending, compared with no fewer than 388 examples of the ending in Latin names. Hehl specifically makes the point that -*aes* is rare in Greek *cognomina*, whereas -*es* in such names is virtually countless. In Latin *nomina* on the other hand he finds only 17 cases of -*es* (most of them late) but 222 of -*aes*.

Hehl (1912: 23) mistakenly seeks to find Oscan influence in the emergence of -*aes*.[234] While the ending is predominantly found in Latin names, it was closely associated with the Greek population, particularly of Rome.[235] This is clear from the frequency with which it appears in the Latin *gentilicia* of those bearing Greek *cognomina* (see above, for example, for the juxtaposition of -*aes* in *gentilicia* with -*es* in Greek *cognomina*). A cursory glance at Roman inscriptions containing -*aes* repeatedly turns up some sort of Greek ambience. Any explanation of the -*aes* form must take its starting point from bilingual Greco-Latin communities. This social background is of crucial importance in explaining the emergence of the form.

We are now in a position to suggest possible sequences of events. One such is as follows:

(1) Servile women of Greek origin, who by manumission had acquired a Latin *nomen* to add to their original Greek name, which became a *cognomen*, reveal a sense of their mixed identity by retaining in their Greek names Greek dative and genitive morphemes in -*e* and -*es* respectively.

(2) In the naming of such women the Greek dative ending -*e* in the Greek name regularly, as we saw, stands alongside the Latin dative ending -*ae* in the Latin name.

---

[234] So too Palmer (1954: 241), Moltoni (1954: 217): i.e conflation of -*ae* and -*as*. Moltoni, though commenting on the Latin character of names with –*aes*, appeared not to know of Hehl's work.

[235] See the geographical distribution of -*aes* as set out by Hehl (1912: 23). There are 284 examples at Rome, whereas in the region which comes second in the frequency of its employment (Ostia) there are only 23 examples.

(3) In Greek names the genitive can be interpreted as formed by the addition of *s* to the Greek form of the dative. On this analogy, the genitive of the Latin name came to be formed by the addition of *s* to the Latin form of the dative. One can set up therefore a proportional analogy *e: es :: ae: aes*.

There is another way of looking at the matter, to which I incline. There was probably some leakage or extension of the *-es* ending from the Greek names (*cognomina*) of such persons into their Latin names (*nomina*) (a leakage that might readily have occurred when Greek name and Latin, in the genitive, were juxtaposed), followed by a superficial Latinisation of the new genitive in the Latin name by means of the replacement of *e* by *ae*. In reference to the dative we observed in the last section the principle that in these hybrid names the digraph *ae* in the written form of the Latin name corresponded to *e* in the Greek name. *ae* was seen in such circles as a Latinate grapheme. It would thus follow that the *-aes* genitive ending represents *Greeks' Latinisation of the Greek* -es *ending effected (appropriately) in Latin names* by the application of the principle of correspondence to which I have referred.

However one looks at it, the *-aes* ending is a Latinate form, found predominantly in Latin *nomina*, but those belonging to Greeks. The form is artificial and restricted to the written language, because in pronunciation it would not have differed from *-es*. Thus we can deduce that Greeks with Greek *cognomina* tended to give their *gentilicia* Greek endings as well, but in the written form of those *gentilicia* the genitive ending was often superficially Latinised. I am concerned in this section only with the *origin* of *-aes*, in the early Empire. In some texts and corpora of inscriptions it showed a rather haphazard tendency to spread from names to other types of words,[236] but its overwhelming predominance, particularly in the early period,[237] is in names, and it is there that its starting point must be sought.

Two further points may be made about the *-aes* ending. First, the emergence of the ending (in writing) cannot be described as a case of direct interference from Greek; rather, it is another example of what was called 'creative' interference, though that interference operates only on the written language. If on the other hand *-es* were used in a Latin name (as it sometimes is), that would be direct interference. In speech

---

[236] See e.g. Battisti (1949: 202), Gaeng (1977: 29), id. (1984: 10), and below, v.3.1.2.
[237] It should be noted that the material in Solin (1982b) is set out in a rough chronological order.

(see above) such interference would have been more apparent, because *ae* had become a monophthong. The *-aes* spelling is a stage beyond direct interference, in that the alien morpheme is partially Latinised in its written form.

Secondly, an observation concerning contact-induced morphological change can be made on this evidence. It is code-switching (retention) that leads to the entry of the alien morpheme *-es* into Latin, in the first instance in Greek names. Having established a firm foothold in one type of name in bilingual communities of freedmen, it spread more widely (see below, v.3.1.2), and in Latin names (and nouns) acquired a Latinised written form *-aes*.

v.3.1.2 Venusia and convergence

I stay with the genitive (in this case that in *-es*), but present in brief a different type of case study, this time based on the Jewish community in Venusia. We have from here seventy-four Jewish epitaphs, dated roughly to the fourth and fifth centuries AD (see Noy (1993), 42–116).[238] About 60 per cent of the inscriptions of this community are in Greek, 30 per cent in Latin and 10 per cent in Hebrew.[239] There is also a bilingual text, in Latin and Hebrew (Noy (1993), 84), and a Hebrew and Greek inscription written entirely in Hebrew characters (Noy (1993), 75; see above, I.VII.2.4). In this small corpus, whether in Greek or Latin language or Greek or Latin script, the genitive singular form of the feminine genitive is almost always *-es* / -ες: 89 *C<a>telles*, 90 *Annes, Maries*, 59, 62, 71 πρεσβιτέρες, 62 Μαννίνες, 65 Φαστίνης, 71 Φαοστινες, 65 νηπίης.[240] It should be noted that not all of the inscriptions in Greek script are in the Greek language. At Noy (1993), 59 πρεσβιτερες stands in a Latin text, whereas at Noy (1993), 62 exactly the same form is in a Greek epitaph.

Various things stand out in the above list of genitives. First, the distinction observable at Ostia between the method of inflecting Greek names and that of inflecting Latin names has been lost. Names even of Latin origin receive the *-es* ending, whatever the language in use. The code-switching inflection of female names as Greek in Latin texts observable at

---

[238] See also Leon (1953–4), and most recently Williams (1999).
[239] See Leon (1953–4: 274).
[240] There are only two other genitive singulars in the feminine declension, Noy (1993), 42 τάφος Βερο[νική]νης, 59 τάφος Βερωνικενις. In both examples the ending derives from the Latin *-e*, *-enis* formation that will be dealt with below, v.3.1.3; at 42 that ending appears with a Grecised final syllable.

Ostia had hardened into regular practice in this community, such that female names of other sorts came to be inflected in the same way.[241] Secondly, though names predominate slightly in the list, there are also some words of other types which are given the same ending. The line of development would therefore seem to have been: generalisation of the Greek ending from Greek names to all female names of the first declension, and the spread of the ending from names to other words. Thirdly, even in inscriptions in Greek script the ending more often than not appears in the form -ες rather than -ης. There were two complementary reasons for that. *Eta* and *epsilon* were confused in koine following the loss of quantitative distinctions in Greek.[242] And the graphemic form of the Greek genitive as it appears in Latin script might have influenced the representation of the genitive in Greek script as well, given that in this small community Greek and Latin were written side by side and in both scripts. Fourthly, πρεσβιτέρες is written with -ες even after *rho* in the Greek inscription Noy (1993), 62, whereas α would have been expected in classical Greek. Again there are several factors which might have contributed to this spelling. First, there is evidence in the koine for the generalisation of the genitive form with *eta* (sometimes replaced by *epsilon*) to environments in which it did not belong in Attic.[243] Secondly, there is likely to have been some input from Latin orthography, once the genitive in -*es* had been established. It is significant that the same form πρεσβιτερες is also found in the Latin inscription Noy (1993), 59 written in Greek letters.

A form of *morphological convergence* had taken place in the feminine genitive singular (with the historically more correct -ης of Attic Greek no more than an occasional variant for -ες) of Greek and Latin among Jews at Venusia. It is not only at Venusia that -*es* in Latin and -ες in Greek are attested, but this is the only corpus known to me in which there is virtually no distinction between Greek and Latin in this respect, though admittedly the figures are small. When two languages are in contact over a long period convergence of one kind or another is not uncommon.[244] It was suggested in the previous paragraph that the influence was bi-directional, at least where the writing of the two languages was concerned. The Greek ending intruded into Latin in Greek names, then spread to other names, and finally non-names. The Latin representation of the Greek genitive

---

[241] The same might have been true at Rome. As we saw, the Latinised written form -*aes* implies the existence of -*es* in Latin names in the spoken language.

[242] Gignac (1976: 242–7).   [243] Gignac (1981: 3–4).

[244] See e.g. Hock and Joseph (1996: 393–417), Aitchison (1991: 110–12).

ending then influenced the way the ending was written in Greek (that is with *epsilon* for the most part rather than either *eta*, or, in appropriate environments, *alpha*).

Although Venusia is in the south, it cannot be assumed that the Greek used there, whether by Jews or gentiles, reflected the lingering influence of earlier Greek colonisation in Magna Graecia. The survival of only one non-Jewish Greek inscription from the area (*IG* XIV.688) does not speak for any currency of Greek outside the Jewish community; indeed, Venusia had been the site of a large Latin colony as early as 291 BC. The Jewish use of Greek there should be seen as independent of the Greek of Magna Graecia.

It is best to think of the seventy-four epitaphs at Venusia as reflecting a long period of Jewish residence in the city. Over the centuries the community might on the one hand have been reinforced by immigrants from the east, who will have bolstered the survival of Greek (and perhaps Hebrew) in a Latin-speaking town, but on the other hand have been so profoundly exposed to Latin that Greek was difficult to maintain. It is of note, for example, that the 'Greek' epitaph Noy (1993), 62 is replete with errors of morphology and syntax and also heavily Latinised (see I.VII.3, 3.XII.I). It was probably written by a Latin speaker with imperfect command of Greek in accommodation to an old Jewish convention of using Greek for funerary inscriptions. Similarly Noy (1993), 59, which begins with the Greek word τάφος and is in Greek script, turns out to be in Latin. The 'Greekness' of the text therefore lies only in the initial key-word and the choice of script (see above, I.VIII). But while these two texts carry a hint that there were Jews at Venusia who could not quite manage to use Greek, the use of the *-es* genitive even in Latin shows that Latin had succumbed to the influence of Greek in this special community.

In the material cited particularly in the previous section the Greek feminine genitive singular morpheme did not enter Latin haphazardly. It made its first appearance in Greek personal names as a deliberate transfer (a code-switch on my interpretation) reflecting the origin or chosen mixed-identity of the referents. As an analogy I would cite a form from the text *ChLA* I.12, discussed briefly below, 5.VII.2.2: *scripsi me recepisse res s(upra) s(criptas) [a Corneli]o Germa[n]o cuius [e]xemplum* **epistules** *habio. actum Puluinos nonar̲[u]m Octobrium isdem co[ns]u̲libus.* Here in a document with another Grecising feature (see below, V.4.2 on the genitive of time) there is also a case of the Greek *-es* genitive singular in a Latin text. But again the transfer is not inexplicable. *Epistula*, though a naturalised Latin word, was of Greek origin (genitive ἐπιστολῆς). Here a Greek, writing Latin, lapsed into a Greek inflection when writing a word that he knew as Greek. We might label the phenomenon as 'interference' in this case, or alternatively as the sort of code-switch described in the first chapter (1.v) as a 'leak'. Much the same thing is to be found in the (Latin) receipt of Aeschines, in the genitive form κλάσσης (see 1.vii.2.3). In these various examples it is possible to see the manner in which the Greek morpheme found its way into Latin. The transfer did not come out of the blue but took place first in lexical items with a Greek association, whether we call the process interference or code-switching.

I append further evidence to do with the *-es* genitive. In a receipt of unknown provenance (*ChLA* 3.204.9) (see 5.vii.2.2 below) there is the expression *ad statione liburnes 'Fides'*. The Greek adjective Λιβυρνίς (sc. ναῦς) ought to have had a genitive form -ίδος, the Latin *liburna* an ending *-ae*. The ending here is neither Latin nor correct Greek. The *-es* ending had acquired some vitality in Latin once it had emerged under Greek influence, such that it could be inflicted on a word current in both languages, in neither of which it should strictly have had this inflection.

v.3.1.3 A new Latin suffix determined partly by contact with Greek

Paradoxically there is in imperial Latin inscriptions a new Latin suffix found in personal names the emergence of which seems to have been caused by the need felt for a Latin inflection of Greek female names with a nominative in -η. As we have seen, in various corpora of Latin inscriptions female *cognomina* of Greek origin are frequently given Greek inflections in the genitive and dative. But a new, Latinised inflection of Greek female names in -η, showing the structure *-e*, *-enis*, also developed in such communities, apparently on the analogy of the Latin masculine formation in *-o*, *-onis*.[245] Thus, whereas at *IPO* A.24 *Tyche* is the Greek dative of the name (*D.M. Antoniae Tyche matri optimae*), at *IPO* A.225 *Tycheni* is used instead as a Latinised form (*D.M. Septimiae Tycheni*). Βερωνικενις at Noy (1993), 59, quoted above, n. 240, is a Latinised genitive of the Greek name Βερενίκη (which is sometimes spelt with an *o* in the second syllable in Latin), with an *epsilon* in the second last syllable under the influence either of Latin orthography or of developments in the koine (cf. -ες for -ης).

---

[245] See Leumann (1977: 459), Väänänen (1966: 86). Battisti (1949: 203) appears to think that the formation is of Greek origin, but where is the evidence for that?

There is no sign of this form in literary texts, and it is not reflected in Romance. An abundance of examples can be found in the nomenclature of slaves and freedmen as set out by Solin (1982b). The formation must have originated in lower-class bilingual communities in the west.

The form alternates with a suffix showing *-eti(s)* in the oblique cases. Thus, for example, for *Ireneni*, see *CIL* VI.19705, and for *Ireneti*, *ICUR* 594; for *Daphneni*, see *CIL* VI.26034, and for *Daphnetis*, *ICUR* 10240. This fact is noted by scholars,[246] but no reason seems to have been offered for the variation. But a complementary relationship between the two suffixes can be deduced from the data collected by Solin (1982b). The suffixes, at least as they are used at Rome, should not be seen as independent of each other, but as interrelated. Sievers (1872) has an extensive discussion of the *-eti(s)* suffix, while disregarding entirely that in *-eni(s)*; that, in my opinion, is a misguided approach.

The following table (derived from the material in Solin (1982b)) shows the incidence of *-eni(s)* and *-eti(s)* in a variety of Greek female names with nominative in -η. The material is set out in two groups, with double spacing after *Tyche*:

	-eni(s)	*-eti(s)*
Acte	6	–
Berenice	3	–
Calliope	2	–
Calliste	14	–
Chreste	21	1 (*Chrestedi*)
Nice	61	1
Philete	14	–
Tyche	52	1
Agne	–	11
Blastiane	–	1
Calligone	–	1
Καρπιανή	–	1
Chrysogone	–	1
Cymine	–	1
Cyrene	–	1
Daphne	3	1
Epigone	4	–
Eutychiane	–	7
Hedone	5	3
Hermione	–	8
Irene	2	30

---

[246] See e.g. Leumann (1977: 460).

Melpomene	–	1
Philumene	–	6
Oenone	–	1
Semne	–	4

While some names display both endings, there is a principle of selection at work.[247] When the ending of the nominative is in *-ne*, *-eti(s)* is preferred (by 78:14), whereas when the nominative has any consonant other than *n* before the final *eta*, it is *-eni(s)* which is overwhelmingly in the majority (by 173:3). Thus, for example, in the name *Irene*, *Ireneti(s)* is preferred by 30:2, whereas in *Nice*, *Niceni(s)* predominates by 61:1. The preference for *-eti(s)* in a name of the type of *Irene* is, loosely speaking, dissimilatory: a sequence of *n*s is avoided if the oblique cases have the structure *-et-*. On the face of it *-eni(s)* looks like the primary form, with *-eti(s)* a dissimilated variant. The primacy of *-enis* is shown by its great frequency, and also by the fact that it displays a rather more marked tendency to intrude into names with nominative in *-ne* than does *-etis* to intrude into names with consonants other than *n* before the final vowel.

But how did the *-etis* formation originate? A purely phonetic explanation (of the type which assumes a dissimilation of the form $n \ldots n > n \ldots t$) will hardly do, because *t* is not a normal phoneme to find in a dissimilatory relationship with *n*. A more precise, morphological, explanation must be sought.

In Greek there was a masculine formation in names, -ῆς, -ῆτος, which entered imperial Latin as *-es*, *-etis* (thus *Apelles*, *Apellen* in Horace (*Epist.* 2.1.239), but *Apelletem* in Petronius (64.4)).[248] But more importantly, in Greek epigraphy, particularly that of Asia Minor, there is also a well-attested *feminine* formation in -ής, -ῆτος, as for example (in the nominative) in the inscription cited by L. Robert at *Bull. épigr.* 1959, 411 **Συντύχης** Στεφάνῳ τῷ ἀνδρὶ μνήμης ἕνεκεν καὶ ἑαυτῇ ζώσῃ. Robert illustrates the type extensively, both in the nominative and oblique cases.[249] Similarly in the Greek inscriptions of Rome various Greek female names of the type we have been looking at turn up with -ῆτι (or -ῆδι) in the dative: e.g. *IGUR* 566 θ(εοῖς) κ(αταχθονίοις) **Ζωτικῆτι** Νεικομήδης ὁ σύμβιος τῇ γλυκυτάτῃ γυναικὶ τίτλον ἔθηκεν, 942 Σόλων Διδύμου **Τυχῆτι** ἐποίησε μνήμης χάριν, *IG* XIV.1738 (Rome) [τῇ γλυκυτάτῃ θυγα]τρ[ὶ]

---

[247] This is alluded to by Helttula (1973: 151–2), but without discussion.
[248] For the Greek masculine formation -ῆς, -ῆτος see Mayser (1906: 274), Gignac (1981: 59–60). On the Latinised form, see Leumann (1977: 460), Sievers (1872: 55–65).
[249] See further *Bull. épigr.* 1961, 737. Mayser (1906: 274, also 179 n.12) alludes to feminines of this form.

Καρπιανῆτι [Σωσί]μη καὶ ᾽Ιούνιος..., *IGUR* 555 [Ε]ὐφ[ρ]οσυνῆδι θ[υ]γατρὶ ἐποίησα. Most of these are unambiguously feminine. It is possible that immigrant Greeks brought with them to Rome the -ής, -ῆτος feminine inflection, and then transferred it into Latin in Latinised form. But if so, when it came into Latin it was not an out-and-out rival of -*e*, -*enis*, but entered into a complementary relationship with it.

It is though a moot point whether (at Rome) the nominative of such names with dative in -ῆτι should be regarded as ending in -ής or -η. Moretti (*IGUR*), influenced by Robert, cites as nominative forms in his index Τυχής and Ζωτικής (see also his notes on *IGUR* 555 and 943), though such nominatives do not seem to be attested in the Roman inscriptions themselves. Solin (1982b), on the other hand, always lists the nominative of such names as ending in -*e*. The example of Τύχητι quoted above is listed by Solin (accented thus) under *Tyche* (vol. 1.441 col. b), that of Ζωτικῆτι under *Zotice* (ii.1113), and that of Καρπιανῆτι under Καρπιανή. Given the frequency of -*e* nominatives in Greek names at Rome (both in Greek and Latin inscriptions), the existence of the type *Tyche*, *Tychenis*, and the complementary relationship of -*etis* to -*enis* (see above), it seems reasonable to think that Greek names at Rome with oblique cases in -ητι(ς) should be assigned a nominative in -η in parallel to the Latin formation -*e*, -*etis*. On this view it might be argued that the oblique cases -ῆτι, -ῆτος at Rome (and, from there, the Latin correspondents -*eti*, -*etis*) originated in the existing Greek formation -ής, -ῆτος, but that the nominative in -ής did not succeed in ousting the usual Roman nominative form of female names.

The relationship between these Latin and Greek inflections of Greek personal names deserves full investigation.[250] One problem, as we have hinted, concerns the *nominative* form of names in -ῆτι in the Greek of Rome. The problem is further complicated by the attestation of a so-called -*n* suffix in Greek names in Greek inscriptions from (e.g.) Macedonia (so O. Masson, *Bull. ép.* 1992, no. 184). One such example (from Morrylos in Macedonia) is worth quoting (M. B. Hatzopoulos, *Bull. ép.* 1991, 397): ᾽Απολλόδωρος καὶ ᾽Αρτεμίδωρος αὐτοῖς ζῶσιν καὶ **Ἡλιοῦνι** τῷ πατρὶ καὶ **᾽Αρτέμινι** τῇ μητρί, μνήμης χάριν. The two datives in -νι of the names Helios and Artemis are typical of the Macedonian material cited by Masson (cf. *Bull. ép.* 1988, 812, 1989, 447). But an ending -νι is not exactly the same as that in -*eni* of the type seen at Rome.

---

[250] Masson was right to say (*Bull. épig.* 1992, 184) that the subject needs further investigation; it is the relationship between the Greek ending found in Greek-speaking areas and the Latin suffixes that is problematical.

Also relevant are Greek names in Latin texts showing either *-uti* or *-uni* in the dative. Solin (1992b), for example, cites and discusses the inscription *Cresces* **Euplunis** *threptus u(ixit) a(nnis) XV. h(ic) s(itus) e(st)*. Note too (e.g.) *CIL* VI.17359 *dis manib.* **Eunuti**. *u(ixit) a(nnis) XXXV. Fortunata conserua contubernali b. m.*[251]

The suffix *-e*, *-enis* seems to be a genuine Latin analogical development. It is a consequence of bilingualism. A female name in -η could be readily Latinised by transfer to the Latin first declension, and many Greek names show just such a modification (e.g. *IPO* A.11 *Hygiae*). The name *Helena* appears more often in Solin's material in the form of a Latin first-declension noun than otherwise. But the great frequency of pure Greek inflections (dative *-e*, genitive *-es*) in Greek servile names in Latin inscriptions (evidence can be found in Solin (1982b); see also above, v.3.1.1) points to the desire of many Greeks to hold on to a remnant of their linguistic identity. The new formation in *-e*, *-enis* is a partial concession to Latin morphological processes, but it also gives a distinctiveness to Greek names which was lost once they passed into the Latin first declension. The emergence in Latin of the feminine in *-e(s)*, *-etis*, however it is to be explained, is also closely related to language contact.

v.3.1.4　The type *Marciane*

A case of mutual morphological influence lies in names with the suffix *-iane* (e.g. *IPO* B.301 *Iunia Marciane*, A.214 *Aelia Saluiane*, *IRB* 59 *Vibia Liuiane*, 62 *Clementiane*).[252] *-iana* is a native Latin suffix, well attested for example in all of the names just cited, but it has been given a Greek ending in *-e* (-η). The form is frequent in Latin inscriptions and also in Greek (e.g. Ἰουλιανή at *IGUR* 330, 372, Μαρκιανή at 779). Greeks appear to have Grecised the Latin suffix by the change of the final vowel, retaining the modified form in Latin (and not only in the nominative: note *CIL* VI.20004 *Iulianes*, 13029 *Marcianes*). Two further developments are worth stressing. First, the *-iane* ending was attached not only to names of Latin origin, but also to those of Greek (e.g. *IGUR* 402, 431 Εὐτυχιανή, 441 Ναρκισσιανή etc.).[253] Such forms are genuine hybrids, in more senses than one: the root and suffix originated in different languages, and the suffix, while fundamentally Latin in origin, had a Greek ending. Secondly,

---

[251] See Solin (1978: 78–81); also id. (1987).
[252] See further Sievers (1872: 67), Schulze (1894 = 1958: 104), Leumann (1977: 460).
[253] Further material can be found in Schulze (1894 = 1958: 104); see also Jannaccone (1950: 59–60).

the suffix *-et-* was sometimes used to augment *-iane* (e.g. *CIL* VI. 26274 *Iulianeti* (so 2562, 31960), 13620 *Marcianeti*).[254]

v.3.1.5 Some concluding remarks

Interference has numerous forms. Direct interference results in the transfer of an element from one language to another. But it has been stressed that a bilingual's contribution to a transfer may be creative (see above on *-aes*).

The retention of Greek morphemes in female names which could have been integrated into Latin goes against the tendency of the literary language (see 3.v.2 for the Latinisation of Greek mythological names). I classify the emergence of the inflection *-e*, *-enis* as contact-induced, but it can only be described as such in a special sense. *-e*, *-enis* was not an alien formation imported into Latin from another language (except, one might argue, in its nominative form). The formation was generated from within Latin itself by a Latin analogy of the form *-o:-e* : :*-onis:-enis*. Though it was of recognisable Latin type (and it is worthy of note that in later Latin *-o*, *-onis* generated another new formation, *-a*, *-anis*, as e.g. *scriba, scribanis, barba, barbanis* 'uncle'),[255] it was nevertheless suitable as a means of integrating Greek names without depriving them completely of their Greek flavour (in that there was a long *e* throughout the paradigm). Here then is a creative morphological process at work among Greek-speaking bilinguals who wanted to express a mixed identity through their nomenclature.

It is remarkable to what extent these various Greek or Grecising inflections congregate in the paradigm of female names. We occasionally find the juxtaposition of Greek endings with Latin in the double names of freedmen (see above, I.VII.2.2 on *IGUR* 616), but more rarely, as far as I can tell. Could there be some significance to the frequency of the phenomenon in female names? Perhaps women of Greek origin were more keen to preserve their Greek identities. The linguistic conservatism of women in immigrant communities has sometimes been noted.

I repeat finally a general point made above concerning the mechanism of some contact-induced language change. A foreign morpheme may first enter a language through code-switching or borrowing from a donor language. If code-switching is common in a category of words (such as

[254] See further Sievers (1872: 67), Leumann (1977: 460).
[255] See e.g. Battisti (1949: 203), Leumann (1977: 460), Väänänen (1981: 109).

names), the morpheme may pass into associated words (such as names of native origin) in the recipient language.

I move on now to some miscellaneous cases of morphological inter-ference.

V.3.2 *Genitive plural*

In Latin texts written in Greek script there are numerous attempts to render the Latin genitive plural (of various declensions). Some examples are scattered about in earlier chapters, discussed from differing points of view; here I bring the evidence together.

A 'correct' transliteration of a genitive plural can be seen at *ICUR* 1867: ᾽Ερμαείσκε φῶς ζῆς ἐν θεῷ κυρείῳ Χρειστῷ **αννωρουμ** X **μησωρουμ** *septe* (for which inscription, see above, 3.VIII). μησωρουμ is not strictly correct, but it has a genuine Latin morpheme, taken over presumably from the previous noun (see *ILCV* index, III.552 for the form *mensorum*). But in many cases such correctness is not achieved. Note for example *IGUR* 1040 δηφουνκτους αννωρουμ ν[.] μησουμ γ´ διου[μ . . .]. Here the -ουμ of αννωρουμ seems to have been interpreted as a genitive marker, and it has accordingly been added to μησ- and δι-.

A more complicated case is at *ILCV* 4954: Βενερωσα αυρων XVII εκουμαριτους μησις XV. This Roman inscription is full of difficulties. αυρων is obviously equivalent to *annorum*, but how is it to be explained? One possibility is that the Greek genitive plural ending -ων has been substituted for the Latin -*orum*, but with an illogical retention of ρ. On this view Greek morphology would have been imposed on a Latin word, but the form would show a feature which might be called 'learner's irrationality' (for which see I.VII.2.3 on the receipt of Aeschines). It is however more likely that the last three letters have been reversed in order, and that the form represents *annor(um)*.[256] Similarly a Greek epitaph from Rome (*ILCV* 4912) expresses the (Latin) name of the dedicator as Βικτρω (= *Victor*). In αυρων the reversal might have been influenced by the fact that Greek genitive plurals ended in -ων.

At *ILCV* 3391 (Rome, AD 269) (κωσουλε Κλυδειω εδ Πατερνω νωνεις Νοβενβρειβους δειε Βενερες λουνα XXIIII Λευκες φειλειε Σεβηρε καρεσσεμε ποσουετε [*sic*] εδ εισπειρειτω σανκτω τουω. μορτουα αννουωρωμ VL εδ μησωρων XI, δευρων X) μησωρων stands for the substandard genitive plural *mensorum* (see on *ICUR* 1867 above), but with

---

[256] I am grateful to David Langslow for drawing my attention to this possibility.

Grecising of the ending by the substitution of the Greek genitive ending -ων for *-um*.

In αννουωρωμ in the same inscription on the other hand the writer has correctly used a Latinate -μ at the end of the word, but otherwise the inflection is even more anomalous. The vowel in the final syllable is long (ω): there has been a contamination of Lat. *-orum* with Gk. -ων, such that the first long *o* is from the Latin ending and the second from the Greek. There is an additional anomaly in the presence of ου before the ending, for which attempted explanations could only be speculative. It is possible that the writer, familiar with the nominative *annus*, analysed the root as *annu-*. *Annorum* (*annos*, *annis*) was constantly abbreviated in Latin epitaphs. The elements of conflation and irrationality which come together in this item suggest that the writer had a poor command of Latin oblique-case morphology.

A conflation identical to that in μησωρων above occurs at *ICUR* 4025 (see above, 3.VIII) (αννωρων).

A feature of these genitive plurals is that they show evidence of false analysis of the Latin ending (thus *annorum* is analysed as *annor-um* rather than *ann-orum*), prompted possibly by the fact that the Greek genitive plural inflection is monosyllabic whereas that of Latin has two syllables. The inability to recognise *-orum* as an inflection implies a lack of competence in Latin morphology. It is additionally significant that all of the examples cited here are written in Greek script. These then are inscriptions written by first-language speakers of Greek who had learned Latin literacy and morphology imperfectly. Under conditions of imperfect learning morphological interference is likely to occur. It is probable too that the use of Greek script had something to do with the errors. The mere fact of using Greek letters for the writing of Latin might have prompted the writers to lapse mechanically into endings of Greek form from time to time (see below, v.3.3). Finally, 'creative' processes are at work again. Usually there has not been a straightforward replacement of a Latin morpheme by a Greek, which would have constituted direct interference. Some superficially similar material will be discussed below, 5.V.3, but there the Latin endings in Greek inscriptions may represent code-switching rather than interference.

V.3.3 Nominative singular

Interference from Greek in the masculine nominative singular has already come up in earlier chapters. In a Latin epitaph of a soldier of the *Legio II Parthica* found at Apamea in Syria we saw (1.VII.4.1) the form *Moucianos*, which as well as morphological interference shows orthographic interference in the first syllable. From the trilingual (Greek, Latin, Punic) Christian community at Sirte in Tripolitania (for which see above, 2.V.6 and below, V.4.4) note Bartoccini (1928), 15 *Balerianos uix(it) an(nos) XXX*. In the bilingual glossary *P. Lond.* II.481 (= Kramer (1983), 13) we have already seen in this chapter an instance of phonetic influence from Greek (V.1.1 ουντε (cf. 1.VII.2.1)), but the main sign of Greek interference lies in the form of masculine nominative singulars. Sometimes the writer used the ου digraph that by convention rendered Latin *-u* (δακτυλους, ρεμους), but he also often wrote the Greek ending -ος (κολουνβος, ειβερνος, βεντος, βιλος = *uillus*). It is as if he had to remember to transliterate the Latin ending. The pressure exerted on him by the inflectional form of the Greek nominative is nicely illustrated in the item κολουνβος. In the second syllable the *u* of Latin is correctly transliterated, but the written form of the Greek morpheme (i.e. the nominative ending) overrode the accepted method of phonetic transcription.[257] In one sense the error might be treated as graphemic; the writer is so used to the Greek nominative form that he slips into it by mistake. Again it is in a transliterated text that we find particularly marked interference (cf. V.3.2 above).

V.3.4 Accusative plural

The scribe of Terentianus' letter *P. Mich.* VIII. 468 wrote (62): *saluta omnes contubernales* **nostrous**. Whether the spelling was a reflection of Terentianus' pronunciation as he dictated the letter, or was an error purely by the scribe, it can at one level (that of the written language) be classified as morphological interference, in that the Greek accusative ending, transliterated into Latin characters, has been imposed on a Latin word. There are comparable examples in Latin texts written in Greek characters, as in Aeschines' δηναριους σεσκεντους (see 1.V, 1.VII.2.3 for further material). Whether morphological transfers of this type occurred in speech as well as writing it is impossible to say on the evidence available. If a Greek pronounced Latin *-os* in an approximation of the Latin manner but wrote it as *-ous*, the 'morphological' interference in the written version would be more appropriately labelled orthographic.

---

[257] On the other hand in the second syllable of δακτυλους the writer was influenced by the graphemic form of the word in Latin script, but he did get the ending right.

v.3.5 Suffixation: some Latinate suffixes in the Greek of Egypt

At the start of this chapter the borrowing of suffixes by one language from another was introduced (II). Here I discuss some further instances from one area. Various Latin suffixes became well established in later Greek, particularly that of Egypt. For example, Greek had functionally parallel suffixes in -τήρ (oxytone) and -τωρ (paroxytone). The latter was far less common and productive than -τήρ, but an interesting late development was 'the rejuvenation of this native suffix [-τωρ] . . . by the introduction of Latin loan-words in -*tor*'.[258] The revival of -τωρ manifests itself not only in loan-words, but in new Greek coinages (e.g. *P. Rein.* 42.12 παραλήμπτωρ, apparently = παραλήπτής).[259] The process is exactly parallel to that seen in the case of -*ianus* (II) and in -*es* (v.3.1): the foreign morpheme enters the language in foreign words, and then takes root. Also productive in later Greek was the Latin suffix -*arius*.[260] The pre-existence of the diminutive suffix -άριον in Greek perhaps favoured the acceptance of the Latin suffix -*arius* (-άριος).[261] Once again it is possible to distinguish between loans from Latin (e.g. λεγιωνάριος, often)[262] and new Greek formations with Greek bases (e.g. *P. Oxy.* XII. 1432.5 ὑποσχεσάριος, 'tax-farmer', third century).[263] What these cases suggest is that if the borrowing language already has a suffix which resembles phonetically a suffix in the contact language, conditions are ideal for the suffix in the contact language to be borrowed. Another illustration of the part played by loan-words in initially familiarising Greeks with a Latin suffix is to be seen in the case of -*ianus*, which turns up in Greek not only in the names of sects (see above, II), but also in Latin loan-words to do with military affairs and civil administration.[264] Of particular interest is the term στρατηλατιανός, discussed by Palmer (1946: 46). This word belongs to the military sphere, but here the base is Greek. The suffix will have become known through Latin technical terms to Greek speakers in contact with the Roman army and administration, and then been adopted (though not extensively) to form Greek technical terms. It is also possible that the suffix was easily accommodated because Greek itself had words in -ανός. Finally, it is worth mentioning Latin -*atus*, the history of which in Greek resembles that of the above suffixes. In the

---

[258] Palmer (1946: 118). See also Jannaccone (1950: 60–1), Cavenaile (1952: 200).
[259] See Palmer (1946: 119), Cavenaile (1952: 200).   [260] See in particular Palmer (1946: 48–9).
[261] See Cavenaile (1952: 201–2); cf. the remarks of Schulze (1894 = 1958: 113).
[262] See Daris (1991a: 65–6).
[263] See Palmer (1946: 48–9), Jannaccone (1950: 57), Cavenaile (1952: 201–2).
[264] See Palmer (1946: 46).

period covered by Palmer (1946) it is found almost exclusively in Latin loan-words (but note κυκλᾶτος 'shod'), but later in Greek 'it struck deep roots and became exceedingly prolific in its new home'.[265]

v.4 Syntax

The artificial imitation of Greek syntactic patterns in literature (on which see above, II) I leave aside here, partly because the subject has been adequately treated (for example by R. Coleman (1975)). While Coleman's paper has to do with imitation in the sense in which I use the word here, to some extent it also deals with syntactic convergences between the two languages (see for example the discussion of *habeo* and ἔχω with both the perfect participle (113–16) and the infinitive (116)), affecting more than the high literature, but very difficult to explain: did one language influence the other, or was there independent development along the same lines? I will not deal at length with such problematic cases.

Syntactic interference from L1 in L2 is a distinctive marker of foreigners' language use. The phenomenon may be illustrated by features of the Latin of Anthimus. Anthimus, as we have seen (above, v.2.3), was a Greek doctor who had moved to Italy where he picked up a colloquial form of Latin, onto which were grafted Grecising features from his first language. The construction found in the preface at p. 3.11 (*nam de potu est quando habent, est quando longo tempore non habent*, 'sometimes they have something to drink, sometimes they do not for a long time') reflects the double ἔστιν ὅτε construction of Greek.[266] Or again, when at 22, p. 11.12f. Anthimus twice used the neuter plural *posteriora* with singular verbs (*nam posteriora ipsorum non praesumatur*,[267] *quia grauat stomachum*), he was probably influenced by the Greek syntax of neuter plural subjects.[268] And at 81, p. 29.15f. (*quia exsucata alia pinguedo lapidis puras efficitur*) (discussed in another connection above, v.2.11) *efficitur* seems to have been treated not as a passive but as a middle used transitively on the model of ἀπεργάζεται.[269] Similarly Claudius Terentianus, though fluent in substandard colloquial

---

[265] Palmer (1946: 45; see too 46); cf. Jannaccone (1950: 58–9).

[266] See Mras (1943–7: 99); on the other hand this construction if found in a translation of a Greek work is mere translationese, and not so interesting; for examples of this type, see Mazzini and Flammini (1983: 28). Mras discusses a number of cases of interference, not all of them from the sphere of syntax.

[267] This is classified by Liechtenhan (1963: 58, 4) as *pass. impers. cum acc.*; but what of *grauat*? It is not clear that the alleged construction exists. For Latin neuter plurals with singular verbs in medical translations, see Mazzini and Flammini (1983: 29), Mazzini (1984: 23).

[268] See Mras (1943–7: 101).

[269] See Mras (1943–7: 101). Liechtenhan (1963) again classifies the usage as *pass. impers. cum acc.*

Latin, shows the influence of a Greek background in various ways. We have seen his taste for local Greek words (see v.2.2), and also his tendency to translate Greek formulae into Latin (see above, I.VII.4.2). There are signs too of Greek syntactic interference in his Latin. His use of *factum est* with dative + infinitive at *P. Mich.* 471.21–2 (*factum est illi uenire Alexandrie*) is not completely normal by Latin standards, but is identical to the Greek construction ἐγένετο with dative and infinitive, which occurs in the papyri: note *P. Mich.* VIII.503.2–3 καταπλέοντί μοι ε[ἰ]ς Ἀλεξανδρίαν διὰ σπουδῆς ἐγέ[ν]ετο γενέσθαι εἰς τὸ καταγώγιον. It is likely that Terentianus unconsciously transferred the idiom/construction into his Latin.[270]

I note in passing that not all syntactic interference which has been identified in antiquity can be accepted as such. Of Cicero's Greek (in the letters to Atticus) it has been remarked (by Dunkel (2000: 127)) that '[t]rue interference...is seen when Greek nouns appear in the exclamatory accusative instead of in the genitive (as is normal in Greek...)'. Various examples are cited, as *Att.* 6.1.18 *o* ἀνιστορησίαν *turpem*. But, as Wenskus (1996: 256) has pointed out, Cicero uses the Latin accusative construction if there is a Latin word in the exclamation; he uses the correct Greek genitive construction if the exclamation is wholly Greek (e.g. 6.1.17).

In the following discussion I will attempt to determine whether it is the writer's first or second language that is affected by a syntactic transfer, and will consider in each case under what heading the example should be classified (interference, etc.). I start with a case study of certain uses of the Greek dative, which illustrate the ways in which bilingualism may influence the syntax of one of the languages in contact.

v.4.1 *Roman Greek again: the Greek dative*

Roman Greek has already come up in this chapter, in the section on loan-shifts (v.2.11); here some syntactic material will be discussed. From the Roman period there are some curiosities in the use of the Greek dative, which acquires certain functions of the Latin ablative which it had not had in the classical period. The evidence though is varied, in that it is sometimes in the writings of native speakers of Latin, and sometimes in those of Greeks. As such it is open to variable interpretations. I start with the Greek dative as it is used by Cicero, as these bring out the nature of the problem well.

---

[270] For a discussion of the Latin construction, see Adams (1977: 63–4); also Cugusi, *CEL* II, p. 172.

Historically there was a marked degree of syntactic overlap between the dative in Greek and the ablative in Latin. The Latin ablative combines the functions of the ablative proper (expressing separation, = 'from'), the instrumental and locative, whereas the Greek dative combines those of the instrumental and locative, as well as the dative. If therefore in a sentence with code-switching in Cicero's letters a Greek dative adjective with instrumental function were made to qualify a Latin noun in the ablative (also with instrumental function), syntactic harmony would be achieved, because the Greek dative and the Latin ablative both carried this function. The one serious discrepancy between the two cases lies in the fact that the Greek dative did not inherit the functions of the Indo-European ablative; in Greek those went to the genitive (often accompanying a preposition). If therefore a Greek adjective in the dative were made to qualify a Latin noun in the ablative with *ablatival* function, then the function of the dative would have been *overextended* (on which term, see above, IV). Such usages one would expect to find in the Greek of Romans, who, starting from the areas of syntactic overlap between the two cases, might have extended the use of the Greek dative into an area in which historically it did not belong.

There is though more to the matter than that. Not only did the Latin ablative and the Greek dative overlap functionally, but they also in effect shared certain endings in the singular, at least in their graphic forms: in the feminine singular *-a* is much the same as -ᾳ, and in the masculine *-o* corresponds to -ῳ. To establish definitely that overextension had taken place, one would ideally have to find Greek datives behaving as ablatives whose endings were not replications of Latin ablative forms. Where there is a graphemic (or, one might equally say, phonetic) correspondence, it is always possible that a Roman such as Cicero wrote the Greek word in Latin script as a loan-word, in which case its ending would be that of the Latin ablative rather than of the Greek dative; or alternatively that, though he wrote the word in Greek form, he was expecting his reader(s) to interpret the ending as ambiguous in form between Greek dative and Latin ablative. I set out below a complete collection from Cicero's letters to Atticus of those examples of the Greek dative standing in agreement with a Latin ablative, or dependent on a preposition or other word (such as a verb) requiring an ablative, arranged according to ending:

(1) Forms ending in -ᾳ
   1.16.18 (SB16.18) quo ornatu, qua τοποθεσίᾳ
   1.16.18 (16.18) historias de'Αμαλθείᾳ

2.1.8 (21.8) in Platonis πολιτείᾳ

4.16.3 (89.3) in πολιτείᾳ

10.8A.1 (199A.1) a ζηλοτυπίᾳ (a letter of Antonius)

14.19.1 (372.1) ex Dolabellae ἀριστείᾳ

16.5.3 (410.3) de ὁμοπλοίᾳ

16.4.4 (411.4) uti ὁμοπλοίᾳ

16.8.2 (418.2) in maiore ἀπορίᾳ fui

16.11.2 (420.2) cum εὐμενείᾳ

(2) Forms ending in -ῳ

5.21.14 (114.14) de ἐνδομύχῳ

6.6.2 (121.2) de Academiae προπύλῳ

10.11.4 (202.4) illo Rhodiorum ἀφράκτῳ nauigans

15.26.1 (404.1) ψευδεγγράφῳ senatus consulto

16.7.3 (415.3) opus est σχολίῳ

16.12 (421) de Ἡρακλειδείῳ

16.15.3 (426.3) ἐν πολιτικῷ genere

(3) Other endings

5.21.2 (114.2) recesserant. ., sed nullo nostro εὐημερήματι

14.13.1 (367.1) ambulatione ἀλιτενεῖ delecter

12.3.1 (239.1) in eodem πάθει

13.21.3 (351.3) ab ἐποχῆ

Thus there are twenty-one examples, of which seventeen have the Greek dative endings -ᾳ or -ῳ. The disproportionate frequency of Greek words in -ᾳ and -ῳ shows that it was the correspondence of form, allied with the correspondence of function, which made certain Greek datives readily substitutable for Latin ablatives in Ciceronian code-switching. It is of particular note that the Greek 'ablatival' datives of the first declension almost invariably have the *alpha* rather than the *eta* ending, even though the *eta* form is far more numerous in Attic Greek. It would seem therefore that Cicero was careful in the first declension to admit only nouns having *alpha* forms with ablative function in his code-switches because of their correspondence of form with the Latin first-declension ablative (but see further below). On their own the seventeen examples would not constitute evidence that Romans' Greek had undergone any modification in the use of the dative. This evidence is incidentally relevant to 'constraints' on code-switching, a subject touched on in the previous chapter (3.III.10). On the whole Cicero code-switches into the Greek dative with ablatival function only if the form of the dative corresponds to a Latin ablative; he puts a constraint on his code-switching, by avoiding for example *eta* forms of nouns with the function of the Latin ablative.

It is the evidence assembled in (3) above that is the most interesting for our purposes. The endings found there if transliterated into Latin script would not give straightforward Latin ablative forms. εὐημερήματι has a short final *i*, which does not constitute a Latin ablative; and the ει ending if transliterated as (long) *i* could only be treated as an ablative form on the assumption that Cicero might have admitted in nouns a confusion of the *i*-stem ablative (cf. *omni*) and the consonantal-stem ablative (*capite*), of the type seen, for example, in *capiti*, which is allowed for metrical reasons in poetry.[271] But in ἐποχῇ at 13.21.3 Cicero has for once departed from his practice as stated above of admitting only *alpha* forms of the Greek dative in ablatival functions. Though a long *e* ending is found in the ablative of the Latin fifth declension (*die*, etc.), ἐποχή would not have gone into that declension if borrowed by Latin, but into the first; and it is moreover obvious from Cicero's near-complete avoidance of -η forms in ablatival contexts that he was distinctly uneasy about according such forms ablatival function.

I turn now to the syntactic interpretation of the material. Examples such as those at 5.21.2 and 14.13.1 (in section (3)), where the case role of the phrase is instrumental, are unremarkable, as we saw, because the Greek dative, like the Latin ablative, had instrumental function. These two examples might not therefore be straightforwardly interpretable as Latin ablatives in *form*, but in *function* at least the Greek case corresponds in this instance to the Latin ablative. It appears then that Cicero when using Greek datives with ablative function first strove to use forms which were ambiguous between Greek dative and Latin ablative, but in the absence of that type of correspondence at least sought a correspondence of function. Similarly there is nothing surprising about the use of *in* with a Greek dative (4 examples), because ἐν, the equivalent of *in*, governed a dative. *De* too with the dative of a Greek word (5 examples) is syntactically almost in line with Greek usage, because (e.g.) περί could be construed with a dative as well as a genitive in Greek; though it has to be said that περί takes a genitive when it has the function of Lat. *de*. Again, the use of *utor* with a Greek dative is tolerable, because the equivalent χράομαι took a dative object. It follows that if a use of the Greek dative corresponds exactly to a use of the Latin ablative, and if in addition there is an inflectional or graphemic correspondence between the case forms of the two languages, Cicero cannot be said to have been doing anything remarkable.

But that is not the end of the story, because in three places (one of them in a letter of Antonius) the prepositions *ab* or *ex* are used with a

---

[271] See e.g. Adams (1995a: 99–100).

Greek dative, and the equivalent Greek prepositions, ἀπό and ἐκ, are used exclusively with the genitive case. Thus Cicero (and Antonius) have used a Greek dative as an equivalent to a Latin ablative *in a context in which Greek would have required a genitive rather than a dative.*[272] This then is an extension of the use of the Greek dative made on the analogy of the functions of the Latin ablative. Also worth noting is the use of *opus est* at 16.7.3 with a Greek dative. Again Greek would have required a genitive in such a context (δεῖ and χρεία ἐστί both take a genitive of the thing needed). Outside the letters, at *Acad.* 2.17 (*nihil esset clarius* ἐνεργείᾳ),[273] Cicero uses the Greek dative as an equivalent to the Latin ablative of comparison, even though it was the genitive that had this function in Greek.[274] However, in almost all of these examples in which the Greek dative appears to be extended in function, the ending of the Greek word corresponds graphically/phonetically to a Latin ablative, and again we see the attempt to achieve, if not correspondence of both form and function, at least a correspondence of one type or the other. There remains only ἐποχῇ at 13.21.3: here Cicero has used a Greek dative with a form which he clearly did not regard as unequivocally ablatival, and with a function which did not belong to the dative. There is though on the face of it a factor which tones down the abnormality of the usage. ἐποχῇ could be put in inverted commas, as it is the word which is under discussion (note Shackleton Bailey's translation: 'That is as far as possible from the Greek ἐποχή'). The dependence of the form on *ab* may thus seem to be lessened. But words (Greek or Latin) discussed in Latin texts are usually not detached syntactically (by being placed, say, in the nominative),[275] but are construed according to the

[272] It is worth noting 5.19.3 (SB 112.3) τὸ νεμεσᾶν *interest* τοῦ φθονεῖν. Here the genitive construction with *interest* is not that normally found with the Latin verb, but that of its Greek equivalent διαφέρει (see Shackleton Bailey on 1.14.4 (p. 309)). The syntax of the Greek dependent word is thus determined not by the Latin governing word, but by its implied Greek equivalent. On that analogy the syntax of a Greek word dependent superficially on Latin *ab* or *ex* might also have been determined by the equivalent Greek prepositions. There is thus a fundamental difference between the relationship between Greek and Latin at 5.19.3, and that in the prepositional examples cited above, with the first showing correct Greek syntax, and the second incorrect. Also of note in this use of *interest* is its allusiveness. Cicero expects the reader to spot the Greek verb behind the Latin, just as (e.g.) he expects Paetus to pick up the Greek behind certain tags rendered into Latin (see 3.III.1, and also above, V.2.11). See also on the passage Wenskus (1996: 244).

[273] Cited by Shackleton Bailey on *Att.* 1.14.4 (vol. I, 309).

[274] The so-called 'dative of comparison' in Latin (see Hofmann and Szantyr (1965: 113–14), a construction which had its starting point in such phrases as *nulli inferior*, would not have provided Cicero with a purely Latin justification for using the dative in this context, as the construction is not genuinely equivalent to the ablative of comparison, and is not classical in prose.

[275] The word could stand in the nominative if it were preceded by a demonstrative 'article' expressing the case required in the context: see Quint. 1.4.8 *in his 'seruus' et 'uulgus'*, and below,

syntax of the phrase in which they occur. Thus Cicero has construed ἐποχῇ syntactically as dependent on *ab*; and that dependence entails giving the dative a separative (ablatival) function.

Cicero was thus capable of pressing the Greek dative into service as an equivalent to the Latin ablative to express a function that in Greek did not belong to the dative but to the genitive. For the most part his use of the dative *qua* ablative is syntactically harmonious, in the sense that the dative already had the same function in Greek itself, but he occasionally went beyond such harmonious uses and extended the Greek dative, but usually only when the extension was supported by a correspondence of form between Greek dative and Latin ablative. The one distinctive example, ἐποχῇ, does not amount to much, but it does bring out the circumstances under which a syntactic change might occur in conditions of language contact.

I offer some conclusions about the nature of the syntactic change that is hinted at in Cicero's use of the Greek dative. First, the extension is in Cicero's second language, and it thus underlines the fact that linguistic change can occur in a bilingual's second language under pressure from or on the analogy of the first. Secondly, the functional extension which the Greek dative undergoes in the example ἐποχῇ does not arise out of nothing, but is facilitated by the pre-existing overlap in both function and form between Greek dative and Latin ablative. The functions of the dative in the second language are extended slightly to replicate those of a case in the first language that already is partially equivalent to the Greek dative. There is an analogy between such syntactic or functional replication, and the semantic replication that underlies a loan-shift (see V.2.11). Thirdly, it is easy to see how such a development might have been peculiar to the second language of just one or a small handful of speakers: interlanguage phenomena, as was stressed at the outset (IV), need not catch on in a whole community, or even show themselves consistently in the output of one speaker/writer. That said, analogous uses of the Greek dative are attested in sources other than Cicero (see below). Thomason and Kaufman (1988: 97–8) stress that 'similarity favours borrowing', and that generalisation could be restated in reference to the present material. When certain cases in two languages have a partial overlap of form and of function, the two cases may further converge functionally, such that one takes on a function of the other which it had not had before. The

n. 313. Here if Quintilian had written *in seruo* the point would have been lost, because he is commenting on gemination of *u*. The Greek article itself was later borrowed by some technical writers to introduce a word or words under discussion (see Wenskus (1995: 189–92)).

functional extension in our material obviously begins in those forms in which the Greek dative had the same form as the Latin ablative; but Cicero's greater boldness in the use of ἐποχῇ points the way to extensions of function even in forms which differed from Latin ablatives. I would finally stress that the material considered in this section is not located in passages of continuous Greek, but in code-switches, and it highlights the restrictions which Cicero was imposing on switches of code in one grammatical case.

v.4.1.1 A use of the dative in the Greek translations of *senatus consulta*

The use of the Greek dative as an equivalent of the Latin ablative can be traced back well into the Republican period, at least as far as the second century BC. In the *senatus consulta* circulated in Greek translations in the Greek world (and drafted it would seem at Rome by first-language speakers of Latin: see above, n. 218) the name of the tribe of Roman citizens (in Latin expressed by an ablative[276] in -*a* attached to the name of the referent and placed after the filiation) is rendered in Greek by the dative: e.g. Sherk (1969), 10B.3 (dated before 135BC) Λεύκιος Τρεμήλιος Γναίου **Καμελλίᾳ** Γάιος Ἄννιος Γαίου **Καμελλίᾳ**, 12.24 (129 BC) Μάαρκος Πούπιος Μαάρκου Σκαπτιᾳ. This document has an extensive accumulation of such ablative/datives from lines 24–47. The phonetic/graphemic similarity of the Latin ablative and Greek dative in such names helps again to explain the usage, but it must be stressed that code-switching (into Latin) is out of the question in such documents. They are translations of a very literal kind (see v.2.12), in which the whole of the Latin document was put into Greek, and it would not do to argue that the tribal designations were envisaged as being in the Latin language: rather, the Latin translators rendered a separative use of the Latin ablative by a Greek dative, feeling no doubt that the usage was justified by the phonetic and graphemic equivalence of the two cases. A proper rendering would have made use of the genitive, or genitive dependent on ἐκ. There is an analogy in Greek to the Latin tribal designations, namely the use of δήμου or ἐκ δήμου attached to a personal name (see LSJ, s.v.), and this construction establishes how the Latin translators should have rendered the Latin ablative of the tribe.

It thus becomes clear that Cicero's tolerance of the -ᾳ 'ablatival' dative has a long-standing precedent.

[276] This ablative is interpreted by Ernout and Thomas (1964: 83) as a type of ablative of origin. It does not seem to be mentioned by most grammars.

v.4.1.2 The dative in consular dates

A translation of a consular date into idiomatic Greek would normally be expected to contain a genitival construction of some sort. Thus Sherk (1969), 22 (*senatus consultum de Asclepiade* of 78 BC) has in line 1 of the Greek version ἐπὶ ὑπάτων Κοίντου Λυτατίου Κοίντου υἱοῦ Κάτλου καὶ Μάρκου etc. corresponding to the ablatival date of the Latin version. Often, however, both in texts originating from Rome itself and in Greek papyri, the Latin consular date is rendered into Greek by means of a dative. Thus in the *senatus consultum de Panamara* of 39 BC (Sherk (1969), 27) in lines 3–4 there is a date in the dative which contrasts with that in the *senatus consultum* just cited: Λευκίῳ Μαρκίῳ Κησωρίνῳ καὶ Γαΐῳ Καλουησίῳ ὑπάτοις. There are also examples in the Greek translation of the *Res Gestae* of Augustus (1.2, 6.1, 12.2, 16.1, etc.).[277] The Latin construction should probably be described as an ablative absolute. The emergence of the Greek construction was again facilitated by the similarity of the endings of the Greek dative and the Latin ablative in many personal names of Latin origin, but the construction is not real Greek, as the more correct rendering quoted above shows. Moreover when the Latin name is of the third declension, the Greek dative does not correspond exactly to the Latin ablative form (e.g. 6.1 Τουβέρωνι, 12.2 [Νέ]ρωνι, 16.1 Αὔγουρι, for *Tuberone, Nerone, Augure*). Again we see the same sort of 'Roman' extension of the range of the Greek dative. In this case though the construction spread from Romans to Greeks, in that it is found in genuine Greek from Greek regions such as Egypt, and also in inscriptions (e.g. *IGUR* 999 = *IG* XIV.2090) and in late writers such as Josephus and Appian,[278] though only in the recording of the names of Roman magistrates (see n.277); in Greek eyes it must have had a certain Romanness about it.

v.4.1.3 The dative of duration of time

I move on from Romans using Greek to Greeks using their own language.

At (e.g.) *IGPorto* 43, p. 63 ὃς ἔζησεν ἔτεσιν ιαʹ, μησὶν εʹ, ἡμέραις IX the dative has been used to express duration of time, whereas in classical Greek it denoted time 'when'. In Latin funerary inscriptions the ablative

---

[277] See Viereck (1888: 62), Meuwese (1920: 59–62). Meuwese, who is cautious about accepting non-classical Greek usages as Latinisms even when they correspond to a Latin original, nevertheless regards this use of the dative as a Latinism. He points out that it is used by Greeks as well as Romans (61), but that it does not spread to dating by means of Greek officials' names (60). It retained its association with the Latin dating system.

[278] See García Domingo (1979: 160–1), Hering (1935: 42).

is constantly used to indicate duration.[279] Here the Greek endings definitely do not resemble Latin ablatives. There are three other Latinate features of this inscription. First, it has a Latin numeral symbol alongside the two Greek symbols (for this type of alphabet switching, see above, 1.VII.4.1). Secondly, it begins with θ(εοῖς) κ(αταχθονίοις), which is a rendering of *dis manibus* (see 1.VII.4.2 (1)). Thirdly, it expresses the age of the deceased in months and days as well as years. That is a characteristic of Latin funerary inscriptions rather than Greek.[280] There can be no doubt that the text is closely modelled on Latin funerary inscriptions. A particularly telling example of this use of the dative is found at *IGUR* 685 ζησάσῃ ἔτεσιν ζ΄ καὶ μηνὶ καὶ **ἡμέρας** ια΄. Here there is a mixture of cases (with the dative alternating with the accusative). Such variation is typical of Latin funerary inscriptions, the most frequent pattern being *annis menses dies*.[281] It is thus particularly obvious here that the case usage of the inscription has been influenced by that of Latin inscriptions, and that the dative is meant to correspond to the Latin ablative of duration of time. The names in these various inscriptions are largely Greek, and they almost certainly come from Greek communities. Kajanto (1963a: 15) also draws attention to a similar variation of cases at *MAMA* VII.323 συμβίῳ συνζησάσῃ ἔτεσι κγ΄ μῆνας [. . .] ἡμέρας κ΄, putting it down to Latin influence exerted in a bilingual setting in an area superficially Greek;[282] it matches exactly *annis menses dies*. Greek inscriptions written in Greek areas sometimes had a bilingual background, and subtle structural features occasionally betray this underlying bilingualism. A case in point is the Bulgarian inscription *IGBulg.* II.692: θ(εοῖς) κ(αταχθονίοις). Καλπουρνίῳ Γαίῳ τῷ καὶ Κάρπῳ ἀνδρὶ πολείτῃ φυλῆς Ἀπολλωνιάδος καὶ γερουσιαστῇ **ζήσαντι ἔτεσιν** ἑξήκοντα καὶ Εὐτυχίδι θυγατρὶ **ζησάσῃ ἔτεσιν** δεκαεννέα Χρήστῃ Χρήστου ζῶσα τὸ μνημεῖον ἐκ τῶν ἰδίων κατεσκεύασεν. This is one of a small group of Greek funerary inscriptions from Nicopolis ad Istrum, which collectively have a range of Latinate characteristics (see 1.VII.4.2 (1)), such as θεοῖς καταχθονίοις and the use of υἱός in a filiation (693 θεοῖς καταχθονίοις. Ἀσκλᾷ Χρήστου υἱῷ νέωι ἥρωι ζήσαντι ἔτη β΄ μνήμης χάριν ὁ πατὴρ Χρῆστος τὴν στήλην ἀνέστησεν), as well as the dative of duration. Elsewhere in Bulgarian inscriptions the accusative ἔτη is very much the norm (e.g. *IGBulg.* II.688, 690, 693, 694, 716, 737). The Latinised group of epitaphs may reflect either a degree of Romanisation and hence bilingualism

---

[279] See for example the discussion of E. Löfstedt (1911: 54–6).   [280] See Kajanto (1963a: 13).
[281] See E. Löfstedt (1911: 54–6).   [282] See further Schulze (1894 = 1958: 107).

on the part of the clients and referents, or the practices of a bilingual workshop of stonemasons influenced by Latin structures.

In the previous sections we saw Romans extending the use of the Greek dative on the analogy of the Latin ablative. The writers of the inscriptions discussed in this section are likely to have been primary speakers of Greek, albeit bilinguals: a funerary inscription would not as a rule have been written in a language alien to its referents. Thus the Greek dative was under pressure to extend its range from two directions: from Latin speakers who associated the case with the Latin ablative because of the similarities of form and the pre-existing functional overlap, and from bilingual Greeks, who made the same association and may have been aware of the use of the case by primary speakers of Latin. I stress that the examples of the Greek dative (expressing duration of time) cited in this section are all overtly Latinate, in the sense that they all occur in Roman inscriptions or Latin-inspired formulae or in expressions for which there is an exact Latin parallel. There can be no room for doubt that the dative in these instances, given the contexts in which it is found, represents the imitation of a mundane use of the Latin ablative. But the dative of duration of time is not restricted to inscriptions. There are also literary examples. Note, for example, Lucian *Dial. Meretr.* 8.2 ταῦτα λέγω πρός σε εἴκοσιν ὅλοις ἔτεσιν ἑταιρίσασα.[283] The discussion by Hering (1935: 38–9) of Appian's methods of expressing duration of time is especially systematic, and brings out the change that had taken place in Greek (or at least some varieties of the language). In Appian the dative of duration outnumbers the accusative by 34:30 (with various prepositional alternatives even less favoured), whereas in Hering's sample of Thucydides, Polybius and Diodorus the dative does not occur. In Josephus it is common, but does not outnumber the accusative (see the table, p. 39). Literary evidence on its own is difficult to interpret, because it is not always possible to separate developments internal to a language from externally motivated changes. But given the explicit contextual parallels between the Latin ablative and Greek dative in inscriptions, the material in Appian falls more clearly into place. Hering has moreover demonstrated that Appian has many Latinisms of other types.[284] Though of Alexandrian birth, Appian was a Roman citizen and resident of Rome, where he practised as an advocate.

In Claudius Terentianus there is a use of πολλοῖς χρόνοις (where χρόνοις = 'years') in a closing formula which corresponds exactly to *multis*

---

[283] See e.g. Sophocles (1888: 43), Radermacher (1925: 133 with n. 1), Blass, Debrunner and Rehkopf (1975: 163–4), García Domingo (1979: 156–7) (this last hardly satisfactory).

[284] See also Famerie (1998).

annis in the equivalent formula in several of his Latin letters: *P. Mich.* VIII.477.44f. ἐρρῶσ]θ[αί σε] εὔχομαι πολ[λοῖς χ]ρό[νοις; for the Latin formula *bene ualere te opto multis annis*, see *P. Mich.* VIII.467.35, 468.64 (see also above, I.VII.4.2 (6)). Terentianus' usage strongly suggests a direct link between the Latin *multis annis* and the Greek πολλοῖς χρόνοις.[285] There are though some complicating factors. A computer search of the papyri turns up more than 300 examples of πολλοῖς χρόνοις, usually in this same formula, which occurs, for example, no fewer than 17 times in the Abinnaeus archive, which is overwhelmingly Greek. Could it be assumed that the Greek formula as used so extensively in Greek settings originated straightforwardly as an imitation of the Latin? That is not impossible, given that many archives of Greek papyri have a Roman military background, in which Latin could have been influential. Even if the ἐρρῶσθαι-formula were earlier in Greek than it appears (see above, I. VII.4.2 (6)),[286] it need not have had πολλοῖς χρόνοις at first.[287] An alternative possibility to that of the Latin origin of the whole formula is that the infinitive formula originated in Greek, was taken over by Latin,[288] but with the addition at some point of the typical Latin construction *multis annis*; then the Latin version could in its turn have influenced the Greek. But there is need of a proper study of the provenance and date of the dative expression in Greek.

I mention in passing another dative temporal construction discussed by Dubuisson (1985: 238–9) under the heading 'Le complément de l'espace de temps' and by Hering (1935: 35–7). Dubuisson cites, for example, Pol. 4.32.8 πλεονάκις... οὐ πάνυ πολλοῖς χρόνοις 'several times in not very many years', noting that classical Greek normally used the preposition ἐν for this purpose but that Polybius and others (including Appian) use a 'Latinate' dative (equivalent to the Latin ablative). There is though an obvious methodological question to be raised here. Was this 'Latinate' usage of the dative of time 'within which' the norm in later Greek? If so, can it legitimately be described as a Latinism when used by monolingual Greeks? Did it enter Greek as a result of Latin influence, or could internal determinants have been in operation as well? I have restricted myself earlier in this section to examples from overtly bilingual communities in which there is good reason to see a link between the usage in question in Greek and Latin, but I am reluctant to argue from these that Latin was the only influence in the new late uses of the Greek

---

[285] See also E. Löfstedt (1956: II, 448).
[286] The 'ἐρρῶσθαι-formula' of Exler (1923:103–7) is different.
[287] Exler (1923: 107–10) does not deal with the phrase.   [288] Thus Cugusi, *CEL* II, p. 144.

dative. More work needs to be done on later literary Greek to assess the acceptability of the term 'Latinate' in reference to such examples.

v.4.1.4 Another use of the dative

In Polybius there is a common use of the dative of relation or respect, as for example at 2.14.4 τῷ σχήματι τριγωνοειδής 'triangular in form'.[289] This usage is discussed by Dubuisson (1985: 237–8), who points out that in classical Greek it is the accusative which has this function (τὰ πολέμια μαλακοί, etc.), but that in later Greek the dative ousts the accusative, most notably in the New Testament. He puts this down to the influence of Latin among bilinguals, noting (see above) that the starting point for such an extension of the use of the dative must have been the degree of overlap (in the locative and instrumental uses) which the Greek dative and Latin ablative had inherited. The case remains unproven on the limited evidence presented.

v.4.1.5 Conclusions

Some of the material presented in the last two sections introduces a new dimension to the discussion of the dative. We saw earlier that Cicero in his letters occasionally extended the use of the dative *in his second language* on the model of the range of uses that the Latin ablative possessed. His first language was responsible for the extension. But an inscription such as *IGUR* 685, quoted above, v.4.1.3, in which the dative of time alternates with the accusative, is a different matter. This inscription cannot have been written by a first-language speaker of Latin. Like the numerous other Greek funerary inscriptions at Rome, it must originate in the Greek population of the city, as it is inconceivable that a native Latin speaker would have been commemorated in Greek. It is probably the writer's first language which is affected. The person who wrote the inscription was familiar with the format of Latin funerary inscriptions (see above), and he set out to imitate that format in Greek, even to the extent of mimicking the alternation of cases. One should speak of 'imitation' again, which we classified above (II) as borrowing. Thus second-language extensions of the range of the Greek dative, and first-language borrowing by Greeks of Latin ablative functions in their use of the Greek dative, come together. The literary examples of the same dative usage in writers such as Appian suggest that 'imitation' hardened into widespread usage (whereas the Grecising syntax in high Latin literature usually remained artificial and

---

[289] See Dubuisson (1985: 238).

not part of the language as a whole). But it would be useful to have statistics from a wider range of later Greek writers showing the incidence of the dative of duration in relation to other equivalent constructions. Miscellaneous examples tell us nothing about the state of the language.

The material assembled in this section allows one to suggest tentatively the steps by which the new uses of the dative entered Greek. First, second-language speakers of Greek, such as Cicero and the translators of the Roman *senatus consulta*, began to use the dative with ablatival functions, thereby imposing on the dative the full range of functions possessed by the Latin ablative. In bilingual communities, such as that at Rome, first-language speakers of Greek would have been in contact not only with Latin but with speakers and writers of Roman Greek (that is, native speakers of Latin whose Greek showed forms of interference from Latin). Secondly, in the Latin-speaking environment of Rome, Greek bilinguals sometimes gave the dative the new function, influenced first and foremost by specific contexts (such as that seen above in the funerary inscription *IGUR* 685) in which there was pressure to imitate the ablatival use of the Latin ablative in a succinct way. Contact with Roman Greek, allied with imitation of Latin syntax in particular contexts, seems to have caused the new use of the Greek dative to take hold, such that eventually it came to be used by later writers, not all of whom need have perceived it as a Latinism; though we have stressed the need for a more systematic study of Greek literature. What makes the Greek dative a revealing case study is the survival of material, such as the letters of Cicero, the translations of *senatus consulta* and the inscriptions of Roman Greeks, which bridges the gap between the classical Greek use of the dative on the one hand and the later literary use (in writers such as Appian, Lucian, etc.) on the other. It is not the later literary use that is specifically Latinate (except historically), so much as usage in the intermediate period, when we can observe on the one hand direct interference (of Latin in the Greek of Latin speakers) and on the other direct borrowing (from Latin in the Greek of Greek speakers). On the interpretation offered here, both native speakers of Latin and native speakers of Greek are implicated in the emergence of the new usage.

V.4.2 Greeks' Latin: the genitive (of time) in Latin

My next example is of the reverse type, that is of Greek interference in the syntax of Latin. The evidence assembled in this section concerns Greek interference in the Latin of Greeks. In ordinary Latin there is no trace of a genitive expressing time, other than in a few old usages (such as *nox* in the Twelve Tables and *trinum nundinum*), the interpretation of which is controversial.[290]

The following is part of the text of a receipt written at an unidentified place *Puluin-* (?), dated 7 October, AD 167, which is published conveniently at *ChLA* 3.204 and *CEL* 156 (for the circumstances of composition of which, see *ChLA* 3, p. 85): *miserat mi[hi] Cornelius [G]ermanus procurator meus quas has res [i] ntra scriptas meas, salbas, sanas recepisse scripsi* **nonarum** Octobrium *ad Puluinos, ad statione Liburnes 'Fides', interueniente Minucium Plotianum triarchum et Apuleium Nepotem scriba. actum Puluinos nonis Octobris* (this and the following text are discussed in another connection below, 5. VII.2.2).

The genitive in Greek may express time 'within which', and it follows that the genitive *nonarum Octobrium* is Greek-determined. Oddly at the end of the text the writer switches into the ablative, though not without a morphological error (*Octobris* for *-ibus*).

Apparently on the same day and at the same place the text *ChLA* 1.12 (= *CEL* 157) was written, of which I quote the last few lines: *scripsi me recepisse res s(upra) s(criptas) [a Corneli]o Germ[a]no cuius [e]xemplum epistules habio. actum Puluinos* **nonar[u]m Octobrium** *isdem co[ns]ulibus.*

Here there is the same Greek genitive construction, this time at the point where the other document had the correct ablative. It is also of note that *epistules* is inflected with the *-es* genitive (cf. ἐπιστολῆς); and *liburnes* in the first text also has the same ending (see above, V.3.1.2). The two texts are formulaic, but even so have been subject to Greek influence.

There is another receipt (for hay) which has a genitive relating to time (*ChLA* 3.203, Fink (1971), 80, *CEL* 150, dated AD 130): *alae uetrane galliga, turma Donaciani, Serenus procurator conductoribus fenaris salute. accipi fenum contur[m]alibus meis* **mensis Iuni** *et naulum s[ustu]li per me et tibi fiunt eccutes triginti.* Here though the genitive could be construed in attachment to *fenum* ('the hay of the month of June').

At *P. Mich.* VII.438.9 (= *ChLA* 5.303, *CEL* 154) the genitive *diei i(nfra) s(cripti)* has been taken as another example of the Greek construction,[291] but the context is too fragmentary to allow certainty. Whatever the case, the usage had certainly entered the language in bilinguals' Latin.

It is no surprise that receipts should sometimes have embodied Greek interference. In Greek environments where there were persons subject to Roman law (as for example in Roman Egypt, where there were Roman

[290] See in general Hofmann and Szantyr (1965: 85), with some bibliography.
[291] See Cugusi, *CEL* II, p. 194.

citizens who did not necessarily have a knowledge of Latin, and in the Roman army, which had units containing men of eastern origin), a first-language speaker of Greek might sometimes have been required (contrary to his usual practice) to write in Latin because of the convention of using Latin for receipts. The consequence of this requirement was seen in the receipt of Aeschines (see 1.VII.2.3). The Greek milieu lying behind the first two texts quoted above is apparent not only in the genitive of time, but also in items of morphology (see above). And in the receipt for hay the spelling *eccutes* for *equites* is also suggestive of the writer's background. *qu* is not infrequently misspelt in Latin as *cu*,[292] as in this word at *CIL* III.14406a (*ecuites*), but in this document the spelling might have been subject to interference from the form which the term had taken on as a loan-word into Greek. Note, for example, Jaussen and Savignac (1914), 14 (ἐκκύης αλα Γετουρῶν), and also 16 (Φολσκιανὸς Σεουέρος ἐκύης δὶς αλε Γετουλῶν). Also of note in the same receipt for hay is *naulum* = ναῦλον 'passage-money, freight'. The word was no doubt a localised borrowing into Latin in this area, though there are stray examples in literary texts (e.g. Juv. 8.97).

In the last line of *ChLA* 3.204 above (*nonis Octobris, Imp(eratore) Vero ter(tio) et Vmmidio Quadrato consulatus*) *consulatus* could be a careless resolution of the abbreviation *cos.*, or some sort of copying error. Or, if it was conceived as a genitive, it might have been influenced by the use of the genitive ὑπατείας in dates: e.g. *P. Harr.* 1.65.1 ὑπατείας τῶν δεσπότων ἡμῶν Κωνσταντίου τὸ γ'...

There is then a cluster of cases of Greek influence in the two or three documents, syntactic, morphological, orthographical and lexical. It is though worthwhile to put these Greek-inspired errors into context. Though the texts were the work of writers used to using Greek, they also admitted usages of types that can be paralleled in the substandard output of monolingual speakers of Latin (see 5.VII.2.2). The texts are thus evidence for the Latin usage of bilingual Greeks familiar with colloquial Latin (see e.g. V.3.3 above (with cross references) on the glossary *P. Lond.* II.481, and V.2.3, V.4 on Anthimus).

V.4.3 The genitive of filiation in Latin
An archaic Latin inscription from Capua (*CIL* I². 400) quoted and discussed in an earlier chapter (2.II.3, p. 136) has a series of filiations (abbreviated) comprising genitive alone without *filius*. In Oscan it was the normal practice to attach the genitive to the name (e.g. Vetter (1953), 11,

---

[292] See Väänänen (1966: 54–5).

12, 13, 137, 142, 150, 151, 156, 163, 168, 196 etc.), and there can be no doubt that in this text it is the influence of Oscan that is the determinant of the structure. It is not possible to determine whether this is a case of imitation or interference.

Sometimes structures of this type represent Greek, rather than Oscan, interference. So at *MAMA* VIII.27 (*Tattis Flaui*) the 'Italo-Lykaonian Tattis writes in Latin, but expresses affiliation in the Greek style' (so the editors). A bilingual funerary inscription from Bulgaria (*IGBulg.* II.600) has the same genitival filiation in the Latin version as in the Greek: *Agathadorus* **Diophanis** *uiuos sibi [f(aciendum)] curauit.* Ἀγαθόδορος Διοφάνου Νεικεὺς ζῶν καὶ φρονῶν ἑαυτῷ ἐποίησεν ἀνεξοδίαστον. Greek seems to have been the writer's primary language, to judge by the greater fullness of the Greek version. The Latin has no ethnic, nor an equivalent of the last word (paraphrased by the editor G. Mihailov as = *qui uendi non debet*). Conversely those writing Greek either as their second language, or under conditions which favoured the imitation of Latin practice, often used υἱός in filiations in violation of the standard Greek practice (see 6.v.1). See also e.g. *MAMA* VIII.367 (from Carik Saray in the Pisido-Phrygian borderland) Κοκκείαν Γαίου **θυγατέρα** Λουκίαν Αὐλόσιος Αὔλου Κεντου **υἱὸς** τὴν ἑαυτοῦ γυναῖκα καὶ Διογένης καὶ Σεύθης οἱ ἀδελφοὶ φιλοστοργίας καὶ μνήμης ἕνεκεν. Some of the names here are of Latin origin. Not infrequently inscriptions of Asia Minor written in Greek betray the bilingualism of the writer (see above v.4.1.3 for another example).

V.4.4 African Latin: the use of the vocative for nominative

Svennung (1958: 395) and others have noted that in African Latin inscriptions the vocative is sometimes used where a nominative might have been expected (e.g. *CIL* VIII.2182 *L. Leli Siluane, sacerdos Saturni, uotum soluit libens animum* [= *animo*], 8670 *DMS Egnati Gemne* [= *Gemine*] *uixit anos LXXXXV*).[293] These examples though do not admit of a straightforward interpretation. They could be genuine vocatives (acclamations), followed by a shift into the third person,[294] or alternatively fossilised vocatives playing the role of nominatives; such fossilisation might reflect the particular frequency with which names are used in address in any language.[295]

---

[293] Svennung was not the first to make this observation. For a brief history of the matter, see Adamik (1987: 1); see further Petersmann (1998: 133).

[294] See Adamik (1987) for a balanced discussion of the problem, and Petersmann (1998: 133–4), discussing some interesting specific cases.

[295] Adamik (1987: 8) notes that in some cases of the *tria nomina* it is only the *cognomen* that has a vocative form. Since the *cognomen* would have been particularly used in vocative address, this oddity is consistent with fossilisation of the most frequently used vocative form.

Nor are vocatives of this type particularly common: Adamik (1987: 4) mentions a figure of seven examples in 30,000 African inscriptions (though it is not clear that he knows of examples from Sirte in texts published by Bartoccini (1928), on which see below).

But there is another dimension to the matter which Latinists seem not to have noticed. As we saw in an earlier chapter (2.V.5.1, V.6), in neo-Punic inscriptions names of Latin origin regularly correspond in their Punic guise to the vocative form of the Latin rather than to the nominative.[296] This may be seen, for example, in the Punic–Latin bilingual from El-Amrouni in Libya (*KAI* 117) which was quoted and discussed above, 2.V.5.1, p. 218. The deceased Q. Apuleius Maximus Rideus has an exclusively Latin name, as do his sons Pudens, Severus and Maximus, and in the Latin version these names have the correct Latin nominative inflection. But in the Punic version the names of Latin origin all correspond to the Latin vocative.

Or again, in the Punic inscription *KAI* 173 the emperor's name corresponds to the Latin *Marce Aureli Antonine Auguste*.[297]

In a catacomb at Sirte (see above) the inscriptions of which were published by Bartoccini (1928) there has been virtual convergence of Latin and Punic in the use of vocative forms for nominative. In neo-Punic texts (written in Latin script) *Mercuri* and *Anniboni* are both found,[298] and in Latin texts vocatives with nominative function abound: Bartoccini (1928), 3 *Flabiane*, 9 *[F]labiane*, 21 *Demetri*, 25 *Rogate*, 51 *Kallibi* (*Cal(l)ibius*). There is also (a further indication of the linguistic complexity of the community) one Latin name which is given a *Greek* nominative ending: 15 *Balerianos uix(it) an(nos) XXX* (see above, V.3.3). The sheer abundance of vocatives, considered alongside this last example in -*os*, and also alongside some nominatives in -*u* (with omission of -*s*), rules out any attempt to explain the usage in Latin as exclamatory (and hence as syntactically vocatival). It would be perverse to take such examples as anything other than fossilisations of the vocative used with nominative function.

Friedrich and Röllig (1970: 100), pointing out that Latin names in -*us* rarely enter Punic in a form derivable from -*us*, but instead almost always have a form representing an -*e* ending (see above, 2.V. 5.1), deny that the latter is a reflex of the Latin vocative; they see its origin rather in the Etruscan ending of the type *Aule* = *Aulus* ('Vielmehr ist wohl eher an Übernahme der bei den Etruskern geläufigen Namensformen

[296] See Donner and Röllig (1966–9: 122), Friedrich and Röllig (1970: 100), and for further bibliography, Chapter 2, n. 428.
[297] See Friedrich and Röllig (1970: 100).   [298] See Bartoccini (1928), 15, *KAI* 180d.

(*Aule* "Aulus", *Marce* "Marcus" . . .) zu denken'). Though the Etruscans had early contacts with the Carthaginians, Latin 'vocative' forms in Punic are attested many centuries after those contacts and after the demise of Etruscan, and it is difficult to believe that there had been continuity in such posited Punic usage between the early Republican period and the late Empire. Friedrich and Röllig (loc. cit.) relate Latin names in *-i* (i.e. those deriving from Lat. *-ius*: see above for examples)[299] to a 'vulgar Latin form in *-i*.[300] On this view the Punic forms representing *-e* are given one origin, but those representing *-i* another, and one must treat it as mere coincidence that each happens to correspond to the appropriate Latin vocative. It is far more economical to assume that the origin of both lay in the respective vocative forms of Latin names in *-us* on the one hand and in *-ius* on the other, and that the Punic evidence is independent of the Etruscan, and those are the assumptions which I make here. The Etruscan material is though of some comparative interest. It is not only the case that Latin (or Italic) names in *-us* (original *-os*) entered Etruscan with the ending *-e* (e.g. *Tite*), but also that some Latin–Italic names in *-ius* (*-ios*) turn up in Etruscan with the ending *-i* (e.g. *Publi, Arri*) or *-ie*.[301] There are two possible explanations of this. Either *-e* and *-i* were pre-existing Etruscan endings (a view advanced by De Simone (1970:142) in reference at least to *-e*), in which case it might well have been the correspondence between the two Latin (Italic) vocative endings and the Etruscan forms which determined the Etruscan category to which the Latin (Italic) loans were assigned. Alternatively, Etruscan might have borrowed the Latin–Italic personal names (if not divine names) in their vocative forms, and those vocative morphemes might then have spread in Etruscan into names of native Etruscan rather than Italic origin.[302] On this second view the morphological borrowing into Etruscan began with the borrowing of lexical items from the donor language(s) which happened to contain the morphemes in question; the morphemes then took on a life of their own in the recipient language. We have seen this phenomenon before.

There are two ways of interpreting the above African data, which are not mutually exclusive. First, the vocative use of names with nominative function might have been well entrenched in African Latin, with the result that Latin names taken over into Punic naturally showed vocative

[299] For full bibliography, see Chapter 2, n. 428.
[300] Presumably of the complex type discussed by Kaimio (1969).
[301] See Rix (1963: 227, 230, 258, 259); id. (1994: 63–4).
[302] See e.g. Rix (1981: 124), id. (1994: 63 n. 32), Steinbauer (1993: 288). I am grateful to John Penney and David Langslow for discussion of this problem.

forms. Alternatively, it might have been first-language speakers of Punic, with imperfect competence in Latin, who falsely assumed that the vocative was the 'normal' form of Latin names, since it is the vocative that is most commonly heard in any language.[303] Quite apart from the Etruscan case dealt with above, in Coptic various names of Greek origin can be interpreted as borrowings of the Greek vocative form.[304] On this second view, it is not necessary to assume that in native speakers' Latin the vocative for the nominative was the norm at all: a false deduction might have been made by second-language speakers of Latin about the form of Latin names. Having borrowed these false base forms into Punic, bilinguals might then have transferred them back into Latin (as nominatives). Both processes might have taken place at the same time, and it is impossible to be sure where the starting point lay. Nevertheless it is of note that in the bilingual text *KAI* 117 referred to above (see 2.V.5.1) the nominative is correctly used in the Latin version, but the vocative form appears in the Punic. This would suggest that vocative forms were associated by literate bilinguals chiefly with Punic, in which case it might be argued that Punic is more likely to have influenced Latin than vice versa. Whatever the case, in the community at Sirte the Latin vocative form is regularly, if not exclusively, used in both Punic and Latin texts, and that represents a (partial) convergence. It is also worth noting that in *Latin* inscriptions from Etruria the *-e* ending is found in Latin names with nominative function (see above, 2.III.6, p. 177), and this might represent a transfer of the 'Etruscan' form back into the Latin of Etruscan speakers, a development which would be parallel to that which (on the second possibility advanced above) might have taken place centuries later in Africa.

V.4.5 *The definite article: Romans' Greek and Roman Latin*

The Greek definite article presented complex problems for Latin speakers, the consequences of which, it might be argued, were twofold. On the one hand in Romans' Greek there might have been interference from Latin (i.e. omission of the article when it might have been expected), and on the other hand in the Latin of those who were in close contact with Greek there will have been pressure to add to the Latin demonstratives an article function. I take first Greek written by Romans. Key documents are Greek translations of Latin *senatus consulta* and the Greek translation of Augustus' *Res Gestae*. The interpretation of the evidence though is not

---

[303] See in general Wackernagel (1926: 309–10).
[304] See the material collected by Heuser (1929: 89–90). I owe this reference to James Clackson.

straightforward, and I discuss the complexities of these documents in some detail.

In reference to the use of the definite article in Greek translations of Latin *senatus consulta* Sherk (1969: 16) asserts that the 'lack of a definite article conditioned the Romans to neglect it when translating into Greek'. He points out (17) that its 'omission is regular in the prescript for the title of the presiding magistrate', and that 'the place of meeting usually lacks it'. For example, the *Senatus consultum et foedus cum Astypalaeensibus* of 105 BC (Sherk, 16) has (line 11) the expression ἐν Καπετωλίῳ, whereas sometimes elsewhere the same phrase has the article (e.g. 22.25).

Sherk was here taking much the same line as Viereck (1888: 60–1). A more judicious discussion of the subject is to be found in Meuwese (1920: 32–55). In the Greek versions of *senatus consulta* and the Greek version of Augustus' *Res Gestae* there are indeed non-classical Greek constructions which correspond closely to the syntax of the Latin, but in many cases later Greek itself also possessed the 'Latinate' construction, perhaps independently of Latin influence. For example, at Sherk (1969), 2.18–19 there is a neuter plural standing as subject of a plural verb in the Greek.[305] The form of agreement must have corresponded to that in the Latin original, but the construction is not for that reason necessarily to be treated as a Latinism, because in Greek as well the neuter plural came to be construed with a plural verb.[306] Or again the use of the subjunctive in such translations (the *coniunctiuus latinus*, in the terminology of Viereck (1888: 68)) where classical Greek would have used the optative or indicative cannot necessarily be put down to Latin influence, because the subjunctive extended its range from the Hellenistic period.[307] The aoristic use of the perfect is not classical in Greek, but it is, for example, common in the Greek translations of *senatus consulta*. However it is not necessarily a Latinism, because there were changes in the use of the perfect in later Greek.[308] Rose (1921: 115) cites some alleged cases of the Greek perfect 'as a historic tense' from Cicero's letters to Atticus (13.20.4, 14.6.2) (the latter is not well chosen), and states that this 'would be particularly natural for a Roman'. His case is not conclusive. Meuwese was prepared to admit the presence of Latinisms in the Greek translations, but in each case he was careful to determine whether later Greek might itself have changed independently along Latin lines.

---

[305] See Viereck (1888: 62).   [306] See e.g. Jannaris (1897: 314), Mayser (1934: 28–30).

[307] See Meuwese (1920: 99). On the decline of the optative in Greek, see e.g. Mayser (1926: 288), Schwyzer and Debrunner (1950: 337).

[308] See the discussion of Meuwese (1920: 85–92). On the aoristic function of the perfect in later Greek, see e.g. Jannaris (1897: 439), Mayser (1926: 139–40), Dubuisson (1985: 240).

Where the article is concerned Viereck (1888: 60) sees the construction (for which see *Res Gestae* 6.1 Gagé) ὁ δῆμος τῶν Ῥωμαίων as 'incorrect' (in contrast to ὁ Ῥωμαίων), but Meuwese (1920: 39) illustrates the type from later Greek. There is though a genuine Latinism in the sphere of such phrases, and that is the type δῆμος Ῥωμαίων (without any article).[309] This construction occurs frequently in the Latin translation of the *Res Gestae* (e.g. 15.1, 26.1 Gagé). The omission on the face of it might be interpreted as a mistake in the writer's second language due to interference from his first. But an expression at Plut. *Galba* 5.2 (στρατηγὸς συγκλήτου καὶ δήμου Ῥωμαίων)[310] gives one pause. Plutarch cannot have been subject to interference from Latin in his Greek (though his Latin shows interference from Greek, see IV above): the form of the phrase has been adopted deliberately on the model of the Latin *senatus populusque Romanus*. It is a case of imitation of the Latin structure in a Roman formula in the writer's first language. Thus we should not automatically assume unconscious interference from Latin in the Greek of the translator above. He may deliberately have imposed the Latin structure on the Greek version (for which process in Greek translations of Latin official texts, see above, v.2.12).

A failure to achieve the correct idiomatic relationship between Greek and Latin in the use of the definite article is to be found in text no. 12 of the archive of Babatha from the Cave of Letters (Lewis (1989)). The document seems to be a Greek translation of a Latin original (report of the town council of Petra). Notable in the inner text is the phrase ἀπὸ ἄκτων βουλῆς Πετραίων, which must be a rendering of *ex (ab) actis senatus Petraeorum*, with total omission of the article in Greek under the influence of the Latin (see above, 2.VII.5).[311] It may be conjectured that the translation was done by a native speaker of Latin, unless a Greek did a word-for-word translation without any attempt to achieve idiomatic character for the Greek. This example may again reflect the deliberate imposition of a Latin structure on Greek made by a Roman in an official document. On the other hand at *O.Claud.* II.360.5 (ἔπεμψα διὰ Δῆβατες κοστωδίας) there is unlikely to have been deliberate imitation of Latin. If the final word is taken as a genitive singular in apposition to the name (see the editor, pp. 200–1), 'l'absence de l'article [est] due ... à l'influence du latin'. This looks more like interference.

On the other hand there emerged in Latin a definite article which passed into the Romance languages (*ipse* and *ille* are the forms reflected

---

[309] See Meuwese (1920: 40–1, 54).   [310] Cited by Meuwese (1920: 41).
[311] See Lewis (1989: 17).

in this function). The question whether Greek influenced Latin or the development occurred independently in Latin has been much discussed. I refer here only to R. Coleman's overview of the question (1975: 117), in which he allows Greek 'influence' (i.e borrowing, in the case of native speakers of Latin, or interference, in the case of native speakers of Greek). Here I restrict myself to some direct evidence of contact (between a Latin speaker and the Greek language) which has not been noticed.

In the prologue to Plautus' *Miles Gloriosus* where the plot is set forth the characters mentioned (the soldier, the *lena*, the young man and his lover) are constantly designated by common nouns (*miles, lena* etc.) + demonstrative (for the most part *hic* and *ille*, but also *iste*): 88 *illest miles*, 105 *illam amicam*, 109 *militi huic*, 110 *illi lenae*, 111–2 *is . . . miles*, 120 *huic . . . militi*, 122 *illam amicam*, 127 *illum . . . meum erum*, 128 *istum militem*, 131–2 *illum . . . meum erum*, 136 *illi amanti suo hospiti*. The frequency of the demonstratives is striking, and it exceeds what might have been expected in Latin. The demonstratives carry no contrastive function in the context to justify their presence. But lying behind this passage is a Greek original, and in the prologues of Greek New Comedy it was conventional to explain the plot, not by using the names of characters, but by giving them a descriptive designation *accompanied by the definite article*: e.g. *Asp.* 109 τοῦ μειρακίου, 114 ὁ γέρων, 122 ὁ θεράπων, 128 ὁ μειρακίσκος, 133 τὴν παρθένον, *Dysc.* 28 ὁ παῖς, 30 ὁ γέρων, τὴν θυγατέρ', *Phasma* 4 τῆ]ς παρθένου τὴν μητέρα, 10 τῆς γαμουμένης.[312] It seems to me likely that Plautus has imitated this practice in the prologue of the *Miles* (given that the nouns themselves without deixis would have expressed their own differentiation of the characters), and in so doing has virtually treated *hic* and *ille* as article-equivalents. What this shows is that in conditions of close contact there will from the earliest period have been pressure on (bilingual) Latin speakers to extend the function of Latin demonstratives such that they might play the role of the definite article.[313] That said, it is important to note that there are distinctions of deixis to be found between *hic* and *ille* in the passage of Plautus. The soldier is twice referred to by means of *hic* (after the first mention of him at 88),[314] whereas the

---

[312] I am grateful to David Bain for information on this point.

[313] Similarly from early Latin onwards a neuter demonstrative is often used in the manner of the Greek article in application to a word under discussion (see also above, n. 275): e.g. Plaut. *Mil.* 27 *illud dicere uolui, 'femur'* (cf. 819). This usage is particularly common in Quintilian: e.g. 1.4.8 *ut in his 'seruus' et 'uulgus' Aeolicum digammon desideratur*. See Colson (1924), ad loc., and id., index p. 205 s.v. 'article'.

[314] There are also single instances of *is* and *iste*, this last apparently anticipating the later encroachment of the word on *hic*.

youth and young woman receive instead *ille*. There is a reason for this: the soldier has already appeared on stage in the previous scene, but the others have not. *Hic* thus marks closer proximity,[315] as we would expect in normal Latin deixis. Plautus has not abandoned normal Latin procedures of deixis,[316] but he has nevertheless drifted under Greek influence into a frequency of demonstratives which goes beyond the norms of the language. The scene does no more than offer a glimpse of the starting point of the long process by which, at least partly under Greek influence, certain demonstratives were to develop into definite articles. The interest of the passage lies in its early date, and in the fact that language contact is unequivocally in the background.

V.4.6 *Bilingualism and the system of gender*

It is not unusual in the output of bilinguals for the gender of a word in the writer's/speaker's first language to influence that of its equivalent in a second language (usually a form of interference). This phenomenon is particularly clear in translation literature. Thus in the Latin translation of the ps.-Hippocratic Περὶ γυναικείων (for which see Mazzini and Flammini (1983)), which was almost certainly done by a native speaker of Greek,[317] *uenter* is used in one place in the feminine under the influence of the word it renders, γαστήρ: 593 *heracleam uentrem, quod dicitur uenter maior.*[318] And at 537–9, in a clause of which the subject understood is *infans*, neuter adjectives are several times used in application to the subject because of interference from the gender of the corresponding noun in the Greek (ἔμβρυον): *est autem et hic magna culpa, ut non in celeritate exponatur, uel **mortuum** uel **apoplecticum** uel si duplicetur.*[319]

Similarly in a Latin account discussed earlier (V.2.2) for its bilingual characteristics (*P. Tebt.* 686 = *ChLA* 5.304), the masculine use of *harundo* in the expression *harundines Graeci* (frg. b, line 5) shows interference from Greek (cf. κάλαμος Ἑλληνικός, cited from *BGU* 776.10 at *ChLA* 5.304, p. 54).

From a different culture a document from the Cave of Letters published and discussed by Cotton (1995) has at line 8 κῆπος followed by the

---

[315] This usage has a parallel in a use of οὗτος in Menander, which in prologues sometimes refers to someone who was recently on stage. See e.g. *Aspis* 110, where the word is used in a prologue by Τύχη in reference to Daos, who had taken part in the preceding opening scene.

[316] It is of interest that in the Latin Bible translations, in exactly the same way, though *hic* often translates the direct article of Greek, it retains its deictic function of indicating what Abel (1971: 56) describes as 'la présence'.

[317] See Mazzini and Flammini (1983: 45).   [318] See Mazzini and Flammini (1983: 22, 28).

[319] See Mazzini and Flammini (1983: 28).

expression σὺν ὕδατος **αὐτῆς**. The last word, according to Cotton (1995: 194) ad loc., 'is influenced by the gender of the Aramaic gnh "orchard"'. In an earlier chapter (2.VIII) we alluded to an Old Latin version of the Psalms in which various Latin words are given the gender of their Hebrew equivalents.

More complex evidence for the effects on the gender system of a language wrought by intense contact with another language is to be found in the potters' community at La Graufesenque. This evidence is discussed in a later chapter (7.V).

VI CONCLUSIONS

In this chapter I have understood 'language change' in an all-embracing sense, to include any deviation from the norms of Greek and Latin, however ephemeral, which can be attributed to the influence of language contact. I have not confined myself to changes which became institutionalised, because that would have meant the exclusion of a good deal of revealing evidence for contact-induced changes which were destined to be overtaken by further events. Thus, for example, the apparent convergence of -ης and -*ae* at Venusia was inevitably to leave no trace because of the abandonment by the Romance languages of inflected genitive forms in favour of the prepositional type. Bilingual communities did not necessarily constitute the majority of the population in any one area, and changes within such a community often did not catch on in a whole area. But such changes may be illuminating in their own right; and they may also have claims to be regarded as regionalisms. Some of the deviations which have been discussed had an even narrower distribution than those affecting a community, in that they were restricted to certain individuals and perhaps even to particular occasions. But they have their interest, first as revealing the pressures faced by bilinguals when they are using a second language, secondly as reflecting the same mechanisms as those behind changes which happened to catch on more widely, and finally as contributing to the diversification of Latin and Greek across the Empire.

It should be clear from much of the material in this chapter that the Latin language cannot be treated as a unity where bilingual transfers are concerned: there are 'languages' within the language Latin. The chapter on contact-induced change in a recent book (Harris and Campbell (1995)) deals exclusively with languages in general, but Latin must be considered as a collection of language varieties. There is the Latin of native speakers of the language, and that of foreigners (mainly Greeks) learning and writing Latin as a second language. The contact phenomena in these two varieties are very different. And even within native speakers' Latin there are variations determined by genre in the acceptability of different types of bilingual transfers. Thus Greek patterns of syntax could be borrowed in Latin poetry, in some other forms of high literature, and in private letters, but not in oratory. Calques were only acceptable in poetry (particularly of the higher genres) and technical registers.

It follows that the partial 'Hellenisation' of Latin came from different sources, and affected different varieties of the language. Writers imitating Greek syntax were Hellenising (up to a point) the literary language, but at a lower social level Latin as the second language of Greeks was subject to Greek interference which was probably often unconscious. Greeks' Latin occupies a significant place in this chapter. Lexical loans too entered Latin in different social strata and in different varieties of the language. There were learned borrowings on the one hand, introduced by educated first-language speakers of Latin, and popular borrowings on the other, introduced in some cases probably by lower-class Greeks acquiring Latin as a second language. A case in point of the latter sort was discussed in the previous chapter (*colaphus* 'blow', which came to Rome not from Attic Greek but from the Greek of Sicily or the south of Italy, transported possibly by Greek slaves or slave dealers: see Chapter 3, n. 100).

Two important points to have emerged from this chapter are worth stressing again. First, apparent interference in a writer's L2 may in fact be deliberate, particularly if the writer is translating a text which carries religious or legal authority (see v.2.12). We should not speak of the 'incompetence' of the translators (into Greek) of Latin texts of this kind, or attempt to establish from their performance features of Roman Greek (though distinctive Roman Greek has come up in other contexts, as in the discussion of loan-shifts and that of the dative). Secondly, the discussion of Cicero's use of the Greek dative in v.4.1 is relevant to the question of the constraints to which code-switching might have been subject (see above, 3.1, III.10). Cicero largely restricts the Greek dative in code-switches to forms and functions which harmonise morphologically and syntactically with the Latin ablative.

VI.1 Contact-induced linguistic change of the creative type

Direct influence results in the transfer of an element from one language to another, whether a word, a morpheme (e.g. *nostrous*), a syntactic structure, a phoneme, intonation pattern or a word-meaning (I refer to loan-shifts).

But it was stressed at the outset that a bilingual's contribution to a language may be creative. The genitive in -*aes* represents a step beyond mere interference (-*es* in a Latin word would qualify for that designation), and can therefore be treated as creative. The Greek who wrote διουμ as the genitive plural of *dies* (v.3.2) made a deduction from αννωρουμ (which he had just written) that -ουμ was the Latin genitive plural ending. Thus a false analysis of one word (facilitated perhaps by the -*um* genitive plural found in some third declension words, and by the monosyllabic character of the Greek genitive plural ending) led to the use of a 'new' morpheme, though it has to be said that this is likely to have been one of those changes restricted to one or two writers or speakers rather than affecting a whole group. False morphological analysis, it has to be said, does not only take place in bilingual settings. The re-analysis, for example, of *Hamburg-er* as *ham-burger* has created a productive new suffix in the catering industry. At *Vitae Patrum* 5.15.29 (*dum autem coepissent eum mittere foras, dicebant ei: exi foras, Aethiops. ille uero egrediens, dicebat: bene tibi fecerunt, cinerente et caccabate*) *cinerente* (vocative) appears to comprise root *ciner*- and suffix -*entus*, whereas historically the expected suffix is -*ulentus*. If *cinerulentus* is segmented as *cinerul-entus* (with the base taken to be the diminutive of *cinis*), a new suffix is created. It is the fact that various adjectives in -*ulentus* are constructed on nouns which happen to have a diminutive in -*ul*- which permitted the interpretation of -*ul* as part of the root (cf. *farina* alongside *farinula*; there is an adjective *farinulentus* which was open to false analysis). It is perhaps significant that in διουμ a fifth declension noun is involved. Greeks learning Latin had trouble with the small set of nouns comprising the fifth declension. The translator of Babrius, for example, wrote *spaearum* as the genitive plural of *spes* (see 8.1). And a new, regularised inflection of *spes* (*spes, spenis*) emerged,[320] showing the -*eni*, -*enis* inflection which first developed in Latin in Greek names and was thus a creation of bilinguals (v.3.1.3). The new inflection of *spes* might well have originated in the Latin of bilinguals. It is indeed attested several times in bilingual or transliterated texts, such as that discussed by Curbera (1997b). The creative inflection of *dies* is a consequence of imperfect learning.

VI.2 Factors facilitating linguistic change in situations of language contact

(1) In a loan-shift, a word A (of language a) which shares a meaning or meanings with a word B (of language b) acquires a new meaning which

[320] See Bindel (1912: 55–6), Leumann (1977: 461).

its partial equivalent in the other language already had. *The pre-existing degree of overlap between A and B facilitates the semantic extension of A.* The extension of meaning may take place in the first or the second language of the bilingual. *Conquiro*, for example, as used in one place by Cicero (see V.2.11), is given a new meaning in his first language modelled on the semantic range of the overlapping item συζητέω in his second. On the other hand the use of μέλι (vocative) as a term of endearment by Martial reflects an extension of the range of the word in his second language (or that of the character in the poem) modelled on a use of *mel* in his first. In a case such as the latter, it is always possible that the new use of μέλι had already been introduced to Greek in Rome by native speakers of Greek, but the generalisation remains true that loan-shifts may be made in the speaker's second language as well as his first.

In some cases of syntactic change there is a similarity to the processes at work in semantic loan-shifts. The Greek dative acquired various functions possessed by the Latin ablative (e.g. a separative function, and the expression of duration of time). But there had always been an overlap between the functions (and forms) of the Greek dative and those of the Latin ablative, and the developments seen in the dative merely extend that overlap.

There are also comparable extensions of the function of suffixes. The borrowing language may extend the role of a native suffix to replicate that of a corresponding suffix in the language in contact (see V.2.11).

(2) It is an important principle that *similarity favours contact-induced change.* 'Similarity' in different senses underlies the phenomena discussed in (1) above. In a loan-shift the words A and B are already similar in their semantic range, and the overlap increases by a degree. The Latin ablative and the Greek dative were similar in their range of functions, and that similarity was extended. Phonetic or graphemic similarity may also play a part in facilitating change. The Latin ablative and Greek dative not only overlapped functionally, but they also shared various forms. It can be no coincidence that the earliest 'ablatival' uses of the dative adopted by native speakers of Latin (translators of *senatus consulta*, Cicero) overwhelmingly involve those forms of the dative which were identical to ablative forms in Latin. The adoption by Greeks of various Latin suffixes was also favoured by the pre-existence in Greek of suffixes of similar form (see V.3.5, e.g. on -τωρ). Even the strange new use of *potare* (IV) rests on the phonetic similarity of the Greek model verb.

(3) A foreign morpheme may first enter a language in words *borrowed* or *otherwise adopted* (by e.g. code-switching) from the donor language. This

point is illustrated by the history of the *-es* Greek feminine genitive in Latin. Similarly various Latin suffixes first entered Greek in Latin loan-words, and then acquired a life of their own in the recipient language.

VI.3 Bilingualism and the diversity of Latin

Bilingualism and language contact were important determinants of the diversification of Latin, as we have already seen in Chapter 2 (see XIV.1). I say 'diversification' here rather than, for instance, 'regional varia-tion', because the diversity of Latin as it was promoted by bilingualism cannot necessarily be equated with regional or dialectal forms of the language.

There are however phenomena discussed in the chapter which may be described as peculiar to particular regions (see also above, 2.XIV.1 for regional diversification). A notable case is the emergence of the form *paraxidi* at La Graufesenque (V.1.3). In extant Latin it is restricted to the one (bilingual) community. The *TLL* cautiously accepts the explanation from language contact. Nor is this the only oddity at La Graufesenque which may be described as a regionalism, and linked in some way with language contact (see below, 7.V). The use of the vocative with nominative function (V.4.4) also seems to be specific to just two regions, and related to language contact.

Other regionalisms determined by language contact were seen at the level of the lexicon. Particularly noteworthy is a coherent group of His-panic words not only attested in Pliny the Elder but also to some extent reflected in Ibero-Romance, which reveal the lexical influence exerted on Spanish Latin by the local languages. A further indication of their significance as markers of regional usage is to be seen in the Spaniard Martial's use of one of them (*balux*), qualified by the adjective *Hispanus*. Or again, *hydreuma* is confined to the Latin of the eastern desert of Egypt, and various Libyan or Punic terms expressing units of measure to the desert of Tripolitania. There is also evidence from the Celtic, Italic and Germanic regions for the entry of substrate words into the local Latin, perhaps contributing to something approaching a dialectal diversity in peripheral areas of the Empire. The point was however made that there is a difference between a regional dialect native, as it were, to an area, with native speakers, and varieties of Latin marked by regional words (*hydreuma* is a case in point) which need not have had native speakers. The Latin-speaking population in eastern areas in particular, such as Egypt, was constituted not by locally born Latin speakers, but by mobile (chiefly military) personnel, who would no doubt adopt 'regional' usages as they came and went.

I move on to some other types of diversity. Latin (as was stressed at VI above), like all other languages, was not monolithic, but an assortment of varieties. A clear-cut variety which has emerged from the material in this chapter is that which I have labelled 'Greeks' Latin'. Determinants of variety include stylistic factors and the social and educational status of the speaker/writer, as well as language contact. I list here some of the contact-induced manifestations of diversity that have come up in this chapter and earlier.

(1) When a language shift, destined to end in language death, is well advanced, the dying language may be imperfectly remembered or learnt, and those attempting to use it are likely to borrow extensively (or admit heavy interference) from the new language. The Umbrian text Vetter (1953), 234 (with Latin morpholology) discussed at 2.II.3, p. 140 belongs in this category, as does one of the Jewish Greek inscriptions from Venusia (Noy (1993), 62).

(2) Imperfect learning of a language which is not dead or dying can also produce extensive interference and also irrational errors in the target language. 'Imperfect learning' embraces a wide spectrum of second-language performance, from the use of what has here been called 'reduced language' (see 1.IX) to fluent command of the target language, but with occasional signs of interference from the other. 'Reduced Latin' and varieties of Latin showing Greek interference are particularly characteristic of Roman Greek communities and military communities in Egypt (see 5.VII.3, VIII). I stress that not all of the interlanguage phenomena in these varieties comprise direct interference. There is an element of the irrational (*Rabennatous* in Aeschines, for example: see 1.VII.2.3) in learners' Latin, as well as creative interference.

(3) Not all change through contact can be put down to imperfect performance in the second language. Speakers sometimes modify their first language in response to a feature of the second language, for various reasons. For example, the Greeks at Rome who made the Greek dative express duration of time in funerary inscriptions were practising a form of imitation of their second language in their first, and thereby contributing to the diversity of the first. The aim was to achieve in Greek as close a replication as possible of the form of the Latin model. In this case it is the prestige of the model in a Latin-speaking society which motivated the imitation (along with the pre-existing degree of functional overlap between Latin ablative and Greek dative).

VI.4 The limitations of language contact as a determinant of language change

I would finally stress the distinction between ephemeral interference (direct or creative), and contact-induced changes which took deeper root. Our material is full of *ad hoc* occurrences of interference perpetrated mainly by language learners, but it is virtually impossible to attribute to language contact alone any long-term changes (apart of course from the adoption of lexical items) of the type which, for example, might have affected the character of the Romance languages in comparison with that of Latin. The construction infinitive + *habeo*, for instance, had a parallel in Greek, but the development of the construction can be traced as a response to determinants internal to Latin itself (see Adams (1991b)). Language change influenced by language contact falls into two main types (see above). First, at a time of language shift learners of a second language rather haphazardly inflict on their new language morphemes and syntactic structures of their first, but this appears to be a relatively short-term phenomenon. As the second language is passed on to later generations the syntactic and morphological interference disappears. Secondly, bilinguals often imitate in their first language structures of a second. But this tends to be an artificial and self-conscious practice, which leaves no lasting impression on the first language as a whole. These limitations on the extent of contact-induced change make a nonsense of some of the pronouncements which have been made about external influences on Latin. There has long been a tendency to look for, say, 'Oscan influence' on the Latin of inscriptions from Oscan-speaking areas (see e.g. Moltoni (1954)), but this is a thoroughly misguided activity unless it can be shown in individual cases either that the writer was a first-language speaker of Oscan, or that he was deliberately imitating structures of one language in the other (as happens for examples in some Oscan legal documents). Most alleged 'Oscanisms' can be shown to represent developments native to Latin, though that is a story for another time.

5

Latin in Egypt

I INTRODUCTION

Latin had only a marginal place in Egypt; it has been estimated that only about 1 per cent of documents from the Roman period that have survived are in Latin, proportionate to those in Greek.[1] Even in military finds only about 10 per cent of texts are in Latin. Bagnall (1986: 5) notes that included in the 76 publication numbers of the texts from Quseir-al-Qadim (military documents of early Imperial date from the Red Sea coast, eight km north of the modern town of Quseir) there are three Latin papyri (18–20), three Latin ostraca (44–6) and perhaps one Latin inscription (66). He observes: 'Latin thus makes up about ten percent of the corpus of Greek and Latin texts. The same ratio is found in the Florida ostraka, and no doubt in both cases we have at least a general reflection of the limited but real role of Latin in the administration of the Roman army in Egypt.' To talk of the Latin *of* Egypt would be misleading, because it might imply that there was an established Latin-speaking population such as might have developed over the generations its own regional features in that language. In fact the Latin which has turned up in Egypt represents a considerable diversity. If a Latin text is discovered in Egypt, that does not mean that its author was of Egyptian origin. An inscription published at *AE* 1955, 238 (now re-edited as Kayser (1994), 102) shows that among the 136 men discharged from the Egyptian legion *II Traiana* in AD 157, at least 107 came from the west and only 25 from the east, with at most one from Egypt.[2] Many finds, such as the ostraca from Mons Claudianus and Wâdi Fawâkhir and the papyrus letters of the Tiberianus archive, are from military environments, and soldiers were extremely mobile. We know little of the origin of those scribes who

[1] See Bagnall (1995: 22).   [2] See Gilliam (1956: 360).

wrote Latin (and Greek) texts for military personnel,[3] or of translators and scribes who drafted Latin legal documents for Greek speakers.[4] I therefore prefer to talk of Latin *in* Egypt, leaving open the possibility that some specimens of 'Egyptian' Latin might even be the work of Italians or Romans.

That is not to say that there were no Latin speakers in Egypt whose families had been there for some time. The soldier Claudianus Terentianus, who, like his father Claudius Tiberianus, certainly knew and used Latin (as well as Greek), seems to have settled in Egypt (Karanis) on his discharge.[5] If his own offspring spoke some Latin, they would, at the very least, have been third-generation speakers of the language. Or again, the house of Socrates at Karanis, recorded as B17, which has recently been studied by Strassi Zaccaria (1991) and Van Minnen (1994: 237–46), contained a mixture of Greek and Latin texts. Socrates was a tax collector and not a Roman citizen. Greek documents predominate in the archive (*P. Mich.* VI. 419, VIII. 505–7, 564). A certain Sempronia Gemella, a Roman citizen and the mother of illegitimate twins registered in a Latin birth certificate *P. Mich.* III.169 (with Greek summary) found in the house (see below, IV.5), seems to have been his wife. There are also the fragmentary remains of what appears to be a recipe in Latin (*P. Mich.* VII.449). The nouns *oleum, ad offa[m], porr..., palm[a], lente...* and *fabal...* can be read, as well as the verb *accipe*. The recipe, if it is such, could as well be medicinal as culinary. But these are not the only Latin texts in the house. There is also an incomplete document to do with a dowry, the exact nature of which is unclear (*P. Mich.* VII. 442 = *ChLA* 5.295). This text has been discussed elsewhere in this book, as it shows a loan-shift determined by Greek (*malum* = 'cheek': see 4.V.2.11), as well as a Greek formulaic structure (an unconstrued nominative use of *lentigo*: see 1.VII.4.2 (9)). It was drawn up, undoubtedly by a first-language speaker of Greek, at Colonia Caesarea in Mauretania (Algeria), where part of the Alexandrian fleet was based to defend the western coasts, before finding its way to the house of Socrates. The document contains the words *C. Valerio Gemello mil(iti) classis Aug(ustae) Alexandrinae libyrni Dracontis*; it is signed individually on the back by seven Roman citizens, who incorporate tribal designations but write in Greek. Van Minnen (1994: 244) comments as follows: 'Among the letters found in B17 is a letter from an army recruit on his way to Algeria [*P. Mich.* inv. no.

---

[3] One or two pieces of evidence can be cited. *IGRRP* 1362 (= Ruppel (1930), Gr 20) from Dakka presents a miltary scribe who signs in Greek: τὸ προσκύνημα ᾿Αντωνίου γραμματέος Φιλῶν, (ἑκατονταρχίας) Καπίτωνος. Note too Baillet (1920–6), 1733, discussed at 1.VIII, p. 85.
[4] However on legal translators, see below, IV.5.   [5] See Lewis (1959: 143).

4711b, unpublished]. Among Socrates' papers we also find a Latin document relating to a marriage agreement of a soldier in the navy drawn up in Algeria [*ChLA* 5.295]. For all we know this document may be related to Gemella. Young Egyptian males served in the Roman army and navy world-wide, and Socrates apparently had contacts with army officials within Egypt itself as well.' The document concerning the dowry is a specimen of Greeks' Latin; it is likely that Socrates mixed in circles in which some Latin was spoken, even though Greek obviously predominated. There are bound to have been some other residents of Egypt bilingual in Greek and Latin (in addition to serving soldiers who came and went), but apart from these few cases it is not possible to identify such people.

But although Latin statistically is insignificant, its importance sociolinguistically should not be underestimated. In the Roman period Latin was, after all, the language of the rulers. Even if the Roman authorities had chosen never to use Latin in Egypt, or indeed never to use Greek, those would have been significant acts, of interest to sociolinguists. Parallels could be found (for instance) for the ruling class using one language but their subjects another, as for example in Russia in the nineteenth century (see below). As it is, Latin was extensively used in Egypt, not only by incoming Romans, but also by Greek speakers who had learnt the language. We will see much indirect evidence in this chapter for Latin learning by Greeks, both within and outside the army (see particularly VII.2.2, VII.3, VIII). Moreover many Latin speakers had some command of Greek, and the question arises what factors determined language choice on any particular occasion.

1.1 Latin, Greek and Egyptian

Bilingualism in Latin and Egyptian (or multilingualism involving the use of the three languages) is virtually unattested, and it is indeed unlikely that Latin speakers of external origin who were only passing through Egypt would have had the opportunity or inclination to pick up any Egyptian, particularly since most of them (those in the army) were in relatively closed Greco-Latin communities. There must however have been some Greco-Egyptian bilinguals or Egyptians who picked up some Latin, the more so the longer the Empire went on. A recently published Coptic text (*P. Kell.* V.20.24–5)[6] refers to a teacher of Latin ('And Piene: the great Teacher let him travel with him, so that he might learn Latin.

---

[6] See Gardner, Alcock and Funk (1999). I owe this reference to James Clackson.

He teaches him well'). On the possible circumstances, see the editors'
note ad loc.: 'one wonders if Priene was being groomed for missionary
work in the west; though, since Manichaean missions often targetted
the highest authorities, perhaps [Latin] may have been regarded as of
some real utility in Egypt'.[7] Two tax receipts from Edfu on ostraca,
published in full for the first time by Zauzich (1984: 79–80), begin with
several lines of Demotic bearing the main information of the receipt,
and then have the name of the contributor, as well as the date, repeated in Latin script. I quote the texts as published by Zauzich, with his
translation:

O. Brooklyn 16.580.253
1 ḥz. t-sp 38 Gysrs
2 ibd 2 šmw sw 23 r-wt
3 Pz-byk sz Pz- ʿḥm-n-sws
4 šmy. t n Tb ʿ sw 1
5 BECES PACHUM
6 SAS I. PAY(NI) XXV

1 Regnal year 38 of Caesar (= Augustus)
2 Payni day 23. Has contributed
3 Pbekis, son of Pachymsasis,
4 for the harvest tax of Edfu 1 (artaba) of wheat.
5 Beces, (son of) Pachum-
6 sas, 1 (artaba of wheat) Pay(ni) (day) 25.

O. Warsaw 139802
1 [ḥz. t-sp ...] Gysrs ibd 2 šmw sw 11
2 [r-wt] Pz-ʿḥm-n-pz-byk sz Pz-dy-ḥr-smz-tz.wy
3 [šmy.t n T]bz sw 2
4 PACHOMBECHIS. PETESTHEO[S]
5 PAYNI. XI

1 [Regnal year ...] of Caesar (= Augustus) Payni day 11.
2 [Has contributed] Pachombekis, son of Petestheus,
3 [for the harvest tax of] Edfu 2 (artabas) of wheat.
4 Pachombechis, son of Petestheus,
5 Payni day 11.

[7] Note too the Latin–Greek–Coptic glossary, *P. Berol.* Inv. no. 10582 = Kramer (1983), 15 (with text, discussion and commentary at pp. 97–108); see also the remarks of Rochette (1999: 329, 333). In this chapter I do not intend on the whole to go so late as the period of Coptic texts. A text with Latin and Demotic, as well as Greek and an unidentified language, is published by Coles (1981). The character of the text has not been fully established, and the Demotic version is not published. The text at least offers evidence that speakers of Latin and of Demotic were not entirely isolated from each other. See further the material cited below, n. 177.

The two documents are receipts for a harvest tax, paid in kind. Zauzich gives the date of the first as 17 June 2 BC. They are not in any sense full bilinguals; it is only the name of the contributor and the day of the month that are in 'Latin'. The language is defective: the term 'Latin' can only be employed in reference to the script and the use of Roman numerals. The texts could not have been written by native speakers of Latin who had learnt Demotic. On the contrary, it is obvious that the writers were Demotic (and Greek) speakers who in the early days of Roman rule for some reason chose to repeat part of the information in Latin letters in an approximation of Latin.

Neither filiation is correct by Latin standards. In neither is there the requisite *filius*, and in the first the name of the father is not inflected. Interestingly, in the second case the filiation is inflected as Greek, and it is Greek in syntax as well, with a genitive attached to the name of the contributor. This can only be the work of a Demotic–Greek bilingual, who was attempting to give the document a Latinate appearance, perhaps in deference to the new ruling power, but knew little or nothing of Latin other than the alphabet and the numerals. He must however have been exposed to some sort of instruction in Latin literacy even if he had not had learnt the language. This is learners' 'Latin' at its most rudimentary. For scripts made to serve as languages, see 1.VIII, p. 91, 2.III.6, p. 175, 2.VIII.

This type of bilingual receipt, but in Demotic and *Greek*, is not uncommon at Edfu.[8] Zauzich (1984: 76–8) cites nine ostraca (tax receipts), which are basically in Demotic, but at the end of which the name of the contributor is repeated in Greek form. Twice (nos. 2 and 8) the name is accompanied by an attached genitive patronymic (e.g. 8 [Αρμεσυνις] Πατεστεος). Clearly the 'Latin' –Demotic texts quoted above belong to much the same category, but they have been given a superficially Latinate character by the use of the Latin alphabet.

The Latin part of the second bilingual document quoted above was published without the Demotic by Cavenaile, *CPL* 296, along with a group of purely Latin texts of much the same type. Most of the latter have an abbreviation (*mat*) which has caused some trouble. The letters were interpreted by Youtie (1949) (followed by Cavenaile) as an abbreviation of *matulas* ('water jugs'), given the find-spot of the texts in a bath house. Zauzich (1984: 80–1), however, explains *mat* decisively as standing for *matia* (Gk. μάτιον, which was taken over from Egyptian md̲z.t). The texts are no doubt receipts for the delivery of goods (probably grain)

---

[8] For a text and discussion of thirteen bilingual tax receipts (in Greek and Demotic) on ostraca of the Ptolemaic period, see Devauchelle and Wagner (1982).

measured in *matia*. I quote some of these Latin texts for the light they throw on the linguistic situation:[9]

283
Apion Apolloniu
mat. V
Hierax Paniscios
mat. III

284
Apion Apolloni
mat. V
et Apolleni II

286
Pachois Pambecios
mat. VI

287
Petheus Arsinios
mat. VII = =

289
Hierax Ptollionis
mat. VII.

The filiations (like that in the second bilingual above) are heavily Grecised. The syntax is Greek (in the absence of *filius*), and the genitive inflection is usually of Greek form (though there are also one or two Latin genitives: note particularly *Apolloni* alongside *Apolloniu*). All four ostraca bearing the name Apion (two of which are quoted above) were written by a single hand,[10] and it is therefore the more remarkable that the language of the filiation varies in one and the same name *Apollonius* in this group of texts. One explanation for the inconsistency might be that the writer's first language was not Latin, and that he was accordingly under pressure when attempting to write the language to switch into his stronger language (cf. below, VII.1, p. 604 on the filiations in Fink (1971), 76). It is indeed obvious that the receipts come from a group of Greco-(Egyptian?) speakers with imperfect command of Latin. There was a Roman garrison at Edfu, and the ostraca surely have some sort of military provenance.[11] Since some of the texts are in effect Greek written

---

[9] For the texts, see also Youtie (1949: 270).
[10] See Youtie (1949: 269).   [11] See Youtie (1949: 268).

in Latin letters and with Latin numerals, there would seem to be evidence here that instruction in Latin literacy was sometimes given in military circles to those who did not really know the Latin language. Much the same phenomenon is observable in the potters' community at La Graufesenque (see Chapter 7). Gaulish potters used Latin letters, numerals and sigla for records which are frequently not in Latin but in Gaulish. Short lists, receipts and the like in one language may be comprehensible to speakers of another language provided that they can read the script, since lists often contain only nouns and numerals and have little syntax.

At the level of public language use the Romans made little effort to address Egyptian speakers through their own language, though a notable exception is to be seen in the trilingual inscription at Philae (in Latin, Greek and hieroglyphics) of the first prefect of Egypt, the poet Gallus (*IG Philae* II.128). The Egyptian version, though fragmentary, might have differed somewhat from the Greek and Latin versions. The Egyptian text is discussed with a partial translation by Erman (1896 = 1986), who, because of the impossibility of producing a definitive translation, summarised the content of the inscription (1896 = 1986: 347) as follows:[12] (1) the date is 20 Pharmuthi of the first year of Caesar; (2) the prince of Egypt has subdued all the barbarians; (3) he conducted a war against the princes of Ethiopia and after that did something in relation to the gods of Philae; (5) the one who did this was the Caesar. The gods of Elephantine (Chnum, Satis and Anukis) and of Philae (Osiris, Isis and Horus) are alluded to.

The Latin and Greek versions of the inscription (the Greek in smaller script)[13] are discussed in the Appendix to this chapter; it is enough to say here that Gallus gave himself prominence in these versions, laying claim to significant military victories in the Thebaid. It used to be thought (so Erman (1896 = 1986: 347)) that, if the priests of Philae who must have been responsible for the hieroglyphic version were supposed to render the Latin as accurately as possible, they had let Gallus down. Erman claimed that they passed over in silence Gallus' campaigns in Egypt, dealt with his actions against the Ethiopians only in a roundabout way, and most strikingly of all apparently excluded the prefect himself from the inscription. But a recent re-reading of the text has re-instated the prefect under the name 'Cornelius'.[14]

---

[12] See also Boucher (1966: 39–40).
[13] See A. Bernand (1969: 35) for measurements; see also Stein (1915: 182).
[14] See Bresciani (1989).

A crucial aspect of this text is that it comes right at the beginning of Roman rule in Egypt, and can be seen as a continuation and extension of an older Ptolemaic tradition (according to which Greek and Egyptian sometimes stood together in public inscriptions: see the texts below discussed by Bowman and Rathbone (1992)), a tradition though soon abandoned by the Romans (but see below on religious inscriptions). By convention in eastern regions of the Empire the Romans regularly used Greek as a lingua franca instead of operating in local languages (see above, 2.VII.5), and Egypt came to be no exception in this respect.

There are some other public inscriptions with 'Roman' content from the Roman period in Egypt which have an Egyptian version or versions. Some of these have been collected with brief bibliography by Daumas (1952: 264–72). The point about them is that they typically occur on temple walls, and present emperors making offerings to Egyptian deities. They should be seen as a form of propaganda setting out the emperors' claims to be legitimate pharaohs of Egypt.[15] They can also be taken as evidence for Romans in a foreign region showing deference to the local religion. Such deference, in the form of linguistic accommodation in religious contexts, will be one of the themes of the chapter (see below, v). Even if the hieroglyphs could not be understood by the Egyptian population, the names and titles of the emperors and the pictorial representations were no doubt comprehensible. Outside the religious sphere Egyptian (hieroglyphic) was not used by the Romans. I list here some relevant examples of 'Roman' hieroglyphic inscriptions found in religious contexts.

(1) Milne (1905: 39), 22129 is a bilingual inscription from Quft of the period of Tiberius, described by Milne in the following terms: 'A stele of Egyptian design, on a rectangular block of stone: the upper part is occupied by a scene of the emperor adoring Horus and Isis, surmounted by a winged sun-disk with uraei: below this are two lines of hieroglyphs.' The Greek inscription is as follows: ὑπὲρ Τιβερίου Καίσαρος Σεβασ[τοῦ . . .] Φ[α]ῶφι ιθ´ Παρθένιος Παμίνεως προ[στάτης ῎Ισιδος]. The date is given of about AD 31. Milne does not print the hieroglyphics.

(2) There is a second dedicatory stele also from Quft and dated 5 July AD 31. The stele is described in detail by Milne (1905: 39–40), 9268.

---

[15] An important article is that of Grenier (1987), who describes the conception of the Pharaonic function of the Roman emperors found in the Pharaonic protocols in temple inscriptions of the Roman period (see 81–2). Though there is some evolution in the form of these protocols (described in general terms and discussed at 102–4), it is nevertheless the case that the names of emperors simply replace those of the Lagides on the walls of sanctuaries, and the Pharaonic system continues to function (81). See further Grenier (1988).

I quote part of the description and print the text of the Greek below:
'... In the centre is Geb, standing to right... Before him is a figure of
the emperor, advancing to left, wearing the royal dress and the crown of
Lower Egypt: in his left hand he holds a staff and baton, and raises his
right hand as if making an offering. Before him is an altar in the form of
a pylon. .... Below the scene is an inscription of two lines of hieroglyphs
cut in relief.'

The Greek inscription, in three lines, is as follows: ὑπὲρ Τιβερίου
Καίσαρος Σεβαστοῦ (ἔτους) ιη´ Ἐπεὶφ ιαʹ Κρόνωι Θεῶι μεγίστωι Παρθένιος Παμ<ί>νεως προστάτης Ἴσιδος.

(3) Another stele of Egyptian form with a bilingual inscription and
of much the same period is published by Milne ((1905: 28–9), 9286).
I quote part of the description of Milne (p. 28): '... In front of the first
Horus stands a figure of the emperor to left, wearing the royal dress and
a triple atef-crown, and presenting with both hands a dish covered with
offerings.' There are two Greek inscriptions accompanying the hieroglyphs, one dated to AD 20–1, the other to 148–9; I quote the former:
ὑπὲρ Τιβερίου Καίσαρος Σεβαστοῦ Ἴσιδι καὶ Ἁρποχράτη καὶ Πανὶ θεοῖς
μεγίστοις τὸν περίβολον Παμῖνις Παρθενίου καὶ Παρθένιος υἱός. (ἔτους)
η´ Τιβερίου Καίσαρος Σεβαστοῦ.

(4) There is also a stele of the period of Vespasian, published by
Schiaparelli (1887), 1670 (p. 411–12). Vespasian makes an offering to
Chnum, Satis and Anukis (see further Daumas (1952: 268)). The hieroglyphic inscription is translated by Schiaparelli (1887: 412). The Greek
text is fragmentary, and there is no point in quoting it here.

(5) Particularly remarkable are the hieroglyphic inscriptions on the
Kalabcha gate, now reassembled in the Ägyptisches Museum in Berlin.[16]
The inscriptions, dating from the early years of Augustus' reign,[17] present
the emperor as pharaoh. In cartouches he is named as 'Autokrator
Kaisaros', with the title expressed in hieroglyphs sound for sound from
the Greek, or 'Kaisaros, the god', or 'Kaisaros, the god, son of a god'.[18]
None of the Ptolemies had allowed himself to be called 'god' in hiero-
glyphic inscriptions.[19]

I mention finally two inscriptions from the precinct of the temple of
Hathor at Denderah, discussed by Bowman and Rathbone (1992: 107).
The first, dated to 12 BC, is trilingual (in Demotic, Greek and hieroglyphs)
(see A. Bernand (1984), 24 for the Greek version),[20] and the second, dated

[16] The gate is discussed with very clear photographs by Winter (1977).
[17] See Winter (1977: 68).   [18] See Winter (1977: 66–7).   [19] See Winter (1977: 68).
[20] See Spiegelberg (1932), 50044 for all of the versions.

23 September AD 1, is in Greek alone (see A. Bernand (1984), 25). The content of both is much the same, but there is a difference between the two in the presentation of the material, and, it might be added, in the language choice. In the first, the *strategos* Ptolemaios makes a dedication of land to Hathor, and in the second there is a dedication of a gateway to Isis and the gods of the same shrine. In the first the emperor is a marginal figure and the role of the *strategos* is given prominence, whereas in the second the dedication is on behalf of the emperor and the *strategos* is mentioned only as part of the dating formula.

I quote Bowman and Rathbone (1992: 107): 'The inscriptions . . . illustrate the radical changes in communal organization and administration which the Romans introduced. . . . The first inscription . . . is almost entirely in the pre-Roman tradition. It is a trilingual dedication with the primary version in Demotic (i.e. Egyptian). Augustus is god, implicitly Pharaoh, and lacks his Roman titles. The *strategos* (governor of the nome) Ptolemaios gives himself obsolete court titles and a string of local priesthoods.' They go on to point out that the second inscription 'reveals a very different situation. The dedication was made on Augustus' birthday, and was finely inscribed in Greek only. The *strategos* Tryphon . . . figures only as an element of the official dating clause standard throughout Roman Egypt; he is just a cog in the Roman administrative machine.'

1.2 Some questions

Given then the limited role of Egyptian in the Roman scheme of things, discussion of the position of Latin in Egypt very much concerns the relationship between Latin and Greek, particularly, if not exclusively, in the army. Questions which suggest themselves are: (1) is there an identifiable diglossic relationship between the two languages? (2) Is there explicit evidence for bilinguals using one language when they had the competence to use the other?; (3) and if so, what might have determined their language choice on a particular occasion? (4) Is there any evidence for the operation of a language policy by the Roman administration or by the army? (5) Is there evidence for language learning in Egypt, and in particular for the acquisition of Latin by Greeks? (6) Is there evidence for bilinguals' or learners' Latin in Egypt, showing for example interference from the other language?

These questions are not independent of one another. (2) and (3) are interrelated, and a linguistic policy, if such existed, would have been bound to influence language choice. Indeed the major issue that is raised by the use of Latin in Egypt is its role *vis-à-vis* Greek and the motivation of language choice by bilinguals. The role of Latin in Egypt has been extensively discussed, most notably by Stein (1915: 132–86), and also by Cavenaile (1952), Kaimio (1979b), Daris (1991b), Rochette (e.g. 1996a, c) and Ghiretti (1996),[21] though the evidence is now considerably greater than it was at the time of Stein. The usual approach has been to attempt to capture the place of Latin by means of some sort of general formulation, of which the following may be quoted as typical (Kaimio (1979b: 27)):[22] 'the language of administration in Egypt before Diocletian was Greek, with the following exceptions: the edicts and decrees of the central government were Latin, when they concerned the Roman army, Roman magistrates or Roman individuals; the correspondence between Roman magistrates was mainly written in Latin; the official language of the Roman army was Latin and the documents of Roman citizens inside the sphere of the *ius ciuile* had to be originally written in Latin.' He continues (28): 'It seems probable that there was not in Egypt any language community where Latin would have been in any normally separated language function the dominant language; the military camps may have formed an exception, but there, too, Greek or probably some kind of pidgin military Greek dominated in most functions.'

Generalisations such as these are on the whole unexceptionable, but do little justice to the complexities of the situation. The view that Latin was in some sense the 'official' language of the army is very persistent, but not tenable without serious modification, as we will see (VII.1).

Much of the chapter has to do with the overriding question of language choice in Roman Egypt and its motivations, from the perspective particularly of the Latin speaker. I would not in any way wish to play down the extent of Greco-Egyptian bilingualism, but that is another story which is not my concern here, since I have chosen to deal with Roman linguistic policy in keeping with the subject of the whole book. I begin with a few general issues which will be relevant in much of the rest of the chapter: the concept of diglossia, and the availability of scribes as a possible determinant of language choice.

1.3 Diglossia

The term 'diglossia' (for which see above, 3.VIII) was introduced to English by Ferguson (1959), though not specifically in reference to

---

[21] For some further bibliography, see Rochette (1994: 316 n. 19).
[22] See also Bagnall (1993: 231).

bilingualism. Ferguson used the word to describe the coexistence in a
society of two varieties of the same language which were *functionally
distinguished*,[23] as for instance in Arabic-speaking countries where both
classical Arabic and colloquial Arabic stand side by side. The other
languages showing this characteristic to which he referred were Modern
Greek, German in Switzerland and Haitian creole in relation to French.
Ferguson classified one of the two varieties in each case as H(igh)
and the other as L(ow). He did not consider the possibility that there
might be other societies in which two language varieties did not fit
into such a neat binary model. The H variety, he argued, was marked
by prestige, and was typically used in the business of government,
political speeches, public lectures, sermons, news broadcasts, newspaper
editorials and poetry, whereas the L variety lacked prestige and was
used for colloquial purposes, for example in ordinary conversations in
the home, in instructions to servants and in folk literature. Ferguson
dealt with language varieties in contact rather than with different
languages standing in a polar functional opposition (though at least
one of his examples, the case of Haitian creole in relation to French,
seems to fall into the latter category). His diglossic model has, however,
often been treated as applicable to some bilingual societies. In an earlier
chapter (3.VIII) it was pointed out that in western Greek communities
there is evidence that Greek was the language of home, whereas Latin
was regarded as that of bureaucracy, and this functional distinction
corresponds closely to Ferguson's H–L opposition. Fishman (1967) had
a good deal to say about different languages falling into the H–L model.
He sought to describe the various possible permutations of diglossia
and bilingualism. There may in theory be bilingualism with diglossia,
in which situation most speakers know both the H and L languages.
Paraguay is often referred to as an example of such a society. Here both
the Indian language Guarani and Spanish are used, in what is said
to be a diglossic relationship.[24] Another possibility is diglossia without
bilingualism, such that two distinct groups within a society speak
different languages. I quote Fasold (1984: 41): 'One [group] is the ruling
group and speaks only the High language. The other, normally a much
larger group, has no power in the society and speaks exclusively the Low
language. . . . An example might be one period in the history of czarist
Russia during which it was fashionable for nobles to speak only French,
whereas the masses of Russians spoke only Russian.' A third possible

[23] On 'function' in this context, see in particular Fasold (1984: 52, also 72–8).
[24] See Rubin (1962), Fishman (1967: 31), Fasold (1984: 13–19).

combination is bilingualism without diglossia. This designation might be applied to the linguistic practice of bilingual groups who switch in and out of two languages in such a way that it is impossible to perceive a clear functional differentiation within the group itself, though a differentiation might become apparent once speakers move outside their closed circle. For example, some Puerto Ricans in New York are reported as mixing Spanish and English haphazardly among themselves as a marker of their mixed cultural identity (see above, 3.1, III.10).[25] The two languages may not have different functions in such interchanges, but if such a Puerto Rican were to write a formal letter to an official such as a government officer, he would (one assumes) be bound to use English, and would thus, in an outward-looking transaction, be according English H status. It is not relevant to the present chapter, but for completeness I mention that Fishman (1967: 36–7) raised the possibility that there might be communities in which there was neither diglossia nor bilingualism.

Problems have begun to be noticed in the applicability of the neat polar opposition H–L to bilingual communities en bloc (though much depends on the particular conditions within the community: we noted above that such an opposition does seem to exist between Latin and Greek as used by some western Greeks in Latin-speaking regions). Functional differentiation does of course exist both within the varieties of a single language, and across languages in contact, but there are two theoretical inadequacies in the explanatory power of the H–L opposition. First, the functional oppositions or contrasts between languages in a multilingual society need not be binary, and secondly, even if they are binary, they need not be readily classifiable into H–L. Fasold (1984: 44–50), for example, discusses more complex cases of what he calls 'double overlapping diglossia', 'double-nested diglossia' and 'linear polyglossia.' In this last case[26] degrees of formality are set up among a variety of languages in Singapore and Malaysia spoken by English-educated Chinese (the languages being various Chinese languages, forms of English, and standard and 'bazaar' versions of Malay). Or of two languages neither may qualify for the designation 'Low'; one, for example, may be H, the other 'super-high' or 'supreme.'[27] Another notion discussed by Fasold

[25] See Poplack (1988: 217): 'code-switching between English and Spanish was [found to be] such an integral part of the community linguistic repertoire that it could be said to function as a mode of interaction similar to monolingual language use'.

[26] See Fasold (1984: 48–50).

[27] See Hamers and Blanc (1989: 174), citing the multilingual situation of Brussels, where 'the supreme languages are the Standard French of France and the Standard Dutch of the Netherlands, over and above the regional high languages, Standard Belgian French and Standard Belgian Dutch'. See further Romaine (1995: 34–6).

(1984: 49), following Platt (1977: 373–4), is that of the 'Dummy High' language. This is a language which some members of a society have some knowledge of, and which is given high prestige, but is little if at all spoken. Fasold (1984: 49) notes that a 'DH owes its significance in the community almost exclusively to the high regard in which the people hold it; it is not used for any real communicative purpose.' He cites as examples Mandarin in the eyes of the English-educated Chinese in Malaysia, and Sanskrit in India.

Another more general shortcoming of accounts of diglossia has been observed by Gardner-Chloros (1991: 190). She notes the drawbacks of excessive concentration on societal language choice, to the neglect of the diversity of influences that may affect interpersonal exchanges. I quote: 'It is a well-recognized danger of the sociolinguistic approach that it disguises important intra-individual variation in seeking to provide a picture of the group. This danger should make us particularly wary of very broad concepts – the classic example being diglossia, which for many years was thought to hold great explanatory power, and is now seen if anything as disguising the subtlety of linguistic hierarchies even in the most archetypal communities.'

It is in fact obvious that the polarity H–L is not straightforwardly applicable to the respective functions of Latin and Greek among bilinguals whose first language was Latin (though the attitudes of those whose first language was Greek were no doubt different again: see above, and 3.VIII). It is inconceivable that an educated speaker of Latin, fluent in Greek, could regard Latin as L, even if he might feel a certain ambivalence about the merits of his language *vis-à-vis* Greek. He might indeed accord Greek high prestige, but that would not mean that Latin was necessarily L. According to Plutarch (*Mar.* 2.2), Marius never used Greek for any matter of real importance, and that would imply that he was in fact attempting to treat Greek as Low.

The Romans' attitude to their language was admittedly complex, with language pride tempered by a certain unease about the possibility that Greek might be a 'richer' language. On a roughly parallel case of language pride in competition with diffidence (in Paraguay), see Fasold (1984: 15): 'Paraguayans have a profound sense of devotion to their language [Guarani]; they want to be proud of it and are. Nevertheless, there is a covert sense of uneasiness about it and a feeling that somehow Spanish is really more elegant and better.' On the one hand Lucretius spoke about the relative 'poverty' of the Latin language in relation to Greek (1.136–45), whereas Cicero felt moved to assert that Latin was in fact the richer language: *Fin.* 1.10 *sed ita sentio et saepe disserui, Latinam linguam*

non modo <non> inopem, *ut uulgo putarent, sed* ***locupletiorem etiam esse quam Graecam*** (cf. 3.5). Cicero was wont to liken Roman Latin to the Attic dialect of Greek (*De orat.* 3.42, *Brut.* 172), an attitude which put city Latin on a par in status with Athenian Greek. Yet on occasions there is acknowledgment in his work of the controversial nature of any assertion that Latin was richer than Greek: note *Fin.* 3.51 *cum uteretur* ***in lingua copiosa*** *factis tamen nominibus ac nouis, quod nobis* ***in hac inopi lingua*** *non conceditur; quamquam tu* ***hanc copiosiorem etiam soles dicere***. Much the same diffidence can be detected in Quintilian's discussion (1.5.58–64) of the inflection of Greek words in Latin. Here the 'ancients' are imagined as being praised by the hypothetical grammarian who is *ueterum amator*, because of their desire to 'increase the power of the Latin language' (1.5.60 *qui potentiorem facere linguam Latinam studebant*). The view that the Latin language had to be made more 'powerful' suggests that there were those who felt that it was inferior to Greek.

What these bits and pieces of evidence show is a keenness on the part of some educated Romans to regard Latin as H, even if they were covertly not convinced of its superiority to Greek. Such uncertainty does not however mean that either Latin or Greek could be classed (in the thinking of such people) as L. And the evidence discussed so far is only part of the story. The disputants were *littérateurs*, interested in the status of Latin *vis-à-vis* Greek as a *literary* language. But Latin was more than a mere literary language; it was potentially a language that might be used symbolically in Greek areas to highlight Roman imperial power.

On the Greco-Latin evidence alone it is obvious that there are limits to the potency of the H–L differentiation. That is not to say that in a bilingual Latin–Greek community there could not be a functional differentiation of the two languages; but in seeking to define any such differentiation one must proceed with an open mind instead of assuming a polar opposition in every case; different communities differed in their language attitudes. In fact the different constructions put upon the role of Latin and Greek by Romans are nowhere better illustrated than in two corpora of material from Egypt, the inscriptions at the Colossus of Memnon on the one hand, and the Abinnaeus archive on the other. Following this introduction I will begin with a discussion of these texts.

1.4 *The availability of scribes as a determinant of language choice*

It is tempting to think that in (e.g.) private letters the language chosen might have depended on the linguistic competence of the scribe available on a particular occasion, given that extensive use was made of scribes especially for letters of military provenance. That might sometimes have been the case, but there is internal evidence in some Egyptian documents to suggest that the writer could, if he had chosen or been instructed to do so, have used the other language. Letter 468 of Terentianus (*P. Mich.* VIII), for example, though it is written in a practised Latin hand, is marked by various instances of orthographic interference from Greek. The spelling *nostrous* (line 62, accusative plural) is a mechanical slip by a scribe, who adopted the spelling of the Greek accusative form (see 4.V.3.4). The same scribe also wrote *utranus* (468.6) for *ueteranus*, under the influence of the common Greek spelling of the Latin loan-word, οὐτρανός. Such interference is only explicable on the assumption that the scribe was also accustomed to writing in Greek. Terentianus must on this occasion have had the choice of dictating a letter in Greek or Latin. One cannot eliminate the possibility that on other occasions he used scribes who preferred to write one language rather than the other. But it does seem unlikely that there were many scribes in Egypt who could only write Latin. For example, in the various archives from veterans' families which have been found in Karanis, Greek is overwhelmingly preferred (except in the archive of Tiberianus).[28] In communities such as this the difficulty if any would have been in finding scribes to write Latin (see the remarks below, IV.5, on the drawing up of the birth certificate registered by Sempronia Gemella); and hence when Latin is used in letters, it will often have been the case that Greek could have been used instead. When Terentianus sent letters in Latin he must surely have had the option of using Greek.

Further evidence for the bi-literacy of some scribes can be seen in those texts in which the letter forms show the influence of the other script (see I.VII.4.1). It must however be pointed out that in bilingual communities there was a tendency towards *convergence* of letter shapes in the two scripts.[29] A person writing (e.g.) Greek letters with Latinate features need not have been conflating scripts himself, but merely reproducing the letter shapes as they had developed in a bi-literate community;[30] though if a community was bi-literate, it must also have been up to a point bilingual.

---

[28] See on these families Alston (1995: 126–42), with the lists of documents in the footnotes at pp. 231–3.

[29] See Norsa (1946), and particularly Rochette (1999), with full bibliography.

[30] See Rochette (1999: 329–30). In bilingual literary exercises from Egypt written by learners of Latin (with Latin literary texts on the left in a column containing no more than three words to the line, and a Greek *ad uerbum* translation on the right) scribes use a script with marked convergences.

Nevertheless interference of types which go beyond mere letter shapes (such as the morphological interference seen in *nostrous*) provides better evidence for the bi-literacy of the writer. In this connection I draw attention to *O. Claud.* 388–408, lists of soldiers in Greek. The editor (F. Kayser) mentions the influence of Latin (pp. 229–30): there is a tendency to write *upsilon* as V, puncta are placed between *gentilicia* and *cognomina*, before patronymics or at the end of the line, some Latin names are transliterated rather than put into their usual Greek form (Κάπιτο at 392, 394, 402 rather than Καπίτων), an *omicron* is sometimes used under Latin influence, as in Ούίκτορ at 388, 389, 390, Πετρόνιος in 390, and μαίορ at 404, and *epsilon* is used at 391 in Πομπέις. These features considered as a whole, involving as they do rather more than letter shapes, point to a writer[31] who was very familiar with the writing of Latin, perhaps more familiar with that language than with Greek. He was making concessions to the primary language of the area. It is indeed a moot point whether the texts are entirely in Greek: note that the Latin adjectives μίνωρ and μαίωρ are several times used in conjunction with a name (390, 392, 393, 400). Filiations, however, are definitely in Greek (406 Φίλιππος 'Ιουλίου). Another piece of significant evidence from Mons Claudianus can be found at *O. Claud.* nos. 239–40, both documents by a certain Piso. He writes in the first (2–3) προσδέχομαι ὑμᾶς ἐν ταῖς κα[λ]άνδαις 'I expect you on the first of the month', but in the second (3) προσδ[έχ]ομαι ὑμᾶς εἰς καλάνδα<ς>. The editor notes that this latter prepositional expression appears to be unique in Greek except in the title of Libanius' speech *Or.* 9, where it means 'in honour of' the Kalends. He observes that the 'expression here must translate the Latin *ad Kalendas*'. The writer may have been a Latin speaker; this looks like a case of interference (from L1) in the use of a prepositional expression in L2.

Further internal evidence will be cited below, from inscriptions/graffiti at Kalabcha (v.3), the Syringes of Thebes (v.4) and on the Koptos–Quseir road (v.6), suggesting that various writers had the competence to use the other language if they had chosen to do so.

II THE EVIDENCE FROM EGYPT

There is no comprehensive collection of Latin material from Egypt, and the evidence is widely scattered.[32] It would be pointless to consider only

---

[31] Note that the editor suggests that most of the lists are in the same hand (p. 229).
[32] But two useful collections with abundant Latin material from Egypt are *CPL* and *CEL*.

documents and inscriptions written in Latin, because in such polyglot communities Greek texts may also betray the influence of Greek–Latin bilingualism. I have taken into account here scattered papyri from the major corpora such as that from Oxyrhynchus, but more particularly the following archives (ostraca and papyri) for the most part of military provenance and usually containing material of relevance to bilingualism: first and foremost the archive of Tiberianus, as well as the Abinnaeus archive (Flavius Abinnaeus was commander of the *ala* at Dionysias in the Fayûm in the 340s),[33] the ostraca from Mons Claudianus, the Florida ostraca (the date of these military documents from Upper Egypt is the second century),[34] *O.Max.*,[35] letters from Latopolis (?),[36] texts from Quseir-al-Qadim (see above, 1),[37] texts from Wâdi Fawâkhir,[38] texts from 'Abu Sha'ar,[39] texts from the Myos Hormos road,[40] and ostraca from Wâdi Hammâmât.[41] Also worth mentioning are *P. Qasr Ibrîm* inv. 78 (Parsons, *P. Rainer Cent.* no. 164) (a Latin letter, of the first century BC, from Nubia and the same deposit as the famous verses of Gallus), *ChLA* 10.434 (a Latin letter in chancellery style addressed to a soldier of the *Legio II Traiana Fortis* and embodying a switch into Greek, though the text is very fragmentary), various documents published in Fink (1971), e.g. 75 (auxiliaries' receipts for money, two in Greek and a third in Latin; all are in different hands) and 76 (see below, VII.1), and the bilingual glossaries conveniently collected by Kramer (1983).

Of inscriptions and graffiti I mention the collection of non-funerary Greek and Latin inscriptions from Alexandria by Kayser (1994), the important and revealing sets of texts from the great pilgrimage or tourist sites of Egypt, namely Philae (*IG Philae*),[42] the Colossus of Memnon,[43] Kalabcha (= Talmis), the site of the famous temple of Mandulis,[44] the Syringes of Thebes,[45] Dakka (= Pselchis),[46] and Deir el-Bahari,[47] and the various other volumes by A. and É. Bernand collecting texts from a variety of areas. Many of these inscriptions were set up by Roman soldiers, in either language. They raise acutely the question of the motivations of language choice, as there are striking differences between soldiers' practice at different sites and in different types of inscriptions.

---

[33] See Bell et al. (1962: 8, 11) on the date.   [34] See Bagnall (1976: 5).
[35] See Bülow-Jacobsen, Cuvigny and Fournet (1994).   [36] Published by Sijpesteijn (1973).
[37] See Bagnall (1986).   [38] See Guéraud (1942).   [39] See Bagnall and Sheridan (1994).
[40] See Meredith (1956).   [41] See Schwartz (1956).   [42] A. Bernand (1969).
[43] See A. and É. Bernand (1960).
[44] The inscriptions may be found in Gauthier (1911), but only as diplomatic transcriptions. There is a selection of the Greek inscriptions at *IGRRP* I. 1331–56, all of which are by Roman soldiers.
[45] These are edited by Baillet (1920–6).   [46] See Ruppel (1930).   [47] See Bataille (1951a).

III LANGUAGE CHOICE AS AN EXPRESSION OF POWER OR ACT OF ACCOMMODATION

The inadequacies which we have seen of the H–L opposition are such that I would like to get away from it for the moment, and to present a more dynamic model of language choice by Romans in Egypt. There are two competing functions of language choice which are relevant to a good deal of the rest of the chapter, that is language choice as a form of accommodation (for which see 2.XIV.6 with cross references, 3.I, 3.III.I, 3.IV.I),[48] and language choice as a manifestation of power (or, one might alternatively say, using the terminology of e.g. Vaahtera (2000: 4–9), 'authority'). To take two over-simple examples. If speaker A adopts the language of speaker B in an exchange, he might, as we have seen (3.IV.I), have been adapting his language choice to suit the linguistic competence of the addressee (see also below, V, 6.V.I). That accommodation might be condescending, but it is just as likely to be an act of deference or politeness, or a gesture of solidarity. On the other hand if A were to speak in the presence of B in his own language A, a language which B did not understand, B would obviously be excluded, and that exclusion (though it might have a variety of motivations) could on occasions be interpreted as an insult or as an attempt to cast B as an outsider lacking control over the situation. The language choice is thus an act of 'power' which reduces B to an inferior position (see above, 3.VI). These two examples are intended merely to show up extremes. Language choice as an exercise in power may have many, rather more subtle, forms, as we will see. I will return to diglossia and its relationship to the opposition set up here in sect. VI.3.

The role which (some) Romans on occasions chose to assign to Latin *vis-à-vis* Greek in Egypt can be nicely illustrated from the inscriptions at the Colossus of Memnon. I will use this case to introduce the discussion of language choice as displaying 'power.' The discussion will then move on to accommodation (V).

IV LATIN AS A LANGUAGE OF POWER

I use the expression 'language of power' in this context in the loosest possible way. In no sense, as has been stressed here, did the Romans make an aggressive attempt to impose their language in any part of the Empire.

---

[48] I refer here to 'accommodation theory', for which see e.g. Giles and Smith (1979); also Gardner-Chloros (1991: 57) for a few remarks on the relevance of accommodation theory to language choice.

We have seen evidence for their acceptance of Greek as a lingua franca in the east (2.VII.5), and in Egypt itself Greek was overwhelmingly the language of daily administration and of the army (see the next section, and below, VII.1). But the Romans were always capable of asserting themselves *ad hoc* by the choice of Latin in circumstances in which linguistic accommodation, particularly to Greeks, would have been expected. It is to this theme that I now turn.

IV.1 Greek and Latin inscriptions at the Colossus of Memnon

Two colossal statues on the left bank of the Nile are the remains of a temple of Amenophis II, dated to the fifteenth or fourteenth centuries BC.[49] These objects, and particularly the northern Colossus, excited awe in visitors, not least because the northern figure emitted a sound at dawn which was believed to be the voice of the god himself. By Greeks and Romans the god was identified with Memnon, the son of Dawn by Tithonus. The Colossus was visited by Romans of the highest status.[50] The prefect Aelius Gallus went there in 24 BC, accompanied by Strabo, and together they heard the sound (Strabo 17.1.46). In AD 19 Germanicus visited the Colossus, as recorded by Tacitus (*Ann.* 2.61). Hadrian's visit, in November 130, was celebrated by the poetess Julia Balbilla (A. and É. Bernand (1960: 28–31)), though for him the god failed to speak.

The Colossus is remarkable for the language choice of the visitors. Whereas at other pilgrimage sites in Egypt which will be discussed below Romans tended to suppress their Latin-speaking identities, at the Colossus Latin bulks much larger.[51] Moreover it is possible to discern a distinctive role that was assigned the language by visitors, contrasting with a rather different role given to Greek. It is essential to attempt to explain the reason for the difference between this site and the others. I would suggest that the function given to Latin at the Colossus is of a more general significance and helps to account for language choice in some other settings.

The legs and feet of the northern Colossus are covered by some 107 inscriptions, in both Greek and Latin, some of them in prose, others

[49] For general background see Casson (1974: 272–8), Bowersock (1984). The standard edition of the inscriptions, with substantial commentary, is by A. and É. Bernand (1960).

[50] Pilgrimage/tourism to this site has often been discussed, usually in brief: see Milne (1916: 78), Hohlwein (1940: 275–6), Bataille (1951b: 349–50), Casson (1974: 260–1, 272–8, 284–5), Bowersock (1984), Théodoridès (1989).

[51] Stein (1915: 180–1) is not at his best on these various sites. He fails to bring out the difference in the matter of language choice between the inscriptions at the Colossus and those in other places.

(mainly in Greek) in verse. The Greek texts number 61 and the Latin 45 (with one bilingual), a distribution which is strikingly different from that at comparable sites elsewhere in Egypt. A second feature of the texts lies in the high status of those whose names they bear. Most of the signatories were either high functionaries of Egypt (including the prefect), or high ranking military officers.[52] Professional poets were sometimes employed, as for example Balbilla (see above). The cult of Memnon gives every appearance of being organised in some way by the authorities;[53] it was not a haphazard affair such that ordinary pilgrims could leave their scrawlings. I quote Casson (1974:275): 'Most [graffiti] . . . are no casual scribblings but veritable inscriptions carved with care; they were probably done by professional stonecutters who were available for hire in the vicinity. Apparently only the *élite* were allowed to leave these elegantly engraved momentoes.'[54] A. and É. Bernand (1960) arrange the inscriptions chronologically into three groups, the pre-Hadrianic (1–15), those of the period of Hadrian himself (16–50),[55] and those from Hadrian to Septimius Severus (51–61). The inscriptions numbered 62–107, many of which are fragmentary, are undated.

Prefects of Egypt had their inscriptions written all but exclusively in Latin at all periods (pre-Hadrianic: 3, 15; also 8, which bears the name of the wife of a prefect, C. Tettius Africanus; Hadrianic: 16, 24, 40; post-Hadrianic: 57). It has been suggested (by A. and É. Bernand (1960: 49)) that the Mettius in whose name Greek verses were written by a poet Παιών (11) might have been M. Mettius Rufus, prefect of Egypt from 89–91. Here at once, in the prominence of Latin, is a significant feature, for in the administration of Egypt prefects regularly used Greek. I dwell on this point briefly, commenting on various texts which show prefects functioning in Greek, before coming back to the Colossus.

For example, É. Bernand (1975), 75 (dated 29 March 54) is a decree of the prefect L. Lusius Geta exempting the priests of a local god from γεωργία. The decree is preceded by a letter to the *strategos* of the Arsinoite nome instructing him to display the decree in suitable places so that everyone may know the prefect's orders, with his words then quoted in Greek, introduced by λέγει. The reason for the choice of Greek is obvious: it is only thus that the order could be disseminated. The most famous such example is the decree of Tiberius Julius Alexander, of

[52] See A. and É. Bernand (1960: 25).   [53] See A. and É. Bernand (1960: 19).
[54] See Bataille (1951b: 349) for much the same point.
[55] During this period there is a particular abundance of inscriptions by administrative personnel: see A. and É. Bernand (1960: 25).

28 September 68. In this Julius Demetrius, *strategos* of the oasis of Thebaid, reveals that he has received the edict, which is then quoted in full, again with λέγει introducing the prefect's words. There is a full list of extant edicts in Chalon (1964), appendix, pp. 251–6, all of them in Greek.[56]

Prefects' dealings with *strategoi* were in Greek,[57] in keeping with a policy of employing Greek as the language of internal civil administration. *P. Oxy.* IX.1185, for example, is a partial copy of several distinct documents, including two letters of the prefect Magnius Felix Crescentillianus in Greek to *strategoi*. *P. Oxy.* IX.1191 is a copy of a letter in Greek from Aurelius Ammonius on behalf of the prefect Hadrianius Sallustius to the *strategos* of the Oxyrhynchite nome with an order; the copy of the original is sent on by the *strategos* to a secretary followed by a letter. *P. Oxy.* XLIII.3129 is a letter of a prefect (Flavius Philagrius) to the *strategos* of the Oxyrhynchite nome in Greek instructing the *strategos* 'to make an investigation into the facts stated in a petition that had been sent to him'. The copy of the petition which must have accompanied the letter is lost. The document is the original issued from the prefect's chancery. As we have seen (3.VI.2), a consular date in another hand is written in Latin, and there is another date in Latin in the margin. There is thus a certain amount of official notation in Latin in what is basically a Greek text (on dates, see 3.VI.2, further below in this section, and IV.6 below).

There are also letters in Greek from prefects to other officials. The sender of the text edited as *P. Oxy.* LV.3794 was the same Philagrius, and the subject (though the text is fragmentary) the supply of craftsmen to praetorian prefects. The addressee in this case is a *curator*. In the left margin there is a Latin notation of the day and place of issue. That is the only use of Latin, though a Latin consular date has no doubt been lost (see the editor, p. 63). The document resembles 3129 above. Note too *P. Oxy.* LXIII. 4376 (AD 368), which is (I quote the edition) 'a covering letter from a magistrate of Oxyrhynchus which once accompanied a copy of an order of the prefect of Egypt Flavius Eutolmius Tatianus. It warns the recipient, a private inhabitant of Oxyrhynchus, [in Greek] that he must comply with the provisions of the order.'

Even veterans were not constrained by any obligation to address the prefect in Latin. *P. Oxy.* XXXVI.2760 is a petition to the prefect in Greek by an ex-cavalryman; this might be a copy of the original. The petitioner was on military business of sorts. He had left Oxyrhynchus 'to deliver

---

[56] See further Stein (1915:151).   [57] See also Stein (1915: 163).

blankets for the use of soldiers of the Egyptian legion, *II Traiana Fortis*'
(p. 39), but had been detained for forty days in an unspecified place, probably Alexandria. He writes asking that the business should be settled.
This document should be contrasted with *ChLA* 3.201, discussed below, iv.6 (1). There a prefect (it can be deduced) had replied in Latin to a
veteran, and his reply is translated into Greek and the translation authenticated by the prefect. Prefects were obviously more likely to use Latin
(or both languages) in addressing veterans or soldiers (see below, iv.2.1)
than in addressing local Egyptian officials.

The employment of Latin by prefects at the Colossus is the more
remarkable because at another pilgrimage site, the Syringes of Thebes,
several prefects have been identified who left graffiti in Greek, not Latin.[58]
For possible prefects visiting the Syringes (on which see below, v.4), see
e.g. 1600, 1356 (on which see below, v.4), 1412 in Baillet's edition (1920–6).
If the identifications are correct, at this place prefects adopted the local
convention, and made no display of their Romanness.

I return to the Colossus. Greek appears definitely under the name of
a prefect only once, in 13.7–8 (AD 92), in a significant context, where two
Greek verses are inserted in a Latin prose text (but cf. the inscription of
Mettius above, which is also in verse). The whole inscription is as follows:

Im(peratore) Domitiano
Caesare Aug(usto) German(ico) XVI c(onsule)
T(itus) Petronius Secundus pr(aefectus) Aeg(ypti)
audit Memnonem hora I pr(idie) Idus Mart(ias)
et honorauit eum uersibus Graecis
infra scriptis:
φθέγξαο Λατοίδα, σὸν γὰρ μέρος ὧδε κάθηται,
Μέμνων, ἀκτεῖσιν βαλλόμενος πυρίναις.
curante T(ito) Attio Musa prae[f](ecto) coh(ortis) II
Thebaeor(um).

The factual part of the text, which names the emperor and gives the date
and identifies the prefect along with his title, is in Latin, whereas Greek
is used as a poetic language appropriate for honouring (note *honorauit*)
Memnon in high-flown terms. The Latin is given a certain detachment
by the use of the third-person singular (notably in *audit*), and it is made
clear at the end that the prefect did not write or oversee the writing of
the inscription himself; that was done by a military officer.

Any attempt to distinguish the two languages here in terms of the diglossic opposition H–L would be wide of the mark. Neither language is L,

---

[58] Casson (1974: 279) refers to 'at least six governors of Egypt' at the Syringes.

but rather each has a distinctive formal function. Latin comes across as the official imperial language, suitable for dating and for expressing military (see further below) and imperial titles (for comparable uses of Latin in mixed-language texts, such as coin legends and milestones, see above 2.XIV.2 with cross references; see also 3.VI.2 on code-switching into Latin in dates), whereas Greek is the language of high literary culture, used in eulogistic verses containing no such titles.[59] Latin is used here in apparent indifference to local (Greek or Egyptian) readership, symbolising, it would seem, the power of Rome. Whereas other places such as the Syringes and the temple at Kalabcha, as we will see, were visited by all sorts of fairly ordinary people, the Colossus was a mecca for the highest classes, who provided a readership for formal inscriptions constructing self-consciously different roles for the two languages.

Latin had from time to time been employed ostentatiously by Romans as a language of power (see below, IV.3), but pragmatism dictated that no serious attempt was ever made to inflict the language on subject peoples at all costs. We simply find occasional attempts to present Latin in a dominant light. As far as Greek is concerned, the language had been treated as the literary language *par excellence* from the beginnings of Latin literature. Fabius Pictor, for example, had written his history in Greek. Those developing literary genres in Latin (e.g. epic, didactic poetry, comedy and tragedy) not only looked to Greek works for subject matter, but also drew in various ways on the Greek language in creating a literary language for Latin. In particular, Greek syntax was deliberately imitated in Latin poetry as a marker of poetic language (see 4.II). At the Colossus it is on stone that Greek is defined as the high literary language (see further below).

The other prefects' inscriptions are all similar to no. 13 above, though no other incorporates Greek, apart from the possible case in the name of Mettius. With the exception of 3, each has a date, either consular or by the year of the reign of the emperor (15 and 16; also 8), and each has *audi(t) Memnonem (audi(ui)* at 3, 40, 57, *audit* at 15, 16, 24). The prefect is given his full name and title.

The roles of the languages distinguishable in prefects' inscriptions can also be discerned in military inscriptions, to which I now turn.

On 7 March AD 134 Q. Marcius Hermogenes, prefect of the Augustan fleet at Alexandria, set up an inscription in Latin recording that he had heard Memnon (A. and É. Bernand (1960), 38): *Q(uintus) Marcius*

---

[59] For this type of opposition, see Dagron (1969); also Rochette (1996c: 66).

Hermogenes praef(ectus) classis Aug(ustae) Alex(andrinae) audit Memnonem hora (prima et dimidia) Nonis Martis Seruiano III *et Varo co(n)s(ulibus).* There is a parallelism between this text and that of the dedications by prefects of Egypt. Hermogenes gives his full name and title in Latin, and also a consular date; as in some of the inscriptions discussed above, the third person of the verb is used.

But Hermogenes also recorded his presence in Greek, this time in verse (A. and É. Bernand (1960), 39), which is fragmentary in the second line:

Μάρκιος Ἑρμογένης ἔκλυον μέγα φωνήσαντος
Μέμνονος, ΑΝΤΕΛΛΟΥ . . . ΔΥΟ βαλόντος

In the Greek Hermogenes does not, it seems, state his title or the date. There is an obvious functional distinction between the Latin and the Greek. The Latin text is described by the editors (A. and É. Bernand (1960: 12)) as banal, in contrast to the Greek verses. We might rather say that Latin is the language used to set out in full the military man's position in the army, and to record the date of the visit, whereas Greek is the language of literary pretension, in which humdrum information is not conveyed. The different roles of the two languages in these two inscriptions are much the same as those in the single inscription which bears the name of the prefect Petronius Secundus. Hemogenes had, as it were, a public or official voice on the one hand, and a literary voice on the other. I would not wish to argue that Hermogenes wrote the Greek himself; it is more likely that there were professional poets on hand to compose Greek verses in this vein. However, even those Romans who had Greek verses written on their behalf were making a language choice, and paying lip service to an interpretation of the appropriate function of Greek; and on the other hand those who instead used Latin for conveying a type of information were putting a construction on the function of Latin.

The two 'voices' of Roman soldiers to which I refer are also discernible in the other military inscriptions. It is illuminating to consider the group of inscriptions (from different periods) written by or in the name of centurions.[60] The inscriptions are: (pre-Hadrianic) 2, 7, 10; (Hadrianic) 25, 44, 45, 47; (post-Hadrianic) 51, 52, 53; (undated) 101. The pattern identified above repeats itself here. All of the Greek inscriptions are in verse, and the Latin in prose.

---

[60] For some remarks on these, see Adams (1999: 128–9).

The Latin inscriptions vary slightly according to period. The three pre-Hadrianic inscriptions all give the full name, title and legion of the centurion (no. 2 records two centurions and a decurion), and a date by day, month and year; no. 7 indeed records a whole series of dates on which Memnon was heard. From the Hadrianic period no. 25 states the full name, *domus* and legions of the centurion, and a consular date, with day and month also noted. The *domus* of the man was Corinth, and he would probably have been a Greek as well as Latin speaker, but Latin was chosen for information of this kind in this setting. The other three Hadrianic (Latin) inscriptions are briefer: they give the name, title and legion of the centurions, but not the date.

The first Greek inscription (no. 51) is post-Hadrianic (8 May 150), and it presents a contrast with what had gone before. The body of the text contains ten hexameter lines (most of them damaged), in a flowery poetic language heavily indebted to Homer.[61] The centurion records his name (Marius Gemellus) and rank in an acclamation (comprising εὐτυχῶς + dative of the name) before the start of the poem, and after the poem he gives a similar acclamation to his wife (Rufilla, also called Longinia). His legion is not stated. A Greco-Egyptian style of date (the month is Pachon) is worked into the poem. This inscription is literary, personal and non-official, in that it is not overburdened with Romanising information. Gemellus establishes his status, but does not locate himself explicitly in the Roman army.

No. 53 is by the same centurion, but its four lines of hexameter verse are fragmentary. This time Gemellus names himself and states his rank (without mention of a legion) in another acclamation at the end of the piece. Again I stress that Gemellus need not have written the Greek himself, though on the usual restoration of 51.9 ([ταῦτ' ἔγραψα]) he claimed to have done so. The fragmentary poem 52 embodies the same name Γ(έ)μελλος, and is attributed to the same centurion by A. and É. Bernand (1960: 27).

The undated piece (101) is in six lines of Homericising hexameters. Here the centurion records only one of his names (᾽Ιούλιος, which is in a verse), and, like Gemellus, he does not specify his legion: he is merely [ἑκα]τόνταρχος λεγεῶνος (6).

The centurions' inscriptions as a group show a parallelism with the pair of texts by the prefect of the Alexandrian fleet discussed above. Greek is the literary language which presumably demonstrates the literary culture

---

[61] See A. and É. Bernand (1960: 133 n. 1).

of the writer or referent; in all of these Greek military inscriptions the soldier's membership of the Roman army is incidental, and information about it is not provided. Latin, on the other hand, is the language which a man chooses, even in a Greek-speaking region, when he wishes to assert his military status.

At other pilgrimage sites (discussed below) soldiers regularly record themselves, with full military details, in *Greek*. It is not therefore merely the military nature of the information which determines the choice of language, but also the setting in which that information was conveyed. Latin was available to the military officer as the formal language of military power when the circumstances warranted symbolic display, but in different circumstances, as for instance in a Nubian temple, such display might have been inappropriate. The Romans had appropriated the Colossus of Memnon as a place to express symbolically to an élite readership their imperial and military power through the use of the Latin language.

The remaining military inscriptions are (in Latin) 4, 6, 9, 14, 26, 46, 56 and 60,[62] and (in Greek) 20. Of the Latin inscriptions, 4, 9, 14, 26, 46, 56 and 60 all provide the full name of the soldier, his rank and his unit; 6 is slightly less informative than the rest, in that, though it states the full name and rank (*praefectus castrorum*) of the soldier and the date of the inscription, it does not indicate his unit. The one Greek inscription (20) breaks the pattern, in giving full military information about the subject, Servius Sulpicius Serenus, of a type for which Latin was normally used. Serenus is known from a bilingual inscription at Thebes (*ILS* 8908),[63] and the evidence suggests that he spent his entire military career in Egypt; possibly he was a native of Alexandria.[64]

Another minor curiosity is no. 14, set up by one Caesellius, *praefectus Gallorum alae* and also *praefectus Berenices*. The first three lines are hexameters:

> Memnonis . . . clarumque sonor[em]
> exanimị inanimẹm mi[ssum] de tegmine bruto
> auribus ipse meis cepi sumsique canorum.

A. and É. Bernand (1960: 55) note that this piece expresses in Latin certain ideas and commonplaces found in the Greek poems in honour of Memnon. They compare, for example, the reference to the sound coming *de tegmine bruto* with expressions in Greek poems (28.1–2, 31.1, 51.8) stating

---

[62] This inscription gives a full *cursus honorum*; not all of the referent's offices were military.
[63] See A. and É. Bernand (1960: 67).   [64] See A. and É. Bernand (1960), loc. cit.

the paradox that the voice of Memnon came forth from rock or stone, a lifeless substance. Caesellius departed from the conventions of language choice at the Colossus, but language choice is never an inflexible matter; however much is known about a bilingual speaker and his addressee and about the circumstances, topic and purpose of an encounter between them, language choice cannot always be predicted. Here was a soldier who was creating a special literary persona for himself by imitating in Latin the Greek verses which he had read at the site.

I turn finally to the inscriptions of civil functionaries. Local officials within the Egyptian bureaucracy (such as three with the title *epistrategos Thebaidos*, two *strategoi* of the nomes of Hermonthite and Latopolite: see A. and É. Bernand (1960: 26)) regularly left inscriptions in *Greek*, in both prose and verse (nos. 18, 19, 21, 23, 27, 34, 35, 36, 43, 62, 67, 73). There is only one such inscription in Latin (partly in verse), by the *epistrategos Thebaidos* Iulius Fidus Aquila (41), who was a native of Numidia (see A. and É. Bernand (1960: 118)). Aquila also left a verse inscription in Greek (42), thereby displaying his bilingualism. There is thus a distinction between the practice of the prefects of Egypt, who used Latin, and lesser functionaries, who almost always used Greek. At this site prefects chose to give themselves a different, Latin-speaking persona as representatives of Rome in Egypt, and thereby asserted their position above that of the local officials. In other circumstances, as we have seen, they accommodated themselves to local officials by using Greek. The Greco-Egyptian officials used Greek regularly as the language of local administration, and similarly they were using it formally at the Colossus.

There was obviously something special about the Colossus which inspired prefects and military officers to use Latin in recording their visits. The grandeur of the site and its attraction to both Greek-speaking and Roman *élites* made it suitable for a public display of Romanness by high-ranking officials and military officers. The Ethiopian Memnon fought on the Trojan side in the Trojan War, being eventually killed by Achilles. This tradition may have enhanced the significance of the site to the Roman upper classes, and prompted expressions of Roman identity through the Latin language (cf. also below, n. 108). It is impossible to know whether the choice of Latin in the inscriptions was the consequence of a decision, or at first an informal response to the nature of the place and of its visitors. If the latter, traditions of language use would soon have developed. But much remains obscure. Who were the stonecutters, and what was the manner of the organisation which seems to have prevented those ordinary tourists (albeit educated and belonging to the wealthier classes) who visited the nearby Syringes in such numbers from leaving their mark to any extent at the Colossus?

It would, as I noted earlier, be implausible to suggest that the language used at the Colossus by *strategoi* and in Homeric-style verse was in any sense Low, but it does seem reasonable to say that Latin trumps Greek by being used on the one hand by the senior Roman official in Egypt and on the other by high-ranking military officers, though Hadrian characteristically had himself presented as a Greek *littérateur*, by having his visit recorded in Greek verse. If one wanted to put the relationship of Latin to Greek in the terms of diglossia, there is no term more appropriate in my opinion for expressing the status and function of Latin at the Colossus than 'super-high', if only in a narrow political sense, in contrast to the H of Greek. Latin seems to be used here as an explicitly political language for bringing out the Romanness of imperial power in Egypt. Greek is the language of lesser power and also of literary culture. The diglossic relationship between Greek and Latin thus differs from that argued earlier (3.VIII) for Roman Greek communities.

IV.2 *The Abinnaeus archive*

A second collection of texts which is relevant to the linguistic expression of power is the Abinnaeus archive. Flavius Abinnaeus, as mentioned earlier, was commander of the *ala* at Dionysias in the Fayûm in the 340s.

Among the numerous items in the Abinnaeus archive there are two letters (one in Greek, the other in Latin) written by Abinnaeus himself, or at least described as from him (see below on the authorship). I leave aside the Greek letter (43), which has no closing greeting and may be a mere draft. More interesting is a petition to the emperors from Abinnaeus written in Latin (no. 1). See Bell et al. (1962: 7) on the circumstances of its composition: 'Their imperial majesties . . . had appointed Abinnaeus to the command of the ala at Dionysias. But when he arrived at Alexandria and handed in the imperial letter of appointment to the bureau of the count of Egypt, he was met with the information that other gentlemen had also arrived with similar letters of appointment to the same command. The petition (possibly presented in person by Abinnaeus) is his successful counter to a situation which . . . was perhaps not uncommon in these times.' The petition was almost certainly not drafted or written by Abinnaeus himself, because it is composed in an official style. But Abinnaeus must have been able to understand it. Note the significance

of the correction (sect. 13) found in the last clause of the document: see
Bell et al. (1962: 7): 'after, or perhaps during, its copying Abinnaeus was
dissatisfied with the wording of its final clause, and had a revised version
written above the line and in the right-hand margin. To this accident
its survival among his papers is due.' If this suggestion is accepted, it
follows that Abinnaeus oversaw the writing of the document, and he
must have had some knowledge of Latin. He had acquired the rank of
protector before being seconded to Dionysias,[65] and at this exalted level a
good knowledge of Latin must have been the norm even among those
who were not native speakers of the language (cf. Ammianus).

There is only one other document in the archive that is in Latin (2; see
below); it is Greek that is regularly used as a formal or 'official' language. Thus, for example, letter 11, in Greek, is a formal piece from a
military officer transmitting to Abinnaeus 'the instructions of an officialis
of the dux Flavius Felicissimus'. The letter begins along these (highly
formal) lines: 'It has become necessary to inform your nobility of the instructions given by (ἀνάγκη μοι γεγένηται δηλῶσε τῇ σῇ καλοκαγαθίᾳ τὰ
γραφέντα ὑπό . . .) the official of my lord the Duke, Flavius Felicissimus.'
Also in Greek is another formal letter, no. 3, written by Flavius Macrinus,
procurator of the Imperial estates, informing Abinnaeus of certain orders
of the *dux*. Greek was clearly standard or commonplace in high-level
communications within the army (on which topic, see the detailed discussion below, VII). Or again, at the level of internal administration, there
is an application for leave written in Greek (*P. Abinn.* 33),[66] whereas at
Vindolanda such applications were written in Latin. And 17 is a letter
'informing Abinnaeus that the imperial notarius is due to pay a visit that
day for the enrolment of recruits' (Bell et al. (1962: 61)).

The other Latin document referred to above (2) is a letter written by
the *dux* of Egypt himself, Valacius.[67] Its content is significant, for it is
a letter of dismissal from the command of the *ala*. Thus the only two
Latin letters in the Abinnaeus archive concern appointment to the post
of commander (so no. 1), or dismissal.

[65] See Bell et al. (1962: 11).

[66] This is not the only extant application for leave written in Greek. Cf. the ostracon published by
Price (1955–6), 2, which is a 'request from one soldier to another for leave of absence for the
following day' (Price (1955–6: 162)). It contains (line 4) the expression λαβεῖν μοι κομ[ί]ατο(ν).
On a leave pass written in Greek (*O. Flor.* 1), see below, VII.1. The document from the Abinnaeus
archive is not however of standard type. A certain Clematius in 'well-turned letters' (so the
editors, p. 84) writes at length on behalf of his kinsman Ision, a non-commissioned officer under
Abinnaeus' charge. It is then a personal rather than an official letter, but its content is formal
and the subject is military.

[67] On this man see *PLRE* I.929. The *dux Aegypti* was the supreme military officer.

On the evidence of this archive, then, Greek was in regular use as an official, formal language, but Latin was available as a sort of 'super-high' language which could be employed either to make obvious the location of supreme power (see further below, VII.2), or in appeal to a supreme authority. There is a similarity between the factors motivating the choice of Latin in this archive, and those at the Colossus. That is not to say that Latin was regularly used when, for example, a superior official addressed a subordinate, or a subordinate addressed his superior. On the contrary, a practical *laissez-faire* attitude seems to have brought it about that even in communications in which the status of the participants was not equal, Greek was regularly chosen, even in the army. But Latin was in the wings, to be called on *ad hoc* for the forceful symbolising of Roman power. It would seem that, when an associate of the *dux* sent orders, Greek was considered acceptable (see above on nos. 3 and 11). But a letter directly from the *dux* exercising his full power inspired the super-high language.

By chance a recently published papyrus text from Oxyrhynchus throws further light on the language choice of the *dux Aegypti* in formal dealings with soldiers.

IV.2.1 P. Oxy. *LXIII.4381*

This is a report of proceedings in camera before Flavius Mauricius, *dux Aegypti*, in August 375 at Alexandria. These, the editor notes, are the only extant proceedings before a *dux*. The *dux* is judge because the plaintiffs are soldiers. The soldiers are appealing against an attempt to exact from them a trade tax (payable in gold and silver bullion) called *collatio lustralis*. The circumstances of the hearing are described as follows (p. 82): 'The proceedings took place in camera because the business was to give a written judgement in reply to a petition. Neither the defendants nor the petitioners were present and there are no advocates' speeches. After the date and location comes a request from the staff of the *dux* for permission to read the petition, and the *dux* gives the instruction for it to be read and inserted in the record. All this is in Latin. Then the petition is read and recorded in Greek, to be followed by the judgement in Latin. This may have done no more than authorize the pursuit of the case in another court.' There is thus the usual Latin framework in the record of the hearing (in this case the preamble giving date and location), but as well language mixing in the hearing itself. The petitioners had applied in Greek to the *dux*, who conducted the hearing around the Greek petition in Latin, giving his decision in that language. The supreme military official in Egypt was willing to receive a petition in Greek, but he responds in Latin, thus apparently symbolising his authority.

As we saw in the previous section, within military units Greek could be used for matters of an official nature (see further below, VII.1), but when a supreme outside official intervened in the affairs of a unit or responded to an appeal from below Latin tended to be used as the super-high language. There is a similar case at *P. Oxy.* VII.1022. This is 'a letter in Latin addressed by the praefect of Egypt, C. Minicius Italus, to Celsianus, praefect of the third Ituraean cohort, announcing the addition to the cohort of six recruits, whose names, ages and distinguishing marks, if any, are given' (p. 150). The date is AD 103.

Interestingly, at the end of the text there is the following subscription: *Auidius Arrianus cornicular(ius) coh(ortis) iii Ituraeorum scripsi authenticam epistulam in tabulario cohortis esse*, which is rendered by the editor as 'I, Avidius Arrianus, adjutant of the third cohort of the Ituraeans, have written out the original letter for the archive of the cohort.' Here is evidence for official record keeping, with the Latin original copied out and kept in the unit; alternatively, the sense may be that the original was in the archive. I will return in section VII to the use of Latin in the army as a super-high language.

I next consider in greater detail the concept of Latin as a 'language of power.'

IV.3 *The past and some miscellaneous texts*

The linguistic attitudes observable at the Colossus and in the last section can be put into historical perspective. There is nothing new about the occasional use of Latin to assert symbolically the power of Rome, in circumstances in which Greek might have been expected to be preferred. According to Valerius Maximus 2.2.2, early magistrates, in their zeal to maintain Roman *maiestas*, used only Latin in giving responses to Greeks, and forced them to speak through an interpreter, not only in Rome itself, but also in Greece and Asia: *magistratus uero prisci quantopere sui populique Romani maiestatem retinentes se gesserint hinc cognosci potest, quod inter cetera obtinendae grauitatis indicia illud quoque magna cum perseuerantia custodiebant, ne Graecis unquam nisi Latine responsa darent. quin etiam ipsos linguae uolubilitate, qua plurimum ualent, excussa per interpretem loqui cogebant non in urbe tantum nostra, sed etiam in Graecia et Asia, quo scilicet Latinae uocis honos per omnes gentes uenerabilior diffunderetur.*[68] The generalisation is to some extent

---

[68] Loeb: 'How carefully the magistrates of old regulated their conduct to keep intact the majesty of the Roman people and their own can be seen from the fact that among other indications of their

borne out by the evidence, but it cannot be taken as a description of an invariable practice. Rather, it expresses an awareness that Latin could be invoked *ad hoc* in Greek settings to underline the power of Rome. The complexity of language choice is underlined by the fact that on occasions Greek itself could be used for the same purpose: a Roman official might condescendingly use Greek in Greece as a form of ostentatious accommodation to his addressees, making it clear that he could use their language even if they could not use his. Condescending accommodation stresses the speaker's complete control of the situation (see further below, V).

Incidents from the Republic which fall into line with Valerius' remark are not difficult to find. Cato at Athens in 191 addressed the crowd in Latin (Plut. *Cato* 12.4–5), leaving it to a subordinate to translate the speech into Greek. The Latin will have been largely incomprehensible to the audience, but of symbolic significance.[69] Gruen (1993: 68–9) comments, rather imaginatively, as follows: '[the speech] signified the superior economy and directness of Cato's native tongue, as against the overblown wordiness of Greek. But Cato's act also carried a further implication. By asserting command of both languages and choosing the better, he announced superiority at yet another level. The Athenian audience knew no Latin and had to receive a translation. Cato had the advantage of them also in this regard. In effect, he declared that Roman ascendancy carried over from the military sphere to the realm of high culture.' L. Aemilius Paullus, the victor at Pydna in 168, announced at Amphipolis the 'decrees concerning Macedonia in Latin in the presence of the representatives of the ten Macedonian peoples, and let his praetor Cn. Octavius translate the decrees into Greek' (Kaimio (1979a: 100)).[70] The incident is strikingly similar to that at Athens in 191: in both cases the Roman commander spoke Latin to the uncomprehending audience, with a translation later provided by a subordinate (cf. the manner in which decisions were expressed in legal hearings before Roman officials in Egypt: above, 3.VI.1). In this way two purposes were served. The translation conveyed the necessary information to the Macedonians (and, earlier,

---

duty to preserve dignity they steadfastly kept to the rule never to make replies to Greeks except in Latin. Indeed they obliged the Greeks themselves to discard their volubility which is their greatest asset and speak through an interpreter, not only in Rome but in Greece and Asia also, intending no doubt that the dignity of Latin speech be the more widely venerated throughout all nations.' Kaimio (1979a: 94–6) argued that Valerius' text represents propaganda from the era of Tiberius, but Dubuisson (1982: 192–210) and Gruen (1993: 235–41) uphold the face value of Valerius' assertion.

[69] See Kaimio (1979a: 98–9), Dubuisson (1982: 200), Gruen (1993: 64–5, 68–9, 237).
[70] Livy 45.29.1–3. See further Gruen (1993: 245).

the Athenians), but not before a foreign language had been forced upon their hearing in a symbolic display of Roman supremacy. Or again, after this affair, Paullus set out on a tour of the major sites of Greece. At Delphi a significant event took place (Plb. 30.10.2, Livy 45.27.7, Plut. *Aem. Paull.* 28.2). I quote Gruen (1993: 246): '... he saw a column or columns erected to hold the sculptured image of Perseus. The Roman might have ordered them destroyed or even left incomplete in order to symbolize the Macedonian defeat. Instead, he took a further and significant step, ordering that his own statue be carved and stationed on top of the column meant for Perseus ... The symbolic import would, of course, be unmistakable. And lest anyone miss it, Paullus, philhellene though he was, had the monument inscribed with the notice of its capture – in Latin' (*ILLRP* 323 *L. Aimilius L. f. inperator de rege Perse Macedonibusque cepet*).[71] We will see a later parallel from Egypt for a Latin inscription with such a function (see IV.7 on the Vatican obelisk).

If we turn to the Empire, a passage in Apuleius (also found in truncated form in the Greek *Lucius or the Ass* 44) eloquently reveals the use to which Latin might be put, *ad hoc*, in a Greek area to place the hearer at a disadvantage. At *Met.* 9.39 a legionary soldier, probably a centurion, comes upon the market gardener who has possession of the donkey Lucius, and demands to know in arrogant tones where he is taking the donkey: *quidam ... miles e legione factus nobis obuius superbo atque adroganti sermone percontatur, quorsum uacuum duceret asinum.* The gardener does not understand Latin, and without replying moves on: *at meus, adhuc maerore permixtus et alias Latini sermonis ignarus, tacitus praeteribat.* For this he is beaten, and is moved to say that through ignorance of the language used by the soldier he could not know what had been said to him: *tunc hortulanus subplicue respondit sermonis ignorantia se, quid ille diceret, scire non posse.* The soldier switches into Greek, and puts his question again (Apuleius of course translates it into Latin, this time using direct speech): *ergo igitur Graece subiciens miles: 'ubi' inquit 'ducis asinum istum?'.*

Although the soldier is bilingual and the confrontation is set in a Greek-speaking part of the Empire, and although the *hortulanus* is a humble local character who could not have been assumed by the soldier to be a Latin speaker, nevertheless the *miles* chose to address him in Latin. Significantly Apuleius describes the form of address as 'arrogant.' There is such abundant evidence from the Empire of linguistic accommodation by the Roman army in the east (see below, V, VII.1) – in the

---

[71] See further Ferrary (1988: 557–60) on the form of the inscription and the significance of the choice of Latin.

form of tolerance of Greek in everyday activities in units containing native Greek speakers, and of the use of Greek in dealings with local civilians – that it comes as a surprise to find Latin used aggressively in a Greek area. The linguistic accommodation to which I refer is revealed through relatively formal or quasi-official texts, but the story in Apuleius takes us into the mundane world of the individual soldier.[72] The initial language choice of the soldier reinforces the aggressive nature of his demands. With obvious symbolism he uses the language of the imperial power as an opening gambit, in disregard of the peasant's likely inability to understand Latin. Thereafter he is prepared to use Greek to make his demands understood, but even that linguistic accommodation might be seen as condescending and a further demonstration of his control of the situation. The parallelism with the incidents at Athens and Amphipolis discussed above (where a translation was eventually provided) is obvious.

It should, finally, be acknowledged that language or language choice is not 'powerful' of itself, but it acquires its power from the listener's recognition of the power invested for other reasons in the speaker.[73] The person who uses language in a way which symbolises power will be powerful for other reasons. The soldier above was no doubt recognisable as a member of the Roman army, and hence as powerful, even before he spoke, but his choice of Latin reinforced the power that he obviously had.

I return to Egypt.

IV.4 Bilingual transcripts of hearings

Reports of hearings before Roman officials in Egypt which display code-switching into and out of Latin were discussed earlier, in the chapter on code-switching (3.VI.I). I merely repeat here that the presence of snatches of Latin either in the hearing itself or in the record seems to have symbolised in various ways the separateness of the Roman administration. On the whole the Romans allowed the use of Greek in such hearings as a form of pragmatically determined accommodation, but not without reminding readers and participants from time to time that they were an outside power. The use of Latin to express decisions is comparable with the function of the language in some of the incidents discussed in the previous section.

---

[72] On the realism of the scene, see Millar (1981: 67–8).
[73] See the remarks of Bourdieu (1991: 67, 72).

IV.5 Latin as a language of power: the citizenship

A state may expect its citizens to be able to speak a language deemed to be official. At the naturalisation ceremony of 'New Australians' an oath of loyalty is taken in English. European history is full of examples of attempts to define nationhood partly through the imposition of a single language on the citizens of the state.[74] The Jacobins at the time of the French Revolution proclaimed the ideal of 'une langue, une nation' and openly 'linked language and politics, claiming that national unity under a new democratic system could be achieved only by abandoning the regional languages of France' (Hoffmann (1991: 203)). 'Linguistic nationalism' of this type seeks to suppress minority languages. The Romans most definitely did not as an act of official policy demand that Roman citizens should speak Latin, but there are occasional signs of an informal expectation that possessors of the *ciuitas* should know the language. Tiberius refused to allow a centurion to speak Greek in the senate (D.C. 57.15.3, Suet. *Tib.* 71), and Claudius is said to have stripped a Greek of the citizenship because he could not speak Latin (D.C. 60.17.4, Suet. *Claud.* 16.2).[75] Claudius was not putting into effect a general policy, but acting *ad hoc* on a whim. There is though an attitude embodied in that whim.

A connection between the citizenship and the Latin language comes to the fore in Egypt in the insistence that certain types of legalistic documents concerning Roman citizens should be in Latin, even if the citizens did not know Latin. The requirement was presumably not particular to Egypt, but it is especially obvious there because of the survival of many legal documents on papyrus, and because there were Roman citizens resident who were Greek speakers. It led to complications in the drawing up of the documents. If a Roman citizen did not know Latin and wanted to write a will, he would have to resort to translators to have the Latin version done; and since he would have to sign, his signature would be in a language different from that of the rest of the document. The result of this linguistic policy is the survival of a cluster of documents in a mixture of languages, with the Latin having official status and the Greek provided only for the information of the Greek speaker. Having such documents drafted must have imposed a burden on Roman citizens, as will be seen from the complicated nature of some of the mixed-language texts discussed in the next section. They will have been aware that a linguistic demand was being made of them which symbolised the authority that

---

74 See for example Hoffmann (1991: 199–204).
75 See also Stein (1915: 136), Rochette (1997a: 107).

Rome exercised over their lives, and the obligations carried by possession of the citizenship.

The names and status of some legalistic translators in Egypt are, incidentally, known. The will of the soldier C. Longinus Castor was translated into Greek by the νομικός L. Lucius Geminianus:[76] *BGU* 1.326 < ... Γάιος Λούκκιος> Γεμινι[ανὸ]ς νομικὸς Ῥωμαικὸς ἡρμήνευσα τὸ <προκείμενον ἀντίγραφον καί ἐστιν> σύμφωνον τῇ αὐθεντικῇ διαθήκῃ. The last clause, claiming the sympathy of the document to the original, makes it clear that Geminianus had translated from Latin into Greek for the benefit of Castor; but he may also (see below on *P. Oxy.* XXXVIII.2857) have put the spoken (Greek) instructions of Castor into the valid Latin form.

For further details of translators of these and other legal documents see Rochette (1994: 318–20), noting that the νομικός was a functionary of the nome, apparently called Ῥωμαικός because he knew Latin.[77] There is a list of relevant documents at p. 318. The formula κατὰ τὸ δυνατόν[78] shows that translators were alive to the difficulty of producing accurate versions, and perhaps conscious of their shortcomings. Those shortcomings might have been more apparent in the Latin versions than in the Greek, if the translators were native speakers of Greek rather than Latin: one thinks for example of an inadequate document concerning a dowry (see VIII (1)).

The two classic document-types which had to be in Latin were birth certificates and wills. I offer a few comments on each before discussing in detail some mixed-language texts in the next section.

For a list of birth certificates, see Schulz (1942–3: i, 78–80).[79] There was a fundamental importance to birth certificates, namely that they provided evidence of Roman citizenship.[80] Birth certificates thus provide an explicit example of the symbolic use of Latin in matters to do with the citizenship. The documents were written in stereotyped form, no doubt by professional scribes.[81] I single out just one interesting example, the birth certificate of Herennia Gemella (AD 128).[82] The name of Herennia Gemella is added at the end of the second outside page in Greek, in the accusative ΕΡΕΝΝΙΑΝ ΓΕΜΕΛΛΑΝ. This must be the file copy, which for ease of reference had the name written in Greek for the benefit of

---

[76] See Taubenschlag (1951a: 362–3), id. (1951b = 1959: 163), Rochette (1994: 319); on the document, see especially Keenan (1994).

[77] See further Rochette (1997a: 120–2), with extensive bibliography.

[78] See Rochette (1994: 319 n. 27).

[79] See also Stein (1915: 148–9), Rochette (1996a: 160 n. 30), id. (1997a: 112, 115).

[80] See Schulz (1942–3: ii, 63).   [81] See Schulz (1942–3: ii, 60).   [82] See Kelsey (1923).

Greek-speaking clerks. Here is an indication that even those charged with the administration of the system of having birth certificates written in Latin might sometimes have been more accustomed to using Greek.[83] The difficulties imposed by the language requirement are also illustrated by a birth certificate of twins registered by one Sempronia Gemella (see above, I), who went to Alexandria to have a text done,[84] either because she could not find a local scribe to do it, or because there were not enough Roman citizens to hand to witness the document.[85] Wills of Roman citizens had to be in Latin until the time of Alexander Severus.[86] Again the requirement is related to possession of the citizenship, because only Roman citizens had the right to make a Roman will.[87] After the period of Alexander Severus wills of Greeks can be found in Greek, as e.g. *P. Oxy.* VI.907, the will of a certain Hermogenes, dated AD 276. Line 2 reveals that it was dictated in Greek (τόδε τὸ βούλημα Ἑλληνικοῖς γράμμασι κατὰ τὰ συνκεχωρημένα ὑπηγόρευσεν), but the editor points out (p. 248) that it nevertheless shows a close adherence to the old Latin formulae, as illustrated for example in the will of Gaius Longinus Castor (see above). The testator would not have dictated the version preserved, which must have been put into this form by an expert drafter.

For a Latin version of a will, see e.g. *P. Oxy.* LII.3692, on which the editor provides a comprehensive bibliography to such documents. *P. Oxy.* XXXVIII.2857 is the draft of a Roman will dated 17 May 134, with a fragmentary Latin text and a Greek version, which will have been of no legal validity but merely a copy for the Greek-speaking testator. Often it is only the Greek copy that survives, as e.g. at *P. Oxy.* XXII.2348.

The drafting of a Latin will for a Greek speaker in, say, Egypt, will have required various stages. As the editors point out at *P. Oxy.* XXXVIII.2857, the testator must first have dictated his requirements in Greek. The Latin will would then have been drawn up, and a Greek translation done.

IV.6 The citizenship: some mixed-language official documents from Egypt

It was not only wills and birth certificates which had to be in Latin. I consider now some other documents involving Roman citizens in which the

---

[83] Note Kelsey (1923: 191): 'a memorandum added for convenience of reference by someone who was more familiar with Greek than with Latin'.

[84] See Schulz (1942–3), 16 = *P. Mich.* III.169.   [85] See Schulz (1942–3: ii, 60).

[86] See Stein (1915: 142–4), Rochette (1990: 334), id. (1996a: 160), id. (1997a: 115). See also the commentary on *P. Oxy.* LII.3692.

[87] See the discussion of E. Meyer (1990: 78–81).

form of linguistic policy introduced in the previous section can be seen at work.[88]

(1) *P. Oxy.* IX.1201 is a 'succession to an inheritance.' The text is in a mixture of Latin and Greek. It contains an application (dated AD 258) to the prefect Mussius Aemilianus from a man whose father has died intestate, asking for the *agnitio bonorum possessionis* or right of succession to the estate. There are four parts to the document. The first comprises the petition in formulaic Latin, of which only four lines survive:

Mussio Aemiliano u(iro) p(erfectissimo) praef(ecto) Aeg(ypti)
ab Aurelio Heudaemone.
rogo domine des mihi b(onorum) p(ossessionem)
[Catilli]i Variani patris mei..

The second section (in a second hand), which confirms the presentation of the petition, has the name of the petitioner (Eudaemon) in Greek, but written for him by a certain Aurelius Theon because Eudaemon was illiterate. Lines 9–11 are as follows: Αὐρήλιος Θέων Ἁρπάλου ἔγραψα ὑπὲρ αὐτοῦ μὴ ἰδότος γράμματα. (ἔτους) ϛ Θὼθ κζ. It is noteworthy that this, the most personal part of the petition, in that it not only has the signatures but also some information about the petitioner (his illiteracy), has a date of Egyptian type ('in the sixth year, Thoth 27') but no Roman date. The petitioner and his assistant were clearly Greek speakers and used to the Egyptian dating system.

The third section (three words only) is the endorsement by the prefect in Latin granting the petition: *ex edicto: legi.* It was standard practice for the Roman official to put his notation in Latin rather than in Greek or in both languages, even though the milieu was Greek and the participants Greek-speaking. So it is that at *ChLA* 3.201, a fragment of a petition addressed by a veteran Aelius Syrion to Aurelius Sanctus, prefect of Egypt, the notation *recognoui* is found after the Greek translation of the prefect's reply (line 36). The editor (*ChLA*) collects other examples of *recognoui*, and observes (p. 73): 'In the light of these parallels, *recognoui* is a visa giving authenticity to a text: here it affirms the authenticity of the Greek translation of the Prefect's reply, which must have been in Latin.'[89] The endorsement of a petition was a formal bureaucratic act, and there seems to have been a convention whereby the official used Latin for this purpose. It might alternatively be suggested that, if the

[88] See also Stein (1915: 142–7), Bagnall (1993: 234 n. 16), and for a comprehensive collection of material, Rochette (1997a: 109–14).
[89] For bibliography on *recognoui*, see the editor's note on line 25.

extant versions of the documents were purely archival, then the prefect's notation would not have been for the eyes of anyone but the prefect's officials, in which case it could not be interpreted as evidence for any sort of (public) language policy. There is however extant at least one document, though not from Egypt (a text from the archive of Babatha, already mentioned at 2.vii.5) in which the Roman official's notation was on the version of the text displayed in public (in an area where Latin was scarcely spoken). I return briefly to this document below (2).

I return to *P. Oxy.* ix.1201. There follows finally the translation into Greek (ἑρμηνεία τῶν ʽΡωμαικῶν) of the (largely missing: see above) Latin version of the petition. This significantly contains a Latin-style consular date translated into Greek, as well as an Egyptian date: π[ρ]ὸ η Καλ(ανδῶν) ʼΟκτωβρίω[ν] Τούσκῳ καὶ Βάσσῳ ὑπάτοις (ἔτους) ζ Θώθ κζ. At the end of this section the endorsement *ex edicto: legi* is also trans-lated (21–2 ἐκ τοῦ διατάγματος· ἀνέγνων).

There is evidence here that the date of Latin type was needed in the official petition, even in the Greek version and even if the petitioner was not a Latin speaker and himself used a different dating system (as emerges from the signature: see above).[90] On this interpretation the Latin date was a requirement of the Roman authorities, whereas the juxtaposed Egyptian date in the Greek version can be seen as a form of conces-sion to the petitioner (on Latin dates in documents otherwise in Greek, see 3.vi.2).[91]

A text such as this shows traces of the exercise of a language policy, in that the office of the prefect required that a petition of this type under Roman law should be submitted in Latin, with some Greek as well if the petitioner knew only that language. There is also the Latin notation. The preparation of documentation for Greek-speaking citizens was obviously a complicated matter, its complexity determined by an insistence on the use of Latin on the one hand, and by a willingness to provide Greek translations on the other.

(2) I return now, by way of illustration of some of the remarks made above, to the text from the archive of Babatha (no. 16). It was noted earlier (2.vii.5) that in Babatha's copy (that which is extant) the official's subscription (a receipt, which validated the tax return), though in Greek, is described as a translation (from Latin). The original version (with the official's notation in *Latin*) was displayed in public. Latin was thus used

---

[90] On the significance of Latin dates in Egyptian documents, see also Stein (1915: 155 n. 1).
[91] On Roman dates in Greek papyri, see in general Sijpestein (1979).

publicly as a form of validation even though the area was not Latin-speaking, and that practice in a mild sense represents the deployment of Latin as the language of power.

(3) *P. Oxy.* IV.720 (cf. *ChLA* 4.269) is a request (dated AD 247) in Latin to the prefect Claudius Valerius Firmus by a woman Aurelia Ammonarion that he appoint Aurelius Plutammon as her guardian in accordance with the *Lex Iulia et Titia*.[92] The seven-line request extant, in formulaic but less than assured Latin (note line 2 *ab Aureliae*), concludes with a Latin consular date: *dat(um) do(minis) no(stris) Philippo Aug(usto) ii et Philippo Caesaris [sic] ço(n)s(ulibus)*. The woman then signs in Greek, and the guardian also accedes to the request in Greek, and there then follows a date of Egyptian type in Greek in another hand: (ἔτους) δ Τῦβι ι. The woman was obviously a Greek speaker, and probably literate, as there is no indication that someone else signed for her. The date associated with her signature is in one dating system, whereas that in the formal petition is in the other (Roman) system.[93] This phenomenon was seen above in (1). The prefect then gives his decision in Latin: *quo ne ab[ ] abeat Pl[utammonem] e leg(e) Iul(ia) et [Titia auctorem] do. cepi* (the last word possibly in another hand). It is likely that a Greek copy of the document has been lost. The practice of giving decisions in Latin, either on its own or with a Greek translation appended, has been seen several times in Egypt (see 3.VI.1 on reports of hearings, and below, (5)), as well as in the Republican period at Amphipolis (IV.3).

(4) *P. Oxy.* VIII.1114, of much the same period (237), is a declaration made to a Roman official by M. Aurelius Saras, a citizen of Oxyrhynichus, 'that his wife had died intestate, and that the inheritance, which passed to their two daughters, was of the value of 200,000 sesterces and free from the *vicesima hereditatium* or succession duty of 5 per cent' (p. 192).[94] The declaration, of some fifteen lines in length, is in Latin. It begins with an elaborate date, stating first the names of the consuls and then that the year was the third of the emperors (who are given very full titles). The declaration is supported by an affidavit (called a *testatio* in the Latin), in Greek, which largely matches the Latin declaration in content, if not phraseology. This is witnessed in Greek in several hands, confirming the fact of intestate death. In the affidavit (16) the date is given by regnal year (ἔτους τρίτου Αὐτοκράτορος Καίσαρος etc.), in conformity with part of

---

[92] See also Stein (1915: 150–1).
[93] Note the uncertainties in the consular date quoted, which has a genitive (*Caesaris*), perhaps under Greek influence.
[94] See Stein (1915: 146).

the date in the Latin portion, with an Egyptian month ('Ἐπεὶφ ιβ) to which there is nothing corresponding in the Latin declaration. There is not a consular date in the Greek affidavit. On the other hand at the end of the document the subscription in Latin by a notary of the office concerned with the tax has a thoroughly Roman date, recording the relevant days of the month, the month and consuls: . . . *secundum adfirmationem insertam pr(idie) non(as) Iul(ias) Perpetuo et Corneliano co(n)s(ulibus) notaui pr(idie) id(us) Iul(ias) co(n)s(ulibus) s(upra) s(criptis).*

In this text then the recording of the consuls is tied to the Latin language. Given the association of consular dating with on the one hand official documents to do with the Roman administration and on the other hand the Latin language, it is not surprising that in official texts in Greek (see above, 3.VI.2) there should sometimes have been a switch into Latin when the consular date was noted.

On the evidence of the three Egyptian texts just discussed (and also, it might be said, the document of Babatha), consular dates at this period seem to have been *de rigueur* in those parts of documents concerning Roman citizens or Roman law which were either in Latin or, if in Greek, were translated from the Latin portions (extant or lost) of the same document. In purely Greek parts, or at least in the signature, there seems to have been no such requirement. The declaration which forms the primary part of the document *P. Oxy.* VIII.1114 above is again in Latin. One assumes that, even though the affidavit is in Greek, Saras would have been made aware that there had to be an official version in Latin. The official's subscription is in Latin.

(5) *ChLA* 5.290 (AD 236) (= *P. Mich.* III.165, but with restorations) is a request for a guardian from a woman addressed to the prefect of Egypt. The fragmentary text begins in Latin as follows: *Meuio Honoratiano praef(ecto) [Aeg(ypti) ab Aurelia Diodora rogo domine des mihi] tutorem auctorem e lege I[ulia et Titia . . .].* The restorations are made on the basis of other such requests (*P. Oxy.* IV.720 (above (3)), XII.1466 (below (6))).

In a second hand there is a repetition of the request from Diodora, this time in Greek: Διοδώρα ἐπιδόδωκα [*sic*] τὰ βιβλ[ίδια ταῦτα αἰτουμένη ὅπως ἐπιγραφῇ κύριος] μου Αὐρήλιος Θέων ὁ καὶ Ἀσκληπιὸ[ς . . .] Ἰ[σιδώρ]ου ἔγραψα ὑπὲρ αὐτῆ[ς μὴ εἰδυίης γράμματα . . .]. The person who wrote on behalf of the woman names himself and gives the reason for his part in the transaction (the illiteracy of Diodora). Finally there are Latin fragments of the prefect's decision.

The situation is straightforward. The petitioner was an illiterate Greek speaker who probably did not know Latin. The official request is put in Latin, drafted by a scribal official, probably with a translation into Greek, spoken or written, provided for the petitioner. The petitioner had to sign the document, ideally in his or her own hand, but in the case of an illiterate the signature might be done by a third party, but in the primary language of the petitioner. Thus a change of language takes place in the *subscriptio* if the petitioner was not a Latin speaker. It was acceptable for the signature to be in Greek, but the official text had to be in Latin even if the matter concerned a purely Greek-speaking Roman citizen.

(6) *P. Oxy.* XII.1466 is a type of document closely related to (3) and (5) above, but interestingly whereas *P. Oxy.* IV.720 (3) is the 'original petition, containing the actual signatures of the applicant and her proposed guardian (both in Greek), with the answer made in the office of the praefect and a remark of assent, probably in the praefect's own handwriting' (see on 1466, p. 193), 1466 is not the original document but a largely Greek copy without autograph signatures and with significant divergences from 720. I describe these divergences, because they are testimony to the linguistic situation. The date is 245, and the prefect petitioned is the same as that in (3) above.

The Latin version of the petition, which for official purposes was the essence of the document, is very brief and shows one significant omission: *Valerio Firmo praef(ecto) Aeg(ypti) ab Aurelia Arsinoe. rogo, domine, [des mihi auctorem e lege Iulia et Titia Aurel(ium)] Erminum.* It will be noted that there is no consular date, and yet the Greek version which follows, described at the outset as a translation of the Latin (ἑρμηνεία τῶν ʻΡω[μαικῶν]), has one. The Latin section must therefore be a summary of a longer original. This conclusion can be confirmed from further features of the text (see below). Thus a short Latin version of this part of the text is provided even for the Greek-speaking Roman citizen, a practice rich in symbolism and making an explicit connection between the Roman citizenship and the Latin language.

Appended to the Latin summary there is an Egyptian date ((ἔτους) β Παχὼν κϛ) and a Greek docket (= 'sheet 94, vol. 1'), said by the editor to give the number of the original petition, which had been entered in the prefect's books. It is suggested (note on line 2) that the Egyptian date belongs to the docket rather than to the Latin text. If this is so, we again see the preference of the prefect's bureau for Greek in making their records easily accessible (see above, IV.5, on the birth certificate of Herennia Gemella), a preference which highlights the artificiality of the language policy in operation.

The next six lines are in Greek. Since this section contains no fewer than four elements (first, a translation of the Latin, as noted above, with the addition of a consular date, secondly, a signature in the name of the petitioner, thirdly, a signature by the man who wrote for the illiterate woman, and finally a signature by Aurelius Herminus consenting to be appointed) and yet is in a single hand, it is obvious that the signatures are not the originals. This section too is a copy.

Finally (line 10) in another hand the prefect's decision is given in Greek: εἰ μὴ ἔχεις ἑτέρου κυρίου δίκαιον ὃν ᾳ[ἰτεῖ κύριον (?) δίδωμι]. This section too must be a copy, because the original document would have had the decision in Latin (cf. (3) above; contrast (1), a text in which the prefect's endorsement granting the petition is in Latin with a Greek translation).

This whole document must have been for the benefit of a Greek speaker, presumably the petitioner. Its existence alongside a text such as 720 shows that record keeping operated on different levels, with the two languages having different roles in different circumstances. In the original, official version the Latin framework was clearly of importance, but for less formal (perhaps private) purposes a Greek copy might be drawn up. But even the copy in this case is not without Latin. The editor suggests (p. 193) that this copy was made in the prefect's office.

(7) I mention finally a different type of document. *ChLA* 4.266 (*P. Oxy.* x.1271) is an application to the prefect for permission to leave Egypt (AD 246). I quote the editor of *ChLA*: 'The text consists of 1) a request for permission to "sail beyond the Pharos", deposed in Greek by *Aurelia Maiciana*[95] of Sidè, probably written by a clerk in a special office, 2) the Latin authorisation, in the form of a letter addressed by the prefect to Asclepiade guard of the Pharos, written by an official of the Prefecture and signed by the Prefect himself.' The second hand (that is, the first Latin hand) is read thus: *Valerius Firmus Asclepiade sal[u]tem, dimitti iusi de p[haro]. comendo t[ibi]*; and the third hand which is said to follow (*Vale iu[si]*) is interpreted as that of the prefect. Then in the second hand again there is a two-line Roman calendar and consular date, preceded by *datum*.

The authorisation in Latin is of note, even though the petition was in Greek.

I conclude this section. In certain petitions made under Roman law by Roman citizens in Egypt Latin had to be used in the primary version of the document. There is a linguistic policy in evidence, but it only affects

---

[95] Corrected to Μαρκιανή by Sijpesteijn (1981: 108).

part of the population (Roman citizens), and mainly in matters based on Roman law. The drafting of such documents was done against a complex linguistic background, with Latin-speaking Roman officials, either bilingual themselves or accompanied by bilingual clerks or interpreters, dealing with Greek-speaking Roman citizens on various legal matters. The petitioners were allowed to sign in their own language if they were literate (or have someone do so on their behalf if they were not), and Greek versions of the relevant parts of the documents were provided, but the Latin language was thrust before the petitioner in various ways. Even in the summary document *P. Oxy.* XII.1466 (6) provided in Greek for the Greek-speaking petitioner some Latin is symbolically included. It was undoubtedly made clear to the petitioner that the primary text which validated the transaction was that in Latin (even if for practical purposes the Greek version might have chronological primacy, in the sense, for example, that a Greek-speaking Roman citizen might first have dictated his testamentary requirements in Greek before the validating Latin version was drawn up).[96] The judgment or notation of the Roman official was written in Latin, even if (as in the case of the text from the archive of Babatha) it was for public display in a Greek- or Aramaic-speaking area. There is finally light thrown on the bureaucratic significance of Latin dates to add to that seen in earlier chapters (2.XIV.2, 3.VI.2; see also in the next section A. Bernand (1977), 37).

IV.7 *Some bilingual inscriptions: building inscriptions*

I mention one further category of examples of the use of Latin as a super-high language in a public domain. I refer to building inscriptions set up by Romans in Egypt. These may be in Latin alone, but are often bilingual.[97] Public building may be presented as an act of imperial patronage or munificence, and is often done in the name of emperors or high-ranking officials such as the prefect.

I begin with the symbolic Latin inscriptions on the so-called Vatican obelisk.[98] The obelisk stood in Alexandria until AD 37, when it was removed to Rome. It was not a Roman imitation of an earlier structure, but an Egyptian original, dedicated to the sun by Amenemhat II, son of Sesostris I, at the temple of Aton at Heliopolis.[99] From there it was removed to Alexandria by the Romans, and became one of the first monuments set up there after the Roman annexation. Cornelius Gallus,

---

[96] See the editor's remarks on *P. Oxy.* XXXVIII.2857.   [97] See Stein (1915: 183).
[98] See in particular Iversen (1965), Kayser (1994), 1, 4.   [99] See Kayser (1994: 5 n. 2).

in establishing the Forum Iulium before he became prefect, put a Latin text on it in bronze letters, which were removed when he suffered a *damnatio memoriae* after his suicide in 26 BC. The reconstitution of the text was due to F. Magi, who used the traces of the holes made for attaching the individual letters to the stone to deduce the wording of the Latin. The text (Kayser (1994), 1) runs as follows: *Iussu Imp(eratoris) Caesaris Diui f(ilii) C(aius) Cornelius Cn(aei) f(ilius) Gallus* vac. *praef(ectus) fabr(um) Caesaris Diui f(ilii)* vac. *Forum Iulium fecit* vac. Kayser (1994: 5) aptly comments on the symbolism, thus: 'Bien que le grec reste la langue officielle, le latin est la langue des nouveaux maîtres de l'Égypte, qui vont y instaurer un ordre nouveau. Ce n'est pas un hasard si notre dédicace apparaît sur un monument typiquement égyptien, que l'on a fait venir exprès d'Héliopolis pour l'installer dans la capitale: le pays change de propriétaires.' The choice of Latin is highly significant.

The first inscription was replaced by another, again in Latin (Kayser (1994), 4): *diuo Caesari Diui Iulii f(ilio) Augusto Ti(berio) Caesari Diui Augusti f(ilio) Augusto sacrum.* The dedication in Latin to Augustus and Tiberius in effect appropriates the Egyptian object for Rome. We saw a parallel in the Republic (IV.3), when a column at Delphi intended for Perseus was appropriated by L. Aemilius Paullus and furnished with a symbolic inscription in Latin. It is important to note that Iversen (1965: 152) has argued plausibly (against traditional opinion) that the second inscription above on the obelisk was inscribed under Tiberius, that is *before the obelisk was taken to Rome.* This then is a case of the assertive use of Latin in Egypt and in an Egyptian cultural context.

A bilingual inscription serves a double purpose. The Greek part makes the local population aware of Roman imperial generosity, and the Latin has typical symbolic value. But there are variations in the way in which the languages are combined.

A. Bernand (1977), 37 (= *ILS* 5741) is a bilingual inscription on a granite altar at Mons Claudianus, marking a *fons* (ὕδρευμα). This is only loosely speaking a 'building' inscription, but worthy of inclusion; the *fons* is explicitly associated with the emperor:

right side	fons felicissimus
	Traianus Dacicus
plinth	Ἄμμωνις
left side	῎Υδρευμα εὐτυχέστατον
	Τραιανὸν Δακικόν.
plinth	Κησωνίου

front	An(no) XII Imp(eratore) Nerua Traiano
	Caesare Aug(usto) Germanico
	Dacico
	per Sulpicium Simi(le)m
	praef(ectum) Aeg(ypti)
plinth	Μαλλίτης.

The inscription is not wholly bilingual. The name on the plinth is only in Greek, whereas the consular date and the reference to the prefect of Egypt are only in Latin. It is not clear who is referred to by the Greek name 'Ammonis Mallites son Caesonius' (see A. Bernand (1977: 87) for discussion), but he is possibly either the designer or the craftsman who made the object. This then seems to be a case of a 'signature' which does not match exactly the language of the rest of the inscription (see 3.III.8, n. 87). Cf. *SEG* 44 (1994), 644 = *ILBulg.* 9, a bilingual in the name of a *primipilaris*, where the name Ἀντωνίνου is interpreted as that of the stonemason. The use of Latin for the date in the text above is another reflection of the bureaucratic status of dates, which, as we have seen, sometimes led to code-switching out of Greek into Latin (see 2.XIV.2, 3.VI.2, and above, IV.6). The appearance of Latin alone in the part of the inscription referring both to the emperor and to the prefect of Egypt recalls the use of that language in the texts of prefects at the Colossus of Memnon, and on various bilingual coins and milestones containing the names of emperors, and also the choice of Latin by soldiers in Egypt honouring emperors, a subject to which I will come below (VII.2.4).

Another bilingual building inscription can be found at *IGRRP* 1.1099 (Schedia): *anno VI im[p. Domitiani] Caesar. Aug. Germanic. sub C. Septimio Vegeto praef. Aeg. foditu est flumen Philagrianu at tria soldu usque ad petras.* ἔτους ς΄ Αὐτοκράτ[ορος] Καίσαρος [Δομι]τια[νοῦ] Σεβαστοῦ Γερμανικοῦ ἐπὶ Γαίου Σεπτιμίου Οὐεγέτου ἡγεμόνος ὠρύγη ποταμὸς Φιλαγριανὸς ἐπὶ τὰ γ΄ στερεὰ ἕως τῆς πέτρας. A curiosity is *petras* / πέτρας, which is accusative plural in the Latin but genitive singular in the Greek. A mistake has been made either in the Greek or the Latin, determined by the identity of form of the Greek genitive singular and the Latin accusative plural. One of the versions must have had chronological primacy; when the translation into the other language was done, the translator failed to adjust the case of *petras*/πέτρας, and retained the graphic form of the ending used in the first version. The ineptitude is suggestive of poor control of one of the languages, and it illustrates the problems which had to be faced by those who required that certain types of inscriptions should be bilingual.[100]

There is a bilingual dedication by the prefect P. Rubrius Barbarus of an obelisk at the Caesareum (Kayser (1994), 2): (ἔτους) ιη´ Καίσαρ[ο]ς Βάρβαρος ἀνέθηκε, ἀρχιτεκτονοῦντος Ποντίου. *a[n]no XVIII Caesaris Barbarus praef(ectus) Aegypti posuit, archetectante Pontio.* The Caesareum at Alexandria was a temple consecrated to Augustus, but as well 'c'était un véritable complexe culturel et administratif, comprenant aussi des portiques, des bibliothèques, des esplanades' (Kayser (1994: 11)).[101] This then was an important monument associated with Roman domination in Egypt, and the Latin has symbolic force, though Greek is also present. The editor (p. 11) notes the peculiar feature that the Greek text comes before the Latin (on the potential significance of the ordering of the versions of bilingual inscriptions, see Levick (1995: 398), and above, 2.IV.2 (1)).[102] It is worth noting that the title of the prefect is given only in the Latin version. That was also the case in the trilingual of Gallus (see the appendix to this chapter).

Kayser (1994), 3 is another bilingual, on a column commemorating the construction of a canal, the *flumen Sebaston.* Here the Latin comes first, and is in larger letters than the Greek.[103] No. 3 bis (on a plaque) is a copy of 3. The genitive ending (-αι) of the *cognomen* in the Greek of 3 bis may also be Latinate (ἐπὶ ἐπάρχου τῆς Αἰγύπτου Γαίου Ἰουλίου Ἀκύλαι), since Ἀκύλα or Ἀκύλου would have been expected (3 has the correct form in -α).[104] Either there is a parasitic iota or the genitive is a transliteration of the Latin genitive form.

I return briefly to purely Latin building inscriptions.[105] Kayser (1994) prints as 104 the following inscription (a dedication of the restoration of a fort), the syntax of which he regularises without justification (= *CIL* III.12048). I give here the text as it is written on the stone: *Imp(eratoris) Caesaris M(arci) Aureli Antonini Aug(usti) praesidium uetustate dilapsum renouauit*

---

[100] Or (to put it another way), on the assumption that primacy belongs to the Greek version, the text shows the difficulty of enforcing a policy that building inscriptions should have a Latin version.

[101] In the same year the same prefect dedicated a temple to Augustus at Philae, in Greek (*IGPhilae* II.140). At traditional Egyptian religious sites Latin was generally not foisted on the Egyptians, as we will see. At Alexandria the Romans seem to have been keener to make their presence felt linguistically.

[102] Kayser cites Stein (1915: 183) on the normal practice of putting the Latin before the Greek.

[103] See Kayser (1994: 13).   [104] See Kayser (1994: 16 n. 1).

[105] I have not exhausted the bilinguals, but merely illustrated the type. See further (e.g.) *ILS* 8908 (Thebes).

sub C(aium) Caluisium Statianum praef(ectum) Aeg(ypti), per Valerium Maximum (centurionem) leg(ionis) II Tr(aianae) Fort(is), VII Kal(endas) Nou(embres), Flacco et Gallo cos. (vac.) anno XV. Curiously, the name of the emperor is in the genitive (changed throughout to the ablative by Kayser). There can be no doubt that the construction is that found in Greek, whereby in a dating by regnal year the name of the Caesar is in the genitive either dependent on ἔτους, or juxtaposed with a number for the year of his reign, with ἔτους understood. Two of the bilingual inscriptions discussed above show the same pattern (adopted in the Latin version as well as the Greek), and it would be easy to cite further examples from Greek: e.g. É. Bernand (1969), 139 (ἔτους) ιη΄ Καίσαρος; see also 139, 142 ((ἔτους) κγ΄ Καίσαρος . . . ἐπὶ Νείλου στρατηγοῦ) (note here the combination of the genitive expression and that with ἐπί), 151, 152, 153 etc. That the writer of the Latin inscription above had the Greek construction in mind is confirmed by the final *anno XV.* In this case *anno XV* comes at the end, where it can be taken as governing the initial genitive. Was it perhaps omitted in error at the start, and put in as an afterthought?

The inscription is interesting for two reasons. It again shows the choice of Latin in a building inscription. Secondly, quite apart from the inept opening genitive construction, there are signs that the writer was struggling with Latin. *Renouauit* (which Kayser changes to *renoua(tum est)*) does not have a subject. *Vetustate dilapsum* was a formula, but the writer has not succeeded in putting the main verb in the passive. The subject may perhaps be understood as the emperor. The use of *sub* with the accusative is also non-classical, but it could be explained from within Latin as a sub-standard use of accusative for ablative with a preposition. The choice of a *sub*-expression in such a context can be paralleled (e.g. Kayser (1994), 102 *missi honesta missione sub M(arco) Sempronio Liberale (vac.) praef(ecto) Aegypti*; see also *IGRRP* I.1099 above), but it probably in origin reflects the influence of the use of ἐπί in Greek. By contrast in Kayser (1994), 3 discussed briefly above (*praefect(o) Aegypti C(aio) Iulio Aquila,* = ἐπὶ ἐπάρχου τῆς Αἰγύπτου Γαίου ᾽Ιουλίου ᾽Ακύλα) the Greek has ἐπί, but the Latin has the old ablatival construction. If the writer of Kayser (1994), 104 was more familiar with Greek, he had made a conscious decision to use his second language, and that decision can only have been determined by the perceived appropriateness of using Latin, with or without Greek, in such public building inscriptions.

The Roman authorities were proud of their building works, and for that reason tended to use Greek as well as Latin for the benefit of local readers. But Latin seems to have been the necessary component of such inscriptions, and sometimes no Greek version was provided. The Latin versions from time to time have ineptitudes.

V ACCOMMODATION: INTRODUCTION

I turn now from power to accommodation. By this term (see further above, III with cross references) I refer to the attempt by a speaker to accommodate his language use in some way to that of his addressee. Fasold (1984: 188) notes that normally 'accommodation takes the form of *convergence*, in which a speaker will choose a language or language variety that seems to suit the needs of the person being spoken to.' But accommodation may be of various types. At its most blatant it is characterised by Fasold's 'convergence', as for example when the speaker chooses the language of the addressee because he is aware that that is the only language which he would understand. More interestingly, the speaker may make subtle modifications to his mother tongue for the sake of the addressee, switching, for example, sporadically into the addressee's language, or even modifying a syntactic pattern of his own language to match a syntactic pattern of the addressee's (see e.g. 3.IV.1, 6.V.1, p. 672). I am not concerned here with subtle modifications, but with language choice itself as a form of accommodation.

If a speaker chooses to use the addressee's language, the accommodation can often be interpreted as polite or deferential (see above, III). There was a long history of Romans making such accommodation to Greek. When Cicero addressed the senate in Syracuse in Greek (*Verr.* 4.147)[106] he was on one level making a display of his own linguistic abilities, but on another was showing deference (particularly in the light of those incidents in which prominent Romans in Greece had publicly addressed Greeks in Latin) which might even be seen by fellow Romans as demeaning; and so it was that he came under attack from Verres' predecessor in Sicily, L. Caecilius Metellus, for having committed something that was more than an *indignum facinus* (for the passage, see above, 1.III). A classic case of such accommodation occurred after the battle of Actium when Augustus addressed the Alexandrians in Greek so that they would understand him (D.C. 51.16.4, and above, 1.III).

Accommodation may on the other hand be characterised not so much by deference or politeness, as by condescension, and condescension is

---

[106] See Kaimio (1979a: 112–13), Gruen (1993: 240–1).

as effective a way of dominating an exchange as is the aggressive use of a language incomprehensible to the addressee (on accommodation as disparagement, see above, 3.IV.I). We have already witnessed this phenomenon several times (see IV.3 on Cato at Athens, and the tale in Apuleius), and further evidence is not difficult to find. For example, after the surrender of Macedon to Rome in 168 BC the defeated Macedonian ruler, Perseus, was promised clemency, in Greek, by the victor L. Aemilius Paullus (Livy 45.7.4–8.8, Val. Max. 5.1.8). I quote Gruen's interpretation (1993: 245) of the event: 'The conversation, of course, was conducted in Greek, in a show both of magnanimity and of cultivation on Paullus' part. Having completed the discourse, Paullus then turned to his own staff and summarized in Latin the gist of the interview... The *imperator* had, therefore, not only reminded the deposed Macedonian of Roman cultural and political superiority, he also engaged in a bit of cultural snobbery toward his own subordinates.' Or, to put it in the terminology of the present chapter, he accommodated his language choice to both parties, in a double act of condescension. The dividing line between accommodation based on genuine deference or politeness, and that based on condescension, is a fine one, and different observers may well put different interpretations on the same act.[107]

V.1 Accommodation in the religious sphere

One sphere in which (deferential) accommodation by Romans is commonplace in Greek areas is the religious.[108] For example, Romans visiting Delos regularly made religious dedications to local divinities in Greek,

[107] Several of the incidents discussed by Gruen (1993), chapter 6, could be interpreted in terms of accommodation theory, though Gruen does not use such terminology.

[108] However, one Greek site at which linguistic accommodation by the Romans was not invariable is Samothrace. In the *theoroi* lists at Samothrace as published by Fraser (1960) Latin and Greek appear almost equally, with twenty-two Greek texts and nineteen Latin, some of the Latin texts being among the earliest extant at the site (see Fraser (1960: 74). Moreover the *lex sacra* (Fraser (1960), 63) is, perhaps uniquely for the Greek world, bilingual (*deorum sacra qui non acceperunt non intrant.* ἀμύητον μὴ εἰσιέναι) (Fraser (1960: 17)). Fraser observes (loc. cit.) that this implies that the proconsular Romans and their staffs were assumed not to be Greek-speaking. To look at it another way, the accommodation is made by Greeks rather than Romans, in contrast for example with the practice in religious dedications at Delos. There seems to have been something special about the cult of Samothrace in Roman eyes. Fraser (1960: 15–16) suggests that it might have been important to Romans because of versions of the Aeneas legend which associated the hero with Rome and Samothrace. It might accordingly have been felt that Romans should assert their identity by the use of the Latin language, much as they did at the Colossus of Memnon, which also had connections with the Trojan legend. On this view it could not be deduced that the choice of Latin implies ignorance of Greek.

in deference to the local convention (on accommodation in religious dedications at Delos, see further below, 6.v.1, pp. 675–6).[109] Sometimes such accommodation was made by Romans of high rank. P. Scipio Africanus left a dedication in Greek at Delphi,[110] and T. Quinctius Flamininus dedicated spoils at Delphi, to which he 'attached Greek verses of his own composition'.[111]

In Egypt religious dedications by Roman soldiers are often in Greek, as we will see below when the major pilgrimage sites are discussed. There are also, as we saw (1.1) a few inscriptions in hieroglyphics which present emperors as making offerings to Egyptian deities. Here by way of introduction I present some miscellaneous Egyptian evidence of linguistic deference in the religious sphere, before moving on to the pilgrimage sites.

A. Bernand (1977), 22, is a dedication at Mons Porphyrites by a centurion Fanius Severus of an altar to Isis of the ten thousand names, in Greek. A. Bernand (1977), 51 is a long dedication in Greek of a sanctuary to Pan in the Wâdi Semna by a tribune Poplius Iuventius Rufus of the *legio III Cyrenaica*, who was also ἔπαρχος of Berenice. A. Bernand (1989), 195 is a dedication in Greek to Sarapis made by a woman Julia on her own behalf and that of her husband Antonius Serenus, a centurion of the *leg. II Traiana Fortis*. É. Bernand (1988), 3 is a dedication in Greek of an altar by a centurion T. Egnatius Tiberianus of the *leg. III Cyrenaica* to Zeus, ὑπὲρ σωτηρίας [καὶ] νείκης of Domitian. Similarly in the same collection no. 19 is a dedication (of a statue) in Greek to Ammon by a commander of the Alexandrian fleet. Note too no. 20: Διὶ Ἡλίῳ μεγάλ[ῳ] Σαράπιδι. Κούρουιος Ροῦφος (ἑκατόνταρχος) λεγεῶνος κβ΄, and see the next paragraph below. The legion is the *leg. XXII Deiotariana*. A. Bernand (1984), 80 is a Greek dedication to Zeus Helios by a soldier: Διὶ Ἡλίῳ θεῷ μεγίστῳ Ἀντώνιος Ἡρακλιανὸς δουπλικιαίριος ἴλης Οὐοκοντίων ἐποίησεν εὐσεβείας χάριν ἐπ' ἀγαθῷ...; and no. 85 is a dedication to the god Hierabolos by a *uexillarius* of the Palmyrene archers. The god is Palmyrene, and it is natural that Greek should have been used by soldiers of Palmyrene origin. At É. Bernand (1975), 99 a Roman citizen (with the *tria nomina*) uses Greek to dedicate an altar to a local god.

---

[109] It is of note that in the inscriptions of the eastern Balkans found between the rivers Oescus and Jatrus Greek predominates in religious dedications, whereas Latin is preferred in funerary inscriptions (see Gerov (1980: 245)). Exactly the same pattern is found in Egypt, as we will see (see below, VII.2.5 on epitaphs). An epitaph was a type of text in which those claiming to be 'Roman' in some sense might hope to fossilise that identity for posterity by the use of the Latin language, whereas religious devotion inspired subservience to local conventions.

[110] See Gruen (1993: 243).   [111] See Gruen (1993: 244); Plut. *Flam.* 12.6–7.

É. Bernand (1981), 124 is a dedication of a sanctuary to Ammon by a veteran (C. Valerius Cottus) of the third Cyrenaic legion. Greek is used. Following the inscription is [Νί]κανδρος ἔγραψε, a rare indication that the writer of the inscription was different from the dedicator (cf. Ruppel (1930), Gr 28, quoted below, v.5, and above, I.VIII). Kayser (1994), 32 is a dedication of a statue in Greek to Isis, by a former prefect of the *Cohors I Flauia*, now a εὐθηνιάρχης.

Only occasionally do we find soldiers or other Romans making religious dedications in Latin in Egypt. At exactly the same spot[112] as the Greek dedication no. 20 in É. Bernand (1988), quoted above, a centurion from the same legion left a Latin dedication to the same deity, Sarapis: 21 *Sarapi C(aius) Rammius Cypronianus (centurio) leg(ionis) XXII Deiot(arianae) u(otum) s(oluit)*. This is at least evidence for bilingualism in the centurionate: officers in the same legion were indifferently using Greek and Latin for the same purpose. Or again no. 93 in A. Bernand (1984) is a dedication to Jupiter Optimus Maximus (*ceterisque diis*) in Latin, by P. Aelius Aemilianus, *speculator legionis secundae Traianae Fortis*, at Coptos. The Roman character of the deity was no doubt the determinant in this case.

On the face of it these inscriptions of religious type display Roman soldiers using Greek because they perceived it as appropriate to the setting, though the last but one (Latin) text gives us pause. Since two officers from the same legion left inscriptions to the same god in the same place, but one in Greek and the other in Latin, it is possible that their linguistic preferences or competences were at issue. The frequency of Greek in such inscriptions makes it likely that a deliberate choice of that language was often made, but to confirm this likelihood we really need evidence in such cases that *some writers had the competence to use the other language if they had chosen to do so*. Evidence of this type will be discussed below in the account of various tourist and pilgrimage sites (see especially v.2–7).

v.2 *Pilgrimage and tourist sites*

There are some differences in the place of Latin *vis-à-vis* Greek at the great Egyptian sites such as Dakka, Kalabcha, Philae, the Syringes of Thebes and the Colossus of Memnon. Tourists had a habit of recording their visit or making a *proskynema* in formulaic terms, much the same formulae tending to be used in both languages. Many of the visitors were in the Roman army, and they often gave details of their rank and

---

[112] See É. Bernand (1988: 35).

unit. But whereas at the Colossus of Memnon there is a substantial amount of Latin, as we saw, at some of the other places Latin is almost non-existent. Not only that, but some of those Romans (I use the word loosely of members of the Roman army and Roman citizens, whatever their provenance) using Greek at places other than the Colossus *reveal by tell-tale signs that they would have been competent to use Latin instead, or indeed more competent to do so.* Their language choice can therefore be put down to deliberate decision. Accommodation is the norm, with the Colossus a case apart for the reasons which we have discussed. In the following sections (v.3–7) I discuss a variety of mainly tourist or pilgrimage sites, attempting to support my contention that those using Greek could in some cases also have used Latin if they had wished to do so.

V.3 Kalabcha (Talmis, the temple of Mandulis)

Kalabcha was a Roman garrison town south of the first cataract deep in Nubia, and the seat of the god Mandulis (Mandaules), this being the hellenised name of Merul or Melul. Under one of the Ptolemies a temple was created to Mandulis, but it was under Augustus that there began the construction of the great temple, which was finished under Vespasian.[113]

Nock (1934: 53–4) suggests that 'Ptolemaic and Roman interest in the temple may have been due to a political purpose, the desire to make it a place at which the nomads would come to worship together with the peaceful subjects of the Empire.' He points out that in any case 'there was no Egyptian settlement at Talmis in Roman times; there are very few Demotic graffiti'. Frankfurter (1998: 108) takes a similar view, stressing that the temple originated 'as an attempt on the part of Ptolemy Philadelphus and then Augustus to establish common holy sites for the military and the nomadic tribes they were supposed to control, since Mandulis was himself a nomadic god and his establishment at Talmis an act of deliberate priestly syncretism.'

The temple 'attracted considerable attention, being new and magnificent and remote. The soldiers quartered there and men who came from a distance . . . made numerous acts of veneration, *proskynemata*, on behalf of themselves and of those near and dear to them, sometimes of their horses and commonly of "whosoever reads this"' (Nock (1934: 54)).

---

[113] See Nock (1934: 53). To be more precise, the northern half of the temple was dedicated to Mandulis, whereas the southern half was dedicated to Osiris and Isis (see Winter (1977: 69)).

The great majority of the inscriptions found here (for which see Gauthier (1911)) are in Greek not Latin (on the rarity of Demotic graffiti, see Nock's remark, quoted above), even though many Roman soldiers left *proskynemata*. There is a selection of the Greek inscriptions in *IGRRP* 1.1331–56; all of these are by Roman soldiers. *Proskynemata* by Roman soldiers are to be found all over Greco-Roman Egypt, almost invariably in Greek; I know of just one certain case in Latin (see below, VI.5, on Dakka). The *proskynema* is a prayer to a specific local deity or more generally τοῖς ἐνθάδε θεοῖς on behalf of someone, or more vaguely an act of adoration with its nature unspecified. Such *proskynemata* were often offered up in letters on behalf of the addressee (see e.g. the archive of Dioscorus at *O.Claud.* II. 224–42), but they are also commonly found in inscriptions, in formulaic language.[114]

Latin fragments can be found at Kalabcha as published by Gauthier, pp. 184, 194, 265, 282. There is also a Latin hymn to Apollo (with whom Mandulis was equated) (*CLE* 271). Latin was not banned, but it was very rare (so Gauthier (1911:184)).

The most remarkable Greek inscription is the so-called 'vision of Maximus', done in the name of a decurion in the Roman army.[115] This is a long poem in Sotadeans, pentameters and hexameters at the south portico, where there are other inscriptions expressing personal devotion to the god.[116] The poem is an acrostic which spells out the name and rank of the man (Μάξιμος δεκουρίων ἔγραψα). Nock (1934: 60) describes the content in these terms: 'Maximus came to this blessed place of quiet with a clear conscience, free from all guilt, and was seized with an inspiration to compose. He fell asleep and dreamed that he was washing in the waters of Nile and that Calliope was singing among the Muses. Then the real impulse to write in Greek free from barbarism came to him from Mandulis, who strode forth from Olympus on the right of Isis . . . His praises follow, in a semicreedal style.' There is a suggestion that Maximus was not a native speaker of Greek, and a strangeness has been detected in the style.[117] Whether he received help is not known. Nock (1934: 61) points out that to carry out the act of piety 'in a difficult style was . . . a mark of divine help.'

---

[114] On *proskynemata*, see in general Geraci (1971), and for discussion of those in letters at Mons Claudianus, see A. Bülow-Jacobsen in *O. Claud.* vol. II, pp. 65–8.

[115] The text may be found as no. 168 in É. Bernand (1969), along with a long discussion (pp. 591–610).

[116] See Nock (1934: 59).

[117] Note É. Bernand (1969: 598): 'Maximus manie assez mal le grec et le parle comme un étranger hellénisé.' See also the note on line 24 (606–7).

Roman soldiers often identify themselves in detail, giving their rank and unit in Greek, e.g. *IGRRP* 1334 τὸ προσκύνημα Μάρκου Ἀντωνείου Οὐάλεντος ἱππέος σπείρης αʹ Θηβαίων ἱππικῆς (the *cohors I Thebaeorum equitata*). Of particular interest for our purposes is *IGRRP* 1339 τὸ προσκύνημ[α] Γαίου Ἰουλίου Ἀμινα[ί]ου καὶ Λουκίου Λογγίνου Φιλώτας στρατιωτῶν σπείρης γʹ **Ιτουραιωρουμ**.[118] Here the writer has switched languages in the final word and used a Latin genitive plural inflection. Another inscription in the name of one of the same men has the same feature: 1340 ἐπʼ ἀγαθῷ τὸ προσκύνημα Γαίου Ἰουλείου Ἀμμειναίου στρατιότου σπείρης τρίτης **Ειτουρεορου** (note here the Latinate omission of the final -*m*, and what might also be a Latinate o for ω in the inflection). The word was readily inflected as Greek: contrast e.g. 1348 σπείρης βʹʹ Ἰτουραίων. In the second of these texts the writer also used the phonetic spelling ε instead of the digraph. If these alien genitive inflections do not represent unintentional slips into Latin (which would then by definition have been the writer's first language), the writer deliberately code-switched in the official title of his unit, perhaps as a marker of its Romanness, thereby advertising some knowledge of Latin. It is clear that he knew the genitive ending not only in written, but also in spoken form, as the phonetic spellings show.

Some further cases of such code-switching/interference can be found in references to the cohort of Spaniards. At 1347 the name appears in correct Greek form: [σπείρη]ς Ἰσπανῶ[ν]. But note the following two examples: 1345 σπείρης **Σπανώρων**, 1346 χώρτης **Ισπανωρουμ** τύρμα Φλώρου. In the first the name is not pure Greek but a hybrid form, conflating -*orum* and -ων (for which see 4.v.3.2). In the second the name is inflected purely as Latin, and the writer also prefers the Latinate χώρτης to σπείρης, and uses τύρμα in what is as likely to be the Latin ablative as the Greek dative (see 3.v.5). The word has a Latinate *upsilon* representing Lat. *u* instead of the usual ου (see below, v.4 for further spellings of this type; cf. εωρυμ = *eorum* at *IGUR* 616, discussed at 1.vii.2.2).

Local priests might have controlled the setting up of inscriptions, and indeed helped in their composition. Nock (1934: 58–9) wonders whether it might not have been 'that a special authorization was necessary for these inscriptions'. But it would be wrong to assume that all such inscriptions were done by the priests themselves.[119] The Latin hymn to

---

[118] For this inscription, see also Gauthier (1911: 264).

[119] For which view see Frankfurter (1998: 109) 'all these inscriptions must have required . . . a priesthood to compose, choose a place for, and inscribe the words'; but contrast the more guarded

Apollo is undoubtedly the composition of a Latin-speaking outsider;[120] and the morphological Latinisms in soldiers' graffiti suggest the work of the soldiers themselves.

It is not difficult to see why Romans would have used Greek at Kalabcha even if their first language was Latin. It was the very alienness of the place that gave it its appeal to pilgrims: note Frankfurter (1998: 108) 'the local distinctiveness of such cults made them no less accessible – and seems indeed to have rendered them increasingly attractive in their peripheral location'. The seeker after 'alien wisdom' would scarcely be moved to put forward aggressively his own identity, but would be more likely to accommodate himself to the prevailing language (or rather the eastern lingua franca in Roman eyes) and forms of expression. The Roman soldier who at a holy site in Nubia recorded his military status in Latin would have been presenting himself as an alien representative of the imperial power, indifferent to the spirituality of the place.

V.4 The Syringes of Thebes

The Syringes were the underground tombs of the Pharaohs in the Valley of Kings. They took their Greek name from the pipe-like character of the underground corridors. There are sixty-one syringes, in ten of which tourists have left graffiti marking their visit in formulaic language,[121] usually near the entrances where there was light to see. The earliest graffiti date from the third century BC, but most are from the Imperial period. Those in Greek and Latin (edited by Baillet (1920–6)) number more than 2,000. Demotic graffiti are extremely rare, as at Kalabcha.[122] Conditions were not ideal for writing, and elaborate literary display or self-advertisement was not an option.[123] The character of the place and its visitors is captured by Casson (1974: 279): ' . . . even as now, tourists liked to go about in company. Families travelled together, as we see from the many instances in which fathers sign for their wives and children as well as themselves. People of like interests travelled together; there are graffiti, for example, left by a group of Neoplatonist philosophers who paid the site a visit *en masse*. Officials went with their entourages: a certain Tatianus, governor of the district of Thebes, left signatures in

statement at 176, in reference to the graffiti on the walls of the temple of Mandulis: ' . . . whether inscribed by priests or the pilgrims themselves'.

[120] See the notes to the text in *CLE* 271, which bring out the writer's knowledge of Virgil and his familiarity with high literary style.

[121] See Bataille (1951b: 350–3).   [122] See Bataille (1951b: 351).

[123] For a good discussion of the Syringes, see Casson (1974: 278–83).

three different places, and nearby are those of at least two secretaries, two assistants, and a friend. Many graffiti include mention of a home town, and these reveal that the fame of the tombs was world-wide ... As we might imagine, the tourists were largely from society's upper crust, people who had time and money for travel. No royalty ever took the trouble to see the tombs, but at least six governors of Egypt did, quite a few district governors, and the inevitable ubiquitous army officers. For intellectuals the 'pipes' seem to have had even more appeal than Memnon: calling cards were left by judges, lawyers, poets, prose writers, public speakers, professors, doctors (no less than twenty-eight of these), and philosophers of various persuasions.'

This then was a very different pilgrimage site from the temple at Kalabcha. Though it inspired awe (see below on the formulae), it was without religious significance. It is then understandable that, though Greek heavily predominates, there is no shortage of Latin. It is remarkable how powerful convention was in determining the form even of graffiti, including those of intellectuals who would have been capable of invention. Again and again the same phrases turn up, most usually of the type 'I saw and wondered.' Those writing Latin by and large adopted the same formulae as the Greek, thereby showing the underlying bilingualism of Latin speakers of the upper classes who were able to travel to the Valley of Kings.

Here are some typical Greek formulaic inscriptions: 1071 Μουσῆς εἰστορήσας ἐθαύμασα, 1418 Ἄμμων θεωρήσας ἐθαύμασα, 1678 Κλ(αύδιος) Κομμοδιανός, χειλίαρχος λεγ(εῶνος) β´ Τραιανῆς Ἰσχυρ(ᾶς), πάσας τὰς σύριγγας ἰδών, ἐθαύμασα (with a date of the regnal-year type). So standard were these types of formulae that they could be mocked: 1613 Ἐπιφάνιος ἱστόρησα, οὐδὲν δὲ ἐθαύμασα, εἰ μὴ τὸν λίθον, 1550 Διοσκοράμμων εἶδον τὴν μανίαν κ(αὶ) ἐθαύμασα.

For much the same formulae in Latin, see e.g. 1408 *Mauricius u(ir) c(larissimus) dux uidi et miratus sum* , 1423 ... *adis, uidi et miratus su[m]*, 1448 *[M.] Vlpius Antiochianus Pulcher, domo Hermesa, tribunus mil(itum) leg(ionis) VII Gem(inae) Fel(icis) et III Aug(ustae) inspexi. Aproniano et Paullo II (iterum) co(nsulibus), pr(idie) idus Nouembres, feliciter, cum Epicteto actori* (AD 168), 1504 *Ianuarius p(rimi)p(ilaris) uidi et miraui locum* (for *inspexi et miraui* (sic) in a fragmentary inscription, see 1827b). Januarius the centurion left various inscriptions, all of them with the same solecism (the active use of *miror*) (cf. 1585, 1620). His fullest inscription is 468 *Ianuarius p(rimi)p(ilaris) uidi et miraui locu(m) cum filia mea Ianuarina. ualete omnes*. Further Latin graffiti are: 1540 *Celer miratus* (?),1822b obscure beginning, but with the formula *inspexi et sum mirat[u]s*, 1835 obscure, but with *uidi*, 469 (name Vitalianus only),

697 (inscription of Marcellus), 719 (Marcellus again), 978 (*M[arc]us Laetus hic fuit*), 983 (fragmentary). For a bilingual, see 1830 Σα[τ]ο[ρ]νῖνος ἱστόρησα – *Saturninus uidi*.

Language choice was flexible. Latin speakers could if they wished use Latin, but there is nevertheless some evidence for Latin-speaking visitors accommodating their language choice to the character of the area. For example, the writer of the graffito 1695 (Εὐτρόπιος Ῥωμᾶος) not only called himself a Roman, but according to the editor he mixed the Greek and Latin alphabets, and used a Latin R. This is not the only evidence for Latin speakers choosing to use Greek, without complete success. At 642 there is a signature Πρόκιλλυς. The editor notes the Latin ending; it is suggested that the name might rather have been *Proximus*, but the ending does not appear to be problematic. Another Latinate nominative ending seems to be found at 1393, Κασᾶνυς ἱστόρησα, if the name is intended to be *Cassianus*. *i* is often omitted in hiatus, as a reflection of the syllabic reduction effected by palatalisation. *Upsilon* is several times found in words or names of Latin origin where the correct Greek or transliterated form should have had ου rendering the Latin *u*: e.g. 1410 Ὑλπίου, 278 Ποστυμίου (significantly in a *proskynema*), 865 Σευῆρος (where *upsilon*, like Lat. *u*, represents a semi-vowel), 1421 Καλπύρνιος Παῦλος ἀφίκομ[αι] (contrast the 'correct' [Κ]α(λ)πτου(ρ)νία at 1923).[124] A striking example of a Latinate spelling is in the signature Ηορτήσιος ἥ[κω] at 846. Here the possessor of a Latin name writes it in Greek form, but with an H at the beginning (and with a Latinate omission of the nasal before *s*). Another man with a Latin name writes (734) Μάρκος Πόρκιος Μάρκελλος Ηιστόρησεν, starting the verb with a Latin H (see below, VII.1 on H in certain Greek receipts in *P. Hamb*. 1.39). It is interesting to note that the same man wrote in Latin at 697 and 719; he was therefore explicitly bi-literate, with Latin his language of primary literacy. At 1205 morphological interference from Latin is discernible in a piece of Greek: Ἄπιος σὺν Νεικέρωτε (followed by a date). The second name, Niceros, has been given a Latin ablative ending in a prepositional expression dependent on σύν.[125] Underlying the construction is the Latin use of *cum* + ablative. The writer must have felt that Greek was the appropriate language to register his presence in the syrinx, but it was obviously his second language. Another Latinate feature is the use of the dative to express origin at 743 (Σίμον Ἀλεξανδρείᾳ) in the manner of the Latin ablative (see 4.V.4.1.1).

---

[124] These spellings are discussed briefly by the editor at p. lxxxiv of the introduction to vol. I.
[125] See the editor, vol. I, introduction p. lxxxv.

Various others using Greek one suspects of being Romans or Latin speakers (1412, 1421, 1688 (an Italian), 1936 (a Massiliote, probably a trader)). Soldiers, who might one assumes have used Latin (and sometimes did: see above on Januarius) tended to use Greek even when giving themselves something of a military identity by mention of their rank (e.g. 875, 1484, 1662, 1678, 1688, 1733, 1738, 1806, 1942).[126]

I conclude that some of the Latin speakers who visited and left graffiti in the Syringes, including soldiers, showed an inclination to write in Greek, even if it was a struggle for them, apparently fitting in thereby with what they thought appropriate to the place. Soldiers show no persistent attempt to convey a Latin identity. Even prefects seem to have been prepared to use Greek (contrast their practice at the Colossus, above, IV.1):[127] note e.g. 1356 Μάξιμος ἔπαρχος. The writer was possibly C. Vibius Maximus, pref. 103–7.

V.5 Dakka (Pselchis)

Dakka (where there was a temple of Hermes) was another site much visited by Roman soldiers, who left *proskynemata*. Here unusually there is a *proskynema* by a soldier in Latin: Ruppel (1930), Gr 28 *Deo magno Mercurio adorauit ue.xillus leg(ionis) II Traiane Fortis nonas Febr(uari)as anno XI Imp(eratoris) Traian(i) Hadri(ani). scripsit C. Cossutius Nigrinus*. The form is modelled on that of Greek. For *deo magno Mercurio*, see e.g. Gr 20 θεὸν μέγιστον Ἑρμῆ. *adorauit* is equivalent to προσεκύνησε. The dative construction was presumably determined by the usual syntactic format of Latin dedications (with dative of the dedicatee). The few other Latin inscriptions at the site are usually acclamations or funerary (for Latin as the language of soldiers' epitaphs, see VII.2.5), and several of them are not explicitly military: Gr 61 *Val(erio) Max[i]mo feliciter*; Gr 72 *C. Iulius Suauis Q(uinti) f(ilius) dec(urio) coh(ortis) II Itur(aeorum) ann(orum) XXXXII ΛF* (last two letters obscure); Gr 92 *Veratio Proculo feliciter cum Achilleo suo*. There remains an honorific inscription on a statue base in Latin to the emperor by a centurion (Gr 100: see below, VII.2.4).

All other dedications by Roman soldiers are in Greek,[128] and here again, as at Kalabcha, there are occasional signs that the writers were familiar with Latin writing. Some Latin sigla are to be found in Greek

<hr>

[126] For a discussion of soldiers writing in the Syringes, see introduction, pp. xliv–xlvii (most use Greek)

[127] See Casson (1974: 279), quoted above.

[128] See nos. 1, 4, 20, 24, 27, 44, 54, 67, 82, 87, 88, 89, 96.

inscriptions. Note Gr 1 Τίτος Σερούλιος στρα[τιώτη]ς λεγεῶνος **III** Κυρηναικῆς χωρογραφήσας ἐμνήσθη τῶν γονέων παρὰ τῷ κυρίῳ 'Ερμ[ῆ]
vac. κα ἔτος Τιβερίου Καί[σ]αρος Σεβαστῆ Με[σο]ρὴ β΄. Here there is a
Latin numeral in the Greek text (see above, 1.VII.4.1 for the significance
of such numerals). In references to Roman military units in Greek inscriptions Greek ordinal adjectives or symbols are usually used. For a
Roman numeral in a soldier's inscription from Philae, see A. Bernand
(1989), 35, quoted at 1.VII.4.1, with some further parallels. Or again,
in Gr 20 (τὸ προσκύνημα 'Αντωνίου γραμματέος Φιλῶν **7** Καπίτωνος
καὶ προσεκύνησα θεὸν μέγιστον 'Ερμῆ καὶ ἐπόησα τὸ προσκύνημα τῶν
ἐμῶν πάντων καὶ φίλων (regnal date)) the century symbol of Latin
has been used in Greek. For this symbol in a Greek text,[129] see also
A. Bernand (1989), 286 (Elephantine), another *proskynema*, by a centurion Antoninus (τὸ προσκύνημα 'Αντωνίου 7).

The convention at Dakka is clear. *Proskynemata* set up by soldiers are
formulaic and almost invariably in Greek. Yet there are Latinate touches,
albeit slight, in some of the Greek inscriptions which imply that the
writers were *au fait* with at least some aspects of the writing of that
language. It is the religious character of the *proskynemata* that seems to
determine the language choice.

Of the miscellaneous (non-religious) Latin inscriptions listed in the
first paragraph above, I would particularly stress the character of two:
one is a soldier's epitaph (72), and the other (100) a dedication by a soldier
to the emperor. These are two domains which regularly inspired the use
of Latin by soldiers in Egypt, as will be shown below.

V.6 Inscriptions on the route from Coptos to Quseir

I refer here to the collection of inscriptions, most of them *proskynemata*,
put together by A. Bernand (1972). Bernand (15) points out that the
inscriptions are basically of the Imperial period, and he concludes that
the region was not frequented in the Ptolemaic period. It was presumably
the Roman army which opened the area up.

Most of the inscriptions are in Greek; the handful of Latin inscriptions
are usually little more than signatures. Many of the Greek texts are by
Roman soldiers.[130] Some of these have a vague military designation, such
as 'soldier', 'decurion', but in several cases (41, 50, 52, 77, 92, 133) more

---

[129] In Greek texts the usual century symbol is χ with subscript or overwritten ρ. See e.g. A. and
É. Bernand (1960), 51.
[130] See nos. 41, 43, 50, 52, 56, 60a, 60d, 62, 63, 64, 65, 77, 92, 106, 112, 115, 127, 133, 143.

precise details of the man's military position are given. A significant text is 82: TO PRSVNHMA. The first four letters of the noun are Latin (A. Bernand (1972: 148)), and apart from that the word is misspelt. This looks like the effort of a Latin speaker who was moved to fall into line with the local convention of using Greek for such adorations.

In the dedication 106 (Σωκράτης υἱὸς Πρίσκου τὸ προσκύνημα) the *upsilon* of υἱός is Latinate in form (see the editor, p. 179), and the filiation is of the Latin type, though not in word order (see further below, 6.v.1; in this case the presence of υἱός is not necessarily Latin-inspired). There is also υἱός in a filiation at 112.

Another of the Greek inscriptions has an error in every word: 65 τὸ προσκύνεμα Γαίω Παπίρο Κυτιανõ. The editor states that the signatory was undoubtedly a soldier, though the writer does not specify that. He has the *tria nomina*. There is an inconsistency about the errors, which at least suggests lack of fluency in Greek.

V.7 Deir el-Bahari

The sanctuary at Deir el-Bahari (see Bataille (1951a)) was dedicated to Imouthes-Asclepius-Amenothis.[131] The *proskynemata* here are entirely in Greek, and usually by Egyptians,[132] which makes the corpus as a whole of less concern in the present context. The most interesting inscription for our purposes is no. 126, by a Roman soldier, a certain Athenodorus, who described himself as *tesserarius* of the first vexillation and from Coptos. The inscription is in Greek, but again there is a tell-tale sign of his knowledge of Latin. The text is very corrupt, but parts of it are clear. I quote one section: ἦλθον ἀπὼ Κοπτοῦ, ᾿Αθηνοδώρου, τεσσεραρίω πριμα ουεξιλλατειωνε, εἰς τὸ ἱερὸν ᾿Ασκληπιοῦ κα[ὶ] ᾿Αμενώθη. It will be noted that πριμα ουεξιλλατειωνε is a Latin ablative.

V.8 Conclusions

In the pilgrimage and tourist material considered in this chapter the Colossus of Memnon and various other sites (particularly the temple of Mandulis at Kalabcha) stand at opposite extremes. At the first, Latin is prominent but at some others it is virtually non-existent. Yet (e.g.) Kalabcha was visited by Roman soldiers, at least some of whom must have been capable of writing in Latin. Indeed, we have seen bits and pieces of evidence in Greek inscriptions, such as the occasional use of

---

[131] See in particular Frankfurter (1998: 158).
[132] On the Egyptian clientele of the cult, see Frankfurter (1998: 158).

Latin inflections, which suggest that some writers would have been able to use Latin instead of Greek. It is no surprise that soldiers visiting such a revered site at a vast remove from areas which were Latin-speaking should have tried to use the eastern lingua franca; after all, Romans had long been used to doing so in Greek regions. More remarkable than the accommodation at Kalabcha is the assertive use of Latin at the Colossus. An attempt has been made to explain the prominence of Latin there as related to the character of the visitors and perhaps to a deliberate policy. This was a site where high-ranking visitors adopted a self-conscious persona for the benefit of their peers, either as representatives of the imperial, military or local administration (with Latin appropriate to prefects and officers in the Roman army, and Greek to the local Greek administrators), or as members of the cultural élite.

At the nearby Syringes of Thebes many tourists of a more middle-class status left their mark. They fell into brief formulae of the 'I was here' type, using Latin or Greek, but overwhelmingly the latter. There is some good evidence here for the choice of Greek by Latin speakers. The *proskynema* obviously had a strong association in the eyes of Roman soldiers and others with the Greek language. At every one of the sites discussed Latinate features in the Greek are to be detected.

I have suggested that the different linguistic behaviour of pilgrims at Egyptian sites reflects the competing influences of language choice as an act of power, and that as an act of accommodation. If the terminology of diglossia is to be retained, neither Greek nor Latin was treated by the Romans as Low. Both languages were High, but Latin was potentially 'super-high' or 'supreme' in a political sense. Greek retained its status in Roman eyes as the primary language of literary culture, and was also the language of religious observance in the east.

VI FURTHER ASPECTS OF DIGLOSSIA IN EGYPT

VI.1 Mundane practical bilingualism: linguistic competence as a determinant of language choice

It is tempting to assume that there must always be a significance to changes of language in a bilingual community, but that assumption is probably not justifiable. Certainly in military settings in Egypt there is evidence for what might be called a mundane practical or transactional bilingualism. We find certain individuals communicating in both languages under (as far as we can tell) unchanging circumstances on the same everyday topics and even with the same addressees. The letters between Claudius Terentianus and his father Claudius Tiberianus do (it can be argued) display some principles of language selection, but not always (see also below, VI.2). What I here call 'mundane practical bilingualism' is the phenomenon referred to earlier as 'bilingualism without diglossia' (1.3). It was suggested that within closed bilingual groups language variation might take place with no discernible principles of selection, simply as a reflection of the fluent polyglot character of the community. Communication with outsiders, though, might generate a functional distinction between the languages.

Letters on papyrus tend to be highly formulaic, and those of Terentianus, both Greek and Latin, are no exception. There is usually a section containing the opening greetings, and a set of farewells, in which greetings may be sent to named individuals via the addressee. Letter 468 (Latin), contains, as well as four lines of greeting at the start, some twenty lines at the end (46–65) in which greetings are transmitted to others. Yet Terentianus could write to the same person in Greek, expressing and transmitting the same types of greetings (e.g. 476.23–4, 477.39–44, 479.19–21). Another common component of letters are statements referring to the receipt or dispatch of goods or money. At a time when transport and carriage were haphazard, those sending or expecting goods were constantly anxious about their safe arrival. Both the Latin and Greek letters of Terentianus refer to the receipt of goods (Latin: 467.4–6, 468.4–11; Greek: 476.5–9), or request that something be dispatched or brought (Latin: 467.17–23, 468.23–7; Greek: 476.27–9, 477.27–8). There is thus a degree of overlap in the topics of the two sets of letters, sent to the same addressee. There might have been different circumstances lying behind the various letters that we cannot now know, but on the face of it Terentianus used either language indifferently in dealing with everyday practical affairs. Much the same formulae and clichés were current in the two languages, and that no doubt facilitated unmotivated switches of language (on such formulae, see above, I.VII.4.2 (2), (5)). I draw attention also to a syntactic structure which recurs in letters in both languages. One of the letters from Latopolis (?) edited by Sijpesteijn (1973) (no. 6, lines 11–12) runs: ἐρωτῶ σε, τέκνον, τὴν παραθήκην, ἣν δωκά σοι, φυλᾶξε. Note here the use of ἐρωτῶ + imperative, a colloquial paratactic construction also found in a letter (published by Bagnall and Sheridan (1994: 117)) from 'Abu Sha'ar, no. 7, line 3 (ἐρωτῶ σε, ἄδελφε, πέμψον), and at *O. Claud.* II.366.11 (ἐρωτῶ σε πέμσον μοι κρειθήν), a letter by a bilingual discussed below. The corresponding Latin construction, *rogo* + imperative, turns up in Latin letters of military provenance, some of them from Egypt, including the Tiberianus archive (e.g. Terentianus, *P. Mich.* VIII.469.17, *O. Wâdi Fawâkhir* 1 *rogo te, frater, . . . scribe mi*; also *Tab. Vind.* II.343.14–15).[133] The structure is not re-markable, but the exact parallelism between the two languages must have assisted low level communication in bilingual communities. I have also referred elsewhere to the various technical terms shared by the two lan-guages in Egyptian military communities, such as *zeucteria, ydreuma*, and *amaxa* (see 4.V.2.2). I conclude that in military camps in Egypt Greek and Latin shared terms and clichés which made it easy for individuals to select either language indifferently for practical dealings. The two lan-guages had undergone a degree of convergence, in vocabulary, clichés and forms of expression.

The archive of Successus at Mons Claudianus (*O. Claud.* 124–36), like that of Terentianus, also presents an individual operating indifferently in the two languages on practical working matters. Successus proba-bly 'filled a position similar to a quartermaster for Mons Claudianus' (Nielsen (1993: 175)). 'Several of the letters sent to Successus are orders for tools and equipment for the quarries. Others concern empty ἀσκοί and some water-supply to the quarries' (A. Bülow-Jacobsen in Bingen et al. (1992: 111)). The one letter of Successus himself is in Greek (136), but otherwise letters sent to him (generally about goods of one kind or another) are written indifferently in Latin (131, 135) or Greek. Paradoxi-cally persons with Greek names (Athenor, Agathon) write to Successus in Latin, whereas 'people with Latin names like Rusticus, Ponticus, Grata and Domitius wrote to him in Greek' (Bülow-Jacobsen in Bingen et al. (1992: 111)). Those writing to Successus made the assumption that he could understand both languages; it was not then *his* language prefer-ence which determined their choice of language, but presumably their own. Nor does the topic of the letters appear to be a determinant of the language choice.

In the second volume of ostraca from Mons Claudianus there are two letters (366, 367), one in Greek, the other in Latin, from the same man (Teres, curator of Raima). Both have the same addressee (Anius Rogatus). Both deal with the receipt and dispatch of goods and one or two other practical matters. Both are in a similar style: the editor (Hélène Cuvigny) points to such similarities as ταχύτερον in one, *celerius* in the other, and a succession of purpose clauses expressed by ἵνα . . . ἵνα in the one, *ut . . . ut* in the other. She asks why one and the same man used different languages

---

[133] See Adams (1995a: 118).

(p. 207), and suggests that Teres may have used a Greek scribe for 366. The problem with this interpretation is that the word ἐππές = ἱππεύς in that text (line 3) seems to display the influence of Latin *eques*, as the editor herself notes (p. 209). Why would a Greek scribe have admitted Latin interference in his Greek? Possibly Teres wrote the Greek letter himself, his first language being Latin. The editor points out (p. 209) that the author of the Latin letter clearly had Latin as his native language. It is fluent and correct, whereas the Greek is not so well spelt. There remains a lingering doubt whether the authors and addressees are the same in the two letters, because the recipient of the Greek letter is called *Anius duplicarius* (written in Greek) and of the Latin letter *Anius Rogatus*, and the sender of the Greek *Teres curator Raima* (in Greek) and of the Latin *Teres curator*. But it is almost inconceivable that the persons could be different in the two letters. Clearly Teres could use both languages. His language choice was not determined by the linguistic ability of his addressee, since the same person is addressed in both languages, nor by the topic of the letters, since both are similar in content. Was some special, extraneous factor of which we could have no knowledge behind his choice, or did bilinguals in military camps choose their language rather haphazardly if the subject could readily be handled in both (see below)?

I conclude that it is sometimes difficult at the level of everyday practical communication to detect any functional differentiation of Greek and Latin among soldiers and ex-soldiers in Egypt. Language choice might sometimes have been determined by such factors as the linguistic competence of the writer or addressee, the competence of scribes, or the whim of the writer on a particular occasion. Competence is an important, but perhaps neglected, factor in language choice. I quote Gardner-Chloros (1991: 50): 'although [a] society may itself be bilingual, each of the individuals who make up that society is bilingual to a different extent; in any given interaction, the interplay of the various speakers' competences is a very significant factor in the determination of language choice and code-switching. In Alsace, for example, where certain "bilingual" individuals are noticeably more competent in French and others in Alsatian, a conversation might well start in French and then move on to Alsatian when one of the participants has trouble expressing something in French or comes to the conclusion that his interlocutor would rather speak Alsatian.' If, for example, Teres preferred Latin but Rogatus Greek, a conflict might have been set up in Teres between his own preference and the desire to be accommodating towards the addressee, and this might have caused the use of a different language on different occasions.

There is a greater complexity to Terentianus' language choice, and I turn again to that.

VI.2 The archive of Tiberianus and the roles of Greek and Latin

The archive of Tiberianus (*P. Mich.* VIII.467–81) presents the most clearcut evidence of Greek–Latin bilingualism in Egypt. In this correspondence Claudius Terentianus, probably the son of Tiberianus, writes five times to his father in Latin and five times in Greek. Such a situation would be out of the question were father and son not bilingual, but one can only speculate about the circumstances that lay behind the bilingualism.[134] There is now, as we have just seen, a parallel from Mons Claudianus for letters written by the same man to the same addressee in Greek on the one hand and Latin on the other (*O. Claud.* II.366–7). Similarly in the archive of Successus (*O. Claud.* I.124–36) there are letters in both Greek and Latin (see above), and Abinnaeus too received letters in both languages (see IV.2). Was Terentianus perhaps the son of a Latin-speaking immigrant who had settled in Egypt and married a Greek speaker? He is also, it seems, referred to in a Greek letter from Valerius Paulinus *né* Ammonas to one Valerius Apollinarius. Terentianus is the carrier of the letter, and is described as a veteran of some means (line 11).[135] The letter offers a picture of the settlement of veterans in the Egyptian countryside,[136] and at least some of these veterans must, like Terentianus, have been Latin- as well as Greek-speaking.

It calls for comment that the same addressee should be the recipient of private letters from the same person in both languages, particularly in view of the close relationship between them. I here consider various possible explanations.

It might seem plausible to suggest that, because the letters of Terentianus were written for him in the usual manner by scribes (the hand varies from letter to letter), his linguistic choice was determined by the linguistic competence of the scribe: i.e. that he used Latin if the scribe available at the time could only write Latin. But letter 468, as we have seen (I.4), though it is written in a practised Latin hand, is marked by various instances of interference from Greek. The interference goes beyond mere letter shapes. This scribe could have written in Greek, and Terentianus must have selected Latin.

---

[134] See Adams (1977: 86).   [135] See Lewis (1959).
[136] On the phenomenon, see the remarks of Lewis (1959: 143).

On internal evidence the editors (Youtie and Winter) suggest a chronological difference between the Latin and Greek letters, with the Latin
thought to predate the Greek (*P. Mich.* VIII, p. 16). If this is true, it opens
the way for other explanations of Terentianus' language choice. Kaimio
(1979a: 190–1; cf. 158) suggests that, given the chronology of the letters,
Terentianus' language choice might have depended on 'the influence of
the army: a young soldier, still proud of his social position, employs its distinguishing characteristic, the Latin language, especially since the recipient also served in the army. But when the time of discharge approaches,
this is no longer important.'

This explanation has its attractions, but it would be more compelling
if one were able to argue that Terentianus was proud of his *recent* acquisition of Latin (in the army), and desirous of displaying his competence
to his father. It would, however, be unconvincing to argue along these
lines. Terentianus writes not as a learner of Latin, but as a fluent user
of a non-standard variety of the language, in which he is capable, for
example, of a heated and dramatic description of events (letter 471). His
Latinity is in stark contrast to that of various genuine learners (see below,
VII.3, VIII), and his knowledge of the language would on purely linguistic grounds be assumed to go back beyond the time of his enlistment.
Moreover it is definitely *not* the case that the Latin letters were written
while Terentianus was in service but the Greek after he had left the army.
The military background to the whole corpus is clear. Letters 467 and
468, in Latin, allude to Terentianus' service in the fleet and to his hopes
of transfer to a cohort, and also request that pieces of military equipment be sent. But on the other hand in the Greek letter 476 Terentianus
requests a sword sheath (9 θήκην μαχαιρίου), and calls himself a legionary
soldier (33 λε(γιῶνος) στρα(τιώτου)). 477 (in Greek) mentions a riot in
Alexandria in the suppression of which (as a soldier) he was involved (lines
29–30), and 478 refers to his inability to 'pass the camp gate' (line 12).

One must also consider, if only to reject, the possibility that early in
his military career Terentianus did not know Greek fluently. Although
his Latin is not marked by Greek interference (other than interference
of a superficial kind which can be attributed to the scribe rather than
to Terentianus himself), there is a Greek feel to some of the formulaic
language of the Latin letters; various formulaic expressions are translated
from Greek (see the previous section, and the editors, p. 18; also above,
1.VII.4.2), and are likely to be the work of a bilingual. On balance it
seems preferable to assume that Terentianus throughout the period of
his extant letter writing had the choice of using either Greek or Latin.

It is a familiar idea that among bilinguals the *domain* of an interaction may determine the choice of language. For example, the domains family, friendship, religion, employment and education may each tend to generate the use of one language rather than the other;[137] this of course is the notion that underlies a diglossic opposition of the H–L type. On this view however it might seem odd that within the family Terentianus chose to use two different languages. But domain in this sense does not operate in isolation; it may interact with other factors, such as the topic of conversation, the degree of formality or seriousness of the speakers at the time, and the circumstances under which the conversation takes place.[138] It is in theory possible that within a family in which, say, Greek was the language normally used, a topic associated particularly with Latin (e.g. a discussion of a matter of Roman law) might cause a switch, partial or total, into that language.

There is, as we have seen (VI.1), a degree of overlap in the topics of the two sets of letters of Terentianus, but there are also some differences which may be significant. Letter 476, in Greek, deals at length with an unusually personal matter. Terentianus 'seeks to win his father's consent to a plan for bringing a woman into his household. [He] anticipates strong opposition and so redoubles his affirmations of filial obedience' (editors, *P. Mich.* VIII, p. 54). The section runs from lines 9 to 20 (twelve lines of a letter of thirty-one lines (on the recto), i.e. about 39 per cent of the whole). There is no such serious or intimate matter dealt with in such solemn tones anywhere else in the correspondence, Latin or Greek, but particularly Latin. It is a possibility that to Terentianus Greek was the appropriate language for dealing with deep personal concerns, or that it was the more 'formal' language (see below for an expansion of this suggestion). The only protracted passage concerning a single topic in the Latin correspondence is in letter 471, but the tone and subject are of a different order. Terentianus complains in bitter terms that he has been made to obtain money from an unnamed individual. As the editors note (p. 37), '[i]ntimately linked with his difficulties are his mother's accouchement, a quarrel about clothing in which Ptolemaeus plays a part, the subsequent departure of Ptolemaeus for Alexandria as escort for a group of recruits, and Saturninus' indifference to his plight'. The letter communicates a good deal of frustration and anger, and is full of vivid quoted direct speech. If Latin was a language of lower prestige or less formality or with family associations in Terentianus' eyes, then

---

[137] See, for example, Romaine (1995:30).   [138] See in general Hoffmann (1991: 177–80).

it might well have been thought suitable for an embittered account of quarrels. It could not be said that the subject of the letter was a matter that was not of personal concern to Terentianus. But Greek might have imparted an element of formality which, while it was not needed in an account of money problems and quarrels, was suited to an anxious request on a subject which Terentianus was uneasy about speaking of. In these two letters Latin seems to be chosen as a direct form of expression for encompassing aggression and complaint, whereas Greek perhaps conveys a more formal distance (see in another connection 3.III.4).

The two other Latin letters which have been preserved in such a way as to be comprehensible (467, 468) are largely banal and miscellaneous in content. Some of the other Greek letters, however, concern serious issues which are beyond the normal run of things as found in the Latin letters. In letter 477, lines 7–17, Terentianus explains to his father at length 'that difficulties have arisen in connection with the registration of a document and urges him to return to Alexandria. Tiberianus is neglecting his affairs by remaining in the country, and Terentianus is ill in Alexandria' (*P. Mich.* VIII, p. 58). The serious tone adopted here, in Greek, when the issue turns on an important official matter, is repeated in two other Greek letters. In 479.10–15 'Terentianus gives directions for the delivery of a letter from the dioecetes to the strategus through Tabetheus, the sister of Tiberianus' (*P. Mich.* VIII, p. 67). Similarly 480, though fragmentary, clearly has the same serious tone in relation to a complicated business matter. 'Terentianus writes to his father regarding conversations with Aemilius, seemingly a business agent or legal adviser. Difficulties have arisen in connection with a group of chirographs, because these can be registered only through the bureau of the archidikastes. Terentianus has addressed a petition to that official and hopes that the affair will soon be concluded' (*P. Mich.* VIII, p. 69).

It is possible that Latin was the mundane family language of Tiberianus and Terentianus. Letter 471, with its quoted speech (in Latin), is significant in this respect. On the assumption that Tiberianus was a westerner who had married a local woman, Latin would have been his mother tongue. It is particularly noticeable that when Terentianus deals with a matter of an official or administrative kind involving in some cases the bureaucracy of the Egyptian state, he uses Greek. As we have seen (see IV.1), Greek was the language regularly used in administration by officials of the type referred to in Greek in letters 479 and 480 (see the previous paragraph), and Terentianus perhaps adopts that language under the the influence of the bureaucratic status of Greek in Egypt in all domains below the highest affairs of the Roman state. There would seem to be a diglossic relationship between Greek and Latin in the correspondence, with a significant element of overlap, but Greek preferred for bureaucratic subject matter concerning the local civilian administration. If so, Terentianus' strategy of using Greek when making the request to introduce a woman into his house falls into place. Instead of using the mundane family language, he erects a barrier of formality between Tiberianus and himself, and converts the request into a semi-official one.

If Terentianus had been a Greek recruited into the Roman army who had learnt Latin only after his recruitment, the diglossic relationship which he set up between the two languages could well have been reversed. Latin might have seemed the formal language of (military) administration, Greek the more banal language of the family. So it is that some Greeks at Rome, as we saw, treated Latin as the bureaucratic language, and Greek as that of the family (see 3.VIII).

VI.3 *Conclusion: diglossia in Egypt*

In sections V–VI I have considered whether there was a diglossic relationship between Greek and Latin in Egypt by examining on the one hand language choice as a display of power, and on the other language choice as a form of accommodation. It is the accommodation of Romans that is most striking in Egypt. Greek was used not only in the local administration, but also in most internal affairs by the prefect. In court hearings advocates and indeed the presiding officials spoke Greek. And at pilgrimage sites, with the exception of the Colossus of Memnon, Roman visitors tended to use Greek. On this evidence it might be said that Greek was considered appropriate to the domains of civil administration, the courts, local religion, and also (at the Colossus) high poetry, all of which were prestigious. If Ferguson's H–L model were to be applied to Egypt, it would be obligatory on this material to classify Greek as H. But where would that leave Latin? Certainly it could not be classified as L. On the contrary, I have argued that Latin was available as a potentially super-high language, to be used occasionally to assert the Romanness of the imperial power controlling Egypt. In the courts, though speeches were in Greek, there was an increasing tendency for the presiding official to use Latin. Latin was also imposed in legalistic documents relating to the Roman citizenship, a policy which had the effect of defining the Latin language as a component of being Roman. And at the Colossus of

Memnon Latin was used to symbolise the military and political power of Rome, whereas Greek was treated as a poetic language and as the language of local administration. The contrast between the language choice of *strategoi* at the Colossus and that of prefects well expresses what I mean by the super-high character of Latin. The highest official uses Latin, his subordinates Greek.

All of the domains mentioned in this section so far could be described as public. But not all language use is public. What was the relationship between Greek and Latin in more private settings?

If we can make the assumption that there is a significance of the type suggested in the previous section to Terentianus' language choice, then it can be seen that within a single society the relationship between two languages may vary according to circumstances and to the backgrounds and motivations of the speakers/writers.

To educated Roman outsiders to Egypt Greek was potentially a language of prestige, associated for example with literature. Latin was not for that reason a language of low prestige; the H–L model is simply inadequate as a means of describing the relationship between the two languages. Latin, as we have seen, in accordance with a long tradition that can be traced well back into the Republic, was liable to be used occasionally by those in authority as an assertion of the Romanness of the imperial power.

But the administrative system of Egypt had more than one layer. There was an overarching Roman administration embodied above all in the prefect, but at a lower level the old Greek-style administration was retained. The titles of the representatives of this system were Greek, and their language also Greek. Thus when such people visited the Colossus of Memnon it was Greek that they chose for their public inscriptions.

Consider the linguistic situation in Egypt from the point of view of an ordinary Greek speaker with no official post, either monolingual in Greek or bilingual in Greek and Latin. The Latin-speaking higher administration might scarcely ever impinge on his daily life, but he might occasionally have dealings with local, Greek-speaking officialdom. Whether he knew Latin or not, Greek would in his eyes be the language of administration. And if he was of Latin-speaking origin, the opposition might have existed to his way of thinking between Greek as the language of public administration, and Latin as the language of the family. The choice by Terentianus of Greek when he raises matters to do with the local authorities suggests that that was precisely how he saw the linguistic situation.

On the other hand, in a remote Roman military outpost in the desert occupied by a mixture of first-language speakers of Greek and first-language speakers of Latin having little contact with the outside world, language choice in mundane daily activities would have had little to do with the symbolic associations of the two languages as those appear in formal public inscriptions. Speakers will have selected a language on a particular occasion according to such factors as their own preferences, those of their addressees or of other bystanders, the language last used in the exchange, the availability of the necessary technical terms in the one language or the other, and even whim.

The failure of Greek and Latin to fall into a neat opposition H–L in Egypt reflects the complexity of the society. To the Roman official Latin might be the language of power, whereas by the humble bilingual Greek might be seen as the language of local administration, and that, as we have stressed, is only part of the story.

VII LANGUAGE USE IN THE ARMY IN EGYPT

VII.1 Latin as the 'official' language of the army?

A good deal of the evidence which has been discussed so far concerns members of the Roman army. We have seen, for example, at Mons Claudianus what I have called a 'mundane practical bilingualism', such that certain individuals operated indifferently in Greek or Latin without the subject of the communication having any apparent influence on language choice. We have also observed soldiers adapting their language choice to (civilian) environments, using for example Greek for *proskynemata* at pilgrimage sites when they had the competence to use Latin. And the archive of Tiberianus has been discussed for its language choice.

A persistent misconception is that Latin was the 'official' language of the army (see further below on the use of the word 'official'). While it is true that service in the army gave recruits, if they were not Latin speakers, the opportunity to acquire the language (see below), and although there might have been pressure on them to do so, in that training in the skills of Latin literacy seems to have been provided, some excessively sweeping generalisations have been made about the role of Latin as the official language of the army. It is not difficult to find assertions of the following kinds: 'It is striking that such letters were written in Latin, *the army's official language*, even when as was sometimes the case, the writer's first

language was Greek, and his command of Latin by no means perfect'
(Watson (1974: 496), my italics), 'Latin was the language regularly used
within the army' (Welles, Fink and Gilliam (1959: 235)), 'The army's internal administrative affairs were commonly carried out in Latin, while
civil affairs were conducted in Greek' (J. R. Rea at *P. Oxy.* L. 3577, p. 193),
'the official language of the Roman army was Latin' (Kaimio (1979b: 27)),
'*In the East* as in the West Latin was the language of the army' (Balsdon
(1979: 131), my italics), 'Latin was the official language of the army in
which most records were written, though Greek was also sometimes used'
(Alston (1995: 138)), 'la langue officielle de l'armée romaine était le latin'
(Rochette (1997a: 147)), 'la langue officielle des documents émanant de
l'armée est latin' (id. (1997a: 149)).[139]

The term 'official' is rather vague. I use it here to refer to language
use in settings which are not personal, but related to the operation of
the army as an institution. Documents to do with record keeping, the
transmission of orders, the application or granting of leave, and also
letters between military men on formal military business, or between
military men and civil officials on matters to do with the army, all fall on
my definition within the category 'official'. On the other hand private
letters between soldiers may be purely personal, and the language choice
irrelevant to any linguistic policy which the army itself might have been
operating.

The Abinnaeus archive, discussed above (IV.2), well illustrates the
superficial nature of assertions of the type quoted above. The archive,
as we saw, has a number of communications in Greek which could be
described as formal or official; Latin is used in only two letters in the collection, both of them concerning appointment to or dismissal from the
command of the unit. The Latin letter of dismissal in particular, from
the *dux Aegypti*, alongside the official Greek documents referred to above,
suggests that the model seen earlier, whereby both Greek and Latin
were 'High', but Latin was available as the 'super-high' language when
a Roman official might wish to pull rank, is applicable to the language
use of the army as well as to certain civilian settings. And we saw (IV.2.1)
another example of the *dux* using not the language of certain petitioners addressing him (Greek), but Latin, apparently in keeping with his
status.

---

[139] For a good account of language use in the army in Egypt, see Stein (1915: 173–80; also 165–6),
stressing (173) that Latin was *not* the exclusive language of the army. See also Kaimio (1979a:
153–62), and the brief remarks of Bagnall (1993: 244).

I consider now some military documents from Egypt with the aim of showing that Greek was acceptable for official purposes. I will then move on to a few cases of the use of Latin as a super-high language by soldiers.

An Egyptian text which undermines any assumption that Latin was the sole official language of the army is *P. Hamb.* 1.39, which in the original edition was not published in full. A complete re-edition can be found in Fink (1971), 76, which I cite here. The document is dated to 179. It is a long papyrus roll forming a book of receipts given by soldiers of the *ala ueterana Gallica* for their hay allowance for the year, all of them addressed to the *summus curator* of the *ala*, Julius Serenus, in formulaic Greek, but replete with spelling errors which suggest that dictation was used (see Fink (1971: 284), citing the editor of *P. Hamb.* 39 (Meyer), p. 161). It is repeatedly stated that someone had written on behalf of the recipient, who 'did not know letters' (e.g. col. iii. 8, 9, 11, 12 etc.). It is unclear whether this last remark refers to genuine illiteracy, or to illiteracy specifically in Greek. The documents are discussed briefly by Stein (1915: 178).

These then are semi-official texts of record keeping, but are in Greek. Fink shows an awareness of the possible significance of the language choice. He states (1971: 284): 'Meyer notes that the language of these receipts is Greek instead of the Latin usual in military texts, but does not comment further. Greek, in fact, seems commoner than Latin in receipts; **74, 75, 78, 80,** and **81** [nos. from Fink's collection], as well as the present one, are either entirely or almost entirely in Greek, though I believe that col. xvi 1–9 of this text shows a tendency to lapse into the Roman alphabet.' Earlier (p. 242), in reference to the receipts in general, he remarks that they 'are almost all in Greek', which 'show[s] that the Romanization of the soldiers did not extend, in Egypt at any rate, to the language which they normally used among themselves.' Note too p. 278: 'the great majority of such military receipts are in Greek; and that fact, as well as the quality of the Greek, gives us a glimpse of the actual speech of the Roman army camps in Egypt'.

These observations are not entirely satisfactory. First, not all of the receipts which he lists are in Greek. 80, a receipt again for hay written by a procurator of the same *ala ueterana Gallica*, is in Latin (see below, p. 605), and in 75 one receipt is in Latin and two others in Greek, all of them in different hands. The other documents, all of them from Egypt, are indeed in Greek. Secondly, while it is undoubtedly true that the Romanisation of soldiers in Egypt 'did not extend to the language which *they normally used*', it is misleading to imply that receipts represent normal language use. For one thing, receipts are formal and stereotyped, and they do not embody creative language use. Even if they were not dictated (and dictation is likely to have taken place), it remains true that many of them were written by one person for another, and the circumstances of their composition were thus artificial.

Fink's point that the writer of xvi. 1–9 shows a tendency to lapse into the Latin alphabet is rather more interesting. Unfortunately he does not give details, other than to print the initial name of the section in the form ηερμιας ηεβερι, showing two examples of the Latin H (for this phenomenon in a Greek text, see above, v.4). There is then at least a hint here that the writer might have been used to writing in Latin.

In fact a close examination of Fink's version of the whole document reveals the constant intrusion of Latin inflections into the Greek,[140] and that fact suggests the bilingual background which must lie behind the texts. Clearly some writers were familiar with Latin morphology, and they could not prevent themselves from lapsing occasionally into Latin inflections even when writing Greek. They could no doubt have used Latin instead; and on that assumption it becomes clear that in this unit there was a policy, perhaps on the part of the *curator* Serenus himself, that Greek should be used for all such receipts. It is enough to stress that the policy was put into effect, without speculating what its motivations might have been. There was no rigid adherence to a policy of using Latin for public documents in the army; on the contrary, there were occasions when a decision was taken to use Greek instead. Since the Latin elements in the document are of some interest as forms of code-switching (or interference), and since virtually no effort has been made by those discussing the text to elucidate this feature, I offer some illustrations and comment.

Recipients are regularly described as being 'of the *ala ueterana Gallica* and of the *turma* of so and so'. At col. ii.5, however (I use throughout the numeration of Fink), part of this formula has the following form: είλης ουατρανα γαλιγα τουρμα. The genitive with which the formula correctly begins gives way to what can only be a string of Latin ablatives (contrast e.g. col. i.2 είλης γαλλικῆς τούρμης . . .). It is out of the question, for example, that they might be interpreted as Greek datives (which would in such words have displayed an *eta* in the inflections). How then is the syntax to be explained? Intriguingly, the answer is to be found in the *Latin* hay receipt originating in the same unit, Fink no. 80 referred to above. The text begins as follows: *alae uetrane galliga turma Ḍoṇaciani.*

[140] Stein (1915: 177) quite rightly refers to the Latinisms in the document, without offering details.

In this type of phrase Latin permitted either the genitive (*alae, turmae*) or the ablative (of origin or description),[141] and the writer of the Latin receipt has conflated the two, shifting in mid-sentence from the genitive to the ablative.[142] The conflation is more dramatic in the 'Greek' receipt *P. Hamb.* 39, because it entails a change of language as well as of case. The principle though is much the same.

Not infrequently the genitive dependent on *turma* is of Latin form. Thus xx.59 has a double Latin genitive at one point (εἴλης οὐετρανῆς γαλλικῆς τούρμης Σερηνι Μελανι),[143] but later (in the same hand) there are correct Greek genitives, one of them in the same name *Serenus* (τούρμης Αἰλίου Σερήνου). Given this latter expression, it could hardly be argued that the writer had deliberately code-switched in the first expression; the switching looks like unintentional interference from the writer's other (perhaps indeed his first) language. The same receipt also has the Latin expression κιτατορ καμπι, inflected again as Latin. This text betrays the writer's inability to maintain Greek morphology throughout.

The change of construction from genitive to ablative discussed in ii.5 above has a parallel in xiii.39 (ἱππεὺς ἴλης γαλλικῆς τουρμα Γαιμελι) (cf. n. 142). This example has the additional interest that the Latin ablative has dependent on it a Latin genitive, which I take to be that of the name *Gemellus*. In the previous receipt (xiii.38) the same name occurs with Latinate inflection, but dependent on a correct Greek genitive form (τούρμης Γεμελι). Exactly the same phenomenon occurs at GG (hand 42) ἱπ[π]εὺς [εἴλη]ς οὐετραγῆ[ς] γαλλικῆς τυρμα Φουρωνι. Here moreover τυρμα has a Latinate *upsilon* rather than ου. And finally in xiii.39 again there is a second example of similar type (ἱππεὺς ἴλης τῆς αὐτῆς τουρμα τῆς αὐτῆς), but here the Latinate τουρμα has a Greek genitive in 'agreement' with it.

Other Latin genitives are at col. iii.10 Αἶλις Καίπιτον ἱππεὺ εἴλης γαλικῆς τούρμης Οππατιανι (here Meyer read γ as the second letter of the name), col. vii.20 τούρμης Σερήνου Μελανι (contrast x.29 Μέλανος), col. viii.25 τούρμης Σωτηριχι (whereas at xix.56 the same name has

[141] See the examples cited by Cugusi on *CEL* 150.1 (II, p. 182).
[142] For the phenomenon of a shift from *alae* to *turma*, see e.g. *P. Fuad* 1.45.1–2 (= *CPL* 189, *CEL* 155, *ChLA* 42.1207): *[Antonius] Heron[ian]us eques alae ueteranae [Gallicae tu]rma . . . i.* This type of conflation is perhaps not an individual's mistake; it seems to reflect a common usage whereby a different case was used for the two nouns *ala* and *turma*. In Fink (1971), 80, and in our text, the conflation carries over into other words. Compare too *ale tertia Assuriorum* in a text discussed below, VII.3 (1).
[143] Fink (1971: 284) draws attention to the variable forms of the genitive of the name *Melas*, without bringing out the fact that that in -*i* is Latinate.

an -ου ending), FF (hand 20) τούρμης Ηρωδιανι. The present set of receipts is not the only document containing a Latin genitive singular dependent on *turma* in a Greek text. Note too Fink (1971), 75 (= *P. Yale* 249), dated May–June 139 and also from Egypt: τουρμα Λογγινι. This text is from a bilingual setting, in that two of the receipts that the papyrus contains are in Greek and the third in Latin.

I return to Fink (1971), 76. It is not only in the context seen in the previous paragraph that Latin genitive inflections are found. Filiations sometimes have a Latin genitive form (for which phenomenon see also 3.V.4, and I.1 above on *CPL* 296): xvi.45 ηερμιας ηεβερι, xvii. 52 Ἀμέριμνος Αμμωνι, 53 Μηνόδορος Μαρκι. Here the morphology is Latin, but the syntax (plain genitive without υἱός) is Greek.

Whereas at vi.16 the (perfectly correct) expression τύρμης Πετρωνίου occurs (though the *upsilon* in the first word for the expected ου is Latinate), at xvii.48 there is an adjectival replacement for the genitive: τούρμης Πετρωνιανα. The writer had in mind the Latin expression *turma Petroniana*, and admitted the adjective in its Latin form (with *alpha* rather than *eta* in the final syllable), but uninflected (in the nominative rather than the genitive: see below, IX, p. 633).

There remain a few other possible Latinisms which are open to different explanations. At iv.11 the genitive expression recording the date by regnal year and Egyptian month is anomalous: ιθ Αὐρηλίω ᾽ Ἀντωνείνω καὶ Κομμόδω τῶν κυρίων αὐτοκρατόρων τῦβι κ. The expected construction can be seen at (e.g.) iv.13 Αὐρηλίων ᾽ Ἀντωνίνου καὶ Κομόδου τῶν κυρίων. It is not clear in the first example whether ν in final position in the first word has been omitted and ω used for ου in the genitive singular, or the Greek conflated with a Latin ablative construction. Or again, at ii.5 (᾽Ἰουλίο Σερῆνο σούμμο κου[ράτορι]), has there been a Greek phonetic confusion between long and short *o*, or is the spelling a graphic representation of the Latin dative form?

Julius Serenus was the keeper of an important set of records of the *ala*. The production of each receipt was by no means straightforward. Scribes had to be on hand for those who were illiterate, and there was an insistence on a formulaic structure which identified the recipient in some detail and gave the date. This insistence must have entailed supervision of the writers such that the correct wording was used, and it is difficult to believe that dictation did not take place. These complicated circumstances of composition underline the formality of the documents. The constant Latinisms show that at least some of the writers were Latin speakers, and capable of writing Latin.

It is a reasonable assumption that for this type of record keeping there was no inflexible army policy requiring the use of Latin. The language choice might have been down to the individual record keeper, and the invariable selection of Greek in this archive suggests that Serenus enforced his own strict policy.[144] The persistent use of Greek would of course be rather less interesting if there were no Latin speakers in the unit.

I would draw attention to various other receipts or sets of receipts (for hay and the like) which support the assumptions of the previous paragraph. Fink (1971), 75, referred to above, is bilingual, with two Greek receipts and one Latin, all in different hands. If the (fragmentary) document represents a similar form of record keeping to that of *P. Hamb.* 39, then clearly the overseer was more flexible in his language policy.

Fink (1971), 80 = *CPL* 114 = *CEL* 150 (*P. Lond.* 482) is a receipt for hay (see also above, and 4.v.4.2) from someone described as *procurator* of the *ala ueterana Gallica*, taking the form of a letter addressed to *conductoribus fenaris*, followed by a list of the thirty *equites* concerned. The document is in Latin throughout. Its genre is not the same as that represented by *P. Hamb.* 39, in that the recipient is not a soldier receiving his wheat within the unit, but an official acknowledging receipt from some sort of military suppliers. Nevertheless the milieu is military, the *ala* is the same as that in *P. Hamb.* 39, and it is Latin rather than Greek which is used. This text is similar to *P. Oxy.* IV.735 (= Fink (1971), 81 = *ChLA* 4.275). This is a receipt for wheat for cavalrymen and infantry. It begins with some fragmentary names in Latin, followed by a letter in Greek, of which I quote the translation of Fink: 'Malochos son of . . . optio, to Victor Comarinus, vicarius of the dispensator Caesarum. The aforenamed cavalrymen, *praitôn* (?),[145] 50 in number (?), have been measured out for the month Thoth of wheat fifty artabas. Year 14 of the Lords Augusti, Thoth 7. Also infantry of the century of Bebeus.' There follow names written in Latin.

The addressee, a *uicarius* of the imperial *oeconomus*, must be a civilian (Fink (1971:335)). The distinctive feature of this text is the mixture of languages. One may deduce that the writer was accustomed to using Latin in the camp in quasi-official documents, and for that reason wrote both lists of names in that language. But Greek must have been the

[144] It is possible that the scribes (or some of them) who wrote for illiterate soldiers were primary speakers of Latin, and that the soldiers themselves on the whole were primary speakers of Greek. The choice of language would on this view reflect the linguistic competence of the soldiers, whereas the scribes (who were better educated) were bilingual.

[145] Corrected now by Sijpesteijn (1981: 107–8) (ἱππεῖς πραι(σιδίου) Σοήν(ης)).

appropriate language for addressing the outside official, either because it was known to be his preferred language, or because of a feeling that Greek was the language of civilian administration. The text hints at the special place of Latin within the army. But though Latin was clearly often used for record keeping and the like, there was no fixed policy at the everyday level. The overall impression given by these various documents is of linguistic flexibility in the conduct of army business.

I move on to other military archives from Egypt which show the acceptability of Greek in the army for formal communications, and the overlapping roles of Latin and Greek. The Florida ostraca are military documents from Upper Egypt dated to the second century (see above, II). There was a degree of bilingualism in this community, as is confirmed by the survival of fragments of three Latin letters along with a more substantial amount of Greek material. Bagnall (1976: 21) notes that '[t]he character of several of our texts as military and official cannot be questioned, and most of the ostraka are in Greek.' One noteworthy quasi-official document in Greek is no. 1, a furlough pass (ἔχεις δέκα ἡμέρας κομμιᾶτεν).[146]

The texts from Quseir-al-Qadim[147] also contain one or two quasi-official documents. Text no. 1 is a roster of soldiers absent, written in Greek, and consisting of name + patronymic (in the genitive): e.g. line 3 Νεμώνιος Μαμμογαίου. Comparable documents (strength reports, or daily reports listing duties, absentees and the like: see below on *O. Claud.* II.191 ff.) are known in Latin (*Tab. Vind.* II.154, *O. Bu Njem* 1–62),[148] but there was clearly no overriding military rule that they should be in that language in Greek-speaking areas or units (but see below, VII.3, on some military lists in Latin, and see the remarks at p. 618). Bagnall (1986: 6) notes that the names in the document are redolent of 'an Egyptian population at least in part': about 25 per cent of the names are Roman, 50 per cent are Greek, 20 per cent Egyptian and one name is Semitic.

By contrast text no. 18 in the same archive is a *Latin* list, and in this the 'eleven names fully or partially preserved ... have a strongly Roman cast; they include a number of names rarely if at all found in Egypt and then in a Roman context ... No name on the list, in fact, is particularly characteristic of the onomastics of Roman Egypt' (Bagnall (1986: 6)).

There is a correlation between the character of the names in the two lists, and the language used for each list. The variation does not suggest a

---

[146] On applications for leave written in Greek, see p. 556.   [147] See Bagnall (1986).
[148] For such documents, see Bowman and Thomas (1991: 63–6).

rigid linguistic policy, but a readiness to accept the language appropriate to the personnel. In Egypt more often than not that language would be Greek. Bagnall (1986: 6) suggests that the Latin names (in the Latin list) may come from a legionary detachment, the Greek names from an auxiliary unit.

There is one further piece of evidence from this corpus that official business might be conducted in Greek. No. 25 is an official letter in Greek to or from a *curator*, probably the *curator* of Leukos Limen.[149]

I turn now to Mons Claudianus, and particularly volume II of the os-traca, which allows some refinements to be added to the general picture.

At 191–210 there are lists of those sick on a certain day: e.g. 191 αἶγροι Ἀθυρ... Τροκουν[δας Ἀ]λέξαν[δρος .. This is a familiar type of semi-official document, found in Latin as well as Greek, as we have just seen. The referents must have been members of the *familia* working at the quarries. Notable is the use of the Latin term αἶγροι in two of the lists (191, 192: see above, 4.V.2.9: *aegri* was standard in Latin lists of this type). The intrusion of the Latin word into Greek lists when there was a current Greek word available probably reflects the influence of a continuing tradition of such Latin record keeping within the army, if not in this unit at this time. Greek seems to have been grafted on to a Latin form of record. What emerges from these lists, and indeed some corresponding ones in vol. I (83–117, which are fully Greek, with ἄρρωστοι rather than αἶγροι), is that despite the strength of that tradition Greek could be employed if the record keepers felt it appropriate to the situation.

It is also of note that the lists 193–210 are all in the same hand, *which has Latin characteristics* (see above, I.VII.4.I): see *O. Claud.* II, p. 22 '... de la même main ... qui pourrait être celle d'un latiniste peu accoutumé à écrire le grec.' The writer seems to have been a Latin speaker, literate in Latin, who could have used Latin for the record. That he did not do so shows that it was not merely the linguistic competence of the scribes available which determined the choice of language. Greek was acceptable for record keeping even if there was a scribe to hand who could have used Latin.

The interchangeability of the two languages in the same sorts of military documents can also be seen from a comparison of *O. Claud.* 304 with *O. Amst.* 8. The former is a military roster, in Latin, written on a whole amphora. The names are all abbreviated. The other is a *Greek* roster, also on an amphora.[150]

---

[149] So Bagnall (1986: 26).   [150] See Clarysse and Sijpestein (1988).

The most important set of documents for present purposes are *O. Claud.* II, nos. 309–36 (see above, 3.VI.3). These again have a quasi-official flavour, in that they belong to the system of transmitting orders at the base. The documents are lists of *uigiles*. I will return to them briefly in the next section, but here it is enough to say that whereas most of the lists are in Greek, no. 355 is in Latin.

I conclude this section. In the Roman army in Egypt matters of an official kind were regularly handled in Greek, both in dealings with outsiders to the unit and in internal record keeping. The choice of Greek might on occasion have reflected the availability of scribes, but by no means always. We have seen evidence for those literate in Latin using Greek. The same kinds of documents turn up now in Latin now in Greek, a fact which suggests that there was not a fixed linguistic policy consistent with claims that Latin was the 'official language' of the army. It was probably the currency of the one language or the other within a unit that determined the language used, as is clear in the two rosters from Quseir-al-Qadim (see above).

That said, Latin was clearly a sort of supreme or super-high language in the army, which was bound to be used in certain circumstances. When Abinnaeus wrote to the emperor he did so in Latin, and when he received his letter of dismissal, that too was in Latin. The *dux Aegypti* Flavius Mauricius did not respond in kind when he received a petition in Greek. Latin was the language of power, which might be used when a superior wished to assert his power over a subordinate, or when a subordinate wished to make a potent appeal to higher authority.

I turn now to various other striking uses of Latin in the army, which point to its occasional supreme status.

VII.2 *Latin as a super-high language in the army*

VII.2.1 *Latin and the transmission of orders*

O.Claud. II.309–36, as was just mentioned, are lists of eight *uigiles* designated for duty at Mons Claudianus, written predominantly in Greek. These have been discussed in the chapter on code-switching (3.VI.3), and I merely reiterate here that in documents otherwise in Greek the passwords are Latin (and inflected as Latin). If Greek in this camp was the language of most of the individuals present, Latin, as represented in the passwords, might in a more abstract sense be described as the language of the army itself. It would seem that there were certain terms related to the command structure of the army which were Latin and without Greek equivalent. There is, as we have seen (3.VI.3), comparable evidence that in the Byzantine army stereotyped orders were given in Latin. Latin passwords used in a Greek unit represent the same phenomenon, that is the use of Latin at key moments to symbolise the Romanness of command. Similarly, as we saw in the same section earlier (3.VI.3), Roman ordinals are used at *O. Amst.* 8 frg. *e* in assigning posts in *stationes*.

VII.2.2 Receipts

The receipts discussed above (VII.1) were for goods received within or by units of the army in Egypt, and in those the choice of language was variable. Different again are receipts for money received by individuals either by way of a loan or in exchange for goods. There were standard formats for such receipts,[151] as we saw in the case of the receipt of Aeschines (1.VII.2.3), and the language apparently had to be Latin. Those who could not write the text in Latin script might use Greek letters,[152] or alternatively have the text written out for them in Latin and then append a summary in their own hand in Greek (see below). In the army even in Greek-speaking regions this convention persisted; Latin, as the language of Roman law, is given super-high status in such documents, and is imposed even on those who did not speak the language.

P. Cairo J72083 (*P. Fuad* 1.45, *ChLA* 42.1207, *CEL* 155) is a declaration from Alexandria dated AD 153 in which a cavalryman Antonius Heronianus of the *ala ueterana Gallica* acknowledges receipt of a loan of 50 denarii from a fellow soldier. The main body of the text is in formulaic Latin running to thirteen lines. It has the formula *fateor me accepisse et debere* . . . as well as other formulaic material in fragmentary state. The place of the transaction is recorded precisely (*actum Alexandriae ad Aeg(yptum)* . . . *in hibernis leg. II Traian(ae) F(ortis) et alae [u]eteranae Gallicae*), and the section concludes with a consular date.

Then follow four subscriptions, three of them in Greek and one in Latin. The first of these is by the debtor himself, written in crude Greek capitals: Ἀντώνιος Ἡρωνιανὸς ἱππεὺς [ὁ προγ]εγραμ<μ>ένος ἔλαβα καὶ ὀφίλω [τὰ προ]κίμενα δηνάρια πεντήκον[τα κ]αὶ ἀπ[ο]δώσω καθὼς πρόκιται.

Of the two witnesses' signatures which follow one is in Greek and the other in Latin (though comprising only one complete word, . . . *etis*

---

[151] See e.g. Andreau (1974: 18–19) on two types of receipts to do with sales by auction (with the texts quoted in the appendix, 312–38).

[152] The fragmentary transliterated document elucidated by Wolf (1982) is worth citing by way of analogy, though it is not (it seems) strictly a receipt.

adfui). The mixture of languages is of some interest. Clearly there was no requirement that the document should be witnessed in a particular language; each witness chose the language of his greater literacy or competence. The switch of languages in (most of) the subscriptions reflects the accomplishments in language or literacy of the participants in the transaction.

The background to this receipt may be compared with that of the receipt of Aeschines discussed in another chapter (1.VII.2.3). That text was written in Greek characters, and that is because the debtor must have been unskilled in Latin writing and yet pressured to use that language. Heronianus too presumably lacked literacy skills in Latin, but a different strategy was used to get around the problem. The Latin text was drawn up by a scribe, which Heronianus authenticated by writing a Greek summary in his own hand. By coincidence we have another (fragmentary) receipt by the same man Heronianus found at Karanis (*P. Mich.* VII.438, = *ChLA* 5.303, *CEL* 154), dated 140, at a time when he was in a different unit. The structure of this document is much the same as that of the first. Again the body of the text is in Latin, and then Heronianus writes in Greek in his own hand.

These documents are a nice illustration of bilingualism in action in a military environment. Those gathered to draw up the texts had differing languages of primary competence. And though the debtor was serving in the Roman army he was by preference a speaker of Greek. This was a Roman-style legalistic transaction, in which Latin had to be used for the primary text.

P. Mich. III.161 = *ChLA* 5.294 is probably a parallel for the above documents, but it is not well preserved. It comes from Caesarea in Mauritania rather than Egypt, but I mention it here for its similarity to the above text. The surviving Latin is as follows:

]ċ[o]s(ulibus) XII K(alendas) Martias
]ṣcribsi me accepisse
]classis Aug(ustae) liburn(a)
]ṣ ex stipendio eis
]ị actum Ḳaesareae

]io
] [ ] ch[e]irographo

The second line shows that this too was an acknowledgment of debt. Line 3 suggests that the context was again military. The first and fifth lines contain elements found in the text discussed above, but their place-ment here differs. The final word (*cheirographo*) must look forward to the subscription of the debtor himself, and it may well have been in Greek.

ChLA 3.204 (= *CEL* 156), a receipt, and *ChLA* 1.12 (= *CEL* 157), a registration of the receipt written on the same day at the same place Pulvinos, are fragments of the same τόμος συγκολλήσιμος and in very similar hands.[153] There are hints in both texts that Roman military per-sonnel were involved in the transactions. The Greek interference in the Latin of both documents has been discussed in an earlier chapter (see 4.V.3.1.2, V.4.2), and its presence suggests again that the writers would have been at home in Greek, but were using Latin in line with a policy. Here I quote the best preserved parts of the texts, and by way of digres-sion say something more about their language in order to bring out the character of this 'bilinguals' Latin' written no doubt by first-language speakers of Greek.

3.204 is better preserved. The first five lines are fragmentary, but the rest of the text (6–12) is clear, and I quote it in full:

miserat mi[hi] Cornelius Germanus procurator meus quas has res [i]ntra scriptas meas, salbas, sanas recepisse scripsi nonarum Octobrium ad Puluinos, ad statione liburnes Fides, interueniente Minucium Plotianum triarchum et Apuleium Nepotem, scriba. actum Puluinos nonis Octobris imp(eratore) Vero ter(tio) et Vmidio Quadrato consulatus.

1.12 is badly damaged. Not much can be made of the first fifteen lines, but I quote from line 16 to the end as the text is set out in *ChLA*:

D]ameto frater minus posso agere
]denarios super scripta et uesti
Lon]ginio Castore centurionem
].. ta super scriptas res et reme
]. mi hic se [a]ccepisse reaque
nona]s Octobres Imp. Aug. III et M. Vmidio Quadrato cos]
]ope scripsi me recepisse res s(uper) s(criptas)
a Corneli]o Germ[a]no cuius [e]xemplum

The sentence then continues to the side:

epistules habio. actum Puluinos nonar[u]m Octobrium isdem co[ns]ulibus.

---

[153] The introduction to *ChLA* 3.204 discusses the circumstances of composition of the two texts.

In the relative clause (which is not logically constructed) of 3.204 there is a redundant demonstrative in agreement with the relative pronoun (*quas has*...). The combination is substandard in Latin, springing probably from *ad hoc* conflations rather than from established usage: cf. e.g. *Mul. Chir.* 164 **quem** *et alii* **hunc** *morbum suspirium dixerunt* (but see above, 4.v.2.12 for a comparable construction which is Hebrew-inspired).[154]

The place name *Puluinos* is used once with the preposition *ad* in locative function, but also without a preposition in the accusative (?) form with the same function; the same phrase *actum Puluinos* is also in the associated document, line 12. For this usage in substandard Latin (in the case of a non-Latin place name), cf. *O. Bu Njem* 81 *ad usus militum morantium* **Golas**.[155]

There is a substandard ablative absolute (where the nominal components are in the accusative): *interueniente Minucium*...*Nepotem*. Usually in such a 'mixed' ablative absolute the nominal element is put in the accusative if it is the underlying object of the verbal element, as e.g. at *Anon. Val.* 63 *postea uero accepta* **uxorem**.[156] Examples of the present type (in which the nominal element inflected as accusative is the underlying *subject* of the verbal idea) are sometimes attested: e.g. Greg. Tur. *Hist. Franc.* 5.34 *discordantibus reges*.[157] Possibly such constructions in the very late period are to be interpreted as conflations of the accusative and ablative absolute,[158] but here it is more likely that the usage is that 'detached' accusative which is sometimes found either in appositions where a case other than the accusative is required, or at the end of lists in another case (see above, 4.v.3.1, p. 477). Here the names in the illogical accusative come after the correctly inflected participle; the writer lapses into one of the two 'default' cases as the thread is lost. Cf. in the subscription to the receipt of Aeschines *pro Aescine Aescine philium* (see above, 1.vII.2.3, n. 146).

In the ablative form of the date there is a morphological error (*Octobris* for -*ibus*).[159] It is common in inscriptions for the case ending of a noun to be influenced by that of a juxtaposed word. So at *ICUR* 1867 (in Greek letters) μησωρουμ is given a second- rather than the third-declension ending under the influence of the preceding αννωρουμ.

Fides, the name of the *liburna*, is in the nominative. It might have been expected to be in the genitive, either in apposition to *liburnes*, or

---

[154] See Ahlquist (1909: 114–15), Hofmann and Szantyr (1965: 556–7).

[155] See Adams (1994a: 110).   [156] See Adams (1976: 99).   [157] See Helttula (1987: 77).

[158] See Helttula (1987: 77) for a different explanation.

[159] Cugusi, *CEL* II, 156.12 suggests that *Octobris* may be a genitive.

as a *gen. definitiuus*. For the latter construction, see Terentianus, *P.Mich.*
VIII.467.25f. *in liburna N[e]ptuni* (cf. also the expression *libyrni Dracontis* in a
document discussed above, I, p. 528).[160] This is a case of the 'nominative
of apposition'. Appositional words have a syntactic detachment, and
there is a tendency in substandard writings for either the nominative or
the accusative (see above) to be used as an appositional case (e.g. *ChLA*
5.298.15 *Diocletiano pater Aug(ustorum)*, *App. Probi* 134 *uico capitis Africae non
uico caput Africae*).[161] I mention finally *triarchum* (= *trierarchum*), a haplology
typical of substandard writings.[162]

The document *ChLA* 1.12 also has some substandard deviations from
'correct' Latin usage. The irregular verb *possum* is regularised to *posso*,
a form found in Terentianus (*P.Mich.* VIII.469.15). Such regularisations
are not uncommon in Egyptian Latin texts. In a letter of recommendation (*P.Oxy.* 1.32 = *ChLA* 4.267.15f.) the infinitive of *refero* is regularised
to *referere*. In a promissory note from Karanis, dated AD 140 (*P. Mich.*
VII.438.5), *reddo* is given an infinitive *[r]eddare*, and similarly Rustius
Barbarus (*O. Wâdi Fawâkhir* 5) writes *redda illi* (imperative). To this category also belongs the participle *obtulitus* at *P. Abinn.* 1, a regularisation
in the sense that the degree of suppletion in the perfect and perfect participle forms of *fero* (*tuli* on the one hand, *latus* on the other) has been
reduced by the reconstruction of the participial form on the perfect
stem. *P.Abinn.* 1, as we saw, is a formal petition to the emperor, no doubt
drafted by a learned scribe. Standardised forms of irregular verbs were
making their way up the educational scale. Though these regularisations come from Egypt, the phenomenon was no doubt commonplace
beneath a certain educational level all over the Empire (cf. e.g. *essere* at
ILCV 3865).[163]

At line 8 of 1.12 (not quoted here) there is a misspelt numeral
[q]uadrincento. There was uncertainty about the form of the higher numerals. A receipt for victuals dated AD 220 from Egypt (*ChLA* 41. 1198 =
CEL 205) has (line 20) *sextaria kastresia sexcenta* (on the analogy of *sex*:
see below, VIII (6)), the receipt for hay (*ChLA* 3.203.7) has the form *triginti* = *triginta* (influence of *uiginti*), and another Egyptian text (*P. Mich.* VII.
435.3) has *nonagen[ta]* = *nonaginta* (influence of *nongenti*). In all of these

[160] See Adams (1995a: 109), Hofmann and Szantyr (1965: 62).
[161] See further Hofmann and Szantyr (1965: 27), commenting explicitly on the use of the nominative
    instead of the *gen. definitiuus*. See also above, 4.V.3.1 n. 227 on a 'default' use of the nominative.
[162] See Leumann (1977: 234) on the general phenomenon. Examples of the form *triarchus* are cited
    at *ChLA* 3.204 (on line 10) from *CIL* X.7291 and XI.3719.
[163] Cf. Väänänen (1981: 136).

cases there has been remodelling on the analogy of a related numeral.[164]
1.12 also shows the locatival use of *Puluinos* seen above. It has an apparent
lapse of concord (*denarios super scripta*), Greek morphology (*epistules*), and
a misspelling of *habeo* (*habio*, with closing of *e* in hiatus).

All of these texts reflect a policy of requiring that receipts/promissory
notes should be written in Latin in military environments, and this points
to the legalistic function of Latin as super-high. The last two texts display
traces of colloquial Latin alongside their Grecisms (see 4.V.4.2). It can be
deduced that the writers were native speakers of Greek who had acquired
Latin first as a spoken language. The mixture of influences is of general
interest, because it hints at the learning of Latin (and literacy in Latin)
by Greek-speaking military personnel (for which see further below, VII.3
(1)). I have digressed slightly to bring out the diversity of the linguistic
situation in Egyptian military communities.

VII.2.3 Diplomata

The super-high status of Latin within the army can also be seen in the
invariable use of that language in *diplomata* or certificates of discharge of
auxiliaries, whatever the language of the individual soldier.[165]

VII.2.4 Dedications to emperors

A Roman soldier might be expected to address himself formally to the
emperor in Latin, even if his first language was Greek. This we saw in
the Abinnaeus archive. Similarly the future emperor Maximinus Thrax
when serving as a soldier once addressed the emperor Septimius Severus
in a language that was almost Thracian, but he made the effort to use
Latin (see 1.V).

There is an analogy between the use of Latin by a Greek-speaking
Roman soldier in addressing the emperor, and the use of Latin in Egypt
by soldiers making dedications to the emperor. Perhaps the most telling
evidence for this latter practice is now to be found in Kayser's collection (1994) of the Greek and Latin inscriptions from Alexandria of the
Imperial period (first to third centuries AD). The collection gives an idea
of the influence of domain (by which is meant in this context the interaction of addressee, dedicator and document-type) in determining
language choice. Most of the inscriptions in the corpus are in Greek,
but of the inscriptions classified by Kayser (102–15) as military almost all

---

[164] The misspellings of numerals discussed by Ihm (1892: 69–70) are not quite the same as these.
[165] On *diplomata* see in particular Roxan (1978, 1985, 1994). For their significance in the present
context, see also Stein (1915: 176).

are in Latin. I list the military inscriptions in Kayser's order with brief description:

102 Statue base set up to an **emperor** by veterans of the *leg. II Traiana*. The inscription contains a long list of the soldiers classified by cohort and century.

103 Dedication to an **emperor** by tribunes of the second legion.

104 A commemoration of building works: dedication of the restoration of a fort (see in general IV.7 above).

105 Similar to 102: a dedication to an **emperor** by veterans of the second legion, again containing a long list of names classified by cohort and legion.

106 Similar again. This time there is a dedication of a statue to an **emperor** by decurions of two legions, again with a long list of names.

106 bis Dedication of a statue of an **emperor** by the *ala ueterana Gallica*.

107 Fragment of a dedication to an **emperor**.

108 An inscription on behalf of the safety of an **emperor**.

109 An inscription to the *genius* of a legion.

110 A Greek fragment mentioning the *decanoi* of the praetorian fleet of Misenum.

111 A fragment mentioning **emperors**.

112 A fragment of a dedication to **emperors**.

113 A fragment mentioning a *praefectus castrorum*.

114 A list of soldiers.

115 An obscure fragment.

For convenience I have only cited the military inscriptions classified as such by Kayser, although there are some other texts in the volume, classified differently, that could be included among the military texts. Nevertheless it is clear that a majority of the above Latin inscriptions are dedications in Latin by soldiers to emperors. In their relationship to the emperor it would seem that soldiers felt impelled to adopt a Latin-speaking persona. There must have been pressure to symbolise the Romanness of the institution to which they belonged when addressing the supreme Roman authority.

At Dakka, we saw (V.5), Roman soldiers almost invariably adopted Greek in *proskynemata*. There is however an honorific inscription on a statue base in Latin to an emperor by a centurion (Ruppel (1930), Gr 100): *pro salute Imp(eratoris) Neruae Traiani Caesaris Aug(usti) Germa(nici) Dacici domuique eius T(itus) Flauius Valens (centurio) cho(rtis) I Aug(ustae) Pr(aetoriae) Lusitano(rum). d(edit) d(edicauit) praefectura Bassi.*

Another comparable Latin inscription from Akôris can be found in E. Bernand (1988), 12, a dedication by a trierarch in honour of the emperors Septimius Severus, Caracalla and Geta. Note too *IG Philae* II.163, an incomplete dedication in Latin to Trajan, without a surviving name of the dedicator. Most of the inscriptions at Philae are in Greek.

In these texts there are complementary determinants of language choice. It was not exclusively the fact that the dedicators were Roman soldiers which determined the choice of Latin; after all, there are numerous inscriptions in Greek by soldiers, as we have seen. Nor was it exclusively the fact that the dedicatees were Roman emperors; there was no reason for run-of-the-mill Greeks to use Latin in inscriptions to emperors. This point is confirmed by Kayser (1994), 14, a dedication in Greek by the city of Alexandria to Caracalla, Julia Domna and the divine Septimius Severus. It was the concatenation of topic, addressee and dedicator which established the language chosen in these inscriptions. The addressees are Roman emperors, the dedicators members of the Roman army, and the nature of the dedication formal and public.

I mention finally an anomalous inscription. Kayser (1994), 15 is a dedication of a statue of Diocletian in Greek by a prefect of Egypt.

VII.2.5 *Some epitaphs*

Another text at Dakka which is in Latin rather than Greek is a soldier's epitaph (Ruppel (1930), Gr 72), as we saw above, v.5. The epitaph was a written form in which a soldier might expect to be commemorated as a member of the Roman army. Latin, either on its own or in conjunction with Greek, is constantly found in soldiers' epitaphs, even in Greek regions of the Empire (see above, n. 109).[166] The choice of Latin was as powerful as the wording in conveying the status of the referent as a Roman soldier. Similarly in another chapter we saw an inscription commemorating a soldier which was in Greek but with a switch into Latin when his rank was recorded (see 3.1; cf. *AE* 1984, 893, discussed at 2.VII.3).

I cite only a small amount of evidence from Egypt, because there is a substantial collection of data in Stein (see n. 166). In É. Bernand's collection (1988) of the inscriptions of Akôris no. 3 is a dedication in Greek of an altar to Zeus by a centurion of the *leg. III Cyrenaica* (see v.1 above). The religious character of the inscription is consistent with the choice of Greek. But in the same collection there is an epitaph of a member of the same legion, and it is in Latin: 172 *M. Terentius Long[us] mil(es) leg(ionis)*

---

[166] For Egypt, see in particular Stein (1915: 181 n. 3). Note also (for other areas) Isaac (1990: 319, 324), and the remarks of Adams (1999: 132). Note too above, 2.VII.3.

III Cuir(enaicae), (centuriae) Arr[e]cini u[i]xit an[n.] . . . men[s. .]. For another
Latin epitaph for a member of this legion, see A. Bernand (1984), 95
T. Messius T(iti) f(ilius) miles leg(ionis) III Cyre(naicae.

Alternatively, such epitaphs are sometimes bilingual. Note e.g. A.
Bernand (1989) 227 (Syene):

Sex(tus) Meuius Sex(ti) f(ilius), Fab(ia tribu), Domittius eques signif(er) ala
Apriana ann(os) XXIV hic situs est
Σέξστος Μήουιος Σέξστου **υἱὸς** Φαβία Δομίττιος ἱππεὺς σημμαφ(όρος)
ἄλης ῾Απριανῆς ἐτῶν κδ' **ἄωρος ἐνθάδε κεῖται.**

Note that the form of the filiation in the Greek version is Latinate. The
two inscriptions are not absolutely identical. ἄωρος is typical of Greek
inscriptions commemorating the young, but there is no ready equivalent
in Latin and so the formulaic conventions of the two languages are
followed.

An epitaph might be seen as the ultimate definition of a person's
identity (see above, 2.VII.3). While soldiers in Greek-speaking areas were
happy to use Greek even in inscriptions which conferred an explicit military identity on them by recording their rank and unit (as for example
in *proskynemata*), a different practice is often followed in epitaphs of much
the same content in the same areas. The soldier's Romanness is formally
expressed for posterity by the presence of Latin.

In this and the preceding sections (see also IV.1, IV.2) the case has been
argued that Greek could be used for some official functions in the Roman
army, but that Latin had super-high status which made it suitable for various symbolic purposes, whether in legalistic documents, or to highlight
the Roman identity of a soldier, or to mark or acknowledge overriding
authority. During the discussion we saw evidence for the learning of
Latin by soldiers of Greek origin (VII.2.2), and I turn now directly to that
subject.

VII.3 Evidence for the learning of Latin in the army

The view that Latin was the official language of the army entails an
assumption that foreign recruits will have learnt Latin as a second language, and thereby acquired degrees of bilingualism with varying competence in the second language. I have attempted to refine this view,
suggesting (1) that many units functioned mainly in Greek, and (2) that
Latin was rarely obligatory, though it had a role as a super-high language.
But however slight the survival of Latin might be in corpora of military

texts, forms of bilingualism or a passive knowledge of Latin must have been widespread. In Chapter 2 we saw evidence for the acquisition of Latin in the army by Germans (2.IX), Palmyrenes (2.VII.2), Thracians (2.XIII), Africans (2.V.7) and Celts (2.IV.3). Even texts in Greek may hint at the bilingualism (and bi-literacy) of the writer, in that interference not infrequently betrays some knowledge of Latin in the background.

The many Latin inscriptions by and dedications to soldiers recruited outside Latin-speaking regions are not conclusive proof of their subjects' bilingualism, because any inscription can be the work of a stonecutter or even of a third party. I now move on therefore to assemble some explicit evidence for (Greek-speaking) soldiers in the process of learning Latin. Such evidence is not inconsistent with the implications of section VII, but considered alongside the evidence collected there leads to a more balanced view of the place of Latin in the army. Latin learning and instruction in Latin literacy took place in the army, but the aim of such learning and instruction was not to enforce the use of Latin in all circumstances.

(1) *ChLA* 18.660 is a list of soldiers of the *ala III Assuriorum*, dated to AD 319–29, its provenance probably Oxyrhynchus. There is unambiguous internal evidence that the writer's language of primary literacy was Greek, and that he had learnt to write Latin only imperfectly. The text shows morphological interference from Greek, some use of Greek letters, and a failure to make the necessary conversions from Greek orthography to Latin. I start with this last feature.

In *prigceps I turmηs* (ii.2) the writer has failed to convert the Greek representation of the velar nasal (i.e. γ in certain environments) into the Latin representation (*n*), but has simply transliterated γ (on this mistake, see above, 1.VII.4.1). This is a peculiarly mechanical error, which could not have been committed by someone with even a minimal reading or writing experience in Latin script. The perpetrator must have been a literate Greek recruited into the army, who had been drafted into service as clerk in a script which he had not mastered. Although it is his imperfect *literacy* in Latin, and the primacy of his Greek literacy, which are in evidence here, it is reasonable to assume that Greek was also his primary *language*; it is inconceivable that he was a first-language speaker of Latin who was more skilled in Greek literacy than Latin. I take it that he was a Greek who was improving his Latin language and writing while serving in the army.

There is much else besides in this text which points to the same conclusion. The Greek digraph αι is not converted into its Latin correspondent *ae* in *Caisar is* (i.3). For such a spelling in a Latin inscription found in Greece, see *ILGR* 55 *Germ[anico] Caisa[ri]*. The same digraph *ai*, which had no currency at this time in Latin, is used to represent not only CL *ae*, but also long *e* (ii.4 *decurionais* = *decuriones*). This misspelling seems to have its basis in later Greek (substandard) orthography where αι is sometimes used for ε (and inversely ε is sometimes used for αι);[167] by analogy in Latin script the writer uses *ai* for Lat. *e* making no distinction between *e* representing long *e* on one hand and short *e* on the other. That is not surprising, given the tendency for long vowels in final syllable to be shortened in Latin, and given the loss of quantitative distinctions in Greek.

The writer made use of the digraph *ei*, which, in so far as it was used at all in Latin by this date, served in formal writings as a representation of long *i* (see I.VII.2.2). In this text though it is used in hiatus for short *i*: ii.17 *actuareius*, 18 *Aṛeius*. This spelling is a familiar one in Greek. See Gignac (1976: 189): 'There is a very frequent interchange of ει and ι (whether long or short etymologically) in all phonetic enviroments throughout the Roman and Byzantine periods. This indicates the identification of the classical Greek /ei/ diphthong with the simple vowel /i/.' Cf. *ILI* 884 *soceio suo fecerunt* (= *socio*).

Turmη̄s (ii.2, above) has a Greek genitive inflection, written moreover with an *eta*. This looks like a case of morphological interference from Greek. *Turma* had been borrowed by Greek, and in Greek its genitive was τούρμης (see e.g. *O.Flor.* 5.7 and above VII.1).

A Greek ending, written in Greek characters, is also found in the Greek name *Diugenη̄s* at ii.14. There is a parallel in an inscription set up in Latin on Andros (*ILGR* 30: see above, I.VII.4.1).

Morphological interference also seems to be found in *summos* (ii.15), where the Greek nominative ending has been imposed on a Latin word. There are also a few other misspellings which might possibly have been Greek-inspired: i.3 *nubilissimis* (*u* for long *o*; for the writing of *upsilon* for *omega* in later Greek, see Gignac (1976: 294)); ii.3 *Diunusius*, 14 *Diugenη̄s* (*u* for short *o*, for which type of misspelling in Greek, see Gignac (1976: 293)).[168]

One or two uncertainties in the use of Latin case inflections tell us nothing about the origin of the writer, but they add to the picture of one who was having difficulty in writing correct Latin. *Nubilissimis* (+ *Caesaris*)

---

[167] See Gignac (1976: 192–3).
[168] These spellings though are not necessarily Grecising. Misspellings showing *u* for *o* (whether long or short) turn up from time to time in Latin, but they are not easy to classify. See B. Löfstedt (1961: 69–75).

at i.3 has a false genitive in -*is*. In *ale tertia Assuriorum* (i.1) the lack of agreement between *ale* and *tertia* recalls the conflated construction *alae uetrane galliga* at Fink (1971), 80 (see also above, VII.1).

On the basis of this and other evidence several stages can be identified in the acquisition of literacy in Latin script by Greeks attempting to write the language (see also above, 1.VII.4.1 for brief mention of the hierarchy of errors proposed here):

(1) Greeks who had picked up some spoken Latin but were uninstructed in Latin script (e.g. Aeschines: see 1.VII.2.3) might use only Greek letters for the writing of the Latin language (complete transliteration).

(2) Once the Latin letters were learnt, an unpractised writer might occasionally switch alphabets unconsciously.

(3) Even those who used only Latin letters might fall into spellings motivated in type by conventions operating in Greek script. Into this class fall the failure to convert Greek digraphs into their Latin equivalents (by using, e.g., *ai* for *ae*), and the wrong choice of letter to render an allophone (e.g. *g* for the velar nasal).

(4) The Greek who had progressed further in Latin literacy might avoid completely errors of types (2) and (3), but still betray his Greekness by (e.g.) syntactic or morphological interference from Greek, or by code-switching into Greek of the type called 'leaks' here (on this stage see further below, pp. 625–6). The writer of our text was guilty of this type of error as well.

(5) A final stage might be marked by control of Latin script, orthography and language such that the writer's first language did not influence at all the way in which he wrote Latin.

Stages (2) and (3) are not mutually exclusive, and they come together in the writer of our military unit. He was clearly a Greek, bilingual up to a point, and more importantly for our present purposes *a learner of Latin serving in the Roman army*. His errors show that he would have been more at ease using the Greek language and script; it is likely therefore that he was required on this occasion to write in Latin. The document suggests that there must sometimes have been circumstances in the army when Latin was considered appropriate for a document even when there was not a fluent Latin writer available to draft the document.[169] Since the learner who wrote the text was not able to avoid rudimentary writing errors of types (2) and (3), he could scarcely have been learning Latin literacy long; and if so it must have been in the army that he had received instruction.

---

[169] We have though seen above (VII.1, pp. 606–7) some military lists written in Greek. The variability of language choice suggests that a good deal of discretion was in the hands of the commanding officer or the clerk who supervised record-keeping.

If certain documents had to be in Latin, in units with few native speakers of Latin instruction in Latin literacy must have been provided.

(2) *P. Vindob.* L2 (= *ChLA* 43.1242, Fink (1971), 34, and especially Kramer (1993), whose text I cite here) is a list of soldiers of the third Cyrenaic legion, dated AD 115–17 (?).[170] The format of the document is as follows. The century symbol is followed by the name of the centurion in the genitive. Then follows a list of legionaries belonging to that century in the nominative.[171] For example:

ii.22 (centuria) Aufri Açulị
    Iulius Rusticus
    Petucaeus Otaus.

Alphabet switching (type (2) above) can be seen in the name *Aga*θo (col. ii. 33). Morphological interference is found in the name *Capiton* (i.16), where the Latin *-o* ending has been Grecised (cf. *-ων*). The writer shows some uncertainty in his treatment of *-on* / *-o*. Thus the ending of *Aga*θo is Latinised (despite the presence of the Greek letter), whereas (e.g.) *Zenon* (i.11) retains its Greek *-n*. Both *Longo* (ii.35) and *Longon* (i.17) appear.

    A striking feature of the text is the chaotic use of Latin cases. Note the following oddities:

(i) ii.35 (centuria) Antoni Longo.

Here the first name is in the expected genitive, but the second name is not declined; the writer reverts to the nominative as a sort of base form (see below, IX, p. 633).[172]

(ii) i.3–5 (centuria) Nini Rufi
        Cereli Rufi
        Cocceus Clemes.

The second pair of names is mechanically put in the genitive when they should be in the nominative. The writer must have taken over the endings from the preceding pair of names. The same thing happens at ii.35–7 (partly quoted above): *Antoni Longo / Paconi Egnati / Iulius Niger*.

(iii) ii.29 Balini Ecateus.

Here the first name (*Balenius*: cf. *CIL* VIII.26480) seems to be in the genitive.

---

[170] See further Watson (1974: 506).
[171] For this type of format, cf. Kayser (1994), 102. On the other hand for the accusative used in a list of recruits written by a prefect, see *P. Oxy.* VII.1022 (discussed above, IV.2.1).
[172] See Kramer (1993: 148 n. 6).

The writer shows no clear understanding of the function of case variations in the list, and his alternations between nominative and genitive are sometimes unmotivated. His command of the Latin morphological system may well have been imperfect. Note Kramer (1993: 148 n. 6) 'Man hat überhaupt den Eindruck, dass dem Schreiber des Papyrus das lateinische Flexionssystem nicht besonders vetraut war.' He was almost certainly a Greek, and he may also have been unfamiliar with the format of the document; a copyist working mechanically without full control of the language might readily have written genitive for nominative or vice versa if he lost the thread of the text.

There is another aspect of the text which is worth noting here. It contains a substantial number of misspellings determined by the sounds of colloquial Latin, and must therefore have been the work of someone familiar with ordinary Latin speech. Note (e.g.) the form *Cladius* = *Claudius* (ii.33; cf. Väänänen (1981: 39) 'Une réduction de *au* en *a*, due à la dissimilation, se produit dans la syllabe initiale, lorsque la syllabe suivante contient un *u*'), and the forms *Flaus* = *Flauius* (i.13, 18) and *Otaus* (ii.24), showing -*aui*- > -*au*- where *i* is unaccented, as in *auispex > *auspex, aucellus, paumentum*, etc.[173] *Otaus* also shows a familiar dissimilation (*Oct-* > *Ot(t)*).[174] The form *Vpis* = *Vlpius* (ii.43, 44) displays in its ending the Greek change -ιος > -ις,[175] but more interestingly 'dark' *l* has been absorbed by the adjacent back vowel *u*. *Dulcis*, for example, is often spelt *ducis* in inscriptions (e.g. *ILCV* 2544A *ducisime*, 2574 *ducis* (cf. 2876, 4648), 4469 δουκις, *IGUR* 350 δουκισιμο); note too *O. Wâdi Fawâkhir* 3.14 *si uut* = *si uult*; and for the original *l* combining as *u* with a preceding *a* to produce *au* diphthong, see *cauculus* = *calculus* (*TLL* III.141.26: e.g. *Mul. Chir.* 228).[176] It appears to be a distinctively Latin feature; the examples of omission of λ in Greek papyri cited by Gignac (1976: 107) are not consistent with a change of *l* to a high back vowel before stops (note *P. Ryl.* 153.46 ὀφθαμόν not ὀφθαυμόν, = ὀφθαλμόν).

The text is thus a hybrid in its influences. For a similar combination of interference errors with colloquially determined features of substandard Latin, cf. the receipts written at Pulvinos (VII.2.2). One may conjecture that the writer was a Greek, literate in Greek, who had first acquired some Latin as a spoken language, and then taken some lessons in Latin literacy.

In one respect these texts differ from *ChLA* 1.12 and 3.204 (see above, VII.2.2). These last have errors of type (4), but not of types (2) and (3);

---

[173] See Battisti (1949: 141–2), Leumann (1977: 97, §103*b*). [174] See e.g. Väänänen (1981: 65).
[175] See Georgacas (1948).
[176] On the phenomenon in general, see in particular Battisti (1949: 166–7).

thus the writers had progressed further in their learning of Latin than the writers discussed in this section. The texts which we have just been considering were written in Latin in military communities, but each provides hints that all was not as it might seem in the matter of the writer's language use. There is reason to think that the writers were Greeks with varying command of the Latin language and literacy in the script of that language.

VIII THE LEARNING OF LATIN IN EGYPT

Evidence for the learning of Latin does not only come from military communities in Egypt.[177] There are also civilian texts dealing with matters (e.g.) related to Roman law in imperfect, Greek-influenced Latin (see also above, IV.6 (3)). I would suggest that the imperial bureaucracy did not have at all times and in all places a ready stock of native speakers of Latin to draft quasi-official Latin texts when the need arose, and that in the time-honoured Roman way Greek clerks or scribes were sometimes used.

(1) I consider first the document *P. Mich.* VII.434, *P. Ryl.* IV.612, *ChLA* 4.249. This legal text in Latin displays a range of Grecising errors and interference phenomena. It is a marriage contract from Karanis, dated to the second century. A 'father, a Roman citizen of three names, gives his daughter in marriage to a Roman also of three names' (Sanders, *P. Mich.* VII, p. 22). The document is witnessed in Greek, though the last witness, according to Sanders, writes in Latin (the text is fragmentary). Though the author was attempting to produce a Latin contract, the items of the dowry are basically designated by Greek terms. It is likely that the parties to the marriage – those who established the components of the dowry – were Greek- rather than Latin-speaking, even though they were Roman citizens. They were not required to use Latin, but by doing so they paraded their Romanness; alternatively, they might have been uncertain of the language requirements concerning the full range of legal documents in the name of citizens. For the compulsory use of Latin under not dissimilar circumstances, cf. the documents to do with citizens discussed earlier (IV.5, 6).

[177] I concentrate here on primary documents as showing signs of imperfect learning, but other evidence of a more literary kind for the acquisition of Latin literary culture in Egypt could be cited. See e.g. the article of Gilliam (1978), especially 128–31 (on a monastery library in the Thebaid which in the fourth century contained at least three Latin texts, including the first two Catilinarians), and also Cameron (1970: 19–21). There are useful remarks in Wilcken (1936). On bilingual exercises containing Latin literary texts with translations into Greek done by Greeks learning Latin, see now Rochette (1999), with bibliography; also id. (1990), (1997a: 177–206).

The orthography of the text is largely correct. There are, as we saw (above, VII.3), texts in which the digraphs of Greek are not converted to the corresponding digraphs of Latin, but that is not the case here. οι is correctly Latinised to *oe* (e.g. 6 *catoecicas*, 13 *lecythoe*), despite the fact that the *oe* spelling of Latin was recherché and scarcely in use (but see below). To judge by the correctness of the spelling, the scribe had been well trained in Latin literacy, though his Latin was imperfect in other respects. He does not commit errors of types (2) and (3) as classified at VII.3, but betrays his Greekness in other ways (see below).

The text has many problematic elements, some of them relevant to the question of bilingual interference. I consider the straightforward before the problematic. I begin with code-switching, then move on to morphological and related phenomena.

The lexicon of the document is heavily infiltrated with Greek terms for which there was a Latin equivalent available. It is clear that the dowry list gave the writer trouble. The list was probably first drawn up in Greek, and then an attempt made to translate it into Latin. The scribe did not have sufficient knowledge of Latin to translate fully. Sometimes he writes out a Greek word in Latin letters, even retaining its Greek inflection (code-switching, or, one might alternatively say, lexical interference/borrowing from the first language), or he may keep the Greek term but attempt (sometimes incorrectly) to Latinise its ending. Code-switching of the type at issue here (if we accept that designation) is that determined by the writer's ignorance of the *mot juste* (on which see 3.11). If on the other hand a Greek term unattested elsewhere in Latin is 'integrated' by means of a Latin ending, the integration may be only surface-deep, and the term cannot necessarily be designated an 'integrated loan-word'. There is little difference between a Greek word inflected as Greek in a Latin text, and a Greek word, otherwise completely alien to the Latin language, inflected as Latin. Both categories of words (at least in this text) reflect the writer's ignorance of Latin, and this ignorance he further betrays by the occasional use of an *incorrect* Latin inflection in a Greek word. I give line numbers from the Michigan fragment as it is printed in *ChLA*. The versions of the document extant are in too fragmentary a state to warrant full quotation; instead I select salient items.

Enotion (8) 'earring' (for which see also 3.11 (2), 4.V.2.2 (3)) is not attested elsewhere in Latin; by contrast in a marriage contract at *PSI* 730 the Latin term *inaures* is used instead. This was an early calque on ἐνώτιον, found from Plautus onwards. *Enotion* retains its Greek ending. *Catoecicas* (6) (< κατοικικός) is not recorded in the *TLL*. *Osyptrum* (12) 'mirror' (usually Gk. εἴσοπτρον; there was an alternative form ὄσοπτρον attested at *P. Oxy.* VI.978)[178] had a ready Latin equivalent (*speculum*), and the Latinised ending gives a false impression of its integration. *Tribacum* (15) (τριβακός) = 'worn' is cited only from this text by the *OLD*. Other Greek terms in the text are *[a]mpelitis* (8), *heratianon* (11), *epi[car]sium* (11–12), *cadium* (12, 13), *cathedran* (14), *pyxidam* (14), *cophinum* (14), *[pa]raferna* (15) (παράφερνα), *lecythoe* (13). Almost every word in the dowry list is of Greek origin, and a number are attested only here. *Cadium* (κάδιον), for example, is not noted by the *TLL*. *Heratianon* has not been decisively explained, though editors cite ἡραχιανόν at *P. Oxy.* XIV.1679.6. The ending has again been left as Greek.

I move on to some morphological features of the text. The essence of the Latinity is captured by *cathedran*, *pyxidam* and *cophinum* in 14, which are all of different types. Both the Michigan and Rylands texts have the form *cathedran*, which has retained its Greek inflection, though the word was well established in Latin. *Pyxidam* on the other hand displays an attempt at Latinisation, but an unsuccessful one. Inflected as classical Greek the accusative form would be *pyxida*, whereas the correct Latin form is *pyxidem*. The writer has either taken the classical Greek accusative form πυξίδα and 'Latinised' it by adding the -*m* of Latin, or (more likely) a later Greek accusative form, πυξίδαν, has been Latinised.[179] On either interpretation the writer obviously did not know the long-established Latin form of the word. Finally, *cophinum* has been fully Latinised.

In *lecythoe* (13) the writer has applied an orthographic conversion rule, according to which the Latin digraph *oe* corresponded to the Greek οι, a rule which, as we saw, was also applied in *catoecicas*. Unfortunately, however, by this period the digraph *oe* no longer had the status in the written language of a nominative plural morpheme. Thus the writer displays a greater understanding of writing conventions than of Latin morphology. The *oe* ending could alternatively be interpreted as the *Greek* ending (with a Latin spelling), and hence as a manifestation of code-switching (or interference) which has been slightly obscured by the spelling.

There is evidence in these cases that it was easier for a Greek learner of Latin to acquire spelling rules which allowed the conversion of Greek into Latin than it was to master the morphology of the target language

---

[178] See the material assembled by S. Eitrem, *P. Osl.* 46.7n.
[179] See Gignac (1981: 45–6) on -αν accusatives in the third declension.

(i.e. errors of type (4) persist when those of types (2) and (3) have been eliminated).

Various alleged Grecisms of inflection (as claimed by the Michigan editor Sanders, pp. 23–4, nn. 2–3) must be rejected. I mention them for the sake of completeness, because they are relevant to the interpretation of an interesting Greek word in the text. In *matrimonio* (3), *uico* (7) and *loco* (6, 16) there is a stroke over the final *o* which is interpreted by Sanders as an abbreviation indicating the accusative (*matrimoniom*, etc.), on which view the accusative could be taken as partially Grecised (*-om* = Gk. -ov). However the editors of *ChLA* 4.249 (p. 50 n.2) are undoubtedly right to take these forms as ablatives, with the stroke marking length.

Statmo (13) is an interesting case. The word is Greek, and there was in Greek an absolute use of the accusative σταθμόν = 'in weight' (LSJ *s.v.* σταθμός III.2). It is therefore tempting in this case (in contrast to those in the previous paragraph) to take the stroke as indicating a final nasal (code-switching, with the word, its form and its syntax all belonging to Greek). It is taken in this way by the *OLD*, s.v. Alternatively, the form might be a Latin ablative, in which case the term would have to be treated as a loan-word which has superficially been integrated into Latin. The scribe wrote the Latin equivalent *pondo* in line 10, and in *statmo* he may have given the Greek word the same ending. However the ending is taken, the word is of some interest purely as a lexical item. *Stathmos* does not appear in Lewis and Short, and it is unlikely ever to have been domiciled in Latin. Its presence in the text is another sign that the writer was operating more with a Greek than with a Latin vocabulary.

I next consider possible errors of gender. Again it is necessary to avoid over-confidence in interpreting the text. The editor of the Michigan text prints (line 7) *a]d eam uico*, and takes this as a mistake of gender. But the duplicate text in the Rylands collection shows that the correct reading is *in eo]dem uico*, which is adopted at *ChLA* 4.249.[180]

In the Michigan version (at 16) the text printed by *ChLA* is *pa]terna iug(er) fr(umentarias) duas*. The editor of *ChLA* 4.249 (p. 50 n. 4) tentatively suggests *iuger(es)* (cf. Sanders, p. 24 n. 6), but it is far from clear how this interpretation is to be squared with his placement of the *er* of *iuger* … in brackets. The original Michigan edition prints *pa]terna[s] iug. fr. duas.* There is obviously some confusion here.

Has *iugera* been used as a feminine (note *duas*)? If so there are two possible explanations: (1) The neuter plural might have been reinterpreted, in

[180] See the review by J. F. Gilliam, *AJP* 71 (1950), 433.

the familiar way, as a feminine singular, opening the way for a new plural *iugerae*; (2) the Latin word might have been influenced by the gender of ἄρουραι. Bilingual interference of gender is not unknown (see 4.v.4.6). The two factors are not mutually exclusive. Whatever the case, is there any justification for the restoration *iugeres*? The *TLL* incidentally cites no feminine *iugera*.

This is the only serious contender for a mistake of gender, but it must remain doubtful, given that the text is fragmentary at this point. *Alter* = *alterum* (13) I would not classify as an error of this type (see below).

There remain a few miscellaneous mistakes.

The lack of agreement at 13 (*cadium alter* = *alterum*) is described by Sanders (p. 25 n. 13) as 'wrong gender for *alterum*'. But even if an (incorrect) masculine gender was intended, the masculine form would have been *alterum* (accusative) not *alter*. It is the case ending as well as the gender that is wrong.

There are two ways of interpreting *alter*. It may simply be an abbreviation (*alter(um)*). This is the view put forward at *ChLA* ad loc. (p. 53, on the Michigan texts); cf. *P. Ryl.* 612.11 *pater(nam)*. The second possibility is that the writer reverted as it were to the base form or unmarked case of the adjective, that is the nominative (masculine).

A similar phenomenon is found at l. 13: *et osyptrum et arca [...]s* **lecythoe duae** *et cadium*... The sentence continues in the accusative. *Arca* can be taken as showing an omission of final *-m*, but *lecythoe duae* can only be a lapse into the unmarked (nominative) case-form. There is one difference between *lecythoe duae* and *cadium alter*. The first is internally consistent, whereas the second is inconsistent: if the noun is masculine accusative, the adjective is masculine nominative (an error of case), and if the noun is neuter (accusative/nominative) the adjective is masculine (an error of gender). Lists in Latin could be written in the nominative or the accusative, and writers occasionally oscillate between the two (note the Myconos *defixio*, *ID* 2534 = *ILLRP* 1150, with the text of Solin (1982a); see below, 6.vi). That is how *lecythoe duae* is to be explained. *Alter* should on balance be taken as an abbreviation.

There is no clear orthographic interference from Greek. Yet in the dowry list the writer shows a lack of familiarity with the Latin lexicon, and operates largely with a Greek vocabulary and also to some extent morphology. It seems clear that he had been trained in Latin script and spelling conventions, including the use of digraphs. But his morphological and lexical knowledge of Latin was imperfect. A parallel of sorts can be found in a translation of Babrius (*P. Amh.* II.26). There too there are signs of lexical ignorance and a limited morphology, but the orthography is without Greek interference (Chapter 8).

A Greek–Latin bilingual who had picked up some Latin as a spoken language might in theory have had a good command of Latin morphology and lexicon, but a poor ability to spell the language, if he had never been taught Latin literacy. By contrast a Greek who could spell in Latin but not control the morphology or vocabulary is more likely to have been a late learner (rather than a long-standing bilingual) who had received formal instruction in the language and its writing *in a certain order, with instruction in basic spelling rules (such as the conversion of the digraphs of one language to those of the other) preceding the extensive learning of vocabulary and morphology.* The distinction between learning a language and learning how to write it is an important one: it is the distinction between language learning, which does not require literacy, and literacy learning, which does not imply fluency in speaking the language being written.

The next text reveals the hand of a different type of learner.

(2) The bilingual Latin–Greek glossary *P. Lond.* II.481 has come up several times in earlier chapters (I.VII.2.1, 4.V.1.1, 4.V.3.3). The Latin which the writer knew was that of colloquial speech, as Kramer's commentaries (1977, 1983) demonstrate. But the text also shows, as we have seen, interference, both morphological and phonetic, from Greek.

I mention finally a few miscellaneous texts which seem to imply Latin learning by Greeks (outside the military sphere).

(3) *P. Mich.* VII.442 = *ChLA* 5.295 is a second-century document from Karanis dealing with a dowry which has been mentioned before (see above, I; also 4.V.2.11 on a loan-shift, and I.VII.4.2 (9) on a Greek-derived structural feature).

(4) In an account from Tebtunis of the second or third century (*P. Tebt.* 686, *ChLA* 5.304) showing interference and unusual borrowings from Greek (see 4.V.2.2, 4.V.4.6) there are also various phonetically inspired contractions, such as *aciscularis* and *materiaris*, which suggest again a familiarity with spoken Latin.

(5) In a bilingual birth certificate (*BGU* VII.1690) there is an appositional usage which does not conform with the norms even of substandard Latin constructions of this type: line 4 . . . *sibi natam esse Longiniam ex Arsute Luci f(ilia) hospitae suae. Hospita* 'guest' was a euphemism for a soldier's concubine (*BGU*, p. 206). For appositional examples of the word, see *CIL* III.2013, 2052, XI.6349.[181] Appositional terms are sometimes in the

---

[181] See *TLL* VI.2–3.3031.66ff.

neutral cases nominative or accusative (see VII.2.2), but a genitive of apposition does not exist as a genuine category. Has the writer lapsed into a Greek-inspired construction based on the case usage of ἐκ?

(6) *P. Cairo* J49503 (= *ChLA* 41.1198, *CEL* 205, *CPL* 137) is a bilingual receipt from Valerius Valentinus, *agrimensor* of the prefect of Egypt, dated 4 March 220, to Titus Valerius Valerianus, εὐθηνιάρχης of the city of Oxyrhynchus (the local *procurator annonae*), recording the receipt of various foodstuffs (no doubt military supplies). I quote the Latin part in full: *Im(peratore) d(omino) n(ostro) Antonino III et Comaszone II co(n)s(ulibus) IIII Nonas Martias. Valerius Valentinus agrimensor prefecti Egypti susc̣[epi] uinum sextaria kastresia sexcenta qu[ad]raginta Tito Flauio Valeriano euteṇiarca [O]xsoricito poleis, qui I et pretium [dedi] in sextario kastrese uno o[b]oḷoṣ quaternos plenos. actum [. . .] et cos. ss.* It is unclear why there is a Latin version, but it is possibly intended as a mild expression of authority.

One of the consul's names is spelt *Comaszone*. The name of the man was *Comazon*. In Greek papyri ζ is sometimes written σζ.[182] A variant Greek spelling has influenced the writing of Latin. The writer has also achieved only a partial Latinisation of *euteniarca [O]xsoricito poleis* (see 3.v.5, p. 382). On the other hand there are Latinate phonetic spellings which allow the reader to hear the sounds of spoken Latin (notably in the omission of *n* in *kastresia* and *kastrese*). The spelling with *k* of these two words is a reflection of the grammarians' rule that *k* should be written before *a*. The omission of the preposition *ab* with the ablative name *Tito Flauio Valeriano* is probably a simple slip. On the substandard numeral spelling *sexcenta* see above, VII.2.2, p. 613. Here then is a writer on whom again diverse influences were acting: the pressure of the literary practices of his other language, colloquial (spoken) Latin, the instruction which he had received in Latin literacy, and perhaps his imperfect competence in the second language.

I conclude, first, that here is yet more evidence that there were Greeks who had picked up Latin, in some cases originally as a spoken medium (despite the common misconception that Greeks disregarded other languages),[183] secondly, that the acquisition of Latin by Greeks must often have taken place well down the social scale (to judge by the features of substandard Latin which intruded into the texts), and thirdly, that degrees of competence in the second language varied, from imperfect knowledge (as in the case of Aeschines (1.VII.2.3), the translator of Babrius (Chapter 8), the writer of the epitaph inflected entirely as Greek

---

[182] See Gignac (1976: 123–4).
[183] For a thorough reassessment of the question, see now Rochette (1997a).

(1.IX (5)) and the slave Cerinthus (3.II (5)) to colloquial fluency. These texts combine features of colloquial Latin which could be paralleled in the writing of monolingual Latin speakers, with interference from Greek which marks the writers as bilingual, and probably native speakers of Greek.

IX CONCLUSIONS

Bilingualism in Greek and Egyptian, a large subject worthy of separate treatment,[184] does not fall within the scope of this book, though in an earlier chapter (1.VII.3) attention was drawn to various Demotic documents from Medinet Madi which show classifiable forms of code-switching into Greek, and earlier in this chapter (1.1) various bilingual texts were quoted which mix Demotic and Greek and also make use of the Latin alphabet and numerals.

There is both direct and indirect evidence for bilingualism in Egypt where one of the languages was Latin. By 'direct' evidence I refer to material which shows individuals using two languages indifferently. The letters of Terentianus are the prime case in point, but there are other users of two languages attested, particularly in military archives, such as the ostraca of Mons Claudianus (I refer to the archive of Successus, and to the correspondence between Annius Rogatus and Teres) and the Abinnaeus archive. There are also one or two explicitly bilingual individuals at the Colossus of Memnon and in the Syringes of Thebes. Code-switching also constitutes direct evidence. Court officials conducted proceedings in Greek, but they switched into Latin from time to time, as we saw in an earlier chapter (3.VI.1). Others used Latin themselves, but were addressed in Greek. Indirect evidence is perhaps more interesting, and about this a good deal has been said in the present chapter. By this phrase I mean performance in one language which betrays (through interference) the writer's knowledge of another. There is interference from Greek in Latin texts (as for example in the receipts from Pulvinos (VII.2.2), various military lists discussed at VII.3, and the marriage contract which has a dowry list intended as Latin but closer to Greek (see VIII)), and on the other hand 'interference' from Latin in some Greek texts. The most distinctive example of the latter kind is the military document *P. Hamb* 1.39, discussed at VII.1, but comparable phenomena are to be found in the Syringes of Thebes, and at Kalabcha and Deir-el-Bahari

---

[184] See for example La'da (1994), referred to at p. 36; also Fewster (forthcoming).

(though in all of these cases the data may be classified as showing code-switching rather than or as well as interference).

It may seem puzzling that there is not only interference from Greek in some Latin documents of military provenance, but also interference from Latin in various Greek military texts. The first phenomenon is easily understandable, because it is in line with the conventional view of linguistic policy in the army: recruits who were Greek-speaking will have been exposed to some Latin and their performance in the second language will often have been imperfect. Not so straightforward is the use of Greek in the army by those who were not completely adept in the language. Did the army ever impose the use of Greek on those who were primarily Latin-speaking? In fact Greek 'military' texts with Latin interference are not homogeneous, but reflect different situations. At pilgrimage sites those Roman soldiers who adopted Greek even though it might have been difficult for them to do so were not conforming with any military policy, but were either acting in accordance with what they felt was appropriate to the site (where an open display of Romanness might have been offensive) or (perhaps) were falling into line with a requirement of local priests. On the other hand the evidence of *P. Hamb.* 39 suggests that in one unit an individual, Julius Serenus, did require Greek from soldiers writing receipts for his book. It is unlikely that the choice of Greek by Serenus reflects anything that could be called an army policy; after all, there is extant a receipt from the same unit in Latin (Fink (1971), 80), and the remains of another receipt book show both languages used indifferently (Fink (1971), 75). It is much more likely that Serenus was imposing his own linguistic policy, perhaps in line with his own linguistic preference or competence.

On this evidence it would seem that the linguistic competence of individuals was one determinant of language choice in the army even when a document with official status was to be composed. The overwhelming predominance of Greek in military archives from Egypt (some 90 per cent of texts extant are in that language) must reflect the high proportion of native speakers of Greek serving in the armies of the east, the presence in the army of at least some native speakers of eastern languages other than Greek or Latin who were forced to communicate in the lingua franca Greek, and finally a *laissez-faire* attitude on the part of the authorities, who were prepared to allow Greek (but not other vernacular languages) in written documents to do with military affairs.

But that said, there are signs even in the limited Latin material extant that instruction in Latin language and literacy must have been provided in the army, at least for some of its members. Literary or anecdotal evidence for Latin-learning in the east has been well documented,[185] but anecdotes cannot always be taken at their face value,[186] as I have suggested in an earlier chapter (see I.III, I.III.1). Primary evidence for language learning in Egypt (including the Roman army in Egypt), minuscule though it might be in quantity, can show us stages of learning in practice, and also take us into the world of the relatively humble learner. Upper-class language learning, which often entails the acquisition of a whole literary culture as well as the language of the literature, has an obvious interest, but the Roman army in the field did not resolve problems of communication by laying on a literary education for recruits. In this chapter I have discussed in detail (VII. 2.2, VII.3) various military documents written in Latin which show varying degrees of Greek-determined error, ranging from what might be called errors of literacy to errors of language. A feature of these texts is that they do not exclusively concern language learning, but reveal the hand of Greek speakers reaching ascending levels of literacy in their second language. Many illiterate recruits into the Roman army no doubt picked up Latin as a spoken medium without ever learning to write the language (for evidence of illiteracy in the army see VII.1 on *P. Hamb.* 1.39). But the existence of military texts in Latin containing errors betraying the early stages of literacy learning does suggest that some illiterate recruits did not remain illiterate. Since the writers were not far advanced in Latin literacy, it was almost certainly in the army itself that they had been given instruction. And since in these documents different degrees of competence are discernible, instruction might have been ongoing, with the result that a camp had within it learners at different levels. Since non-native speakers were used as scribes for the writing of official documents, there must have been a shortage in some units of native Latin speakers who could carry out such tasks. Given that, as we have repeatedly seen, the Roman army was prepared to allow the use of Greek for many official documents, it is particularly interesting to find evidence that some largely Greek-speaking units felt the need to teach some Latin. Signs of a linguistic policy thus emerge. Greek was usually acceptable, but a unit could not get by on Greek alone. In a unit largely using Greek circumstances might at any time arise requiring the use of Latin, as for example when Abinnaeus had to make his appeal to Rome. Language and literacy learning in Latin must have been taking place in the background even in units whose records

---

[185] See Rochette (1997a), chapter 3.
[186] See the remarks of J. Geiger in his review of Rochette (*JRS* 89 (1999), 232–3).

were mainly in Greek. What the army did not require is that in pre-dominantly Greek-speaking units Latin should under all circumstances be used, but it clearly did require that some learning of Latin was going on so that the language could be used when necessary.[187] The policy is subtle and not at all doctrinaire.

I have not in this chapter attempted a survey of the linguistic features of the Latin documents found in Egypt. The focus has been on bilin-guals' or learners' Latin rather than on the performance of users of the language who were either monolingual or native speakers and thus not subject to interference from the other language. Fluent (substandard) Latin texts from Egypt do of course have their interest (the letters of Rustius Barbarus from Wâdi Fawâkhir are a case in point,[188] and also some Latin material from Mons Claudianus and Myos Hormos[189]), but not strictly in the present context. I would single out here just two further features of bilinguals' texts.

First, it is worth noting the frequency with which the nominative is used as a sort of base form instead of other cases.[190] In 1.1 we saw a Demotic receipt with Latin letters and numerals at the end expressing a name and date. The filiation is not inflected. This document is more complex than it appears, because it is possible that the writer knew nothing of Latin other than the alphabet, and that he may in fact have been using *Greek* in the Latinate part, though he was surely aspiring to write Latin. In *P. Hamb.* 1.39 (above, VII.1) one writer switches from a Greek genitive (τούρμης) to a Latin nominative (Πετρωνιανα). Thus he was under pressure not only to switch into the nominative, but also to revert to his first language. There is a further example in the military list discussed at VII.3 (2). The dowry list discussed at VIII is meant to be in the accusative, but there is one unambiguous case of a lapse into the nominative. I leave aside the 'nominative of apposition' as seen in the receipt *ChLA* 3.204 (VII.2.2) because, though attested in bilinguals' texts (as e.g. the African Latin *defixio* in Greek letters (Audollent (1904), 270) discussed at I.VII.2.2), it is merely substandard and not necessarily a consequence of imperfect learning. Unconstrued nominatives have not received much attention.[191] It is understandable that an imperfect learner of a second language might sometimes have lapsed into the case which

---

[187] But the vernacular languages of the Empire, unlike Greek, were definitely not acceptable in record keeping. The learning of Latin must have been rather more extensive in units with (e.g.) large numbers of Africans or Palmyrenes.

[188] See Cugusi (1981).   [189] See Bülow-Jacobsen, Cuvigny and Fournet (1994).

[190] For this usage in Greek, see above, 2.V.7.

[191] For a discussion of some cases, with bibliography, see Adams (1994a: 96–102).

he had learnt as the base-form of a word. Unconstrued nominatives are not however homogeneous, and cannot always be attributed to imperfect learning. I stress the important point here that learners' irrational errors must be distinguished from commonplace colloquial deviations from an educated norm.

Secondly, while code-switching which was conscious (or, if not conscious, determined by fluent bilingual skills) is attested in Egypt (e.g. in hearings before officials), some of the most striking texts discussed in this chapter display language mixing of the type described in an earlier chapter (3.II) as code-switching caused by imperfect competence in the second language (or perhaps we should call the phenomenon 'interference'). I am thinking particularly of the receipt-book *P. Hamb.* I.39 which is intended to be in Greek but has uncontrolled lapses into Latin. The other side of the coin is represented by the dowry list (VIII), which is meant to be in Latin but is mainly in (transliterated) Greek. Much of the contract would have had a standard format, and the writer will merely have had to copy out an exemplar. But the dowry list was an original part of the document, and there the drafter had difficulties. It is of interest that both of these specimens of language mixing are in formal documents. The drafting of legal and military documents was not exclusively in the hands of educated bureaucrats with fluent bilingual skills. The fact that imperfect second-language learners had to be employed is a result of low rates of literacy and the shortage of learned scribes capable of doing a job properly. It may be conjectured that in this society a good deal of communication took the form of mixed-language utterances by speakers who had to get by as best they could in a second language.

It was mentioned above that Roman linguistic policy in the army was subtle and adaptable. I move on now to set out in summary form what has emerged in this chapter about Roman linguistic policy in Egypt (though in referring to Egypt I am aware that if the evidence were more extensive in other eastern areas it would probably be justifiable to refer to a single Roman linguistic policy in the whole of the eastern Empire).[192] One obvious question which ought to be faced is whether policy (if there were such) changed in time.

I summarise the most straightforward conclusions that can be drawn from the material assembled here. First, Greek was used extensively as the

---

[192] Kaimio (1979b) argues that there was nothing special about Egypt when compared with the other eastern provinces in the matter of language choice and policy. See too Rochette (1997a: 125–6) (and particularly the comparative table at 126 showing language choice in a variety of documents in Egypt compared with that in the same sorts of documents elsewhere in the east; there are no differences).

administrative language, as we saw for example in prefects' dealings with other officials (IV.1). This practice was in line with a widespread Roman view of Greek as a suitable lingua franca in the east. The appropriateness of Greek even in informal discussions of matters to do with the civil administration is reflected in the correspondence of the Latin speaker Terentianus, who used Greek when he dwelt on affairs which concerned the local administration (VI.2). Secondly, if there were Latin speakers who knew Demotic we do not know of them. Certainly no use was made by the Romans (after the very early period from which the trilingual inscription of Gallus dates) of Egyptian in formal documents, apart from religious inscriptions in hieroglyphics in temple precincts in which the emperors are portrayed as pharaohs. Thirdly, the most distinctive and positive form of policy which we have seen concerns the insistence on the use of Latin in certain types of legal documents relating to possessors of the citizenship (IV.5, 6).

It has become a commonplace that the amount of Latin used in Egypt (and in the east in general) increased under Diocletian.[193] But an examination of Rochette's discussion (1997a: 118–19) in this connection of reports of judicial hearings before Roman officials (for which see 3.VI.1 and, in brief, above, IV.4) suggests in my opinion that this view is rather weakly based. In this book such documents have been dealt with at length in the chapter on code-switching, and very briefly in this chapter in connection with language use as an assertion of power (IV.4). The placement of the two discussions is quite deliberate. I reiterate the features of the texts in order to bring out my own view of them. First, the framework of the written report, comprising a brief preamble and introductions of the speakers (often merely *d(ixit)* and a name), is often in Latin. Numerous such (fragmentary) reports come from the post-Diocletianic period (see Rea's list at *P. Oxy.* LI.3619). But the skeleton framework in Latin of the written record of a hearing is not to be confused with the hearing itself. These Latin parts of the record are usually very skimpy and unobtrusive. Their presence must reflect a policy determining the format of records, but that policy, symbolic though the Latin might be, has virtually nothing to tell us about a possible shift of attitude by the imperial administration to the role of Latin in administration. The records may, after all, have been purely for the administrators themselves. Moreover we discussed at Chapter 3, VI.1 the record of a hearing

---

[193] See for example Turner (1961), but above all the extensive discussion of Rochette (1997a: 116–26), with abundant bibliography; also id. (1999: 325 with n. 4). Also worth noting is J. Rea on *P. Oxy.* LI.3619.

before Caracalla held at Antioch in 216 which shows the same type of
Latin framework enclosing Greek speeches, but antedating Diocletian
by more than fifty years. The possibility that the format might have been
a Diocletianic innovation is thus ruled out. Secondly, there are signs of
code-switching into Latin by the officials when they address one another.
Thirdly, there is one abnormal hearing reported (with a parallel in the
Theodosian Code) in which the *praeses* spoke Latin but the advocates
Greek. This document is after the time of Diocletian. Finally, decisions
seem to have been given first in Latin, but with a translation sometimes
provided.

Basing himself on this evidence, Rochette (1997a: 119; cf. 118) concludes that it was Diocletian's intention to introduce a reform, whereby
Latin was to become the normal language of tribunals and 'perhaps
even of the entire provincial administration' ('Cette réforme, voulue par
Dioclétien, qui visait à introduire le latin comme langue usuelle des
tribunaux et peut-être même dans l'ensemble de l'administration provin-
ciale . . . '; cf. 118 'Dans l'usage officiel et administratif, le latin tend à se
substituer de plus en plus au grec. Les audiences judiciaires des gou-
verneurs se déroulent en latin'). The evidence does not in my opinion
support such conclusions. For one thing, there was nothing unusual in
giving decisions in Latin. We saw this phenomenon centuries earlier at
Amphipolis (IV.3). It is also a vital fact that the Latin spoken in these hearings took the form of code-switching. An official policy might attempt to
impose a single language on proceedings, but code-switching is an *ad hoc*
and variable phenomenon which could not possibly be the subject of any
official proclamation. The variability of the switching even in the limited
number of documents extant suggests the personal linguistic behaviour
of various individuals in a bilingual community, not the operation of a
formal policy. If we were right to argue that the switching was motivated
by a desire to exclude monolingual Greeks from time to time, then it
was a manifestation of language use as a symbolic show of power. The
choice of Latin on occasions before Greeks as an act of power was not
a Diocletianic invention, but had its roots back in the Republic. Even
in Egypt we have observed the phenomenon well before the time of
Diocletian, at the Colossus of Memnon (IV.1). Instead of attempting to
set up a Diocletianic reform, I would prefer to stress that the practice on
the one hand of linguistic accommodation to Greek, particularly in the
religious sphere, and on the other of using Latin assertively in political
contexts, can be traced back into the Republic. Moreover the texts discussed in this chapter which exemplify language learning in progress do

not only come from the period after Diocletian. The learning of Latin had no doubt been going on informally in Egypt for a long time; it might well have been more widespread in the fourth century than earlier, but if so that need have had nothing to do with an official policy.

I would though concede that I am restricting myself in this discussion to the material from Egypt, and would suggest that a re-examination of all of the relevant evidence from the whole of the eastern Empire concerning a possible change of linguistic policy under Diocletian would be a useful undertaking. There is, for example, a valuable collection of inscriptional material in Sironen (1997: 53; cf. 63).

I would draw attention finally to the conclusions earlier in this chapter (VI.3) about possible diglossia in Egypt. The old diglossic opposition H–L does not apply to the relationship between Latin and Greek in Egypt, because both languages were High in different senses, with Latin available, as it always had been in Greek areas, as a super-high political language. I mentioned in this connection the Colossus of Memnon, the archive of Abinnaeus, court hearings, and documents under Roman law concerning Roman citizens. We saw that in the inscriptions of Alexandria soldiers regularly used Latin in dedications to emperors. By contrast those soldiers making dedications to local deities in the same corpus regularly used Greek. Latin thus symbolises the relationship between soldier and emperor, but again soldiers show linguistic accommodation in the religious sphere. This ancient evidence ought to be added to the general critique of conventional diglossia that is now under way.

It must though be added that the functional relationship between Greek and Latin depended on the native language of the speaker and on the dominant language of the society in question. Greeks at Rome treated Latin as the H language (of bureaucracy) and Greek as the L, whereas in Egypt Terentianus seems to have regarded Greek as the administrative language, and Latin as that of the family.

APPENDIX: THE TRILINGUAL INSCRIPTION OF GALLUS

IGPhilae ii.128, *CIL* iii.14147

C(aius) Cornelius Cn(aei) f(ilius) Gallu[s, eq]ues Romanus, poṣṭ reges a Caesare deiui f(ilio) deuictos praefect[us Alex]andreae et Aegypti primus, defectioni[s] Thebaidis intra dies XV, quibus hostem u[icit bis a]cie, uictor, V urbium expugnator, Bore[se]os, Copti, Ceramices, Diospoleos Meg[ales, Op]hieu, ducibus earum defectionum inter[ce]ptis, exercitu ultra Nili catarhacte[n transd]ucto, in quem locum neque populo Romano neque regibus Aegypti [arma s]unt prolata, Thebaide communi

omn[i]um regum formidine subact[a], leg[atis re]gis Aethiopum ad Philum auditis,
eo[dem] rege in tutelam recepto, tyrann[o] Tr[iacontas]choe(ni) in fine Aethiopiae
constituto die[is] patrieis et Nil[o adiut]ori d(onum) d(edit).

'C. Cornelius Gallus, son of Cn., Roman knight, after the kings were
defeated by Caesar son of the divine (Caesar), as the first prefect of
Alexandria and Egypt, defeater of a defection of the Thebaid within
fifteen days, in which he defeated the enemy twice in battle, taker of five
cities, Boresis, Coptos, Ceramice, Diospolis Magna, Ophieum, with the
leaders of those defections cut off, with his army led across beyond the
cataract of the Nile, into which place neither by the Roman people nor
by the kings of Egypt have arms been carried, with the Thebaid, the
common scourge of all kings, reduced, with legates of the king of the
Ethiopians heard at Philae, with the same king received into guardianship, with a ruler set over the land of the thirty schoenoe on the frontier
of Ethiopia, made this dedication to the ancestral gods and to the Nile
his assistant.'

[Γ]άιος Κορνήλιος Γναίου υἱὸς Γάλλ[ος, ἱππεὺ]ς ‘Ρωμαίων, μετὰ τὴν
κατάλυσιν τῶν ἐν Αἰγύπτωι βασιλέων πρῶτος ὑπὸ Καίσ[αρος ἐπὶ]
τῆς Αἰγύπτου κατασταθείς, τὴν Θηβαίδα ἀποστᾶσαν ἐν πεντεκαίδεκα
ἡμέραις δὶς [ἐν παρ]ατάξει κατὰ κράτος νικήσας, σὺν τῶι τοὺς ἡγεμόνας
τῶν ἀντιταξαμένων ἑλεῖν, πέν[τε τε πό]λεις τὰς μὲν ἐξ ἐφόδου, τὰς
δὲ ἐκ πολιορκί[ας] καταλαβόμενος, Βορῆσιν, Κόπτον, Κεραμικὴ[ν,
Διόσπ]ολιν μεγάλην, ’Οφιῆον, καὶ σὺν τῆι στρατιᾶι ὑπεράρας τὸν
καταράκτην, ἀβάτου στρατία[ις τῆς χώρ]ας πρὸ αὐτοῦ γενομένης, καὶ
σύμπασαν τὴ[ν] Θηβαίδα μὴ ὑποταγεῖσαν τοῖς βασιλεῦσιν [ὑποτάξ]ας,
δεξάμενός τε πρέσβεις Αἰθιόπων ἐν Φίλαις καὶ προξενίαν παρὰ τοῦ
βασιλέως λ[αβών, τύ]ραννόν τε τῆς Τριακοντασχοίνου τοπαρχία[ς]
μιᾶς ἐν Αἰθιοπίαι καταστήσας, θεοῖς πατρ[ῴοις, Ν]είλῳ συνλήπτορι
χαριστήρια.

'Gaius Cornelius Gallus, son of Gnaeus, Roman knight, after the disso-
lution of the kings in Egypt, appointed by Caesar as the first man over
Egypt, having conquered by force the Thebaid (which was in revolt) twice
in battle in fifteen days, along with the capture of the leaders of those who
opposed him, having seized five cities, some by assault, some by a siege,
Boresis, Coptos, Ceramice, Diospolis Magna, Ophieum, having crossed
the cataract with his army, though the place had been inaccessible to
armies before him, having subdued the whole of the Thebaid which had
not been subdued by the kings, having received the ambassadors of the
Ethiopians in Philae and accepted a compact of hospitality from the king,

having appointed a ruler of the Triacontaschoenus, which constituted a single district, in Ethiopia, (made) a thank-offering to the ancestral gods and to the Nile which supported him.'

I offer some miscellaneous comments on the inscription.

(1) With its long string of ablative absolutes, all of them claiming triumphs of one sort or another, followed by an expression of thanks to the ancestral gods, the Latin version resembles the returning general's prayer of thanksgiving as parodied at Plaut. *Pers.* 753ff. *hostibus uictis, ciuibus saluis, re placida, pacibus perfectis, / bello exstincto, re bene gesta, integro exercitu et praesidiis, / quom bene nos, Iuppiter, iuuisti, dique alii omnes caelipotentes, / eas uobis gratis habeo atque ago, quia probe sum ultus meum inimicum.*[194] Note here *iuuisti*, and compare the terminology applied to the Nile in the inscription (*adiutori* is a restoration, but justifiable from the Greek). Another similar passage in Plautus, again with ablative absolutes, though this time more in the nature of a military report announcing victory (*Amph.* 188ff.), also has *uictores*, as well as juxtaposition of the participles *uictum* and *expugnatum* (cf. the juxtaposition of *uictor* and *expugnator* in the inscription): *uictores uictis hostibus legiones reueniunt domum, / duello exstincto maxumo atque internecatis hostibus. / quod multa Thebano poplo acerba obiecit funera, / id ui et uirtute uictum atque expugnatum oppidum est.* Here *uictor* and the verb *uinco* are juxtaposed, as is virtually the case in the inscription. And both Plautine passages and the inscription have the verb phrase *hostes (-em) uincere.*

(2) The Greek version lacks a word for *praefectus*, which in Greek would have been ἔπαρχος.[195] Is there some polemical point at issue here, or has the word been inadvertently left out by the stonecutter? πρῶτος does not seem entirely convincing construed with the participle κατασταθείς.

Strabo travelled in Egypt a few years after the setting up of the inscription. At 17.1.53 he adopts some of the wording of the Greek version: Γάλλος μέν γε Κορνήλιος, ὁ πρῶτος κατασταθεὶς ἔπαρχος τῆς χώρας ὑπὸ Καίσαρος, τήν τε Ἡρώων πόλιν ἀποστᾶσαν ἐπελθών. It is of note that here πρῶτος is accompanied by the expected word for 'prefect'. Did he emend the text that he saw on the inscription?[196]

(3) Some of the discrepancies between the Greek and Latin may be explained as due to a rather mundane setting out of details in the Greek where the Latin has a graphic or even poetic phrase. Thus, in describing the capture of the five cities, the Latin has the stylish -*tor* noun *expugnator*,

[194] See Laughton (1964:102).　　[195] See Magie (1905: 25–6).
[196] On the passage of Strabo, see Boucher (1966: 42), though not discussing this point or the source of the wording.

whereas the Greek (πέν[τε τε πό]λεις τὰς μὲν ἐξ ἐφόδου, τὰς δὲ ἐκ πολιορκί[ας] καταλαβόμενος), with its balanced reference to assault and siege, is superficially more precise in a banal way, but lacks the stylistic markedness of the Latin. Similarly the *-tor* noun *uictor* with dependent genitive (*defectioni[s] Thebaidis*) corresponds to a verbal construction in the Greek (τὴν Θηβαίδα ἀποστᾶσαν . . . κατὰ κράτος νικήσας). One might compare *Res Gestae* 3.1 Gagé **uictor**que *omnibus . . . ciuibus peperci*, where the Greek translation has a verbal construction: [νεικ]ήσας τε πάντων ἐφεισάμην . . .

É. Bernand's (1969) summary of the different aims of the Latin and Greek versions is set out at pp. 46–7. The Latin version supposedly expresses pride in Gallus' victories and is calculated to please the prefect and his men and to convey the glory of the Empire,[197] whereas the Greek is a concession to the language of the Ptolemaic administration and to the defeated people, and does not abuse the departed regime. But it has been pointed out by Hauben (1976) that at least one of the crucial passages does not support this conclusion at all. The reference to the crushing of the Thebaid takes the following form in the two versions: σύμπασαν τὴ[ν] Θηβαίδα μὴ ὑποταγεῖσαν τοῖς βασιλεῦσιν [ὑποτάξ]ας; *Thebaide communi omn[i]um regum formidine subact[a*. The Latin has a stylish expression, *formidine* = 'source of fear', used in apposition to *Thebaide*. For this usage, see e.g. Hor. *Sat.* 1.8.4 *maxima formido furum*. In no sense could this expression be taken as hostile to the previous administration, given its vagueness. The clear statement in the Greek of the inability of the Ptolemies to subjugate the Thebaid could surely be taken as a greater insult to the Greek-speaking population (so Hauben (1976: 189)): 'the Greek version goes much further in belittling the Ptolemies than the Latin'). Indeed Bernand's discussion of the passage (43–4) is at variance with his general thesis described above. He states (44): 'Il est plus vraisemblable que l'auteur de l'inscription grecque a travesti quelque peu la réalité et grossi l'importance des révoltes de la Thébaide sous les Ptolémées, pour mieux vanter les mérites de l'occupation romaine et spécialement ceux du premier préfet.' On this view the Greek (at this point) is more polemical and pro-Roman than the Latin.

One way to explain the discrepancy would be to argue that the Latin version was the work of a stylist (perhaps even Gallus himself) who had no wish to overdo the precision of the text, and that the Greek version

---

[197] 46 'Elle est faite pour plaire au préfet victorieux et à ses hommes.' For a few remarks on discrepancies between the versions, see also Marrone (1976: e.g. 320–1).

was a rendering of the Latin by an official who had no claims to literary style but a desire to make the vague phrases of the original as precise as he could.

(4) The Greek version has the Latinate filiation with υἱός, and that is a hint, though not in itself a proof, of the primacy of the Latin version.

(5) An interesting feature of the Latin version is the inflection of the place names. There is no consistency here. Most are given a Greek inflection, but *Copti* is inflected as Latin. For an explanation of the variability, see above, 3.V.2, n. 141.

(6) There are several similarities of ideas and wording between the Latin version and the *Res Gestae* of Augustus (which was written somewhat later). There can obviously be no direct connection between the two texts; but both writers were working within a tradition of self-advertisement by great men (cf. the Scipionic elogia), and in such a tradition clichés or patterns of thought may proliferate. Note *Res Gestae* 2 Gagé *uici bis acie* (in the Greek of Augustus δὶς ἐνείκησα παρατάξει; cf. the Gallus inscription δὶς [ἐν παρ]ατάξει . . . νικήσας), 16.1 *id primus et solus omnium . . . feci* (the commonplace claim to have been the first to have done something; cf. *praefectus . . . primus*), 26.4 *quo neque terra neque mari quisquam Romanus ante id tempus adit* (the claim to have been the first to go with an army to a previously inaccessible place; cf. *in quem locum neque populo Romano neque regibus Aegypti*), 30.1 *Pannoniorum gentes, quas ante me principem populi Romani exercitus nunquam adit, deuictas per . . .* (much the same sort of claim), followed by the participle *deuictus* that is also in the Gallus inscription).

6

Bilingualism at Delos

Delos provides an interesting case study of bilingualism in the public domain in a trading community in which Romans and Italians were prominent in the last centuries of the Republic.[1] Trade is an activity in which cross-language communication is essential. Two separate trading or commercial communities, in which Roman linguistic attitudes differed markedly, are the subject of chapters in this book. In the pottery at La Graufesenque there is no sign of Italians learning Gaulish. Gaulish went on being used by Celts, but there are indications that they were also learning Latin. But on Delos the Roman/Italian attitude to the other language was far more deferential. Italians were happy to have themselves presented as Greek-speaking in formal texts, though the situation was complex, as we will see.

Delos was the site of the earliest and largest Roman–Italian commercial community in the Greek world. After 167 the senate expelled the Delians and the island became a free-trade centre under nominal Athenian supervision.[2] Many inscriptions, in Greek, Latin and both languages, distributed for present purposes from the second century BC onwards into the early Imperial period, attest the activities of Latin-speaking, or, one should more accurately say, bilingual, *negotiatores*, and raise fundamental questions about the relationship between the two languages, the motivations of language choice, if only in public documents (for 'private' language use, see the discussion below (VI) of the Myconos curse tablet), and the character of the bilingualism of the traders. The Romans/Italians are referred to in the inscriptions variously as ʿΡωμαῖοι

---

[1] On bilingualism at Delos see Touloumakos (1995: 114–21) and Siebert (1999), who studies in detail the Greek and Latin inscriptions in the Agora of the Italians.
[2] See e.g. Gruen (1984: 311), Rauh (1993: 1–3).

or Ἰταλικοί (*Italicei*). These are terms of controversial meaning, to which I will come in due course (III).

A good deal is known about individuals who made up the 'Italian' presence at Delos and about their origins in Italy, though not as much as has sometimes been suggested. Solin (1982a:111–12) rejects Hatzfeld's belief (see e.g. 1919: 239–42) in the 'prevalenza dell'Italia meridionale nel novero degli Italici di Delo'.[3] It would also be wrong to classify the Italians as exclusively or predominantly monolingual Latin speakers who either had to learn, or to adopt strategies for communicating in, Greek. Neither Italy nor Rome was monolingual in Latin in the Republican period. There were Greeks (of diverse eastern origins) not only in the servile class, but also in the Greek settlements of Italy (*Magna Graecia*). The *negotiatores* resident at Delos were not ethnically or socially homogeneous.[4] Romans, even if in some cases they might have been monolingual in Latin, were assisted by slaves or freedmen of Greek origin,[5] either brought from Italy or employed from Delos itself. Greek speakers from *Magna Graeca* also traded on the island. The pattern will have repeated itself whenever 'Romans' traded in eastern areas. Those who did not know Greek could readily have found Greeks from Rome or elsewhere in Italy to make up their entourage. Moreover Roman trade on Delos was not short-lived: 'Certain families flourished on Delos through several generations' (A. Wilson (1966: 116)), and these will have become bilingual, even if they did not begin as such.

A few salient examples will bring out the complexity of the Italian group at Delos. A prominent figure was the banker Philostratus, who was a citizen of Naples but had originally come from Ascalon (see *ID* 1724).[6] Another such person was Simalos of Tarentum (*ID* 1755), who probably had connections with Cyprus (see *ID* 1533, 1534).[7] These two cases suggest that Greek-speaking 'Italians' working at Delos might have had

---

[3] Note especially (Solin 1982a: 117): 'Ho cercato di dimostrare che la grande massa degli Italiani di Delo non può essere costituita esclusivamente da persone originarie dall'Italia meridionale; il ruolo dell'Italia centrale, soprattutto di alcuni grandi centri del Lazio come Praeneste, e della stessa Roma non deve essere sottovaluto.'

[4] See Rauh (1993: 33), and for an account of the Italians and their origins, A.Wilson (1966: 105–11).

[5] See the bilingual inscription *ID* 1771 (discussed by Touloumakos (1995: 81–2); see further below, IV.2), which is dedicated to Zeus Eleutherios by four slaves and a freedman, all with Greek names. The five men were all members of the Italian entourage.

[6] See Mancinetti Santamaria (1982), Leiwo (1989).

[7] For the possible identification of the referent of 1755 with that of 1533 and 1534 (who was from Salamis in Cyprus), see the editor on *ID* 1755. See further Rauh (1993: 33), Hatzfeld (1912: 79), A.Wilson (1966: 115).

roots in Greece itself before they found themselves in Italy or the Italian community on Delos. Less complicated are natives of Greek-speaking parts of Italy, such as the banker Heracleides of Tarentum (*ID* 1716), or the Neapolitan Serapion (*ID* 1755). There are 221 'Ρωμαῖοι of identifiable status in the inscriptions, according to Hatzfeld (1919: 247),[8] of whom 88 are freeborn (and of these 27 are from southern Italy). No fewer than 95 others are freedmen, and a further 48 are slaves, many of whom were no doubt of eastern origin and native speakers of Greek (see below).

Sometimes we can identify the Greek freedmen of a Roman or probable Roman at Delos. Thus at *ID* 2013 a freedman with the name Ἀριστόμαχος honours in Greek his patron Seius (marble block): Γναῖον Σήιον Γναίου υἱὸν ʽΡωμαῖον Γάιος Σήιος Γναίου Ἀριστόμαχος, Ἀπόλλωνι. Aristomachus was a first-language speaker of Greek. At 2245 he honours his mother, a Greek, in Greek (white marble statue base; on the implications of the accusative in such a context, as constantly in the Delian inscriptions, see below, III.3): Κλεοπάτραν Φιλοστρά[τ]ου Ἀραδίαν τῶν ἀπὸ Μαράθου Γάιος Σήιος Γναίου ʽΡωμαῖος Ἀριστόμαχος *v.*τὴν ἑαυτοῦ μητέρα ʽΑγνῇ Ἀφροδίτη Συρίᾳ θεῷ. The mother was from Aradus, which was was 'the main city of north Phoenicia, on the island of Awad' (*OCD*³), and Marathus was one of its dominions. Aristomachus calls himself a Roman here, presumably because on manumission he became a Roman citizen (on this use of ʽΡωμαῖος, see below, III.2). Either the mother had been brought to Rome, giving birth to Aristomachus into a bilingual environment, or Aristomachus himself had come to Rome as a slave. The second possibility seems the more likely. It would have been linguistically advantageous for Roman *negotiatores* trading in Greece to take with them from Rome slaves or freedmen of Greek origin. I would also point out in passing (it will become relevant later) that in the first inscription Aristomachus uses υἱός to express the filiation of the Roman, but the plain genitive to express his relationship to his patron; on this distinction, see below, V.1.

At *ID* 1802 Q. Tullius Q. f., who was an Apolloniast (on this term, see below, IV.2) *c.* 125 BC, is honoured in a bilingual inscription by three of his freedmen, who have Greek names; one of them, Q. Tullius Heracleo, is known to have been a competaliast (on which title, see below, IV.2) *c.* 108 (1761). The inscription is on a statue base found in a private house, the house of Q. Tullius.[9] At lines 2–4 of the Greek, Κόιντος Τύλλιος

---

[8] See also A.Wilson (1966: 106).

[9] On which see Rauh (1993: 195–9). On the inscription and the problem of identifying the referent, see Rauh (1993: 198–9).

Ἀλέξανδρος καὶ Κόιντος Τύλλιος Ἀρίσταρχος οἱ Κοίντου corresponds (with a change of order) to *Q. Tullius Q. l. A[ristarchus], Q. Tullius Q. l. Ale[xander]* in the Latin; note the absence of an equivalent in the Greek to *libertus*, and see above on 2013. The bilingualism of the inscription seems to contain on the one hand a display of deference to Tullius, and on the other an expression of the freedmen's linguistic identity as a contrast to that of their patron.[10] They put the Greek version first. The text could have been written exclusively in Latin or Greek, and inscriptions of both types could be paralleled (see e.g. 2013, quoted above).

II LINGUISTIC INTEGRATION OF ROMANS/ITALIANS ON DELOS

There is evidence for a considerable degree of linguistic integration of Romans in the Greek-speaking community of Delos. To judge by certain dedications written in Greek, Romans were fully participant in the primary language of the area. There can be no question of Roman *negotiatores* practising anything resembling the linguistic nationalism attributed by Valerius Maximus 2.2.2 (see 5.IV.3) to Roman magistrates in Greek areas. In this section I discuss some evidence for this willingness on the part of the Italians to be seen as Greek-speaking.

Sometimes Romans honour Greeks in Greek. At *ID* 1724 the banker Philostratus receives a dedication from a group of three Romans with the *gentilicium Egnatius*: [Φιλ]όστρατον [Φ]ιλοστρά[του] Νεαπολίτην [τ]ὸν πρότερον [χ]ρηματί[ζ]ον[τα Ἀ]σ[κα]λωνίτην, τραπεζιτε[ύοντα] ἐν Δήλῳ, [Π]ό[π]λιος καὶ Γάιος καὶ Γναῖος Ἐγνά[τι]οι Κοίντου Ῥωμαῖοι τὸν ἑαυτ[ῶν] εὐεργέτην, Ἀπόλλωνι. Philostratus, as we saw, was a Greek, and the choice of language can be interpreted as a form of deference to his mother tongue (and that of the community at large). Latin might in theory have been used instead by a group of Romans determined to maintain a linguistic aloofness from the local population. There is one linguistic detail which is of note here: the patronymic of the Romans is expressed by the genitive alone (Κοίντου) rather than by genitive + υἱός, a usage which would have reflected the Latin structure genitive +*filius*. There is evidence, as we shall see (see especially v.1), for the currency of genitive + υἱός in the nomenclature of Romans/Italians as expressed in the Greek language, adopted in imitation of the Latin method of

[10] Touloumakos (1995: 90) puts a very similar interpretation on the text: 'Man hat den Eindruck, dass die drei griechischen Freigelassenen durch die lateinische Fassung lediglich ihre Bindung zu ihrem italischen Patron manifestieren wollten (oder mussten), während sie durch die Voranstellung der griechischen ihr griechisches Selbstgefühl bekundeten.'

expressing filiation. Here the Egnatii were content to have their filiation written in the Greek style, and that is suggestive of a degree of accommodation to Greek ways.

Rather more strikingly, at *ID* 1842 P. Cornelius Scipio Aemilianus Africanus (cos. 147, 134 BC) is honoured by L. Babullius, a Roman, in Greek (statue base of white marble). The honorand is described as φίλον:

[Πόπ]λ[ιον Κορνήλιον Ποπλίου]
[Σ]κιπίων[α] Ἀ[φρικανόν,]
[σ]τρατηγὸν [ὕ]πα[τον ʽΡ]ωμα[ίων]
Λεύκιο[ς] Βαβύλλιος [Τ]ιβ[ερίου]
ʽΡωμαῖος τὸν ἑαυτοῦ φίλο[ν] ... [11]

Visiting Roman dignitaries were usually accorded Latin in such dedications (see below, III.2, IV.1), either on its own or along with Greek, but on this occasion the dedicator (who, being an individual Roman, contrasts with the dedicators of the inscriptions to be discussed below at III.2 and IV.1, in that these latter are collective groups of Greeks and Romans) acts entirely as if he were a local Greek. Greeks in Greek areas regularly honoured Roman worthies in Greek,[12] but for a Roman individual to do so implies a special linguistic situation on the island, and a distinctive linguistic identity adopted by the dedicator. It is however only fair to acknowledge a potential difficulty in the interpretation of such texts: the possibility cannot be ruled out in every case that an inscription extant in a single language was originally bilingual, with one of the versions now lost. This particular statue base though is well preserved. Nevertheless, even if one version had been lost, the presence of the Greek alongside Latin would not be without significance. If Roman writing to Roman uses Greek either on its own or in conjunction with Latin, he is presumably seeking to address Greek readers as well as the honorand, and that would seem to imply his integration into local society; at the very least he is not portraying himself as detached from local Greek speakers. Alternatively he may be attempting to present a distinct identity to the Roman honorand.

A dedication published at *ID* 1688 does not (unlike the above inscription) involve an outsider: Γάιον Ὀφέλλιον Μαάρκου υἱὸν Φέρον Ἰταλικοὶ δικαιοσύνης ἕνεκα καὶ φιλαγαθίας τῆς εἰς ἑαυτούς, Ἀπόλλωνι (there follow in Greek the names of the sculptors).[13] The dedication,

---

[11] Citing this inscription, Siebert (1999: 96) remarks: 'Des actes de consécration entre Romains s'expriment plus d'une fois par la seule langue grecque.'

[12] See, e.g. Fraser (1960), 18 for a dedication in Greek to L. Calpurnius Piso, governor of Macedonia in 57–55 BC; and see especially below, IV.1.

[13] Discussed briefly by Touloumakos (1995: 119).

dated *c.* 100 BC, is from the so-called 'Agora of the Italians';[14] the honorand is a Roman merchant active on Delos and belonging to a well-known family of *negotiatores*, and the dedicators are *Italici.* The inscription is from an area particularly associated with 'Italians'. There are 22 inscriptions published in *ID* which can definitely be assigned to the Agora, of which 10 are in Greek, 6 in Latin and 6 are bilingual.[15] Whatever language Italians might have used in private, this inscription and others from the same site would suggest that as a group they were not averse from using Greek as a formal public language even when addressing one another. Siebert (1999: 97) observes that the major dedications in the Agora, those on the Doric porticoes, 'sont faites en grec et en grec seulement, du moins pour les ailes Nord et Ouest'. One of these Greek texts is by the Greek Philostratus, but another more interestingly (in the present context) is (apparently) by the same Roman C. Ofellius (*ID* 1683). There is evidence here of an acceptance of Greek by the Italians, and of their immersion in Greek-speaking Delian society. There is no sign of a doctrinaire insistence on Latin, though there is more to be said on the matter. I move on now to a few further signs of this linguistic assimilation.

It was noted above (1) that in *ID* 2013 a Greek freedman sets up an inscription in honour of his Roman patron in Greek, thereby, it would seem, implying that the referent was, or had been, at home in a Greek-speaking culture. Similarly at 1728 a freedman (of unknown origin) honours his patron, a Roman banker (see also 1729), in Greek: Λεύκι[ον] Αὐφίδιον Λευκίο[υ υἱ]ὸν ῾Ρωμαῖον τραπεζ[ιτε]ύσαντα ἐν Δήλωι, [Λ]εύκιο[ς Α]ὐφίδιος Λευκίου . . . τὸν ἑαυτοῦ [πάτρωνα κ]αὶ εὐεργέτην. And at 2001 L. Orbius, known from 1742, in which he is referred to as a *mag(ister)* (of one of the *collegia*: see below, IV.2), receives a dedication in Greek from his 'friends' (φίλοι), in honour of Apollo. If his friends were Romans or Italians, they had adopted Greek in formal address among themselves; if they were Greeks, they were treating Orbius as one of themselves; and if they were both Roman and Greek, they constituted a unified group in which Greek could be used as a common public language. On all three interpretations Orbius was linguistically assimilated into a Greek-speaking society. 1842, quoted above, has φίλον used in an address of one Roman by another.

---

[14] See the editors on the nature of the inscription: 'Base de statue qui occupe une niche du côté Ouest [of the Agora of the Italians]. . . . Les trois premières lignes [those quoted here] sont gravées sur la corniche.'

[15] See Siebert (1999: 96) for statistics and a classification.

Two other inscriptions (on identical white marble plaques) from the Agora of the Italians, *ID* 1690, 1691, have a Roman making a dedication 'to Apollo and the Italians', in Greek: Αὖλος Νούιος Λευκίου ʿΡωμαῖος ᾿Απόλλωνι καὶ ᾿Ιταλικοῖς. Here again the filiation of the Roman is expressed in the Greek manner.

Frequently too Romans are linked with Athenians and Greeks in dedications written in Greek, with the dedicatee sometimes a Roman (these inscriptions are found mainly at *ID* 1642–82). Several Roman bankers are honoured in Greek by such combined groups (see 1726, 1727). At *ID* 1659 a Roman proquaestor, 'probably serving with L. Cornelius Sulla during the Mithridatic war' (Rauh 1993: 15), Μάνιον Α[ἰ]μύλιον Μανίου υἱὸν Λέπεδον,[16] is honoured on a statue base of white marble, ἀρετῆς ἕνεκεν καὶ δικαιοσύνης καὶ τῆς πρὸς τοὺς θεοὺς <ευσ>εὐσεβείας, by a combined group expressed by the commonly recurring formula ᾿Αθηναίων καὶ ʿΡωμαίων καὶ τῶν ἄλλων ʿΕλλήνων οἱ κατοικοῦντες ἐν Δήλωι ... The Roman has his filiation expressed in the Latin style. Honorific inscriptions in the name of this collective group or containing several other similar collective formulae start to appear in the 120s BC; A.Wilson (1966: 114) suggests that '[s]ome sort of committee may have taken the decision to honour benefactors in the name of the various groups'. If so (and the suggestion seems plausible), Roman members of such committees were obviously happy with the use of Greek as the collective language.

Similar to the above joint dedication, though with a different collective formula, is that at *ID* 1694 (statue base).[17] The dedicatee is described as a quaestor: Λεύκιον Κορνήλιον Σερουίου υἱὸν Λέντελον ταμίαν ʿΡωμαίων, ᾿Ιταλοὶ καὶ῞Ελληνες (see further below, IV.1). The name of the sculptor is also given, Δημόστρατος Δημοστράτου ᾿Αθηναῖος ἐποίει. Artists' signatures on Delos are always in Greek.[18] Note that the patronymic of the Athenian sculptor is given in the Greek style (cf. 1688), whereas that of the Roman magistrate is in the Latin manner, rendered into Greek. For another Roman official (a proconsul, unidentified) honoured in Greek, this time by Romans resident and working on Delos, see *ID* 1679, on the plinth of a marble statue from the Agora of the Italians:[19] Γάιον Κλούιον Λευκίου υἱὸν στρατηγὸν ἀνθύπατον ʿΡωμαίων οἱ ἐν Δήλωι ἐργαζόμενοι καὶ κατοικοῦντες (see below, IV.1).

---

[16] This man was consul in 66, but the date of his proquaestorship is unknown: see the editors ad loc.

[17] See also Touloumakos (1995: 119).

[18] As Siebert (1999: 100) puts it, 'l'art était aux yeux des familiers de l'agora des Italiens une affaire de Grecs'. For artists' signatures in a different language from that of the main part of the text, see above, 5.IV.7.

[19] See Siebert (1999: 98).

Also worth noting is the 'complementary' bilingual text 1736 (for which type of text, see Chapter 2 at e.g. XIV.4): *L. L. Orbieis L. l. mag(istreis) laconicum Italiceis*; Λεύκιος ῎Ορβιος Λευκίου Λικῖνος καὶ ῎Ορβιος Λευκίου Δίφιλος 'Ερμαισταὶ γενόμενοι *v.* 'Ιταλικοῖς. Neither version gives complete information. The reader needs the Latin to know what has been dedicated (a *laconicum*: see below, III.2), and the Greek to know in what sense the dedicators were *magistri* (of the *collegium* referred to as the 'Ερμαισταί: on which see further below, IV.2).[20] Therefore the two versions are not simply provided for readers with different linguistic competence, but have to be read together to make the message comprehensible.[21] The writer has made an assumption that the potential readers will have been bilingual.

These various cases seem to show Romans thoroughly assimilated into the Greek-speaking life of the community, though it has to be said that there is a difference between a joint dedication such as those above (where Greeks might have taken the lead in having the inscription drafted), and individual dedications of the type illustrated earlier.

In the presence of such evidence one might be tempted to think that the linguistic identity of various Italians and Romans had been submerged at Delos, with Greek widely adopted. It should however be stressed that the *negotiatores* had certainly not lost their identity as outsiders; they are constantly referred to even in monolingual texts as 'Ρωμαῖοι, 'Ιταλικοί or 'Ιταλοί. Public dedications may be an indication of the public or formal language of a community, but not of its private language(s). And in any case the texts cited above are not the sole evidence for formal language use at Delos: the place of Latin has not yet been considered. Nevertheless, Romans/Italians were remarkably accommodating in allowing themselves to be given a Greek-speaking identity. This was not always the case in Greek areas. At Samothrace, for example, Romans seem under some circumstances to have been keener to present themselves as Latin-speaking (see 5.V.1, n. 108).

III *ITALICI*, 'Ρωμαῖοι AND IDENTITY: A TYPE OF INSCRIPTION

I turn now to questions of identity, and to some aspects of bilingualism. A suitable starting point is a bilingual dedication to Q. Marcius Rex set up by *negotiatores* at Argos (*CIL* III.7265 = *ILLRP* 376):*Q. Maarcium Q.*

[20] This complementary relationship between *magistri* in the Latin version and the collective name of the group also obtains in the collegial bilinguals *ID* 1731, 1732, 1733 (but contrast 1751, 1753).
[21] See Poccetti (1984: 649) for a discussion along these lines.

[f. Regem] Italicei quei negotian[tur Argeis]; Κόιντον Μαάρκιο[ν Κοίν]του υἱὸν ʻΡῆγαʼἸταλ[ικοί]. Though not from Delos, it is relevant because it is formulaic and can be paralleled at Delos, and is straightforward and useful as an introduction.

Q. Marcius Rex was probably consul in 68 BC, and he was almost certainly honoured by the Italian *negotiatores* because of his activities against pirates at this period.[22] There are several features of this inscription which deserve comment. First, it is formulaic. Secondly, it contains the term *Italici*. Thirdly, it has an unusual syntactic structure (at least by Latin standards), with the honorand in the accusative case and no verb expressed. Fourthly, the name *Marcius* has a spelling with gemination of the vowel in both the Greek and Latin versions. And finally it is bilingual, or, to put it slightly differently, it has a Latin version as well as a Greek. I intend to comment on all of these points in the next section, relating them to the Delian evidence. Also of interest is the form which the filiation has in the Greek versions; I will return to this matter in a later section (V.1).

III.1 *Formulaic structure*

First, for the formulaic structure one might compare (e.g.) at Delos *ID* 1698 = *ILLRP*369: *A. Terentium [.] A. [.]f. Varro[nem legatum] Italicei et Graecei quei [.] Delei negoti[antur].* [Α]ὖλον Τερέντιον Αὔλου υἱὸν Οὐ[άρρωνα πρεσβυτὴν ʻΡ]ωμαίων ʼΙταλικοὶ καὶ ῞Ελληνες οἱ κατ[οικοῦντες ἐν Δήλῳ]. Here the same conventions are observed: presence of *Italici*, the accusative structure, and virtually the same relative clause, introduced by an old spelling of the relative pronoun, and containing the same verb *negotiantur* with locative of the place name. The inscription is also bilingual. Or again, in a different place in the Greek world (Aegium in Achaea), there is *ILLRP* 370 (*Italicei quei Aegei negotiantur P. Rutilium P. f. Nudum q(uaestorem)*), which differs from the other inscriptions only in its word order. Another inscription from Argos (cf. that of Marcius Rex cited in the previous section) has most of the formulaic elements (but not the accusative of the honorand): *CIL* 1².746 = *ILLRP* 374 *Q. Caecilio C. f. Metelo imperatori Italici quei Argeis negotiantur.*[23] An inscription from Sicily in the name of the *Italici* (*ILLRP* 320) also has an unmistakable affinity with our formulaic type: *Italicei L. Cornelium Sc[ip]i[one]m honoris caussa.*[24] This

[22] See Degrassi on *ILLRP* 376; also A.Wilson (1966: 149).
[23] On these inscriptions from Argos, see Touloumakos (1995: 122–3).
[24] For an inscription of a different type mentioning *Italici* in Sicily (more precisely, *fugiteiuos Italicorum*), see *ILLRP* 454. The reference must be to slaves of the Italian traders.

may be as early as 193 BC.[25] Here again is the same accusative structure, in a Greek-speaking area, but generations (it seems) before the examples from Delos. Also worth noting is *ID* 1699 = *ILLRP* 343 (*[C. Marium C. f. legat]um Alexandreae Italicei quei fuere [uirtut]is beneficique ergo.* Ἀγασίας Μηνοφίλου ʾΕφέσιος ἐποίει), which differs slightly from some of the other inscriptions in that it does not have the verb *negotiantur*, but the other elements are there, such as the accusative construction, the presence of *Italici*, the *ei* spellings in the same places, and a relative clause with locative of the place name. This inscription is of interest because the *Italici* in this case had been at Alexandria before erecting a statue at Delos.

The *negotiatores* who described themselves as *Italici* must have been some sort of loose collective presence in Greek-speaking areas in the last centuries of the Republic, with networks and contacts such that the formula, with its distinctive spelling and phraseology, could spread across a whole area and linger over a long period. Indeed the last example mentioned provides evidence for members of the group styling themselves as *Italici* moving around the Greek-speaking world and using formulaic Latin in public inscriptions. The repeated use of the term *Italici* suggests that the *negotiatores* perceived themselves as having a corporate identity, and accordingly I now turn to this term.

III.2 Ῥωμαῖοι *and* ʾΙταλικοί

The terms Ῥωμαῖος and ʾΙταλικός have been much discussed, most notably by Solin (1982a: 114, 116), who shows that Ῥωμαῖος indicated a Roman citizen in the juridical sense, or an inhabitant of the city of Rome, whether free or servile,[26] while ʾΙταλικός designated on the one hand Roman citizens, in which sense it was synonymous with Ῥωμαῖος, or on the other hand Italians in the modern sense.[27] In addition Ῥωμαῖοι could be used by Greeks as a general designation of Italians whatever their place of origin (see below). These definitions are no doubt correct. Indeed there is a bilingual inscription from Gytheum with some verbal and structural similarities to the inscriptions so far quoted, which revealingly has Ῥωμαῖοι in the Greek part but *ciues Romani* in the Latin: *ILGR* 40 *C. Iulium Lacharis f. Euruclem* **ciues Romani** *in Laconica qui habitant, negotiantur*

---

[25] See Brunt (1988: 117).

[26] See Solin (1982a: 114): 'Tutti i casi apparentemente irregolari, riportati dallo Hatzfeld, possono essere spiegati con le due accezioni che, a mio vedere, il termine Ῥωμαῖος ha: cittadino romano o abitante della città di Roma, compresi anche gli schiavi romani.'

[27] See Solin (1982a: 116): 'Per questo, credo, il termine *Italici* ʾΙταλικοί designava nell'Oriente sia cittadini romani, ed era per questo rispetto alquanto equivalente a Ῥωμαῖοι, sia Italici nel senso moderno.' See further Poccetti (1984: 647), Rochette (1997a: 36–8).

benifici ergo. Γάιον ᾽Ιούλιον Λαχάρους υἱὸν Εὐρυκλέα ʿ**Ρωμαῖοι** οἱ ἐν ταῖς πόλεσιν τῆς Λακωνικῆς πραγματευόμενοι τὸν αὐτῶν εὐεργέτην. Note again the accusative structure, the relative clause with *negotiantur*,[28] and the use of *ergo* preceded by a genitive (cf. *ID* 1699 above).

There are however two fundamental differences between the ways in which the two words ʿΡωμαῖος and ᾽Ιταλικοί/*Italici* are used at Delos, and these do not seem to have been brought out in discussions of the terms.

First, ᾽Ιταλικοί/*Italici* is used exclusively in the plural, whereas ʿΡωμαῖος is regularly used in the singular as well as the plural. There is not a single example at Delos of *Italicus* in the singular. Its consistent use is in reference to the group of Italian *negotiatores*, and this fact supports the contention that the *Italici* had a collective identity. ʿΡωμαῖος on the other hand when used in the plural often behaves quite differently from *Italici*. It may be applied to small groups of individuals who are separately named, as at *ID* 1724, quoted above, II (see also 1527), or it may in effect be equivalent to *populus Romanus*, as for example at *ID* 1859 (Γάιον ʿΡαβήριον Γαίου υἱὸν ἀνθύπατον ʿΡωμαίων; cf. e.g. 1878 τοῦ δήμου τοῦ ʿΡωμαίων). The Roman people were located at Rome and not in the Greek world. The *Italici* by contrast operate at Delos and elsewhere in Greece.

Secondly, ʿΡωμαῖος, or rather its Latin synonym *Romanus*, is never found in a Latin inscription at Delos, whereas *Italici* is regularly used in Latin and bilingual texts; the only exception in inscriptions of *negotiatores* of the type in question that I have found is the bilingual *ILGR* 40, quoted above, which contains the phrase *ciues Romani*, but it is not from Delos. If an individual or a group designated 'Roman' makes a dedication at Delos, whether to Greek or fellow Roman, or receives a dedication, whether from Greek or Roman, the language used is always Greek. For example, in the first volume of *ID* containing inscriptions from the period after 166 BC I have noted about 82 examples of ʿΡωμαῖος, both in the singular and plural, in Greek inscriptions, but not a single case of *Romanus* in a Latin inscription. These figures in part reflect the integration of individual Romans into Delian society, but they also to some extent imply a Greek perception of the Italian *negotiatores*. To Athenians and others they were 'Romans', even if they did not come from Rome itself (see above, p. 651). In this respect the following inscription is revealing, though it is not from Delos: *CIL* I². 2259 = *CIL* III.7242 = *ILLRP* 961 *Q. Auile C. f.*

---

[28] For further examples of *ciues Romani* in association with *negotiantur*, see Pârvan (1909: 11), citing e.g. *CIL* III.7160 *ciues Romani qui Mytileneis negotiantur*, and also Cic. *Att.* 5.21.6 *Q. Volusium … misi in Cyprum … ne ciues Romani pauci qui illic negotiantur ius sibi dictum negarent.*

Lanuine salue. Κόιντε ᾿Αουίλλιε Γαίου υἱὲ ῾Ρωμαῖε χρηστὲ χαῖρε.[29] The Latin version has the precise *Lanuine*, which is generalised to 'Roman' in the Greek. The numerous joint dedications at Delos in Greek, by 'Athenians, *Romans* and other Greeks' (see above, II, and below, IV.1), employ a formula which might have been devised by Athenians, and which as such might originally have embodied an Athenian perception of the Italians.

Italici/᾿Ιταλικοί on the other hand occurs four times in inscriptions which, as they stand, are in Latin alone (*ID* 1620, 1695, 1696, 1742), ten times in inscriptions which are in Greek alone (1683, 1688, 1689, 1690, 1691, 1717, 1718, 1722, 1757, 1758),[30] and seven times in bilingual inscriptions (1685, 1686, 1687, 1698, 1699, 1735,[31] 1736).[32] Of 28 cases of the two words *Italici/*᾿Ιταλικοί, 11 are in Latin and 17 in Greek. About 40 per cent of cases of *Italici/*᾿Ιταλικοί are in Latin texts, whereas 100 per cent of the references to 'Romans' are in Greek texts. There seems to be at least a superficial association here between the 'Italians' and the Latin language,[33] but that is a possibility which must be subjected to closer scrutiny (see below). It is also possible that some of the purely Greek inscriptions at Delos to or by ᾿Ιταλικοί were originally bilingual.

Whatever the case, the consistent plural use of *Italici* suggests that the Italians saw themselves as a group, with the public use of the Latin language perhaps one potential marker of their collective identity. Romans on the other hand tended rather to be individuals or collections of individuals, except when the Roman state was at issue. A. Wilson (1966: 117) asserts that 'the ῾Ρωμαῖοι were a body with a sense of separate identity', but in so doing he fails to observe the fundamental distinction between ῾Ρωμαῖοι and ᾿Ιταλικοί: it was the latter who had the clearest collective identity, and not only at Delos.

The picture must though be refined somewhat. Clearly the *Italici* did not use Latin willy-nilly in public inscriptions. We have suggested above that Romans/Italians seem to have been well integrated linguistically into Delian society; and even the inscriptions containing the word *Italici/*᾿Ιταλικοί are more often in Greek than in Latin. The circumstances behind an inscription, such as the nature of the honorand, the position of

---

[29] See Solin (1982a: 114).   [30] Also perhaps 1727 (conjectural).
[31] See *ILLRP* 750 (d). *ID* does not accept the word here.
[32] I include 1699 among the bilingual, as distinct from monolingual Latin, inscriptions with some hesitation. See Degrassi *ILLRP* 343.
[33] It is also worth stressing that the four inscriptions (quoted above, p. 650) set up in the name of *Italici* from areas of the Greek world other than Delos are all in Latin or have a Latin version.

the inscription, and perhaps the date, must also be taken into account as potential influences on language choice. I turn to these additional factors.

In the inscriptions listed above containing explicit reference to Italians the word *Italici*/ Ἰταλικοί is variously in the nominative or the dative. If it is in the dative, the Italians were in some sense recipients of a dedication, and not necessarily in control of language choice. If on the other hand it is in the nominative, then the dedication is explicitly by the *Italici* themselves, and it may be assumed that the dedicators made the choice of language. Accordingly I offer some comments on those inscriptions which have nominative forms. Of the four purely Latin inscriptions listed above, three have the nominative (*ID* 1620, 1695, 1696), whereas of the ten certain purely Greek inscriptions, only two have the nominative (1688, 1722). These figures on their own are suggestive, for they seem to imply that the *Italici* when acting on their own behalf tended to prefer Latin; there is though more to it than that, as we will see. Finally, of the seven bilinguals, two have the nominative (1698, 1699).

There is a distinction between those inscriptions with the nominative which contain a Latin version, and those which do not. The only two inscriptions which are in Greek alone reflect the activities of Italians as insiders, as it were, in Delian society. At *ID* 1688 the Ἰταλικοί make a dedication in the Agora of the Italians to a local *negotiator*, C. Ofellius Ferus. And at 1722 the dedication is to the Greek banker, Philostratus. By contrast in every single inscription by the Italians (nominative) containing a Latin version the dedication is to a Roman official who was an outsider to Delos (Latin: *ID* 1620 L. Licinius Lucullus, *c*. 84–80, 1695–6 L. Munatius Plancus, *c*. 88; bilingual: 1698 A. Terentius Varro, *c*. 82, 1699 C. Marius, *c*. 99). It is also the case that the four dedications in Latin by *Italici* (nominative) found in places other than Delos (quoted above) all honour Roman officials. It may be suggested that within Delian society itself the *Italici* were usually happy to be seen as Greek-speaking,[34] but that when their dealings were with outside Roman officialdom they were careful to project a Latin-speaking, or at least bilingual, identity. There is possibly also a chronological dimension to the language choice in these inscriptions. Those with a Latin version come from the late Republican period when Delos was under threat from various quarters and reliant on Rome (as personified by such visiting officials) for protection.[35] However, it is not easy to pin down date as a determinant, because we do

---

[34] They were, for example, honorands of inscriptions in Greek set up not only by the Greek Philostratus (1717), but also by the Roman Aulus Novius (1690, 1691).

[35] See Touloumakos (1995: 120).

not have for comparison inscriptions by the *Italici* from an earlier period honouring prominent visiting Romans. There are Greek inscriptions of earlier date addressed to Roman dignitaries, but these are not in the name of the *Italici* (note 1842, discussed above, ii).

I next consider the inscriptions in which 'Ιταλικοί/*Italici* is not in the nominative. Of those with a Latin version, all without exception come from the Agora of the Italians, and are either inscriptions on the architraves recording the dedication of porticoes to the *Italici* by groups of persons, or are explicitly in the name of *magistri* of the *collegia* into which the Romans and Italians had formally organised themselves on the island (for which see further below). Unfortunately most of these inscriptions are fragmentary, and are not worth quoting in full. The inscriptions are as follows: *ID* 1742 (a *magister* L. Orbius dedicates to the *Italici* 'une statue en forme d'Hermès, représentant un homme couvert d'une peau de lion et tenant à la main une feuille (d'acanthe?)'), 1685–7 (all on architraves of the Agora of the Italians, and all, though fragmentary, obviously listing individuals dedicating porticoes to Apollo and the *Italici*), 1735 (if the word is to be read here (see above, n. 31), again named persons, this time categorised as *magistri* if the conventional restoration is to be accepted, dedicate a portico in the Agora of the Italians), 1736 (two *magistri* dedicate a *laconicum*, a type of vapour-bath (Vitr. 5.10.5), to the *Italici*).

The eight inscriptions without a Latin version in which 'Ιταλικοί is in the dative rather than the nominative do not differ radically from those with a Latin version, but there are some distinctions to be made. All eight are once again in the Agora of the Italians, a fact which underlines the significance of the place to the group so styled.[36] Just as two of the purely Greek inscriptions containing the nominative (discussed above) honour insiders to Delos, one of them an Italian *negotiator*, the other a Greek, so three of the inscriptions with the dative are dedicated to the Italians and (in two cases) Apollo (1689, 1717, 1718) by *Greeks*. Twice the Greek dedicator is the same Philostratus honoured himself in Greek by the 'Ιταλικοί (see above). Two inscriptions are dedications by an individual, A. Novius, to Apollo and the Italians (1690–1); Novius is described as a 'Roman', a word which, we have seen, never occurs in a Latin text. The remaining three texts do not seem to differ from the Latin inscriptions discussed in the previous paragraph. One (1683) is on an architrave. The other two (1757, 1758) are dedications to Heracles and the Italians, and Apollo

---

[36] For a detailed discussion of the significance of the Agora of the Italians, see Coarelli (1982) and Rauh (1993: 289–338), in which many of the inscriptions discussed in this section are commented on.

and the Italians respectively, by the combined *collegia*, the *Hermaistai*, *Apolloniastai* and *Poseidoniastai* (on which groups see below). The inscriptions by the *collegia*, as we will see (IV.2), are often bilingual, and one wonders in these cases whether a Latin version has been lost.

There is a loose connection between the presence of the 'Italians' in an inscription and the choice of the Latin language. It is not though straightforwardly the case that reference to the Italians automatically triggers the use of Latin (whether on its own or along with Greek). Several other factors have to be taken into account as complementary determinants of language choice. When the Italians presented themselves as making dedications (usually in the form of inscriptions on statue bases) to distinguished Roman *outsiders*, they made a point of using Latin at least as one of the versions of the text (see further below, IV.1). The language choice both makes a linguistic accommodation to the addressee (if only partially, in the bilingual texts), and gives the Italians themselves a 'Roman' (i.e. Latin-speaking) identity which might be seen as politically expedient. The willingness of Greeks for their part to be included as dedicators in such Latin texts (they tend to be associated with the *Italici* in the inscriptions) no doubt reflects their pragmatism and pro-Roman feelings at this period.[37] When the subject of an inscription by the *Italici* was an *insider*, Greek could be used. When a dedication was made *to* the Italians, both languages are attested. Greek on its own appears mainly when the dedicator is an insider apparently acting as an individual (Novius), or a Greek (insider),[38] whereas a Latin version is present particularly when the inscription is set up by a person or group of persons associated with the *collegia* (on the language use of the *collegia*, see below, IV.2). The Italians thus presented themselves, or were perceived, as Latin-speaking either when their dealings were with outside Roman officialdom, or in the formal context of the activities of the *collegia*, which no doubt gave them their most formal identity on the island. The determinants of language choice in this small group of inscriptions are thus complex, with addressee, dedicator, placement of the text and possibly its date, all potentially interacting. Clearly the Italians were putting Greek on a par with Latin as a formal public language, and that implies that in everyday life they were mixing freely with native Greek speakers through the medium of Greek; but they were nevertheless holding on to Latin under certain circumstances. This language maintenance constitutes one aspect of their identity. It has been stressed by Gabba (1994: 108) that at

[37] See the general remarks of Touloumakos (1995: 124).

[38] 1757 and 1758 have an anomalous look to them, as we saw, and may be incomplete.

this period protection was afforded by the Roman government indifferently to Roman citizens, Latins and Italians, and indeed the reliance of the *Italici* on the protection of the *magnitudo populi Romani* is made very clear at Sall. *Jug.* 26.1, which will be quoted below. The Italians in potentially hostile environments sought to use linguistic strategies to underline their connection with the Roman state.

Our use of *Italici* was not confined to inscriptions in the Republican period. There are several examples of the word in Sallust's *Jugurtha* which match closely the use of the term at Delos. At 26.1 it is used in the plural not of Italians in any vague general sense, but specifically of Italian *negotiatores* who act together in defending Cirta in Numidia against Jugurtha: *ea postquam Cirtae audita sunt,* **Italici**, *quorum uirtute moenia defensabantur, confisi deditione facta propter magnitudinem populi Romani inuiolatos sese fore . . . ; Iugurtha . . . Numidas atque* **negotiatores** *promiscue . . . interfecit.* The passage has the additional interest that it displays the unity of the group, as Gabba (1994: 108) has noted. There is another relevant passage at *Jug.* 47.1, where Sallust uses instead a circumlocution, *Italici generis multi mortales*, but again the reference is to *negotiatores*: *erat haud longe ab eo itinere quo Metellus pergebat oppidum Numidarum nomine Vaga, forum rerum uenalium totius regni maxume celebratum, ubi et incolere et mercari consueuerant* **Italici generis multi mortales**.

The term *Italici* was to develop a powerful symbolism, as is shown by the fact that the Italian rebels at the time of the Social War renamed their capital, Corfinium, *Italica*,[39] though that may not be relevant to our cases. That the group at Delos (and other groups elsewhere in Greece) used the term *Italici* of themselves may rather be related to the fact that, while they must have embraced many Romans, there was also a substantial element of non-Romans. A comprehensive designation was required.

It is also relevant, if only as part of the general background, that for some time now Italian élites, and the Italians at Delos were certainly to some extent members of important local Italian families, had been assimilating themselves to Roman norms,[40] and in the matter of language that meant the abandonment of local languages and the adoption of Latin. One thinks of the story in Livy (40.42.13) that in 180 BC the people of Cumae asked the senate that they might be allowed to use Latin in certain public affairs. This story suggests, first, that the local upper classes were according Latin a high prestige, and secondly that they wanted to be seen by Rome to be using the Latin language, because there was no

---

[39] See Strabo 5.4.2, Vell. Pat. 2.16.4; note Gabba (1994: 118): 'a name rich in symbolism'.
[40] See e.g. Gabba (1994: 109).

legal requirement that they should ask permission of the Roman senate
to do so (see 2.II.1). Similarly at Delos and elsewhere in Greece the *Italici*
are seen by prominent Romans to be holding on to Latin as a feature of
their public identity.

III.3 Accusative of the honorand

The third feature of the Marcius Rex inscription which I mentioned
earlier was the accusative of the honorand. This, as we saw several times
in the first two chapters, is the standard Greek construction in honorific
inscriptions (see especially above, 2.VII.2), with a verb of some sort (see
below) understood, but it is not the normal Latin construction. It is found
typically on the base of statues which represent the honorand (as often at
Delos), and can be interpreted as originally meaning 'X (set up a statue
of) Y',[41] though it must have been subject to reinterpretation as having
simply a verb of honouring understood (a problem which might repay
investigation). In Latin the most usual construction is the dative of the
honorand, with a completely different verb understood, such as *fecit* or
posuit. The different conventions of the two languages can be seen in the
bilingual inscription *CIL* III.8, quoted above, I.VII.1, p. 38.[42] The distribution of the accusative construction in Latin texts is of some interest. It
can be stated categorically that it occurs with any frequency only in inscriptions which there is reason to believe were influenced by the Greek
pattern. The most obvious group comprises those which are explicitly
bilingual, and in which the Greek syntactic pattern has been used in the
Latin as well as the Greek.[43] This is the case in the Marcius Rex inscription, and also in various bilingual texts at Delos, such as *ID* 1698 = *ILLRP*
369 and *ID* 2009 = *ILLRP* 363. It spread from honorific to funerary inscriptions, and again turns up in Latin in bilingual texts of this genre, as
at Speidel (1994a), 688a, quoted and discussed above, I.VII.1 (with cross
references to other examples of the usage).[44] A second group comprises
texts in Latin only either found in Greek-speaking areas or showing some
other association with Greek speakers. Note for example the dedication
by a centurion on an Alexandrian statue base honouring a praetorian

---

[41] See Veyne (1962: 68), and for the non-elliptical construction (with the verb of setting up expressed),
see below, n. 49.

[42] Comparable examples can be found in Touloumakos' collection of bilingual inscriptions
(e.g. 1995: 108–9).

[43] A number of such cases can readily be found in Touloumakos (e.g. 1995: 106).

[44] See further Kajanto (1963a: 19), Adams (1998).

prefect, Domitius Honoratus (*CIL* III.12052; cf. III.14127):[45] *[L(ucium) Domitium] Honoratum, prae(fectum) praetor(io)* vac. *em(inentissimum) u(irum)* vac. *Pacilius Tychianus (centurio) leg(ionis) II Tr(aianae) F(ortis) [G(ermanicae) Seuer(ianae)]*. The centurion (who has a Greek name) seems to have chosen the Greek structure in line with the Greek convention in a Greek city.

A particularly interesting group of examples of the accusative construction is found in Rome itself. I refer to the dedications on the Capitoline Hill to Jupiter Capitolinus and the Roman people set up by various Asiatic kings, cities and communities.[46] Their date is controversial (period of Sulla, or second century BC?).[47] These texts are bilingual, or in one or two cases in Greek or Latin alone (but these last may be incomplete). The accusative of the honorand occurs throughout the corpus: e.g. *ILLRP* 175 *[. . . populum R]omanum cognatum, amicum, sociu[m, uirtutis et beniuolent]iaei beneficique erga Lucios in comu[ne]*; *ILLRP* 177 *populus Laodicensis af Lyco populum Romanum, quei sibei salutei fuit, benefici ergo, quae sibei benigne fecit*; ὁ δῆμος ὁ Λαοδικέων τῶν πρὸς τῷ Λύκῳ τὸν δῆμον τὸν ʿΡωμαίων γεγονότα ἑ[αυτῷ] σωτῆρα καὶ εὐεργέτην ἀρετῆς ἕνεκεν καὶ εὐνοί[ας] τῆς εἰς ἑαυτόν. There are also one or two other similarities with some of the Delian inscriptions, as in the archaic use of *ergo* preceded by a genitive, corresponding to genitive + ἕνεκεν in the Greek version (see 177, and cf. the Delian inscription 1699, quoted above, III.1). The dedicators presumably used native Latin speakers to draft the Latin versions, but determined the structure themselves, perhaps merely by providing the Greek versions and requesting that the structure be reproduced. The Greek versions underline the dedicators' Greekness, but the flattery had to be in Latin as well to achieve its full effect. Romans thus had the opportunity to become familiar with the Greekness of this type of construction in Rome itself.

I have mentioned that *bilingual* dedications at Delos have the accusative construction. More interestingly, the same is true also of purely Latin dedications, such as *ID* 1699 = *ILLRP* 343 (Latin, but with the artist's signature in Greek), *ID* 1620 = *ILLRP* 362 and *ID* 1695 = *ILLRP* 359; from places other than Delos, note too *ILLRP* 370 (Aegium) and *ILLRP* 320 (Sicily); both of these inscriptions have been quoted above (III.1). It should be noted that in each of these texts the *Italici* appear among the

---

[45] For the text, see now Kayser (1994: 69–73), 19.
[46] For texts see *ILLRP* 174–81; also Mellor (1978).
[47] See Degrassi, *ILLRP* I, 114–17, Mellor (1975: 203–6), id. (1978), Lintott (1978), Gruen (1984: 187 n. 187). I owe these references to John Briscoe.

dedicators. There is only one purely Latin inscription at Delos which has the dative (*ID* 1712 = *ILLRP* 344 *C. Iulio C. f. Caesar[i] pro co(n)s(ule) olearii*), and this is not in the name of the *Italici*, but of the oil sellers (this text will be discussed below, IV.1). All honorific inscriptions connected with the *Italici*, whether bilingual or monolingual in Latin, have the accusative. Since the same is true of inscriptions by *Italici* from Greek regions other than Delos, there must be a convention deliberately adopted by the *Italici* at work here. I stress that, though the Italians in these dedications are often associated with Greeks, that is not always the case, as can be seen from the Marcius Rex inscription and that from Sicily (*ILLRP* 320), and also *ID* 1699 = *ILLRP* 343. The participation of *Graeci* was not therefore the determining factor in the choice of the accusative construction. Nor, I stress in passing, was the participation of Greeks a determinant of the language choice. When *Romans* are associated with Greeks, Greek is always used, as at *ID* 1659 Ἀθηναίων καὶ Ῥωμαίων καὶ τῶν ἄλλων Ἑλλήνων οἱ κατοικοῦντες ἐν Δήλῳ... Μάνιον Α[ἰ]μύλιον Μανίου υἱὸν Λέπεδον ἀντιταμίαν ἀρετῆς ἕνεκεν καὶ δικαιοσύνης καὶ τῆς πρὸς τοὺς θεοὺς <ευσ>εὐσεβείας..., but when *Italici* make a joint dedication with Greeks, Latin is always one of the languages.[48] In the inscription just cited Romans are associated with Athenians and other Greeks, but when at *ID* 1620 = *ILLRP* 362 (*[L. Licinium L. f.] Lucullum pro q(uaestore) p[opulus Athe]niensis et Italicei et Graece[i que]i in insula negotiantur*) the *Italici* rather than Romans are linked with Athenians and Greeks, the language is Latin (see further below, IV.1). This last inscription is particularly revealing evidence for the influence of the *Italici* in determining the use of Latin when they were overtly included among the dedicators of a public inscription to an outside dignitary: the dedicators were virtually the same in the Greek and Latin texts, save for the replacement of 'Romans' by 'Italians' in the Latin.

The use of the accusative can at one level be seen as a form of accommodation to Greek practice, but it is doubtful if it would have been perceived by Greeks as such, because a Greek would not necessarily have remarked the abnormality of the usage. One assumes however that it would have appeared somewhat abnormal to a Latin speaker, and moreover it is precisely in inscriptions which honour prominent Romans that it is found. Would the honorand have been struck by the alienness of the construction? I am tempted to speculate that the usage was deliberately adopted by the *Italici* in their public inscriptions as a mark

[48] See *ID* 1620, 1695, 1696, 1698 (the last bilingual).

of their complex identity; when used at Rome in public inscriptions in the Republican period (in the Capitoline dedications: see above) the construction is in texts which have an explicit Greekness about them, conferred both by the presence of Greek versions and by the Greekness of the dedicators. It is interesting that it is distributed over the long period 193 BC to 68 BC across Greek areas in inscriptions containing the word *Italici*. On this view the frequent use of Latin in formal public inscriptions served to define the *Italici* in the eyes of Greeks, including slaves (see below, IV.2), whereas the use of an alien construction in their Latin might have defined them in the eyes of Latin-speaking outsiders to the region.[49]

III.4 Gemination of vowels

The fourth feature of the Marcius Rex inscription to which I referred was the spelling of *Marcius* with gemination of the vowel. It has now become something of a commonplace that the Latin of the Delos inscriptions is the Latin not of the city of Rome, but of Campania,[50] and this notion is supposed to accord with the view that many of the *negotiatores* were Campanians. It must though be noted that Hatzfeld's view that the *negotiatores* were basically southern Italians has now been rejected by Solin (1982a: especially 111–12; cf. A.Wilson (1966)), to whom Vine (1993: 163) does not refer (see further below, p. 677). Solin (1982a: 112) refers to Hatzfeld's inadequate understanding of Latin onomastics.

It has been argued by Lazzeroni (1956) that Latin, as distinct from Oscan, inscriptions which have gemination are predominantly found in Oscan areas of Italy. This view has now been supported by Vine from newer attestations of gemination not appearing in *CIL* I².[51] Moreover Vine has been able to demonstrate close similarities between the nature of gemination in Oscan texts, and that in Latin inscriptions. For example,

---

[49] A similar type of syntactic imitation of Greek found in two bilingual inscriptions (discussed by Poccetti (1984: 651) lies in the use of *statuo* + name in the sense 'set up (a statue) of someone' or 'set up someone (as a statue)'. See *ID* 1750, where *Maiam statuerunt* corresponds to τὴν Μαίαν ἀνέθηκαν, and 1771, where *Iouem Leiberum statuerunt* corresponds to Δία 'Ελευθέριον ἀνέθηκαν. Poccetti points out that where there is no Greek version, *signum* + genitive stands as object of the verb (2247 *hisce signum Volcani merito statuerunt*). Pocceti thus declares the Latin construction to be 'un calco sintattico' on the Greek. It is interesting to see that the new construction obviously first entered Latin in bilingual texts. Once a construction came in in such an explicitly bilingual context, it could in theory take on a life of its own, as happened with the accusative of the honorand, though that construction retained its Greek feel, as can be seen from the contexts in which it is admitted.

[50] See Vine (1993: 163).   [51] See Vine (1993: 270–2).

aa is the most common type in both Oscan and Latin, and gemination is predominantly found in initial syllables in both languages.[52] There are also correspondences of detail between the Oscan material and the Latin. The spelling *Maarcius*, for example, found in the Marcius Rex inscription, might be compared with Osc. **Maak-**,[53] and the occasional Latin form *aara* has an exact correspondent in Osc. **aas-**.[54]

It is possible then that vocalic gemination found its way into written Latin first of all in Oscan areas. But that does not mean that it would be justifiable to argue that such spellings were deliberately adopted by the *negotiatores* as part of an attempt to construct for themselves a regional Italian identity. In the Delian *Latin* inscriptions there is in fact only one such form (*aaram* at *ID* 1750 = *ILLRP* 751), which may indeed reflect the non-urban origin of the composer. But a single example would not provide grounds for assigning an ideological significance to the spelling of the *negotiatores*. Gemination is for the most part found at Delos in *Greek* inscriptions, overwhelmingly in the *praenomen* Μάαρκος, which is of course always abbreviated in Latin.[55] There is also a case of Μαάρκιος (*ID* 1731), which contrasts with the *non-geminated* form of the same name in the Latin inscription *ID* 1692. And *Marcellus* is spelt *without* gemination in both the Latin and Greek versions of *ID* 1685. Granted the likely Oscan origin of such gemination, the fact is that it had spread beyond Oscan-influenced Latin[56] (and Greek). In the Roman names *Marcus*, *Marcius* and *Marcellus* gemination became commonplace for some reason in Greek inscriptions in the second century BC.[57] For example, in the Greek versions of *senatus consulta* circulated in the Greek world (see Sherk (1969)) gemination is widespread in these names,[58] and there is no reason to think that the documents were drafted anywhere but in Rome. In Greek documents gemination begins to fade out in the first century BC, and is scarcely found after about 50 BC.[59] I attach no significance for our purposes to the spelling, given its almost complete restriction at Delos to a single name and to *Greek* inscriptions, and given the wide distribution of αα in Roman names in Greek inscriptions of this period. The question of

---

[52] Vine's detailed discussion of the various issues occupies the whole of Chapter 11.
[53] See Vine (1993: 277).   [54] See Vine (1993: 278).
[55] There are numerous examples of the Greek form of the name with gemination in *ID* 1685, 1732, 1733, 1753, 1754.
[56] Witness the recommendations of Accius (see Terentius Scaurus, *GL* VII.18.12, and cf. Lucil. 351–5).
[57] See Eckinger (1892: 8–11), Threatte (1980: 136–7).
[58] Numerous examples can be found in the index of *nomina Romana* in Sherk (1969: 390–2).
[59] See Eckinger (1892) and Threatte (1980), locc. cit.

regionalisms in the Latin at Delos will be discussed briefly in a later section (v.2).

I conclude that the *Italici*, at least those who were from prominent families as distinct from slaves (see IV.2), associated themselves with Rome and Romans in the maintenance of Latin under certain circumstances, much as the Cumaeans in 180 BC adopted a formal, Latin-speaking identity in the period of Italian aspirations before the Social War. But they also resorted to linguistic strategies, such as the use of bilingual texts and of Greek-inspired syntax, to construct a separateness from Roman outsiders, and a partial assimilation to Greek ways.

IV FURTHER ASPECTS OF LANGUAGE CHOICE

IV.1 Dedications to Roman dignitaries

As we have seen, high-ranking Romans visited Delos and were honoured from time to time. It was noted above that when *Italici* made a dedication to a visitor of this kind, they predominantly used Latin or Latin alongside Greek, and their motivations were discussed. But not all inscriptions dedicated to such persons are in the name of the *Italici*, and I turn now to some other dedicators in order to determine whether any principles of language selection can be identified. Was the origin of the honorand a factor, or do we have to consider as well the identity of the dedicator? Is the date of an inscription relevant to its language?

A text which seems to display a linguistic accommodation to the honorand is *ID* 2009, a bilingual in which two Melians honour C. Fabius Hadrianus, who is taken by Degrassi (*ILLRP* 363) to be the praetor of 84 or his son. Greeks might well have used Greek in such a dedication (see above, n. 12, and below):*[C. Fabiu]m C. f. Q. n. Hadrianum [Herm]olucus et Apollonius [Apo]lloni f. Me[li]ei benefici ergo. Apollini*; Γάιον Φάβι[ον] Γαίου υἱὸν ᾿Αδριανὸν ῾Ερμόλυ[κ]ος καὶ᾿Απολλώνιος οἱ ᾿Απολλωνίου Μήλιοι, τὸν ἑαυτῶ[ν] εὐερ[γ]έτην *v.* ᾿Απόλλωνι.

But this inscription is unusual. Greeks, or Athenians and Greeks along with Romans, or generalised inhabitants of the island, use Greek to Roman outsiders even in the late Republican period (cf. above, II, for a few relevant items discussed in a different connection), if we leave aside the inscriptions of the *Italici* (see below). Whereas at 1847 C. Iulius Caesar (the father of the dictator) was the subject of an inscription in Latin,[60]

---

[60] The inscription is fragmentary, and no dedicators are named.

at 1701 the same man (so the editors, and Degrassi on *ILLRP* 345) was honoured in *Greek* by Delians: Γάιον Ἰούλιον [Γαίου] υἰὸ[ν] Καίσαρα Δήλιοι τὸν ἑαυτ[ῶν] πάτρωνα Ἀπόλλω[ν]ι Ἀρτέμιδι *vac.* Λητοῖ. He was proconsul in Asia between 99 and 89. At *ID* 1710 C. Billienus is the honorand of an inscription in Greek set up by οἱ ἐν Δήλωι ἐργαζόμενοι, dated by the editors as earlier than 88. At 1854 the same man is honoured in Greek on a statue base by an individual Greek, conjectured on the basis of 1689 to be [Μίδας Ζή]νωνος Ἡράκλειος. Billienus is given his title στρατηγὸν ἀνθύπατον. The same name Βιλλιῆνον appears in the fragmentary inscription 1632 where the dedicators are ὁ δῆμος [ὁ Ἀθηναίων] καὶ οἱ τὴν ν[ῆσον κατοικοῦντες]. Q. Pompeius Q. f. Rufus, consul with Sulla in 88, is the honorand of a fragmentary Greek inscription 1849; the dedicators are not known but are bound to have been a Greek or collective group. At 2002 (a marble plaque from a statue base) two Greek individuals, one of them an Athenian, make a dedication in Greek to A. and P. Gabinius, the former 'peut-être un tribun militaire de l'armée de Sulla vers 85' (editors). In an inscription of uncertain date (1679) an unidentified C. Cluvius, στρατηγὸν ἀνθύπατον Ῥωμαίων, is honoured by οἱ ἐν Δήλωι ἐργαζόμενοι καὶ κατοικοῦντες. Two somewhat earlier inscriptions (110/109) in Greek, set up by groups of Greeks, are dedicated to Servius Cornelius Lentulus, another proconsul (1845, 2000). And then there are some of the inscriptions in the name of Ἀθηναίων καὶ Ῥωμαίων καὶ τῶν ἄλλων Ἑλλήνων οἱ κατοικοῦντες ἐν Δήλωι. Of these, 1659 is dedicated to Manius Aemilius Lepidus (see above, II), and 1660 to T. Manlius Torquatus (perhaps of much the same date). At 1604bis, an inscription found at Paros but certainly of Delian origin, ὁ δῆμος ὁ Ἀθηναίων honours L. Caecilius Metellus, στρατηγὸν ὕπατον, *c.* 85. An unidentified person Lucius Cornelius Lentulus, described as ταμίαν Ῥωμαίων, receives a dedication of uncertain date on a statue base at 1694 from a group referred to as Ἰταλοὶ καὶ Ἕλληνες (see above, II). Finally, there are three inscriptions (*c.* 69) in Greek dedicated to C. Valerius Triarius, a legate of Lucullus, by Greek contingents who had fought with him (1855–7); another Greek inscription to the same man is extant (1858) in which the name of the dedicator(s) is missing (see also 1621).

It follows that Greeks, or groups embracing both Greeks and Romans, whether described explicitly as such or merely by implication of mixed composition (as in the case of the generalised references to those inhabiting or working on the island), were content to go on using Greek in the first half of the first century BC on statues dedicated to prominent Roman outsiders. They made no linguistic accommodation to their addressees. The language choice is not then determined by the origin of the honorand, or by the historical circumstances (and hence the date), but reflects the preferences of the dedicators. Romans were ready to be associated with their Greek colleagues in this way, without feeling any need to assert their identity linguistically merely because the addressee was Roman. Again their integration is obvious. The exceptional inscriptions in this respect (if one leaves aside isolated cases such as 2009, discussed above) are two categories of Latin or bilingual texts which bring together Greeks and Romans in a particular form as dedicators. I refer of course first and foremost to the texts set up by *Italici et Graeci* (see above, III.2), and secondly to the single text in the name of Athenians and Greeks and *Italici* (1620, discussed above, III.3). The conclusion is obvious. The presence of the *Italici* in a dedication overrules the normal practice adopted in collective honorary inscriptions of using Greek in addressing high Roman officials. We have further confirmation here of the role played by this particular group in determining language choice.

I turn now to a few other Latin inscriptions. *ID* 1712 honours C. Iulius Caesar, the father of the dictator, *c.* 100: *C. Iulio C. f. Caesar[i] pro cos. olearii.* The *olearii* (ἐλαιοπῶλαι) perhaps turn up in two other inscriptions (1713, 1714). *ID* 1713 is an inscription recording the setting up of a temple by a group conjectured to be the [᾽Ελαι]οπῶλαι (a similar conjecture is made in 1714). These two inscriptions are in Greek alone. The dedicators of 1713 are a mixture of Greeks (Ζήνωνος καὶ Θέωνος τῶν ῞Ερμωγος ᾽Ελεατῶν), Romans (Σπορίου ᾽Αρίου τοῦ Δέκμου ῾Ρωμαίου) and possibly Italians (Εἰρηναίου τοῦ Ζωίλου ᾽Αζωτίου). In this last expression the editors take the ethnic to be derived from Azetium in Apulia rather than Azotos in Syria, but that must be considered speculative. Whatever the case, the group was clearly ethnically (and linguistically) mixed. On this evidence they seem to have been prepared to use Greek in their internal affairs; the switch into Latin in 1712 might have been motivated by the (Roman) identity of the honorand. In 1713 there was no insistence by the Latin-speaking member or members of the group on the use of Latin alongside Greek, and that is a further sign of the integration of Romans into local life. But it has to be acknowledged that the textual uncertainties of the Greek inscriptions make it unwise to press the interpretation of the group of texts too far.

Various other Latin inscriptions from the first century BC merely name the honorand without indicating the identity of the dedicators (1847, 1848, 1850, 1858 bis). It is unsafe to base conclusions on such material. It is true that, as we have seen (II), at an earlier date (the second half of the second century) Scipio Aemilianus was the recipient of an inscription *in Greek* from a Roman, but the scrappy Latin material above dated to several generations later does not establish decisively a change of linguistic policy on the part of 'Romans' setting up inscriptions to visiting Roman dignitaries, not least because the dedicators are unknown. The survey of material undertaken in this section serves to support the special character of the inscriptions by *Italici*.

IV.2 A social dimension to language choice: the collegia

There is also a social dimension to language choice at Delos, in that the social composition of the group setting up an inscription sometimes played a part. This factor is nowhere clearer than in the inscriptions of the *Competaliastai*.

It should be stressed that it is by no means only in inscriptions containing the word *Italici* that Latin is used. One notable context in which Latin regularly turns up is in the formal inscriptions of the *collegia* which the *negotiatores* had set up on the island on the model for example of the *collegia* of Capua.[61] The *collegia* in the conventional manner bore the names of gods, and we have inscriptions in the name of the groups called *Hermaistai*, *Poseidoniastai* and *Apolloniastai*. These inscriptions sometimes, but not always, end with a dedication to the *Italici*, as at *ID* 1736 (*L. L. Orbieis L. l. mag(istreis) laconicum Italiceis.* Λεύκιος Ὄρβιος Λευκίου Λικῖνος καὶ Λεύκιος Ὄρβιος Λευκίου Δίφιλος Ἑρμαισταὶ γενόμενοι v. Ἰταλικοῖς), though it has to be said that the dedicators are a pair of *magistri* rather than a whole *collegium*.[62] There are about thirty inscriptions attributed to the *Hermaistai*,[63] the *Poseidoniastai*[64] and the *Apolloniastai* (1730), either as groups acting separately or of all three acting collectively,[65] and of these

---

[61] On the *collegia*, see Flambard (1982: 71); also Degrassi, on *ILLRP* 747–62, Hatzfeld (1919: 267, 1912: 184–5); for Capua, see *CIL* x.3772–91; among the *magistri* (of *collegia*) at Capua can be identified two *Italici* who were in comparable groups at Delos (see Flambard 1977: 138).

[62] On *Orbeis* as a nominative plural, see below, v.2.

[63] *ID* 1731–50; of these 1731–7 are certainly by the *Hermaistai*, 1738–49 are probably so, and 1750 is conjectured to be.

[64] 1751 and 1752. The presence of Latin in these two inscriptions is the more interesting in that the inscriptions of the *Poseidoniastai* of Beirut also found at Delos are in Greek (see *ID* 1772–85), and that despite the fact that Beirut was an island of Latin culture in the east.

[65] For the collective dedications, see 1753–8; also probably 1759.

sixteen or seventeen are either bilingual[66] or in Latin,[67] but the remaining Greek inscriptions are almost without exception very fragmentary, and it is likely that in at least some cases the original inscriptions were bilingual. There is a remarkably high incidence of Latin in the inscriptions of the *collegia*, which suggests that in their most formal mode of behaviour – and *collegia* represent a form of institutionalised collective activity – the Italians felt some pressure to express a Latin-speaking (or at least bilingual) identity.

It is worth noting that the majority of the inscriptions with a Latin version are dated by the editors to a relatively early period (the second half of the second century BC, with several as early as 150–125). This applies to the eight bilinguals of the *Hermaistai* (1731–3, 1735–6, 1738–9, 1750), the bilingual (1751) and Latin (1752) inscriptions of the *Poseidoniastai*, and the two bilinguals of the three *collegia* acting together (1753–4). 1756, a Latin fragment published by the editors among the inscriptions of the combined *collegia*, is attributed to *c.* 100. So the Latin inscriptions by the *magister* L. Orbius (1742–3) are both dated to *c.* 100. Of the inscriptions which, as they stand, are in Greek alone, two are definitely also early (1734, 1741) and some are of uncertain date (1740, 1744–9). 1755 survives only in manuscript, but is dated by the editors to *c.* 100. 1757 is dated 97, but is incomplete. But 1758, a long Greek inscription on a white marble base which may be complete, is as late as 74, and the partial bilingual 1737 (see n.66) is even later (57/6). It is, as we saw, bilingual only in name, for the main text is in Greek but is preceded by a double date. Can any conclusions be drawn from this material about a possible change of linguistic policy on the part of the *collegia*? The last two inscriptions hint at a change from strict insistence on the inclusion of a Latin version in the earlier period, to a more relaxed policy in the first century, but there is no more than a hint of such a shift. Too many of the texts are fragmentary or undated to allow firm conclusions to be drawn. Nevertheless this chronological survey does have its interest. It emerges that in the second century the *collegia* were definitely holding on to a Latin-speaking identity in a Greek world; and in this they are obviously to be compared with

---

[66] 1731–3, 1735–6, 1737 (but only partially bilingual: see below), 1738–9, 1750, 1751, 1753, 1754, and possibly 1759. Of these, 1737 is the latest inscription of the *Hermaistai* (dated 57/6), and is partially bilingual in that it begins with a consular date in Latin, then has the same date in Greek, and finally presents its main text in Greek alone. Dates, as we have seen, are often in other places expressed in two languages, or alternatively in a language different from that of the main text (see 3.VI.1, p. 388, 3.VI.2, 5.IV.6). However the former practice is to be explained, it is probably related on occasions to a desire for precision in record keeping.

[67] 1742–3, 1752, 1756.

the *Italici*. The *collegia* and the group called *Italici* no doubt had much the same membership, with the texts of the one body tending to be early and of the other somewhat later. When Italians/Romans adopted a collective persona in public as members either of colleges or of the *Italici* they showed a marked tendency to use Latin; the frequency of Latin in their daily commercial activities was probably much lower than it is in these official documents.

There was also a fourth college, the inscriptions of which add the *social* dimension referred to in the title of this section to the language choice of the *negotiatores*. This group is that of the *Competaliastai*.[68] Their name has a Latin base (*compitum*; the ε of the second syllable reflects the openness of Latin short *i* as it was heard by Greek speakers[69]), to which is attached a Latin suffix (*-alis*), followed by the same Greek suffix as in the other names. They are likely to have been an organisation with Italian roots, and it has been argued that they fulfilled the same function as the *magistri uicorum* of Italy.[70] There are about eleven dedications by this group, which are long and well preserved, not a single one of which uses Latin either on its own or alongside Greek. Moreover, unlike the other *collegia*, the *Competaliastai* never included the *Italici* in their dedications, and while the other three groups sometimes acted jointly in setting up inscriptions, the *Competaliastai* are never included in any joint inscription. This then was a group which adopted a Greek persona in public documents. The reason for this becomes clear from the composition of the *Competaliastai*. Whereas the other three *collegia* were composed largely of freemen or freedmen, the *Competaliastai* were predominantly slaves or freedmen,[71] with Greek names very prominent in the lists. These were the servile entourage of the *Italici*, drawn from the slave population of Rome and Italy (see e.g. 1761, 1763 for natives of Naples) or acquired directly from the east, many of whom would have been native speakers of Greek. It might be argued that, just as the *collegia* with free membership used Latin to give themselves a distinctive public character, so the Greeks of the *Competaliastai* sought to establish their own exclusivity *vis-à-vis* the other groups by holding strictly to Greek in the formal documents of their college.

Language use in private is of course an entirely different matter. It cannot be assumed that in private slaves or freedmen of Greek origin will

[68] For the inscriptions of the *Competaliastai*, see *ID* 1760–70. The bilingual 1771 is not necessarily by the *Competaliastai*. On the *Competaliastai*, see in particular Flambard (1982: 68–72); also id. (1977: 133–40, especially 136).

[69] See Allen (1974: 61), and cf. Λέππεδον at 1659.   [70] See Flambert (1982: 70–1).

[71] See A.Wilson (1966: 117), Flambard (1977: 136), id. (1982: 68), Rauh (1993: 110).

have been resistant to the learning and use of Latin. On the contrary, the acquisition of Latin was a necessary step on the path of social or material advancement (including manumission). We have already seen (1) a case of three Greeks of servile background presenting themselves (in addressing their patron) not only as Greek-speaking but also as users of Latin (*ID* 1802). Interestingly, one of them (Q. Tullius Heracleo) is known to have been a competaliast (see 1761); his (bilingual) linguistic behaviour as a private individual thus differs from that of the institution to which he belonged. The Greeks in 1802 put the Greek version of their dedication first in keeping with their origins, but perhaps as an act of deference (or display) to their patron they then moved on to a Latin version.

A similar text (referred to above, n. 5) can be found at *ID* 1771:

Μάαρκος Γράνιος Μαάρκου ʿΗρακ(λέων?)
Διόδοτος Σήιος Γαίου καὶ Γναίου
ʾΑπολλώνιος Λαίλιος Κοίντου
Πρέπων ῎Αλλιος Μαάρκου
Νίκανδρος ʿΡασέννιος Μαάρκου
Δία ʾΕλευθέριον ἀνέθηκαν.

M. Granius M. l. Her(acleo)
Diodotus Seius C. Cn. s.
Apollonius Laelius Q. s.
Prepon Alleius M. s.
Nicandrus Rassenius M. s.
Iouem Leiberum statuer(unt).

Here, as the Latin but not the Greek version makes clear (for which phenomenon, see below, v.1), the dedicators of a statue to Zeus Eleutherios comprise one freedman and four slaves, all of them Greeks. The context is thoroughly Greek, in that the deity is Greek, but they neverthless felt moved to give themselves a secondary Latin-speaking identity; once again the Latin version follows the Greek. What they were attempting to demonstrate is unclear,[72] but they must have had some purpose in going to these lengths, and their linguistic identity was evidently at issue. We may conclude that the adherence by the *Competaliastai* to an exclusively Greek identity in their institutional inscriptions masks the realities of the linguistic behaviour of the Greek slaves and freedmen in the Italian entourage on Delos, and must therefore have been a matter of deliberate choice.

---

[72] For a discussion of the inscription, with bibliography, see Touloumakos (1995: 81–4).

V SOME LINGUISTIC FEATURES OF THE INSCRIPTIONS

V.1 Uses of υἱός : *aspects of imitation, accommodation and code-switching*

The interaction between Greek and Latin at Delos can be studied through expressions of filiation and an analogous expression. I begin with a classification of various usages.

(1) In some early bilingual inscriptions, in which the Latin version distinguishes in the usual way between filiation (genitive + *f(ilius)*) and the relationship of freedman to patron (genitive + *l(ibertus)*), the Greek version has name + genitive to express both relationships. *ID* 1733 (*c.* 125 BC) begins in the two versions as follows: *M. Pactumeius* **M. f.**, *M. Tuscenius L. f. Nobilior, D. Foluius D. f., D. Gessius* **D. l.** . . . Μάαρκος Πακτομήιος **Μαάρκου**, Μάαρκος Τοσκήνιος Λευκίου Νοβε(ιλίωρ), Δέκμος Φόλουιος Δέκμου, Δέκμος Γέσσιος **Δέκμου**. . . . 1732 (150–125 BC) shows the same phenomenon: Λεύκιος Ὄππιος Λευκίου corresponds to *L. Oppius L. f.*, and Αὖλος Πλώτιος Μαάρκου on the other hand to *A. Plotius M. l.* The same Greek imprecision is also found in the following bilinguals: 1750 = *ILLRP* 751 (dated by Degrassi to the period 142/1 to 135/4) and 1753 (dated by the editors to 113 BC). In these texts the Greek and Latin versions clearly follow their own conventions, with no influence observable of the one language on the other.

(2) The above Greek system was not ideal in inscriptions naming a variety of freedmen and freemen with filiation. In response to this ambiguity we find some inscriptions, bilingual or Greek only, in which in the Greek υἱός is used with the genitive to express filiation, whereas the plain genitive is retained as a correspondent to the Latin genitive in association with *l(ibertus)*. Thus in 1754 (end of the second century BC) υἱός is used throughout in the Greek version, but there are cases of the plain genitive where the Latin has *libertus*: *C. Heius* **T. f.** *Libo,* . . . *Q. Saufeius* **P. f.** *Treb(ianus),* . . . *D. Ampius* **Q. l.** . . . Γάιος Ἥιος **Τίτου υἱὸς** Λίβων, . . . Κόιντος Σαυφήιος **Ποπλίου υἱὸς** Τρεβιανός . . . Δέκμος Ἄμπιος **Κοίντου**. The same distinction is found in 1758 (not a bilingual text; 74 BC), 1802, discussed and quoted in part above, 1 (Κοίντου υἱόν contrasts with οἱ Κοίντου, which collectively renders a string of examples of *Q. l.* in the Latin), and 2013 (Γναῖον Σήιον Γναίου υἱὸν ῾Ρωμαῖον Γάιος Σήιος Γναίου ᾿Αριστόμαχος, ᾿Απόλλωνι; quoted and discussed above, 1). In the last a Greek freedman honours his Roman patron, with the relationship freedman to patron expressed by a genitive dependent on the name of the patron; the filiation of the Roman on the other hand has genitive + υἱός.

This economical new system in Greek owes its origin in part to the influence of Latin, whether because bilingual Latin speakers introduced the use of υἱός to their Greek, or because Greeks adopted the practice from Latin. The two possibilities are not mutually exclusive. In this case a Latin convention influences Greek, whereas in the matter of the accusative of the honorand (see III.3) the influence was in the reverse direction.

It would be wrong to give the impression that in Greek outside Delos patronymic expressions always comprised name + genitive without υἱός; but this was certainly the normal usage. It may well be that elsewhere υἱός with the genitive sometimes came into vogue independently of any Latin influence,[73] but at Delos the influence of Latin was certainly the decisive factor in causing the spread of the type of expression with υἱός. In other texts too the influence of Latin can sometimes be observed. Dionysius of Halicarnassus uses υἱός in expressing the filiation of Romans (e.g. *Ant.* 6.69.3 (numerous examples in a list), 8.87.2). In the Entella tablets from Sicily (Hellenistic period), note 4.4–5 Τεβέριος Κλαύδιος Γαίου υἱὸς Ἀντιάτας, with Loomis (1994: 143). In the Roman inscription *IG* XIV.1680 (Γάι]ος Ἰούλιος Θεμίσων [Τρ]αλλιανὸς ἰατρός, [Τι]βερίου Ἰουλίου Ἀρώγου [υἱ]ὸς Τραλλιανοῦ), which no doubt springs from one of the bilingual communities of the city, we again find the Latin practice transferred into Greek, but this time with some ineptitudes: the full three names of the father are expressed in the genitive, instead of the *praenomen* alone. One set of texts in which υἱός is commonly used under the influence of the Latin pattern are the Greek versions of Latin *senatus consulta* dating from about the second century BC onwards (Sherk (1969)). In these υἱός is definitely the norm in expressing the filiation of Romans, but practice is not absolutely standard. In the *Senatus consultum de agro Pergameno* of 129 BC (?) (Sherk no. 12), for example, there is a long list of Roman names from line 23 onwards in which υἱός does not occur. Isolated omissions of the word may be put down to carelessness on the part of Greek stonecutters, but in no. 12 the drafter must have followed a deliberate policy of expressing filiation in a Greek text in the Greek

---

[73] In Greek papyri of the Roman and Byzantine periods υἱός is commonly inserted in expressions of filiation (see Thomas (1971: 283), Hagedorn (1990)). This development seems to have been independent of Latin influence, because the word regularly *precedes* the name of the father in the genitive (see the examples quoted by Hagedorn). In a Greek–Lycian–Aramaic trilingual text from Xanthos of the fourth century (drawn to my attention by I. C. Rutherford) the Greek runs at lines 1–2 Πιξώδαρος Ἑκατόμνω υός (see Neumann (1979: 45), 320). The Lycian has an equivalent of υἱός (*Pigesere Katamlah tideimi*; *tideimi* means 'son'), and this may have influenced the Greek.

manner. In such texts it is not surprising to find Greeks named with the Greek method of filiation (as at no. 10, B line 4 Τηλέμαχος Μάτρωνος, Λέων Λέοντος), but even Greeks are sometimes named in the Latin style (e.g. 15, line 7 Δημ]οχάρης Δη[μοχάρου] υἱός). A case such as the last shows the primacy of the Latin text, which would have had *filius* whatever the ethnic origin of the referent. I conclude that the influence of the Latin method of filiation on Greek, mainly but not exclusively in the naming of Romans, was widespread, but that consistency of practice was not established.

(3) Finally, in many purely Greek inscriptions filiation is expressed by genitive + υἱός when the referent is Roman, but by the plain genitive when the referent is Greek. Thus at *ID* 1694 the filiation of the Roman honorand has the form Κορνηλίου υἱόν, whereas that of the Athenian sculptor on the same stone has the conventional Greek form of name + genitive (Δημόστρατος Δημοστράτου ’Αθηναῖος ἐποίει). This example is of limited interest, because the drafters of the two parts of the text were probably different. More striking is *ID* 2009, quoted above, IV.1. Two Greeks (Melians) set up a bilingual inscription in honour of C. Fabius Hadrianus. In the Greek version Roman practice is followed in the filiation of the Roman (Γαίου υἱόν), but Greek practice in that of the Melians (οἱ ’Απολλωνίου). It is important to note that the dedicators are Greeks, not Romans. It would arguably be less surprising if a native speaker of Latin when writing a formal Latin name in Greek should have translated *filius* into Greek. That Greeks should have done so reveals not only a knowledge of the Latin practice but also a readiness to accommodate their Greek usage to it. Similarly in the inscriptions which have the formula ’Αθηναίων καὶ ‘Ρωμαίων καὶ τῶν ἄλλων ‘Ελλήνων οἱ κατοικοῦντες ἐν Δήλωι or a variant Greeks are regularly named without υἱός in the filiation (e.g. 1649, 1652, 1653, 1656), whereas Romans are given this word (1659, 1660). Note, for example, the following two inscriptions: *ID* 1659 ’Αθηναίων καὶ ‘Ρωμαίων καὶ τῶν ἄλλων ‘Ελλήνων οἱ κατοικοῦντες ἐν Δήλω... Μάνιον Α[ἰ]μύλιον **Μανίου υὸν** Λέπεδον ἀντιταμίαν ἀρετῆς ἕνεκεν καὶ δικαιοσύνης...; *ID* 1661 ’Ασκληπιάδην **’Αντιόχου** ’Α[θη]ναῖον οἱ κατοικοῦντες ἐν Δήλω ’Αθηναίων καὶ ‘Ρωμαίων καὶ τῶν ἄλλων ‘Ελλήνων... Even in joint dedications to Romans in which there is no explicit Roman dedicator υἱός may occur in the filiation, as at 1622: ὁ δῆμος ὁ ’Αθηναίων καὶ οἱ τὴν νῆσον οἰκοῦντες Κόιντον ’Ορτήσιον Κοίντου υἱόν,... (this inscription is relatively late; the referent is probably Q. Hortensius, son of the orator and governor of Macedonia in 44 BC); or more strikingly at 1603,

where the dedicators are outsiders from Prostaenna in Pisidia: ὁ δῆμος ὁ Προσταεννέων Πισιδῶν Μάαρκον Ἀντώνιον Μαάρκου υἱὸν ταμίαν ἀντιστράτηγον Ῥωμαίων, ἀρετῆς ἕνεκεν καὶ εὐνοίας τῆς εἰς ἑαυτόν. This inscription is earlier than the previous one: the referent is the famous orator M. Antonius, who was in Asia in 113 BC.

The nomenclature of the Romans in these inscriptions is the more remarkable if it is put into historical perspective. A recent paper (Baslez (1996)) has studied the ways in which Romans are named in the inventories and accounts from the sanctuary at Delos. These give an idea of the manner in which Greeks referred to Roman dedicants from a much earlier date than that of most of the inscriptions which are discussed in this chapter. Romans turn up in the documents as early as the third century, and gradual changes in nomenclature can be traced. In the earliest documents (third century) Romans are referred to simply by *praenomen* + Ῥωμαῖος (e.g. *ID* 399 B.141 Κοίντου Ῥωμαίου).[74] At the time of the second Macedonian war the Delians used this form of reference even for Roman commanders: thus, for example, 'Titus, Roman', is none other than the illustrious Titus Quinctius Flamininus.[75] In the early second century BC a change is apparent. Romans are now named by *praenomen, gentilicium* and title.[76] The *tria nomina* never appear in the Delian archives, except in the case of the Scipios, Publius and Lucius.[77] Baslez does not deal explicitly with filiations, but usage is clear. When a patronymic is given (and none is found in the earliest documents) it almost always takes the Greek form of plain genitive: e.g. 442 B.102 (181 BC) Πόπλιος Ποπλίου Κορνήλιος στρατηγὸς ὕπατος Ῥωμαίων; 442 B.147 στέφανον χρυσοῦν ἐπιγραφὴν ἔχοντα 'Μινάτος Μινάτου Τήιος Ῥωμαῖος ἐκ Κύμης ἀνέθηκεν'.[78] The degree of accommodation found in some of the Greek inscriptions of later date quoted in the previous paragraph and elsewhere in this chapter now becomes apparent. Not only do Romans come to be given their *cognomina*, but their filiations also are in the Latin style. The early bilingual inscription cited above (1) (1733), even though it is set up by the Italians themselves (*Hermaistai*), has not yet fully adopted in its Greek version the Latin style of nomenclature. Though it contains *cognomina*, filiations take the Greek form. The

[74] Baslez (1996: 219–24) documents in chronological order all of the Romans who appear in the Delian archives. This Quintus is no. 3 in her list.
[75] See Baslez (1996: 216), and, for documentation, no. 10 in the list.
[76] See Baslez (1996: 216), citing nos. 9, 15–19.
[77] See Baslez (1996: 217), pointing out that the Delians knew the significance of the *cognomen*.
[78] See further e.g. 1403 Bb II.91, 1429 A.II.23–4 (with τοῦ), 1416 B.II.7. An exceptional case of υἱός is found at 442 B.103 Κόιντος Φάβιος Κοίντου υἱὸς στρατηγὸς Ῥωμαίων.

omission of υἱός is remarkable, as it demonstrates a keenness on the part of Romans in the relatively early period of the trading community to get their Greek right. The intrusion of the Latin pattern even into the Greek of Italians thus seems to have been gradual.

Linguistic accommodation among bilinguals takes many forms (see above, 3.IV.1, 5.V). We have seen that at its most obvious it may entail the use by the speaker of the addressee's primary language as a form of deference. An adult (e.g.) addressing a child may talk down to the child, or use baby-talk. Another strategy is seen in code-switching by the speaker into the addressee's primary language. In the present material a syntactic pattern from the honorand's (one might say, the addressee's) primary language is introduced into the speaker's/writer's language in deference to the honorand. The whole inscription of the Melians (2009) referred to above is a striking display of accommodation, in that it has as well a Latin version, in which, it should be noted, filiation of both the Roman and the Greeks is expressed in the Latin manner (*[C. Fabiu]m C. f. ... [Her]molucus et Apollonius [Apo]lloni f. Me[li]ei*. The dedicators thus did not impose a Greek structure on Latin even in their own nomenclature.

Though the Latin pattern of filiation intrudes frequently into Greek inscriptions at Delos, practice was not uniform, and both a *chronological* and *sociolinguistic* dimension may be discerned to the variations. I am concerned henceforth particularly with inscriptions by Romans/Italians rather than Greeks. If Greeks name a Roman in Greek without υἱός, as for example at *ID* 1604bis (ὁ δῆμος ὁ Ἀθηναίων Λεύκιον Καικέλιον Κοίντου Μέτελλον), it would not do to attach significance to the omission. They were after all merely adhering to the conventions of their own language. As far as the *chronology* of the usage of Romans is concerned, it was noted above (1) that in some early bilingual inscriptions of the *collegia*, υἱός is regularly absent from the Greek version. It would seem that in the early period Italians were content to follow the separate conventions of the two languages, without attempting to exploit the expressive potentialities of mixing the conventions. In the early dedication by a Roman to Scipio Aemilianus (*ID* 1842, quoted above, II), Greek practice is adhered to in the naming of both the dedicator and honorand, if the restoration of the text is correct. Similarly in an early (Greek) inscription of the Apolloniasts (1730, *c.*125) we find, for example, Κ[ό]ιντος Τύλλιος Κοίν[του], in reference to the same Q. Tullius Q. f. who, in the bilingual inscription 1802 (on a statue base, and set up by three of his freedmen: see I), receives υἱός in his filiation in the Latin manner. There was probably a gap in time beween the official inscription and that on the statue base,[79] during which the convention may have changed.

Once the use of υἱός had come into vogue, it was open to Romans to vary their usage for effect, and this possibility I refer to as the '*sociolinguistic* dimension'. On the one hand (e.g.) in the bilingual inscription 1698 (*A. Terentium [.] A. [.] f. Varro[nem legatum] Italicei et Graecei quei [.] Delei negoti[antur].* [Α]ὖλον Τερέντιον Αὔλου υἱὸν Οὐ[άρρωνα πρεσβυτὴν ʻΡ]ωμαίων ʼΙταλικοὶ καὶ ″Ελληνες οἱ κατ[οικοῦντες ἐν Δήλῳ]; see above, III.1) the referent A. Terentius Varro (the date is *c.* 82 BC) has the patronymic Αὔλου υἱόν, whereas at *ID* 1724 ([Φιλ]όστρατον [Φ]ιλοστρά[του] Νεαπολίτην [τ]ὸν πρότερον [χ]ρηματί[ζ]ον[τα ʼΑ]σ[κα]λωνίτην, τραπεζιτε[ύοντα] ἐν Δήλῳ, [Π]ό[π]λιος καὶ Γάιος καὶ Γναῖος ʼΕγνά[τι]οι Κοίντου ʻΡωμαῖοι τὸν ἑαυτ[ῶν] εὐεργέτην ʼΑπόλλωνι; see above, II) three Romans setting up an inscription to the banker Philostratus employ Κοίντου alone as their filiation. The presence of υἱόν in the first inscription would convey to the Greek reader that Varro was an outsider, whereas the omission of υἱοί by the Romans in their own nomenclature in the other inscription, if it is not to be taken merely as a stonecutter's slip, suggests that they wished to be seen as insiders, participating on an equal footing with Philostratus in the language and culture of a Greek island. There are thus cases on the one hand of Greeks (see above on the Melians at 2009) according a Roman a patronymic containing υἱός, in deference to the practice of his own language, and Romans on the other depriving themselves of υἱός, in deference to the practice of their addressee's language (see below on religious dedications). Accommodation was thus complex and many-sided at Delos, and it was both Greeks and Romans who were accommodating, and for different motives. The conventional view of Roman linguistic arrogance simply is not applicable to the situation in Delos.

It might be argued that the omission of υἱός in reference to Romans (as e.g. in *ID* 1724 above) could be merely the error of a Greek stonecutter unfamiliar with the Latin system. That is a possibility which cannot be ruled out in every single case, but I would draw attention to one sphere in which the word is regularly, as distinct from occasionally, left out. In private dedications to local divinities, Syrian, Oriental and Greek, which are common at Delos, Romans regularly express their filiation without υἱός, as do Greeks.[80] One possible reason for this is that the act of

---

[79] That is the view of the editors, on 1802, though their note has some inaccuracies.

[80] See e.g. *ID* 2379 Σπόριος Στερτίνιος Σπορίου ʻΡωμαῖος ʼΑρτέμιδι Σωτείρᾳ; cf. e.g. 2266, 2269, 2346, 2355, 2401, 2407, 2409, 2449.

making a dedication to a local god defined the dedicator as participating in the local culture, and he might accordingly be keen to follow the local convention (on Roman accommodation in the sphere of religion, see above, 5.V.1). By contrast in those inscriptions in which a Roman is referred to, or refers to himself, in civilian, as distinct from religious, contexts, the filiation is more likely to be expressed in the Latin style. The regularity of the practice in the religious inscriptions tells against haphazard copying errors.

I would draw attention finally to *ID* 1713, quoted above, IV.1. It was noted that the ἐλαιοπῶλαι (?) responsible for the inscription were of mixed Greek and Italian origin. The Roman in the passage quoted there conspicuously does not have υἱός in his filiation, and that is suggestive of the degree of integration into Greek culture of this group.

(4) A statue base with a Latin inscription (*ID* 2440) has the two expressions *Philologus Aprodisiu* and *Archibius Aprodisiu* (see above, 3.V.4 for the full text). The form *Aprodisiu* ('Ἀφροδισίου) apparently exhibits the type of code-switching referred to in connection with a Sicilian *defixio* and other texts dealt with in this book (3.V.4), whereby a filiation is inflected in a different language from that of the rest of the text. Possible reasons why in some cases the name of the offspring is inflected in Latin but that of the parent(s) in Greek were discussed at 3.V.4. There is though, it must be acknowledged, a question mark hanging over *Aprodisiu* (though Degrassi, *ILLRP* 289, treats it without equivocation as a filiation). In fact almost every other person named in the main body of the text is a freedman, as indicated in each case by *l(ibertus)* after the name. Why should just two persons be given a filiation? It is also an additional oddity that the name of the father is in both cases the same. We saw above (1) that in some Greek versions of bilingual inscriptions the relationship of freedman to patron was indicated by name + genitive, whereas in the Latin versions the genitive was made to hang on *libertus*. Could it be that, within a basic Latin text, there are two switches into the Greek system motivated by the Greekness of the referents? On this view the patron would be the same in both cases.

The aim of this section and of III.3 above has been to present some specific cases of interaction between the two languages at Delos. On the face of it these seem to display the 'influence' of the one language on the other, Latin on Greek in the case of υἱός, and Greek on Latin in the cases of the accusative of the honorand and the morphology and function of the patronymic (?) expressions just discussed. But such a blanket term as 'influence' fails to capture the diversity of the processes at work, which include forms of deference or accommodation, imitation (by the *Italici* in using the accusative construction to their own countrymen) and code-switching of the type referred to elsewhere as retention (possibly in *Aprodisiu*). There are moreover sometimes different ways of looking at one and the same usage. Thus, for example, the omission of υἱός in a filiation where the referent is a Roman could in theory be interpreted in one way in an inscription written by a Greek, and in another way in an inscription written by a Roman. I return to some of these matters briefly in the conclusion (VII).

V.2 Regionalisms (?)

It is, as we saw (III.4), sometimes stated that the inscriptions of Delos reveal features of 'Campanian' Latin.[81] Vine (1993: 163) lists four features in support of this contention: the spelling *irc* for *erc* (as in forms of *Mercurius*), the nominative plural *-e(i)s*, spellings showing 'geminatio uocalium', and the dative in *-a*.[82] He adds that Lazzeroni's conclusion that the Latin of the *negotiatores* in Greece is the Latin of Campania 'can be further supported on the basis of onomastic and historical data'. Unfortunately he does not know of A.Wilson (1966) or Solin (1982a), who have questioned the views of Hatzfeld about the proportion of southern Italians among the traders at Delos. In what follows I concentrate, in accordance with the subject of this chapter, on Delos rather than Greece in general, but there is no reason to think that the *negotiatores* at Delos were any different in origin or linguistic behaviour from those in other parts of Greece; and indeed those who wish to impose 'Campanian' Latin on the *negotiatores* devote their attention mainly to Delos, because that is where the best evidence is found.

Of the four features listed above, one (gemination of vowels) has already been dealt with (III.4). It does not amount to much. A single example in a Latin word at Delos tells us nothing. The gemination of *a* in *Greek* texts in the names *Marcus*, *Marcius* and *Marcellus* is curious, but it can be associated with Rome rather than Campania through the Greek translations of *senatus consulta*.

The plural in *-eis* (*-es*) in second declension words and some pronouns is more common. It is found in *magistreis* (*ID* 1732, 1733, 1753, 1754), in a plural *nomen* in reference to a pair of brothers (1736 *L., L. Orbieis*) and also

---

[81] See Lazzeroni (1974: 306) 'Il latino dei *negotiatores* in Grecia [for which the best evidence of course comes from Delos] è il latino della Campania', quoted with approval by Vine (1993: 163).
[82] He is following Lazzeroni (1974: e.g. 294).

three times in pronouns, at 1753 (*eisde(m)*), 1750 (*eisdem*) and 2440 (*hisce*). The claim that it is 'dialectal' (in distribution; its origin is a different matter) is not convincing. Lazzeroni (1974: 294) lists fifty-two examples (the list is by no means complete: see below), of which (e.g.) six come from Campania, thirteen from Latium, one from northern Italy and two from Spain. Ten, however, are from Rome itself, and consequently to maintain its dialectal status one must have recourse (with Lazzeroni) to some such argument as that the Roman inscriptions must be the work of outsiders to the city. Four are in official acts, and are explained away by the assertion that such documents contain not only archaisms, but also dialectalisms. It should be obvious that there is a good deal of special pleading at work here. 'Campanian' Latin has supposedly swamped many areas. Recently Bakkum (1994) has collected many more examples of the ending (in pronouns as well as nouns and names: he cites more than fifty instances in nouns and a substantial number in pronouns), on the basis of which he concludes (1994: 19): 'They are found throughout the area where Latin was written, including Spain and the Latin-speaking traders' communities in Greece. There are no indications that they belonged to any dialect in particular. Literary attestations of these forms occur in the comedies of Plautus and Terence, with one stray example in a speech of Livy.' It must however be noted (as Bakkum acknowledges) that literary examples consist entirely of pronouns, and Vine (1993: 216–17) suggests that nominal and pronominal examples need not be considered on the same footing. Whatever the case, it emerges clearly from the discussion of Bakkum, and also that of Vine (1993: 215–39), which is independent of Bakkum's, that nominal examples have clear functional restrictions: they are 'virtually restricted to *gentilicia, magister*, and several professional or social designations' (Bakkum 1994: 20), and are 'distributed according to a "resumptiveness"-parameter: the *s*-nominative is used where an enumeration is resumed by a common denominator in the nominative plural' (Bakkum 1994: 25). The vexed question of the origin of the form does not concern me here;[83] I would merely conclude that on the strength of a distribution such as this it is unacceptable to argue that the form as used at Delos is indicative of a non-city dialect of Latin.

The first declension dative in -*a* is attested twice at Delos: *CIL* I².2233 = *ILLRP* 53 *C. Nrius Eros Apolline et Iouei et Neptuno,* **Minerua** *et Mircurio, ID* 1732 = *ILLRP* 748 *magistres Mircurio et* **Maia** *donu d.* There are

---

[83] See Vine, Chapter 8, Wachter (1987: 253–4).

two cases at Rome (*CIL* I². 477 *Amor med* **Flaca** *dede*, 460 *[Me]nerua dono de[d . .]*),[84] but more outside in Latium and at Pisaurum.[85] The methodology whereby regional variations are set up on the basis of a handful of instances in inscriptions of unknown date and by unidentifiable dedicators is far from satisfactory. How much weight is to be attached to the two Roman examples in a small corpus?

The spelling of *Mercurius* with an *i* in the first syllable occurs four times at Delos (see *CIL* I². 2233, quoted in the previous paragraph; also *ID* 1732, 1733, 1753). This form is not certainly attested at Rome, but is found at Praeneste (*CIL* I².553, 564), at Firmum Picenum (1920) and in Dalmatia (2295), (cf. Osc. **mirikui** = *Mercurio* at Vetter (1953), 136). The attestations are few (8). Wachter (1987: 266, §110 (f)) merely places the form in a brief comment on the general variability in the writing of short *i* and *e*, thereby perhaps rejecting the temptation to see it as a regionalism, but the spelling with *i* in this particular phonetic environment does seem to be non-Roman.[86] It would though be useful to have comparative statistics showing the frequency of the conventional spelling at Rome; and it is also necessary to avoid the circular argument (of Vine (1993:163)) that the form is dialectal because it occurs at Delos ('The "dialectal" status of the **Mirc-/Mirq-** forms emerges with particular clarity from the attestation of four such forms in Latin inscriptions from Delos').

Given the diverse origins of the *negotiatores* at Delos it would not be surprising if they sometimes committed spellings associated with regions of Italy. But the evidence on which is based the attempt to find at Delos a markedly 'Campanian' form of Latin is rather weak. The ability of scholars of antiquity to detect 'regional' or 'dialectal' spellings and the like in inscriptional material is inversely proportionate to the size of the corpus of inscriptions. In a small corpus, such as that of the south Picene inscriptions or those of Oscan, regionalisms are readily found. But in the vast corpus of Latin inscriptions of the Roman Empire regionalisms of spelling and morphology are virtually impossible to prove. Spelling variation emerges for what it is, a complex phenomenon related to many determinants. I conclude that even if there are at Delos occasional Latin regionalisms, there are no grounds for assuming any ideological intent on the part of 'Campanians' in adopting 'Campanian' Latin in public inscriptions.

[84] Lazzeroni (1974: 294) claims that 'esso è ignoto al latino di Roma', but see Vine (1993: 349) with bibliography.
[85] See Vine loc. cit., Lazzeroni (1974: 295), Wachter (1987: 483–4).
[86] See Vine (1993: 162–3).

VI THE MYCONOS CURSE TABLET

The evidence which has been looked at so far relates predominantly to public or official language use. An important text, the so-called Myconos curse tablet, which was found in the necropolis of Rheneia but is now in the museum at Myconos, takes us closer to private language use (*ID* 2534 = *ILLRP* 1150). I begin by printing the improved text of Solin (1982a: 102):

L. Paconium senem,
Q. Tullium Q. f. [...ca 6] A [ca 4] + (...)
N. Cottius N. f. + [...]
C. Seium C. f. Cheilonem,
[...]ium Aristomachum,
+ Caecilium L. f. + [...]
Q. Samiariu M. f. Arc[...]
M'. Satricanium Arc[...]
A., Q. Paconios M. f. [...]
Heracleide, Antipatrum [...]
Heliodo*rum* [...] TIV [...]
Demetrius, Caium,
Se[u]them pragmaticum,
Serapion Serapionis f.,
P. Granius Alexandruṣ
[...]tius D. f. Aeg[...]
[...]cius Neiceporus,
Cn. Paconius Apolḷọni[us],
Maṛaị(os?) Gerrillanos [...]
N., M. Raios, et sei quiṣ alius erit
inimeicus Tito Paconio.

Despite its provenance, this *defixio* obviously concerns members of the business community at Delos. It can be dated to about 100 BC (see the editors of *ID* and also Solin 1982a:102). Whether it was written by a scribe or by T. Paconius himself is of course unclear. Solin (1982a: 103, 108) draws attention to what he calls (108) 'numerosi grecismi' (of an orthographical kind), but in fact the document is notable for the relative absence of Greek influence. The use of the digraph *ei* in Greek names (*Cheilonem, Heracleide*) is unremarkable (*Neiceporus* is hypercorrect),[87] and reveals nothing more than that the writer knew the spelling of the names in their Greek form. We have seen repeatedly that a name may retain

---

[87] So Solin (1982a: 108).

morphological or orthographic features from its language of origin when it is transferred into another language. Moreover this is a text in which the digraph *ei* is several times used in Latin words (in *inimeicus* and *sei*) as a marker of long *i*. Solin (1982a: 108), though acknowledging that the spelling of *inimeicus* is not 'in fondo un grecismo', nevertheless goes on to say that 'in ogni caso s'inserisce tra simili grafie influenzate dall'ambiente greco di Delo'. The Greek ambience is immaterial in these cases. The use in Latin of the *ei* digraph, which was on the one hand a grammarians' strategy to render a long *i* and partly a means of conferring an archaic colour on a text (see above, I.VII.2.2 on *IGUR* 616), is well attested at Delos in Latin words. It is found in *Italicei*, *Graecei* and *quei*, which are the standard spellings on the island, in the names *Papeirio* and *Hercolei* at *ID* 1753, and in *Leiberum* at 1771. Solin (1982a: 108–9) is also inclined to see Greek influence in the gemination in *Gerrillannos*, but false geminates are common in Latin as well and are rarely decisive as linguistic evidence.

The Myconos tablet starts off with the names in the accusative, and then in line 3 switches into the nominative. It then proceeds again in the accusative, with some further nominatives later in the text. *-os* forms such as *A., Q. Paconios* are manifestly accusative plurals. Basically the list is in the accusative, with sporadic lapses into the nominative. It is not surprising that the names of the victims of the curse should be placed in the accusative, as the objects of an implied verb of cursing or the like. The *defixio* Audollent (1904), 139 = *CIL* I². 1012 = *ILLRP* 1144 makes explicit the way in which such an ellipse takes place. A name in the accusative (*Rhodine(m)*) is first of all object of the verb-phrase *tibi commendo*, and then there follows a list of accusatival names: *Rhodine tibi commendo, uti semper odio sit M. Licinio Fausto; item M. Hedium Amphionem, item C. Popillium Apollonium, item*... The accusative of the victim is in fact analogous to the accusative of the honorand. But equally it was not unusual to list the names of the victims in the nominative, as in the mixed Latin–Oscan *defixio* Vetter (1953), 7 = *CIL* I². 1614 = *ILLRP* 1146 (discussed above, 2.II.3), or in the long text *CIL* I². 2765 = *ILLRP* 1148, which consists exclusively of names without any verbs (see also 5.VIII, p. 627 for the nominative of names in lists). Similarly on the *defixio* Audollent (1904), 135 (*Malcio Nicones oculos*...) Solin (1995: 572) remarks that the person cursed is without doubt *Malchio* son of *Nico*, and that *Malcio*, often taken to be a dative, is in fact a 'fixed' nominative lying outside the syntax of the text, as is often the case in *defixiones*. Looked at another way, the nominative is not so much fixed, as a heading naming the victim, after which the curse proper is set out. In the Myconos tablet Paconius or his writer has lapsed from time to time into the alternative convention of naming the victim in the nominative.[88]

The interest of the text is that it takes us into the intimate world of the *negotiatores*, with Latin used for what is inherently a private purpose. The choice of Latin in such a context contrasts with the use of Greek from time to time by the *negotiatores* in more formal, public texts. Latin was both the language of formality in public inscriptions which sought to set the Italians apart from the Greeks under special circumstances, and the language of intimacy among primary speakers of Latin. Greek was no doubt often used to Greeks; but if addressed to first-language speakers of Latin (as occasionally in public inscriptions) it had a certain showiness about it.

VII CONCLUSIONS

The Romans acted as if only two languages (Greek and Latin) existed in the administration of the Empire and the conduct of trade. There is a great difference between the language attitudes observable in the two commercial communities discussed in this book, La Graufesenque and Delos. At La Graufesenque, as we will see, there was an expectation that the Gauls would learn Latin, even if no aggressive attempt was made to stamp Gaulish out. Instruction in Latin literacy was an instrument of Romanisation. At Delos on the other hand Greek was given roughly equal status to Latin, and there is abundant evidence for the Italians and Romans using that language. I refer of course mainly to public language use in inscriptional form and not to speech, but public inscriptions require preparation and thought, and are by their very nature expressive of the formal identity which the writer sees as appropriate to his referents; and if Greek was esteemed by Romans such that they were happy to use it in such texts, then it is reasonable to assume that they sometimes used it as well in private (in addressing primary speakers of Greek). Moreover not all of the Greek inscriptions (or inscriptions with Greek versions) discussed in the chapter relate to the activities of institutions or collective groups, such as the *collegia* or the *Italici*. There are more personal Greek dedications by Greek to Roman, Roman to Greek and even Roman to Roman, and these imply that Greeks and Romans were mixing freely and using Greek among themselves.

Linguistically there was give and take between Romans and Greeks, with growing familiarity leading to mutual accommodation. In the

---

[88] See also Jeanneret (1918: 133).

earliest period as represented in the archives of the sanctuary Romans are treated as strangers by the Delians, who show no appreciation of Latin naming practices. Romans, like other outsiders, are named simply by single name + ethnic. There are occasional references in the archives to 'Latin letters' on dedications, but Latin is not quoted: e.g. *ID* 1439 Ca. 8 στλεγγίδιον χρυσοῦν ἐπὶ βάσεως, ἐφ' οὗ ἐπιγραφὴ 'Ρωμαικοῖς γρ[άμ]μασιν. As Delian familiarity with the Romans increases in the second century, Romans are given not only their full names (minus *cognomina*) in the archives, but also from time to time titles, and that suggests that the Delians were now showing a greater interest in them and their culture. By the first century BC radical changes are in evidence. Greeks not only use Greek in formal address of Romans, but also occasionally Latin (as in the bilingual dedication by three Melians). In Greek inscriptions there is a subtle appreciation of Roman naming practices, marked particularly by the imitation in Greek of the Latin formula of filiation. At this period too Greeks begin to appear in joint dedications with Italians written in Latin. Athenians and other Greeks had not in any sense abandoned their linguistic identity, because we simply do not find them using Latin on its own on their own behalf when they are not explicitly associated with *Italici* as joint dedicators of an inscription. But the accommodation seen in filiations shows that they had come a long way since the early archival inscriptions, and suggests that they probably knew Latin informally.

The linguistic concessions made by the Romans and Italians were undoubtedly greater. They appear in joint Greek dedications (as for example those of the 'Athenians, Romans and other Greeks resident on the island'), and also they use Greek (or Greek with Latin) to Greeks and even to fellow Romans/Italians (see II). Texts of this last type, and also the bilingual inscriptions to Roman outsiders which have a Greek structure even in the Latin version (the accusative of the honorand), imply that these Italian traders were proud of their acquired Greekness and keen to parade it before outsiders. On Delos itself there is abundant evidence of their fitting in linguistically, and it is reasonable to deduce from their use of Greek in public inscriptions that they will have conducted a good deal of their public business in Greek. The servile members of the Italian entourage openly projected a Greek identity in their collective inscriptions (those of the *Competaliastai*), and also in private dedications to their masters or patrons. Into the second category fall two bilingual dedications by slaves/freedmen in which the Greek version comes first; though the addition of the Latin does at least constitute a concession to the master/patron. It is also noteworthy that whereas in Latin inscriptions of the first century addressed to Roman officials a Greek epigraphic construction is imposed on Latin (the accusative of the honorand), in the earliest bilingual inscriptions of the *collegia* the Italians were careful not to inflict on Greek the Latin formula of filiation, even though there was a resultant ambiguity in the Greek versions. The Italians thus began by showing a desire to adhere to 'correct' Greek, despite its drawbacks. And in religious dedications to local divinities Romans used Greek exclusively, and avoided completely the Latinate filiation formula, thereby immersing themselves totally in the local cult as insiders.

All of this shows that linguistically Greek had the upper hand, as it were, in that, though there were mutual accommodations and language learning on both sides, Italians conceded more than Greeks. The linguistic attitudes apparent at Delos differ not only from those at La Graufesenque, but also from those displayed from time to time by Roman officials in their dealings with Greeks. Officials sometimes humiliated their Greek subjects by parading their incomprehensible language before them and then making the concession of providing a translation. Trade was a different matter, in which symbolic gestures were likely to be counterproductive. The linguistic integration of the Italians was made easier in that some of them were from Greek-speaking parts of Italy, and others had bilingual Greeks among their slaves and freedmen.

That said, the Italians did *not* give up Latin entirely on the island. It is highly likely (given the relatively limited evidence for Greek concessions to Latin) that in day to day intercourse Greek was the predominating language, but the Italians held on to Latin for symbolic purposes in two spheres: in the formal inscriptions of the *collegia* (particularly in the earlier period), and in the collective inscriptions in which they acted under the name *Italici*. There were good reasons for this. The *Italici* were *negotiatores* who operated all over the Greek-speaking world and elsewhere in the Republican period. Their sense of identity is obvious, as is their reliance on the protection of Rome in times of trouble (see above, III.2, on the passage of Sallust). It was appropriate that they should express their separateness (and 'Romanness') in a Greek-speaking world by the maintenance of Latin in the types of formal inscriptions which conferred a public identity on them. And as for the *collegia*, they were an Italian institution (though with Greek names), and their formal activities probably preserved the Italians' connection with their roots. They did not act as secret societies by insisting entirely on an alien language, but there was an insistence on Latin at least alongside Greek.

The inscriptions of Delos offer us no more than glimpses of bilingualism, and that in its most formal guise. Nevertheless they do raise several issues of a general kind. On the basis of some of the material at Delos it is possible to suggest a difference between some syntactic imitation and syntactic accommodation. The phenomena I have in mind are fundamentally of the same kind, but can be distinguished on the basis of their intention. Consider first the use of the accusative of the honorand in Latin inscriptions. The choice of this construction instead of the normal Latin dative could not have been unconscious. If the addressee or honorand were a Greek, it might be argued that the accusative was chosen as a form of linguistic deference or accommodation (on which see below), but the inscriptions we have seen mostly honour Romans. I would use the term 'syntactic imitation' to describe this procedure. The Greek pattern is deliberately imitated, much as Latin poets imitated Greek syntax (see above, 4.II). It is usually difficult to relate syntactic imitation in poets to the particular context of the poem; a smattering of Greek syntax, particularly of a poetic kind, can be seen as a defining feature of the Latin poetic register, cultivated by poets from Ennius onwards. The imitation of a Greek syntactic pattern in Latin at Delos, and indeed elsewhere in the Greek world in inscriptions set up by *negotiatores*, can be interpreted not so much as a defining feature of a particular register, but rather as one side of the mixed identity which the *negotiatores* were displaying. The usage probably struck Roman readers as unusual for Latin.

By 'accommodation' is meant, as we have frequently seen, the adjustment of speech (or in our case writing) in some way to suit that of the addressee. The employment by Greeks writing Greek at Delos of the Latin style of filiation (υἱός + genitive) in reference to Romans was described earlier as a form of accommodation on the part of the Greeks. It is also a form of imitation, in that a Latin pattern is deliberately imitated in Greek. But in this case the aim is different. The intention is not to make the Greek sound odd, but to accord Romans their full naming formula in a different language. Imitation thus becomes accommodation, with the intended effect on the reader the defining distinction between the two forms of imitation. The accusative of the honorand in Latin addressed by Romans to another Roman introduces a discordant note, whereas the use of υἱός addressed in Greek by Greeks to Romans is in harmony with the expectations of the Romans. Accommodation of this type expresses solidarity, whereas the other type of imitation has the appearance of a method of distancing writer from addressee slightly.

Linguistic accommodation on the island worked in both directions. The bilingual inscriptions of the Italian *collegia* arguably manifest in their very bilingualism a form of accommodation to the Greek environment, though the mixed composition of the *Italici* was possibly an influence as well. And where filiations are concerned, Romans sometimes, in Greek, used the distinctively Greek type of filiation of themselves as a sign of their complete absorption into Greek culture, not least in religious dedications. Mutual accommodation at Delos implies a well integrated Greco-Latin society.

7

Bilingualism at La Graufesenque

I INTRODUCTION

The imperfect bilinguals or second-language learners who have been identified so far belonged largely to groups resident in areas in which two or more languages were in contact, such as the city of Rome. But language contact with its consequent bilingualism did not only take place in static populations. One environment, for example, in which speakers of different languages mixed together was the army; but language learning in the army is a topic in itself (see above, 5.VII.3).

Another group in any population who come into contact with foreign language speakers are traders purveying goods across language boundaries. In many cultures the trading classes have proved adept at acquiring enough of the foreign languages needed to carry on business, and there is no reason to think that Roman traders and their trading partners will have been any different. Language learning was no doubt a two-way process, in the sense that Latin-speakers wishing to exploit a province would have come into contact with provincial languages, and on the other hand provincial traders moving into Latin-speaking areas or dealing with Latin speakers will have picked up some Latin.

We have already seen one example of this second form of contact. The Greek-speaking Milesian slave-trader Aeschines (see I.VII.2.3), while trading in the west, was required to write out in his own hand a legalistic document in Latin. It can be deduced from some of his misspellings that he was familiar with the sounds of substandard varieties of the Latin language. Other spellings, though wrong, reveal a recognition of the function of Latin morphemes.

It would be easy to produce further evidence for provincials or Romans who had acquired respectively some Latin or another language in the interests of trade. There is explicit evidence for the bilingualism of some of the *negotiatores* on Delos, as we saw in the last chapter. Cicero says that Gaul was full of *negotiatores* (*Font.* 11), and there must have been some second-language learning on at least one side at this period. *CIL* XIII.2448 is a bilingual (Greek–Latin) inscription (late second century AD) from Lyons recording the career of a *negotiator* from Syria who traded in the products of Aquitaine and Lyons.[1] The inscription was set up by his 'brother' Avidius Agrippa, who was possibly his real brother.[2] As a Syrian the man (Thaemus) was no doubt primarily a speaker of Greek or Aramaic (or both). As a trader in Gaul he must have spoken some Latin. He would not normally have learnt Latin in Syria,[3] though there was certainly one pocket of Latin culture in the Near East (Beirut).[4] It is likely, but not provable, that he learnt, or improved, his Latin while dealing in the western provinces. The languages chosen for the epitaph advertise on the one hand his eastern origins, and on the other his acquired Latin culture. A special type of bilingual *negotiator* seems to be attested in an inscription from Boldog in S.W. Slovakia, quoted and discussed above, 2.IX. The referent, a military interpreter dealing, it would seem, with Germans, was also a *negotiator*. Perhaps the pattern was a common one: a language acquired or exploited in the army was later put to use in a new career.

II LA GRAUFESENQUE

But by far the most important evidence that we have concerning bilingualism and language acquisition among the commercial classes comes from the extraordinary collection of texts found at La Graufesenque in Gaul, which have recently been edited by Marichal (1988). These present us with language contact in a commercial enterprise. They have light to throw not only on bilingualism in a general sense, but more particularly on language mixing (i.e. code-switching on such an extensive scale that

---

[1] On this man, see Lambrechts (1937: 38), Rougé (1966: 283 n. 8, 305), Biville (1989b: 105).

[2] See Rougé (1966: 305).

[3] Exceptions of course can be found, such as the historian Ammianus Marcellinus (on whose origin, see now Matthews (1994)). At the upper levels of society in Antioch it was no doubt well recognised that a knowledge of Latin was essential for an imperial administrative career, and instruction in the language must have been available, as the Latin literary culture of Ammianus amply shows. For some other cases of upper-class Latin-speaking bilinguals, see Matthews (1989: 71), e.g. the spy Antoninus (Amm. 18.5.1), and the praetorian prefect Strategius (Amm. 15.13.1; see also Drijvers (1996)). Libanius' great-grandfather was versed in Latin, so much so that it was rumoured that he came from Italy (Libanius, *Autobiography* 3). This anecdote tells us not only that Latin was sometimes known in Antioch, but also that such an accomplishment was considered unusual in the place at that time; see also Millar (1993a: 258). There is now a good survey of the evidence for Latin literary culture in Antioch by Geiger (1999: 613–17).

[4] See Millar (1990: 10–23), id. (1993a: 527–8).

the base language is sometimes difficult to determine) as a stage in language shift.

La Graufesenque was the site of an important Gallic–Latin pottery, some 2 km from Millau (Aveyron), on the left bank of the Dourbie. The pottery produced on a vast scale so-called Samian wares which were of Italian rather than Gallic type, in the style of Arretium in N. Italy.[5] The close imitation of Arretine models, particularly in the early period, is consistent with 'direct immigration of certain potters from Arezzo to South Gaul' (Oswald (1956: 107)).[6] The heyday of the pottery was roughly between AD 20 and 120, and many of the texts which we have can be dated to about the middle of the first century. The labour of local Gallic potters was used. The names of the potters at La Graufesenque, many of which are attested, are partly Gallic and partly Latin.

In the pottery it was the custom to fire in a single oven the products of more than one maker at a time. At the firing a list was scratched on the base of a plate of the type of pots to be fired, and the numbers of items for which each craftsman was responsible.[7] This plate was then fired with the rest of the pots to provide a record. More than 160 such texts in varying states of preservation have been published together by Marichal, and there are various other types extant which bring the total up over 200. These documents are a priceless indication of the linguistic situation in a Gallo-Roman commercial community.

Many of the texts are in Celtic, and some are in Latin. Others again present a mixture of elements from both languages, and it is these last which are potentially of greatest interest here. Marichal (1988: 57–102) has provided an impressive description of the linguistic features of both the Celtic and Latin texts, which includes a synthesis of the views of Celticists on the numerous problems thrown up by the Celtic texts. Flobert (1992) has also written an excellent article on linguistic aspects, in which he stresses particularly the bilingualism of the community of potters. In this chapter I will not be saying anything new on points of linguistic detail, but an attempt will be made to assess the documents as products

---

[5] For detailed illustrations showing the influence of Arretine wares on South Gaulish potters, see Oswald (1956); also A. Vernhet in Bémont and Jacob (1986: 96–101).

[6] See also M. Passelac in Bémont and Jacob (1986: 37–8): 'L'influence romaine se manifeste partout très fortement à travers la typologie, le contenu et la forme des timbres, la technique de fabrication, même quand il s'agit de céramique à vernis non grésé. Son origine peut même être précisée dans certains cas: Étrurie ou Italie du Nord pour Bram, Arezzo pour La Graufesenque, Pouzzoles pour Montans et Narbonne. Elle s'est exercée à deux niveaux, par l'immigration de potiers et l'organisation de circuits commerciaux.' On the problem of the relationship between the local Gallic potters and the Italian potteries, see also Woolf (1998: 190).

[7] For further details of the record keeping, see Marichal in Bémont and Jacob (1986: 18).

of a bilingual community in keeping with the terminology and concepts on which this book is based, and to bring out the character of the code-switching as compared with that seen already elsewhere in this book.

There is no need to go into detail here about the evidence for the survival of Gaulish into the Roman Empire. There is literary (anecdotal) evidence[8] as well as some primary material.[9] The motivating forces behind the spread of Latin and its paths of development in Gaul remain controversial.[10] Woolf (1998: 22 n. 74, with bibliography), talking of the spread of Roman culture in general rather than specifically of that of the Latin language, notes the tendency of scholars to pit a deliberate policy by the Romans of Romanising their subjects against emulation of Roman culture by the locals themselves, and states that his own approach 'is to reject the opposition of compulsion and choice . . . and instead to explore the roles played by Romans, Gauls and those who were in some sense both, in constructing Gallo-Roman culture'. I would agree that the positions which he attacks are doctrinaire, and, where the learning of Latin is concerned, take no account of the diversity of the contacts which will have taken place between primary speakers of the two languages. Differing degrees of fluency in Latin will have been acquired under many different circumstances by different individuals and groups.

---

[8] A collection of *testimonia* may be found (e.g.) in Schmidt (1983: 1010). See further Vendryes (1925), Whatmough (1944: 68–73), Barrud (1976), Lee (1993: 68–9). One must though be wary of taking at their face value all references to 'Celtic'. Note the following passage of Sidonius Apollinaris: *Epist.* 3.3.2 *mitto istic ob gratiam pueritiae tuae undique gentium confluxisse studia litterarum tuaeque personae quondam debitum quod sermonis Celtici squamam depositura nobilitas nunc oratorio stilo, nunc etiam Camenalibus modis imbuebatur.* (3) *illud in te adfectum principaliter uniuersitatis accendit, quod, quos olim Latinos fieri exegeras, barbaros deinceps esse uetuisti.* Ecdicius (late fifth century) had inspired the *nobilitas* of the Arverni (region of Clermont) to take up Latin studies (note *oratorio stilo, Camenalibus modis*). The passage has been interpreted in different ways. According to Vendryes (1925: 270) the reference is to the final abandonment of Celtic by the nobility of the Arverne at the time of Sidonius ('Sidoine Apollinaire laisse entendre qu'à son époque la noblesse arverne venait seulement de se débarrasser complètement des restes de la vieille langue nationale'; in country districts, it is suggested, Celtic would have been more persistent). But on another view Ecdicius had established rhetorical and poetical studies in this part of Gaul (see Sofer (1941: 114), Weisgerber (1939: 27), = id. (1969: 153)); the expression *sermonis Celtici squamam depositura* would therefore refer to the improvement of the Latin style of the élite and their rejection of any traces of a 'Gallic' Latin accent. The phrases *oratorio stilo* and *Camenalibus modis*, which refer to higher literary studies, would seem to favour an interpretation of this second kind, and it is indeed possible to find clearcut references to 'Gallic' Latin, as e.g. at Pacatus, *Pan.* 1.3, Sulp. Sev. *Dial.* 2.1.3–4, p. 181.2. A similar difficulty of interpretation hangs over Sulp. Sev. *Dial.* 1.27.2, p. 179 *tu uero, inquit Postumianus, uel Celtice aut, si mauis, Gallice loquere, dummodo Martinum loquaris* (for various views see Whatmough (1944: 72),Weisgerber (1939: 27), = id. (1969: 153)). It is possible that in *Gallice* there is a pun on the addressee's name (*Gallus*) (see Weisgerber, locc. cit.), in which case *Gallice* may simply be a witty rephrasing of the point already expressed by *Celtice*, which, on the evidence of the passage of Sidonius Apollinaris above, could refer to Gallic Latin rather than Celtic.

[9] See Lejeune (1988).

[10] See Herman (1983: 1045–6) on the difficulties of the problem.

Local élites, for example, may from an early date have been moved by the prestige of the Latin language and culture to learn, or have their children taught, the language. At an early date Caesar (*Gall.* 1.19.3) relates how on one occasion in Gaul he had his usual interpreters (i.e. Celtic speakers) removed, and dealt with a Gaul using a Gallic noble as interpreter (see also above, 2.IV.1): *Diuiciacum ad se uocari iubet et cotidianis interpretibus remotis, per C. Valerium Troucillum, principem Galliae prouinciae, familiarem suum, cui summam omnium rerum fidem habebat, cum eo colloquitur.*[11] There is some reason to think that the Romans themselves might, in an informal and non-aggressive way, have encouraged such acculturation in the Celtic provinces.[12] There is evidence, for example, in Tacitus that schools existed which might teach Latin to the offspring of provincial élites. At Agricola 21.2 Tacitus describes Agricola's policy in Britain (in AD 79) of having the sons of local aristocrats trained in the liberal arts: *iam uero principum filios liberalibus artibus erudire, et ingenia Britannorum studiis Gallorum anteferre, ut qui modo linguam Romanam abnuebant, eloquentiam concupiscerent.* Significant here is the relative clause. Until now the provincials in question did not know Latin and even rejected it, but now it is the aim that they should aspire even to eloquence in that language. A twofold development seems to be envisaged here, both the teaching of Latin as a second language, and the learning of the art of rhetoric. Roman encouragement of the process is implicit in the passage, as is a change of attitude on the part of the provincials themselves, from hostility to the new language to a desire for second-language fluency. On this Tacitean view of things neither member of the opposition 'compulsion–choice' referred to above would adequately express the driving force behind the language learning. There was to be give and take, assistance from one side and a readiness to learn on the other. The second language is presented not simply as a means of communication, but as a cultural instrument.[13] The noble British youth are to esteem Latin and the *artes* associated with *eloquentia*. There is a difference between compulsory language instruction, and instruction which is merely available to those who might have reason to esteem the product of that instruction. There is a much more

[11] On the passage, see e.g. Schmidt (1983: 1004). The man has a hybrid name, with his Gaulish name inserted within a Roman framework as a *cognomen*. He was a Roman citizen from Gallia Narbonensis. But the anecdote may have a regional, and not purely a social, dimension. The point is not necessarily that Troucillus was a noble and hence knew Latin, but that he came from the Romanised area Narbonensis, where a knowledge of Latin might already have spread down the social scale. Outside Narbonensis Celtic was still obviously spoken, and Latin not understood.

[12] See e.g. Brunt (1976).

[13] But the interpretation of the clause *ingenia . . . anteferre* is far from clear: see Ogilvie and Richmond (1967: 227).

subtle policy, if it is such, at work here than one of compulsion. It is of note that it is the *filii* of the nobles who are to be so instructed. It is easy to understand how local nobles might have desired for their sons something which they regarded as a cultural attainment presenting potential advantages in the future.

This is not the only evidence for schools of the Latin liberal arts in the western provinces. Tacitus himself mentions at *Ann.* 3.43.1 a school at Autun where the offspring of Gallic nobles were educated:[14] *Augustodunum, caput gentis, armatis cohortibus Sacrouir occupauerat, <ut> nobilissimam Galliarum subolem, liberalibus studiis ibi operatam, et eo pignore parentes propinquosque eorum adiungeret.* According to Plutarch, *Sert.* 14.2–3, Sertorius had the sons of Spanish nobles educated at Osca, and he put in charge of them teachers of both Greek and Latin learning (διδασκάλους . . . ʽΕλληνικῶν τε καὶ ʽΡωμαϊκῶν μαθημάτων). One such teacher, L. Appuleius, may be mentioned at Suet. *Gramm.* 3.5: *L. Appuleium ab Aeficio Caluino equite Romano praediuite quadringenis annuis conductum ut **Oscae doceret** (but *Oscae doceret* is an emendation).[15] The passage goes on to note that *grammatica* had penetrated into the provinces, particularly *Gallia togata*: 6 *nam in prouincias quoque grammatica penetrauerat ac nonnulli de notissimis doctoribus peregre docuerunt, maxime in Gallia togata, inter quos Octauius Teucer et Sescenius Iacchus et Oppius Chares.*[16] Such grammarians as there were in the western provinces in the late Republican and early Imperial periods (and their significance should not be exaggerated) need not, indeed in most cases would not, have been teachers of Latin as a second language. The implication of these various snippets of information is rather that there were some teachers of liberal studies (grammar, rhetoric) at a more advanced level. But if the sons of provincial élites in the relatively early period were in some places at least in a position to learn rhetoric and the like, those élites must already have acquired fluency in Latin as such. The anecdotes at least imply an attitude: that it was desirable for provincial nobles to assume the culture of Rome. This ambition must have entailed the elevation of the Latin language to prestigious status, with consequent bilingualism among the élite, followed eventually by the complete abandonment of the vernacular languages in such circles.

But it cannot be deduced from a few anecdotes such as these that Celtic élites were earlier or more avid learners of Latin than lower-class Gauls, or even that they had better opportunities to learn the language

---

[14] See further Woolf (1998: 72–3).   [15] See Kaster (1995: 84).

[16] For a comprehensive discussion of the passage, see Kaster (1995: 84–6). For rhetoric and the Gauls, see also Tac. *Hist.* 4.73.1, Juv. 7.148, 15.111.

than those further down the social scale. It is only the upper classes who surface in high literature; a silence in literature about lower-class activities does not mean that the lower classes were engaged in no activities. There were no doubt various forms of less exalted contact between Celts and Latin speakers, most notably among those engaged in trade.[17] It is time now to let some socially humble documents speak for themselves as evidence for the linguistic consequences of language contact in a commercial community, and as evidence for the attitude of the two groups to second-language learning and instruction. A detailed examination of aspects of the language of the documents will now be undertaken, along with a discussion of the implications of the evidence for language attitudes and policies. I do not intend to discuss linguistic phenomena for their own sake, but only in so far as they relate to bilingualism in the community. For further details about the spelling and implied phonology of the documents, Marichal (1988) and Flobert (1992) must be consulted.

III LANGUAGE DIFFERENTIATION

Although the texts consist mainly of technical terms, names and numerals, there are enough elements of other kinds to show that at least some speakers/writers at La Graufesenque were capable of *language differentiation*. There is not a single, mixed language in evidence, but two distinct languages can be distinguished across various documents. I illustrate this contention by quoting in full and discussing the features of four texts, two of them in Celtic (Gaulish: I use the two terms indifferently in this chapter), two in Latin. Woolf (1998: 96), drawing partly on Marichal (1988) and partly on Meid (1983), conveys a good deal of uncertainty about the character of the language of the documents. Commenting on certain Gallo-Latin inscriptions which do not concern us here, he states that they 'do not represent either a transitional stage between Gallo-Greek and Latin epigraphy or *the written record of languages half way between Celtic and Latin. The only texts that might fall into the latter category are the late first century AD graffiti from the pottery kilns of La Graufesenque*' (my italics). It follows from what I have already said that I do not accept the suggestion of this second sentence.[18] It is important to note that a text may

---

[17] See above, 4.v.2.6, on two Celtic words, *bedox* and *tossea* in a document (*Tab. Vind.* II.192) purporting to list goods received from a man with a Celtic name, Gauo. Behind this document must inevitably lie contact between the Roman military and a local trader.

[18] Similarly in a footnote on the same page (n. 46) Woolf observes that Marichal does not discuss Meid's 'contention that these and other Gallo-Latin texts represent a popular fusion between the two languages'.

contain a mixture of languages without necessarily representing an institutionalised 'fusion', that is a single language embracing elements of two or more others. Any text written basically in what can be identified as a matrix language may embody in differing degrees bits and pieces of code-switching into a second language without in any sense qualifying for such designations as an 'institutionalised mixed language' or 'fusion'. Any utterance with code-switching on a superficial level might appear to be in a 'mixed language' (on the problems raised by this term, see above, 3.XII.1), but in fact it will be possible on a closer examination to separate the two distinct languages which are mixed together in its formation. It is not then in a 'mixed language' but in a 'mixture of languages', which the speaker would almost certainly be able to distinguish on interrogation. If then at La Graufesenque it proves possible to establish criteria for distinguishing between some texts which are unequivocally in Latin and others which are unequivocally in Gaulish, then both languages as separate entities must have been in use in the pottery; and it follows that if there should be further texts which display some sort of 'mixture', an attempt should first be made to explain that mixture as a consequence of code-switching (that is, the *ad hoc* mixing of two separate languages) instead of making the assumption that the potters in this transitional period of Romanisation were incapable of speaking anything other than a single language (a 'popular fusion' or the like) made up of elements of two pre-existing languages. I turn then to the evidence for language differentiation, quoting first four texts with their numbers in Marichal's edition (1988). The first two are in Gaulish, the second two in Latin:

2.   Tuθo . tr[itios
                casidani . TRI . MON[TANOS
                    AGEDILIO . MATUR . c[an(astri)
                    MASUETOS . canas S = CCC .
                    eti . canast . = = CCC .
                    REGENOS . pe XXXV .
                    eti . mortari . pe . XIIX .
                    atramitari . CCCLXX .
                    mortari . S = CL
                    eti . mort . = = CL
                    MASUETOS . panias . S = DCCLXX .
                TRITOS . PRIVATOS . licuias . VIII
                MASUETOS . paraxidi . (I)(I)
                TRITO . PRIVA . parax (I)CD .
                DEPROSAGI . FELIX . paraxi . (I)CCC[

catili . FELI . DEPRA . IIII C(I)
TERTI . catili . (I) .
acitabli . VIII

19.
          Tυθος sextametos
      cassidanno MONTANOS
A]GEDILLI canastri S = CCCXX
 canastri = = CCL
 pannas   S = DC
 uinari XXC
 pedalis LX
 licuia S = LXX
 ṃortari S = CL
 ]mortari = = CC
 [[[u]inari XXC]]
 ]FELIX catilli LIII
 ]MASUETOS cạṭilli DCL
 T]RITOS LXXXIV licu̦[ia
        A]GIOS par(
        ]Ṣ acitạ[bli
          ] . . . [

47.
Priḍ[. . . . .]es . oneraui . furnum [
              mortarii
       TET[IO. . . . .] = = DL = = CL S = CL̦[
       VER[EC]U̦NDUS . panạs . [
GALUS catila . (I)(I)(I)D[
M[E]LUS . [p]araxides . (I)(I)(I)(I)[
       ]STUS acitablạ VI
CAL]VUS . catil[a] (I)(I)(I)CC[
              ] . [p]anas . (I)
                 ] . res . D
          cati]la . DC
             ca]tila . (I)[
          paraxi]des . bẹ[ssales

74a.
              Flamine . [
                 ESCENTE III[
              Furnus secun[dus
       IUCUNDUS pan (X)CD[
       GEMINUS pannas D . [pan-]
       nas DC APRIMAN[
BURRUS ped IX bes C[
 uinaria CCC itus CL[
 ria CC PRIMULUS cat[

        ALBANUS catil bur
        STEPANUS catil (X)DL APRI[
            catil DCCC BELANIO ca[
        CRESCENS catilla (X)DL L[
            catilla   (X)
          VILIESIUS par (X)(X)C[
          ]..PINUS CC[
          ] . R[

b.   Fu]rnus secundus
            ] . Idus Maias
            CRES]CES k

The structure of the texts, whatever their language, is straightforward. The words in capitals are the names of the potters, standing in the nominative, sometimes in abbreviated form (*Deprosagi* = *Deprosagios*). The other nouns designate the vessel-types produced by the various potters for the particular firing. These nouns are overwhelmingly of Latin, or Greco-Latin,[19] origin.[20] The names of vessels are accompanied by numerals and measurements, these latter either in the form of sigla or words, written in full or abbreviated (on these see below).

Both 2 and 19 begin with a Celtic heading comprising *tuθo(s)* + ordinal. *tuθos* (with various spellings) occurs throughout the texts. On the sense see Marichal (1988: 97): the word has 'un suffixe -*tos* et une racine **tŭs* signifiant: "groupe, masse, total", d'où le sens de "compte, addition, facture, équipe"'. The word thus indicates the assemblage (of pots) fired on a particular occasion. Of particular note in the Celtic texts as a whole is the rich evidence for Celtic ordinals (*cintux, al(l)os, tr(itios), petuar., pinpetos, suexos, sextametos, oxtumetos, namet(os), decametos*).[21]

In line 2 in both of these texts the term *casidanos*, of Celtic root *dan* which is variously glossed in Latin as *iudicem, curator, magister* (see also above, 4.V.2.6),[22] has been illuminated by the Latin text 74, where *flamine (Cr)escente* appears to be an equivalent.[23] The *casidanos* was then some sort of priest, the expression being a form of dating of Latin type. The Latin expression has a (correct) ablative absolute, the presence of which

---

[19] By this I refer to words of Greek origin which had been long since borrowed by Latin, e.g. *paropsides*, which is almost invariably in a debased form, as we will see.

[20] There is a comprehensive discussion of these terms by Marichal (1988: 80–92). There are a few Celtic terms as well (see Flobert (1992: 104)).

[21] See Marichal (1988: 96).

[22] See Marichal (1988: 98).   [23] See Marichal (1988: 98).

implies that there had been some Latin speakers at La Graufesenque at some time who were familiar with the role of that construction in dating formulae. If Marichal is right (1988: 78) in arguing that *tri* is an abbreviation for the name *Tritos*, it follows that *casidani Tritos Montanos* must be a nominative construction functioning like the Latin ablative absolute, but without an explicit marker of its syntactic function. The same nominative construction is found at 19.2.[24] The form *casidani* is of some morphological importance. A plural in *-i* is common in the Celtic texts, but for the most part it is in words of Latin origin (which were usually neuter in Latin).[25] As such its origin is open to question: Latin masculine from an original neuter, or Celtic ending? But the word *casidani* is unambiguously Celtic, and in a Celtic text its ending too is certainly Celtic. In *o*-stem nouns in Gaulish the pronominal nominative plural **-oi* had been generalised to nouns, as in a variety of other Indo-European languages, including Old Irish.[26] The expected diphthong *-oi* must have been monophthongised.[27]

Another Gaulish element in 2 is the use three times of *eti* ('and also': 2.5, 7, 10; in Latin texts the equivalent is *item*, e.g. 54; cf. Gk. ἔτι, Lat. *et*).[28] It must be stressed that in 2 and 19, as in the other texts, both Gaulish and Latin, the sigla (S = equivalent to *bes(s)alis*, = = equivalent to *triantalis*, meaning respectively two-thirds and one-third, of a foot, *pes*),[29] which indicate the measurement (probably diameter) of the vessels, and the terms of measurement themselves when written in full or abbreviated (*pes* and its divisions *bes* and *triens*, which are usually in adjectival form: *pedalis*, *bessalis*, *triantalis*, the *a* in the second syllable of this last possibly due to Gaulish interference),[30] and finally the numerals are all Latin. Thus, for example, 2 has various sigla and two cases of *pe*, and 19 has sigla and one case of *pedalis* written in full. This is an interesting cultural phenomenon. The Gaulish record keepers had clearly received rather more than a rudimentary training in a Latin-based literacy. They did not merely know Latin letters, but could also use the Latin numeral

---

[24] See Marichal (1988: 78) on the possibility that *cassidanno* in 19 might be a dual.
[25] For details, see Marichal (1988: 75–6).
[26] See e.g. Sihler (1995: 261), Dottin (1920: 117), Lambert (1995: 49, 53). Thus OIr. *fir* nominative plural 'men', < **wiroi*.
[27] See Marichal (1988: 76); also Lambert (1995: 53), Flobert (1992: 110 n. 11).
[28] See e.g. Thurneysen (1946: 549–50), Marichal (1988: 100–1). For examples of *item*, and its equivalence to *eti*, see Marichal (1988: 95).
[29] See Marichal (1988: 51–2).
[30] On *triantalis*, see Marichal (1988: 58); on the measures, see Marichal (1988: 92).

symbols up to very high figures,[31] and had been taught Latin sigla. Yet in conjunction with these Latin symbols they used, and were permitted to use, elements of their own language. In texts which are basically lists it is admittedly only a restricted form of language that is in use, with nouns, numbers and no verbs (but see further below on verbs), but that restricted language is arguably Celtic not only in vocabulary but also morphology (on which see further below). On this evidence it would seem that there was a relaxed attitude to language choice in the record keeping. There is no sign of any rigorous attempt to impose Latin on the Gallic potters, or indeed of any persistent attempt by the potters themselves to stick to Latin, and if Celtic predominated in the relatively formal domain of record keeping it is likely to have predominated in informal speech in the community itself. Provided that the Latin technical vocabulary and symbols were adopted, Celtic vocabulary and morphology were accepted, and most of the texts, as we have seen, can indeed be assigned to the Gaulish language rather than to Latin (see above, II). Nevertheless the locals had obviously received a strong dose of Latin literacy training, and had had imposed on them alien names for most of the objects which they were making. The pattern of teaching Latin literacy to provincials repeats itself in other parts of the western Empire where Latin came into contact with and eventually ousted vernacular languages. Thus in N. Africa Punic came in its last days to be written in Latin script (see above, 2.v.6), and the same thing happened to Etruscan (see 2.III.6). It seems likely that the Celtic writers had been trained to use the new script not in the writing of their own language, but in the writing of the new language. It is hard to believe that Italian potters came to Gaul and altruistically taught the locals how to write Celtic in Latin script (even if they had known any Celtic); they will have given them training in how to write in a Latinate way the names of the vessels and the numbers and measurements which were the essential part of the record keeping, and then left them to their own devices in using the Latin letters for the writing of Celtic words in the other parts of the documents if they so wished (see above, 2.XIV.3). The use of the Latin letters, sigla and numerals thus implies that training in Latin writing had taken place, and although that training need not in any way imply an aggressive attempt to suppress the Celtic language, the Latin literacy which the potters had acquired along with smatterings of the Latin language, and the prestige

---

[31] Oddly, Marichal (1988: 101) says that 'les comptables ne savent probablement pas compter en latin'. Contrast Flobert (1992: 113 n. 16).

which will inevitably have been attached to their accomplishment (see further below), will have provided an ideal framework facilitating a gradual extension of their knowledge of the new language.

I turn briefly to the Latin texts quoted above, but will come back to the Celtic texts to conclude this discussion of language differentiation.

The most obvious, but by no means the only, feature which marks 47 and 74 as Latin lies in the opening expression. 47 begins (it seems) with a date (*prid[*) and a Latin verb-phrase (*oneraui furnum*), with interpuncta between words in the Latin manner. 74 has a three-line Latin opening, consisting first of the ablative absolute *flamine [Cr]escente* mentioned above, and then of the expression *furnus secun[dus]*, which is clearly the Latin correspondent of Celtic expressions combining *tuθos* with a Celtic ordinal adjective. *Furnus secundus* occurs again at the end of the document, where there is also a Latin date. *Furnus*, it should be noted, does not mean exactly the same thing as *tuθos*,[32] though its function in the context is the same. Here is the phenomenon seen in some bilingual texts of idiomatic corresponsion. Users of two languages in contact may employ idiomatic expressions in the two languages to convey a single idea, instead of attempting to force non-idiomatic translationese on one of the languages.

These are the clearest language-specific usages which set the two pairs of documents apart, but further examination shows that there is also a subtle morphological differentiation to be seen in the treatment of the names and technical nouns which are to some extent common to the two groups of texts.

I take first personal names in the nominative which are written with an ending (as distinct from abbreviated, a common practice). In the Celtic texts 2 and 19 there are thirteen such names, all of which are given the Celtic nominative ending of the *o*-declension, *-os*.[33] I include in this figure *Agedilio* and *Trito*, in both of which final *-s* has been omitted (on which phenomenon, see below). It makes no difference whether a name is of Latin origin (thus *Masuetos, Priuatos, Montanos*) or Celtic (thus *Agedilio, Tritos*).[34] On the other hand in the Latin texts 47 and 74 there are

---

[32] See Marichal (1988: 97). On *furnus*, see further Flobert (1992: 105 n. 4).

[33] See e.g. Evans (1967: 421–2) on the Gaulish ending *-os* in personal names, and its Latinised substitute *-us*.

[34] The last is the Celtic equivalent of Lat. *Tertius*: see Marichal (1988: 94), Flobert (1992: 111). A number of the Celtic names at La Graufesenque have Latin equivalents also attested there: e.g. *Allos = Secundus, Cintugenos = Primigenius* (Marichal (1988: 94)). The habit had developed among the Gauls, through contact with Latin speakers, of translating their Gaulish names into Latin, a clear sign of Romanisation (see further below, IV.2).

thirteen names of the second declension, of which twelve have the Latin nominative ending -*us* (the exception is *Belanio* at 74). Again the origin of the name (Latin or Celtic) is not a determinant of its ending: names which are Latin and Celtic alike are assigned the Latin ending (thus e.g. *Verecundus, Geminus, Iucundus* on the one hand, *Melus* on the other).

In these texts there is thus no sign of the type of code-switching which we have seen in some Greco-Roman documents, whereby in texts ostensibly written in Latin Greek names were often given a Greek inflection. Here at La Graufesenque, at least in the four documents under discussion, it was clearly the scribe's sense of the language which he was writing which determined his choice of the endings -*os* or -*us*, and not any attempt to match the ending to the etymology of the name. This in turn is subtle evidence that two languages were distinguished, at least by the present writers.

I move on now to the morphology of vessel-names in the four documents. In the two Celtic texts Latin loan-words which in their Latin form would (or could) have been neuters (and hence inflected in the plural with the -*a* ending) invariably have an -*i* nominative plural (some fourteen examples in the two texts: e.g. *mortari, acitabli, uinari*). I include in this figure four examples of *catilli*, because, though *catillus* is normally masculine in Latin, it does have a neuter by-form, and there is reason to think that Latin writers at La Graufesenque thought of it as a neuter (see below). By contrast in the Latin texts 47 and 74 there are seven examples of the Latin neuter ending -*a* in such words (including *catil(l)a*), compared with only one masculine nominative form, *mortarii* at 47, and that seems to be in another hand,[35] and it also has a 'Latinate' form -*ii* as distinct from -*i*. Thus we find for example, *uinari* in the Celtic text 19 (twice), but *uinaria* in the Latin text 74; *acitabli* (< *acetabulum*) in the Celtic text 2, but *acitabla* in the Latin text 47, and *catil(l)i* in both the Celtic texts, but *catil(l)a* in both the Latin.

There is again here evidence for language differentiation by the scribes. Though the names of pots to be found in both Celtic and Latin texts were basically the same, those writing Latin (in the texts which we have seen) retained a feeling for the neuter, whereas those writing Celtic had transferred such terms to the masculine, presumably because Gaulish was further advanced in the loss of the neuter than was non-standard Latin.[36] If there had been just a single, mixed, language

---

[35] See Marichal (1988:75).

[36] See Marichal (1988: 75–6). The neuter plural in -*a* is however attested in Gaulish (Lambert (1995: 54)), if rarely. Is the evidence of La Graufesenque to be treated as a new and extensive contribution to the question, or was usage there abnormal?

spoken at La Graufesenque, one would not have expected such a clear-cut differentiation. It is on the whole true across the whole corpus of texts that -*i* is preferred in the Gaulish, -*a* in the Latin (but see further below).[37]

My third example of language differentiation lies in the loss of final -*s*. In the Celtic texts 2 and 19 final -*s* is omitted four times, usually in the nominative singular (-*o* for -*os*), but once also in the form *licuia* = *licuias* (19).[38] This last (-*as*) ending is common in certain *a*-stem nouns at La Graufesenque (*pannas*, *licuias*),[39] and is probably to be interpreted not as a Latin accusative (or nominative: see the next footnote) plural, but as the Celtic nominative plural.[40] In the Latin texts 47 and 74, on the other hand, there is only one possible example of omission of -*s* (74 *Belanio*), but this name perhaps has the ending -*o*, -*onis*.[41]

Figures showing the relative frequency with which -*s* is written/omitted in this group of texts bring out more clearly the distinction between the two pairs of documents. In the Celtic texts -*s* is written 18 times (and omitted 4: -*s* predominates by 4.5: 1), whereas in the Latin texts -*s* predominates by 28: 0 (or by 28: 1: see above).

These distributions, taken in conjunction with the fact that in the texts as a whole the Celtic ending -*os* is often reduced to-*o*, whereas the Latin ending -*us* is virtually never reduced to -*u*,[42] allow various deductions to be made. Final -*s* is known from plentiful evidence to have been relatively stable in early non-standard Latin,[43] whereas in Gaulish, at least in the nominative singular, there is evidence that it tended to be lost.[44] The consistent writing of -*s* in the Latin texts discussed above, and its occasional omission in the Celtic, suggest a perception among the writers that Latin and Celtic differed in this respect. This perception might, however, have been morphological rather than phonetic. Bilinguals hearing

[37] See Marichal (1988: 75). [38] On which term see Marichal (1988: 88).
[39] Details can be found in Marichal (1988: 74).
[40] See Lambert (1995: 57); but the matter is complicated by the fact that both *pannas* and *pannias*, and *licuas* and *licuias*, are attested: see Marichal (1988: 74). Whatever the reason for this, Marichal's assertion (loc. cit.) on the matter is not compelling: 'les désinences en -*as* sont "latines"; les désinences "gauloises" sont en -*ias*, mais les deux désinences se sont influencées et on est enclin à penser que les formes *pannas* des "gaulois" sont des emprunts aux "latins"'. It is worth noting that in non-standard Latin an -*as* nominative is well attested (see above, 2.II.1; also Gaeng (1977: 46–51), and especially Bakkum (1994); Flobert (1992: 109) is mistaken in asserting that if '-*as* est latin, il ne peut représenter à cette date qu'un accusatif pluriel'). -*as* lies behind the feminine nominative plural in some Romance languages, including French (e.g. *filias* > *filles*). Given the co-existence of a substandard Latin nominative in -*as* with Gaul. -*as*, conditions in Gaul were obviously ideal for the survival of -*as*.
[41] See Marichal (1988: 74).
[42] See Marichal (1988: 68), Flobert (1992: 108–9).
[43] See, e.g. Väänänen (1966: 81), Adams (1994a: 106–7).
[44] See, e.g. Lambert (1995: 50).

and speaking Latin and Celtic might, it is true, have been conscious that -*s* was pronounced in the one language, but often imperceptible in the other, and this awareness might indeed have affected their writing of the two languages. But it seems rather more likely that -*us* was perceived as the Latin masculine nominative singular morpheme, and the alternatives -*os* and -*o* as the Celtic equivalents. The invariable writing of the Latin form as -*us* rather than -*u* supports this explanation.

The writers of the texts considered in this section show a feeling for the distinction between Latin and Gaulish. Of the various pieces of evidence assembled here perhaps the most interesting is the use of -*i* as the nominative plural ending in Celtic texts of loan-words that were neuter in Latin (or Greek). There is evidence elsewhere that Gaulish preserved the neuter, but such evidence has hitherto been so slight that the place of the neuter in Gaulish should now be re-assessed on the basis of the documents from La Graufesenque.

IV CODE-SWITCHING

But Latin and Gaulish are not so consistently differentiated in all texts. The question which must be faced is whether those texts showing a mixture of the elements kept separate in the four documents discussed earlier provide evidence for the currency in the pottery of some sort of institutionalised mixed language, or on the contrary merely display mixing consistent with a basic language differentiation which has been blurred by systematic or at least classifiable forms of code-switching. I will argue that, although the texts are by no means homogeneous in their linguistic character but fall into several groups sharing various characteristics, certain patterns can be identified which may be treated as code-switching from one language into the other.

IV.1 Intra-phrasal switching

The text numbered 14 is undoubtedly to be assigned to Gaulish. It contains *tu[θos]* in the heading, and *eti* occurs twice, along with two examples of *duci*.[45] Vessel-names which might by Latin standards have been in the neuter regularly have the -*i* ending discussed in the previous section (nine examples, no exceptions). And above all in the right-hand margin there is what appears to be a Gaulish sentence:

[45] On which, see Marichal (1988: 101). *Duci* regularly in Celtic texts links the names of two potters, a function given to *et* in Latin texts.

sioxti · Albanos

panna · extra tuθ CCC

Lambert (1995: 133), following a suggestion of Thurneysen, compares *sioxti* with OIr. *siächt* (=‘il a cherché’), and translates: ‘Albanos a recherché des “panna” ... à l’extérieur de la fournée, trois cents.’ Whatever one makes of *sioxti*, it must be a Gaulish verb.[46] *Panna*, according to Lambert, is perhaps not inflected, but it is surely more likely to represent the Gaulish accusative plural *-as* with omission of *-s*. But what is of particular interest is the prepositional phrase *extra tuθ*. This, embedded in a Celtic sentence, comprises a Latin preposition and a Celtic noun. There is an outside possibility that the preposition was also Celtic, but alleged cognates do not suggest that a pure Gaulish form would have had this ending.[47] The switch is not merely intra-sentential, but within the phrase. Code-switching between preposition and noun phrase has been noted in other situations of language contact.[48] It will take place as a general rule only if the contact languages both have prepositions.[49]

It is of some interest that this Gaulish sentence is written with inter-puncta of the Latin sort, and that the numeral is also Roman. Here again we see evidence that Celts had been taught Latin literary practices and left to employ them in the writing of their native language. 14 will come up again in the next section.

IV.2 Code-switching in names

In the texts discussed in III (2, 19, 47, 74) names of the *o*-declension are consistently given an *-os* ending in the Celtic documents, and a *-us* ending in the Latin, whatever the etymology of the name in question. In 14, discussed in the previous section, however, there is the expected profusion of *-o(s)* endings (given that the language is Celtic), but also three cases of *-us* (*Secundus, Albinus, Vindulus*). Two of these names were current

---

[46] Marichal (1988: 79) rejects the explanation of Thurneysen, and remarks: ‘Le sens paraît être “ajouter”.’

[47] See Marichal (1888: 79), who asserts categorically, ‘Il s’agit certainement du lat. *extra*.’ So Flobert (1992: 111) takes the phrase to be of mixed language.

[48] See, e.g. Romaine (1995: 127), on Spanish–English.

[49] See Romaine (1995: 126) on the ‘equivalence constraint’, which ‘predicts that code switches will tend to occur at points where the juxtaposition of elements from the two languages does not violate a syntactic rule of either language. That is, code-switching will tend to occur at points where the surface structures of the two languages map onto each other.’ She goes on to note (1995: 127) that incompatibilities ‘will arise at any site where a switch involves any two adjacent constituents which are ordered differently in the two languages concerned, e.g. prepositional *vs.* postpositional phrases’, and gives various examples of such incompatibility.

in Latin (*Secundus*, *Albinus*), but the third, *Vindulus*, is of Celtic origin.[50] The inconsistent usage of this document is further brought out by the fact that various names of Latin origin, in contrast to *Secundus* and *Albinus*, are inflected in the nominative with -*os* (*Cornutos*, *Albanos*, *Masuetos*, *Castos*). The writer seems to have switched backwards and forwards between Celtic and Latin morphology, with no obvious motivation for doing so (but see further below). It may be worthwhile to examine the whole corpus of texts to see whether any principles can be detected in names. I will return to the inflection of the names in 14 later in this section.

I begin with texts 1–23, all of which are heavily Celtic. Here there are about 141 names in -*os*, compared with only thirteen in -*us*, and of the latter one (in text no. 8) may be disregarded, as it is the ending only (-*rus*) which survives, and there can be no certainty that this was originally part of a name.[51] The 141 names in -*os*, which are indifferently of Latin and Celtic origin, provide overwhelming evidence that the Gaulish potters used the Gaulish inflection if they felt that they were writing Gaulish, whether or not the referents had Celtic names. It also seems likely that in daily life they will have used this inflection among themselves. The thirteen names in -*us* are worthy of closer examination.

It is, first, a remarkable fact that the Celtic name *Vindulus* has a -*us* ending not only in 14, but also twice in 12 and once in 13. The anomaly is particularly obvious in the long text 12, in which there are ten names in -*os*, of both Latin (e.g. *Castos*, *Masuetos*, *Priuatos*) and Celtic (e.g. *Cotutos*, *Tritos*) origin, with two examples of *Vindulus* in the space of two lines. There is no certain example of the expected form *Vindulos* anywhere in the corpus. Lambert (1995: 131), who translates and discusses text no. 13, observes the anomalous ending (line 12 *Tritos duci Vindulus*), and offers the view that it is not a (Latin) nominative singular at all, but an oblique case ('une forme fléchie de thème en -*o*-'), whether an accusative plural or instrumental plural. He concludes: '*Vindulus* doit donc être gaulois aussi bien par la désinence que par la base.'

This explanation will not do. There is no evidence that the admittedly obscure connective *duci* took an oblique case (note, e.g. 3 *Scota duci Felix*), and it is patently obvious from 12.15, when compared with the previous line, that *Vindulus* is a nominative form in -*us*:

---

[50] See, e.g. Evans (1967: 387), Marichal (1988: 270). It is treated by Flobert (1992: 111) as a hybrid (that is, presumably, with Celtic root and Latin diminutive suffix). Contrast Evans (1967: 387): 'It is a derivative (diminutive?) in -*ulo*... of Gaul. *Vindus*.'

[51] I do not include in the figure of thirteen the name *Malciu*, which occurs once in 7 and four times in 20. There are no certain examples of -*u* for -*us* in names (see Marichal (1988: 68 with n. 37)) and one cannot be sure of the nominative form of the name.

Priuatos · paraxidi · (I)(I)(I)DCCCL
Vindulus · paraxidi · (I)C(I).

Clearly *Vindulus* is functionally parallel to *Priuatos*.

One is obliged to treat the spelling *Vindulus* as deliberate rather than as a chance aberration, because it is so consistently used. I would tentatively suggest that one should look not to the etymology of the name,[52] but to the origin or character of its bearer, to explain the-*us* ending. In some Latin texts we have observed cases of code-switching in Latin names (i.e. the use of a Greek ending in a name of Latin origin) when there was reason to believe that the bearer of the name was perceived (or perceived himself) to be Greek (note e.g. the inflection of Aeschines' Latin name *Flauianus* in the receipt discussed at 1.VII.2.3). It is not impossible that the potter Vindulus, unlike many of his colleagues, was widely regarded as a primary speaker of Latin or as heavily Romanised or as intent on expressing some sort of 'Roman' identity, and insistent on the Latinate spelling of his name (particularly if it had a Latin suffix). Interesting evidence can be brought to bear on the matter of the -*us* ending from La Graufesenque itself, and I turn now to that evidence.

Personal names are not only found in the records of firings that we have been looking at; they also occur in profusion as makers' stamps on the pottery produced. These stamps have typical forms, such as genitive of the maker's name, or nominative, or nominative + *fecit*. There is a large collection of material assembled by Oswald (1931). It is a remarkable fact that in these stamps not only is the -*us* ending almost universal, but Celtic names themselves are virtually eliminated.[53] Thus for example *Cintusmos* gives way to *Primus* or *Primulus*, *Allos* to *Secundus*, *Tritos* to *Tertius*, *Petrecos* to *Quartus*, *Matugenos* to *Felix* and *Vindulus* to *Albus*, the Latin name in each case being a translation of the Celtic (see also n. 34). The explanation for this can only be that potters went on using Celtic names and the -*os* ending to a considerable extent in their own community, or alternatively Latin names with the -*os* ending (as the abundant Latin names with the -*os* ending in documents 1–23 suggest), but that their products intended for an outside world were felt to require a Latinate stamp. The language choice is determined by the expected readership. Implicit in the decision to use the Latin morpheme (and language) outside the pottery is in effect a grading of the two languages in terms of their status and function, with Latin treated more as an international or imperial language, but Gaulish

[52] Though if it could definitely be regarded as a hybrid, its Latin suffix would be potentially significant.
[53] See Marichal (1988: 93–4).

as provincial and unsuited for use in the wider world.[54] Here again is
a trace of the polar diglossic opposition H–L. In many cultures names
have a special power to express status or claims to membership of an
ethnic or social group. A Gaul who used a Latin form of his name for
outside consumption was giving himself a Romanised identity. It is also
significant (as we have seen) that, whereas -*os* is often reduced to -*o*, there is
no unambiguous example so far of -*u* < -*us*. Since a Celt pronouncing -*us*
would have been just as likely to drop final -*s* as he would in pronouncing
-*os*, -*us* must have had a learned character which caused those using it in
writing consciously to retain its full Latinate form. This special character
of -*us*, which, we are suggesting, will have prompted status-conscious
Gauls to indulge in code-switching on occasions in naming themselves
(I am referring of course to writing and not to speech), offers a hint of the
prestige of Latin itself, which was ultimately to lead to a language shift
in the whole of Gaul. And that brings me back to Vindulus. He had not
gone so far as to abandon his Gaulish name by switching in the pottery
to *Albus*, but he had adopted a partially Romanised identity. It is also
worth reverting briefly to the text 14, discussed above and at IV.1. It is
arguably the most Celtic of all the documents in the collection, in that it
contains not only the phenomena identified as Celtic in III, but also a full
Gaulish sentence. Yet it also has a mixture of endings in names which
in the opening paragraph of this section were by implication treated
as chaotic. We are now in a better position to see a pattern behind
the chaos. What has happened is that, just as potters' stamps use the
-*us* form, and just as that ending is preferred in reference to a certain
Vindulus in Celtic texts, so in 14 there are a few cases of switching into
the prestigious Latinate ending, once indeed in the name *Vindulus* itself.
Given that this could happen in a heavily Celtic text, in which even Latin
names usually have -*os*, and given that the etymology of the name is thus
not the crucial determinant of the ending chosen, it emerges that the
Gaulish potters were showing a tendency to switch into the -*us* ending
from time to time when writing names, whether the names were Latin or
Celtic. The switching can be interpreted as revealing the same attitude
to the Latinate morpheme as that which may be deduced from the form
of the names adopted in the potters' stamps.

I move on to the remaining eight cases of -*us* in texts 1–23. A majority
(six) of the names were Latin (or Greco-Roman) in origin: *Albanus* in 4,

[54] Or, as Dottin (1924: 73) puts it, 'Les noms en -*us* semblent plus savants, car ils figurent presque
exclusivement dans les estampilles, tandis que les noms en -*os*, plus populaires, dominent dans
les graffites.'

Lucanus in 7, *Secundus* and *Albinus* in 14, and *Summacus* and *Masuetus* in 17. The exceptions are two instances of *Tritus* in 17. The evidence is not extensive, but there are possibly grounds here for thinking that code-switching in names was occasionally motivated by a feeling for the origin of the name. This is of course a phenomenon repeatedly seen in Latin inscriptions, whether transliterated or not: that is, names of Greek origin are often given a Greek inflection in a Latin text. But it must be admitted that on the basis of the material available it is very difficult to distinguish code-switching as determined by the etymology of a name, and that determined by the prestige discussed above which was attached to the Latin ending. In 14 in particular, as we have just seen, the cluster of Latin names in -*os* undermines any attempt to explain away *Secundus* and *Albinus* purely on the basis of their etymologies. These various potters might have been responding not simply to the origin of their names, but to the status of the Latinate form.

I conclude this section. From the Celtic texts 1–23 it is obvious that the Gaulish potters regularly used the -*os* ending of their names in the pottery, whether they retained a Gaulish name or had taken on a Latin name. But outside the pottery they preferred the Latin -*us* ending and Latin names, making the assumption that the Latin form had higher status and should therefore be used outside as conferring a certain cachet on their products. Within the pottery those who were attempting to write in Latin rather than Gaulish usually used the -*us* form, as we saw (III). But one individual, Vindulus, is persistently given the -*us* ending even in Celtic texts, and that suggests that he insisted on that form. In these Celtic texts there are occasionally found other names in -*us*, a phenomenon which may reflect either a feeling for the Latinate character of certain names, or the same sort of motivation as that influencing Vindulus, or a combination of both factors. It is a form of code-switching.

IV.3 *Names, continued: the possible influence of the etymology of a name on the selection of its ending*

Of the texts so far cited, 17, which has four names in -*us*, only two of them of (Greco-)Latin origin, is the most interesting and problematic. I leave it aside for the moment in order to consider further the possibility raised above that code-switching might sometimes have been determined by the etymology of a name. A theme of this section will be that the collection of texts is not homogeneous but reveals different hands and linguistic perceptions.

Text 34 cannot confidently be assigned to either language because of its fragmentary state. One name, of Latin origin (*Florus*), has a Latin ending, while another, of Celtic (*Coros*),[55] has the Celtic ending. Another fragmentary text (45), which certainly has a Celtic heading, has a Latin name with Latin ending (*[Primig]enius*). 27, which is fragmentary but should probably be assigned to Celtic, has two Celtic names in -*os* (*C]otutos*, *M]eθθilos*), and one Latin name in -*us* (*Albus*). A fairly complete Latin text (169), which is an account not of a firing at the pottery, but of miscellaneous works effected between 22 July and 23 August by slaves of a certain Atelia, seems to display the other side of the coin. After a run of Latin or Greco-Latin names in-*us*, the name *Vigedos*, which is presumably Celtic, has the -*os* ending.

This is the extent of the evidence that might be taken to show that the etymology of a name sometimes caused a switch of codes. I return now to the complications raised by 17, which was referred to above.

17 begins with a Celtic heading, *TuÐÐos petuaṛ[.]*, where *petuaṛ-* is the Celtic ordinal = 'fourth' (cf. Welsh *pedwarydd*).[56] It ends, on the other hand, with a Latin word (in the right margin), *summa* (followed by XXXC). Most of the vessel names are abbreviated, but *atramentari* (14) has the typical 'Celtic' form. There are four names in the text in -*us*, but none in -*os* (*Summacus*, *Tritus*, *Masuetus*, *Tritus*). Two of these names are (Greco-)Latin, but *Tritus*, which is elsewhere repeatedly assigned the -*os* ending,[57] is the Celtic equivalent of Lat. *Tertius*. The code-switching here seems to be rather more haphazard, and indeed the text is not unambiguously in either Latin or Celtic. I postpone further consideration of the nature of the switching until further relevant material has been assembled later in the chapter.

The fragmentary text 93 seems to be in Gaulish. The heading is lost, but there are three certain cases of the connective *eti*, and another two conjectural cases. Yet all the definite *o*-stem names end in -*us*. Two of these admittedly are Latin (*Fuscus*, *Cornutus*), but *Cosojus* and *Lousjus* are probably Celtic.[58] Text 66, on the other hand, appears to have been in Latin: part of the heading is legible, containing the expression *furnus one[ratu]s XVI*, which, as we saw, is the Latin equivalent of *tuθos* + Celtic ordinal. Two of the three names in the text are inflected according to etymology, the (Greco-)Latin *Callistus* with -*us*, and the Celtic *Meooillos* (i.e. *Meθθil(l)os*) with -*os*. The third name, however, is Latin, and yet it has

---

[55] See Marichal (1988: 265).   [56] See Lambert (1995: 131).
[57] See Marichal (1988: 269) for a list of examples.
[58] See Marichal (1988: 265, 267).

a Celtic *-os* ending (*Laetinos*).[59] 76, finally, retains a fragment of its Latin heading (*onera[..]*). It contains six names in *-us*, of both Celtic (*Cintusmus*, *Vebrullus*) and Latin origin (*Amandinus*, *Secundanus* twice, *Maturus*), but *Luceios*, a good Latin name (*Lucceius*), has an *-os* ending.

In the texts 34, 45, 27 and 169 it can, as we saw earlier in this section, be argued that the names are inflected according to etymology. But if two of the names in 66 and two of those in 17 are left aside, then it must be conceded that the spellings cited in the previous paragraph and those in text 17 cannot be explained exclusively from the etymologies of the names in question, any more than they can be explained from the language of the document. There is though a preference to be observed even in these rather messy texts (i.e. 17, 93, 66 and 76). Whether the text is in Latin, Celtic or is of indeterminate language, the *-us* ending is heavily preferred, by 15:3, with *-us* used in Celtic as well as Latin names.

The evidence which we have seen so far concerning the choice of *-us* can accordingly be reduced to three patterns: (1) there is a marked tendency for *-us* or *-os* to be selected according to the matrix language of the text (as in 2, 19, 47 and 74, and in the Celtic texts 1–23); (2) there is a possible tendency for names to be inflected according to etymology, as in the case of six names in *-us* in 1–23, and in a group of names in 34, 45, 27 and 169, though this determinant has proved difficult to pin down decisively; and (3) where neither of these factors can be invoked, as wholly or partly in 17, 93, 66 and 76, and in the instances of the name *Vindulus*, *-us* rather than *-os* predominates. We are surely to see here evidence for Romanisation, in the sense that the prestige as discussed above accorded to the *-us* ending caused it to intrude unexpectedly from time to time. If the intrusion had been of a different type (that is, if for example *-os* had shown a persistent tendency to intrude into Latin texts), then we might in theory have been justified in finding signs of a resistance by Gauls to assimilation: Gauls who had had Latin names foisted on them or who were forced to write in Latin might have been holding on to an aspect of their identity. But as it is, Latin names are inflected as Gaulish for the most part only in Celtic texts, and it is mainly the *-us* ending that finds its way into contexts where it cannot be justified either by etymology or the language of the text. This use of the Latin morpheme in places where it does not belong might be interpreted as the very beginning of a language shift. I leave names now and turn to some other matters.

[59] On which name see Kajanto (1965: 261).

Texts 17 and 93, which, as we saw, prefer the -*us* form of names, whatever their origin, share another interesting item. In both *acetabulum* is
spelt in the Latin manner with *e* rather than *i* in the second syllable: *acet*
(abbreviation) at 17.15, and the same abbreviation at 93.9 (following the
Celtic word *eti*). In the corpus as a whole *i* is overwhelmingly preferred
in the second syllable, and that is a reflection of the fact that in Gaulish
original long *e* and *i* merged as a close front vowel written as *i*.[60] *Acit-*
occurs forty-one times, *acet* only nine times, according to Marichal
(1988: 58). Marichal finds four cases of *acet-* in Latin texts, three in heavily
Latinised Gaulish texts (our texts 17 and 93, and also 30), one in a Gaulish
text (92), and one in an indeterminate text. I would modify these figures
slightly. 30, a text to which we will come in the next section, has at least
as much claim to be assigned to Latin as to Gaulish, with a marked
element of code-switching. And 92, classified as Celtic by Marichal, is
so fragmentary that it is impossible to be certain about the language it
was written in. There are thus only two examples of *acet-* in texts displaying marked Gaulish characteristics, and those are the two texts under
discussion here.

It is an interesting fact that the two Celtic texts display not only the
-*us* ending even in Celtic names, but also the Latinate spelling *acet-*. It
cannot of course be deduced from the spelling that the writers would
have pronounced *acetabl-* in the Latin way, but the phenomenon may
be described as a form of 'orthographic' code-switching. Both writers
perceived *acetabl-* as of Latin origin, and both chose to use the 'correct'
Latin spelling in a Celtic text against the practice normally followed
around them by other scribes writing Celtic. Given that the spelling is
self-consciously Latinate and abnormal for the pottery, and given too that
the -*us* endings are self-consciously Latinate, it can be seen that there has
been a deliberate grafting on to Celtic writing of some features of Latin
writing. The prestige of Latin is the determinant of the code-switching,
whether this be classified as phonetic, orthographic or morphological.
The scribe of 93 was particularly well versed in Latin literacy practices.
He not only makes regular use of interpuncta in the Latin style, but he
also twice, in Celtic (?) names, employs the Latin I-longa apparently to
mark the semi-vowel [j] (*Cosojus, Lousjus*).[61]

---

[60] See Dottin (1920: 96), Lambert (1995: 41), Flobert (1992: 107): e.g. *rex* > *rix*.
[61] See Marichal (1988: 60–5) for a comprehensive discussion of the use of I-longa at La Graufesenque; also Flobert (1992: 106), noting that 'cela [I-longa] révèle le soin avec lequel on enseignait
l'écriture dans les écoles de campagne gallo-romaines'.

IV.4 Inter-sentential switching

Text 30 is classified by Marichal (1988: 57, 58, 76) as Gaulish, but 'Latinised'. I would put it rather differently. I quote the text in full:

Tuθos . LV . .[. . . .] .pe . argant [. . .] ebi . .[
TERTIUS . catinos . S = . CDLXXX[
idem . TERTIUS . catinos . triantes . [. . .]
COPPIUS . panae . satlla̧ [. . . . . .]XVII
idem . COPPIUS . pana[e .] ped . sigl.[. . .]..
VERECUNDUS . pana . satll[
idem . VRECUNDUS . mortaria . S = [. .]CXXX
BALBUS . catilla .   (I)(I)D
idem . BA[L]BUS . catilla̧ [.] ḑeupros [.] DCL
CORNTUS . cat[i]lla .   III C
..]ANDUS . paraxides .   (I)(I)D
VA]BIRO . parax[ides .] ţrocliati . CC[
id]em . VABIRO . aceţ[abu]la . duisom[. . . .]ÇC
. . .] . LOS .   para̧[xi]des.   (I)
        ]acit[abula
          ].

          ]CXX[

The only Gaulish element here is the heading *tuθos*. In all other respects the language is overwhelmingly Latin. There are ten names with the *-us* ending, and only one possible name in *-os* (the fragmentary *-los* in 14). *Idem* (= *item*) rather than *eti* recurs throughout (five times). Vessel-names have the *-a* ending rather than *-i*. Remarkably, *panae* (4)[62] is the Latin nominative plural form, the only such example in the corpus; elsewhere, even in Latin texts (cf. 47, 74), the Celtic/non-standard Latin nominative in *-as* is preferred (if we are right to see this as a nominative rather than an accusative). Also significant is the ending of *paraxides* (two examples, and another conjectural). Although it could be Gaulish as well as Latin,[63] its distribution suggests that it was regarded by scribes as Latin. The most common form of the word (when it is not abbreviated) is *paraxidi*.[64] *Paraxides* is attested in just six texts, eight times (30, 34, 47, 49, 53, 60). All of these should in my opinion be classified as Latin, with the exception

---

[62] On this difficult word, see above, 4.V.2.6 n. 160.
[63] See Marichal (1988: 76).
[64] A full collection of examples, classified according to form, is given by Marichal (1988: 274). See also Flobert (1992: 110) on the endings of this word.

of 34, which is indeterminate.[65] There is finally the case of *catinos* (twice), which on the face of it appears to be a Latin accusative plural. The form is, however, problematical. In theory it might be a Gaulish accusative plural as well,[66] but attestations seem to be lacking. The only certain instances of the lexeme *catinus* in the corpus are all in the form *catinos*, whether in Celtic or Latin texts.[67] However the form is to be explained,[68] it was clearly fossilised at La Graufesenque, and was not language-specific.

Thus the heading, which as extant consists of only one word, is Celtic, but the body of the text is Latin. Given the bulk of the Latin in comparison with the Celtic, it is less than satisfactory to assign the document to the base language Gaulish, as Marichal does. It might be argued that the Celtic word at the start is no more than a hackneyed heading consisting of a Celtic loan-word which had entered the Latin of the area. It should be noted that in this case the number with *tuθos* is a Roman numeral symbol rather than a Celtic ordinal; there is not therefore in evidence a 'creative' use of Celtic, and it is indeed possible that this particular writer had integrated the word into his Latin (as a loan-word). Another possibility is that one person wrote the heading and another completed the document.

IV.5 *Morphological code-switching*

Interchanges between -*us* and -*os* were treated above as forms of morphological code-switching. These cases are not the only type of code-switching at La Graufesenque. The Latin neuter plural ending in -*a* and the 'Celtic' -*i* also sometimes alternate, though not to such an extent that the distinction between Latin and Celtic is in this respect blurred. The section will also contain a brief terminological discussion in which types of morphological code-switching will be distinguished.

Sometimes -*a* appears in a Celtic text, sometimes -*i* in a Latin. Note-worthy examples of the first type are found in a group of texts (21, 22, 23; also 25, though its classification as Celtic is not certain) which share other characteristics as well. 21 has *uinaria* alongside *catili* and *acitabli*. 22

---

[65] It should be noted that Marichal (1988: 76), discussing this same point, describes both 30 and 34 as Gaulish.

[66] See the paradigm of Lambert (1995: 49).

[67] See Marichal (1988: 273) for a collection of the evidence.

[68] It has caused some comment, albeit brief. See, e.g. Dottin (1924: 74), Marichal (1974: 100).

again has *uinaria*, but several cases of nouns in *-i*. 23 has *inbratarija* on the one hand, but *catili* and *acitabli* on the other. And 25 has both *uinaria* and *mortaria* (twice).

It is worth dwelling on the various shared features of this group of texts. *Vinari* occurs seventeen times in the corpus, alongside just five examples of *uinaria*, three of which are in 21–5. Another is in a Latin text (74), and the last is in a text of indeterminate language (165).[69]

The heading of 25 is missing, but the other three texts all begin with *tuθθos*, spelt with a double θθ. There are twenty-nine texts which begin with a form of *tuθos*,[70] and of these only four have θθ.[71] Outside our three texts, *tuθθos* occurs only in 24, an extremely fragmentary text consisting almost entirely of numerals; its character cannot therefore be grasped. The form has also been restored in 20, a text which can be associated with 21–3 (see below), and 26.

Scattered throughout our group of texts there are examples of a bizarre form *catilus*, which is interpreted by Lambert (1995: 53) as a Gaulish accusative plural of the *o*-stem (= *-ūs*). It occurs at 22.3 and 5 (*catili* twice in the same text), at 23.13 (this time in the form *catiljus*; *catili* twice in the text, immediately before and after *catiljus*), and three times in 25. There is moreover an example in 20 (*catili* three times), a text which we suggested above should be grouped with 21–3. These seven examples of *catil(j)us* are the only instances in the corpus.[72] It should also be noted that 20, apart from *catilus*, also has a comparable form *uinarijus*.

Finally, in 20–3 (and note again that 20 is to be associated with the other texts in the group) the form *parasidi* is invariable (nine examples), despite the fact that in the corpus as a whole *parax-* is overwhelmingly preferred. Marichal (1988: 274) lists about fifty-four cases of *parax-*, but apart from the nine examples of *parasidi* in 20–3 there are only six examples of the form in the corpus (27.2, 3, 28.6, 7, 8, 125.2).

The features shared by 20–5 are thus so marked that they point to the activity of a single scribe or a closely associated group of scribes. Whereas in other Celtic texts scribes sometimes switched from *-os* to *-us*, in personal names in 20–5 the Celtic ending is rigidly adhered to, if *Malciu* is left aside (some twenty-eight examples in names of both Latin and Celtic origin, but not a single example of *-us*). Yet it is only here in the whole Celtic corpus that vessel-names in *-a* are admitted.[73] In

---

[69] A full collection of examples is given by Marichal (1988: 274).
[70] For a list, see Marichal (1988: 96; also 278).   [71] See Marichal (1988: 278).
[72] See the list in Marichal (1988: 274), s.v. *uxedi*.   [73] See the table in Marichal (1988: 75).

fact the morphology of vessel-names in 20–5 is much more varied than
that elsewhere in either Celtic or Latin texts: both *-us* and *-i* in *catilus*,
uinarius and *uinaria* but never *uinari*, *acitabli* (20, 21, 22, 23) but never
acitabla, *mortaria* (25) but never *mortari* (usually the word is abbreviated),
and the possible Latinism *catinos* throughout (21.2, 3, 4, 23.2, 3, 25.1, 3).
There are patterns of a sort here, but they are difficult to explain: why,
for example, *uinaria* but not *acitabla* or *catila*?

Whatever one is to make of these variations, it is obvious that even
texts which can be classified as Celtic are not linguistically homogeneous.
Some of the features specific to 20–5 might conceivably be dialectal
(e.g. the assimilated form *parasidi* as opposed to *paraxidi*), whereas the
morphological code-switching may reflect a higher than normal degree
of exposure to Latin culture on the part of the scribe(s).

But this is mere speculation. It is enough to say that there was a
greater readiness in Celtic writing at La Graufesenque to use the Latin
-us ending in personal names than the Latin neuter plural *-a* in common
nouns, and that must reflect a particular prestige attached to Latinate
names. The occasional use of Latin morphology in common nouns (in
20–5) is entirely consistent with bilingual practice as observed in other
cultures.[74] We should see here the special bilingual performance of an
individual or small group of scribes.

It may be worthwhile to define further the nature of morphological
code-switching as seen in this section and in IV. 2–3 above, particularly
since the distinction between morphological code-switching and morphological interference is problematic. Morphological code-switching is
itself, as we have seen (p. 27), virtually indistinguishable from morphological borrowing. A distinction can be made between various categories
of switches; I use here the criteria developed in earlier chapters:

(1) A morpheme from language B may be used in a word of language
A when the language being spoken or written is language A. Thus in the
Celtic text 93 (A) the Celtic name *Lousjus* (A) has the Latin morpheme *-us*
(B). Is this morphological interference or code-switching/borrowing? In
an earlier chapter we saw in the receipt written by the Milesian Aeschines
two Latin words (A) in a Latin text (A) inflected as Greek (B) (δηναριους σεσκεντους), and classified the phenomenon as interference. But
there was reason to believe that Aeschines scarcely knew Latin, and that
that was why he kept lapsing into the morphology of his first language.

---

[74] See, e.g. Romaine (1995: 123). Romaine cites from the British Panjabi community an example
of an English word with Panjabi inflectional morphology (*shoppā* 'shops').

Interference on the view adopted in this book usually consists in an unconscious switch from L2 into L1. It seems reasonable to make a distinction between the errors of a learner, such as Aeschines, who had imperfect command of the second language, and switches of the kind noted in *Lousjus* above. The writer of the Gaulish text 93 must have been a native speaker of Gaulish, and he has therefore switched in the name from L1 into L2 rather than the reverse. A Gaulish–Latin bilingual who used the Latin morpheme *-us* (B) in a Gaulish name (A) in a Gaulish text (A) must have done so consciously and deliberately (e.g. because of the prestige he attributed to Latinate names), and not because he had imperfect command of Gaulish (surely an inconceivable situation in a potters' community in Gaul). It may not always be possible to distinguish clearly between the learner's reversion to the morphology of his first language (morphological interference) and the bilingual's switch from the morphology of language A to that of B (morphological code-switching/borrowing), but the distinction is well worth making.

(2) A morpheme from language B may be used in a word of language B when the language being spoken or written is language A. So, for example, in the Celtic text 22 (A) the Latin word *uinaria* (B) is assigned the Latin morpheme *-a* (B) rather than the expected 'Celtic' ending *-i*. In this type of switching the language (i.e. origin) of a particular lexical item overrides, as it were, the language of the utterance as a whole, and causes the lexical item to be assigned the morpheme appropriate to its language of origin. This type of code-switching has been illustrated extensively from the use of personal names elsewhere in this book, and possible examples in names have also been observed in this chapter. It would seem that, whereas common nouns were easily integrated from one language into another, personal names tended to resist integration, such that their language of origin was remembered far more readily. The potter who wrote *uinari* in a Celtic text might not have been aware of the Latin origin of the word; whereas that same potter might have perceived the Celtic flavour of *Meθθilos* or the Latin flavour of *Albus*.

In the above twofold classification it has been assumed that the base language of an utterance can be identified. But that may not always be the case, and the problem of classification may be acute. However, many utterances of mixed language are divisible into segments belonging unambiguously to the one language or the other. The difficulty then is not so much that of identifying the language of each segment, but that of assigning a dominant language to the utterance as a whole.

I turn now to the other side of the coin as alluded to at the start of this section, that is to the use of the *-i* morpheme in Latin neuters in Latin documents.[75] The following examples occur:

47   mortarii
66   mortariji uxẹ[di
83   acetabli

Switching of this type would be particularly easy to understand if those responsible for the 'Latin' texts at La Graufesenque were predominantly Celts with an acquired Latin culture; the 'code-switching' would thus be virtually indistinguishable from morphological interference (see above (1)). All three of these examples display an interesting combination of a 'Latin' feature with the 'Celtic' *-i* ending, a combination perhaps betraying an attempt to use a Latinate form which was not entirely successful. In *acetabli* there is the Latin *e* in the second syllable (see above), and both 47 and 66 have a bookish Latin *i* in hiatus (*-ii*, *-iji*) as distinct from the plain *-i* ending which is the norm in the consistently Celtic texts. *Mortari* occurs thirty-three times, twenty-four times for example in texts 1–19; *mortari(j)i* on the other hand occurs only in 47 and 66 above, and 121.

IV.6 Some formulae

The mixed-language expression *mortariji uxe[di]*, quoted above from the Latin text 66, was discussed in an earlier chapter (4.v.2.6). There is not straightforward intra-phrasal code-switching (Latin noun + Celtic adjective) here. The same phrase occurs repeatedly in Celtic texts, in which it can be interpreted as wholly Celtic, given that *mortari* had been borrowed by Gaulish in this area. Thus a whole phrase had been transferred from one language (Celtic) to the other. A phenomenon described as 'formula-switching' was identified in Greco-Latin epitaphs (see 1.v, p. 22). Just as Greek and Latin epitaphs were highly formulaic, so too record keeping in both Celtic and Latin at La Graufesenque was stereotyped. A formula which etymologically might be attributed to language A could without confusion be transferred to a stereotyped document in language B, its etymology of no consequence to the writer.

Another expression with *uxedios* is *summa uxedia* (five examples, all of them in Celtic texts), which seems to have meant *summa summarum*

---

[75] Since substandard Latin was itself over a long period losing the neuter, it may seem contentious to treat *-i* forms in Latin texts as Celtic-influenced; but the fact of the matter is that in this linguistic community *-a* was strongly associated with Latin and *-i* with Celtic.

(see 4.v.2.6). When it was first coined this phrase definitely would have exhibited intra-phrasal code-switching, whatever the language in which it was used, since it comprises a Latin noun qualified by a Celtic adjective. But it had no doubt acquired formulaic status, such that the etymology of its components was no longer felt. Nevertheless the fact that such a formula, of mixed language, could be coined at all points to the bilingualism of the potters and to the prevalence of code-switching.

IV.7 Conclusions

The forms of code-switching that have been identified at La Graufesenque establish unequivocally that there was a bilingual community in residence. Any attempt, however, to find a chaotically mixed language in use at the pottery would be a failure. On the whole Latin and Gaulish are differentiated, and the code-switching not completely haphazard but revealing of at least some patterns. It is though worth stressing that the material surveyed falls into different groups, each showing its own characteristics. The potters' stamps are uniformly in Latin. The four texts quoted at the start (2, 19, 47, 74) show a language differentiation, with the Latin documents distinguishable from the Celtic on at least four criteria. The group 21, 22, 23, 25 are in Celtic, but with a Latinate feature (-*a*) which is not otherwise common in Celtic texts. And 30 stands out as peculiar in various ways. There were different writers at work, and it is possible that their individual peculiarities shine through. It is worth recalling a point made by Gardner-Chloros (1991: 190), quoted earlier (5.1.3). Commenting on the drawbacks of excessive concentration on societal language choice, to the neglect of the diversity of influences that may affect interpersonal exchanges, she observes: 'It is a well-recognized danger of the sociolinguistic approach that it disguises important intra-individual variation in seeking to provide a picture of the group.' There is no reason why we should expect to find the same type of bilingual performance in all of the documents at La Graufesenque. Different individuals were no doubt prone to different degrees and types of code-switching. There will have been different degrees of competence in the second language, and different attitudes to the outside culture and the language which it brought. Those impressed by the status of the new language might have been more ready to adopt its morphemes even when they were writing Gaulish. The very diversity of the language differentiation and mixing in the groups of texts just listed would make unconvincing any attempt to find a single institutionalised 'mixed language' current in the pottery representing some sort of transitional stage in the Romanisation of the area. There is though in endangered languages (i.e. those in the process of dying) a dramatic increase in the amount of code-switching into the dominant language.[76]

Intra-sententially the mixed phrases *extra tuθ* and *summa uxedia* are telling and typical signs of a bilingual community, even though at least one of them probably had acquired formulaic status. Switching of this kind was facilitated by structural similarities between the two languages (both had the structure preposition + noun, and both had feminines marked by *-a*). Though such mixed phrases are not numerous (*mortariji exedi* as used in a Latin text could perhaps be added), it should be remembered that the vocabulary of the texts is extremely limited, and our few examples may represent the tip of an iceberg.

Another type of switching which falls within the sentence is that which we have called morphological, that is switches within word boundaries. In this category there is the use of the Latin morpheme *-a* in Celto-Latin vessel-names in Celtic texts,[77] and of the Celtic ending *-i* in Latin texts. Remarkably little switching of this type has been observed. If one leaves aside the special text 30 (see below), *-a* for *-i* in Celtic is confined to the bizarre group of texts 20–5. Nor is *-i* for *-a* in Latin texts numerous, but in fact given the paucity of Latin documents extant it would not be unreasonable to say that such morphological switching is as marked in Latin as in Celtic documents. This could reflect the fact that the dominant language even of those writing texts in Latin was Celtic.

The use of *-us* for *-os* in Celtic texts is more extensive (see above IV.1 on 14, IV.2 on *Vindulus* and *Tritus*, and IV.3, particularly on the texts 17 and 93), and in line with the power, which we have observed in other bilingual communities, of personal names to inspire code-switching. By contrast the use of *-os* for *-us* in Latin names in Latin texts is rare (for isolated cases, see above IV.3 on 66 and 76). Morphological code-switching in names belongs to two or three types at La Graufesenque. The language in which a name originated, Latin or Celtic, could, it seems, sometimes cause it to be given the ending appropriate to that language, even if the language of the text as a whole was different: the language of the name takes precedence over the language of the document as a determinant

[76] See Crystal (2000: 22).
[77] I call the vessel-names 'Celto-Latin' rather than simply 'Latin', because, whatever the origin of such terms, they had become the technical terminology of the pottery, their origins of no consequence. The endings which they are given, *-a* or *-i*, are determined by the language of the particular document, not by the etymology of the word itself.

of its ending. Personal preferences could also lead to the regular use of an ending inappropriate to the language in which a document as a whole was written. Thus *Vindulus*, a Celtic name, regularly has a Latin ending even in Celtic texts. Finally, there were scribes writing Celtic documents (see particularly 17 and 93) who had a preference for the Latin *-us* ending even in Celtic names. We have ascribed this to the prestige that Latinate forms of names were acquiring. No evidence is so revealing in this respect as the regular choice of *-us* in potters' stamps placed on objects for circulation in the outside world. Since it is names that are implicated in the choice, personal identity is also at issue. The potter who marked his wares with a Latin name, though he might have used in the pottery a Gaulish equivalent with Gaulish morphology, was giving himself a Romanised identity. The aspirations which seem to underlie the language choice help to explain the language shift which took place later in Gaul. Even in this lower-class community the Gauls had been provided with the tools of Latin literacy, and although they often used those tools to write Gaulish, they were revealing in various ways a regard for the status of Latin, and an awareness of its commercial advantages. Given these attitudes, knowledge of Latin was bound to spread, assisted by the framework of literacy which had already been put in place.

There remains inter-sentential code-switching, as exemplified in text 30, which has a (brief) Celtic part and a Latin part. The significance of the switching here is obscured by the fragmentary state of the heading (the Celtic section). A single-word Celtic heading attached to a Latin text need be no more significant than the insertion of a Celtic formula (cf. *mortariji uxedi*) into a Latin text. *Tuθos* (in Celtic texts) did, however, tend to have variable complements (such as different Celtic ordinal adjectives), and this variability makes it unlike a fixed formula of the type to which *mortariji uxedi* belongs. Moreover it is clear from the extant corpus that there were Latin equivalents to *tuθos* + complement in use at the pottery (various expressions containing *furnus*: e.g. *furnus secundus* at 74); the scribe of 30 thus had a choice open to him, and he selected a Celtic heading, followed by a Latin text. He could have chosen a Latin heading with a Latin text, or a Celtic heading with a Celtic text. That he blended the two possibilities (keeping, it should be noted, the two languages quite distinct: there is no haphazard switching in the Latin section) shows not only the bilingualism of the pottery but also that in at least one domain (record keeping *within* the pottery) the two languages were functionally interchangeable. It is often the case in bilingual societies that the two languages are used in different functions and domains.

V LATIN AT LA GRAUFESENQUE

Brief as the remains of Latin are at La Graufesenque, they display one or two regionalisms determined by the influence of Gaulish, which are relevant to the development of Gallo-Romance. The most noteworthy item is *paraxidi (-es)*, < *paropsides* (παροψίδες), which, as we saw (4.v.1.3), seems to reflect a Gaulish change *ps > x(s)*. It was noted that *paraxidi (-es)* is attested not only in Celtic texts, but also in Latin. It was suggested earlier that some of those using Latin for record-keeping at La Graufesenque 'Latinised' *paraxidi* by giving it the termination *-es*. The fact that they failed to reintroduce the 'correct' *ps*-spelling suggests that Latin in the pottery had taken on a life of its own, uninfluenced by contact with native speakers of Latin from outside. If the writers of Latin records had been first-language speakers of Latin of Italian origin one would have expected the *ps*-spelling in Latin texts. Those writing Latin at La Graufesenque might in the main (but see further below) have been Gauls whose bilingualism could be traced back over the generations to the time of an original influx of Italian potters. The spelling *parabsidi* found at 154 in a text of uncertain language nicely illustrates the degree to which the original form of the word had been forgotten at the pottery. *Parabsidi* can be interpreted as a conscious 'Latinisation' of the word, in that the Latin prefix *ab* has been inserted probably into the assimilated form *parasidi*. Such a Latinisation betrays a striving for correctness; if the writer had known the genuinely correct form, he would have used it.

Another sign of Celtic influence on the Latin of the region is to be seen in the merging of long *e* and *i* as a form of *i*.[78] *Acitab-* is found not only in Celtic texts, but also in Latin (47), though there are, as we noted above, traces of the retention of the more open vowel in Latin or Latinate texts.

In Latin texts the neuter plural form *catil(l)a* is standard (30, 47, 74: also in fragmentary texts probably in Latin, e.g. 49), as compared with the form *catilli* which is the norm in Celtic texts.[79] *Catilla* is of some interest. In classical Latin the word is masculine, with a rare neuter variant.[80] 'Correct' writers of Latin should therefore have retained the form used in Celtic texts. *Catilla* should probably be interpreted, not as further evidence for the existence of a neuter by-form of *catillus*, but as a reaction against the perceived 'Celtic' form *catilli*. Writers of Latin clearly followed a rule whereby the termination *-i* as used in Celtic texts should

---

[78] See further Marichal (1988: 58), Flobert (1992: 107).
[79] See Marichal (1988: 273).   [80] See *TLL* III.618.69ff.

be converted into -*a* in Latin. But in the case of *catilla* this rule led to the creation of a neuter form which was hypercorrect. In effect contact with Celtic has disturbed the Latin gender system, not as a result of borrowing or interference from the substrate language, but as a reaction against the form which a Latin word borrowed into the substrate had acquired there. Again, as in the case of the forms of *paraxides* used in Latin texts (I refer both to $x = ps$ and the falsely Latinised form with -*ab*-), we see a sign that the Latin of La Graufesenque had a life of its own, in detachment from the mainstream language in which *catilla* would have been anomalous. The conversion rule (-*a* for -*i* in vessel-names in Latin texts) has the look of an artificial rule of thumb which would have been laid down as part of a policy of teaching Latin formally. If there are features in the Latin of La Graufesenque which had evolved in isolation over a period (*paraxides*), the use of *catilla* in Latin texts would seem to reflect the coaching of Gauls in the writing of Latin imparted by Latin-speakers who were themselves cut off from mainstream Latin. I repeat the suggestion made above that speakers/writers of Latin at La Graufesenque were probably on the whole Gauls rather than recent immigrants from Italy. There are, however, as we will see, one or two Latin documents at La Graufesenque which reflect a higher cultural standard (see below).

I turn finally to a point of syntax. A curiosity of both the Celtic and Latin texts is to be found in the syntax of lists. Names of the potters responsible for the objects listed are usually in the nominative, with occasional genitives (5.10; some possible cases could be abbreviations). This is what might have been expected: in lists and accounts without an expressed verb, personal names, at least in Latin, regularly go into the nominative, if the person can be interpreted as an agent of some sort of verbal action.[81] A nice set of examples can be found now in a 'letter relating to missing lances' from Carlisle, published by Tomlin (1998: 55–6) as text no. 16. Here in a list the names (of those who have lost their lances) are in the nominative, with the words for 'lance' (as the object of the process) in the accusative, as e.g. at line 26, *Felicio lanciam [pug]natoriam*. We would expect the accusative of personal names in a list only if the referent was perceived as patient of a process, as e.g. as the object of a curse. The Myconos *defixio*, for example, predominantly has the names of those cursed in the accusative (e.g. line 1 *L. Paconium senem*), though it also displays lapses into the nominative (see above, 6.VI). Another such accusative list can be found at *P. Oxy.* VII.1022, where an implied governing

---

[81] See Adams (1995a: 115).

verb is easy to supply. The nominative of names is also used when a list
records members of a group who are not necessarily seen as agents of
any action but are simply named for their membership of that group
(see e.g. the military lists Kayser (1994), 102, and Fink (1971), 34 = *ChLA*
43.1242).

   But in the documents of La Graufesenque the goods made by each
potter are also usually in the nominative, and that is certainly anomalous
by Latin standards, where one might have expected the accusative, or
genitive (dependent on a quantity term).[82] The nominative in Celtic texts
is represented by the numerous nouns in *-i*. *Pannas* and other words in *-as*
should also probably be regarded as nominative, both in Celtic and Latin
documents (e.g. 74): both Gaulish and non-standard Latin had an *-as*
nominative plural. In Latin texts the nominative can be seen in *panae* (30),
a 'correct' alternative to *-as*, and in *mortari* (47) and *acetabli* (83). Possible
accusatives are the oddity *catinos*, which is frequent in Celtic texts and is
also, it seems, in the Latin text 83; and *catilus*, etc. (a Celtic accusative?:
see above, IV.5). But the nominative outnumbers these isolated forms,
at least in Celtic texts. It has to be admitted that in Latin the frequent
neuters in *-a* could be either nominative or accusative.

   In other respects the lists in both languages have a markedly Latinate
appearance. Roman numerals and sigla, as we saw, are used throughout,
and interpuncta are not uncommon. One may conjecture that at an
early stage in the history of the pottery the Italian immigrants imposed
what was basically a Latin structure on the record-keeping. Crucial requirements of any such lists were that the potters should be identified,
and their output specified and numbered. The 'language' of the lists, as
indicated by the inflectional morphology (and also the headings), was
of lesser importance, though, as we have seen, scribes tended to adhere
to one language or the other. Because the structure, the numbers, sigla
and basic terminology were more important than the inflectional morphology, it is possible that the hypothetical immigrants made no attempt
to impose a Latinate accusatival form on the goods named. The preference for the nominative may reflect Gaulish practice; if so its use in
Latin texts constitutes another anomalous feature of the Latinity of the
pottery determined by the influence of Celtic. For anomalous uses of the
nominative in the writing of learners of a second language, see above,
5.IX, with cross references.

---

[82] See Adams (1995a: 114–15). For a few unusual examples of the nominative in lists, see Svennung
   (1935: 178, 192).

It was mentioned above that there is at least one Latin text extant which reflects a higher cultural level, namely (169), an account of works effected between 22 July and 23 August:

> ATELIAE puerorum ex XI August[is
> in X K(alendas) Septebres
>]CUNDUS, AGILEIUS dies XIIII s(emis) ar[gilam
>]dierum XXX, IIII ad Capuries, XI[
> CA]LISTUS
>   O]NESIMUS ad Sabros III, ad Crau[cinam
>   ]ad Craucinam III it(em) ONESIMUȘ[
> mat]eriem erigenda I
>]dierum XXX
>   ]ae III, CALISTUS ad samiandum[83]
>]...NOS, VIGEDOS III mercatu a[d
>   em
>   ]s materi erigedam[
>   ]argilam [III] di[es
>   ]
>   ]s ad A[
> mulio CANDIDI URI d(ies) XXV
>   ar[gilam?
>   ad m[ercatum?
>   ad Saḅr[os
>   ].ales
>   ]. dies XIIX.

The Latin here has a more complicated syntactic structure than that of the potters' list.[84] I draw particular attention to a 'default' use of the accusative which occurs throughout the text. The nature of the work of various slaves, or the sphere of their activities, is specified by various nouns in the accusative (3 *Agileius dies XIIII s(emis) ar[gilam]*,[85] .. *Vigedos III mercatu* (= *-um*)) without prepositions or governing verbs.[86] Marichal (1988: 228) translates: 'Agileius: 14 jours 1/2 à l'argile ... Uigedos: 3 jours au marché'. This accusative, in contrast to the anomalous nominatives in lists discussed above, has an idiomatic, though substandard, look to it. In Vindolanda tablets there are one or two cases of 'unconstrued'

---

[83] On this verb, see Flobert (1992: 112), translating *samiare* as 'purifier l'argile' (< *Samia* (*testa*)). Was this another Latin regionalism?

[84] See Marichal (1971: 197) for some remarks on the structure.

[85] The restoration of the last word seems justified by line 13, *]argilam [[III]] di[es]*.

[86] See Marichal (1971: 197–8) on this usage; he compares a use of *calcem* at ChLA 1.7, p.17 (*P. Gen. Lat.* 1).

accusatives whose purpose seems to be to introduce a new subject.[87] Another unmotivated accusative can be found in a list of soldiers published most conveniently by Fink (1971), 36 and at *CPL* 109 and *ChLA* 10.426. The entries comprise name, filiation, tribe and *origo*. The *origo* is sometimes (predictably) in the ablative (e.g. line 9 *Adrymeto*, line 14 *Altino*), but twice it is accusative (lines 1, 5 *Pessinuntem*), though here there may simply have been a hypercorrect addition of *-m*.

---

[87] See Adams (1995b: 116–17).

8

*The Latin of a learner (*P. Amh. *II.26): a case study*

I A TRANSLATION OF BABRIUS

It was noted earlier that the acquisition of *literacy* in the script of a second language can be divided into stages (see 5.VII.3), several of which are identified through various types of errors. Learners also commit different categories of errors in the acquisition of a second *language*, whether they are learning that language by contact at the level of speech, or by formal instruction with the help of writing.[1] Some research has been devoted to the question whether sequences can be identified in second-language acquisition.[2] I would not wish to claim that I have any contribution to make on the general issue of whether such sequences may be detected across a broad spectrum of languages; indeed it seems to me that where formal instruction is involved, the sequence will be determined by the nature of the instruction. Nevertheless, there is one Latin text extant which is relevant to the matter. I refer to a Latin translation of parts of two fables of Babrius which is preserved at *P. Amh.* II.26. The document is dated by the editors (p. 26) to the late third or early fourth century. In this chapter I offer a discussion of the Latinity of the translation, paying attention not only to its substandard features, but also to its numerous errors, many of which cannot be explained merely as displaying typical substandard or vulgar usages. There can be no doubt that the author was a Greek learner of Latin as a second-language. A distinction, as we will see (note particularly the commentary below, line 5), should be made between the author (i.e. the translator), and a later scribe who copied out the text and introduced a further degree of error; but by no means all of the errors in the text can be attributed to scribal corruption. Some of the mistakes reveal the areas of the translator's deficiencies in

---

[1] On 'error analysis' discussed in relation to the learning of Latin, see Adams (1994a: 91 with n. 29).
[2] See e.g. Cook (1993: 25–50).

725

the learning of the language, and allow deductions to be made about the order in which he was acquiring Latin morphology (see above, 1.IX (1) on the sequence whereby Phonen acquired Greek verb morphology). In a second section of the chapter I will discuss the (verb) morphology of Claudius Terentianus and some letters from Vindolanda, to bring out the distinction between fluent colloquial Latin, and the reduced Latin of an imperfect learner. The translation was probably done as an exercise in language learning. I quote the text in full, along with the relevant parts of the text of Babrius, taken from the edition of Perry (1965):

Col. I

luppus autem auditus anucellam uere dictu[m
putatus m[a]nsit quasi parata cenaret
dum puer quidem sero dormisset
ipse porro esuriens et luppus enectus u̦er̦[e
rediuit frigiti<s> spebus frestigiatur
luppa en̦im̦ eum coniugalis interrogabat
quomod[o n]ihil tulitus uenisti s[i]cut sole[bas
et il̦l̦e̦ [dix]it q̦u̦o̦m̦o̦d̦o̦ enim quis m̦ulieri cr̦[edo
. . . .

Col. II

. . . .
bulpecula inio̦n̦f̦o̦rtunam binearisq[ue h]ort[isque
peregrina uolens circomitti quis șa̦e̦u̦i̦[tia
codam su[c]census et linei quidem a[ll]igatus
sinuit fu[ge]re [h]anc șpeculator genius malus
infra aruras missuro procedebat
ignem babbandam erat autem tempus sectilis
et pulcheri fructus spaearum sorsus
oportet ergo serenae magis aut in^{a}equa irasci
nec uidit eius ariis Cereris
est quidam ira ultricis quem custodiamus
ip̦sișmet ipsis nocentiam ferentes animosali[bus

Babrius 16.3ff.
λύκος δ' ἀκούσας τήν τε γραῦν ἀληθεύειν
νομίσας ἔμεινεν ὡς ἕτοιμα δειπνήσων,
ἕως ὁ παῖς μὲν ἑσπέρης ἐκοιμήθη,
αὐτὸς δὲ πεινῶν καὶ λύκος χανὼν ὄντως
ἀπῆλθε νωθραῖς ἐλπίσιν παρεδρεύσας.
λύκαινα δ' αὐτὸν ἡ σύνοικος ἠρώτα
'πῶς οὐδὲν ἦλθες ἄρας, ὡς πρὶν εἰώθεις;'
ὁ δ' εἶπε 'πῶς γάρ, ὅς γυναικὶ πιστεύω;'

A wolf heard this and, believing that the old woman meant what she said, stayed to enjoy a dinner all but served; until at last the child at evening fell asleep and our hero, hungry and foolishly agape, as the veritable wolf in the proverb, went away, after standing by in attendance on idle hopes. Then the she-wolf who was his wife questioned him, saying: "Why have you come back without bringing anything as you used to do?" And he replied: "What can you expect, when I put my trust in a woman?".

Babrius 11

> ’Αλώπεκ’ ἐχθρὴν ἀμπέλων τε καὶ κήπων
> ξένη θελήσας περιβαλεῖν τις αἰκείῃ,
> τὴν κέρκον ἅψας καὶ λίνου τι προσδήσας
> ἀφῆκε φεύγειν. τὴν δ’ ἐπίσκοπος δαίμων
> εἰς τὰς ἀρούρας τοῦ βλαβόντος ὡδήγει
> τὸ πῦρ φέρουσαν. ἦν δὲ ληίων ὥρη,
> ποίη δὲ καλλίκαρπος ἐλπίδων πλήρης.
> ὁ δ’ ἠκολούθει τὸν πολὺν πόνον κλαίων,
> οὐδ’ εἶδεν αὐτοῦ τὴν ἅλωα Δημήτηρ.
>   Χρὴ πρᾶον εἶναι μηδ’ ἄμετρα θυμοῦσθαι.
> ἔστιν τις ὀργῆς νέμεσις, ἢν φυλαττοίμην,
> αὐτοῖς βλάβην φέρουσα τοῖς δυσοργήτοις.[3]

Someone caught a fox, the enemy of his vines and garden. Wishing to punish him with a new kind of torment, he set fire to his tail, after tying some tow upon it, and let him loose to run. But the spirit of Retribution that keeps watch over such acts guided the fox with his burden of fire straight into the grain fields of the man who had done him hurt. It was the season of standing crops, and the grain was fruitful, fair, and full of promise. The owner ran after the fox, bewailing the loss of his hard work, and the grain never saw his threshing floor.

One must be calm and not unbounded in one's anger. There is a certain retribution for anger – and may I guard against it – bringing loss upon such men as lose their tempers. (Translations from Loeb)

The translator had learnt Latin letters, including the correct form of digraphs (e.g. *ae* is correctly written, though imperfect Greek learners of Latin not infrequently wrote *ai*: see 5.vii.3). Notable is the superscript *a* in the second syllable of *inaequa*, itself a hypercorrect form. The writer recomposed *iniquus*, used a 'phonetic' spelling *inequa*, and then 'corrected' it. Latin case inflections are often correctly used. The only clear morphological error in the case system is to be seen in the genitive plural *spaearum* = *sperum*; the ablative plural *spebus* is correctly written at col. 1.5.

---

[3] It should be noted that the Greek text which the translator had (and which is partly preserved in the papyrus) differed in a few respects from that printed here. One such difference will be germane to the discussion below (see n. 7).

The Latin fifth declension, which was not recognised by ancient grammarians as a separate category until late,[4] and did not contain many members and was not surprisingly absorbed by other declensions, posed particular problems for bilinguals/learners. In various transliterated texts (which almost by definition were written by Greek learners of Latin), there are anomalous forms of *dies* which show the difficulties faced by learners attempting to use words of this type (e.g. *IGUR* 718 διον = *diem*, *ILCV* 3391 δευρων, genitive plural; cf. 1.IX (5)), and *spes* itself developed an inflection in *n* (*spenis, speni*: see 4.VI.1). Some syntactic errors in the use of cases occur in the last few lines as the text is printed above (*serenae, ariis, Cereris*), but textual corruption is likely here, as we will see.

It is in the handling of the verb system that the writer reveals his imperfect learning of Latin. Some verb-forms are correctly used, but others are not, and it is the nature of the errors which is significant.

I take first correct forms. There are, first, twelve correct active indicative forms used with correct function, distributed across three tenses, the present, imperfect and perfect: *m[a]nsit, rediuit,*[5] *interrogabat, uenisti, sole[bas], [dix]it, cr[edo], sinuit* (on which see below), *erat, oportet, uidit, est*. Most of these are in the third person singular, but there is also at least one second person singular, and possibly a first person singular. I have classified *sinuit* as 'correct', because though it is a vulgar form,[6] it does not represent a learner's error but shows that the writer had not acquired Latin exclusively from bookish sources. The contrast between the vulgar *sinui* and the ps.-correct *rediuit* immediately points to two different sources of the translator's Latinity: the popular language, and grammar-book paradigms. *Procedebat* finally is a correct active indicative form, but it has been forced to bear a transitive meaning.

Secondly, there are three correct active subjunctive forms: *cenaret, dormisset* (but see further below, line 3 on this simplex), *custodiamus*. Again three tenses are represented, the present, imperfect and pluperfect.

---

[4] See Law (1997: 72).

[5] This form is in fact hypercorrect for CL *rediit*; there is a hint here that the learner has learnt an artificial, bookish paradigm in *-iui*.

[6] The perfect suffix *-ui* (like *-si*), was very productive in Vulgar Latin (see e.g. Grandgent (1908: 180–1), Bourciez (1946: 83–4), Leumann (1977: 595), Adams (1977: 53)). Among the earlier perfect formations which it replaced were (1) those whose perfect marker was long grade of the root (*uenui = *ueni*, *capui = *cepi*); (2) those with reduplication (*parcui = *peperci*, *cadui = *cecidi*); and (3) those without an explicit perfect marker (*bibui = *bibi*). The perfect of *sino* had a long vowel in the root; moreover it could not be directly associated with the infectum because its second consonant was different. *-ui* has been attached to the root of the infectum (cf. *capui above). *Sinui* is attested in inscriptions (see Ihm (1902: 150)), and was no doubt a genuine popular usage.

Thirdly, there are two correct present participle forms, in the nominative singular: *esuriens, uolens.* To these could perhaps be added one other
correct participle, the perfect passive *enectus* (col. 1, line 4): *esuriens et luppus
enectus ụẹṛ[e];* cf. Babrius 16.6 πεινῶν καὶ λύκος χανὼν ὄντως. *Enectus*
could be used hyperbolically in the sense ' "killed" by hunger', i.e. starving (see *TLL* v.2.563.54, e.g. Livy 21.40.9 *fame frigore inluuie squalore enecti*).
The rendering is thus not literal, but appears to be idiomatic Latin. The
writer might, however, have known *enectus* virtually as an adjective =
'starving' rather than as a participial form of the verb *eneco.* As such
it should probably not be included in an account of the verbal forms
used in the text.

Finally, there are three correct present infinitive forms: *circomitti,
fu[ge]re, irasci.* Of these the first is the only genuine passive, rendering quite
idiomatically an active (aorist) infinitive in the Greek (11.2 περιβαλεῖν).

Of the twenty-one correct verb forms (I omit *enectus*), only one is passive
(*circomitti*), though *irasci* has a passive form. Sixteen of the twenty-one
are finite forms, and only five non-finite. Genuine (present) participles
are used only in the nominative singular form, and infinitives only in
the present tense. One might conclude that the writer had command
of finite active forms of verbs, and that he had some understanding of
non-finite forms.

His errors reveal the limitations of his Latin learning, and considered
in conjunction with the correct forms listed above, point to the order in
which he had acquired his knowledge of the verb system.

There are ten clear mistakes in the use of verbs, *nine of which are in
non-finite forms, all of them participial.* Here is a classification of these errors.

First, five perfect participles are used, not as they should have been,
as passives, but as actives. *Auditus* renders the Greek active aorist
ἀκούσας (16.3), *putatus* renders νομίσας (16.4), *tulitus* (on which see below)
renders ἄρας (16.9), *succensus* renders ἄψας (11.3), and *a[ll]igatus* renders
προσδήσας (11.3).

The writer was able to cope, up to a point, with the present active participle, but he had failed to grasp the difference which existed between
the Latin perfect participial system, most members of which were passive, and the Greek aorist participial system, which offered distinctions
between active, middle and passive. He had learnt the correct form
of various Latin perfect participles but did not understand their function. It is impossible to explain these various usages internally, from
developments within ordinary substandard varieties of Latin itself. Nor

could they possibly have arisen through surface corruption. The type of error repeats itself so consistently that it can only reflect the writer's misconception of an aspect of the verb system. In one sense the errors might be said to display interference from Greek, in that the writer has assumed that, since Greek possessed past participles which were active in voice, so too the Latin past participles must be active. But they are perhaps more interesting for the light which they throw on the stages of the writer's learning of the verb system. Clearly he had a surer grasp of the relationship between the form and function of finite forms of verbs than of participial forms, and within the participial system he was more *au fait* with the function of present active than with that of perfect passive forms. I conclude that he had come to the learning of the participial system after that of the finite (active) verb system. His use of the perfect participles listed above would suggest that he did not necessarily learn function concurrently with form.

A second error lies in the rendering of an aorist active participle in the genitive: col. II, line 29 *infra aruras* **missuro** *procedebat*; cf. 11.5 εἰς τὰς ἀρούρας τοῦ βλαβόντος ὡδήγει).[7] On a charitable view it might be said that a possessive dative has been substituted for the genitive of the Greek, but *missurus* belongs to the wrong tense. Again the writer reveals his ignorance of the function of non-present participial forms; he was, however, able to call up an existing (future) participial form, and to give it a case ending which might be justified by the context.

In the next line there is another mistake in the rendering of an oblique-case participle. The Greek runs thus (11.4–6):

> τὴν δ' ἐπίσκοπος δαίμων
> εἰς τὰς ἀρούρας τοῦ βλαβόντος ὡδήγει
> τὸ πῦρ φέρουσαν.

Here φέρουσαν is in agreement with τὴν at the start of the sentence, which picks up ἀλώπεκ'. The expression underlined is translated by *ignem babbandam*. It might seem that a gerundive form (on an incomprehensible root) has been brought into play to render a participle, but it is more likely that textual corruption is behind this bizarre form (*portantem* ?).[8]

The last two lines of Babrius 11 are rendered by Perry (1965), 'There is a certain retribution for anger – and may I guard against it – bringing

---

[7] The translator had a variant reading βαλόντος for βλαβόντος.
[8] See Ihm (1902: 150), also suggesting *baiulantem*.

loss upon such men as lose their tempers.' The Greek is translated thus (col. II, lines 34–5):

> est quidam ira ultricis quem custodiamus
> ịpsịṣṃet ipsis nocentiam ferentes animosali[bus.

The first line here is astray both in case usage and agreement of gender. *Ira* ought to be in the genitive (cf. ὀργῆς), and *ultricis* in the nominative, if it is intended as a rendering of νέμεσις (see the commentary below, line 18). The masculine *quidam* (a mechanical translation of τις) has nothing to agree with: both *ira* and *ultricis* are feminine. Again a participle seems to be erroneously used. *Ferentes* on the face of it would seem to be a plural (nominative?), which ought to agree with whole or part of the complex *quidam ira ultricis*. It is probably a misspelt genitive singular agreeing with *ultricis*.

A final error in the use of a non-finite form is to be seen in the rendering of the infinitive ἀληθεύειν at 16.3: λύκος δ' ἀκούσας τήν τε γραῦν ἀληθεύειν / νομίσας, 'A wolf heard this and, believing that the old woman meant what she said . . . ' (Perry (1965)). This is translated (col.I, lines 1–2): *luppus autem auditus anucellam uere dictu[m] / putatus. Anucellam* ought to be the subject accusative of an active form of the infinitive of *dico* (either *dicere* or *dixisse*). Instead the writer has used the perfect *passive* expression *uere dictum*. Taken in isolation this expression might be regarded as a meaningful impersonal passive, and indeed one wonders if the writer had seen or heard *uere dictum est/esse* somewhere. But with a subject accusative it is intolerable that there should be an impersonal passive verb. It almost looks as if the writer has translated word by word, without concerning himself with the syntactic relationship of one word to another. Thus γραῦν motivates *anucellam*, and *uere dictum* is chosen as a phrase-book rendering of ἀληθεύειν which is acceptable only if its relationship to *anucellam* is disregarded. *Vere dictum* could only be made meaningful within the wider structure of the sentence if *anucellam* were (incorrectly) taken as 'object' of *auditus*, and *(uere) dictum* as an impersonal passive dependent on *putatus*, i.e. 'thinking that it had been truly said'. The presence of τε after τήν makes it clear that such an interpretation would be incorrect, and it is difficult to believe that a Greek speaker could have construed Babrius thus. It is preferable to believe that the translator, when confronted with a 'difficult' non-finite form, could at best come up with a one-to-one Latin correspondent to the Greek which theoretically might have been acceptable in some contexts; but that he was incapable of fitting that correspondent to the context at hand. Alternatively, *dictum* might be a corruption of *dictam*, in which case a perfect passive form would have been used with active meaning, in much the same way as *auditus*, etc.

Our nine non-finite errors (or eight, if *babbandam* is eliminated from consideration) thus involve either the perfect (strictly passive) participles of Latin, or participles in cases other than the nominative (singular). I conclude that, while the writer had some command of finite verb-forms and of the case system which allowed him to write grammatical sentences provided that the verb was finite and active (e.g. *ipse porro esuriens et luppus enectus uer[e]/rediuit*), he was all at sea with the Latin participial system. The one error in a finite verb lies in the use of *procedebat* (on which see above).

The script of the translation, according to the editors (*P. Amh.* II, p. 26), is very fair, and hence they deduce that 'the writer can hardly have been in the early stages of his education' (though a distinction must be made between the writer/scribe, and the original translator). I would suggest that the sources of the translator's knowledge of Latin were various. First, he had acquired some Latin at a subliterary level: the influence of substandard spoken varieties of the language is easy to detect in the translation (see the commentary below). Secondly, he must have moved on to formal instruction in literacy and in morphology, but the instruction which he had received, as we have seen, was obviously incomplete. It is of note that, whatever the errors and vulgarisms in the text, the writer on the whole spells correctly; final -*m*, for example, is consistently written, and the hypercorrection in *inaequa* and *spaearum* points to a desire to get the digraph *ae* correct. It may be conjectured that the Latin which he was capable of speaking was a reduced form of the language, in that he will have preferred active forms of verbs to passives, and finite forms to non-finite. Learners often have to adopt a strategy of avoidance: each utterance has to be structured in such a way that they can make use of the morphology and syntax which they know. It is when circumstances (as, in this case, the demands of a formal translation exercise) require them to make an attempt at structures which they do not fully command that they are likely to fall into bizarre errors. A third source of the author's Latinity was some sort of bilingual glossary (see the commentary below, particularly on line 5).

I move on now to a systematic examination of the language of the translation, with the aims of establishing a claim made above (that the writer was in contact with colloquial spoken varieties of Latin), and of illustrating further the learners' errors which the text contains.

II.1 Commentary

1, 4 *luppus*, 6 *luppa*. Notable examples of expressive gemination;[9] for this phenomenon in an animal-term, cf. *Appendix Probi* 110 *draco non dracco* (cf. *CIL* III 8238 *Draccenae, Dracco*). It is possible that the spelling reflects an expressive pronunciation with which the name of the animal providing the subject of the fable might have been articulated. Some expressive geminations caught on and passed into the Romance languages, but others were no doubt *ad hoc* and determined by the special circumstances of an utterance. Was there an affected and expressive manner of delivering a fable?

1 *autem*. As in many translated texts, δέ is explicitly translated, here (cf. Babrius 16.3) and at 14 (Babrius 11.6) by *autem*, and at 6 (*luppa enim eum*) by *enim* (cf. Babrius 16.8 λύκαινα δ' αὐτὸν; for another particle rendering δέ, see below on 4). These renderings illustrate the failure of the Latin particles to maintain their classical nuances. In translation texts and stylistically pretentious later narrative many are used indifferently as equivalents of δέ.[10]

1 *anucellam*. The use of this diminutive for *anus* was not motivated by the Greek version (16.3 γραῦν). Old age and childhood inspired the use of diminutives in Latin.[11] *Anicula* was the standard diminutive in early and classical Latin, but the evidence of Varro (*Ling.* 9.74), who mentions both *anicula* and *anicilla*, shows that the *-ella* / *-illa* form must already have been in existence at a subliterary level. An advantage of the diminutives was that they showed their gender, whereas *anus* did not, and for that reason it must have been under threat in ordinary speech (note *Appendix Probi* 172 *anus non anucla*). The suffix *-ellus*, originally a double diminutive formation (<*porc-el-elos*> *porcellus*),[12] seems to have been more intensive in diminutive meaning than *-ulus*; it is the implication of Varro, *Ling.* 9.74 that *canis, catulus, catellus* expressed comparative degrees of smallness (note *ubi magnitudo animaduertenda sit in unoquoque gradu*). *-ellus* no doubt was capable of greater affective force than *-ulus* (note Plaut. *Asin.* 667–8), and that caused it sometimes to encroach on and even displace the alternative in *-ulus*:[13] note e.g. *Appendix Probi* 50 *catulus non catellus*. So, for example, it is *porcellus* and *lancella* rather than *porculus* and *lancula* which survive in the Romance languages. The suffix *-ellus*, unlike *-ulus*, also had that

---

[9] For which phenomenon, see in general Graur (1929: 89–100), Väänänen (1981: 59–60).
[10] See, e.g. Adams (1995b: 629–31).   [11] See Baehrens (1922: 20).
[12] See Leumann (1977: 143; also 306).
[13] See Baehrens (1922: 121–2), Väänänen (1966: 100–2), Adams (1995a: 106, 107).

desirable property of a popular suffix that it carried the accent of the word.

Neither *anicella* nor *anicula* survives in Romance, perhaps because of a homonymic clash with *annicellus* and *anniculus*, both of which do have reflexes, and which carry a meaning almost at a polar remove from that of *anicula, anicella*.

The writer's choice of *anucella* instead of *anus* (or *anicula*) strongly suggests that he was influenced by (spoken) colloquial Latin, and that his sources of knowledge were not entirely bookish.

Another diminutive unmotivated by the Greek is *bulpecula* (9) (cf. Babrius 11.1 ἀλώπεκ'). *Vulpecula* is rare in extant Latin (< *uulpes*), but reflected in Romance (see *REW* 9463).

3 *dum puer quidem sero dormisset*. The writer continues with his crude translation method of using (almost invariably) one word in Latin for every word in the Greek (see 4.V.2.12 for this translation technique). So here *quidem* is used for μέν (Babrius 16.5 ἕως ὁ παῖς μὲν ἑσπέρης ἐκοιμήθη).

In the same line it is not the learned word *uesper* but *sero* which is used to translate ἑσπέρης. This is another usage which the writer had picked up from speech. The adverb *sero*, which in reference to time of day is sometimes indistinguishable in sense in Classical Latin from 'in the evening' (e.g. Cic. *Att.* 7.21.1 *eo die Lentulus uenit sero*), lies behind Fr. *soir*, Log. *sero*, etc.; cf. *sera* (*dies*) > It. *sera*. For some parallels which may be roughly contemporary, see *SHA, Gord.* 6.5, *Hel.* 28.6.

Dormisset has to be given the sense 'had fallen asleep', and is an imprecise rendering (cf. *addormio, addormisco, dormisco*).

4 *ipse porro esuriens et luppus enectus uer[e*. The structure is again identical to that of the Greek (Babrius 16.6 αὐτὸς δὲ πεινῶν καὶ λύκος χανὼν ὄντως. Here it is *porro*, forced to bear virtually an adversative function,[14] which corresponds to δέ.

On the idiomatic use of *enectus*, see above. Used of hunger (which has not caused death in the literal sense), *enectus* is not only hyperbolical but elliptical, in that the idiom is generated by deletion of a complement (*fame*). Note Cic. *Diu.* 2.73 *fame enecta*, Nonius p. 556.34 L. *maestum, enectum fame*.[15]

5 *rediuit frigiti(s) spebus frestigiatur*. For the omission of final -*s* before a word beginning with *s*, see e.g. Catull. 116.8 *dabi(s) supplicium*, Claudius Terentianus, *P. Mich.* VIII. 471.21 *pater meu(s) sopera*.[16]

---

[14] See Hofmann and Szantyr (1965: 491), citing this passage.

[15] On *neco* and compound used in reference (literally and hyperbolically) to starvation, see Adams (1990a: 250), id. (1991a: 105–7).

[16] The phenomenon is widespread, and may be seen as simplification of a geminate across word boundaries; as such it should not be confused with the issue of whether, when and in what registers

The spelling of *frigidus* with *t* rather than *d* is probably not a hyper-correct reaction against any tendency which there might have been for intervocalic voiceless stops to be voiced; it may represent the intrusion of the familiar participial ending -*itus* into an adjective. Here again, as in the case of *enectus* above, the translation (*frigidae* with *spes*) is not mechanical (Babrius 16.7 νωθραῖς ἐλπίσιν) but idiomatic (metaphorical).[17]

Frestigiatur is meaningless (Gk. παρεδρεύσας). Ihm (1902: 150) observed that παρεδρεύω is glossed by *praestolor* at *CGL* II.397.31, and convincingly suggested *praestolatus*, which would give exactly the right meaning. Since even a translator labouring under the disadvantage of poor command of Latin is unlikely to have written such gibberish, we see that a second layer of error must be assumed in the text, inflicted by an incompetent copyist of the original translation. There is textual corruption, in addition to the errors of translation caused by the translator's imperfect Latin. The editors of *P. Amh.* II.26 themselves argued for this additional layer of surface corruption, drawing attention not only to this case but also to *inionfortunam*, *babbandam* and *sorsus*. They remark (p. 26): 'The Latin version ... is extraordinarily bad, giving the impression of having been composed by a person who knew very little Latin, and copied by another who knew less.' Ihm's discovery of a point of contact between the translator's word choice and the bilingual glossaries is of particular interest, and he was moreover able to reinforce the connection with further evidence (see Ihm (1902: 151), and below on 12 and 18). His observations point unmistakably to one of the sources of the translator's Latinity: he must have had before him some sort of Greek–Latin glossary.[18]

6 *luppa enim eum coniugalis interrogabat*. The word order is again exactly that of the Greek (Babrius 16.8 λύκαινα δ' αὐτὸν ἡ σύνοικος ἡρώτα).[19]

7 *quomod[o n]ihil tulitus uenisti s[i]cut sole[bas*. Cf. Babrius 16.9 'πῶς οὐδὲν ἦλθες ἄρας, ὡς πρὶν εἰώθεις;'. Notable here is *tulitus*, which is not only used as if active, but is also morphologically anomalous. The participle is based on the perfectum. There is a parallel (but used 'correctly' as a passive) at *P. Abinn.* I.7 (*obtulitis*, on which see the editors' note ad loc.; see also above, 5.VII.2.2, p. 613), a fact which suggests that the term might have had some currency at a subliterary level. It is of course the

---

final -*s* was omitted (see also above, 2.II.3, p. 130). See further Väänänen (1966: 79), Adams (1977: 30).

[17] *Frigidus* is sometimes coordinated with *inanis* (e.g. Plin. *Epist.* 4.17.4), which is sometimes linked to *spes* (*TLL* VII.1.825.83ff).

[18] For similarities between glosses in *CGL* and those in glossaries on papyrus from Egypt, see e.g. Kramer (1988: 142), Rochette (1989, 1990: 340).

[19] σύνοικος is printed by Perry (1965), but the translator probably had σύνευνος: note *CGL* II.445.45 σύνευνος *coniunx*, and see Ihm (1902: 151).

irregularity of the verb (and the relative infrequency of the past participle compared with the perfectum *tuli*) which lies behind the remodelling.[20] A small number of structural parallels can be cited, all of them in verbs which might have been perceived as irregular: **uixutus = uictus, pepercitus, fefellitus*.[21] Alternatively, and perhaps more frequently, a remodelled participle might be based on the infectum: thus Petronius' *uinciturum* (45.10) = *uicturum*, where the nasal infix is from the infectum.

Additional interest is given to *tulitus* by the fact that it renders ἄρας rather than a form of φέρω. *Tulitus* is based on *tuli*, but clearly the writer has taken *tuli / tulitus* as parts of *tollo*.[22]

8 *et ille [dix]it quomodo enim quis mulieri cr[edo*. This line follows the Greek word for word, and would be incomprehensible without it: Babrius 16.10 ὁ δ᾽ εἶπε 'πῶς γάρ, ὃς γυναικὶ πιστεύω;'. This use of *quomodo enim* is a good example of the literal rendering of an idiom of one language into another, with meaningless results. It is also of note that the translator has used *quis* for *qui* as a relative pronoun, for which usage cf., e.g. Sen. *Apoc.* 9.5 *censeo uti diuus Claudius ex hac die deus sit, ita uti ante eum quis optimo iure factus sit*.[23]

9 *bulpecula inionfortunam binearisq[ue h]ort[isque*. Cf. Babrius 11.1 ἀλώπεκ᾽ ἐχθρὴν ἀμπέλων τε καὶ κήπων. On *bulpecula*, see above, on 1. *Binearis* is of some interest. If the restoration of the end of the line is correct (and the Greek suggests that it is), then *binearis* (= *uineariis*) must be a substantivised adjective translating ἀμπέλων. The origin of the substantivisation lies in the ellipse of *hortus* in the adjective-noun combination *hortus uinearius* (found in the plural at *Dig.* 50.16.198 = 'vineyards'). *Vinearius* is indeed reflected in this sense in Prov. *vinier* (see *REW* 9352). It is therefore likely that the translator had encountered the usage in spoken Latin.

Inionfortunam should almost certainly be read as *importunam* (= ἐχθρήν). The word is well attested in comparable senses in reference to animals: see *TLL* VII.1.664.1 ff. (quoting this passage).

---

[20] As a general principle it may be suggested that an irregular verb-form will tend to be maintained if it is in common use; but if it is rare it is more likely to be replaced. This point will be developed further later in this chapter. On 'frequency' and the issues it raises, see now Bybee and Hopper (2001).

[21] For the latter two participles, see Marx (1906–8: 88).

[22] *Fero* in classical Latin has the fairly neutral meaning 'carry away' (*OLD* s.v. 35), but *tollo* the unambiguous meaning 'steal' (*OLD* s.v. 11). An example such as that at *Tab. Sulis* 47.3 (*si liber hoc tulerit*), which in the context refers to theft, could just be interpreted as part of the verb *fero*, but in the translation of Babrius the association with *tollo* is made explicit by the Greek. See further Ihm (1902: 149 n. 2), Adams (1995b: 565).

[23] On which passage see Russo (1964: 95) ad loc. See further e.g. Hofmann and Szantyr (1965: 554), Petersmann (1977: 267). A freedman at Petron. 50.7 says *quid* for *quod*, a usage which editors (e.g. K. Müller (1995), following Muncker) tend to emend away (but see Petersmann (1977: 269)).

10 *peregrina uolens circomitti quis saeui[tia.* Further translationese. The word order is identical to that of the Greek (11.2 ξένη θελήσας περιβαλεῖν τις αἰκείη), and *quis* has been pressed into service to translate τις. *Quis* can of course be indefinite (e.g. after *si* or *ne*), but here it was *quidam* which was required. This, like *quomodo enim* above, could be classified as an interference error.

11 *codam su[c]census et linei quidem a[ll]igatus.* The writer uses the phonetic spelling *codam = caudam,* another indication of his familiarity with spoken Latin. He construes it ineptly as object of what is strictly a passive participle. Educated Latin had *linea* or *lineus* (adjective). Here we have a substantivised neuter adjective *lineum* (which is attested in the *Vetus Latina* and a few times elsewhere in later Latin: *TLL* VII.2.1442.77ff.). *Linei quidem* renders λίνου τι. *Quidem* has been confused with *quid(d)am,* if the reading is correct.

12 *sinuit fu[ge]re [h]anc speculator genius malus.* On *sinuit,* see above, n. 6. *Speculator genius malus* translates ἐπίσκοπος δαίμων (11.4). Of note here is the idiomatic use of a noun in -*tor* virtually with adjectival/participial function. Such uses of substantives in -*tor* (originating in appositions) are associated particularly with translation literature and colloquial texts under the Empire.[24] Ihm (1902: 151) notes again that a rendering (of δαίμων by *genius*) can be paralleled in glossaries (see *CGL* III.290.54) (see further the case cited at 18 below).

13 *infra aruras missuro procedebat,* renders εἰς τὰς ἀρούρας τοῦ βαλόντος ὡδήγει (11.5). This line is full of oddities. *Missuro* = βαλόντος has been commented on above. *Infra,* translating εἰς + accusative, has been confused with *intra* + accusative, a familiar conflation in substandard Latin.[25] The translator presumably did not know a Latin equivalent of ἀρούρας, and he accordingly retained the Greek word, which had no currency in Latin. Retentions (or, one might say, code-switches prompted by a writer's or speaker's ignorance of the *mot juste*) are a feature of imperfect second-language learning (see 3.II).

The transitive use of *procedebat* (ὡδήγει) is unlikely to have had any basis in genuine Latin. The translator could not come up with an appropriate transitive verb.

14f. *erat autem tempus sectilis / et pulcheri fructus spaearum sorsus.* Cf. Babrius 11.6f. ἦν δὲ ληίων ὥρη, / ποίη δὲ καλλίκαρπος ἐλπίδων πλήρης. The syntax of *sectilis* is problematical. Is it, like *lineum* above (11), a substantivised adjective (i.e. a form *sectile*), or alternatively an adjective in

---

[24] See Hofmann and Szantyr (1965: 157–8).
[25] See, e.g. Hofmann and Szantyr (1965: 231), with bibliography, and *TLL* VII.1.1485.4ff.

agreement with *fructus*? On the first interpretation the Latin could be made to match the structure of the Greek, in which a colon ends at ὥρη, and the sentence continues with a new nominative phrase. If the Latin is to be given the same structure as the Greek, *pulcheri fructus* would have to be in the nominative plural. It is alternatively possible that the translator has compressed two cola into one, with *sectilis et pulcheri* a pair of genitive adjectives agreeing with *fructus*. Whether *sectilis* is taken thus, or as a neuter substantive (which on balance seems more plausible, given the Greek), it must refer to a crop fit for reaping. *Secare* survives in Romance as a specialised verb = 'reap' (It. *segare*). Perhaps the writer was familiar with this use of the verb, and had it in mind when attempting to translate ληίων.

The -*er* adjectives of the second declension tended to assume a -*us* ending which either replaced -*er* or was attached to it, as in *pulcheri*. Note on the one hand *Appendix Probi* 138 *teter non tetrus*, and on the other (possibly) *CIL* IV. 2250 *miserus* = *miser*.[26]

I cannot explain *sorsus* (= πλήρης).

16 *oportet ergo serenae magis aut inaequa irasci*. This corresponds to Babrius 11.10 χρὴ πρᾶον εἶναι μηδ' ἄμετρα θυμοῦσθαι, but is neither syntactic nor meaningful as it stands. The text must be corrupt: it is noteworthy that here for once there is not a word for word correspondence between original and translation, and that at least raises the possibility that something has gone wrong with the text. *Haut* would be an improvement on *aut*, and *esse serenum* would render πρᾶον εἶναι (taking *ergo* as a corruption of *esse*).

17 *nec uidit eius ariis Cereris*. This line is out of position: it should precede 16. It obviously corresponds to Babrius 11.9 οὐδ' εἶδεν αὐτοῦ τὴν ἅλωα Δημήτηρ, but again it is not meaningful. *Cereris* should be subject, and *ariis* object, of *uidit*. Should we emend to *aream Ceres*, assuming a corruption, or put the wording down to the incompetence of the writer? I return briefly to the matter of corruption in such a text in the conclusion to this section.

18 *est quidam ira ultricis quem custodianus*. In *ira ultricis* the translator seems to have reversed the order of the components of the original expression. The Greek ὀργῆς νέμεσις means 'retribution for anger', but the Latin phrase means 'anger of Nemesis', a sense which is established by Ihm's observation (1902: 151) that *ultrix* and νέμεσις are equated in a glossary (*CGL* II.201.37). It is unclear why the reversal has taken place. The antecedent of the masculine relative *quem* (= ἥν) is feminine. The masculine

---

[26] The reading is not absolutely certain (see *TLL* VIII.1100.2).

form of the relative pronoun was to displace the feminine, and *qui* for *quae* is not uncommon in substandard texts.[27]

19 *ipsismet ipsis nocentiam ferentes animosali[bus.* Cf. Babrius 11.12 αὐτοῖς βλάβην φέρουσα τοῖς δυσοργήτοις. *Ipsismet ipsis* corresponds to αὐτοῖς. On *ferentes*, see above. *Nocentia* is quoted by Lewis and Short only in the sense 'guilt' (Tertullian; cf. *nocens, in-nocentia*), but here, translating βλάβην, it has been associated semantically with its verbal root (*noceo* 'harm'). The writer's source was a bilingual glossary: note *CGL* II.257.51 *no[n]centia* βλάβη.

Animosali[bus], = δυσοργήτοις, is an augmented form of *animosus*. The suffix -*alis* (like various other stress-bearing adjectival suffixes) was sometimes used in substandard Latin to augment an existing adjective without change of meaning (e.g. *aestiualis* = *aestiuus*).[28] Either *animosalis* was the translator's own coinage, in which case it would display some feeling for Vulgar Latin word formation, or it was a popular, subliterary form.

Alongside the imperfect learning discussed in the first part of this chapter, exemplified particularly in the poor command of non-finite verb-forms, and some additional cases of bizarre usage illustrated in the commentary (e.g. *dormisset, procedebat, sectilis*), we have been able to identify on the one hand a few idiomatic or inventive usages not determined by the Greek original (*enectus* 'starving', the metaphorical use of *frigidus* (-*tus*)), and on the other a good deal of Latinity of a type which, though not classical, might have had a place in substandard colloquial varieties of the language (the expressive gemination seen in *luppus* and *luppa*, various diminutives, *spaearum, tulitus, uinearius* (substantive), *sinuit, infra* = *intra*, *quis* = *qui, quem* = *quam*, the form *pulcheri, animosalis*). There are also usages which display crass interference from Greek, as *quomodo enim*. I conclude that the translator was a Greek who spoke a reduced form of colloquial Latin. In the chapter on Egypt we saw (5.VII.3, VIII) evidence for Greek learners of Latin grafting Latin literacy on to a (limited) knowledge of spoken, as distinct from literary, Latin, and the translator of Babrius belongs to the same category, though his Latin morphology was especially imperfect. In speech, it was suggested above, he would have resorted to avoidance strategies to conceal the inadequacies of his morphological knowledge, restricting himself for example to active, finite verb-forms. If he had first learnt some Latin as a spoken language, he must then have moved on to the acquisition of literacy and to more formal learning of the

---

[27] See Hofmann and Szantyr (1965: 440), E. Löfstedt (1911: 132), and for new (early) evidence of the phenomenon, Adams (1995a: 101).

[28] See, e.g. Adams (1995b: 530–41).

language. The present exercise, with its rather literary flavour, suggests that he might have been receiving some instruction, and that impression is reinforced by the clear signs that he was using a glossary.

There can be no doubt that the translator was a primary speaker of Greek attempting to learn Latin, rather than a primary speaker of Latin attempting to learn Greek. If he had been a learner of Greek, one would have expected errors of translation but meaningful Latin verb morphology. The non-Latin, active use of a whole set of perfect participles could not possibly be the work of a native speaker of Latin, who would inevitably have used present active participles to render Greek aorist actives. Nor would a native Latin speaker have perpetrated such things as *missuro* = βαλόντος, transitive *procedebat*, *quis* = τις etc.

The errors in the text must sometimes have been due to textual corruption (as we have seen above), and it therefore has to be assumed that the extant text is not in the hand of the translator but is a copy of someone else's translation. There is nothing surprising about this; there is at least one other exercise extant (*P. Ness.* 1) in which a scribe was copying an earlier text and introducing corruptions.[29] But the Latinity of *P. Amh.* II.26 cannot simply be explained as the consequence of corruption. Forms such as *auditus* and *putatus* reflect unmistakably a poor knowledge of Latin morphology: they are correct in form but not function, and could not under any circumstances be put down merely to scribal corruption. If an incompetent scribe is to be brought into the picture, there was certainly as well an incompetent translator in the background, and his efforts shine through a certain amount of surface corruption.

I have concentrated particularly on verb morphology, because it is in that area that the writer's deficiencies are most marked. The translation may be compared with the letter of Phonen in Greek which was discussed in an earlier chapter (1.IX (1)). In that too the writer's imperfect morphology can be classified quite precisely. He had begun by learning the present tense, in which he had a good command of the endings, but in the aorist he knew only the stems, and generally used a single morpheme for all of the persons in both numbers. The imperfections of the translator of Babrius do not match exactly those of Phonen, but they are similar. He knew finite forms of verbs adequately, but in the non-finite forms his performance is chaotic.

[29] See Casson and Hettich (1950: 12), noting that it 'is better to assume that he [i.e. the writer of the Latin-Greek glossary of the *Aeneid*, *P.Ness* 1] was almost certainly innocent of Latin and relatively illiterate in Greek, and that he was copying from a worn and faulty exemplar'.

It would be wrong to imply that all native users of a language employ the full range of (e.g.) verb morphology. Where Latin was concerned the active is far more common in many texts than the passive, and not all Latin verb morphology was to pass into the Romance languages. There is some correlation between the frequency in colloquial texts of a verbal category, and its survival into Romance. An infrequent category, such as the gerund, was less likely to survive than a form in frequent use (see n. 20 above).

To put the verb usage of the translator of Babrius into perspective, I am now going to examine the verb morphology of Claudius Terentianus. In his writing too some verbal categories are far more frequent than others, and in those that are infrequent there is a greater degree of error. But Terentianus' 'errors' cannot be ascribed to imperfect learning of a second language; they are rather to be related to features of colloquial usage and can be seen as foreshadowing developments in Romance. The errors in the translation discussed above will emerge in the course of the comparison as of a different order.

II VERB-MORPHOLOGY IN CLAUDIUS TERENTIANUS AND SOME VINDOLANDA TEXTS

An unsatisfactory feature of almost all work on 'Vulgar Latin' is that there is a concentration on usages, morphology, spellings, syntax etc. regarded as aberrational by the standards of classical Latin, with little attempt to assess the degree of overlap between the language of a text seen as 'sub-standard', and that of a classical text. There is much to be said for putting aberrations in perspective by relating their frequency to that of non-aberrational forms, and by identifying those areas (e.g. of morphology and syntax) in which aberrations are most often found. Such an approach will be adopted in this section, and the significance of Terentianus' deviations from the 'norm' (as represented in classical texts) will be further assessed by means of a comparison of his Latinity with that of some contemporary documents from the opposite end of the Empire (letters from Vindolanda). This evidence will then be related to that of the translation.

I consider here the verb-morphology of Terentianus, taking statistics from the best preserved letters, *P. Mich.* VIII.467, 468, 469 and 471. The aim will be as much to identify areas in which his correspondence with educated norms is most marked, as to find those areas in which he had less control over the morphology which might have been used by an educated writer.

Finite verbs, active and passive

I give statistics here for verb-forms correctly used, first in the indicative and then in the subjunctive.

	Indicative	
	active	passive
present	54	I
future	7	I
imperfect	4	–
perfect	27	5
future perfect	4	–
pluperfect	I	–
totals	97	7

Various observations may be made about these statistics.

(1) The only genuine synthetic passive form is *adfertur* at 467.24. I have included as a future 'passive' *uidebitur* at 468.24, but it is of course a deponent, without a conspicuous passive semantic function. Similarly a deponent is included among the five perfect passives (467.8 *optime scis et tu quantum col[legis suis m]entitus*), but it is odd that there is no auxiliary, and the reconstruction of the text is no better than a guess (read *sit* for *suis?*). The genuine (periphrastic) perfect passives are *postae sunt* (467.23), *sublata mi s[unt]* (468.13), *inu[e]ntus est* (468.44) and *factam est* (471.27). Particularly interesting among these is that at 468.13: *et me iacentem in liburna sublata mi s[unt]*. I take it that *sublata* here is focussed, and that the enclitic pronoun has been attached to the focal term, thereby effecting a separation of the participle from its auxiliary. This type of separation (though not necessarily with an enclitic pronoun acting as the separating element) sometimes occurs in classical prose when the participial element of the periphrastic passive is strongly emphatic.[30] The Latin of Terentianus at this point has an idiomatic look to it.

(2) At 468.39 *fiet* may be a vulgarism for *fit*,[31] though I am less confident about that interpretation than I once was. In any case it has been omitted from the above table because it is not passive in the strict morphological sense.

(3) There is a correctly constructed periphrastic future-equivalent at 467.23, *missurus es*.

(4) It should be noted in passing that, though there is one example of a periphrastic future-equivalent, the synthetic future is still very much

---

[30] See Adams (1994b: 40–2).   [31] See Adams (1977: 51).

in use. The replacement of the inflected future by *habeo* + infinitive is a development which, though its seeds were sown relatively early, very much belonged to late Latin or even beyond.[32] It is though noticeable that in one place what looks like a future form is used where a present tense was intended: 471.33 *ueni*, **dicet**, *Alexandrie et dabo t[i]bi*. This misspelling of the present reflects the merger in spoken Latin of CL long *e* and short *i* as a close *e*, with the *e*-spelling representing the new pronunciation of short *i*. So in 468 the forms *uolueret* (36) and *aiutaueret* (41) are written for *uoluerit* and *aiutauerit*. Similar misspellings are common at Pompeii.[33] In the early period such misspellings are often as here located in final syllables, where the merger may have begun.[34]

	Subjunctive	
	active	passive
present	26	I
imperfect	3	–
perfect	–	–
pluperfect	I	–
totals	30	I

The only passive form is *mute[t]ur* (467.24).

What most stands out in these two tables is the great preponderance of active forms over passive (127: 8), and the handful of passives would be further reduced if deponents were excluded. Most of the genuine passives are not synthetic forms, but periphrastic perfects. It has been observed that passive verbs are relatively infrequent outside high literature (in which their frequency depends on the type of text and various pragmatic factors),[35] and that impression is abundantly confirmed by these figures. Moreover the synthetic passive was a casualty in the transition from Latin to the Romance languages,[36] in which the passive represents an expansion and reinterpretation of the Latin periphrastic passive formation. It will be seen that the practice of Terentianus offers an illuminating background to these developments. The inflected passive was virtually not in use in his idiolect. If his practice reflected that of ordinary speakers over a long period it is not difficult to see why the inflected passive should have been lost. It is no doubt significant that it is the periphrastic formation which shows signs of continued vitality, not only in the sense that it does

---

[32] It is interesting to note that the future periphrasis ἔχω + infinitive occurs in one of the Greek letters of Terentianus (476.12): see the editors ad loc.

[33] See Väänänen (1966: 22).

[34] There is a cluster of such examples in the unpublished Vindolanda letter Inv. no. 1575.

[35] See E. Löfstedt (1956: II. 71), Väänänen (1981: 129).   [36] See e.g. Vincent (1988: 47–8).

turn up from time to time, but also in that in one place it is employed in a non-mechanical, pragmatically determined manner.

The predominance of the active over the passive in Terentianus certainly does not mean that he was an imperfect learner of Latin, because, as we will see (below), the same phenomenon is to be found in colloquial texts from elsewhere in the Empire. However, the virtual non-existence of passive forms in Terentianus does put in perspective the inability of learners to use such forms. A Greek learning Latin as a spoken language would not on this evidence often be confronted by the passive. It can also be assumed that those formally instructing Greeks in Latin would not give a high priority to the teaching of the passive.

I turn now by way of comparison to some Vindolanda letters, those which make up the archive of Cerialis (*Tab. Vindol.* II. 225–90). These, consisting of letters both by Cerialis and to him, have the advantage that they can, up to a point, be placed socially. The writers belonged to the officer class at Vindolanda.

	Indicative	
	active	passive
present	28	2
future	4	–
imperfect	–	–
perfect	12	3
future perfect	2	–
pluperfect	3	–
totals	49	5

	Subjunctive	
present	21	I
imperfect	2	–
perfect	I	–
pluperfect	–	–
totals	24	I

The similarity between the archives of Cerialis and Terentianus is striking. Despite the fact that the correspondence of Cerialis belongs to a higher social milieu than that of Terentianus, there is the same overwhelming preponderance of active over passive verb-forms. Any possibility that the frequency of passives in Terentianus might be attributed to imperfect learning of Latin as a second language is thus out of the question: the passive simply did not have much currency below the level of the high literary language. All of the passive forms in the Cerialis archive are either present-tense forms, or periphrastic perfects, and this distribution matches closely that in Terentianus. Again there is evidence that the synthetic future was still in use, but again there is an example of the periphrastic substitute comprising *-urus* + *esse* (248 *acturus es*).

I turn now to *errors* (by classical standards) in the verb morphology of Terentianus. These may be classified into five categories:

(1) The irregular verb *possum* has a first-person present indicative form *posso* at 469.15.

(2) At 468.40 *ualeo* is given the third-person present indicative form *ualunt* for *ualent*.

(3) There are three errors in future infinitive forms. Twice in future active infinitives the participial component is incorrect by the norms of classical Latin (468.22 *missiturum*, 37 *[u]iciturum* = *uicturum*), and at 468.38, where the sense requires a future passive infinitive, the present passive is used instead (*[tra]nsferri*).

(4) In 471.31 the bizarre form *exiendo* is used where the sense requires a dative of the present participle: *attonitus exiendo dico illi* (cf. earlier (26) *Saturninus iam paratus erat* **exire**; in the first passage quoted *illi* refers to Saturninus). I take it that Terentianus did not make a clear distinction between the present participle in an oblique case form, and a 'gerund' form; though that 'gerund' is morphologically incorrect, because the dative/ablative form in classical Latin would have been *exeundo*.

(5) The form *collexi* (471.12) is a typical substandard remodelling of a long-vowel perfect.[37] It is a similar type of vulgarism to *sinui* in the translation of Babrius.

No errors of these or other types are found in the Cerialis archive. I conclude then that Terentianus' Latin *was* substandard when assessed alongside another specimen of non-literary military Latin of the same period, and that its non-standard appearance cannot merely be attributed to superficial misspellings inflicted by scribes.

The substandard features in verb morphology are not, however, peculiar to Terentianus or to texts from Egypt. They can constantly be brought into line with phenomena attested elsewhere (in the west as well as the east), and it can also be argued (from Romance evidence) that it was precisely in a number of these areas of verb morphology that one would expect to find errors. This point will be further explained below. I conclude therefore that the deviations listed above in Terentianus were

---

[37] See Adams (1977: 53).

in no sense oddities or 'learners' errors', but must have been common-place. They are indicative of various pressures exerted on the Latin of those below a certain educational level. These pressures came partly from analogy, but a crucial factor serving as the background to some of the errors was the fact that various verbal categories were scarcely in use in everyday Latin. Writers such as Terentianus who were not conversant with the literary language were clearly prone to analogical 'errors' within these categories.

I take then the errors in turn, offering some explanations and relating them to comparable phenomena elsewhere.

(1) Random, non-systematic regularisation of parts of irregular verbs was a widespread phenomenon, by no means peculiar to Terentianus. Examples have been collected elsewhere in this book (5.VII.2.2, p. 613).

(2) *-unt* for *-ent* (as *ualunt*) in second-conjugation verbs is not confined to Terentianus, nor was it an ephemeral phenomenon. *Debunt* is used repeatedly at Vindolanda in the *renuntium* reports, which there is reason to think were written by *optiones*, and there is now a case of *habunt* in a letter at Vindolanda written by a *decurio*.[38] By contrast in an account at Vindolanda the correct form *debent* is used (181). It would seem that various lower-ranking officers at Vindolanda were in the habit of saying *-unt* for *-ent*.

In no sense does this represent a wholesale conflation of the second and third conjugations. It must be significant that in different parts of the Empire it is the third person plural form *-unt* which is implicated. By contrast in another person (469.20 *habemus*) Terentianus was able to use the conventional inflection of the second-conjugation verb.

It may not be fanciful to see an analogy between the use of *-unt*, and the source of the *-ons* ending in the first person plural of French verbs of whatever conjugation. *chantons* for example, must derive from a form **cantumus*. Since the only verbs in classical Latin which had an *-umus* ending were *sumus*, its compound *possumus*, and the auxiliaries *uolumus* and *nolumus*, it is possible that, at least in French, the *-umus* ending of a small group of frequently used auxiliaries was generalised to other verbs.[39]

Could it be significant that the small group of verbs so far attested in early texts with the *-unt* ending for *-ent* are all themselves auxiliaries, or at least have auxiliary uses (*debunt, ualunt, habunt*)? Had they, in some

---

[38] For the text see Bowman and Thomas (1996: 324) (Inv. no. 93.1544, lines 13–15 *ceruesam commilitones non habunt quam rogo iubeas mitti*); see also Adams (1995a: 102–3).

[39] See Elcock (1960: 121–2).

varieties of Latin up to a certain social level, taken on the ending of *sunt?* In this connection I draw attention to a curious use of *habeo* in Terentianus: 467.18 *nem[i]nem* **habeo enim** *karum nisi secundum deos te.* What is odd here is that *enim* is forced into third position by *habeo.* In other words, the colourless verb *habeo* has behaved as a clitic. Similarly the verb 'to be' can even in classical prose take precedence over *enim.*[40] Here then is a point of contact between the verbs *esse* and *habere* which may help to explain how by analogy one acquired an ending of the other, though it has to be acknowledged that there are serious uncertainties in any attempt to explain *habunt,* etc. It is though clear that there is nothing overly peculiar about Terentianus' *ualunt.* Fr. *ont* reflects a form **aunt* (< *habunt*).[41]

The *-unt* ending in second conjugation verbs is reflected in Italian,[42] whereas in Spanish it is *-ent* which has survived.[43] In Provençal *-ent* was the predominating form, with *-unt* an occasional variant.

However *ualunt* and the like are to be explained, we may conclude, first, that, at least in this early period, it was only the third-person plural, present indicative form of second conjugation verbs that was subject to modification,[44] and secondly that this was by no means a phenomenon peculiar to Egypt. The evidence from Vindolanda shows that the intrusion of *-unt* into the second declension was commonplace in the speech of military officers below the highest level. The phenomenon provides evidence of the piecemeal way in which linguistic change takes place. There has been no sudden and systematic readjustment of verb-morphology, such as a conflation of two conjugations; change has affected just one ending.

(3) No fewer than three of Terentianus' verbal errors involve the use of the future infinitive, both active and passive. What is significant here is that the CL future participle and infinitive did not survive into Romance.[45] If Terentianus could make a number of errors in this one verbal category, that would seem to imply that, like the inflected passive, this category was not widely used beneath the high literary language; and if a category was not in widespread use, it was likely eventually to be eliminated. The practice of Terentianus can thus be seen as a general background to Romance developments, if not as anticipating them in precise details.

---

[40] See Watt (1980).   [41] See Elcock (1960: 128).
[42] Elcock (1960: 123).   [43] Elcock (1960: 120–1).
[44] At a later period things might have been different. See, e.g. Väänänen (1981: 136) on the form *misco,* a thorough-going alternative to *misceo* in some texts.
[45] See Elcock (1960: 110), Vincent (1988: 48).

Once again Terentianus' errors can be paralleled elsewhere. A modified future active infinitive form is found in Petronius (*uinciturum = uicturum*
at 45.10), and the use of the present passive infinitive for the future passive
is widespread.[46]

It is a curiosity that Terentianus constructs the periphrastic future indicative *missurus es* (467.23) with a correct form of the future participle,
but that when the future infinitive of the same verb is used the incorrect
missiturum is adopted. What is to be made of this inconsistency? It might
seem logical to deduce that Terentianus did not equate the -*urus* form
used in the future finite periphrasis with that used in the infinitive. Or
was there a different input from different scribes? Was the -*urus* participle kept alive (in certain verbs) chiefly through its use in finite future
periphrases, whereas the infinitival use was all but dead, with the participle form exposed to analogical remodelling by the uneducated whenever
an attempt was made to use a future infinitive?

The learner who attempted to translate Babrius into Latin made an
error of a different type in using the future participle of the same verb.
He wrote the form *missuro*, which is morphologically correct, but since it
translates the aorist active participle βαλόντος the writer clearly had no
understanding of the function of the -*urus* form.

(4) *Exiendo = exeunti* cannot be paralleled, and is not easy to account
for. This is the only 'gerund(ive)' form in the letters and it does not
have a proper gerund(ive) function, but appears to function as a present
participle in the dative case. It may be relevant that there survived into
Romance only a single gerund form, technically an (instrumental) ablative (in -*do*), which ousted the present participle?[47] The encroachment of
the ablative of the gerund on the present participle (in subject function)
is already apparent in classical Latin,[48] but there is a difference between
our case, where *exiendo* has to be given a dative function, and a case
such as Vitr. 2. 8. 20 **recipientes** *umorem turgescunt, deinde* **siccescendo**
contrahuntur, where the ablative *siccescendo* is interchangeable with a
nominative present participle. Could it be that *exiendo* has been used as
a sort of fossilised present-participle equivalent, with a dative function
in the context?

However it is to be explained, this usage does seem to reveal an uncertainty on Terentianus' part in the general area of the gerund(ive) / present

---

[46] See Hofmann and Szantyr (1965: 358).
[47] See, e.g. Elcock (1960: 111), Väänänen (1981: 140). For an explanation of the form along these
lines, see B. Löfstedt (1983: 460).
[48] See Väänänen (1981: 140).

participle, which would fit in with the reduction in gerund / present participle uses in the Romance languages, and with the conflation of the two categories.

Terentianus uses only two present participles (in the formal, morphological sense), *iacentem* at 468.13, where the construction is confused,[49] and *pergentes* at 470.21.

III CONCLUSIONS

Terentianus had a good command of verb morphology, certainly in the active voice. The disappearance of the inflected passive by the time of the Romance languages must be related to its lack of currency in ordinary, non-literary Latin over many centuries.

Terentianus' deviations from classical norms in verb morphology suggest various conclusions:

(1) These are sufficient to show that Terentianus' Latin belongs some way down the social scale (and the parallels to be found at Vindolanda in the letter of a *decurio*, and in some documents probably written by *optiones*, should be recalled); it is not the 'correct' educated standard buried beneath superficial spelling errors inflicted by scribes.

(2) Most of his deviations are analogical (*posso, collexi, ualunt*). They do not reflect major remodelling of the verb system, but marginal regularisations or remodellings of one kind or another.

(3) It is possible to parallel most of these deviations elsewhere, both in Egypt and beyond. These are deviations belonging to the real, non-literary, language, and not to some artificial 'learners'' variety peculiar to Egypt.

(4) Various errors affect areas of verb morphology the components of which, in their classical form, were not to survive in the Romance languages: future infinitives, active and passive, and the present participle in an oblique case. It might be suggested (*a*) that where a verbal category was not in widespread use, it was more likely to generate errors in those unversed in the literary language who were attempting to use it; and (*b*) that such verbal categories, unsupported by currency, were likely either to disappear or to be modified in some way.

There is a superficial similarity between Terentianus' verb morphology and that of the learner who translated the two fables of Babrius into Latin. The learner was only able to use active (finite) forms of verbs

[49] See Adams (1977: 53).

correctly, and, like Terentianus, when he attempted to use non-finite forms he committed errors of various kinds. But the similarities should not be exaggerated, because the degree of error is much higher in the translation. Whereas Terentianus' deviations reflect a living colloquial language, the deviations perpetrated by the translator, despite the signs in his Latin of some exposure to the colloquial language, betray extensive ignorance of basic Latin forms and their functions. Terentianus' non-standard forms are meaningful and explicable from analogy, and may well have been more widespread in everyday Latin than their classical counterparts, whereas errors such as the use of passive participles in the active show that the translator did not understand an area of the verb system. Terentianus by contrast regularly uses perfect participles correctly in the passive, either in periphrastic passive formations or in pure participial functions (467.17, 23, 468.9, 13, 471.22, 27). Terentianus was a fluent speaker of a non-standard variety of Latin which hints at things to come in the transition to Romance, whereas the translator was a learner who had not progressed far in the second language.

9

Some concluding remarks

I INTRODUCTION

In this final chapter I refer briefly to some of the themes scattered through-out the book without attempting to be comprehensive. Other topics, such as accommodation, regional variation determined by language contact, language mixing etc. are discussed particularly in the concluding sections to various chapters, and can be followed up through the index.

II IDENTITY

It is often argued in linguistic literature that language is the most impor-tant marker of identity that there is (see e.g. Crystal (2000: 40)). Even monolinguals living in a monolingual society where they have little or no contact with other languages may be conscious that it is their lan-guage which gives them a special identity in the world. The English, for example, constantly express pride in their language, and in doing so they are implicitly presenting the English language as one of the markers of their achievements as a people. Attempts by the French to eliminate 'Franglais' from the French language are reported with alacrity in the British press, with the implication that the English language is now doing what the English people have ceased to do, that is colonising foreign terri-tory. The fading of French as an international educated language in the face of English is reported from time to time with satisfaction. Articles in the press regularly speak of the 'richness' and 'subtlety' of English, usually without acknowledgment that the 'richness' of its vocabulary is largely due to its reception of foreign loan-words over a long period. If English is rich, other languages are by implication less rich, and this English richness enhances the native speaker's feeling of cultural dominance and hence of his special place in the world.

This book is overwhelmingly about identity, and that is because bilin-guals of different types are often particularly aware of the conflicts of identity determined by their belonging to more than one speech community. The peoples who turn up in the book were sometimes passing from one language to another, or were under pressure to do so. Sometimes they had acquired (or were in the process of acquiring) a second language which did not replace, but stood alongside, their primary language in a variety of relationships. Depending on the circumstances of their acquisition of the second language, their language attitudes, social circumstances and a variety of other factors, bilingual speakers may variously be conscious of their identity as fluent users of a second language, or proud of the new (dual) identity that the second language gives them, or worried about the potential loss of an aspect of their identity (at a time of language shift), and so on. The defiant use of an Hispanic language during interrogation under torture by a Spaniard hostile to the Romans as reported by Tacitus (see 2.x) reveals a resistance to Romanisation as symbolised by language use: here was a speaker determined not to move an inch towards abandoning his inherited linguistic identity. More often speakers under Roman rule accepted the new alongside the old. The inclusion of an Oscan formula (e.g. *brat. datas*) in an inscription otherwise in Latin (see 2.II.3) can be interpreted as an attempt to hold on to an older identity at a time of language shift. Jews in the west probably knew in most cases little or no Hebrew, but a Hebrew tag such as *shalom* at the end of a text in Greek or Latin effectively symbolises the Jewishness of the writer or referent (see 2.VIII, p. 271). All over the Empire Palmyrenes serving in the Roman army left funerary inscriptions in Aramaic (2.VII.2), as well as Latin, despite the fact that recruits into the Roman army from non-Latin speaking regions were usually submerged linguistically. To Palmyrenes the language Aramaic was a strong marker of ethnic identity. It did not matter that in the places where such Aramaic inscriptions have turned up they would not have been understood. On the other hand those Greek- or vernacular-speaking soldiers who were commemorated partly or wholly in Latin, as was constantly the case, were symbolising an acquired professional identity rather than their ethnic origins. Professional identities we have seen marked by the use of one language (associated with the profession) alongside another (as in bilingual military inscriptions, or in doctors' inscriptions with a Greek version), or by code-switching from the everyday language into key terms of the 'professional' language.

Identity as expressed through language comes out particularly in the usage of names. The dedication to the Etruscan deity Turan made in the Etruscan language but with the name of the dedicator in Greek and Greek script (see 2.III.3) reveals the dedicator's determination to retain both his ethnic and linguistic identity in an alien environment. There is a comparable dedication at Carthage (see 2.V.5.1), the main part of which is in Punic, but with the name of the dedicator in Greek and Greek script. At a time of language shift in a bilingual community names are a significant indicator of the sense of identity of their bearers. As a language dies the names of those with roots in the old culture tend to be changed in various ways. New names belonging to the new language may replace the old, or old names may be adapted morphologically to the new language. If a speaker shifts to the new language and changes the inflection of his name (or the name itself) as well, he has become partly or fully assimilated to the new culture. On the other hand during a language change he may resist full assimilation, by keeping for example the original inflection of his name even when using the new language. Greek women in the western Empire constantly have their Greek names inflected as Greek even in Latin inscriptions. There are Latin inscriptions from the Venetic territory (see 2.II.3, p. 143) which sometimes have personal names inflected as Venetic, and sometimes as Latin. Those of the first type reveal the bearer's unwillingness to abandon entirely his inherited linguistic identity, and the mixture of languages has the effect of giving him a mixed identity. Alternatively in bilingual communities a person may have two names or sets of names, one appropriate to one of his languages and the other to the other (see 2.III.6 on double names among the Etruscans, and particularly 2.V.5.1 on the situation in north Africa, where changes in naming practices can be plotted across several generations in certain families). The use of two languages (expressing names) side by side to give the referents a mixed identity is perhaps nowhere clearer than in the coin legends on issues from towns of Punic origin under the Roman Empire (see 2.V.3). The use of neo-Punic in naming the town subtly draws attention to the Punic origins of the place; whereas the use of Latin in naming the emperor symbolises its acquired Romanness.

Though name-changing and second-language acquisition go hand in hand, chronological primacy cannot necessarily be given to one or the other. In Sardinia there is a pure Punic inscription (see 2.V.4) in which the names are Latin, whereas in some north African inscriptions written in Latin names are mainly Punic (see 2.V.5.3). It is though likely that new names would only have been taken on by those shifting languages.

III DIGLOSSIA

There was not a uniform diglossic relationship between Greek and Latin under the Roman Empire. We have seen as many as four different functional relationships between the two languages dependent on the nature of the community.

First, lower-class Greeks at Rome treated Latin as the language of bureaucracy and Greek as the language of the family (see 3.IV, VIII). This in fact is classic diglossia, with Latin having High function and Greek Low.

It is now well established that the polar opposition H–L, once thought to have great explanatory power, may disguise the subtleties of the hierarchies operating in bilingual societies (see 5.I.3). Whereas those above were first-language speakers of Greek who had moved to the west, first-language speakers of Latin who were running the eastern Empire had a different view of the relationship between the languages. There was no movement to belittle Greek, but Latin was used from time to time to assert Roman political supremacy symbolically, and we have classified it as 'super-high' in relation to the H of Greek. Or to put it another way, there was a tendency at least among administrators in Egypt to define Greek as the language of culture but Latin as the language of political dominance (see 5.I.3, IV.I).

In some military communities in Egypt there seems on the face of it to be bilingualism without diglossia. There is evidence for the same persons writing to the same addressees on the same topics indifferently in Greek and Latin (5.VI.I). We cannot of course know the full circumstances behind such linguistic acts, but in working communities engaged in humdrum physical activities there does seem to have been a degree of convergence between the two languages in the use of clichés, formulaic structures and technical terms which would have made it easy within such closed groups for communication to take place in either language indifferently on mundane practical matters.

Finally, in the archive of Tiberianus, though Terentianus up to a point uses both languages for the same purposes to the same addressee, he does seem to have been treating Greek as the bureaucratic language of civil administration, and Latin as the family language. Thus, within family correspondence to do with official civil matters, it was Greek which was H; but it may be conjectured that Latin could become H if the subject (e.g. a military matter) were different and the addressee a high-ranking soldier rather than his father. Thus the relative status and functions of the two languages were constantly shifting according to the circumstances.

The polar opposition H–L is also implicit in the use of names by the potters at La Graufesenque. Latin names with Latin inflections are used on the makers' stamps on products intended for the outside world, whereas there is a profusion of Celtic names with the Celtic ending *-os* in the material intended only for the consumption of the pottery itself (see 7.IV.2). The potters thus gave themselves a Latin identity for the sake of the outside world, but (often) a Gaulish identity within the pottery; they were thereby setting up a hierarchic relationship between the languages.

IV LANGUAGE ATTITUDES

Under the Empire there is evidence for a wide range of vernacular speakers (and also Greeks) learning Latin (2.XIV.5), but virtually none for Latin speakers learning any language other than Greek, though we cannot know what was happening among ordinary speakers of the type usually excluded from upper-class literature who resided in regions where speakers of vernacular languages were present. In the Republic by contrast upper-class Romans are reported as being students both of Etruscan and Punic (see 2.III.5,V.2), though it would not do to exaggerate Roman knowledge of these languages (particularly Punic); there is after all some evidence for suspicion on the part of the Romans of those such as Carthaginians who were considered to be gifted linguists (see 2.V.2 with n. 381), and that attitude implies an awareness that they themselves were not great language learners. But Etruscan and Punic did have a special place among the languages with which the Romans came into contact, in that both had associated literate cultures and literary works which the Romans in the early period esteemed. Early Italy was far more complex linguistically than it was to become. Nothing is more revealing in this respect than the Pyrgi tablets, which show (by implication) Phoenicians and Etruscans communicating with each other. As far as the Romans are concerned, there was probably a change of attitude during the Republic, as Latin spread and its speakers became more powerful. Henceforth the only language which they evaluated alongside their own was Greek. The contrasting attitudes of the Romans to Greek and to a vernacular language (Gaulish) can be observed in the two trading communities studied in this book, Delos and La Graufesenque (see 6.I). At the first the Romans made various concessions to Greek, whereas at the other the pressure was entirely on Gauls to learn Latin literacy practices and Latin itself. There is no sign of native Latin speakers learning Gaulish. Not that there is any suggestion that compulsion was applied to the Gauls to drop Gaulish, but some instruction in Latin literacy must have been given, and the Gauls themselves must have taken the initiative in responding to the prestige of Latin.

Romans had mixed feelings about Greek. Greek culture and language were admired, but the use of Greek in public, as in a speech, particularly if there were Greeks in the audience, might be considered demeaning, in that it could be interpreted as an act of deference out of key with the political dominance of the Romans (see 3.III.1). In fact the Romans display signs of what can be called 'linguistic insecurity' in their attitude to Latin alongside Greek (see 5.I.3). They were keen to assert their Romanness through the use of the Latin language in their administrative dealings with Greeks from time to time, but this assertiveness goes hand in hand with an underlying sense that Greek might in some way be a 'superior' language (5.I.3). But whatever the attitudes of upper-class Romans to Greek in public when they were acting as representatives of the Roman state (and I am referring to Valerius Maximus 2.2.2, and to the occasional assertive use of Latin in the hearing of Greeks), Delos presents a very different picture. Here Romans were willing to present themselves as integrated into a Greek-speaking society. In the context of trade they were happy to moderate their language use to fit in with their partners, but in more political contexts Latin could be forced on Greeks as a symbolic gesture.

Punic is the one language other than Greek which elicits (up to a point) mixed attitudes from speakers of Latin during the Empire. On the one hand there is some disparagement of Punic speakers who cannot speak fluent Latin (see 2.V.10), but on the other Augustine's attitude, though defensive, is deferential, and he was surely not alone among Latin-speaking African Christians.

There is not a lot of evidence for the language attitudes of vernacular speakers, but we have collected some bits and pieces of information the gist of which is entirely in line with what might have been expected in those provinces or regions which were to undergo language death: there is occasional assertiveness in the use of the vernacular language on the one hand, but an attitude of deference to Latin on the other. At La Graufesenque the use of Latin on makers' stamps implicitly grants Latin the prestige of an international language (7.IV.2). Punic speakers in particular show mixed attitudes to their language. On the one hand the emperor Septimius Severus was embarrassed by his sister's lack of fluency in Latin (2.V.8), an attitude which accords higher prestige to

Latin, but on the other in the early Empire the prominent urban family the Tapapii (see 2.V.5.2), though they had adopted Latin, display signs of language pride in their attempt to keep Punic free from alien elements when Roman officialdom is mentioned. Such language pride was one of the factors lying behind the long currency of the language under Roman rule. Pride in a native language and a feeling of embarrassment about it are in direct opposition; pride fosters language maintenance, whereas embarrassment is one of the factors leading to language death (see Crystal (2000: 81)). For linguistic pride among vernacular speakers during the Roman Empire there is other evidence. Palmyrene soldiers held on to their native tongue while learning Latin. Oscan was used on some coin issues at the time of the Social War (2.II.1), and there is inherent in that act an assertion of identity through language. The Spaniard interrogated under torture defied his inquisitors by speaking his vernacular language at a time of advanced Romanisation in Spain (see above). According to an anecdote in Gellius the poet Ennius evaluated the three languages Latin, Greek and Oscan equally (2.II.1). Attention was sometimes paid to the literary form of Oscan inscriptions. And the *Tabula Bantina* is on the standard view an aggressively 'Oscan' document, in which the choice of language has symbolic intent (2.II.1). Certain Punic (see 2.V.3) and Spanish towns (2.X) display a pride in their earlier linguistic origins. It cannot be assumed that linguistic Romanisation took place without resistance from vernacular speakers, and it was only in the west in any case that language death occurred under Roman influence (see further below, VI).

V LANGUAGE POLICIES

It has been pointed out that 'the nations which are most monolingual in ability and attitude are those with a history of major colonial or religious expansion – their roles, in the West, reflected chiefly in the former or present-day widespread use of Arabic, Dutch, English, French, German, Italian, Potuguese, and Spanish' (Crystal (2000: 45)). Curiously, one cannot accuse the Romans of being monolingual in the administration of their Empire, because, in contrast (e.g.) to the English and French, they operated in two languages, Latin and Greek. Speakers of non-prestigious languages (in Roman eyes) either had to pick up Latin (which happened in the west), or communicate through Greek. What obviously made Greek acceptable was its prominent place in the upper-class Roman education system, and the prestige which it had taken on through its admired literature. Although the Romans asserted themselves linguistically by using Latin under some circumstances in the hearing of Greeks, in no sense did they make the attempt to impose Latin systematically in their eastern administration (see 5.IV). Rather it was used only from time to time symbolically. In the east Greek was generally used by the Romans as a lingua franca (2.VII.5).

Little concession was made to vernacular languages, except in Egypt. The Romans had their emperors represented as pharaohs in Egyptian temples through the medium of the Egyptian language in religious inscriptions, in which the emperor is shown making offerings to Egyptian deities. Romans were always ready to show accommodation in religious contexts by dropping Latin, though in this case there is an element of propaganda as well. This sort of religious accommodation usually only operates if one of the local languages is Greek (see the examples in 5.V); with the exception of the above hieroglyphic texts we do not, as far as I know, find religious dedications in vernacular languages by Romans.

There does not seem to have been an explicit official policy (based on the sort of linguistic nationalism which has often surfaced in the history of Europe) that subject peoples should learn Latin. There was however an expectation that Roman citizens, even if they were Greek speakers, should learn the language, and certain types of documents concerning citizens, for a period at least during the Empire, had to be in Latin, even if the citizen to whom the document applied did not know the language (wills, birth certificates, and various other types of legal text: see 5.IV.5, 5.IV.6). In the west the onus was on locals to learn Latin if they wanted to get on, as their masters treated vernacular languages as if they did not exist.

The question whether Roman policy towards the use of Greek in the administration of the eastern empire changed in time or from one emperor to another is a difficult one given the state of the evidence, and I have preferred to concentrate here on certain timeless attitudes and forms of behaviour (such as the occasional aggressive use of Latin as a symbolic gesture, amid much use of Greek adopted out of simple pragmatism) rather than getting bogged down in the details of individual emperors' policies (or lack thereof). Certainly it became acceptable for citizens to write wills in Greek after 212 (5.IV.6), but I am less than persuaded (see 5.IX) that Diocletian was responsible for a change of policy (a greater insistence on the use of Latin). There is discussion of such matters in Dagron (1969), Kaimio (1979a) and Rochette (1997a), among others.

VI LANGUAGE DEATH

In the last two centuries BC Roman Latin came to be treated particularly by outsiders to the city as a superior variety of the language, and there was a tendency to disparage regional varieties (see 2.II.6, p. 153). There is some comparable evidence for a condescending attitude to Oscan by Latin speakers, though the evidence is slight. The most compelling item is a passage of Lucilius which appears to mock a piece of Oscanised Latin (see in general 2.II.6). The complete disregard, if not open contempt, shown by the Romans (at least under the Empire) for languages other than Greek will have placed great pressure on speakers of vernacular languages to switch to Latin (or Greek) once the Romans had established power in their territories. Septimius Severus' embarrassment about his native language Punic, the public application by the Cumaeans for permission to switch to Latin in certain domains, and the use by the potters of La Graufesenque of Latin for their makers' marks all point to the prestige of Latin in the eyes of vernacular speakers (despite their occasional displays of linguistic nationalism: see above, IV), and it is this attitude, rather than any aggressive policy on the part of the Romans themselves, which provides the background to language death in the western provinces. Worth noting too are the language attitudes of the (Greek) servile class at Rome as revealed by language choice and mixing (3.IV, p. 349). To such Greeks Latin had High status, and that is one reason why they will have been motivated to learn the language, however much they attempted to maintain Greek.

Four bilingual inscriptions set up by Palmyrenes at Rome (see 2.VII.6 for a summary of the details) in various mixtures of Aramaic, Greek and Latin show a correlation between the adoption of Latin and the dropping of various other indicators of Palmyrene identity, such as Palmyrene names and long genealogies. Languages in the process of dying tend to 'lose domains': they come to be used for an ever decreasing range of purposes (see Crystal (2000: 83)). The process can be observed in these Palmyrene bilingual inscriptions, and in some of the other material cited and discussed in Chapter 2. Palmyrenes at Rome used their native language largely in the domain of religion; religion is usually the last domain to be affected in a language shift (Crystal, loc. cit.). Similarly among Jews at Venusia 'Greek' was probably restricted to the domain of funerary commemoration (see I.VII.3, 3.XII.1, 4.V.3.1.2).

VII THE ARMY

The army was polyglot, and it was recognised that there might be problems of communication and cohesion caused by this linguistic diversity (see I.V with n. 61, 2.IX). It is possible that in some auxiliary units the majority of men were not Latin-speaking, but their commanders would have had to know Latin. Interpreters were an important group in the imperial army (2.VII.5 with n. 556, 2.IX), and these will have combined Latin with a variety of languages, such as forms of Germanic and Aramaic (see 2.IX). A German- or Aramaic-speaking interpreter would however almost invariably have been a German or easterner recruited into the army and not a native Latin speaker who had picked up Germanic or Aramaic. Moreover the story from Jerome's *Vita Hilarionis* (2.VII.5) suggests that often (perhaps usually) in eastern areas the army would have communicated with locals through the lingua franca Greek (see too the material from the archive of Babatha cited there), rather than through vernacular languages translated by military interpreters.

While some recruits at low levels might have stuck to their vernacular languages without acquiring much Latin, there is explicit evidence for various language groups in the army, quite apart from Greeks, learning Latin (for Palmyrenes see 2.VII.2, Africans, 2.V.7, Germans, 2.IX, Thracians, 2.XIII; see too 2.IV.3 for Celts). Latin became a marker of Roman military identity for those soldiers who were originally speakers of Greek or of another language. Thus we saw (3.I) the case of the Greek soldier who was commemorated in Greek, but with his rank written in Latin. A Greek soldier writing to another in Greek might attach a Latin greeting to the letter as an acknowledgment of that identity (3.VII), and a soldier addressing a Greek peasant might do so first in Latin to underline his military status.

We have questioned the common belief that Latin was in a sweeping sense the 'official' language of the army (5.VII.1). Certainly there was extensive learning of Latin in the army by foreigners, as we have just mentioned, and among Greek speakers there are signs of different degrees of competence in Latin as a second language (5.VII.3) suggestive of different stages in the process of learning. But that is not to say that Latin was without exception used for official purposes. Greek is constantly used rather than or as well as Latin in documents which are formal or official in content. The same type of document may appear now in Latin and now in Greek, and it is necessary therefore to allow a certain amount of discretion in language choice to record keepers, scribes and others in military communities. But just as in political contexts Latin was sometimes in the hearing of Greeks used to symbolise Roman authority, so in the army, though Greek was the predominating daily language in eastern areas, Latin was available to confer particular authority on the user or to symbolise Roman military identity in the most potent way or to underline under special circumstances the Romanness of the institution. In other words it was capable of use as a super-high language (see above, III) if the user felt that such symbolism was appropriate to the circumstances. The need felt to symbolise Romanness or power will have depended on the attitudes of the participants in a particular transaction and on other extraneous circumstances which we cannot know, and for that reason it is not possible simply to list mechanically documents which had to be in Latin as against those which could be in Greek. Language choice has to be seen as dynamic rather than mechanical, in the sense that it was related to the relationships being negotiated on particular occasions between writer/speaker and addressee.

Language policy in the army is discussed at 5.IX. Vernacular languages such as Palmyrene were not acceptable in formal documents, but Greek often was. The use and learning of Latin might not have been enforced, but some Latin learning was going on even in eastern units which were regularly using Greek. A unit could not get by on Greek alone, because a situation might arise at any time requiring the use of Latin, as for example when Abinnaeus had to appeal to the emperor. Thus it is that we find some official texts in Latin written not by fluent scribes but by imperfect second-language learners.

The Roman army was undoubtedly the most potent force during the Roman Empire behind the learning of Latin by speakers of Greek and vernacular languages, and behind the consequent spread of bilingualism.

VIII SLAVERY

Another institution which was influential in the spread of bilingualism was that of slavery. Although slaves of many nationalities were represented at Rome (see Bang (1910), Gordon (1924), Harris (1980)), Roman households will almost certainly have preferred Greek speakers both because those from (e.g.) Syria, Asia, Lycia and Pamphylia were relatively urbanised, and because Greek, unlike many other languages, was widely understood in the city (see MacMullen (1993: 50–1)). In a large house-hold with numerous Greek-speaking slaves and a *dominus* who knew that language as well, the 'life of service . . . need do little to inculcate Latin or Roman ways' (MacMullen (1993: 51)). There is a passage of Juvenal (see 1.III.1, 3.V, n. 130) which suggests that a *dominus* at Rome would often have had to address a slave in Greek. Because the Roman upper classes esteemed Greek and wanted it taught to their children, the language would often have survived in servile families beyond the generation of immigration, but degrees of bilingualism must eventually have devel-oped. We have seen a good deal of evidence, literary and primary, for servile bilingualism (I refer here to freedmen as well as slaves). At Delos there are slaves and freedmen attested using both languages (see, e.g. 6.1). One of the freedmen in Petronius is a marked code-switcher (see 1.V). Slaves in Plautus sometimes switch into Greek (see 3, n. 100), and also use some distinctive loan-words suggestive of their background (e.g. *cola-phus*: see 3, n. 100). On language mixing in a lower class Roman epitaph (*IGUR* 501) springing from the population of former slaves, see 3.V, p. 363. A letter by a certain Cerinthus (see 3.II (5)) reveals the hand of a Greek slave who had acquired some Latin in imperfect form. Particu-larly noteworthy is a Republican inscription in the name of a freedman the Latin element of which is conspicuously bad (1.IX (5)).

IX 'HELLENISATION' OF THE LATIN LANGUAGE (?)

If the Latin language was indeed 'Hellenised', the processes would not have been homogeneous. A distinction must be made between the native speaker of Latin importing Greek elements into his first language, and the native speaker of Greek importing Greek elements into his second language. Among native speakers of Latin social class must be taken into account: there is no reason why the linguistic behaviour of the educated should have been the same as that of the uneducated. In this book much has been said about both native speakers of Latin and native speakers of Greek, and the evidence considered has also come from different social strata.

I start with the upper classes who spoke Latin as their first language. Hellenising structures were to some extent an optional extra which the speaker or writer could select or reject at will. The speaker whose pro-nunciation of *Amphionem* could not be understood by a *rusticus testis* (1, Appendix, 4.II) switched into a Latinate pronunciation to make himself understood. There is a social dimension to the story, in that an explicit contrast is made between the pronunciation of the rustic and that of the educated orator. The orator's Grecising pronunciation of the Greek name was an affectation which could be dropped if necessary, and the 'Hellenisation' in this case was thus extremely superficial. It also influenced a Greek word and not a Latin, and on this evidence we would not be justified in arguing for any sort of change to the Latin language itself. Nevertheless in the matter of pronunciation there is some evidence for the imposition of Greek sounds even on Latin words (see 1, Appendix). But the evidence makes it clear that such practices were considered artificial and that they were rejected by some as pretentious. A good deal of the Grecising of Latin is artificial in exactly this way. It affects the higher literary genres rather than the speech or writing of the relatively uneducated, it is avoided in some genres and by some educated writers, and it had no lasting effect on Latin as it developed into Romance. To this general category belong above all the imitation of Greek syntactic structures in poetry and poeticising prose (see 4.II), and the humorous use of Greek morphemes on Latin bases, as in *facteon*, *uinoeo* and *betizo*. Such forms were coined in speech (*betizo*) as well as literature, but they were stylistically marked, and an aspect of the bilingual games which the educated classes were keen to play with Greek and its relation to Latin. That is not to say that no Greek structures entered Latin in a wider sense. Where the borrowing of morphemes was concerned, if there was heavy lexical borrowing of terms with a particular suffix, that suffix might eventually be taken into Latin and used creatively on Latin roots (see 4.II). Similarly constant code-switching in lexical items of a particular type (e.g. in Greek names of genitive form) could lead to the spread of the foreign morpheme found in the code-switch into associated words of native origin (4.V.3.1.1). In the sphere of syntax there does seem to have been a need for more than mere borrowing to cause what originally might have been an alien structure to extend beyond the higher literary genres in which educated Romans indulged in artificial Grecising. In this I agree with the gist of Coleman's article of 1975, and also with Löfstedt in his chapter on the subject in *Syntactica*. The earliest uses of Latin demonstratives with article function directly imitate Greek usages, as for example in Plautus and in those writers who mimic the Greek use of τό + lexeme in discussion of the lexeme (4.V.4.5). In translation literature too (see, e.g. Abel (1971)) demonstratives could be pressed into service to render the Greek article. But it was centuries after Plautus that the article function was established in non-Grecising Latin, and it has to be assumed that there were influences additional to mere imitation of Greek. The causes are difficult to pin down, but the development of demonstratives into articles in other languages is not uncommon even without external pressures, and it must be allowed that some such development within Latin itself, enhanced perhaps by input from Greek, lay behind those usages which foreshadow the emergence of the definite article in the Romance languages. Or again, where the use of *habeo* + infinitive as an exponent of futurity is concerned, the evidence is clearcut that native Latin structures had long been leading in that direction (see Adams (1991b)), even if the development was given impetus by the equivalent construction in later Greek.

I have nothing to say here about lexical borrowings. The Latin language in virtually all of its varieties was full of Greek loan-words, a subject which has been extensively studied, and certainly in this sense the language was heavily Hellenised. We have dealt briefly (see 4.V.2.11) with what might be called 'indirectly Grecising' lexemes, that is terms whose components are exclusively Latin but the combination of which has Greek inspiration. Calques, though they were coined in higher registers rather than everyday speech, were sometimes influential in the educated language in the longer term (e.g. *substantia*). Phrasal lexemes with a Greek base, such as Ennius' *dicti studiosus*, belong rather with the allusive use of Greek structures (see above on syntax) which the learned writer expected his learned readers to recognise for what they were.

Native speakers of Greek who learnt Latin were a different matter. These were subject to interference from L1 in L2, and their Latin forms a neglected variety of the language which we have called 'Greeks' Latin' (see the next section). The dietary writer Anthimus was a case in point (4.V.2.3, 4.V.4). Greeks were seen to have a distinctive accent in Latin (4.V.1.1). They introduced Greek morphemes into their Latin and conflated Greek and Latin endings (see 4.V.3.2), and also admitted Greek syntactic structures in Latin (4.V.4, 4.V.4.2). But the alien elements imposed on Latin were not necessarily pure Greek; they might derive from false morphological analysis of Latin forms (4.VI.1), or reflect complex processes including forms of 'creativity'. In this latter matter the distinctive Latin of Roman (and some other western) Greeks is nicely revealed in the use of the oblique case inflections of names (4.V.3.1.1). Greeks tended to code-switch into Greek when using their Greek names, particularly in the dative and genitive cases, and from that starting point introduced the Greek genitive morpheme into their Latin names. The morpheme then tended to be Latinised in the written form of the language (into *-aes*), a feature which we have called 'creative'.

X VULGAR LATIN

A good deal of this book has in effect been about Vulgar Latin, or at least about a particular form of substandard Latin. I refer to Greeks' Latin (see above). Greeks in the army, at Rome, in Egypt and in the pursuit of trade picked up spoken varieties of Latin and then attempted to graft literacy on to their new language (see below, XI). Their written output in Latin, such as receipts found in Egypt written by soldiers or traders, combines syntactic and morphological interference from Greek with Vulgar Latin features (5.VII.2.2, VII.3). The morphology of a piece of 'Latin' may indeed by entirely Greek (see 1.IX). But in addition to vulgarisms and Grecisms imperfect learners commit irrational errors (see 1.VII.2.3), tend to use cases chaotically with no principles discernible (5.VII.3 (2)), and to use the nominative as a sort of base form (5.IX, p. 633). See further 3.V.4 on the *manumissio inter amicos* which has wrong (pointless) Latin inflections and unsystematic switches into Greek inflections, as well as syntactic interference from Greek (in a filiation), 4.V.1.1, V.3.3, 1.VII.2.1 on the glossary Kramer (1983), 13, 1.VII.2.3 on the document of Aeschines, 3.II (5) on the letter of Cerinthus, and also the conclusion to 5.VIII.

XI LITERACY

The acquisition of literacy may have a bilingual dimension (usually neglected in discussions of ancient literacy) in that a learner or speaker of a second language may have to use a second script to write in the second language. We have seen that the learning of a second language may go hand in hand with the learning of the second script (5.VII.3, VIII), such that errors of language combine in interesting ways with errors of literacy. A hierarchy of language and literacy errors was set up at 5.VII.3, and it is possible to place different learners at different points on the scale as they progress in the learning of the second language and script. It was easier for a Greek learning Latin to learn spelling rules (such as the conversion of digraphs from one language to the other) than to master the morphology of the second language (see 5.VIII (1)), just as it was easier to learn morphemes than it was to master their functions (see 8.1). The dowry list written by a Greek and discussed at 5.VIII (1) shows ignorance not only of Latin morphology but also of the lexicon (a feature it shares with the translation of Babrius: see Chapter 8), and yet it is without spelling errors. Deductions can be made about the order of the instruction in Latin language and literacy which the writer had received: he must have begun with the use of letters and digraphs. Some second-language users did not even attempt to learn the script of the new language (see I.VII.2.3): a language may, after all, be acquired exclusively as a spoken medium. That Greeks learning Latin sometimes began by using Latin in spoken form can be deduced from those texts showing second-language and/or literacy errors but also the influence of spoken Latin on the writers: they must have picked up Latin as a spoken language before learning to write it.

Another theme of the book has been the acquisition of Latin literacy by vernacular speakers who then used the Latin script to write their native language. This phenomenon was seen in Etruria, Africa, Spain, the Venetic territory and Gaul. It presumably reflects a policy by Roman officialdom in the western provinces of giving instruction in Latin literacy (and therefore by definition in Latin itself), and leaving the learners if they wished to use the new script for their old language as expertise in the old script declined.

Bibliography

Abel, F. (1971), *L'adjectif démonstratif dans la langue de la Bible latine* (Tübingen)

Adamik, T. (1987), '*Romaniane vivat* (Bemerkungen zum Gebrauch des Vokativs und zur afrikanischen Latinität)', in Herman (1987), 1–9

Adams, J. N. (1976), *The Text and Language of a Vulgar Latin Chronicle (Anonymus Valesianus II)* (*Institute of Classical Studies, Bulletin Supplement*, 36) (London)

———— (1977), *The Vulgar Latin of the Letters of Claudianus Terentianus (P. Mich. VIII, 467–72)* (Manchester)

———— (1981), 'Ausonius *Cento Nuptialis* 101–131', *SIFC* 53, 199–215

———— (1982), *The Latin Sexual Vocabulary* (London)

———— (1990a), 'The uses of *neco* I', *Glotta* 68, 230–55

———— (1990b), 'The Latinity of C. Novius Eunus', *ZPE* 82, 227–47

———— (1991a), 'The uses of *neco* II', *Glotta* 69, 94–123

———— (1991b), 'Some neglected evidence for Latin *habeo* + infinitive: the order of the constituents', *Transactions of the Philological Society* 89:2, 131–96.

———— (1992), 'British Latin: the text, interpretation and language of the Bath curse tablets', *Britannia* 23, 1–26

———— (1993), 'The generic use of *mula* and the status and employment of female mules in the Roman world', *RhM* 36, 35–61

———— (1994a), 'Latin and Punic in contact? The case of the Bu Njem ostraca', *JRS* 84, 87–112

———— (1994b), *Wackernagel's Law and the Placement of the Copula* esse *in Classical Latin* (Cambridge)

———— (1995a), 'The Latin of the Vindolanda writing-tablets: an interim report', *JRS* 85, 86–134

———— (1995b), *Pelagonius and Latin Veterinary Terminology in the Roman Empire* (Leiden)

———— (1996), 'The interpretation of *souxtum* at Tab. Vindol. II.301.3', *ZPE* 110, 238

———— (1998), 'Two notes on RIB', *ZPE* 123, 235–6

———— (1999), 'The poets of Bu Njem: language, culture and the centurionate', *JRS* 89, 109–34

Adams, J. N. and Mayer, R. G. (eds.) (1999), *Aspects of the Language of Latin Poetry* (*Proceedings of the British Academy*, 93) (Oxford)

Ahlquist, H. (1909), *Studien zur spätlateinischen Mulomedicina Chironis* (Uppsala)

767

Aitchison, J. (1991), *Language Change: Progress or Decay?*, 2nd edn (Cambridge)

Al-As'ad, Kh. and Teixidor, J. (1985), 'Quelques inscriptions palmyréniennes inédites', *Syria* 62, 271–80

Albrecht, M. von (1973), 'M. T. Cicero, Sprache und Stil, II A 3. Ciceros Briefe', *RE Supplementband* 13, 1271–86

Allen, W. S. (1965), *Vox Latina. A Guide to the Pronunciation of Classical Latin* (Cambridge)

(1974), *Vox Graeca. A Guide to the Pronunciation of Classical Greek*, 2nd edn (Cambridge)

Alston, R. (1995), *Soldier and Society in Roman Egypt. A Social History* (London and New York)

Amadasi Guzzo, M. G. (1967), *Le iscrizioni fenicie e puniche delle colonie in occidente* (Rome)

(1979), 'Osservazioni sull'iscrizione Tripol. 32', *Studi Magrebini* 11, 27–35

(1986), 'L'onomastica nelle iscrizioni puniche tripolitane', *Rivista di studi fenici* 14, 21–51

(1988), 'Cultura punica e cultura latina in Tripolitania. Osservazioni in base alle iscrizioni puniche e alle iscrizioni bilingui', in Campanile, Cardona and Lazzeroni (1988), 23–33

(1989), 'Stato degli studi sulle iscrizioni latino-puniche della Tripolitania', *L'Africa Romana* 7, 101–8

(1990), *Iscrizioni fenicie e puniche in Italia* (Rome)

Ammassari, A. (1987), *Il Salterio latino di Pietro, I. Introduzione e commento del Salterio latino tradotto dall'ebraico da Pietro, terzo nell'ordine del Salterio quadruplo, secundo il Codice Latino Cassinese 557* (Rome)

Ampolo, C. (1981), 'I gruppi etnici in Roma arcaica: posizione del problema e fonti', in *Gli Etruschi e Roma. Atti dell' incontro di studio in onore di Massimo Pallottino, Roma, 11–13 dicembre 1979* (Rome), 45–67

Anderson, J. G. C. (1938), *Cornelii Taciti de Origine et Situ Germanorum* (Oxford)

Anderson, R. D., Parsons, P. J. and Nisbet, R. G. M. (1979), 'Elegiacs by Gallus from Qaṣr Ibrîm', *JRS* 69, 125–55

André, J. (1956), *Lexique des termes de botanique en latin* (Paris)

(1967), *Les noms d'oiseaux en latin* (Paris)

(1971), *Emprunts et suffixes nominaux en latin* (Geneva and Paris)

(1985), *Les noms de plantes dans la Rome antique* (Paris)

(1991), *Le vocabulaire latin de l'anatomie* (Paris)

Andreau, J. (1974), *Les affaires de Monsieur Jucundus* (Rome)

Antonini, R. (1977), 'Iscrizioni osche pompeiane', *SE* 45, 317–40

Appel, R. and Muysken, P. (1987), *Language Contact and Bilingualism* (London)

Arena, R. (1969), 'Di un complesso mitico greco e dei suoi riflessi in area italica', *PP* 24, 437–61

Arnott, W. G. (1996), *Alexis: the Fragments. A Commentary* (Cambridge)

Aronen, J. (1996), 'Dragon cults and νύμφη δράκαινα in *IGUR* 974', *ZPE* 111, 125–32

Audin, A. (1979), *Lyon, miroir de Rome* (Paris)

Audollent, A. (1904), *Defixionum Tabellae* (Paris)

Austin, R. G. (1948), *Quintiliani Institutionis Oratoriae liber XII* (Oxford)
 (1964), *P. Vergili Maronis Aeneidos Liber Secundus* (Oxford)
 (1977), *P. Vergili Maronis Aeneidos Liber Sextus* (Oxford)

Baehrens, W. A. (1922), *Sprachlicher Kommentar zur vulgärlateinischen Appendix Probi* (Halle an der Saale)

Bagnall, R. S. (1975), 'The Roman garrison of Latopolis', *BASP* 12, 135–44
 (1976), *The Florida Ostraka. Documents from the Roman Army in Upper Egypt (GRBS Monograph, 7)* (Durham, N. Carolina)
 (1986), 'Papyri and ostraka from Quseir al-Qadim', *BASP* 23, 1–60
 (1993), *Egypt in Late Antiquity* (Princeton)
 (1995), *Reading Papyri, Writing Ancient History* (London and New York)

Bagnall, R. S. and Sheridan, J. A. (1994), 'Greek and Latin documents from 'Abu Sha'ar, 1992–1993', *BASP* 31, 109–20

Bagnall, R. S. and Worp, K. A. (1978), *The Chronological Systems of Byzantine Egypt* (Zutphen)

Bailey, C. (1947), *Titi Lucreti Cari De Rerum Natura libri sex*, 3 vols. (Oxford)

Baillet, J. (1920–6), *Inscriptions grecques et latines des tombeaux des rois ou syringes à Thèbes* (Cairo)

Bakkum, G. C. L. M. (1994), 'The second-declension nominative plural in *-eis, -es, is*, and the first-declension nominative plural in *-as*', in J. Herman (ed.), *Linguistic Studies on Latin. Selected Papers from the 6th International Colloquium on Latin Linguistics (Budapest, 23–27 March 1991)* (Amsterdam and Philadelphia), 19–39

Baldwin, B. (1992), 'Greek in Cicero's letters', *Acta Classica* 35, 1–17

Balsdon, J. P. V. D. (1979), *Romans and Aliens* (London)

Balty, J. C. (1988), 'Apamea in Syria in the second and third centuries AD', *JRS* 78, 91–104

Balty, J. C. and Rengen, W. van (1993), *Apamea in Syria. The Winter Quarters of Legio II Parthica. Roman Gravestones from the Military Cemetery* (Brussels)

Bang, M. (1910), 'Die Herkunft der römischen Sklaven', *Mittheilungen des Kaiserlich Deutschen Archaeologischen Instituts, Römische Abteilung* 25, 223–51

Barr, J. (1966–7), 'St Jerome's appreciation of Hebrew', *BJRL* 49, 281–302

Barr, W. (1973), 'Juvenal's other elephants', *Latomus* 32, 856–8

Barrud, G. (1976), 'La résistance des substrats préromains en Gaule méridionale', in Pippidi (1976), 389–405

Bartelink, G. J. M. (1965), *Etymologisering bij Vergilius* (Amsterdam)
 (1980), *Hieronymus, Liber De optimo genere interpretandi (Epistula 57). Ein Kommentar* (Leiden)

Bartoccini, R. (1928), 'Scavi e rinvenimenti in Tripolitania negli anni 1926–1927', *Africa Italiana* 2, 187–200

Baslez, M.-F. (1996), 'La première présence romaine à Délos (vers 250–vers 140)', in Rizakis (1996), 215–24

Basset, A. (1952), *Handbook of African Languages*, Part I. *La langue berbère* (London, New York and Toronto)

Bataille, A. (1951a), *Les inscriptions grecques du temple de Hatshepsout à Deir el-Bahari* (Cairo)

(1951b), 'Thèbes gréco-romaine', *C d'É* 26, 325–53

Battisti, C. (1949), *Avviamento allo studio del latino volgare* (Bari)

Bauer, J. B. (1983), 'Semitisches bei Petron', in P. Händel and W. Meid (eds.), *Festschrift für R. Muth* (Innsbruck), 17–23

Beaujeu, J. (1973), *Apulée, Opuscules philosophiques (Du dieu de Socrate, Platon et sa doctrine, Du monde) et fragments* (Paris)

Beaulieu, A. and Mouterde, R. (1947–8), 'La grotte d'Astarté à Waṣṭa', *Mélanges de l'Université Saint Joseph* 27, 1–20

Becatti, G. (1954), *Scavi di Ostia*, vol. II, *I Mitrei* (Rome)

Bell, H. I. (1937), 'A Latin registration of birth', *JRS* 27, 30–6

Bell, H. I. et al. (1962), *The Abinnaeus Archive: Papers of a Roman Officer in the Reign of Constantine* (Oxford)

Bémont, C. and Jacob, J.-P. (eds.) (1986), *La terre sigillée gallo-romaine. Lieux de production du Haut Empire: implantations, produits, relations* (Paris)

Bénabou, M. (1976), *La résistance africaine à la romanisation* (Paris)

Benelli, E. (1994), *Le iscrizioni bilingui etrusco-latine* (Florence)

Bentahila, A. and Davies, E. E. (1998), 'Codeswitching: an unequal partnership?', in Jacobson (1998a), 25–49

Berger, P. (1895), 'Le mausolée d'El-Amrouni', *Rev. Arch.*, 3rd ser. 26, 71–83

Bernand, A. (1969), *Les inscriptions grecques et latines de Philae*, II. *Haut et bas empire* (Paris)

(1972), *De Koptos à Kosseir* (Leiden)

(1977), *Pan du désert* (Leiden)

(1984), *Les ports du désert* (Paris)

(1989), *De Thèbes à Syène* (Paris)

Bernand, A. and É. (1960), *Les inscriptions grecques et latines du Colosse de Memnon* (Paris)

Bernand, É. (1969), *Inscriptions métriques de l'Égypte gréco-romaine. Recherches sur la poésie épigrammatique des grecs en Égypte* (Paris)

(1975–81), *Recueil des inscriptions grecques du Fayoum*, 3 vols. (I (1975) Leiden, II–III (1981) Cairo)

(1988), *Inscriptions grecques et latines d'Akôris* (Cairo)

Berthier, A. and Charlier, R. (1955), *Le sanctuaire punique d'El-Hofra à Constantine* (Paris)

Bertinelli Angeli, M. G. (1969), 'Termini romani, pubblici e sacri, in epigrafi "latino-libiche"', in *Studi di storia antica in memoria di Luca de Regibus* (Genoa), 217–24

Bertoldi, V. (1931a), 'Fenomena basco-guascone attestato da Plinio?', *Archivum Romanicum* 15, 400–10

(1931b), 'Problèmes de substrat. Essai de méthodologie dans le domaine préhistorique de la toponymie et du vocabulaire', *BSL* 32, 93–184

(1937), 'Contatti e conflitti di lingue nell'antico Mediterraneo', *ZRPh* 57, 137–69

(1950), *Colonizzazioni nell'antico Mediterraneo occidentale alla luce degli aspetti linguistici* (Naples)

Best, E. E. (1966–7), 'The literate Roman soldier', *CJ* 62, 122–7

Beszard, L. (1910), *La langue des Formules de Sens* (Paris)

Bindel, H. (1912), *De declinatione latina titulorum quaestiones selectae* (Jena)

Bingen, J. et al. (1992), *Mons Claudianus, Ostraca Graeca et Latina*, I *(O.Claud. 1 à 190)* (Cairo)

Bingen, J. et al. (1997), *Mons Claudianus, Ostraca Graeca et Latina*, II. *O. Claud. 191 à 416* (Cairo)

Birch, R. A. (1981), 'The correspondence of Augustus: some notes on Suetonius, *Tiberius* 21.4–7', *CQ* n. s. 31, 155–61

Bird, D. G. (1984), 'Pliny and the gold mines of the north west of the Iberian peninsula', in T. F. C. Blagg, R. F. J. Jones and S. J. Keay (eds.), *Papers in Iberian Archaeology, BAR International Series*, 193 (i), 341–68

Birley, E. B. (1953), *Roman Britain and the Roman Army: Collected Papers* (Kendal)

Biville, F. (1989a), 'Grec et latin: contacts linguistiques et création lexicale. Pour une typologie des héllénismes lexicaux du latin', in Lavency and Longrée (1989), 29–40

(1989b), 'Les hellénismes dans les inscriptions latines paiennes de la Gaule (1er – 4ème s. ap. J.-C.)', in *La langue des inscriptions de la Gaule. Actes de la Table-ronde tenue au C.E.R.G.R. les 6 et 7 Octobre 1988 (Université Lyon III)* (Paris), 99–115

(1990), *Les emprunts du latin au grec. Approche phonétique*, Tome I. *Introduction et consonantisme* (Louvain and Paris)

(1991), 'L'emprunt lexical, un révélateur des structures vivantes des deux langues en contact (le cas du grec et du latin)', *RPh* 55, 45–58

(1992), 'Le grec parlé en latin vulgaire. Domaines lexicaux, structures linguistiques d'accueil', in Iliescu and Marxgut (1992), 25–40

(1995), *Les emprunts du latin au grec. Approche phonétique*, Tome II. *Vocalisme et conclusiens* (Louvain and Paris)

(1996), '"*Sophos!*" *uniuersi clamamus* (Pétrone 40, 1). Acclamations grecques et latines dans les loisirs des Romains', in J.-M. André, J. Dangel and P. Demont (eds.), *Les loisirs et l'héritage de la culture classique* (Brussels), 310–18

(2000), 'Bilinguisme gréco-latin et créations éphémères de discours', in *La création lexicale en latin (Lingua latina. Recherches linguistiques du Centre Alfred Ernout)* (Paris), 91–107

Blass, F., Debrunner, A. and Rehkopf, F. (1975), *Grammatik des neutestamentlichen Griechisch*, 14th edn (Göttingen)

Bloch, O. and Wartburg, W. von (1968), *Dictionnaire étymologique de la langue française*, 5th edn (Paris)

Bloomfield, L. (1933), *Language* (New York)

Boeft, J. den, Hengst, D. den and Teitler, H. C. (1991), *Philological and Historical Commentary on Ammianus XXI* (Groningen)

Bognetti, G. P. (1954), 'Les inscriptions juives de Venosa et le problème des rapports entre les Lombards et l'Orient', *CRAI* 193–202

Bonfante, L. (1990), *Etruscan* (London)

Boucher, J.-P. (1966), *Caius Cornélius Gallus* (Paris)

Bourciez, E. (1946), *Éléments de linguistique romane*, 4th edn (Paris)

Bourdieu, P. (1991), *Language and Symbolic Power*, translated by G. Raymond and M. Adamson (Cambridge)

Bowersock, G. W. (1984), 'The miracle of Memnon', *BASP* 21, 21–32

Bowman, A. K. and Rathbone, D. (1992), 'Cities and administration in Roman Egypt', *JRS* 82, 107–27

Bowman, A. K. and Thomas, J. D. (1991), 'A military strength report from Vindolanda', *JRS* 81, 62–73

(1994), *The Vindolanda Writing-Tablets (Tabulae Vindolandenses II)* (London)

(1996), 'New writing-tablets from Vindolanda', *Britannia* 27, 299–328

Boyancé, P. (1956), 'La connaissance du grec à Rome', *REL* 34, 111–31

Boyce, B. (1991), *The Language of the Freedmen in Petronius'* Cena Trimalchionis (Leiden)

Bradley, G. (2000), *Ancient Umbria. State, Culture, and Identity in Central Italy from the Iron Age to the Augustan Era* (Oxford)

Brand, P. (2000), 'The languages of the law in later Medieval England', in D. A. Trotter (ed.), *Multilingualism in Later Medieval Britain* (Cambridge), 63–76

Bresciani, E. (1989), 'La stele trilingue di Cornelio Gallo: una rilettura egitto-logica', *Egitto e vicino oriente* 12, 93–8

Bresciani, E., Pernigotti, S. and Betrò, M. C. (1983), *Ostraka demotici da Narmuti*, 1 (Pisa)

Bresciani, E. and Pintaudi, R. (1987), 'Textes démotico-grecs et greco-démotiques des Ostraca de Medinet Madi: un problème de bilinguisme', in Vleeming (1987), 123–6

Breyer, G. (1993), *Etruskisches Sprachgut im Lateinischen unter Ausschluss des spezifisch onomastischen Bereiches* (Leuven)

Briscoe, J. (1973), *A Commentary on Livy Books XXXI–XXXIII* (Oxford)

(1981), *A Commentary on Livy Books XXXIV–XXXVII* (Oxford)

Brixhe, C. (1988), 'La langue de l'étranger non grec chez Aristophane', in R. Lonis (ed.), *L'étranger dans le monde grec* (Nancy), 113–38

Brock, S. (1979), 'Aspects of translation technique in antiquity', *GRBS* 20, 69–87

Brogan, O. (1964), 'The Roman remains in the Wadi el-Amud', *Libya Antiqua* 1, 47–56

Brown, D. (1992), *Vir Trilinguis. A Study in the Biblical Exegesis of Saint Jerome* (Kampen)

Brown, P. and Gilman, A. (1968), 'The pronouns of power and solidarity', in Fishman (1968), 252–75

Brown, P. and Levinson, S. C. (1987), *Politeness: some Universals in Language Usage*, 2nd edn (Cambridge)

Browne, G. M. (1969), 'Note on BGU XI 2112', *ZPE* 4, 45–6

Brüch, J. (1913), *Der Einfluss der germanischen Sprachen auf das Vulgärlatein* (Heidelberg)

Brugsch, H. (1888), 'Vier bilingue Inschriften von Philä', *ZÄS* 26, 57–69

Brunt, P. A. (1976), 'The Romanization of the local ruling classes in the Roman Empire', in Pippidi (1976), 161–73

(1988), *The Fall of the Roman Republic and Related Essays* (Oxford)

Buck, C. D. (1904), *A Grammar of Oscan and Umbrian* (Boston)

Buecheler, F. (1907), 'Neue italische Dialektinschriften v', *RhM* 62, 554–8

Bülow-Jacobsen, A., Cuvigny, H. and Fournet, J.-L. (1994), 'The identification of Myos Hormos. New papyrological evidence', *BIFAO* 94, 27–42

Burnett, A. (1998), 'The coinage of the Social War', in A. Burnett, U. Wartenberg, and R. Witschonke, (eds.), *Coins of Macedonia and Rome: Essays in Honour of Charles Hersh* (London), 165–72

Bybee, J. and Hopper, P. (2001), *Frequency and the Emergence of Linguistic Structure* (Amsterdam and Philadelphia)

Calderini, R. (1953), 'De interpretibus quaedam in papyris', *Aegyptus* 33, 341–6

Callebat, L. (ed.) (1995), *Latin vulgaire – latin tardif. Actes du 4ᵉ colloque international sur le latin vulgaire et tardif. Caen, 2–5 septembre 1994* (Hildesheim, Zurich and New York)

Cameron, A. (1931), 'Latin words in the Greek inscriptions of Asia Minor', *AJP* 52, 232–62

Cameron, Alan (1965), 'Wandering poets: a literary movement in Byzantine Egypt', *Historia* 14, 470–509

(1970), *Claudian. Poetry and Propaganda at the Court of Honorius* (Oxford)

(1973), *Porphyrius the Charioteer* (Oxford)

Campanile, E. (1976), 'La latinizzazione dell'osco', in *Scritti in onore di Giuliano Bonfante* (Brescia), I, 109–20

(1985), 'Questioni metodologiche nell'analisi dei testi oschi', in E. Campanile (ed.), *Lingua e cultura degli oschi* (Pisa), 11–20

(ed.) (1988a), *Alle origini di Roma. Atti del Colloquio tenuto a Pisa il 18 e 19 settembre 1987* (Pisa)

(1988b), 'Per una definizione del testo epigrafico bilingue', in Campanile, Cardona and Lazzeroni (1988), 17–21

(ed.) (1991a), *Rapporti linguistici e culturali tra i popoli dell'Italia antica (Pisa, 6–7 ottobre 1989)* (Pisa)

(1991b), 'Limiti e caratteri del bilinguismo romano', *Il bilinguismo degli antichi* (Genoa) [no editor], 9–23

(ed.) (1993), *Caratteri e diffusione del latino in età arcaica* (Pisa)

Campanile, E., Cardona, G. R. and Lazzeroni, R. (eds.) (1988), *Bilinguismo e biculturismo nel mondo antico. Atti del Colloquio interdisciplinare tenuto a Pisa il 28 e 29 settembre 1987* (Pisa)

Cantineau, J. (1932), *Inventaire des inscriptions de Palmyre*,VIII (Beirut)

(1933), 'Tadmorea', *Syria* 14, 169–202

Carnoy, A. (1906), *Le latin d'Espagne d'après les inscriptions*, 2nd edn (Brussels)

Casson, L. (1974), *Travel in the Ancient World* (London)

Casson, L. and Hettich, E. L. (1950), *Excavations at Nessana*, vol. II. *Literary Papyri* (Princeton)

Castrén, P. (1975), *Ordo Populusque Pompeianus. Polity and Society in Roman Pompeii* (Rome)

Cavenaile, R. (1951), 'Influence latine sur le vocabulaire grec d'Égypte', *C d'É* 26, 391–404

(1952), 'Quelques aspects de l'apport linguistique du grec au latin d'Égypte', *Aegyptus* 32, 191–203

Cèbe, J.-P. (1972), *Varron, Satires Ménippées*, 1 (Rome)

(1974), *Varron, Satires Ménippées*, 2 (Rome)

(1975), *Varron, Satires Ménippées*, 3 (Rome)

(1980), *Varron, Satires Ménippées*, 5 (Rome)

(1983), *Varron, Satires Ménippées*, 6 (Rome)

(1987), *Varron, Satires Ménippées*, 8 (Rome)

Cervenka-Ehrenstrasser, I.-M. and Diethart, J. (1996–2000), *Lexikon der lateinischen Lehnwörter in den griechischensprachigen dokumentarischen Texten Ägyptens*, 2 vols. (Vienna)

Chabot, J.-B. (1917), 'Punica', *JA* (onz. sér.)10, 5–79

(1932), 'Nouvelle inscription Palmyrénienne d'Afrique', *CRAI*, 265–9

Chabot, J.-B. (1940), *Recueil des inscriptions libyques* (Paris)

Chalon, G. (1964), *L'Édit de Tiberius Julius Alexander. Étude historique et exégétique* (Olten and Lausanne)

Chantraine, P. (1933), *La formation des noms en grec ancien* (Paris)

Charpin, F. (1978), *Lucilius Satires*, Tome I. *(Livres I–VIII)* (Paris)

Clackson, J. (2000), 'A Greek papyrus in Armenian script', *ZPE* 129, 223–59

Clackson, J. and Meissner, T. (2000), 'The poet of Chester', *PCPS* 46, 1–6

Clarysse, W. and Sijpesteijn, P. J. (1988), 'A military roster on a vase in Amsterdam', *AncSoc* 19, 71–96

Coacci Polselli, G. (1978), 'Per un corpus delle iscrizioni latino-puniche', in *Atti del I° convegno italiano sul vicino oriente antico (Roma, 22–24 Aprile 1976)* (Rome), 231–41

(1979), 'A proposito di alcune iscrizioni latino-puniche', *Studi Magrebini* 11, 37–42

Coarelli, F. (1982), 'L'"Agora des italiens" a Delos: il mercato degli schiavi?', in Coarelli, Musti and Solin (1982), 119–45

Coarelli, F., Musti, D. and Solin, H. (eds.) (1982), *Delo e l'Italia (Opuscula Instituti Romani Finlandiae* II) (Rome)

Cohen, D. (1985), 'Paroles arabes et charmes éthiopiens. Hypothèses à propos du langage médico-magique', in C. Robin (ed.), *Mélanges linguistiques offerts à Maxime Rodinson* (Paris), 147–59

Cohen, S. J. D. and Frerichs, E. S. (eds.) (1993), *Diasporas in Antiquity* (Atlanta)

Coleman, K. M. (1988), *Statius* Siluae *IV* (Oxford)

Coleman, R. G. G. (1971), 'The monophthongization of /ae/ and the Vulgar Latin vowel system', *TPhS* (1971), 175–91

(1975), 'Greek influence on Latin syntax', *TPhS* (1975), 101–56

(1989), 'The formation of specialized vocabularies in philosophy, grammar and rhetoric: winners and losers', in Lavency and Longrée (1989), 77–89

(1990), 'Dialectal variation in Republican Latin, with special reference to Praenestine', *PCPS* n.s. 36, 1–25

Coles, R. A. (1966), *Reports of Proceedings in Papyri (Pap. Brux. 4)* (Brussels)

(1981), 'A quadrilingual curiosity in the Bodleian Library in Oxford', in R. S. Bagnall et al. (eds.), *Proceedings of the Sixteenth International Congress of Papyrology (New York, 24–31 July 1980)* (Ann Arbor), 193–6

Colin, G. S. (1926), 'Étymologies magribines', *Hespéris* 6, 55–82

(1927), 'Étymologies magribines (II)', *Hespéris* 7, 85–102

Colonna, G. (1981), 'Quali Etruschi a Roma', in *Gli Etruschi e Roma. Atti dell'incontro di studio in onore di Massimo Pallottino, Roma, 11–13 dicembre 1979* (Rome), 159–72

(1987), 'Etruria e Lazio nell'età dei Tarquini', in Cristofani (1987), 55–66

Colonna, G. et al. (eds.) (1970), *Pyrgi: scavi del santuario etrusco (1959–1967), N.Sc. 24, Suppl.* II

Colson, F. H. (1924), *M. Fabii Quintiliani Institutionis Oratoriae liber I* (Cambridge)

Colvin, S. (1999), *Dialect in Aristophanes. The Politics of Language in Ancient Greek Literature* (Oxford)

Cook, V. J. (1993), *Linguistics and Second Language Acquisition* (Basingstoke and London)

Cooke, G. A. (1903), *A Text-book of North-Semitic Inscriptions* (Oxford)

Cornell, T. J. (1989), 'Rome and Latium to 390 B.C.', *The Cambridge Ancient History*, 2nd edn, vol. VII.2 (Cambridge), 243–308

(1995), *The Beginnings of Rome. Italy and Rome from the Bronze Age to the Punic Wars (c. 1000–264 BC)* (London and New York)

Corominas, J. (1956), 'New information on Hispano-Celtic from the Spanish Etymological Dictionary', *ZcPh* 25, 30–58

(1961), *Breve diccionario etimológico de la lengua castellana* (Madrid)

Corominas, J. and Pascual, J. A. (1980–91), *Diccionario crítico etimológico castellana e hispaníca*, 6 vols. (Madrid)

Cotton, H. M. (1993), 'The guardianship of Jesus son of Babatha: Roman and local law in the province of Arabia', *JRS* 83, 94–108

(1995), 'The archive of Salome Komaise daughter of Levi: another archive from the "Cave of letters" ', *ZPE* 105, 171–208

Courtney, E. (1980), *A Commentary on the Satires of Juvenal* (London)

(1995), *Musa Lapidaria. A Selection of Latin Verse Inscriptions* (Atlanta)

(1999), *Archaic Latin Prose* (Atlanta)

Courtois, C. (1950), 'Saint Augustin et le problème de la survivance du punique', *Revue africaine* 94, 259–82

Cox, M. G. (1988), 'Augustine, Jerome, Tyconius and the *lingua Punica*', *Studia Orientalia* 64, 83–105

Crawford, M. H. (ed.) (1996), *Roman Statutes*, 2 vols. (London)

Cristofani, M. (ed.) (1987), *Etruria e Lazio arcaico. Atti dell'Incontro di studio (10–11 novembre 1986)* (Rome)

Crystal, D. (2000), *Language Death* (Cambridge)

Cugusi, P. (1981), 'Gli ostraca latini dello Wâdi Fawâkhir. Per la storia del latino', in *Letterature comparate, problemi e metodo. Studi in onore di Ettore Paratore*, II (Bologna), 719–53

    (1983), *Evoluzione e forme dell'epistolografia latina* (Rome)

    (1992), *Corpus epistolarum latinarum papyris tabulis ostracis servatarum*, 2 vols. (Florence)

    (1996), *Aspetti letterari dei* Carmina Latina Epigraphica, 2nd edn (Bologna)

Curbera, J. B. (1997a), 'The persons cursed on a defixio from Lilybaeum', *Mnemosyne* 50, 219–25

    (1997b), 'Graecolatina', *ZPE* 118, 235–6

Dabène, L. and Moore, D. (1995), 'Bilingual speech of migrant people', in Milroy and Muysken (1995), 17–44

Dagron, G. (1969), 'Aux origines de la civilisation byzantine: langue de culture et langue d'État', *Revue historique* 241, 23–56

Daris, S. (1960), 'Il lessico latino nella lingua greca d'Egitto', *Aegyptus* 40, 117–314

    (1991a), *Il lessico latino nel greco d'Egitto*, 2nd edn (Barcelona)

    (1991b), 'Latino ed Egitto romano', in *Il bilinguismo degli antichi* (Genoa), 47–81

Daumas, F. (1952), *Les moyens d'expression du grec et de l'égyptien comparés dans les décrets de Canope et de Memphis* (Cairo)

Davies, A. M. (1987), 'The Greek notion of dialect', *Verbum* 10, 7–28

Davies, O. (1935), *Roman Mines in Europe* (Oxford)

Décourt, J.-C. (1993), 'χαῖρε καὶ ὑγίαινε: à propos de quelques inscriptions lyonnaises', *RPh* 67, 237–50

De Jonge, P. (1935), *Sprachlicher und historischer Kommentar zu Ammianus Marcellinus XIV 1–7* (Groningen)

de Lange, N. (1996), *Greek Jewish Texts from the Cairo Genizah* (Tübingen)

Delisle, J., Lee-Jahnke, H. and Cormier, M. C. (eds.) (1999), *Terminologie de la traduction* (Amsterdam)

Della Corte, F. (1976), 'Il 'Geticus sermo' di Ovidio', in *Scritti in onore di Guiliano Bonfante* (Brescia) I, 205–16

Del Tutto Palma, L. (1990), *Le iscrizioni della Lucania preromana* (Padua)

    (ed.) (1996), *La Tavola di Agnone nel contesto italico: convegno di studi, Agnone 13–15 aprile 1994* (Florence)

Deman, A. (1981), 'Le terme de parenté germanique *suecerio/socerio* dans les inscriptions latines', *AC* 50, 198–208

Depauw, M. (1997), *A Companion to Demotic Studies (Pap. Brux. 28)* (Brussels)

Descoeudres, J.-P. (ed.) (1990), *Greek Colonists and Native Populations (Proceedings of the First Australian Congress of Classical Archaeology held in honour of Emeritus Professor A. D. Trendall, Sydney 9–14 July 1985)* (Canberra, A.C.T. and Oxford)

De Simone, C. (1968), 'Zur altetruskischen Inschrift aus Rom (*ni araziia laraniia)*', *Glotta* 46, 207–12

    (1970), *Die griechischen Entlehnungen im Etruskischen*, II. *Untersuchung* (Wiesbaden)

    (1975), 'Etruskischer Literaturbericht: neuveröffentliche Inschriften 1970–1973', *Glotta* 53, 125–81

(1980), 'Italien', in Neumann and Untermann (1980), 65–81

(1988), 'Gli imprestiti etruschi nel latino arcaico', in Campanile (1988a), 27–41

(1991), 'I rapporti linguistici tra gli etruschi e gli italici', in Campanile (1991a), 129–47

de Ste. Croix, G. E. M. (1981), *The Class Struggle in the Ancient Greek World: from the Archaic Age to the Arab Conquests* (London)

Detschew, D. (1957), *Die thrakischen Sprachreste* (Vienna)

Devauchelle, D. and Wagner, G. (1982), 'Ostraca ptolémaïques bilingues d'Edfou', *ASAE* 68, 89–101

Devoto, G. (1933), 'Contributo alla teoria del sostrato osco-umbro', *Revue de linguistique romane* 9, 229–45

(1956–7), 'La romanisation de l'Italie médiane', *Cahiers d'histoire mondiale* 3, 443–62

(1968), *Geschichte der Sprache Roms*, translated by I. Opelt (Heidelberg)

Dickey, E. (2001), 'ΚΥΡΙΕ, ΔΕΣΠΟΤΑ, *DOMINE*: Greek politeness in the Roman Empire', *JHS* 121, 1–11

(2002), *Latin Forms of Address from Plautus to Apuleius* (Oxford)

Dionisotti, A. C. (1982), 'From Ausonius' schooldays? A schoolbook and its relatives', *JRS* 72, 83–125

Dittenberger, W. (1871), 'Römische Namen in griechischen Inschriften und Literaturwerken', *Hermes* 6, 129–55, 281–313

Di Vita, A. (1966), *La villa della 'Gara delle Nereidi' presso Tagiura: un contributo alla storia del mosaico romano; ed altri recenti scavi e scoperte in Tripolitania (Supplements to Libya Antiqua* II) (Tripoli)

Domergue, C. (1972–4), 'À propos de Pline, *Naturalis Historia*, 33,70–78, et pour illustrer sa description des mines d'or romaines d'Espagne', *AEA* 45–7, 499–525

(1990), *Les mines de la péninsule ibérique dans l'antiquité romaine* (Rome)

Dommelen, P. Van (1998), 'Punic persistence: colonialism and cultural identities in Roman Sardinia', in R. Laurence and J. Berry (eds.), *Cultural Identity in the Roman Empire* (London and New York), 25–48

Donderer, M. (1995), 'Merkwürdigkeiten im Umgang mit griechischer und lateinischer Schrift in der Antike', *Gymnasium* 102, 97–122

Donner, H. and Röllig, W. (1966–9), *Kanaanäische und aramäische Inschriften, mit einem Beitrag von O. Rössler*, 2nd edn, 3 vols. (Wiesbaden)

Dottin, G. (1920), *La langue gauloise. Grammaire, textes et glossaire* (Paris)

(1924), 'La langue gauloise dans les graffites de La Graufesenque', *REA* 26, 73–7

Douglas, A. E. (1966), *M. Tulli Ciceronis Brutus* (Oxford)

Draeger, A. (1882), *Ueber Syntax und Stil des Tacitus* (Leipzig)

Drijvers, J. W. (1996), 'Ammianus Marcellinus 15.13.1–2: some observations on the career and bilingualism of Strategius Musonianus', *CQ* n.s. 46, 532–7

Dubuisson, M. (1980), '"Toi aussi, mon fils!"', *Latomus* 39, 881–90

(1981), '*Utraque lingua*', *AC* 50, 274–86

(1982), 'Ya-t-il une politique linguistique romaine?', *Ktèma* 7, 197–210

(1985), *Le latin de Polybe. Les implications historiques d'un cas de bilinguisme* (Paris)

(1992), 'Le grec à Rome à l'époque de Cicéron. Extension et qualité du bilinguisme', *Annales E.S.C.* 47, 187–206

Dunbar, N. (1995), *Aristophanes Birds* (Oxford)

Dunkel, G. E. (2000), 'Remarks on code-switching in Cicero's letters to Atticus', *MH* 57, 122–9

Durante, M. (1978), 'I dialetti medio-italici', in A. L. Prosdocimi (ed.), *Lingue e dialetti dell'Italia antica* (Rome), 789–823

Dyck, A. R. (1996), *A Commentary on Cicero, De Officiis* (Ann Arbor)

Eckhardt, K. A. (ed.) (1962), *Pactus Legis Salicae (MGH, Leges Nationum Germanicarum* IV.1) (Hanover)

Eckinger, T. (1892), *Die Orthographie lateinischer Wörter in griechischen Inschriften* (Zurich)

Edmondson, J. C. (1989), 'Mining in the later Roman Empire and beyond: continuity or disruption?', *JRS* 79, 84–102

Eger, O. (1921), 'Eine Wachstafel aus Ravenna aus dem zweiten Jahrhundert nach Chr.', *Zeitschrift der Savigny-Stiftung für Rechtsgeschichte, Romanistische Abteilung* 42, 452–68

Elcock, W. D. (1960), *The Romance Languages* (London)

Elmayer, A. F. (1983), 'The re-interpretation of Latino-Punic inscriptions from Roman Tripolitania', *Libyan Studies* 14, 86–95

(1984), 'The reinterpretation of Latino-Punic inscriptions from Roman Tripolitania', *Libyan Studies* 15, 93–105

(1985), 'The *centenaria* of Roman Tripolitania', *Libyan Studies* 16, 77–84

Erman, A. (1896 = 1986), 'Zu der hieroglyphischen Inschrift', appendix to H. G. Lyons and L. Borchardt, 'Eine trilingue Inschrift von Philae', *Sitzungsberichte der königlich-preussischen Akademie der Wissenschaften zu Berlin* 1, 474–8, = A. Erman (1986), *Akademieschriften (1880–1928)* (Leipzig) 1, 344–8 (the reprint is cited in this book)

Ernout, A. (1909), *Les éléments dialectaux du vocabulaire latin* (Paris)

(1930), 'Les éléments étrusques du vocabulaire latin', *BSL* 30, 82–124 (= id. (1946), 21–51, the latter version cited here)

(1946), *Philologica*, I (Paris)

Ernout, A. and Meillet, A. (1959), *Dictionnaire étymologique de la langue latine*, 4th edn (Paris)

Ernout, A. and Thomas, F. (1953), *Syntaxe latine*, 2nd edn (Paris)

Eska, J. F. (1987), 'The language of the Latin inscriptions of Pompeii and the question of an Oscan substratum', *Glotta* 65, 146–61

(1989), 'Italic *e/iste*, Hispano-Celtic *isTe*', *Emerita* 57, 317–21

(1991), 'The demonstrative stem **isto-* in Continental Celtic', *ZcPh* 44, 70–3

(1998), '*Tau Gallicum*', *Studia Celtica* 32, 115–27

Evans, D. Ellis (1967), *Gaulish Personal Names* (Oxford)

Exler, F. X. J. (1923), *The Form of the Ancient Greek Letter. A Study in Greek Epistolography* (Washington)

Famerie, E. (1998), *Le latin et le grec d'Appien* (Geneva)

Fasold, R. (1984), *The Sociolinguistics of Society* (Oxford)

Feltenius, L. (1977), *Intransitivizations in Latin* (Uppsala)

Ferchiou, N. (1989), 'Le Mausolée de Q. Apuleus Maximus à El Amrouni', *PBSR* 57, 47–76

Ferguson, C. A. (1959), 'Diglossia', *Word* 15, 325–40

Ferrary, J.-L. (1988), *Philhellénisme et impérialisme. Aspects idéologiques de la conquête romaine du monde hellénistique, de la seconde guerre de Macédoine à la guerre contre Mithridate* (Rome)

Février, J.-G. (1951–2a), 'La bilingue de Guelaa bou Sba', *JA* (1951–2), 38–43
    (1951–2b), 'Une corporation de l'encens à Althiburos', *Semitica* 4, 19–24
    (1953a), 'La ligne néopunique de l'inscription bilingue: *I.R.T.*, 305', *REA* 55, 358–9
    (1953b), 'La prononciation punique des noms propres latins en -*us* et en -*ius*', *JA* 241, 465–71

Février, J.-G. and Fantar, M. (1963–6), 'Les nouvelles inscriptions monumentales néopuniques de Mactar', *Karthago* 12, 43–59

Fewster, P. (forthcoming), 'Bilingualism in Roman Egypt', in J. N. Adams, M. Janse and S. C. R. Swain (eds.), *Bilingualism in Ancient Society: Language Contact and the Written Word* (Oxford)

Fink, R. O. (1971), *Roman Military Records on Papyrus* (*Philological Monographs of the American Philological Association*, 26) (Cleveland)

Fischer, K.-D. (1977), 'Ionisms – a trademark of the ancient medical profession?', *LCM* 2, 185

Fischer, W. and Rix, H. (1968), 'Die phönizisch-etruskischen Texte der Gold-plättchen von Pyrgi', *Göttingische Gelehrte Anzeigen* 220, 64–94

Fishman, J. A. (1967), 'Bilingualism with and without diglossia; diglossia with and without bilingualism', *Journal of Social Issues* 23.2, 29–38
    (ed.) (1968), *Readings in the Sociology of Language* (The Hague)

Fiske, G. C. (1920), *Lucilius and Horace. A Study in the Classical Theory of Imitation* (Madison)

Flambard, J.-M. (1977), 'Clodius, les collèges, la plèbe et les esclaves. Recherches sur la politique populaire au milieu du Ier siècle', *MEFRA* 89, 115–56
    (1982), 'Observations sur la nature des *magistri* italiens de Délos', in Coarelli, Musti and Solin (1982), 67–77

Fleuriot, L. (1991), 'Celtoromanica in the light of the newly discovered Celtic inscriptions', *ZcPh* 44, 1–35

Flobert, P. (1992), 'Les graffites de La Graufesenque: un témoignage sur le gallo-latin sous Néron', in Iliescu and Marxgut (1992), 103–14
    (1995), 'Le latin des tablettes de Murécine (Pompéi)', *REL* 73, 138–50

Font, A. (1894), *De Cicerone Graeca uocabula usurpante* (Paris)

Fordyce, C. J. (1961), *Catullus, a Commentary* (Oxford)

Fraenkel, E. (1960), *Elementi plautini in Plauto* (Florence)

Frank, T. (1935), '*Tau Gallicum*, Vergil, Catalepton II, 4', *AJP* 56, 254–6

Frankfurter, A. (1998), *Religion in Roman Egypt. Assimilation and Resistance* (Princeton)

Fraser, P. M. (1960), *Samothrace. The Inscriptions on Stone* (London)

Frederiksen, M. (1984), *Campania* (Rome)

Frei, P. (1958), *Die Flexion griechischer Namen der 1. Deklination im Latein* (Zurich)

Friedrich, J. (1919), 'Das Attische im Munde von Ausländern bei Aristophanes', *Philologus* 75, 274–303

Friedrich, J. (1947), 'Griechisches und Römisches in phönizischem und punischem Gewande', in J. Fück (ed.), *Festschrift Otto Eissfeldt zum 60. Geburtstage 1. September 1947* (Halle an der Saale), 109–24

(1953), 'Vulgärpunisch und Vulgärlatein in den neupunischen Inschriften', *Cahiers de Byrsa* 3, 99–111

(1957), 'Punische Studien', *Zeitschrift der Deutschen Morgenländischen Gesellschaft* 107, 282–98

Friedrich, J. and Röllig, W. (1970), *Phönizisch-Punische Grammatik*, 2nd edn (Rome)

Gabba, E. (1994), 'Rome and Italy: the Social War', *The Cambridge Ancient History*, 2nd edn, vol. IX (Cambridge), 104–28

Gaeng, P. A. (1968), *An Inquiry into the Influences of the Germanic Superstratum on the Vocabulary and Phonetic Structure of Gallo-Romance* (Upper Montclair)

(1977), *A Study of Nominal Inflection in Latin Inscriptions. A Morpho-Syntactic Analysis* (Chapel Hill)

(1984), *Collapse and Reorganization of the Latin Nominal Flection as Reflected in Epigraphic Sources* (Potomac)

Gagé, J. (1977), *Res Gestae Diui Augusti*, 2nd edn (Paris)

Gal, S. (1988), 'The political economy of code choice', in Heller (1988), 245–64

Galand, L. (1966), 'Inscriptions libyques', in Galand, Février and Vajda (1966), 1–77

Galand, L., Février, J. and Vajda, G. (1966), *Inscriptions antiques du Maroc* (Paris)

Gallo, P. (1989), 'Ostraca demotici da Medinet Madi', *Egitto e vicino oriente* 12, 99–123

Gamillscheg, E. (1970), *Romania Germanica: Sprach- und Siedlungsgeschichte der Germanen auf dem Boden des alten Römerreiches*, Bd. 1: *Zu den ältesten Berührungen zwischen Römern und Germanen; Die Franken*, 2nd edn (Berlin)

Garbini, G. (1974), 'Dieci anni di epigrafia punica nel Magreb (1965–1974)', *Studi Magrebini* 6, 1–36

(1986), 'Venti anni di epigrafia punica nel Magreb (1965–1985)', *Rivista di studi fenici* 14, *Supplemento*

Garcia y Bellido, A. (1972), 'Die Latinisierung Hispaniens', *ANRW* 1.1, 462–500

García Domingo, E. (1979), *Latinismos en la koiné (en los documentos epigráficos desde el 212 a. J. C. hasta el 14 d. J.C.). Gramatica y léxico griego-latino, latino-griego* (Burgos)

García-Hernández, B. (ed.) (1998), *Estudios de lingüística latina. Actas del IX Coloquio Internacional de Lingüística Latina (Universidad Autonóma de Madrid 14–18 de abril de 1997)* (Madrid)

Gardner, I., Alcock, A. and Funk, W.-P. (1999), *Coptic Documentary Texts from Kellis*, I: *P. Kell.* V (Oxford)

Gardner-Chloros, P. (1991), *Language Selection and Switching in Strasbourg* (Oxford)

(1995), 'Code-switching in community, regional and national repertoires: the myth of the discreteness of languistic systems', in Milroy and Muysken (1995), 68–89

Garnsey, P. (1974), 'Aspects of the decline of the urban aristocracy in the Empire', *ANRW* II.1, 229–52

Garrucci, P. R. (1853), 'L'ambulatio e i programmi popolari in Pompei', *Bullettino archeologico napolitano* n.s. 19, 148–52

Gauthier, H. (1911), *Les temples immergés de la Nubie. Le temple de Kalabchah*, Tome premier.*(Texte)* (Cairo)

Geiger, J. (1996), 'Titulus crucis', *Scripta Classica Israelica* 15, 202–7

(1999), 'Some Latin authors from the Greek East', *CQ* 49, 606–17

Geller, M. J. (1997), 'The last wedge', *Zeitschrift für Assyriologie und Vorderasiatische Archäologie* 87, 43–95

Gelsomino, R. (1959), 'Il greco e i grecismi di Augusto – la vita privata', *Maia* 11, 120–31

Georgacas, D. J. (1948), 'On the nominal endings -ις, -ιν, in later Greek', *CP* 43, 243–60

Geraci, G. (1971), 'Ricerche sul proskynema', *Aegyptus* 51, 3–211

Gerov, B. (1980), *Beiträge zur Geschichte der römischen Provinzen Moesien und Thrakien. Gesammelte Aufsätze* (Amsterdam)

Gershevitch, I. (1979), 'The alloglottography of Old Persian', *TPhS* (1979), 114–90

Ghiretti, E. (1996), 'Note sul bilinguismo greco-latino dell' Egitto romano', *Aevum Antiquum* 9, 275–98

Giacalone Ramat, A. (1995), 'Code-switching in the context of dialect/standard language relations', in Milroy and Muysken (1995), 45–67

Giacomelli, G. (1963), *La lingua falisca* (Florence)

Giard, J.-B. (1965), 'La monnaie de Capoue et le problème de la datation du denier romain', *Congresso internazionale di numismatica, Roma 11–16 settembre 1961*, vol. II. *Atti* (Rome), 235–60

Gibson, J. C. L. (1982), *Textbook of Syrian Semitic Inscriptions*, vol. III. *Phoenician Inscriptions* (Oxford)

Gifford, D. J. and Hodcroft, F. W. (1966), *Textos lingüísticos del medioevo espanol*, 2nd edn (Oxford)

Gignac, F. T. (1970), 'The pronunciation of Greek stops in the papyri', *TAPA* 101, 185–202

(1976), *A Grammar of the Greek Papyri of the Roman and Byzantine Periods*, I. (*Phonology*) (Milan)

(1981), *A Grammar of the Greek Papyri of the Roman and Byzantine Periods*, II. *Morphology* (Milan)

Giles, H. and St. Clair, R. N. (eds.) (1979), *Language and Social Psychology* (Oxford)

Giles, H. and Smith, P. M. (1979), 'Accommodation theory: optimal levels of convergence', in Giles and St. Clair (1979), 45–65

Gilliam, J. F. (1956), 'The veterans and *praefectus castrorum* of the *II Traiana* in AD 157', *AJP* 77, 359–75

(1978), 'Some Roman elements in Roman Egypt', *ICS* 3, 115–31

Giuliani, E. (1985), 'Note su alcuni calchi nel *De medicina* di Cassio Felice', in Mazzini and Fusco (1985), 313–19

Godefroy, F. (1888), *Dictionnaire de l'ancienne langue française*, V (Paris)

Gómez Pallarès, J. G. (1991), 'Nombres de artistas en inscripciones musivas latinas e ibericas de *Hispania* (1) (2)', *Epigraphica* 53, 59–96

Gomme, A. W. and Sandbach, F. H. (1973), *Menander, a Commentary* (Oxford)

Goodchild, R. G. (1950), 'The Latino-Libyan inscriptions of Tripolitania', *Antiquaries Journal*, 30, 135–44

   (1954), 'La necropoli romano-libica di Bir Ed-Dréder', *Quaderni di archeologia della Libia* 3, 91–107

Gordon, M. L. (1924), 'The nationality of slaves under the early Roman Empire', *JRS* 14, 93–111

Grandgent, C. H. (1908), *An Introduction to Vulgar Latin* (Boston)

Grant, M. (1946), *From Imperium to Auctoritas. A Historical Study of Aes Coinage in the Roman Empire 49 B.C. – A.D. 14* (Cambridge)

Gratwick, A. S. (1971), 'Hanno's Punic speech in the Poenulus of Plautus', *Hermes* 99, 25–45

Graur, A. (1929), *Les consonnes géminées en latin* (Paris)

Green, D. H. (1998), *Language and History in the Early Germanic World* (Cambridge)

Green, R. P. H. (1991), *The Works of Ausonius* (Oxford)

Green, W. M. (1951), 'Augustine's use of Punic', *Univ. Calif. Stud. in Sem. Philol.* 11, 179–90

Grenier, J.-C. (1987), 'Le protocole pharaonique des empereurs romains (analyse formelle et signification historique)', *Revue d'Égyptologie* 38, 81–104

   (1988), 'Notes sur l'Égypte romaine (1,1–7)', *C d'É* 63, 57–76

Griffin, M. (1994), 'The intellectual developments of the Ciceronian age', *The Cambridge Ancient History*, 2nd edn, vol. IX (Cambridge), 689–728

Gruen, E. S. (1984), *The Hellenistic World and the Coming of Rome* (Berkeley)

   (1993), *Culture and National Identity in Republican Rome* (London)

Guéraud, O. (1942), 'Ostraca grecs et latins de l'Wâdi Fawâkhir', *BIFAO* 41, 141–96

Gummerus, H. (1932), *Der Ärztestand im römischen Reiche nach den Inschriften* (*Soc. Scient. Fennica, Comment. hum. lit.* 3.6) (Helsinki)

Gumperz, J. J. (1982), *Discourse Strategies* (Cambridge)

Hadas, M. (1929), 'Oriental elements in Petronius', *AJP* 50, 378–85

Hagedorn, D. (1990), 'Zur Verwendung von υἱός und θυγάτηρ vor dem Vatersnamen in Urkunden römischer Zeit', *ZPE* 80, 277–82

Hahn, L. (1906), *Rom und Romanismus im griechisch-römischen Osten* (Leipzig)

Hall, R. A. (1974), *External History of the Romance Languages* (New York)

Hamers, J. F. and Blanc, M. H. A. (1989), *Bilinguality and Bilingualism*, revised edn (Cambridge)

Harrauer, H. and Sijpesteijn, P. J. (1985), *Neue texte aus dem antiken Unterricht* (Vienna)

Harris, A. C. and Campbell, L. (1995), *Historical Syntax in Cross-Language Perspective* (Cambridge)

Harris, W. V. (1971), *Rome in Etruria and Umbria* (Oxford)

(1980), 'Towards a study of the Roman slave trade', *MAAR* 36, 117–40

(1989), *Ancient Literacy* (Cambridge, Mass.)

Harrison, S. J. (1994), 'Yew and bow: Vergil *Georgics* 2.448', *HSCP* 96, 201–2

Hassall, M. W. C. and Tomlin, R. S. O. (1993), 'Inscriptions', *Britannia* 24, 310–22

Hatzfeld, J. (1912), 'Les Italiens résidant à Délos mentionnés dans les inscriptions de l'île', *BCH* 36, 5–218

Hatzfeld, J. (1919), *Les trafiquants italiens dans l'Orient hellénique* (Paris)

Hauben, H. (1976), 'On the Gallus inscription at Philae', *ZPE* 22, 189–90

Healey, J. F. and Lightfoot, C. S. (1991), 'A Roman veteran on the Tigris', *EA* 17, 1–7

Healy, J. F. (1999), *Pliny the Elder on Science and Technology* (Oxford)

Hehl, A. (1912), *Die Formen der lateinischen ersten Deklination in den Inschriften* (Tübingen)

Heim, R. (1893), *Incantamenta magica Graeca Latina* (*Jahrbücher für classische Philologie*, 19. Supplementband, 463–576) (Leipzig)

Heller, M. (ed.) (1988), *Codeswitching. Anthropological and Sociolinguistic Perspectives* (Berlin, New York and Amsterdam)

(1995), 'Code-switching and the politics of language', in Milroy and Muysken (1995), 158–74

Helttula, A. (1973), 'Onomastica', in V. Väänänen (ed.), *Le iscrizioni della necropoli dell'autoparco vaticano* (Rome), 139–55

(1987), *Studies on the Latin Accusative Absolute* (Helsinki)

Heraeus, W. (1930), 'Ein makkaronisches Ovidfragment bei Quintilian', *RhM* 79, 253–78

(1937), *Kleine Schriften von Wilhelm Heraeus zum 75. Geburtstag am 4. Dezember 1937*, ed. J. B. Hofmann (Heidelberg)

Herescu, N. I. (ed.) (1958), *Ovidiana. Recherches sur Ovide* (Paris)

Hering, J. (1935), *Lateinisches bei Appian* (Leipzig)

Herman, J. (1983) 'La langue latine dans la Gaule romaine', *ANRW* II.29.2, 1045–60

(1966), 'Recherches sur l'évolution grammaticale du latin vulgaire: les emplois "fautifs" du nominatif', *Acta Classica Univ. Scient. Debreceniensis* 2, 109–12 (= Herman (1990), 321–5)

(ed.) (1987), *Latin vulgaire – latin tardif. Actes du Ier Colloque international sur le latin vulgaire et tardif (Pécs, 2–5 septembre 1985)* (Tübingen)

(1990), *Du latin aux langues romanes. Études de linguistique historique*, ed. S. Kiss (Tübingen)

(1991), 'Spoken and written Latin in the last centuries of the Roman Empire. A contribution to the linguistic history of the western provinces', in R. Wright (ed.), *Latin and the Romance Languages in the Early Middle Ages* (London and New York), 29–43

Hernando Balmori, C. (1935), 'Sobre la inscripción bilingue de Lamas de Moledo', *Emerita* 3, 77–119

Heurgon, J. (1964), *Daily Life of the Etruscans*, translated by J. Kirkup (London)
(1966), 'The inscriptions of Pyrgi', *JRS* 56, 1–15
(1976), 'L'agronome carthaginois Magon et ses traducteurs en latin et en grec', *CRAI* (1976), 441–56

Heuser, G. (1929), *Die Personennamen der Kopten* I (Leipzig)

Hillers, D. R. and Cussini, E. (1996), *Palmyrene Aramaic Texts* (Baltimore and London)

Hintze, F. (1964), 'The Latin inscription from Musawwarat es Sufra', *Kush* 12, 296–8

Hock, H. H. (1986), *Principles of Historical Linguistics* (Berlin, New York and Amsterdam)

Hock, H. H. and Joseph, B. D. (1996), *Language History, Language Change, and Language Relationship: an Introduction to Historical and Comparative Linguistics* (Berlin)

Hoffmann, C. (1991), *An Introduction to Bilingualism* (London and New York)

Hofmann, J. B. (1951) *Lateinische Umgangssprache*, 3rd edn (Heidelberg)

Hofmann, J. B. and Szantyr, A. (1965), *Lateinische Syntax und Stilistik* (Munich)

Hohlwein, N. (1940), 'Déplacements et tourisme dans l'Égypte romaine', *C d'É* 15, 253–78

Holford-Strevens, L. A. (1988), *Aulus Gellius* (London)
(1992), '*KAI* for *ET*', *CQ* 42, 284–7
(1993), '*Vtraque lingua doctus*: some notes on bilingualism in the Roman Empire', in *Liverpool Classical Papers* No. 3. *Tria Lustra: Essays and Notes Presented to John Pinsent Founder and Editor of Liverpool Classical Monthly by some of its Contributors on the Occasion of the 150th Issue* (Liverpool), 203–13

Homeyer, H. (1957), 'Some observations on bilingualism and language shift in Italy from the sixth to the third century BC', *Word* 13, 415–40

Hopkins, M. K. (1961), 'Social mobility in the later Roman Empire: the evidence of Ausonius', *CQ* n.s. 11, 239–49

Horrocks, G. C. (1997), *Greek: a History of the Language and its Speakers* (London and New York)

Horsfall, N. (1979), 'Doctus sermones utriusque linguae ?', *EMC* 23, 79–95
(1983), 'Some problems in the "Laudatio Turiae"', *BICS* 30, 85–98

Horsley, G. H. R. (1989), *New Documents Illustrating Early Christianity*, volume V. *Linguistic Essays* (Sydney)

Housman, A. E. (1972) = J. Diggle and F. R. D. Goodyear, (eds.), *The Classical Papers of A. E. Housman*, 3 vols. (Cambridge)

Houston, G. W. (1990), 'The altar from Rome with inscriptions to Sol and Malakbel', *Syria* 67, 189–93

Hunink, V. (1997), *Apuleius of Madauros Pro se de Magia (Apologia)*, 2 vols. (Amsterdam)

Hutchinson, G. O. (1998), *Cicero's Correspondence. A Literary Study* (Oxford)

Ihm, M. (1892), 'Vulgärformen lateinischer Zahlwörter auf Inschriften', *ALL* 7, 65–72
(1902), 'Eine lateinische Babriosübersetzung', *Hermes* 37, 147–51

Iliescu, M. and Marxgut, W. (eds.) (1992), *Latin vulgaire – latin tardif III. Actes du IIIème Colloque international sur le latin vulgaire et tardif (Innsbruck, 2–5 septembre 1991)* (Tübingen)

Isaac, B. H. (1990), *The Limits of Empire. The Roman Army in the East* (Oxford)

Iversen, E. (1965), 'The date of the so-called inscription of Caligula on the Vatican obelisk', *JEA* 51, 149–54

Jacobson, R. (1998a), *Codeswitching Worldwide* (Berlin and New York)

 (1998b), 'Conveying a broader message through bilingual discourse: an attempt at Contrastive Codeswitching research', in Jacobson (1998a), 51–76

Janko, J. (1910), '*Melca*', *Glotta* 2, 38–49

Jannaccone, S. (1950), *Recherches sur les éléments grecs du vocabulaire latin de l'empire* (Paris)

Jannaris, A. N. (1897), *An Historical Greek Grammar, chiefly of the Attic Dialect* (London)

Jaussen, R. P., and Savignac, P. P (1914), *Mission archéologique en arabie*, II (Paris)

Jeanneret, M. (1918), *La langue des tablettes d'exécration latines* (Paris and Neuchâtel)

Jocelyn, H. D. (1972), 'The poems of Quintus Ennius', *ANRW* I.2, 987–1026

 (1973), 'Greek poetry in Cicero's prose writing', *YCS* 23, 61–111

 (1999), 'Code-switching in the comoedia palliata', in G. Vogt-Spira and B. Rommel (eds.), *Rezeption und Identität. Die kulturelle Auseinandersetzung Roms mit Griechenland als europäisches Paradigma* (Stuttgart), 169–95

Jordan, D. (2000), 'Ephesia grammata at Himera', *ZPE* 130, 104–7

Kahle, W. (1918), *De vocabulis Graecis Plauti aetate in sermonem Latinum vere receptis* (Münster)

Kaimio, J. (1969), 'The nominative singular in *-i* of Latin gentilicia', *Arctos* n.s. 6, 23–42

 (1975), 'The ousting of Etruscan by Latin in Etruria', in *Studies in the Romanization of Etruria (Acta Instituti Romani Finlandiae*, vol. V) (Rome), 85–245

 (1979a), *The Romans and the Greek Language* (Helsinki)

 (1979b), 'Latin in Roman Egypt', *Actes du XVe Congrès International de Papyrologie*, III (Brussels), 27–33

Kajanto, I. (1963a), *A Study of the Greek Epitaphs of Rome* (Helsinki)

 (1963b), *Onomastic Studies in the Early Christian Inscriptions of Rome and Carthage* (Helsinki)

 (1965), *The Latin Cognomina* (Helsinki)

 (1966), *Supernomina. A Study in Latin Epigraphy* (Helsinki)

 (1980), 'Minderheiten und ihre Sprachen in der Hauptstadt Rom', in Neumann and Untermann (1980), 83–101

Kajava, M. (1999), ''Ἄρκτος: ἀρκτεύω and the like', *Arctos* 33, 15–65

Kapsomenos, S. G. (1953), 'Das Griechische in Ägypten', *MH* 10, 248–63

Kaster, R. A. (1995), *C. Suetonius Tranquillus, De Grammaticis et Rhetoribus* (Oxford)

Katičić, R. (1980), 'Die Balkanprovinzen', in Neumann and Untermann (1980), 103–20

Katz, J. T. (2000), 'Egnatius' dental fricatives (Catullus 39.20)', *CP* 95, 338–48

Kayser, F. (1994), *Recueil des inscriptions grecques et latines (non funéraires) d'Alexandrie impériale (Ier - IIIe s. apr. J.-C.)* (Cairo)

Kearns, J. M. (1990), 'Σεμνότης and dialect gloss in the *Odussia* of Livius Andronicus', *AJP* 111, 40–52

Kearsley, R. A., with the collaboration of Evans, T. V. (2001), *Greeks and Romans in Imperial Asia. Mixed Language Inscriptions and Linguistic Evidence for Cultural Interaction until the End of AD III* (Bonn)

Keenan, J. G. (1994), 'The will of Gaius Longinus Castor', *BASP* 31, 101–7

Kelsey, F. W. (1923), 'A waxed tablet of the year 128 AD', *TAPA* 54, 187–95

Killeen, J. F. (1974), 'Tau Gallicum (Vergil, *Catalepton* 2, 4)', *Orpheus* 21, 57–9

Kohlstedt, H. (1917), *Das Romanische in den Artes des Consentius* (Erlangen)

Kolník, T. (1978), 'Q. Atilius Primus – interprex centurio und negotiator. Eine bedeutende Grabinschrift aus dem 1. Jh. u. Z. im Quedischen Limes-Vorland', *Acta Archaeologica Academiae Scientiarum Hungaricae* 30, 61–75

Konjetzny, G. (1906–8), 'De idiotismis syntacticis in titulis latinis urbanis (C.I.L. vol. VI.) conspicuis', *ALL* 15, 297–351

Kossmann, M. (1999), *Essai sur la phonologie du proto-berbère* (Cologne)

Kotansky, R. (1991), 'Incantations and prayers for salvation on inscribed Greek amulets', in C. A. Faraone and D. Obbink (eds.), *Magika Hiera. Ancient Greek Magic and Religion* (New York and Oxford), 107–37

Kramer, J. (1977), 'Sprachlicher Kommentar zum lateinisch-griechischen Glossar P. Lond. II 481', *ZPE* 26, 231–8

  (1983), *Glossaria bilinguia in papyris et membranis reperta* (Bonn)

  (1984) 'Testi greci scritti nell'alfabeto latino et testi latini scritti nell'alfabeto greco: un caso di bilinguisimo imperfetto', *Atti del XVII Congresso Internationale di Papirologia*, III (Naples), 1377–84

  (1988), 'Griechisches und lateinisches Glossar *de moribus humanis*', *Tyche* 3, 141–5

  (1990), 'Zwei neue Augustalpräfekten auf einem lateinischen Protokoll', *Tyche* 5, 41–3

  (1993), 'Die Wiener Liste von Soldaten der III. und XXII. Legion (P. Vindob. L2)', *ZPE* 97, 147–8

  (1999), 'Zwei lateinische Alphabete für Griechischsprachige. Neuausgabe von P. Ant. 1, fr. 1 Verso', *APF* 45, 32–8

Kroll, W. (1912), 'Der lateinische Relativsatz', *Glotta* 3, 1–18

  (1933), *Die Kultur der ciceronischen Zeit*, 2 vols. (Leipzig)

Kruschwitz, P. (2000), 'Die sprachlichen Anomalien der Werbeinschrift CIL X 7296', *ZPE* 130, 239–40

Kühner, R. and Stegmann, C. (1955), *Ausführliche Grammatik der lateinischen Sprache: Satzlehre*, 3rd edn revised by A. Thierfelder (Leverkusen)

Lachmann, K. (1848), *Die Schriften der römischen Feldmesser*, 1 (Berlin)

La'da, C. A. (1994), 'One stone: two messages (CG 50044)', in A. Bülow-Jacobsen (ed.), *Proceedings of the 20th International Congress of Papyrologists, Copenhagen, 23–29 August, 1992* (Copenhagen), 160–4

Lambert, P.-Y. (1995), *La langue gauloise* (Paris)

Lambrechts, P. (1937), 'Le commerce des "Syriens" en Gaul du Haut Empire à l'époque mérovingienne', *AC* 6, 35–61

Lambrino, S. (1958), 'Tomis, cité gréco-gète, chez Ovide', in Herescu (1958), 379–90

Lancel, S. (1981), 'La fin et la survie de la latinité en Afrique du nord. État des questions', *REL* 59, 269–97

(1985), 'Y a-t-il une *Africitas?*', *REL* 63, 161–82

Landgraf, G. (1914), *Kommentar zu Ciceros Rede Pro Sex. Roscio Amerino*, 2nd edn (Leipzig and Berlin)

Langslow, D. R. (2000), *Medical Latin in the Roman Empire* (Oxford)

(forthcoming), 'Approaching bilingualism in corpus languages', in J. N. Adams, M. Janse and S. C. R. Swain (eds.), *Bilingualism in Ancient Society: Language Contact and the Written Word* (Oxford)

Laoust, E. (1920), *Mots et choses berbères. Notes de linguistique et d'ethnographie. Dialectes du Maroc* (Paris)

La Regina, A. (1976), 'Rivista di epigrafia italica', *SE* 44, 283–8

Laughton, E. (1964), *The Participle in Cicero* (Oxford)

Laurand, L. (1936–8), *Études sur le style des discours de Cicéron*, 4th edn (Paris)

Lavency, M. and Longrée, D. (eds.) (1989), *Actes du Ve Colloque de Linguistique latine* (*Cahiers de l'Institut de Linguistique de Louvain*) (Louvain-la-Neuve)

Law, V. (1997), *Grammar and Grammarians in the Early Middle Ages* (London and New York)

Lazzeroni, R. L. (1956), 'La "geminatio vocalium" nelle iscrizioni latine', *ASNP* 25, 124–35

(1965), 'Il dativo "sabellico" in -*a*. Contributo alla conoscenza della latinizzazione dei Peligni', *SSL* 5, 65–86

(1974), 'Contatti di lingue e di culture nell'Italia antica: il patronimico nella formula onomastica', *SSL* 14, 275–306

(1976), 'Differenze linguistiche nel territorio dell'Abruzzo e del Molise in epoca italica', in *Scritti in onore di Giuliano Bonfante* (Brescia) I, 389–99

(1991a), 'Contatti di lingue e di culture nell'Italia antica: un bilancio', in Campanile (1991a), 177–88

(1991b), 'Osco e latino nella *Lex sacra* di Lucera: fra competenza linguistica e valutazione metalinguistica', *SSL* 31, 95–111

Lee, A. D. (1993), *Information and Frontiers. Roman Foreign Relations in Late Antiquity* (Cambridge)

Leiwo, M. (1989), 'Philostratus of Ascalon, his bank, his connections and Naples in *c*. 130–90 BC', *Athenaeum* 77, 575–84

(1995a), *Neapolitana. A Study of Population and Language in Graeco-Roman Naples* (Helsinki)

(1995b), 'The mixed languages in Roman inscriptions', in Solin, Salomies and Liertz (1995), 293–301

Lejeune, M. (1949), 'Sur le traitement osque de *-ā* final', *BSL* 45, 104–10

(1952a), 'Notes de linguistique italique: V–VII. Les inscriptions de la collection Froehner', *REL* 30, 87–126

(1952b), 'Problèmes de philologie vénète: VII–X', *RPh* 26, 192–218

(1953a), 'Notes de linguistique italique: VIII–XI. Les urnes cinéraires inscrites d'Este', *REL* 31, 117–74

(1953b), 'Les plaques de bronze votives du sanctuaire vénète d'Este (Étude épigraphique)', *REA* 55, 58–112

(1954), 'Notes de linguistique italique: XII. Les dédicaces du sanctuaire de Làgole', *REL* 32, 120–38

(1970), 'Phonologie osque et graphie grecque', *REA* 72, 271–316

(1972), 'Venetica, XV–XVII', *Latomus* 31, 3–21

(1974), *Manuel de la langue vénète* (Heidelberg)

(1976a), 'Rivista di epigrafia italica', *SE* 44, 290–1

(1976b), *L'Anthroponymie osque* (Paris)

(1988), *Recueil des inscriptions gauloises (R.I.G.)*, volume II – fascicule 1. *Textes gallo-étrusques, textes gallo-latins sur pierre* (Paris)

(1992), 'En marge de la Sententia Contrebeensium', *REL* 70, 43–55

Lendle, O. (1992), 'Vitruv als Übersetzer aus dem Griechischen', in Müller, Sier and Werner (1992), 189–200

Leo, F. (1883), 'Lectiones Plautinae', *Hermes* 18, 558–87

(1912), *Plautinische Forschungen zur Kritik und Geschichte der Komödie*, 2nd edn (Berlin)

Leon, H. J. (1953–4), 'The Jews of Venusia', *JQR* n. s. 44, 267–84

Leumann, M. (1947), 'Die lateinische Dichtersprache', *MH* 4, 116–39

(1977), *Lateinische Laut- und Formenlehre*, 6th edn (Munich)

Levick, B. (1995), 'The Latin inscriptions of Asia Minor', in Solin, Salomies and Liertz (1995), 393–402

Levi Della Vida, G. (1935), 'Due iscrizioni imperiali neo-puniche di Leptis Magna', *Africa Italiana* 6, 1–29

(1951), 'The neo-Punic dedication of the Ammonium at Ras El-Haddagia', Appendix I to R. G. Goodchild, 'Roman sites on the Tarhuna plateau of Tripolitania', *PBSR* 19, 65–8

(1963), 'Sulle iscrizioni "latino-libiche" della Tripolitania', *Oriens Antiquus* 2, 65–94

(1965), 'Parerga Neopunica', *Oriens Antiquus* 4, 59–70

Levi Della Vida, G. and Amadasi Guzzo, M. G. (1987), *Iscrizioni puniche della Tripolitania (1927–1967)* (Rome)

Lewis, N. (1959), 'A veteran in quest of a home', *TAPA* 90, 139–46

(1970), '"Greco-Roman Egypt": fact or fiction?', in D. H. Samuel (ed.), *Proceedings of the Twelfth International Congress of Papyrology* (Toronto), 3–14

(1984), 'The Romanity of Roman Egypt: a growing consensus', in *Atti del XVII Congresso Internazionale di Papirologia*, III (Naples), 1077–84

(1989), *The Documents from the Bar Kokhba Period in the Cave of Letters. Greek Papyri* (Jerusalem)

Lewis, P. R. and Jones, G. D. B. (1970), 'Roman gold-mining in north-west Spain', *JRS* 60, 169–85

Liechtenhan, E. (1963), *Anthimi De obseruatione ciborum ad Theodoricum regem Francorum epistula* (Berlin)

Lindner, T. (1996), *Lateinische Komposita. Ein Glossar vornehmlich zum Wortschatz der Dichtersprache* (Innsbruck)

Lindsay, W. M. (1894), *The Latin Language* (Oxford)

Lintott, A. W. (1978), 'The Capitoline dedications to Jupiter and the Roman people', *ZPE* 30, 137–44

Löfstedt, B. (1961), *Studien über die Sprache der langobardischen Gesetze* (Uppsala)
(1983), 'Rückschau und Ausblick auf die vulgärlateinische Forschung. Quellen und Methoden', *ANRW* II.29.1, 453–79

Löfstedt, E. (1911), *Philologischer Kommentar zur Peregrinatio Aetheriae* (Uppsala)
(1932), 'Lateinisch-griechische Parallelen', in *Symbolae Philologicae O. A. Danielsson octogenario dicatae* (Uppsala), 171–82
(1936), *Vermischte Studien zur lateinischen Sprachkunde und Syntax* (Lund)
(1950), *Coniectanea. Untersuchungen auf dem Gebiete der antiken und mittelalterlichen Latinität* (Uppsala and Stockholm)
(1956), *Syntactica. Studien und Beiträge zur historischen Syntax des Lateins*, vols. I 2nd edn, II (Lund)
(1959), *Late Latin* (Oslo)

Lomas, K. (1993), *Rome and the Western Greeks 350 BC – AD 200. Conquest and Acculturation in Southern Italy* (London and New York)

Loomis, W. T. (1994), 'Entella tablets VI (254–241 BC) and VII (20th cent. AD?)', *HSCP* 96, 127–60

Lot, F. (1946), 'La langue du commandement dans les armées romaines et le cri de guerre français au moyen âge', in *Mélanges dédiés à la mémoire de Félix Grat*, I (Paris), 203–9
(1948), *Naissance de la France* (Paris)

Lozovan, E. (1958), 'Ovide et le bilinguisme (avec une *Note* de N. I. Herescu)', in Herescu (1958), 396–405

Lunelli, A. (ed.) (1980), *La lingua poetica latina. Saggi di Wilhelm Kroll, Hendrikus Hubertus Janssen, Manu Leumann*, 2nd edn (Bologna)

MacBain, B. (1982), *Prodigy and Expiation: a Study in Religion and Politics in Republican Rome* (Brussels)

McClure, E. (1998), 'The relationship between form and function in written national language–English codeswitching: evidence from Mexico, Spain, and Bulgaria', in Jacobson (1998a), 125–50

Mackey, W. F. (1968), 'The description of bilingualism', in Fishman (1968), 554–84

Maclean, I. (1992), *Interpretation and Meaning in the Renaissance. The Case of Law* (Cambridge)

MacMullen, R. (1966), 'Provincial languages in the Roman Empire', *AJP* 87, 1–17
(1993), 'The unromanized in Rome', in Cohen and Frerichs (1993), 47–64

Machado, J. P. (1967), *Dicionário etimológico da língua portuguesa*, 2nd edn, 3 vols. (Lisbon)

Magie, D. (1905), *De Romanorum iuris publici sacrique vocabulis sollemnibus in graecum sermonem conuersis* (Leipzig)

Mallon, H. (1952), *Paléographie romaine* (Madrid)

Mancini, M. (1988), 'Sulla "defixio" osco-latina Vetter 7', *SSL* 28, 201–30

Mandilaras, B. G. (1973), *The Verb in the Greek Non-Literary Papyri* (Athens)

Maniet, A. (1972), 'La linguistique italique', *ANRW* I.2, 522–92

Marichal, R. (1971), 'Quelques graffites inédits de La Graufesenque', *CRAI* 1971, 188–212

(1974), 'Nouveaux graffites de La Graufesenque, IV', *REA* 76, 85–110

(1988), *Les graffites de La Graufesenque* (Paris)

(1992), *Les ostraca de Bu Njem* (Assraya al Hamra, Tripoli)

Mariner Bogorra, S. (1952), *Inscripciones hispanas en verso* (Barcelona and Madrid)

(1973), *Inscripciones romanas de Barcelona (lapidarias y musivas)* (Barcelona)

Mariotti, S. (1988), 'Enn. *Ann.* 120 Skutsch (126 Vahlen²)', in N. Horsfall (ed.), *Vir bonus discendi peritus. Studies in Celebration of Otto Skutsch's Eightieth Birthday (Institute of Classical Studies, Bulletin Supplement,* 51) (London), 82–5

Marrone, G. Cresci (1976), 'Sulla traduzione in alcune epigrafi bilingui latino-greche del periodo augusteo', in *Contributi di storia antica in onore di Albino Garzetti* (Genoa), 315–30

Martelli, M. (1981), 'Rivista di epigrafia etrusca', *SE* 49, 243–6

(1982), 'Rivista di epigrafia etrusca', *SE* 50, 287–90

(1984), 'Rivista di epigrafia etrusca', *SE* 52, 316

Martin, R. H. (1976), *Terence Adelphoe* (Cambridge)

Marx, F. (1904–5), *C. Lucilii Carminum Reliquiae,* 2 vols. (Leipzig)

(1906–8), 'Fefellitus sum', *ALL* 15, 88

Mastino, A. (1985), 'Le relazioni tra Africa e Sardegna in età romana: inventario preliminare', in A. Mastino (ed.), *L'Africa romana. Atti del II convegno di studio Sassari, 14–16 dicembre 1984* (Sassari), 27–89

Mateescu, G. G. (1923), 'I Traci nelle epigrafi di Roma', *EphDacor* 1, 57–290

Matthews, J. F. (1989), *The Roman Empire of Ammianus* (London)

(1994) 'The origin of Ammianus', *CQ* 44, 252–69

Mattingly, D. J. (1987), 'Libyans and the "limes": culture and society in Roman Tripolitania', *Antiquités africaines* 23, 71–93

Maurach, G. (1995), *Lateinische Dichtersprache* (Darmstadt)

Mayser, F. (1906), *Grammatik der griechischen Papyri aus der Ptolemäerzeit,* I. *Laut- und Wortlehre* (Leipzig)

(1926), *Grammatik der griechischen Papyri aus der Ptolemäerzeit,* II.1 *Satzlehre, analytischer Teil* (Berlin and Leipzig)

(1934), *Grammatik der griechischen Papyri aus der Ptolemäerzeit,* II.3 *Satzlehre, synthetischer Teil* (Berlin and Leipzig)

Mazzini, I. (1984), *De observantia ciborum. Traduzione tardo-antica del* περὶ διαίτης *pseudoippocratico* (Rome)

Mazzini, I. and Flammini, G. (eds.) (1983), *De conceptu. Estratti di un'antica traduzione latina del* περὶ γυναικείων *pseudoippocratico* (Bologna)

Mazzini, I. and Fusco, F. (eds.) (1985), *I testi di medicina latini antichi. Problemi filologici e storici (Atti del I Convegno Internazionale, Macerata – S. Severino M., 26–28 aprile 1984)* (Rome)

Meid, W. (1983), 'Gallisch oder Lateinisch? Soziolinguistische und andere Bemerkungen zu populären gallo-lateinischen Inschriften', *ANRW* II.29.2, 1019–44

(1996), *Heilpflanzen und Heilsprüche. Zeugnisse gallischer Sprache bei Marcellus von Bordeaux* (Innsbruck)

Meinersmann, B. (1927), *Die lateinischen Wörter und Namen in den griechischen Papyri* (Leipzig)

Meiser, G. (1986), *Lautgeschichte der umbrischen Sprache* (Innsbruck)

(1987), 'Pälignisch, Latein und Südpikenisch', *Glotta* 65, 104–25

Mellor, R. (1975), ΘΕΑ ΡΩΜΗ. *The Worship of the Goddess Roma in the Greek World* (Göttingen)

(1978), 'The dedications on the Capitoline Hill', *Chiron* 8, 319–30

Mengarelli, R. (1936), 'Il luogo e i materiali del tempio di ″HPA a Caere', *SE* 10, 67–86

Meredith, D. (1953), 'Annius Plocamus: two inscriptions from the Berenice road', *JRS* 43, 38–40

(1956), 'The Myos Hormos road: inscriptions and ostraca', *C d'É* 31, 356–62

Meuwese, A. P. M. (1920), *De Rerum Gestarum Diui Augusti uersione Graeca* (Buscoduci)

Meyer, E. A. (1990), 'Explaining the epigraphic habit in the Roman Empire: the evidence of epitaphs', *JRS* 80, 74–96

Meyer, G. (1895), *Neugriechische Studien*, III: *Die lateinischen Lehnworte im Neugriechischen* (*Sitzungberichte der philosophisch-historischen Classe der Kaiserlichen Akademie der Wissenschaften* 132) (Vienna)

Migliorini, P. (1981), 'Κόλποι e *sinus* nella lingua medica greca', *Prometheus* 7, 254–62

Milik, J. T. (1954), 'Le graffito phénicien en caractères grecs de la grotte d'Astarté à Waṣṭa', *Mélanges de l'Université Saint Joseph* 31, 3–12

(1967), 'Inscription araméenne en caractères grecs de Doura-Europos et une dédicace grecque de Cordoue', *Syria* 44, 289–306

Millar, F. G. B. (1968), 'Local cultures in the Roman Empire: Libyan, Punic and Latin in Roman Africa', *JRS* 58, 126–34

(1981), 'The world of the *Golden Ass*', *JRS* 71, 63–75

(1990), 'The Roman *coloniae* of the Near East: a study of cultural relations', in Solin and Kajava (1990), 7–58

(1993a), *The Roman Near East 31 BC – AD 337* (Cambridge, Mass.)

(1993b), 'Ovid and the *Domus Augusta*: Rome seen from Tomoi', *JRS* 83, 1–17

(1995), 'Latin in the epigraphy of the Roman Near East', in Solin, Salomies and Liertz (1995), 403–19

Milne, J. G. (1905), *Catalogue général des antiquités égyptiennes du Musée du Caire. Greek Inscriptions* (Oxford)

(1916), 'Greek and Roman tourists in Egypt', *JEA* 3, 76–80

Milroy, L. and Muysken, P. (eds.) (1995), *One Speaker, Two Languages. Cross-disciplinary Perspectives on Code-Switching* (Cambridge)

Milroy, L. and Wei, L. (1995), 'A social network approach to code-switching: the example of a bilingual community in Britain', in Milroy and Muysken (1995), 136–57

Minnen, P. Van (1986), 'A change of names in Roman Egypt after AD 202? A note on P. Amst. I 72', *ZPE* 62, 87–92

(1994), 'House-to-house enquiries: an interdisciplinary approach to Roman Karanis', *ZPE* 100, 227–51

Mirecki, P., Gardner, I. and Alcock, A. (1997), 'Magical spell, Manichaean letter', in P. Mirecki and J. BeDuhn, *Emerging from Darkness. Studies in the Recovery of Manichaean Sources* (Leiden), 1–32

Mitchell, S. (1976), 'Requisitioned transport in the Roman Empire: a new inscription from Pisidia', *JRS* 66, 106–31

Moltoni, V. (1954), 'Gli influssi dell' osco sulle iscrizioni latine della Regio I', *RIL* 87, 193–232

Mommsen, T. (1877), 'Die pompeianischen Quittungstafeln des L. Caecilius Jucundus', *Hermes* 12, 88–141

Moretti, L. (1972), *Inscriptiones Graecae Urbis Romae* II (Rome)

Morey, C. R. and Ferrari, G. (1959), *The Gold-Glass Collection of the Vatican Library* (Rome)

Mørland, H. (1932), *Die lateinischen Oribasiusübersetzungen* (Oslo)

Mouritsen, H. (1988), *Elections, Magistrates and Municipal Élite. Studies in Pompeian Epigraphy* (Rome)

(1998), *Italian Unification. A Study in Ancient and Modern Historiography* (London)

Mouterde, R. (1956), '*Jupiter Heliopolitanus rex et regulus*', *CRAI* 45–8

Mras, K. (1927–8), 'Randbemerkungen zu Lucilius' Satiren', *WS* 46, 78–84

(1943–7), 'Anthimus und andere lateinische Ärzte im Lichte der Sprachforschung', *WS* 61–2, 98–117

Müller, C. W., Sier, K. and Werner, J. (eds.) (1992), *Zum Umgang mit fremden Sprachen in der griechisch-römischen Antike* (Stuttgart)

Müller, K. (1995), *Petronii Arbitri Satyricon Reliquae*, 4th edn (Stuttgart and Leipzig)

Mueller-Goldingen, C. (1992), 'Cicero als Übersetzer Platons', in Müller, Sier and Werner (1992), 173–87

Mura, P. and Prosdocimi, A. L. (1978), 'Umbro *preplohotatu* (*TI* VIb 60; VIIa 49)). A proposito di osco *plavtad*', *SE* 46, 205–11

Muysken, P. (1995), 'Code-switching and grammatical theory', in Milroy and Muysken (1995), 177–98

Myers-Scotton, C. A. (1993), *Social Motivations for Codeswitching* (Oxford)

(1998), 'Structural uniformities vs. community differences in codeswitching', in Jacobson (1998a), 91–108

Nencioni, G. (1939), 'Innovazioni africane nel lessico latino', *SIFC* 16, 3–47

Neumann, G. (1979), *Neufunde lykischer Inschriften seit 1901* (Vienna)

Neumann, G. and Untermann, J. (eds.) (1980), *Die Sprachen im Römischen Reich der Kaiserzeit* (Cologne and Bonn)

Nicolas, C. (1996), *Utraque lingua. Le calque sémantique: domaine gréco-latin* (Louvain and Paris)

Niedermann, M. (1937), *Consentii Ars De Barbarismis et Metaplasmis; Victorini Fragmentum De Soloecismo et Barbarismo* (Neuchatel)

Nielsen, B. E. (1993), Review of *Mons Claudianus. Ostraca graeca et Latina I (O. Claud. 1 à 190)*, *BASP* 30, 173–7

Nock, A. D. (1934), 'A vision of Mandulis Aion', *HTR* 27, 53–104

Norsa, M. (1946), 'Analogie e coincidenze tra scritture greche e latine nei papiri', *Miscellanea Giovanni Mercati* VI (*Studi e testi* 126, Vatican City), 105–21

Noy, D. (1993), *Jewish Inscriptions of Western Europe*, volume I. *Italy (excluding the City of Rome), Spain and Gaul* (Cambridge)

(1995), *Jewish Inscriptions of Western Europe*, volume II. *The City of Rome* (Cambridge)

(1999), ' "Peace upon Israel": Hebrew formulae and names in Jewish inscriptions from the western Roman Empire', in W. Horbury (ed.), *Hebrew Study from Ezra to Ben-Yehuda* (Edinburgh), 135–46

(2000), *Foreigners at Rome. Citizens and Strangers* (London)

Nutton, V. (1968), 'A Greek doctor at Chester', *Journal of the Chester Archaeological Society* 55, 7–13

Oakley, S. P. (1998), *A Commentary on Livy Books VI–X*, vol. II. *Books VII–VIII* (Oxford)

Oates, D. (1954), 'Ancient settlement in the Tripolitanian Gebel, II: the Berber period', *PBSR* 22, 91–117

Ogilvie, R. M. and Richmond, I. (1967), *Cornelii Taciti De Vita Agricolae* (Oxford)

O'Hara, J. J. (1996), *True Names. Vergil and the Alexandrian Tradition of Etymological Wordplay* (Ann Arbor)

O'Sullivan, N. (1986), 'Two notes on [Vergil] *Catalepton* 2', *CQ* n. s. 36, 496–501

Oswald, F. (1931), *Index of Potters' Stamps on Terra Sigillata 'Samian Ware'* (East Bridgford)

(1956), 'Arretine and early South Gaulish potters', *JRS* 46, 107–14

Oxé, A. and Comfort, H. (1968), *Corpus Vasorum Arretinorum. A Catalogue of the Signatures, Shapes and Chronology of Italian Sigillata* (Bonn)

Pabón, J. M. (1939), 'El griego, lengua de la intimidad entre los Romanos', *Emerita* 7, 126–31

Pallottino, M. (1968), *Testimonia Linguae Etruscae*, 2nd edn (Florence)

(1979a), 'Lo sviluppo socio-istituzionale di Roma arcaica alle luce di nuovi documenti epigrafici', *Studi Romani* 27, 1–14

(1979b), 'Rivista di epigrafia etrusca, 29', *SE* 47, 319–25

Palmer, L. R. (1946), *A Grammar of the Post-Ptolemaic Papyri*, I. *Accidence and Word-formation*, Part I. *The Suffixes* (London)

(1954), *The Latin Language* (London)

Palmer, R. E. A. (1981), 'The topography and social history of Rome's Trastevere (southern sector)', *Proc. Am. Philos. Soc.* 125, 368–97

Panciera, S. (1967), 'La genesi dei documenti epigrafici secondo Mallon. A proposito di una nuova iscrizione metrica', *Atti della Accademia Nazionale dei Lincei. Rendiconti, classe di scienze morali, storiche e filologiche* ser. 8, 22, 100–8

Pandolfini, M. (1983), 'Rivista di epigrafia etrusca', *SE* 51, 254–68

Parlangèli, O. (1960), *Studi messapici* (Milan)

Pârvan, V. (1909), *Die Nationalität der Kaufleute im römischen Kaiserreiche* (Breslau)

Paul, G. M. (1984), *A Historical Commentary on Sallust's Bellum Jugurthinum* (Liverpool)

Pease, A. L. (1920–3), *M. Tulli Ciceronis De Diuinatione libri duo* (*University of Illinois Studies in Language and Literature*, vol. VI (1920), 161–500, vol. VIII (1923), 153–474) (repr. 1973, Darmstadt)

Pellegrini, G. B. and Prosdocimi, A. L. (1967), *La lingua venetica*, 2 vols. (Padua)

Penney, J. H. W. (1988), 'The languages of Italy', *The Cambridge Ancient History*, 2nd edn, vol. IV (Cambridge), 720–38

    (1999), 'Archaism and innovation in Latin poetic syntax', in Adams and Mayer (1999), 249–68

Perry, B. E. (1965), *Babrius and Phaedrus* (Cambridge, Mass. and London)

Peruzzi, E. (1962), 'Testi latini arcaici dei Marsi', *Maia* 14, 117–40

Pestman, P. W. (1977), *Recueil de textes démotiques et bilingues*, I (with the collaboration of J. Quaegebeur and R. L. Vos) (Leiden)

Petersmann, H. (1977), *Petrons urbane Prosa. Untersuchungen zu Sprache und Text (Syntax)* (Vienna)

    (1995), 'Soziale und lokale Aspekte in der Vulgärsprache Petrons', in Callebat (1995), 533–47

    (1998), 'Gab es ein afrikanisches Latein? Neue Sichten eines alten Problems der lateinischen Sprachwissenschaft', in García-Hernández (1998), 125–36

    (1999), 'The language of early Roman satire: its function and characteristics', in Adams and Mayer (1999), 289–310

Pfiffig, A. J. (1965), *Uni-Hera-Astarte. Studien zu den Goldblechen von S. Severa/Pyrgi mit etruskischer und punischer Inschrift* (Vienna)

    (1969), *Die etruskische Sprache. Versuch einer Gesamtdarstellung* (Graz)

Pfister, M. (1972), 'Die sprachlichen Berührungen zwischen Franken und Galloromanen', *ZRPh* 88, 175–93

    (1973), 'La répartition géographique des éléments franciques en gallo-roman', *Revue de linguistique romane* 37, 126–49

Pippidi, D. M. (1976), *Assimilation et résistance à la culture gréco-romaine dans le monde ancien. Travaux du VIᵉ Congrès International d'Études Classiques (Madrid, septembre 1974)* (Bucarest and Paris)

Pirson, J. (1901), *La langue des inscriptions latines de La Gaule* (Brussels)

Pisani, V. (1977), 'Rivista di epigrafia italica', *SE* 45, 346–7

Planta, R. von (1892–7), *Grammatik der oskisch-umbrischen Dialekte*, 2 vols. (Strasburg)

Platt, J. T. (1977), 'A model for polyglossia and multilingualism (with special reference to Singapore and Malaysia)', *Language in Society* 6, 361–78

Poccetti, P. (1979), *Nuovi documenti italici* (Pisa)

    (1980), 'Elementi culturali negli epitafi poetici peligni, I: questioni ortografiche', *AION* 2, 89–98

    (1981), 'Elementi culturali negli epitafi poetici peligni, II: modelli formulari', *AION* 3, 259–70

    (1982a), 'Il testamento di Vibio Adirano', *RAAN* 57, 237–45

    (1982b), 'Minima Paeligna', *SSL* 22, 183–7

    (1982c), 'Elementi culturali negli epitafi poetici Peligni, III: La struttura metrica', *AION* 4, 213–35

(1984), 'Romani e Italici a Delo. Spunti linguistici da una pubblicazione recente', *Athenaeum* n. s. 62, 646–56

(1993), 'Aspetti e problemi della diffusione del latino in area italica', in Campanile (1993), 73–96

Polomé, E. C. (1983), 'The linguistic situation in the western provinces of the Roman Empire', *ANRW* II. 29.2, 509–53

Poncelet, R. (1957), *Cicéron, traducteur de Platon. L'expression de la pensée complexe en latin classique* (Paris)

Poplack, S. (1980), 'Sometimes I'll start a sentence in Spanish Y TERMINO EN ESPAÑOL: toward a typology of code-switching', *Linguistics* 18, 581–618

(1988), 'Contrasting patterns of code-switching in two communities', in Heller (1988), 215–44

Poplack, S. and Sankoff, D. (1984), 'Borrowing: the synchrony of integration', *Linguistics* 22, 99–135

Porzio Gernia, M. L. (1970), 'Aspetti dell'influsso latino sul lessico e sulla sintassi osca', *AGI* 55 (1970), 94–144

Poultney, J. W. (1959), *The Bronze Tablets of Iguvium* (Baltimore)

Powell, J. G. F. (1995), 'Cicero's translations from Greek', in J. G. F. Powell (ed.), *Cicero the Philosopher, Twelve Papers* (Oxford), 273–300

(1999), 'Stylistic registers in Juvenal', in Adams and Mayer (1999), 311–34

Prachner, G. (1980), *Die Sklaven und Freigelassenen im arretinischen Sigillatagewerbe* (Wiesbaden)

Price, P. I. (1955–6), 'Some Roman ostraca from Egypt', *JJurPap.* 9–10, 159–67

Priuli, S. (1984), 'Una lapide sepolcrale di Roma con iscrizione incisa nel recto e minuta dello stesso testo graffita nel verso', *Epigraphica* 46, 49–63

Prosdocimi, A. L. (1976), 'Sui grecismi dell'osco', in *Scritti in onore di Giuliano Bonfante* (Brescia), II, 781–866

(1978), 'Contatti e conflitti di lingue nell'Italia antica: l'elemento greco', in A. L. Prosdocimi (ed.), *Lingue e dialetti dell'Italia antica* (Rome), 1029–89

(1979), 'Rivista di epigrafia etrusca', *SE* 47, 385

(1983), 'Puntuazione sillabica e insegnamento della scrittura nel venetico e nelle fonti etrusche', *AION* 5, 75–126

(1989), 'Le lingue dominanti e i linguaggi locali', in *Lo spazio letterario di Roma antica*. II. *La circolazione del testo* (Rome), 11–91

Radermacher, L. (1925), *Neutestamentliche Grammatik. Das Griechisch des Neuen Testaments im Zusammenhang mit der Volkssprache*, 2nd edn (Tübingen)

Rauh, N. K. (1993), *The Sacred Bonds of Commerce. Religion, Economy, and Trade Society at Hellenistic Roman Delos, 166–87 B.C.* (Amsterdam)

Rawson, E. (1978), 'Caesar, Etruria and the *disciplina Etrusca*', *JRS* 68, 132–52

(1985), *Intellectual Life in the Late Roman Republic* (London)

Rea, J. (1979), 'The letter of Phonen to Aburni', *ZPE* 34, 147–62

Reichenkron, G. (1961), 'Zur römischen Kommandosprache bei byzantinischen Schriftstellern', *BZ* 54, 18–27

Reynolds, J. M. and Ward Perkins, J. B. (1952), *The Inscriptions of Roman Tripolitania* (Rome and London)

Ricci, S. de (1904), 'A Latin deed of manumission (AD 221) in the collection of The Right Hon. Lord Amherst of Hackney, F. S. A.', *Proceedings of the Society of Biblical Archaeology* 26, 145–52, 185–96

Ridgway, F. R. S. (1990), 'Etruscans, Greeks, Carthaginians: the sanctuary at Pyrgi', in Descoeudres (1990), 511–30

Rix, H. (1956), 'Die Personennamen auf den etruskisch-lateinischen Bilinguen', *BN* 7, 147–72

(1963), *Das etruskische Cognomen* (Wiesbaden)

(1981), 'Rapporti onomastici fra il panteon etrusco e quello romano', in *Gli Etruschi e Roma. Atti dell'incontro di studio in onore di Massimo Pallottino, Roma, 11–13 dicembre 1979* (Rome), 104–26

(1984), 'Etr. *mec rasnal* = lat. *res publica*', in *Studi di antichità in onore di Guglielmo Maetzke* (Rome), II, 455–68

(1991), *Etruskische Texte. Editio Minor*, 2 vols. (Tübingen)

(1994), *Die Termini der Unfreiheit in den Sprachen Alt-Italiens* (Stuttgart)

(1996), 'Variazioni locali in osco', in Del Tutto Palma (1996), 243–61

Rizakis, A. D. (ed.) (1996), *Roman Onomastics in the Greek East. Social and Political Aspects (Proceedings of the International Colloquium on Roman Onomastics, Athens, 7–9 September 1993)* (Athens)

Robert, L. (1989), *Opera Minora Selecta* V (Amsterdam)

Rochette, B. (1989), 'Le *P. Vindob.* L150 et les "glossaires" virgiliens', *C d'É* 64, 231–4

(1990), 'Les traductions grecques de l'*Énéide* sur papyrus. Une contribution à l'étude du bilinguisme gréco-romain au Bas-Empire', *Les études classiques* 58, 333–46

(1994), 'Traducteurs et traductions dans l' Égypte gréco-romaine', *C d'É* 69, 313–22

(1996a), 'Sur le bilinguisme dans l'Égypte gréco-romaine', *C d'É* 71, 153–68

(1996b), 'Marginalia Vergiliana', *ZPE* 114, 97–8

(1996c), 'Papyrologica bilinguia Graeco-latina', *Aegyptus* 76, 57–79

(1997a), *Le latin dans le monde grec* (Brussels)

(1997b), 'Sur le bilinguisme dans les armées d'Hannibal', *Les études classiques* 65, 153–9

(1999), 'Écrire en deux langues. Remarques sur le mixage des écritures grecque et latine d'après les papyrus littéraires bilingues d'auteurs classiques', *Scriptorium* 53, 325–34

Rodinson, M. (1950), 'Une inscription trilingue de Palmyre', *Syria* 27, 137–42

Röllig, W. (1980), 'Das Punische im Römischen Reich', in Neumann and Untermann (1980), 285–99

Rönsch, H. (1874), *Itala und Vulgata. Das Sprachidiom der urchristlichen Itala und der katholischen Vulgata* (Marburg)

Rössler, O. (1962), 'Die lateinischen Reliktwörter im Berberischen und die Frage des Vokalsystems der afrikanischen Latinität', *BN* 13, 258–62

(1980), 'Libyen von der Cyrenaica bis zur Mauretania Tingitana', in Neumann and Untermann (1980), 267–84

Rohlfs, G. (1954), *Die lexikalische Differenzierung der romanischen Sprachen* (Munich)
(1958), 'Messapisches und Griechisches aus dem Salento', in *Sybaris: Festschrift Hans Krahe* (Wiesbaden), 121–8
(1959), 'Am Kreuzweg der Sprachen (Neues aus Südostitalien)', *Die Sprache* 5, 172–82
(1966), *Grammatica storica della lingua italiana e dei suoi dialetti. I. Fonetica* (Turin)

Romaine, S. (1995), *Bilingualism*, 2nd edn (Oxford)

Rose, H. J. (1921), 'The Greek of Cicero', *JHS* 41, 91–116

Rosén, H. (1999), *Latine loqui. Trends and Directions in the Crystallization of Classical Latin* (Munich)

Rossi, L. E. (1973), '*Qui te primus "deuro de" fecit* (Petr. 58.7)', *SIFC* 45, 28–45

Rossi, M. and Garbini, G. (1976–7), 'Nuovi documenti epigrafici dalla Tripolitania romana', *Libya Antiqua* 13–14, 7–20

Rougé, J. (1966), *Recherches sur l'organisation du commerce maritime en Méditerranée sous l'empire romain* (Paris)

Roussel, P. and Launey, M. (1937), *Inscriptions de Délos* (Paris)

Roussel, P. and Visscher, F. de (1942–3), 'Les inscriptions du temple de Dmeir', *Syria* 23, 173–200

Roxan, M. M. (1978), *Roman Military Diplomas 1954–1977* (London)
(1985), *Roman Military Diplomas 1978–1984* (London)
(1994), *Roman Military Diplomas 1985–1993* (London)

Rubin, J. (1962), 'Bilingualism in Paraguay', *Anthropological Linguistics* 4 (1), 52–8

Rudd, N. (1986), *Themes in Roman Satire* (London)

Ruppel, W. (1930), *Les temples immergés de la Nubie. Der Tempel von Dakke*, III. *Die griechischen und lateinischen Inschriften von Dakke* (Cairo)

Russell, D. A. F. M. (ed.) (2001), *Quintilian, the Orator's Education*, 5 vols. (Cambridge, Mass. and London)

Russell, J. (1980), 'Julius Caesar's last words', in B. Marshall (ed.), Vindex Humanitatis. *Essays in Honour of John Huntly Bishop* (Armidale), 123–8

Russo, C. F. (1964), *L. Annaei Senecae Diui Claudii* ΑΠΟΚΟΛΟΚΥΝΤΩΣΙΣ, 4th edn (Florence)

Rutgers, L. V. (1995), *The Jews in Late Ancient Rome: Evidence of Cultural Interaction in the Roman Diaspora* (Leiden)

Sabbah, G. (1985), 'Observations préliminaires à une nouvelle édition de Cassius Félix', in Mazzini and Fusco (1985), 279–312

Sacco, G. (1984), *Iscrizioni greche d'Italia. Porto* (Rome)

Salmon, E. T. (1967), *Samnium and the Samnites* (Cambridge)
(1982), *The Making of Roman Italy* (London)

Salonius, A. H. (1927), *Die Griechen und das Griechische in Petrons Cena Trimalchionis* (Societas Scientiarum Fennica, Commentationes Humanarum Litterarum II.1, Helsinki)

Sanders, H. A. (1941), 'The origin of the Third Cyrenaic Legion', *AJP* 62, 84–6

Sandy, G. (1997), *The Greek World of Apuleius. Apuleius and the Second Sophistic* (Leiden, New York and Cologne)

Sanie, S. (1970), 'Inscriptio bilinguis tibiscensis. A. Pars palmyrena', *Dacia* n. s. 14, 405–9

Santamaria, G. Mancinetti (1982), 'Filostrato di Ascalona, banchiere in Delo', in Coarelli, Musti and Solin (1982), 79–89

Šašel, A. and J. (1963), *Inscriptiones latinae quae in Iugoslavia inter annos MCMXL et MCMLX repertae et editae sunt* (Ljubljana)

Šašel Kos, M. (1979), *Inscriptiones Latinae in Graecia repertae. Additamenta ad CIL* iii (Faenza)

Schiaparelli, E. (1887), *Museo archeologico di Firenze. Antichità egizie*, pt. i (Rome)

Schickinger, H. (1897), *Die Gräcismen bei Ammianus* (Nikolsburg)

Schmidt, K. H. (1983), 'Keltisch-lateinische Sprachkontakte im römischen Gallien der Kaiserzeit', *ANRW* ii.29.2, 988–1018

Schnorr v. Carolsfeld, H. (1884), 'Das lateinische Suffix ânus', *ALL* i, 177–94

Schopf, E. (1919), *Die konsonantischen Fernwirkungen: Fern-Dissimilation, Fern-Assimilation und Metathesis* (Göttingen)

Schramm, F. (1911), *Sprachliches zur Lex Salica. Eine vulgärlateinisch-romanische Studie* (Marburg a. L.)

Schulz, F. (1942–3), 'Roman registers of birth and birth certificates', i, *JRS* 32, 78–91, ii, *JRS* 33, 55–64

Schulze, G. (1894 = 1958), *Orthographica et Graeca Latina* (reprinted, with preface by E. Fraenkel) (Rome)

Schwartz, J. (1956), 'Deux ostraca de la région du wâdi Hammâmât', *C d'É* 31, 118–23

Schwarzlose, W. (1913), *De titulis sepulcralibus Latinis quaestionum capita quattuor* (Halle)

Schwyzer, E. and Debrunner, A. (1950), *Griechische Grammatik auf der Grundlage von Karl Brugmanns griechischer Grammatik*, ii (Munich)

Sedley, D. (1999), 'Lucretius' use and avoidance of Greek', in Adams and Mayer (1999), 227–46

Sevenster, J. N. (1968), *Do You Know Greek? How much Greek could the First Jewish Christians Have Known?* (Leiden)

Seyrig, H. (1941), 'Inscriptions grecques de l'agora de Palmyre', *Syria* 22, 223–70

Shackleton Bailey, D. R. (1962), 'L.S.J. and Cicero's letters', *CQ* n. s. 12, 159–65
(1963), 'L.S.J. and Cicero's letters', *CQ* n. s. 13, 88
(1965–70), *Cicero's Letters to Atticus*, 7 vols. (Cambridge) [cited by name of author only, without dates]

Sheets, G. A. (1981), 'The dialect gloss, Hellenistic poetics and Livius Andronicus', *AJP* 102, 58–78

Sherk, R. K. (1969), *Roman Documents from the Greek East: senatus consulta and epistulae to the Age of Augustus* (Baltimore)

Shipp, G. P. (1953), 'Greek in Plautus', *WS* 66, 105–12
(1979), *Modern Greek Evidence for the Ancient Greek Vocabulary* (Sydney)

Siebert, G. (1999), 'Dédicaces déliennes et culture bilingue', in R. G. Khoury (ed.), *Urkunden und Urkundenformulare im Klassischen Altertum und in den orientalischen Kulturen* (Heidelberg), 95–101

Sier, K. (1992), 'Die Rolle des Skythen in den *Thesmophoriazusen* des Aristophanes', in Müller, Sier and Werner (1992), 63–83

Sievers, O. (1872), 'Quaestiones onomatologicae', *Acta Societatis Philologae Lipsiensis* 2, 53–106

Sihler, A. L. (1995), *New Comparative Grammar of Greek and Latin* (New York and Oxford)

Sijpesteijn, P. J. (1973), 'Letters on ostraca', *Talanta* 5, 72–84
  (1979), 'Some remarks on Roman dates in Greek papyri', *ZPE* 33, 229–40
  (1980), 'Wiener mélange', *ZPE* 40, 91–110
  (1981), 'Small notes on bilingual papyri', *ZPE* 42, 107–10
  (1984), 'Nachlese zu Wiener Texten II', *ZPE* 56, 93–6

Sironen, E. (1997), *The Late Roman and Early Byzantine Inscriptions of Athens and Attica* (Helsinki)

Sittl, K. (1890), *Die Gebärden der Griechen und Römer* (Leipzig)

Skutsch, O. (1974), 'Notes on Ennius', *BICS* 21, 75–80
  (1985), *The Annals of Quintus Ennius* (Oxford)

Smith, M. S. (1975), *Petronii Arbitri Cena Trimalchionis* (Oxford)

Smolicz, J. (1981), 'Core values and cultural identity', *Ethnic and Racial Studies* 4, 75–90

Snellman, W. J. (1914–19), *De interpretibus Romanorum deque linguae latinae cum aliis nationibus commercio* (Leipzig)

Sofer, J. (1941), 'Der Untergang der gallischen Landesprache und seine Nachwirkungen', *ZcPh* 22, 93–132

Solin, H. (1971), *Beiträge zur Kenntnis der griechischen Personennamen in Rom*, I (Helsinki)
  (1978), 'Varia onomastica', *ZPE* 28, 75–81
  (1982a), 'Appunti sull'onomastica romana a Delo', in Coarelli, Musti and Solin (1982), 101–17
  (1982b), *Die griechischen Personennamen in Rom. Ein Namenbuch*, 3 vols. (Berlin and New York)
  (1983), 'Juden und Syrer im westlichen Teil der römischen Welt. Eine ethnisch-demographische Studie mit besonderer Berücksichtigung der sprachliche Zustände', *ANRW* II.29.2, 587–789
  (1987), 'Varia onomastica VI. Eupluti', *ZPE* 67, 200–6
  (1992), 'Varia onomastica X. Euplunis', *ZPE* 91, 183–4
  (1995), '*Corpus defixionum antiquarum*. Quelques réflexions', in Callebat (1995), 569–76

Solin, H. and Kajava, M. (eds.) (1990), *Roman Eastern Policy and Other Studies in Roman History. Proceedings of a Colloquium at Tvärminne 2–3 October 1987* (Helsinki)

Solin, H., Salomies, O. and Liertz, U.-M. (1995), *Acta Colloquii Epigraphici Latini Helsingiae 3.-6. sept. 1991 habiti* (Helsinki)

Sophocles, E. A. (1888), *Greek Lexicon of the Roman and Byzantine Periods (from B. C. 146 to A. D. 1100)* (New York and London)

Sotgiu, G. (1961), *Iscrizioni latine della Sardegna*, I (Padua)

Soubiran, J. (1972), *Cicéron, Aratea. Fragments poétiques* (Paris)

Sourvinou-Inwood, C. (1995), *'Reading' Greek Death* (Oxford)

Speidel, M. P. (1994a), *Die Denkmäler der Kaiserreiter. Equites singulares Augusti* (Cologne)

(1994b), *Riding for Caesar. The Roman Emperors' Horse Guards* (London)

Spiegelberg, W. (1932), *Die demotische Denkmäler*, III. *Demotische Inschriften und Papyri* (Berlin)

Starcky, J. (1949), *Inventaire des inscriptions de Palmyre*, X (Damascus)

Steele, R. B. (1900), 'The Greek in Cicero's epistles', *AJP* 21, 387–410

Stein, A. (1915), *Untersuchungen zur Geschichte und Verwaltung Aegyptens unter roemischer Herrschaft* (Stuttgart)

Steinbauer, D. (1993), 'Etruskisch-ostitalische Lehnbeziehungen', in H. Rix (ed.) *Oskisch-Umbrisch. Texte und Grammatik* (Wiesbaden), 287–306

Steinmetz, P. (1992), 'Gellius als Übersetzer', in Müller, Sier and Werner (1992), 201–11

Strassi Zaccaria, S. (1991), 'Prosopografia e incarichi amministrativi a Karanis nel II sec. d. C. Proposte interpretative', *ZPE* 85, 245–62

Sturtevant, E. H. (1907), 'Some unfamiliar uses of *idem* and *isdem* in Latin inscriptions', *CP* 2, 313–23

Susini, G. (1973), *The Roman Stonecutter: an Introduction to Latin Epigraphy*, edited with an introduction by E. Badian, translated by A. M. Dabrowski (Oxford)

Svennung, J. (1935), *Untersuchungen zu Palladius und zur lateinischen Fach- und Volkssprache* (Lund)

(1958), *Anredeformen. Vergleichende Forschungen zur indirekten Anrede in der dritten Person und zum Nominativ für den Vokativ* (Uppsala)

Syme, R. (1969), 'Pliny the procurator', *HSCP* 73, 201–36

(1978), *History in Ovid* (Oxford)

Szemerényi, O. (1975), 'The origins of Roman drama and Greek tragedy', *Hermes* 103, 300–32

Sznycer, M. (1958), 'Remarques sur le graffito phénicien en caractères grecs de la grotte de Waṣṭa', *Semitica* 8, 5–10

Taubenschlag, R. (1951a), 'The interpreters in the papyri', in *Charisteria Thaddaeo Sinko* (Warsaw and Vratislava), 361–3

(1951b), 'The legal profession in Greco-Roman Egypt', in *Festschrift Fritz Schulz* (Weimar), II, 188–92

(1959), *Opera Minora*, II (Warsaw)

Taylor, D. G. K. (forthcoming), 'Bilingualism and diglossia in late antique Syria and Mesopotamia', in J. N. Adams, M. Janse and S. C. R. Swain (eds.), *Bilingualism in Ancient Society: Language Contact and the Written Word* (Oxford)

Teixidor, J. (1979), *The Pantheon of Palmyra* (Leiden)

Tekavčić, P. (1972), *Grammatica storica dell'italiano*, I. *Fonematica* (Bologna)

Terzaghi, N. (1966), *C. Lucili Saturarum Reliquiae*, 3rd edn (Florence)

Théodoridès, A. (1989), 'Pèlerinage au Colosse de Memnon', *C d'É* 64, 267–82

Thomas, J. D. (1971), 'Notes on documentary papyri (P.Oxy. 1572 and 2561, BGU 2118)', *ZPE* 8, 278–84

Thomason, S. G. and Kaufman, T. (1988), *Language Contact, Creolization, and Genetic Linguistics* (Berkeley)

Thomsen, P. (1917), 'Die römischen Meilensteine der Provinzen Syria, Arabia und Palaestina', *Zeitschrift des Deutschen Palästina-Vereins* 40, 1–103

Threatte, L. (1980), *The Grammar of Attic Inscriptions*, volume 1. *Phonology* (Berlin and New York)

Thumb, A. (1901), *Die griechische Sprache im Zeitalter des Hellenismus. Beiträge zur Geschichte und Beurteilung der KOINH* (Strasburg)

Thurneysen, R. (1923), 'Irisches und Gallisches', *ZcPh* 14, 1–12

(1946), *A Grammar of Old Irish*, revised edn, translated by D. A. Binchy and O. Bergin (Dublin)

Thylander, H. (1952), *Inscriptions du Port d'Ostie*, 1 (Lund)

Tobler, A. and Lommatzsch, E. (1975), *Altfranzösisches Wörterbuch*, X.3 (Wiesbaden)

Tomlin, R. S. O. (1998), 'Roman manuscripts from Carlisle: the ink-written tablets', *Britannia* 29, 31–84

Touloumakos, J. (1995), 'Bilingue [griechisch-lateinische] Weihinschriften der römischen Zeit', TEKMHRIA 1, 79–129

Tovar, A. (1980), 'Das Vulgärlatein in den Provinzen', in Neumann and Untermann (1980), 331–42

Townend, G. B. (1960), 'The sources of the Greek in Suetonius', *Hermes* 88, 98–120

Traina, A. (1989), 'Le traduzioni', in *Lo spazio letterario di Roma antica*, II. *La circolazione del testo* (Rome), 93–123

Tranoy, A. (1981), *La Galice romaine. Recherches sur le nord-ouest de la péninsule ibérique dans l'antiquité* (Paris)

Treffers-Daller, J. (1998), 'Variability in code-switching styles: Turkish – German code-switching patterns', in Jacobson (1998a), 177–98

Turner, E. G. (1961), 'Latin versus Greek as a universal language: the attitude of Diocletian', in *Language and Society. Essays presented to Arthur M. Jensen on his Seventieth Birthday* (Copenhagen), 165–8

Ullman, B. L. (1935), 'Two Latin Abecedaria from Egypt', *AJP* 56, 147–8

Untermann, J. (1961), *Die venetischen Personennamen* (Wiesbaden)

(1968), Review of Pellegrini and Prosdocimi (1967), *Kratylos* 13, 137–45

(1975), *Monumenta Linguarum Hispanicarum*, I. *Die Münzlegenden* (Wiesbaden)

(1979), 'Literaturbericht italische Sprachen', *Glotta* 57, 293–324

(1980a), 'Hispania', in Neumann and Untermann (1980), 1–17

(1980b), 'Alpen – Donau – Adria', in Neumann and Untermann (1980), 45–63

(1983), 'Die althispanischen Sprachen', *ANRW* II.29.2, 791–818

(1990), *Monumenta Linguarum Hispanicarum*, III. *Die iberischen Inschriften aus Spanien*: 1. *Literaturverzeichnis, Einleitung, Indices*; 2. *Die Inschriften* (Wiesbaden)

(1997), *Monumenta Linguarum Hispanicarum*, IV. *Die tartessischen, keltiberischen und lusitanischen Inschriften* (Wiesbaden)

(2000), *Wörterbuch des Oskisch-Umbrischen* (Heidelberg)

Vaahtera, J. (2000), *Roman Augural Lore in Greek Historiography. A Study of the Theory and Terminology* (Turku)

Väänänen, V. (1965), *Étude sur le texte et la langue des* Tablettes Albertini (Helsinki) (1966), *Le latin vulgaire des inscriptions pompéiennes,* 3rd edn (Berlin) (1981), *Introduction au latin vulgaire,* 3rd edn (Paris)

Vainio, R. (1999), *Latinitas and Barbarisms according to the Roman Grammarians. Attitudes towards Language in the Light of Grammatical Examples* (Turku)

Valvo, A. (1988), *La 'Profezia di Vegoia'. Proprietà fondiaria e aruspicina in Etruria nel I secolo a. C.* (Rome)

Vanoni, L. C. (1965), 'Rivista di epigrafia etrusca', *SE* 33, 500–4

Vattioni, F. (1968), 'Sant'Agostino e la civiltà punica', *Augustinianum* 8, 434–67 (1976), 'Glosse puniche', *Augustinianum* 16, 505–55

Vendryes, J. (1925), 'Celtique et roman', *Revue de linguistique romane* 1, 262–77

Venini, P. (1952), 'Le parole greche nell'epistolario di Plinio', *Istituto Lombardo di Scienze e Lettere, Rendiconti* 85, 259–69

Versnel, H. S. (1970), *Triumphus. An Inquiry into the Origin, Development and Meaning of the Roman Triumph* (Leiden)

Vetter, E. (1953), *Handbuch der italischen Dialekte* (Heidelberg)

Veyne, P. (1962), 'Les honneurs postumes de Flavia Domitilla et les dédicaces grecques et Latines', *Latomus* 21, 49–98

Viereck, P. (1888), *Sermo Graecus quo senatus populusque Romanus magistratusque populi Romani usque ad Tiberii Caesaris aetatem in scriptis publicis usi sunt examinatur* (Göttingen)

Vincent, N. (1988), 'Latin', in M. Harris and N. Vincent (eds.) *The Romance Languages* (London), 26–78

Vine, B. (1993), *Studies in Archaic Latin Inscriptions* (Innsbruck)

Vives y Escudero, A. (1924), *La moneda hispánica,* III (Madrid)

Vleeming, S. P. (ed.) (1987), *Aspects of Demotic Lexicography (Acts of the Second International Conference for Demotic Studies, Leiden 19–21 September 1984)* (Leuven)

Wachter, R. (1987), *Altlateinische Inschriften. Sprachliche und epigraphische Untersuchungen zu den Dokumenten bis etwa 150 v. Chr.* (Bern)

Wackernagel, J. (1926), *Vorlesungen über Syntax,* II, 2nd edn (Basel)

Wagner, M. L. (1936), *Restos de latinidad en el norte de Africa* (Coimbra)

Walbank, F. W. (1957), *A Historical Commentary on Polybius,* I (Oxford) (1967), *A Historical Commentary on Polybius,* II (Oxford) (1979), *A Historical Commentary on Polybius,* III (Oxford)

Walde, A. and Hofmann, J. B. (1938), *Lateinisches etymologisches Wörterbuch* I, 3rd edn (Heidelberg)

Wallace, R. (1988), 'Dialectal Latin Fundatid, Proiecitad, Parentatid', *Glotta* 66, 211–20

Walsh, P. G. (1958), 'The negligent historian: "howlers" in Livy', *GR* n. s. 5, 83–8

Warmington, E. H. (1940), *Remains of Old Latin,* IV. *Archaic Inscriptions* (Cambridge, Mass.)

Watkins, C. (1955), 'The phonemics of Gaulish. The dialect of Narbonensis', *Language* 31, 9–19
    (1995), *How to Kill a Dragon. Aspects of Indo-European Poetics* (New York and Oxford)
Watmough, M. T. (1997), *Studies in the Etruscan Loanwords in Latin* (Florence)
Watson, G. R. (1974), 'Documentation in the Roman Army', *ANRW* II.1, 493–507
Watt, W. S. (1980), '*Enim* Tullianum', *CQ* n.s. 30, 120–3
Weinreich, U. (1953), *Languages in Contact. Findings and Problems* (New York)
Weis, R. (1992), 'Zur Kenntnis des Griechischen im Rom der republikanischen Zeit', in Müller, Sier and Werner (1992), 137–42
Weisgerber, L. (1939), 'Zur Sprachenkarte Mitteleuropas im frühen Mittelalter', *Rheinische Vierteljahrsblätter* 9, 23–51
    (1969), *Rhenania Germano-Celtica, Gesammelte Abhandlungen* (Bonn)
Welles, C. B., Fink, R. O. and Gilliam, J. F. (1959), *The Excavations at Dura-Europos. Final Report V, Part I* (New Haven)
Wenskus, O. (1993), 'Zitatzwang als Motiv für Codewechsel in der lateinischen prosa', *Glotta* 71, 205–16
    (1995), 'Triggering und Einschaltung griechischer Formen in lateinischer Prosa', *IF* 100, 172–92
    (1996), 'Markieren der Basissprache in lateinischen Texten mit griechischen Einschaltungen und Entlehnungen', *IF* 101, 233–57
    (1998), *Emblematischer Codewechsel und Verwandtes in der lateinischen Prosa. Zwischen Nähesprache und Distanzsprache* (Innsbruck)
    (2001), 'Wie schreibt man einer Dame? Zum Problem der Sprachwahl in der römischen Epistolographie', *WS* 114, 215–32
Wessely, C. (1902), 'Die lateinischen Elemente in der Gräzität der ägyptischen Papyrusurkunden', *WS* 24, 99–151
Westendorp Boerma, R. E. H. (1949), *P. Vergili Maronis Libellum qui inscribitur Catalepton*, I (Assen)
Whatmough, J. (1944), 'Κελτικά, being prolegomena to a study of the dialects of ancient Gaul', *HSCP* 55, 1–85
    (1970), *The Dialects of Ancient Gaul* (Cambridge, Mass.)
Wigtil, D. N. (1982a), 'The ideology of the Greek "Res Gestae"', *ANRW* II. 30.1, 624–38
    (1982b), 'The translator of the Greek *Res Gestae*', *AJP* 103, 189–94
Wilcken, U. (1936), 'Ueber den Nutzen der lateinischen Papyri', in *Atti del IV Congresso Internazionale di Papirologia* (Milan), 101–22
Williams, M. (1999), 'The Jews of early Byzantine Venusia: the family of Faustinus I, the father', *JJS* 50, 38–52
Wilson, A. J. N. (1966), *Emigration from Italy in the Republican Age of Rome* (Manchester)
Wilson, R. J. A. (1996), 'Sicily, Sardinia and Corsica', *The Cambridge Ancient History*, 2nd edn, vol. X, 434–48

Winter, E. (1977), 'Das Kalabsha-Tor in Berlin', *Jahrbuch preussischer Kulturbesitz* 14, 59–71

Wolf, J. G. (1982), 'Aus dem neuen pompejanischen Urkundenfund: Graeca leguntur', *ZPE* 45, 245–53

Woolf, G. (1998), *Becoming Roman. The Origins of Provincial Civilization in Gaul* (Cambridge)

Wouters, A. (1976), ' "Latijns Grieks" en "Grieks Latijn" ', *Hermeneus* 48, 179–91

Wright, R. (1982), *Late Latin and Early Romance in Spain and Carolingian France* (Liverpool)

Wuilleumier, P. (1942), '*Socerio*', *REL* 20, 47–49

(1963), *Inscriptions latines des trois Gaules (France)* (Paris)

Youtie, H. C. (1949), 'Records of a Roman bath in Upper Egypt', *AJA* 53, 268–70

(1981–2), *Scriptiunculae Posteriores*, 2 vols. (Bonn)

Youtie, H. C. and Winter, J. G. (1951), *Michigan Papyri*, VIII. *Papyri and Ostraca from Karanis* (Ann Arbor)

Zamudio, R. Jiménez (1986), *Estudio del dialecto peligno y su entorno lingüístico* (Salamanca)

Zauzich, K.-Th. (1984), 'Zwischenbilanz zu den demotischen Ostraka aus Edfu', *Enchoria* 12, 67–90

Zevi, F. (1976), 'Monumenti e aspetti culturali di Ostia repubblicana', in P. Zanker (ed.) *Hellenismus in Mittelitalien* I (Göttinge(Göttingen), 52–83

Zilken, F. (1909), *De inscriptionibus latinis graecis bilinguibus quaestiones selectae* (Bonn)

Zilliacus, H. (1935), *Zum Kampf der Weltsprachen im oströmischen Reich* (Helsinki)

(1941), *Vierzehn Berliner griechische Papyri. Urkunden und Briefe* (Helsinki)

Subject index

abbreviations in epigraphy
in Greek, imitated from Latin, 45 with
n. 120, 101 n. 223; in neo-Punic, imitated
from Latin 231
Abinnaeus archive
78, 382, 397, 555–7, 600
ablative
ablative forms where dative required 104,
211; ablative absolute in Oscan and
Umbrian 134 with n. 111, 142, 156;
ablative absolute with nominal element in
accusative 612; in Gallus inscription and
prayers of thanksgiving 639; ablative
attached to name as matronymic in Latin
of Etruria 178, 286
accents, regional, foreign
Spanish in Latin 16; affecting of Greek by
Latin speakers 108–10, 432; of Greeks
in Latin 432–7; of 'city' Latin 114; 'rustic'
in Latin and in Etruscan 168; Gaulish in
Greek/Latin (?) 191; African in Latin 237,
437; Gallic in Latin 356 with n. 109, 690
n. 8
Accius
inflection of Greek names in 371
acclamations   406–7
accommodation
nature of 295–6, 545 (contrasted with
divergence as act of power), 576–7; as
'convergence' 301, 351; in conventions of
naming 171; in the form adopted of a
filiation 674, 675–6; of Etruscan to Latin
in funerary formulae 173; of Latin to
Etruscan 173–4; marked by
code-switching 295, 300, 316, 351–6; as
act of deference to referent 295; as
response to circumstances, setting of an
exchange etc. 295, 321; as response to
origin of addressee 656; as 'talking down'
to the addressee 350; as sarcastic,
threatening, humorous, offensive 353–5;

'ironical over-accommodation' 356;
offensive accommodating use of Aramaic
by Roman official 268; in the form of
condescending translation into Latin of
decision given in Greek 388; as
condescending repetition in second
language of what has been said in a
language incomprehensible to addressee
559, 561, 576–7; in the sphere of religion,
to local linguistic practice 577–9, 578
n. 109, 579, 583, 589, 675–6; in the
adoption of a syntactic structure 660–1; in
language choice 576, 663; at Delos, by
Italians using Greek to suit the setting
645–9; mutual, by Greeks and Italians at
Delos 683–4, with Romans making more
concessions than Greeks 683–4
accusative
plural, Greek in Latin word 25, 28, 56–7,
400, 494; of honorand 37, 103, 254–5,
259, 260, 650–1, 658–61; of apposition 62
n. 146, 227, 613; with prepositions (for
ablative) 14, 62 n. 146, 477, 575; in lists 62
n. 146, 477, 627, 721–2; of place name,
with locative function 612; 'default', in list
477, 621 n. 171; in ablative absolute 612;
'default' use of at La Graufesenque
723–4; of the victim, in curse tablets 681;
for ablative, expressing *origo* 724
acquisition, second-language
17–18; stages of, according to Ovid 18; order
of acquisition of elements of 97, 104, 628,
725 (sequences determined by nature of
instruction received), 740, 750; second
language 'corrupting' first 17 with n. 49,
277, 435–6; Romans as second-language
learners 9–12, 151, 201, 293, 295; of
Etruscan 166–7; of Punic 204–6, 293; of
Aramaic 268–9, 294; of Hebrew (Jerome)
273; of forms of Germanic 276–7;
learning a barbarian language as 'funny'

acquisition (*cont.*)
277; language learning associated with migration 188–9, 248–54, 291–2, 365, 375; Greeks as learners of Latin 15–16, 35–6, 54–63, 101–2, 103, 436–7, 617–30, 632, 725 and Chapter 8 *passim*; as 'late learners' 628; learning by means of instruction 628 and Chapter 8 *passim*; resorting to 'avoidance strategies' through imperfect competence in L2 732, 739; in army 617–23, 632; in Egypt 623–30; Venetic speakers as learners of Latin 125–6; Italic speakers learning Latin 151–4 with cross references; Gauls as learners of Latin 185, 188–9, 190, 197, 290, 691 with n. 11, Chapter 7 *passim*; Etruscans as learners of Latin 168, 169–79; Germans as learners of Latin 20, 275–6; African Christians as learners of Punic (?) 238; Punic speakers as learners of Latin 206 n. 381 (Republican period), 209–29; Palmyrenes as language learners 247; as learners of Latin 33–4, 248–58, 260; eastern Hebrew speakers learning Latin 273–4; Hispanic speakers learning Latin 281–3; speakers of 'Libyan' learning Latin 346; Thracians as learners of Latin 283–4, 305; second-language learners imposing ephemeral changes on target language 285, 286; language learners making false analogies 178, 285–6, 720–1; primary speakers of Oscan, Venetic, Etruscan, Punic, Gaulish, Germanic, Hispanic, Aramaic and Thracian learning Latin 293, and various language/ethnic groups learning Latin in army, summary of 760; *see also* 'competence', 'imperfect learning', 'Greeks'
adnominal phrases in Latin
with *cum*, standing for Greek compound 461
adverbs, Greek, in -ῶς in Latin 327 with n. 58
ae
Latinate digraph in Oscan 138, 141, 142, 155; as hypercorrect for short *e* 179 with n. 278
Aemilius Paullus, L.
assertive use of Latin by 559–60; and linguistic accommodation 577
-*aes* genitive
473, 478, 479–83; not influenced by Oscan 481; origin of 481–2; geographical distribution of 481 n. 235
Aeschines Flavianus from Miletus 53–63
African Latin 232, 245, 437–8, 454–5, 512–15; *see also* 'regional variation'

Albucius, T.
10, 19 n. 59, 300; mocked by code-switching 353
alphabet switching *see* 'character switching'
'allusive Grecisms' 19, 77 with n. 173, 315, 431 n. 54, 460–1, 501 n. 272
Ammianus
10 with n. 31, 268; on German speakers in Roman army 275, 294; as user of Grecising syntax 425; loan-shifts in (?) 464, 467; origin of 688 n.3
amulets
transliterated 44; in Hebrew language with Greek script 66; with Latin and Ethiopic 194; in Hebrew language in west 272
anaptyxis 120 n. 42, 157
ancestry, expressions of in Semitic inscriptions 212, 214, 223 n. 448, 225, 252
anecdotal evidence 9–14, 166–8, 204–6
Annius Cimber, T. 191
Anthimus
influence of Greek and Germanic on Latin of 448–9; of Greek on Latin of 463 (loan-shift); Greek syntactic interference in 496
Antioch Latin at 688 n. 3
Antonius Julianus, Latin accent of 16
Apamea in Syria, inscriptions of 72, 74
Apollonius Molo 10, 13
Appian
427; Latinate idioms in 472; dative of duration in 506; other Latinisms in 506; difficulty of interpreting evidence of 508–9
applications for leave 556 with n. 66
Apuleius
errors of Greek in 5; on broken Latin of Punic speaker 105; on poor Latin of African 237; on assertive use of Latin by soldier 383, 414, 560–1; on letter in Greek written by woman 220, 416
Aramaic
bilingual inscription with Greek 39; Palmyrene 32, 33–4, 247–71; Nabataean 264
Aristophanes, 'foreigner talk' in 97–100
Arminius code-switcher in Tacitus 20
army, Roman
polyglot, and Latin not necessarily known by all 20 n. 61, 275; officers as necessarily knowing Latin 20 with n. 61, 275, 276; German units retaining knowledge of first language (?) 20 with n. 61, similarly Palmyrenes (*see* 'Palmyrenes'); bilingual members of 262, 264, 275 (in form of

Egyptian Demotic (*cont.*)
  referring to Roman emperors as pharaohs
  534–6
Egyptians learning Latin and literacy in
  Latin 529–30
'embarrassment' as factor in language shift
  294
Ennius
  'three hearts' of 116–17, 153; of Messapic
  origin (?) 117; sources of Latin of 117, 153;
  on *Bruttaces* 149; Gaulish word in 185;
  inflection of Greek names in 371 with
  n. 135; imitation of Greek syntax in 422;
  calques on Greek in 460; 'allusive' phrasal
  renderings of Greek compounds in 460–1;
  'Oscanisms' in (?) 117
epitaphs
  84–7, 89, 90; of soldiers, in Latin and
  Palmyrene 253, 255–8; of soldier, in Latin
  at Palmyra 262; Latin funerary inscription
  as fossilisation of soldier's identity 262,
  578 n. 109, 616–17; Latin in soldiers'
  epitaphs for symbolic purposes 37, 262,
  299 with n. 10, 586, 616–17; bilingual, in
  Latin and Greek 37, 38, 87, 617; in Greek
  and Aramaic 39; code-switching from
  Greek into Latin to record military
  rank or unit 299; significance of epitaphs
  as evidence for code-switching
  409–10
errors
  of translation: in literary texts 4 with n. 7, 5,
  431 n. 54 (deliberate, by 'paronomasia');
  in inscriptions 87–8, 573; of
  second-language learners/users 7, 55 (in
  text copied from exemplar), 58–9, 69,
  94–105, 472, 525, 725–6 (revealing order
  of acquisition of morphology of L2),
  749–50 (distinguished from banal Vulgar
  Latin deviations from educated language);
  in fifth-declension nouns by Greeks
  learning Latin 102, 522, 728; in non-finite
  forms of verbs by Greek learning Latin
  729–31, including active use of perfect
  participles 729; deliberate errors in Greek
  composed by Roman 11; Roman apologies
  for errors in Greek 12 n. 37; inexplicable,
  irrational errors, usually of learners of L2
  58, 59, 62 with n. 146, 382, 472 (*tituli* for
  titulum), 477 (accusative for ablative), 525,
  737 (*procedebat*), 739; 'comprehensible', by
  L2 user, as revealing knowledge of L2 59;
  distribution of errors in formulaic text as
  revealing method of composition 59–60;
  in inscriptions (reflecting activities of
  client, composer or stonemason?) 86, 88,

92; of scribes, revealing bi-literacy 542–3;
of morphology, determined by ending of
juxtaposed word 492, 612; in higher
numerals in substandard Latin 613; errors
in verb morphology of Claudius
Terentianus as background to
developments in Latin language 745–8,
749; 'error analysis' 725 with n. 1 (for
'errors' of idiom in 'Romans' Greek', *see*
'translation')
Eshmun Merre 210
Este 126
eta intrudes into Latin texts 73, 76
Etruscan
  alongside Phoenician in tablets of Pyrgi
  202–3; in Rome 160–3; palatalisation in
  161; naming patterns in 161–2; suffixes
  (*-erna, -ennus, -enna*) in Latin 164–5;
  voiceless stops in 164; Roman boys
  learning Etruscan 'letters' 167; Etruscan
  disciplina 167; bilingual Etruscans in Livy
  168; 'rustic' accent in 168; bilingual
  inscriptions in Etruscan and Latin
  169–79; origins of endings in names such
  as *Tite, Publi* 514
euphemism
  311, 330–5; 'distancing' as sub-category of
  332–4
exclamations
  21, 27; exclamatory accusative/genitive in
  Cicero 497

f converted to aspirate by Greek speaking
  Latin 108
false morphological analysis 492–3, 522
fifth declension, Latin learners' errors in 102,
  522, 728
filiation, expressions of
  34 (inadequately expressed in Latin by
  learner), 128, 131, 134–5, 145; Oscan with
  Umbrian order 135, with n. 119; Oscan
  pattern in Latin 136, 158, 285, 511–12;
  Oscan with Latin genitive inflection 136;
  Greek with Latin genitive 136, 376, 604;
  Latin with Greek genitive 377–8, 676;
  reasons for switch of language in filiation
  379–80; summary of Latin patterns in
  Italic 155–6; in Etruscan-Latin bilinguals
  169, 170, 173; not compulsory in Etruscan
  171–2; *clan* = *filius* in Etruria 172; Latin
  with Etruscan genitive 177; Greek word
  for 'son' in Phoenician filiation 240;
  Semitic word for 'son' in Greek–Punic
  inscription 241; genitive without *filius* in
  Latin version of Latin–Palmyrene
  bilinguals 255, 257; *filius* with uninflected

Latin
    ineptly expressed 35 n. 99, 575; written with
    phonetic spellings 57, 62; with Greek
    endings 101, 103, 475–7; accent of Rome
    114, 154; Latin in Umbria 152; in Oscan
    territories before Social War 150–4; that
    with Oscan interference representing
    performance of L2 users 122; 'Campanian'
    153, 677–9; of Etruria 177, 178;
    supposedly 'Etruscanised' 173 n. 260; at
    Palmyra 33–4, 260; features of as spoken
    by Greeks 432–5; prestige of Roman
    Latin 114, 154; Latin in soldier's epitaph
    as marker of identity 262, 299 (*see also*
    'epitaphs'); harsh directness of compared
    with pleasant effects of Greek 331 n. 67;
    used to express decisions in legal hearings
    and appeals in Egypt and the east 384,
    387, 388, 557–8, 567, 568, 570; as
    language of a prefect's authorisation 570;
    as language of authority at Rome 414; in
    Egypt, symbolising Roman power,
    aloofness or 'Romanness' 387, 550, 553;
    assertive or ostentatious use of 550,
    558–61 (in Republic and as reported in
    literary sources), 589; Latin texts with
    Greek obscenities 361–2; Greek sexual
    terms borrowed by Latin 405; Greek
    suffix associated with female purveyors of
    sex borrowed by Latin 420; other Greek
    suffixes in Latin 419, 420, 422; Latin
    suffix extended in function on analogy of
    overlapping Greek suffix 467–8; Greek
    morphemes in Latin 421, 475–7 (*see also*
    'morphemes'), as 'supraregional' or 'link'
    language 425–6; not a unity, but
    comprising native speakers' Latin, the
    Latin of learners and numerous varieties
    520–1, 525; 'Hellenisation' of Latin
    language (?) 521, and the distinction
    between the contribution of L1 and L2
    speakers in this matter 762–4; marginal
    place of in Egypt 527; role of in Egypt
    537, 635–7; alleged role of as official
    language from Diocletian onwards 635–7;
    role of in legal documents to do with
    Roman citizens 562–71; as 'rich' or
    'impoverished' in Roman eyes 540–1; in
    Egypt, sources of information about
    543–4; as 'super-high' language in
    Roman eyes 555; as 'super-high' language
    of army 557; Latin as official language of
    Roman army (?) 599–608; Latin
    inscriptions symbolically appropriating
    objects for Rome 560, 572

'Latinisation'
    of Oscan 133–4, 137–8, 139–40, 154; of
    Venetic 143; of Latin literary language
    372 n. 142
Latinisms in Greek writers to suit 'Roman'
    subject matter   423, 472, 517
'Latino-Punic' inscriptions   230–5
'learners' Latin/Greek'
    7, 54–63, 64–5, 93–105, 379, 472, 581
    ('vision of Maximus'), 617–30; *see also*
    'acquisition, second-language', 'Greeks',
    'reduced languages', 'Vulgar Latin'
learning a second language   *see* 'acquisition,
    second-language'
letter names   42
letter shapes, convergence of in Greek and
    Latin   74–5, 542–3, 607
Lex Osca Tabulae Bantinae   115, 134 n. 111, 137,
    138, 151, 154, 156
'Libyan'   245–6
lingua francas   265, 266, 267, 294
lists, syntax of   *see* 'accusative', 'nominative'
literacy
    in two scripts 44–52, 765; not necessarily
    easy to master in second script 41–2;
    literacy of writer in second script revealed
    by way in which first is used 44–50, 52,
    543; literacy in one script only 53–63;
    stages in the acquistion of literacy in a
    second language 71–2, 620, 765–6;
    imperfect literacy in second script 617–23;
    literacy learning and its relation to
    language learning 40–1, 107, 533, 618,
    632, 698–9, 765; training in Latin literacy
    as instrument of Romanisation 176 with
    n. 264, 184 (Etruria), 290, 698, 722 (La
    Graufesenque); loss of literacy in the
    scripts of vernacular languages such as
    Etruscan 66, 182, Punic 66, 231, 235,
    Venetic 66, 143, Oscan and Umbrian 66,
    and varieties of Hispanic 66–7, 281; Latin
    literacy practices used in writing of
    Gaulish 698, 710; Latin literacy learning
    in western provinces 290; in Roman army
    533, 617–23, 632; learning a degree of
    'literacy' in script of a second language
    without learning the language 533;
    illiteracy of some participants in legal
    documents and its consequences 565,
    568–9, 610; *see also* 'script'
literary tags   *see* 'proverbs'
Livius Andronicus   122 n. 55, 372 n. 142
Livy
    misunderstandings of Greek in 4; on Cumae
    affair 113; on Etruscan 166–8; on spies

Word index

GREEK

LATIN (this list also contains numerous loan-words used in Latin)

OSCAN

UMBRIAN

PAELIGNIAN

VENETIC

ETRUSCAN

GAULISH

IBERIAN

CELTIBERIAN

PHOENICIAN

PUNIC

ARAMAIC

THRACIAN

GERMANIC

BERBER